Elizabeth Coon (Phenix) Copperthite - Kramer, Jr. (BAP)

In my pin # for At+t calling card!!!

I American Telephone & Telegraph
(I purchased 1,000.00 worth of At+t stock when At+t stock was @ 16 1/4. I, then, purchase 1,000.00 worth of At+t stock when the (At+t) stock had gone up to 33 or 34.)

INTRODUCTION TO
AMERICAN GOVERNMENT
THE NATIONAL GOVERNMENT

When Peter Verfurth was my Financial Engineer — Pete Verfurth almost Engineered me out of my money. Why —? Pete Verfurth was taking a course in Real Estate — Virginia-Side of Potomac River — And — Therefore did not pay attention to my Return of Capital — I lost money @ Dean Witter Reynolds!!!

I did the above investment with Dean Witter Reynolds — when Pete Verfurth (456 — another West Pointer, Class of 1956) was my Investment — what(?) —
1.) Manager(?)
2.) Financial Protector(?)
3.) Financial Engineer(?)

Introduction to
AMERICAN GOVERNMENT
THE NATIONAL GOVERNMENT

by

FREDERIC A. OGG

Professor Emeritus of Political Science
in the University of Wisconsin

and

P. ORMAN RAY

Professor Emeritus of Political Science
in the University of California

NINTH EDITION
THOROUGHLY REVISED

APPLETON-CENTURY-CROFTS, INC.
NEW YORK

PREFACE

This book is identical with the complete ninth edition of our *Introduction to American Government* except only for the omission of two concluding parts (fourteen chapters in all) dealing with the government of states and local areas. Part I provides a broad, over-all picture of the American constitutional and political system, with emphasis on such matters as constitutional origins and foundations, federalism and inter-level relations and trends, citizenship, civil rights, and instrumentalities of popular participation and control. Part II analyzes the national government in terms of structural arrangements, functions, powers, processes and procedures, trends, and problems of reorganization and improvement.

Every effort has, of course, been made to bring the volume completely abreast of the times. Events have no regard for the convenience of authors or printers; and much will have happened while the pages were in press. In general, however, it has been possible to square the book's contents with situations as of the beginning of 1948, and occasionally a little later. Speaking broadly, the seventh edition, published in 1942, had to do with a prewar government; the eighth, published in 1945, was focused on a government at war; the ninth deals with a government liberated from the immediate impact of war, yet confronted at every turn with tasks and problems which war had thrust upon the country and the world.

As heretofore, a large amount of space—more than one-fifth of the total—is devoted to chapter bibliographies and foot-note materials, the latter including not only citations of constitutions, statutes, and court decisions, but references to books and articles pertinent to matters under discussion in the text, together with illustrative or explanatory comment. Obviously, no teacher, and certainly no student, can make use of any very large part of the literature indicated. Wide opportunity for selection is, however, afforded; and even fleeting glimpses of the nature and variety of available materials on various topics should have some value.

For numerous criticisms and suggestions received from persons who have used earlier editions of the book—both teachers and students—we continue to be grateful; and special thanks are due many busy people in public positions in Washington and elsewhere who have responded generously to requests for materials and information.

F.A.O.
P.O.R.

v

CONTENTS

PART I

THE FOUNDATIONS OF GOVERNMENT IN THE UNITED STATES

1. *The Constitutional Basis*

2. *The Federal System*

3. *Citizenship and Civil Rights*

4. *Instrumentalities of Popular Control*

PART II

THE NATIONAL GOVERNMENT

1. *Organization, Powers, and Procedures*

2. *Functions and Services*

INTRODUCTION TO
AMERICAN GOVERNMENT
THE NATIONAL GOVERNMENT

CHAPTER I

GOVERNMENT IN THE MODERN WORLD

The Nature of Government

No experience of mankind is more customary than living under government; people everywhere, and in all ages, have found some form of political authority resting upon them and have submitted, willingly or otherwise, to controls imposed by it. To be sure, in tribal groups of North American Indians, among the Eskimaux, and in African jungles, government has commonly been a very rudimentary affair. In essence, however, it has existed, or still does; and in the more civilized world every nation, state, and community has developed it in more or less elaborate forms. Nor is there a more perennial human interest than devising, adopting, amending, and operating plans of governmental organization. For government, even among the most advanced peoples, is not something which, once constructed, goes on indefinitely according to pattern; on the contrary, like all other human institutions, it is subject to continual change, whether with revolutionary abruptness, as in France in 1789 or Russia in 1917, or by slow processes stretching through the centuries as in England, or at least through decades as in the United States. The world of today is not unique in being prolific in situations involving the rise of new governments (*e.g.*, in Germany, Austria, Italy, the Baltic and Balkan states, India, Japan); in others in which, as in France, older governments are being extensively reconstructed; and in still others everywhere (including the United States) in which the tide of quieter change flows on endlessly as in the past. *[margin: Governments change; government endures]*

What, then, is this matter of government, so enduring and yet so pliable? The truth is that, under differing conditions, it is, or may be, many things, not always compatible, and that while countless books could be brought together discussing it, no entirely satisfactory definition of it ever has been, or probably ever will be, formulated. The essence of it, however, is authority exercised through some given channel over the lives and affairs of a given body of people; authority expressing itself, too, on lines that may broadly be termed political as contrasted with simply religious or social—not the authority of a father over his family or of a clergyman over his parishioners or of a business man over his employees, but authority of a *public* character resting upon all of the people of a given area as being, for this purpose, an integrated unit, perchance an empire, a nation, a state, a county, or a municipality. The channel through *[margin: What is government?]*

1

which government operates may, of course, be a tribal chief, a king, or an emperor; it may be a dictator or some sort of oligarchy; or it may be a complicated mechanism set up and controlled by the people themselves; and by the same token it may operate independently and arbitrarily or as an instrument of the public will. In any event, however, it will involve the exercise of certain indispensable functions or powers almost indistinguishably blended in a primitive or despotic government, but in all modern governments of the more liberal sort recognized as basically dissimilar, and in the United States deliberately separated so as to be exercised by different authorities.

Three necessary elements   As reflected in the familiar three branches of government in this country, the indispensable functions referred to are: legislative, executive, and judicial. In the legislative function, broadly viewed, is included everything pertaining to the determination and declaration of public policy, *e.g.*, the framing of constitutions and the enactment of laws and ordinances; and in modern governments generally, the function is exercised by parliaments, congresses, legislatures, municipal councils, constitutional conventions, and sometimes with the people participating directly by means of the initiative and referendum. Aside from certain appropriate activities such as managing foreign relations, the executive function naturally is that of seeing that legislative decisions are carried out through the agencies of administration provided—departments, boards, commissions, and the civil service. And finally the judicial function is not only that of providing machinery and procedures for the settlement of disputes between private individuals, corporations, and the like, but especially that of backing up law-enforcement by providing means for compelling offenders against the law to conform or by bringing them to justice for proved infractions. A few moments' reflection on the essential task of any government will show that there is little or nothing that cannot be brought within one or another of the categories enumerated; and government in general is simply a composite of the three, though with plenty of differences in concepts and arrangements.

Concepts of Government's Functions

Some different schools of thought   In the modern world, there have been many different philosophies of government, springing not only from contrasting ideas on the degree, if any, to which the people should be allowed control, but also from opposing views on the amount of authority that government, however operated, ought to be permitted to exercise over people's affairs. Taking the different quantitative views in ascending order, we encounter first the anarchists, who, regarding government as by nature an instrument of arbitrary coercion, would dispense with it altogether, except in so far as men might voluntarily pool their energies for common protection. Not as much is heard of them as half a century ago, but they are not extinct. Next we find the communists, plentiful in these times, and of many different hues, but, if strictly orthodox, looking ultimately for the day when "political" government will wither away, leaving a classless, stateless world-society liberated from controls save those arising directly out of the new economic order envisaged. Then there are the "rugged individualists," conceding that government is a practical necessity and even useful, but wanting to confine its activities—aimed chiefly at preserving "law and order" and preventing people from injuring one another—largely to those of the policeman and umpire. For the next group, there is hardly an accepted name (perhaps we may call them the "regulationists"); but anyway they look upon government, not negatively as do the individualists, but positively and as a supreme agency of initiative, control, and service—an active, aggressive, expanding, regulating force, ever seeking new ways not only of protecting people, but of advancing their economic, social, and moral well-being. Finally, we have the socialists, agreeing with the foregoing school as far as it goes, but—attributing most of the ills of society to the inequalities of wealth and opportunity characteristic of a capitalistic, competitive order—bent upon doing away with private ownership and control of the instrumentalities for producing and distributing goods and upon installing the state as over-all owner, employer, and manager. The full gamut, therefore, runs all the way from no government control at all to government as a veritable colossus of managerial authority.

Anarchists have never had much of a chance to see their ideas tried in a civilized community; nor are they likely to have. Communists have contrived a few sporadic experiments, although looking upon the present order in the U. S. S. R. and its satellite states as representing only a transitional socialist stage preliminary to full communism later on. Individualists had their day in the eighteenth and earlier nineteenth centuries, when *laissez faire* was the watchword and when in our country the Jeffersonian political philosophy was dominant. Regulationists came into their own after the Industrial Revolution, and moved from triumph to triumph as later economic and social conditions emerged, with the American "New Deal" as one of their topmost achievements. Socialists (who in point of fact differ widely among themselves on the lengths to which they would press the program indicated above, and who in any event will gladly accept half a loaf when more is not to be had) have risen to power in countries here and there—most recently in Great Britain— and have had the added satisfaction of seeing modern governments everywhere adopt policies of public ownership and control identical with theirs, and in increasingly wide fields of action. In any event, the transcending fact is the general tendency toward strong government in a regulative type of state.

The trend toward strong government

Factors in Government's Modern Growth

1. The contribution of inventions

How did government arrive at its present extraordinary importance? In a sense (in the Western world at all events), the development started on a Sunday morning in 1765 when James Watt, strolling across a Scottish golf-field, was observed to break into a mysterious smile. The upshot of that smile was the steam-engine, and after it the remarkable series of inventions and practical applications giving rise to what historians describe as the *technological* revolution. A world of stage-coaches, sailing ships, and hand-looms became, in time, a world of railroads, oil-burning leviathans, telegraphs, telephones, motor-cars, air-planes, submarines, radio, television, and talking-pictures.

2. Effects of increasing socio-economic complexity

These inventions alone would have meant much for government. New instruments were given it with which it could assert authority instantly at any distance, mobilize a nation almost overnight, make war with machine guns, submarines, airplanes, and tanks, and utilize all the processes and techniques of science for whatever purposes it had in hand. From the technological revolution, however, flowed other changes even more momentous. Men could not use the new tools placed in their hands and yet go on living and working as before; and from their adjustments to the situations and opportunities opened up—adjustments known collectively as the *industrial* revolution—sprang a new society. A world of country-dwellers and villagers became a world of teeming urban populations. A world of petty farmers and traders became a world of engineers and machinists, of electricians and aviators, of scientists and technicians, of huge industries and businesses, of professions and crafts undreamt of in any earlier age. And the effect was to open to government not only further avenues to power, but an ever-expanding area of novel obligations, duties, tasks, and challenges.

A hundred years ago, the structure of society, even in the most advanced countries, was relatively simple. In America, it was largely that of a small-farmer, trading population in New England, a planter-slave-holding population in the South, a frontier agricultural population west of the Alleghenies. The growth of numbers, however, together with the impact of railroads, machinery, expanding business, professional organizations, and general mobility of economic life, has in later days produced a social pattern of such intricacy that scholars can spend a lifetime analyzing it without exhausting the problems that it offers. Think for a moment of the social relationships of almost any person of your acquaintance. He has a home and is a member of a family. That alone means much. He belongs to a club or a lodge, perhaps to several. He is a church member, and is affiliated with a political party. There is also his trade union, employers' association, or other professional organization. There are the people to whom he sells, and those from whom he buys. And in most of these directions his tangible and immediate connections are only the initial stages or steps in a ramification of radiating relationships which neither he nor any one else can trace out to their limits. Consider, furthermore, the interrelations, not merely of individuals or of individuals with groups, but of group with group, of interest with interest, which our modern civilization entails—of great businesses and professions, of corporations and trusts, of churches and universities, of philanthropic and propagandist organizations, of federations of labor, of political parties, of other huge social structures, national and international, each competing with or otherwise impinging on the rest. To be sure, most of these relationships are not primarily of a political nature. Yet hardly one of them has failed to be brought within the orbit of public regulation. In the train of steam, electricity, machinery, and science came new industrial procedures needing control, new social relationships calling for adjustment, new forms of crime requiring repression, new activities (like radio-broadcasting) needing regulation—new labors and problems at every turn for legislator, administrator, and judge.

But power gained from inventions and from regulatory authority springing from industrial development still falls short of completely explaining the importance that government now has. Time was when the functions of the state hardly extended beyond police, taxation, diplomacy, and defense. To these were gradually added, under the impetus described, a wide variety of controls applying to industrial production, agriculture, trade, transportation, communications, banking, insurance, and what not; and thus to the police state succeeded the regulatory state. To the regulatory state, however, has now succeeded the *service* state, based on a conception of government as existing not merely to keep the peace and provide defense, nor yet merely (in addition to these things) to order or control economic life in the interest of fairness and opportunity, but to take systematic and continuous measures to promote and protect the education, health, comfort, security, and general well-being of the mass of the people. Implicit in this view of governmental functions are newer ideas of social justice, strongly tinged with humanitarianism; and in pursuance of them we find steadily widening public provision for education on all levels (carried even to such lengths as free lunches for school children), publicly owned and operated utilities, multiplied facilities for public recreation, compulsory sickness and accident insurance, old-age pensions, maternity and child welfare legislation, unemployment insurance—a program of publicly provided protections and benefits pointed up in this country most spectacularly, even though with manifest limitations, in the momentous Social Security Act of 1935. In most of the fields mentioned, private agencies help, but the principal burden falls on government. A major tendency of government in our generation has, indeed, been to become less purely political and more socio-economic.

3. The rise of the service state

Finally, government's expansion to present dimensions has been power-

4. Effects of depression and war

fully accelerated by the devastating effects of economic depression and war. The point need not be elaborated here; abundant illustrations from the experience of the United States will attract attention as we proceed. But the impact upon government of a full generation of perilous world experience—World War I, years of hazardous readjustment, a decade of economic disaster and social distress, another and greater war, and the peculiarly painful and explosive resulting situations amid which we live today—can hardly be over-estimated. Never was government called upon to undertake more than during the past three or four decades; never did it, in an equally brief period, assume more new functions and launch more new ventures.

An irrepressible trend

He would be a bold man, indeed, who would attempt to draw up a list of the functions and powers that governments in these days may exercise, even under normal peacetime conditions. There are, of course, certain purposes which any and all governments serve—certain tasks which any government worthy of the name performs. Such are the raising of revenue, the maintenance of public order, and (in the case of national governments) the management of foreign relations and of arrangements for defense. Beyond this, nothing is fixed or final. Wherever one goes, one finds government doing things that no one a generation ago would have expected of it—nay more, things of which no one a generation ago had even so much as heard. William McKinley had no notion of government regulation of transportation through the air; Theodore Roosevelt hardly dreamed of a government licensing radio stations, prescribing their hours of operation, and fixing their wave-lengths; Herbert Hoover, when in the White House, would hardly have thought it possible that government should tell the farmer how many acres of corn or cotton he might plant. And so it will be in the future. Further technological advances, changing ideas on social and economic subjects, hard experience in a score of directions, will go on bringing into play one new governmental activity after another. To be sure, criticism of this inexorable trend is heard every day. Believers in individualism deplore it; persons who dislike some particular form of regulation, e.g., the anti-trust laws, talk in terms of disapproval of all "centralization"; "big government" is condemned as bureaucratic, wasteful, and destructive of the people's liberties. But nothing is more quickly learned from the history of government in all modern times than that for every form of activity given up, two or three new ones find places in the ever-lengthening list. Ground once occupied by government is rarely surrendered.

Our constant contact with government

Let it then be emphasized that in our coming study of American government—its structure, what it does, how it does it, and the extent to which it controls, and is controlled by, the people it serves—we shall be dealing, not with something remote and theoretical, but with something very real and present—something that surrounds and permeates us even as the air we breathe, and almost as essential to our well-being. Day in and day out, it is government that protects our lives and property, validates and upholds our business dealings, and regulates the conditions under which many of us work. It is government that constructs our highways, builds our school-houses, enfranchises the gas and electric companies and other public utilities that serve us, licenses (or at least permits) us to practice a profession, authorizes us to run our automobiles, keeps us from drinking contaminated water, and protects us from eating impure food. We cannot bring a law-suit, have a deed recorded, inherit an estate, ship a consignment of goods, deposit money in a bank, marry or be divorced—nay, even buy a package of cigarettes—without dealing with government or complying with regulations which government has laid down. Government meets us at birth and records our arrival; government follows us to the end of the journey and issues the permit for our burial; government, indeed, is not content until it has seen such possessions as we leave behind us disposed of in accordance with rules which it has laid down.

To be sure, there is nothing, except perhaps the weather, which people are more prone to complain of than government. It is of the very essence of government to regulate, to restrain, to control, to *govern*. But it is human nature to dislike being regulated; to resent being told that one may not park one's car at some especially convenient spot; that one may not put up an apartment house at some location promising uncommon profits; that one must pay some new tax. Of course it is all right to find that the city council will not allow cars to be parked so that one cannot get into one's own drive-way; that the health department is quarantining a house where there is a contagious disease; that a policeman has risked his life to prevent a bank robbery. Moreover, let calamity befall—an epidemic, a fire, a flood, a drought, a riot, a depression—and the first thing that the average person does is to call upon government to come to his protection or relief. And if the country is assaulted by a foreign foe, as when Japan loosed her attack at Pearl Harbor in December, 1941, he realizes that government alone can mobilize and direct the national defense. Indeed, if he thinks about the matter at all, he perceives that, in one way or another—in fact, in many ways at one and the same time—he not only needs, but is completely dependent upon, services which government alone can render. Sometimes, in truth, people show an almost childlike faith in the ability of government to work miracles.

And our dependence upon it

Forms of Government—Democracy

Throughout the centuries, government has taken many forms, ranging from the autocracies of ancient Egypt and Babylonia (and of recent Nazi Germany and Fascist Italy) to the direct democracies of certain present-day Swiss cantons; and a twentieth-century Aristotle seeking to classify the scores of governments now extant or emerging would have a difficult task indeed. Everywhere except in Great Britain, a written constitution undertakes to outline governmental structure, distribute functions, and

Substance more important than form

in some degree define the relations between government and people. Yet of the realities of a governmental system, a constitution often tells little; and in any case, as illustrated by the "crowned republic" of Great Britain, and the ostensibly democratic institutions of Soviet Russia, forms and mechanisms frequently are the matters of least significance. What one really wants to know about a government in these days is not whether there is a monarchy or a republic, a federal or a unitary form of organization, a cabinet or a presidential system (important as these things are), but the extent and nature of popular control—in other words, how *democratic* the system is; and even though various totalitarian régimes throughout the world have lately been beaten down by defeat in war and are being superseded, this is a test that not all governments (particularly those of Russia and Russian-controlled states) can as yet meet. Moreover, the spirit of fascism is still abroad in the world; that of subversive communism too; and even sober people in apparently well-entrenched democracies, impressed by the growing extent to which government in this technological age must deal with matters which the general run of men can know little or nothing about, are wondering whether political forms and methods will not in future have to be reshaped so as to give more weight to expertness and less to popular control. One may confidently believe that full scope for expertness is not incompatible with over-all control of policy by the people—provided the people do not insist upon choosing the experts. But in any case democratic institutions and processes are not so securely established, even in countries like the United States and Great Britain, that public apathy about preserving them can safely be risked.

What is democracy?
  People sometimes use the term "democracy" with only a shallow conception of what it really means. Properly understood, it denotes not simply a form of government under which many are allowed to vote, but—quite beyond that—a general scheme or manner of thought and life. Implicit in it are such concepts as the dignity and worth of the individual, the equality of all men (not in capacity and condition, but in title to respect as human beings), the right to freedom of person, of thought, and of action except as restricted in the common interest by laws bearing alike upon all. Democracy is therefore at bottom a matter of moral values and relationships, with broad social, intellectual, and economic, as well as political, implications; and achievement of it on political lines, as perhaps a necessary prerequisite, has in most countries—certainly in the United States—been followed by efforts to attain it more completely on the levels of social amenity, intellectual tolerance, economic opportunity, and industrial coöperation. The democracy with which we are principally concerned in this book is, however, political; and, as influenced heavily from abroad yet developed mainly by ourselves to meet our own conditions, needs, and ideals, it has a content that will readily become apparent as we proceed. To begin with, all political power is regarded as residing ultimately in the people, who indeed necessarily delegate much of it to

governments which they create, but who also fix, in fundamental laws, or constitutions, the general conditions under which power may be exercised. In line with this basic popular sovereignty, substantially all adult citizens—both men and women—are at least potential voters. The great policy-framing agencies of government—the federal Congress and president, the state legislatures, and even county boards and municipal councils—are elective. Opportunity to seek election is wide open, and elections are regulated and guarded to insure fairness and honesty. Quite rightly, multitudes of executive and administrative, and some judicial, officials are not popularly chosen; but in the case of at least the more important ones, the authorities (president, governor, mayor, and the like) who appoint them have themselves been placed in power by the people, to whom they are responsible. Further, the people have rights and freedoms (long lists of them) which no government may deny or violate—as well as duties and obligations also, since citizenship in a democracy is no one-way street but something to be earned and paid for in terms of attention, loyalty, and service. All these and other features of our American democracy will be described in later chapters. As we shall see, in practice they have their limitations and raise plenty of problems. Taken together, however, they yield us a political order at once strong and liberal, and enable us to hold our place as the world's most powerful bulwark of freedom.

Why Study Government?

The last thirty or forty years have seen, in this country, a significant increase of popular interest in government and a great growth of systematic study of its history, workings, and problems. National, regional, and local organizations devoted to such study steadily grow more numerous; serious literature on different aspects of the subject pours from the presses, and journals serving various segments of the field multiply; municipal, university, and other research bureaus take their places in an ever-lengthening list; college and university departments of "political science" offer more and more courses to more and more students. Why the effort? Why study government? In particular, why study it in college? Reasons of many sorts might be offered, but for present purposes four must serve, and briefly. (1) In the first place, as emphasized above, government envelops, serves, and controls us all; no one of us can escape having his life largely molded by it; and it would seem the part of prudence to know as much as we can about it. (2) As citizens of a democracy, we have the high privilege of helping determine what kind of government we shall have, who shall frame public policies on the various levels, and even what those policies shall be; and to do these things intelligently, we need the clearest possible insight, not merely into current candidacies and issues, but into the entire governing process and the principles and conditions underlying it. (3) Up to now, man has been a good deal more success-

Four major reasons

ful in harnessing the forces of nature than in controlling human relations; the loosing of the atomic bomb, on the one hand, and the sorry spectacle presented by a postwar world groping precariously for security, on the other, are dramatic illustrations of a social and political lag frightful to contemplate. Yet if the gap is ever closed, it will have to be through instrumentalities provided or operated by government; and the moral is clear that people who hope to see government achieve this crowning triumph cannot know too much about political processes and modes of influencing and expediting them. (4) On all levels of government, people get honesty, efficiency, economy, and service in proportion to the civic interest and intelligence that they display—the first requisite of a successful democracy being an alert and informed body politic. Not all citizens have the education or the time to follow public affairs in more than a very broad and general way. Efforts of even this limited sort are not to be discounted; the instincts of the great mass of relatively uninformed voters are frequently sound. But the body politic must also be heavily leavened with people who have seriously pondered and weighed the processes and problems of government, and who, moreover, can supply a liberal share of the leadership required for carrying democracy toward its goals. Upon none does obligation at these points more obviously rest than upon the youth coming up through our colleges and universities—youth to whom, preëminently, will be presented the challenges of an unfolding future.

REFERENCES

M. E. Dimock, *Modern Politics and Administration; A Study of the Creative State* (New York, 1937), Chaps. I-IV, VII.

J. A. Corry, *Elements of Democratic Government* (New York, 1947), Chaps. I, III.

C. A. Beard [ed.], *Whither Mankind?* (New York, 1928), Chap. VI.

————, *The Economic Basis of Politics* (rev. ed., New York, 1945).

C. A. and M. R. Beard, *The American Spirit; A Study of the Idea of Civilization in the United States* (New York, 1942).

E. M. Sait, *Political Institutions: A Preface* (New York, 1938).

M. C. Swabey, *Theory of the Democratic State* (Cambridge, Mass., 1937).

E. S. Griffith, *The Modern Government in Action* (New York, 1942).

A. N. Holcombe, *Government in a Planned Democracy* (New York, 1935).

C. E. Merriam, *Political Power; Its Composition and Incidence* (New York, 1934).

————, *The New Democracy and the New Despotism* (New York, 1939).

————, *On the Agenda of Democracy* (Cambridge, Mass., 1941).

————, "The Assumptions of Democracy," *Polit. Sci. Quar.*, LIII, 328-349 (Sept., 1938).

C. Becker, *Modern Democracy* (New Haven, 1941).

D. Bryn-Jones, *Toward a Democratic New Order* (Minneapolis, 1945).

R. H. Gabriel, *The Course of American Democratic Thought* (New York, 1940).

S. K. Padover [ed.], *Thomas Jefferson on Democracy* (New York, 1946). Selections from Jefferson's writings.

E. E. Robinson, *The New United States* (Stanford Univ., 1946).

L. D. White, *The Future of the Government of the United States* (Chicago, 1942).

R. S. Woodward, *You Are the Government* (New York, 1945).

H. J. Laski, *Where Do We Go From Here?* (New York, 1940).

S. McK. and L. R. Rosen, *Technology and Society* (New York, 1941).

PART I

THE FOUNDATIONS OF GOVERNMENT IN THE UNITED STATES

1. THE CONSTITUTIONAL BASIS

CHAPTER II

OUR FIRST STATE AND NATIONAL GOVERNMENTS

Colonial and Revolutionary Backgrounds

Organized government in this country reaches far into the past. The national government, centering in Washington, is now in the latter half of its second century. Several of the state governments—based upon colonial governments established two or three hundred years ago—are even older. The county dates from 1634 in Virginia and 1643 in Massachusetts; and New York became the first chartered municipality as long ago as 1686.[1] In its characteristic New England form, the town, or township, existed practically from the date of the first settlement on Massachusetts Bay. More than this: American political institutions have a rich European background. County, borough, parish; popular election and representative legislature; limited executive and the common law; jury trial, *habeas corpus*, the right of petition and of assembly—all were carried to our shores from across seas, being rooted in the England of the Bill of Rights, of *Magna Carta*, and even of Norman-Angevin administration.[2]

English and colonial origins of American political institutions

The first governments on American soil which have any bearing on our present subject of study were those of the thirteen colonies; although they are of concern only as paving the way for the later state governments, and as sources of influence on the shaping of national constitutions—first the Articles of Confederation, and afterwards the basic instrument of government under which we live today. Established under widely varying conditions, by dissimilar groups of people, and at intervals covering more than a century and a quarter, the colonies naturally started off with a considerable variety of political arrangements. Except with respect to the areas and agencies of purely local government, there was, however, as time went on, a tendency toward substantial uniformity.

The governments of the thirteen colonies

[1] In fact 1652, if a Dutch charter is counted.
[2] This phase of our national development is treated fully in E. P. Cheyney, *The European Background of American History, 1300-1600* (New York, 1904).

11

Every colony except Rhode Island, Connecticut, Maryland, Pennsylvania, and Delaware ultimately became a "royal province," administered by a governor appointed by the king; and even the five enumerated eventually acquired charters providing for governments in most respects like the others. All had legislatures, which steadily strove, with varying success, to gain more power. All had the same common law, and practically the same judicial organization and procedure.

Colonial autonomy

In theory, the colonies were controlled in all important matters from the mother country. Three thousand miles of salt water, however, separated the settlements from the English seat of authority, and even if there had been any colonial office, or similar integrated establishment, charged with enforcing the king's prerogatives, the exigencies of life in a frontier world, combined with eighteenth-century conditions of communication, would have frustrated anything approaching continuous and effective overseas control. As it was, the colonists early grew accustomed to doing pretty much as they pleased. They made their own laws, and paid little attention to the few regulations—relating chiefly to trade—which Parliament sought to impose; they paid no taxes to the home government; and, except in times of emergency, they looked after their own defense.

Attempts at firmer control lead to independence

After the French and Indian War, the ministers of George III felt that the time had come to tighten the reins, and it was decided not only to enforce various long-evaded commercial regulations, but also to station British regulars in the colonies, as part of a permanent system of imperial defense, and to ask the colonists to pay taxes to help meet the costs entailed. From the English point of view, this was a reasonable plan. But the colonists did not like it. Now that the French power had been broken, they anticipated no more need for military assistance; they disliked the idea of paying taxes not voted by their own chosen representatives; they resented the effort to restrict their commerce to the closed system of the Empire; they recognized no sovereignty except that of the Crown, and totally rejected the notion that Parliament had any general right of legislation over them such as it enjoyed in the mother country. Inadequately informed on the state of mind prevailing in the dependencies, the king's government went ahead with its plans, and when halted by unexpected opposition, merely tried different methods (meanwhile meeting disobedience with reprisals) without abandoning the general policy. The upshot was a series of events—familiar to every American schoolboy—which steadily widened the breach until, in April, 1775, debate gave way to action. From the ministers' ill-advised decisions flowed the Revolutionary War, the independence of the thirteen colonies, and the establishment of a new trans-Atlantic English-speaking nation.

The aristocracy and the "people"

We are prone to think of the Revolution as simply a contest for independence from Great Britain. But it was a great deal more than that. Once started, it brought into view sharp cleavages within the colonies themselves between the well-to-do and privileged on the one hand and the "people"—the unenfranchised small freehold farmers, tenants, artisans, and laborers—on the other; and the new pattern of politics to which it gave rise proved almost as significant as the fact of independence itself. Government in the mother country was in those days far from democratic; and in the new world, despite the leveling effects of frontier life, it was hardly more so. Every one of the thirteen, on the eve of the Revolution, had a property qualification for voting. In five, ownership of personal property sufficed; but in seven, no one could vote unless he owned real estate. In various instances, there were also moral, religious, and racial qualifications. Office-holders were required to meet property and other tests, and legislatures were hedged about with restrictions. Altogether, the people, taken in the mass, certainly did not rule.

When the Revolution came on, many of the more educated and privileged (clergymen, officials, landowners, merchants) who had joined in protest against the imperial policies nevertheless remained loyal to the mother country; indeed, if these elements had been able to keep the upper hand, there would have been no armed revolt, and no separation, at all. Sooner or later, however, they lost their grip in all of the colonies; and the movement which they had helped to launch was carried forward by other men, on lines that led not only to independent nationality, but to the infusion of new elements of democracy into the existing social and political order.

Some of these later leaders were, to be sure, men of means and of conservative temper; one thinks instantly of Washington, reputed the richest man in the colonies. In the main, however, they and their supporters were people owning little property and having but limited business experience, with only here and there a figure of the type of Jefferson, who, although a plantation-owner and slaveholder, was inclined to a broad liberalism in politics. They were, in general, people who risked little by change; the chances were that they would gain something from it, both socially and politically. They did not stop with arguments for constitutional rights as colonists, or even for independence. Drawing upon the great streams of English liberal thought in the seventeenth century—especially as they flowed together in the pages of John Locke— they turned their minds to what they conceived to be the general and universal rights of man, and to reconstructing government and politics in America in accordance with such rights. *Political liberalism in the saddle*

Many, indeed, advanced to the conclusion that government is hardly better than a necessary evil. Life and property must be protected; social order must be maintained. But this, many considered, was about as far as government ought to be permitted to go. Better run the risk of occasional riots and other disturbances than have too much government. The oft-quoted remark of Jefferson that that government is best which governs least expresses the idea that underlay, not only the Declaration *Dislike of too much government* of Independence, but the early constitutions of the states as well; and it is no cause for surprise that, motivated by such a philosophy, the makers of our first national constitution, the Articles of Confederation, planned a system which, when put to a test, quickly broke down. Bitter experience showed that the revulsion against governmental authority had gone too far.

The Revolutionary State Constitutions

Origins   After war broke out, in 1775, many royal governors and other officials left the country, and in one colony after another control of affairs passed into the hands of rump legislatures, specially chosen "conventions," and other more or less irregular bodies. Under these circumstances, the Continental Congress—even before independence was declared—advised that each colony reconstruct its own government on lines believed most likely to meet its particular needs. More than a hundred years previously, Connecticut and Rhode Island had obtained exceptionally liberal charters, and they now found it necessary to make only a few minor changes in order to adapt these to the new situation. But other colonies—or *states*, as they were now beginning to be called—required something more; and, by one means or another, all of these framed and adopted new fundamental laws, or constitutions, Massachusetts closing the list in 1780. Some of the new instruments were drawn up by assemblies chosen solely, or at any rate mainly, for this specific purpose. Most of them, however, were made and put into operation by bodies selected rather for the general management of affairs; and in only two states—Massachusetts and New Hampshire—were they the handiwork of conventions which confined their labors to this one task. In half a dozen states, the new constitutions were submitted to a popular vote, though in only two—again Massachusetts and New Hampshire—was final adoption made dependent upon ratification in this manner.[1] Notwithstanding that they thus were brought into being by rather undemocratic, and even irregular, procedures, the majority served their purpose, with few changes or none, for as long as fifty or seventy-five years. Massachusetts, indeed, did not give her original constitution a general overhauling until 1917-18.

General features   Although differing widely in detail, these Revolutionary state constitutions, and the governments organized under them, had many important features in common. First, the people were proclaimed to be the sole source of authority: the rule of the king was gone; sovereignty had passed to the politically organized populations of the states. Second, the new governments had only such powers as were expressly bestowed upon them, or at all events were not prohibited to them by the constitutions under which they operated. And since it was considered that government, by its very nature, tends to become oppressive, powers were conferred sparingly,

---

[1] In the case of New Hampshire, the constitution of 1784 is meant—not the provisional instrument of 1776.

and with means provided by which misuse of them could be prevented or punished.

Third, for what was then believed to be the better protection of the people's liberties, the powers conferred were deliberately divided among three separate and coördinate departments or branches of government— executive, legislative, and judicial. Distinct, however, as these branches were to be, they were not to function in water-tight compartments. Over against the principle of separation of powers was set that of "checks and balances"; and so vigorously was it brought into play that each branch of government, far from being allowed full freedom of action, was tied up with the others and made liable to restraint by them at many different points. Particularly was this true of the relations between the executive and legislative branches. *Separation of powers; checks and balances*

Another significant feature of the constitutions was the prominence given to guarantees of civil rights and liberties. Several states prefixed "bills of rights" to their constitutions, and in all cases it was made plain that the individuals composing the sovereign people had rights—freedom of speech and of assembly, trial by jury, *habeas corpus*, etc.—which every agency of government must at all times respect. Many of these rights were embedded firmly in the common law brought over from England. But most of the states thought it worth while to reënforce this safeguard by full enumeration also in their written constitutions. *Civil rights*

Finally, notwithstanding a steady growth of liberal opinion, the doctrine of popular sovereignty was not construed to imply full political democracy. On the contrary, it was still thought best to restrict the suffrage to men having some material stake in the community—practically, therefore, to property-holders. A property qualification for voting was adopted in every state except Vermont, and in most instances it operated to debar more than half of the adult male population. High property qualifications were set up also for membership in legislatures, and for office-holding generally. *Limitations upon democracy*

Early State Governments

The governments under the new constitutions rested on a basis different from that of the previous colonial governments, and often were actuated by a different spirit. Structurally, however, they showed little change. In every case there continued to be a governor, a legislature, a system of courts, and appropriate machinery for local administration.

Under the colonial régime, the governor, although somewhat differently situated in various types of colonies, had always been the outstanding political figure. In practice, to be sure, his prerogatives were sometimes not as impressive as they looked on paper; instructions from London often left him little leeway, and the power of the purse as wielded by the legislature sometimes placed him at grave disadvantage. As a rule, however, he had sufficient authority to cause him to be regarded as an *1. The governor* autocrat; and it is not to be wondered at that when, after 1776, the colonists came into a position to institute governmental systems constructed according to their own ideas, one of the first things that they did was to strip the governor of the greater part of his powers. In many instances, indeed, he was deliberately subordinated to the legislature, being, in fact, elected by that body in all except four states,[1] where he was chosen by the people. In ten states, his term of office was restricted to a single year. In Massachusetts alone did he retain an independent veto power; although before 1800 four other states put this weapon back in his hands.[2] Everywhere the appointing power was shared with a council or with the assembly.

2. The legislature   On the other hand, the legislature, as a body standing close to the people, was endowed with rather extensive authority. From the opening of the eighteenth century, every colony had an elective assembly, variously termed "house of burgesses," "house of commons," or "house of representatives"; and in all except three instances this assembly formed the lower branch of a legislature whose upper chamber was the governor's council. Pennsylvania adhered until 1790 to the unicameral form of legislative organization inherited from colonial days; and Georgia, adopting that form in her new state constitution of 1777, kept it until 1789.[3] Elsewhere, when the colonies became states the bicameral plan continued, with no important change except that the governor's council, in becoming a senate, became also popularly elective. Elections to the lower house were annual except in South Carolina, where they were biennial; and existing local-government areas were employed as electoral districts, subject to occasional reapportionment of seats in accordance with changes of population. In New England, the town was—as it still is, except in Massachusetts—the unit of representation; elsewhere, the county was employed.

3. The judiciary   Patterned closely after the English system, arrangements for the administration of justice were substantially the same in all of the colonies, and were carried over into the states with relatively little change. There were commonly three grades of tribunals. At the bottom stood the justices of the peace, named as a rule by the governor (although in some instances elected by the freeholders), with individual jurisdiction extending only to petty offenses and to civil cases involving small amounts. Above these stood the county court, or court of quarter sessions, consisting of the justices in each county sitting together, with criminal jurisdiction over all except capital cases, and jurisdiction over civil cases involving varying, but relatively large, sums. At the top stood a court of appeals, which, in

---

[1] New Hampshire, Vermont, Massachusetts, and New York.

[2] In Massachusetts, measures could be passed over the governor's veto by a two-thirds vote in both houses of the legislature. In New York, the veto power was shared by the governor and council, and a veto could be similarly overridden in the legislature.

[3] Vermont entered the Union in 1791 with a unicameral legislature, which it retained until 1836. The state's experience with the system is analyzed in D. B Carroll, *The Unicameral Legislature of Vermont* (Montpelier, Vt.. 1933).

colonial days, consisted commonly of the governor and council, but which, after the colonies attained statehood, gradually came to be a specially chosen group of judges similar to our present supreme courts. All of the colonial courts recognized and enforced not only colonial statutes, but the common law and such acts of Parliament as had been made to apply to America; and English judicial procedure, including trial by jury, was universally adhered to. In most cases, the severing of connection with England made necessary some new arrangement for the selection of judges. Some states, *e.g.*, Rhode Island, New Jersey, Virginia, and the Carolinas, introduced election by the legislature; an almost equal number, *e.g.*, Massachusetts, New York, Pennsylvania, and Maryland adopted appointment by the governor, with or without confirmation by the council or the senate. Only in later times did the state judiciary become generally elective, as it is today.[1]

4. Local government

With even less change than in the higher levels of government, colonial areas and institutions of local government and administration were perpetuated in the new states. These areas and institutions were, in turn, based largely upon those familiar in England. However, conditions of life in a frontier world made it necessary to improvise a good many novel features. Furthermore, physical surroundings differed from colony to colony, and more diversity arose in local government than in other parts of the political system.

The New England town

Devoted to small-farming and to trade, needing protection against Indian attacks, and desiring to remain in close fellowship with the religious congregations to which they belonged, the people of New England settled in compact communities, and therefore had as their main unit of local government the town; counties existed, but served only minor purposes. To be sure, the New England town was not necessarily, nor even usually, an "urban" center. Rather, it was what Middle Westerners of later days would have called a "township"—often entirely rural, although likely to contain at least a village. At all events, it was small, and its people could come together easily and frequently for worship, for social intercourse, and for political action. The governing authority was a primary assembly of voters known as the town-meeting, which convened at least once a year and made by-laws on various matters, levied taxes, voted appropriations, and elected not only the town's representative (or representatives) in the colonial assembly, but also officers—chiefly a board

---

[1] One of the principal contributions of these early state courts was the practice of judicial review. In no one of the state constitutions was the power expressly conferred; but as early as 1780 certain of the courts began inquiring into the constitutionality of statutes and refusing to enforce any found deficient. The right to do this was challenged, but the judges stood their ground; and judicial review, as a device for keeping legislatures within the bounds supposed to have been fixed for them, developed into a major feature of the American governmental system. See pp. 57-58 and 540-546 below, and E. S. Corwin, "The Establishment of Judicial Review," *Mich. Law Rev.*, IX, 102-125, 283-316 (Dec., 1910, and Feb., 1911). Cf. D. O. McGovney, "The British Origin of Judicial Review of Legislation," *Univ. of Pa. Law Rev.*, XCIII, 1-49 (Sept., 1944).

of "selectmen"—to manage the town's affairs during the ensuing twelve months. As a rule, these little governments went along with no interference from the colonial and English authorities, and the experience which the people gained in looking after their community interests, even though within modest limits, was of inestimable value in the era of self-government on higher levels ushered in by the Revolution.

The county In the Southern colonies, the situation was different. The plantation system there prevailing caused the population to be scattered thinly over wide areas, with the result that the county, rather than the town, became the principal local-government unit. Broadly, the county was organized like its prototype in the mother country. There was no popular assembly, and most of the officers—lieutenant, sheriff, coroner, and justices of the peace—were appointed by the governor, commonly on nomination by the justices, who, as at that time in England, were administrative as well as judicial authorities. In the Middle colonies, a mixed system of town and county government grew up, although after 1688 the town was gradually overshadowed by the county, especially in Pennsylvania.

The Beginnings of National Government

The Continental Congress Scattered along a seaboard almost 1,300 miles in length, the colonies developed little machinery for coöperative action until forced to do so by the widening breach with the mother country. To consider measures required by the new situation, a body of delegates, known in history as the First Continental Congress, held sessions in Philadelphia in the autumn of 1774; and a second Congress, meeting in the same city in May, 1775, although later moving from place to place as the exigencies of war required, served as the country's sole organ of national government until March, 1781.

Need for a stronger government Without some such unifying authority as the Continental Congress, the war for independence could never have been carried to a successful conclusion. As an agency of government, however, the Congress left much to be desired. Starting as only a voluntary intercolonial conference, it remained to the end a revolutionary assembly, resting on no basis of law and exercising powers only by virtue of having assumed them with the tacit consent of the governments and peoples of the states. To meet a temporary emergency, makeshift arrangements such as these might possibly have served. But the war gave promise of lasting many dreary years; if successful, it would leave the country confronted with the problem of a permanent national government; and in any event, finance, commerce, and foreign relations, to say nothing of military and naval operations, called for management at the hands of a government resting on some regular basis, endowed with definite powers, and assured of some degree of permanence. And out of this practical situation arose the idea of a genuine and enduring union of the states under a national constitution— in other words, that concept of American nationality which gradually broadened and deepened until it found expression in the Articles of Confederation, the constitution of 1789, and eventually the vast and complicated mechanism of national authority and management which we know today as the government of the United States.

The Articles of Confederation

On June 7, 1776, Richard Henry Lee, of Virginia, introduced in the Continental Congress his famous resolution declaring the colonies "free and independent states," and at the same time moved the appointment of a committee to draw up "articles of confederation." Scattered proposals looking in these directions had previously attracted little support. By this time, however, Congress had come to a point where it could no longer evade or postpone either issue. Hence on June 11 a committee was appointed to draft a declaration of independence, and on the following day another to draw up a plan for a more substantial union. The result in the one case was the eloquently phrased Declaration of Independence, adopted by the Congress on July 4; in the other, the preparation of the first constitution for a united America, *i.e.*, the Articles of Confederation. The latter instrument, brought forward by the committee on union in the brief space of eight days, was, however, not approved by the Congress until November 15, 1777, and did not secure the endorsement of the last necessary state, *i.e.*, Maryland, until three and one-half years later. When, therefore, it finally went into operation, the war which had called it into being was fast approaching an end.

The Articles drafted and ratified

Under the Articles,[1] the United States at last achieved a government resting on a written constitution and endowed with definite powers—a government which, it must not be forgotten, was considerably superior to the extra-legal Continental Congress, even though it, in turn, proved inadequate and eventually had to be replaced. Three main features characterized it. The first was the continued sovereignty of the states, unequivocally asserted in the document. The states, to be sure, delegated to the national government the right to exercise certain powers and denied certain powers to themselves. But they retained all powers and rights not expressly delegated or prohibited; the union was only a loose confederation, or league; and, notwithstanding that the Articles spoke of it three times as "perpetual," the states plainly regarded themselves as entitled to withdraw if they desired.

Continued sovereignty of the states

A second feature was the concentration of all national powers in a Congress of one house, meeting annually, and composed of delegates appointed in each state in whatever way the legislature thereof should direct. Each state paid its own delegates, and could recall them and appoint others at any time; and no person might serve more than three

The Congress

---

[1] The text of the Articles will be found in many places, *e.g.*, J. M. Mathews and C. A. Berdahl, *Documents and Readings in American Government* (rev. ed., New York, 1940), 27-34.

years out of any six. A state might send any number of delegates from two to seven. But voting was by states, and each state had one vote. Committees might, of course, be set up, and subordinate officers appointed. But there was no executive branch, and also no national judiciary.

Powers
and
limita-
tions

Not only was machinery thus simple, but, in the third place, powers and functions were few and severely restricted. Far from being a general lawmaking authority like our present Congress, the Congress of the Confederation was, in effect, only a grand committee of the states charged with executive and managerial functions, such as looking after foreign relations, declaring and conducting war on land and sea, building and equipping a navy, carrying on dealings with the Indian tribes, borrowing money, issuing bills of credit, regulating weights and measures, and making requisitions upon the states for soldiers and for funds. It could not reach down past the state governments to control the people in any effective way. It could adopt resolutions and issue commands, but it had only limited means of enforcing them—none at all through judicial process except by resort to the courts of the states. And some of the most important powers definitely possessed—for example, fixing the size of the military and naval forces, making treaties, and borrowing money— could be exercised only if the delegations of as many as nine states concurred.

Difficul-
ties en-
coun-
tered:

As has been said, the Articles finally went into effect on March 1, 1781. Momentarily, there was improvement. The new Congress, while not a distinguished body, was superior to its predecessor; and it addressed itself courageously to the performance of its difficult tasks. Notwithstanding some notable achievements, however, inherent defects of the new frame of government quickly produced distressing results. Four main difficulties

1. Lack
of money

appeared. The first was the lack of effective power to raise money, in particular, to tax. The amounts needed would seem small in these days of immense national disbursements, but they were distressingly large for the time. Interest payments on sums borrowed for the prosecution of the war were in arrears; officers and soldiers, who in many cases had received nothing for their services except certificates of indebtedness, were clamoring for their pay; a new army was needed to repel possible British or Spanish attacks and to hold the Indians in check, and a navy to protect commerce from the depredations of the Barbary pirates; the current expenses of the new government must, of course, be provided for.

Obstacles
to obtain-
ing it

Congress had only two ways of obtaining funds, namely, by borrowing and by making requisitions on the states. The possibilities in the first direction had already been pretty well exhausted—although optimistic Dutch bankers continued to extend small loans which quite possibly saved the country from utter bankruptcy. Requisitions upon the states were likewise a hazardous resource. Congress could apportion sums (in proportion to land values in the several states) and request remittances, but it had no way of compelling a state to turn over a penny. There was widespread objection to land values as the basis of apportionment; people disliked sending off the proceeds of local taxation to a distant government; and a state naturally hesitated to meet obligations in full while others were shirking them. The result was that, after a brief period, some states fell into the habit of contributing hardly anything, others paid irregularly, and only two or three—chiefly New York and Pennsylvania—made any genuine effort to come forward with all that was asked of them.

A second main difficulty was the lack of power to control commerce. Congress, to be sure, had authority to regulate trade with the Indian tribes and to conclude treaties of commerce with foreign nations. But it had no power to regulate commerce between the states; it could not lay duties on exports or imports; and it had no means of preventing the states from levying duties, or even prohibiting the exportation or importation of goods, as they severally desired. The consequences were disastrous. No money for national use could be raised from tariff duties; no uniform commercial policy could be adopted; and the states laid duties, granted favors, and set up barriers as their individual interests dictated, sacrificing by their jealousies and bickerings splendid opportunities for advancing the struggling new nation's trade, wealth, and prosperity. Enmeshed in a network of interstate duties and tolls, trade languished; healthy commercial competition gave way to downright commercial warfare. *2. Inability to regulate commerce*

Lack of power to raise money by taxation and to regulate commerce on uniform lines would alone have been enough to insure the failure of the new government. Coupled with these obstacles were, however, two further fundamental weaknesses: (1) the government of the Confederation rested only upon the states and not upon the people, and (2) it was wholly without power to enforce its authority, even upon the states. From the first circumstance flowed many unhappy results, in addition to inability to lay and collect taxes. Congress could not make laws and enforce them upon the people; it could only pass resolutions, advise and admonish the state authorities, and hope that such agencies would give heed. It had no power to raise armed forces independently, even when— as during the Shays rebellion in Massachusetts in 1786—the new order was gravely imperiled. *3. A government of states and not of men*

Equally serious was the lack of power to compel the states to live up to their obligations. Not only did they frequently fail to comply with requisitions for money and for armed forces, but some of them freely violated the Articles by making treaties with Indian tribes, by entering into alliances among themselves without the consent of Congress, by ignoring obligations created by treaties negotiated by Congress, and by seeking to make their issues of paper money legal tender. Congress was powerless to prevent these infractions by military, judicial, or other means; and its moral authority carried little weight. *4. State infractions of the Articles*

Meanwhile, general economic conditions steadily deteriorated. Real money was scarce; paper currency issued by the confederation and by the states was plentiful, but of such doubtful value that prices in terms of it soared to almost incredible heights; depression and inflation are no experiences peculiar to our own time—the American of a hundred and sixty years ago had both; amid hardship and discontent, many short-sighted people clamored for still more borrowing and "cheap" money as aids to "prosperity," as numbers have been known to do in much more recent days.

The Movement for Revision

Revision proposed

Even before the Articles took effect, men who had the country's welfare at heart—among others, Washington, Hamilton, Madison, Jay—felt that a government so devoid of power could not succeed. The most they could hope for was that a brief trial of the plan would convince the people of its futility and lead to the stronger system from which the states as yet drew back. A few years of experience fully vindicated the doubts entertained; and suggestions for an amending convention gradually grew in favor. Every effort to bring about a change by simple agreement having been blocked, Congress itself, in 1784, began to talk about a convention; and in the following year the Massachusetts legislature formally requested that a call be issued, although the state's representatives in Congress refused to present the resolution. Matters were fast going from bad to worse, and in 1786 Congress, in making a final appeal for an oft-proposed amendment conferring power to lay import duties, frankly told the people of the "almost disunited states" that the government was at the end of its tether and that only immediate action could save the country from ruin.

Virginia and Maryland negotiate on the navigation of the Potomac

Meanwhile, a chain of events started which led, somewhat deviously, to the long-talked-about convention. From as far back as 1777, Virginia and Maryland had been trying to arrive at an understanding concerning the navigation of the Potomac river, forming their common boundary. Washington and Madison were especially interested in the matter, and at their instigation Virginia appointed commissioners in 1784 to renew the negotiations. Maryland took similar action in 1785, and at length, in a conference held at Washington's Mt. Vernon home, the desired agreement was reached. The Maryland legislature thereupon suggested that other issues between the two states be taken up. If navigation questions could be settled by conference, why not tariff difficulties? Furthermore, if two states could advantageously confer, why not four—especially in view of the fact that Pennsylvania and Delaware were vitally concerned with some of the problems to be considered? The upshot was that, early in 1786, Madison piloted through the Virginia legislature a resolution appointing commissioners to meet such representatives as might be named by any other states to survey the trade of the country and "to consider how far a uniform system in their [the states'] commercial regulations may be necessary to their permanent harmony." A formal invitation was thereupon issued to all of the states to send as many delegates as they might desire to a convention to be held at Annapolis in the following September.

At the designated time, representatives appeared from only five states. Four others had, indeed, appointed delegates, who failed to attend; four had taken no action at all. This was a discouraging showing, and the persons present agreed that it would not be worth while to go ahead with the contemplated discussions. Some felt that the project might as well be dropped. Madison and Hamilton, however, thought otherwise; and before disbanding, the delegates unanimously adopted a report prepared by the latter calling attention afresh to the critical situation of the country and proposing that delegates from all of the states meet at Philadelphia [1] on the second Monday of May, 1787. The purpose in mind, furthermore, was no longer merely to promote agreement on commercial regulations. Rather, the gathering was "to take into consideration the situation of the United States," with a view to recommending to Congress changes in the Articles sufficient to make them genuinely effective. How sweeping such changes would probably have to be, the authors of the proposal discreetly refrained from saying.

The Annapolis convention (1786)

By this time, Congress was grasping at straws, and on February 21, 1787, it resolved that the proposed convention should be held "for the sole and express purpose of revising the Articles of Confederation, and reporting to Congress and the several legislatures such alterations and provisions therein as shall, when agreed to in Congress and confirmed by the states,[2] render the federal constitution adequate to the exigencies of government and the preservation of the Union." Congress had itself fallen into disrepute. But the activities of Washington, Madison, Hamilton, Franklin, and others in behalf of the plan gave it weight, and all of the states except Rhode Island eventually followed Virginia's example and named delegates, although New Hampshire failed to act until the convention was well under way. In some cases, the legislature elected, in others it authorized the governor to appoint; in no instance were the delegates chosen directly by the people. Little or nothing was said about making a new constitution. The instructions given the delegates plainly assumed that nothing would be done beyond revising the Articles; indeed, in most instances they expressly limited the delegates' powers to this one object, and Delaware went so far as to forbid her representatives to agree to any proposal that would take away the equal vote of the states. If any persons expected a new constitution to be made—and probably some did so—they were tactful enough to keep their ideas to themselves, lest apprehensions be aroused and the project ruined. Never-

The Philadelphia convention called

---

[1] Philadelphia, it will be recalled, was the country's "federal city," or capital, under the Articles of Confederation, as also during most of the first decade under the later constitution.

[2] By their own provision, the Articles could be amended only with the consent of *all* of the states, as well as of Congress.

theless, most men must have felt with Madison that unless "some very strong props" were applied, the existing union would "quickly tumble to the ground."

REFERENCES

C. A. and M. R. Beard, *The Rise of American Civilization* (New York, 1927), I, Chaps. II, V.

C. B. Swisher, *American Constitutional Development* (Boston, 1943), Chap. I.

C. Becker, *The Eve of the Revolution* (New Haven, 1918), Chaps. II-IV.

——————, *The Declaration of Independence; A Study in the History of Political Ideas* (New York, 1922).

J. P. Boyd, *The Drafting of the Declaration of Independence* (Princeton, N. J., 1944).

C. M. Andrews, *The Colonial Background of the American Revolution* (2nd ed., New Haven, 1931).

——————, *The Colonial Period of American History*, 4 vols. (New Haven, 1934-38).

C. H. Van Tyne, *The American Revolution* (New York, 1905), Chaps. IX, XI.

C. E. Merriam, *History of American Political Theories* (New York, 1903), Chaps. I-II.

R. G. Gettell, *History of American Political Thought* (New York, 1928), Chaps. III-IV.

J. A. Fairlie and C. M. Kneier, *County Government and Administration* (New York, 1930), Chaps. I-III.

J. Fiske, *The Critical Period of American History* (Boston, 1888), Chaps. III-IV.

A. C. McLaughlin, *A Constitutional History of the United States* (New York, 1935), Chaps. IX-XIII.

——————, *The Confederation and the Constitution* (New York, 1905), Chaps. IV-XI.

H. C. Hockett, *The Constitutional History of the United States* (New York, 1939), I, Chaps. VII-X.

C. Bridenbaugh, *Cities in the Wilderness; The First Century of Urban Life in America, 1625-1742* (New York, 1938).

E. C. Burnett, *The Continental Congress* (New York, 1941).

B. F. Wright, Jr., "The Early History of Written Constitutions in America," in C. Wittke [ed.], *Essays in History and Political Theory* (Cambridge, Mass., 1937).

W. C. Webster, "A Comparative Study of the State Constitutions of the American Revolution," *Annals of Amer. Acad. of Polit. and Soc. Sci.*, IX, 64-104 (May, 1897).

R. G. Adams, *The Political Ideas of the American Revolution* (Durham, N. C., 1922).

C. H. McIlwain, *The American Revolution; A Constitutional Interpretation* (New York, 1923).

J. F. Jameson, *The American Revolution Considered as a Social Movement* (Princeton, N. J., 1926).

A. Nevins, *The American States During and After the Revolution, 1775-1789* (New York, 1924).

E. B. Greene, *The Provincial Governor in the English Colonies of North America* (New York, 1898).

——————, *The Revolutionary Generation, 1763-1790* (New York, 1943).

M. Jensen, *The Articles of Confederation; An Interpretation of the Social and Constitutional History of the American Revolution, 1774-1781* (Madison, Wis., 1940)

CHAPTER III

MAKING AND ADOPTING THE NATIONAL CONSTITUTION

The convention was announced to meet on the second Monday of May. When that day arrived, however, only a few delegates had reached Philadelphia; and since it was useless to start until a majority of the states were represented, the opening session did not take place until May 25. Though characterized by Jefferson as "an assembly of demigods," the convention naturally contained men of widely differing temperaments, abilities, and aptitudes. There were members of great personal force and political sagacity: Washington and Madison of Virginia, Franklin and Wilson of Pennsylvania, Alexander Hamilton of New York, John Dickinson of Delaware.[1] There were delegates of fair, but not exceptional, ability: Rufus King of Massachusetts, Roger Sherman and Oliver Ellsworth of Connecticut, Gouverneur Morris of Pennsylvania, William Paterson of New Jersey, George Mason and Edmund Randolph of Virginia, John Rutledge and Charles Pinckney of South Carolina. And there were a few members of narrow vision and limited talent, except perhaps as politicians: Lansing and Yates of New York, Elbridge Gerry of Massachusetts, and Luther Martin of Maryland. Lawyers predominated; and several of the delegates were reasonably well acquainted not only with the history of English law and politics, but with the governmental systems of Continental Europe. About half were college graduates. Practically all had been active in the government and politics of their respective states. Many had helped frame constitutions, sat as members of legislatures, or held executive or judicial office. Half had been members of Congress. Men of age and maturity were included, notably Franklin, who was almost eighty-two. But a large proportion of the most active and influential delegates were comparatively young: Madison, the master-builder, was thirty-six, Gouverneur Morris thirty-five, Hamilton thirty, Charles Pinckney twenty-nine.

Furthermore, the men who now held the country's political destinies in their hands were not, in the main, those who had led in bringing on the Revolution and in declaring independence. In general, they were a more conservative and cautious group. Patrick Henry "smelt a rat," and refused to attend. John Hancock was not there; nor were Richard Henry Lee, Samuel Adams, and Thomas Paine. Almost to a man, the delegates were drawn from the professional and propertied classes, chiefly in the

___

[1] Jefferson was on a diplomatic mission in Europe; otherwise he undoubtedly would have been a member. The same is true of John Adams of Massachusetts.

25

seaboard towns where such wealth as existed was largely concentrated. Forty of the fifty-five who actually attended owned public securities; fourteen or more had acquired land for speculative purposes; twenty-four were loaning money at interest; eleven had mercantile, manufacturing, or shipping connections; fifteen were slave-owners. Not one represented, in his immediate personal economic interest, the debtor, small-farming, or wage-earning class. Few were as conservative as Hamilton, who wanted to see a highly centralized and definitely aristocratic political system set up. But few, also, were democrats in the sense in which that term is nowadays understood. Plenty of disagreements were bound to arise, once the delegates had started their discussions. Upon the objective chiefly to be aimed at, however, there was, first and last, little difference of opinion —namely, a government of sufficient strength to withstand agrarian-debtor agitation, preserve social order, and keep the country on an even keel. And it is not to be wondered at that a constitution coming from a group thus inclined (although, to be sure, providing for a more truly popular plan of government than could at that time have been found in any other important country of the world) should have been devised deliberately—by means of checks and balances, indirect elections, tolerant acceptance of the suffrage restrictions of the states, presidential veto, and the implicit principle of judicial review—to keep the restless forces of democracy from capturing control of affairs.[1]

Organi-
zation
and pro-
cedure

The convention's sessions were held in the old brick State House in Philadelphia, probably in a room directly above that in which the Declaration of Independence was signed. Seventy-four delegates, in all, were appointed,[2] but only fifty-five ever attended; of these, some were present only part of the time, and the average attendance seems not to have exceeded thirty. At the opening meeting, Washington was unanimously chosen to preside; and this prevented him from taking an active part in

---

[1] The members of the convention are characterized briefly, one by one, in M. Farrand, *The Framing of the Constitution* (New Haven, 1913), Chap. II; and the correlation between their economic interests and their political ideas and aims is discussed illuminatingly in C. A. Beard, *An Economic Interpretation of the Constitution of the United States* (new ed., New York, 1935), 74-149, 189-216, although with rather too much emphasis, considering that the Declaration of Independence —a more radical document than the constitution—had also been the work largely of men of means. A somewhat facetious "Who's Who" of the members of the convention, written by one of the delegates—William Pierce of Georgia—is reprinted in J. Butzner [comp.], *Constitutional Chaff* (New York, 1941), and in *Amer. Hist. Rev.*, III, 310-334 (Jan., 1898); and a good deal of information about them (including their careers subsequent to the convention) will be found in H. Lyon, *The Constitution and the Men Who Made It* (Boston, 1936), espec. Chap. XVII. Viewed from abroad, the constitution as adopted was no doubt, as Professor Merriam has termed it, "one of the most revolutionary documents of its day—a shock to the sense of propriety in the established political and economic order of the time." *The Written Constitution and the Unwritten Attitude*, 1. From the viewpoint of contemporary American radicalism and democracy (such as existed), it was, however, a stabilizing, cautious, conservative instrument; the advocates of cheap money, the spokesmen of the debtor elements, the people who were willing to play fast and loose with the obligations of contracts, had no part in making it. On the "interests" and the convention, see particularly H. Lyon, *op. cit.*, Chap. XII.

[2] From twelve states; Rhode Island was at no time represented.

the debates. Indeed, so far as is known, he addressed the convention only twice, on the opening and closing days. With the possible exception of Franklin, he, however, was less dependent on speech-making than any other delegate. He performed his duties as moderator in a manner to allay strife; in private conversation and informal conference, his opinions and advice were always to be had; and it is doubtful whether, on the whole, any member exerted greater influence.

Having full power to make its own rules, the convention early decided, not only that each state should have one vote, as in the Congress of that day, but that, in order to enable the members to speak freely and plainly and to protect them against outside criticism and pressure, the sittings should be behind closed doors, and that nothing should be put into print or otherwise made public until the work was finished; and this injunction of secrecy was observed with remarkable fidelity. A secretary was appointed, and a journal kept. When, however, in 1819, this official record was printed by order of Congress, in the hope that it would throw light on the way in which various provisions of the constitution then in controversy should be interpreted, it proved to be only a bare and not wholly accurate enumeration of formal motions and of the votes by states.[1] Happily, one of the most vigilant and efficient delegates, sensing the importance of what was being done, planned to keep a record of his own. This was Madison. Fragmentary memoranda were left by a few other members, and something can be learned from letters written by certain delegates to their friends. But what we know today about the convention's discussions, as distinguished from its formal actions, comes mainly from the clear and candid *Notes* laboriously compiled—sometimes to the extent of three or four thousand words a day—by the learned and methodical Virginian.[2]

[1] For the official journal, printed directly from manuscript, see *Documentary History of the Constitution, 1786-1870* (Washington, D. C., 1894-1905), I, 48-308. It may be commented that the convention's work was done largely in committee of the whole, and that its decisions were the product of serious discussions, not of oratory.

[2] This was in addition to his exacting labors as, in effect, convention "floor leader." Madison's papers were purchased by the national government after his death in 1836, and those containing the *Notes* were first published in 1840. Of several editions, the best are: G. Hunt [ed.], *Writings of James Madison* (New York, 1900-10), III-IV, and G. Hunt and J. B. Scott [eds.], *The Debates in the Federal Convention of 1787 Which Framed the Constitution of the United States of America* (Internat. ed., New York, 1920). Professor A. C. McLaughlin has rightly stressed the significant fact that during our first half-century under the constitution, politicians, statesmen, and judges relied for such information as they had about the proceedings at Philadelphia upon sources that were highly fragmentary and sometimes prejudiced. "The great decisions of John Marshall, the speeches of Hayne and Webster, the theories and pronouncements of Calhoun, were all made with nothing like the information that might have been gained had Madison's *Notes* been published." *A Constitutional History of the United States,* 154. The *Notes* and all other contemporary materials relating to the work of the convention are conveniently assembled in M. Farrand [ed.], *The Records of the Federal Convention,* cited on p. 39 below.

The Constitution Framed

The convention's main problem

Deliberations had not gone far before the delegates were brought face to face with a truly challenging question. Should they merely revise the Articles of Confederation, or should they make a new constitution? There was no getting away from the fact that their instructions looked only to revision, or from the suspicion that the proposal for a convention would have failed had the people of the states supposed that anything more drastic would be undertaken. On the other hand, many thoughtful persons agreed with Washington when he confessed the hope that the convention would "adopt no temporizing expedients," but would "probe the defects of the constitution [i.e., the Articles] to the bottom and provide a radical cure, whether they are agreed to or not." Both points of view commanded lively support among the delegates participating, and a plan based on each was quickly presented for consideration.

The Virginia plan

The first scheme to appear came logically from the state that had taken the initiative in causing the convention to be held, i.e., Virginia. Madison was its principal author, although Governor Edmund Randolph presented it; and it embodied the best thought of the convention's ablest student of political, and especially federal, institutions. The plan did not explicitly repudiate the Articles. But it looked to a general reconstruction of the system of government existing under them, and the fiction that a mere revision was intended was soon dropped. A national executive was to be established; also a national judiciary; and, finally, a legislature, with a lower house elected directly by the people and an upper one chosen by the lower from persons nominated by the state legislatures. Thus basically reconstructed in three coördinate branches (after the pattern prevailing in the states), the national government was to have greatly increased powers, among them that of vetoing state legislation when considered contrary to the Articles or to a treaty, and that of calling forth the militia against any member of the union "failing to fulfill its duty." Presented on May 29, in the form of fifteen resolutions, this plan gave the convention something to go to work on forthwith; and for two weeks the delegates, sitting in committee of the whole, discussed it zealously.

The New Jersey plan

One feature of the plan strongly objected to by members particularly sensitive about the "rights" of their states was the proposal to substitute for the existing equal voting power of the states in Congress an arrangement under which, in both branches, voting power should be apportioned in accordance with numbers of free inhabitants or in some similar manner; and to forestall such a change, certain interested members decided to present a counter-plan based on a "purely federal" principle. Cast in the form of nine resolutions, this alternative project was laid before the convention on June 15 by William Paterson of New Jersey. It did not shrink from certain significant changes. For example, it allowed Congress power to raise money from duties on imports and from stamp taxes, and to regulate commerce, and it invested acts of Congress with the character of "supreme law of the respective states." It even envisaged a national executive in the form of a council chosen by Congress, and a national judiciary composed of a "supreme tribunal." Congress, however, was still to consist of but a single house, with all states retaining an equal voice.

The New Jersey plan was advocated ably by Paterson and other members, and it enlisted the support of about half of the states. The introduction of it, indeed, split the convention sharply into two groups, one representing the large states and the other the small states. One wanted political power proportioned to the ability of the states to aid in bearing the public burdens, and was not afraid of a strong national government; the other held that the states, as sovereigns, were equals, and argued that if the small states gave up their existing equal voice in public affairs, they would find themselves ruinously subordinated to their more populous neighbors. Happily, it was not necessary that either group have its way completely. The delegates were, after all, practical-minded patriots, accustomed in their business relations and in their home politics to the saving principle of give and take. They expressed their widely differing views freely, sometimes acrimoniously. But, having done so, most of them were not averse to compromise; and the constitution upon which they finally agreed was, clause after clause, a product of mutual concession. Compromise the only solution

Fortunately, however, the bulk of the delegates were essentially united on matters of decidedly larger significance than those on which they differed, and compromise was resorted to only after certain vital decisions had been reached. The most important of these was to cast aside the Articles and to establish a government resting on a more truly national basis. Some delegates were of the opinion that the instructions given by the states were binding literally, and that if the convention wanted to do more than merely revise the Articles, its members ought to go back to their constituents and ask for appropriate authority. But the majority were, as Randolph later put it, "not scrupulous on the point of power," and felt, as he further testified, that "when the salvation of the republic was at stake it would be treason to our trust not to propose what we found necessary." Within five days after the convention began work, a resolution was adopted in committtee of the whole "that a national government ought to be established consisting of a supreme legislative, executive, and judiciary"; and Madison, Hamilton, and other delegates made it perfectly clear that this meant a government embodying one supreme power, with "complete and compulsive operation." The small-state elements protested, saying at first that they would have no part in such a union; the large-state delegates declared they would accept nothing less. The small-state people, as we have seen, brought forward the New Jersey plan; yet at the final test only three states voted for it. From first to last— sometimes at grave risk of driving the convention on the rocks—the Decision in favor of a strong national government initial determination was wisely adhered to. The time for compromise had not yet come.

From this key decision flowed, also, certain great corollaries: (1) the powers of the national government should be decidedly increased; (2) the machinery of government should be enlarged, as indeed was proposed in all of the plans; (3) the national government, equally with the state governments, should operate directly on the people, through its own laws, administrative officers, and courts; and (4) the new constitution should be "the supreme law of the land," enforceable in the courts like any other law, and paramount over all other constitutions, laws, and official actions, national or state. Mere mention of these points should impress the fact that, while from one point of view a "bundle of compromises," the constitution as it emerged was to a far greater extent a pattern of fundamental, and often almost unanimous, agreement.

A national government resting directly upon the people

Adoption of the third principle, in particular, meant that the national government was to be put on a wholly new basis. Instead of resting almost entirely upon the semi-independent states, and having little control over the people except through the uncertain medium of state authorities, it was thenceforth to be a government of a single body politic, with power to levy and collect taxes and to make and enforce laws by its own direct action. Thereafter, as James Wilson pointed out to the convention, over each citizen there were to be two governments, both "derived from the people," both "meant for the people," and both operating by an independent authority upon the people. This decision, as Madison subsequently explained in a letter to Jefferson, relieved the convention of one of its most delicate problems. If the experience of the Confederation indicated anything, it was that states might fail to live up to their obligations; and every plan thus far presented to the convention had embraced or assumed some arrangement for coercing states proving delinquent. The nature and method of coercion to be authorized would, however, have stirred grave differences of opinion; and members must have been relieved to find that in providing for a national government endowed with power to enforce its authority directly upon *people*, they had—so, at least, it was supposed—made the coercion of *states* unnecessary. Two generations later, the Civil War was prosecuted by President Lincoln and Congress on the theory that the object was to suppress rebellion on the part of individual men and women, not of states; although any one familiar with the policies pursued toward the Southern states and their governments during the era of Reconstruction will not need to be told that, under the stress of party and sectional politics, this theory largely broke down.

The great compromises:

These fundamentals settled, the large-state forces were ready to make concessions; and the first and most notable one related to voting power in Congress. The large states wanted representation and voting power proportioned to population; the small states insisted upon equality in voting; spokesmen of each group threatened more than once to withdraw unless their demands were met. At a very critical point in the proceedings, the delegates from Connecticut—a middle-sized state firmly attached to the idea of a stronger union—brought forward a proposal for equal representation in the upper house, combined with representation in proportion to numbers in the lower house; and after heated debate, the deadlock was broken and the compromise adopted. This eminently sensible disposition of the matter had been casually suggested early in the session and did not originate with the Connecticut delegation; Franklin, indeed, was probably its actual author. Dr. Johnson and his colleagues, however, deserve credit for putting it formally before the convention, with an array of unanswerable arguments; and the agreement has ever since been known as the "Connecticut compromise." It removed the greatest single obstacle to harmony. *1. The "Connecticut compromise"*

The decision in favor of proportioned representation in the lower house, however, made it necessary to determine how population should be computed; and difficulty at this point was produced by the existence of slavery. Should slaves be regarded as persons or as chattels? If the former, they ought to be counted in; if the latter, they ought to be left out. With a view to increasing their quotas in Congress, the Southern states naturally wanted the slaves included; the Northern and Middle states, having few slaves, quite as naturally wanted them disregarded; and much lively discussion ensued. A possible solution was, however, already in men's minds when the convention met. When asking the states for additional funds in 1783, Congress had proposed changing the basis of requisitions from land values to numbers of population, so computed as to include three-fifths of all slaves. This "federal ratio" was early incorporated in the Virginia plan as an amendment; it found a place also in the New Jersey scheme; and, notwithstanding individual differences of opinion, it was ultimately adopted by the convention as being, in the words of Rufus King, "the language of all America." There was no defense for it in logic. But it represented the closest approach to a generally satisfactory arrangement that a body of practical-minded men could discover. The slave states received less representation than they thought their due. They found compensation, however, in a provision that direct taxes laid by Congress should be apportioned on the same reduced basis as representation—although, in point of fact, direct taxes were actually imposed by the national government only three times before slavery was abolished. *2. The three-fifths clause*

Still another compromise pertained to the powers of Congress over commerce. The states north of the Potomac had large commercial interests; and, having suffered most from the commercial anarchy of the Confederation period, they wanted Congress to have full power to regulate trade and navigation. The four states farther south, however, were agricultural, and their delegates feared that Congress would levy export duties on Southern products and in other ways discriminate against the *3. Commerce and the slave trade* non-commercial section. Furthermore, there was the question of the slave trade. The Northern states would have been willing to see the traffic abolished immediately, and Maryland and Virginia, being well stocked, had no great interest in it. But Georgia and the Carolinas wanted it to continue, and the convention was told firmly that these states would never accept the new plan "unless their right to import slaves be untouched." The outcome was an agreement which pacified all elements. Congress was to have broad powers to regulate navigation and foreign trade, including power to lay duties on imports. But duties on exports were forbidden, and the importation of slaves was not to be interfered with by the national government (except to the extent of a head-tax not exceeding ten dollars) prior to the year 1808.

The constitution completed

Many other important matters claimed the attention of the delegates through the sultry mid-summer days during which the convention patiently pursued its labors. The nature and powers, and especially the mode of selection, of the executive absorbed much time and thought, the more by reason of the fact that plans gradually took form for a chief executive different from any that the world had ever known. The manner of electing senators—whether by the people, by the state legislatures, or by some agency especially devised for the purpose—proved difficult to decide. The appointment and status of the national judiciary provoked ardent discussion. The broadened powers to be vested in Congress, the mode of admitting new states, the control of the national government over state militia, the manner of amending the new constitution—these and a score of other topics required painstaking consideration; and the convention, as Franklin testified, spent a great deal of time "sawing boards to make them fit." From first to last, the Virginia plan, and amendments thereto, formed the main basis of discussion. First, the essentials of the plan, as embodied in the Randolph resolutions, were threshed out in committee of the whole. Then, after being reported back to the convention considerably altered, they were again debated in full. Next, the growing document was turned over, near the close of July, to a committee of detail, which worked it into a balanced constitutional text; and the convention spent upwards of six weeks more in discussing this draft. Finally, Gouverneur Morris, aided by his fellow-Pennsylvanian James Wilson, wrote out with his own hand the completed fundamental law, putting it into the lucid English for which it has ever since been notable among great documents; and on September 17, thirty-nine delegates, representing the twelve states participating, signed it.

The test ahead

To a group of delegates, Franklin, whose contribution had been chiefly that of wise suggestion and quiet conciliation, remarked while the signatures were being affixed that "often and often" during the session he had looked at a sun painted on the president's chair without being able to tell whether it was rising or setting. "Now, at length," he added hopefully, "I have the happiness to know that it is a rising, and not a setting, sun."

The real test, however, was yet to come. The convention had ignored the instructions given most of its members, and, instead of patching up the Articles, had prepared a new and very different frame of government. Would the people of the states approve what it had done? Even the delegates were not very enthusiastic about their handiwork. Three of those present when the document was signed refused to put their names to it. Of thirteen who were absent, at least four are known to have been critical if not actually hostile. Few, if any, were entirely satisfied: Franklin, although optimistic, had misgivings; Hamilton admitted that he signed mainly because he felt that the proposed scheme of government could not possibly prove worse than the existing one.

The Struggle Over Ratification

In laying the results of its labors before Congress, the convention made two significant recommendations: (1) that in each state the instrument be submitted to a convention chosen by the people, and (2) that steps be taken to put it into effect whenever as many as nine states should have approved it. The object of the first proposal was, as Hamilton explained, to give the new plan of government a more popular basis than it would have if ratified merely by the state legislatures.[1] The aim of the second was, of course, to enable the plan to go into operation when endorsed by a good working majority of the states, without waiting for the unanimity which it had taken three and one-half years to obtain in the case of the Articles. With scant show of enthusiasm, Congress assented to both suggestions; and on September 28 the constitution was transmitted to the states without recommendation or other comment. *Procedures agreed upon*

The controversies that had stirred the convention were now transferred to the country at large; and from New England to Georgia, the new frame of government was circulated and discussed, dissected, explained, praised, denounced. Objections arose in many quarters; scarcely a feature of the plan, indeed, escaped attack. There were men who, like Patrick Henry and Samuel Adams, were so imbued with the Revolutionary concepts of liberty that they took instant offense at any proposal looking toward a centralization of authority.[2] On the other hand, some people thought that the new plan did not provide for as much centralization as was needed. The paper-money elements were aroused by the clause which forbade the states to issue bills of credit. Many Northerners considered that too much was conceded to the slaveholding interests; many Southerners felt that these interests had been dealt with unfairly. Large inland elements—small farmers, backwoodsmen, pioneers—feared the effects of the commercial powers given to Congress; men of property, although *Objections to the new plan*

---

[1] *The Federalist,* No. XXII (Lodge's ed., 135). In addition—and this was probably the main motivation—it was thought that the proposed conventions would be more likely to act favorably than would the state legislatures.

[2] "I look on that paper" [the proposed constitution], said Patrick Henry, "as the most fatal plan that could possibly be conceived to enslave a free people."

generally favorable, wondered how freely the new taxing powers would be used.[1] Everywhere the complaint was voiced, and rightly, that the document, although touching upon *habeas corpus*, jury trial, and bills of attainder, failed to take any express notice of numerous fundamental rights and liberties—freedom of speech, freedom of the press, freedom of assembly, right of petition, religious liberty, and security against unreasonable searches and seizures—which had been so carefully guaranteed in the bills of rights prefixed to a majority of the state constitutions; Jefferson himself thought this omission the most serious defect of the convention's work. No single group of dissenters could have prevailed by its own efforts; but in most states the various hostile elements tended to merge into an opposition extremely difficult to convert or overcome.

In the Philadelphia convention, the interests hardest to appease were the small states. The conclusions arrived at were, however, on the whole favorable to those states, which accordingly became the first to ratify. Delaware "came under the federal roof" on December 7, 1787; New Jersey, on December 18; Georgia, on January 2, 1788, and Connecticut one week later. Pennsylvania, although a large state, was centrally located and federally inclined, and its convention ratified early, *i.e.*, on December 12. This rapid pace, however, could not be maintained. In Massachusetts, Virginia, New York, and other states, time was required to rally support; and while there was never much doubt that as many as nine states would eventually ratify, there was grave danger lest some state which was indispensable to the proposed union because of its location and general importance should remain obdurate. By cleverly appeasing Samuel Adams and John Hancock, to whom the "Anti-Federalists" of the interior looked for leadership, the supporters of the new system won in Massachusetts, February 7, 1788, although by an extremely close vote, and only after agreeing to a series of suggested amendments aimed at reducing the power of the central government. Between April and June, Maryland, South Carolina, and New Hampshire followed, each after a hard contest. This brought up the number to the required nine.[2] But no one supposed that the new government could be launched successfully on this minimum basis. Even after Virginia gave a favorable decision (following an exceptionally bitter fight in which Patrick Henry led the irreconcilables), the battle was but half won; New York was still outside, and New York was a pivotal state without which the union would be a mere caricature.

Moreover, the opposition in New York, especially in the rural sections,

Ratification by nine states

---

[1] On the controlling influence of the professional and propertied classes in adopting, as well as framing, the constitution, see C. A. Beard, *Economic Interpretation of the Constitution,* cited above, and O. G. Libby, *Geographical Distribution of the Vote of the Thirteen States on the Federal Constitution* (Madison, Wis., 1894).

[2] Some of these ratifications became possible only after leaders like Madison had given assurance that, once the new government was in operation, amendments constituting in effect a federal bill of rights would be adopted—a pledge made good when the first ten amendments became effective in 1791.

was very formidable. Knowing it to be so, the friends of the constitution made every effort before the state convention met at Poughkeepsie to convince the people that the proposed plan of government was moderate, safe, and workable. The most active champion was Hamilton, who, after having been regarded somewhat skeptically at Philadelphia on account of his ultra-conservative views, now came into his own as a leader in the campaign for ratification, as also later in the effort to start off the new government in a manner calculated to develop vigor and inspire respect. He it was who conceived the idea of printing in the leading newspapers of the state a systematic exposition and defense of the constitution in the form of a series of brief public letters, associating with himself for the purpose another able New Yorker, John Jay, and also the most convincing expounder outside of New York, namely, Madison. The result was the remarkable group of papers, eighty-five in number, appearing over the pen-name "Publius," but known ever since to students of American history as *The Federalist*. The letters were prepared in haste and published, at the rate of three or four a week, as campaign documents.[1] But their authors—all young and vigorous—were full of their subject and knew how to write; and, taken as a group, the papers, though frankly propagandist and presenting only one side, have never been surpassed as examples of direct, lucid, and convincing exposition. Gathered in book form even before the series was completed and constituting one of the world's few really great treatises on government, the collection has passed through more than thirty editions.[2] Better than anything else—unless possibly Madison's *Notes*—it shows what the constitution meant to the men who made it.

Whether because won over by Hamilton and his collaborators or because of being unwilling to see the state remain outside the union after all but two of the others had joined, the New York convention finally ratified, on July 26 (1788), although by a margin of only three votes. Meanwhile, on July 2, it was officially announced in Congress that the ninth state had ratified, and attention was turned to preparations for putting the new government into operation. The states were called upon to choose presidential electors, senators, and representatives, and New York City was selected as the temporary seat of government. Then the old Congress, expiring prematurely for lack of a quorum, disappeared, leaving the field clear for its successor. The new House of Representatives was organized on April 2, 1789; the Senate came together three days

Margin notes: Ratification in New York: *The Federalist* / The constitution put into effect

[1] Hamilton alone wrote upwards of sixty of them. Madison contributed some fifteen and Jay about half a dozen. A few were prepared by Hamilton and Madison jointly. These two men were destined to draw far apart on questions of constitutional interpretation in later days, but in the present fight they stood shoulder to shoulder.

[2] The title of the first edition was *The Federalist; A Collection of Essays Written in Favor of the New Constitution* (New York, 1788). The best editions for present use are those of H. C. Lodge (New York, 1888) and P. L. Ford (New York, 1898). C. A. Beard, *The Enduring Federalist* (Garden City, N. Y., 1948), is a well edited abridgment.

later; and on April 30, Washington took the oath of office as president.[1] Seven months afterwards, North Carolina, appeased by the decision of Congress to submit to the states a series of constitutional amendments guaranteeing civil liberties, and threatened with being treated commercially as though a foreign country, ratified the new fundamental law; and similar action by Rhode Island in the spring of 1790 made the union complete.

A remarkable record of survival

The new "supreme law" which the founding fathers thus arduously devised and hopefully adopted has served as a charter of free government in this country for over a century and a half. Within this time, it has seen thirteen states increase to forty-eight, less than four million people grow to more than one hundred forty-four million, a simple frontier existence develop into the bewilderingly complex life and economy of the present day. Nowhere else is there a written constitution with so imposing a record. To be sure, the instrument has undergone change by the addition of twenty-one different amendments, lengthening its text by fully one-half. To be sure, too, its terse but pregnant phrases have in many instances proved only starting points for interpretation, usage, legislation, administrative action, and judicial decision from which have flowed ever-widening streams of new constitutional law and practice. Without such flexibility, it would never have survived; indeed, there are people who would have it completely overhauled and rewritten in our day. Despite all, however, the constitution as it came from the hands of the framers still lives, and the broader features of the plan of government for which it provided are as yet intact.

The Constitution's Characteristics and Sources

The constitution as a document

"This paper," wrote Robert Morris in commending the constitution to a friend, "has been the subject of infinite investigation, disputation, and declamation. While some have boasted it as a work from Heaven, others have given it a less righteous origin. I have many reasons to believe that it is the work of plain honest men, and such, I think, it will appear." Herein lies the reason why the instrument, once adopted, succeeded and survived beyond the hopes of its most ardent sponsors. First, as constitutions go, it was a brief and simple document. Even with the later amendments, its approximately six thousand words fill only twelve or fifteen pages of print; one can read it through in leisurely fashion in half an hour. Had the text been fuller and more detailed, some doubts and controversies of later days would unquestionably have been averted. Excess of detail, however, could easily have proved a handicap. The arrangement of subject-matter has sometimes been criticized as not wholly logical. The fault, however,—if it be one—has been of no practical significance.

[1] The launching of the new government is described in C. B. Swisher, *American Constitutional Development* (Boston, 1943), Chap. III, and in J. S. Bassett, *The Federalist System* (New York, 1906), Chap. I.

Following a brief preamble (important as a statement of general purpose, but having no legal force), three main articles are devoted to the legislative, executive, and judicial branches, respectively. Four lesser articles deal, in order, with the position of the states, the modes of amendment, the supremacy of national power, and ratification. Finally come the amendments, appended at the end and numbered serially.

Thanks to the committee of detail, and especially to Gouverneur Morris, the language of the original document is clear, direct, and concise; there is not an unnecessary word or an intentionally ambiguous phrase.[1] To be sure, some clauses, *e.g.*, those authorizing Congress to "lay and collect taxes . . . to . . . provide for the general welfare of the United States," and to "regulate commerce . . . among the several states," leave plenty of room for differences of opinion (in the instances cited, about the scope of "welfare" and "commerce"); and the conflicts and decisions arising out of such differences make up a considerable part of the country's constitutional history in the past hundred and sixty years. Nevertheless, our greatest constitutional controversies are traceable rather to omissions than to provisions of doubtful meaning. In part, these omissions are traceable to the natural concentration of the framers' interest and effort upon the big fundamentals of the new system, to the exclusion of relatively minor matters. In part, they are accounted for by the impossibility of foreseeing technological advances and social and economic developments which in later days have put a new aspect on the functions of government—for example, the changes in transportation and communication resulting from the introduction of steam-power, electricity, aviation, and radio-broadcasting. But in part also they arose from the unwillingness of the constitution's architects to jeopardize their work by forcing decisions on delicate matters which it was possible to pass over in silence. Could a state, by its own volition, withdraw from the new Union? The constitution did not undertake to say. It could be argued plausibly that the Union was intended to be permanent, and that no member had a right to secede. On the other hand, the "sovereignty" of the states was nowhere expressly denied, and the thrice-repeated assertion of the Articles that the Union was to be "perpetual" found no place in the new instrument. The matter was glossed over, not because men of insight like Madison and Hamilton were unconcerned about it, but because of the inexpediency of pressing it at a time when the preservation of a central government of any kind whatsoever was hanging in the balance. The "plain honest men" of whom Morris wrote were bent on an immediate practical remedy for the defects of the existing government, not on anticipating and providing for every contingency that might later arise. They did, however, endow Congress with powers capable of broad interpretation; they also provided modes of constitutional amendment; and thus, significantly, they left the way

The saving quality of flexibility

[1] It might, however, have been a little more explicit on the subject of citizenship. See pp. 140-141 below.

open for the national government in subsequent times to concern itself with multifold interests and problems—agriculture, labor, banking, corporations, immigration, education, and what not—which in the constitution itself went entirely unmentioned.

The constitution's sources

It follows that the fathers did not go out of their way to invent political forms. Nor did they borrow far afield. Some of them were students of Vattel, Montesquieu, and other Continental writers; some had read history and could cite the failures of ancient confederacies or draw illustrations from the experiences of France and other Continental states. But, as some one has remarked, this knowledge taught them rather what to avoid than what to adopt; and in so far as they drew upon European sources at all, those sources were the common law, the principles of *Magna Carta* and the Bill of Rights, the writings of Locke and Blackstone, and other significant products of their English motherland. In the main, however, this rich heritage had passed to America far back in colonial days, and, at the time when the national constitution took form, was already deeply embedded in the constitutions, laws, and usages of the states. In a very true and literal sense, therefore, the new instrument grew out of the political life of Americans themselves in the colonial, Revolutionary, and post-Revolutionary periods. "Experience," said John Dickinson, "must be our guide; reason may mislead us." Fortunately, our forefathers had accumulated enough political experience by 1787 to serve as a rich and adequate resource.

The constitution as an instrument of democracy

Through the descending years, the constitution has been venerated as a bulwark of American democracy. But it also has been disparaged as a bulwark of special interests, particularly those of property. There can be no denying that, in its origin and intent, it was not, by present-day standards, democratic. Speaking broadly, it was made by the well-to-do; it presupposed the property (or as we might say today, the capitalist) system; it had as a main objective the safeguarding of social order and stability, always fervently desired by the propertied classes; as a proposed frame of government, it was never submitted to a direct vote of the people, who quite possibly might have rejected it; the state conventions which so arduously, and in some cases so narrowly, ratified it had behind them only the highly restricted electorates characteristic of the period.

This, however, does not tell all. The eighteenth century, in general, was not democratic by today's standards. The nineteenth was the century of ripening democracy, in America no less than in Europe. The constitution's authors did not foist their product upon helpless states; every state was free to accept or reject it, and to permit as many of its inhabitants as it liked to help choose those who were to make the decision. The great objectives of law, order, and stability sought by those who supplied the driving force were bound, in the long run, to be to the advantage of the masses as well. Still more important, the constitution, while itself conservative and cautious, interposed no immovable barriers to the progressive unfolding of democracy in response to changing conditions and ideas in later generations. If we have democracy today, it is democracy *under the constitution,* and well within the limits of the instrument's potentialities from the beginning.

REFERENCES

C. A. and M. R. Beard, *The Rise of American Civilization* (New York, 1930), 1, Chap. VII.

A. C. McLaughlin, *A Constitutional History of the United States* (New York, 1935), Chaps. XIV-XV.

—————, *The Confederation and the Constitution* (New York, 1905), Chaps. XII-XVIII.

H. C. Hockett, *The Constitutional History of the United States* (New York, 1939), I, Chap. XI.

C. B. Swisher, *American Constitutional Development* (Boston, 1943), Chap. II.

C. A. Beard, *An Economic Interpretation of the Constitution of the United States* (new ed., New York, 1935), Chaps. III-XI.

B. J. Hendrick, *Bulwark of the Republic; A Biography of the Constitution* (Boston, 1937), Pt. I.

C. Van Doren, *The Great Rehearsal; The Story of the Making and Ratifying of the Constitution of the United States* (New York, 1948).

H. Lyon, *The Constitution and the Men Who Made It; The Story of the Constitutional Convention, 1787* (Boston, 1936).

M. Farrand, *The Framing of the Constitution* (New Haven, 1913). The best general account.

—————— [ed.], *The Records of the Federal Convention,* 3 vols. (New Haven, 1911), rev. ed., 4 vols. (New Haven, 1937).

C. Warren, *The Making of the Constitution* (Boston, 1928). Criticizes the views of Beard and other "economic historians."

R. L. Schuyler, *The Constitution of the United States; An Historical Survey of Its Formation* (New York, 1923).

C. E. Stevens, *Sources of the Constitution of the United States* (New York, 1894).

S. G. Fisher, *The Evolution of the Constitution of the United States* (Philadelphia, 1900).

O. G. Libby, *Geographical Distribution of the Vote of the Thirteen States on the Federal Constitution* (Madison, Wis., 1894).

J. Butzner [comp.], *Constitutional Chaff; Rejected Suggestions of the Constitutional Convention of 1787, with Explanatory Argument* (New York, 1941).

A. J. Beveridge, *The Life of John Marshall* (Boston, 1916), I, Chap. IX on the state ratifications generally and Chaps. X-XII on ratification in Virginia.

S. B. Harding, *The Contest Over the Ratification of the Federal Constitution in the State of Massachusetts* (New York, 1896).

C. E. Miner, *The Ratification of the Constitution by the State of New York* (New York, 1921).

G. Hunt and J. B. Scott [eds.], *The Debates in the Federal Convention of 1787 Which Framed the Constitution of the United States of America* (New York, 1920). Contains Madison's *Notes.*

J. Elliot [comp.], *Debates in the Several State Conventions on the Adoption of the Federal Constitution* ...5 vols. (2nd ed., Washington, D. C., 1854).

The Federalist. Editions by H. C. Lodge (New York, 1888) and P. L. Ford (New York, 1898).

CHAPTER IV

HOW THE NATIONAL CONSTITUTION DEVELOPS

A document with a long life, but a brief biography

As already remarked, our written national constitution has been in operation more than a century and a half—longer than any other one in the world.[1] Moreover, if Madison and Hamilton could look over it as it has emerged from the years, they would have no difficulty in recognizing it. For although those who made it realized that it was not perfect, and wisely provided ways of amending it, the document has undergone a good deal less textual change than might have been expected. A few short passages—amounting to perhaps one-seventh of the whole—have been rendered obsolete by repeal or replacement, and enough new matter has been inserted to fill four or five pages of print. As measured, however, against the full and rich content of the nation's history, the biography of the constitution as a document is brief. Several pages of numbered articles and sections still stand exactly as they left the fluent pen of Gouverneur Morris.

The real constitution more than a document

From this must not be inferred, however, any lack of actual constitutional growth and change—of which, indeed, there has been an immense amount. The moment the new fundamental law took effect, executive officers, lawmakers, and courts began interpreting and applying its provisions; and the resulting decisions and actions forthwith began to amplify and fill out those provisions by adding—usually not in the document, but in accumulating practice based upon it—a wealth of ever-expanding detail. Furthermore, as the country developed and the tasks of government grew more complex, decisions and usages—still presumably based upon pertinent articles and clauses, but not actually incorporated into them—carried over into new and wider areas (including many not envisaged at all by the constitution's framers), until they were found involving no longer mere detail in any proper sense, but matters of fundamental significance as well. With this sort of thing going on for a century and a half, the constitutional text, even with twenty-one formal amendments added, became only a sort of core (or, to change the figure, skeleton) of the actual operating constitutional system; and while we still may properly enough refer to the document itself as "the constitution," in a larger and truer sense the constitution is the document as enveloped in a vast, living, changing complex of interpretations and usages—an accumulation of constitutional principles and practices so extensive that scholars

---

[1] The constitution of Massachusetts ostensibly dates from 1780, but has been largely rewritten in later times.

40

undertaking to set forth our national constitutional law, even in the relatively concise form of a textbook, rarely succeed in covering the subject in less than a thousand pages. The English constitution is supposed to be the most flexible on earth because of being the most largely unwritten and the easiest to change. The American, however, has proved also about as flexible as it needs to be in order to serve the purposes of a great and growing nation. Actually, it is changing all of the time under our very eyes.

Turning now for a closer look at the ways in which the national constitution—the constitution in the broader sense—develops, we start with formal amendment of the basic text, but soon come also to legislation, judicial construction, and other processes for which the document merely provides guide-posts marking points of departure.

Methods of Constitutional Amendment

Even if the constitution's makers had considered the new fundamental law satisfactory in all respects when it came from their hands, they would have been statesmanlike enough to realize that under changing conditions and ideas it would not long remain so. They had had experience with one national constitution, and also with some state constitutions, which had proved nearly impossible to amend, and they did not want the new instrument to suffer from such rigidity. On the other hand, they did not want it to be capable of being amended too swiftly or lightly. Accordingly, they devised somewhat difficult, but not impossible, amending procedures as follows: "The Congress, whenever two-thirds of both houses shall deem it necessary, shall propose amendments to this constitution, or, on the application of the legislatures of two-thirds of the several states, shall call a convention for proposing amendments, which in either case shall be valid to all intents and purposes as part of this constitution, when ratified by the legislatures of three-fourths of the several states, or by conventions in three-fourths thereof, as the one or the other mode of ratification may be proposed by the Congress." [1] The only restriction placed upon the free operation of these procedures (aside from a temporary one relating to the slave trade) is that no state may be deprived of its equal representation in the Senate without its consent.

The amending clause

Although two methods of initiative and two methods of ratification are provided for, all amendments thus far adopted have been proposed in the same way, i.e., by joint resolution of the two branches of Congress, and all except the Twenty-first (repealing national prohibition) have likewise been ratified in the same manner, i.e., by action of the state legislatures. Any proposed amendment receiving a two-thirds vote in both House and Senate (quorums being assumed [2]) is transmitted by

Stages in the amending process:

1. Initiation

[1] Art. V.
[2] That two-thirds of a quorum in each house, rather than two-thirds of the entire membership, meets the requirement was definitely established in the National Prohibition Cases, 253 U. S. 350 (1920).

the secretary of state to the governors of the several states, to be laid by them before the legislatures or conventions. The president will naturally have an interest in whatever is proposed, but he has no veto upon it, and in fact amendments, not being legislative acts,[1] are not officially submitted to him at all.

The national convention an unused device

This does not mean that there has been any lack of attempts to secure the launching of amendment proposals by the alternative method of a national convention. On the contrary, in one period or another the legislatures of considerably more than two-thirds of the states have called upon Congress to convoke a convention for the purpose. Sometimes such a request has been made in behalf of a particular proposed amendment, as, for example, in more than a score of earlier instances in which the object sought was the popular election of United States senators, or, as in a group of later instances, the repeal of the Eighteenth Amendment. Sometimes the aim has been more general, as in the case of appeals voiced by different states at the time of the nullification controversy of 1832, and again in 1859-60 when civil war was imminent. The opinion has sometimes been advanced that every request for a convention made at any time by a state is to be regarded as pending indefinitely, and that whenever two-thirds of the states are found to have made such a request (a situation that has long existed) Congress should forthwith call a convention. This "cumulative" view, however, is not generally accepted. Even though there never has been any official determination of the period of time at the end of which a request from a state should be regarded as having lapsed, it is hardly conceivable that Congress would act unless petitions were received from the necessary number of states within a sufficiently limited period to create an appearance of concerted demand; and, in practice, such concurrence would be likely to lead Congress of its own accord to place the desired amendment before the states, as in the instance of prohibition repeal. If a convention were once convoked, it presumably could go as far as it liked in proposing amendments, and might even put before the country a completely rewritten fundamental law.[2]

2. Ratification

Whether a given amendment shall be acted upon within the states by the legislatures or by conventions specially chosen for the purpose is determined entirely by Congress. It is more economical to employ the legislatures; and although the original constitution was ratified by conventions, the legislative method was adhered to uniformly for amendments until the Twenty-first was submitted in 1933. Conventions, how-

---

[1] Hollingsworth *et al v.* Virginia, 3 Dallas 378 (1798). In submitting an amendment, said the Court, Congress is not legislating. Neither is a state legislature doing so when ratifying—with the result that the governor has no veto on ratifications.

[2] For twenty-five years, books have been appearing voicing proposals for a general constitutional revision through the medium of a convention. Among them may be mentioned W. MacDonald, *A New Constitution for a New America* (New York, 1921); W. K. Wallace, *Our Obsolete Constitution* (New York, 1932); W. Y. Elliott, *The Need for Constitutional Reform* (New York, 1935); H. Hazlitt, *A New Constitution Now* (New York, 1942); and A. Hehmeyer, *Time for Change; A Proposal for a Second Constitutional Convention* (New York, 1943).

ever, are likely to give quicker results, and they have the further advantage of being chosen by the people with reference solely to the proposal upon which they are to act. As recognized belatedly by both of the major political parties, the prohibition question was one on which it was peculiarly appropriate to use the convention method; and it was resorted to at the time of repeal, although not at that of original adoption. On the other hand, when submitting an amendment in 1947 imposing a limitation upon presidential tenure, Congress reverted to the legislatures as ratifying agencies.[1] Whichever plan is employed, reports of actions taken are sent by the governors to the Department of State, which, if and when the necessary three-fourths majority is attained, proclaims the amendment effective as part of the constitution.[2]

What of a proposal that fails to secure the necessary three-fourths? Until rather recently, the view was that, rejection never being officially proclaimed, a proposal in this position remains "outstanding" and might be pushed across the line decades, or even generations, afterwards by belated ratifications; in 1869, the Ohio legislature solemnly ratified an amendment submitted eighty years previously! Beginning with the Eighteenth Amendment, however, a new procedure appeared. By its own terms, that proposal was to remain before the states no longer than seven years; if not ratified by the requisite number within that period, it was to be regarded as dead. The Twentieth and Twenty-first Amendments contained a similar provision; [3] and inasmuch as, when the principle of limitation was challenged, the Supreme Court upheld it as valid and the seven-year period as reasonable,[4] it is to be presumed that, even when containing no express limitation, amendment proposals will henceforth tend to be regarded as "alive" only for something like a seven-year period. A child labor amendment submitted in 1924 has, nevertheless, been acted upon by state legislatures as recently as 1937; and in recognizing it as still pending in 1939, the Supreme Court indicated that the question of how long a proposed amendment shall remain subject to ratification, being of a "political" nature, is one for Congress, not the courts, to decide.[5]

How long does a proposal remain before the states?

Can a state, once having ratified an amendment, change its mind while the proposal is still pending and reverse its action? By decision of Congress, confirmed in 1939 by the Supreme Court,[6] the answer is in the negative. New Jersey, Ohio, and Oregon undertook to withdraw their ratifications of the Fourteenth Amendment, New York her ratification of

Can a ratification be withdrawn?

---

[1] See pp. 429–430 below.

[2] *Rev. Stat. of U. S.* § 205; G. Hunt, *The Department of State*, 168–178. In Dillon v. Gloss, 256 U. S. 368 (1921), the Supreme Court has said that an amendment becomes effective the moment when the last of the required number of states ratifies.

[3] Likewise the amendment relating to presidential tenure submitted in 1947. See p. 429 below.

[4] Dillon v. Gloss, 256 U. S. 368 (1921).

[5] Coleman v. Miller, 307 U. S. 443 (1939). The view is logical since it is Congress that submits the amendment in the first place.

[6] In Coleman v. Miller cited.

the Fifteenth, and Tennessee hers of the Nineteenth. On the first occasion, two of the three ratifications involved were necessary to the required number; Congress ordered that they be counted; and the precedent has ever since been followed, with the Supreme Court, as indicated, later adding the weight of its authority, even though recognizing that the question is inherently one for Congress to decide. As a result, every ratification reported to the Secretary of State at Washington is regarded and counted as final. On the other hand, there is nothing to prevent a state which has rejected an amendment from later reversing its decision and ratifying.[1] Finally, under judicial interpretation of Article V, ratification must be literally by state legislatures or conventions, as Congress may ordain, and not by the people acting directly. In 1918, Ohio amended her state constitution so as to provide that after her legislature should have ratified a federal amendment the voters should be given an opportunity through a referendum to confirm or reverse the decision. A test case being brought, the federal Supreme Court held that the term "legislature" as employed in Article V means literally an elected representative body, and not the people acting directly.[2]

The Twenty-one Amendments

Number of amendments proposed and adopted

The states were not yet safely gathered under the "New Roof," as the constitution was popularly termed in early days, before proposals began to be made for "extensions of the eaves" and other more or less significant alterations. In all, no fewer than 1,964 drafted amendments (many of them identical, of course, or at all events relating to the same matters) were introduced during the first hundred years of the constitution's history, and 2,056 others found their way to the clerks' tables between 1889 and 1941.[3] Nowadays, anywhere from forty to seventy-five pro-

---

[1] In 1937, the Kentucky court of appeals denied the right of the state legislature to ratify the child labor amendment after a previous legislature had rejected it and after more than one-fourth of the states had similarly rejected it, unless the amendment were resubmitted by Congress. Wise v. Chandler, 108 S.W. (2nd) 1024. But the federal Supreme Court, in Coleman v. Miller, upheld the supreme court of Kansas in ruling that that state's ratification of the amendment in 1937 was entirely valid notwithstanding a previous rejection; and this, of course, represents the actual law on the subject.

[2] Hawke v. Smith, 253 U. S. 221 (1920). There is no constitutional obstacle to an "advisory referendum" on a proposed amendment before the legislature votes; and such a test of public opinion has been made in a number of states. Official decision, however, must be by legislature or convention. See W. A. Robinson, "Advisory Referendum in Massachusetts on the Child Labor Amendment," Amer. Polit. Sci. Rev., XIX, 69-73 (Feb., 1925). It may be added that where the convention method of ratification is employed, delegates are likely to be instructed by their constituents as to how they shall vote, and that to a degree this attains the same object as a referendum on the lines attempted in Ohio.

[3] The proposals between 1789 and 1889 are classified and described in the monograph by H. V. Ames listed on p. 59 below; those between 1889 and 1929 are similarly classified in M. A. Musmanno, "Proposed Amendments to the Constitution," 70th Cong., 2nd Sess., House Doc. 551 (1929); and the 740 introduced between 1926 and 1941 are listed in E. A. Halsey [comp.], Proposed Amendments to the Constitution of the United States Introduced in Congress December 6, 1926-January 3, 1941 (Washington, D. C., 1941). Amendments proposed from year to year will be found

posals are presented in the prescribed form during an average session. The total number of amendments actually endorsed by the two houses since 1789 is, however, only twenty-seven, and the number ratified by the states only twenty-one. Indeed it would hardly be erroneous to say that only eleven actual amendments have been adopted, because the first ten so-called amendments were, to all intents and purposes, contemporary addenda to the original constitution rather than amendments to a finished document. A good deal of trouble would have been saved if they had been incorporated at the outset.

As submitted to the states in 1787, the new fundamental law contained no bill of rights, and indeed not a great deal bearing directly on what we are accustomed to think of as civil liberties. To be sure, the framers did not fail to consider the subject. But since eight of the existing state constitutions contained bills of rights or their equivalent,[1] and since, in addition, the federal government was to have only delegated powers—none of which, it was believed, would carry authority over matters which a federal bill of rights could reach—inclusion of provisions on the subject was decided to be superfluous. "Why," asked Hamilton, "declare that things shall not be done which there is no power to do?"[2] In this, however, the convention misjudged the temper of the country. The deficiency was promptly seized upon by the fault-finders and made a leading argument against ratification; and of the 124 amendments formally proposed by seven of the states when ratifying, the great majority had to do with this matter. After ratification, little time was lost in rectifying the error. In Virginia, Madison was chosen to the first Congress under pledge to use his influence to bring about the adoption of a federal bill of rights; and in June, 1789, he introduced a long series of proposals looking to that end. Of seventeen amendments voted by the House, twelve were endorsed by the Senate, and ten were ratified by the states. Eight of the number embodied most of the desired express guarantees of personal and property rights;[3] the Ninth provided that the enumeration of certain rights in the constitution should not be construed "to deny or disparage

The first ten amendments

listed in the appropriate volumes of the *Statutes at Large*. It is hardly necessary to add that the annual grist contains many that are trivial and some that are palpably ridiculous.

[1] Georgia, New Jersey, New York, South Carolina, and Virginia adopted theirs later.

[2] *The Federalist*, No. LXXXIV (Lodge's ed., 537).

[3] As adopted, the eight amendments protecting expressly-named liberties applied to the federal government only; and so they do today, except as certain of them have been made indirectly applicable to the state governments by judicial construction in later years extending the due process clause of the Fourteenth Amendment into the sphere of state action. It is interesting to note that as offered by Madison all were to apply to the state legislatures as well as to Congress, and that the House of Representatives approved them in that form. Greatly to the Virginian's disappointment, the Senate, however, struck out this feature. It is equally interesting to observe that Madison's proposals entirely omitted a right which nowadays is considered one of the most important, *i.e.*, that of freedom of speech. Notwithstanding, however, that no state constitution then had a clause on the subject, the first federal amendment as adopted expressly forbade Congress to "make any law . . . abridging the freedom of speech." Cf. Chap. IX below.

others retained by the people"; and the Tenth was intended to clear up lingering doubts as to precisely what powers were reserved to the states or to the people.

Eleventh Amendment
The next two amendments were adopted to overcome certain practical difficulties arising early in the constitution's history. In the case of Chisholm *v.* Georgia,[1] the Supreme Court held, in 1793, that a state could be sued without its consent by a citizen of another state or of a foreign state. To people of strong states' rights views, this was shocking doctrine; and under their influence the Eleventh Amendment was adopted, in 1798, stipulating that "the judicial power of the United States shall not be construed to extend to any suit in law or equity, commenced or prosecuted against one of the United States by citizens of another state, or by citizens or subjects of any foreign state." The amendment's primary object was to protect the states against suits for debt.

Twelfth Amendment
Whether this amendment was desirable depended on the point of view. But the threatened breakdown, in 1800, of the system of electing the president, because of a tie between Jefferson and Burr, brought a change which—even though resisted stoutly at the time—looks from this distance to have been a practical necessity. The nature of the crisis, and the device adopted to prevent it from recurring, will be explained at a later point.[2] Suffice it to say here that the Twelfth Amendment, ratified in 1804, provided for separate balloting for president and vice-president.

The Civil War amendments
The first half of the nineteenth century saw many new state constitutions framed and many older ones revised; but, apart from the amendment just mentioned, no change took place in the national written constitution, notwithstanding that hundreds of proposals made their appearance in Congress. Then, however, came the Civil War, and as a result of it, three amendments designed primarily to define and protect the rights of the recently emancipated Negroes, and all forced upon the Southern states as conditions of their restoration to their former places in the Union. One—the Thirteenth (1865)—prohibited slavery; another—the Fourteenth (1868)—defined citizenship, laid important new restrictions upon the states in the interest of civil rights, and penalized states denying the suffrage to male inhabitants except for participation in rebellion or other crime; and the third—the Fifteenth (1870)—forbade both state and federal governments to abridge or deny the right to vote on account of race, color, or previous condition of servitude. All were important; and although the penalty prescribed in the Fourteenth for withholding the suffrage has never been enforced,[3] the "privileges and immunities," "due process," and "equal protection" clauses contained in this same amendment have influenced our social and economic development almost beyond computation.

[1] 2 Dallas 419 (1793).
[2] See pp. 255-256 below.
[3] See pp. 195-196 below.

Forty-three years now elapsed without further change in the written fundamental law, and people interested in various reforms began to wonder whether amendments would ever again be found possible unless easier amending procedures were introduced—an objective itself attainable only through an amendment. A period of great national growth witnessed, however, momentous changes in political, economic, and social conditions and attitudes; and in the space of twenty years (1913-33) the constitution was amended no fewer than half a dozen times. First came an express grant of authority for federal taxation of incomes. Notwithstanding that a federal income tax had once been sustained as an indirect tax,[1] an act of 1894 providing for such a levy was construed by a sharply divided (five to four) Supreme Court [2] as imposing a direct tax which, under the terms of the constitution, must be apportioned among the states "according to their respective numbers"—a thing which obviously could not be done in the case of a tax of this nature. For a time, existing sources of federal revenue (principally the tariff) proved adequate, and further effort was not made. Eventually, however, more income was needed; and in 1909 Congress, with a view to clearing the way, submitted to the states a proposal that the federal government be authorized to "lay and collect taxes on incomes, from whatever source derived, without apportionment among the several states, and without regard to any census or enumeration." The response was slow, but in 1913 this unequivocal provision—the basis of our present drastic federal taxation of incomes—was added to the constitution as the Sixteenth Amendment. The amendment does not undertake to say whether an income tax is or is not a direct tax; it simply authorizes such a tax to be laid without reference to apportionment.

Sixteenth Amendment

The Seventeenth Amendment, providing for direct popular election of senators, dates also from 1913. This mode of election found few supporters in the convention which framed the original constitution. But it was advocated as early as 1826; and from 1893 onwards the House of Representatives repeatedly passed resolutions favoring it. The Senate remained obdurate until 1912, when, however, it finally yielded; and in 1913 the amendment became effective.[3]

Seventeenth Amendment

The next two amendments date from shortly after the First World War and in part owed their adoption to wartime experiences. One, the unlucky Eighteenth, launched a gigantic experiment in the regulation of human behavior by undertaking to do away with the liquor traffic; the other, the Nineteenth, nationalized woman suffrage. A movement for suppressing the transportation and sale of intoxicating liquors had been under way for decades, and by 1917 eleven states' had constitutional prohibition, ten had statutory prohibition, and five others were about to pass under prohibition laws or amendments. As soon as we entered the

Eighteenth Amendment

[1] Springer v. United States, 102 U. S. 586 (1880).
[2] Pollock v. Farmers' Loan and Trust Company, 158 U. S. 601 (1895).
[3] See p. 299 below.

war, Congress forbade the manufacture and importation of all spirituous liquors for beverage purposes for "the duration"; and shortly afterwards a constitutional amendment was submitted to the states providing that "after one year from the ratification of this article the manufacture, sale, or transportation of intoxicating liquors within, the importation thereof into, or the exportation thereof from the United States and all territory subject to the jurisdiction thereof for beverage purposes is prohibited." Ratified by the necessary thirty-six states, the amendment was proclaimed in January, 1919, and in due time—after the end of the war which had given it impetus—it took effect.

Nine-
teenth
Amend-
ment

The background of the Nineteenth Amendment, dealing with woman suffrage, will be reviewed when we later come to the subject of qualifications for voting.[1] A resolution submitting the proposal was passed by the House of Representatives early in 1918. Despite earnest support from President Wilson, the Senate twice refused to concur. A year later, however, agreement was reached; and ratification by the states proceeded with such alacrity that on August 26, 1920, the amendment was ready to be proclaimed. Like the Fifteenth, and in almost the same language, the Nineteenth Amendment restricts both federal and state control over the suffrage—in the case of the Nineteenth, by forbidding the right of citizens of the United States to vote to be denied or abridged on account of sex.

Twen-
tieth
Amend-
ment

Until a little over a decade ago, our national political calendar preserved the tempo of a stage-coach age. A president elected in November did not take office until the following March; a Congress chosen at the same time did not (unless sooner convoked in special session) meet until thirteen months had elapsed, and could not in any case start work within less than four months. Meanwhile, with a new Congress chosen and endowed with a fresh mandate from the voters, the old one, cluttered up with "lame ducks" who had failed of reëlection, sat in more or less perfunctory and futile session from December until the close of its term on March 4. For a decade, Senator George W. Norris of Nebraska led a movement aimed at correcting this glaring defect; and on February 6, 1933, the Department of State was able to proclaim the Twentieth (or so-called "Lame Duck") Amendment, moving back the date for inaugurating a new president from March 4 to January 20, and fixing the term of a new Congress to begin even a little earlier, i.e., on January 3, on which day, unless provided otherwise by law, the two houses now assemble and start work. "Short"—or "lame duck"—sessions became a thing of the past.[2]

Twenty-
first
Amend-
ment

The Fourteenth Amendment has never been completely enforced, but the first and only one of the series actually to be repealed was the Eighteenth. Although ratified by the legislatures of forty-six states, and un-

---

[1] See Chap. x below.

[2] The Twentieth Amendment contains provisions also relating to succession to the presidency. See p. 277 below.

shaken by attacks upon it in the courts on every possible ground, constitutional prohibition on a nation-wide basis lasted less than fourteen years, *i.e.*, only until 1933. The task of regulating the personal habits of a vast, heterogeneous, far-flung population—much of it still under the influence of European traditions—proved one of the most difficult that our national government has ever undertaken, and public sentiment turned so decisively against the amendment, and especially against the Volstead Act and other enforcement measures, that in December, 1932, a resolution for repeal passed both houses of Congress by the necessary two-thirds, with votes to spare. "The Eighteenth Amendment," ran the proposal, " . . . is hereby repealed." And then, in order to protect states which had prohibition laws and wished to retain them: "The transportation or importation into any state, territory, or possession of the United States for delivery or use therein of intoxicating liquors, in violation of the laws thereof, is hereby prohibited." The proposal was to remain before the states not longer than seven years, and, as we have seen, was to be acted upon in them, not by the legislatures, but by conventions chosen particularly for the purpose. Starting in Michigan and Wisconsin in April, 1933, the amendment swept through the resulting conventions with such speed that the thirty-sixth state to ratify (Utah) was reached on December 5; all, indeed, eventually ratified except two—the Carolinas. Accordingly, on the date mentioned, the Twenty-first Amendment was duly proclaimed, and the ill-fated "noble experiment" launched by the Eighteenth—having demonstrated how inadvisable it is to put into the constitution anything in the nature of police regulations not clearly supported by public opinion—passed into history.[1]

Looking over the twenty-one adopted amendments as a group, one notes three or four significant facts. (1) They are considerably more concerned with denying powers, or placing restraints upon the exercise of powers, than with bestowing new powers. Sometimes (as in the first ten or eleven) it is the national government that is restricted; sometimes (as

Observations on the amendments as a group

---

[1] For a convenient account of the Eighteenth and Twenty-first Amendments, see C. B. Swisher, *American Constitutional Development*, 703-722. Cf. H. L. McBain, *Prohibition, Legal and Illegal* (New York, 1929); C. Merz, *The Dry Decade* (New York, 1930); and E. S. Brown, "The Ratification of the Twenty-first Amendment," *Amer. Polit. Sci. Rev.*, XXIX, 1005-1017 (Dec., 1935). Over half of the conventions which ratified the Twenty-first Amendment were elected on a state-wide basis, several by districts, and a few by a combination of the two methods. In size, they varied from ten members in New Hampshire to 329 in Indiana.

With repeal, the Volstead Act and other enforcing legislation collapsed, except as applying to strictly federal territory. On the other hand, state prohibition and local option laws antedating, or at least independent of, the Eighteenth Amendment, were not affected; and when confronted with the question, the Supreme Court (in McCormick *v.* Brown, 286 U. S. 131, 1932) ruled that the Webb-Kenyon Act of 1913 (withdrawing protection from liquor shipped through interstate commerce with a view to violating state laws) was similarly intact. At the time of repeal, twenty-eight states had independent prohibitory laws of one kind or another. Subsequently, practically all relaxed or rescinded their legislation on the subject, and today none is "bone-dry" except Mississippi, although Kansas and Oklahoma permit the sale of no intoxicants except beer. In six other states (all Southern), more than half of the counties bar spirits by local option.

in the Civil War group) it is the state governments. But in any case most of the amendments are prohibitive rather than creative. (2) The amendments, accordingly, are to only a relatively slight extent directly responsible for the phenomenal growth of national powers and functions witnessed in recent decades. From one of them, to be sure, the national government derives the tremendously important power to tax incomes; and from the Eighteenth it, of course, once drew power to enforce—or at least to *try* to enforce—prohibition of the liquor traffic. This last authority, however, has now been withdrawn; and even the remarkable expansions of federal power associated with carrying out the Roosevelt Administration's program of national recovery, and also with our participation in World War II, came without any change whatsoever in the written fundamental law. (3) At the same time, the amendments of the past eighty years have, in general, by imposing restrictions on the states, contributed to national uniformity, solidarity, and priority, and in this sense may be said to have had a pronounced nationalizing tendency. Without adding anything, in so many words, to national powers as such, amendments making it impossible for the states to legalize slavery, requiring them to respect interstate citizenship and due process of law, and forbidding them to deny the suffrage to Negroes and to women, unquestionably weight the scales against the states in the ever-shifting balance of federal-state relations; after all, the amendments are themselves national instrumentalities. (4) The amendments have introduced relatively few changes in the machinery and procedures of the federal government. As a result of them, the president and vice-president are voted for separately rather than otherwise; Negroes are counted equally with whites in apportioning congressional seats among the states; senators are elected by the people instead of by the state legislatures; qualified women have become voters in all parts of the country. But that is all—aside, at least, from the creation of new machinery to administer the income tax (and to enforce prohibition when the Eighteenth Amendment was in effect).

Amendments now pending:

1. Presidential tenure

Two amendments duly submitted by Congress are now (1948) before the states for consideration. One, imposing a ban upon child labor, has been pending for almost a quarter of a century. The other, submitted as recently as 1947, proposes restriction of the maximum tenure of a president to ten years, and while by no means assured of the requisite number of ratifications, has (at least for the time being) diverted attention from other oft-proposed amendments variously contemplating a single term of six years or a maximum of two regular four-year terms. Further comment on the proposal may, however, be deferred to a later point where the general subject of presidential tenure receives consideration. [1]

[1] See pp. 429-430 below; and for complete texts of the two amendments, (see Appendix).

Balked by the Supreme Court in its attempt to restrict child labor, first 2. Child labor in 1916 by prohibiting the shipment in interstate commerce of goods produced by such labor,[1] and again in 1919 by taxing the products of such labor,[2] Congress in 1924 made a bid for the authority which it apparently lacked by submitting an amendment authorizing it directly to "limit, regulate, and prohibit the labor of persons under eighteen years of age," and suspending state laws in so far as not compatible with federal legislation on the subject. To the close of 1937, twenty-eight states ratified the proposal. This, however, was eight short of the requisite number; and (although the Supreme Court as recently as 1939 recognized the amendment as still pending) there have been no additions since. To a degree, the desired reform was achieved in the Fair Labor Standards Act of 1938, whose restrictions upon child labor were, in 1941, upheld by the Supreme Court in a decision sharply reversing the Hammer v. Dagenhart verdict of 1918.[3] Since, however, this measure does not reach the labor of children (a) in establishments whose products are handled exclusively in intrastate commerce, or (b) in agriculture, there is still room for the laggard amendment. The outlook for its ultimate adoption is, however, not bright.[4]

Rarely is there a time when proposals for amendment of the constitu- Others proposed tion on various lines are not being agitated in some quarter; as already mentioned, every session of Congress sees a number introduced, even though many receive (and deserve) little attention. Now and again it is suggested, indeed, that a convention be assembled to undertake an overhauling of the entire document—although of this there is no present prospect. Several recurring specific proposals (apart from the two now before the states) are, however, to be regarded as having some vitality, and even some limited chance of ultimate adoption; and included among the number are: (1) an amendment doing away with the system under which people vote only for presidential electors, and not for presidential candidates directly;[5] (2) an "equal rights" amendment sponsored for nearly a generation by the National Woman's party, unfailingly introduced in every session of Congress since 1923, and reading: "Equality of rights under the law shall not be denied or abridged by the United States or by any state on account of sex;"[6] (3) an amendment—advocated by

[1] Overruled in Hammer v. Dagenhart, 247 U. S. 251 (1918). This decision was by a bare majority of the Court, and Mr. Justice Holmes voiced what has ever since ranked as a classic dissent.

[2] Likewise overruled in Bailey v. Drexel Furniture Company, 259 U. S. 20 (1922).

[3] United States v. Darby Lumber Co., 312 U. S. 100.

[4] For a fuller survey, see G. Abbott, "Federal Regulation of Child Labor, 1906-1938," Social Service Rev., XIII, 409-430 (Sept., 1939). Cf. P. T. David, Barriers to Youth Employment (Washington, D. C., 1942); Nat. Child Labor Committee, The Long Road (New York, 1945)

[5] See pp. 278-280 below.

[6] The object, of course, is to put an end to many older laws (in some twenty-six states) placing women, in one way or another—as to employment, jury service, and the like—on a different basis from men. In the national nominating conventions of 1940, both major parties were urged from some quarters to declare for, and from others to remain silent upon, the proposal. The Republicans declared, if not directly

at least three recent presidents and supported by some leaders in all parties—making all bonds and other securities issued by federal, state, and local governments liable to federal taxation; [1] (4) another reducing the quota of senators necessary to assent to the ratification of treaties from two-thirds to a simple majority, or, as an alternative, requiring treaties to be submitted to both branches of Congress, with a majority in each sufficing for assent; [2] (5) another prohibiting poll-tax qualifications for voting; [3] and (6) still another empowering Congress to straighten out the tangle of existing marriage and divorce laws by enacting uniform legislation on the subject. [4]

Criticism of the Amending Process

1. On the ground that it is too slow and difficult

Madison believed that the modes of amendment agreed upon by the framers guarded "equally against that extreme facility which would render the constitution too mutable and that extreme difficulty which might perpetuate discovered faults;" and, on the whole, history has sustained his judgment. Chief Justice Marshall, however, characterized the amending machinery as "unwieldy and cumbrous;" and many times later it has been criticized sharply, on one or another of four principal grounds: (1) that procedures under it are too slow and difficult; (2) that, on the contrary, they are too easy; (3) that they are too far removed from direct action by the people; and (4) that they afford too much opportunity for minority dictation. Thirty-five or forty years ago, the notion was prevalent that no more amendments would be found possible unless the amending process were made easier; and farmer and labor interests, anxious for legislation which the Supreme Court seemed likely to block as long as the constitution's definition of congressional powers stood unchanged, were prolific in proposals for reducing the majorities in Congress requisite for submitting amendments (usually to simple majorities), or the number of states required for ratification (commonly to two-

---

for the amendment, at least for submission of it to the states, while the Democrats refrained from taking any stand on the subject. In 1944, the platforms of both parties declared for submission. Women's organizations are divided sharply, the opposition being led by the National Consumers League and the League of Women Voters of the United States, and contending that if the amendment were adopted, women would lose (especially in connection with protective labor laws) more than they would gain. Able jurists, too, have pointed out that adoption, with no standards specified, would give rise to chaos in nearly all fields of law. In the Senate, submission to the states was defeated July 19, 1946, by a vote of 38 for to 35 against, *i.e.,* 26 short of the necessary two-thirds. See "The Proposed Equal Rights Amendment to the United States Constitution" [Symposium], *Cong. Digest,* XXII, 99-128 (Apr., 1943).

[1] It is doubtful, however, whether an amendment is necessary for this purpose. See pp. 89-90 below.

[2] See p. 788 below.

[3] Although there is Southern contention to the contrary, an amendment seems unnecessary for achieving this purpose so far as federal elections are concerned; and, as pointed out later, bills dealing with the matter by ordinary legislation have long been pending in Congress (see p. 193 below). If, however, poll-tax qualifications were to be banned in *all* elections, an amendment would be essential.

[4] See pp. 95-96 below.

thirds), or both. Unquestionably, obstacles presented by the amending process have operated, over the years, to stimulate judicial review as an alternative means of keeping the fundamental law abreast of changing conditions. The adoption, however, of four amendments of large economic and social import within the space of seven years (1913-20), and of two others of much significance in the single year 1933, proved that, after all, the constitution's provisions are less immutably "frozen" than many had imagined.

Hamilton devoted almost an entire number of *The Federalist* to arguing that the amending process could not have been made any easier without inviting constitutional instability; [1] and the speedy ratification of the Eighteenth Amendment by legislatures of states in which, both before and after the advent of national prohibition, the people in state-wide referenda voted against the plan led many persons to believe that in point of fact the amending process was easier than it ought to be. For some years, therefore, proposed changes looked rather in the direction of making it more difficult. However, people who were disturbed because of the ease with which the Eighteenth Amendment swept through the state legislatures were happy over the equal facility with which the amendment repealing it was carried; and of late little has been heard of the earlier complaint.

2. On the ground that it is too easy

There has been the criticism, also, that in the absence of any provision for direct popular initiation of amendments or for submission of amendments to popular vote, the system is insufficiently democratic; and in 1912 the elder Senator La Follette brought forward a now forgotten plan designed to meet the objection. Submission of the Twenty-first Amendment to conventions in the states chosen for the sole purpose of acting on the proposal, and composed of delegates prepared to vote as instructed, put the fate of that amendment very definitely in popular hands. There is, however, no guarantee that this procedure will be followed again; certainly when submitting the presidential-tenure amendment of 1947, Congress ignored an excellent opportunity to establish a future presumption in its favor.[2] Besides, there are still those who would prefer that action on amendments be taken by the people directly [3] rather than even by specially elected and instructed convention delegates; and several amendments looking to that end have been proposed.

3. On the ground that it is not sufficiently democratic

The amending process has been criticized also because, at the final decisive stage of ratification, all states, regardless of population, have an equal voice—the objection being that this opens a way for the outcome to be determined by popular minorities. So great are the inequalities of population among the states that ratification of an amendment might be

4. On the ground that minorities may control

[1] No. LXXXV (Lodge's ed., 544-552).

[2] See pp. 429-430 below.

[3] As it is on amendments to state constitutions in all states except Delaware. Cf. *Hearings on Sen. Joint Res. 134,* 75th Cong., 3rd Sess. (1938), 1-85 ("Ratification of Constitutional Amendments by Popular Vote").

accomplished by thirty-six states containing among them considerably less than half of the inhabitants of the country; and in this way an amendment might be forced by a minority. Conversely, under the three-fourths rule, it is possible for a small number of less populous states to defeat an amendment desired by a vast majority of the people. Thirteen states can prevent any amendment from being adopted; and thirteen could be found which together would contain hardly one-twentieth of the population of the country—less, indeed, than half of the population of New York State alone. Should such a grouping actually take place on any proposed amendment, the remaining nineteen-twentieths of the people would be helpless. To be sure, the difficulty is largely theoretical; because, unless in the highly improbable event of an amendment definitely harmful to small states as such, states both large and small will be found on both sides of every proposal. It does, nevertheless, remain true that, without any sharp alignment of small states against large, (1) a sufficient number of states mostly less populous can give effect to an amendment not desired in states with a greater aggregate of population, and, on the other hand, (2) an amendment favored by states having such an aggregate may be defeated by a more or less fortuitous combination of hardly more than a quarter of the forty-eight containing decidedly fewer people. In amending the constitution, as in voting in the Senate, the mainly agricultural states of the West and South enjoy a distinct advantage over the industrial East.

Changes in procedure improbable

Taking into account all aspects of the situation, and especially the developments of the past thirty years, it would seem that changes in amending procedure such as would require the rewriting of Article V are unlikely. In the first place, we have discovered that the constitution can, after all, be amended with reasonable facility; six major amendments within twenty-one years (1913-33) is no mean record. In the second place, decided improvements have been achieved within the limits of the amending procedure as it now stands: (1) a principle concerning reasonable time limits for ratifications has been worked out and applied; (2) after lying unused for nearly a century and a half, the device of ratification by conventions, rather than by legislatures, has been brought into play, suggesting some presumption that hereafter Congress will, on each occasion, at least weigh the relative advantages of the two methods before prescribing either of them.[1] In the third place, while the Supreme Court has ruled that a popular referendum *after* a legislature has acted

[1] The almost total unfamiliarity of both senators and representatives with the convention plan of ratification as displayed when the presidential-tenure proposal of 1947 was debated is, however, not encouraging. Even a representative who introduced an amendment to the resolution providing for submission to conventions thought that the method had been followed in the case of the Eighteenth Amendment, whereas of course it was the Twenty-first. The Senate judiciary committee did indeed report a similar amendment, but was able to answer few questions about how the plan would operate. See E. S. Brown, "The Term of Office of the President," *Amer. Polit. Sci. Rev.*, XLI, 447-452 (June, 1947).

cannot be allowed to upset a ratification, popular mandates to conventions when such are employed, and "advisory" referenda as guides for action by legislatures when these are used, would seem to furnish about as much democratic control as can reasonably be asked. Finally, the arrangements permitting of undesirable, but actually rare, minority decisions are so inherent in the federal system that they can hardly be eliminated as long as that system stands.[1]

Other Modes of Constitutional Growth

To this point, our attention has been fixed upon the constitution as a *Expansion by interpretation* document—upon the ways in which its provisions can be, and have been, changed to achieve ends deemed politically or socially desirable. But if one sets out to discover the full sweep of the constitutional principles and rules under which we live, the document alone, even as amplified by amendment, will not carry him far. To be sure, when it says that the term of the president shall be four years, that the Senate shall be composed of two senators from each state, and that a member of the House of Representatives shall be at least twenty-five years of age, no room is left for any doubt or difference of opinion. When, however, it says that the privilege of the writ of *habeas corpus* shall not be suspended "unless when in cases of rebellion or invasion the public safety may require it," that Congress shall have power to "regulate commerce . . . among the several states," and that no person shall be deprived of life, liberty, or property "without due process of law," scores of questions at once arise which have to be answered before one can know what the provisions mean and how they apply—questions, however, to which no direct answers are supplied in the document. Who may suspend the writ of *habeas corpus?* When is a situation serious enough to justify suspension? What is included in "commerce among the states"? At what point in a commercial transaction may regulation by Congress begin? What is commerce, anyway? And what is "due process of law"? Who is to say? And on what lines is the principle to be applied to the bewilderingly varied interrelations and dealings of individuals and corporations?

The answers to these and scores of other questions like them, once *Who interprets* arrived at, are seldom written into the formal constitutional text. Nevertheless, they just as truly become effective parts of the fundamental law; indeed, most of our constitutional system as operating today, save only for its broader outlines, rests upon precisely such a basis. In one way or another, the answers are supplied, too, by nearly every operating branch of the government—even by instrumentalities like political parties which function largely outside of the government. In the exercise of broad

[1] For a vigorous demand, nevertheless, for "amending the amending process," see H. Hazlitt, *A New Constitution Now*, Chap. XIII. Cf. A. Hehmeyer, *Time for Change*, Chaps. III-V, suggesting, among other aids to constitutional revision, a constitutional convention convoked by joint resolution of Congress and having power, not of course to submit amendments to the states, but simply to report to Congress general revisions or particular amendments for that body to consider and perhaps propose.

discretionary powers which the courts have recognized as belonging exclusively to him, the president, by decisions and orders, contributes heavily. Heads of executive departments, commissions and boards, and even subordinate administrative authorities, interpret and apply the constitution's principles as related to their respective functions. Every time that Congress passes a bill, it in effect interprets the constitution and may add something to the ever-growing body of constitutional law and practice. Even the people who elect members of Congress may in so doing, and intentionally or otherwise, impart a slant to constitutional development. Finally, the courts, although dependent for their opportunity to construe and apply constitutional terms and provisions upon actual cases coming before them, have hundreds of chances every year to say what the law is and to give it the meaning and effect which their experience, predilections, and surroundings influence them to read into it. Here—in orders, rules, statutes, decisions, together with custom or usage— is the truly flexible, and ever-changing, part of our constitutional system; here is mainly where the constitution grows.[1]

Two or three of these remarkable processes may well be looked into a little more closely.

1. Statutory elaboration

Desirous of avoiding what one of them called "a too minutious wisdom," the framers of the original constitution outlined clearly enough the general framework and functions of the new government, but wisely left a multitude of matters to be taken care of, as need should arise, by Congress, and even in a subsidiary way by the state legislatures. For example, they assumed the existence of executive departments, and twice referred in the constitution to the heads of such establishments, yet left Congress not only to create the departments but to determine how many there should be, what they should be called, how they should be organized, and what should be their functions and interrelations. Other great regulative and administrative structures, standing outside of the executive departments, e.g., the Interstate Commerce Commission and the Federal Trade Commission, have originated, and their broad powers have been defined, in the same way. The composition of the two houses of Congress was prescribed carefully, but the times, places, and manner of electing both senators and representatives were left to be fixed by the state legislatures, subject to control by Congress itself;[2] and in a comprehensive statute of 1842 on the election of representatives, and another of 1866 on the election of senators, Congress amplified the constitutional law of this subject in much detail. Again, the judicial power of the United States was vested in

---

[1] Save for the wide scope for constitutional expansion through the channels indicated—resulting in "the swelling tide of constitutional development as it has flowed down through the years"—the written document undoubtedly would have been amended many more times than it has been; indeed, it might not have survived.

The constitutions of the states have developed in similar ways, but with formal amendment, including total revision, playing a larger part. See Chap. xxxvii in complete edition of this book.

[2] Except that Congress might not regulate the places of electing senators.

"one Supreme Court, and in such inferior courts as the Congress may from time to time ordain and establish." [1] Aside from the Supreme Court, therefore, the entire federal judicial establishment rests upon acts passed from time to time by Congress. A very large part of the actual working governmental system, indeed, has been created, and powers, duties, and limitations defined, by statutes passed under authority of constitutional provisions and of administrative regulations issued, in turn, under authority of statutes. As remarked above, whenever Congress enacts a law, it in effect interprets the constitution. If a given measure touches some hitherto unsettled problem, or carries the power of the government into an area not previously penetrated, it not only interprets but adds. And while such creative acts may be tested in the courts, the great majority are not—which to that extent leaves Congress the undisputed author of whatever new constitutional refinements and devices may be involved.

Mention of the courts suggests a second major mode of constitutional growth, *i.e.*, judicial construction or interpretation. How such action comes about must already be apparent.[2] Congress, or a state legislature, passes a law, or a national or state official performs an act, which is challenged as exceeding proper authority by some citizen or group of citizens affected adversely. A case is brought in the courts, and the law or action is attacked as being unconstitutional; whereupon the judges must decide whether the charge is well founded—in other words, whether the measure is or is not in conformity with constitutional stipulation or reasonable construction. To do this, it is, of course, necessary to determine what the pertinent constitutional provisions mean; and this high task the courts boldly and habitually assume. There is hardly any limit to the constitutional expansion and adaptation that may arise in this way. A disputed phrase of the constitution is interpreted in such a manner as to give it a content and application beyond that formerly attributed to it. This, in turn, furnishes a point of departure for a further elongation when the next similar case comes up. And so the process goes on, the lines of development being "pricked out by one decision after another until the last has carried matters a long way from the point at which the interpreting process began." [3] Nearly all of the more important implied powers of Congress, as distinguished from the modest list of eighteen powers enumerated in the eighth section of the first article, are traceable to this source; [4] and these implied powers have never been projected more boldly into new areas than in the past decade. The most important single reason why the written constitution has not been amended more frequently is that from an early stage in the nation's history the federal Supreme Court has sat as a "continuous constitutional convention,"

2. Judicial construction

[1] Art. III, § 1.
[2] On the historical development of it, see pp. 72-73 below.
[3] W. B. Munro, *Government of the United States* (5th ed.), **71**.
[4] See pp. 67-70 below, and for references, p. 75.

interpreting, developing, and expanding the basic law. One almost may say that every time the Court hands down one of its weekly batches of decisions, we have a constitution in some respects new.

3. Growth by usage

"Time and habit," remarked Washington, "are at least as necessary to fix the true character of governments as of other human institutions;" and so it comes about that another mode by which our national constitution expands and develops is usage or custom. This method of change attracts less attention than the others; it does not—at all events immediately—result in amendments, laws, or judicial decisions. Superimposed, nevertheless, upon the instrument of 1787 and its formal amendments, upon the laws that amplify and the decisions that extend it, is a great and steadily developing "unwritten constitution," consisting of usages determining actual governmental practice quite as truly as do the stipulations of written law—in fact sometimes more truly, considering that no small number of such usages have had the effect of turning written law into unintended channels, or even of reducing it to a dead letter. Plenty of illustrations will come to view as we proceed; for the present, it must suffice merely to mention the manner in which the electoral college functions in choosing the president, the extensive use of "executive agreements" in lieu of treaties, the assembling of the department heads in the advisory body known as the cabinet, the caucus and committee systems in Congress, the custom requiring members of the House of Representatives to be residents of the districts in which they are elected, and substantially all of the apparatus—caucuses, conventions, committees, platforms, funds—of political parties.

"The living word and deed of living men"

The general theme need not be elaborated farther. The upshot of all that has been suggested is that the bare outline of a governmental system contained in the written constitution as it came from the hands of the fathers, and as it still can be read in the books, has been amplified and filled in—by amendment, executive action, statute, judicial construction, usage—until it has come to be one of the most elaborate and complicated plans of political organization and procedure known to history. And the process goes on unceasingly. This does not prevent some people from clamoring for a "modernization" of the constitution, or even for "a new constitution now." What they fail to recognize is that we actually *have* a new constitution now, and shall have another tomorrow, and still another the day after. For the actual constitution at any given time is what citizens, lawmakers, administrators, and judges think it is; it is, in a sense, "a state of mind, and can be changed by changing our mind." [1] Certainly we change our mind (or the judges change it for us) with remarkable facility. To be sure, there are periods in which little seems to happen—in which the written fundamental law looks like a strait-jacket. People bent upon innovations then grow impatient. But if our experience

[1] C. E. Merriam, *The Written Constitution and the Unwritten Attitude* (New York, 1931), 3.

teaches anything, it is that other periods follow in which momentous changes tread upon one another's heels. Of late, we certainly have been living in such a period. Formal amendments do indeed come rather infrequently; during the most recent decade and a half of swift and fundamental change, there have been none at all. And if we were dependent upon such, we should either have to go over to something like the English system, in which any constitutional change can be made by simple act of Parliament, or, as an alternative, see our constitution snap under the strain and be replaced with something else. But (except of course at certain points) there is hardly any limit to what can take place without formal amendments at all; often, indeed, by the time when formidable sentiment for an amendment can be built up, new lines of interpretation and action will be found to have rendered the amendment itself unnecessary. As "the living word and deed of living men," the constitution of our day is the handiwork of John Marshall, Andrew Jackson, and Abraham Lincoln—of Woodrow Wilson, Mr. Justice Holmes, Senator Norris, and Franklin D. Roosevelt—no less truly than of Hamilton, Madison, Franklin, and Morris. When the fundamental law no longer lives and grows, flexibly and spontaneously, the nation which it serves will have become a memory.

REFERENCES

A. N. Christensen and E. M. Kirkpatrick, *The People, Politics, and the Politician; Readings on American Government* (New York, 1941 and 1947), Chap. III.

B. F. Wright, *The Growth of American Constitutional Law* (Boston and New York, 1942), Chaps. v-vi, ix-x.

C. B. Swisher, *American Constitutional Development* (Boston, 1943), Chaps. xxix, xxxix.

————, *The Growth of Constitutional Power in the United States* (Chicago, 1947), Chaps. i, iv.

W. W. Willoughby, *Constitutional Law of the United States* (2nd ed., New York, 1929), I, Chap. xxxvii.

R. E. Cushman, *What's Happening to Our Constitution?*, Pub. Affairs Pamphlets, No. 70 (New York, 1942).

W. A. Platz, "Article Five of the Federal Constitution," *Geo. Washington Law Rev.*, III, 17-49 (Nov., 1934).

H. V. Ames, "The Proposed Amendments to the Constitution of the United States During the First Century of Its History," *Annual Report of Amer. Hist. Assoc.* (Washington, D. C., 1896), II.

D. P. Myers, *The Process of Constitutional Amendment* (76th Cong., 3rd Sess., Sen. Doc. No. 314, 1940). Sets forth the legal problems arising in connection with the adoption of successive amendments.

T. H. Reed [ed.], "The Constitution in the Twentieth Century," *Annals of Amer. Acad. of Polit. and Soc. Sci.*, CLXXXV (May, 1936). An extensive series of articles, including a convenient bibliography by E. W. Carter and C. C. Rohlfing.

C. A. Beard, "The Dear Old Constitution," *Harper's Mag.*, CLX, 281-291 (Feb., 1930).

————, *The Supreme Court and the Constitution* (New York, 1912).

L. B. Orfield, *The Amending of the Federal Constitution* (Ann Arbor, Mich., 1942).

E. S. Corwin, *The Constitution and What It Means Today* (10th ed., Princeton, N. J., 1948).

——————, *Constitutional Revolution, Ltd.* (Claremont, Calif., 1941).

P. T. Fenn, *The Development of the Constitution* (New York, 1948).

C. Warren, *Congress, the Constitution, and the Supreme Court* (Boston, 1925).

F. Frankfurter, *Mr. Justice Holmes and the Constitution* (Cambridge, Mass., 1927).

N. B. Lasson, "The History and Development of the Fourth Amendment to the United States Constitution," *Johns Hopkins Univ. Studies in Hist. and Polit. Sci.*, LV, 223-360 (1937).

H. E. Flack, "The Adoption of the Fourteenth Amendment," *ibid.*, Extra Vol. XXVI (Baltimore, 1908).

J. M. Mathews, "Legislative and Judicial History of the Fifteenth Amendment," *ibid.*, XXVII, Nos. 6-7 (Baltimore, 1909).

E. K. Ketcham, *The Sixteenth Amendment* (Urbana, Ill., 1926).

E. S. Brown, *Ratification of the Twenty-first Amendment to the Constitution of the United States; State Convention Records and Laws* (Ann Arbor, Mich., 1938).

W. B. Munro, *The Makers of the Unwritten Constitution* (New York, 1930).

C. E. Merriam, *The Written Constitution and the Unwritten Attitude* (New York, 1931).

H. W. Horwill, *The Usages of the American Constitution* (London, 1925).

W. K. Wallace, *Our Obsolete Constitution* (New York, 1932).

W. MacDonald, *A New Constitution for a New America* (New York, 1921).

W. Y. Elliott, *The Need for Constitutional Reform* (New York, 1935).

H. Hazlitt, *A New Constitution Now* (New York, 1942).

A. Hehmeyer, *Time for Change; A Proposal for a Second Constitutional Convention* (New York, 1943).

The Constitution of the United States of America as Amended to January 1, 1938 (70th Cong., 2nd Sess., Sen. Doc. No. 232). Elaborate annotation of the twenty-one amendments.

2. THE FEDERAL SYSTEM IN TRANSITION

CHAPTER V

FEDERALISM AND THE PRINCIPLE OF NATIONAL SUPREMACY

As planned by the constitutional fathers and developed through the years, American government acquired three predominating features—popular sovereignty, federalism, and separation of powers. To be sure, the system did not start off in a setting of thoroughgoing democracy. The men who made the original constitution were not elected by the people; the people did not directly vote on its adoption; no very large proportion of them were voters in any case. Nevertheless, according to the document's opening words, "we the people" ordained it; the government for which it provided rested fundamentally on popular consent; and by leaving the states free to regulate and expand the suffrage as they chose, the constitution opened wide the road for progressive attainment of the broad democracy that we know today. Notwithstanding qualifications and limitations that will occur to any one, our government is of, by, and for the people.

Three great principles of American government: 1. Popular sovereignty

In the second place, it is a federal government. The people of the country are not thrown into a single mass, under simply one government endowed with full powers wielded from one center. On the contrary, while all are directly under one national government for certain purposes, they also are under one or another of forty-eight state governments which are not mere arms of the national government, but instrumentalities of original, separate, and to a considerable extent independent, political units. There is government on the national level, government on the state level, and of course government on local levels as well. And as we shall see, no other circumstance introduces so much complexity into our constitutional and political system as especially the national-state division or dichotomy.

2. Federalism

Finally, there is cleavage vertically as well as horizontally; national, state, and many local governments are organized on the constitutional principle of separation of powers. The idea that government analyzes into three main functions, executive, legislative, and judicial, and that prudence requires the three to be placed in different hands, is as old as Aristotle; Locke, Montesquieu, Blackstone, and other seventeenth- and eighteenth-century authorities who influenced our constitution's makers expounded it persuasively; separation found recognition in the colonial governments, and in state governments under the Revolutionary constitutions it was conspicuous; and the planners of our present system took it quite for granted as a proper and necessary safeguard against excessive con-

3. Separation of powers

centration of power, with resulting invitation to tyranny. Recognizing, however, that *complete* separation would result in deadlocks and breakdowns, the constitution's authors also introduced "checks and balances" calculated to make executive, legislative, and judicial branches nevertheless work as one government. All of the three basic principles enumerated will receive abundant comment and illustration as we proceed—the first to be followed up in some detail being that of federalism.

Nation and states Rumor has it that, at a critical moment in the proceedings of the Philadelphia convention, Alexander Hamilton, irked by obstacles to the national centralization which he desired, petulantly exclaimed that the states ought to be abolished. Of course neither Hamilton nor any one else ever for a moment supposed any bold step like that to be possible. Far to the contrary, if there was one thing above all else that the constitution's makers were bound to do, it was to keep a place in the new system—and a very important one at that—for the states, whose delegates they were, and without whose approval their work might as well never have been done. All of the existing states were carried over from the old constitutional régime into the new one, with their names, boundaries, and governments unchanged, and with functions and powers curtailed to be sure, but nevertheless still extensive and fundamental. Furthermore, the constitution authorized Congress to admit new states to the Union; and from 1791 onwards this power was exercised, as the Southern and Western portions of the country filled with population, until in 1912 the admission of New Mexico and Arizona brought the number to the present forty-eight.

When, however, the constitution's framers wisely decided upon a national government resting directly upon the people, as the state governments also did, they opened up a question around which much of our later history has revolved, namely, that of the legal and practical relations existing between nation and states. Indeed, out of differences of view upon this matter arose long and bitter disputes which not only tested to the utmost the Supreme Court's capacity for constitutional interpretation, but at one stage plunged the country into devastating civil war. Never yet has the question been answered at all points, nor in truth can it ever be; for in a dynamic, changing society governmental powers simply cannot be defined and circumscribed with such precision and finality as to prevent people from construing them differently in the face of new circumstances and needs. In a country like England, with all public authority concentrated in a single national government,[1] no difficulty arises. But our system is "federal," not "unitary;" except in a few fields such as foreign relations, powers are divided, or distributed, by fundamental law between a national government and forty-eight state governments. And no legerdemain of constitutional phraseology can prevent

---

[1] Though of course exercised to a considerable extent through counties, boroughs, and other units of local government.

the division from giving rise to endless doubts and challenges. In America, as elsewhere, federalism has proved an exciting adventure.[1]

Historic Problem of the Nature of the Union

Weighty as are many of the questions of national power and state power brought to the fore, for example, by experiences under the New Deal and in World War II, such questions have, after all, related only to the distribution of power within a political order the ultimate basis and nature of which are matters of general agreement. But there was a time when dispute went farther than that. Throughout the first half of our national history, it reached to the very nature of the Union itself. Was the United States, under the constitution, a true and indivisible nation; or was it only a league of sovereign states as before 1789? The question may sound hollow to our ears, but it once stirred the profoundest thought and emotion of American political leaders. That the states were not mere administrative subdivisions, nor yet simply subordinate areas with a limited autonomy conferred by the central government, was conceded by all. They were, as everybody knew, distinct, original, indestructible political entities, with broad surviving inherent powers. But did this mean that they were "sovereign"? Or were their people so merged in a common, superior, national fabric that the states also, as political units, had become inextricably embedded in it?

The fundamental issue

Happily, the logic of events has gone far toward clearing up all reasonable doubt on this score. As every student of our history knows, the trend since 1789 has been decidedly in the direction of a strong national government based on an indissoluble union of the states. In a remarkable series of decisions in cases turning on constitutional questions, the Supreme Court, notably during John Marshall's long tenure as chief justice (1801-35), consistently—and with powerful effect—gave its support to the nationalist view. The denial and total extinction of the alleged right of a state to nullify acts of Congress and decisions of federal courts, notwithstanding momentary successes of nullificationists in South Carolina and Georgia in 1829-32, worked to the same end. And—passing over a great number of other contributing factors—the failure of secession in 1860-65, and the general acceptance of the doctrine that a state cannot secede, clinched the victory of nationalism and stamped the union with the quality of permanence which it unmistakably possesses in our own day.

Triumph of the nationalist view

[1] The advantages and disadvantages of federalism are considered at some length in J. W. Garner, *Political Science and Government* (New York, 1932), 346-356, 412-422, and J. Bryce, *The American Commonwealth* (4th ed., New York, 1910), Chaps. XXVII-XXVIII. Canada, Australia, Switzerland, Brazil, Argentina, and Mexico have federal systems; although outside of the United States, the most interesting federal arrangements are perhaps those prevailing in the U.S.S.R. The only modern book devoted specifically to federalism is K. C. Wheare, *Federal Government* (London and New York, 1946), which, however, is marred by somewhat imperfect understanding of the American system.

The verdict of history is that the ultimate, *i.e.*, sovereign, authority in this country is, not each particular state in its own separate sphere, nor yet the nation itself as embodied in a government, but rather the general mass of people standing back of both state and national governments.[1] In line with the famous assertion of the Declaration of Independence that "governments derive their just powers from the consent of the governed," they—the people—have the final word on the kind of government they will have, the powers it shall possess, and how these powers shall be exercised; [2] if enough of the people so desired, they could abrogate both state and national governments as we know them and put something entirely different in their places. Under our so-called divided system of government, it is not sovereignty itself that is divided; if divided, it would hardly continue to be *sovereignty*. What is divided is, rather, the exercise or use of sovereign powers—powers inherent in the sovereign people, but for convenience intrusted to governments, national and state, as agencies for exercising them. For obvious reasons, the people cannot, in the mass, execute laws, operate public services, or administer justice. They can, and in some states occasionally do, legislate, through the medium of the popular initiative and referendum.[3] Even the most enthusiastic advocates of those twin devices of direct democracy regard them, however, only as "guns behind the door," to be brought out for use when legislatures fail to give desired results; normally, legislation will in any case be by bodies of representatives chosen for the purpose. What happens under our system is, then, (to repeat) that the sovereign people, through constitutional provisions, parcel out the exercise of authority— executive, legislative, and judicial—to agencies which we know as the national and state governments; and, aside from making provisions for the structure, and to some extent the workings, of the national government, the federal constitution is devoted mainly to drawing boundary lines between the powers which the governments on the two levels are required, permitted, or forbidden to wield.

The Distribution of Powers

Three or four major aspects of this distribution of powers call for emphasis. The first is that the national government is strictly limited to powers delegated to it or reasonably implied therein. Such was the almost inescapable presumption from the language of the constitution as originally adopted. Some doubt, however, having arisen on the point, the Tenth Amendment, ratified in 1791, fixed the principle beyond all

---

[1] "Sovereignty" is a tricky word. As some one has remarked, the history of it in the United States illustrates the familiar fact that in all argument, if you insist on making certain words mean what you want them to mean, you can always reach the conclusion you wish to reach. With easy fluency, the states are today sometimes spoken of sentimentally, even by the courts, as "sovereign."

[2] Cf. Marshall's vigorous assertions in McCulloch *v.* Maryland, 4 Wheaton **316** (1819).

[3] See pp. 900-904 below (in complete edition of this book).

possible challenge. Specific grants of power (and some of more general character) are made in the constitutional text to Congress, to the president, to the courts; but, says the Amendment, "all powers not delegated to the United States by the constitution, nor prohibited by it to the states, are reserved to the states respectively or to the people." [1] No reader of this book will need to be told that the powers wielded by the national government are immeasurably greater today than in the times of Washington and Jefferson. At some points, they appear to a good many people to have been carried considerably beyond the grants contained in the constitution. In the eye of the law, however, whatever expansion has taken place— except in taxation and one or two other areas where changes have been authorized by constitutional amendment—has resulted solely from progressively wider and more penetrating applications of powers already possessed. President, Congress, and courts have no proper authority except such as can be found somewhere (as express provision or by reasonable implication) within the four corners of the constitution.[2]

A second fact, already indicated, is that the state governments, on the other hand, have powers that are original, inherent, and largely undefined—derived from and authorized by the people of the respective states, of course, but at any rate not dependent on the national constitution. A certain number of powers belonging to state governments are, to be sure, alluded to in the national constitution. But there is no attempt to present a list. Carrying over into the new system the great bulk of powers which they possessed under the old one (and they would never have ratified the constitution unless permitted to do this), the original states have ever afterwards enjoyed the ample and undefined range of powers guaranteed in the Tenth Amendment—a range of powers which, although curtailed at some points by nationalizing amendments, and in effect also by legislation and judicial decisions, has expanded considerably more than it has contracted, notwithstanding the common impression that it is the powers of the national government alone that have been magnified

State powers

---

[1] In the federal system of Canada, the principle of distribution was intended to be precisely the opposite. Influenced to some extent, it would appear, by the recent spectacle of civil war in the United States, the authors of the British North America Act of 1867 undertook to assign to the provinces only enumerated powers, leaving everything else to the Dominion government. In actual practice, however, the whole subject of delegated and residual powers has become so beclouded by judicial decisions that no one knows precisely where the lines of division fall. See J. E. Hodgetts, "Problems of Canadian Federalism," *State Government*, XVIII, 95-99 (June, 1945).

[2] The view of Theodore Roosevelt and others that all powers of a *general* nature, *i.e.*, affecting the nation as a whole, properly belong to it, even though not definitely granted, was expressly rejected by the Supreme Court in Kansas *v.* Colorado, 206 U. S. 46 (1902). With respect to the field of international relations, however, the Court has more recently recognized (in United States *v.* Curtiss-Wright Export Corporation, 299 U. S. 304, 1936) that even if the constitution were silent on the point (which it is not), the power to carry on diplomatic intercourse and to make war and peace would belong to the federal government as being "necessary concomitants of nationality." In other words, such powers could (*if necessary*) be inferred from the very fact of the United States being an independent nation, as obviously predicated in the constitution.

in these later decades.[1] And of course, under the principle of state equality, all states subsequently admitted to the Union are entitled to, and possess, a similar range of authority.

No government endowed with unlimited powers A third fact is that no government in our system has unlimited powers. The national government has only the powers delegated to it, expressly or by implication; the state governments, although with powers undefined and unenumerated, are restricted at many points by the federal constitution and at still more by the state constitutions; and measures enacted by either Congress or a state legislature (acts, too, performed by executive or administrative authorities), if regarded as exceeding the limits of powers constitutionally fixed, are practically certain sooner or later to be challenged in the courts, and may be held null and void.

This is but another way of saying that by no means *all* power has been intrusted by the people to government of any kind. Plenty of powers are withheld from the national government, simply by not being conferred in the national constitution; many are withheld from state governments by being prohibited in state constitutions. But—and this is the present point —some also are withheld from both national and state governments, either by being forbidden to both in the national constitution (*e.g.*, depriving a person of life, liberty, or property without due process of law) or by being prohibited to national and state governments concurrently by the respective constitutions (as in the case of taking private property for public use without compensation). Taken together, the federal and state constitutions thus leave, and in fact create, "spheres of anarchy"—of no government, so to speak, within which people may not be interfered with at all by any public authority.[2] As suggested by the above illustrations, these areas of immunity are associated mainly with civil rights and liberties; and the Ninth Amendment gives them a significant flexibility by stipulating that the enumeration of certain rights in the federal constitution "shall not be construed to deny or disparage others retained by the people."

The resulting pattern Viewed in the large, the arrangements relating to powers under our national constitution work out somewhat as follows:

A. Powers possessed:
1. Powers conferred on the national government exclusively (*e.g.*, conducting foreign relations, regulating foreign and interstate commerce);
2. Powers possessed by the states exclusively—appropriate to their status and not forbidden (*e.g.*, creating counties, chartering cities);

[1] To confirm this fact of the enormous growth of state powers, one has only to compare the list of things that his own state is now doing—in the fields of taxation and finance, education, public health and safety, social insurance, conservation of resources, regulation of transportation and trade, control of elections, and what not— with the activities of any one of the states a hundred, or even fifty, years ago. Cf. Chap. XLII below (in complete edition of this book).

[2] C. A. Beard, *American Government and Politics* (4th ed., New York, 1924), 102.

3. Powers possessed by national and state governments concurrently—conferred on the former and not withheld from the latter (*e.g.*, levying taxes, borrowing money).

B. Powers withheld:

1. Powers forbidden to the national government only (*e.g.*, levying direct taxes otherwise than in proportion to population [1]);

2. Powers forbidden to the state governments only (*e.g.*, making treaties, coining money);

3. Powers forbidden to both national and state governments (*e.g.*, passing *ex post facto* laws, abridging the right of United States citizens to vote on account of color or sex, infringing certain civil liberties guaranteed in the first ten amendments to the national constitution [2]).

Implied Powers

The careful phrasing of the constitution did not prevent—no linguistic niceties could have prevented—differences of opinion concerning the limits of both national and state powers, and sharp controversy ensued before the new system had been in operation a year. In 1790, Alexander Hamilton, secretary of the treasury, proposed the establishment of a national bank. Opponents of further centralization at once objected that the constitution, in enumerating the powers of Congress, said nothing about a bank; they could show, indeed, that its authors had deliberately refused to give Congress, by direct grant, even limited authority to create corporations. Hamilton and others who supported his policy replied that while the constitution did not, to be sure, authorize Congress in so many words to create a bank, the power to do so could easily be deduced from certain grants of authority about which there could be no question— particularly those relating to currency and other aspects of national finance, not to mention the "sweeping clause" with which the constitution's enumeration of the powers of Congress concludes, and in which the two houses are authorized "to make all laws which shall be necessary and proper for carrying into execution the foregoing powers, and all other powers vested by this constitution in the government of the United States, or in any department or officer thereof." [3] The Hamiltonian view prevailed, and the bank was established. Opinion on the matter, however—undoubtedly reflecting honest, and more or less doctrinaire, differences of interpretation, but rooted also in practical considerations of

(marginal note: How the question arose)

[1] For income taxes (often considered direct), the Sixteenth Amendment waives this limitation.

[2] On their face, these amendments restrict the federal government only, but Supreme Court interpretations of the due process clause of the Fourteenth Amendment have in later days made the restrictions relating to speech, press, religion and assembly applicable to the states also. Cf. p. 154, note 1, below.

[3] Art. I, § 8, cl. 18. One will not be surprised to be told that this spacious clause became a principal basis for the entire development of implied powers in later times.

personal interest and party strategy [1]—continued divided; and from this beginning the issue of "implied powers" broadened out until it became the topmost one (except that of secession for a decade or two) in the entire constitutional history of the country.

Led by Jefferson, the strict constructionists argued that the national government had no powers except such as were expressly conferred upon it in the constitution, or, at most, such as could be shown to be indispensably involved in the exercise of these delegated powers. To take a single step, urged the vigilant Virginian (in a letter in which he gave Washington his views on the constitutionality of the proposed bank), beyond the boundaries "specially drawn" around the powers of Congress by the Tenth Amendment "is to take possession of a boundless field of power, no longer susceptible of any definition." On the other hand, the loose or broad constructionists, such as Hamilton, contended that the national government had all powers which could by any reasonable interpretation be regarded as implied in the letter of the granted powers, and also that it had a right to choose the manner and means of performing its functions, even though involving the employment of agencies not necessarily *indispensable* for its purposes.

A practical necessity

On purely legal grounds, Jefferson's argument was plausible; and events proved him right in predicting that the doctrine of implied powers, once accepted, would lead to endless expansion of the national government's activities—often at the expense of powers originally considered as belonging to the states. The logic of practical necessity lay, however, with the Hamiltonian view. If the national government, perennially confronted with new conditions and unforeseeable problems, was to attain the ends for which it was established, it must without fail have the benefit of all authority that could reasonably be deduced from the grants that had been made to it; otherwise, it would be halted at points where inaction would be ruinous. This was eventually conceded, although grudgingly, by the Jeffersonians themselves; and when they gained control of the government in 1801, they soon were found availing themselves of implied powers almost, if not quite, as freely as had their Federalist rivals. On no other basis, for example, could Louisiana have been annexed in 1803 or an embargo laid on foreign trade in 1807—actions for which there was only the same kind of indirect constitutional warrant as for Hamilton's bank.

Chief Justice Marshall's historic pronouncement

In the course of time, the question reached the Supreme Court; and in a memorable series of nationalizing decisions between 1809 and 1835 that tribunal—while acknowledging limits beyond which powers could not properly be inferred—lent the doctrine the full weight of its authority. Classic expression was given the Court's views by Chief Justice Marshall in the case of McCulloch *v.* Maryland, in 1819, as follows: "This govern-

---

[1] Certainly, for example, the business and propertied elements favoring Hamilton's policies had an economic interest in seeing them carried out.

ment is acknowledged by all to be one of enumerated powers. The principle that it can exercise only the powers granted to it is now universally admitted. But the question respecting the extent of the powers actually granted is perpetually arising and will probably continue to arise as long as our system shall exist. . . . The powers of the government are limited, and its powers are not to be transcended. But we think the sound construction of the constitution must allow to the national legislature that discretion with respect to the means by which the powers it confers are to be carried into execution, which will enable that body to perform the high duties assigned to it in a manner most beneficial to the people. Let the end be legitimate, let it be within the scope of the constitution, and all means which are appropriate, which are plainly adapted to that end, which are not prohibited but consist with the letter and spirit of the constitution, are constitutional." [1]

The doctrine here laid down gained general acceptance and is today firmly embedded in our constitutional law. Not only so, but, as a result of social and economic changes, of wartime and depression crises, and of growing belief in the usefulness of government regulation, the doctrine is nowadays applied in directions and in situations of which Marshall and his black-robed colleagues never dreamed. Remarkable indeed are the multifold activities for which it has supplied the sole legal justification. To cite a familiar illustration: From the constitution's terse grant of power to "regulate commerce with foreign nations and among the several states," Congress has drawn authority to control not only the transportation of goods by rail, water, motor, and air, but the carriage of passengers, the transmission of electric current, the moving of oil through pipe-lines, and the communication of ideas by telegraph, telephone, and radio; and not only to control, but even to prohibit, as in the case of the interstate transportation of commodities manufactured with the aid of child labor. Again: Starting with what appears a modest grant of authority to "establish post-offices and postroads," Congress is found providing for transportation of mail by railroad, steamship, and airplane; prohibiting interference with the mails; placing armed guards in railway mail cars; subsidizing and providing federal supervision of a national highway system; authorizing non-military road-building by the national government itself; excluding seditious, salacious, and fraudulent matter from the mails; and maintaining a federal express business in the form of what we know as the parcel post. Once more: The constitution has nothing to say about unemployment compensation and old-age pensions. The delegates who rode into Philadelphia by stage-coach and on horseback could not possibly have foreseen the development of our present complicated industrial society. They did, however, write a "general welfare" clause into the constitution in connection with the power to tax and borrow and spend. And when Congress in 1935 passed a Social Security Act extending

Implied powers a prolific source of government action

[1] 4 Wheaton 316. For an explanation of the case, see p. 87, note 5, below.

the advantages of unemployment allowances and old-age insurance to multiplied millions of people, the Supreme Court found in that clause ample authority for its doing so.

Sometimes, to be sure, the executive and legislative branches embark upon policies involving the exercise of powers which the courts hold *not* to be warranted by the constitutional phraseology from which they were deduced. In this way, for example, an act of 1894 laying a federal tax on incomes—also a child labor act of 1916 and another of 1919—was rendered of no effect.[1] A similar fate befell the National Recovery Act and the Agricultural Adjustment Act of 1933. Speaking generally, the judges have been inclined to give the national government the benefit of a broad and liberal construction of the constitution's provisions. A decade or so ago, there was loud complaint, in government circles and outside, that the "nine old men" then on the Supreme Bench were, by taking too restricted a view of implied powers, perversely obstructing the social and economic program associated with the New Deal; and an enlargement of the Court's membership with a view to "liberalizing" the tribunal's attitude became the uppermost political question of 1937.[2] In a message to Congress, President Roosevelt contended that the founders of our government expected and intended that a liberal construction of the constitution in later years would give Congress the same relative powers over new national problems that they themselves had envisaged with respect to the national questions of their day. Others, however, were of the opinion that acceptance of so broad and general a principle would tend to break down the fundamental safeguard of limited powers, and believed that, rather than stretch implied powers to such lengths, the constitution should itself be amended to cover the matters most gravely at issue. The number of justices was not increased. But some change of heart was evidenced in a series of newer decisions; "liberals" succeeded to a number of seats falling vacant; and after the flurry subsided broad construction of implied national powers quietly went on transforming the country's constitutional pattern.

Ultimate Supremacy of the National Government

Under our federal system, the national government is supreme within the sphere assigned to it, the states no less so in the sphere reserved to them. Contrary, however, to a view once widely held and still occasionally cropping up,[3] this does not mean that nation and states stand on a footing of equality. Such a notion, indeed, ought (it would seem) to be completely dispelled by one clause of the constitution, if no other. "This constitution," we read, "and the laws of the United States which shall be made in pursuance thereof, and all treaties made, or which shall be made, under

---

[1] As we have seen, however, the Supreme Court reversed itself on the child-labor issue in 1941. See p. 51 above.

[2] See pp. 546-549 below.

[3] As, for example, in K. C. Wheare, *Federal Government* (London, 1946), 2.

the authority of the United States shall be the *supreme law of the land;* and the judges in every state shall be bound thereby, anything in the constitution or laws of any state to the contrary notwithstanding." [1] In other words, while the state governments may be, and are, supreme within their reserved spheres, these spheres are circumscribed not only by the delegation of numerous vital powers to the national government, but by the basic operating principle that whatever the national government ordains—within the broad and still expanding area of its authority— is *supreme law,* enforceable as such and binding no less upon state executives, legislatures, courts, and people than upon officers and people of the nation itself. Nothing of this sort can be said for the laws or other governmental actions of any state. So long, to be sure, as these go unchallenged by federal authority, or indeed if, upon being challenged, they are held to be not inconsistent with that authority, they may be said— so far as the national government is concerned—to flow from "supreme" power within the boundaries of the state. If shown, however, to be incompatible with any legitimate exercise of power by the national government, they lose all claim to validity; and many have in this way been rendered of no force and effect.

But who is to say whether a state government—or for that matter the national government—has overstepped the bounds marked out for it? To this question, the constitution gives only a partial answer; and there has always been difference of opinion as to what the framers intended. To be sure, there was a proposal in the Philadelphia convention that, as a means of upholding the "supreme law" and protecting the Union, Congress be given power to disallow, or veto, any act passed by a state legislature. But although at one time this was agreed to without dissent, so much opposition developed that the idea was abandoned. And for two reasons, the decision was a wise one—first, because the broad grant proposed would have enabled Congress to interfere with state legislation, in a wholly undesirable manner, on political as well as on constitutional grounds (that is, merely on grounds of policy, whether or not any constitutional question was involved), and second, because in the "supreme law" clause the constitution's authors already had in a measure supplied the answer: if state judges were to be "bound" by the national constitution, laws, and treaties as supreme law, "anything in the . . . laws of any state to the contrary notwithstanding", it manifestly would be their duty to declare unconstitutional and unenforceable any state legislation conflicting with such supreme law. To this extent, even if somewhat indirectly,

Who is to decide in cases of dispute?

[1] Art. VI, § 2. "This clause," observes a distinguished historian, "may be called the central clause of the constitution [other writers have called it the linchpin], because without it the whole system would be unwieldy, if not impracticable. Draw out this particular bolt, and the machinery falls to pieces. In these words the constitution is plainly made not merely a declaration, a manifesto, dependent for its life and usefulness on the passing will of statesmen or of people, but a fundamental law, enforceable like any other law in courts." A. C. McLaughlin, *The Confederation and the Constitution* (New York, 1905), 247.

the national constitution provided for—or at least assumed—judicial review as a means of protecting the federal-state balance.[1]

But who was to guard against *Congress* overstepping constitutional bounds? And would the watchfulness of the state courts prove a sufficient safeguard against transgression by state legislatures? In other words, were the federal courts also to have power of review, applying to both federal and state legislation? The Virginia plan had proposed to associate with the national executive a council of revision which should scrutinize every measure passed by Congress, with any objected to taking effect only if subsequently reënacted by a two-thirds vote in both houses. Presumably a measure might be questioned on constitutional as on other grounds, although manifestly that was not what the authors of the plan were thinking of primarily; and in any event the convention's final decision was to give the veto of acts of Congress to the president alone.[2] This left open the question of review by the federal courts. But the constitution as adopted said nothing on the point; and in consequence there have always been people who maintained that the fathers did not intend that the federal tribunals should have such power, and that the exercise of it by them is not only unsupported by the letter, but contrary to the spirit, of the fundamental law, and therefore sheer usurpation.

A different view, however, won more general acceptance. From the records, it appears that the constitution's makers did not remain silent on the subject simply because they had not thought of it, nor yet because they considered it unimportant, but only because they regarded inquiring into the constitutionality of legislation as necessarily involved in, and going along with, the work not only of the state courts already existing (which, as we have seen, were currently exercising the function), but equally of the national courts remaining to be established. In other words, it was simply taken for granted that the forthcoming national courts would, as an incident of judicial power, refuse to enforce as law any act of a state legislature "contravening," as Roger Sherman put it, "the authority of the Union," or, for that matter, any act of Congress transcending the proper powers of that body; and in so doing, they would simply be upholding the principle of federalism fundamental to the entire governmental system. In line with this argument, indeed, judicial review becomes, for the judiciary, comparable to the great "resulting" powers of

[1] Within the brief period of their existence, state courts already had declared state legislation void as being incompatible with state constitutions (*e.g.*, in the New Jersey case of Holmes *v.* Walton in 1780 and the Rhode Island case of Trevett *v.* Weeden in 1786).

[2] Of course, he too is not precluded from passing judgment on a measure's constitutionality, and may veto any that he considers unconstitutional. President Taft vetoed the Webb-Kenyon Act (penalizing shipments of liquor into prohibition states) in 1913 on this ground. The president's judgment, however, has no finality; Congress may reënact a measure over his veto, as happened in the instance cited. And this puts him in the position of being obliged to enforce a law which he regards as contrary to the constitution. To a degree, the Supreme Court eased the situation for Taft by pronouncing the Webb-Kenyon Act constitutional.

Congress [1]—a power arising from the very nature of the judicial process when operating under a system of government based upon limitation of powers and distribution of them between two sets of authorities inevitably tending to encroach upon one another.[2]

As is so often the case, however, fact is here more important than theory; and the fact is that not only did the Judiciary Act passed by the very first Congress in 1789 authorize the federal Supreme Court to review any case in which a state court had upheld a state law alleged to be in conflict with the constitution, with a statute, or with a treaty of the United States, but the power was early brought into play, steadily broadened in scope and application, and has been employed with tremendous effect for more than a century and a quarter. An act of Congress was first held void by the Supreme Court on the ground of unconstitutionality in the case of Marbury v. Madison, decided in 1803; [3] state statutes were declared void, on constitutional grounds, in a long line of cases beginning with Fletcher v. Peck in 1810.[4] And thus was built up in the federal domain—paralleling a similar development in the states— a function which sharply differentiates our American courts from the courts of Great Britain and most other countries. Judicial review has, indeed, been termed America's distinctive contribution to the science of politics.[5]

From judicial review as developed by the federal Supreme Court arises a situation of major importance with respect to the boundary lines between federal and state powers. In all disputes touching this subject, the last word is, or may be, spoken by nine (indeed by a majority of *five*) federal judges in Washington—which is tantamount to saying that in conflicts of authority between national and state governments, the *national* government makes and enforces the decision, subject only to possible, but improbable, reversal by a constitutional amendment.[6] As once remarked, the Supreme Court has throughout our history been "as impartial an umpire in national-state disputes as one of the members of two contending teams could be expected to be." [7] As an organ of the

The national government as judge of its own powers

[1] See p. 342 below.

[2] In No. LXXVIII of *The Federalist,* Hamilton expressly indicates that the courts were intended to exercise the function of review, and in his *The Supreme Court and the Constitution* (New York, 1912), C. A. Beard analyzes the opinions of the delegates to the federal convention and reaches the same conclusion.

[3] 1 Cranch 137. To be more exact, that part of the Judiciary Act of 1789 which authorized the Supreme Court to issue a writ of mandamus under certain circumstances.

[4] 6 Cranch 87.

[5] The nature and effects of judicial review are discussed more fully in a later chapter dealing with the federal judiciary. See pp. 540-546 below. In Britain, there is judicial review of rules, orders, and other "subordinate legislation," but not of statutes.

[6] It should be observed, too, that the states as such may not challenge the acts of the national government, but must rely upon suits brought by individual citizens or corporations considering themselves injured by such acts.

[7] O. P. Field, "States versus Nation, and the Supreme Court," *Amer. Polit. Sci. Rev.,* XXVIII, 233 (Apr., 1934).

national government, it has, however, undeniably shown predisposition, if not downright favoritism, toward that government. "The states," continues the writer quoted, "have had to play against the umpire as well as against the national government itself. The combination has been too much for them." Over against the clear principle that the national government is a government of limited powers stands the hard fact that not a limitation on its authority in relation to state authority is fixed in the fundamental law which Congress, the president, and the Supreme Court—indeed, merely Congress and the Court—acting concurrently, may not override if they wish. Of course, this is speaking legally, rather than practically; actually, and as a matter of political expediency, Congress will shrink from giving the impression that it is playing fast and loose with constitutional limitations; and if it should grow careless, it is likely to be brought to book by the Supreme Court. Marvelous discoveries of previously unsuspected national power have, however, been made; others are no doubt impending; and, irrespective of all future uncertainties, the frontiers of national authority will unquestionably prove to have been widened permanently since 1933 as in few, if any, other periods in the nation's history. All experience, too, goes to show that national power, once asserted and safely past the hurdle of the courts, is almost never relinquished. No important instance of surrender of a peacetime power so fortified can be cited except abandonment of the prohibition of the liquor traffic; and that retrenchment came about only because the national government itself, driven by public opinion, experienced a change of heart on the subject.[1]

How national authority is enforced

How is the supremacy of national authority maintained and enforced? Normally, of course, by the ordinary processes of legislation and administration, operating directly upon the people irrespective of states and state governments. When, however, these processes are challenged or obstructed, the courts may be brought into play to determine in how far the actions taken or contemplated are constitutionally legitimate; and, once it is established (whether through judicial decision or otherwise) that the laws under which the national authorities are claiming to act are valid, the president may, indeed must, proceed to execute them, by military

[1] No man ever asserted more unequivocally that the national government is not final judge of its own powers than did Thomas Jefferson, e.g., in the Kentucky Resolutions of 1798. On the other hand, no major political group has ever sponsored policies and measures predicated on a more daring concept of national supremacy than did the reputedly Jeffersonian Democratic party under the leadership of Franklin D. Roosevelt in the earlier days of the New Deal—even though numerous "Jeffersonian Democrats" were forced into open revolt. The paradox is not mentioned in a spirit of criticism, but merely to emphasize the distance that we have traveled in a century and a half. Other times, other ideas!

National powers developed to meet special situations, e.g., in wartime, may, of course, lapse into disuse. So long as kept on the books, however, they can always be invoked again—except in the rare instance of a Supreme Court reversal of an earlier supporting decision. A good illustration of this sort of carry-over is afforded by various powers developed during World War I and promptly put into effect again after Pearl Harbor. See p. 813 below.

means if necessary. Both the Virginia and New Jersey plans as presented to the Philadelphia convention provided for forcible coercion of any state opposing or preventing the execution of national laws or treaties. When, however, it was settled that the new national government was to operate directly upon the people, and not simply upon states, this idea of coercing states as such was given up; and, as observed elsewhere, the Civil War itself was prosecuted by the Lincoln Administration on the theory that its object was to repress rebellious *people*, not rebellious *states*. In dealing with concrete situations requiring forcible execution of national law, it is not always easy, or even possible, to ignore the existence and actions of state governments. Certainly the theory underlying the Civil War became considerably blurred in the Reconstruction measures adopted after Lincoln's death. The principle that national power acts compulsorily upon people, not upon governments, is, however, clear; and effort is commonly made to adhere to it in practice.[1]

REFERENCES

The Federalist, Nos. XLI-XLVI.

H. L. McBain, *The Living Constitution* (New York, 1927), Chap. II.

B. F. Wright, *The Growth of American Constitutional Law* (Boston and New York, 1942), Chaps. II, III, VI, XI.

C. B. Swisher, *American Constitutional Development* (Boston, 1943), Chaps. IV-XII.

————, *The Growth of Constitutional Power in the United States* (Chicago, 1947), Chaps. II, IV-V.

W. W. Willoughby, *Constitutional Law of the United States* (2nd ed., New York, 1929), I, Chaps. III-X.

A. C. McLaughlin, *The Courts, the Constitution, and Parties* (Chicago, 1912), Chaps. I, IV.

————, *A Constitutional History of the United States* (New York, 1935), Chaps. XXIII, XXX.

————, *The Foundations of American Constitutionalism* (New York, 1932).

H. C. Hockett, *The Constitutional History of the United States* (New York, 1939), I, Chaps. XII-XIII.

C. G. Haines, *The American Doctrine of Judicial Supremacy* (Berkeley, Calif., 1932). Revised edition of a book first published in 1914.

————, *The Rôle of the Supreme Court in American Government and Politics, 1789-1835* (Berkeley, Calif., 1944).

I. Brant, *Storm Over the Constitution* (Indianapolis, 1936).

H. A. Wallace, *Whose Constitution? An Inquiry into the General Welfare* (New York, 1936).

C. A. Beard, *The Supreme Court and the Constitution* (New York, 1912).

E. S. Corwin, "The Establishment of Judicial Review," *Mich. Law Rev.*, IX, 102-125, 283-316 (Dec., 1910, and Feb., 1911).

————, *The Doctrine of Judicial Review* (Princeton, N. J., 1914).

[1] This does not mean that the federal government does not have plenty of dealings with states as such. At bottom, however, such dealings usually rest on voluntary, coöperative agreements rather than compulsion, a good example being afforded by the various forms of federal aid to the states (see pp. 108-117 below). Out of such arrangements may, of course, arise a good deal of actual federal control, as certainly is true in the field of federal aid. On federal-state coöperation, see especially Chap. VII below.

D. O. McGovney, "The British Origin of Judicial Review of Legislation," *Univ. of Pa. Law Rev.*, XCIII, 1-49 (Sept., 1944).

C. Warren, *Congress, the Supreme Court, and the Constitution* (Boston, 1925).

G. C. S. Benson, *The New Centralization; A Study of Intergovernmental Relationships in the United States* (New York, 1941).

E. M. Patterson [ed.], "Federal versus State Jurisdiction in American Life," *Annals of Amer. Acad. of Polit. and Soc. Sci.*, CXXIX, 1-167 (Jan., 1927).

O. P. Field, "State versus Nation, and the Supreme Court," *Amer. Polit. Sci. Rev.*, XXVIII, 233-245 (Apr., 1934).

J. Story, *Commentaries on the Constitution of the United States* (4th ed., Boston, 1873), I, §§ 306-457, 518-545.

CHAPTER VI

THE CONSTITUTIONAL POSITION OF THE STATES

The power and prestige of the national government must not be permitted to blind us to the immense importance of the states in our constitutional and political system. After all, our nation is the *United States* of America; and while the activities of the national government attract more attention and get more headlines in the newspapers, the states, on their part, now perform more tasks, spend more money, and provide more services than at any time in the past. Operations of the national government come close to the average citizen a good deal more frequently than they once did—for example, when he pays his federal income tax, makes his social security contribution, is drafted for military service, or even mails a letter. But the governments which chiefly guard and control him from the cradle to the grave are rather those of his state and its subdivisions; and he ought to show more interest in these than he commonly does. Vast as is the machinery of government centering in Washington, it would be vaster still, and its operations more cumbersome and congested, if the states did not, in their respective spheres, take care of by far the larger portion of the work to be done. The states, too, provide means by which, within limits, Vermonters, Virginians, Iowans, and Californians can have governments and laws to their own taste, instead of being subjected to a single uniform pattern. Moreover—and this is particularly significant—they can pioneer and experiment, "under the urge of a local opinion that does not have to wait to convert the entire nation to its hopes and beliefs." Oregon can try the popular initiative and referendum; Arizona can experiment with the recall of judges; Nebraska can test the merits of a one-house legislature; Illinois can find out the advantages of a new plan of administrative consolidation. In many legislative and administrative fields, indeed, *e.g.*, in the regulation of railroads and other utilities, in enacting labor laws, and in promoting social insurance and public health, various states have gone far before others even started, perchance before the national government recognized any need for action at all.[1]

But the states have still another vital aspect. Not only would county, city, and other local governments lose all legal basis if state constitutions and laws on which they rest were extinguished, but many necessary

Importance and uses of the states

---

[1] On the other hand, of course, the federal government sometimes leads, as for example in civil service reform, in several phases of social security and labor legislation, and in the conservation of natural resources.

operations of the national government itself would come to a halt. The president is chosen by electors grouped by states and themselves elected by the people of states; senators are chosen likewise by the people of states; congressmen are selected in districts laid out by states and under state election laws administered by state officials; and in the main the states determine who may vote in all of these elections. Constitutional amendments, too, require state action; and at bottom political parties are organized on a state pattern, with coördinating agencies like the national committees and conventions forming only a sort of super-structure. Nation, state, local areas—all, indeed, are interlocked, not only geographically, economically, and socially, but also politically, under a system of government which, however diverse its parts, must still be regarded as basically a unit.

Aspects to be considered here
The ways in which the states, viewed internally, are organized and governed will be dealt with in due time.[1] For the present, we are concerned, rather, with a closer look at the place which the forty-eight jurisdictions occupy in the country's governmental system considered as a whole. In the present chapter, attention will be focused upon formal constitutional provisions regulating their relations with the nation and with one another; in the chapter that follows, we shall be interested in seeing how these relationships have developed as a matter of experience and practice. In this latter connection, many things will come to light that the constitution's makers certainly did not anticipate.

Admission of New States

First of all, there is the question of how a state becomes a state. To be sure, until rather recently, the question might have seemed rather academic; even now, no new state has been added to the list in thirty-six years. In 1944, however, both major political parties went on record for eventual statehood for Alaska, Hawaii, and Puerto Rico; the first two, at least, have strong backing for the coveted promotion, locally and in government circles in Washington; "enabling acts" in behalf of Alaska and Hawaii have been introduced in Congress a number of times—one for the admission of Hawaii passing the House of Representatives in July, 1947; and one or more of the three territories will probably be admitted comparatively soon, with the chances for priority strongly favoring Hawaii.[2] There is, too, some remote possibility of the eventual creation of one or more new states by dividing existing ones.

"Original" and "admitted" states
What has happened in the past is, of course, known to every student of our national history. The thirteen "original" states became members of the Union by participating together in the Revolution and ratifying the Articles of Confederation and the present constitution. The other thirty-five were brought in, one by one, by acts of Congress. Considered from

---

[1] In Part III of the complete edition of this book.
[2] See pp. 845-846 below.

the point of view of previous status or condition, these later commonwealths fall into four groups: (1) five which were formed by separation
from other states, i.e., Vermont set off from New York in 1791, Kentucky
from Virginia in 1792, Tennessee from North Carolina in 1796, Maine
from Massachusetts in 1820, and West Virginia from Virginia in 1862-63;
(2) one, i.e., Texas, which before its admission in 1845 was an independent
republic; (3) one, i.e., California, which was formed—also without
passing through the territorial stage—out of a region ceded by Mexico
in 1848; and (4) twenty-eight which prior to admission were organized
territories.

The constitution confers on Congress general power to admit new   Process
states, subject only to the restriction (1) that no state may be erected   of admis-
within the jurisdiction of any other state except with the consent of the   sion
latter's legislature—such as was obtained, for example, from the legislature of Virginia when Kentucky was admitted in 1792 and from that of
Massachusetts when Maine was admitted in 1820—and (2) that no state
may be formed by the union of two or more states or parts of states
without consent of the legislatures of all states concerned as well as of
Congress.[1] Ordinarily, the procedure of admission is started by the
people of a territory, who, if a substantial proportion desire statehood,[2]
petition Congress, through their territorial assembly or territorial delegate, or both, to specify and authorize the steps necessary to be taken
(commonly simply the framing of a constitution) in order that the territory may be received into the Union as a state. If receiving the
petition favorably, Congress passes an "enabling act" under which the
people of the territory elect a convention and frame their constitution;
and if the resulting instrument meets the approval of the territorial population when submitted for adoption, it goes to Congress for inspection.
If Congress, in turn, finds it acceptable, all that remains is to pass a
joint resolution recognizing the territory as a new member of the Union
as soon as its elected senators and representatives shall have been seated.
Occasionally (as, for example, when a western area ceded by North Carolina became the state of Tennessee in 1796), a territory has omitted the
initial petition and gone at once to Congress with its proposed constitution; and a few times controversies have ensued (in the case of Missouri
over the slavery question and in that of Michigan over a question of
boundaries) entailing long delays in the final stages.

If, as has happened several times, Congress finds something in the   Special
constitution as submitted that it dislikes, or fails to find something that   condi-
it thinks should be there, it will communicate its criticism to the author-   tions
  may be
  imposed

---

[1] Art IV, § 3, cl. 1.

[2] Sentiment on the subject may be tested by putting the question directly to the
people in a territorial election—either with a view to an immediate request of Congress or as a means of sounding out opinion that may lead to a request eventually.
Such plebiscites have been held in all of the territories recently agitating statehood,
i.e., Hawaii. Alaska, and Puerto Rico.

ities of the territory, either in the form of a suggestion or in that of a definite requirement to be met as a condition of admission. In the latter situation, there is nothing for the territory to do but comply—or wait for a possible change of opinion in the two houses; for without the consent of Congress no territory can become a state, and there is no way of compelling that consent to be given. In this manner, several incoming states have been subjected to requirements not imposed upon others. Ohio, for example, was required in 1802 as a condition of admission to agree not to tax for five years any public land sold within its borders by the United States; Nevada, in 1864, to bind herself never to deny the suffrage to persons of color; Utah, in 1896, to write into her constitution a clause prohibiting polygamy; Oklahoma, in 1907, to undertake not to move the state capital from Guthrie to any other city before 1913.[1] The president, too, can take exception to a proposed constitution, and can veto a resolution providing for admission.

Yet all
states
legally
equal

Such minor differences as arise in this way do not, of course, prevent the states from being true equals in the eye of the law. In size, population, wealth, and general importance they, of course, vary enormously. The largest, Texas, has an area of 265,780 square miles; the smallest, Rhode Island, contains only 1,250. The most populous, New York, had 13,479,142 inhabitants in 1940; the least populous, Nevada, had 110,247. Average density of population varied, at the same date, all the way from 674.2 per square mile in Rhode Island to 1.0 per square mile in Nevada. Some states are almost wholly agricultural, others are mainly industrial and

[1] Naturally, incoming states do not relish such treatment; and a considerable amount of political and constitutional controversy has resulted. Nor, indeed, have conditions so imposed always been lived up to, once the state was safely in the fold, and with no possibility of its admission being revoked. The capital of Oklahoma, for example, was actually moved to Oklahoma City by legislative act of 1910; and when so palpable a violation of the terms of the state's admission was challenged, the federal Supreme Court (in Coyle v. Smith, 221 U. S. 559, 1911) ruled that while Congress is free to impose any conditions initially that it chooses, once a state is admitted, there is no way of compelling fulfillment of them if they are of such a nature as to compromise the independence of the state in managing its own internal affairs—otherwise, said the Court, Congress might impose all sorts of unreasonable conditions, resulting in different classes of states with widely varying powers. When, in 1910, the people of Arizona, yielding to the objections of President Taft and many members of Congress, voted to eliminate the recall of judges from their proposed constitution, it was locally understood that the surrender was to be only temporary. And so it turned out. In his very first message, the governor of the new state recommended a constitutional amendment restoring the recall; and forthwith such an amendment was adopted by the legislature and approved by the voters. President Taft and Congress to the contrary notwithstanding, Arizona has had recall of judges ever since. Nor, in the light of the Oklahoma decision, was it worth while for the national government to attempt to do anything about the matter. On the other hand, a requirement that the state of Minnesota impose no tax on lands belonging to the United States, and no higher tax on non-resident proprietors than on residents, was upheld in 1900 (Stearns v. Minnesota, 179 U. S. 223)—on the ground that it was a contractual agreement respecting a matter of property and not affecting the state's political freedom. In the same way, New Mexico was balked in 1919 (Ervien v. United States, 251 U. S. 41) in an attempt to use proceeds of the sale of public lands in a manner different from that specified in the terms of the state's admission. Whether, therefore, an imposed condition is enforceable after admission depends entirely upon the nature of the condition.

commercial. Some are of great weight in the councils of the nation, others count for comparatively little. Some are more able to provide the services expected of modern governments than are others. All have their separate and more or less differing constitutions, laws, courts, systems of taxation, and arrangements for local government. Nevertheless, in their constitutional and legal status they are equal.

Obligations of the National Government Toward the States

By way of further defining the position of the states in the federal system, the constitution requires of the national government a number of significant guarantees in their behalf. To start with, that government must scrupulously respect every state's geographical unity and integrity. As already indicated, it may neither instigate, promote, nor sanction the erection of any state within the jurisdiction of an existing state except with the consent of the latter's legislature;[1] nor may it allow a state to be formed by uniting two or more states or parts of states unless the legislatures of all states affected signify their approval. In other words, a state cannot be deprived of its separate existence, or even of territory, without its consent. If, for example, it were undertaken to set off Chicago and its environs as a separate state (as has at times been suggested), nothing could be done without the assent both of Congress and of the Illinois legislature,[2] with the latter certainly not likely to look favorably upon the heavy loss of tax revenue sure to result.

1. Respect for geographical and unity identity

A second obligation resting upon the national government is to protect every state against invasion and (when requested) against domestic violence.[3] An invasion of a state by a foreign enemy is, of course, also an invasion of the United States, and the right and duty of the national government to repel such attack is clear, quite apart from any action independently taken, or any request made, by the state or states affected. Repression of insurrections, riots, and other domestic violence is, however, a different matter. One of the things that the government of a state is expected to do is to maintain order; and unless such a government, finding itself unable to cope with a disturbance, calls for assistance, national authorities will not intervene, so long, at all events, as national laws are not violated, national functions (*e.g.*, carrying the mails) interfered with, or national property endangered. If, however, assistance is

2. Protection against invasion and domestic violence

---

[1] The closest approach to a violation of this guarantee was the formation of the state of West Virginia from loyal western Virginia counties during the Civil War. Consent in this case was given merely by a minority of the Virginia legislature representing the seceding counties. As viewed by Congress, however, this group of members constituted the only "legislature" having a claim to recognition.

[2] The Indiana legislature also if, as would be probable, a small metropolitan corner of that state were to be included in the plan. See C. E. Merriam, S. Parratt, and A. Lepawsky, *The Government of the Metropolitan Region of Chicago* (Chicago, 1933), Chap. XVIII, where an argument for such a solution of Illinois' problem of metropolitan-"down-state" relations is presented. It has often been proposed also that New York City be set off as a separate state.

[3] Art. IV, § 4.

requested, the president will comply, unless he is of the opinion that the state can and should handle the situation alone; and if national interests are menaced, he will act without invitation, and even against the wishes of the state authorities.[1]

3. Guar-
antee of
a repub-
lican
form of
govern-
ment
A third requirement made of the United States is that it shall guarantee to every state a republican form of government.[2] The men who framed and adopted the constitution had no desire to see monarchy or oligarchy arise within the limits of the new nation; and, having lately witnessed the Shays rebellion and other subversive movements, they were determined to put it within the power—indeed to make it the solemn duty—of the national government to prevent any form of political organization other than republican from establishing itself anywhere in the country. They did not define the term "republican," and it is clear that they did not contemplate requiring any one precise governmental set-up, to the exclusion of all others. There were at the time considerable differences from state to state; yet all of the existing governments were regarded as republican. Madison assured the people that they had a right to "substitute other republican forms" whenever they chose and to claim the federal guarantee in behalf of them.

Who
decides
whether
a state
govern-
ment is
repub-
lican?
The final judge of whether the government of a state is republican is not the people of the state, but the national government. The constitution does not, however, say what branch of the national government shall make the decision. Conceivably, it might be the courts. In handling cases turning on the nature of republicanism, the Supreme Court, however, has always held that the question is of a political nature, and hence one to be decided, not by the judiciary, but by the government's political branches. This leaves it to the president or Congress, or both. As for the president, he undoubtedly might pronounce the government of a given state to be other than republican, and might use force to dispossess it. Indeed, in the single instance in which the guaranty clause was invoked down to the Civil War, i.e., the Dorr rebellion in Rhode Island in 1841-42, President Tyler recognized the old government of the state as the rightful government and took steps to give it the aid which it asked against a rival government set up by an insurrectionary element led by Dorr. The really decisive factor in the national government's handling of the Rhode Island situation was, however, the action of Congress in continuing to receive the state's elected senators and representatives. This, said the Supreme Court when a case growing out of the dispute came before it, constituted valid and final recognition of the state's government as being republican.[3] It was Congress, too, that at the close of the Civil War forced the Southern states, as a condition of regaining representation, to adopt suffrage (and other) arrangements which the radical Republican majority

[1] See p. 450 below.
[2] Art. IV, § 4.
[3] Luther v. Borden, 7 Howard 1 (1849).

at Washington professed to consider essential to a republican form of government. Certainly its power to cut off a state from any share in controlling national policy, enacting national laws, and raising and appropriating national money gives Congress the whip-hand in the matter.

In the Reconstruction period, the term "republican" was construed arbitrarily and narrowly. At all other times, however, it has been interpreted broadly and liberally. Thus, when a generation or so ago, opponents of the popular initiative and referendum as newly adopted devices of direct legislation in Oregon sought to make out that republican government means only *representative* government, with all laws enacted by elected assemblies, the Supreme Court said simply that the question was one for the political arms of the government, and that as long as Congress continued to receive senators and representatives from the state, it (the Court) would be satisfied.[1] And Congress itself took the sensible view that as long as representative institutions are maintained by a state, it does not matter if they are *supplemented* by provision for occasional direct action by the people. More recently, some Northern opponents of the poll-tax qualification for voting found in seven Southern states have charged that so many people are kept from the polls that the governments of those states are no longer "republican in form." Even though the qualification be regarded as inherently unjustifiable, however, the point is not well taken.

Tendency to liberal construction

Constitutional Limitations Upon the States

As we have seen, the federal constitution distributes powers between nation and states on the general principle that whatever is not conferred exclusively upon the national government remains to the states—with one obvious qualification, namely, that it does so only if not forbidden to them. Much, in point of fact, is forbidden, in the interest of national unity and effective national government, giving rise to the "constitutional limitations" about which the lawyers talk; and while one large group of such limitations, having to do with the protection of civil liberties, calls for separate treatment in a later chapter,[2] certain additional ones of major importance require attention here.

It is, of course, the intent of the constitution that official relations with foreign powers shall be conducted only through the national government, and one will not be surprised to find the states unequivocally forbidden to enter into "any treaty, alliance, or confederation."[3] A state, to be sure, may enter into an "agreement or compact" with a foreign power, but only with the consent of Congress, and only, of course, if not having the effect of creating an "alliance or confederation," *i.e.*, a relationship of a political character. Except for an agreement between New York and

1. Foreign and interstate relations

---

[1] Pacific States Tel. and Tel. Co. *v.* Oregon, 223 U. S. 118 (1912).
[2] See Chap. ix below.
[3] Art. I, § 10, cl. 1.

Canada relating to an international bridge, no such agreements or compacts have ever been concluded.

Inter-
state
compacts   Agreements or compacts among the states themselves is a different matter. These, too, are authorized, subject in general to the consent of Congress; and so useful has the device been found that upwards of a hundred such "interstate compacts"—concluded usually by governors or through specially appointed commissioners—are now on record. For more than a hundred years, agreements were few and had to do almost exclusively with boundary lines. In the last quarter-century, however, they not only have grown more numerous, but have dealt with a steadily widening range of interstate interests. To cite but a few illustrations: (1) an agreement of New York and New Jersey in 1921 creating the present Port of New York Authority charged with developing the facilities of New York harbor; (2) a Colorado River Compact of 1922 (finally effective in 1928) allocating rights to the waters of the Colorado among seven states containing portions of the river's basin; (3) a four-state compact, first authorized by Congress in 1935 (with numerous other states later adhering), for the conservation of oil and gas resources; (4) an Atlantic States Marine Fisheries Compact, assented to by Congress in 1940 and adhered to by upwards of a dozen states, with a view to promoting better utilization of marine fisheries; and (5) a compact of New England states in 1947 for control of water pollution. Other varied matters with which compacts have dealt include park and parkway development, flood control, tobacco production, inland fisheries, minimum wages, and supervision of parolees and probationers. According to the nature of the subject, the states involved may be contiguous or closely grouped, or on the other hand widely scattered—though with a tendency to agreements of regional scope, and often entailing some sort of advisory or directive interstate commission for carrying them out. Opponents of centralization, it has been remarked, see in such devices "a kind of intermediate arrangement which avoids the centralizing tendencies of federal regulation, whereas the advocates of centralization consider compacts a basis for possible evolution of control from the state to the region and then from the region to the nation." [1]

When
congres-
sional
consent is
necessary   The constitution seems to make all interstate agreements contingent upon the consent of Congress. In practice, however, there is no such rigid requirement. Without going to Congress about the matter at all, two or more states may agree to clean up a disease-producing district on their common border; some years ago, New York, New Jersey, and Connecticut settled in this manner a long-standing dispute concerning sewage pollution

[1] J. P. Clark, "Interstate Compacts and Social Legislation," *Polit. Sci. Quar.*, L, 503 (Dec., 1935). The article cited, of which there is a concluding instalment in the same periodical, LI, 36-61 (Mar., 1936)—with both embodied in the same author's *The Rise of a New Federalism* (New York, 1938)—is the best extended discussion of one large and growing group of compacts. Cf. E. M. Johnson, *Interstate Compacts on Labor Legislation in the United States* (Geneva, 1936).

in New York harbor. In 1931, Maryland, Virginia, and West Virginia similarly adjusted fishing rights on the Potomac. In 1941, six Midwestern states signed an agreement aimed at higher standards in the dairy industry. As construed by the courts, the requirement of congressional consent applies only to agreements "tending to increase the political power of the states, which may encroach upon or interfere with the just supremacy of the United States." [1] Furthermore, where consent is necessary, it may be given either before or after the agreement is entered into, and may be either express or implied. Indeed, blanket permission to make agreements on a given subject may be given in advance; in 1936, for example, acts of Congress authorized any two or more of fourteen specified states in New England and of eight specified states in the Ohio Valley to enter into compacts for the abatement of pollution in interstate streams.[2]

In general, defense, like foreign relations, is a national rather than a state function; and without the consent of Congress no state may keep troops or ships of war, or "engage in war unless actually invaded or in such imminent danger as will not admit of delay." [3] The prohibition, however, was never intended to preclude the states from maintaining organized militia, for use primarily in repressing domestic disorder; and, as we shall see, such militia, although long since assimilated to the armed establishment of the nation, remains basically a state instrumentality. 2. De-
fense

Speaking generally, the states are free to levy and collect taxes as they choose, for revenue or with other objectives in mind; and many differing tax systems have resulted. There are, however, constitutional limitations— either expressly imposed or implied in general clauses, or even in the inherent nature of the federal-state relation. The restrictions expressly stipulated are that no state shall, without the consent of Congress, lay (1) "any imposts or duties on imports or exports, except what may be absolutely necessary for executing its inspection laws," or (2) any duty on tonnage.[4] Import and export duties laid by state authority are subject to revision and control by Congress; and, further to discourage such taxation, all net proceeds are required to be turned over to the national treasury. State-imposed import and export duties—tonnage duties like- 3. Taxa-
tion (a) Ex-
port, im-
port, and
tonnage
duties

---

[1] Virginia v. Tennessee, 148 U. S. 503 (1893). The Supreme Court has habitually been well disposed toward the interstate compact as a device for alleviating or averting conflicts. More than once, it has suggested to states engaged in litigation that it would be better for them to adjust their differences by compact or agreement; and the advice has not always gone unheeded. For a study of the effectiveness of compacts, see M. E. Dimock and G. C. S. Benson, *Can Interstate Compacts Succeed?* (Chicago, 1937).

[2] A full list of the interstate compacts of the period 1936-43—twenty-eight in number—will be found in Council of State Governments, *The Book of the States, 1943-1944* (Chicago, 1943), 52-57. New compacts entered into are reported in successive editions of this manual. At least three new compacts and a renewal of the oil and gas compact for four years were assented to by Congress in the 1947 session.

[3] Art. I, § 10, cl. 3.

[4] Art. I, § 10, cls. 2-3. Ships as property may be taxed, but not their tonnage, or carrying capacity, *i.e.,* not as instruments of commerce and navigation.

wise—were not uncommon in the earlier decades under the constitution, but nowadays are almost unknown.

(b) General constitutional provisions

Among clauses of general application which have bearing on the taxing power are those forbidding a state (a) to deprive any person of ... property without due process of law, or deny to any person within its jurisdiction the equal protection of the laws; (b) to pass any law "impairing the obligation of contracts"; also the well-known clauses stipulating (a) that "the citizens of each state shall be entitled to all privileges and immunities of citizens in the several states," and (b) that no state shall make or enforce any law which shall abridge the privileges or immunities of citizens of the United States." The taxing power may no more be employed in violation of these blanket provisions than may any other power.

(c) Exemption of federal property

But there are also restrictions arising, not from specific constitutional provisions, but from interpretations placed upon the inherent nature of our federal system. One of these relates to federal property, which, in spite of much local demand for a different policy, is to all intents and purposes completely immune from state taxation. To be sure, Congress in 1864 authorized the states to tax national bank stock and also the physical property belonging to national banks. Such property, however, is in reality private rather than public; and every effort of a state to tax real estate or other property belonging directly to the national government has met with defeat.[1] Certain Southern states in which the Tennessee

---

[1] When, indeed, in 1937, the city of Springfield, Mass., undertook to assess land acquired and for a time used by the federal government for a post-office but subsequently leased to private parties for use as a bus depot, the federal Supreme Court, in City of Springfield v. United States, 306 U. S. 650 (1939), held that not only federal property in general, but such property when leased to private users, is tax exempt. In a case in 1944 involving an attempt in Pennsylvania to tax gun-making machinery belonging to the federal government but leased to a private manufacturer of munitions, it said the same thing. United States of America and Mesta Machine Company v. County of Allegheny, Pennsylvania, 322 U. S. 174. On the other hand, when the federal government sought to have voided tax liens on lands which it had acquired in Alabama, the Supreme Court held (in United States v. Alabama, 313 U. S. 274, 1941) that the liens remained good, even though Alabama could hope to enforce them only after the lands in question should have passed from the federal government to private owners. And in 1946 the Court upheld a Minnesota tax upon land sold by the federal government, but as yet only partly paid for and with the federal government still holding the title. S. R. A., Inc., v. United States, 327 U. S. 558. By repealing an earlier prohibitory statute, the Wisconsin legislature in 1946 subjected to state taxation federally-owned machinery and equipment coming under the state's definition of real estate. Precedent, however, would indicate that the federal Supreme Court would not uphold this action.

The situation as to federal taxation of state property and activities is, in general, that such may not be taxed if involved in discharging a state's "ordinary functions as a government," but may be taxed if involved in "the carrying on of an ordinary private business," e.g., the sale of liquor. South Carolina v. United States, 199 U. S. 437 (1905). Thus in 1946 the Supreme Court upheld federal excise taxes on state sales of mineral waters taken from Saratoga Springs. New York v. United States, 326 U. S. 572. A bill introduced in the national House of Representatives in 1947 would require the federal government or any federal agency owning property leased for private use (the amount of such has increased greatly in later years) to make payment to local taxing bodies equal to the taxes that would be paid under private ownership; but enactment of the proposal is doubtful.

Valley Authority has acquired large stretches of land were formerly so handicapped that in 1940 the Authority was required by act of Congress to start paying a percentage of its gross electric power income to states and counties in lieu of the tax revenues lost.[1]

In deciding a case in 1873, the Supreme Court said: "It is of national importance that over the subject [interstate commerce] there should be but one regulating power; for if one state can directly tax persons or property passing through it, or tax them indirectly by levying a tax upon their transportation, every other may, and thus commercial intercourse between states remote from each other may be destroyed." [2] In pursuance of this principle, a state may not impose any tax on the carrying of goods across its borders or on sales of such goods, or indeed on any *transactions* in interstate commerce whatsoever, although property (*e.g.*, railroads) employed in such commerce may be taxed in proportion to the amount located in a state, and "compensating" taxes on the *use* of goods purchased in a different state to evade sales taxes in the home state may be levied.[3]

(d) Immunity of interstate commerce

Until 1939, there would have been added to the foregoing a restriction preventing the states from taxing federal "instrumentalities" such as bonds and other securities (or the income therefrom), franchises granted by the federal government, and salaries of federal officials and employees. On its part, the federal government was considered equally debarred from taxing state officials' salaries, as well as income from state and municipal bonds, and other state "instrumentalities." [4] Under force of the reasoning employed by Chief Justice Marshall in McCulloch *v.* Maryland in 1819,[5] these reciprocal immunities were long regarded as flowing inevitably from

(e) Exemption of federal "instrumentalities":

[1] A. T. Edelman, "Public Ownership and Tax Replacement by the T.V.A.," *Amer. Polit. Sci. Rev.*, XXXV, 727-737 (Aug., 1941). In the special situation of the District of Columbia, the substantial federal contribution made annually to the cost of operating the local government is explained primarily by the vast amount of tax-exempt federal property located in Washington and its environs. The share of total costs thus assumed has, however, of late been declining.

[2] Reading Railroad Co. *v.* Pennsylvania, 15 Wallace 232 (1873).

[3] Henneford *v.* Silas Mason Co., 300 U. S. 577 (1937). On "use taxes," see p. 980 below (in complete edition of this book).

[4] The Supreme Court so held in Collector *v.* Day, 11 Wallace 113 (1870).

[5] In 1818, the state of Maryland imposed a stamp tax on the circulating notes of all banks or branches thereof located in the state and not chartered by the legislature. The Baltimore branch of the United States Bank refused to pay the tax. Suit was brought against the cashier, McCulloch, and the state court rendered judgment against him; whereupon the case was taken to the federal Supreme Court. Pronouncing the law imposing the tax unconstitutional, Marshall declared (in a decision cited elsewhere as helping to establish the doctrine of implied powers) that, otherwise unlimited as is the power of a state to tax objects within its jurisdiction, that power does not "extend to those means which are employed by Congress to carry into execution powers conferred on that body by the people of the United States . . . powers . . . given . . . to a government whose laws . . . are declared to be supreme." 4 Wheaton 316 (1819). As indicated above, national-bank stock and the physical property of national banks are taxable; but this is because such property is private rather than public and, further, on the theory that, falling on property rather than on operations, the taxes do not impair the capacity of the banks to serve the national government according to the intent of the laws establishing them.

the very nature of the federal system, and as being inviolable unless terminated or altered by federal constitutional amendments. Growing budgets and need for new sources of revenue—combined with the greatly increased numbers of people living on government salaries and the retreat of mounting sums of money into tax-exempt securities—gradually led, however, within the past two or three decades, to a different view of the matter. Federal salaries *were* taxed by the federal government and state and local salaries by state governments. But why should a state salary be any more exempt from federal taxation than a salary paid by a private corporation, or a federal salary any more exempt from state taxation? In other words, why should not people living from salaries drawn from government sustain tax burdens on the same basis (*i.e.*, pay income-tax levies on salary to both nation and state) as people obtaining their liveli-, hood from private employment? How could such taxation be construed as a burden upon *governments* as such? And why should not the Sixteenth Amendment, empowering Congress to lay and collect taxes on incomes, "from whatever source derived," be taken, at face value, to include the taxation of state and local salaries and, for that matter, of income from state and local bonds? [1] Long before 1939, exemption of government officials and employees from taxation of their salary income seemed to many people unfair; and as for incomes from government securities, at least three Republican presidents (Harding, Coolidge, and Hoover) had agreed with Secretary of the Treasury Mellon in his characterization of their exemption as "an economic evil of the first magnitude." [2]

The upshot was that when, in 1938 and 1939, President Franklin D. Roosevelt, returning to a subject on which he had previously spoken with feeling, urged Congress to wipe out all inter-governmental tax immunities enjoyed by salaries and by income from securities, he was successful in securing the Public Salary Tax Act of 1939 [3] giving effect to his recommendations in so far as relating to salaries, although not income from securities; and with little delay the Supreme Court—which for a good while had been gradually narrowing the actual tax immunity of state and

Federal salaries no longer immune

---

[1] When the income-tax amendment was pending in 1912-13, many people opposed the phrase cited because they considered that it would open the way for precisely such forms of taxation. Among them was Charles E. Hughes, then governor of New York.

[2] Such exemption, according to Mr. Mellon (speaking, of course, under conditions antedating the recent war period), has three harmful consequences: (1) by making it easier for federal and other governments to sell bonds, it encourages the growth of public indebtedness; (2) it tends to divert capital from productive enterprise; and (3) it "enables a very large class of investments to escape their just share of taxation." In January, 1939, the under-secretary of the treasury estimated that the sum of sixty-five billion dollars was then invested in tax-exempt securities issued by the state and local governments, and that removal of such exemptions would net the national government about $300,000,000 a year. See A. L. Powell, *National Taxation of State Instrumentalities* (Urbana, Ill., 1936); M. Philipsborn, Jr., and H. Cantrill, "Immunity from Taxation of Governmental Instrumentalities," *Georgetown Law Jour.*, XXVI, 543-573 (Mar., 1938).

[3] 53 *U. S. Stat. at Large*, 575 (1939).

local salaries [1]—overruled a long line of earlier decisions and upheld the new legislation as constitutional.[2] The federal government now, therefore, taxes state and local salaries, and (this being the point immediately relevant here) the states are reciprocally free to tax federal salaries [3]— which most of them, if employing income taxes at all, are now doing.

Income derived from securities of the national government, even when issued not to raise money for the government's own use, but only to obtain funds to be lent to farmers and home-owners, is still (1948) exempt from state taxation, with income from state and local securities reciprocally exempt from federal taxation.[4] To the end, the Roosevelt Administration remained committed to federal taxation of all future issues of state and local securities. Notwithstanding, however, that in their national platform of 1940 the Democrats declared against the future issuance of tax-exempt governmental securities on any level, and despite a vigorous presidential recommendation to Congress on this same line in 1942, not even the extreme pressures for revenue incident to wartime spending led to action. It nevertheless seems safe to predict that sooner or later the federal government will be found taxing state and local issues—whereupon the present restraint of the states from taxing federal issues naturally will terminate. Whether favorable or not to the objective, most state attorneys-general, and others also, contended—contrary to the view of President Roosevelt—that reciprocal taxation of salaries could properly be authorized only by a constitutional amendment, not by mere legislation. The Supreme Court thought otherwise; and, while the same argument will be, and is, heard in relation to intergovernmental taxing of income from securities, the language of the pertinent decisions leaves little

Income from federal securitie; still exempt

[1] For example, in 1938, the Court had sustained federal taxation of salaries received from the Port of New York Authority, a corporation (as indicated above) jointly created by New York and New Jersey. This was quite at variance with a ruling in the early case of Collector v. Day (11 Wallace 113, 1870) denying the right of Congress to tax the salary of a Massachusetts judge—a ruling completely overthrown in 1938 in a case involving an attorney of the Home Owners' Loan Corporation.

[2] Graves v. People of the State of New York ex rel. O'Keefe, 306 U. S. 466 (1939). Cf. State Tax Commission of Utah v. Van Cott, 306 U. S. 511 (1939). The point to these decisions was, not that national and state governments may tax each other, but only that the taxing by either of salaries paid by the other imposes no burden upon any government, but merely one upon the persons who pay the tax.

When the act of 1939 was passed, there were approximately 2,600,000 state and municipal employees, with salaries aggregating $3,600,000,000. Because many salaries, however, were so low that exemptions left nothing to tax, the total federal income tax from this source was only about $16,000,000—until later when wartime lowering of exemptions operated to increase the figure.

[3] "The United States," said the act of 1939, "hereby consents to the taxation of compensation, received after December 31, 1938, for personal service as an officer or employee of the United States . . . by any duly constituted taxing authority." At the time there were 1,200,000 federal employees, with an aggregate payroll of two billion dollars, much of which, however, was received by federal employees living in states not taxing incomes.

[4] Formerly, the federal government did not tax income from its own securities, but in 1941 the secretary of the treasury announced, on authority of Congress, that thereafter no new federal issues would be tax-exempt; and since the date mentioned income from all such securities has been taxed.

doubt that only an act of Congress would be required for achieving the purpose.[1]

4. Commerce

The clause of the constitution giving Congress authority to "regulate commerce..."[2] is at once a fertile source of power for the national government and a sharp restriction upon the states.[3] To be sure, over commerce that is strictly intrastate the several states have substantially complete control. To come under this head, however, it must originate, end, and have its entire course in a single state; if at any stage a transaction takes on an interstate aspect, it is subject to federal regulation from the moment it begins until it is completed. In exercising its police power, a state may impose regulations affecting interstate as well as intrastate commerce (*e.g.*, forbidding railroads to employ color-blind engineers on either local or through trains, or limiting the speed of trains within city limits). The object, however, must clearly be to promote public safety and welfare, with the effect upon interstate commerce entirely incidental. Restrictions upon state taxation of interstate commerce have already been mentioned.

5. Currency

One of the main advantages of union is a common currency system. Hence the federal constitution gives the national government full control over the country's currency and forbids the states to coin money, to emit bills of credit, or to "make anything but gold and silver coin a tender in payment of debts."[4] Under their reserved powers, the states can charter banks; and banking institutions so created exist beside and compete with national banks in all of the states. Furthermore, the states can authorize these banks and banking associations to issue notes for circulation as currency, although not as legal tender. In 1866, however, this latter power was stripped of all practical significance by an act of Congress laying taxes up to ten per cent on such notes and thereby making it unprofitable to issue them. The Supreme Court upheld the measure,[5] and as a result, state bank currency has passed entirely out of existence.

6. Contracts

Society exists and business is carried on by virtue of a network of human relations which find expression in agreements, or contracts; and little thought is required to show how insecure and otherwise difficult our every-day existence would be if these agreements could be disregarded with impunity. It is not strange, therefore, that the framers of the national

---

[1] On the general subject, see K. M. Williamson, "The Case for Taxation of Governmental Securities," *Annals of Amer. Acad. of Polit. and Soc. Sci.*, CCXIV, 68-72 (Mar., 1941). For counter-arguments (emphasizing increased difficulties of local financing and added burdens on local taxpayers that would result), see C. H. Chatters, in *ibid.*, 73-77, and P. V. Betters, "The Case Against Taxing Income from Governmental Securities," *Law and Contemporary Problems*, VII, 222-234 (Spring, 1940). Cf. debate of the issue in E. H. Foly and H. Epstein, "Shall We Tax Government Bonds?," *Nat. Mun. Rev.*, XXX, 674-688 (Dec., 1941).

[2] Art. I, § 8, cl. 3.

[3] See Chap. xxvii below, where one will be impressed with the progressive narrowing of state control because of judicial construction of the term "commerce" to include manufacturing, mining, and other operations of production.

[4] Art. I, § 10, cl. 1.

[5] Veazie Bank *v.* Fenno, 8 Wallace 533 (1869).

constitution put into that instrument a clause explicitly forbidding the states to pass any law impairing the obligation of contracts,[1] *i.e.*, weakening their effect or making them more difficult to enforce. They did not lay a similar prohibition on the national government; but this was mainly because they expected business relationships to be controlled by the state governments rather than by Congress.

A contract may be defined as an agreement enforceable at law; and no state legislation which weakens the obligations arising from such an agreement is valid unless considerations of public health, safety, or morals demand it and compensation is rendered for the injury done.[2] Both the definition and the rule are, however, easier to state than to apply. Ordinary agreements, executed in due legal form, between individuals or groups of individuals, *e.g.*, to pay a debt, are obviously included. But how about a charter granted by a state to a bank or a railroad company? Or an appointment to a public office? Or a license to practice medicine? These and many similar questions have been passed upon in numerous judicial decisions, with results which must be stated briefly. In the Dartmouth College case, in 1819, the Supreme Court held that the charter of the college, granted by the English crown, was a contract which the state of New Hampshire, as represented by its legislature, had no power either to revoke or to impair without the college's consent.[3] This was tantamount to saying that franchises and charters issued to private corporations by public authorities, including state legislatures, were protected by the constitutional guarantee against ever being withdrawn or altered without consent of the holders; and corporations long tried to maintain that any withdrawal or curtailment of privileges once granted them was an illegal impairment of contract. If this contention could have been sustained, the results would have been serious. But later the courts took the common-sense view that charters and franchises are, after all, only a species of property, and as such can be modified, or even revoked, with compensation rendered—or even without compensation when it can be shown that a corporation's business is "affected with a public interest" and that such public interest demands state intervention. Furthermore, it is open to legislatures, when granting new charters, to insert in them clauses making them revocable, or at least limiting their duration to a period of years; and this is now usually done. Indeed, a state constitution may cover the matter blanketwise (as does that of Wisconsin) by making *all* acts of the legislature subject to

Status of charters and franchises

---

[1] Art. I, § 10, cl. 1. The original object was to prevent the states from passing laws to relieve debtors of their legal obligation to pay their debts, but as we shall see, the clause is now given a far broader interpretation.

[2] As established by the courts, the reason for the exception indicated is that a state has no right to bargain away the interests of public health, safety, and morals. Stone *v.* Mississippi, 101 U. S. 814 (1879). A state's police power is superior to any contract, just as it also is superior to "due process."

[3] Dartmouth College *v.* Woodward, 4 Wheaton 518 (1819). The case arose out of an attempt of the state to take control of the college out of the hands of its trustees.

alteration or repeal. Having taken precautions on some such lines, a state can amend or abrogate a charter or franchise at will, subject only to the provision of the Fourteenth Amendment that no person (individual or corporation) may be deprived of life, liberty, or property without due process of law—which means, among other things, that while a corporation may be extinguished, the tangible property interests of the stockholders cannot simply be wiped out.[1]

By judicial determination, the charters of public corporations, *e.g.*, cities and towns, investing them with governmental powers are not contracts within the meaning of the "obligation" clause. Such local units are merely agencies of the state created for purposes of practical convenience, and so far as the national constitution is concerned, the state legislature can rescind or amend their charters in any way at any time, or even extinguish the units themselves. Various forms of agreement between a state and its citizens are construed also not to be contracts. Thus a person appointed to a public office, even for a fixed term and at a stipulated salary, acquires no vested right in it; no contract is violated if the state subsequently abolishes the office outright. Furthermore, a license issued by a state, or by one of its political subdivisions, to engage in a vocation or profession, *e.g.*, to practice medicine, is not a contract, but only a grant of privilege which legally can be revoked at any time. For example, a license to sell liquor automatically lapses if the state adopts a prohibition law.

7. Privileges and immunities of citizens of the United States

As will be explained presently, the constitution makes it the duty of every state to extend the privileges and immunities of its own citizenship to citizens of other states coming within its jurisdiction.[2] To this, the Fourteenth Amendment adds the provision that a state may not make or enforce any law abridging the "privileges and immunities of citizens of the United States." Originally designed primarily for the protection of the recently liberated Negroes against discriminatory treatment under laws of Southern states, this clause has caused the courts a good deal of trouble. What are the privileges and immunities of citizens of the United States? Do they include all of the civil rights appertaining to citizenship in general under our system, *e.g.*, freedom of speech, freedom

---

[1] That even the contract clause of the constitution can be bent from its ordinary meaning in time of emergency was revealed in 1934 when, by a five-to-four decision, the federal Supreme Court sustained a Minnesota law giving embarrassed property-owners the right to apply in court for a two-year extension of the time otherwise open to them for redeeming property about to be taken under foreclosure of mortgage. Without trying to deny that the statute did violence to the obligation of mortgage contracts, the Court held that the impairment was a justifiable exercise of the state's police power under the unusual conditions created by the economic depression. Home Building and Loan Association *v.* Blaisdell *et al.*, 290 U. S. 398 (1934). As recently as 1945, indeed, and in the face of the argument that the emergency originally inspiring the legislation no longer existed, the Court upheld a New York moratorium law dating from 1933, several times renewed, and suspending the right of foreclosure of mortgages, although providing for the payment of interest and for amortization of the debt. East New York Savings Bank *v.* Hahn, 326 U. S. 230 (1945).

[2] See p. 96 below.

of religion, and the like? If so, state guarantees of such rights are in effect swallowed up in federal guarantees, rights are almost completely nationalized, and state responsibilities in the area are of no very great importance. Starting with decisions in the so-called Slaughterhouse cases of 1873, the Supreme Court has refused to concede that the authors of the clause meant thus to transform the character of the federal system,[1] and has held that the "privileges and immunities" contemplated are limited to such as not only are expressly conferred by the federal constitution, laws, and treaties, but manifestly are attributes of *national* citizenship alone, as opposed to *state* citizenship—*e.g.*, the right to engage in interstate and foreign commerce, the right of free migration from place to place throughout the country, the right to become a citizen of any one of the states, the right of access to the federal courts and to all other agencies of the national government, the right to protection when travelling or living abroad, and the right of expatriation—and not the great bulk of ordinary rights derived from or recognized in state law, even as reënforced by the earlier amendments to the federal constitution. In principle, privileges and immunities attaching specifically to United States citizens *as such* may not be infringed by any state. The Supreme Court's interpretation, however, has considerably devitalized the relevant constitutional clause: the list of privileges and immunities covered has been kept as narrow as possible; state legislation entailing palpable infringements has been invalidated sparingly or not at all; and altogether the guarantee has less practical importance than a reading of it in the constitutional text would suggest.

Obligations of the States in Their Relations with One Another

Every state is legally separate from every other state, and each has jurisdiction only within its own boundaries.[2] Massachusetts cannot project her laws into Connecticut; an Illinois state judge cannot hold court in Indiana. Every state, however, must constantly have dealings with other states, and the populations of all of the forty-eight are perpetually commingling in pursuit of the various trades and professions. It therefore becomes a practical necessity that the states accept in common certain obligations toward one another. Four specific obligations were, indeed, imposed by the national constitution as originally adopted. One

[1] There is, however, a good deal of evidence that this is precisely what they did intend.

[2] Slight exceptions are afforded by a good many state laws permitting law-enforcement officers, in "hot pursuit" of an alleged offender, to follow him across the border, arrest him, and turn him over to the local police.

The growing importance of air transport promises to lead to certain exceptions also of a different nature. Wisconsin and Minnesota, for example, have enacted legislation authorizing counties of any adjoining state to acquire and operate airports within the enacting state, provided the adjoining state reciprocates by granting equal privileges to the political subdivisions of the enacting state. In some respects, such out-of-state airports are to be subject to regulations of the enacting state and in others to those of the state in which they are located.

of them—the duty to deliver up fugitive slaves escaping from one state into another—became obsolete when the Thirteenth Amendment abolished slavery in 1865. The other three continue in effect, and pertain to (1) recognition of legal processes and acts, (2) interstate citizenship, and (3) rendition of persons accused of crime.

1. Recognition of legal processes and acts

"Full faith and credit," says the constitution, "shall be given in each state to the public acts, records, and judicial proceedings of every other state." [1] This does not mean—so the Supreme Court has held—that one state is obliged to aid in enforcing the penal laws of another state.[2] But it does mean that records of deeds, wills, contracts, mortgages, charters, legislative enactments, and other legal papers or instruments must, when duly authenticated according to forms prescribed by Congress, be recognized and accepted at their face value in every other state precisely as in the state from which they emanated. It means also that the authorities of Illinois (for example) must recognize and carry out the decisions of the courts of Michigan in civil cases, on presentation of certified copies of the relevant records, exactly as they would honor decisions of the courts of their own state. Thus a will made in Michigan but probated in Illinois is just as good in the latter state as in the former, no matter how widely the laws of the two states on the subject of wills may differ. Or, to take another illustration: A and B are residents of Detroit. A brings suit against B and gets a judgment in the amount of $500. Without paying, B moves to Chicago, taking his property before it can be attached. Under the "full faith and credit" clause, A can go into a court in Illinois, and with simply the judgment of the Michigan court as evidence, obtain a decree against B for the amount of the judgment. B may challenge the authenticity of the record; and he may demand a new trial on the ground that the Michigan court did not have jurisdiction. But on no other grounds can he secure a reopening of the case. An obligation—whether as debtor, partner, trustee, guardian, party to a contract, husband, or what not—cannot be evaded by the easy method of simply moving from one state into another.

On numerous subjects, the laws of the states, even in the same section of the country, differ widely. Some progress has been made in bringing about uniform legislation on such matters as commercial transactions; [3]

---

[1] Art. IV, § 1.

[2] Wisconsin v. Pelican Insurance Company, 127 U. S. 265 (1888). As will be pointed out presently, a state may surrender an accused person to the state from which he has fled; but it will not try him or enforce a penalty imposed upon him elsewhere. In 1934, Congress expressly authorized "any two or more states to enter into agreements or compacts for coöperative effort and mutual assistance in the prevention of crime and in the enforcement of their respective criminal laws and policies, and to establish such agencies, joint or otherwise, as they may deem desirable for making effective such agreements and compacts." (48 U. S. Stat. at Large, 909). In pursuance of this, nearly all of the states have become parties to a compact under which parolees and probationers may be permitted to leave the jurisdiction of the sentencing state and be supervised by the parole or probation authorities of a different state.

[3] See pp. 921-922 below (in complete edition of this book).

but the obstacles are many, and as long as our federal system exists, the authorities of any one of the states will have to be prepared to coöperate in giving "full faith and credit" to actions taken under laws of other states differing sharply in content and spirit from their own. Impelled by considerations of comity, most states, as a matter of fact, habitually give the benefit of the doubt to acts of other states even in situations where not judicially compelled to do so, and where the methods or principles involved are perhaps very different from those to which they themselves adhere.

An illustration or two of the workings of "full faith and credit" will be in point. Why is it that so many businesses, no matter in what parts of the country they operate, are incorporated under the laws of Delaware? The answer is simple: the laws of that state are probably the least rigorous in the country concerning the issuance of stocks and bonds and the obligations of corporations to their stockholders and the public. Other states with stricter regulations, however, have, in practice, no alternative to recognizing and accepting Delaware-incorporated businesses operating alongside any that they may themselves have incorporated.[1] *Some illustrations*

Again, there is the matter of divorce—perhaps the most troublesome that the states have encountered in this field. Marriage—at all events if not of divorced persons—raises few difficulties; if contracted legally in a given state, it is accepted in all other states as valid, regardless of how different their marriage laws may be. Divorce, however, is not so simple.[2] One state, South Carolina, permits its courts to grant no divorces at all; other states have rules of such strictness as to admit of but few; still others leave wide latitude, Nevada requiring two years as the period for establishing "legal residence" for other purposes, but only six weeks for purposes of a divorce. For a good while before 1942, a Supreme Court decision of 1906[3] maintained a reasonably adequate standard with respect to divorces which the states were bound in common to recognize. At that date, however, people who felt deeply about the matter received a shock. A North Carolina man and woman went to Nevada, lived in an auto court as transients, filed suit for divorce from their respective spouses as soon as the Nevada law permitted, were married, and returned to their native state to live; and when a prosecution for bigamous cohabitation reached the Supreme Court, the verdict was that, under the "full faith and credit" clause, the two divorces must be accepted as valid by North Carolina and of course by all other states.[4] To the objection, furthermore, that the ruling would enable any state with lax divorce requirements to enforce *The troublesome matter of divorce*

---

[1] On the right to exclude corporations from doing business in a state, see p. 97, note 1, below. To exclude all Delaware corporations from a state would, however—even if otherwise desirable—wreck its business structure.

[2] Very early in the country's history, indeed, each individual divorce required the passage of a special act by a state legislature.

[3] Haddock v. Haddock, 201 U. S. 562 (1906).

[4] Williams v. North Carolina, 317 U. S. 287 (1942).

its standards on states with strict ones, the judges (or most of them) could make no more comforting reply than that such a result is "part of the price of our federal system." [1] This, however, was not the end of the story; for when the defendants were again haled into court, the state of North Carolina, basing its case this time on the charge that the courts of Nevada had no proper jurisdiction over the parties because of the inadequate and fraudulent character of their residence in the state, a majority of the justices accepted the contention and ruled that the divorces were not of such validity that North Carolina (or any other state) must necessarily recognize them.[2] For at any rate the present, therefore—with every state entitled to challenge the validity of a domicile acquired in another state solely for the purpose of a divorce—"full faith and credit" does not cover divorces under all circumstances, leaving in a somewhat precarious position persons who have been divorced after the manner of the unlucky North Carolinians.[3]

2. Interstate citizenship   The framers of the national constitution rightly thought that no state should be allowed to discriminate, in favor of its own citizens, against persons coming into its jurisdiction from other states. To do so would be inherently unjust, and would seriously interfere with genuine national unity. Hence it is provided that "the citizens of each state shall be entitled to all privileges and immunities of citizens in the several states." [4] In general, this means that citizens of any state may move freely about the country and settle where they like, with the assurance that as newcomers they will not be subjected to discriminative taxation, that they will be permitted to carry on lawful occupations under the same conditions as older residents, and that they will not be prevented from acquiring and using property, or denied the equal protection of the laws, or refused access to the courts. It does not mean that privileges of a political nature, *e.g.*, those of voting and holding office, must be extended forthwith. Nor is a state prevented from imposing quarantine or other police regulations which will have the effect of denying free ingress or egress or the right to bring property in or to take it out. But such police restrictions must be justified by provable public necessity; furthermore, they must be so framed as to fall alike upon the citizens of the given state and those of all other states. It is hardly necessary to add that a citizen of New York, migrating to Pennsylvania, does not carry with him the rights which he

---

[1] The decision stirred wide protest and gave added point to demands long heard that the federal constitution be amended to empower Congress to enact uniform legislation on marriage and divorce. There is, however, no present promise of such action at any early date.

[2] Williams *v.* North Carolina, 325 U. S. 226 (1945).

[3] T. R. Powell, "And Repent at Leisure; An Inquiry into the Unhappy Lot of Those Whom Nevada Hath Joined Together and North Carolina Hath Put Asunder," *Harvard Law Rev.*, LVIII, 930-1017 (Sept., 1945). For conveniently assembled data on the marriage and divorce laws of all of the states, see R. V. Mackay, *Law of Marriage and Divorce Simplified* (New York, 1947).

[4] Art. IV, § 2, cl. 1.

enjoyed in New York. The point is rather that he becomes entitled to such rights as the citizens of Pennsylvania enjoy.[1]

A third obligation resting upon a state is the rendition of fugitives accused of crime. "A person charged in any state with treason, felony, or other crime," says the constitution, "who shall flee from justice, and be found in another state, shall, on demand of the executive authority of the state from which he fled, be delivered up, to be removed to the state having jurisdiction of the crime." [2] The object is, of course, to prevent criminals from "beating the law" by taking refuge on soil over which the states from which they have fled have no jurisdiction and on which they can execute no processes.[3] Rendition as practiced among the states is similar to, and was suggested by, extradition as carried on from very early times in the domain of international relations. There are, however, important differences. Nations are sovereign authorities and, as such, they practice extradition only within rather rigid limits. In the first place, they will rarely or never hand over a fugitive unless they have a reciprocal extradition agreement with the nation demanding him. In the second place, they will not surrender him unless the crime of which he is accused is one of those enumerated for extradition purposes in the agreement. Furthermore, nations usually refuse to extradite their own citizens or subjects; and by almost universal usage, political offenders, *e.g.*, persons accused of participating in a rebellion, are exempted. Finally, it has become an accepted rule that an extradited person cannot be tried for

3. Rendition:

---

[1] R. Howell, "The Privileges and Immunities of State Citizenship," *Johns Hopkins Univ. Studies in Hist. and Polit. Sci.*, XXXVI, No. 3 (1918). Notwithstanding that, in law, corporations are "citizens," at least of a qualified sort, the courts have ruled that they have no *right* of interstate migration. Those created in one state, and seeking to do business in another, may have restrictions imposed upon them in the other state which do not apply to domestic corporations, or (unless engaged in interstate commerce or aiding in the performance of federal functions) may be excluded altogether. The status of such "foreign" corporations was recently reviewed by the Supreme Court in Asbury Hospital *v.* Cass County, 326 U. S. 207 (1945).

During the depression decade, interstate migration—with more than two million persons crossing state lines every year in quest of work—created exceedingly difficult social and economic problems, especially for states (most of all, California) receiving the heaviest influx; and in twenty-seven states restrictive legislation of one sort or another was enacted. In 1941, a California statute making it a misdemeanor to "bring or assist in bringing into the state any indigent person who is not a resident of the state, knowing him to be an indigent person," was declared unanimously by the federal Supreme Court (in Edwards *v.* People of State of California, 314 U. S. 160) to exceed the police powers of the state and to violate the commerce clause of the federal constitution (four justices found it also violating a privilege of United States citizenship), and hence to be unconstitutional. The effect, of course, was to upset the "Okie" laws of all twenty-seven states having them. The general principle of freedom of migration as a privilege of United States citizenship seems clear. In practice, however, it has not prevented some states from successfully maintaining restrictions upon it—in the form, for example, of arbitrary regulations relating to vehicles with out-of-state licenses. See S. M. Cohen, "State Regulation of Migration of Indigent Persons," *Bill of Rights Rev.* II, 119-126 (Winter, 1942); H. Roback, "Legal Barriers to Interstate Migration," *Cornell Law Quar.*, XXVIII, 281-312, 483-526 (Mar., June, 1943).

[2] Art. IV, § 2, cl. 2.

[3] The refuge state has no jurisdiction in such a situation, but only the state in which the alleged offense was committed.

any offense other than that named in the warrant of extradition. Rendition as practiced by the states, on the other hand, is provided for by the national constitution, not by interstate agreements; the offenses for which an accused person is to be delivered up are broadly defined as treason, felony, and "other crimes;" states commonly give up their own citizens on proper demand; and there is no rule against trying a person so delivered up for an offense other than that with which he was charged when his delivery was requested.

Procedure

The constitution says that the demand for the surrender of a fugitive from justice shall be made by the "executive authority", *i.e.*, the governor, of the state from which the person fled; and an act of Congress provides that after the accused has been duly indicted, the demand shall be addressed to the executive authority of the state in which the accused has been apprehended. If, therefore, A kills a man in Ohio and flees into West Virginia and is there placed under arrest, the governor of Ohio will send a requisition, accompanied by a certified copy of the indictment, to the governor of West Virginia asking the return of A so that he may be placed on trial in an Ohio court. If the requisition is honored, the fugitive will be turned over to the Ohio police officer (commonly a sheriff) who has been dispatched to bring him back.

Limitations

There is no certainty, however, that the demand will be complied with. To be sure, the constitution says plainly that the fugitive "shall . . . be delivered up"; and the act of Congress says, with equal directness, that it "shall be the duty" of the executive authority to cause him to be handed over. But despite such lucid and mandatory language, many cases of refusal are on record. The governor upon whom the demand is made may (perhaps after a hearing) decline to comply—on the ground that the person wanted is not actually a fugitive, or that the evidence against him is not sufficient to establish a presumption of guilt, or that he will not get a fair trial if returned, or that the alleged offense is not known to the law of the refuge state, or that there has been unreasonable delay in making the requisition; the actual reason may be something still different—perchance a mere whim, or even a personal grudge. But in any event there is no way by which a refusal can be overcome; no court will issue a writ of mandamus to compel compliance; and the fugitive is safe so long as he remains where he is and no change of mind takes place in the governor's office.[1] In the final analysis, the constitutional mandate is effective only in so far as chief executives choose to make it so. Yet this does not mean that it is a dead letter, or even that it is commonly ignored;

---

[1] "The words 'it shall be the duty,'" declared Chief Justice Taney, "were not used as mandatory and compulsory, but as declaratory of the moral duty which this command created, when Congress had provided the mode of carrying it into execution. The act does not provide any means to compel the execution of this duty, nor inflict any punishment for neglect or refusal on the part of the executive of the state; nor is there any clause or provision in the constitution which arms the government of the United States with this power." Kentucky *v.* Dennison, 24 Howard 66 (1861).

on the contrary, it is obeyed in the great majority of cases, and when not obeyed, is usually evaded for reasons that have substantial merit.[1]

Disputes Between States

The history of the Confederation was filled with controversies between states regarding boundaries, commercial regulations, and other matters; and the makers of the constitution were not so naïve as to suppose that under the new frame of government the members of the Union would always live in perfect accord. Among sovereign nations, disputes have traditionally been settled by (a) direct agreements reached through negotiation, (b) arbitration undertaken by some neutral ruler or similar authority, (c) adjudication in an international court, or (d) in the last resort, by war. The states of the Union are not supposed to make war on one another—although they did so in 1861-65. They may, and do, reach agreements through direct negotiation. But the method of settlement chiefly contemplated by the constitution's authors was that of judicial determination; and in pursuance of this intent, the judicial power of the United States is extended to all "controversies between two or more states," with the further stipulation that in all cases in which a state is a party (regardless of the character of the opposing party) the Supreme Court shall have original jurisdiction.[2] The road to amicable adjustment of interstate differences by regular judicial process is thus always open, and many troublesome disputes relating to boundaries, water diversions, fishing rights, and other matters have been cleared up by resorting to it.[3]

Modes of settlement

REFERENCES

W. B. Graves, *American State Government* (3rd ed., New York, 1946), Chap. i.
————, *Uniform State Action* (Chapel Hill, N. C., 1934).
A. W. Bromage, *State Government and Administration in the United States* (New York, 1936), Chap. iii.
A. F. Macdonald, *American State Government and Administration* (3rd ed., New York, 1945), Chaps. ii-iii.
J. M. Mathews, *The American Constitutional System* (2nd ed., New York, 1940), Chaps. vi, xxv, xxxi.
W. W. Willoughby, *Constitutional Law of the United States* (2nd ed., New York, 1929), I, Chaps. xi-xvi.

[1] A long list of heated controversies between governors over rendition questions includes that between the chief executives of New York and Pennsylvania with respect to Harry K. Thaw more than a generation ago; one between the governors of Kentucky and Indiana (about the same time) over the fugitive Kentucky chief executive Taylor, accused of the assassination of a political rival; and a later one between the governors of Georgia and New Jersey over Robert E. Burns, author of *I Am a Fugitive from a Chain-Gang* (1932).

[2] Art. III, § 2, cl. 2.

[3] Down to 1940, some eighty suits were brought by one state against another in the Supreme Court, with every state except Maine either plaintiff or defendant in at least one. A full record to 1918 will be found in J. B. Scott [ed.], *Judicial Settlement of Controversies Between States of the American Union*, 2 vols. (New York, 1918). The judicial character of controversies between states is discussed at length in Kansas *v.* Colorado, 185 U. S. 125 (1902).

C. P. Curtis, *Lions Under the Throne* (Boston, 1947), Chap. xiv.

C. Warren, *The Supreme Court and Sovereign States* (Princeton, N. J., 1924).

B. F. Wright, *The Contract Clause of the Constitution* (Cambridge, Mass., 1938).

R. L. Hale, "The Supreme Court and the Contract Clause," *Harvard Law Rev.*, LVII, 512-557, 621-674, 852-892 (Apr., May, July, 1944).

R. H. Jackson, *Full Faith and Credit; The Lawyer's Clause of the Constitution* (New York, 1945).

T. R. Powell, *Indirect Encroachment on Federal Authority by the Taxing Powers of the States* (New York, 1918).

A. L. Powell, *National Taxation of State Instrumentalities* (Urbana, Ill., 1936).

A. G. Buehler, "Discriminations in Federal Taxation of State and Local Government Securities," *Amer. Polit. Sci. Rev.*, XXXVI, 302-312 (Apr., 1942).

R. L. Olson, *The Colorado River Compact* (Los Angeles, 1926).

F. Frankfurter and J. M. Landis, "The Compact Clause of the Constitution—A Study in Interstate Adjustments," *Yale Law Jour.*, XXXIV, 685-758 (May, 1925).

J. P. Clark, "Interstate Compacts and Social Legislation," *Polit. Sci. Quar.*, L, 502-524 (Dec., 1935), and LI, 36-61 (Mar., 1936).

M. E. Dimock and G. C. S. Benson, *Can Interstate Compacts Succeed?* (Chicago, 1937).

J. B. Moore, *Extradition and Interstate Rendition*, 2 vols. (Boston, 1891).

J. A. Scott, *Law of Interstate Rendition* (Chicago, 1917).

J. B. Scott, *The United States of America; A Study in International Organization* (New York, 1920).

———— [ed.], *Judicial Settlement of Controversies Between States of the American Union*, 2 vols. (New York, 1918).

Council of State Governments, *The Book of the States, 1945-1946* (Chicago, 1945).

The Constitution of the United States of America as Amended to January 1, 1938 (70th Cong., 2nd Sess., Sen. Doc. No. 232). Elaborate annotation of Art. IV on states' relations.

CHAPTER VII

CHANGING FEDERAL-STATE-LOCAL RELATIONS

The conditions under which the United States became a nation pre-destined it to federalism; and although in these days we often hear it mournfully asserted that the national government is preëmpting everything and leaving the states impotent, our system is still federal, with distribution of powers among three great levels of government—national, state, and local—its most conspicuous characteristic. If we could imagine ourselves planning a new constitutional pattern with no states to start with, we possibly should not create any. But the states exist; they have more machinery, spend more money, and perform more functions than ever before; and while often opening the way for friction, divided responsibility, and paralysis of action, the federal plan has, on the whole, served us well. Certainly we could have got our start on no other basis; certainly, too—in spite of people who would like to see federalism go, and of others who consider it already gone—there is no prospect of our ever becoming anything other than federal. *The basic fact of federalism*

Our federalism today is, however, very different from that with which we began. The national government has grown enormously in power; the states serve purposes and exercise controls undreamt of in earlier times; federal-state relations (and, for that matter, state-local and certainly federal-local relations) present novel patterns. In a hundred and sixty years, we have advanced from the position of a small and struggling nation with a simple agricultural society to that of the most highly industrialized and powerful of the great nations of the world; and as we have moved from milepost to milepost, our political, economic, and social institutions, responding to altered conditions and needs, have cut new channels and developed new forms. Deeply involved in resulting readjustments have been the relations between nation and states—defined in the constitution on certain simple and fundamental lines, to be sure, yet always a matter of considerable fluidity. In the convention of 1787, the question of this relationship overshadowed everything else; no sooner was the new constitution in operation than it again came to the fore; in some periods more than in others, but always in some significant degree, politics, legislation, judicial actions, and administrative procedures revolved around it as our history unfolded in the nineteenth and twentieth centuries; and never since the Civil War has it stirred greater interest or stronger feeling than in the decade and a half since the launching of President Roosevelt's New Deal. "The question of the relation of the *Federal-state relations a continuing problem* states to the federal government," declared Woodrow Wilson forty years ago, "is the cardinal question of our constitutional system. It cannot be settled by the opinion of any one generation, because it is a question of growth, and every successive stage of our political and economic development gives it a new aspect, makes it a new question." [1]

Growing predominance of the national government

The topmost development taking place has, of course, been the rise of the national government to its present paramount position. From the outset, to be sure, that government was always present in the states, enforcing laws, collecting taxes, making judicial decisions, operating the postal system, and doing other things. In early days, however, the states— both meriting and receiving the greatest popular allegiance—considered themselves, and in most respects actually were, rather more than equal members of the federal-state partnership. Seeking in 1788 to reassure people troubled about the outlook for the states in case the new constitution were adopted, Hamilton indeed expressed the opinion that it would "always be far more easy for the state governments to encroach upon the national authorities than for the national government to encroach upon the state authorities;" [2] and most men of his day agreed with him. The trend of experience, nevertheless, has been completely to the contrary; for although in their broad reserved powers the states have potentially a marvelously rich resource, even this has failed to counterbalance the fewer but more transcendant powers conferred upon the national government, interpreted ultimately, as they have always been, by national authorities. In an expanding national economy, all of our governments, state and local as well as national, have developed numerous and significant new controls.[3] But the national government has gained quite disproportionately.

Some Factors in the Growth of National Power

1. "Big nation, big government"

Any analysis of the reasons for the national government mounting to its present preëminence must start with the remarkable economic and social transformation of the country itself. In early times, the people lived mostly on farms, in villages, and in small towns. Their interests and activities were largely local, and most needs for government on any higher level were met by the states. To be sure, a national government was necessary for some purposes—to conduct foreign relations, to coördinate defense, even to regulate, on simple lines, the carrying on of interstate commerce. But, relatively, the government over which Washington and Jefferson presided had little to do. In time, however, the country expanded to include the Louisiana territory, the regions thence westward to the Pacific, and eventually Alaska and islands of the seas. Gradually, and after 1850 rapidly, population grew. Cities developed; industry was

[1] *Constitutional Government in the United States* (New York, 1908), 173.
[2] *The Federalist*, No. XVII (Lodge's ed., 98).
[3] Except only at the lowest levels, where the township, for example, has lost importance and in some places totally disappeared.

built up; railroads penetrated the great West; wealth increased; people moved about; life became more complex; state lines were increasingly transcended. After the Civil War, a collection of more or less isolated and self-sufficient states became a nation, in which matters more and more had to be handled on national lines. The era of "big business" dawned. Commerce, transportation, communication, linked the country from coast to coast. So did corporations, holding companies, labor unions. States tried to regulate and control, but things got out of hand. People wanted services that states could not—or did not—provide. Wars came, and only the nation could act. Depressions came, and the states were baffled. Older states—especially in the ever-jealous South—clung to their "rights"; in newer states—many of them carved out of the national domain, admitted to the Union by act of Congress, and lacking the background of separateness dominating the traditions of the older states—most people could not even recognize their state flag when they saw it. Finding in the constitution powers originally dormant, often quite unperceived, the national government gathered new functions and edged into new controls; and one day—though not until the nineteenth century was far spent—the country awoke to find the old federal-state balance toppled and a government at Washington ensconced, even if sometimes a bit precariously, in the seat of the mighty. Some did not like what had happened, but there was little that they could do about it. By building a big populous country in an age of swift technological advance, Americans had made big, centralized government inevitable.

A second major factor, supplying political implementation for economic and social change, has been the expansion of national power through legislative action, backed by judicial interpretation. Here, as we have seen, is chiefly where the constitution grows, and here is chiefly where the preponderance of the federal government over the states has found its way into the operating constitutional system. The main medium of expansion is, of course, the device of implied powers, without which the federal government could not possibly meet the demands of our age upon it, and in the absence of which the venerated fundamental law adopted a century and a half ago would long since have gone the way of the Articles of Confederation. To elaborate the point would be but to repeat things said in earlier chapters, or to anticipate others to be said later. Suffice it merely to remind ourselves how, in great domains like finance, commerce, agriculture, labor, defense, and social security, Congress has started with often the most meager phrases in the constitution's text, or indeed none of direct application at all, and, spinning a web of inference and deduction, has projected a presumed regulating authority into the deepest recesses where the states live and move and have their being; and how the courts have followed, hearing protests, weighing the validity of powers asserted, and usually, although of course not invariably, giving the stamp of approval, and perchance of finality, to new federal-

2. Legislation and judicial interpretation

state frontiers evolved. Of course it is not to be assumed that in all this the federal government is simply building itself up by taking things away from the states. Many of the great powers exercised—regulating interstate and foreign commerce, waging war, and the like—never belonged to the states at all. Others, *e.g.*, the taxing and spending powers, have from the first belonged to nation and states alike. In other words, the national government has, to quite an extent, developed its present mighty volume of authority entirely within its own sphere, on lines plainly laid down in the constitution, and without preventing the states, *in their spheres,* and equally under constitutional warrant, from likewise expanding their own powers and controls. And the present disposition of the Supreme Court is to decide disputed constitutional questions in such ways as to leave a maximum of power in the hands of *both* the federal government and the states. In scores of instances, nevertheless, a main or incidental effect of national legislation and judicial action has been, if not to "encroach" on the states in the somewhat invidious sense contemplated by Hamilton, at any rate to curtail jurisdictions, withdraw or restrict powers, and otherwise tip the traditional federal-state balance in the federal government's favor.[1]

3. Constitutional amendment

A third factor, of minor importance yet calling for mention, is constitutional amendment. To be sure, most of the twenty-one amendments thus far adopted have curbed rather than extended national powers. But the Fourteenth definitely nationalized citizenship and imposed restrictions upon the states at many points at which they previously had been free; the Fifteenth and Nineteenth took significant steps in the direction of nationalizing the suffrage, once solely under state control; the Sixteenth made possible an effective system of taxing the incomes of the people of the states; and the Eighteenth—although eventually repealed—for a time abrogated a traditional state control by empowering the national government to prohibit the manufacture, sale, and transportation of intoxicating liquors. Other amendments of similar purport, *e.g.*, on the subject of child labor, have been proposed though not adopted.

4. Federal state coöperation

In general, extensions of federal power resulting from legislation and judicial action are, so far as the states are concerned, compulsory; that is to say, the states as such have no option but to accept and make the best of them. There are, however, procedures which, although also entailing

---

[1] Especially fruitful in this connection has been the extension (on the basis of both express and implied powers) of *interstate* regulation to the point where it is separated from *intrastate* control by only the thinnest sort of wavering line. In this, the national government has been abetted by the whole development of transportation, communication, and corporate industry on a nation-wide basis, rendering it increasingly difficult, if not impossible, to regulate interstate aspects without at the same time controlling intrastate phases with which they are intermingled. In their efforts to retain control over the railroads, telegraph and telephone lines, and radio networks within their boundaries, the states have long been waging a losing fight; and even over manufacturing, mining, lumbering, and the like they lost a good deal of control when, a decade ago, the Supreme Court began to consider these as within the orbit of federal regulation in so far as their products flow through the channels of interstate and foreign commerce. See p. 619 below.

federal influence and even control over the states, have at the same time more of a voluntary or even contractual character, in that the states, at least ostensibly, may coöperate in them or not as they choose. The best illustration is afforded by the prevailing system of grants-in-aid— although before we turn to this, a few other forms of the same sort of relationship may be noted.

First of all, federal influence, and to some extent control, flows into the states through certain administrative channels. In enforcing its own direct authority upon the people, the national government has, of course, from the beginning had full right to maintain in every state whatever administrative personnel and processes are required for the purpose. Moreover, as its laws become more numerous and penetrating, entailing new offenses and penalties, administrative machinery blankets the states with increasing weight. The federal invasion here in mind, however, takes rather the form of a tie-up between the national government and the states for the joint performance of certain administrative functions; it is invasion, even though the spirit be one of coöperation rather than of domination. One phase presented takes the form of assumption by the national government of a share in the enforcement of certain state laws. Such an arrangement does not often arise, but a good illustration is furnished by the action of Congress in accepting the wild-game statutes of the states in lieu of laws on the subject which Congress would itself have no power to enact [1] with the result that, while state officials are, of course, not precluded from administering their local laws, federal officials participate by bringing to justice persons who transport or offer for transportation in interstate commerce game killed in violation of whatever laws the state concerned may have on the subject. Another instance is the very common commissioning of federal forest officers as state deputy fish and game wardens. *(a) Administrative relationships*

In various numbers of *The Federalist,* Hamilton and Madison expressed the opinion that the national government would rely heavily, if not mainly, upon state officials for carrying out its powers. In practice, there has been less such reliance than predicted; speaking generally, nation and states have maintained their own separate administrative personnel, with originally few, to be sure, but now swarms of federal officials and employees found at work in every corner of the land. From far back, however, federal elections have been conducted by state officers under state law, and state courts have nationalized aliens under federal law; and in later days state officials have had authority to help enforce the federal Employers Liability Act and to assist in enforcing the Migratory Bird Act, the Motor Carrier Act, the Pure Food and Drugs Act, the Wages and Hours Act, and (when they were in effect) the Volstead Act, the National Recovery Act, and the Agricultural Adjustment Act of 1933. County agricultural agents, too, are in the employ of both the state and *Federal use of state administrative officials*

[1] Except in the case of migratory animals—a matter of interstate commerce.

the nation, as well as of the local unit.[1] And, but for arrangements such as these, it would be necessary for the federal bureaucracy to become even more numerous and costly than it already is. On several occasions, the courts have upheld the right of Congress to confer powers and duties on officials of the states,[2] and although it is generally considered that such officials cannot be compelled in this way to act in a dual capacity, "serving two masters," the authority has been exercised repeatedly, and thousands of officials have performed a wide variety of resulting duties. On their part, the states very commonly forbid stipulated (chiefly higher) officials on their payrolls to hold federal office if carrying a stipend. But the constitutional provisions invariably use the term "office" in a technical sense, leaving the way open for federal utilization of any and all persons on state payrolls whose work is in the nature of *employment* rather than the holding of office.[3]

(b) Federal research as a service to the states

Another widening channel of federal influence in the domain of the states is research. Simultaneously with the extension of government's long regulating arm into social and economic affairs, those affairs grew more complex and the problems relating to them more technical. For purposes both of enacting wise laws and achieving intelligent administration, a vast amount of painstaking investigation became necessary— much of it of a highly scientific character. Even a small town has need of the latest and best information on such matters as public health and education; and practically all state and more important municipal governments have set up agencies and spent money for investigative purposes. Localized research on this basis, however, has the disadvantage that frequently it cannot be pursued on such a scale as to yield the best results, and that, in any event, it involves wasteful duplication of effort. More and more, therefore, the country has come to rely upon the large-scale and expanding research activities of the national government, even in fields like education which are not, except to a limited extent, within that government's jurisdiction. Utilized by the national government in its own ever-widening activities throughout the land, the results of large-scale investigative work carried on, for example, by bureaus in the Departments of Agriculture and Labor, the Bureau of Standards in the Department of Commerce, the Public Roads Administration in the Federal Works Agency, and the Office of Education in the Federal Security Agency, are turned to their own uses by the states and often become the basis for widely standardized state legislation and administrative policy.

[1] The extensive federal use of state officials in wartime will be mentioned later. See p. 828 below.

[2] *E.g.*, United States *v.* Jones, 109 U. S. 513 (1883); Selective Draft Law Cases, 245 U. S. 366 (1917).

[3] Reciprocal federal-state employment of officials is treated at some length in J. P. Clark, "Joint Activity Between Federal and State Officials," *Polit. Sci. Quar.*, LI, 230-269 (June, 1936). Cf. A. N. Holcombe, "The States as Agents of the Nation," *Southwestern Polit. Sci. Quar.*, I, 307-327 (Mar., 1921); D. Fellman, "Some Consequences of Increased Federal Activity in Law Enforcement," *Jour. of Crim. Law and Criminology*, XXXV, 16-33 (May-June, 1944).

For coöperation between federal and state governments, indeed, a new atmosphere has happily been created. The old idea—Hamilton emphasized it in his day--was that nation and states were necessarily competitive and, at least potentially, always in conflict. To this has succeeded, even in the thinking of the legally-minded Supreme Court, the concept of nation and states as rooted in the same American traditions, possessing many vital interests in common, and capable of friendly coöperation for promotion of the general good.[1] Of such coöperation there has come to be a great deal, beyond the forms already mentioned; and, among other results, it has carried federal influence (amounting sometimes to substantial control) deeply into the realm of state affairs. In multiplying instances, it rests upon formal contracts or agreements, initiated by either party, and embodied in federal or state legislation (or both). The secretary of the interior, for example, is authorized to enter into contracts with any state with a view to education, medical assistance, and agricultural aid for Indians living in the state. The federal Bureau of Prisons can make agreements with state authorities for the care of federal prisoners. The Tennessee Valley Authority has an arrangement with seven states within its area for a joint program of agricultural development, water-shed protection, and other activities. Starting with New York in 1928, nearly all states have relinquished their right to license airplane pilots flying solely within their boundaries, requiring them instead to take out federal licenses, and thereby turning a federal administrative service to state use. Congressional assent to interstate compacts is, of course, another illustration; and federal financial aid to the states for a great variety of purposes (to be spoken of presently) is a most conspicuous example. On the other hand, such coöperation may be maintained simply as a matter of comity and without any legislative or other formal contract at all. Thus, many state agricultural experiment stations carry on investigative work in conjunction with bureaus of the federal Department of Agriculture. The Federal Bureau of Investigation aids state and local police forces through its finger-print service, its training school, and its uniform crime reports. State and local police may, and frequently do, join with federal authorities in apprehending violators of either federal or state law.

The advantages accruing from all such federal-state coöperation are many. In particular, (1) concurrent federal and state legislation may be virtually indispensable to well-rounded regulation of a given type of activity; (2) both nation and states may be enabled to profit reciprocally from administrative arrangements worked out, or even information made available; and (3) the federal government may be enabled to acquire a wholesome supervisory or directive influence over activities of

---

[1] This view was given notable expression by Mr. Justice Cardozo in an opinion which he wrote for the majority of the Court in 1938 upholding the constitutionality of the Social Security Act of 1935. Steward Machine Co. v. Davis, 301 U. S. 548.

states, while still permitting some useful independence of state and local planning and management.[1]

Federal Aid to State and Local Activities

Two main forms
One of the most important means by which the national government has gained a hand in state (and of late also local) affairs, thereby further enhancing its own preëminence, takes the form of spending money for purposes of "federal assistance." During the depression of the thirties, the national government embarked upon heavy outlays in the states for provision of employment and other forms of relief—outlays sometimes made directly and without the intervention of state authorities. With better times returning, and employment at length rising to top levels as a result of the defense effort launched in 1940 and the later war starting in 1941, it became possible to bring this form of assistance gradually to an end. The federal assistance with which we are here concerned is of a more permanent nature—the "grant-in-aid," as commonly termed, under which federal money, earmarked for particular activities, is turned over to state treasuries to be expended by state agencies, or is paid to such agencies directly, or even nowadays to local governments. Federal assistance in this quasi-contractual form has become an established feature of our governmental system and a principal factor in determining actual day-to-day federal-state relations.

Earlier grants of land and money
Grants by the federal government to the states are no novelty; on the contrary, they go back almost to the beginning of our national history. Starting with Ohio in 1802, Congress made a regular practice of bestowing on newly admitted states public land within their boundaries equivalent to one section in every township, to be used for the development of permanent school funds—in fact, two sections after 1848, and even four in the cases of Utah, Arizona, and New Mexico. In the famous Land Grant College [Morrill] Act of 1862, it set aside still more land for the benefit of the states,[2] specifying that the proceeds should be used by each in endowing and maintaining one or more colleges devoted primarily, although not exclusively, to instruction in "such branches of learning as are related to agriculture and the mechanic arts;" and funds derived from this source help support many of our "land-grant" colleges today. In 1887, furthermore, such funds began to be supplemented by regular yearly lump-sum allotments of federal money to help the states develop experiment stations in connection with their agricultural colleges; and simultaneously an office of experiment stations was started in the federal Department of Agriculture to work with the states in supervising the colleges and stations. Meanwhile not only other land but money also

---

[1] J. P. Clark, *The Rise of a New Federalism; Federal-State Coöperation in the United States* (New York, 1938); E. S. Corwin, "National-State Coöperation; Its Present Possibilities," *Yale Law Jour.*, XLVI, 599-623 (Feb., 1937).

[2] Allotted in the proportion of 30,000 acres for every senator and representative that a state had in Congress.

(in periods of surplus revenues) was bestowed, and not only for education, but likewise for roads and canals.

Starting with a Smith-Lever Act of 1914 for the promotion of agricultural extension work, Congress eventually developed a new form of *conditional* grant which in time became a standard pattern. Referred to commonly as a "grant-in-aid," its cardinal principle is that Congress will appropriate money for the promotion of a specified service or activity carried on by the states, apportioning the sum for any given purpose among the whole number of states on some fixed basis, but permitting a state to share in the subvention only, as a rule, on four conditions—(1) that the state shall spend the federal money only for the exact purpose indicated and under whatever specifications may have been attached; (2) that the state itself, or its subdivisions, shall make concurrent appropriations for the given purpose (usually in amounts at least equal to its share of the national grant); (3) that the state shall create, or at all events maintain, a suitable administrative agency—highway commission, extension director, vocational education board, or whatever it may be—with which the federal government can deal in relation to the activity to be carried on; and (4) that, in return for the assistance received, the state shall recognize the federal government's right (with suitable regard for local conditions) to approve plans and policies, interpose regulations, fix minimum standards, and inspect results—for inevitably "control follows the dollar." Often, of course, it will be necessary for states to enact new legislation in order to qualify for sharing in a given grant; almost always, administrative machinery will have to be reconstructed so as to open a way for supervision by national officers over activities that previously—if undertaken at all—were entirely in the state's own hands. Ostensibly, no compulsion is exercised. A state may, if it likes, decline to meet the conditions imposed, in which event it simply does not participate in the federal subsidy; and this voluntary aspect of the plan has been of great help to the courts in getting around the constitutional difficulties which some of the legislation, dealing with matters far out on the rim of federal authority, presents. Compliance by the states is, however, less voluntary than appears. For the federal funds represent the proceeds of taxes paid by the people of the entire country, and if any state refuses to go into a given arrangement, it thereby cuts itself off from benefits which its taxpayers are helping to bestow on the states that participate. Naturally, it will be reluctant to do this; and the same considerations that initially induce a state to accept its share of a grant commonly impel it to live up to the standards and specifications required rather than run the risk of having its subvention withheld. Practically all existing forms of grants-in-aid are shared in by all, or substantially all, of the states.

Prior to the depression of the thirties, federal grants-in-aid, although significant, were on a rather modest scale. In 1920, they aggregated only $77,115,000; in 1930, approximately $135,000,000. By 1937, however, the

The later pattern of conditional grants

Mounting totals

states, as a group, were deriving more of their revenue (fourteen per cent) from this source than from any other except gasoline taxes (fifteen per cent) and general sales taxes (sixteen per cent); and in 1939 grants of the kind were made for no fewer than twenty-one different state or local purposes, while the total outlay mounted to $582,519,000—an increase of more than three hundred per cent in ten years. Even this huge figure, however, was destined to be topped later: in 1941—the last year before the war disrupted activities like highway construction—it rose to $851,005,000; in 1944, with the war in progress, it fell to $649,758,000; but in 1946, with more normal conditions restored—it shot up to $1,100,-000,000.[1] If a growing movement for a nation-wide, or even more limited, system of grants for assistance to elementary and secondary education eventually prevails (as almost certainly it will), further substantial increases may be expected—with still others to come in case a general scheme of health insurance now fairly certain of adoption within a few years proves to have been organized on the grant-in-aid pattern. Meanwhile, some of the principal forms taken by the huge grants of today may be briefly reviewed.

1. Defense—the National Guard

In 1916, a National Defense Act,[2] carrying farther the invasion of state autonomy begun by a Militia Act of 1903, discarded the old term "militia," substituted the significant name "National Guard" (already more or less in use unofficially), and welded the various bodies of state troops into a unified, nationally organized force auxiliary to the Regular Army and closely tied in with it. From as early as 1808, Congress appropriated money almost every year to assist the states in arming and equipping their militiamen, and gradually some slight federal controls began to be exercised. Not until after the legislation of 1916, however, did grants become large or controls extensive. Nowadays, federal aid is provided liberally,[3] and federal standards of equipment, training, and discipline are rigorously enforced. As an organized militia, the National Guard still serves the states; but it has likewise become (as its complete mobilization by the national government in both World Wars I and II so forcefully illustrated) an integral part of the war machine of the nation.[4]

2. Highways

A Federal Aid Road Act of 1916[5] provided for appropriations rising by stages to $25,000,000 in 1921, to be expended by the Bureau of Roads (then in the Department of Agriculture),[6] in coöperation with the highway departments of the several states, in the construction of rural postroads; and here reappeared the lately invented device of requiring the

---

[1] Current figures are given in the Census Bureau's annual publication entitled *State Finances*. Emergency relief grants and the like are not included in the statistics cited above.

[2] 39 *U. S. Stat. at Large*, 197.

[3] Not in any fixed ratio; but in 1939 (a typical prewar year) state expenditure was $11,861,000 and federal $43,376,000.

[4] See pp. 804-805 below.

[5] 43 *U. S. Stat. at Large*, 653.

[6] The present authority is the Public Roads Administration in the Federal Works Agency.

states to match evenly the amounts allotted to them if they wanted to share in a subsidy. As was to be expected, the scheme proved popular in what already was beginning to be an automobile age. Every state accepted the provisions of the act; the national grant (distributed according to three equally weighted factors—area, population, and rural delivery route mileage) was increased repeatedly, reaching $161,730,958 in 1939; and under the federal impetus, road construction went forward on a scale never before witnessed in this or any other country. State highway legislation, conforming to federal requirements, grew voluminous; and state indebtedness incurred in carrying out the joint program rose in some instances to alarming proportions. During American participation in World War II, non-military road-building almost completely ceased. Resumption of such building on a large scale after the war was, however, envisaged in an act of 1944 authorizing the appropriation of $500,000,000 a year, on a sixty-forty basis the first year, but fifty-fifty thereafter, for each of three postwar years for federal aid in the construction of interstate highways, secondary or "feeder" roads, and highways in metropolitan areas.[1]

With a view to ameliorating conditions of existence for various classes of handicapped or otherwise unfortunate people, and putting even larger numbers in a better position to meet the vicissitudes of life, the Social Security Act of 1935 [2] instituted a broad permanent federal-state program of social welfare. One major feature, i.e., old age insurance, was made exclusively a federal enterprise, and another, i.e., unemployment compensation, was planned to be financed entirely from payroll taxes on employers and employees, except that the national government was to bear the cost of administration. Practically all other features, however, were developed on a basis of federal grants-in-aid. For assistance to the needy aged, such aid (to a maximum of twenty-five dollars monthly per beneficiary) is granted on condition of equal sums being contributed by the states. Aid on a fifty-fifty basis is provided for the care of dependent children, and, on the same basis, up to a limit of twenty-two and one-half dollars per person monthly for assistance to the blind. And while no federal program of general health insurance has as yet been adopted, the legislation of 1935 extends aid to the states for strengthening and improving state and local public health services. One would be justified in assuming that henceforth social security and well-being in this country are to be the joint concern of the federal and state governments, with the former meeting much of the cost, largely determining how the money shall be spent, and therefore holding the whip-hand.

During World War I, state employment offices throughout the country

3. Social welfare (margin note)

---

[1] The power of Congress to appropriate money for highways can be deduced from the post-offices and postroads clause of the constitution, the authority to provide for the national defense, and presumably—if it were necessary—from the general welfare clause.

[2] 49 *U. S. Stat. at Large*, 620. See Chap. XXXII below.

4. Employment offices

began to be supplemented with federally maintained offices under supervision of a U. S. Employment Service. The federal system did not develop impressively, and although a Wagner-Peyser Act of 1933 reinvigorated it, the same measure instituted a plan of federal non-matched grants to the states in aid of their own offices. Taken over by the national government during World War II (1942), the state offices were restored to state management late in 1946; and federal aid to them was resumed.

5. Conservation of national resources

From 1911, the federal government incurred small direct expenditures in the states for forest-fire protection, and in 1924 it instituted contributions on a grant-in-aid basis, with activities extended to include the distribution of forest plant-stock among farmers. Grants on the same basis for the support of agrcultural experiment work contributing primarily to the conservation of resources began as early as 1887, and for support of various forms of agricultural extension work in 1914.

6. Education

Although education has traditionally been looked upon as a state and local function, federal aid, as we have seen, started at a very early date in the form of grants of land for school purposes, including those later provided for in the Morrill Act of 1862 and aimed at promoting vocational education in the fields of agriculture and the mechanic arts. The federal grants-in-aid for the support of agricultural experiment stations and extension services referred to above have, of course, their educational, as well as their conservational, aspects; and further provision for vocational education for the physically handicapped, on a grant-in-aid basis, and in the fields of agriculture, trade, industry, and home economics, was made in the Smith-Hughes Act of 1917, with later increases (as under the Social Security Act of 1935) of the amounts expended.[1]

The problem of a general system of educational grants-in-aid

Financial difficulties of both urban and rural areas during the depression of the thirties seriously affected the public schools and prompted demand for a general system of grants-in-aid for the benefit of both elementary and secondary education, and especially to enable poorer states to pay teachers and provide equipment on a scale comparable to more favored ones; and discussions then taking place (although the subject had received some attention earlier) have thrust upon the country one of its largest and most baffling domestic problems. The federal government already does something for general education. Its Office of Education (in the Federal Security Agency), dating from 1867, carries on research, collects statistics, publishes reports, prepares and distributes teaching materials, and coöperates with other federal agencies and with state and local authorities as opportunity arises. What increasing numbers of school men, educational organizations like the National Education Association, and thoughtful citizens have in mind, however, is something far beyond this—nothing less, indeed, than a general, nation-wide system of grants to the states for the same leveling up of educational services that has been sought in other fields through grants for old-age assistance and the

[1] M. E. MacDonald, *Federal Grants for Vocational Education* (Chicago, 1944).

like. The existing situation is high-lighted by startling disparities among the states in what they spend per pupil on education, what they pay their teachers, how many months per year their children are in school, and what results they get, or can hope to get, in terms of training for their future citizens. Ironically, the poorer states make a relatively greater effort to support education than do the richer ones. But it is not enough, and their meagerness of resources precludes doing more. Education, however, is an interest of national, not merely state and local, scope; and it is to implement this interest and bring the country to a more generally satisfactory condition educationally that the grant-in-aid program is proposed. Among obstacles are apprehensions lest federal support turn out to mean federal domination; doubts about how an equitable system could be worked out for states of the most widely differing needs; anxiety lest the distribution of funds become entangled with discriminations on grounds of race or color; complications raised by the unfavorable attitude of Catholics and the Catholic parochial schools; besides objections advanced against the grant-in-aid system generally, to be touched upon presently. But as long ago as 1938, an Advisory Committee on Education appointed by President Roosevelt reported favorably on the proposal;[1] hardly a major general educational organization in the country is not on record for it; Congress has been flooded with bills on the subject (ten pending at one time in 1946, and several in 1947, with hearings held on some[2]); and although many difficult angles of the problem remain to be smoothed out, it is probably at this point—unless a nation-wide system of health insurance should gain priority—that the grant system will next be significantly expanded.[3]

With the development of the grant-in-aid system has come new relationships not only between the federal government and the states, but between that government and subdivisions of states such as counties and cities. There was a time when the government at Washington was supposed to have, and speaking generally did have, virtually no direct relations with

Federal grants to local author- ities

[1] *Report of the Advisory Committee on Education, Floyd W. Reeves, Chairman* (Washington, D. C., 1938).

[2] A measure providing for educational aid to low-income states in amounts rising to $250,000,000 a year was reported favorably by the Senate committee on education and labor in 1946, but not passed.

[3] The arguments pro and con, with much relevant material, will be found in J. E. Johnsen [ed.], *Federal Aid for Education* (New York, 1941). Cf. E. R. Rankin, *Federal Aid to Education* (Chapel Hill, N. C., 1934); G. F. Zook, *The Rôle of the Federal Government in Education* (Cambridge, Mass., 1945); "Should Financial Aid be Extended to Public Schools?" [Symposium], *Cong. Digest*, XXIII, 35-64 (Feb., 1944; "The Quest of Federal Funds for Public Schools—Pro and Con" [symposium], *ibid.*, XXV, 35-64 (Feb., 1946).

Several forms of federal aid not touched upon in the foregoing summary include (1) grants (or loans) in the as yet somewhat chaotic field of public housing; (2) matched grants for the construction and development of airports; (3) grants (under legislation of 1946) for assistance to the states and territories in providing hot lunches for school children—the states matching federal funds dollar for dollar during the first three years, but with the federal share decreasing from then on, and as a matter of fact actually reduced in 1947; (4) a program, started in 1920, and with matching of funds, for vocational rehabilitation; and (5) aid to a few states which maintain schools for training officers for the American merchant marine.

local governments—outside, at all events, of the District of Columbia and the territories; the relations of such governments reached upwards only to the states in which they were located. In the first instance, it was mainly the depression of the thirties that brought a different situation. Problems of relief and unemployment with which the states proved incapable of dealing effectively had to be taken over by the federal government; and in handling them that government often simply by-passed the states, reaching down to local areas and dealing with them directly. Cities all over the country were given or loaned sums for water-works, sewerage, street improvements, airports, and public buildings; federal money was made available to municipal housing authorities; insolvent cities were given means of reaching agreements with their creditors in federal bankruptcy courts. With the return of better economic conditions, most of these activities came to an end. But a pattern of direct federal-local relations had been established, and to a considerable extent it persists today in the handling of grants-in-aid. In some instances, all that happens is that federal money granted to the states, but necessarily to be expended locally, is channeled directly to local authorities without passing through state hands. In states that have so authorized, for example, federal funds for old-age assistance, aid to needy children, aid to the blind, and development of airports go directly to the counties. In other instances, too, the states are by-passed, largely if not completely. Only New York and a few other states have housing authorities properly set up for administering federal housing grants; hence such grants commonly go directly to local housing agencies. Similarly, in making and supervising grants for airport development under the Federal Airport Act of 1946, the Civil Aëronautics Administration deals only with cities and other localities unless a given state requires the funds to be channeled through its own authorities. Through the soil-conservation service of the Department of Agriculture, the federal government also directly assists local soil-conservation districts in their soil-conservation and erosion-prevention activities; and county agricultural agents, usually appointed by the county board, are paid partly by the federal government, to which naturally they have some responsibility. Whenever a new form of grant-in-aid is introduced, indeed, a question that has to be settled is whether the federal subsidy shall be paid in lump sums to the states to be distributed or instead shall be paid directly to localities. In so far as new forms of federal-local relations—financial or otherwise—are so conducted as to "short-circuit" the states, the traditional federal-state equilibrium tends to be upset in the federal government's favor; although fairness requires it to be added that, in general, due regard for state constitutions and laws has been shown and local authorities have not been put in leading strings from Washington.[1]

[1] C. E. Merriam, "The Federal Government Recognizes the Cities," *Nat. Mun. Rev.*, XXIII, 107-109 (Feb., 1934); P. V. Betters, "The Federal Government and

The rise of the present towering structure of federal financial assistance to states and local areas is no isolated phenomenon. Practically every modern government has found it increasingly necessary to extend central aid to subordinate governments; [1] and our system of federal assistance is paralleled by similar systems of state aid to local units. Fundamentally, the explanation in our country is the decline of the general property tax in a period of swiftly increasing outlays, especially upon highways, education, and social services.[2] Adequate new sources of local revenue not having been found, state governments, and ultimately the national government, have been compelled to come to the rescue. Starting with only a few small scattered grants a generation ago, the federal grant-in-aid system has grown into a huge device of joint financing, basic to the fiscal operations of nation and states alike, and, for better or worse, curtailing much of the local autonomy of former times in favor of planning and control from Washington.

A phase of a general trend

In earlier years, the grant-in-aid policy was opposed vigorously on such grounds as (1) that under it the national government practiced a species of bribery, i.e., in effect bought the right of prescribing and supervising activities over which it otherwise would have no control; (2) that the system coerced the states (however gently) into overloading themselves with expenditures and obligations; (3) that it encouraged manipulation and vote-trading in Congress for special favors for particular causes or interests; (4) that it tended to create masses of voters dependent on federally aided enterprises, thereby assuring the party in power an unfair initial advantage in elections; (5) that, in addition to depriving the states of their proper powers, it engendered the habit of relying on doles, encouraged the demoralizing notion that the government at Washington owed every business and profession a living, and if adhered to meant "the gradual breakdown of local self-government in America"; (6) that "federal aid" was a misnomer, since all that the federal government did was to take money from the people of the states in the form of taxes, put it in the general fund, draw it out again, and give it back, in proportions not always easy to justify; (7) that the richer states—in which opposition to the policy largely centered—were made to bear most of the burden and progressive states were penalized for the benefit of more backward ones; and (8) that, if grants were to be made at all, they might

Some earlier arguments:

1. In criticism

the Cities; A Problem in Adjustment," *Annals of Amer. Acad. of Polit. and Soc. Sci.,* CXCIX, 190-199 (Sept., 1938). For an excellent survey of the general subject, see C. M. Kneier, *City Government in the United States* (rev. ed., New York, 1947), Chap. VIII.

[1] On the vast system of grants-in-aid built up in Great Britain during the past hundred years, see H. R. Bowen, *English Grants-in-Aid; A Study in the Finance of Local Government* (Iowa City, Iowa, 1939).

[2] See pp. 972-977 (in complete edition of this book).

[3] For a full statistical picture of the grant-in-aid system as of fairly recent date, see Council of State Governments, *Grants-in-Aid and Other Federal Expenditures Within the States* (rev. ed., Chicago, 1946), covering the situation during the fiscal year ending June 30, 1946.

better be "block," or lump-sum (rather than functional) grants, to be spent by the states entirely at their own discretion.

2. In defense

To all this there was, of course, a rebuttal, running somewhat as follows: (1) the system encouraged the states to undertake social services which many of them otherwise would ignore or feel that they could not afford; (2) it enabled minimum national standards to be set up in fields of social and economic regulation in which the people of the entire country had a vital interest; (3) it divided burdens which states were often unable to bear alone, quite justifiably requiring the richer states to help the poorer ones improve conditions in which all had a common concern; (4) it made for economical expenditure of federal funds, and, by imposing reciprocal obligations, checked the scramble for public money which frequently took place when such money was bestowed without imposing local responsibilities, as was the practice, for example, in making river and harbor appropriations; (5) the initiative and responsibility left to the states kept the scheme elastic and furnished all necessary safeguards against undesirable dictation from Washington; (6) legally at least, no state was obliged to subject itself to the operation of the system unless it desired to do so; and (7) in the final analysis, the grant-in-aid system was the only alternative to an enormous expansion of direct federal control on lines that would be still more damaging to state power and pride.[1]

Some major facts

In the last twenty years or so, the critics have been largely silenced by the expanding conception of the services that government ought to render and by the manifest need of the states for increased funds with which to undertake them. And today certain facts are clear. (1) The grant-in-aid system is here to stay. Not only so, but it will continue to grow in magnitude and importance. Even if it should not be extended into new fields of governmental activity, existing grants—especially for old-age assistance, maternity and child welfare, and other social services—will almost certainly mount to higher levels. New extensions, however—as already indicated, in such domains as public health and education—are practically inevitable. (2) The time-honored objections to the system still hold with some people; yet, speaking broadly, opposition has melted away. Specific proposals draw attack, but usually only because the critics would like to deflect attention to different ones. The Supreme Court is committed to the grant-in-aid principle;[2] and so far as one can see there

---

[1] Incidental effects included (1) opening a way for improvement of state personnel practices, through authority conferred in 1939 on the Social Security Board to require of the states, as a condition of receiving grants under the Social Security Act, that they establish and maintain merit systems in their unemployment insurance and public assistance agencies (see pp. 750-758 below), and (2) greatly broadening the impact of the Hatch legislation of 1940 (see p. 226 below) curtailing the political activities of state and local officials and employees whose compensation is derived in any degree from the federal government.

[2] Massachusetts *v.* Mellon and Frothingham *v.* Mellon, 262 U. S., 447 (1923), in effect sustaining the Federal Child Hygiene [Sheppard-Towner] Act of 1921 and by inference the grant-in-aid system generally; also cases cited on p. 758, note 1, below, sustaining the Social Security Act of 1935.

is no limit to the lengths to which grants may in future be carried except only the resources of the United States Treasury. But (3) there is need for a more coherent policy concerning the matter, and for better federal supervision and administration. One almost may say that up to now there has been no general, over-all policy at all. Certain state activities, *e.g.*, the development of airports, have been made beneficiaries because of manifest practical national interests involved; others, *e.g.*, highways, partly at least in response to persuasive lobbying; still others, *e.g.*, various forms of social welfare, because of pressures exerted by socially-minded people envisaging a program obviously beyond the capacity or disposition of the states to carry out. But the structure lacks logic and symmetry; in 1946, the Senate committee on education and labor frankly called it "chaotic." Twenty years ago, lack of a general policy did not greatly matter; subsidies were few and small. But the mammoth proportions lately assumed, with prospects for still farther growth, now call for a thoroughgoing appraisal of the entire resulting situation, to be followed by more or less formal adoption of a general, consistent, and rational line of policy under which both existing and proposed grants would be tested by accepted norms and cut off, reduced, or increased—or initially refused—according to principle rather than simply as dictated by casual concern or by pressure group. Similarly, the federal government's rôle of inspection and supervision should be discharged more consistently and efficiently than at present; and for bringing this about, more adequate financial provision should in certain cases be made.[1]

The General Problem of Centralization

A time-honored issue in the United States is certainly that of "centralization;" loose constructionists and strict constructionists were arguing over it before the constitution had been in operation a twelvemonth. An old question assuredly, but also ever new; and no one needs to be told that fierce fires of controversy have raged around it in the last three decades of rapidly growing federal power, and particularly in the era of emergency and reform measures associated with the New Deal.

On the one hand, it is contended (1) that the only feasible plan for a land of continental proportions and a people of vast numbers and divergencies is one—such as the makers of our constitution had in mind— *Criticism of the present trend*

[1] In 1947, a critical study of the existing system in both its financial and administrative aspects was undertaken by the Council of State Governments, the National Association of State Budget Officers, and the Governors' Conference, and a report was expected within a year.

For various books dealing with federal aid, see p. 127 below. The most generally useful now is that by J. A. Maxwell. Arguments against the system are presented cogently in C. Warren, *Congress as Santa Claus* (Charlottesville, Va., 1933). A plea for a more systematic policy is contained in J. P. Harris, "Should Grants-in-Aid Have a Policy?," *State Government*, XIII, 107-108, 115-117 (June, 1940); and some of the deeper financial implications are considered in W. Kilpatrick, "Neglected Aspects of Intergovernmental Fiscal Relations," *Amer. Polit. Sci. Rev.*, XLI, 452-462 (June, 1947). As a rule, information on current developments is obtainable from successive issues of Council of State Governments, *The Book of the States*.

which allows a large measure of local and regional autonomy, restricts centralized, uniform, national control over social and economic matters to a minimum, and encourages and nourishes the responsibilities of local government; (2) that even if Congress has the constitutional right to extend its regulating activities in certain of the present and proposed directions, it is not wise, or even safe, for it to insist upon going farther than it has already gone, especially in the broad domain of the police power, once supposed to be occupied mainly or entirely by the states; (3) that the national government has already (especially as a result of depression-time measures and of the later war) become overgrown, top-heavy, unwieldy, with the people in danger of finding themselves hopelessly weighed down with a vast, professionalized federal bureaucracy, not too careful about the ways of democracy; (4) that in many large fields the state governments are still the more natural and effective agencies of control, because closer to the problems involved and especially to the people concerned; (5) that it is no less desirable now than in the past that the states be left wide latitude for serving as testing grounds and "experiment stations"; and (6) that in seeking to enforce nation-wide standards through an ever-widening network of federal law, backed up by steadily expanding federal administrative machinery, the national government is assuming and trying to accentuate a uniformity of American life that does not and cannot exist, meanwhile strangling the states and reducing them to mere local areas charged only with "the neat and humble care of detail in obedience to a nationally determined policy."

Counter-
argu-
ments

In opposition to all this, it is maintained (1) that time, inventions, and other forces have so thoroughly nationalized the United States that most fundamental social and economic interests are no longer local, but instead cut across state and sectional boundaries, and are of common concern to the entire country; (2) that along with this great change of conditions has gone a corresponding change of political thought, so that people no longer expect or desire the state or regional autonomy that prevailed in earlier and simpler days, but, on the contrary, are prepared to see the competitive federalism of the past give way increasingly to the *coöperative* federalism of the future; (3) that the states have not been so efficient as to have demonstrated their right to be let alone in matters of wide national concern; and (4) that so long as social and economic conditions arise which, if they are to be regulated effectively at all, must be regulated by the national government, it is of no use to say that the national government is unfitted to take on more responsibilities, the proper course being, rather, to improve that government so as to remedy the deficiency, if it exists.[1]

[1] In 1932, Franklin D. Roosevelt, campaigning for the presidency, assailed the Republicans for "committing themselves to the idea that we ought to center control of everything in Washington as rapidly as possible." Twelve years later, the Republican party, and in particular a group of Republican state governors (including the party's candidates for both the presidency and the vice-presidency) warmly advo-

Here again, out of a wealth of *ex parte*, and often emotional, argument arise certain conclusions. The first is that the subject is not one upon which to dogmatize. The proper attitude is not a generalized condemnation or a generalized approval, but willingness to consider each proposed extension of national activity on its own merits. A second point is that centralization and decentralization are not mutually exclusive principles, only one of which can be adhered to at a given time. Large business establishments have found that efficiency requires uniformity and concentration in certain of their operations and quite the reverse in others. So it is with governments. A high degree of centralization in one field is not incompatible with no centralization at all in other fields. In the third place, the growth of national control—quite apart from the special circumstances that have stimulated it so powerfully in this country during the past twelve or fifteen years—is inevitable, however one may feel about it. It is the universal experience, once national unity has been attained; and the device of federalism can no more stop it in the United States than in the old German Empire and Republic, in Switzerland, or in other countries that started with highly decentralized systems. Let social and economic activities and problems develop to a point where they are no longer bounded by state lines, but are of regional or national scope, and any attempt to keep up a monopoly of state regulation not only is hopeless, but, if persisted in, will certainly precipitate damaging conflict between state power and national power. "The outcome of such a conflict can never be long in doubt. The greater will prevail over the lesser." [1]

Some broad conclusions

The Outlook for the States

What, then, of the states? Are they to be completely overborne by the advancing supremacy of the national government? Have they become so enamored of federal aid as to have lost their constitutional vigor and self-respect? Are they, indeed, worth saving? Notwithstanding all that they obviously still mean in our national life, and in spite of impressive displays of vitality during World War II, there undoubtedly are people who regard them as completely eclipsed; indeed, there are those who look hopefully to the day when the "waste and confusion" of forty-eight separate state governments will be no more.[2] Charges are brought that,

Some serious charges

cated a revival of states' rights, so disastrously subverted, it was alleged, by the policies and measures of the Rooseveltian New Deal! On the level of practical political argument, at least, as opposed to more rarefied constitutionalism, one would not be far wrong in concluding that the "ins," whoever they are, are likely to incline to federal centralization and the "outs"—as long as they remain "outs"—to deplore it. Nor is this any new phenomenon. A century and a half ago, Jefferson created the Republican party—forerunner of the present Democratic party—to oppose an increase of centralized power, and then when he became president reversed himself and fostered the very development he had resisted.

[1] W. MacDonald, *A New Constitution for a New America*, 169.

[2] See W. Y. Elliott, *The Need for Constitutional Reform*, Chap. ix (New York, 1935).

A decade ago, a friendly English critic (writing, as will be surmised, from a

as resulting from history, existing states commonly do not correspond to economic or social unities; that provincial viewpoints of their populations and restrictive clauses in their constitutions too often prevent them from coöperating for the public well-being, either with one another or with the national government—in a period, too, when public problems are increasingly taking on a nation-wide aspect; that often they fail to deal vigorously and effectively with even their purely internal affairs. And remedial proposals include such drastic suggestions as (1) redrawing the map of the country so as to bring state boundaries into better accord with the present distribution of population, and with other social and economic conditions; (2) displacing the states for many, if not most, purposes by superimposing upon them a smaller number of political divisions laid out to correspond to socio-economic *regions;* and (3) maintaining the system of states more or less as now, but giving the national government power not only to regulate *all* commerce, protect *all* natural resources, and the like, but undivided authority to legislate on health, safety, morals, and the general welfare, even though such "police power" is now the states' most distinctive feature and their principal reason for existence.

1. Redrawing the map of the states

Before turning to some conclusions and constructive comments, we may pause briefly on each of these three suggestions. The point to the first is not simply that the present forty-eight commonwealths are extremely unequal in area, population, and resources; of itself, this does not seriously trouble anybody except a few people who profess to worry about the equal representation of the states in the United States Senate.[1] The matter of concern is, rather, that most state boundary lines are purely artificial and the resulting divisions consequently often lacking in topographic, social, and economic unity. More than one person has amused himself by working out a system of state boundaries presumed to be more in accord with the present-day actualities of population, social viewpoint, and economic interest.[2] In particular, a great deal has been said, and with considerable plausibility, in behalf of organizing metropolitan areas like New York, Philadelphia, Chicago, and Detroit into separate states, which, as such, would be free from the "upstate" or "downstate" restraint and domination that nowadays give rise to so much friction and dissatisfaction.[3] California might be divided into northern and southern

---

socialist viewpoint) expressed the opinion that the states and state powers had been all well enough in the old days of an expanding capitalism and a vigorous individualism, but that now, in an age of capitalist contraction and decline they have become mere instruments of capitalism for obstruction and evasion of legitimate control of our economy by the central government, with no functions of their own which that government could not better perform. H. J. Laski, "The Obsolescence of Federalism," *New Republic,* XCVIII, 367-369 (May 3, 1939).

[1] See pp. 296-298 below.

[2] See, for example, a map in *Chicago Tribune,* Jan. 5, 1930, pt. 11, p. 5.

[3] The arguments for separate statehood are particularly cogent when, as in the cases of New York and Chicago, the metropolitan area extends into two or more states. See W. B. Graves, in *Amer. Polit. Sci. Rev.,* XXX, 41-45; and for an argument for

commonwealths (even though such a division of Dakota is of questionable value); Texas might be split into any number of states up to the five envisaged as a maximum by the joint resolution of admission in 1845; the surveyor's line between Vermont and New Hampshire might simply be erased. Other possibilities suggest themselves, with, in some cases, a certain attractiveness—until one recalls the stentorian injunction of the constitution that no new state may be erected within the jurisdiction of any other state, nor formed by the union of two or more states or parts of states, without the consent of *the legislatures of the states concerned* as well as of Congress. How (historical backgrounds, public attitudes, and vested interests being what they are) such consent could be obtained in cases like those mentioned—to say nothing of a general reshuffling of state boundaries—no one has yet risen to explain. In general, the proposal, therefore, is not very realistic.

A second suggested line of attack primarily by way of geography is even more radical, contemplating as it does the displacement of the states largely or wholly by regional commonwealths of greater size and essentially different nature. One idea is that all state boundaries be entirely erased, or at best preserved as lines having merely historical associations. More commonly, however, the thought is to leave the states *in situ*, and even with governments exercising some present functions, but to interpose between them and the nation a series of regions with governments exercising superior, or at least different, authority. It would be possible, it is argued, to cut the country into a number of broad areas having genuine unity, and for the governments of such areas to function for many purposes more economically and efficiently than do the present state governments. Years ago, a leading historian, Frederick J. Turner, wrote: "We in America are really a federation of sections rather than of states. State sovereignty has never been influential except as a constitutional shield for a section. In political matters, the states act as groups rather than as individual members of the Union. They act in sections and are responsible to the respective interests and ideals of these sections." [1] Translating "section" into "region," the National Resources Committee, in a report submitted in 1935, proposed ten or twelve regions of a socio-economic nature as a basis for national planning and for coördination of federal administrative services.[2] The Committee expressly disclaimed suggesting any new form of political jurisdiction; the states were to go on as before. But numerous writers, showing less restraint, have proposed and advocated regionalism as a more or less

2. Replacing the states with "regions"

---

statehood for the Chicago area, C. E. Merriam, S. D. Parratt, and A. Lepawsky, *The Government of the Metropolitan Region of Chicago* (Chicago, 1933), 179-180. The objection to statehood for cities most often heard is that it would undermine the tax structure of the state or states affected by withdrawing the areas of greatest taxpaying capacity.

[1] "Sections and Nation," *Yale Rev.*, XII, 1-21 (Oct., 1922), 6. Cf. the same author's *The Significance of Sections in American History* (New York, 1932).

[2] *Regional Factors in National Planning and Development* (Washington, D. C., 1935)

complete substitute for the present state system. Only by such a change, asserts one who has already been quoted, can our "drooping federalism" be revived and the steady march of centralization be stayed.[1] People taking this approach naturally do not agree upon the number of regional commonwealths to be set up, upon their boundaries, or upon their powers and functions. The number most commonly suggested is nine;[2] the particular area most frequently marked off as one of the series is New England. Even more surely, however, than the plan of merely rearranging state boundaries, the scheme of erecting new regional governments—with functions and powers presumably drawn from both the federal government above and the state governments below—is, for an indefinite time to come, relegated to utopia by state pride—to say nothing of constitutional restraints.[3]

3. Full police power for the national government

The third proposal mentioned approaches the problem, not geographically, but functionally. As indicated above, police power, *i.e.*, power to restrict the rights of liberty and property in the interest of public health, safety, morals, and general welfare—not only is vested in the states, but furnishes their main reason for being. On the theory that the matters to which it mainly relates are so closely bound up with local conditions and opinion that they ought to be regulated state by state, and sometimes even locality by locality, the constitution's framers made no direct grant of authority of the kind to the national government, but instead left the states in possession, on the basis of their broad reserved powers; and the commonest instances of police regulations are found in state legislation and municipal ordinances. To be sure, a certain amount of police power long ago began to develop in the national government as well; after all, the constitution authorizes that government to tax and spend, to regulate interstate commerce, and, in the broadest possible language, to "provide for the general welfare of the United States;" and from these grants of power have, as time advanced, flowed ever-broadening streams of regulatory actions (anti-crime acts, pure food and drugs laws, labor laws, public

---

[1] W. Y. Elliott, *op. cit.*, 195. Cf. A. Hehmeyer, *Time for Change* (New York, 1943), Chap. XI.

[2] See, for example, W. K. Wallace, *Our Obsolete Constitution*, 185.

[3] At the same time, it is to be observed that we do make some use of the regional principle. The TVA operates in a region covering parts of seven states; and other similar "valley authorities" may come into being. The Federal Reserve System functions through banks situated in twelve large districts into which the country is divided; and numerous other federal activities are carried on in sets of districts overlapping and crisscrossing one another the country over. States are linked into regional groups for one purpose or another under interstate compacts. In short, the federal-state pattern is not absolute or exclusive, but rather is plastered over with jurisdictions conforming to patterns of their own. See J. W. Fesler, "Federal Administrative Regions," *Amer. Polit. Sci. Rev.*, XXX, 257-268 (Apr., 1936).

Extended discussions of regionalism (although not on purely political lines) include H. W. Odum and H. E. Moore, *American Regionalism; A Cultural-Historical Approach to National Integration* (New York, 1938), and D. Davidson, *The Attack on Leviathan; Regionalism and Nationalism in the United States* (Chapel Hill, N. C., 1938). Cf. National Resources Committee, *The Future of State Planning* (Washington, D. C., 1938); "A Symposium on Regional Planning," *Iowa Law Rev.*, XXXII, 193-406 (Jan., 1947).

health acts) belonging by their very essence in the category of police legis-lation. Meanwhile, as demand mounted for progressive legislation on these and similar lines, the states fell under criticism for being hesitant or negligent; and not only did the federal government outstrip many of them, enacting great regulatory measures on independent lines or taking the lead in coöperative action under (for example) the Social Security Act of 1935, but people concerned about social and economic reforms came by the idea that the way of advance lay through integrated, uniform, nation-wide legislation rather than through hazardous and piecemeal action by the states.[1] From this, it was for some but a step to the notion that the federal police power—already far extended, yet in most areas confined to the *interstate* aspects of things—might advantageously be broadened so as to become applicable to substantially all social and economic activi-ties and relationships, and in their *intrastate* aspects as well as interstate. In McCulloch *v.* Maryland, John Marshall asserted that "no political dreamer was ever wild enough to think of breaking down the lines which separate the states, and of compounding the American people into one common mass." He would hardly make that observation today; for the proposed broadening of the federal police power would at least be a very long step in that direction. The step is, however, not at all likely to be taken. Extensive constitutional amendments would be required; states that balked at even a child labor amendment would certainly not be prepared for the great surrender involved; and although future exten-sions under the existing constitutional régime are likely to prove no less astonishing than some already recorded, the federal-state problem will hardly be solved—at least in the foreseeable future—by reducing the states to impotence.

On the whole, it is safe to assume that, however much farther their posi-tion may be undermined in certain directions by constitutional amend-ment and interpretation, and by legislation and practice in such matters as federal aid (which, however, commonly tends to increase rather than diminish state activities), the states will persist, not merely as geo-graphical and political entities, but as custodians of the greater part of their present powers and functions, together with new ones springing from ever-continuing development of technology, economic relationships, and social policies. Hardly anything short of sheer dictatorship could enable the map of this country to be remade as that of Germany was remade by ruthless Nazi officials after 1933. Not only so, but even after their harrowing experiences of the depression decade, the states have grounds for facing the future with assurance. Their fundamental position in the constitutional system is secure as long as they do not themselves choose

The states not yet "finished"

---

[1] Simultaneously, decisions of the Supreme Court a decade ago construing the national authority to regulate commerce as extending, not merely to commerce in the older and narrower sense, but also to manufacturing, mining, and other forms of production opened greatly broadened avenues for federal action. See p. 619 below.

to relinquish it; the United States, reaffirmed the Supreme Court in 1936 [1] (employing the historic language of Chief Justice Chase), is still "an indestructible union of indestructible states." As observed above, the states nowadays carry on more activities, spend more money, have more employees, and do more for their people than at any time in the past.[2] Even if they could be abolished, something—as all regionalists concede— would have to be put in their places. As semi-autonomous political units regulating the activities and relations of their citizens by laws of their own devising, they unquestionably have lost some ground; in larger matters of social and economic control, they probably will continue to lose. As areas of administration, however, they have gained; and even though, as seems likely, they in future may function more and more, in their administrative work, as collaborators with, and even as agents of, the national government, they need not on that account suffer loss of genuine vitality—even if there were not always going to be plenty of things for them to decide upon and undertake independently.

Some ways of strengthening their position:

There are ways, too, in which they can definitely improve their present position. One of these is to keep up the intelligent and fearless overhauling of governmental machinery and procedures which has been going on encouragingly in later years. Notwithstanding a good record achieved during the late war, prestige and power have been lost, over the decades, because (to no small extent) of failure of the states to deal effectively with difficult problems thrust upon them by the exigencies of the times. To be sure, a good deal of what has happened has flowed from circumstances beyond the states' control. By setting their houses in order, however,—regenerating their legislatures, toning up their civil services, improving their administrative methods, modernizing their county and other rural local governments, and utilizing the newer techniques of long-term planning—they may still, to a considerable degree, stem the tide that has been running against them. The best way to preserve state power is to increase state competence.

1 Overhauling their own governments

2. Removing interstate barriers and curbing interstate rivalries

A second promising line of action is the breaking down of certain barriers arising perhaps naturally from the legal separateness of the states, yet interfering with their own best interests as well as with the free life of a united nation. Most serious of these obstructions have been those erected against the movement of goods and services across state lines. To be sure, the federal constitution, correcting a grievous deficiency of the Articles of Confederation, forbids the states to levy tariff duties on imports or exports or to discriminate against the commerce, shipping, or citizens of other states. In the depression era, however, states, and even localities, were in many cases persuaded to come to the aid of their own

---

[1] In United States v. Butler (297 U. S. 1), invalidating the Agricultural Adjustment Act of 1933.
[2] A reading of Chap. XLII (in complete edition of this book) will surely leave the impression that the states are still busy and important.

hard-pressed producers by setting up obstacles to the admission of competing products from outside sources; and a great variety of ingenious devices resulted, ranging all the way from mere organized campaigns to promote the buying of local products to (1) laws giving preference to such products in all state purchases, (2) laws forbidding the sale of electric power beyond state lines, (3) quarantine and inspection laws grounded ostensibly on the police power of protecting health, morals, and safety, but really designed to set up discriminations against goods produced outside of the state, (4) measures creating "ports of entry" to administer restrictions calculated to discourage interstate trucking, and, above all, (5) employment of the taxing power (a) to discriminate against corporations chartered in other states, "foreign" insurance companies, nation-wide chain-store systems, and interstate purchases of goods,[1] and (b) to protect "domestic," as opposed to out-of-state, products, as, for example, in the case of states imposing tax burdens (in the interest of local butter producers) on margarine, or (in the interest of local cotton growers) on "foreign" ingredients used in place of cottonseed oil in manufacturing that commodity.[2]

For a good many years, however, there has been growing realization that the supposed advantages accruing from interstate trade barriers are deceptive. Individuals profit, of course; but for every one who gains, many lose. The cost of intrastate products to the consumer is increased; other states are driven to retaliatory measures which cut off extrastate markets; ill-will and recrimination are engendered all around. Although too often behaving like competitive nations, the states in reality are bound up in one nation-wide economy, and in the long run can prosper, not alone and individually, but only jointly and collectively. And it is gratifying to know that, largely as a result of a persistent publicity and educational campaign launched by the Council of State Governments and its affiliated organizations in 1939, there was, even before the war, a decided slackening in trade-barrier legislation, accompanied by fairly rapid repeal of existing discriminative laws. Wartime need for the fullest mobility of shipping and trade accelerated the trend (one will recall Secretary Hull's fervent appeal to all state governors in 1940 for collaboration in doing

---

[1] This last-mentioned procedure has commonly taken the form of imposing "use taxes," *i.e.*, taxes on the use of goods bought outside of a state with a view to avoiding the sales taxes which would have had to be paid if the articles had been purchased at home. See p. 980 below. To the surprise of many who expected use taxes to be held unconstitutional as imposing a burden upon interstate commerce, the Supreme Court has sustained them. Henneford *v.* Silas Mason Co., 300 U. S. 577 (1937).

[2] Many cases involving interstate discriminations not only by taxation but by other means have, of course, reached the courts. The general disposition has been to give the states the benefit of the doubt and to overrule only measures manifestly having restriction of interstate commerce as their dominant objective. Thus a Florida law requiring inspection of all cement brought into the state, but not of the locally-produced product, and imposing an inspection fee sixty times the actual cost of inspection, was naturally declared unconstitutional. Hale *v.* Bimco Trading Co. 306 U. S. 375 (1939).

away with state barriers to the free flow of interstate commerce, followed by nation-wide abandonment, at least for the duration, of burdensome restrictions upon truck transportation); and we may anticipate a considerably improved situation in the future—unless perchance another era of economic depression should unfortunately lead to a revival of the discriminative practices of the thirties.

3. Coöperation in other ways

Coöperation need not, however, be confined to the removal of barriers and the curbing of rivalries. By enacting uniform legislation on business practices and other appropriate subjects, states may not only raise the general level but counteract arguments for national, or perchance regional, regulative action. By reciprocally extending rights and privileges to each other's citizens, as, for example, in the practice of the professions, they may obviate jealousies and promote the general well-being; in the domain of taxation, in particular, they may serve the ends of justice by mutually refraining from imposing double or triple burdens.[1] Information may be exchanged, common problems discussed in conferences, joint investigations carried on, voluntary interstate organizations maintained for a wide variety of purposes. And of course interstate compacts link varying groups of states in helpful ways.

Many new instrumentalities have come into existence to facilitate coöperation on such lines. The Council of State Governments, dating from 1933 and already mentioned, links the governments of all of the states in a voluntary league for the promotion of coöperative action; the 7,455 members of state legislatures have been brought together in a professional American Legislators' Association; different types of state and local executive and administrative officials—governors; auditors, comptrollers, and treasurers; chiefs of police; city managers; housing officials; etc.—have formed similar nation-wide organizations;[2] interstate commissions on social security, crime, and conflicting taxation have been set up; and a strong consciousness of common interests and reciprocal obligations has been developed among state legislative and administrative groups the country over. All told—through this series of activities and in other ways—the chances for friendly and intelligent solution of problems transcending state lines have been considerably improved; and in so far as matters that otherwise the national government would be tempted or compelled to take over are cared for through such channels of interstate comity and coöperation, the outlook for the states themselves will have been brightened.

[1] A familiar form taken by this sort of comity is the recognition all around of one another's motor vehicle licenses.

[2] All of these, and other, organizations, such as an American Municipal Association and an American County Association, have headquarters in a building located at 1313 East 60th St., Chicago, with, in some cases, branch offices in Washington, D. C., and other cities.

REFERENCES

A. N. Christensen and E. M. Kirkpatrick, *The People, Politics, and the Politician; Readings on American Government* (New York, 1941 and 1947), Chaps. v-vi.

C. B. Swisher, *The Growth of Constitutional Power in the United States* (Chicago, 1947), Chap. ii.

A. W. Bromage, *State Government and Administration in the United States* (New York, 1936), Chaps. iii, xxiv.

A. F. Macdonald, *American State Government and Administration* (3rd ed., New York, 1945), Chap. ii.

W. B. Graves, *American State Government* (3rd ed., New York, 1946), Chaps. i, xxi, xxiii.

————, "The Future of the American States," *Amer. Polit. Sci. Rev.*, XXX, 24-51 (Feb., 1936).

————, *Uniform State Action* (Chapel Hill, N. C., 1934), Chap. xix.

———— [ed.], "Intergovernmental Relations in the United States," *Annals of Amer. Acad. of Polit. and Soc. Sci.*, CCVII, 1-218 (Jan., 1940).

R. H. Wells, *American Local Government* (New York, 1939). Largely on federal-state relations.

J. P. Clark, *The Rise of a New Federalism; Federal-State Coöperation in the United States* (New York, 1938).

G. C. S. Benson, *The New Centralization; A Study of Intergovernmental Relationships in the United States* (New York, 1941).

D. Fellman, "Federalism," *Amer. Polit. Sci. Rev.*, XLI, 1142-1160 (Dec., 1947).

J. A. Maxwell, *The Fiscal Impact of Federalism in the United States* (Cambridge, Mass., 1946).

J. E. Kallenbach, *Federal Coöperation with the States Under the Commerce Clause* (Ann Arbor, Mich., 1942).

W. Anderson, *Federalism and Inter-Governmental Relations; A Budget of Suggestions for Research* (Chicago, 1946).

F. E. Melder, *State and Local Barriers to Interstate Commerce in the United States* (Orono, Me., 1937).

J. V. Van Sickle, *Planning for the South; An Inquiry into the Economics of Regionalism* (Nashville, Tenn., 1943).

A. F. Macdonald, *Federal Aid; A Study of the American Subsidy System* (New York, 1928).

H. J. Bitterman, *State and Federal Grants-in-Aid* (Chicago, 1938).

E. A. Williams, *Federal Aid for Relief* (New York, 1939).

M. E. MacDonald, *Federal Grants for Vocational Education* (Chicago, 1944).

V. O. Key, Jr., *The Administration of Federal Grants to States* (Chicago, 1937).

S. E. Harris, *How Shall We Pay for Education?* (New York, 1948).

M. V. Burr, "Arguments For and Against Federal Aid to Education," *State Government*, XX, 307-312, 320 (Dec., 1947).

C. L. Dearing, *American Highway Policy* (Washington, D. C., 1941).

F. L. Paxson, "The Highway Movement, 1916-1935," *Amer. Hist. Rev.*, LI, 236-253 (Jan., 1946).

C. Warren, *Congress as Santa Claus* (Charlottesville, Va., 1933).

National Resources Committee, *Regional Factors in National Planning* (Washington, D. C., 1935).

Council of State Governments, *The Book of the States, 1945-1946* (Chicago, 1945).

State Government. Published monthly at Chicago by the Council of State Governments.

3. CITIZENSHIP AND CIVIL RIGHTS

CHAPTER VIII

THE PEOPLE OF THE UNITED STATES—CITIZENS AND ALIENS

Declining rate of population growth

The sixteenth census showed the population of the continental United States as of April 1, 1940, to be 131,409,881; and the federal Census Bureau's estimate for October 1, 1947, was 144,708,000. These are large numbers of people; among the countries of the world, only China, India, and the U.S.S.R. contain more. The average density per square mile in 1940 was, however, only 44.2; and notwithstanding the comparative sparseness that this figure suggests, the rate of population increase has for upwards of a generation been slowing down, being only about seven per cent in 1930-40, as compared with 16.1 per cent in the preceding decade and as high as 21 per cent in 1900-10. To be sure, the pace has quickened in the decade presently to end; in the first five years (1940-45) alone, it raised the total by 6.6 per cent. This showing, however, is ascribed wholly to the accelerated birth-rate commonly associated with wartime conditions,[1] and already the rate has gone back almost to the prewar level. In part, the longer-term downward trend is to be explained by the falling off of immigration, under our quota system, to a mere trickle.[2] In larger degree, however, the reason lies in a persistent decline of the birth-rate, observable from as far back as 1924, and only momentarily interrupted during the war years—a decline from 27 births per thousand of population in 1910 to 17.6 in 1940. Nor is this decline expected ever to be reversed, except perhaps temporarily. On the contrary, students of population problems, peering into the future, see it continuing until, around 1970 or 1980, a peak equilibrium will be reached, with the figure at something like 165,000,000—after which there may set in an actual recession. Throughout our history, national prosperity has always been predicated on rapidly expanding population, as well as fast-growing industry and markets. The day is at hand, however, when the nation's business can no longer count on that favoring factor. This does not necessarily mean less prosperity and lower living standards in the future. But it does mean that business, industry, and agriculture have a job of preparing for changed conditions.

Changing distribution: rural and urban elements

Not only is the country's population growing more slowly, but significant changes are taking place in its distribution and character. During a generation and a half marked by great industrial expansion, the population of

[1] Among the reasons are economic prosperity induced by defense activity, and marriages hastened by prospect of war service.

[2] See pp. 132-133 below.

towns and cities increased far faster than that of rural areas—at an average rate, indeed, of 33 per cent in the period 1890-1930, as compared with a rural rate of 7.2 per cent; and as a result, the proportion of the country's inhabitants living in towns and cities of over 2,500 rose from 35.4 per cent at the earlier date to over 56 per cent at the later one. During the decade 1930-40, however, the shift of population from farm to city levelled off sharply, urban increase being at the surprisingly low rate of less than eight per cent, as compared with a rural increase of somewhat over six per cent. In other words, American cities were, for the first time in a century, growing at a pace scarcely faster than rural areas, or than the country as a whole. Many cities, indeed (including twenty-six important ones in the industrial Northeast alone) actually contained fewer people in 1940 than in 1930. Diminished immigration and a declining birth-rate, of course, afford explanation in part. But lessened opportunities for work and wages during the depression years, together with a tendency toward the decentralization of industry, were influential—as was also the movement of people everywhere from older crowded urban areas into newer and more attractive suburbs, made possible by the automobile and improved highways.

After 1940, the picture naturally was changed by the defense effort and war. Not only did literally hundreds of smaller places become "boom towns" thronging with workers in munitions plants and other war industries (many such boom towns, indeed, sprang up where none had been before), but middle-sized and larger cities received an inflow swelling their populations (mainly in 1940-42) by anywhere from twenty to fifty per cent.[1] While this was going on, however, other cities declined; and although it is still too early to forecast the ultimate and lasting consequences of so vast a dislocation of population, it is reasonable to expect that the long-term slowing down of urban growth will prove to have been reversed only temporarily—particularly if depression conditions should recur, leading workless people to turn once more to the countryside (where, however, new limitations are imposed by the mechanization and otherwise increased efficiency of agriculture, enabling one-fifth as many workers to produce a given volume of foodstuffs and materials as seventy-five years ago[2]). In general, it is fair to assume that in days ahead, cities will remain static or actually decline, that farm populations also will drop, and that while the West Coast, the Southwest, and Florida will gain, the Northeast will continue to lose, along with a tier of states beginning with North Dakota and ending with Oklahoma.

[1] See B. Bolles, "The Great Defense Migration," *Harper's Mag.*, CLXXXIII, 460-467 (Oct., 1941), and W. F. Ogburn, "Whither Population?," *State Government*, XVI, 27-28, 38-41 (Feb., 1943). It may be mentioned, too, that between July 1, 1940, and July 1, 1942, there was a shift of two and one-half million civilian war-workers, together with men in military training, and also women auxiliaries, to the Southern and Western portions of the country, while the North-Central and Northeastern sections were suffering a net loss of half a million.

[2] Cf. p. 670 below.

Signif-
icance
for
govern-
ment   The over-all declining growth of urban population is, of course, not
without its significance for city planning, for education, and for party
procedures, elections, representation in Congress and in state legislatures,
and other political processes; in particular, the movement of people out
into suburban districts has created tax difficulties for many municipalities.[1]
More than half of the people of the country, however, are still to be
found in urban areas; and this remains a cardinal factor in our political
life. Municipal government has gained enormously in importance; a new
type of population grouping—the metropolitan community, best illustrated
in the New York, Boston, Chicago, and Detroit areas, but to be observed
wherever a constellation of towns is clustered around a dominating metropolitan center—has risen to complicate governmental relationships; new
and baffling problems of rural local government have been created, not
only by the transition from an ox-cart to a motor age, but by the depletion
and impoverishment of great stretches of the countryside, and by the
frequently defective distribution of population in relation to economic resources. Even the question of how, and to what extent, government may
intervene to bring about a sounder population distribution has come into
the picture.[2]

Race and
nativity   Then there are the matters of racial texture and ratio of native elements to foreign-born. Viewed racially, our population in 1940 was 89.8
per cent white, 9.8 per cent Negro, 0.3 per cent Indian, 0.1 per cent
Chinese, and 0.1 per cent Japanese, with quite a number of other very
small groups. Taking the heavily dominant white element alone, 63.7
out of every hundred were native-born of native parentage; 17.5 were
native-born of foreign or mixed parentage; and 8.6 were foreign-born.[3]
Analysis of the many complicated data involved goes to show that the
country is steadily becoming more "American," in the sense that native-
born whites of native parentage—now outnumbering all other persons
by nearly three to two and all other whites by two to one—have for
some time been increasing at a considerably faster rate than the total
population.[4] Here again is a fact of political as well as social significance,
giving promise of a more homogeneous population than that which fifty
years ago created problems of serious import, especially in the government

---

[1] P. M. Hauser, "How Declining Urban Growth Affects City Activities," *Pub.
Management*, XXII, 355-358 (Dec., 1940). Cf. M. Jefferson, "The Great Cities of the
United States," *Geog. Rev.*, XXXI, 479-487 (July, 1941).

[2] Under the direction of the federal Resettlement Administration and the Farm
Security Administration which succeeded it in 1937, many thousands of people were
moved from inhospitable to better favored areas. See p. 688 below. Appointment
of a committee on urbanism by the then existing National Resources Committee
some years ago bore fruit in an interesting report. *Our Cities; Their Rôle in the
National Economy* (Washington, D. C., 1937). Cf. S. A. Queen and L. F. Thomas,
The City; A Study of Urbanism in the United States (New York, 1939).

[3] For the figures, see *Statistical Abstract of the United States, 1942* (Washington,
D. C., 1943), 19.

[4] *Recent Social Trends in the United States* (one-vol. ed., New York, 1933), 19.
Today, nine out of ten children born in this country have native-born American
parents, as compared with only five out of ten a generation ago.

of cities. In 1940, the largest group among the foreign-born was Italian, with Germans second, peoples from Russia (mainly Jews) third, and Poles fourth.[1]

The Regulation of Immigration

Historically, the United States is, of course, an immigrant country; Earlier
policies all of our people except the Indians have come from foreign lands or are descended from those who did so at some time after the beginnings of European settlement on our soil. In the eighteenth and nineteenth centuries, our fast-growing population was fed steadily by immigrant streams flowing in earlier days principally from Great Britain, Ireland, Germany, and Scandinavia (Negroes, too, from Africa), but later also from Italy and Slavic Europe, and to a less extent from Latin America and Canada.[2] To be sure, from early times the inflow was to some extent checked by restrictions against undesirables; and for half a century it was chiefly the states, like Massachusetts and New York, that acted. In 1849, however, the Supreme Court held that the matter was one for federal regulation exclusively;[3] and such it has remained. In a series of cases between 1875 and 1884, the Court declared such jurisdiction incidental to the power of Congress to regulate foreign commerce; and in 1889 it further based it upon the right of any sovereign nation to control its own foreign relations.[4] For a long time, however, our policy was to encourage, and even to stimulate, the coming of home-seekers, laborers, and refugees. Only when the influx from southern and central Europe—the so-called "new" immigration, in contrast with English, German, and the like—grew startlingly large and sentiment against the admission of Chinese laborers reached a high pitch on the Pacific coast did we definitely embark upon a different course. In 1882, the first Chinese Exclusion Act was passed; in the same year, paupers, insane persons, and other undesirables, from whatever country, were excluded; three years later, laborers under contract to individuals or corporations were debarred; and thereafter one group after another (e.g., anarchists in 1903) was added to the ineligible list, until by 1917 the laws enumerated no fewer than thirty different grounds for exclusion. In the year mentioned, still another was added, when Congress enacted (over two vetoes by President Wilson) that thenceforth no

[1] Other interesting facts about the country's population are that it contains approximately 200,000 more females than males, and—what is socially and politically more significant—that, as a result of falling birth-rates and death-rates, the population is "growing older," with a present median age of 30 expected by the year 2000 to reach 37. The increased proportion of people of advanced age obviously affects the problem of social (particularly old-age) insurance. See pp. 753-755 below.

[2] The coming of forty million Europeans to our shores in little more than a century has no parallel in the history of mankind. To them, the United States represented a haven of refuge and opportunity; to us, they represented a reservoir of human wealth which enabled us to exploit our vast natural resources, to expand our population, and to attain great power at home and abroad.

[3] Passenger Cases, 7 Howard 282 (1849).

[4] Chinese Exclusion Case, 130 U. S. 581 (1889). Cf. Fong Yue Ting v. United States, 149 U. S. 698 (1893).

migrants over sixteen years of age should be admitted who could not read English or some other language or dialect.[1]

Adoption of the quota system

Despite the impediments imposed, the inflowing tide of foreigners reached the high level of 1,200,000 in 1913;[2] and when, following a sharp recession during the ensuing war, indications of a new flood appeared, Congress, believing that such numbers were too large for assimilation, decided (in 1921) that mere personal defects and racial origins would no longer suffice as grounds for restriction and superimposed upon the existing regulations a "quota" system under which even the fully qualified were to be admitted to a total of only 357,803 in any year, apportioned to the various immigrant countries on the basis of three per cent as many migrants as there were people of the respective nationalities residing in the United States in 1910.[3] Designed to be merely preparatory to more fully considered permanent legislation, the act of 1921 operated for three years, and then was replaced by broadly similar provisions of a general Immigration Act of 1924[4] which (with some changes made in 1929) have continued in effect to the present day—except, of course, as thrown out of focus by the recent war. When Europe's new boundaries are finally fixed by a complete set of peace treaties, a new scheme of quotas will have to be put into operation. The general policy of not only limiting the quantity of immigration, but selecting it qualitatively in terms of national stocks, undoubtedly has, however, become a fixture.

The national origins system in operation

Under the national origins plan as thus adhered to for nearly a quarter of a century, the salient features of our immigration policy have been: (1) aliens not eligible for naturalization have been debarred, including most Asiatics until, in 1943, China was allowed an annual quota of 105 and in 1946 India a quota of 100;[5] (2) immigrants from countries in the Western Hemisphere have been admitted without restriction except as the laws exclude categories such as anarchists, criminals, and paupers; (3) immigrants from European countries have been admitted (subject, of

---

[1] For a consolidated collection of these measures, see *Code of the Laws of the U. S.* (1940), Title 8. This same act of 1917 contained a "barred-zone" provision under which all immigrants from a list of areas mainly in Southeast Asia were excluded. By and large, the influence operating most powerfully in favor of immigration restriction has been organized labor, the object being, of course, to prevent the impairment of wage-levels and of the workingman's standard of living through the influx of workers willing to accept meager wages and accustomed to "un-American" living conditions. It is not without significance that the administration of the immigration laws was from 1913 to 1940 vested in the Department of Labor. Transfer of it at the latter date to the Department of Justice evidenced a shift of emphasis —at a time of anxiety about subversive activities—from the labor aspect to regulation in the interest of national unity and security.

[2] Our heaviest immigration in any single year was 1,285,349 in 1907.

[3] Quota Act, 42 *U. S. Stat. at Large*, 5 (1921).

[4] 43 *U. S. Stat. at Large*, 153 (1924).

[5] Asiatic travellers, students, business-men, and professional people might be admitted for limited periods. As "nationals" of the United States, Filipinos were, in general, free to enter the country until 1936, when, under terms of the Philippine Independence Act of 1934, they were cut to a quota of fifty—a figure which, however, was doubled after the Islands attained their independence in 1946.

course, to the same general rules of eligibility) on a national origins basis, and to a yearly maximum (since 1929) of 150,000, the quota allotted to each nationality being "a number which bears the same ratio to 150,000 as the number of inhabitants in continental United States in 1920 having that national origin . . . bears to the number of inhabitants in continental United States in 1920," with a minimum quota of 100. Almost eighty-five per cent of all whites in the United States in 1920 represented strains originating in northwestern Europe. Hence the largest quotas have gone to Great Britain and Northern Ireland (65,721), Germany (25,957), and the former Irish Free State—present Eire (17,853). Far below have come Poland with 6,524, Italy with 5,802, and other countries each with 3,330 or less.[1]

The national origins system in this form was hardly in operation before the United States was overtaken by the economic depression starting in 1929, and the combined effect was to reduce immigration to its smallest dimensions in many decades; years ensued in which the number of aliens entering the country for permanent residence was actually smaller than that of those departing, voluntarily or by deportation. The outbreak of European war in 1939 temporarily stimulated some flight to America, and in the fiscal year ending June 30, 1940, a total of 51,997 alien immigrants from quota countries were admitted. In the following year, however, the number dropped to 36,220; and with the entrance of the United States into the war, in December, 1941, all immigration from enemy countries (chiefly Germany and Italy) came to an abrupt stop,[2] and that from other European lands fell to negligible proportions.

One result of the war for this country was to bring up again the general question of immigration policy (not simply the readjustment of quotas), at least for the period of postwar readjustment. On the one hand, large numbers of Europeans who had lost everything might be expected to want to make a fresh start in America; in particular, there were more than a million "displaced persons" (850,000 forced by the Nazis into Germany alone) who never would be able to return to their old homes in Russia, Poland, Yugoslavia, and other countries because of their hostility to political régimes prevailing there—people, furthermore, to whose support in refugee camps the United States was contributing $180,000,000 a year. On the other hand, the United States was confronted with huge tasks of economic reconversion and haunted by fear of a declining prosperity, with resulting large-scale unemployment. Assuming that the long-time, over-all policy of controlled immigration would in no wise be abandoned, people who thought about the matter developed widely differing ideas as to what it was wise or safe to do for the immediate future. Some considered that

Postwar problems

---

[1] It must be remembered that in every year large numbers of "non-immigrants" are admitted, *i.e.*, government officials, temporary visitors for business or pleasure, students, and the like. They, of course, do not figure in the quotas. Thus in 1946, when immigrants numbered 108,721, non-immigrants numbered 203,469.

[2] The immigration of alien enemies was definitely prohibited by presidential proclamation of December 7, 1941.

our prospects of population decline, in contrast with potential rivals like Russia, would justify letting down the bars rather freely; that the danger to workingmen standards of living no longer exists in these days of strong unions; that the effect upon employment, in an economy of fifty-eight million workers, could not be serious, especially in view of the high proportion of immigrants in these times who are women and children; that normal qualitative selection would protect us against opponents of our form of government and other undesirables; and that, while the interests of the United States must not be overlooked, we none the less must have regard for our obligations to mankind, accepting our fair share of responsibility for promoting world-wide well-being. Persons of such views were likely to advocate, concretely, (1) that unfilled quotas of 1940-46—aggregating over 900,000—should forthwith be declared still valid, opening a way for an equivalent number of migrants who *might* have come during these years to do so now, and (2) that over a period of four years we should provide a haven for 400,000 (upwards of half) of the displaced persons referred to above. In opposition, however, to this general line of reasoning, it was contended that such enlarged immigration would take away jobs from American workers, lower our standards, aggravate our housing problem, and damage our economy, and that some of our own pressing economic and social problems must be solved before we accepted any further large numbers of immigrants. And people of such opinion proposed receiving no immigrants outside of the regular quotas, with perhaps the quotas themselves reduced by from fifty to ninety per cent; or suspending all immigration for a specified period; or suspending it during all periods when the unemployed should number more than a million—which would be a disguised mode of having no immigration at all.

At the date of writing (January, 1948), the question was still open. President Truman had directed that every effort be made to facilitate the immigration of displaced persons under the quota laws;[1] and a bill introduced by Congressman William G. Stratton of Illinois, warmly supported by the President, and proposing admission of 100,000 of the displaced in the first year and 300,000 additional in three succeeding years had commanded wide support of press and public.[2] The first session of the Eightieth Congress, however, had ended with no legislation enacted; and although the matter was certain to come up again in the following session, there was no assurance of favorable action. Meanwhile, the quota system continued to operate in so far as unsettled conditions permitted, but with the problem of its revision looming ahead, and other questions, too, such as whether to repeal the provision of the act of 1924 debarring aliens not eligible to naturalization (a clause considered by Asiatics as

---

[1] *Department of State Bulletin,* Dec. 23, 1945.

[2] Under encouragement from an International Refugee Organization, Great Britain, France, Belgium, and various other countries were receiving considerable numbers of the displaced, and it was argued that the United States should do its part toward relieving the situation.

tantamount to a gratuitous proclamation of their inferiority), and likewise whether, after official restoration of peace, the Japanese, if permitted entry at all, should be placed on a quota basis like Filipinos, Chinese, and the peoples of India.

Originally left mainly to state authorities, enforcement of the immigration laws has since 1891 been in charge of a staff of federal commissioners of immigration, stationed at the various ports of entry and assisted by inspectors, interpreters, and other subordinates, with supervision centralized in an Immigration and Naturalization Service (formerly in the Department of Labor but since 1940 in the Department of Justice) and headed by a commissioner. Until some two decades ago, little effort was made to sift prospective migrants before departure from their old homes; those desiring admission to the country simply presented themselves at our ports, where they were examined and accepted or rejected. The number of rejections was large, and many hardships resulted. Beginning in 1924, we wisely shifted most of the work of inspection to foreign centers from which immigrants come. Experienced officers assigned to American consulates in the capacity of technical advisers on immigration interview intended migrants, counsel them, and determine whether they would probably be admitted; indeed, since 1927 those who would enter the country have been required to provide themselves with an American consular "visa" before embarking. How effective the reform has been is indicated by the fact that in the later prewar years not more than from five to seven per cent of those seeking entrance at our ports were turned back. With the quota system in operation, immigration officials stationed on our own soil have for a good while been occupied more largely with deportations than with admissions, except in the case of a border patrol, mounted and otherwise, which is charged with preventing the smuggling of aliens into the country from Canada, Mexico, and near-by islands. Aliens who consider that they have been unjustly denied admission to the country (as also those resisting deportation) are entitled to have their cases reviewed by three-man boards of special inquiry and ultimately by a board of immigration appeals in the Department of Justice.[1]

Administration of the immigration laws

Aliens—Rights and Restrictions in Peace and War

Speaking broadly, every inhabitant of the United States is either a citizen or an alien—if an alien, presumably a citizen of some foreign state living temporarily or permanently in our midst. In times past, no one knew how many aliens there were in the country or where they were located except as disclosed every ten years by the census. Growing tenseness of the international situation in the later thirties, however, combined with the increasingly difficult task of curbing subversive activities and

Numbers and registration

[1] From the vast literature on immigration and immigration policies, some selected titles are indicated on p. 149 below. On postwar aspects, see E. G. Harrison, "Immigration Policy of the United States," *For. Policy Reports*, XXIII, No. 2 (Apr. 1, 1947).

influences, and climaxed by the outbreak of a major war in Europe in 1939, led in 1940 to a decision to require every alien over fourteen years of age to register and be fingerprinted within a stipulated period, and thereafter to keep the federal authorities informed of his address and occupation.[1] The resulting registration revealed a total of 4,921,452 aliens fourteen years of age or over in a total population (by the census of April 1 of the same year) of 131,409,881, or about three and one-half per cent. One effect of the European, and later global, war was to make American citizenship uncommonly attractive; and as a result of more numerous naturalizations, combined with an almost complete cessation of immigration during the war years, the number of aliens dropped to 3,050,803 by the middle of 1945—the smallest known figure in thirty-five years. The decline has since continued, and in the spring of 1947 the number was estimated at well under 3,000,000.

Status in peacetime

In many respects, it does not greatly matter—under ordinary peacetime conditions—whether a person is an alien or a citizen. He must obey the laws and pay his taxes in any case; even though an alien, he is entitled to "the equal protection of the laws," and may sue and be sued in the courts, enter into contracts, and send his children to the public schools; and unless he happens to belong to a racial group that has been made ineligible, he may be naturalized, thereby acquiring full citizenship status. There are, however, limitations. An alien cannot vote or hold public office; [2] seldom can he act as a juror; his right to own land is almost as broad as a citizen's, but not quite, because California, Minnesota, Missouri, and a few other states impose varying restrictions; [3] and while, in general, he can engage in any gainful occupation or profession not requiring a license, increasing numbers of businesses and professions have been put under license requirements, and in virtually every state there are laws debarring aliens from receiving certain kinds of licenses.[4] The alien, further, may be excluded from employment on public works and in munitions plants; increasingly, too, he is prevented—rather unjustly—from sharing in various benefits, such as workmen's compensation and old-age pensions; [5] and

---

[1] The same Alien Registration Act (54 *U. S. Stat. at Large,* 670) requires all newly arriving aliens to register also.

[2] In as many as twenty-two states and territories, aliens who had declared their intention to be naturalized have, at one time or another, been allowed to vote. Constitutional amendments gradually withdrew this privilege, however, and a state supreme court decision of 1926 terminated it in the last state (Arkansas) in which it survived.

[3] D. O. McGovney, "The Anti-Japanese Land Laws of California and Ten Other States," *Calif. Law Rev.,* XXXV, 7-60 (Mar., 1947); E. E. Ferguson, "The California Alien Land Law and the Fourteenth Amendment," *ibid.,* XXXV, 61-90 (Mar., 1947).

[4] For example, to practice law or medicine or dentistry. Such discriminative laws must run the gantlet of the courts on the ground of reasonableness, but even in the legal and medical professions the alien has been largely shut out.

[5] Sometimes, however, a state goes too far in enacting such legislation. Thus when Arizona undertook to require that any individual or corporation employing more than five workers at one time should employ not less than eighty per cent qualified electors or native-born citizens of the United States, the federal Supreme Court held that such a requirement was unconstitutional as involving a denial of the equal pro-

of course if he goes abroad, he cannot claim protection from our government as can a citizen.[1]

Indeed, even here at home, an alien may fail to receive protection of person and property to which legally he is as much entitled as is a citizen. At various times, "foreigners" have been the victims of mob violence;[2] and as matters stand, with the states primarily responsible for maintaining law and order, such injured persons, or their relatives, have recourse only to state authorities (including grand juries and courts), which may easily be influenced by local sentiment to deny justice due. At least four presidents have asked Congress to give the federal courts jurisdiction in such cases, but to no avail, and meanwhile the national government continues in the uncomfortable and undignified position of being responsible under international law for protecting aliens, but unable under our system of constitutional law either to punish the perpetrators of outrages or to compel negligent states to assume the burden of damages. What usually happens is that after the federal government, pressed by the envoy of the foreign nation concerned, tries but fails to induce state authorities to act, Congress, on request of the president, votes a sum of money to be awarded *ex gratia*, and the affair ends. *(margin: Inadequate protection against mob violence)*

As our immigration laws grew stricter, the grounds on which aliens, once admitted at our ports, might be deported to the country of their origin multiplied;[3] and whereas formerly deportees were usually mental or physical defectives, criminals or immoral persons, persons who had become public charges, or persons who had entered the country illegally, the range has now been broadened to include a wide variety of people regarded as objectionable because of holding views, or advocating methods, regarded as inimical to the political system, laws, and institutions of the United States. Fear of subversive influences after the Russian Revolution of 1917 led Congress in 1918 to authorize the expulsion of alien revolutionists, anarchists, and advocates of sabotage, assassination, and other forms of violence; and under this authority the Department of Justice in 1919-20 conducted a sensational drive against "reds" and suspected "reds," whose wholesale deportation aroused considerable protest against what many considered an unfortunate surrender to popular hysteria.[4] For a good while, *(margin: Deportations)*

---

tection of the laws. Truax *v.* Raich, 239 U. S. 33, 41 (1915). See B. O'Connor, "Constitutional Protection of the Alien's Right to Work," *New York Univ. Law Quar. Rev.*, XVIII, 483-497 (May, 1941).

[1] On the general subject, see M. R. Konvitz, *The Alien and the Asiatic in American Law* (Ithaca, N. Y., 1946), Chaps. v-vii; E. W. Puttkammer [ed.], *War and the Law* (Chicago, 1944), 38-47; W. M. Gibson, *Aliens and the Law; Some Legal Aspects of the National Treatment of Aliens in the United States* (Chapel Hill, N. C., 1940); and N. Alexander, *The Rights of Aliens Under the Federal Constitution* (Montpelier, Vt., 1931).

[2] Perhaps the most serious incident of this nature was the lynching of eleven Italians at New Orleans on March 14, 1891.

[3] Except for the notorious Alien Act of 1798, the right was first asserted in the Chinese Exclusion Act of 1882.

[4] L. F. Post, *The Deportations Delirium of 1920* (Chicago, 1923); Z. Chafee, *Free Speech in the United States*, Chap. v. There were 26,427 deportations in 1921-25 and 64,123 in the next five years.

too, there was doubt about the propriety of deporting a person who, although not at the moment a member of any subversive organization, had been such when admitted to the country or at some subsequent time; and in 1939, the Supreme Court held an alien not deportable because of having once belonged to the Communist party.[1] New provisions in the Alien Registration Act of 1940, however, covered the matter explicitly, and aliens may now be deported not only for advocating, but for ever having advocated, or ever having belonged to any party or other organization advocating, "revolutionary" doctrine or "doctrines of violence."[2] No sooner, indeed, was this legislation on the books than the Department of Justice started a systematic combing of the alien registration returns with a view to ferreting out cases of illegal entry, criminality, falsifying information, membership in subversive organizations, and other deportable offenses, with Communist, Fascist, and Nazi activities aimed at undermining the government and security of the United States a major ground for action. Throughout the period between the wars, the number of deportees (deported under warrants or allowed to depart at their own expense and without warrants) averaged from 15,000 to 20,000 a year; after 1939, it was smaller only because, with sailings to Europe practically restricted to Great Britain, there were no means of returning the bulk of persons liable to deportation to the countries of their origin. Thousands detained during the war were started on their way after peace returned.[3] The point is important, however, not only that an alien against whom deportation proceedings are brought may appeal to the board of immigration appeals in the Department of Justice, but that he has access also to the courts for judicial determination of his rights.[4]

[1] Kessler, District Director of Immigration, v. Strecker, 307 U. S. 22.

[2] Even earlier, the Supreme Court had held (Mahler v. Eby, 264 U. S. 32, 1924) that the prohibition of ex post facto laws does not apply to deportations—the deporting power being limited only by treaty obligations. The general principle is that aliens are in the country only by sufferance and can be expelled for any reason specified by Congress, and at any time.

[3] In 1946, 14,375 persons were deported and 101,945 adjudged deportable were allowed to depart voluntarily. In the war year 1942, 3,709 were deported and 6,904 left voluntarily.

[4] On the general subject, see M. R. Konvitz, *The Alien and the Asiatic in American Law,* Chap. ii. Earlier discussions include "Report on the Enforcement of the Deportation Laws of the United States," *Report of the National Commission on Law Observance and Enforcement,* No. 5 (May 27, 1931), and J. P. Clark, *The Deportation of Aliens from the United States to Europe* (New York, 1931). An alarmist discussion of the menace (to a degree a genuine one) arising from the presence of unfriendly foreign agents in the country will be found in M. Dies (former chairman of the House of Representatives Committee for the Investigation of Un-American Activities), *The Trojan Horse in America* (New York, 1940), and a less sensational one in H. Lavine, *Fifth Column in America* (New York, 1940). The most notable deportation case of recent years involved a West Coast labor leader of Australian antecedents, Harry Bridges, against whom deportation proceedings, based on his alleged connections with the Communist party, were begun as early as 1938. In 1945, the Supreme Court reversed an order for his deportation, on the ground that he had not been proved a member of the Communist party, and that his associations with Communist groups "seemed to indicate no more than coöperative measures to obtain objectives which were wholly legitimate"; and later in the same year the accused was granted citizenship papers. For a review of the case, see M. R. Konvitz, *op. cit.,*

When war comes, aliens immediately fall into two categories—those of neutral or friendly nationality and those of enemy nationality, or in other words "alien enemies." The war in which we became involved in 1941 (and alien status during war can be indicated most concretely in terms of what happened during that conflict) had no very important effect upon the legal position of aliens in the former category. If they desired to leave the country, they must secure a permit prior to departure; those having assets amounting to more than one thousand dollars must report them. But, in general, there was no sharp differentiation from citizens; even military service was exacted, as from the latter.[1] To be sure, many lost their jobs—though only because over-cautious industrial establishments preferred not to employ non-citizens at such a time.

The case of alien enemies [2] was, of course, quite different. Obviously, one of the first things to be done was to obtain means of identifying them; and under a proclamation of the president, issued January 14, 1942—five weeks after we entered the war—all alien enemies over fourteen years of age were required to register again at their local post-offices, to be fingerprinted, to deposit three photographs of themselves, and to receive certificates of identification (to be carried at all times) in the form of booklets resembling passports. The number revealed was approximately a million—Germans, Italians, and Japanese; although, as of the following October 19, some 600,000 Italians, because of their generally recognized loyalty to the United States, were removed *en masse* from the classification. Drawing most of the necessary authority from an Alien Enemy Act dating from as far back as 1798 and authorizing alien enemies to be "apprehended, restrained, secured, or removed," the government pursued a course of action embracing the following main features: (1) negotiation (through neutral intermediaries) with the enemy governments for reciprocal humane treatment of civilians in enemy territory; (2) imposition of various restrictions, such as forbidding alien enemies (a) to enter "restricted" or "prohibited" areas (*e.g.*, prescribed zones around army camps, navy yards, and munitions plants), or, indeed, to travel at all beyond very limited distances without permission, (b) to change their jobs without giving advance notice, or (c) to have in their possession firearms, shortwave radios, cameras, military maps, or other designated articles; (3) arrest of alien enemies with dubious records or for other reasons subject to suspicion, with hearing boards set up in all of the eighty-four federal judicial districts to recommend to the attorney-general whether a given

Alien status during war:

1. Aliens of friendly nationality

2. Aliens of enemy nationality

61-76; and cf. J. M. Landis, *In the Matter of Harry Bridges* (Washington, D. C., 1939).

[1] W. W. Fitzhugh and C. C. Hyde, "The Drafting of Neutral Aliens by the United States," *Amer. Jour. of Internat. Law*, XXXVI, 369-382 (July, 1942).

[2] With a view to discouraging a repetition of the anti-alien hysteria of 1919-20, the government sought to soften the opprobrium attaching to "alien enemy" by using only the designation "of enemy nationality." The shorter and more usual term may, however, be employed here.

alien should be released unconditionally, paroled, or interned for the duration of the war, and with the official mentioned making the final decision; [1]
(4) removal in 1942, on joint congressional-presidential authority and
under military auspices, of 110,000 Japanese—citizens as well as aliens—
from military zones adjacent to the Pacific Coast, followed by resettlement
of them, under direction of a civilian War Relocation Authority, in ten
inland "relocation centers," from which those found loyal to the United
States were permitted to go to other parts of the country in quest of homes
and employment; (5) "freezing" of enemy funds and investments in the
United States, followed by general sequestration (not confiscation) of
billions of dollars worth of enemy-owned private property—banks, stores,
warehouses, and what not—which from then on, for the duration, was in
the care of an Alien Property Custodian. Some of the policies adopted
raised debatable issues—most of all, that relating to the Japanese evacuation, which now appears to have been dictated rather more by anti-
Japanese bias and hysteria on the West Coast than by the national danger
which was its ostensible motivation.[2] Considering, however, the numbers
of alien enemies involved, all told, and the unfortunate consequences that
might have followed from mishandling it, the problem may be said, on the
whole, to have been dealt with intelligently and successfully.[3]

Citizenship and How It Is Acquired

Citizen-
ship as
defined
in the
constitu-
tion—its
dual
aspect

Curiously, there long was a great deal of doubt in this country as to
precisely who were entitled to be regarded as citizens, and of what jurisdictions. In its original form, the constitution used the term no fewer than
seven times, but without ever once defining it. In some clauses, it spoke
of citizens of states, and in others of citizens of the United States; and
nowhere were the relations between the two (if they were different)
made clear. Adding to the confusion, the Supreme Court, in the famous
Dred Scott case of 1857,[4] voiced the view, through Chief Justice Taney,

---

[1] The first year of the war saw only 12,071 persons taken into custody; and of the
number, more than one-fourth were released. Experience showed plainly the fallacy
of assuming that any national of an enemy state was *per se* loyal to the enemy.

[2] In Korematsu *v.* United States (323 U. S. 214, 1944), a divided Supreme Court
sustained the action taken, but in *Ex parte* Endo (323 U. S. 283, 1944) a unanimous
Court held that Japanese citizens of proved loyalty could not be detained indefinitely
in relocation centers. On these and related cases, see M. R. Konvitz, *op. cit.*, Chap. xi;
and cf. E. V. Rostow, "The Japanese-American Cases—A Disaster," *Yale Law Jour.*,
LIV, 489-533 (June, 1945).

[3] L. V. Howard and H. A. Bone, *Current American Government*, Chap. viii; D. O.
Walter, *American Government at War*, Chap. v; R. R. Wilson, "The Treatment of
Civilian Alien Enemies," *Amer. Jour. of Internat. Law*, XXXVII, 30-45 (Jan., 1943).
A good brief account of the evacuation of the Japanese will be found in E. W. Puttkammer [ed.], *War and the Law*, 58-70, and a full discussion in C. McWilliams, *Prejudice; Japanese-Americans: Symbol of Racial Intolerance* (Boston, 1944), Chaps.
iv-v. The latter author considers the Japanese evacuation understandable (with the
West Coast early thought of as a possible theater of war), but nevertheless unnecessary and ill-advised; and the opinion is shared by practically all writers on the
subject.

[4] Dred Scott *v.* Sandford, 19 Howard 393.

that there were two entirely separate citizenships, and that a person could perfectly well be a citizen of a state without being a citizen of the United States—which, indeed, was the position to which the decision clearly relegated all Negroes capable of being regarded as state citizens, as well as any other persons upon whom states might choose to confer their own citizenship. Such persons would have no *national* citizenship at all, and consequently no status internationally. Only the Civil War availed to straighten out the tangle. From it came the Fourteenth Amendment; and in that momentous extension of the original constitution we find citizenship at last defined, clearly and precisely. "All persons," it says, "born or naturalized in the United States, and subject to the jurisdiction thereof, are citizens of the United States and of the state wherein they reside." Even this recognizes two citizenships, capable of being separated. But it plainly specifies who are to be considered national citizens; it makes all national citizens residing in any state citizens of that state; and it contemplates no state citizens who are not also national citizens.[1] The only point at which the two citizenships do not go together is in the case of national citizens living in the District of Columbia, in a territory, or in a foreign country, and therefore having no state citizenship. Legally, therefore, we still have dual citizenship—national and state. National citizenship, however, is primary and basic, state citizenship only secondary and incidental.[2]

Citizenship is acquired in various ways in different countries; but the most important are the two mentioned in the Fourteenth Amendment, *i.e.*, birth and naturalization. Citizenship by birth arises from the operation of one or the other of two quite different principles. Under the first— known as *jus sanguinis* ("law of blood or parentage")—a child takes the nationality of its parents, regardless of the place of its birth; under the second—called *jus soli*—nationality is determined by the place of birth, irrespective of the citizenship of the parents. The historical and fundamental rule of the United States, in common with other English-speaking, and also Latin American, countries, is *jus soli* ("law of soil

(margin note: How citizenship may be acquired:*)*

(margin note: 1. By birth*)*

---

[1] Such are not absolutely precluded, but there are no longer any important groups of the kind.

[2] The Supreme Court's general concept of citizenship is as follows: "Citizenship is membership in a political society and implies a duty of allegiance on the part of the member and a duty of protection on the part of the society. These are reciprocal obligations, one being a compensation for the other." Luria *v.* United States, 231 U. S. 9 (1913).

Speaking strictly, citizens are individuals only. Corporations, however, are "persons" within the meaning of various clauses of the constitution, and are regarded judicially as citizens of the states in which they are chartered. But they are at best only quasi-citizens, being not entitled to all the "privileges and immunities" which the constitution guarantees to the individual citizen. See C. H. Maxson, *Citizenship*, Chaps. XI-XII. One encounters also the term "nationals," which is not to be confused with "citizens." In a general way, it denotes all persons who, for purposes of international intercourse, are identified with a given nation; the Nationality Act of 1940 defines it as denoting persons "owing permanent allegiance to a state." The term is therefore broader than "citizen;" for example, the people of the Philippine Islands, prior to independence, were nationals of the United States, but never citizens thereof.

or place") ; [1] and the rule is construed to be applicable even to children born on American soil to alien parents, *e.g.*, Japanese, who are themselves ineligible to citizenship.[2] The phrase of the Fourteenth Amendment requiring that a person be not only born or naturalized in the United States, but "subject to the jurisdiction thereof," gives rise, however, to at least one exception: children born to foreign diplomatic representatives stationed in this country are not American citizens, because even though born on our soil, they are considered subject to the jurisdiction of the state which the ambassador or minister represents, and not to the jurisdiction of the United States.[3] On the other hand, persons born abroad *before* May 24, 1934, are citizens if the father had American citizenship and resided in the United States or its outlying possessions at some time before the child's birth; and persons born abroad *after* the date mentioned are such if either of the parents was an American citizen who before the child's birth resided ten years or more in the United States or its possessions, at least five years of which were after attaining the age of sixteen—although in this latter case the child must reside in the United States not less than five years between the ages of thirteen and twenty-one. In any event, an oath of allegiance must be taken at the age of twenty-one.

2. By naturalization:

The second main way in which citizenship is gained is by naturalization, which means the conversion of aliens into citizens by some kind of official act. Naturalization may be either collective or individual. The

(a) Of inhabitants of annexed territories

most usual form of collective naturalization is the extension of citizenship to the inhabitants *en bloc* of regions acquired by purchase or conquest.[4] Down to 1898, the United States regularly conferred citizenship upon the general mass of inhabitants of the territories which it annexed; [5] and as

[1] As applying to the United States, the statement must be qualified by saying that, as indicated below, in connection with *our own* nationals abroad, and children born to them, our government has leaned strongly toward *jus sanguinis.*

[2] United States *v.* Wong Kim Ark, 169 U. S. 649 (1898). In Perkins *et al. v.* Elg and Elg *v.* Perkins *et al.*, 307 U. S. 325 (1939), the Supreme Court held (contrary to what previously would have been supposed) that a woman born in the United States did not lose her American citizenship merely because when she was four years old her parents returned to their native Sweden and renewed their allegiance there. For purposes of citizenship, the "soil" of the United States includes the continental area, Alaska, the Hawaiian Islands, Puerto Rico, the Virgin Islands, all American embassies and legations, American war vessels, and (since 1940) American merchant ships.

[3] In former times, another exception to the operation of *jus soli* was furnished by Indians living in tribal relations. Although born in the United States, such Indians were regarded as subject to the "jurisdiction" rather of their tribes, and, until 1924, could become citizens only by naturalization, as in the case of other "aliens;" at the date mentioned, a full third of the Indian population of the country still lacked citizen status. An act of Congress then gave citizenship to all native-born Indians.

[4] A different form was the collective naturalization of Negroes under the Fourteenth Amendment; also the naturalization of Indians in 1924 (preceding footnote).

[5] Except the non-white inhabitants of Alaska and persons not Hawaiian citizens in Hawaii. In the case of Louisiana, Florida, and Alaska, the treaties of cession provided that the inhabitants should be admitted "as soon as possible to the enjoyment of all the rights, advantages, and immunities of citizens of the United States." In the case of Texas, all citizens of the previously independent republic were made citizens of the United States by resolution of Congress. American citizenship was conferred on the citizens of the former Hawaiian Republic by an act of 1900 which established a territorial government in the new dependency.

recently as 1927 (ten years after annexation) citizenship was similarly bestowed collectively upon all inhabitants of the Virgin Islands who did not elect to retain their Danish citizenship. On the other hand, the treaty of peace with Spain in 1898 by which the United States acquired Puerto Rico, Guam, and the Philippines expressly provided that the cession of those islands should not of itself operate to naturalize their native inhabitants, whose civil status and political rights were left to be determined by Congress. In later statutes, Congress declared the Puerto Ricans and Filipinos citizens of their respective islands, and conferred upon the former most, and upon the latter some, of the privileges and immunities of citizens of the United States. Furthermore, the Supreme Court held that Puerto Ricans were not aliens in the sense in which the term is used in the immigration laws.[1] So that, although full American citizenship was withheld, both Puerto Ricans and Filipinos became, in international law, "nationals," no less entitled to the protection of the United States than were full-fledged citizens; and in constitutional law the distinction—at least in the case of the Puerto Ricans—was in nearly every respect one without a difference. Finally, in 1917, the Puerto Ricans were made "citizens of the United States"—the Filipinos remaining nationals only, until even that status was terminated in 1946 by independence.

Naturalization is, however, usually individual, rather than collective; and as practiced in all countries it involves the granting of citizenship by a court, or more often by some administrative officer, after the applicant has fulfilled certain prescribed conditions. Our national constitution authorizes Congress to "establish an uniform rule of naturalization;" and although it was at first supposed in some quarters that naturalization was one of the concurrent powers to be exercised by the states as well as by the nation, this view was gradually perceived to be unwarranted. In 1817, Chief Justice Marshall was able to declare that it was not, and "certainly ought not to be," doubted that the power is vested exclusively in Congress.[2]

(b) Of individual aliens

The first act of Congress relating to the naturalization of individual aliens—dating from 1790—assigned the work to the courts; and under supervision of the Immigration and Naturalization Service in the Department of Justice it is now carried on by courts of designated grades, i.e., all federal district courts (in states or territories), the supreme court of the District of Columbia, and all state and territorial courts of record which have a clerk and a seal and have jurisdiction in actions at law or equity in which the amount in controversy is unlimited. The original law was brief and general, and for a hundred years much was left to chance, or at all events to the discretion of the naturalization authorities. In most states, it was necessary to be a citizen in order to be a voter. Party organizations and candidates were, therefore, under strong temptation to

[1] Gonzales v. Williams, 192 U. S. 1 (1904).
[2] Chirac v. Chirac, 2 Wheaton, 259.

procure the naturalization of all alien residents whose votes they thought they could control; and plenty of grave abuses resulted. Following an extensive investigation by a commission appointed by President Theodore Roosevelt, Congress in 1906, however, enacted a far more adequate statute, under which—as revised and in part superseded by a comprehensive Nationality Act approved October 14, 1940 [1]—the work is now carried on in a considerably improved fashion.

Present
mode of
naturali-
zation

The stipulated procedure is more complicated and tedious than in most other countries, and involves three main steps. The first—commonly referred to as "taking out first papers"—is a declaration of intention to become a citizen, which must be filed with the clerk of a duly authorized federal or state court at least two years before the applicant is given his final examination.[2] The second is the filing of a petition with the court (not less than two years nor more than seven years after the declaration), affirming that the applicant has been a resident of the United States for at least five years continuously and of the state or territory in which he applies for at least six months, that he is not an anarchist or opposed to organized government, and that he expects to remain permanently in this country and is loyal to it and its institutions. Full information must be given about both the candidate and his family (if he is married); and the application must be supported by affidavits of two citizens testifying to the applicant's period of residence, his moral character, and the general accuracy of the claims made in his petition. The third step, taken not less than thirty days after the petition is filed, is a public hearing and examination by the judge, after which, if all goes well, that official authorizes the clerk of the court to issue letters of citizenship, or "final papers." During the interval, the petitioner's claims (when being presented to a *federal* court) are investigated by a naturalization examiner, who may merely submit his findings in writing, but may also appear at and take part in the hearing; and in nearly every case, the commissioner's findings determine the action taken by the court. In some jurisdictions, the candidate is heard by the examiner only, and appears before a judge only after he has been given clearance for taking the oath of allegiance.[3]

---

[1] 54 *U. S. Stat at Large,* 1137. See C. C. Hyde, "The Nationality Act of 1940," *Amer. Jour. of Internat. Law,* XXXV, 314-319 (Apr., 1941), and for full text of the act, *ibid.,* "Documents" section, 79-124, and 79th Cong., 2nd Sess., Sen. Doc. No. 207, containing amendments through March 31, 1946. This major statute now constitutes the general law on the subject; but both earlier and later laws will be found brought together in E. A. Lewis [comp.], *Naturalization Laws* (Washington, Govt. Printing Office, 1946).

[2] The applicant must be at least eighteen years of age.

[3] The language of this oath is as follows: "I hereby declare, on oath, that I absolutely and entirely renounce and abjure all allegiance and fidelity to any foreign prince, potentate, state, or sovereignty of whom or which I have heretofore been a subject or a citizen; that I will support and defend the constitution and laws of the United States of America against all enemies, foreign and domestic; that I will bear true faith and allegiance to the same; and that I take this obligation freely without any mental reservation or purpose of evasion: So Help Me God." 54 *U. S. Stat at Large,* 1157.

As already indicated, after 1939 war in Europe and the later realized threat of

Although tightened up considerably of late in respect both to qualifica- tions for naturalization (as freshly defined in the Nationality Act of 1940) [1] and methods of actual administration, the system still leaves a good deal to be desired. The examination by the judge, or even the examiner, may be as thorough, or as perfunctory, as he cares to make it. The applicant must swear that he "speaks English;" but ability to utter "yes" and "no" sometimes suffices, and indeed one judge is reported to have been satisfied with a candidate who merely "nodded his head in English." [2] The law presumes intelligence, but provides no standards by which that somewhat flexible qualification is to be judged. It presupposes some knowledge of the form of government of the United States, but leaves the way open for the widest latitude in testing such knowledge.[3] "Final papers" cannot be issued within sixty days preceding any federal or state election; nevertheless, over-zealous ward-leaders and other politicians have sometimes contrived, by plenty of sharp practices, to get tractable aliens

---

global war powerfully stimulated the interest of aliens resident in this country in gaining the advantages of American citizenship. The number of naturalizations rose to 275,000 in 1941, 318,000 in 1943, and 441,979 in 1944. In 1946, it fell back to 150,062. In the Second War Powers Act of 1942, Congress relaxed certain naturalization requirements in favor of aliens serving honorably in the armed forces of the country. Even alien enemies who had started on the road to naturalization at least two years before a war began can complete the process without interruption.

[1] Sec. 305 of this statute goes into much detail in debarring opponents of organized government, persons advocating overthrow of the government of the United States, and persons evidencing tolerance toward violence and sabotage.

[2] The appearance of Dr. Albert Einstein before a citizenship examiner in Princeton, New Jersey, in the summer of 1940 was hailed by the paragraphers with considerable hilarity. It is a matter of record that he acquitted himself rather more creditably than the Italian who, after a judge had lectured him on the significance of the American flag, replied, in answer to a question asked him in desperation, What flies over City Hall?—"Peejuns."

[3] One of the questions which a candidate must answer when making his application is: "If necessary, are you willing to take up arms in defense of this country?" Much discussion of the status of "pacifists" in relation to this requirement was stirred by the case of Rosika Schwimmer in 1929 and those of Douglas C. MacIntosh and Marie Bland in 1931, in all of which a divided Supreme Court, on appeal, denied the right to be naturalized. United States v. Schwimmer, 279 U. S. 644; United States v. MacIntosh, 283 U. S. 605; United States v. Bland, 283 U. S. 636. Madame Schwimmer, a high-minded and sincere woman of Hungarian birth, declared herself opposed not only to military service but to the entire system of "common defense" which, as the Court remarked, is "one of the purposes for which the people established and ordained the constitution." Dr. MacIntosh, a Canadian professor of theology at Yale University and a chaplain in the First World War, disclaimed being a pacifist, but confessed to holding religious views which prevented him from promising in advance to bear arms in any war in which the country might be involved, whether or not he believed it to be morally justified. Miss Bland, also a Canadian, refused to pledge herself to defend the constitution and laws except with written interpolation of the words, "as far as my conscience as a Christian will allow." In 1943, a Canadian by the name of Girouard filed a petition in Massachusetts for naturalization, and to the question about willingness to take up arms answered flatly in the negative, explaining that to do so would be contrary to his convictions as a Seventh Day Adventist, although he would be willing to serve in the Army as a non-combatant. On the ground that the prescribed oath of allegiance says nothing about taking up arms and that Congress has nowhere expressly made willingness to do this a prerequisite of citizenship, the Supreme Court (again sharply divided) sustained the action of a district court in admitting the candidate to citizenship, and thus in effect reversed its own earlier position. Girouard v. United States, 328 U. S. 61 (1946). On the series of cases, see M. R. Konvitz, op. cit.. 97-107.

through the mill in time to round them up at the polls. For the courts, the work of naturalization is a sideline activity which they carry on as effectively as they do only because of being provided with the assistance (in the case of the federal courts, where most naturalizations take place) of the "naturalization examiners." The entire naturalization process being essentially a matter of fact-finding, and therefore by nature administrative rather than judicial, it has been suggested that full power to admit to citizenship be transferred to such examiners, with merely a right of appeal to the courts on questions of law.[1]

Aliens who are ineligible   Not all aliens, it must be observed, are eligible for naturalization, but only such as, in addition to meeting all other requirements, are white persons, persons of African nativity or descent, Chinese, Filipinos, or persons descended from races indigenous to the Western Hemisphere or to India. Chinese (both older residents and the few newcomers legally admissible as immigrants) have been eligible only since 1943; persons descended from races indigenous to India only since 1946; and other Asiatics (except Filipinos)—Japanese, Koreans, Burmans, etc.—still are excluded either by the "barred-zone" provision of the act of 1917 or by judicial interpretation as not falling within any of the categories mentioned above.[2] As we have seen, however, children born of Asiatic parents resident in the United States and subject to its jurisdiction—even though the parents themselves are ineligible for naturalization—are citizens by birth.

Other Aspects of Citizenship

Citizenship of married women   Formerly (from 1855 to 1922), an alien woman marrying a native-born or naturalized American citizen automatically became herself (if a person eligible for naturalization) an American citizen; and, conversely (from 1907 to 1922), an American woman marrying an alien forthwith lost her citizenship. In other words, a married woman's status was determined entirely by that of her husband. As a result of persistent agitation led by various women's organizations, this is no longer true. Prompted by unhappy experiences of women under the operation of the rule during the World War of 1914-18, and by growing recognition of women's claim to their own individuality as members of the body politic, Congress in 1922, 1930, and 1931 conferred upon them progressively expanded rights of

[1] The best discussion of naturalization in all of its aspects is L. Gettys, *The Law of Citizenship in the United States* (Chicago, 1934), Chaps. III-IV, VI.

[2] Among decisions, see Ozawa v. United States, 260 U. S. 178 (1922): Toyota v. United States, 268 U. S. 402 (1924). In the case of persons of mixed racial origin, they must, in order to be eligible, "possess ... a preponderance of blood of one or more of the eligible classes." The Supreme Court explicitly held Japanese ineligible in the cases mentioned; and the Immigration Act of 1924 debarred them (and all other aliens ineligible for naturalization) from further admission to the country. In 1944, the then retiring commissioner of immigration and naturalization called attention to the fact that, outside of Nazi Germany, the United States was the only country in the world practicing racial discrimination in matters relating to naturalization.

independent citizenship, and finally, in 1934, made nationality rights as between the sexes equal and uniform in all essential respects. An alien woman marrying a citizen of the United States now becomes a citizen only if naturalized (on somewhat easier terms than in the usual case) ; and an American woman marrying an alien retains her American citizenship (even though her husband is ineligible for naturalization) unless she chooses to renounce it.[1]

Citizenship, once possessed, becomes a constitutional right and cannot be abrogated except by procedures that are themselves constitutional, *e.g.*, in accordance with due process of law. Whether acquired by birth or by naturalization, it, however, may be voluntarily relinquished, or simply lost, or, if obtained by naturalization, may be cancelled as a punishment or penalty. Although doubt long hung about the matter, Congress in 1865 expressly recognized the right of a citizen to "expatriate" himself, except at a time when the country is engaged in war; [2] and in 1907 it provided explicitly how this may be done, *i.e.*, by being naturalized in, or by taking an oath of allegiance to, any foreign state. Citizenship is forfeited, too, if a naturalized American lives continuously for at least two years in a foreign state of which he was formerly a national (providing that through such residence he has acquired the nationality of the foreign state) ; also if he lives as long as five years in any other foreign state.[3] Naturalized persons, also, may be "denaturalized" by court action, *i.e.*, have their certificates of citizenship canceled, if it develops that there was anything fraudulent about their admission to the country or their naturalization, or for disloyal utterances or acts, the presumption in this case being that they did not take the oath of allegiance in good faith. Legislation of 1906 covering this matter was invoked several times during World War I; there were further provisions on the subject in the Nationality Act of 1940; and in the first year alone of World War II forty-two members of the German-American Bund and other naturalized citizens found to be disloyal were denaturalized, three hundred other cases were brought into the courts, and 2,500 additional persons under suspicion were investigated.[4]

How citizenship may be terminated

---

[1] For an excellent brief review of the subject, see L. Gettys, *The Law of Citizenship in the United States,* Chap. v, and for discussion in a broader setting, S. P. Breckinridge, *Marriage and the Civic Rights of Women* (Chicago, 1931).

[2] The Nationality Law of 1940 discarded this exception.

[3] Under the operation of this rule, hundreds of Americans trapped in enemy countries during World War II and unable to return promptly after its close suffered at least a temporary loss of citizenship.

[4] L. Preuss, "Denaturalization on the Ground of Disloyalty," *Amer. Polit. Sci. Rev.*, XXXVI, 701-710 (Aug., 1942). Much interest was aroused in 1943 by the government's attempt to revoke the citizenship of a certain William Schneiderman on the sole ground that at the time of his naturalization in 1927 he was an active member of the Communist party, and, being such, could not sincerely declare adherence to the constitution of the United States. In Schneiderman *v.* United States (320 U. S. 118, 1943), the Supreme Court frustrated the effort by reversing a circuit court of appeals decision, mainly on the ground that it had not been established that belief in communism was, at least as matters stood in 1927, incompatible with attachment to the American system of government. In setting aside the denaturalization

Dual
citizen-
ship

Nations adhering to the principle of *jus sanguinis* have been inclined to claim as citizens children born abroad to parents who were citizens of the nation making the claim. Nations, however, following the principle of *jus soli* have claimed such children as their own citizens; and out of such conflicting claims has arisen the troublesome question of "dual citizenship," or multiple nationality.[1] Not that nations have commonly *recognized* any such thing as dual citizenship; each has been wont to recognize only its own citizenship as having validity. Such rival claims, nevertheless, can easily bring hardship to the persons involved. The principal significance of the matter for the United States in later times has been in connection with the position of certain Japanese residents before the recent war. Japan followed *jus sanguinis;* and although in 1924 she modified her citizenship law in the direction of accepting the principle of *jus soli* for Japanese born thereafter in any one of several designated countries (including the United States), she continued to consider as Japanese citizens any such persons declaring an intention to adhere to Japanese nationality or registered by their parents at a Japanese consulate as being of that nationality. As a consequence, large numbers of Japanese on the Pacific coast were, when the war began, not only citizens of the United States, but, under Japanese law, and in many cases without having been aware of the fact, citizens of Japan as well; and the same was true in Hawaii.[2] Wartime hysteria was responsible for proposals in Congress to revoke the American citizenship of many, or even all, of the more than 70,000 Japanese possessing it. Fortunately, no such ill-advised step was taken; and without much doubt the position into which Japan has come as a result of her war experience will lead to final abandonment of all citizenship claims from Tokyo upon Japanese enjoying citizen status in this country.[3]

Educa-
tion for
citizen-
ship

Recognition not only that the country can offer no higher privilege than citizenship, but also that new citizens ought to be encouraged and helped to prepare themselves for proper discharge of their obligations, has led

---

of a German shown to be an admirer of Nazism, the Court, in 1944, gave him the benefit of the doubt as to the sincerity of his loyalty to the United States before the Nazis came to power. Baumgartner *v.* United States, 322 U. S. 665. On the Schneiderman, Baumgartner, and other cases, see M. R. Konvitz, *op. cit.*, 119-147.

Contrary to general impression, conviction of crime (other than treason), followed by imprisonment, does not abrogate citizenship. What the offender loses, along with his personal liberty, is merely his civil and political privileges, including the privilege of voting. See E. S. Brown, "The Restoration of Civil and Political Rights by Presidential Pardon," *Amer. Polit. Sci. Rev.*, XXXIV, 295-300 (Apr., 1940).

[1] The term "dual citizenship" is sometimes employed also to designate the national-state aspect of citizenship, which, of course, is quite a different matter from that here in mind.

[2] A few months before Pearl Harbor, some 30,000 Hawaiian "dual citizens" petitioned the government at Washington for relief, in some fashion, from Tokyo's claims upon them. See C. H. Coggins, "The Japanese-Americans of Hawaii," *Harper's Mag.*, CLXXXVII, 75-83 (June, 1943); C. McWilliams, "Dual Citizenship," *Far Eastern Survey*, XI, 231-233 (Nov. 16, 1942).

[3] It has been suggested, and from some quarters urged, that all non-citizen Japanese of demonstrated loyalty now in the United States be made eligible for naturalization.

in recent years to various special efforts aimed at civic education for the foreign-born. To prepare applicants for the examination that they must undergo, as well as to furnish a fund of pertinent general information, the Immigration and Naturalization Service has for some time given wide distribution to a *Federal Textbook* and to "readers" or handbooks for candidates for naturalization, bearing such titles as *Introduction to America* and *Our Constitution and Government*. Planning still more ambitiously, it in 1940 procured presidential approval for launching a nation-wide citizenship education program, to involve the expenditure of millions of dollars and to supplement and amplify citizenship education projects already operating in many of the states, with emphasis naturally in areas where heavy alien populations indicated special need. Under the supervision of an advisory board, operating largely through state offices, teacher-training programs were instituted, special teaching aids devised, and classes organized which, although interfered with by the war, were expected eventually to reach at least a million of the foreign-born.[1] Congress, too, took cognizance of the problem when, in 1940, it set aside the third Sunday in May of each year as "Citizenship Day," with the idea that appropriate local ceremonies designed not only for the recently naturalized, but also for native-born citizens lately attaining the age of twenty-one, would prove interesting and stimulating to the body politic in general.

REFERENCES

1. POPULATION AND IMMIGRATION

Recent Social Trends in the United States (New York, 1933), I, Chaps. I, XI. These chapters of a report of a commission appointed by President Hoover give the best general view of the subject as envisaged a decade and a half ago. Developments associated with the recent war and its aftermath will make a new study of the kind, in due time, highly advisable.

W. S. Thompson and P. K. Whelpton, *Population Trends in the United States* (New York, 1933). A monograph supplementing the foregoing report.

F. Lorimer and F. Osborn, *Dynamics of Population* (New York, 1934), Chap. I.

————, *Population: Problems and Trends of Our Changing Population* (Pamphlet, Washington, D. C., 1943).

Our Cities; Their Rôle in the National Economy (Washington, D. C., 1937). A report of the Urbanism Committee to the National Resources Committee.

Statistical Abstract of the United States, 1947 (Washington, D. C., 1947), §§ 1, 4.

L. H. Chamberlain, *The President, Congress, and Legislation* (New York, 1946), Chap. IX. A history of immigration legislation, 1880-1940.

C. P. Howland [ed.], *Survey of American Foreign Relations* (New Haven, 1929), 415-518. An excellent survey of American immigration policy and regulation to the date of publication.

A. E. Reitzel, "The Immigration Laws of the United States—An Outline," *Va. Law Rev.*, XXXII, 1099-1162 (Nov., 1946).

[1] See F. L. Burdette, "Education for Citizenship," *Public Opinion Quar.*, VI, 269-279 (Summer, 1942).

M. R. Davie, *World Immigration, with Special Reference to the United States* (rev. ed., New York, 1933).

M. Kohler, *Immigration and Aliens in the United States* (New York, 1936).

M. L. Hansen, *The Immigrant in American History* (Cambridge, Mass., 1940).

Annual report of the attorney-general of the U. S. (containing reports of the Immigration and Naturalization Service).

2. The Status of Aliens

L. V. Howard and H. A. Bone, *Current American Government* (New York, 1943), Chap. VIII.

D. O. Walter, *American Government at War* (Chicago, 1942), Chap. V.

M. R. Konvitz, *The Alien and the Asiatic in American Law* (Ithaca, N. Y., 1946).

N. Alexander, *The Rights of Aliens Under the Federal Constitution* (Montpelier, Vt., 1931).

W. M. Gibson, *Aliens and the Law; Some Legal Aspects of the National Treatment of Aliens in the United States* (Chapel Hill, N. C., 1940).

W. C. Van Vleck, *The Administrative Control of Aliens* (New York, 1932).

J. P. Clark, *The Deportation of Aliens from the United States* (New York, 1931).

C. McWilliams, *Prejudice; Japanese-Americans: Symbol of Racial Intolerance* (Boston, 1944).

H. Lavine, *The Fifth Column in America* (New York, 1940).

3. Citizenship

W. W. Willoughby, *Constitutional Law of the United States* (2nd ed., New York, 1929), I, Chaps. XVIII-XX.

C. H. Maxson, *Citizenship* (New York, 1930), Chaps. I-XIV.

L. Gettys, *The Law of Citizenship in the United States* (Chicago, 1934).

F. A. Cleveland, *American Citizenship as Distinguished from Alien Status* (New York, 1927).

C. B. Moore, *Our American Citizenship* (New York, 1936).

H. M. Beck, *How to Become an American Citizen* (Philadelphia, 1941).

W. E. Waltz, *The Nationality of Married Women* (Urbana, Ill., 1937).

R. W. Flournoy, "Revision of Nationality Laws of the United States," *Amer. Jour. of Internat. Law,* XXXIV, 36-46 (Jan., 1940).

F. G. Franklin, *The Legislative History of Naturalization in the United States* (Chicago, 1906).

M. E. Dimock, "Administrative Standards for Improving Naturalization Procedure," *Amer. Polit. Sci. Rev.,* XXXVII, 81-90 (Feb., 1943).

E. M. Borchard, *Diplomatic Protection of Citizens Abroad* (new ed., New York, 1927).

F. S. Dunn, *The Protection of Nationals; A Study in the Application of International Law* (Baltimore, 1932).

A. J. Lien, *Privileges and Immunities of Citizens of the United States* (New York, 1913).

R. Howell, *The Privileges and Immunities of State Citizenship* (Baltimore, 1918).

J. L. Cable, *Loss of Citizenship; Denaturalization—The Alien in Wartime* (Washington, D. C., 1943).

C. Seckler-Hudson, *Statelessness, with Special Reference to the United States* (Washington, D. C., 1934).

C. Brinkman, *Recent Theories of Citizenship in Its Relation to Government* (New Haven, Conn., 1927).

CHAPTER IX

CIVIL RIGHTS AND HOW THEY ARE PROTECTED

In the great war which so recently drenched the earth in blood, two Two opposing theories of government diametrically opposed theories, or concepts, of government were struggling for world mastery; and this, rather than any mere competition for control over territories or peoples, was the most deeply significant phase of the conflict. One theory was that of the Italian Fascists, the German Nazis, the Japanese warlords, and of fascist-minded people everywhere, for whom the state was something over and above, separate from and superior to, the men and women living under it—exempt from ordinary moral laws and standards, responsible to nobody, an end in itself. And from this it followed not only that the general mass of the people should have no control over governmental policies and actions, but that they were merely tools or agencies which the state might use for its own purposes, with no "rights" or "liberties" which they, individually or collectively, could assert against it. The other theory, adhered to in democratic countries like the United States, Great Britain, and France, was rather that of the state as a sort of social framework within which government operates with only such authority and powers as the sovereign people, by direct act or tacit consent, have conferred upon it, with government itself subject to popular control, and with individuals and groups retaining rights and liberties which they are entitled to assert and uphold against any governmental agency. Basically, the antithesis was between *authority* and *liberty*, concepts which must have clashed from the beginning of man's political experience. To be worthy of the name, a government must have authority; yet if it is not to be arbitrary and tyrannical, there must be restrictions upon how far it may go in regulating the actions and relations of those living under it. The "authoritarians," or "totalitarians," would have only *authority*, independently arrived at and with no restrictions; the democratically-minded would have a substantial measure of authority, yet conditioned on public consent and steadfastly confined within retaining walls beyond which stretch broad areas of human freedom. No problem in the entire range of political science is more basic than that of working out and maintaining a proper balance between two objectives which, after all, when viewed sensibly, are not incompatible—authority and liberty.

In the United States, we adhere to the doctrine of limited, responsible government. National and state (including, of course, local) governments alike are not sovereign institutions, but merely agencies or instrumental-

The
situation
in the
United
States—
how civil
liberties
arise

ities created by the only sovereign that we recognize, *i.e.*, the people. Powers have been conferred or assented to—many of them—but not *all* powers. To put it differently, the people have reserved to themselves large areas of freedom which government is forbidden to invade—forbidden in some cases negatively through the simple omission of any constitutional authorization, in other cases positively through express injunctions and prohibitions contained in constitutional "bills of rights," both national and state. On the one hand, a person owes the various governments resting upon him loyalty, obedience, and service; on the other, he has a valid claim upon them for observance and protection of rights and liberties which often are thought of as having been granted to him, but which, more truly, he has reserved for himself.[1]

General Aspects of the American System of Civil Rights

Enough must have been said about citizenship in the preceding chapter to leave the impression that the subject is one of considerable complexity. Even more complicated is our system of civil rights. To begin with, there are rights—including the "privileges and immunities of citizens of the United States" of which the constitution speaks—which can be claimed by national citizens only; others which, under state constitutions and laws, attach to state citizens only; and still others—many of them— to which all "persons," aliens included, are alike entitled.[2] In the second place, there are rights which are applicable only to natural persons, as human beings, and others (relating particularly to property) which apply, as well, to "artificial persons" such as corporations. The main complicating circumstance, however, is, of course, our federal form of government; for from this it results (1) that there are rights guaranteed as against the national government only, others as against state governments only, and still others—many indeed—as against both national and state govern-

---

[1] *Rights and liberties,* be it observed, rather than *privileges.* Confusion often arises here. One has a right, as we shall see, to freedom of speech, religious liberty, and due process of law. He has no such right to vote, to hold public office, to practice medicine, or to drive a motor-car on the public highways. One may vote only if given the privilege, hold office only if appointed or elected thereto, practice medicine or drive a car only if licensed to do so. One's *rights* in such matters are confined to seeking the privilege in the first place, and to exercising it, when once attained, without restraint except as duly prescribed by law.

Nor is the "GI Bill of Rights" germane to the present discussion. It does not have to do with fundamental general constitutional guarantees, but only with benefits of various kinds pledged to ex-servicemen under terms of an ordinary act of Congress— the Servicemen's Readjustment Act of 1944 (see p. 758 below). The last two of President Roosevelt's famous "four freedoms"—freedom of speech and religion, freedom from want and fear—are likewise of only potential relevance, because as yet they have no constitutional or statutory basis and are not recognized and enforced by the courts. It is to be noted, however, that a Human Rights Commission set up by the United Nations was at work in 1947 on an international bill of rights which all member states were to be asked to adopt if and when approved by the organization's General Assembly. The United States might in this way incur some new legal obligations in the matter, although it did not seem likely that many rights would be envisaged which were not already given protection in our domestic constitutions and laws.

[2] The status of aliens has been touched upon above (pp. 136-140).

ments; (2) that of rights which can be asserted as against state governments, some rest upon restrictions laid down in the national constitution, others upon restraints embodied in state constitutions, and still others upon the mere absence of any granted or implied authority on the part of any government to interfere with them; and (3) that consequently there is not complete uniformity of rights the country over, but on the contrary some variation from state to state, even though in practice such differences as exist are rarely of much significance.

A second fact is that if any one of us were to undertake to compile a complete and definitive list of the civil rights to which he individually is entitled, he would be doomed to failure. He could carry his catalogue to a considerable length, but in the end he would become lost in doubts and obscurities. Naturally, he would turn to the national constitution, and afterwards to the constitution of his state. But what would he find? In the former, he would discover—chiefly in the first eight amendments [1]— a long and impressive list, followed, however, by the baffling provision of the Ninth Amendment that "the enumeration . . . of certain rights shall not be construed to deny or disparage others retained by the people." What others? No man can say conclusively. Similarly, he would find in all of the state constitutions articles and sections in form or in effect comprising bills of rights, besides scattered clauses pertinent to his inquiry. But in no instance would he come upon any indication that the rights mentioned form an exact and exhaustive list. Quite the contrary. Nor would he be helped out of his dilemma by consulting judicial decisions; for although the Supreme Court, in the Slaughterhouse cases in 1873,[2] went into the matter in some detail, it made no pretense to covering it exhaustively. On the contrary, the Court, speaking of guarantees contained in the federal constitution, said that interpretation of them must be "a gradual process of judicial inclusion and exclusion;" and the same principle holds for rights guaranteed by constitutions of the states. The truth is that there is nowhere, in the constitutions or outside of them, any enumeration that purports to be complete. The national government has limited and delegated powers. The state governments have powers both delegated and residual—but nevertheless limited. As against these governments, taken together, the people have whatever rights and liberties are expressly guaranteed to them, and, in addition, all that are not definitely denied or otherwise inconsistent with the instrument under which they are claimed.

Even, however, if one had a complete picture of rights and liberties as they exist today, it would not hold true tomorrow; far from being fixed and static, the conditions and concepts determining the nature and scope of established rights (especially as construed by courts prone to differ among themselves, and not above reversing their own positions) are perennially undergoing change. As a single illustration may be cited the

2. No full enumeration possible

3. Changes constantly going on

[1] Also in Art. 1, § 9, cls. 2-3; Art. III, § 2, cl. 3, and § 3.
[2] 16 Wallace 36.

fact that whereas formerly the states were free, so far as the federal constitution was concerned, to go as far as they liked in restricting freedom of religion, speech, press, and assembly, the federal Supreme Court has now for some two decades held that the due process clause of the Fourteenth Amendment makes the guarantees of these four liberties, as set forth in the First Amendment, no less applicable to the states than to the national government.[1] Indeed, the entire function of protecting civil liberties has been reoriented as a result of federal safeguards being pushed, by judicial construction, into areas not previously covered. The states are still partners in the protection of liberties; but they have less freedom of action in the matter than formerly.

4. Nevertheless a fairly coherent system

Notwithstanding all of the complications referred to, civil rights in this country can still be recognized, defined, and classified with sufficient thoroughness and accuracy to serve most practical purposes. In fact, to a very considerable extent they constitute a single coherent system. Rights which protect the individual from encroachment by the national government are, of course, uniform the country over. The same is true of those flowing from restrictions imposed in the national constitution upon the dealings of the states with their inhabitants. And although, as indicated above, those resting merely upon state constitutional provisions naturally differ somewhat from state to state, they are nevertheless sufficiently similar to enable one to say that civil rights are approximately the same for all of our people.

5. Rights not absolute

Liberty is not license, and rights are relative, not absolute. After all, one of the main purposes of government is to prevent the safety and well-being of the many from being jeopardized by one or a few. Freedom of speech and press does not carry with it any right to incite persons to crime or panic, to voice slander or to print libels; freedom of assembly does not entitle any group to interfere with public order and safety. To be validly claimed, a right must be exercised so as to entail no infraction of law and no impairment of the same or any other right possessed by others.[2]

---

[1] Gitlow v. New York, 268 U. S. 652 (1925). This step was so significant that we well may note what the Court said: "For present purposes, we may and do assume that freedom of speech and of the press—which are protected by the First Amendment from abridgment by Congress—are among the fundamental personal rights and liberties protected by the due process clause of the Fourteenth Amendment from impairment by the states." The Gitlow case involved a Communist convicted under a New York "criminal anarchy act" for publishing a subversive pamphlet; and the Supreme Court sustained the conviction. The Court's view, first announced as to speech and press in the Gitlow decision, and somewhat later extended to religion and assembly, is that the four liberties "are so indispensable to the democratic process and to the preservation of the freedom of our people that they occupy a preferred place in our scheme of constitutional values." R. E. Cushman, "Civil Liberties," Amer. Polit. Sci. Rev., XLII, 42 (Feb., 1948). Other guarantees have not been so assimilated into the concept of liberty in the due-process clause of the amendment cited.

[2] "The liberty of the individual to do as he pleases, even in innocent matters," said the Supreme Court in Adkins v. Children's Hospital (261 U. S. 525, 1923), "is not absolute. It must frequently yield to the common good; and the line beyond which the power of interference may not be pressed is neither definite nor unalter-

Here and there, the makers of written constitutions have undertaken to list not only civil *rights* but civic *duties* as well; at the close of World War I, the authors of the ill-fated Weimar constitution of Germany did this, although to no avail. In no American constitution is anything of the kind attempted; nor would there likely be any gain from such a procedure. From the very nature of a state and of government, duties and obligations of subjects or citizens—of those governed—naturally flow. Loyalty, obedience, service, are to be presumed. And under a free government, "of, by, and for the people," with extraordinarily extensive guarantees of individual liberty such as ours in the United States, it is the more to be presumed that rights carry with them, one by one, duties for those enjoying them. The right to equal protection of the laws would be meaningless unless the laws were obeyed. The guarantee of freedom of speech, press, and religion entails an obligation not to abuse such precious rights or to interfere with their enjoyment by others. The right to protection by one's government against evil-doers, including aggressive nations, can be maintained only by contributing to the support of police forces and armies. To be loyal, to pay taxes, to render military service if called upon, to obey the laws, to assist in law enforcement, as by jury duty and by serving with a posse if summoned by a sheriff or police chief—these are only a few of the more obvious ways in which the citizen is obligated, by law and honor alike, to acknowledge and make return for the rights and privileges he possesses. And it would be well if, in our thinking about our rights under government, we paid more attention to this reverse side of the shield.

6. Duties inseparable from rights

Freedom can always be abused, and it is not difficult to see why, with the country at war and its life perhaps at stake, civil rights (especially those relating to speech, press, and assembly) are likely to come in for some curtailment. Contrary to an impression sometimes encountered, such rights are not automatically suspended by the mere fact of war. Rarely, indeed, are they legally suspended at all. But under the urgency of wartime situations they may, in practice, become attenuated, even almost to the vanishing point. Sometimes there is more whittling down—more repression—than necessary, as, for example, during the First World War, when, playing fast and loose with the terms of an Espionage Act of 1917 and a Sedition Act of 1918, the Department of Justice not only ferreted out and brought to punishment persons who by any reasonable standards were guilty of offenses against the national morale, but embarked upon, and for a time after the end of hostilities kept up with even greater vigor, a veritable "witch-hunt" in the course of which grievous wrongs were committed, especially as related to aliens. The record during World

7. The special problem of civil rights in wartime

----

able, but may be made to move within limits not well defined, with changing need and circumstance." "Neither property rights nor contract rights," said the Court again, in the case of Nebbia v. New York, 291 U. S. 502 (1934), "are absolute... Equally fundamental with the private right is that of the public to regulate it in the common interest."

War II was considerably better. The Espionage Act of 1917 was, to be sure, called back into operation; a drastic code of regulations embodied in the Alien Registration Act of 1940 and reviving many of the provisions of the Sedition Act of 1918, was in full effect; and both nation and states enacted new protective regulations. Properly enough, there was tightening up, especially as against suspected "fifth columnists." On the other hand, both the president and the Department of Justice insisted that the excesses of World War I be avoided; the Supreme Court, although often dividing on a right wing-left wing pattern, commonly upheld the liberties claimed in cases coming before it unless palpable abuse could be shown; and, as no less vigilant a guardian in this field than the Civil Liberties Union has conceded, on the whole a commendable record was achieved. Unquestionably, the fabric of rights was subjected to its severest strain— not only in World War II, but in the entire history of the country—when, in 1942, all Japanese residents of designated areas adjacent to the Pacific Coast—loyal as well as disloyal, citizen as well as alien (and two-thirds were citizens)—were uprooted from their homes and businesses and herded into remote relocation centers; although even this action, based on alleged military necessity, was, when tested before the Supreme Court, held to have been constitutional, given the circumstances existing.[1]

Numerous and varied as they are, civil rights fall rather naturally into (1) those relating to personal status, and (2) those having to do with property. On a different basis of classification, they also are either (1) *substantive, i.e.,* pertaining to the fact and essence of freedom, or (2) *procedural, i.e.,* relating to the methods by which freedom is protected. The brief survey that can be presented here will follow these broad categories.

Rights of Personal Liberty: I. Substantive

So long as Negro slavery prevailed within our borders, no general immunity from personal servitude was, or could be, asserted. The

---

[1] See p. 140, note 2, above; and cf. pp. 811-814 below. As Professor Robert E. Cushman has pointed out, World War I found legislatures, courts, and people inexperienced and unprepared in this important field of wartime procedure, and bad mistakes were made. By 1941, we had the advantage of extensive, and some costly, experience, and were prepared to approach the whole matter more sanely. See "Civil Liberties" [during our first year in World War II], *Amer. Polit. Sci. Rev.*, XXXVII, 49-56 (Feb., 1943). The principal lapses during the later war took the form of efforts to purge the federal service of officers and employees regarded in certain quarters as holding subversive views; various discriminations against Negroes, *e.g.,* in war industries; and certainly the Japanese evacuation. For an excellent survey of the country's earlier experiences with wartime civil liberties, see C. B. Swisher, "Civil Liberties in Wartime," *Polit. Sci. Quar.*, LV, 321-347 (Sept., 1940), and for a full study of the impact of World War II, E. S. Corwin, *Total War and the Constitution* (New York, 1947), Chap. III. Cf. R. E. Cushman, "Civil Liberty After the War," *Amer. Polit. Sci. Rev.* XXXVIII, 1-20 (Feb., 1944), a thoughtful wartime analysis of the strains to which civil liberties might be (and to some extent have been) subjected after the war. See also O. K. Fraenkel, *Our Civil Liberties* (New York, 1944), Chap. III; A. G. Hays, "Civil Liberties in Wartime," *Bill of Rights Rev.*, II, 170-182 (Spring, 1942); and *Iowa Law Rev.*, XXIX 379-480 (Mar., 1944), a symposium on civil liberties in wartime.

Thirteenth Amendment, however, dating from 1865, prohibits throughout the United States and in all places under its jurisdiction not only slavery but every form of "involuntary servitude except as a punishment for crime whereof the party shall have been duly convicted." According to the Supreme Court, involuntary servitude does not arise when a person is held against his will to the completion of a period of service upon which he has entered (*e.g.*, as a seaman), but on the other hand does arise if a laborer who is indebted to his employer is required, on penalty of going to jail, to work out the debt in the employer's service.[1] A federal statute forbids this form of peonage, and so do various state constitutions and statutes; many state constitutions, indeed, forbid imprisonment for debt under any circumstances. Involuntary service in the Army, or compulsory work on the highways—falling within the legitimate exercise of the military or police power—does not constitute "servitude;" nor does compulsory jury or posse service.

1. Immunity from slavery and involuntary servitude

The First Amendment forbids Congress to make any law "respecting the establishment of religion or prohibiting the free exercise thereof;" and the same restriction is imposed upon the states, not only by similar provisions in the constitutions of all of them, but by judicial construction in later years making the Fourteenth Amendment's due process clause applicable to state actions in this field. The Supreme Court has held that these guarantees of religious liberty do not confer any right to violate a criminal statute in the name of religion; for example, they do not entitle a Mormon to practice polygamy.[2] Likewise, they confer no license to perpetrate fraud, *e.g.*, by extracting money from the ill with promises of supernatural cure.[3] But so long as there is no violation of law or breach of the peace, freedom of belief and worship must be unrestricted. Many difficult questions, however, arise. Some two decades ago, a Tennessee statute prohibiting the teaching of the theories of evolution in the public schools was attacked on the ground of being inconsistent with a section of the state constitution which forbade giving preference by law to "any religious establishment or mode of worship." The highest court of the state, however, held that since people of all faiths are divided in their attitude on evolutionary doctrines, no "religious establishment or mode of worship" was discriminated against or jeopardized by the measure challenged.[4]

2. Freedom of religion

More recently, questions of religious liberty (in some instances involving also freedom of the press) have been brought to the fore by the beliefs and practices of an aggressive sect known as Jehovah's Witnesses—an organization which in a decade has been responsible for more judicial decisions

The troublesome Jehovah's Witnesses

[1] The latter principle has rather recently been reaffirmed in Taylor *v.* State of Georgia, 315 U. S. 25 (1942), a case involving a Negro held to labor under the Georgia contract labor law—a law, said the Court, violating the Thirteenth Amendment.

[2] Reynolds *v.* United States, 98 U. S. 145 (1878); Church of Jesus Christ *v.* United States, 136 U. S. 49 (1890).

[3] United States *v.* Ballard, 322 U. S. 78 (1944).

[4] Scopes *v.* State, 154 Tenn. 105 (1927).

touching the subject [1] than were recorded in the entire previous history of the country. Not even an outline of this extraordinary chapter (which promises to continue indefinitely) can be presented here. But it may be noted (1) that whereas in 1940 the federal Supreme Court held that school boards might exclude from public schools pupils who refuse to salute the American flag, "symbol of our national unity," regardless of religious scruples on the part of the children or their parents [2] (the sect referred to opposes such salutes as savoring of idolatry), three years later it reversed itself by holding invalid a regulation of the state of West Virginia requiring the salute from school children, on penalty of expulsion; [3] and (2) that, while refusing to countenance disturbances of the peace or other infractions of reasonable police regulations, the Court, in numerous cases, has sustained appeals against municipal ordinances requiring the sect's canvassers to take out peddler's licenses before distributing their books and tracts and soliciting contributions from door to door. In a notable case in 1942, the Court did, indeed, hold that, since the canvassers were in effect selling their literature, their activities were primarily commercial rather than religious, and therefore might properly be subjected to license and payment of fees.[4] The decision, however, which was of the hair-line variety (five to four), was widely regarded—even by people who considered the Witnesses a public nuisance—as reactionary; and in the following year a Court with a slightly changed personnel reversed it,[5] so that the sect is now allowed free scope so long as disturbances are not created or reasonable police regulations violated.[6] The situation in general is that the interests of religious freedom are being satisfactorily protected, even though, in practice, some favoritism is often shown Christianity, as, for example, in laws relating to Sabbath observance or requiring Bible-reading in the public schools.[7]

---

[1] Some twenty-five by the federal Supreme Court alone to the autumn of 1947.

[2] Minersville School District v. Gobitis, 310 U. S. 586 (1940).

[3] West Virginia State Board of Education v. Barnette, 319 U. S. 624 (1943).

[4] Jones v. Opelika, 316 U. S. 584 (1942).

[5] Murdock v. Pennsylvania, 319 U. S. 105 (1943).

[6] On this interesting chapter in our civil-rights experience, see V. Rotnem and F. G. Folsom, Jr., "Recent Restrictions upon Religious Liberty," Amer. Polit. Sci. Rev., XXXVI, 1053-1068 (Dec., 1942); H. W. Barber, "Religious Liberty v. The Police Power: Jehovah's Witnesses," ibid., XLI, 226-247 (Apr., 1947); and comments by R. E. Cushman in Amer Polit. Sci. Rev., XXXVII, 278-280 (Apr., 1943), and XXXVIII, 277-284 (Apr., 1944). Cf. O. K. Fraenkel, Our Civil Liberties, Chap. vi; H. Stroup, The Jehovah's Witnesses (New York, 1945).

[7] For comment on these latter matters, see G. I. Haight and C. H. Lerch, "Freedom of Religion," Bill of Rights Rev., II, 111-118 (Winter, 1942), and A. W. Johnson, The Legal Status of Church-State Relationships in the United States, with Special Reference to the Public Schools (Minneapolis, Minn., 1934).

In wartime, a troublesome situation arises from the unwillingness of some persons, (Quakers, Seventh Day Adventists, etc.), because of religious scruples or on other grounds of conscience, to render military service. Legally, of course, such dissenters are no less obligated to such service than are other people. As an act of grace, however, Congress has, in our last two great wars, authorized draft boards to call "conscientious objectors" only for non-combatant service in the Army, or in the case of those opposed even to that form of service, for employment in park improvement or other useful work in civilian camps. Far from being penalized for their beliefs,

Cultural achievement and democratic government alike presuppose wide freedom of the people to express opinions orally, to write, and to print; and in the First Amendment to the federal constitution, as well as in nearly all of the state constitutions, will be found clauses intended to protect political discussion and criticism, along with the interchange of ideas and opinion generally, against censorship and repression such as that which used to stifle all dissenting thought and expression under the Nazi and Fascist dictatorships of Europe. No guarantee of a right better illustrates, however, the presumption of propriety and rationality upon which all civil rights are predicated. It was manifestly not intended that freedom of speech and press should extend to the utterance or publication of libels, blasphemies, and indecencies, the incitement of insurrection, the encouragement of disobedience to law, the defamation of the government, or giving aid and comfort to foreign states making war upon the United States; and the federal constitution had been in operation less than a decade before Congress passed a Sedition Act (1798) laying heavy penalties upon encouraging insurrection or other disorder, publishing "false and malicious writings" against the government, or inciting any foreign power to make war upon the country. This particular measure flowed from an unfortunate outburst of Federalist partisanship, and after the Jeffersonian Republicans came into power they not only allowed it to lapse (it had, indeed, expired on the day before Jefferson was inaugurated, and simply was not renewed), but liberated the prisoners held under it and repaid the fines that had been assessed.

For more than a century thereafter, legislation on similar lines was enacted only to meet temporary wartime situations. During the Civil War, the "war powers" of the government were construed to extend to the suppression of newspapers, the arrest and imprisonment of editors, and the punishment of speakers, accused of encouraging rebellion or seeking

3. Freedom of speech and press

---

therefore, such persons are, on account of them, excused from the hazards of combat and, in a sense, given preferential treatment—although some, failing to understand or appreciate the government's leniency, protest that they are being discriminated against or even "persecuted." On the other hand, conscientious objectors have been improperly discriminated against in other ways, as when the law examiners of Illinois excluded one of the number, otherwise qualified, from admission to the bar and the federal Supreme Court rather unaccountably upheld the action. *In re* Summers, 325 U. S. 561 (1945).

Much interest was stirred in 1947 by a five-to-four Supreme Court decision in a case (Everson *v.* Board of Education, 67 Sup. Ct. 504) turning on the question of whether New Jersey school funds raised by taxation could lawfully be used to pay for transporting children to parochial, as well as to public, schools. On being challenged, the power was denied by a lower court, but upheld by the highest state court. On the ground that the law permitting the payments amounted to public benefit legislation, and that no person might properly be barred from such benefit because of his religion, and, further, that, far from contravening the separation of church and state, the law merely averted discrimination in a public service, the federal Supreme Court sustained the favorable state decision—although the dissents were vigorous, mainly on the ground that compelling people to pay taxes to help support Catholic education violates the First Amendment. In any event, the voters presently settled the question for themselves by approving (on November 4, 1947) a new state constitution legalizing free school-bus transportation for all children, including those attending parochial and private as well as those attending public schools.

to weaken the morale of Unionist supporters. And during the First World War an Espionage Act of 1917 and a supplementary Sedition Act of 1918 laid heavy penalties, not only on all persons who, by speaking or writing, sought to turn sentiment against the war, but on all who wrote, printed, or published any "disloyal, scurrilous, or abusive" language about the constitution or form of government of the United States. Although regarded by many people as unnecessary, and unquestionably working injustice in some instances, these measures were enforced vigorously (nearly five thousand persons were prosecuted under them, and some two thousand convicted) ; and when tested in the courts, they were in nearly every instance sustained—although Justices Holmes and Brandeis, in dissenting opinions, developed a doctrine of "clear and present danger" according to which repression was justifiable only when shown to be "immediately required to save the country." [1]

The act of 1918 was repealed in 1921. But the 1917 measure was still on the statute-book, ready to be invoked, when we entered World War II. In the meantime, two significant things had happened. In the first place, as indicated above, the Supreme Court, after long hesitation, had in 1925 construed the due process clause of the Fourteenth Amendment as making the fundamental guarantees of the First Amendment covering speech and press applicable to the states—which meant that the rights involved had been "nationalized," with the states no longer free, as in the past, to abridge or destroy them.[2] In the second place, a vigorous drive dating from the 1920's had led to inclusion in the Alien Registration Act of 1940 of a series of five sections comprising our first *peacetime* sedition law since that of 1798, and placing the most drastic national restrictions on freedom of speech and press in our history.[3] Of course, this measure was adopted at a time when the country's well-being was thought to be particularly imperiled by subversive elements. Nevertheless, its enactment, when we were still at peace, and, more particularly, its strong terms, startled a good many people. At all events, when war burst upon us in 1941, we had on the books most of the legislation deemed necessary for the new emergency, the principal addition thereafter taking the form of a section of the First War Powers Act (1941) under which President

[1] Although appearing first in an opinion delivered by Mr. Justice Holmes, speaking for the Court, in Schenck *v.* United States, 249 U. S. 47 (1919), this significant doctrine naturally has been asserted oftenest in dissenting opinions holding that circumstances did not warrant given actions taken. In later years, however, it has come to represent a substantially agreed principle, especially for application in cases involving abridgment of freedom of speech and of the press; legislation entailing such abridgment is now *presumed* to be unconstitutional unless shown to be justified by "clear and present danger."

[2] Gitlow *v.* New York, 268 U. S. 652 (1925) ; Near *v.* Minnesota *ex rel.* Olson, 283 U. S. 697 (1931).

[3] Not only did this legislation make speech and publication punishable if construed as tending to have illegal consequences at any possible future time, as well as at the moment, but it abandoned the doctrine that guilt is purely personal and made it an offense to be associated with any organization or society regarded as having subversive purposes.

Roosevelt set up an Office of Censorship charged with prescribing regulations for the press and for radio-broadcasting and with inspecting all private communications entering or leaving the country by mail, cable, radio, or other means.[1] Although armed with ample powers, the national government—to which the states were persuaded to leave nearly the whole task of dealing with sedition, espionage, and related matters—pursued a considerably more moderate course during World War II than during the earlier conflict; in general, the press and radio networks complied voluntarily with Office of Censorship regulations; and prosecutions, through the Department of Justice and its police arm, the F. B. I., were relatively few.

Hardly any problem of government presents greater difficulty than that of drawing a line between what is permissible and what is not in the matter of speech, communications, and publication. The general principle is clear; fundamentally, speech and press are free. Even in normal times, however, there are limits: freedom must not be allowed to become license; character and reputation must be protected against slanderous attack; where individual right clashes with the interest of public order or security—perchance even with the authority of the government itself— it must give way. And in wartime, the bounds to which curtailment may go seem to be fixed only by the dictates of national defense and military necessity.[2]

Congress, further says the First Amendment, shall make no law abridging "the right of the people peaceably to assemble, and to petition the government for a redress of grievances;" and state constitutions commonly lay the same restraint upon state legislatures. Like other

4. Right of assembly and petition

[1] See p. 818 below; B. K. Price, "Governmental Censorship in Wartime," *Amer. Polit. Sci. Rev.*, XXXVI, 837-849 (Oct., 1942). For a brief discussion of freedom of speech and press in wartime, see E. W. Puttkammer [ed.], *War and the Law* (Chicago, 1944), 17-37.

[2] The federal government's control over the press is, of course, reënforced by its exclusive operation of the mails. Ordinarily it is futile to publish what cannot be given postal circulation; and indecent, fraudulent, and seditious matter can at any time be denied all postal privileges. An interesting case arose in 1943 when the postmaster-general revoked the second-class permit of *Esquire* magazine as being a publication not contributing "to the public good." In Hannegan v. *Esquire*, 237 U. S. 146 (1946), the Supreme Court unanimously reversed the action. The case turned, however, rather on interpretation of the postal laws than on any direct question of "freedom of the press." Efforts of the newspaper industry to persuade the Supreme Court that freedom of the press entails immunity from the operation of such statutes as the Sherman Anti-Trust Act and the National Labor Relations Act have been unsuccessful. See Oklahoma Press Publishing Co. v. Walling, 327 U. S. 186 (1946).

The principal books on free speech are Z. Chafee, *Freedom of Speech* (New York, 1921)—inspired by the experiences of 1917-20—and the same author's *Free Speech in the United States* (Cambridge, Mass., 1941). On freedom of the press, one notes especially *A Free and Responsible Press; A General Report on Mass Communications* (Chicago, 1947), and W. E. Hocking, *Freedom of the Press; A Framework of Principle* (Chicago, 1947)—the first being the report of a Commission on the Freedom of the Press financed by the publisher of *Time* and *Fortune* and appointed by Chancellor Robert M. Hutchins, of the University of Chicago, and the second a supplementary essay by a member of the Commission. M. L. Ernst, *The First Freedom* (New York, 1946), is in some respects an even more thorough discussion. See also F. Thayer, *Legal Control of the Press* (Chicago, 1944), especially Chap. III.

rights, that of holding public meetings is not absolute; a meeting cannot be allowed to block traffic on city streets, to spread disease, to become riotous, or to be employed for purposes of agitation against law and government. In cities, therefore, it is usual to require a permit from the mayor or other officer for holding any meeting in the streets or parks; and while there is supposed to be no restraint except that which a reasonable exercise of police power entails in the interest of public health, safety, morals, and convenience, over-zealous authorities undoubtedly make it difficult at times for people of radical inclinations to hold meetings of actually innocent character.[1] As for petition, the main question arising in the past has been that of whether the right to present a petition involves the right to have it heard and considered. Theoretically, such a deduction would seem obvious, but in practice it does not follow. Congress, every year, is flooded with petitions and memorials on all sorts of subjects. Received without objection, printed in the *Congressional Record,* and usually referred to appropriate committees, they, however, are almost invariably pigeonholed and never heard of afterwards; otherwise, the two houses would have time for little else.

5. Right to keep and bear arms

"A well regulated militia," says the Second Amendment, "being necessary to the security of a free state, the right of the people to keep and bear arms shall not be infringed;" and more or less similar provisions are found in many of the state constitutions. The arms referred to are those of the soldier. Under the police power, the "bearing" of arms intended for private use may be regulated and restricted by both the federal government and the states; and, as is well known, there are plenty of laws forbidding the carrying of concealed weapons (pistols, revolvers, dirks, bowie-knives, sword-canes, etc.) and the sale, possession, or use of sawed-off shot-guns and other weapons not employed for military purposes but habitually used by criminals.[2] Back of the federal guarantee, as originally conceived, was the notion of a free and peaceful nation depending for defense chiefly or wholly upon locally organized militia drawn directly from the people; and that is what we still might prefer if the times in which we live did not require a substantial national army in addition. But

---

[1] The right of assembly, in this aspect, received notable vindication in 1937 in the case of DeJonge v. Oregon (299 U. S. 353), in which the federal Supreme Court reversed the supreme court of Oregon, which had upheld police arrests of persons attending a peaceable meeting under the auspices of the Communist party. In doing this, the Court for the first time brought freedom of assembly expressly under the protection of the due process clause of the Fourteenth Amendment—as in Gitlow v. New York, 268 U. S. 652 (1925) it had already done in the case of freedom of speech and press. In 1939, a Jersey City ordinance under which practically all meetings of leftist organizations were being prevented was held unconstitutional in Hague v. C. I. O., 307 U. S. 496. On the general subject, see J. M. Jarrett and V. A. Mund, "The Right of Assembly," *N. Y. Univ. Law. Quar. Rev.,* IX, 1-38 (Sept. 1931); Anon., *Freedom of Assembly and Anti-Democratic Groups* (Washington, D. C., 1941); and cf. Whitney v. California, 274 U. S. 357 (1927).

[2] See United States v. Miller, 307 U. S. 174 (1939), for a Supreme Court decision upholding the constitutionality of the National Firearms Act of 1934. Cf. G. I. Haight, "The Right to Keep and Bear Arms," *Bill of Rights Rev.,* II, 31-42 (Fall. 1941).

in any event the people have a right to arm themselves for protection against both domestic disorder and foreign dangers.

No state, says the Fourteenth Amendment, may "deny to any person within its jurisdiction the equal protection of the laws." The original intent of this provision hardly extended beyond protecting the lately emancipated Negroes against discriminative treatment at the hands of the Southern states. In practice, it has developed into a general guarantee against arbitrary classification and other forms of discrimination, and as such it is applicable alike to all persons (citizens and aliens, individuals and corporations), and to all kinds of civil rights. Furthermore, although the Fourteenth Amendment lays the injunction upon the states only, equal protection is regularly construed as contained within the broad concept of due process of law, and therefore as binding upon the federal government as well. On its face, the provision might seem to preclude all grouping or classification of persons or things with a view to differing status or treatment under the law.[1] But of course such literal construction would be an absurdity. As an American jurist has remarked, the very essence of legislation is classification; and as the courts have repeatedly asserted, the purport of the "equal protection" clause is merely to require that when statutory classifications are made, they shall be reasonable with respect to the end sought and compatible with the purposes of good government, and that all persons or things standing in substantially the same relation to the law shall be treated alike. People of large income may be taxed at higher rates than people of low income, but higher rates for Protestants than for Catholics would be inadmissible. Negroes may not, as such, and by legislation, be prevented from serving on juries, from renting or buying homes in specified sections of cities, or from voting in primaries.[2] But the Southern states are held to be justified—with a view to minimizing racial antagonisms and promoting public order—in sanctioning, or even by law requiring, the segregation of white and colored people on railway trains and in hotels and restaurants—provided always that substantially equal accommodations are made available to both racial elements.[3] Similarly, Negroes cannot, as such, be excluded from public schools, but may be required to attend separate

6. Equal protection of the laws

[1] It is to be observed that, in general, the restriction applies only to discrimination practiced by governments, or by public authorities as their agents—not as practiced by private individuals, businesses, and the like, e.g., railroads, hotels, and theaters. Civil Rights Cases, 109 U. S. 3 (1883). Thus when in Washington, D. C., the property-owners in a block of a certain street entered into a "white covenant" barring selling or leasing houses in the block to Negroes, their action was judicially sustained. Rights as related to various forms of social and economic discrimination are most adequately treated in M. R. Konvitz, *The Constitution and Civil Rights* (New York, 1947).

[2] On primaries, see pp. 189-192 below.

[3] In 1946, to be sure, a "Jim Crow" law of Virginia segregating white and colored bus passengers was held invalid by the federal Supreme Court, but on the ground of imposing a burden of inconvenience upon interstate carriers rather than as a matter of "equal protection." Morgan v. Virginia, 328 U. S. 373. Cf. Southern Pacific Co. v. Arizona, 325 U. S. 761 (1945).

schools maintained for them if of approximately equivalent standard.[1]

In the next place, every one is protected against the possible danger of being adjudged a traitor under impetuous or partisan acts of Congress or through procedures of over-zealous prosecutors or courts; for treason against the United States is defined by the constitution, and neither Congress nor any law-enforcing authority has power to add to the definition. As so defined, treason consists only in levying war against the United States or adhering to the country's enemies, giving them aid and comfort. Furthermore, no person may be convicted of treason except on the testimony of two witnesses to the same overt act or on confession in open court;[2] and while Congress fixes the penalty, it cannot in doing so impose any disability upon the convicted person's heirs or descendants.[3] It is to be observed, however, that sedition is closely related to treason, and that Congress may go as far as it likes not only in making acts seditious, but in providing for the punishment of persons committing them. Treason trials in the federal courts of the United States have been neither numerous nor (except perhaps in the case involving Aaron Burr) dramatic; and the death penalty was never imposed for the offense until 1942, when four German-born American citizens (one in Detroit and three in Chicago) were convicted and condemned to be hanged. In point of fact, there have, to the date of writing (1948), been no actual executions; for the president, in 1943, commuted the sentence of the convict in Detroit to life imprisonment, and the ultimate fate of the Chicago trio is still awaiting the outcome of appeals. John Brown, of Harper's Ferry fame, was executed for treason; but he was tried in a Virginia court and convicted of treason against "the commonwealth." Each state may not only define treason for its own purposes, but prescribe such penalties as it sees fit.[4]

---

[1] Plessy v. Ferguson, 163 U. S. 537 (1896). For a case relating to the admission of a Negro to the law school of the University of Missouri, see Missouri ex rel. Gaines v. Canada, Registrar, 305 U. S. 337 (1938). The Court held that Missouri must either admit Negroes to its existing law school or set up a separate law school for them; and the state did the latter. The Court, too, has repeatedly held that a Negro is constitutionally entitled to be indicted and tried by juries from which Negroes have not been excluded on grounds of race; in 1935, it held void an indictment of a Negro in Alabama (Norris v. Alabama, 294 U. S. 587), and in 1942 set aside the conviction of a Negro in Texas (Hill v. Texas, 316 U. S. 400), because it found that they had been victims of such discrimination; late in 1947, also, it ordered a new trial of a Mississippi Negro condemned to the electric chair, on the ground that in a county where Negroes composed more than one-third of the population, no Negro name had appeared on grand and petit jury lists in more than thirty years.

[2] Art. III, § 3, cl. 1. In other words, one cannot commit treason simply by talking or conspiring against the government; he must actually do something, and there must be witnesses to what he does.

[3] Bigelow v. Forrest, 9 Wallace 339 (1869).

[4] In Cramer v. United States (325 U. S. 1, 1945), the Supreme Court for the first time in its history reviewed a conviction for treason; and in so doing it authoritatively analyzed the nature of the crime and the kind and amount of evidence required to prove it. The case turned on Cramer's fraternization in New York City with two of the Nazi saboteurs referred to on p. 168, note 1, below (i.e., "adhering to enemies" of the United States), and, on the ground that the only overt acts testified to by two witnesses were insufficient to prove treasonable intent, the Court,

Rights of Personal Liberty: II. Procedural

During the political struggles of the seventeenth century in England, persons were "attainted" of treason and sent to the scaffold, or otherwise severely punished, by simple act of Parliament, with no judicial trial. Often, too, their descendants were made ineligible to hold public office, and otherwise deprived of rights and privileges. Properly enough—considering that similar practices had been by no means unknown in the American colonies—the authors of our national constitution took the position that, aside from removal from office as a result of impeachment, punishment ought to be inflicted only in pursuance of the verdict of a court of proper jurisdiction. Hence, national and state legislative bodies alike are forbidden to pass bills of attainder in any form.[1] ^{1. Bills of attainder forbidden}

Similarly, there is full protection against *ex post facto*, *i.e.*, "after the fact," legislation.[2] As defined by the Supreme Court, an *ex post facto* law is one which "makes an action done before the passing of the law, and which was innocent when done, criminal, and punishes such action;" or one which "aggravates a crime, or makes it greater than it was when committed;" or one which "changes the punishment, and inflicts a greater punishment than the law annexed to a crime when committed;" or, finally, one which "alters the legal rules of evidence and requires less, or different, testimony than the law required at the time of the commission of the offense, in order to convict the offender."[3] *Ex post facto* legislation is therefore criminal legislation passed after the alleged crime was committed, which, if brought to bear against an accused person, would be to his disadvantage; and the enactment of such legislation is expressly forbidden to both the nation and the states. Retroactive legislation on civil matters, and retroactive criminal legislation which is not detrimental to an accused person, *e.g.*, a law reducing a penalty, is, however, permissible. ^{2. Ex post facto laws forbidden}

---

by five to four, reversed his conviction at the hands of a lower tribunal. For a summary, see *Amer. Polit. Sci. Rev.*, XL, 236-238 (Apr., 1946).

To the foregoing list of substantive personal guarantees may be added two others appropriately dealt with in an earlier chapter: (1) the provision of Article IV of the federal constitution that "the citizens of each state shall be entitled to all the privileges and immunities of citizens in the several states," and (2) the stipulation in the Fourteenth Amendment that "no state shall make or enforce any law which shall abridge the privileges or immunities of citizens of the United States." See pp. 96 and 92 above.

[1] Art. I, § 9, cl. 3. Proposing to "purge" from the federal service employees alleged to be disloyal or subversive, Congress in 1943 undertook to oust Robert M. Lovett, secretary of the Virgin Islands, and Goodwin B. Watson and William E. Dodd, Jr., employees of the Federal Communications Commission, by cutting off their salaries. In United States *v.* Lovett, 328 U. S. 303 (1946), the Supreme Court held that, apart from the highly dubious authority of Congress to effect removals (actually, the officials stayed on), the action taken was tantamount to a bill of attainder, and therefore unconstitutional.

[2] Art. I, § 10, cl. 1.

[3] Calder *v.* Bull, 3 Dallas 386 (1798). Originally, it was supposed that the constitution's clause applied to legislation of all kinds, but in the case cited the Court ruled that it was applicable to *penal* legislation only.

It is an axiom of Anglo-American jurisprudence that a person suspected or accused of crime shall have a fair trial, according to humane methods, and with the burden of proof resting on his accusers; and in both the federal constitution and the constitutions of the states the entire process of criminal justice is surrounded with restrictions to this end. Pettifogging lawyers and spineless judges too often try the public patience by twisting these restraints to the advantage of hardened criminals. The fault lies, however, with those who abuse the sheltering provisions, rather than with the provisions themselves; administered properly, the safeguards erected are wholesome barriers against the conviction of innocent persons and against other miscarriages of justice. Reënforced by stipulations of similar purport in state constitutions in behalf of persons accused of violating state laws, the national constitution throws around those accused of violating federal law the following broad blanket of guarantees: [1] (1) a person in civil life may be held to answer for "a capital or otherwise infamous crime" only on "a presentment or indictment of a grand jury;" (2) the privilege of the writ of *habeas corpus* may be denied only when the public safety, in times of rebellion or invasion, requires its suspension; (3) the accused is entitled to a speedy trial, by an impartial jury of the state and district in which the crime has been committed; (4) he has a right to be confronted with the witnesses against him, to have counsel for his defense, and to avail himself of compulsory process for obtaining witnesses in his favor; (5) he may not be compelled to give evidence against himself, either orally or by producing books or papers; (6) he is given security against "unreasonable searches and seizures;" (7) he may not be "deprived of life, liberty, or property without due process of law;" (8) excessive bail may not be required, nor excessive fines imposed, nor cruel and unusual punishments inflicted; and (9) a person may not be twice put in jeopardy of life or limb for the same offense (except under separate federal and state authority).

Some of these guarantees call for a word of comment. Indictment by grand jury came into American usage as a highly valued English common-law procedure, and originally was provided for not only in the federal constitution but in all of the state constitutions as well. To this day, no person may be proceeded against under federal authority for "a capital or otherwise infamous crime, unless on a presentment or indictment of a grand jury, except in cases arising in the land or naval forces, or the militia, when in actual service in time of war or public danger." [2] Presided over by the judge functioning within the given jurisdiction, a federal grand jury consists of from twelve to twenty-three persons, before whom the

---

[1] In Art. I, § 9, cl. 2, and Amendments V–VIII. The provisions noted do not apply to cases arising in the Army, Navy, or Air Force, or in the militia when in the service of the United States.

[2] Amendment V. As defined by the Supreme Court, an "infamous crime" is one punishable by imprisonment, by loss of civil or political privileges, or by hard labor. *Ex parte* Wilson, 114 U. S. 417 (1885).

public prosecutor (normally a district attorney) makes accusations of crime, which thereupon are weighed privately by the jurors and either dismissed as being insufficiently supported by the evidence or made the basis of indictments charging specified persons with committing stipulated crimes. The object is, of course, to insure that no one will be inconvenienced and humiliated by being held for trial unless a substantial number of his fellow-citizens agree with the prosecutor that there is good reason for it being done. The procedure, however, tends to be cumbersome, slow, and otherwise unsatisfactory, and several of the states (amending their constitutions in so far as necessary) have substituted, all around or for certain types of cases, a simpler process under which the grand jury is dispensed with and the prosecutor (usually a county attorney) merely files an "information," or affidavit, against a person under suspicion. And in reply to argument that this constitutes a denial of the due process of law guaranteed by the Fourteenth Amendment, the Supreme Court has said that while due process was once supposed to require indictment by grand jury, the new method is none the less due process simply because of being new.[1] The grand jury, however, could not be displaced in *federal* procedure without amending the national constitution.

The privilege of the writ of *habeas corpus*—"the most important single safeguard of personal liberty known to Anglo-American law"—is guaranteed or assumed, within the appropriate spheres, by both national and state constitutions. By virtue of it, any person arrested or otherwise detained on suspicion of crime may demand an immediate hearing in court with a view to determination of whether there is adequate ground for his detention. The writ is addressed by the court (federal or state, as the case may be) to the officer having custody of the suspect and directs that the petitioner's "body" be brought into the court's presence. If it develops that the prisoner is being held contrary to law, he will be given his freedom; otherwise, he will be held for trial, with or without release on bail.[2] Under constitutional provision, the privilege of the writ may be suspended by federal authority only "when in cases of rebellion or invasion the public safety may require it." [3] On the question of *who* may suspend, the constitution is silent; and usage has varied. Largely supported, however, by the Supreme Court in the famous Civil War case of *Ex parte* Milligan,[4] the best opinion is that the function properly belongs

(b) *Habeas corpus*

---

[1] Hurtado *v.* California, 110 U. S. 516 (1884).

[2] Bail is money or property deposited by an accused person, or by his sureties, as a pledge that he will appear for trial. The federal constitution stipulates, as do most of the state constitutions, that excessive bail shall not be required.

[3] Art. I, § 9, cl. 2. The only situation normally regarded as justifying suspension is one in which the regular courts are not in operation and martial law has been proclaimed. See R. S. Rankin, *When Civil Law Fails* (Durham, N. C., 1939).

[4] 4 Wallace 2 (1866). Milligan had been court-martialed in Indiana—far from the theater of war, and where the regular courts were in full operation—and had been convicted of treason and sentenced to death, although the sentence had not yet been executed when the war ended and the *habeas corpus* privilege, where suspended,

to Congress, but that, under proper conditions, it may be exercised by the president in pursuance of express congressional authorization. Some of the states, within their own spheres, have forbidden the writ's suspension altogether.[1]

(c) Jury trial

Like indictment by grand jury, trial by "petit" (petty), or trial, jury passed into American usage with the English common law. The federal constitution provides for it in three different clauses,[2] and no state constitution fails to provide for it also. In the federal field, the constitution requires it to be employed in "the trial of all crimes, except in cases of impeachment," and "preserves" it as a right, too, in civil cases in which the value in controversy exceeds twenty dollars. It is, however, by common law that a federal jury must consist of twelve persons and must arrive at its verdict by unanimous vote. It is also by common law that the right of jury trial does not apply to cases in courts of equity, to cases in contempt of court, and to petty offenses, or misdemeanors, punishable only by small fines. Formerly it was supposed that wherever applicable under constitutional provision or common law, jury trial must prevail. The federal Supreme Court has now held, however, that since the device is intended fundamentally for the accused's protection, he may, if he considers it to his interest to do so, waive the right in federal proceedings; and many states allow the same discretion.[3] The Court, moreover, has ruled that where juries are employed, they must not be made up deliberately to exclude workingmen, Negroes, or any other particular class of persons.[4]

(d) Searches and seizures

Another treasured inheritance from English common law is grounded upon the ancient maxim that every man's house is his castle. "The right of the people," says the Fourth Amendment, "to be secure in their persons, houses, papers, and effects against unreasonable searches and seizures

---

was restored. The Court held that President Lincoln had no authority to suspend the writ independently of the provision of an act of Congress regulating such suspension, or therefore to authorize persons to be court-martialed in the circumstances existing, *i.e.*, with the regular courts in operation; and a majority of the justices contended that not even Congress could have conferred authority so to act in the face of those circumstances. In connection with his various suspensions of the writ, Lincoln said that he believed them legal, but that in any case it was better to violate one legal provision of the constitution than to permit collapse of the entire national structure on which our legal system rested.

[1] In July, 1942, seven Nazi saboteurs, apprehended after entering the country surreptitiously, and being, by presidential direction, brought to trial before a special military commission, appealed to the federal Supreme Court for a ruling entitling them to writs of *habeas corpus* opening the way for substitution of civilian trials. The Court, however, held unanimously (Justice Murphy not participating) that the president had acted within his proper powers and denied the appeal. Attorney-General Biddle successfully contended that the accused were enemy combatants properly charged with violating the laws of war, and therefore not entitled to the procedural protections applying to ordinary criminals. See R. E. Cushman, "The Case of the Nazi Saboteurs," *Amer. Polit. Sci. Rev.*, XXXVI, 1082-1091 (Dec., 1942); E. S. Corwin, *Total War and the Constitution* (New York, 1947), 117-121.

[2] Art. III, § 2, cl. 3, and Amendments VI and VII.

[3] Patton *v.* United States, 281 U. S. 276 (1930). Cf. J. A. Grant, "Felony Trials Without a Jury," *Amer. Polit. Sci. Rev.*, XXV, 980-995 (Nov., 1931).

[4] Among various cases, Thiel *v.* Southern Pacific Co., 328 U. S. 217 (1946)

shall not be violated;" and state constitutions commonly say much the same thing. The language employed suggests that there are searches and seizures which are *reasonable;* and the Fourth Amendment goes on to define them as being such as are conducted in pursuance of warrants (1) issued "upon probable cause, supported by oath or affirmation," and (2) "particularly describing the place to be searched and the persons or things to be seized." The Supreme Court has, however, recognized situations in which the police may legitimately make searches and seizures without a warrant. Thus if it is known or thought probable that a person guilty of a felony or breach of the peace has taken refuge in a certain house, officers of the law may go in after him without waiting for written authority. Likewise, if a search is to be made of a boat, automobile, airplane, or other vehicle which could take advantage of delay in order to move out of the officers' reach, a warrant is held to be unnecessary.[1]

Underlying and cementing together the long list of judicial guarantees enumerated is that of "due process of law." The Fifth Amendment to the federal constitution forbids that under the operation of the national government any person shall be "deprived of life, liberty, or property" without due process; in 1868 the Fourteenth Amendment imposed the same general restriction upon the states [2]—a restriction which in point of fact is also laid upon themselves by all of the states in their own constitutions. Operating as a limitation equally upon executive, administrative, legislative, and judicial branches of government on every level, due process has therefore become a paladium of individual and corporate rights as against all governmental authority in the country. *(e) Due process of law*

---

[1] For a famous prohibition case in which the Supreme Court sustained the admission of evidence obtained surreptitiously by "wire-tapping," see Olmstead *v.* United States, 277 U. S. 438 (1928). The Federal Communications Act of 1934 forbids any person, without authorization by the sender, to intercept and divulge any communication; and in Nardone *v.* United States, 302 U. S. 379 (1937), the Court held that the restriction applies equally to public officers and to private individuals. In a number of later cases, the Court has held evidence obtained by wire-tapping (or its equivalent) admissible, so long as the *sender* suffers no disadvantage. In 1943, the restraints upon the use against an accused person of evidence secured by questionable methods on the part of law-enforcement officers seemed to be tightened by decisions in Anderson *v.* United States, 318 U. S. 350 (1943), and McNabb *v.* United States, 319 U. S. 41 (1943). On the other hand, a five-to-four decision of 1947, in the case of Harris *v.* United States (67 Sup. Ct. 1098) upheld a conviction based upon evidence obtained without authority of a search warrant, notwithstanding that extenuating circumstances such as those indicated above were not involved. Agents of the F. B. I., while unsuccessfully ransacking the defendant's apartment in Oklahoma City for two stolen cancelled checks thought to have been used in a fraud scheme had accidentally come upon draft classification notices and draft registration certificates unlawfully in the defendant's possession. Duly armed with a warrant in connection with the checks, the searchers of course had none relating to the draft documents. Notwithstanding, however, that there was no connection between the two matters, the defendant was convicted in a federal district court for possession of the documents; and his conviction, resisted on the ground of unreasonable search and seizure, was sustained, not only in the circuit court of appeals, but in the Supreme Court as well.

[2] With narrower content, however, in that whereas due process as applied to the federal government includes the criminal procedures specified in the Fifth and Sixth Amendments, *e.g.,* indictment by grand jury and jury trial, as applied to the states it does not—although, in an over-all way, it *does* require "fair trial."

The term
nowhere
fully
defined
Notwithstanding its great significance, the term has never been fully and conclusively defined. Broadly equivalent to the "law of the land" as guaranteed in *Magna Carta* and to the "rule of law" upon which English jurists have traditionally placed the utmost stress, it has, like those phrases, been subject to steadily broadening and deepening interpretation. Certainly the constitutions do not fix its bounds, and no more do the courts. Efforts to apply it to the multifold actions and relationships of life have given rise to a stupendous amount of litigation and to an unending stream of judicial decisions; more cases find their way into the courts involving the due process clause than any other provision of the federal constitution. But, though sometimes pressed to do so, the judges have never cared—or dared—to try to frame any complete definition. Rather, they have preferred, as the highest federal tribunal has said, that "the full meaning of the term should be gradually ascertained by the process of inclusion and exclusion in the course of decisions in cases as they arise." [1]

No other policy would indeed have been feasible, because the endless shadings taken on by the rule as new situations bring it into play would make it impossible to frame a definition that would long have any claim to exactness, and because the interests of justice and social well-being demand that this rule, more than any other, be kept flexible and adaptable. Happily for the courts, due-process questions usually come to them in such form as to call for only a negative sort of definition. An individual or a corporation objects to some administrative or legal action on the ground that deprivation or loss has been suffered through due process not being observed; and the thing that the court is called upon to determine is, not the scope of due process in general, but simply whether the action in question was or was not, so far as it went, in accordance with due process. In other words, the courts say that *this* is due process and that the *other* is not, but leave the way open to make further rulings subsequently in either direction.

Due
process
and
proce-
dural
rights
On looking into the ways in which the term has actually been applied, one finds that sometimes it is invoked in defense of rights of a procedural character and at other times in behalf of those that are by nature substantive. In earlier days, it was thought applicable (as in England) to procedural matters only. The Supreme Court so construed it in 1856,[2] and the view stood until the last quarter of the century, when decisions of the same tribunal turned it also to the defense of substantive rights, giving it a scope and importance which it had never before possessed. Quite apart from due process, the rights of a person accused of crime are, as we have seen, rather extensively protected by guarantees such as those of indictment by grand jury, trial by petit jury, and exemption from self-incrimination. Contrary to what might be supposed, due process does

---

[1] Twining *v.* New Jersey, 211 U. S. 78 (1908).
[2] Murray's Lessee *v.* Hoboken Land and Improvement Co., 18 Howard 272

not directly confirm or strengthen these particular rights. What it does is rather to require, on even more fundamental lines, that an accused person be given a speedy, public, and *fair* trial before a court of proper jurisdiction, with opportunity to confront the witnesses against him, to have the assistance of counsel, and to secure favorable evidence by compulsory process. If in a given circumstance, this means jury trial, due process requires it; if the end can better be attained by some other procedure, due process does not insist upon a jury.[1] In civil cases, the situation is in principle the same: due process requires merely (but of course this is the nub of the matter) a regular proceeding before a proper court, with a fair hearing for both parties.

It was, however, when due process ceased to be a weapon merely against arbitrary and unfair judicial procedure and was turned to the curbing of arbitrary and unfair governmental action of any kind that the rule came into its own. As indicated above, the change occurred during the closing decades of the nineteenth century, in a period during which the states were vigorously meeting new conditions and problems (arising from rapid expansion of their industrial life) with drastic regulation of business, trade, and labor, and when disapproval or downright fear of what was happening gradually swung the courts to the view that the principle of due process might properly be invoked as a norm or test for determining the validity of the acts in question. Under the due process clause of the recently adopted Fourteenth Amendment, the police power of the states came in for rigorous restraint, and simultaneously the corresponding clause of the Fifth Amendment was interpreted afresh to enable new restrictions to be placed upon federal power as wielded through legislation by Congress. *Due process and substantive rights*

For many years now, there have been plenty of due process cases turning on the question of whether a given act of Congress deprives an individual or corporation of life, liberty, or property—freedom of person, liberty of contract, or what not—in a manner to be construed as violating due process. But the principal field in which the rule operates today is that occupied by the police power of the states; in that area, cases and decisions involving applications of it are legion. The matter is complicated by the fact that, just as the courts refuse to attempt any general definition of "due process," so they find it impracticable to mark out any very definite boundaries for the police power, preferring, rather, to decide when controversy arises whether any given act is to be construed as coming within the scope of that power. Under commonest usage, however, the police power is viewed as including all regulative authority exercised *Due process and the police power of the states*

[1] In the case of Powell *v.* State of Alabama (287 U. S. 45), the Supreme Court, in 1932, held for the first time that the due process clause guarantees the defendant in a criminal proceeding the right to counsel and an opportunity to prepare for trial. This was the famous Scottsboro (Ala.) case, in which the Court reversed a lower tribunal that had convicted and sentenced to death eight Negro youths within a week after their arrest for rape, and notwithstanding that they entirely lacked counsel prepared to defend them.

for the protection and promotion of public health, safety, morals, order, convenience, and general welfare—in short, authority to restrict and control individual and corporate freedom of action and use of property, in the interest of the public well-being. When, however, a state, in pursuance of this residual and basic authority, undertakes to regulate the rates and services of public utility corporations, or to protect the health of women and children by restricting the number of hours a week that they may lawfully be employed in a factory, or to restrain citizens from making use of their property in ways considered deleterious to public health or morals, it is not unlikely to find itself accused of having deprived individuals or corporations of liberty or property, or both, without due process of law; and, a test case being brought, it falls to the courts to determine whether or not the contention is well founded. Manifestly, great latitude of judgment is open to the judicial authorities in handling cases of this type. Due process is nowhere precisely defined; the same is true of the police power; and the variety of considerations that will have to be taken into account is simply limitless. In consequence, there is wide opportunity for the personal opinions, susceptibilities, and social philosophies of the judges to influence the decisions rendered, and a court today may take a position diametrically opposite to that taken by it at an earlier time. From having originally been simply the modes of procedure which were *due* at common law, due process of law has come to mean, in effect, whatever has the approval of the Supreme Court as reasonable (regardless of what a legislature may think about it). And enforcing it becomes not merely a matter of settling disputes at law, but a matter as well—and a most important one—of fixing public policy.[1]

Varying attitudes of the Supreme Court

For several decades, the Supreme Court—although sometimes handing down decisions both unexpected and difficult to harmonize with previous ones in due process cases—was inclined to hold the states within narrower bounds in the exercise of their police power than they would have observed of their own accord. Thus, when the legislature of New York, in 1897, passed an act forbidding employees to work in bake-shops more than sixty hours a week or ten hours a day, a "conservative" Court held the provision unconstitutional, on the ground that it was an "unreasonable, unnecessary, and arbitrary interference with the right and liberty of the individual to contract in relation to labor." [2] This "right and liberty," it was considered, had been taken away in violation of due process; although, twelve years later, an Oregon law restricting the hours of labor in manufacturing establishments to ten, and applying to both sexes, was upheld

[1] "Originally," writes Professor E. S. Corwin, " 'due process of law' meant simply the modes of *procedure* which are due at the common law....Today, 'due process of law' means 'reasonable' law, or 'reasonable' procedure, that is to say, what a majority of the Supreme Court find to be *reasonable* in some or other sense of that extremely elastic term. In other words, it means, in effect, *the approval of the Supreme Court;* but...this approval will sometimes be extended on easier terms than at others." *The Constitution and What It Means Today* (10th ed., Princeton, N. J., 1948), 170.

[2] Lochner *v.* New York, 198 U. S. 45 (1905).

by a Court that had been "liberalized." [1] Again, when the legislature of Kansas sought to make it a misdemeanor for an employer to threaten to discharge an employee because he was a member of a trade union, the Court pronounced the statute invalid.[2] When Arizona undertook to forbid the use (under certain circumstances) of injunctions in connection with labor disputes, that measure also was overthrown.[3] An Oregon minimum-wage law for women was sustained in 1917 only by the narrowest possible margin, *i.e.*, a four-to-four division of the court; [4] and a similar law enacted by Congress for the District of Columbia was set aside as "unreasonable" and "arbitrary" in 1923.[5] In 1932, an Oklahoma statute requiring those engaged in the manufacture, sale, and distribution of ice to obtain a state license was overthrown; [6] although two years later a New York statute undertaking to establish a milk-control board with power to fix prices of milk charged by stores to customers was upheld.[7]

Manifestly, in applying the due-process principle to state legislation— and federal legislation as well—the Court wields tremendous power over social and economic policy (Senator William E. Borah once termed it "the economic dictator of the United States"); and dissatisfaction with the prevailingly conservative temper displayed by the judges in ruling on what a state might and might not do was long a principal motivation of popular demand for curbing the tribunal's authority. Appointment of a number of younger and more liberal justices by President Franklin D. Roosevelt led, however, to a different attitude; and nowadays the policy functions of both nation and states are construed with a breadth and tolerance rendering due process as a substantive restriction on government control of property far weaker than it used to be, and imparting a wholly new slant to our constitutional law. As a single illustration may be mentioned the Court's reversal, in 1937, of its 1923 decision on minimum-wage legislation for women.[8]

Rights of Property

Civil rights extend to the protection of property interests as well as of personal freedom, and in some of the constitutional provisions the two

---

[1] Bunting *v.* Oregon, 243 U. S. 426 (1917).

[2] Coppage *v.* Kansas, 236 U. S. 1 (1915). Similar laws of fourteen other states were made void by this same decision.

[3] Truax *v.* Corrigan, 257 U. S. 312 (1921).

[4] Stettler *v.* O'Hara, 243 U. S. 629 (1917).

[5] Adkins *v.* The Children's Hospital, 261 U. S. 525 (1923).

[6] New State Ice Co. *v.* Liebman, 285 U. S. 262 (1932).

[7] Nebbia *v.* New York, 291 U. S. 502 (1934).

[8] West Coast Hotel *v.* Parrish, 300 U. S. 379. Cf. Highland Farms Dairy *v.* Agnew, 300 U. S. 608 (1937); Olsen *v.* Nebraska, 313 U. S. 236 (1941). For fuller discussions of due process, see J. M. Mathews, *The American Constitutional System* (2nd ed.), Chaps. xxvi-xxx, and other works cited on pp. 176-177 below; and on the weakening of substantive due process as a limitation upon social legislation, taxation, rate-making, and regulatory action generally, R. J. Harris, "Due Process of Law," *Amer. Polit. Sci. Rev.*, XLII, 32-42 (Feb., 1948).

are bracketed together. Due process, for example, applies to deprivation of property no less than to that of life and liberty; so likewise do the guarantees pertaining to interstate citizenship. State constitutions abound in provisions relating mainly or solely to property rights; and the national constitution, leaving the states generally free to say what constitutes property,[1] simply throws around it, as severally defined by them, a further shield of protective stipulations.

Limitations upon the power to take private property:

Government everywhere has power to take private property from individuals and corporations; otherwise it would have no adequate means of subsistence. As a rule, it takes property (usually in the form of money) by procedures constituting one form or another of taxation. Sometimes, however, it finds itself in need of some particular piece of property, *e.g.*, a plot of ground suitable for a public building, and possesses itself of it—irrespective of whether the owner wants to part with it—by virtue of the right of "eminent domain." A word must be said about civil rights as related to each of these procedures.

1. By taxation

The taxing power of both nation and states is broad and undefined. In the case of the states, the national constitution forbids laying imposts or duties on imports or exports except as necessary for the execution of inspection laws, and also the laying of tonnage duties; and judicial construction prohibits the taxing of certain (although no longer all) federal instrumentalities.[2] Otherwise, the states are free, so long as their tax laws and procedures keep within the bounds of due process, equal "privileges and immunities" for the citizens of the United States, and other broad requirements already indicated in the present chapter. Taxation by the national government likewise is subject to any and all limitations that may arise from the operation of due process. In addition, it is expressly restricted by constitutional provision (1) that no tax may be imposed upon articles exported from any state;[3] (2) that all direct taxes (apart from income taxes, if they be regarded as direct) shall be apportioned among the several states in accordance with the respective numbers of their inhabitants;[4] (3) that all indirect taxes, such as customs and excises, shall be uniform—that is, shall fall upon the same kinds and amounts of property with equal weight in all parts of the country;[5] and (4) that no money may be drawn from the public treasury except in pursuance of "appropriations made by law."[6] Whatever comfort the taxpayer may be able to derive from these restrictions he is clearly entitled to, because his property cannot constitutionally be levied upon in violation of any of them.

---

[1] Except that under the Thirteenth Amendment a state may not establish or recognize property in man or man's labor—in other words, legalize slavery or involuntary servitude. It may be added that through its exclusive power to grant patents and copyrights, the national government in effect defines property in inventions and publications.

[2] See pp. 86-90 above.

[3] Art. I, § 9, cl. 5.

[4] Art. I, § 2, cl. 3.

[5] Art. I, § 8, cl. 1.

[6] Art. I, § 9, cl. 7.

The power of eminent domain is one which every government must have. In the absence of constitutional restraints, however, it would be peculiarly liable to abuse: compensation might be altogether inadequate; indeed, it might be denied altogether. Hence, the Fifth Amendment not only forbids private property to be taken by the national government for public use without due process of law, but requires that "just compensation" be rendered; and state constitutions commonly impose the same restrictions (sometimes in a more detailed way) upon state and local governments.[1] To be sure, the courts have usually interpreted eminent-domain clauses very broadly. For example, they uphold the taking of land not only for purposes which are strictly governmental, *e.g.*, the erection of a court house, but for purposes which have any clear relation to governmental functions, *e.g.*, the creation of a park; and they raise no objection to the exercise of the power by railroads or other corporations to which the government has delegated it, provided that such corporations are engaged in a business "affected with a public interest"—provided, too, that the property sought is essential to the corporation's activities, and so long as the same conditions are observed that the government itself would be required to meet.[2]

What is to be regarded as just compensation in any particular instance is likely to be a matter for judicial or administrative determination. The government or corporation will ordinarily make the owner an offer. This is very likely to be refused. Counter-proposals and mutual concessions may lead to an agreement, as in an ordinary sale. But if they do not, the owner can appeal to the courts, which will fix the amount that he may receive and must accept; or the decision may be reached by commissioners or other administrative boards. All that is necessary to meet the requirements of the constitution is that the dissatisfied seller shall have an opportunity to be heard and to present such evidence concerning the value of his property as he may desire to bring forward.[3]

[1] Even if they fail to do so, the due-process clause of the Fourteenth Amendment is sufficient to impose the obligation of compensation. Chicago, B. & Q. Ry. Co. *v.* Chicago (166 U. S. 226, 1897).

[2] Property deemed necessary for national defense can be conscripted, just as men are conscripted, although of course only in pursuance of law. On a requisitioning provision of the National Defense Act of 1916, see p. 813 below.

[3] United States *v.* Jones, 109 U. S. 513 (1883). Condemnation laws of the federal government and of many states permit taking possession of land before the property-owner has actually been paid, under safeguards requiring the condemning government to deposit cash with the court or put up an equivalent bond, so that the property-owner will be protected against any possibility of being unable to get his money. Thereafter, the sum to be paid may be determined by negotiation, or by a jury trial if the property owner so desires. Illinois is one of a number of states requiring a condemning government to refrain from taking possession of land until the sum to be received by the owner has been either fixed by agreement or set by a jury. Finding that under this rule the carrying out of Chicago super-highway projects was being obstructed, the state government in 1947 planned to ask for suitable amending legislation.

Still another form of protection for private property is the prohibition which rests upon the states—although not upon the national government—to "pass any law impairing the obligation of contracts." This matter, however, has been considered in an earlier chapter (see pp. 90-92 above).

REFERENCES

C. A. Beard, *The Republic; Conversations on Fundamentals* (New York, 1943), Chaps. x-xii.

J. M. Mathews, *The American Constitutional System* (2nd ed., New York, 1940), Chaps. xxiii-xxxi.

W. W. Willoughby, *Constitutional Law of the United States* (2nd ed., New York, 1929), III, Chaps. xci-cv.

E. S. Corwin, *Total War and the Constitution* (New York, 1947), Chap. iii.

C. B. Swisher, *The Growth of Constitutional Power of the United States* (Chicago, 1947), Chap. vii.

C. P. Curtis, Jr., *Lions Under the Throne* (Boston, 1947), Chap. xvi.

M. R. Konvitz, *The Constitution and Civil Rights* (New York, 1947). Confined to rights as related to various forms of social and economic discrimination.

R. E. Cushman, *Safeguarding Our Civil Liberties*, Pub. Affairs Pamphlets, No. 43 (New York, 1940).

————, *Our Constitutional Freedoms; Civil Liberties—An American Heritage* (New York, 1944). Basic American Concepts Series.

————, "The Impact of War on the Constitution," in R. E. Cushman *et al.*, *The Impact of the War on America* (Ithaca, N. Y., 1942), Chap. i.

————, "Civil Liberty After the War," *Amer. Polit. Sci. Rev.*, XXXVIII, 1-20 (Feb., 1944).

————, "Civil Liberties," *ibid.*, XLII, 42-52 (Feb., 1948). A review of developments during 1937-47.

E. W. Puttkammer [ed.], *War and the Law* (Chicago, 1944), 17-37.

J. P. Shalloo and D. Young [eds.], "Minority Peoples in a Nation at War," *Annals of Amer. Acad. of Polit. and Soc. Sci.*, CCXXIII (Sept., 1942).

M. Hallgren, *Landscape of Freedom* (New York, 1940).

C. Becker *et al.*, *Safeguarding Civil Liberty Today* (Ithaca, N. Y., 1945).

O. K. Fraenkel, *Our Civil Liberties* (New York, 1944).

H. Vreeland, *Twilight of Individual Liberty* (New York, 1945).

R. K. Carr, *Federal Protection of Civil Rights; Quest for a Sword* (Ithaca, N. Y., 1947).

F. J. Stimson, *The American Constitution as It Protects Private Rights* (New York, 1923).

T. M. Cooley, *Treatise on the Constitutional Limitations Which Rest Upon the Legislative Power of the States* (8th ed., Boston, 1927), Chaps. ix-xiii.

E. Freund, *The Police Power; Public Policy and Constitutional Rights* (Chicago, 1904).

N. B. Lasson, "The History and Development of the Fourth Amendment to the United States Constitution," *Johns Hopkins Univ. Studies in Hist. and Polit. Sci.*, LV, 223-360 (Baltimore, 1937).

H. Brannon, *The Rights and Privileges Guaranteed by the Fourteenth Amendment to the Constitution* (Cincinnati, 1901).

G. T. Stephenson, *Race Distinctions in American Law* (New York, 1910).

C. S. Mangum, *The Legal Status of the Negro* (Chapel Hill, N. C., 1940).

W. Lippmann, *American Inquisitors* (New York, 1928).

————, *The Method of Freedom* (New York, 1934).

Z. Chafee, *Free Speech in the United States* (Cambridge, Mass., 1941).

————, *Government and Mass Communications; A Report from the Commission on Freedom of the Press*, 2 vols. (Chicago, 1947).

W. E. Hocking, *Freedom of the Press; A Framework of Principle* (Chicago, 1947). An essay supplementary to the above Commission's report.

M. L. Ernst, *The First Freedom* (New York, 1946).

F. Thayer, *Legal Control of the Press* (Chicago, 1944).

J. R. Mock, *Censorship 1917* (Princeton, N. J., 1941).

V. Rotnem and F. G. Folsom, Jr., "Recent Restrictions Upon Religious Liberty," *Amer. Polit. Sci. Rev.,* XXXVI, 1053-1068 (Dec., 1942).

H. W. Barber, "Religious Liberty *v.* The Police Power: Jehovah's Witnesses," *ibid.,* XLI, 226-247 (Apr., 1947).

R. J. Harris, "Due Process of Law," *ibid.,* XLII, 32-42 (Feb., 1948). A review of developments during 1937-47.

R. L. Mott, *Due Process of Law* (Indianapolis, 1926).

To Secure These Rights; Report of the President's Committee on Civil Rights (Washington, Govt. Printing Office, 1947).

P. Nichols, *The Law of Eminent Domain,* 3 vols. (2nd ed., Albany, N. Y., 1917).

The Constitution of the United States of America as Amended to January 1, 1938 (70th Cong., 2nd Sess., Sen. Doc. No. 232). Annotation of Amendments I-IX.

Bill of Rights Review (New York). A quarterly journal launched in 1940 under the auspices of the Bill of Rights Committee of the American Bar Association, but discontinued in 1942.

G. H. Fuller [comp.], *A Selected List of References on the Bill of Rights* (Washington, Govt. Printing Office, 1940).

4. INSTRUMENTALITIES OF POPULAR CONTROL

CHAPTER X

THE PEOPLE AS VOTERS

Popular government basic to our system

At a time when popular government was not very widespread over the earth, the founders of this nation dedicated it to the principle of rule by the people; and in days when democracy, under *some* sort of definition, is professed by the adherents of almost every political system the world over (including the Soviet), there are still few if any countries in which the assertion rings more true. Through constitutions freely made and amended, through party organization and elections, and by the force of public opinion, an electorate potentially embracing almost ninety-seven per cent of the adult population creates its own governments, endows them with powers, fixes the limits of their authority, chooses lawmakers and other policy-framing officials,[1] and determines the broad objectives and currents of public action.

Some limitations

To be sure, any one having some acquaintance with American political history, and not altogether blind to what goes on around him, knows that, even among us, the democratic process has its limitations. He is aware, for example, that the federal constitution was put into operation without ever being submitted to a popular vote; that amendments to it have commonly been adopted or rejected by state legislatures acting in the matter without instructions from the people; that presidential candidates sometimes win with only a minority of the popular ballots; that rarely more than seventy per cent, and sometimes hardly more than fifty-five per cent, of the potentially qualified electors go to the polls, even when a president is being elected; that some of our cities (happily far fewer than in the past) are still dominated by bosses, rings, and "interests;" that the fate of many a significant bill in Congress is determined by seniority traditions governing committee chairmanships, by log-rolling maneuvers, lobbying activities, and legislative by-play (including filibustering in the Senate) over which the voters have at least no direct and immediate control. He knows, in short, that if the people rule, they rule a good deal of the time at rather long range and by decidedly roundabout means and processes.[2]

---

[1] As well as numerous officials who, not being policy-determining, might better be appointed rather than elected. All told, the people elect the president and vice-president, 531 members of Congress, 10,000 state legislators and officers, 54,000 county officers, 66,000 city councillors and officers, and upwards of 750,000 town, school, and miscellaneous officers—a total of some 880,500.

[2] C. A. Beard, "The Fiction of Majority Rule," *Atlantic Mo.*, CXL, 831-836 (Dec., 1927); J. Dickinson, "Democratic Realities and Democratic Dogma," *Amer. Polit. Sci. Rev.*, XXIV, 283-309 (May, 1930).

Nevertheless, at bottom, our profession of popular rule is valid. Ours *is* a government of the people, in the sense that (1) the great bulk of adult citizens, men and women, have the ballot, at least potentially, (2) in general, voters are free from intimidation by public authorities and may choose (as the voter cannot, for example, in Soviet Russia) between different candidates and among different political programs, and (3) the entire political order is so set up as to make the citizenry the supreme and final authority, with power not only as a matter of law, but in practical fact, to make the government what they want it to be and to compel it, at least eventually, to do what they want it to do. All this is equally true whether one is thinking of the national government alone or of the governments of the states and their political subdivisions as well; and we shall be better equipped to study these different governments as going concerns if we first bring somewhat fully into view the groundwork of popular control on which they rest. Four matters, chiefly, call for attention: (1) the composition and characteristics of the electorate, (2) the organization of the electorate in political parties, (3) the influence of non-party organizations and of public opinion, and (4) the nomination and election of candidates for public office.

Yet a mental funda- reality

Basis and Nature of the Suffrage

By the electorate, we mean, of course, those of the people who are entitled to vote. The matter, however, is less simple than it sounds, because under our federal system every one of the forty-eight states is left largely free to adopt its own suffrage regulations, including whatever age, residence, tax-paying, literacy, or other qualifications it may care to prescribe; in other words, every state, through provisions written into its constitution, creates its own particular electorate. To be sure, this freedom is not quite absolute; for the Fifteenth and Nineteenth Amendments to the federal constitution forbid a state (or the United States) to deny or abridge the "right" of citizens of the United States to vote on account of (a) race, color, or previous condition of servitude, or (b) sex. But to this extent only is the suffrage regulated on a uniform, nation-wide basis.[1] The federal constitution confers the privilege of voting on no one; it merely stipulates certain grounds on which people otherwise qualified shall not be denied the privilege—with the result that the electorate for national purposes becomes simply the aggregate, or sum total, of the more or less differing electorates maintained in the individual states. Any one who can vote for a member of the "most numerous branch" (*i.e.*, the lower house) of his state legislature can vote also for the only members of the national government who obtain their positions by popular election, namely, representatives, senators, and (in effect) the president and

The con- stitutional aspect

---

[1] A clause of the Fourteenth Amendment penalizing the states for abridging the suffrage except for participation in rebellion or other crime has bearing on the matter, but has never been enforced. See pp. 195-196 below.

vice-president,[1] and also commonly (by state regulation) for officers of his county, city, town, or village as well.

The suf-
frage a
<u>privilege,</u>
not a
rightNotwithstanding that the constitutional amendments cited refer to the "right" to vote, the suffrage is to be regarded as not properly a right but rather a privilege. It is, no doubt, a right—a *legal* right—for those who have been endowed with it—so long as they do not disqualify themselves by, for example, committing a crime or going insane. But there is no inherent right to be so endowed. To be sure, people urging an extension of the suffrage in one direction or another have always been prone to picture voting as a natural, if not also a constitutional, right. The argument was heard repeatedly during the long campaign for the enfranchisement of women. A sober view of the matter, however, suggests that, in the last analysis, who may vote and who may not is properly to be determined by considerations of general policy and expediency, and not on the theory that any particular class or classes of the people have an inherent right to be included. Even citizenship, as our courts have declared repeatedly, carries with it no such right.[2] To be sure, no state now allows non-citizens to vote. But children are citizens; and no one proposes that they be made voters.

Historical Development

Disap-
pearance
of prop-
erty and
religious
qualifi-
cationsThe history of the suffrage, particularly in the older states, has been in the main a record of progressive extension of voting privileges to new groups of people—non-property-holders, small taxpayers, ex-slaves, women—although interpersed with extensions have also been contractions arising from the introduction of new tests, as for example that of literacy. Originally, voting was confined almost entirely to male property-holders, with occasionally a religious test in addition. The period from 1815 to the Civil War, however, saw property qualifications lowered and finally to all intents and purposes abandoned, taxpaying requirements given up in all but a few states, religious tests abolished, and in many states aliens somewhat imprudently allowed to become voters as soon as they declared their intention to be naturalized. Influenced by the "Know-Nothing" movement, Connecticut in 1855 and Massachusetts in 1857 adopted reading and writing tests designed to disqualify the illiterate foreign-born. Nevertheless, by 1860 most states had arrived at what may fairly be termed manhood suffrage for whites.

Enfran-
chisement
of Ne-
groesSince the Civil War, the suffrage has been broadened mainly by the enfranchisement of Negroes and of women. A few Negroes voted in certain Northern states (mainly in New England) before 1860. General

[1] This plan is prescribed for the choice of representatives by Art. I, § 2, cl. 1, of the federal constitution; for that of senators, by the Seventeenth Amendment; and for that of presidential electors (regarded as state officers), by state constitutional or statutory provisions.

[2] United States *v.* Anthony, 24 Fed. Cases No. 14459; Miner *v.* Happersett, 21 Wallace 162. These decisions were rendered, in 1873 and 1874, in cases in which the question at issue was the right of women as *citizens* to vote.

enfranchisement of people of color came only, however, as a result of new state constitutions and laws adopted, under pressure from the radical Republican majority in Congress, during the era of Reconstruction; and voting privileges for ex-slaves and their descendants, as indeed for Negroes in every part of the country, were supposed to be guaranteed for all time by the Fifteenth Amendment.

Enfranchisement of women

Demand for the enfranchisement of women was heard as early as the Jacksonian era, and here and there it was pressed rather vigorously during the later stages of the Abolition movement. No legislature or constitutional convention, however, in this period gave serious attention to the petitions presented on the subject; if noticed at all, they evoked only ridicule. After the Civil War, the situation changed. The Negro had been enfranchised; nearly all men were voters; and the advocates of votes for women could no longer be simply laughed out of court. The first notable triumph of the cause was in Wyoming, where in 1869 women were given the privilege of voting for territorial officers on the same terms as men.[1] On being admitted to the Union in 1890, this territory continued its woman suffrage arrangements; and before the close of the century Colorado, Idaho, and Utah also became equal suffrage states. The movement then slackened. But about 1906 it gathered fresh momentum, and in five years (1910-14) the number of equal suffrage states mounted to eleven.[2]

Meanwhile the suffragists turned to the larger objective of a general nation-wide enfranchisement. To this end, some urged amendment of the national constitution so as to require a state to submit the question of woman suffrage to its electorate on petition of as few as eight per cent of the voters. Others, considering that this "states' rights" method was too slow and uncertain, threw their support to the "Susan B. Anthony amendment" (first brought forward in 1869), forbidding the United States or any state to withhold the ballot on account of sex. The movement finally centered upon this latter plan; and a few years of vigorous agitation (dramatized at one stage by picketing of the White House because President Wilson continued to favor state action only—though in the end he changed his position) brought complete success. The Nineteenth Amendment, embodying the Susan B. Anthony proposal, was adopted by Congress in 1919 and ratified by the requisite three-fourths of the states during the next fourteen months. Proclaimed August 26, 1920, it met its first test at the national and state elections of the following November.[3]

[1] Kentucky in 1838 and Kansas in 1861 began permitting women to vote in school elections. Other states gradually took similar action, and in 1887 Kansas conferred full municipal suffrage.

[2] In addition to the four states named, Washington (1910), California (1911), Arizona (1912), Kansas (1912), Oregon (1912), Montana (1914), and Nevada (1914). In Illinois (1913), women were given the right to vote at elections to all offices within the control of the legislature, including most local offices, a few state offices, and the office of presidential elector.

[3] For good brief accounts of the adoption of the amendment, see C. B. Swisher,

Women's
part in
the politi-
cal life
of the
nation

The women of the entire country—or such of them as possess the necessary age and other qualifications—have thus had the suffrage a little over a quarter of a century. It would be interesting to know precisely how they have voted during this time, and to what extent they have influenced electoral results. Unfortunately, such information is not to be had; for while an industrious person can get significant information on relative degrees of political interest by counting the numbers of men and women, in any electoral area, whose names appear on the lists of registered voters, and even the numbers of those who present themselves at the polls at a given election, nowhere are the ballots cast by women and by men tabulated separately.[1] Such evidence as exists, however, indicates that, by and large, women voters are not very different from men voters, and that therefore they have not much changed the over-all quality of the electorate. Some are vigilant and intelligent, many are uninformed and apathetic; some make up their own minds, others merely do as a ward leader, a member of their family, or a clergyman, tells them; many go to the polls voluntarily and with scrupulous regularity, many go but seldom and only when pressed to do so, and many do not go at all.[2] In no part of the country does it appear that they have been responsible for any change in the relative strength of the different parties. Suffrage for women is sound in principle, and entirely correct as a matter of policy, but it has not worked, and should never have been expected to work, a revolution.

Participation of women has, however, added some new and interesting features to the political life of the nation. It has more than doubled the potential electorate and considerably increased the cost of registering voters, carrying on campaigns, and conducting elections. In party conventions, on party committees, and in the rough and tumble of electoral campaigns, women increasingly share almost every form of activity engaged in by men.[3] Laws (particularly relating to social reform) have

---

American Constitutional Development (Boston, 1943), 691-703, and E. M. Sait, *American Parties and Elections* (3rd ed., New York, 1942), 76-96.

[1] An ingenious attempt to study the matter on the basis of a single municipal election (in Portland, Oregon, in 1914) is reported in W. F. Ogburn and I. Goltra, "How Women Vote," *Polit. Sci. Quar.*, XXXIV, 413-433 (Sept., 1919).

[2] In the presidential election of 1920, women, it was estimated, cast about twenty-five per cent of the total vote (they were enfranchised too late to be registered in some states). In the next five presidential elections, their estimated vote varied between thirty-five and forty-three per cent of the total. During World War II, the country's population, both male and female, was heavily dislocated, but of course the male portion far more than the female; and notwithstanding arrangements for soldier voting, the number of women in a position to vote considerably exceeded that of men so situated. In the congressional elections of 1942, women cast an estimated fifty-three per cent of the ballots. In advance of the presidential election of 1944, some women leaders predicted that the female vote would run as high as sixty per cent of the total. No exact statistics will ever be available, but the actual figure was considerably lower—probably not greatly in excess of fifty per cent. Quite apart from wartime conditions, women of voting age outnumber men by half a million or more.

[3] Since soon after their enfranchisement, women have been represented equally with men in the national committees of the two major parties, and in numerous

been enacted, in Congress and especially in state legislatures, that might not have prevailed without the driving influence supplied by women— even though not necessarily by women *as voters*. In addition to appointment to sundry administrative posts, both in the states and at Washington,[1] women have been elected to high public offices, including two governorships (in Texas in 1924 and 1928 and Wyoming in 1924) and a United States senatorship (in Arkansas) in 1932 [2]—although the rather remote dates mentioned indicate no present trend toward increased service on such levels, and women seem generally to expect, if not to prefer, to vote for men. Since 1930, from five to nine members of the national House of Representatives have been women (nine were elected in 1944 and seven in 1946),[3] and the 1946 elections brought a total of approximately two hundred women into state legislatures, well distributed over the country except in the South. The country is dotted with non-partisan state and local leagues of women voters, linked up since 1918 in an active and influential national organization with some 62,000 members—known today as the League of Women Voters of the United States—and concerned primarily with educating women (and incidentally men also) to vote with intelligence and discrimination, and with securing administrative reforms and remedial legislation, national, state, and local. A National Woman's party is working for full legal equality of women with men, to be attained through an "equal rights" amendment to the national constitution, followed by the requisite federal and state legislation.[4]

state and local committees as well. In the Republican national convention of 1944, there were 99 women delegates and 264 women alternates; in the Democratic convention, 174 women delegates and 332 women alternates; and in both conventions women were represented equally with men on committees—in the Democratic convention, on all major committees, and in the Republican, on the committee on platform and resolutions. See M. J. Fisher and B. Whitehead, "Women and National Party Organization," *Amer. Polit. Sci. Rev.*, XXXVIII, 895-903 (Oct., 1944).

[1] In 1933, Miss Frances Perkins, of New York, became the first woman to serve as head of a federal executive department (*i.e.*, Labor), with of course a seat in the cabinet. In the same year, Mrs. Ruth Bryan Owen, as minister to Denmark, became the first woman to be sent as an envoy by the United States to a foreign nation. A few women are serving as chiefs or directors of bureaus in the executive departments or other establishments at Washington, *e.g.*, the Women's Bureau in the Department of Labor and the Children's Bureau in the Social Security Administration; and a few others are members of agencies such as the Civil Service Commission. There is also one woman federal circuit judge. On women in the federal civil service, see p. 492 below.

[2] Three women have held senatorships for brief periods by virtue of temporary appointment.

[3] A. Paxton, *Women in Congress* (Richmond, Va., 1945), unfortunately covering only superficially a topic inviting careful study.

[4] See p. 51 above. Although calling itself a "party," the organization does not put candidates in the field and is really non-partisan. It was the chief proponent of an act of Congress which in 1934 established complete equality of the sexes in matters relating to citizenship (see p. 146 above).

For a sober appraisal of the rôle of women in government and politics, see E. M. Sait, *American Parties and Elections*, 96-106; and cf. C. C. Catt and N. R. Shuler, *Women Suffrage and Politics* (2nd ed., New York, 1926). Conflicting views are presented in J. G. Ross [pseud.], "Ladies in Politics," *Forum*, XCVI, 209-215 (Nov., 1936), and E. R. Richardson, "Women's Rise to Power," *ibid.*, XCVII, 28-32 (Jan., 1937). Informative pamphlets include L. E. McMillin, *Women in the Federal Service* (3rd ed., U. S. Civil Service Commission, 1941); *Women in the Congress of the*

The Suffrage Today

General
qualifica-
tions:
age,
citizen-
ship,
residence

Looking over the electoral systems of the several states at the present time—under which nearly sixty-five per cent of the total population can qualify to vote, as compared with only six per cent during the Revolutionary period—one notes suffrage qualifications that are found in all states and others that are encountered only here and there. Three that are universal and basic have to do with age, citizenship, and residence.[1] Until lately, the voting age in this country was uniformly twenty-one; it is still so except (1) in Georgia, where, by constitutional amendment, it was reduced in 1943 to eighteen, and (2) in South Carolina, where, after the regular primary law was repealed in 1944, the Democrats organized their own "private" primary system and fixed the voting age at eighteen.[2] The reasons assigned by Georgia's governor for the change in that state included the "need of the body politic for the fresh viewpoint of youth" and the gain to accrue to young people from acquiring active political experience.[3] Transcending these considerations in the minds of a good many people, especially in wartime, was, however, the thought that if eighteen-year-olds were mature enough to wear their country's uniform (to say nothing of teaching, engaging in business, and making legal contracts), they were mature enough also to be permitted some voice in determining the country's policies. And it is not surprising that proposals for lowering the voting age to eighteen were brought forward during 1943 in the legislatures of no fewer than thirty states (actually passing one house of the legislature in Arkansas, New York, and Wisconsin), or that three or four constitutional amendments aimed at making the plan nation-wide attracted some attention in Congress. No action, however, resulted, and since the war interest in the matter has slackened. One argument, among others, sometimes advanced against the plan is that among people already enfranchised, the age group most guilty of neglecting to vote is that between twenty-one and thirty. There are,

---

U. S. (Public Affairs Information Service, 1940). Cf. M. J. Fisher and B. Whitehead, "Women and National Party Organization," cited above.

[1] The requirement that the voter be registered might seem to belong in the list. Registration, however, is not strictly a "qualification," but rather only a means of compiling and maintaining accurate voting lists. See pp. 240-241 below.

Certain categories of people are, of course, almost everywhere debarred, *e.g.,* persons convicted of felony or other crime and inmates of asylums for the feeble-minded and insane; and in various states offenses against the election laws (*e.g.,* bribery), malfeasance in office, and vagrancy or pauperism are further grounds for debarment. The Council of State Governments is authority for the assertion that, in one state or another, the privilege of voting can be denied for "any one of fifty or more reasons," with an average of six or seven per state. A foolish demand from some conservative quarters during the worst years of the depression of the thirties that *all* persons on relief be debarred—on a nation-wide basis—did not prevail.

[2] By state law, the voting age for *elections* in South Carolina is still twenty-one. Since, however, in a one-party state nomination is equivalent to election, the reduced voting age applies in the only contests that count.

[3] E. G. Arnall, "Admitting Youth to Citizenship" (*sic*), *State Government,* **XVI,** 203-204 (Oct., 1943).

indeed, people who would raise rather than lower the prevailing age qualification, on the ground that society and government have grown so complex that voters need even greater maturity than in the past.[1]

Since Arkansas fell into line in 1926, citizenship is everywhere a prerequisite for voting, even though as a result of the uncertainties sometimes surrounding that status, a good many non-citizens actually contrive to visit the polls. The commonest requirement relating to residence is that the voter shall have lived in the state at least one year, some stipulated portion of which (frequently three or six months) must have been spent in the county, and some briefer portion (sometimes not more than ten days) in the district in which one's ballot is to be cast.[2] No one may vote in a given election in more than one place; and this place must be the voter's legal residence, however little of his time he may actually spend there.

Taxpaying—once a widely prevalent qualification—has been generally discarded as such except in the South, where payment of a poll tax of one or two dollars annually, and by a specified date, is required of the voter in seven states,[3] partly in aid of school or other special funds, but also with a view to keeping down the Negro and "poor white" vote.[4] In six additional states, some kind of tax qualification applies to persons who vote on bond issues or special assessments, but not to voters in general elections.[5]

More special qualifications: 1. Payment of taxes

In earlier times, educational, or "literacy," qualifications were uncommon. Today, however, they are in use, in some form, in nineteen states (including seven in the solid South and four in New England), and are authorized by constitutional provision in two or three others where the legislature has not yet seen fit to introduce them.[6] Indeed, educational

2. Literacy

[1] "Should the Legal Voting Age Be Reduced to Eighteen Years? Pro and Con" [Symposium], *Cong. Digest*, XXIII, 193-222 (Aug.-Sept., 1944); F. L. Burdette, "Lowering the Voting Age in Georgia," *So. Atlant. Quar.*, XLIV, 300-307 (July, 1945); J. E. Johnsen, *Lowering the Voting Age* (New York, 1944).

[2] For a complete tabular view of residence requirements, see *The Book of the States, 1945-1946*, 88-89; also W. B. Graves, *American State Government* (3rd ed., New York, 1946), 122. The "model state constitution" recommended by the National Municipal League provides for residence in the state for at least one year preceding an election, in the county for the last ninety days of the period, and in the election district for the last thirty days. At all elections, residence requirements operate to bar many people from the polls, especially non-home-owners moving about in quest of work. But they are necessary as safeguards against the importation of "floaters" into districts to turn the electoral tide.

[3] Alabama, Arkansas, Mississippi, South Carolina, Tennessee, Texas, and Virginia. Early in 1943, the legislature of Tennessee repealed the half-century-old poll-tax law of that state, but a few months later the state supreme court held the act unconstitutional. In as many as twelve states (including some Northern ones), the constitution either levies such a tax or requires one to be levied; but in some the tax is not made a qualification for voting. Such a tax is constitutionally forbidden in only four states.

[4] See pp. 192-193 below.

[5] In Mississippi, all property taxes must have been paid; and ownership of property worth three hundred dollars and payment of taxes on it is an alternative to literacy in Alabama and South Carolina.

[6] In about a dozen additional states, there is an indirect literacy test in the sense that no provision is made for assistance to illiterates in casting ballots. Most of the

qualifications may be said, broadly, to have succeeded to the position once held by property qualifications, although, popular education having attained its present level, they operate to debar a far smaller proportion of the people. In three states, the test is confined to ability to read in English (commonly a few lines of the national or state constitution); in all others, it covers also ability to write—though in five instances ability to sign one's name suffices. Applied usually at the time of registration, the test may be conducted perfunctorily, or even perverted, by careless or scheming registration officials;[1] and a far better arrangement is one introduced in New York (in pursuance of a constitutional amendment adopted in 1921) under which reading, interpreting, and writing tests for first voters—planned by a group of educational psychologists to approximate the attainments of a sixth-grade pupil in the public schools—are prepared and administered throughout the state every year, not by registration or election officials, but by the state educational department.[2] Assuming honest administration, there is much to be said for the principle of the literacy test. The electorate having now been expanded almost as far as possible (except perhaps for lowering the age qualification), the next step would seem to be to "trim it at the edges" by eliminating the least fit. Ascertainment that a citizen can read and write no more guarantees that he will always vote wisely than testing an applicant for an automobile driver's license insures that he will invariably manage his car with safety for himself and others. But it is as effective a means as we have of debarring people who, by and large, are most likely to be unfit. And while at first glance the plan might seem undemocratic, and consequently out of harmony with American principles,[3] the fact that nearly all of the states now make it possible for practically any man or woman, even of low intelligence, to receive an elementary education without cost—in evening schools, if in no other way—relieves it of any such opprobrium. Even though it might be difficult to prove that the quality of government is any higher where literacy tests prevail than where they

---

nineteen states referred to make literacy an absolute qualification, but in some (mainly in the South) it is insisted upon only if some tax or other alternative qualification cannot be met.

[1] J. H. Pollack, "Literacy Tests: Southern Style," *Amer. Mercury*, LXIV, 590–594 (May, 1947).

[2] Only those first voters are required to submit themselves to examination (by designated school teachers, and in school buildings) who cannot present as proof of literacy a certificate showing completion of the sixth grade in a school (or second year in an evening school) in which English is the language of instruction. For all purposes of the law, "literacy" means ability to read a paragraph or two of fairly simple English and to answer in writing questions designed to show some comprehension of what has been read, the whole procedure occupying about five minutes. Introduction of the literacy test greatly stimulated the interest of the foreign-born in evening-school instruction. Women are slower to submit themselves to the test than are men, but are more successful in passing it—the proportion of failures, all told, being usually about ten per cent.

[3] Practical politicians often make much of this, arguing that it is unjust to exclude from the ballot people who pay taxes, sometimes render military service, and often discharge other civic obligations.

do not, the road to the ballot-box may nevertheless very appropriately lead through the school-house.[1]

The Problem of Negro Voting in the South

At the close of the Civil War, the Southern states were compelled to give the freedmen the ballot as a condition of being restored to their previous position in the Union, and the Fifteenth Amendment sought to insure permanence for the new situation by prescribing that the right of citizens to vote should not be "denied or abridged by the United States *or by any state* on account of race, color, or previous condition of servitude."[2] Unhappy results followed, especially where control of legislatures by inexperienced and gullible Negroes, abetted by Southern "scalawags" and Northern "carpet-baggers," brought on an orgy of financial extravagance and foolish legislation; and it is not to be wondered at that, once the white populations regained the upper hand, they began looking for ways in which the Negro could be quietly but effectively—and by less rough methods than Ku Klux Klan terrorism—deprived of political power. The main hurdle to be surmounted was, of course, the Fifteenth Amendment; so long as it endured (and there was not the slightest chance of securing repeal of it), no Negro could, *simply as a Negro*, be kept from the polls.

The search for a method of disfranchisement

Negroes, however, were commonly illiterate, and also poor; and this opened a way out of the dilemma. In 1890, Mississippi set the pace for her sister states by writing into her constitution clauses under which, in order to vote, one not only must have lived two years in the state and one year in the election district, but must have paid all taxes assessed against him (including a poll tax of two dollars), and must be able either to read any section of the state constitution or to understand it when read to him and to give a reasonable interpretation of it. And these requirements very well served their purpose. The exceptionally lengthy period of residence barred large numbers of Negroes accustomed to drift from plantation to plantation. Even if a colored man succeeded in paying his poll tax on time (and it was artfully required to be paid a year before

The Mississippi plan

---

[1] F. G. Crawford, "The New York State Literacy Test," *Amer. Polit. Sci. Rev.,* XVII, 260-263 (May, 1923), XIX, 788-790 (Nov., 1925), and XXV, 342-345 (May, 1931); A. W. Bromage, "Literacy and the Electorate," *ibid.,* XXIV, 946-962 (Nov., 1930); W. B. Munro, "Intelligence Tests for Voters," *Forum,* LXXX, 823-830 (Dec., 1928). Variations of definition are responsible for widely differing estimates of the total number of illiterates in the United States. But the census of 1930 reported 4,283,753 people ten years of age or over unable to write in any language. The 1940 census did not check illiteracy directly, but only school attendance; and it showed that out of a total of 74,775,836 persons twenty-five years of age or over, 10,104,612 had not gone beyond the fourth grade, 2,799,923 never having attended school at all. Of the larger number mentioned, 4,200,000 were native-born whites, 3,100,000 foreign-born whites, and 2,700,000 Negroes. New York, with 1,020,197, had the largest total. During the first year's operation of the Selective Service Act of 1940, a quarter of a million men otherwise fit for active service were rejected because of lacking the necessary literacy or mentality.

[2] Under the definition laid down in the Fourteenth Amendment, former slaves were now clearly citizens.

election time), he was likely to be careless enough to be unable to produce his tax receipt when called for. Few Mississippi Negroes could read, and still fewer could give an interpretation of a perhaps craftily selected passage from the state constitution likely to be accepted as "reasonable" by a white official with a strong predisposition against Negro voting. If, too, in replying to searching personal questions a candidate for registration was detected deviating an iota from the truth, he became guilty of perjury, for which also he could be disfranchised. Although every one knew that the primary purpose of the regulations was to keep the Negro from the polls, not a word was said in them about "race, color, or previous conditions;" and when the federal Supreme Court passed upon them in a test case, it was unable to find that they in any manner violated the Fifteenth Amendment.[1] Clauses of similar purport accordingly found their way into the constitutions of most other Southern states—all going to show how ingenious men can become when trying to find a way around legal provisions not backed by local public sentiment.

"Grand-father clauses"
There was, however, one drawback: while a secondary object of the tests was in some instances to curb the effects of radical (chiefly Populist) inclinations among poor whites, the restrictions operated to debar too large a proportion of whites along with the Negroes. But for this, also, a remedy was found—in the famous "grandfather clauses" adopted at one time or another, as constitutional amendments, in no fewer than seven states. South Carolina led off in 1895 by exempting for three years from her literacy and property tests all men, otherwise qualified, who were voters, or lineal descendants of persons who were voters, on January 1, 1867. The first act of Congress forbidding disfranchisement of Negroes in the Southern states (the Reconstruction Act) became law on March 2 of the year mentioned. No Negro, therefore, could avail himself of the new provision. But the poorest and most illiterate white could do so—commonly because of being the son or grandson of a voter of the earlier date. The devices employed in other states differed in details, but the object was always the same, i.e., to open a way for whites to get on the voters' lists without at the same time letting down the bars for Negroes. In all cases, the clauses were only temporary. Having served their purpose, all have long since disappeared. The last to go, i.e., one incorporated in the constitution of Oklahoma by popular initiative and referendum in 1910, differed from the others in being without limitation of time, but was overthrown by the Supreme Court on the ground of incompatibility with the Fifteenth Amendment.[2] Contrary to common impression, the grandfather clauses

[1] Williams v. Mississippi, 170 U. S. 213 (1898).
[2] Guinn v. United States, 238 U. S. 347 (1915). The Oklahoma legislature followed up this decision with a statute of 1916 requiring electoral registrars to enroll as voters only persons who were voters in 1914 (when few, if any, Negroes were such), together with such others as should apply for registration during a specified twelve-day period; but, on the ground that the registration period was inadequate and the

did not disfranchise Negroes. That object had already been largely attained by specially contrived literacy, tax, residence, and other requirements under which, as they stand today, in some states hardly one Negro in a hundred ever casts a ballot, and perhaps not more than ten per cent of the adult black population of the entire South is on the registration lists.[1] Thousands of Southern whites, however, became voters only by virtue of being gathered into the electorate on the strength of their grandfathers' political status; and this is the end which the "grandfather clauses" were mainly intended to serve.

Later days have brought to the fore two issues that have stirred much controversy and are still unsettled. One is that of the future of the "white primary;" the other, that of abolishing the poll-tax qualification. In most Southern states, the Democratic party is so dominant that nomination in a Democratic primary is equivalent to election—which means that if Negroes are to be deprived of political power, it is at least as important to keep them from voting in primaries as in the later elections.[2] And in as many as ten states, the majority party at one time or another procured the enactment of "white primary" laws with this object in view, the favorite method being the rather obvious one of giving each party the right to prescribe for voting in its primaries qualifications additional to any laid down in the state constitution and statutes,[3] nothing being said about Negroes, but the expectation being that the added qualifications would, in the case of the majority party, be found to be possessed only by white Democrats. One state, i.e., Texas, tried to go farther by placing on its statute-book, in 1923, a measure specifying that in no event should a Negro be eligible to participate in a Democratic

The question of the "white primary"

measure as a whole designed to perpetuate the old discriminations, the federal Supreme Court eventually nullified the effort, in Lane v. Wilson, 307 U. S. 268 (1939).

[1] As shown by Professor Paul Lewinson, in his Race, Class, and Party (New York, 1932), the proportion of colored voters in such border states as West Virginia, Kentucky, Tennessee, and Arkansas is relatively high, but in the states of the solid South extremely low. Large numbers of Negroes, it may be added, have been enfranchised in later years as a result of migration to Northern cities; and outside of the South Negro voting is distinctly encouraged, all parties seeking to turn it to their advantage, especially in states like New Jersey, Pennsylvania, Ohio, Illinois, and Missouri where the white vote is close. Indeed, in some Northern cities more Negroes vote, in proportion to their numbers, than whites. A complete list of suffrage qualifications in effect in the Southern states a decade and a half ago will be found in Lewinson, op. cit., 222-245. As a result of recent developments in connection with the "white primary" (about to be described), the number of Negro voters in the South is now steadily increasing.

[2] Outside of Virginia, North Carolina, and border states like Kentucky there are so few Republican voters in the South that Republican primaries are rarely held—never in the "Black Belt." In states like South Carolina and Mississippi there are almost no Republican candidates for congressional and state offices. In Florida, Louisiana, Mississippi, South Carolina, and Texas in 1947 there was not a single member of a state legislature who was not a Democrat—even though the percentage of popular votes cast for Dewey as presidential candidate in 1944 was, respectively, twenty-nine, nineteen, seven, four, and eighteen.

[3] It should be noted that two states outside of the South, i.e., Delaware and Idaho, have done this also.

The
earlier
experi-
ence of
Texas
party primary held in the state. This bold statutory provision—expressly excluding Negroes *as such*—was promptly challenged, and for more than two decades issues relating to the matter were intermittently before the courts. First, the federal Supreme Court, reversing a district court, unanimously held the 1923 statute unconstitutional as being in conflict with the clause of the Fourteenth Amendment which guarantees the equal protection of the laws.[1] Next, the Court, in a close vote, and on the same ground, overthrew a substitute law giving the state executive committee of every political party in Texas the power to prescribe qualifications of party membership, and consequently for participating in party primaries.[2] Persistence, however, sometimes brings its reward; and in the present instance, when the Texas Democrats, giving up as a bad job the effort to attain their ends by the legislation described, repealed the existing state primary law and fell back, in 1932, upon the expedient of a one-party, "white primary" system instituted by their state convention and operated exclusively by the party, the Court gave its unanimous approval—on the ground that the convention is the highest authority (as the executive committee is not) of a party, which, after all, is a voluntary organization entitled to determine its own membership.[3] And on this basis the matter seemed settled.

Congress
held to
have
power
to control
nomina-
tions
In a few years, however, so optimistic a conclusion was completely shattered. To begin with, there arose, in 1940, a case in which an election commissioner in a Louisiana congressional district was charged with altering and falsely counting ballots cast in a congressional primary, and when it reached the federal Supreme Court, that tribunal startled the country (and doubtless the defendant) by ruling not only that the commissioner had been properly indicted, but that Congress has authority, if it chooses to employ it, to protect the right to participate and have one's vote counted, not only in congressional elections, but in congressional primaries as well.[4] The decision was startling for the reason that ever since the Supreme Court had seemed so to hold in 1921,[5] Congress had been supposed to have no authority to deal with *nominations*, but only

---

[1] Nixon *v.* Herndon, 273 U. S. 536 (1927). In its clause guaranteeing equal protection of the laws, the Fourteenth Amendment, said the Court, offered so simple and obvious a basis for a decision that there was no need to consider the bearing of the Fifteenth Amendment upon the case. The plaintiff, Nixon, was an educated Negro physician of El Paso, Texas.

[2] Nixon *v.* Condon, 286 U. S. 73 (1932).

[3] Grovey *v.* Townsend, 295 U. S. 45 (1935). Excluding Negroes from primaries was regarded as merely tantamount to denying them party membership. See O. D. Weeks, "The Texas Direct Primary System," *Southwestern Soc. Sci. Quar.*, XIII, 1-26 (Sept., 1932), and "The White Primary," *Miss. Law. Jour.*, VIII 133-153 (Dec., 1935).

[4] United States *v.* Classic, 313 U. S. 299 (1941). The electoral process, said the Court, is essentially unitary; a congressional primary held at state expense, and therefore acknowledged as having a *public* character, is an integral part of it, and as such subject to the federal control to which congressional elections have always been at least potentially subject.

[5] Newberry *v.* United States, 256 U. S. 232. For the circumstances of this case, see p. 300, note 2, below.

with elections.[1] The two houses have as yet not seen fit to exercise their new-found power; but, manifestly, if they were to do so, the entire "white primary" system—already undermined (as about to be explained) by further judicial decision—undoubtedly would be extinguished.

For more was to follow. In another surprise move, in April, 1944, the federal Supreme Court squarely reversed its position of nine years earlier by holding, eight to one, in a case of identical nature, that, notwithstanding all laws and party rules to the contrary, Negroes were entitled to vote in Democratic primaries in Texas.[2] Under the Fifteenth Amendment, now said the Court, citizens are guaranteed the right to take part in choosing elective officials without restriction by any state on account of race, a primary is a part of the electoral process, and "the right to vote in such a primary for the nomination of candidates without discrimination by the state, like the right to vote in a general election, is a right secured by the constitution;" a state law which, without itself imposing restriction, intentionally opens the way for a private organization, *i.e.*, a political party, to do so, has the effect of making the action of such organization the action of the state itself; and in failing to perceive and assert this in the 1935 decision, the Court had simply been "in error."

A new Texas case further weakens the "white primary"

Naturally, the new turn of events [3] stirred reverberations not only in Texas, but (the Court's ruling being potentially of general application) throughout the entire South; and with the justices a month later refusing to reconsider their action, the search began for ways and means of preventing the decision from having its intended consequences.[4] One state—South Carolina—promptly met the challenge by repealing all legislation relating to primaries, the idea being to clear the way for the state Democratic organization, as a private agency, to institute its own primaries and run them as it pleased; and in the next year or two there were proposals to do the same thing in Alabama, Mississippi, and other states. For a dispassionate observer, however, it was difficult to see how, in the long run, this procedure could accomplish the desired purpose in

The aftermath in the South

---

[1] In the Newberry case, four of the justices thought Congress had power to regulate primaries; four thought otherwise; the ninth, non-committal on this point, tipped the scale in the defendant's favor on an entirely different consideration. So the decision on the main point was certainly not very conclusive, though it stood until United States v. Classic.

[2] Smith v. Allwright, 321 U. S. 649 (1944). The case arose when Smith, a Negro resident of Houston, sued for damages after being refused a ballot in the primary of July 27, 1940, for the nomination of Democratic candidates for Congress and for state offices. In conformity with Grovey v. Townsend (1935), the lower federal courts simply dismissed the claim. See R. E. Cushman. "The Texas 'White Primary' Case—Smith v. Allwright," *Cornell Law Quar.*, XXXX. 66-76 (Sept., 1944).

[3] On the whole, however, expected by students of constitutional law after the basic decision in the Classic case.

[4] Even people who thoroughly endorsed the decision's purport could see some point to the sarcastic condemnation of it by the single Supreme Court justice (Roberts) who refused to concur in it. to the effect that it tended to bring the Court's adjudications "into the same class as a restricted railroad ticket, good for this day and train only."

the face of the Supreme Court's unequivocal assertion of the basic right of all enfranchised citizens to participate in both primaries and elections; and the doubt was confirmed when, in July, 1937, a federal district judge in Charleston held, in a case brought against a Democratic county committee by a Negro storekeeper who had been denied enrollment, that Negroes in South Carolina were entitled to be permitted to vote in Democratic primaries. Meanwhile, since the Smith *v.* Allwright decision of 1944 Negroes have actually been voting in limited, yet increasing, numbers in both primaries and elections in most Southern states, notably in Texas, Alabama, Florida, Georgia, and Mississippi. In Alabama, five thousand were permitted to register in 1946 (out of a total adult Negro population of 500,000; in Georgia, where the "racial issue" since 1944 has been particularly acute, 125,000 registered for and 100,000 voted in the 1946 primaries—although only one-fifth of the potential Negro electorate; [1] in 1946, in a senatorial primary in Mississippi some five thousand Negroes were registered (out of a total Negro population of over a million), although only a thousand actually voted, and in 1947 an amendment to the state primary law authorizing any voter (not excluded by regulation of the state executive committee) to be challenged at the polls in connection with his "party principles" received its first test in a state-wide Democratic primary, with many Negro applicants rejected yet a considerable number permitted to cast their ballots.[2]

The problem of the poll tax

The new "white primary" ruling of 1944 came at a time when feeling was running high over still another effort to frustrate Southern debarment of Negroes from voting. As indicated above, seven Southern states make the payment of an annual poll tax a qualification for the exercise of the suffrage. To be sure, the chronology of the adoption of poll-tax requirements [3] correctly suggests that the restriction was originally motivated to no small degree by a desire to curb the electoral consequences of the spread of Populism among whites of low economic status—this chapter of suffrage history having started, not back in the Reconstruction period, but a full generation later. Negro voting, however, was in mind also; and the tax requirement, once introduced, has ever since operated as an additional restriction. In Southern poll-tax states, voting is only about one-third as heavy as in neighboring states without

---

[1] A "white primary" measure repealing the state primary law and resting all control in the party was passed by both houses of the legislature early in 1947 and signed by a claimant to the governorship (Eugene Talmadge), but killed by veto of another claimant (M. E. Thompson) after his accession.

[2] Cf. D. S. Strong, "The Rise of Negro Voting in Texas"—an article unpublished when these lines were written, but scheduled to appear in the *Amer. Polit. Sci. Rev.*, June, 1948. The author reports an estimate that at least 75,000 Negroes (fourteen per cent of the potential Negro electorate) voted in Texas primaries in 1946, and expresses the opinion that Negro voting is "on its way toward complete acceptance in the state." Another article expected to appear in the journal (and issue) mentioned was O. D. Weeks, "The White Primary, 1944-1948."

[3] Florida (1889), Mississippi and Tennessee (1890), Arkansas (1892), South Carolina (1895), Louisiana (1898), North Carolina (1900), Alabama and Virginia (1901), Texas (1902), and Georgia (1908).

the tax. By opening a way for blocks of poll-tax receipts to be bought up for distribution among people whose votes can in that way be corralled, the requirement likewise has made for political corruption. Four states—North Carolina in 1920, Louisiana in 1934, Florida in 1937, and Georgia in 1945—have abolished it outright.[1]

Growing opposition to the tax as a suffrage qualification led to several attempts to have it outlawed by judicial action. The Supreme Court, however, refused to be persuaded that employment of the tax in this manner was ever more than incidental to the main object of raising revenue;[2] and eventually the attack shifted to Congress, where in recent years, it has precipitated bitter controversy in an atmosphere heavily charged with partisanship. When enacting a measure in the autumn of 1942 to facilitate absent voting by men and women of the armed forces and their auxiliaries, Congress wrote into it a clause forbidding any such persons, for the duration of the war, to be deprived of their votes because of having failed to pay any poll tax. But the House of Representatives was prepared to go farther. For more than a year, a Pepper-Guyer bill, supported by President Roosevelt, and permanently outlawing poll-tax requirements in all federal elections, had been reposing in a pigeonhole of the Southern-dominated House judiciary committee; and the measure was now not only recalled from the committee but passed, by a heavy vote, over vigorous Southern protest. In the Senate, however, the bill was prevented, by a Southern filibuster, from coming to a vote; and the same thing happened to bills on the subject passed by the House in three of the next five years.[3] People who favor the proposed legislation contend not only that the poll-tax qualification is contrary to the spirit of American institutions, but that Congress has full power to fix the qualifications for voting for federal office or, if not that, at least power to prevent fraud in federal elections.[4] For purposes of public discussion, Southern opponents place most stress upon constitutional considerations associated with states' rights. Every one understands, however, that the actual objective is the maintenance of "white supremacy."[5]

The question in Congress

---

[1] A state abandoning the tax as a qualification for voting may, of course, retain it for purposes of revenue, as did North Carolina.

[2] In the case of Breedlove v. Suttles (302 U. S. 277, 1936), the Court, however, unanimously sustained Georgia's poll-tax requirement as a legitimate qualification for voting in state elections, which of course validated it also for federal elections.

[3] At the date of writing (January, 1948), the most recent measure of the kind to reach a Senate calendar was one passed by the House after a sharp parliamentary battle, on July 21, 1947, by a vote of 290 to 112. Seventy-three Northern Democrats and one American Labor member joined with 216 Republicans in supporting the bill; ninety-eight Democrats voted against it, including substantially all of those from the Southern states, whether poll-tax states or not. Carrying over on the Senate calendar, the measure was in line for consideration in the ensuing session, but with no certainty of any outcome different from that on previous occasions.

[4] In the case of United States v. Saylor et al., 322 U. S. 385 (1944), the Supreme Court held that "stuffing ballot-boxes, even in the absence of any federal legislation touching the matter, is a federal crime."

[5] A realistic study of the subject will be found in D. S. Strong, "The Poll Tax— The Case of Texas," Amer. Polit. Sci. Rev., XXXVIII, 693-709 (Aug., 1944); and

For some decades after the Civil War, the suffrage policies of the Southern states stirred lively discussion and protest in other sections of the country. Eventually, as it came to be realized that Southerners of all parties looked upon the restrictive system as politically and socially indispensable, and that—with, of course, many exceptions—the disfranchised were not greatly concerned about political rights, Northern disapprobation declined; in 1912, the Republican party significantly stopped putting in its national platform the time-honored denunciations on the subject. The issue, however, was always smouldering, with developments like the poll-tax controversy capable of fanning it to a flame; and in 1944 the Republican party returned to it with a platform plank declaring for "immediate submission" of a constitutional amendment making it illegal to impose a poll-tax qualification for participation in federal elections—an amendment, of course, in line with one which the Republicans were currently sponsoring in the Senate. The ultimate outcome of the anti-poll-tax drive and of the Supreme Court's new attitude on the white primary cannot as yet be foreseen, and meanwhile one may say simply that the restrictive regulations still prevailing—particularly as administered by sometimes prejudiced and incompetent registration and election officials—are indisputably objectionable in so far as they set up discriminations based on considerations of race and deliberately evade the fundamental law of the country. Moreover, Negro education has now advanced to a point such that some of the Southern states might well adopt a more generous attitude, as indeed one or two of them (notably North Carolina) have done. Many Southern Negroes, however, are still poorly qualified for political power; many of them manifest no desire to vote, considering rather that "politics is white folks' business" (or at any rate that it is dangerous colored folks' business); and with people of color numerically rivaling the white populations in a number of states,[1] the latter can be expected to give up only slowly and grudgingly the idea that their security depends upon maintaining some sort of restrictionist policy. A generation that attaches increasing importance to literacy as a qualification for voting can hardly repress the conviction

---

for an excellent general analysis, see J. E. Kallenbach, "Constitutional Aspects of Federal Anti-Poll Tax Legislation," *Mich. Law Rev.*, XLV, 717-732 (Apr., 1947). Most of the voluminous literature on the subject is propagandist, but mention may be made of F. P. Graham *et al., The Poll Tax* (Washington, D. C., 1940); J. Perry, *Democracy Begins at Home; The Tennessee Fight on the Poll Tax* (Philadelphia, 1944). Not only bills on the subject, but constitutional amendments as well, have been introduced in Congress, one such, brought forward in 1944, being sponsored by substantially the entire Republican membership of the Senate. President Truman's Committee on Civil Rights, reporting in 1947, recommended that poll-tax requirements for voting be abolished "by the states or by Congress;" and support was given the recommendation by the President himself.

[1] The closest approach is in Mississippi, where in 1940 Negroes formed 49.2 per cent of the population. Of course there are many counties in various states in which blacks outnumber whites two, or even three, to one. Throughout the South as a whole, about one-fourth of the potential electorate is colored.

that the initial mistake was made when the Southern states were in effect compelled by national authority to enfranchise Negroes *en masse* three quarters of a century ago.[1]

With a view to penalizing states restricting the suffrage, the Fourteenth Amendment provides that if a state denies or abridges the right of any of its male inhabitants, being twenty-one years of age and citizens of the United States, to vote, "except for participation in rebellion, or other crime," the basis of representation in such state shall be reduced in the proportion which the number of unenfranchised male citizens bears to the whole number of male citizens twenty-one years of age in the state. Attempt has been made to show that this provision is pertinent only in cases of denial of the suffrage because of race or color. But the phraseology of the amendment admits of no such interpretation: New York is precisely as liable to a reduction of its quota of representatives in Congress because of its literacy test as is Alabama on account of its restrictions aimed at the Negro. In point of fact, this provision—although in form and tone no less mandatory than any other part of the constitution—has never been enforced, and probably never will be. Largely because of Negro disfranchisement, the average number of voters in the South who elect a representative to Congress is very much smaller than the average number in other parts of the country; and there has been a good deal of complaint, mainly from Northern Republicans. Any attempt to enforce the constitutional penalty would, however, raise embarrassing questions and precipitate political controversies which most people prefer

Penalty for denial of franchise not enforced

[1] A weighty factor in the perpetuation of Negro disfranchisement in the South is the prevalence of the one-party system in that section, too often reducing politics to mere factionalism in which personal preferment and spoils supplant programs of policy as dominating considerations. If there were two evenly balanced parties, each would not only place more emphasis on programs, but also covet the advantage of the Negro vote (as parties now do in the North), and fairly rapid relaxation of the existing restrictions might be expected. To complete the vicious circle, however, the Negro question is the principal reason for the one-party system.

A new element in the general picture is supplied by the postwar efforts of the A. F. of L. and the C. I. O. to organize Southern (including Negro) workers in the industries which have developed so notably in the section. With its emphasis on political as well as economic action, the C. I. O. in particular is encouraging Negro as well as other workers to join parties, pay their poll taxes, and vote in primaries. This may contribute to forcing Southern politicians to change their attitudes in order to win elections.

The best general studies of suffrage and politics in the South are those of G. Myrdal and P. Lewinson, cited above; and the constitutional and legal aspects are presented admirably in C. S. Mangum, *The Legal Status of the Negro* (Chapel Hill, N. C., 1940), Chap. xviii. An excellent briefer discussion is E. M. Sait, *American Parties and Elections* (3rd ed.,), Chap. iii. The traditional Southern white viewpoint is presented in E. G. Murphy, *Problems of the Present South* (New York, 1904), Chap. vi, and F. G. Caffey, "Suffrage Limitations at the South," *Polit. Sci. Quar.,* XX, 53-67 (Mar., 1905). Cf. W. F. Nowlin, *The Negro in American Politics Since 1868* (Boston, 1931); S. D. Smith, *The Negro in Congress, 1870-1901* (Chapel Hill, N. C., 1940); R. W. Logan, *The Attitude of the Southern White Press Toward Negro Suffrage, 1932-1940* (Washington, D. C., 1940).

It is only fair to record that many individuals and organizations in the South are working for a more general enfranchisement of Negroes, and in particular for repeal of poll-tax qualifications.

to avoid. Consequently, every one of the many bills on the subject that have appeared in Congress has fallen by the wayside.[1]

The Electorate's Tasks—Non-Voting

Such are the complex and devious lines on which our country determines who shall have the political power that goes with voting. What is there for the electorate as thus defined to do? From state to state, there is a good deal of variation. In every state except Delaware, a new constitution or constitutional amendment must be submitted to a popular vote. In twenty-two states, the voters may ratify or veto measures that have passed the legislature, and in twenty they may also directly initiate laws.[2] In hundreds of municipalities, they occasionally exercise similar powers of direct decision on proposals. In all states, they elect the members of both branches of the legislature,[3] the governor and varying numbers of other state officials (including many judges), and widely differing—but usually extensive—lists of county, city, town, and other local officers and boards. By discussion, petition, criticism, and other more or less indirect means, they help the policy-framing authorities discover the public will and carry it out. In the domain of the national government, their tasks are fewer. They agitate for or oppose constitutional amendments, but do not directly vote upon them.[4] There is no national initiative or referendum for ordinary laws. Aside from formulating and expressing opinion (through political parties and in other ways), the voters, indeed, merely elect officers. And the number that they elect is not large, i.e., only the president and vice-president and the members of Congress. No administrative subordinates, and no members of the judiciary, are elective. So far as the national government is concerned, any given elector, therefore, votes only for (1) a set of presidential electors in his state—virtually, of course, for president and vice-president, (2) the two senators of his state, and (3) a representative of his district in the House of Representatives, together with one or more congressmen-at-large if his state, at any given time, is entitled to such [5]—actually and normally, a total of five officers only.[6] In the national government, we obviously have—and have had from the beginning—a "short ballot," whatever must be said to the contrary in the case of the state and local governments.

Officers and measures voted on

[1] Such a measure was defeated in a strongly Republican House of Representatives in 1921 by a vote of 285 to 46.

[2] See pp. 900-904 below (in complete edition of this book).

[3] Except in Nebraska, where there is only one house.

[4] See p. 53 above for proposals to apply the initiative and referendum to amendments.

[5] See p. 291, note 2 below.

[6] One might be tempted to add the delegates to conventions in the states to act on amendments to the federal constitution—a procedure actually employed for the first (and as yet only) time in 1933 in connection with the repeal of the Eighteenth Amendment. Such conventions, however, are, like the legislatures themselves, instrumentalities of the states and not of the nation.

How generally do those of our people to whom it falls, as voters, to supply the popular control which our system of government presupposes live up to their responsibilities? Thereby hangs a somewhat dismal tale. The census of 1920 showed the total population of the continental United States to be 105,710,620. Of this great body of people, somewhat more than 54,000,000 were citizens twenty-one years of age or over. Of this latter number, many (no one knows precisely how many) were, of course, ineligible to vote, because of inability to meet the qualifications imposed in their respective states. When, however, it is observed that in the presidential election of that year only a little over 26,500,000 men and women voted for any candidate for the highest office in the land, we come upon one of the most surprising, and many people would say one of the most discreditable, aspects of our political life. Many of the non-voters had failed to register; many who registered neglected to go to the polls; many who went to the polls voted only for certain offices and not for all. In 1924—notwithstanding unusual effort to "get out the vote"— the proportion was almost exactly the same as four years previously. On the other hand, the exceptionally spirited Hoover-Smith campaign of 1928 yielded a popular vote for president of over 36,879,414, out of a total electoral registration of slightly more than 43,000,000; the almost equally lively Hoover-Roosevelt campaign of 1932 brought out a vote of 39,816,522, out of a registration of some 47,500,000; the reasonably vigorous Roosevelt-Landon campaign of 1936 brought out a vote of 45,646,817, out of a registration of nearly 55,500,000; and the heated Roosevelt-Willkie contest of 1940, with third-term and New Deal issues dominant, yielded a record-breaking vote of 49,815,312, out of a registration of 60,576,979. On the last-mentioned occasion, the number of potential voters (*i.e.*, citizens twenty-one years of age and over) outside of the District of Columbia was estimated by the Census Bureau at 79,863,451. While, therefore, the figure representing the total vote appears impressive, fully a quarter of the adult men and women of the country failed to register,[1] and of those who registered, one out of every six neglected to go to the polls. With about eleven million men and considerable numbers of women in the armed services (millions of them overseas),[2] and with the country's population further dislocated by the exigencies of war industry, the election of 1944 was held under such abnormal conditions as not to be statistically comparable with preceding ones. The civilian vote, however—stimulated by an unusual get-out-the-vote effort —proved heavier than expected, and the same was true of the soldier vote, with a resulting total of 48,025,684.[3]

---

[1] Many, of course, were ineligible to do so, because of lack of the prescribed voting qualifications.

[2] Some two million of these, however, were not of voting age.

[3] *I.e.*, for president. In the same election, the total vote for members of the national House of Representatives was 45,103,023 and for senators (with, of course, no election in some states), 34,973,613.

The reasons for so great an amount of non-voting in the United States are many. To begin with, no elections are held in the District of Columbia, and more than a quarter of a million men and women are kept from the polls because they have no legal residence outside of that area. Large numbers at every election, especially in the cities, are debarred because of not having resided long enough in the state, county, or election precinct. Most of the Southern states to all intents and purposes have but one party, and because of the lack of genuine contests, together with the limitations upon Negro voting, yield an exceedingly small vote; in South Carolina in 1936, only about fourteen per cent of the potential electorate exercised the suffrage, and in a block of nine Southern states (all then having the poll-tax qualification) the average was hardly above twenty-four per cent. Many voters in all parts of the country are prevented from casting their ballots by bad weather, illness, or other legitimate reasons; although it should be noted that, even before World War II prompted extensive new arrangements for voting in the armed services, all but three states had laws largely removing one serious impediment of earlier days, i.e., absence from the voting precinct.[1] To some extent, voters are discouraged or thwarted by legal and administrative obstacles —too great crowding at the polls, too short hours for voting, too much red-tape in absent voting, and of course non-registration. To some extent, they are deterred by the lack of vital issues in an election, by belief that their vote would not affect the result, by fear that employers or others will find out how they voted, by disgust with politics and parties, or even by contempt for political methods of action in general. An obstacle, too, is the "jungle ballot" with which the voter is too often confronted— crowded with names of candidates he never heard of, seeking offices he knows nothing about. After all allowances are made, however, one is tempted to surmise that the most common cause is no one of these things, but simply indifference and inertia; and an extensive first-hand study of non-voting in the city of Chicago, based on the local municipal election of 1923, bears out this opinion.[2] Sometimes indifference is manifested

---

The most trustworthy computations for American elections during the period 1856-1920 will be found in A. M. Schlesinger and E. M. Erickson, "The Vanishing Voter," *New Republic*, XL, 162-167 (Oct., 15, 1924). Figures differing appreciably from those given in this article will be found in many places, but are likely to be erroneous because of insufficient allowance for ineligibles. It must be noted, too, that non-voting usually runs decidedly higher when only state and local officers are to be voted for.

[1] On absent voting, especially as affected by the war, see pp. 243-244 below. Except in the armed services, the number of persons taking advantage of absent-voting privileges has never been large.

[2] C. E. Merriam and H. F. Gosnell, *Non-Voting; Causes and Methods of Control* (Chicago, 1924), Chap. VII. Cf. B. A. Arneson, "Non-Voting in a Typical Ohio Community," *Amer. Polit. Sci. Rev.*, XIX, 816-825 (Nov., 1925); C. H. Titus, *Voting Behavior in the United States* (Berkeley, Calif., 1935), with particular reference to California; J. K. Pollock, *Voting Behavior; A Case Study* (Ann Arbor, Mich., 1940), based on 26,000 voting records in Ann Arbor; G. M. Connelly and H. H. Field, "The Non-Voter—Who He Is, What He Thinks," *Pub. Opinion Quar.*, VIII, 175-187 (Summer, 1944).

toward a particular election only—a colorless local contest, or even a state or national contest barren of challenging issues and commanding personalities. But more often it extends to elections generally; and the Chicago investigation shows it to be especially prevalent among younger voters, in poorer neighborhoods, and among housewives, but only slightly more so among people of foreign than among those of native birth.

Whatever the factors involved, the stay-at-home vote is still of such proportions as to attract a good deal of attention. Every important election brings a fresh round of remorseful and hortatory discussion of the subject; some people go so far as to say that democracy has failed. Two main considerations, however, are always to be borne in mind. The first is that, contrary to a very common assumption, there is no particular virtue in mere numbers of votes. Most get-out-the-vote efforts begin and end in an attempt to induce men and women to go to the polls regardless of whether they know anything about the issues or the candidates. The thing to be aimed at is not simply voting, but intelligent and interested voting; and energy spent upon getting ballots into the hands either of persons who are insufficiently informed to make intelligent decisions or of persons who are informed but have no clear opinions is misdirected. The second consideration is that the solution for the problem lies, not in dragging unwilling electors to the polls, but in improving the electoral system, raising the tone of political life, and laying more stress on broad civic education from early youth through adult years. "What we most need," writes one of the keenest students of the subject, "is to make registration less of an irksome task, the ballot simpler (with provision for the representation of minorities), elections less frequent, the issues clearer, party cleavages more distinct and vital, the party programs less evasive, and, above all, to organize our campaigns of civic education so that they will be more comprehensive, more persistent, and more effective in reaching those sections of the electorate which have enough intelligence to understand what it is all about."[1]

Suggested remedies

A more direct and drastic solution has sometimes been suggested, in the form of legislation making voting compulsory. Let people who will not vote of their own accord, it is urged, be coerced to go to the polls by some penalty (in the form of a fine or eventual disfranchisement) for failure to do so without valid excuse. Several foreign countries—Australia, New Zealand, Switzerland, Belgium, Denmark, the Netherlands, Czechoslovakia, Argentina, and others—have experimented more or less successfully with this procedure, and the constitutions of two of our own states, *i.e.*, Massachusetts and North Dakota, authorize laws on

Proposal for compulsory voting

---

[1] W. B. Munro, "Is the Slacker Vote a Menace?," *Nat. Mun. Rev.*, XVII, 86 (Feb., 1928). Cf. H. F. Gosnell, "Motives for Voting as Shown by the Cincinnati P. R. Election of 1929," *ibid.*, XIX, 471-476 (July, 1930); C. Eagleton, "A Defense of the Non-Voter," *South Atlantic Quar.*, XXVII, 341-354 (Oct., 1928), reprinted in A. N. Christensen and E. M. Kirkpatrick, *The People, Politics, and the Politician* (New York, 1941 and 1947), 228-238.

the subject whenever the legislature sees fit to enact them.[1] The plan, however, offers many practical difficulties. At best, it could be proceeded with only state by state; and to affix appropriate and easily administered penalties would certainly not be easy. Moreover, the policy of drafting voters for an election runs counter to our concept of personal liberty—to say nothing of the consideration that voting is worth while only when interested and intelligent—and the American mind is not likely to be won over to it.

REFERENCES

E. M. Sait, *American Parties and Elections* (3rd ed., New York, 1942), Chaps. ii-iv, xxv.

V. O. Key, *Politics, Parties, and Pressure Groups* (2nd ed., New York, 1947), Chap. xvi.

P. H. Odegard and E. A. Helms, *American Politics; A Study in Political Dynamics* (2nd ed., New York, 1947), Chaps. xii-xiii.

R. C. Brooks, *Political Parties and Electoral Problems* (3rd ed., New York, 1933), Chap. xiv.

A. W. Bromage, *State Government and Administration in the United States* (New York, 1936), Chap. vi.

W. B. Graves, *American State Government* (3rd ed., Boston, 1946), Chap. iv.

A. F. Macdonald, *American State Government and Administration* (3rd ed., New York, 1945), Chap. v.

American Institute of Public Opinion, *The Gallup Political Almanac for 1946* (Princeton, N. J., 1946). Valuable for recent electoral statistics.

K. H. Porter, *History of Suffrage in the United States* (Chicago, 1918).

————, "Suffrage Provisions in State Constitutions," *Amer. Polit. Sci. Rev.*, XIII, 577-592 (Nov., 1919).

H. F. Gosnell, *Democracy; The Threshold of Freedom* (New York, 1948), Chaps. ii-vi.

A. J. McCulloch, *Suffrage and Its Problems* (Baltimore, 1929).

J. E. Johnsen [comp.], *Lowering the Voting Age* (New York, 1945).

A. W. Bromage, "Literacy and the Electorate," *Amer. Polit. Sci. Rev.*, XXIV, 946-962 (Nov., 1930).

W. B. Munro, *The Invisible Government* (New York, 1928), Chap. ii.

C. E. Merriam and H. F. Gosnell, *Non-Voting; Causes and Methods of Control* (Chicago, 1924).

H. F. Gosnell, *Getting Out the Vote; An Experiment in the Stimulation of Voting* (Chicago, 1927).

C. H. Titus, *Voting Behavior in the United States* (Berkeley, Calif., 1935).

L. H. Bean, *Ballot Behavior; A Study of Presidential Elections* (Washington, 1940).

E. H. Litchfield, *Voting Behavior in a Metropolitan Area* [Detroit] (Ann Arbor, Mich., 1941).

J. K. Pollock, *Voting Behavior; A Case Study* (Chicago, 1939).

D. Anderson and P. E. Davidson, *Ballots and the Democratic Class Struggle; A Study in the Background of Political Education* (Stanford University, 1943).

W. MacDonald, *A New Constitution for a New America* (New York, 1921), Chap. xii. Advocates a uniform suffrage law for national elections.

---

[1] In several other states, *e.g.*, California and Oregon, compulsory-voting measures have been rejected by the electorate, and the Missouri supreme court, in 1896, held such a measure unconstitutional.

B. H. Nelson, *The Fourteenth Amendment and the Negro in the United States* (Washington, D. C., 1946).

J. M. Mathews, "Legislative and Judicial History of the Fifteenth Amendment," *Johns Hopkins Univ. Studies in Hist. and Polit. Sci.*, XXVII, Nos. 6-7 (1909).

P. Lewinson, *Race, Class, and Party; A History of Negro Suffrage and White Politics in the South* (New York, 1932).

G. Myrdal, *An American Dilemma; The Negro Problem and Modern Democracy,* 2 vols. (New York, 1944), especially I, Chaps. xx-xxiii.

W. F. Nowlin, *The Negro in American Politics Since 1868* (Boston, 1931).

C. S. Mangum, *The Legal Status of the Negro* (Chapel Hill, N. C., 1940).

J. S. Allen, *The Negro Question in the United States* (New York, 1936).

R. W. Logan [ed.], *What the Negro Wants* (Chapel Hill, N. C., 1944).

C. C. Catt, *Woman Suffrage by Constitutional Amendment* (New York, 1917).

————— and N. R. Shuler, *Woman Suffrage and Politics* (2nd ed., New York, 1926).

E. C. Stanton, S. B. Anthony, and M. J. Gage [eds.], *History of Woman Suffrage,* 6 vols. (New York, 1887-1922).

I. H. Irwin, *The Story of the Woman's Party* (New York, 1921).

CHAPTER XI

POLITICAL PARTIES—NATURE AND ORGANIZATION

Channels of Popular Control Over Government

The broad field of politics

Eighty-five million men and women potentially endowed with the ballot constitute an enormous reservoir of political power.[1] Even such power, however, would merely scatter, frustrate itself, and fail of significant achievement unless harnessed and directed; and we now turn to some of the ways in which the political ideas and energies of our huge electorate are galvanized and channeled into political action. Other portions of this book are concerned primarily with matters of public law, and with the workings of government as an operating mechanism. Here we pause for a glance into the pulsating, often exciting, realm of politics —a term designating that entire segment of our public life embracing the machinery and processes by which the people, under the principle of democracy, express themselves on what they want done and select those of their number who are to be intrusted with carrying out the mandates voiced.

Five main agencies for giving coherence and direction to what otherwise would be only a disordered mass of separate, discordant, and futile individual wills, and for translating an ascertained collective will into governmental action, may be mentioned: (1) public opinion, and the instrumentalities by which it is formed and made articulate; (2) groups and associations of many kinds having political interests and objectives, though not of the nature of political parties; (3) political parties; (4) nominations and elections, as means by which the people choose among programs and candidates put before them usually by the parties; and (5) executive officials, legislatures, and sometimes courts, placed in power by electoral majorities (or pluralities) to carry programs and policies into effect. Among these, our principal concern in the present chapter is with political parties; nominations and elections will occupy us in the two chapters that follow; and from there on, our attention will be fixed mainly on government in action.

Public opinion

Public opinion, as a factor in the political process, is something that in later years has come in for a great amount of investigation and study, by people ranging all the way from enterprising newspaper-men taking

[1] The total number of men and women *of voting age* on January 1, 1944, was reported by the Census Bureau as 88,666,555. The figure, however, included aliens and large numbers of other ineligibles.

"polls" during electoral campaigns to serious students of social psychology and political phenomena. It means, in general, attitudes shared, and perhaps expressed, by some substantial portion, presumably a majority, of the people of a community—the "community" being a village, a city, a state, a nation, or even the world, as the case may be. On some matters, *e.g.*, respect for law and order, the same general attitude is taken by almost everybody, and on these public opinion rates close to unanimity. On others, there is a heavy preponderance for a given view, but nevertheless a dissenting minority. On still others—many in fact—there is sharp and perhaps almost equal division; and in this category are likely to fall many, if not most, of the issues that come up in electoral campaigns, in legislative bodies, and in general political discussion. The most basic political technique, indeed, consists in trying to win the skeptical or the hesitant to acceptance of a given principle, policy, program, or candidate—in other words, to build a public opinion widely enough held to tip the balance in a favorable direction. Another such technique is the attempt to concentrate a stream of vocal public opinion upon Congress or a legislature in behalf of a pending measure, or upon executive authorities urging them to speed up action to some desired end, *e.g.*, bringing to settlement a wave of damaging strikes. Powerful molders of public opinion, on general lines, include the schools, the press, radio-broadcasting, motion pictures, the authors and publishers of pamphlets and books, and of course a wide variety of individuals and organizations (including political parties) engaged in systematic and protracted propaganda in behalf of ideas, "causes," interests, movements, reforms, and what not. All of these instrumentalities can be, and are, used extensively for political purposes—with precisely what results it is usually difficult to determine, although the aggregate effects must be considerable. At all events, public opinion, however formed and influenced, is—especially when giving evidence of solidarity and intensity—bound to be a factor of major importance in shaping the course of political events.[1]

Public opinion is, of course, for the most part unorganized and more or less incoherent; except when given a definite outlet, on political matters, at election time, it can, on controversial subjects, be discerned and appraised in only rather haphazard ways. Americans, however, have

Non-party organizations having political interests

---

[1] Public opinion as a factor in government is conveniently surveyed in E. M. Sait, *American Parties and Elections* (rev. ed., New York, 1939), Chap. v, and E. L. Shoup, *The Government of the American People* (New York, 1946), Chap. x. Fuller general studies include H. L. Childs, *An Introduction to Public Opinion* (New York, 1940); H. Cantril, *Gauging Public Opinion* (Princeton, N. J., 1944); G. Gallup, *Public Opinion in a Democracy* (Princeton, N. J., 1939); and W Lippmann, *Public Opinion* (New York, 1930). Useful readings on the subject will be found in A. N. Christensen and E. M. Kirkpatrick, *The People, Politics, and the Politician* (New York, 1941 and 1947), Chap. x. For a concrete illustrative study of the rôle of public opinion in the court reorganization controversy of 1937, see F. V. Cantwell, "Public Opinion and the Legislative Process," *Amer. Polit. Sci. Rev.*, XL, 924-935 (Oct., 1946). The principal center in this country for serious study of public-opinion phenomena is the American Institute of Public Opinion at Princeton, N. J., which publishes the major journal devoted to the subject, *i.e.*, the *Public Opinion Quarterly*.

a strong propensity for forming and joining clubs, associations, leagues, orders, societies, and other bodies, and the national scene is overlaid with organizations which in some instances have no political interests or implications at all, but which more frequently exist mainly or solely to exert political influence, or have political interests subsidiary to others, or at least are prepared on occasion to support or oppose suggested legislation or other phases of public policy. The American Medical Association is, in general, non-political, yet ever ready to throw its weight energetically against government policies looking toward "socialized medicine." The American Bankers' Association has plenty to say about the relations of the Treasury Department and the Federal Reserve System to fiscal and banking practice. The Civil Liberties Union watches for laxness on the part of national and state governments in upholding personal liberties guaranteed by the respective constitutions, and the National Association for the Advancement of Colored People fights the poll-tax laws of Southern states and other discriminative legislation, wherever appearing. The Single Tax League works for a tax system under which the only taxes would be those on the economic rent of land, and the Chamber of Commerce of the United States urges public policies favorable to the interests of business. The National Woman Suffrage Association prepared the way for the Nineteenth Amendment, and the League of Women Voters of the United States pushes vigorously for administrative reforms, national, state, and local, for legislation on many subjects of wide concern, and for a strong policy of international coöperation. No public policy relating to agriculture can be considered without stirring to action the National Grange, the American Farm Bureau Federation, and perhaps the National Council of Farm Coöperatives. And as for the field of labor, no one needs to be told how exceedingly active are the A. F. of L., the C.I.O., and the great railroad brotherhoods in all that relates to protective and regulative labor legislation and to the labor policies and actions of the executive and judicial arms of the government— a situation dramatized climactically in the spring of 1946 when for weeks John L. Lewis, head of the United Mine Workers of America (then a branch of the A. F. of L.) had the national government by the throat and released it from this humiliating situation only after seeing a wasteful strike settled on terms agreeable to him and his supporters.[1] Finally may be mentioned the P.A.C. (Political Action Committee), formed in 1944 as a unit within the C.I.O. expressly to promote the reelection of President Roosevelt and of congressmen favorable to labor, as energetic in the campaign of that year as any political party could possibly have been, and (after having suffered considerable rebuffs in the congressional elections of 1946) poised again for an active rôle in 1948.[2]

---

[1] Another coal-miners' strike was called the following November, and again the power of the UMW, and especially of its leader, was demonstrated.

[2] During the 1944 campaign, it became necessary for the P.A.C. to sever its

Plenty of other illustrations could be cited, but even the list given is sufficient to bring out the significant, if not startling, fact that, in addition to contributing as it may to the force of public opinion, belonging to political parties, and participating in the processes of nomination and election, an exceedingly large share of the American electorate has avenues of influence and control over national and state governments through the medium of voluntary associations rarely calling themselves political, yet prepared to employ political power to their utmost when considering it to their interest to do so. Needless to say, it is these organizations—or at any rate many of them—that are primarily responsible for most of the lobbying that goes on in Washington and the state capitals.[1]

The Nature and Uses of Political Parties

However influential it may be, no organization like those mentioned can claim to represent the country as a whole, or amass enough power to take over control of the government and run it. Associations able to do these things are likely to be, rather, what we know as political parties. And in saying this, we are not thinking of monopolistic instruments of tyranny calling themselves parties—Fascist, National Socialist, and the like—such as those existing under the dictatorial régimes with which Europe was recently cursed. We refer rather to parties in the truer sense as found in all democratic states. The term "political party," as thus employed, is not easy to define; but essentially it designates some portion of the electorate consciously bound together by at least traditional adherence to certain political principles, by at least some common attitudes toward questions of public policy, and unfailingly by a desire to gain control of the offices, by peaceful, constitutional methods, in order that a program conceived in the nation's, as well as the party's, interest may be carried into effect. A party may be large or small, national or sectional,[2] harmonious or discordant, tightly organized or not so. But more

Essential features

---

formal connection with the C.I.O., in order to evade restrictions of law upon campaign contributions. Cf. J. Gaer, *The First Round; The Story of the C.I.O. Political Action Committee* (New York, 1944). Unfortunately, this book is almost totally lacking in objectivity.

[1] See pp. 407-411 below.

[2] For purposes of statutory regulation of party activities, it, however, becomes necessary to have some standard for determining what groups are, and what ones are not, to be considered parties. To this end, the laws of a state usually fix as a criterion the polling of some definite percentage of the state's entire vote in a previous election, sometimes as low as two per cent, sometimes considerably higher. In some states, too, a minor party gets on the ballot by means of a petition signed by some specified proportion of the voters, *e.g.*, in Oklahoma five per cent, in Ohio fifteen per cent. Even where such requirements can be met, however, a party may be debarred for reasons having to do with its tenets or affiliations: and in a number of states the Communist party (in some instances, any "un-American party") has been outlawed on such grounds. A California supreme court decision of 1942 overthrew a statute of 1940 in so far as banning the Communist party by name, but sanctioned exclusion from the ballot of any party advocating forceful overthrow of the government or accepting the "control and direction of a foreign government." See H. F. Ward, "The Communist Party and the Ballot," *Bill of Rights Rev.*, I,

important ones nearly always operate on a national scale, and commonly permeate all levels of government. Moreover, in democracies any number of parties may spring up and contend freely with one another; a main characteristic of democracy is, indeed, free party life.

Parties criticized and deplored

To be sure, the political party, like many another useful device, has been the object of a great deal of suspicion and criticism, in our own country as elsewhere. When, during the presidency of Washington, the people were unexpectedly found grouping themselves, under the leadership of Hamilton and Jefferson, respectively, in rival Federalist and Republican parties, thoughtful men deplored what was happening; and Washington himself felt it necessary, in his Farewell Address, to affirm that the "common and continual mischiefs of the Party are sufficient to make it the interest and the duty of a wise people to discourage and restrain it." The period from Madison's presidency to that of Jackson has been painted as a golden age of "good feeling" for the simple reason that (despite plenty of local and personal political strife) parties had for the time being largely disappeared. And after party rivalries again grew vigorous, and especially in the decades following the Civil War, critics and reformers aimed their shafts, not only at rings and bosses and spoils, but at parties themselves as being perhaps the basic public evil of the time. Even today, one sometimes hears it charged that party names and platforms mean little, that principles receive mere lip-service, that policies are adopted or discarded mainly with a view to winning votes, that leadership is bankrupt, that indeed most parties are mere shams.[1]

Some uses enumerated

Sordid as are many chapters in their history, parties, however, are both inevitable and necessary—inevitable because the voters of not even a city or a county (to say nothing of a country as a whole) can ever be expected to be of one mind upon political principles and policies, or to agree upon the persons who should be placed in the public offices; necessary, because—while so-called non-partisan elections have proved their worth in jurisdictions of limited area and for the choice of certain types of officials, such as judges—no one has been able to show how the democratic process could be carried on over a wide expanse like a state or nation except with the aid of party organization and activity. Thinking of the matter particularly in relation to our own country, parties serve

---

286-292 (Summer, 1941), and B. Moore, "The Communist Party of the U. S. A.; An Analysis of a Social Movement," *Amer. Polit. Sci. Rev.*, XXXIX, 31-41 (Feb., 1945). Minor parties naturally complain of the laws which operate to debar them and consider themselves victims of a conspiracy of the major parties. Among groups vigorously advocating revision of electoral laws in this regard are the Socialists and the Prohibitionists, who, however, in 1944 got candidates on the ballot in twenty-eight and twenty-seven states, respectively. There were only eleven states in the year mentioned on whose ballots no minor parties appeared.

[1] See, for example, H. J. Laski, "The Bankruptcy of Parties," *The Nation*, CLXIII, 582-584 (Nov. 23, 1946). For interesting suggestions on how parties in the United States could be made more virile and effective, see *Amer. Polit. Sci. Rev.*, XXXIX, 1151-1157 (Dec., 1945).

a variety of useful purposes. (1) They help keep the people informed on public affairs; even though their propaganda be one-sided, they afford voters an opportunity to hear different sides and make up their minds. (2) In this way, parties stimulate opinion, and not only opinion but also action, since the thing that most often prompts the average voter to go to the polls at election time is party incentive. (3) Parties not only formulate policies and platforms, but select candidates for the public offices, thereby enabling voters holding the same general views to pool and concentrate their electoral power in a manner most likely to achieve results. (4) They stand, to some degree, as sureties for the satisfactory performance of official duties by persons elected under their sponsorship. (5) They (at all events those out of power) provide constant watchfulness over and criticism of the conduct of government, a criticism often merely captious, it is true, yet on the whole serving usefully to keep the "ins" on their mettle. (6) Still another point often made in their favor is that they introduce a harmonizing element in government, particularly in a system such as ours, based upon the principle of separation of powers. To be sure, they may tend rather to promote discord when, for example, the president is of one party and Congress dominated by a different one. But when, as most often happens, president and majorities in both branches of Congress—or, in the states, governor and majorities in both branches of the legislature—are of the same party, such harmony of political affiliation and viewpoint makes powerfully, as a rule, for expeditious and effective conduct of affairs. Still other uses of parties will occur to any one who thinks about the matter—for example, the fashion in which they bridge the cleavages and soften the frictions in our society, serving (to change the figure) as a sort of cement holding together people of divergent race, religion, culture, and occupation throughout the broad expanse of the country.[1]

From the foregoing, it follows that any one desiring something more than merely a superficial knowledge of the American system of government must study two distinct yet mutually interdependent sets of political institutions. One may conveniently be described as the machinery of government; the other, as the party system. The first includes the formal organization or structure of our national, state, and local governments, with their executive, legislative, and judicial branches. These formal governmental institutions are outlined more or less fully in the national and state constitutions, in municipal charters, and in national and state statutes which amplify constitutional provisions. But a study restricted to documents like these would leave one quite uninformed upon the actual workings of government in the United States. A main reason is that the formal institutions with which the documents deal frequently do not operate as one would be led to suppose, or indeed as originally intended;

Two sets of political institutions

[1] Cf. C. A. Beard, *The Republic; Conversations on Fundamentals* (New York, 1943), Chap. xviii, "Political Parties as Agencies and Motors."

and as often as not the reason, in turn, why they do not do so is the rise
and growth of political parties. Constitutions and statutes create machinery and confer powers; but flesh is put upon the dry bones and energy
imparted to the mechanism largely by the instrumentalities and driving
force of parties.

The Party Pattern in the United States [1]

Factors
influenc-
ing party
affiliation

Many attempts have been made to explain why people divide on party
lines in the manner they do, and even why they divide at all. There is a
theory that men go in different directions politically because of innate
dispositions or qualities, causing some to become conservatives and
others liberals or radicals. But there is the difficulty that the same
individual may be conservative on some matters and quite otherwise on
others. In the case of the United States, an explanation has been found
in the basic issue of centralized national government versus states' rights.
Yet recent political history shows how easily the same party may, within
a short period, be found on both sides of that question. The truth is that
there is no single explanation. Why are some Americans today Republicans, some Democrats, and others something else? Some because their
fathers and grandfathers were such, and they have grown up in the
tradition; some because they live in a community or region where it is
the normal and natural thing to belong to a given party; some because
they believe a given party more friendly to their race, or even creed;
some because they think it expedient to go along politically with their
employers; some because of deliberate choice grounded upon disinterested
belief in a given set of political principles or devotion to a given leader
or group of leaders.

The
economic-
sectional
basis of
American
politics

Viewing the developing party pattern over the entire stretch of American history, however, the most competent students of party phenomena
have been almost unanimous in finding the basic ground for party cleavage, not in psychology, nor in constitutional theories, nor in any of the
specific motivations just enumerated, but rather in interests and reactions of an economic and sectional nature. It was on this basis primarily
that parties started in the early years of the Republic—the backbone of
the Federalist party being the commercial, financial, and industrial elements of New England and the Middle States; that of the Jeffersonian
Republican party, the agrarian interests (planters and farmers) of the
South and rural North. Moreover, in a general way the pattern thus
initiated projected itself down the course of time in the lineage of Fed-
eralists-Whigs-Republicans (Hamilton, Webster, Lincoln, McKinley,

---

[1] It is not proposed to introduce in the present edition of this book any historical
sketch of American political parties. Such an outline, if desired, will, however, be
found in the 5th edition (1935), pp. 167-178. Interpretative books, with emphasis upon
economic factors, include A. N. Holcombe, *The Political Parties of Today* (2nd ed.,
New York, 1925); *The New Party Politics* (New York, 1933), and *The Middle Classes
in American Politics* (Cambridge, Mass., 1940); also W. E. Binkley, *American Political Parties; Their Natural History* (New York, 1943).

Theodore Roosevelt, Hoover) and, over against it, that of Jeffersonian Republicans-Democrats (Jefferson, Jackson, Cleveland, Wilson, Franklin D. Roosevelt)—the one line associated with high protective tariffs, centralized banking, currency based on gold, a large navy, taxes bearing lightly on wealth, strong national government devoting itself to the promotion of commercial, manufacturing, and business interests; the other line associated equally with states' rights, low tariffs, state banks, "free silver," anti-imperialism, graduated taxation of incomes.

Even a hundred years ago, however, this broad characterization had only rough and approximate validity. No one party ever enlisted the undivided support of any entire economic interest or group or of any entire geographical section; too many other motivations for party alignment cut across economic and sectional lines and blurred the picture. From its beginnings, nearly a hundred years ago, the Republican party attracted heavy support in the rural and agricultural North; on the other hand, as newer industries arose, they sometimes, for varying reasons, were drawn into the Democratic orbit. And today the scene is confused indeed. Economic life has grown infinitely more complex; in capital invested, value of product, and numbers of people employed, agriculture has been displaced by industry and trade; the interests of agriculture, industry, and trade overlap and dovetail in novel ways; sections are no longer so sharply identified with either agriculture or industry—the latter, for example, having undergone notable development in the South itself, as well as, of course, in the once almost wholly agricultural Middle West. And all this has been reflected in the warping and twisting of the traditional party pattern into almost unrecognizable forms. For reasons associated with the aftermath of the Civil War, with the Negro problem, and with loyalty to tradition, the South remains a Democratic stronghold.[1] But elsewhere new lines have been drawn, or at least old ones shattered or obliterated. Industry, grown huge, is divided against itself, with heavy representation in both parties; Democratic hostility to protective tariffs has softened into a program of "trade agreements," for which there is also considerable Republican support; farmers are predominantly Republican, industrial laborers predominantly Democratic, but not so decisively as a generation ago; world developments over which we had no control cast the Democrats in the strange rôle of the party of nationalism, strong armies and navies, international intervention, and war, leaving the Republicans—at least for the time being—to the less glorious and less familiar rôle of advocating caution, restraint, and isolationism.

Today, both of the leading parties are notoriously conglomerate and disunited. Even so, they are not properly to be written off as merely two bottles carefully labeled but empty, as James (later Lord) Bryce asserted

The picture blurred in recent times

[1] M. D. Irish, "The Southern One-Party System and National Politics," *Jour. of Politics*, IV, 80-94 (Feb., 1942).

of the parties of thirty-five years ago. By and large, they still stand for some distinctive things—in traditions, attitudes, principles, and policies. Cutting through all strata of society, penetrating all geographical sections, enlisting in some degree all economic interests, they, however, must increasingly be all things to all men in order to hold, or hope to gain, power. Some significance attaches to polls during the presidential campaigns of 1940 and 1944 showing the Democratic candidates enjoying the support of only a little over one-third of the voters in the upper income groups, of a little over half of those in the middle group, and of seven-tenths of those in the lower groups, with the Republican candidates preferred by almost three-quarters, a little under half, and only three-tenths of the different groups, respectively. This, however, only emphasizes the composite nature of both parties and leaves the way wide open, not only for sharp differences of view between income groups within the same party, but for the divergencies and conflicts widely existing among geographical, occupational, or other elements within income groups taken individually.[1]

The two-party system—minor parties

Despite all that has happened, the mass of American voters have consistently been able to give their support to one or the other of two major parties, with the result that we have always had a bi-party system, as indeed has been true of English-speaking peoples generally.[2] To be sure, from the first quarter of the nineteenth century onwards, dissatisfied elements have been prone to launch independent, or "third-party," movements. There were the Anti-Masons of 1826 and after; the Liberty party, appearing about 1840; the Free Soil party, active in the election of 1848; the Native-American, or "Know-Nothing," party which flourished in the fifties; the Republican party itself, which began as a third party in 1854-56; the Prohibition party, dating from 1872; the Greenback party of the seventies; the People's, or "Populist," party of the nineties; the Socialist party, starting about 1897; the National Progressive party of 1912; the Farmer-Labor and Communist parties formed about 1920; the Progressive party, launched by the elder Senator LaFollette, which made an impressive showing in 1924; the Progressive party which existed in Wisconsin from 1934 to 1946; the Farmer-Labor party in Minnesota which in 1944 joined with the Democratic party to form the present Democratic-Farmer-Labor party; and, more recently, the American Labor party and an offshoot, the Liberal party, local to New York State and largely New York City.[3] Some of these parties momentarily attained

---

[1] The economic and sectional aspects of American parties are dealt with illuminatingly in the books of A. N. Holcombe listed on p. 228 below. Cf. W. F. Ogburn and L. C. Coombs, "The Economic Factor in the Roosevelt Elections," *Amer. Polit. Sci. Rev.*, XXXIV, 719-727 (Aug., 1940).

[2] After the rise of the Labor party early in the present century, Great Britain had three major parties, and in a sense this is still true, although the gradual withering of the Liberal party gives promise of full restoration of the bi-party system eventually.

[3] As these pages went to press, a new party was taking form under the leadership of Henry A. Wallace, whose presidential candidacy in the 1948 elections had been announced.

sufficient strength, especially in pivotal states, to affect the results of even a presidential election,[1] and one—the Republican—grew into a major party. Since 1924, however, all minor parties combined have never polled more than from one-half to two and one-half per cent of the total popular vote in presidential elections (in 1940, 0.5 per cent and in 1944, 0.4); and, over the years—free to cultivate ideas rather than worry about power—they have as a rule found their importance mainly in revealing and crystallizing dissenting opinion (usually on economic and social matters), and as threats to the rather evenly balanced major parties, compelling them, however reluctantly, to take up issues and assume positions calculated to find favor with elements of the population chiefly appealed to by a given third-party movement. A remarkably large proportion, indeed, of leading party issues in the past several decades—the income tax, the regulation of railroads and other corporations, the use of injunctions in labor disputes, woman suffrage, prohibition, and others—were more or less forced upon the major parties in this way. Minor parties are commonly (although not invariably) more or less to the left of, *i.e.*, more radical than, the old-line organizations; and frequently the internal rivalries and frictions handicapping the latter are more than matched by the discord plaguing minor groups—which supplies part of the reason, along with the appropriation of their issues by major parties, and sometimes inept leadership, why so few third parties achieve much importance, or even survive.[2]

Mr. A may avow himself, or be understood to be, a Democrat, Mr. B a Republican, Mr. C a Socialist; and this is taken to mean that they are "members" of their respective parties. Party membership in this country is, however, for most people a rather vague and elusive matter. A person "belonging" to almost any other kind of association—a church, a lodge, a professional society—expects to go through some definite procedure of "joining," to declare formal allegiance to some creed or code or set of principles, to make contributions or even pay "dues," to abide by a code of regulations, perchance to serve on committees, hold offices, and otherwise participate in the organization's work. Minor political parties, being

Party membership

[1] The political history of New York affords several examples. In 1844, the Liberty party's poll in that state was sufficient to throw the state's electoral vote to James K. Polk, the Democratic candidate, and so to insure his election over the Whig candidate, Henry Clay; in 1848, the Free Soil party drew away so many votes from Cass, the Democratic nominee, that the Whig candidate, General Taylor, carried the state; in 1884, the Republicans held the Prohibitionists responsible for loss of the state and the resulting election of Grover Cleveland; and in 1944 the American Labor party and its offshoot, the Liberal party, both supporting the Democratic candidate, President Roosevelt, gave him the margin of victory in the state. In 1912, the National Progressive party, a Republican seceding element supporting Theodore Roosevelt, and in 1924 the Progressive party supporting Senator LaFollette, sharply split the bulk of the popular vote throughout the country (with 35 and 17.1 per cent polled, respectively), but without deflecting the eventual result from what it would certainly have been in 1924, and probably in 1912, in any case.

[2] J. D. Hicks, "The Third-Party Tradition in American Politics," *Miss. Valley Hist. Rev.*, xx, 3-28 (June, 1944); W. B. Hesseltine, *The Rise and Fall of Third Parties; From Anti-Masonry to Wallace* (Washington, D. C., 1948).

recruited usually from people having a missionary zeal for some program or cause, also tend to definite organization on such lines; at all events, they (the Communists, for example) usually have a regularly enrolled membership subscribing to certain purposes and doctrines and pledged to contribute to the party fund. Of the major parties, however, nothing of the kind can be asserted. They have no procedure or ceremony of "joining" (except as one may join a political club or other such auxiliary); they have no general roll of members, but only such lists as result, in less than half of the states, from pre-primary enrollments.[1] They get no signatures to their programs of policy; they collect no dues (though efforts have sometimes been made to institute a system of regular contributions); they enforce no rules; they have no means of disciplining a "member" or expelling him—except as he may be disciplined by failure of support if he chooses to run for office. The picture that one gets is that of a series of concentric circles. At the center is a core of party officers, organizers, voluntary and paid workers, public office-holders, office-seekers, partisan newspaper editors, persons receiving or hoping for favors at the party's hands—in other words, people who not only are Democrats or Republicans, but "work at it." Outside of this is a far wider circle containing people who, without being active full-time participants, nevertheless are regular adherents, in that they consistently go along with the party, register as belonging to it, vote for its candidates, join clubs supporting it, and give it the weight of whatever influence and prestige they may have in their communities. Still farther out is a circle of "in and out-ers"—people who commonly go along, yet often disagree, criticize, vote for opposition candidates, and otherwise prove not dependable. And finally there is a wide periphery of voters who, even though at times they may prove active supporters, do not accept the party name at all and are clearly to be classed as independents.[2] In the election of 1944, Franklin D. Roosevelt polled 25,602,646 popular votes

[1] For most people at least, such enrollments are not a means of *joining* a party, because they are designed primarily to ascertain who the party members *already are* and who therefore are entitled to participate in the primary of a given party. Of course, more or less accurate local lists are likely to be compiled by local committees or managers for local use. But these are nowhere assembled in general lists, and the nearest approach to dependable state lists are such as can be made up, in some states, from the pre-primary enrollments mentioned.

[2] Independence in politics first challenged attention on a considerable scale in the later nineteenth century, when in revolt against the evils encouraged or condoned by the parties of their day, many men of lofty civic ideals not only cut loose from party affiliations, but preached the doctrine that all good citizens should stand ready to uphold principle and support good candidates without regard to party label. And although most people still have rather fixed, if not inflexible, party affiliations, the number of genuine independents is probably larger in our time than ever before, to say nothing of the even greater number who, although normally identified with a given party, have no hesitation about "scratching" tickets and voting from time to time for candidates put up by the opposition. The American Institute of Public Opinion estimates that 5,500,000 independents voted for Roosevelt in 1940 and 3,500,000 for Willkie; 6,000,000 for Roosevelt in 1944 and 4,000,000 for Dewey. *The Gallup Political Almanac for 1946*, p. 205. If these figures are approximately correct, the independent vote in the years mentioned amounted to roughly one-fifth of the total.

and Thomas E. Dewey 22,017,592. But this does not mean that the two parties at that time had those respective numbers of *members*. It means only that the given numbers of votes were amassed *from all sources*, numerous Democrats voting for Dewey, numerous Republicans for Roosevelt, and doubtless still larger numbers of independents for one or the other as they chose. One is a Democrat or a Republican if he says he is (for example, when filling out a blank registering as a voter, or when challenged at a closed primary), or at any rate if he consistently supports the one party or the other; and that is all there is to it. Furthermore, he may change his mind and allegiance as often as he wishes. How many "members" either party has is anybody's guess—and still would be even if there were more trustworthy criteria for determining who is to be regarded as a "member" and who is not.[1]

Parties and the Different Levels of Government

Parties have attained their present significant position not only without constitutional recognition, but without ever becoming parts of the governmental system in any proper sense. In the national constitution, not a word is said about them, and nearly all state constitutions are equally silent. For a hundred years, furthermore, their activities were but little regulated by the states; and although long an arena of party combat, Congress passed its first law touching them in any important manner not much over a generation ago, *i.e.*, in 1907. Notwithstanding a good deal of federal, and especially state, law on the subject today, to a degree investing them legally with a public status, parties are still basically private, largely autonomous and self-governing, organizations.[2]

The legal status of parties

Aside from occasional "third" parties operating on a state, or even a local, basis, *e.g.*, the Farmer-Labor party in Minnesota, the Progressive party of 1934-46 in Wisconsin, the American Labor party in New York State, and a City Fusion party in New York City, parties in this country are nation-wide in name, membership, and scope. They also are nationally organized, and their national programs, candidates, and activities take priority in public attention. A Democrat or Republican thinks of himself primarily as identified with a national party. Nevertheless, viewed structurally, the basic constituent elements of a major party are *state* parties, each ramifying throughout counties, cities, towns, villages, wards, and voting precincts. In other words, state parties are federated over the country *upwards* into national parties, and within their respective areas are subdivided *downwards* into the localities, resulting in the characteristic permeation of our parties through all levels of public organization.

Permeation of all levels of government

[1] On the general subject, see C. A. Berdahl, "Party Membership in the United States," *Amer. Polit. Sci. Rev.*, XXXVI, 16-50, 241-262 (Feb. and Apr., 1942).
[2] J. R. Starr, "The Legal Status of American Political Parties," *Amer. Polit. Sci. Rev.*, XXXIV, 439-455, 685-699 (June and Aug., 1940).

This unity of party, running up and down through all layers of government, is an important factor in promoting coöperation of federal, state,
and local authorities and in binding the nation together. It nevertheless
results in the projection of national politics into state and local affairs
in ways that to many people seem wholly undesirable; and certainly it is
not always easy to see any logical connection between the conduct of
state, county, and municipal government, on the one hand, and Republican and Democratic policies relating to national affairs, on the other.
Explanations for the permeation and overshadowing of state by national
politics are, however, not difficult to discover. To begin with, the manifest
priority of the national government, the far-reaching significance of
national party issues, the exalted position of the presidency, the dramatic
and often spectacular methods employed in national campaigns, the
powerful attraction of occasional national leaders, and the varied and
fervent appeals to the electorate, combine to arouse a keener interest and
to stimulate a larger participation in national than in state and local
elections. To the national party with which the citizen is identified in
such campaigns, there springs up an instinctive attachment, an abiding
loyalty, perchance a zealous devotion, against which state or local parties,
when launched on independent lines, have always found it difficult or
impossible long to prevail. In the second place, from the viewpoint of
national party leaders, the habitual and active participation of national
party organizations in state and local elections is a measure of preparedness for the great presidential battles occurring every four years, and
also for the hardly less important congressional campaigns falling both
in presidential years and midway between them. State and local officers
also are often chosen simultaneously with national officers, as well as in
the intervals between national elections; and national party activity in
connection with the nomination and election of state and local officers
serves to keep the party in its nation-wide aspect more alert and active,
recruited more nearly up to its maximum strength, the different parts
better articulated and running more smoothly, than if it were called to
battle only once in two or four years. Moreover, a steadily increasing
proportion of people in most states now live in cities; and a party's
chances of winning the great national contests will be materially improved
if the national organization can maintain from year to year, in every
important city, well-organized units led by veterans trained in local
political skirmishes.

Many people, however, remain convinced that the injection of national
party cleavages and activities into state and local politics has been productive of more evil than good, and that, in particular, it has been
largely to blame for the existence in populous communities of unscrupulous and corrupt political machines operating comfortably behind the
protective screen of a Democratic or Republican label. As one method of
breaking the undesirable connection, many states have made provision

for holding state and local elections, so far as practicable, in intervals between national elections, with the idea that this will enable state or local issues to be considered on their own merits, even though candidates continue to run and be elected as Republicans, Democrats, or Socialists. Resorting to still more drastic measures, several states have adopted for state, or at least authorized for local, elections a non-partisan form of ballot, *i.e.*, a ballot bearing no indication of the party affiliations of candidates; and many county and city officers, judges of state or local courts, together with some state executive officials and the members of the legislature in Minnesota and Nebraska, are now nominated and elected in this way. Wherever the non-partisan ballot has been adopted, it has been generally assumed by its advocates that the influence of national party organizations will be entirely eliminated, or at any rate reduced to a minimum. In many instances, this has turned out to be the result, especially in relatively small communities. In states or large cities having highly organized national party machines operating the year around, however, the outcome is likely to be, and often has been, quite different. Each political organization is almost certain to have favored representatives on the non-partisan ballot, and the word is passed around—sometimes publicly, at other times in whispers—that such and such men are the "organization" candidates, with the result of the persons named receiving partisan support almost equally with candidates publicly bearing the party label. Too great hope of regenerating state and municipal politics must not, therefore, be staked upon the mere removal of national party labels from the ballot. After all, it is to be remembered, too, that while Democratic and Republican labels may not signify much in state or local elections, they at least give the ordinary voter some idea of the forces or organizations behind the candidates; whereas, with a non-partisan ballot, he may be left quite in the dark. Obviously, a poor clue under such circumstances is better than none at all.

State and Local Party Organization

Although overshadowed by the national party organizations superimposed upon them, the state organizations are, in a real sense, primary and basic. Formed independently in the several states, they are regulated (in so far as regulated at all by anything except their own rules) entirely by state law. The national organizations must accept and work with them as they are, with no authority to dictate to them, even when they prove rebellious. Those organizations have also to abide by whatever state regulations may have bearing on their own activities within any particular state. In spite of all this, however, a party's national organization may in reality hold the whip-hand in that, being usually far more able to raise campaign funds, and having wider access to offices and favors, it is in a position to furnish or withhold the sinews without which the efforts of state organizations would be likely to prove weak and unavailing.

The state convention

In earlier days, the highest party authority in a state was a state convention elected, in counties or other districts, by the party voters or by local conventions; and this body nominated candidates for state offices, adopted platforms, and in general regulated the affairs of the party. In many states, however, the rise of the direct primary [1] as a device for nominating candidates has robbed the convention of one of its main reasons for existence; and even in other states the increased regulation of party activities by statute has contributed to the decline of a once vigorous institution; indeed, in a good many states it has been abolished altogether, although likely to be replaced with some new sort of party council or caucus, particularly for the preparation of the party platform. Here and there, however, the state convention retains considerable significance; and one will recall how the Supreme Court (although changing its mind later) not so long ago recognized the right of the Democratic convention in Texas, as the supreme governing body of the party, to exclude Negroes from Democratic primaries. [2] In general, however, the states now have other more important party machinery.

The state central committee

In every state, the two major parties, and in some states minor parties as well, maintain a central committee which, under a chairman, serves as the true head of the state party organization. In size, composition, and powers, these central committees vary greatly, as also do the subordinate committees farther down the scale. Such matters are now regulated by law in most states; but in the absence of law, party rules govern. Members of the state central committee commonly represent either counties or legislative or congressional districts, and are either elected directly by the voters of the respective areas or chosen by local conventions—with women in nearly all states sharing equally with men. When the convention system held undisputed sway, the state central committee, or a group within it, often exerted decisive influence upon the action of the state convention in selecting candidates; but in states that have adopted the direct primary, the committee's influence upon nominations has declined, or at all events has become much less conspicuous and decisive. Nowadays, the committee's energies are concentrated upon promoting election of party candidates (national and state) and maintaining efficient party organization throughout the state between elections. In some instances, it chooses the party delegates to the national convention; and occasionally it formulates the party platform.

Subordinate committees

Subordinate to the state committee, and operating in a more restricted sphere, are often similarly constituted committees in congressional, legislative, or senatorial districts. But in any event, of special importance are the county committees, with their chairmen—found in practically every county, and city central committees, found in almost all cities, and especially influential in the largest municipalities. Nearly every city

[1] See pp. 235-237 below.
[2] See p. 190 above.

ward and voting precinct also has its dual or triple set of party committees—at all events, its ward leader and precinct leader or captain;[1] and the same is true of almost every village and township. Members of county and other local committees are usually elected directly by the party voters in the subdivision concerned. Originally, all such committees consisted exclusively of male voters; but with the adoption of woman suffrage, many committees have expanded their membership so as to admit women; while in other instances the hierarchy of men's committees is paralleled with a series of women's committees.[2]

With a view to bringing about the nomination of an "organization slate," or ticket of candidates favored by those in control of a given committee or series of committees, committee activities sometimes begin long in advance of the primaries or conventions in which candidates are to be nominated. The greater part of committee work, however, has to do directly or indirectly with the conduct of the campaign starting shortly after nominations are made. State and local committees are particularly active in seeing that new residents and first-voters are properly registered; in assisting aliens to qualify by obtaining naturalization papers (though under the naturalization laws this has to be done a good while before the election); in instructing voters as to registration formalities, the location of polling places, and the proper way to mark a ballot or operate a voting-machine; in raising campaign funds in the local field; in making canvasses of voters before election day in order to ascertain the drift of public sentiment; in assigning speakers, distributing cam-

Committee activities

[1] S. Forthal, *Cogwheels of Democracy; A Study of the Precinct Captain* (New York, 1946).

[2] It should be understood that the party machinery here described is normally quite a different thing from the political "machines" of which we often hear: every state, county, and local subdivision has its committees, chairmen, and the like as outlined; and some have nothing more. Occasionally, however, a state, and fairly often a larger city, has also a political "machine" (with commonly a "boss"), which may operate more or less independently of the regular party organization upon which it is superimposed, or may be practically identical with that organization, or at all events in full control of it. Thus, the Tammany machine is itself the Democratic organization in New York county, and the Republican machine in Philadelphia is the Republican organization of that city. Sometimes, indeed, the party organization for an entire state falls under the dominance of, or in effect itself becomes, a "state machine." Thus there used to be a "Hill machine" controlling the Democratic state organization in New York, and a "Quay machine" and a "Penrose machine" similarly dominant in the Republican state organization of Pennsylvania. Usually, however, a machine is of more local character, with possibility of more than one in a single state. Additional examples of local machines (although, of course, having important connections with state politics) include the Nash-Kelly organization in Cook county (Chicago), the Pendergast machine in Kansas City, the Hague machine in Hudson county (Jersey City), and perhaps the strongest (and at the same time most respectable) of the group, the Crump machine in Shelby county (Memphis), Tennessee. Cf. H. Zink, *City Bosses in the United States* (Durham, N. C., 1930); J. T. Salter, *Boss Rule* (New York, 1935). In the elections of 1946, all of the Democratic machines mentioned except the last one fared badly. E. J. Flynn, *You're the Boss; My Story of a Life in Practical Politics* (New York, 1947), is a revealing political autobiography by the Democratic boss of the Bronx (in New York City), who also was at one time chairman of the Democratic national committee. The author ardently defends the rôle of "good" bosses like himself, castigates all party irregularity, upholds the spoils system as inevitable and proper, and in general gives a frank, if not startling, exposition of what he terms "the political facts of life."

paign literature,[1] and employing every other known means of kindling the enthusiasm and quickening the loyalty of the rank and file;[2] in appointing party watchers to serve at the polls, and often also virtually appointing precinct election officials. Once the party has won, the committees may further serve the cause by seeing that faithful workers are rewarded with places on the public payroll, that legislation is enacted which will strengthen the hold of the party upon the voters, and that administrative policies are developed which, in one way or another, will reflect credit upon the party generally.

Party Organization on the National Level [3]

The national convention

As has been observed, the rise and spread of the direct primary, together with other changes, has left the state party convention with considerably diminished importance. On the national level, however, there have been no corresponding developments, and the supreme organ of the national party is still definitely the national convention. When studying shortly the subject of presidential nominations and elections,[4] we shall have to look somewhat closely into the nature of the national convention, and hence it must suffice here to observe merely that the convention of a major party is a large representative body, composed of delegates chosen in various ways, convoked in every presidential election year, and with authority not only to nominate candidates and adopt platforms for particular campaigns, but to control the party's fundamental organization and rules, or "constitution." Over it, too, as over the national, congressional, and senatorial committees to be mentioned, the national government exercises no control, except incidentally in connection with campaign expenditures.

The national committee:

1. Membership

The convention meets only every four years and naturally must have an arm or agency to carry on, more or less in its name, during the long intervals. The result is a standing executive committee known as the national committee; and just as the convention itself is a federally constructed body, composed of delegations representing the party in the

---

[1] A few states have laws which require the printing and mailing to every voter before primaries and elections of "publicity pamphlets" in which are to be found statements by the various party committees or candidates bearing upon their respective claims to favorable consideration.

[2] To influence voters, party committees employ many devices and methods, including mass meetings or "rallies"; parades, barbecues, and fireworks; paid and volunteer campaign speakers and glee-clubs; lawyers', merchants', workingmen's, and many other temporary clubs; organizations of colored voters, of Irish, Jewish, Italian, Scandinavian, Polish, German, and other foreign-born voters; leagues of college and university students; tons of campaign literature; an immense amount of advertising in newspapers and magazines and on billboards; and extensive radio-broadcasting. A recent, although not very satisfactory, book on practical campaigning is H. Gauer, *How to Win in Politics* (Boston, 1947).

[3] The following comment applies to the two major parties. Minor parties, even when national in scope, show some variations. Party organization in Congress (dealt with in later chapters on the legislative process) is likewise not covered here. See Chaps. xv, xvii, xix below.

[4] See Chap. xiii below.

various states, territories, dependencies, and District of Columbia, so the national committee is also federally constituted, in that all such units are represented equally in it—formerly by one member each, but now by two (a man and a woman). Prior to 1912, members of both Republican and Democratic national committees were "nominated" by the several delegations in the national convention and formally "elected" by the entire convention. Subsequently, the wide adoption of state direct primary laws led to some modification of this practice, although in theory the national convention continues to elect. Where state laws require committeemen to be chosen in a party primary or in some other specified manner (as by a state convention), the persons so designated are regarded as "nominated" to the national convention, and the convention proceeds to elect them to the national committee as a matter of form.

The principal functions of the national committee are to decide, several months in advance, upon the time and place of holding the national convention, to issue the formal call for the election of delegates, to appoint local committees to make preliminary arrangements for the convention, to make up the temporary roll, and, after the convention adjourns, to select a national chairman (in consultation with the presidential candidate, who really makes the choice) and assist him in the conduct of the campaign. Between presidential elections, the committee usually falls into a state of suspended animation until the approach of the time for the next national convention. In recent years, to be sure, permanent headquarters, in charge of a limited staff and with a publicity bureau, have been maintained continuously between presidential elections. But the committee is large and cumbersome, and during such intervals it has very little relationship with, and virtually no control over, the actions of either the president or the party members in Congress.[1] *2. Functions*

At the head of the national committee, and serving as commander-in-chief of the party's forces throughout the campaign, is the national chairman, nominally elected by the committee, but in reality the personal choice of the presidential candidate; and upon him the committee devolves full authority and responsibility for managing the campaign, although naturally assisting in such ways as it can in carrying out the plans and policies which he (in conjunction with the presidential candidate) formulates. The principal auxiliary officials include one or more vice-chairmen (elected by the national committee or appointed by its chairman), a secretary and an assistant secretary, and a treasurer. An executive committee is usually named by the national chairman, with the members serving as his staff officers and advisers during the campaign; and the work carried on under the national committee's auspices is handled by a dozen or more bureaus, departments, or divisions, *The national chairman and other officers*

---

[1] Its members may be active enough in connection with patronage matters in their respective states.

including a speakers' bureau, a publicity department, a purchasing department, an advisory committee, a congressional committee, a foreign-language division, a research division, a commercial travelers' bureau, a labor division, a farm division, a club division, and colored women's, colored men's, and colored speakers' bureaus.

Congres-
sional
and sena-
torial
campaign
commit-
tees

Comparatively inconspicuous in presidential campaigns, but prominently active in connection with congressional and senatorial elections occurring between presidential elections, are the congressional and senatorial committees which assist in the election of members of Congress bearing their respective party labels. The Republican congressional committee is composed of one congressman from each state having a Republican member in the House of Representatives, nominated by the state delegation and formally elected by a caucus of the Republican representatives. The Democratic congressional committee consists of one member from each state. He or she is usually a member of the House of Representatives, and if so, is selected by the delegation from that state. But if the state is without a Democratic representative, the committee chairman may appoint some one, usually an ex-member, to represent it. Since the adoption of popular election of senators, similar committees—usually of six or seven members—have been instituted by both parties to assist in the election of party candidates for the Senate; and although these committees are reorganized every two years, the members are generally retained as long as they remain in Congress and are willing to serve, unless they become candidates for reëlection, in which case they retire from the committee during that campaign.

Upon the opening of a presidential contest, these congressional and senatorial committees place all of their resources at the disposal of the national committee and become its close allies, foregoing much of their own initiative, even in what concerns the election of senators and representatives. After all, in "presidential years" practically all elections follow the fortunes of the contest for the presidency. But in "off years" the committees are much more conspicuous; they then have entire charge of the congressional campaign, relying, of course, upon the coöperation of state and local committees. They distribute political literature, maintain speakers' bureaus, and raise and disburse money in considerable amounts, giving special attention to doubtful states or districts; and they often intervene to smooth out local factional differences. During intervals between elections, too, they keep more or less in touch with the central and district committees in the different states, endeavoring in every way to promote the party's interests.

Party Finances—Corrupt Practices Legislation

Forceful and efficient conduct of any political campaign in which a large number of voters must be appealed to—especially a presidential or a state campaign, or even one restricted to a single large city—requires the collection and disbursement of large sums of money; indeed, the first, and often the principal, task of many of the party committees mentioned above is to raise "campaign funds." As a rule, the burden devolves primarily upon the treasurer of the national or other committee most directly concerned, although in states and localities it may be assigned to a director of finance, with perhaps a committee on ways and means; and such officials leave no stone unturned in their search for "the sinews of war." Appeals go not only to people of wealth, but to any and all party adherents considered likely to respond.

No official records of expenditures in connection with national campaigns were published until 1908. Since that date, however, there has been something more substantial to rely upon than mere estimate or conjecture; for full publicity was voluntarily given to both contributions and expenditures in the year mentioned, and since 1910 such publicity has been required by national law. There is, however, the difficulty that the regular channel for expenditure of money on a national campaign, *i.e.*, the national committee of the party, is by no means the only one through which money contributes, directly or indirectly, to the support of such a campaign; state and local committees also spend money which at least indirectly assists the national effort, and, especially of late, all sorts of voluntary, unofficial committees and organizations raise and spend sometimes even larger sums. Taking, however, what was reported officially to have been paid out, the Hoover-Smith campaign of 1928 saw more money raised and expended than on any previous occasion—more than $10,000,000 in the case of the Republicans and nearly $7,500,000 in that of their leading opponents. Four years later, the country was in the depths of depression, and the amounts fell to $2,900,052 and $2,245,975, respectively.[1] In 1936, however, outlays again reached an all-time high, the Republicans spending $14,198,202 and the Democrats, $9,228,406.[2] In 1940 (the second Hatch Act [3]—passed as the campaign was getting under way—having fixed three million dollars as the maximum that any party committee might spend in any calendar year), the Republican and Democratic national committees paid out $3,451,310 (including old bills unpaid) and $2,783,654, respectively—but with *total* expenditures (national and state committees, voluntary groups, and individuals, though without figures from county and other local committees) mounting to $14,941,142 and $6,095,357, respectively.[4] Finally, in 1944, under the same restrictions on the national committees, the reported expenditures

Expenditures in recent presidential campaigns

[1] L. Overacker, "Campaign Funds in a Depression Year," *Amer. Polit. Sci. Rev.*, XXVII, 769-783 (Oct., 1933).

[2] Sen. Rep. No. 151, 75th Cong., 1st Sess., "Investigation of Campaign Expenditures in 1936." Cf. L. Overacker, "Campaign Funds in the Presidential Election of 1936," *Amer. Polit. Sci. Rev.*, XXXI, 473-498 (June, 1937).

[3] See p. 226 below.

[4] Senate Report No. 47, 77th Cong., 1st Sess. (1941), p. 142. Cf. L. Overacker, "Campaign Finance in the Presidential Election of 1940," *Amer. Polit. Sci. Rev.*, XXXV, 701-727 (Aug., 1941).

by the committees themselves were $2,828,652 and $2,056,122, respectively, with the actual over-all totals estimated at $13,195,377 and $7,441,800, respectively.[1]

The experience of the Republicans in several campaigns would seem to indicate that national elections cannot be won with "big money." And in point of fact, the apprehensions of people who deplore the expenditure of sums such as those mentioned, as being fraught with sinister possibilities for our democratic institutions, are not well founded. Uninformed as a rule concerning the legitimate cost of conducting a national campaign—to say nothing of more than two-score state campaigns and a stupendous number of municipal and other local campaigns—the public is prone to regard outlays on the present staggering scale as presumptive evidence of widespread attempts to debauch the electorate. And rival party organizations, or candidates, especially if having more restricted financial resources, habitually take advantage of this popular suspicion and loudly denounce the "slush funds" of their opponents. Yet any fair-minded citizen who will investigate the facts will find that it takes only a few items of a perfectly legitimate nature to account for outlays running into the millions. Like other forms of publicity or advertising, campaigning has come to be tremendously expensive. One reason is that the electorate has been more than doubled by the extension of suffrage to women; so that, allowing five cents for stationery, printing or typing, and postage, more than three million dollars would be required merely to prepare and mail one circular letter addressed to all of our sixty million registered voters of 1940. A nation-wide campaign necessarily involves the expenditure of hundreds of thousands, if not millions, of dollars, in the aggregate, for the rental of headquarters and places for holding political meetings, for printing and distributing campaign literature, for the traveling expenses of speakers and the higher party officials, for a small army of organizers, canvassers, clerks, copyists, typists, tabulators, and addressers, to say nothing of the cost of advertising in newspapers, in magazines, on billboards, and by radio.[2] When all of these entirely proper objects of expenditure are duly listed and footed up, it will not be difficult to understand why, in spite of extended and searching investigations by Senate special committees in connection with every presidential campaign from 1920 to 1944 inclusive, almost no evidence has come to light justifying suspicion of extensive corruption in the national politics of recent years.

[1] L. Overacker, "Presidential Campaign Funds, 1944," *Amer. Polit. Sci. Rev.*, XXXIX, 899-925 (Oct., 1945). Cf. Miss Overacker's summary treatment of the entire subject in her *Presidential Campaign Funds* (Boston, 1946); also J. K. Pollock, *Party Campaign Funds* (New York, 1926).

[2] In 1944, when both major parties spent more than ever before on radio-broadcasting, the Democratic outlay through the national committee alone was $750,000 (over thirty-six per cent of total disbursements, and not including $175,000 more paid in 1945 on radio bills largely chargeable to the 1944 campaign); and the Republican outlay was $841,600—more than thirty per cent of the total.

Whence come the funds with which to meet outlays on such a scale? Speaking broadly, from anybody who can be induced to give. Party officials and candidates and party office-holders are, of course, expected to dig into their pockets. Contributors during recent campaigns are circularized and invited to help. A decade or so ago, widely heralded efforts were made, especially by the Democrats, to get the general rank and file to manifest interest by contributing a dollar apiece, or some similar small amount. The results were never impressive, though in the aggregate a good many party members do give something (rarely very much) out of more or less disinterested desire to see the party, or perhaps a favorite candidate, win. All this, however, would not carry a major party far toward the vast sums required. And, by and large, the money comes, in more generous quantities, from people who have, or think they have, something at stake—usually, of course, some business or other economic interest—in the success or defeat of a given party; and these are the "prospects" on whom the party treasurers and members of finance committees work in their campaigns of solicitation. Corporations are forbidden by law to contribute. But this does not stand in the way of gifts by officers, directors, and stockholders, acting as individuals; and any list of larger contributors to especially the Republican coffers (in lesser degree to the Democratic also, at least until 1936 [1]) is studded with the names of representatives of big business—Du Ponts, Mellons, Rockefellers, Guggenheims, McCormicks, Milbanks, Pews—and people, too, of less conspicuous yet substantial business interests and connections. Likewise, since 1943 labor unions have been forbidden to contribute; [2] but this did not prevent an auxiliary of the C. I. O., the Political Action Committee, from approaching the campaign of 1944 with a fund of $675,000 to be spent in the interest of President Roosevelt's reëlection, and with a promise of more if needed, or from actually spending $949,351. To be sure, even in days when no efforts had as yet been made to restrict the size of donations, the number of really large individual gifts to the national committees was insignificant—in 1936, only three of over $50,000. One-thousand-dollar contributors, however, are fairly plentiful— 2,349 in 1936 and 1,008 (549 Republican and 450 Democratic) in 1944. The Democrats commonly get contributions, in smaller average amounts, from more people—from 54,739 in 1944, compared with a Republican figure (12,500) less than one-fourth as large.

Manifestly, the raising and spending of money for winning elections opens possibilities of abuse; and both nation and states now have laws, known as "corrupt practices acts," regulating campaign contributions and outlays; such laws, indeed, have been a principal means by which parties and their activities have been brought within the orbit of state,

[1] The business world's aversion to the New Deal was reflected in that year in the conspicuous abstention of bankers and manufacturers from support of the Roosevelt candidacy.

[2] See p. 224 below.

and to a certain extent federal, statutory control.[1] The corrupt practices legislation of forty-eight states is too diverse to be described in detail here; although it may be said that the principal things provided for are: (1) restriction of sources and amounts of contributions, (2) limitation of expenditures, in both primaries and elections, (3) prohibition of bribery, treating, intimidation or impersonation of voters, stuffing ballot-boxes, tampering with voting-machines, and other corrupt practices, and (4) publicity for contributions, or expenditures, or both.[2]

Regulations imposed by Congress, and applicable, of course, only to campaigns and elections involving the choice of president, vice-president, senators, and representatives, may be summarized under four heads. (1) *Limitations on the raising of money.* Under federal civil-service law, persons on the federal payroll may not be solicited for contributions for political purposes by any officer or employee of the government. An act of 1907 forbids any national bank or other corporation organized under national law to contribute to any campaign fund whatsoever, and also makes it unlawful for any corporation (organized under state law) to contribute to such a fund in connection with the election of president, vice-president, senators, or representatives. In a clause irrelevant to the general purposes of the legislation, the War Labor Disputes [Smith-Connally] Act of 1943 extended these restrictions to labor unions; and a few days before that measure expired by its own terms on June 30, 1947,[3] the Labor-Management Relations [Taft-Hartley] Act more than took up the threatened slack by prohibiting, under severe penalties, contributions by labor unions or other organizations (equally with banks and corporations) in connection with not only federal elections, but all primaries, caucuses, and conventions held in connection therewith.[4] Under the Hatch Political Activities Act mentioned below, no contributions from relief

[1] The corrupt practices legislation dealt with in the remainder of this chapter might appropriately be treated in the following chapter on nominations and elections, but is included here for the sake of unity in covering the general subject of money in politics.

[2] The subject is discussed at length in E. R. Sikes, *State and Federal Corrupt Practices Legislation* (Durham, N. C., 1928); and somewhat more recent information will be found in H. Best [comp.], *Corrupt Practices at Elections*, 75th Cong., 1st Sess., Sen. Doc. No. 11 (1937).

[3] The act provided that it should cease to be effective six months after the termination of hostilities as proclaimed by the president; and such termination was proclaimed as of December 31, 1946.

[4] In the election of 1944, the C. I. O., for example, could not contribute directly to the Democratic campaign fund, but, as pointed out, the Political Action Committee, an auxiliary, could and did do so; and this would still be possible under the 1947 legislation. Under the Smith-Connally Act, a union could engage in any political activity, including the use of money in connection with primaries, so long as it did not contribute directly to party funds used to promote the election of candidates for president, vice-president, or seats in Congress. Under the Taft-Hartley Act, however, union funds not only may not be used in connection with caucuses, conventions, or primaries (in addition, of course, to elections in the stricter sense), but, if collected as dues, may not be employed in publishing pamphlets or special editions of newspapers having political purposes, on the theory that union members should not be compelled to see their dues deflected to propaganda against candidates whom they individually may favor. In a test case, a federal district court in Washington, D. C., in March, 1948, held the Taft-Hartley ban unconstitutional.

workers (when there are such) are to be received, and no individual, committee, or corporation may donate more than $5,000 in any calendar year to the campaign of any candidate for a federal office (exclusive of any contribution to a state or local committee). (2) *Restrictions on amounts that may be spent.* The Federal Corrupt Practices Act of 1925 limits the expenditures of a candidate for the Senate to $10,000 and of a candidate for the House to $2,500, unless a lower maximum is fixed by law of the candidate's state, in which case that law is to govern. A candidate has a right, however, to the benefit of an alternative rule under which he may spend up to three cents per vote cast for all candidates for the given office in the last preceding general election, with a maximum of $25,000 for a senatorial candidate and $5,000 for a candidate for the House. In line with the Supreme Court's implication in the Newberry decision of 1921 that Congress had power to regulate elections only, and not nominating procedures,[1] the act specifically exempts primaries from its provisions—which, of course, leaves a big loophole,[2] and in the Southern states, where the Democratic primary invariably determines the outcome of the election, this means that there really are no federal controls at all. One other restriction, found in the Hatch Political Activities Act, is that no "political committee" operating nationally may receive or expend more than three million dollars in any calendar year. (3) *Limitations on the purposes for which money may be spent.* State laws on this subject are usually quite ample, but federal restriction does not extend much beyond prohibition of the more obvious types of corrupt practice; indeed, in limiting the amount of expenditure as mentioned above, the law expressly exempts outlays of candidates on travel, subsistence, stationery, postage, circulars, telegraph and telephone service, and for "personal" items, thereby failing (at least under the last-mentioned category) to close another sizable loophole. (4) *Requirement of publicity.* This takes two main forms. First, every candidate for the Senate or House is required to file with the secretary of the Senate or the clerk of the House, as the case may be, a full report of all contributions received in support of his candidacy and an itemized statement of expenditures. Second, all party committees (and likewise all other committees, organizations, and associations which receive donations or spend money for political purposes in two or more states) must make full periodic reports, under oath, of their financial operations. The difficulty with these requirements is that they have never been very adequately enforced; the reports of many organizations are very casual and unsystematic, and even when otherwise, little actual publicity is likely to·be given them.

With a view, among other things, to bolstering and extending the

---

[5] An implication completely reversed in 1941 in the case of United States *v.* Classic (see p. 190, note 4, above).

[2] Another such loophole is the total absence of any restriction upon outlays made independently in behalf of a candidate by his friends or by organizations or interests supporting him.

earlier and in general not too effective federal corrupt practices laws, Congress in 1939 passed an act (sponsored by Senator Carl A. Hatch of New Mexico) to "prevent pernicious political activities," and in 1940 amended and expanded it in a second "Hatch Act"—the Hatch Political Activities Act already mentioned.[1] To a considerable extent, this legislation has to do with political activities of civil servants on lines other than strictly financial; and these aspects of it will be discussed more appropriately at a later point.[2] As already indicated, however, it contains two principal provisions pertinent here, i.e., (1) the restriction of collections or expenditures by any national political committee to a maximum of three million dollars during any calendar year, and (2) the limitation of individual or collective gifts to national campaign funds to $5,000 in any year.[3]

At their first test (in the campaign of 1940), the foregoing presumed limitations upon contributions and expenditures in national campaigns proved weak reeds upon which to lean. To be sure, the current outlays of the national committees were kept under the legal ceiling of three million dollars. But the actual known expenditures on the campaign of the two major parties were not only the largest on record, but actually some eight million dollars in excess of those of 1936. What happened was, of course, very simple, and without a word in the new legislation to circumvent it. On both the Republican side and the Democratic, all sorts of new "committees," "clubs," "associations," and the like—some of them loudly proclaiming themselves "non-political"—sprang up and raised funds which they independently poured into the respective campaigns, supplementing the efforts of the national committee and enabling the committees to keep their expenditures within the law, yet actually helping push the campaigns with full vigor. The Associated Willkie Clubs of America alone acknowledged an outlay of $1,356,604. While as for individuals—having contributed or loaned up to $5,000 to a national committee, they then made further contributions to the separate organizations mentioned, or often to one or more state committees, which thereupon used the funds to take care of expenses previously assumed by the national committee.[4] The same things happened in 1944, when even larger proportions of the total outlays were accounted for by organizations separate from the national committees. This time, on the Republican side, the Republican Finance Committee of Pennsylvania spent

---

[1] 53 U. S. Stat. at Large, 1147; 54 ibid., 767.

[2] See pp. 511-513 below.

[3] For the text of the consolidated law as it now stands, together with that of the Federal Corrupt Practices Act of 1925 as amended, see H. M. Megill [comp.], Federal Corrupt Practices Act and the Hatch Political Activity Act (Washington, D. C., Govt. Prtg. Off., 1946). Two cases decided in 1947 (although not involving the provisions mentioned above) gave the Supreme Court opportunity to sustain the Hatch legislation. See p. 513, note 1, below.

[1] Another expedient was "family" gifts, several different members of a donor's family each contributing up to $5,000. In 1944, the Republicans listed twelve such contributing groups.

$939,934 and the United Republican Finance Committee of Metropolitan New York, $1,260,593; and on the Democratic side, the Democratic Campaign Committee of Philadelphia spent $228,745, the One Thousand Club, $200,194, and the Political Action Committee and its affiliates, a total of over $1,327,000—while individuals contributed (by splitting among different committees and organizations) amounts up to $125,000 and beyond.

From such experience, it could readily be deduced that if the laudable objects sought in the contributions-expenditures provisions of the Hatch legislation were ever to be attained, laws would have to be enacted that could not so easily be evaded. In disgust, the senator whose name the legislation bore came out with a proposal not only for repeal, but for trying it again with a plan which was drastic indeed, *i.e.*, limiting the outlay of every party in a national campaign to one million dollars and having the national government itself furnish the funds. The idea had a certain attractiveness, and some people endorsed it. Sober second thought, however, raised questions—even beyond that of whether so revolutionary a scheme as government-financed political campaigns would ever commend itself to the country. What *is* a national campaign, and precisely what activities are to be regarded as embraced in it? Could a party be expected to finance a national campaign on only one million dollars—or double that amount? Could private organizations and groups ever be prevented from raising money and spending it on campaigns? If they could not, was it worth while to try to fix ceilings at all? Probably in time there will be new legislation. But it will hardly follow the proposal mentioned. The truth is that the subject is not one on which the people at large feel deeply. They like showy campaigns; it takes big money to run such campaigns; and while there is lip-service for the general objectives of the Hatch legislation, there is no deep popular concern about curbing lavishness on the part of either givers or spenders able to practice it. In default of such concern, regulation with teeth in it will be difficult to enact, and still more difficult to enforce. Over the years, many extremely useful restraints upon the collection and use of money for political purposes have been imposed, and most of them are reasonably well observed. The task which the Hatch legislation undertook, however, is probably the most difficult of all; and the country may be a long time finding out how to perform it.[1]

What next?

[1] In April, 1947, the chairman of a Senate special committee which investigated the campaign expenditures of 1944 (Allen J. Ellender), with bipartisan support from members of his committee, introduced a "Federal Corrupt Practices and Pernicious Political Activities Act of 1947" (1) repealing the federal Corrupt Practices Act of 1925 and all of the Hatch legislation (including the three-million-dollar restriction on campaign committees and the $5,000 limitation on individual donors), (2) redefining "elections" to include primaries and nominating conventions, (3) raising the amounts which senatorial and congressional candidates may spend to $25,000 and $6,500 respectively, with alternative limits of $50,000 and $12,000, respectively, if calculated in terms of total votes cast in the previous election for the office in question or for state governor, and (4) requiring the publication of national committee

REFERENCES

C. A. Beard, *The Republic; Conversations on Fundamentals* (New York, 1943);
Chap. XVIII.

————, *The American Party Battle* (New York, 1928).

E. L. Shoup, *The Government of the American People* (Boston, 1946), Chaps. IX
XIII.

V. O. Key, Jr., *Politics, Parties, and Pressure Groups* (2nd ed., New York, 1947),
Chaps. II-XII, XV.

E. P. Herring, *The Politics of Democracy; American Parties in Action* (New York,
1940), Chaps. VIII, XV-XVII.

E. M. Sait, *American Parties and Elections* (3rd ed., New York, 1942), Chaps. VIII-
XV, XXII-XXIV.

P. H. Odegard and E. A. Helms, *American Politics; A Study in Political Dynamics*
(2nd ed., New York, 1947), Chaps. I-XI, XIV-XV, XXIII.

R. C. Brooks, *Political Parties and Electoral Problems* (3rd ed., New York, 1933)
Chaps. I-VIII.

C. E. Merriam and H. F. Gosnell, *The American Party System* (3rd ed., New York
1940), Chaps. I-VII, XIX-XX.

E. E. Schattschneider, *Party Government* (New York, 1942).

A. N. Holcombe, *The Political Parties of Today* (New York, 1924).

————, *The New Party Politics* (New York, 1933).

————, *The Middle Classes in American Politics* (Cambridge, Mass., 1940).

W. E. Binkley, *American Political Parties; Their Natural History* (New York, 1943).

T. W. Cousens, *Politics and Political Organization in America* (New York, 1942).

H. F. Gosnell, *Grass-Roots Politics* (Washington, D. C., 1942).

S. Forthal, *Cogwheels of Democracy; A Study of the Precinct Captain* (New York,
1946).

J. A. Farley, *Behind the Ballots; The Personal History of a Politician* (New York,
1938).

————, *Jim Farley's Story; The Roosevelt Years* (New York, 1948).

H. L. Childs, *An Introduction to Public Opinion* (New York, 1940).

C. A. Berdahl, "Party Membership in the United States," *Amer. Polit. Sci. Rev.*,
XXXVI, 16-50, 241-262 (Feb., Apr., 1942).

J. R. Starr, "The Legal Status of American Political Parties," *ibid.*, XXXIV, 439-455,
685-699 (June, Aug., 1940).

E. R. Sikes, *State and Federal Corrupt Practices Legislation* (Durham, N. C., 1928),
Chaps. VI-VIII.

J. K. Pollock, *Party Campaign Funds* (New York, 1926).

L. Overacker, *Money in Elections* (New York, 1932).

————, *Presidential Campaign Funds* (Boston, 1946).

W. S. Myers, *The Republican Party; A History* (New York, 1928).

F. R. Kent, *The Democratic Party; A History* (New York, 1928).

G. E. Mowry, *Theodore Roosevelt and the Progressive Movement* (Madison, Wis.,
1946).

contributions and expenditures in two or more leading newspapers in each state.
Legislation on these lines failed of enactment in the session of the Eightieth Congress finally terminating on December 19, 1947. But the proposals evoked favorable comment, as being more realistic than existing regulations, and with another presidential election looming in 1948 there seemed some chance that action, more or less of the sort suggested, would be taken to prevent the country from being compelled to undergo again the farcical experiences of 1940 and 1944. Meanwhile, the Labor-Management Relations Act of 1947 had at least served the useful purpose of merging primaries into elections in connection with campaign contributions.

K. C. MacKay, *The Progressive Movement of 1924* (New York, 1947).

J. Oneal and G. A. Werner, *American Communism; A Critical Analysis of Its Origins, Development, and Programs* (new ed., New York, 1947).

E. W. Browder, *The Communist Party of the United States of America; Its History, Rôle, and Organization* (New York, 1941).

H. W. Laidler, *American Socialism; Its Aims and Practical Program* (New York, 1937).

H. A. Bone, "Political Parties in New York City," *Amer. Polit. Sci. Rev.*, XL, 272-282 (Apr., 1946).

W. B. Hesseltine, *The Rise and Fall of Third Parties; From Anti-Masonry to Wallace* (Washington, D. C., 1948).

R. V. Peel and T. C. Donnelly, *The 1928 Campaign* (New York, 1931).

————, *The 1932 Campaign* (New York, 1935).

P. H. Odegard, *Prologue to November, 1940* (New York, 1940).

American Institute of Public Opinion, *The Gallup Poll Almanac for 1946* (Princeton N. J., 1946). Convenient statistical summaries.

CHAPTER XII

NOMINATIONS AND ELECTIONS

Political parties in a democracy serve a variety of purposes, but chiefly that of providing channels through which candidates for public office can be selected, programs of public action formulated and announced, and candidates and policies urged upon the voters who make the final choices at the polls. From parties and voters, as considered in the previous two chapters, we therefore turn naturally to nominations and elections.

Impor-
tance

Here, of course, is where the stored-up political power of the people is brought to bear most directly in controlling the conduct of government. And in this country it is an impressive power indeed, not only because of the vastness of the electorate, but because of the very great number of elective offices to be filled, the number and frequency of elections held, and the intensity with which electoral contests commonly are carried on. Precisely how many elective officers of all kinds we have in the United States, no one can say. But, as indicated in an earlier chapter, it is at least 880,000—hundreds on the national level, thousands on the state level, and hundreds of thousands on the humbler level occupied by counties, cities, towns, townships, villages, and districts.[1] Elections occur, too, with a good deal of frequency. Hardly a voter escapes being called to the polls (whether or not he actually goes) at least once a year; with both primaries and elections counted, he may indeed be called three or four, or even more, times. And when he goes, he is likely to be confronted with a ballot on which he is expected to vote for a dozen, a score, or even a larger number of candidates, for as many different offices. Rarely will the number of positions he is asked to help fill, over a two- or four-year period, be less than fifty, and often—depending on where he lives— it will exceed a hundred.

Constitutional and Legal Regulation

Prima-
rily a
state
function

As is true of party activities generally, nominations and elections are left to be regulated principally by the states. To begin with, the selection of purely state and local officers is almost completely state-controlled. Congress does not legislate on the matter, except as regulations relating to the choice of officials on the national level may incidentally affect the selection of state and local officials chosen at the same elections; and local governments commonly have only the function of administering election laws rather than making them, except that cities under home-rule systems

[1] See p. 178, note 1, above.

usually have a right to enact electoral ordinances for themselves, even to the extent of installing special electoral devices such as proportional representation. For their own elections, and those of their subdivisions, states determine who shall have the ballot (subject to the federal constitutional amendments touching the subject), and provide for the registration of voters, the conditions which parties must meet (most frequently in terms of votes polled in the previous election) in order to get a place on the ballot, the processes of nomination (including the conduct of primaries), the types of ballots employed, the methods of casting and counting ballots and determining and reporting results, the definition and punishment of corrupt practices, and many other things; and full power of legislatures to exercise such authority, in conformity with constitutional provisions, has almost invariably been sustained by the courts.

National, state, and local elections, however, while technically distinct, are in practice inextricably bound up together: the voters in all of them are the same people; to a large extent, the elections are held at the same time, and as a single procedure; and even the choice of presidential electors and the nomination and election of members of Congress are in most respects governed by the states (with the regular state electoral machinery employed)—as also, in many states, the selection of delegates to national nominating conventions and of members of party committees. To be sure, there is federal regulation as well. In the matter of the suffrage, the states are, of course, restricted by the provisions of the Fifteenth and Nineteenth Amendments. The times, places, and manner of electing senators and representatives are regulated primarily by state legislatures; but Congress may make or alter regulations so made,[1] and indeed has ordained, not only that senators and representatives shall be chosen on the first Tuesday after the first Monday in November of every even-numbered year,[2] but also that representatives shall be chosen by secret ballot (voting machines are construed to be tantamount to the same thing), and by districts except in the case of congressmen-at-large.[3] Congress is authorized also to fix a uniform date for the popular choice of presidential electors throughout the country, and likewise a date for the casting of the electoral votes;[4] and this it has done, with the same first Tuesday after the first Monday (every fourth year) established for what are popularly regarded as "presidential elections." Congress, further, has provided for the settlement of contested elections, regulated campaign contributions and expenditures, and in other ways legislated against corrupt practices. Significant, too, is the fact that,

The federal government's share

---

[1] Art. I, § 4, cl. 1. Congress may not control the places of choosing senators; but this provision lost point when senators ceased to be elected by state legislatures.

[2] Unless the constitution of a state fixes a different date. Maine is now the only state in which this is the case; congressmen, as well as other officers, are there elected on the second Monday of September.

[3] See p. 291, note 2, below. From 1901 until 1929, districts, too, were variously required to be "compact," formed of "contiguous" territory, etc. See p. 290 below.

[4] Art. II, § 1, cl. 4.

whereas formerly nominations, even by direct primary, were not considered to be "elections," and hence were regarded as beyond the power of Congress to regulate, a Supreme Court decision of 1941 construed them to be a feature or aspect of the electoral process, and accordingly subject, after all, to congressional control equally with final elections [1]— even though the power has not as yet actually been exercised. Finally, as we have seen, there is demand that Congress forbid payment of a poll tax to be made a condition for voting in federal elections (thereby expanding federal restrictions upon the states in suffrage matters), although vigorous Southern opposition is manifested on constitutional and other grounds.

State election laws

The general principle emerging is that the states have full control over electoral matters of all sorts, on all levels, except with respect to the suffrage, and except as in other aspects authority is vested in and exercised by Congress. As will be explained later, not even the complications raised by the problem of servicemen voting during World War II resulted in any permanent expansion of federal control—much less anything approaching a single, uniform national ballot. With their own elections almost completely in their own hands, and with federal elections very largely so, all states necessarily maintain collections or codes of election laws, frequently making up a rather sizable volume. And, although few people ever have the courage to wade through the detailed provisions of these codes, the intelligence and care with which the laws are framed and enforced are matters of vital importance. The ballot-box is the one point at which most people can exercise any direct control over their governments; and proper regulation and management of every circumstance and procedure surrounding the electoral process is no mere matter of tedious mechanics, but an indispensable condition of the free and full operation of our democracy.

The Nomination of Candidates

Significance of the nominating process

In any outline of an electoral system, the first phase to be given attention is the method of selecting candidates. To be sure, under our electoral laws, candidates do not have to be "selected," or nominated, at all in order to be elected; any qualified person may be elected to any office without nomination and, so far as that is concerned, without his name appearing on any ballot given the voters at the polls; and to facilitate such independent election, practically all states expressly permit the voter to "write in" names (in some cases to paste in stickers bearing printed names), with space provided on the ballots for the purpose. Very few people, however, ever attain office in this way; almost invariably, the winner in any electoral contest will have been placed before the voters in some manner—even if only by self-announcement—before the polling. In small communities and for minor local offices, such as mem-

[1] See p. 190 above.

bership in the board of a school-district, nothing more, in fact, is usually entailed than self-announcement; on the entire local level, indeed, mere declaration of intent, or "filing," is perhaps commoner than any other procedure. In places of some size, however, and for practically all offices on the higher levels, some mode of actual selection needs to be, and quite regularly is, employed; and this brings into play some kind of formal nominating machinery—usually party machinery, although where non-partisan elections prevail (as in two states and in numerous cities like Boston and San Francisco), nominations are at least presumed to be independent of party connections.[1] To be sure, the making of nominations is, in a sense, only a preliminary incident in the realization of a political party's ultimate objective, i.e., winning (or retaining) control of the government of the jurisdiction concerned. It is, nevertheless, of prime importance; because whether or not we have honest and efficient elected officials naturally depends almost entirely on the character and qualifications of the persons who receive nomination. Particularly true is this in not a few of our states where nomination by a strongly predominant party is usually tantamount to election, e.g., in such "one-party" states as Vermont and most of the Southern states; also in such cities as Philadelphia. The matter, too, is vital, not only to the people, but to political leaders and bosses, who want public officials with whom they can work, and who, to that end, are likely to exert all possible influence to turn nominations in favorable directions.

Even in colonial times, it was common enough for a few leading people of a town to put their heads together and decide who should be supported for the offices; and out of this practice developed a device of considerable importance in our political history, i.e., the caucus. No law was ever passed providing for caucuses, or regulating them. In the absence of other machinery for picking candidates, they arose spontaneously; but in earlier times most nominations were made by means of them. Always more or less informal, and sometimes meeting in secret, they developed typically as small conclaves of party leaders in townships, cities, or other minor areas, with sometimes a standing committee to convoke meetings and perform other services. Frequently, too, these gatherings designated some of their members to confer with representatives of similar caucuses in the choice of candidates for county offices; and eventually it became the customary thing for delegates to be chosen in local caucuses, in accordance with some agreed plan of representation, to attend county or city nominating conventions. Thus, with the local caucus continuing to nominate for offices within its own area, it also became a cog in an

Early nominating machinery—caucus and convention

---

[1] Even with party nominations prevailing, additional nominations can nearly always be made by petition, i.e., by voluntary groups of voters complying with simple requirements of law as to the requisite number (varying from a few hundred to many thousand) or, alternatively, as to the proportion (varying from one to as high as twenty-five per cent) of signers, and the formalities of filing. This, indeed, is the method by which all nominations are made in Great Britain and the British dominions, with only ten signers required.

expanding party mechanism which did not reach its limits until it embraced state nominating conventions and eventually national ones as well. With functions thus enlarged, the caucus also grew less spontaneous. More was now at stake, and politicians reached downwards through their lieutenants to control it, often blandly handing it a slate of names which it was expected to endorse. In time, indeed, it fell to low esteem among sensitive people. For over a hundred years, however, the caucus-convention system dominated American politics.

Before conventions were developed on a state and national scale, however, a special form of caucus played an important rôle, *i.e.*, a caucus drawn from members of a legislature. While as yet there was no other machinery for the purpose, party delegations in state legislatures simply took it upon themselves to "caucus" when a state election was approaching and to decide upon slates of candidates to be "recommended" to the voters; and as soon as parties took on a nation-wide aspect, the same practice arose in Congress for selecting candidates for the presidency and vice-presidency. The legislative caucus, on both the state and federal levels, fell, however, into disfavor, not only because the delegations acted without any conferred authority, leaving the people with no control over the choices made, but because their rôle in picking men to be voted upon for the executive positions was manifestly out of keeping with the spirit of our system of separation of powers. The upshot was that in the states the legislative caucus gradually gave way, especially after 1820, to state-wide conventions for nominating to state offices; while for selecting candidates for the presidency and vice-presidency, parties turned from congressional caucuses to national conventions. By 1835, and for upwards of eighty years thereafter, the representative convention was the almost exclusive device for selecting party candidates for all offices above those of townships, villages, and other minor local areas. Caucuses continued to function in voting precincts and other primary political units; from these, delegates went up to city or county conventions; from these, in turn, delegates went to state, and perhaps legislative- and congressional-district, conventions; and from these higher bodies went the delegates composing the topmost party conclave, the "presidential" convention.

At its advent, the convention system was hailed as a decided improvement upon earlier nominating methods, as indeed it was—if for no other reason, because it applied to the selection of party candidates the principle of representation upon which all government in America was supposed to be based. Theoretically, the voice of each voter could be transmitted up the scale, from delegates on one level to those on the next, helping make selections as it ascended, until finally it registered itself for some candidate for the highest office in the land. And to this day party leaders, as a rule, look upon the convention as the ideal means for selecting candidates. In their eyes, it periodically revitalizes the party organization, brings usefully into the open the party's strength or weakness in various portions of the state or district concerned, provides unexcelled opportunity for appraising and comparing the qualifications and general "availability" of candidates, dramatizes party activity and stirs party enthusiasm, promotes harmonizing of factions by "balanced" or compromise tickets, and furnishes the most natural means for drafting and adopting party platforms.

In operation, however, conventions—especially on state and lower levels —commonly disclosed serious defects. For one thing, they were usually too large to permit of effective deliberation. More serious, boss-ridden caucuses and other local political agencies too often resulted in an inferior order of delegates, with men representing the best type of citizenship rarely included; even when chosen as delegates, such better men often turned over their credentials to "proxies" named by party or factional leaders. Many conventions were completely boss-controlled and became mere "market-places of politics," where trades were consummated by the purchase, sale, or transfer of delegates from one candidate to another. Convention proceedings, too, frequently were marred by disorder and fraudulent practice. Altogether, the influence of the ordinary voter in selecting his party's candidates was likely to be hardly greater than under the legislative caucus; and it is not to be wondered at that—except on the national level, where the convention has been relatively free from the more grievous shortcomings enumerated—the convention system not only came in for vigorous criticism, but, after 1900, was very generally discarded, both for congressional and state nominations and for nominations for county and municipal positions. Where the system survives today, it is likely to be employed only (as in New York, Indiana, and three other states) for nominations to a few principal state offices.[1] In its place, a different nominating device—the direct primary—has been adopted, in one form or another, in all but two states (Connecticut and Rhode Island)—although it, too, is not without shortcomings.[2]

Disadvantages

The essence of the direct primary is, of course, the selection of candidates, not indirectly through conventions, but by direct action of the voters themselves; and the procedures employed are so similar to those used in the final elections that the primary becomes, in effect, a preliminary election—often designated, with entire appropriateness, a *direct primary election*. Primaries of the different parties are commonly held on the same day, and at the places where the regular elections are held later on; they are presided over by the regular election officials, with all

The direct primary— nature and workings

[1] In a few states—Arkansas, Delaware, Georgia, Virginia, and South Carolina, for example—conventions *may* still be employed if a given party so decides; and in Iowa they are used for nominating candidates for any offices, state or local, for which no person has received as much as thirty-five per cent of the primary vote, with South Dakota following the same plan in connection with the offices of governor, United States senator, and representative in Congress.

[2] For fuller discussion of the rise and defects of the caucus-convention system, see M. Ostrogorski, *Democracy and the Party System* (New York, 1910), Chaps. II–V, VII; E. C. Meyer, *Nominating Systems* (New York, 1902), Pt. I, Chap. V; and F. W. Dallinger, *Nominations for Elective Offices in the United States* (New York, 1897).

costs met out of the public treasury; the ballots are like those used in regular elections, and the same corrupt-practice laws and other safeguards apply.[1] Persons seeking nomination to an office may get their names on a primary ballot simply by self-announcement and payment of a fee. The commonest method, however, is to file a petition signed by some specified proportion of the voters in the area, the proportion being gauged roughly in accordance with the importance of the office, and varying all the way from one-half of one per cent to as high as ten per cent.[2] And ordinarily a candidate receiving the largest number of votes for a given office is declared the party nominee for that office, even though, with often three or four persons seeking the same nomination, the victor may win by virtue of only a plurality, rather than a majority, of the votes. Several Southern states,[3] and also Utah, however, require a majority; and if at the first balloting no candidate for a given position receives the requisite vote, a second, or "run-off," primary is held, with the voters choosing between the two candidates standing highest at the first test.[4] In any event, winners in the respective party primaries automatically get their names on the ballots placed in the voters' hands at the later regular elections.

Spread of the system

Following some limited experiments in various states with nomination by this method, Wisconsin, in 1903, adopted the first state-wide direct primary law;[5] and, with reaction against convention nominations sweep-

---

[1] Exceptions, however, appear in Southern states in which only Democratic primaries are held, and in which these either have always been, or since the repeal of primary laws following the Smith v. Allwright decision of 1944 (see p. 191 above) have become, private affairs, conducted and paid for by the party.

[2] California, in 1927, simplified the plan by substituting for petitions signed by a large number of voters declarations of candidacy signed by "sponsors," the number ranging from ten to twenty for the lowest offices up to from sixty to one hundred in the case of the highest. A few states have experimented with "pre-primary" conventions composed of delegates chosen in preliminary primaries and designed to agree upon lists of persons to be placed on the subsequent regular nominating-primary ballots. Massachusetts, Minnesota, and South Dakota have abandoned the plan; but Utah adopted it in 1947, Colorado adheres to a similar one. preferring, however, the term "pre-primary assembly," and in Nebraska, beginning in 1946, there are pre-primary conventions, with opportunity for names to be added by petition, or by simple declaration, to slates prepared by such bodies.

[3] The list formerly was: Mississippi, Texas, North Carolina, South Carolina, Georgia, Louisiana, Florida, Alabama, Arkansas. South Carolina repealed her primary laws in 1944, and the same step has been under consideration in other states.

[4] In Tennessee also a run-off primary is authorized in the case of a tie vote. It is logical enough for the Southern states to employ the run-off primary, for the reason that the winner in a primary of the only party that counts—the Democratic—is pre-destined to eventual election; in other words, it is the primary that determines final results. In order to approximate majority nominations, a number of states have tried the preferential system of voting, under which each voter is given an opportunity to express his first, second, and sometimes his third, choices among the candidates. In Iowa, and for certain positions in South Dakota (as has been indicated), if none of the candidates for a given office receives thirty-five per cent of the total party vote in the primary, the selection of a candidate for that office is left to the action of a delegate convention. Cf. O. D. Weeks, "Summary of the History and Present Status of Preferential Voting in State Direct Primary Systems," Southwestern Soc. Sci. Quar., XVIII, 64-67 (June, 1937).

[5] See A. F. Lovejoy, LaFollette and the Establishment of the Direct Primary in Wisconsin, 1890-1904 (New Haven, 1941).

ing the country, thirty-two states, by 1917, enacted similar legislation covering all state offices and in many cases local offices as well; indeed (though with a few states, *e.g.*, New York and Indiana, reverting to the convention system for certain principal offices), the movement went on until the primary became the sole or main mode of nomination the country over except in Connecticut and Rhode Island, and not only for state offices, but for those of the great majority of counties and cities, and also for members of Congress. In addition, the device has in many states been turned to account in selecting candidates for party offices and committee posts and for service as convention delegates.

In earlier days, when political parties were looked upon as merely private organizations, the ways in which they selected candidates for office were regarded as purely their own concern; and individuals wishing to announce their candidacy independently of any party were similarly exempt from conditions or controls. A basic defect of the historic caucus-convention system was, indeed, its almost total lack of regulation by law. In the period of growing dissatisfaction with conventions, some efforts were directed to curbing abuses by statutory action; and in so far as conventions survive today, they are commonly subject to a good deal of public control. The development, however, which first brought the nominating process widely and fully under public regulation was rather the rise of the direct primary; and nowadays—with parties themselves viewed as organizations of a public nature, subject to much state, and some federal, control relating to legal status, machinery, finances, and methods of operation—primaries have come in for regulation almost if not quite as extensive as that applying to regular elections—regulation actually by state legislatures and potentially (under the Supreme Court's ruling of 1941) by Congress as well. Formerly, every state, indeed—with or without primaries—had laws to which the naming of candidates, on national, state, and local levels alike, must conform; and this is still true except for South Carolina, which, as we have seen, has repealed her direct primary laws.[1]

The primary and public regulation

The direct primary usually presupposes elections on a party basis, and consequently is itself partisan, in the sense that persons seeking nomination do so as Republicans or Democrats and are so listed on the ballots used. Where, however, non-partisan elections have been introduced (as in Minnesota and Nebraska, and in many cities and some counties), they usually are preceded by a non-partisan primary conducted in all respects like an ordinary party primary, except that the ballots carry no indication of the party affiliation of the persons to be voted for, and that no question as to the voters' own affiliations is raised. Partisan and non-partisan primaries, for different offices, may indeed be held at the same time and place, with separate ballots employed for the two. In any event, the two candidates on the non-partisan ticket polling the highest number

Partisan and non-partisan primaries

[1] See p. 191 above.

of votes for each office get their names on the non-partisan ballot used at the ensuing election, the primary thus becoming "a sort of qualifying heat which eliminates the weaker contestants from the final race" and at the same time assures ultimate election by majority rather than mere plurality. Primaries of this nature may, however, be considerably less non-partisan than appears; for not only are the contestants likely to be known to the voters as Republicans or Democrats (and voted for accordingly), but they may actually have a good deal of more or less undercover party backing. Even so, the system somewhat enhances the freedom of voters to express their own preferences, and of independent-minded persons to capture nominations.

"Closed" and "open" primaries

Partisan primaries, in turn, fall into two categories, "closed" and "open," distinguished by the conditions laid down for participating in them. The closed primary not only is partisan, but is supposed to be participated in only by bona fide party members, and therefore to be protected against "raiding" by opposition voters who otherwise might vote its ballot simply in order to bring about the choice of a candidate weak enough to be defeated more easily later. Two methods of guarding against such raiding are employed. One—required by law in nineteen of the states (including New York, Pennsylvania, and California) is an enrollment of voters, sometimes at the primary itself, but in more instances well in advance, with every voter's party affiliation made a matter of record, so that separate Republican and Democratic primary ballots may be given at the polls only to persons whose names appear on the respective party lists. The other method, employed in most of the remaining states, involves no advance enrollment, but contemplates some procedure for challenging voters who call for the ballot of a party with which they are not known to be identified. Such voters may, for example, be asked to say whether they supported a given party at the last election, or at all events half of its candidates, or perchance whether it is their expectation to adhere to it in the future. Either of the two procedures can be flouted by persons of easy conscience if there is sufficient motive; the second is particularly weak. By and large, however, a closed primary of a given party is participated in only by more or less habitual adherents of that party.

But large numbers of voters shift their party allegiance in perfectly good faith; certainly this was true in the troubled decade of the thirties. And eight states frankly accept the fact and maintain "open" primaries operated with no attempt to put the voters' party preferences on record.[1] Instead of asking for and being handed a Republican or a Democratic ballot when he presents himself at the polls, a voter in any one of those states is given either a blanket ballot (in four of the states) listing the

[1] Idaho, Michigan, Minnesota, Montana, North Dakota, Utah, Washington, and Wisconsin. After trying the plan, Arizona, Colorado, Massachusetts, Missouri, Nebraska, and Vermont abandoned it; and in California and Oregon it has been declared unconstitutional.

candidates of the respective parties in separate columns or a sheaf of ballots (in the other four states) containing one for each party. In any event, he votes the ticket of his choice, with no one the wiser. Republicans may take a hand in Democratic nominations, and *vice versa;* and something of the kind often happens. To some, the system seems indefensible. It also, however, has its advantages (especially that of secrecy) ; and it is not to be forgotten that some states ostensibly having the closed form of primary really have the open form, since the tests which they prescribe notoriously fail to prevent voters from shifting temporarily from one party to another.[1]

As evidenced still in the national nominating conventions of the various parties, one of the advantages of the old convention system was the opportunity afforded not only for nominations to be made and platforms formulated, but for the two tasks to be performed in some relation to one another. The primary carries with it, of course, no provision for platform-making; and where it prevails, various means of filling the gap have been introduced. As has appeared, half a dozen states, while employing primaries, also make some use of state nominating conventions; and here the problem is simple. In fourteen others, variously constituted party conclaves—in Wisconsin, for example, consisting of the candidates for state and legislative office together with all hold-over state senators—are employed for the purpose. In four others, the function is performed by the state committee. Something on the order of the Wisconsin plan, deliberately placing the making of platforms in the hands of persons who will be expected to carry them out, has widely conceded superiority over the rather casual and drab type of platform "convention" commonly encountered. *Party platforms under the direct-primary system*

The direct primary method of choosing party candidates unquestionably affords the rank and file of a party opportunity for more direct and decisive influence in controlling nominations than ever exists when candidates are picked merely by delegate conventions. Beyond this point, however, the supporters and opponents of the device hold widely varying views as to its superiority over the convention system. The former argue that, even though the popular turn-out at primaries is commonly disappointing and sometimes pathetically scant, the voters at least respond somewhat more generously than when asked to come out merely to choose convention delegates under the old system; that the primary has materially weakened machine control of nominations; that it affords *Merits and defects of the direct primary*

[1] About half of the states tacitly permit a member of one party to run in the primary of a different party, although a winner of two nominations may usually accept only one. California expressly authorizes running in the primary of a second party, but permits acceptance of two nominations only if one of them comes from the candidate's own party. On the other hand, the constitutionality of a New York [Wilson-Pakula] law of 1947 prohibiting a candidate from entering the primary of a party in which he is not enrolled without permission of the appropriate party committee was upheld by the state court of appeals. The law was aimed at Vito Marcantonio, a county chairman of the American Labor party, who had kept himself in the national House of Representatives by running on the tickets of other parties.

opportunity to bring forward superior candidates, at all events a better chance to defeat conspicuously unfit ones; and that corruption, which often was a decisive factor in determining the selection of candidates by convention, is robbed of most of its potency. Opponents of the direct primary, on the other hand, are in the habit of denying outright most of these assertions, and of arguing that the direct primary has produced no better officials, involves added costs and therefore leads to increased taxation, imposes greater expense upon candidates, favors candidates with plenty of money to spend, weakens party organization, destroys or impairs party responsibility, intensifies machine control, multiplies the number of candidates, and favors populous centers at the expense of rural sections. Obviously, most of the arguments employed, both ways, are matters of opinion, and cannot simply be brushed aside by categorical counter-assertion. Under widely differing laws prevailing in different states, results vary from state to state, and even from time to time and place to place within the same state; and on this account the only trustworthy method of appraising the system is to compare results under it, state by state, with conditions prevailing in the same states under the convention régime.[1]

Election Machinery and Processes

Registration of voters

In early days, when the voters in a village or other district were few and well known to one another, it was possible to get along by merely identifying them as they presented themselves at the polls. But as numbers increased and people moved more frequently from place to place, it became necessary to adopt some plan for enrolling the properly qualified in advance of election day. Hence the rise of varying systems (provided for by law in each state) for preparing and keeping official voters' lists. Such lists, now required in every state, are used in both primaries and elections, and no one whose name does not appear on them is permitted to vote, at all events unless certain formalities prescribed by law are complied with. All but two states (Arkansas and Texas[2]) have

[1] A digest of state primary laws (not, of course, up to date) will be found in *Annals of Amer. Acad. of Polit. and Soc. Sci.*, CVI (Mar., 1923). Significant later changes are summarized in notes by L. Overacker in *Amer. Polit. Sci. Rev.*, XXIV, 370-380 (May, 1930); XXVIII, 265-270 (Apr., 1934); XXX, 279-285 (Apr., 1936); and XXXIV, 499-506 (June, 1940). The principal treatise on the subject is C. E. Merriam and L. Overacker, *Primary Elections* (New York, 1928); and much information will be found in C. A. Berdahl, "Party Membership in the United States," II, *Amer. Polit. Sci. Rev.*, XXXVI, 241-262 (Apr., 1942). Merits and defects are discussed at some length in E. M. Sait, *American Parties and Elections* (3rd ed.), 516-528. The state most recently adopting the direct primary is New Mexico, where the system has been in use since 1940, with results set forth fairly favorably in P. Beckett and W. L. McNutt, *The Direct Primary in New Mexico* (Santa Fé, 1947)—although leading political figures in the state are urging the law's repeal. For a less encouraging account of the system's operation on the county level in an older Midwestern state, see K. H. Porter, "The Deserted Primary in Iowa," *Amer. Polit. Sci. Rev.*, XXXIX, 732-740 (Aug., 1945).

[2] In Arkansas, curiously, personal registration is prohibited by the constitution. In Texas, the eligibility of voters is established by poll-tax receipts. The constitution permits registration in cities of over 10,000, but no system exists.

personal registration, in the sense that one who desires to vote must appear in person before the proper registration official at a county seat or other designated place and establish his right by giving whatever information and assurances the law requires. In a majority of the states until fairly recently, registration was periodic, which meant that the voter might keep his name on the list only by re-registering at yearly or other fixed intervals; and many still think this the surest method of keeping the lists free from the names of persons who have died, moved away, or for any reason become disqualified. A good deal of inconvenience, however, is caused the voters; many fail to register; and thirty-eight of the states have now introduced systems of "permanent" registration (either state-wide or for cities above a given population), under which a voter, once registered, remains on the list as long as it is not discovered that he should be removed.[1] With all of the names arranged conveniently on cards or loose-leaf sheets, registration officials, who, in addition to whatever other duties they may have, are prepared to give attention to registration matters the year around, keep ceaselessly revising the lists as new voters report for registration and old ones drop out. Whatever plan may be in use, the task of guarding against fraud is a difficult one, and the officials in charge need to be persons not only of intelligence but of high integrity; honest registration is the first line of defense against corrupt elections.[2]

Still other preliminary work is necessary before an election can be held. A division of the voters, on geographical lines, must be worked out, so that each will be able to vote in his proper district or precinct—which in rural regions may be a fairly large area, but in towns and cities is likely to be a ward or some subdivision thereof containing a maximum voting population of from two hundred in California to from five to eight hundred in Illinois.[3] Polling places must be designated, with preference in these days for school-buildings, police and fire stations, and other locations of a little more dignity and attractiveness than the livery stables, barber shops, and other places commonly employed before the feminine touch was added to our politics. Polling officers must be appointed, commonly on a bipartisan basis and from residents of the precinct; polling hours and places must be duly advertised; sample and official ballots must be printed and distributed; other polling equipment, down to lead pencils, must be made ready. In large cities, these functions are performed as a

Further preparations for elections

---

[1] In some states, permanent registration is confined to urbanized communities.

[2] A very complete analysis of the registration system of all states will be found in *Registration for Voting in the United States* (rev. ed., Chicago, Council of State Governments, 1946). The principal work on the subject is J. P. Harris, *Registration of Voters in the United States* (Washington, D. C., 1929). The author offers a model registration system; and such a system is outlined in a supplement to the *National Municipal Review*, XVI (1927). Cf. J. B. Johnson, *Registration for Voting in the United States* (rev. ed., Chicago, 1945); and J. K. Pollock, *Permanent Registration of Voters in Michigan* (Pamphlet, Ann Arbor, Mich., 1937).

[3] It is not to be understood that these arrangements are made afresh for every election, although changes may be fairly frequent.

rule by special election boards, appointed by the governor or otherwise; elsewhere, they commonly fall to county authorities, such as boards of supervisors or commissioners. Few people realize the magnitude of the preparations entailed in a major city or even a populous county.

Polling officials

On election day, the polls in each district or precinct are in charge of the polling officials previously appointed. Varying in number, titles, terms, method of selection, and rate of compensation—from state to state, and even in different parts of the same state—such officials usually include an inspector, who has general charge; two judges, who help decide disputes; two or more clerks, who have custody of the voters' lists, initial, number, and pass out the ballots, and check off the voters to whom ballots have been issued; and as a rule one or two police officers, although the duty of quelling possible disturbances and maintaining general decorum may be left to regular sheriffs' deputies or police. Not strictly as election officers, but with a view to looking after party interests, recognized party organizations, and even individual candidates, are allowed to be represented by "watchers" or challengers, who are entitled to see everything that is done by the election authorities at both the casting and the counting of the ballots. Their main function, of course, is to detect illegal voting which otherwise might somehow escape the officials. At first glance, the duties of polling officers may seem so simple and so purely clerical that almost any person can perform them. Certainly this is the theory on which the officials are nowadays too often selected; in many places, the posts are simply distributed by local politicians among their friends as political favors. Full knowledge of the election laws—no simple matter—ought, however, to be possessed, as well as the intelligence and judgment necessary to deal satisfactorily with doubts and controversies which almost inevitably arise. The electoral system could be considerably improved by raising the standard for polling officials, possibly by the use of qualifying examinations, such as were authorized in Milwaukee in 1937 and in Minnesota in 1940. Circulars of instructions are generally distributed in advance to persons who are to serve, but that is about as far as present precautions commonly go.[1]

Casting the ballots

When, on election day, the voter enters the polling place, he takes his turn in identifying himself to the clerks, carries a blank ballot to a screened compartment, or "booth," marks the ballot according to his preferences, folds the ballot with its number and the clerk's initials on the outside, and, emerging, deposits it in the ballot-box, and is duly checked off as having voted. Under only one circumstance may his privacy in the voting booth be invaded: if on account of blindness, illiteracy, or other handicap, he asks for assistance, one clerk of each party may, under the laws of most states, enter the booth to give it, although without trying in any way to influence his decisions.

[1] See M. H. Shusterman, "Choosing Election Officers," *Nat. Mun. Rev.*, XXIX, 188-193 (Mar., 1940); *Mun. Year Book* (Chicago, 1941), 532.

Not all elections involve the literal use of ballots. There is an ingenious Voting
machines contrivance known as a voting machine; and more than half of the states have authorized some use of it.[1] Where such machines are employed, the voter identifies himself at the polls in the usual way, but instead of receiving a printed ballot, is directed to a curtained space in which stands a mechanism showing on its face the candidates' lists which the ballot would contain if one were used, and where he votes by merely pulling levers—a single master lever if voting a straight ticket. Automatically recording the votes, and also adding them up, the voting machine has the great advantages of accuracy, complete secrecy, economy of time, and full tabulation of results the moment the polls are closed. Aside from hesitancy to adopt new ways, and perhaps in some cases the lukewarmness of politicians toward a device that cannot be manipulated,[2] the main obstacle to wider use of voting machines is the cost of the machines themselves—something like a thousand dollars apiece. Use of them in more populous areas is, however, steadily growing.[3]

Not all voters are so situated, at a given election, as to be able to Absent
voting present themselves at the polls. The number who cannot do so is, of course, particularly large in wartime; and as far back as the Civil War, provision (although not very effective) was made for soldiers to cast their ballots *in absentia*. In addition to soldiers and sailors, there are, however, the ill and the disabled, students in attendance at distant colleges and universities, persons engaged in operating trains, migrant workers, people away from home on business trips, and many other persons "unavoidably" or "necessarily" absent (as the laws put it) from their voting precincts at election time. Considering it unjust that people so situated should be compelled to lose their votes, Vermont led off in 1896 with a statute making general provision for absent voting; and by 1940 all states except Kentucky and New Mexico had laws on the subject,[4] although in some instances applying only to certain elections rather than to all. Procedures vary in detail, but in general the voter concerned makes application to the proper home official for the privilege of voting *in absentia,* receives a ballot directly or through an official in charge of elections where the voter is, and—after validating himself before a notary or other official—marks his ballot and mails it to the proper home authority.[5]

[1] In 1946, voting machines were employed extensively in Connecticut, Florida, Indiana, Iowa, New Jersey, New York, Pennsylvania, and Washington, and in a few urban areas in a dozen other states. On the general subject of voting machines, see S. D. Albright, *The American Ballot* (Washington, D. C., 1942), Chap. IV.

[2] This is not to say that voting machines have never been tampered with. But in their improved forms they are fairly immune from that sort of thing.

[3] J. P. Harris, *Election Administration in the United States,* Chap. VII; S. D. Albright, *Ballot Analysis and Ballot Changes Since 1930* (Chicago, 1940), 18-23.

[4] New Mexico was authorized by its constitution to enact such legislation, but had not yet done so.

[5] See J. K. Pollock, *Absentee Voting and Registration* (Pamphlet, Washington, D. C., 1940), and cf. *State Absentee Voting and Registration Laws, Sept., 1942* (Washington, D. C., Govt. Prtg. Office, 1942).

Voting in
the armed
services
during
World
War II
World War II naturally raised a problem of absent voting on a scale never before experienced: multiplied millions of men (many women also) of voting age were in training camps or overseas; hundreds of thousands of others were more or less temporarily employed in war plants far from their accustomed abodes. With the congressional and state elections of 1942 coming on, Congress passed an act designed to reënforce state absent-voting laws—although the results were meager, with only an insignificant number of service people requesting ballots. The presidential election of 1944 offered more of a challenge, not only because of its greater significance, but because the number of men and women in service (approximately nine millions) was by that time almost double the 1942 figure. President Roosevelt favored taking care of the entire situation by a simple, uniform national law. Congress, however, fell into heated controversy over rival plans, and the upshot was a rather confused Armed Services Vote Act [1] under which service people were normally to vote under the absent-voting laws of their own states, but with opportunity in given situations to vote an alternative federal "short ballot" (for president, vice-president, senators, and representatives only). This time, the service vote was heavier than expected—a total of some 2,700,000. Only twenty states, however, permitted federal ballots to be counted, as being in accord with their existing election laws, and the number of such ballots cast was only 109,479. The general tenor of the 1944 statute and of experience under it was to assume and emphasize the basic authority of the states over the electoral process; and in 1946, with the war over, Congress adopted new legislation abandoning the use of federal ballots, urging all states to enact any laws needed for enabling persons in the armed services or the merchant marine to vote when absent from their state, and pledging federal assistance in the form of printed materials and free use of the mails. [2]

Tabu-
lating
and
reporting
electoral
results
Reverting to regular electoral procedures, we next note that when the polls close, the results are canvassed and tabulated, usually by the regular polling officials, although about a dozen states, including Iowa, Kansas, Nebraska, Missouri, and West Virginia, have a "double election board" system under which the "receiving board" has charge of the polling, and a "counting board" confines its labors to reckoning up results, usually starting its work while the voting is still going on. If voting machines are employed, there is little to be done except to open them and find what they have recorded. In the majority of cases, however, there are printed ballots to be counted—perhaps a huge number of them; and the authorized persons attack the job—sometimes, as in New York, in the presence of any voters who care to look on, but usually with only the polling officials present. The task completed, all ballots, used and unused, including spoiled and defective ones, together with the

[1] 58 *U. S. Stat. at Large,* 136 (1944).
[2] 60 *U. S. Stat. at Large,* 96 (1946).

poll-books and tally-sheets, are placed in sealed packages or in sealed ballot-boxes; and all are preserved and carefully guarded for a specified period, after which the ballots are destroyed. Meanwhile, the chief election officer sees that "return blanks" are filled out in duplicate or triplicate, showing the exact number of votes received by each candidate; and, his signature having been affixed, one set is sent off to the city or county clerk or to a board of elections, while another goes to some higher canvassing authority, i.e., the county board of supervisors in California and other states, the judges of the court of common pleas in Pennsylvania, the county clerk assisted by two justices of the peace of the county in Illinois, and the board of election commissioners in most large cities. By telephone, or otherwise, the results are reported to the press and party leaders the moment they are ascertained; and, consolidated with others pouring in from all over the electoral area, they enable an interested, and perhaps excited, public, hovering before radio sets and loudspeakers, to know how things are coming out.

On a day fixed by law, the canvassing bodies in each county or city *Final stages of the count* proceed officially to add up all the votes cast and, in so far as state and national offices are involved, certify the results to some state official (usually the secretary of state), who is required to consolidate and transmit the returns to a state convassing board. The last stage in the process is reached when the state and county canvassing boards file their reports with the officials designated by law, usually the county clerk in the case of county offices and the secretary of state in that of state (and national) offices; whereupon these officials issue to each person declared elected a certificate of election which is *prima facie* evidence of the legal right of that person to hold the office and perform the duties connected with it.

Such a certificate is not, however, conclusive; for all state election *Disputed elections* laws include detailed provisions for "contested elections," that is, for disputes arising when a defeated candidate alleges that he has been illegally denied a certificate of election. Such cases are commonly determined in the courts, although in some states, *e.g.*, Illinois, the legislature is the authority which decides conflicting claims to the highest state offices. Where such contests involve a seat in the state legislature or in a city council, the legislative house or the council concerned almost invariably has the power of decision. By constitutional stipulation, too, disputed seats in Congress are awarded by the appropriate branch.[1]

Forms of Ballots

In sharp contrast with the days when voting was oral and public, *The Australian ballot in general use* secrecy is now everywhere provided for, either in the state constitution or by statutes; and it has been effectually attained through the adop-

[1] Full treatment of practically all aspects of the conduct of elections will be found in J. P. Harris, *Election Administration in the United States* (Washington, D. C., 1934).

tion since 1888 of the so-called Australian ballot in every state except South Carolina.[1] The essence of the Australian system is that the only ballots allowed to be used at the polls are prepared by responsible public officials at public expense, in accordance with forms prescribed by law, and hence can be cast without possibility of detection of the ticket for which one has voted. The ballot is normally in blanket form, *i.e.*, bearing on a single sheet the complete list of offices to be filled and of candidates, although when national, state, and city elections are being held simultaneously, the names of candidates for presidential elector, and also of candidates for municipal offices, are sometimes printed on separate sheets.[2]

Chief ballot forms The arrangement of the names of candidates on the ballot varies in different states, but usually conforms to one or the other of two major plans. In the party-column type of ballot, introduced in Indiana in 1889, and now used in twenty-seven states, candidates of the different parties have their names printed in separate columns, at the head of which appear, in each case, the party name and a "party circle" or "party square," and sometimes a party emblem, or vignette. The voter has merely to place a single cross in this circle or square (or, if voting machines are used, pull the lever once) to vote for all of the candidates of a given party. This obviously facilitates what is called "straight-ticket" voting, and accordingly the plan is regarded with high favor by party leaders. Wyoming and a few other states, although retaining the party column for the guidance of voters, omit the party square or circle at the head of the column, so that there is no possibility of voting a straight ticket merely by making a single cross.

In twenty states, including Massachusetts, New York, and California, a different arrangement is employed—an "office group" scheme which puts less stress on party regularity and more on the weighing of individual candidates. The names of candidates of all parties are grouped together alphabetically according to the offices for which they are running, the designation of the party to which each candidate belongs appearing alongside his name. There is no way of voting a straight party ticket with a single cross or a single pull of a lever; on the contrary, to vote a straight ticket, a voter must place a cross (or pull a lever) opposite the name of every candidate of a given party. For this reason, the Massachusetts type of ballot, as this form is called (because it was employed first in that state, in 1888), is regarded as favoring independent, or "split-ticket," voting. Pennsylvania ballots retain the grouping of candidates by offices, as in Massachusetts, but also provide in the left-hand margin a list of the parties represented on the ballot; and a single cross placed opposite one of these party names is counted as a vote for

---

[1] In that state, there is no statute requiring use of the Australian ballot. The Democratic party, however, requires use of it in its own primaries—which, in a one-party state, invariably predetermine the results of elections.

[2] In twenty-two states, however, the names of presidential electors do not appear on ballots at all.

every candidate nominated by that party—a device which, of course, makes straight-ticket voting quite as easy as where the party-column ballot is employed.[1]

Recall Elections

Normally, elections are held only when officers' terms are about to expire, or occasionally to fill a vacancy arising from the death or resignation of an incumbent. One sometimes hears, however, of an election precipitated by an attempt to "recall" an official in the midst of his term. Appointive officials who prove incompetent or otherwise remiss can usually be removed by the appointing authority; although in the states the power of removal as vested in the governor and principal local officials is often so hedged about with restrictions as to be almost useless. Elective officers on higher levels, including state judges, are usually subject to impeachment. In particular situations, however, there may be reasons for wishing to get rid of such officers, though hardly justifying resort to a procedure so drastic as impeachment; besides, those dissatisfied would be helpless unless the impeaching authorities, *i.e.*, the two houses of the legislature, were prepared to act. Back in the early part of the present century, therefore—in a period when the tide of "direct" popular government was running strong, with the popular initiative and referendum winning their way in state after state, especially in the West—many people became enamored of the idea that the voters themselves ought to be in a position to institute recall proceedings against an official (especially one whom they had themselves elected), subjecting him to the test of reëlection in competition with any candidates who might want to compete against him; and as a result, in a dozen or more states a recall procedure was instituted for use against state officers, sometimes both elective and appointive, and especially against city officers under the commission form of municipal government.[2]

Except for the manner in which it is initiated, a recall election does not differ greatly from any other one. When a movement to oust a given official gets under way, a paper setting forth the charges against him, and known as a "petition," is circulated in a quest for signatures; and if the requisite number (varying from ten to thirty-five per cent of the electorate of the area concerned) is obtained, the city clerk or other official with whom it is filed sets a date for a recall election (unless a regular election is about to take place). If the official whose recall is

Purposes

Procedure

[1] On the general subject of the ballot, see E. C. Evans, *A History of the Australian Ballot System in the United States* (Chicago, 1917); S. D. Albright, *Ballot Analysis and Ballot Changes Since 1930* (Chicago, 1940), and *The American Ballot* (Washington, D. C., 1942).

[2] Oregon (1908), California (1911), Washington, Colorado, Idaho, Nevada, and Arizona (1912), Michigan (1913), Louisiana and Kansas (1914), North Dakota (1920), and Wisconsin (1926). Actually, however, Idaho was without the recall until 1933, inasmuch as the legislature failed for more than twenty years to pass the legislation necessary to make the authorization of 1912 effective. In only eight of the states named does the recall apply to judges. The device made its first appearance in a municipal charter of Los Angeles in 1903.

sought chooses not to face the issue, he may simply resign. If, however, he prefers to fight for vindication, his name is placed on the ballot along with the names of any other persons nominated (usually by petition) to succeed him. The voters then render the verdict. If the incumbent polls the largest number of votes, he continues in office. But if one of his opponents outstrips him, the victor forthwith assumes the office and fills out the remainder of the term, the incumbent being, of course, "recalled." A safeguard usually provided is that no petition for a recall election may be filed against an official until he has served for a specified period, commonly six months; and as a rule an official cannot be subjected to a recall election more than once during a given term.

Results   As in the case of the initiative and referendum,[1] the hopes of the reformers have not been fully realized. To be sure, there is no way of measuring the moral effect upon office-holders of their awareness that the gun is behind the door. But one can hardly believe that the few instances in which the device has been successfully invoked by dissatisfied voters represents all of the situations in which officials deserved to be ousted. A number of municipal officers have been recalled, especially in California.[2] But in only two instances have officials chosen by the voters of an entire state been reached;[3] and it is significant that there have been no new state adoptions of the plan in more than twenty years. The record may be ascribed in part to public inertia. Other shortcomings are, however, more or less inherent: first, the fact that recall elections are ordinarily carried on in the same atmosphere of partisanship, misrepresentation, and confusion that characterize other elections; and second, the circumstance that the issues, growing out of the official's performance of his duties, are often too complex and technical to be passed upon intelligently by a mixed and preoccupied electorate. Where the uppermost question is the relatively simple one of whether an official has truly represented or reflected the opinion of those who chose him, the recall has undoubted validity; and this may well hold true for members of state legislatures, for city councilors and commissioners, and for more conspicuous executive and administrative officers like governors, attorneys-general, and mayors. But where the conditions and character of the work to be performed are less familiar to the general run of voters, other modes of getting rid of the unfit will usually be preferable—even though none is without objectionable features.[4]

[1] See pp. 900-904 below (in complete edition of this book).

[2] For example, the mayor of Los Angeles was recalled in September, 1938. A mayor was recalled also in Detroit in June, 1930, and one in Seattle in July, 1931.

[3] In 1921, the governor, attorney-general, and commissioner of agriculture in North Dakota were recalled because of their connection with developments growing out of the Non-Partisan League movement; and the next year, two members of the state public utility commission of Oregon (one elected by the entire state and one from a district) were recalled because of popular dissatisfaction with certain rate increases which the commission had authorized.

[4] More than two hundred recall movements in California are dealt with in F. L. Bird and F. M. Ryan, *The Recall of Public Officers* (New York, 1930). Cf. J. D.

The Electoral System Criticized—Some Proposed Changes

Despite notable improvements in the past thirty or forty years, the electoral system outlined in the present chapter still encounters, and properly, a good deal of criticism—not only on the ground of excessive, wasteful, and occasionally corrupt, use of money, but with respect also to such features as the frequency of primaries and elections, the holding (too often) of local, state, and national elections simultaneously, the unnecessarily large number of offices filled by popular election, and the almost invariable practice of electing by plurality vote. Each of these latter grounds of objection may receive a word of comment.[1]

Concerning the frequency of elections, nothing more need be said than to call attention to the familiar fact that the election of president and vice-president and of various officers of a number of states occurs every four years; that some state officers are elected triennially, and others, along with congressmen and most county officers, biennially; that many county and local offices are filled annually; and that practically all of these elections are preceded by primaries or nominating conventions. Not only do these frequently recurring primaries and elections impose a heavy financial burden upon the taxpayers,[2] and give more scope than is desirable to the professional politician, but they make it impossible for the average preoccupied citizen to keep up an intelligent interest, and to take an active part, in the nomination and election of the men who in various ways act for him in the conduct of public affairs. *1 Frequency of elections*

National, state, and local elections often fall on the same day, with the result that the names of candidates for offices of all three kinds, or at least for national and state offices, are not infrequently printed on the same ballot. This tends seriously to confuse national with state and local issues, commonly to the detriment of state and local government. A remedy has been sought in many states by arranging elections so that the most important state and local contests will be held in years in which presidential and congressional elections do not occur. Some states, indeed, have not stopped here, but have also separated purely local from state elections. Separation on this line may, however, be carried so far as unreasonably to increase the number of elections occurring in a single year, as has happened in Illinois, where in some years the voters are called to the polls as many as seven times. *2. Simultaneous national, state, and local elections*

Of far greater seriousness than either of the foregoing defects is the long and confusing ballot with which most voters are confronted when they go to the polls at presidential elections and at many state and local *3. The long ballot*

Barnett, *Operation of the Initiative, Referendum, and Recall in Oregon* (New York, 1915).

[1] It may be mentioned, too, that with primaries sometimes held as early as April or May, the period of the electoral campaign is unduly prolonged. Candidates are unnecessarily burdened and voters become surfeited and apathetic.

[2] On the cost of elections as of a decade and a half ago, see J. P. Harris, *Election Administration in the United States*, Chap. x.

elections as well. The bewildering list of candidates to be voted on is accounted for partly by the number of offices now filled by popular election, partly by national, state, and local elections falling at the same time, and partly by the fact that there are usually two or more candidates for every office to be filled. The result is that ballots bearing from one hundred to two hundred or more names (or sheafs of ballots aggregating such a number) are by no means uncommon.[1] Certain serious consequences are entailed. For one thing, it is extremely difficult, if not impossible, for a majority, or even a considerable minority, of the voters to form an intelligent opinion as to the merits of the candidates, especially when elections take place frequently. Consequently, there is a great deal of blind voting, especially in the form of straight-ticket voting. Another result is that the merits of the candidates for only a few principal offices are considered seriously, even by well-informed voters. Popular interest is usually concentrated upon candidates for president, governor, and mayor, to the almost complete neglect of the remainder of the ticket. At best, in other words, there is more or less intelligent voting for a few prominent offices and blind voting for the great majority of minor positions. Taking advantage of popular preoccupation with the most conspicuous offices, politicians are often able to get wholly unfit candidates into minor, though not unimportant, positions.

Need for shortening the ballot

The remedy for much of this blind voting is to shorten the ballot by sharply reducing the number of elective positions.[2] Officers who have a share in translating public opinion into law, or who enjoy large discretionary powers in the administration of laws—in other words, all policy-determining officials—should continue to be elective. But there are surprisingly few of these. The president, the members of both branches of Congress, the governor and members of the legislature, and the mayor and members of the city council are obviously policy-determining officers. To a less extent, this is true of boards of county commissioners or county supervisors. But here the list practically ends; very few other officials have anything to do with the formulation of public policy in the field of either legislation or administration. On the contrary, their respective

---

[1] In addition, in states in which the popular referendum prevails, anywhere from two or three to a dozen or more legislative measures may be submitted to the voter's judgment. A few years ago, Indiana had the dubious distinction of having the largest ballot of any state—a total of fourteen square feet! But in 1946 Omaha voters were handed a ballot thirteen feet long, listing, besides candidates, fifty-six measures to be voted upon. "Blanket ballots," carrying all the offices and all initiated and referred measures, are used in twenty-four states; elsewhere there are separate ballots for offices and measures, and occasionally also for offices on different levels of government.

[2] A few states have to some extent done this. Thus New York, as long ago as 1925, adopted a constitutional amendment making the offices of secretary of state, state treasurer, and state engineer appointive, and three years later Virginia did the same thing for the offices of secretary of state, state treasurer, commissioner of agriculture and immigration, and superintendent of public instruction. The national government presents no problem at this point, except in the sense that the names of candidates for presidential elector help clutter up the ballot unless printed separately, or unless, as in twenty-two "presidential short ballot" states, they do not appear at all.

official duties are set forth minutely in the national or state constitution Offices that should be appointive or statutes, or in the city charter and ordinances; so that all that they have to do is to study the laws relating to their positions, do what the laws require of them, and do it in the manner prescribed. In this category fall such officers as secretary of state, state engineer and surveyor, state superintendent of public instruction, state treasurer or comptroller, county auditors or comptrollers, sheriffs, county clerks and court clerks, city clerks and city treasurers, and a host of others whose candidacies now encumber our ballots. Choosing these by popular election yields no advantage which is not more than offset by the evils traceable to the resulting lengthening of the ballot. Although it is customary to sneer at the political experts called professional politicians, they are nevertheless indispensable so long as we continue to identify multiplicity of elective offices with genuinely democratic government. But the fact is that many, if not most, of our elections now mean little more than the ratification of one or the other of two slates of candidates previously arranged by irresponsible and unofficial party managers, operating more or less in secret.

The recent adoption of commission and manager government in several hundred cities has been accompanied by a noteworthy reduction in the number of elective municipal officers, and thus has familiarized many voters with the advantages of a shorter ballot. In state and county governments, on the other hand, comparatively slight progress has been made —one of the reasons being the necessity for constitutional amendments before numerous elective offices can be made appointive, and another being the natural hostility of professional politicians to changes that obviously would lessen their importance and power.[1]

The last of the several criticisms of our system of elections mentioned 4. Plurality elections above is directed against the plurality rule in deciding elections. Whenever there are three or more candidates for the same office, the successful one—that is, the one receiving the most votes—is very likely to have been elected by only a minority of the voters. This seems inconsistent with the commonly accepted theory that in a democracy the majority The preferential ballot rules. In national, state, and county elections, practically nothing has been accomplished toward remedying the situation. In city elections, however, a partial solution has been found in "preferential" voting. Since 1909, more than fifty cities have done away with primary elections and substituted nomination by petition, followed by the use of a preferential ballot on election day.[2] On this ballot, names of candidates are grouped

---

[1] G. W. Spicer, "Relation of the Short Ballot to Efficient Government and Popular Control," *Southwestern Polit. and Soc. Sci. Quar.*, XI, 182-192 (Sept., 1930); J. K. Pollock, "New Thoughts on the Short Ballot," *Nat. Mun. Rev.*, XXIX, 18-20 (Jan., 1940).

[2] Notably San Francisco, Spokane, Portland, Denver, and Columbus. In Cleveland, also, the preferential ballot was used for some years prior to the substitution of proportional representation in 1922 (in turn later abandoned). In San Francisco, the preferential ballot is no longer used, owing in part to the small number of voters who indicated more than one choice on their ballots, and in part to the introduction of voting machines.

by offices, as in the Massachusetts type of ballot, and the voter may indicate his first, second, and other choices. If any candidate is found to have received a majority of the first-choice votes, he is forthwith declared elected. If no one has a majority, the result is usually determined by adding the second-choice votes to the first choices. If even then no candidate has a majority, to the first- and second-choice votes are added the third choices, and the candidate who now has the *highest* number is declared elected. The plan does not absolutely guarantee, but strongly promotes, election by majority. Additional points urged in its favor are (1) that, by giving the voter a wider range of choices among candidates, it tends to emphasize issues rather than personalities, and (2) that by eliminating the cumbersome and costly primary system, it obviates the necessity of bringing the voters to the polls on two different days.[1]

Propor-
tional
repre-
sentation

Another electoral device sometimes brought into play, but with a different objective, is proportional representation. Applicable only to situations in which three or more members of a board, commission, or legislative body are being chosen in each of a number of districts, its object is, not to promote majority election of any party slate in a district as a whole, but rather to open a way for the district's quota of seats to be distributed among the various candidates in approximate proportion to the votes polled by each, and thereby to increase opportunities for minority representation. No state has seriously considered adopting the plan. But fourteen cities, of various sizes, are using it—although the prospect for further adoptions is obscure.[2]

---

[1] For an interesting special application of the principle of preferential voting, see H. M. Dorr, "The Nansen System: A Michigan Experiment in Voting" [in Marquette, Mich.], *Papers of Mich. Acad. of Sci., Arts, and Letters*, XXVIII, 613-621 (1943).

[2] The fourteen municipalities are Cambridge, Lowell, Worcester, Saugus, Medford, Quincy, and Revere, Mass.; Cincinnati, Toledo, and Hamilton, O.; Yonkers, N. Y.; Wheeling, W. Va.; Hopkins, Mich.; and Coos Bay, Ore. The system has been held constitutional in New York (1937) and unconstitutional in California (1922) and Rhode Island (1939). For further comment and references, see pp. 891-892 below (in complete edition of this book).

In connection with the lower house of the Illinois legislature, effort is made to promote minority representation, not through a proportional system, but by a plan of "cumulative" voting under which a voter has three votes and may distribute them as he likes among candidates for the three seats to which his district is entitled. By concentrating all votes on a given candidate, a minority may carry him to victory.

Notwithstanding adoption of a new constitution in 1945, Georgia retains an archaic electoral system giving rural inhabitants considerably more than their due in state and congressional elections. Under law of 1917, each county is assigned a quota of "unit" votes roughly on the basis of population—the eight most populous having six such votes each, the next thirty four each, and the remaining 121 two each. A candidate for state or congressional office polling a plurality of the popular vote in a county receives all of the county's unit votes; and the candidate receiving the most unit votes over the state wins the Democratic nomination, tantamount to election— except that in the case of governor and United States senator, he must receive a majority, with a "run-off" if no one obtains such. Under this system, candidates often win by piling up unit votes in the numerous rural counties, though lagging far behind in popular votes in counties with urban populations and throughout the state as a whole. In 1946, for example, Eugene Talmadge captured the governorship with 105 unit votes and 297,245 popular votes, as against James V. Carmichael with only

REFERENCES

A. N. Christensen and E. M. Kirkpatrick, *The People, Politics, and the Politician; Readings in American Government* (New York, 1941 and 1947), Chap. XII.

V. O. Key, Jr., *Politics, Parties, and Pressure Groups* (2nd ed., New York, 1947), Chaps. XII, XIV, XVII-XIX.

E. M. Sait, *American Parties and Elections* (3rd ed., New York, 1942), Chaps. XVIII-XXVII.

P. O. Ray, *Introduction to Political Parties and Practical Politics* (3rd ed., New York, 1924), Chaps. IV-VI, XIII, XVII.

R. C. Brooks, *Political Parties and Electoral Problems* (3rd ed., New York, 1933), Chaps. X, XII, XV, XVIII.

T. W. Cousens, *Politics and Political Organizations in America* (New York, 1942), Chaps. IX, XIII.

C. E. Merriam and H. F. Gosnell, *The American Party System* (3rd ed., New York, 1940), Chaps. XIII, XV-XVII.

P. H. Odegard and E. A. Helms, *American Politics; A Study in Political Dynamics* (2nd ed., New York, 1947), Chaps. XVI-XXI.

A. W. Bromage, *State Government and Administration in the United States* (New York, 1936), Chap. VI.

W. B. Graves, *American State Government* (3rd ed., New York, 1946), Chap. V.

A. F. Macdonald, *American State Government and Administration* (3rd ed., New York, 1945), Chap. V.

J. M. Mathews, *American State Government* (2nd ed., New York, 1934), Chaps. VII-IX.

C. A. Berdahl, "Party Membership in the United States," *Amer. Polit. Sci. Rev.,* XXXVI, 16-50, 241-262 (Feb., Apr., 1942).

C. E. Merriam and L. Overacker, *Primary Elections* (New York, 1928).

J. K. Pollock, *The Direct Primary in Michigan* (Ann Arbor, Mich., 1943).

————, "Election Administration in Michigan," *Nat. Mun. Rev.,* Supp., XXIII, 343-359 (June, 1934).

J. P. Harris, *The Registration of Voters in the United States* (Washington, D. C., 1929).

————, *Election Administration in the United States* (Washington, D. C., 1934).

S. D. Albright, *Ballot Analysis and Ballot Changes Since 1930* (Chicago, 1940).

————, *The American Ballot* (Washington, D. C., 1942).

Ill. Const. Conv. Bull., No. 5, "The Short Ballot" (Springfield, Ill., 1920).

National Municipal League Committee on Election Administration, "A Model Election Administration System," *Nat. Mun. Rev.,* Supp., XIX, 625-671 (Sept., 1930).

H. M. Rocca, *A Brief Digest of the Laws Relating to Absentee Voting and Registration* (Washington, D. C., 1928).

Council of State Governments, *Soldier-Sailor Voting* (2nd ed., Chicago, 1944). A digest of state and federal laws to July, 1944.

B. A. Martin, "The Service Vote in the Election of 1944," *Amer. Polit. Sci. Rev.,* XXXIX, 720-731 (Aug., 1945).

F. L. Bird and F. M. Ryan, *The Recall of Public Officers* (New York, 1930).

Bureau of the Census, *Elective Offices of State and County Governments* (Washington, D. C., 1946).

---

44 unit votes but 313,389 popular votes. In the same year, a federal district court refused to hold the system unconstitutional, and, on appeal being taken to the federal Supreme Court, that tribunal, by a vote of six to three, dismissed the case without opinion.

CHAPTER XIII

NOMINATING AND ELECTING A PRESIDENT

Every two years, the people of the United States elect 435 members of the national House of Representatives, one-third or more of the ninety-six senators, and multiplied thousands of state and local executives, administrators, lawmakers, and judges. Every four years, they choose, in addition, a president and a vice-president—or at all events the 531 "electors" who later, meeting in the various state capitals, go through the formality of registering and confirming the popular verdict. It is in nominating and electing these topmost officials that parties are stirred to liveliest action and voters drawn in largest numbers to the polls; and in considering how our loftiest official of all reaches the White House, we are not only paving the way for a later study of his powers and functions, but also bringing into sharper focus the popular basis on which our government is supposed to rest.[1]

The pageant of a presidential election

The pageant of a presidential election in the United States is, indeed, the most remarkable thing of its kind anywhere. Hardly is a new chief executive settled in the White House, with four long years of toil and anxiety ahead of him, before plans are afoot for the next supreme test of electoral strength; and as the red-letter date approaches, potential candidates emerge, "booms" are launched, personal and party groups spar for advantage in the press, on the floor of Congress, and in the swirls and eddies of congressional, state, and local politics. Four or five months before the choice is to be made, tumultuous national conventions battle over nominations and platforms. A pause intervenes for taking stock and for throwing the nation-wide party machinery into high gear; then the fight is on. With steady crescendo, the drama advances from scene to scene, until at length, on election day, forty to fifty million people go to the polls and settle the fate of the candidates. Thousands of speeches have been made, floods of ink spilled, millions of dollars spent.

An Electoral System That Did Not Work as Intended

The system originally adopted

Needless to say, this is not at all the sort of thing that the framers of our national constitution had in view. Having decided against election of the president (1) by Congress, on the ground that if so chosen he would not be sufficiently independent, or (2) directly by the people, because of fear of "tumult and disorder" and apprehension lest the voters,

---

[1] Congressional, senatorial, and other elections will be dealt with at appropriate points below.

scattered thinly over what already seemed a large country, would not be able to inform themselves on the qualifications of candidates, the convention—after taking no fewer than thirty different votes on the subject—finally accepted Hamilton's plan for indirect popular election through the filtering medium of an "electoral college." The decision seemed a happy one, and the resulting provisions became one of the few features of the new constitution that did not have to be defended during the contest over ratification. Each state was to have as many electors as it had senators and representatives; and after such electors had been chosen in all of the states, in whatever way the respective legislatures should ordain, they were to meet and each cast a ballot for two persons, at least one of whom should be a resident of a different state. The votes from all of the states having been assembled and counted, the person receiving the largest number, if a majority, was to be declared president. If more than one person received a majority, and had an equal number of votes, the House of Representatives, voting by states (a concession to the small states), should choose between them. If, on the other hand—as was expected to happen frequently—there was no majority at all, the House (again voting by states) should choose from among the five highest on the list. In every case, after the presidency was settled, the person having the next largest number of electoral votes should be vice-president, with the proviso that in the event of a tie, the Senate should, by individual ballot, choose between those having equal numbers.[1] The people, it was assumed, would, directly or through their legislatures, choose the electors from among the most capable and trustworthy men of the respective states;[2] the electors, in turn, when convoked for the purpose in each state, would look over the country at large and each cast a ballot for any two eligible persons seeming to him best fitted for the nation's highest office, at least one of the two not being a resident of his own state.

For a short time, the plan worked as its authors intended. In 1789, and again in 1792, every elector wrote the name of Washington on his ballot, with second names scattered. In 1796, Washington indicated his desire to retire, and thirteen different persons received electoral votes. In 1800, however, every elector except one, the country over, wrote on his ballot the names of either Jefferson and Burr or Adams and Pinckney. What had happened was that in the meantime two political parties—Federalist and Republican—had come into existence, and each had taken steps in advance of the popular election to agree upon particular "candidates" for the presidency and vice-presidency, and also to put before the voters of the several states lists of men who, it was understood, would, if chosen by the people (or legislatures), cast their electoral ballots in all cases

Effect of the rise of political parties

---

[1] Art. II, § 1. It seems to have been expected that the vote would usually be so split up that the election would be thrown into the House—"nineteen times in twenty," thought George Mason.

[2] For a good while after 1789, the electors were chosen in several states (until 1860 in South Carolina) by the legislature.

for the persons supported by the party to which the given electors belonged. Reduced by this wholly unanticipated development to a "row of ciphers"—a mere recording machine—the electoral college kept on functioning in form, as it does to this day. But never in nearly a century and a half has it served the one real purpose for which it was created; and many people now consider that it might as well be abolished. There is no better illustration of how the actual working constitution changes without a hand being laid on the written fundamental law.

The Twelfth Amendment (1804)

One effect of the changed position of the electors was to make it not unlikely that a tie would result between the two candidates of a winning party; and almost immediately such a situation arose, in 1800, when Jefferson and Burr received the same number of electoral votes. The constitution provided a way out: a tie was to be broken by the House of Representatives, voting by states; and in this manner Jefferson was finally elected. The opposition, however, came near to thwarting the intention of the victors by maneuvering Burr into the highest office; and before the next election came around any repetition of the difficulty was wisely made impossible by an amendment to the constitution specifying that thereafter electors should in all cases "name in their ballots the person voted for as president, and in distinct ballots the person voted for as vice-president." Thenceforth the issue between presidential candidates would have to be settled between them alone, and similarly that between vice-presidential candidates—although, of course, an election might still be thrown into the House (or, in the case of the vice-president, into the Senate).[1]

Machinery for Nominating Candidates—The National Convention

Nominations become a necessity

The next significant development had to do with a matter for which the framers of the constitution made no provision, i.e., the nomination of candidates. As originally set up, the electoral system did not, indeed, contemplate "candidates" at all. When, however, political parties arose, one of their foremost objects naturally came to be to capture control of the presidency. To do this, they must concentrate their support upon given individuals, which, in turn, they could do only if such individuals,

---

[1] It remained legally possible for the president and vice-president to be members of different parties; and this is still possible. The firmly established custom requiring every elector to cast ballots for both the presidential and vice-presidential candidates of his party can be depended upon, however, to avert so awkward a contingency. Incidentally, the rise of parties and the adoption of the Twelfth Amendment relegated the vice-presidency to a lower level in popular esteem than had been intended for it. Originally, all candidates were to be considered, presumably, with reference to their fitness for the presidency. But after 1804 vice-presidential candidates became a species apart, their qualifications inevitably being judged on different and less rigorous lines. In this respect, the new system was a change for the worse.

It may be added that on a few occasions, some electors have cast their ballots for candidates other than those of their party. In the early stages of the 1944 campaign, it was predicted that some Southern Democratic electors would not vote for President Roosevelt for a fourth term; but the threatened bolt did not materialize. At the date of writing, President Truman, as a 1948 candidate, was similarly threatened.

or candidates, were agreed upon in advance; and hence arose the need for machinery for selecting them.

The first device hit upon was the one easiest to contrive, *i.e.*, a caucus composed of the (national) senators and representatives of a given party; and it was employed straight along from 1800 to 1824. There were, however, serious objections to it. The caucus acted only by assumed authority; it provided little or no voice for party members in states in which the party was in a minority; and it gave members of the legislative branch an influence in selecting the chief executive which they clearly were not intended to have. In a period of steadily broadening democracy, some change became inevitable; and in 1831 both the National Republican and Anti-Masonic parties turned for a substitute to popularly chosen nominating conventions, already employed acceptably in state elections. Candidates were nominated and platforms adopted; and in 1832 the Democrats fell into line with a convention of their own. Many political leaders, including Webster and Calhoun, opposed the new device on the ground that it gave too much power in party matters to the rank and file. Nevertheless, by 1840 the national convention became the generally accepted means of putting both candidates and platforms before the voters; and such it has remained.

From congres- sional caucus to national conven- tion

To understand the way in which presidential and vice-presidential candidates are nominated nowadays, it is necessary, therefore, to know something about the national convention—how it is called, of whom it is composed, how it is organized, how it goes about its work, and what are its merits and defects.

The national conventions of the two major parties, and likewise of such minor parties as have built up a permanent organization, are held on call of the national party committee. A year or more preceding a presidential election, the committee meets (commonly in Washington in the case of the Republicans and Democrats), decides upon the place and date of the coming convention, and authorizes the party organizations in the states and territories to see that delegates and alternates are chosen in accordance with an apportionment set forth in the call. The Republicans commonly hold their convention about the middle of June, the Democrats two or three weeks later; and the place is selected (usually from a list of cities competing for both the advertising and the business that such a meeting brings) with an eye not only to practical matters like hotel and convention-hall facilities and donations toward expenses, but also to the preferences of influential candidates and of leading politicians, the need for stirring enthusiasm in a given state or section, and other considerations of party interest or strategy.[1]

Arrange- ments for con- ventions: time and place

---

[1] Chicago, centrally located and with excellent hotel and auditorium accommodations, draws more of the conventions than any other city; but St. Louis, Kansas City, Cleveland, Baltimore, and especially Philadelphia usually stand some chance of being selected. The 1948 conventions of both major parties were held in the last-named city.

Conven-
tion
member-
ship
Except in so far as state laws regulate the method of electing delegates, every party determines for itself how its conventions shall be made up; national law has nothing to do with the matter. In earlier days, the party forces in each state were commonly allowed a quota of votes (and of delegates) equal to the state's electoral vote, or, to put it differently, the number of its senators and representatives in Congress. From 1852 to 1872, the state delegations in the Democratic convention consisted of double this number, but each delegate had only a half-vote. After 1872, the number was determined in the same way, but each delegate had a whole vote; [1] and this likewise was the Republican plan from 1860 until after the convention of 1912. In both parties, the regular practice long was to allow each state (a) four delegates-at-large, with two others for each congressman-at-large, if any, and (b) two district delegates for every congressman representing a district.

Earlier
incon-
gruities
It would seem an elementary principle that seats in a representative body should be apportioned according to the numbers and location of the people to be represented. Manifestly, however, the national nominating convention has been constructed on no such plan. Before changes made in the last two or three decades, a Northern state containing few Democrats was entitled to quite as many delegates in a Democratic convention as a Southern state, of equal total population, containing ten or twelve times as many. Similarly, Southern states yielding few Republican popular votes (and, with rare exceptions, no electoral votes at all) sent to Republican conventions more delegates than Northern states, of less total population, which unfailingly rolled up substantial Republican majorities; slender Southern Republican minorities had great weight in selecting candidates and making platforms, but contributed little or nothing to party victory. [2]

Repub-
lican
reforms
For many years, protest among Republicans against these illogical arrangements was fruitless. But after the defeat of 1912—following a party split aggravated by the South's gross over-representation in the nominating convention—the matter was belatedly taken up; and eventually, in 1923, the national committee (acting on instructions from the 1920 convention) introduced a scheme under which each state became entitled to (a) one district delegate from each congressional district; (b) an additional delegate from each congressional district casting 10,000 or more Republican votes for president or congressman in the last preceding election; (c) four delegates-at-large; (d) two additional delegates-at-large for each congressman-at-large that a state might happen to have; and (3) three further delegates-at-large (as a sort of bonus) if the state

---

[1] Except that in all of the conventions from 1924 to 1944 inclusive each state was allowed eight delegates-at-large (half being women), each with a half-vote.

[2] Thus, in the convention of 1912, Georgia, which had cast only 41,692 Republican votes four years previously, had 28 delegates, whereas Iowa, with 275,210 Republican votes in 1908, had only 26; and Alabama, Louisiana, Mississippi, and South Carolina, with a total Republican vote of 42,592 in 1908, had 82 delegates, while "rock-ribbed" Pennsylvania, with a Republican vote of 745,779, had only 76.

had cast its electoral vote for the Republican presidential nominee in the last preceding presidential election or had elected a Republican senator in the ensuing off-year election. Under this somewhat complicated plan, many states—chiefly in the South—continued to be over-represented. In the convention of 1944, however, the situation was further improved by a rule (adopted by the 1940 convention) under which only districts which cast at least 1,000 Republican votes in the preceding presidential or mid-term congressional election were entitled to any delegate at all.[1]

With only minor modifications in a few instances, the Democrats adhered to the traditional mid-nineteenth-century plan until 1940. Under a rule then adopted, however, every state (beginning in 1944) carried by the Democrats in the preceding presidential election became entitled to a bonus of two extra convention votes—an arrangement designed primarily to compensate the Southern states for their loss of a virtual veto on nominations when, in 1936, a new regulation provided for nomination thereafter by simple majority instead of by the previous two-thirds.[2]

Speaking strictly, the composition of a national convention is defined in terms of votes, rather than of delegates; for although since 1872 the normal arrangement has been for each delegate to have one vote—the Republicans adhering to this usage fairly consistently—there has been nothing to prevent a state from sending a number of delegates exceeding the number of votes to which it was entitled, each delegate in such a case casting only a fractional vote. The motive for doing this has usually been to provide good convention-floor seats for the "boys from home;" and in Democratic conventions the practice developed into a great abuse. To the Democratic convention of 1940 at Chicago, one Mississippi district sent fifty-four delegates to cast its two votes (each delegate shouldering the frightful responsibility of one-twenty-seventh of a vote!), and the state of Texas sent 132 delegates to cast a total of forty-six votes; all told, 1,844 delegates appeared—although to cast only 1,100 votes. On complaint of officials in charge of seating arrangements, the 1940 convention decreed that thenceforth no state might send delegates in excess of twice its quota of votes; and in 1944 the total fell to 1,176. But in any event—recalling that for every delegate there is an alternate holding himself in readiness to take part whenever needed as a substitute— one can see that a national convention is bound to be a decidedly

The Democrats take up the problem

Numbers

---

[1] Some 75 districts, almost wholly in the deep South, consistently fail to meet this minimum requirement.

[2] See p. 267 below; and *Proceedings of the Democratic National Convention, 1940,* pp. 200-202, 341-356.

By courtesy, representation is given also by both parties to the District of Columbia and to various territories and dependencies, although these have no part in the final election. The allotments are: Republicans—Puerto Rico, two delegates, and District of Columbia, Alaska, and Hawaii, three each, or five in the case of Alaska and Hawaii if the territorial delegate is a Republican; Democrats—Virgin Islands, two, and District of Columbia, Puerto Rico, Alaska, Hawaii, and the Canal Zone, six each. The Republicans formerly allowed the Philippines two delegates and the Democrats six, but with the Islands independent this has come to an end.

numerous body. Even the Republican convention of 1944 contained 1,055 delegates and the same number of alternates.[1]

Methods of choosing delegates

Originally, delegates to national conventions were chosen in several different ways—by mass-meetings, by caucuses, by district and state conventions, even by state party committees. Gradually it became the practice of the Republicans to elect delegates-at-large in state conventions and district delegates in conventions held in the several congressional districts; and by rules adopted in 1884 and 1888 the national committee made this plan obligatory. Viewing the state as the basic unit of representation, the Democrats, however, were more likely to authorize selection of all delegates at a state convention or by the state committee.

Rise of the presidential primary

Shortly after 1900, the direct primary began to be used in various states in nominating candidates for state and local offices, and inevitably the question arose of applying the new device, by state law, to the choice of delegates to national conventions. This was first done by Wisconsin in 1905, and so rapidly did the idea take hold that in 1916 more than half of the entire number of delegates of both of the leading parties were chosen, in more than a score of states, under the primary plan.[2] Some states, beginning with Oregon in 1910, provided not only for popular election of delegates but for an expression of the voters' preferences among persons seeking nomination; some even sought to bind the delegates to be guided by preferences so expressed. From time to time, too, the suggestion was broached that the presidential primary, in some one of the numerous forms that it had assumed, be made nation-wide by federal law. In his first annual message (1913), President Wilson, indeed, went so far as to propose that Congress enact legislation under which candidates for the presidency and vice-presidency should be nominated by direct nation-wide action of the people, and that the national convention be transformed into a gathering merely of party officers and nominees for the purpose of declaring and accepting the verdict of the primaries and formulating the platform. Even had Congress been favorably disposed, however, it would probably not have been regarded as having the necessary power; eight years later, indeed, the Supreme Court became responsible for a ruling construed to mean that Congress had no authority to control nominating procedures at all.[3]

A device that proved disappointing

As it was, after starting off with apparently irresistible force, the presidential primary movement lost momentum. Since 1916, no additional states have adopted the device in mandatory form; more than that, eight

[1] In 1947, the Republican national committee indicated that the number of delegates in the 1948 convention at Philadelphia would be 1,093.

The number of women members has undergone some decline since 1924. In the Democratic convention of 1944, 174 women were present as delegates and 269 as alternates; in the Republican convention, the numbers were 99 and 264 respectively.

[2] The Republican convention of 1912 refused to seat certain delegations chosen under direct primary laws, on the ground that long-established party rules required choice by conventions. But of course this attitude could not be maintained in the face of the undeniable right of the states to regulate matters of the kind.

[3] See p. 300, note 2, below.

have abandoned it.[1] Direct primaries, in general, have not met all expectations; and when employed in selecting delegates to national nominating conventions, they have disclosed many serious shortcomings. One fault has been the very great cost to a presidential candidate seeking to carry on a primary campaign throughout the country; a second, the fact that primaries are held at different dates in the various states, which results in one state often having undue influence upon the voting in other states; a third, that some of the strongest candidates usually decide not to enter the primaries in certain states, leaving the voters in such states opportunity to choose only among the weaker ones. In short, with primaries held in less than half of the states and, where held, showing many defects, the plan has furnished no genuine solution for the difficult and important problem of making the national convention a body truly representative of the party.

Nor does the future of the device look promising. Those who believe in it (and many people do so) very properly argue that it has never been given a fair nation-wide test. But the only way in which it could be given such a test would be by virtue of an act of Congress; and notwithstanding that the way seems to have been cleared constitutionally for such legislation,[2] neither Congress nor people is sufficiently convinced of the intrinsic merits of the plan. Nor are the taxpayers prepared to shoulder the expense that would be entailed in disentangling the presidential primary from the primaries for state and local offices and operating it as a separate piece of political machinery. Still further, while such a defect as the scattering of primaries over three or four months might be remedied rather easily, others—such as the cost of candidacy—could not. As for the recording of popular preferences among the candidates, that also has its limitations—especially if the attempt is made to pledge delegates to vote for the popular choice. Candidates may withdraw before the balloting; new ones may enter the race; in any event, the ultimate selection will usually be a matter of give and take on such lines that a delegation will be greatly handicapped and embarrassed unless it has a free hand. Meanwhile, with the presidential primary surviving in mandatory form in only fourteen states (though the list includes several of the most populous ones, *e.g.*, New York, Pennsylvania, and Illinois), the delegates of thirty-four states continue normally to be chosen in state and district conventions or by state central committees. Except in 1912, it has not seemed to make much difference in the final

A doubtful future

---

[1] Iowa and Minnesota in 1917, Vermont in 1921, Montana in 1924, North Carolina in 1927, Indiana in 1929, Michigan in 1931, and North Dakota in 1935. In addition, a law on the subject was declared unconstitutional in Texas in 1916, and an Alabama law was abandoned when the attorney-general of the state rendered an opinion to the effect that it also was unconstitutional. Alabama, Michigan, Florida, and Georgia, however, now have laws under which primaries may be employed when so ordered by the state committee of a party.

[2] By the Supreme Court's decision in United States *v.* Classic (1941). See p. 190, note 4, above.

outcome whether delegates were chosen by primary or by convention; and even on that occasion the drift of Republican opinion in favor of Theodore Roosevelt, as revealed in the primaries, did not enable him to win in the Chicago convention.[1]

The National Convention at Work

Surrounding conditions   Composed mainly of state and local party leaders and workers, business men, lawyers, and journalists, with a liberal admixture of governors of states, senators and ex-senators, congressmen and ex-congressmen, and state legislators,[2] the convention of a major party meets in a large hall, lavishly decorated with flags, bunting, and portraits, and capable of seating usually from fifteen to twenty thousand people. The thousand or more delegates are accommodated on the main floor, grouped around placards bearing the names of their states; the equally numerous alternates are seated directly back of them; representatives of the press, together with radio reporters and commentators, are given generous space (about 1,300 seats in the conventions of 1944); the galleries are packed with intermittently interested and restless spectators; radio "hook-ups" are in readiness to carry the proceedings to every corner of the land.[3] Except during principal speeches and at occasional tense moments, there is a general buzz of conversation; bands fill in intervals with popular airs; deafening "demonstrations" break forth from frenzied supporters of "favorite sons" or other candidates; sheer chaos sometimes prevails for an hour at a stretch. Small wonder that, many years ago, the late Lord Bryce was moved to remark that the setting seems hardly compatible with the deliberative work to be performed;[4] and indeed it

---

[1] A similar Democratic drift toward Champ Clark did not prevent the nomination from going to Woodrow Wilson. In 1916, Hughes was nominated by the Republicans although he had been a primary candidate in only one state; also, in 1920, Harding, beaten in every state in which a primary had occurred except in Ohio. Results of primaries in 1928 foreshadowed the nomination of Hoover and Smith, who, however, would almost certainly have been nominated had there been no primaries. The primaries of 1932 to 1944 inclusive had, on the whole, little significance except perhaps, for the fact that in 1944 an unfavorable result in an early Wisconsin primary nipped in the bud a candidacy for the Republican nomination which had been expected to acquire formidable proportions, i.e., that of Wendell L. Willkie. For an excellent treatment of the entire subject, see L. Overacker, *The Presidential Primary* (New York, 1926); and cf. her "Direct Primary Legislation, 1936-1939," *Amer. Polit. Sci. Rev.*, XXXIV, 499-506 (June, 1940).

[2] Formerly, the delegates always included a large number of postmasters, revenue-collectors, and other federal office-holders. The Hatch Act of 1939 (see p. 511 below), prohibiting political activity on the part of such office-holders (except the relatively few having to do with framing policy), now operates to debar them from serving. The constitution (Art. II, § 1, cl. 2) forbids members of Congress to act as presidential electors; but, contrary to the spirit of the provision, they take part freely in selecting presidential candidates—which has come to be a far more important matter than serving as an elector.

[3] Radio-broadcasting first assumed importance in the conventions of 1924. The Republican convention of 1940 was signalized by the earliest use of television on such an occasion, although the service was available in only a restricted area. Both major conventions in Philadelphia were telecast in 1948.

[4] *The American Commonwealth* (4th ed., 1910), II, 193-194. Cf. E. P. Herring, *The Politics of Democracy* (New York, 1940), Chap. XVI.

is only because practically all of the problems are thrashed out and decisions made behind the scenes—in committee rooms, in the smoke-filled suites of influential delegates, indeed wherever private conferences can be held and understandings reached—that the body performs its functions effectively at all.[1]

Although, under wartime conditions, the conventions of 1944 were streamlined to cover only three days, such gatherings usually last four or five days—sometimes longer. On the first day (with procedure normal), the meeting is called to order by the chairman of the national committee, who, after prayer has been offered and the call for the convention read, announces the temporary officers agreed on in advance by the national committee; whereupon—the list having been accepted by the convention, usually as a matter of routine—the temporary chairman delivers a "keynote" speech (prepared before the convention met) eulogizing the party, drawing applause by referring to the great names associated with its past, assailing the record and ridiculing the promises of its opponents, urging harmony, and in general sounding a call to battle. Pending permanent organization, the rules of the convention held four years previously are adopted; and the day's work may close with a roll-call of the states and territories, each delegation nominating, through its chairman, one of its members (in the case of the Democrats, two) to serve on each of the four great committees [2] (1) credentials; (2) permanent organization; (3) rules and order of business; (4) platform and resolutions—although the less wearisome plan is generally followed of permitting the chairmen of the several delegations merely to hand in written lists of proposed committee assignments.

Temporary organization

The next sessions, extending over at least one day, are devoted to receiving and acting on the reports of these committees. The committee on rules and order of business submits a set of rules based on those of the House of Representatives and more or less similar to those of the previous convention, together with an order of business also adhering closely to past practice; and its report is usually accepted with little or no discussion. The committee on credentials has the difficult task of deciding who shall have seats for which there are rival claimants, doing it, however, supposedly on the basis of evidence filed in advance with the national committee. Sometimes, as in the Republican convention of 1912, contests are numerous; and according as they are decided, the scale may

Committee reports

---

[1] For a scathing indictment of national conventions by a journalist who had attended twenty of them, see S. G. Blythe, "A Decadent Institution," *Sat. Eve. Post,* CCV, 6-7 ff. (Aug. 27, 1932). The pandemonium at the Democratic convention of 1924 has probably never been exceeded. A contemporary realistic description is quoted in J. M. Mathews and C. A. Berdahl, *Documents and Readings in American Government* (New York, 1928), 139-144.

[2] The Democratic quota of two is accounted for by the extension to women, in 1940, of equal representation with men on the platform and resolutions committee, followed in 1944 by application of the same arrangement to the entire group of committees. In the last-mentioned year, the Republicans introduced the plan also, but as yet for the platform and resolutions committee only.

be turned for or against control by a given element of the party, or for or against the nomination of a given candidate. Hence, although the validated list of delegates as made up and reported by the committee is usually accepted, heated controversy may arise and the committee may be overruled.[1]

Perma-
nent
organi-
zation

The next step, normally—although sometimes it is taken before the list of approved delegates is fully made up—is to effect permanent organization. The committee on that subject reports, nominating a list of permanent officials; and ordinarily the persons named are elected without debate, although it was only after a sharp contest on the floor that Senator Walsh was chosen permanent chairman of the Democratic convention of 1932. The permanent chairman will have many difficult decisions to make, and he must be both a master of parliamentary law. and a man of energy and decision. Not infrequently, he is a United States senator.

Framing
and
adopting
the
platform

Following a lengthy, and usually more restrained, speech by the new presiding officer, the convention is ready for a report from the committee on platform and resolutions.[2] Starting commonly at least two or three days before the convention meets, and working day and night over a vast array of platform proposals—bombarded also with suggestions and demands from both delegates and outsiders [3]—the committee will usually have succeeded in whipping together a document which it can report unanimously; [4] and while there is commonly some show of discussion on the floor, and occasionally lively conflict, only rarely is anything finally voted that the committee has not proposed. As approved by the convention, the platform is likely to be a document filling ten or

---

[1] In the interest of harmony, two contesting delegations from a state are sometimes admitted, each member being allowed a half-vote. This, for example, was the plan followed by the Democratic convention of 1944 in dealing with rival delegations from Texas—although the "regular" delegation walked out of the convention in protest. Two delegations from Texas appeared also in the Republican convention of 1944, and, both being seated with the customary half-votes for delegates, both accepted the arrangement. Most contests in Republican conventions come from the Southern or border states—in 1940, 49 out of a total of 54.

[2] Prior to 1932, the Democrats customarily nominated candidates before adopting a platform. During 1932-44, however, they adopted their platform first (as the Republicans have regularly done); and it seems safe to assume that this will be their practice hereafter.

[3] Especially from organized economic, business, professional, and reform groups such as the A. F. of L. and the C.I.O., the American Farm Bureau Federation, the American Legion, and the Chamber of Commerce of the United States. "Lobbying" by special interests, as we shall see, is by no means confined to the halls of Congress and of state legislatures. A president having his party's support for reëlection naturally has a great deal to say about the platform on which he will run. Before being submitted to the Philadelphia convention, the Democratic platform of 1936 was approved in every particular by President Roosevelt, and a later version of it was rushed to him by airplane and further amended by him before being adopted. There was also nothing in the 1940 and 1944 platforms to which he had not given his advance endorsement—except that in 1940 he disliked an anti-war plank included and in his acceptance speech completely ignored it.

[4] Although formally elected only after the convention opens, the platform committee, or at any rate a sub-committee of it, will have been constituted informally in advance, in order that it may thus begin work early.

a dozen pages of print and touching upon a wide variety of topics.[1] On some matters it will make emphatic and unequivocal pronouncements; on others—usually *most* others—it will be wordy and evasive; on still others, although perhaps of vital public concern, it will be completely silent, for the reason that anything that could be said would probably alienate votes. But there will be plenty of generalities, glibly extolling the party's achievements, unsparingly indicting the opposition, and voicing platitudes of hoary antiquity. By and large, the platform is viewed by the sophisticated, not as a program to be carried out if the party wins, but rather as a bid—required by custom, and couched in the familiar catch-phrases—for the confidence and support of the more susceptible elements in the electorate.[2] Fully understanding this, people are rarely so naïve as to take a platform seriously—or even to read it. Sometimes, indeed—as in 1928 and 1932—platforms are so overshadowed by the personalities and announced policies of the candidates that, once the campaign is under way, they almost fade out of the picture.[3]

At last, by the third or fourth day, the convention arrives at its main objective, *i.e.*, the nomination of candidates. The secretary calls the roll of states, beginning with Alabama, and each delegation, in its turn, has an opportunity to place a favorite son or other person in nomination. If the delegates of a state which stands near the top of the list choose to do so, they may yield to a delegation which under alphabetical order would not be called until later; and this opportunity to get a candidate's name officially before the convention in advance of others, and to touch off a demonstration in his behalf, may prove a decided advantage. Anywhere from two or three to upwards of a dozen names may be presented, each in a vigorous, eulogistic, and sometimes flamboyant nominating speech followed by briefer seconding speeches by delegates carefully picked to give an impression of widely distributed support;[4] and no effort is spared by either the orators or the delegates

Nomina tion of candi- dates

---

[1] The brief, crisp platform (1,600 words) adopted by the Democrats at Chicago in 1932 is a notable exception. The Democratic platform-makers of 1944 started off by promising a document even briefer, but in the end succumbed to pressures from groups demanding that this or that be included.

[2] Woodrow Wilson himself, after being nominated for a second presidential term by a party which four years previously had declared for only one term, bluntly asserted: "A platform is not a program."

[3] In 1944, the Institute of Public Opinion found that, three weeks after the Republican convention, not one voter in ten had any idea of what was in the party's platform on world affairs and not one farmer in twelve knew anything about the planks on agriculture. A month after the convention, the Republican candidates, Dewey and Bricker, met with a score of other Republican governors in a two-day conference at St. Louis and with them drew up a fourteen-point statement of policy considerably more explicit than the party platform and designed to receive (as it did) quite as much attention in the coming campaign. In point of fact, in the campaign both principal candidates devoted their attention so largely to attacking the Roosevelt Administration and its record that neither the party platform nor the St. Louis declaration received a great deal of emphasis.

[4] There have been instances in which convention oratory rose to the level of genuine eloquence. Robert G. Ingersoll's "plumed knight" apostrophe, placing Blaine in nomination at Cincinnati in 1876, is a case in point; also the "cross of gold" speech

and spectators favoring a given candidate to whip up enthusiasm for him. At the proper psychological moment, delegates and alternates may break forth with all manner of vocal and mechanical noise, seize flags and standards and start parading around the hall, and plunge the assemblage into pandemonium from which it can be extricated only when the enthusiasts have reached a state of exhaustion an hour or more later. Occasionally such demonstrations are genuinely spontaneous; but usually they are staged according to careful prearrangement, and, being known to be so, are viewed by spectators with mild amusement or growing impatience and quite fail in their purpose of sweeping the convention off its feet.[1]

Voting on the candidates

When, finally, all of the names have been presented, the convention proceeds to vote. The roll of states is called again, and the delegations, through their chairmen, announce their votes. Under early Republican

The Democratic "unit" rule

procedure, each delegate might usually vote as he liked; in any case, he had a right to have his vote recorded separately. The Democrats followed the different plan of permitting the state convention to require the delegates to the national convention to cast their votes in a block for one candidate; and even if no such requirement was imposed, the delegation itself might, by majority vote, determine how the votes of all of its members should be recorded. This historic "unit rule" conformed to the states' rights antecedents of the Democratic party, and had the practical advantage of augmenting the power and importance of a state in the convention's proceedings. The rise of the presidential primary made it necessary for the Republicans to look more tolerantly on instructed delegations, and, on the other hand, forced the Democrats to permit numerous exceptions to their unit rule. In so far as feasible, both parties still hold to their earlier procedures. In practice, however, on one basis or another, most delegates are now free to vote as individuals.

The Democratic "two-thirds" rule abandoned

Until rather recently, another important difference between Republican and Democratic procedure was that whereas a simple majority of all votes cast was sufficient to nominate in a Republican convention, the Democrats required two-thirds. The Democratic rule dated from 1832, being at first applied to the vice-presidency only; in 1836, however, it was extended to presidential nominations as well. Although of certain theoretical merit, it, as well as the unit rule (with which it was closely associated), came in for vigorous criticism in later days, and party opinion increasingly demanded the abrogation of both.[2] As already pointed

---

which won William Jennings Bryan an unexpected nomination at Chicago in 1896. Emotionalism and bombast are, however, far more frequent. The Democratic convention of 1940 restricted nominating speeches to twenty minutes and seconding speeches (not to exceed four) to five minutes.

[1] Sometimes, however, the spectators themselves become demonstrative, as notably in behalf of Wendell L. Willkie during the Republican convention of 1940.

[2] The two-thirds rule was responsible for numerous convention deadlocks, and more than once—as in 1924—it prevented the party's strongest candidate from receiving the nomination.

out, the unit rule partially collapsed under the impact of the direct-primary, instructed-delegation plan of choosing delegates; and a movement for doing away with the twin regulations failed at the Chicago convention of 1932 only because of reluctance to change the rules while the game was being played, *i.e.*, while a contest for nomination was actually going on. The Philadelphia convention of 1936, however, found itself in a position to act; President Roosevelt was about to be renominated without opposition, and hence the chances of no candidate would be in any way affected. The convention, therefore, rescinded the historic two-thirds requirement and prescribed that thenceforth nomination— for both the presidency and vice-presidency, of course—should be by simple majority. No action was taken on the unit rule; but eventually its complete abandonment is likely to prove necessary as a means of preventing nominations from being too much controlled by a few of the most populous states.[1]

After the votes of all of the states have been recorded and counted, the result is announced. Sometimes—especially when a president is being renominated—a single ballot suffices.[2] But often the votes are so divided among a number of candidates that no one obtains the requisite majority, and additional ballots must be taken. In the course of these—while, off in secluded spots, party leaders and chairmen of key delegations dicker, make deals, and toss whole blocks of votes around—weaker candidates drop out; and eventually some one of the contestants (or, perchance, a "dark horse" agreed upon behind the scenes) emerges a victor. Sometimes the balloting (and bartering) is very prolonged, the extremest case on record being the nomination of John W. Davis by the Democrats in 1924 on the 103rd ballot, after a deadlock lasting nine days. With a Democratic candidate, however, no longer obliged to muster a two-thirds vote in order to win, there will hardly be another experience so trying. *The balloting*

The nomination for the presidency having been made, the weary delegates hurry their labors to a conclusion. A candidate for the vice-presidency is still to be named; and the same procedure—roll-call, nominating and seconding speeches, and balloting—is followed. But the contest is usually not very keen, and a decisive vote is soon reached.[3] As a rule, *The nomination for the vice-presidency*

---

[1] Abrogation of the two-thirds rule deprived the South of the control over nominations previously enjoyed by that section, and—as was evidenced in the 1944 convention—there is demand in that section for a restoration of the former system.

[2] No printed or written ballots are employed; all voting is oral. The term "ballot" is, however, commonly used to designate a vote. Occasionally a candidate has been nominated by acclamation, without a roll-call even being completed. The forces in the Democratic convention of 1940 supporting Franklin D. Roosevelt for a third term hoped to accomplish his nomination in this way, but were frustrated by third-term opponents.

[3] The nomination of Henry A. Wallace for the vice-presidency in the Democratic convention of 1940 stirred unusual excitement because many of the party leaders were opposed to him and resented President Roosevelt's virtual dictation that the Secretary of Agriculture be made his running mate. Equal excitement was stirred in the Democratic convention of four years later, when, with Mr. Wallace vigorously supported by liberal and radical elements for a renomination, the President gave

the grounds on which the selection is made leave a good deal to be desired. The prize—such as it is—may be used to placate an important element in the party that has lost in the fight over the presidential nomination or over the platform, or to enhance the chances of capturing a pivotal state. It will usually be bestowed also with a view to balancing the ticket: an Eastern presidential nominee calls for a Western vice-presidential nominee; a dyed-in-the-wool conservative must ordinarily be counterbalanced with a man of known liberal views, or *vice versa*.[1] Every sort of consideration, indeed, may contribute to the decision except the one that ought to dominate, *i.e.*, that the person nominated stands a very fair chance of being summoned by fate to the White House. Despite the melancholy fact that this has happened seven times in our history, and that on some occasions it resulted in a weak or unsuccessful administration, the vice-presidency is still, as some one has remarked, "lightly esteemed and carelessly bestowed."[2]

The convention's closing acts

Two final tasks remain (or used to do so), one important, the other not at all so, and neither very arduous. The convention, or party congress, meets only once in four years, and there must be an accepted party authority to carry on during the interval and in due time to convoke and arrange for the next convention. This authority is the national committee, consisting, as we have seen, of two members—a man and a woman —from each state and territory. Since, however, these persons are in all cases designated (in theory, "nominated") either by the state delegation or by a state primary or convention, election of the committee by the convention is only a matter of form.[3] The other task remaining, formerly at all events, has been to designate (usually by authorizing the convention chairman to appoint) two committees, each consisting of one representative from each state and territory, to carry the news of their nomination to the respective candidates. Although giving the nominees opportunity to deliver more or less significant speeches of acceptance, the old-style "notification" ceremonies were expensive and rather perfunctory; and these days of quick and easy travel by air and communication by radio will probably see them permanently abandoned. Franklin D. Roosevelt got his first campaign off to a dramatic start in 1932 by climbing into an airplane at Albany and a few hours later descending from

him only a gesture of assistance and in the end threw his support to a successful rival, Senator Harry S. Truman. In contrast with what usually happens, the 1944 convention devoted almost a full day—and its most strenuous one—to the vice-presidential nomination.

[1] This sort of thing did not happen in the Democratic convention of 1940, but only because President Roosevelt insisted upon, and contrived to bring about, the nomination of a man holding views similar to his own. There was probably not much difference in liberalism, too, between the Republican nominees of 1944.

[2] The nadir was reached in 1904 when the Democrats nominated a wealthy but undistinguished senator eighty-one years old! In all, ten out of thirty-four vice-presidents have gone on to the presidency, although only seven without being directly elected to the higher office.

[3] The Republicans sometimes elect this committee at an earlier stage of the convention.

the skies at Chicago to accept his nomination forthwith; in 1936, also, he appeared at Philadelphia and accepted his nomination as the closing feature of the convention; and in 1940 and 1944, without actually going to the Chicago conventions, he accepted his third and fourth nominations by radio-broadcast—in the second instance, from a railway car on a siding near a naval station on the West Coast. Until 1944, the Republicans clung to the traditional notification ceremonies. In that year, however, Thomas E. Dewey, duplicating Mr. Roosevelt's feat in 1932, journeyed from Albany to Chicago by air and accepted his nomination (as his running mate had already done) from the convention rostrum.

The Presidential Campaign

At an early date, the new national committee meets and organizes for work during the coming campaign and the ensuing four years. A chairman is chosen, nominally by the committee, but always to meet the wishes of the presidential candidate; and while the latter sometimes— as in the case of both of the Roosevelts—largely determines the strategy to be employed, the chairman is officially, and as a rule actually, the campaign manager. Under his direction, subcommittees and auxiliary committees are set up; a treasurer is appointed and the quest for funds begun; headquarters are opened, usually in both an Eastern and a Western city, with auxiliary offices in a few other centers; a "campaign textbook" (containing the platform, notification and acceptance speeches, biographies of the candidates, statistics and quotations backing up party claims and arguments, and other miscellaneous materials) is published and given wide distribution; a speakers' bureau is organized; and an appeal for votes is launched which, once the campaign has got actively under way (usually by early September), is kept up with increasing resourcefulness and fervor to the day of reckoning. Campaigns for the election of senators and congressmen, state officials and members of state legislatures, and municipal and other local officials are, of course, going on simultaneously, stirring all party machinery, from national committees to precinct organizations, to new vigor and activity.

No aspect of American political life is more familiar, even to younger people, than presidential campaigns; few have been written about more profusely by journalists, politicians, and scientific students of political behavior. Comment here may therefore appropriately be brief. To begin with, it costs a great deal of money to run a presidential campaign; and while ideally the sums needed should be obtained from the rank and file of party adherents and supporters in the form of modest contributions from many contributors, efforts to operate on such a basis have never been very successful. As a consequence, the parties must invariably rely mainly upon substantial gifts by people of substance, even though this opens a way for charges of undue influence of such people and the interests they represent, both upon the conduct of campaigns and upon

Machinery

Funds

the policies pursued by successful candidates once they are in office.[1] A good deal of the money spent (although relatively less now than before radio-broadcasting was introduced) goes for the preparation and distribution of party "literature." In addition to the campaign textbook, each party showers pamphlets, leaflets, posters, cartoons, and what not upon the press, upon local party workers, and upon the general public. Some of the materials are meaty, terse, interesting, and worth while, but many are only reprints of unreadable speeches and compilations of undigested statistics, pretty much a dead loss—except for collectors of waste-paper! It is a fair assumption that the great majority of voters read little or nothing relating to a campaign and its issues except what they find in their favorite newspaper.[2]

Then there is campaign oratory. The "stump" is the vantage point from which office-seekers and party workers have bombarded the voters from the time when popular elections began, and the later stages of a presidential campaign find literally thousands of men and women going up and down the land haranguing audiences in great halls, in stadiums, in court-house yards, in school-houses, and in fact wherever crowds can be assembled, with sometimes accompanying parades and other colorful demonstrations designed to rally the faithful and impress the hesitant. Ordinarily, a president seeking reëlection stays fairly close to the White House and makes only a few speeches, Wilson in 1916, Hoover in 1932, and Franklin D. Roosevelt in 1936 being the principal exceptions; as president, he can keep the public eye and make the front page simply by his official acts and reported press conferences, with perhaps an occasional published letter to a party leader or other form of manifesto. A challenger, on the other hand—a Roosevelt in 1932, a Landon in 1936, a Willkie in 1940, a Dewey in 1944—is likely to go on speaking tours taking him into all, or nearly all, principal sections of the country, particularly if, as in the cases of Landon and Willkie, he had not previously been widely known. It is, however, a matter of opinion whether any candidate gains more than he loses by dashing around the country. Such traveller-candidates as Bryan and Willkie failed to reach the White House; Charles E. Hughes would almost certainly have beaten Woodrow Wilson in 1916 if he had stayed away from California.[3]

---

[1] See p. 223 above.

[2] H. A. Bone, *Smear Politics; An Analysis of 1940 Campaign Literature* (Washington, D. C., 1941); T. M. Black, *Democratic Party Publicity in 1940* (New York, 1941).

[3] During a three-day campaign visit to the state, Mr. Hughes made the mistake of paying no attention to Governor Hiram Johnson, a very popular Progressive Republican then running for the Senate in competition with an "organization" candidate; and the slight was deeply resented. The two men were once in the same hotel in Long Beach for two hours, although without Hughes knowing it at the time. Johnson won a smashing victory; Hughes lost the state by four thousand votes, and with it the presidency. Willkie, in the 1940 campaign, travelled 18,759 miles by rail, 8,884 miles by air, and 2,000 by motor-car, and spoke in 34 states—in all, 540 times. Cf. J. Chamberlain, "Candidates and Speeches," *Yale Rev.*, XXX, 45-61 (Autumn, 1940).

Also there is the radio. In part, the disparaging remarks made above *Radio-broad-casting* about campaign literature were inspired by the fact that in these later days voters depend more upon the ear than upon the eye—more upon what they hear than upon what they read. In the United States as in no other country, radio-broadcasting has revolutionized electoral techniques. Formerly, candidates and other campaign orators could reach by voice only those people who would take the trouble to attend their meetings; nowadays, they project themselves into the voters' homes, competing, to be sure, with sport and entertainment features, but certainly getting a hearing far beyond the limits of their visible audiences. Broadcasting time is limited and expensive; and this makes for more carefully prepared speeches. The same speech, furthermore, cannot be used twice. At all events, the ablest speakers that the parties can enlist may be heard and their arguments compared in twenty-five million homes the country over.[1] Small wonder that in 1944 more than thirty per cent of the total outlay of the Republican national committee, and over thirty-six per cent of that of the Democratic committee, went to broadcasting companies in payment for access to the air.

Still another newer campaign feature is advance polling of the voters, *Polls and surveys* by the sampling method, carried on most extensively some years ago by a now extinct weekly publication, the *Literary Digest,* and employed with rather remarkable success in the most recent campaigns by the American Institute of Public Opinion (established in 1935 and conducting the well-known "Gallup poll"), the magazine *Fortune,* and other private agencies. The ebb and flow of popularity of the candidates is measured and reported upon through the press, usually weekly; and, although always in some danger of being misled, candidates and party managers alike derive information which may lead to important decisions concerning issues to be emphasized or soft-pedaled and areas in which effort is useless or, on the other hand, should be redoubled. The published results, and the forecasts based on them, may also considerably influence campaign contributions. In addition to polls, there are "surveys," leading also to eagerly awaited forecasts grounded upon poll results, press estimates, studies of historical trends, and other factors, and most commonly conducted by newspapers like the *New York Times,* the *Washington Star,* and the *Chicago Tribune.*[2]

---

[1] In 1940, the Republican candidate, Wendell L. Willkie, introduced the new technique (not utilized since) of employing radio time for reading and answering, in conversational style, questions addressed to him from over the country—in short, a sort of long-distance round-table.

[2] In 1940, *Fortune's* poll forecasting 55.2 per cent of the total popular vote for Roosevelt proved erroneous by only one-half of one per cent. The Gallup poll underestimated his vote by 2.7 per cent. Even before the nominating conventions were held, Mr. Louis H. Bean, economic adviser to the Secretary of Agriculture, predicted, on the basis of study of the available statistical and other data, that the Democratic candidate would receive between 54 and 55 per cent of the popular vote—the actual figure turning out to be 54.7. In 1944, the closest estimate was that of *Fortune,* which came within 0.2 per cent of the actual results. The Gallup poll, missing by 2.5

Casting and Counting the Electoral Vote

Presidential electors

What happens after the last local "spellbinder" has descended from the rostrum, the last national "hook-up" has brought the leading candidates' appeals to the voter at his fireside, and the last rosy forecast has been given out by an at least outwardly confident party chairman? Early in the campaign, party conventions or primaries, in each state, made up the respective "slates" of presidential electors, and in due course ballots were prepared on which (in twenty-seven states) the list of electors were printed in parallel columns, under the familiar party symbols.[1] When the people finally go to the polls, they think of themselves as voting for president and vice-president; and, barring certain contingencies very unlikely to arise, they do actually determine who shall fill these two high offices. In form, however, they vote only for electors, even though they usually do not know or care who the individuals personally are; and in twenty-one "presidential short-ballot" states, the names do not even appear on the ballots. On the other hand, in Alabama, Louisiana, and four other states the electors' names appear without those of the presidential and vice-presidential candidates.[2]

Choice by legislatures gives way to choice by the people

To many persons it would come as a surprise to be told that presidential electors were not always chosen exclusively, or even mainly, by popular vote. A national law dating from 1845 requires that they be elected in all cases on the Tuesday following the first Monday in November; but as for the mode of selection, there has never been any nation-wide rule except a simple constitutional provision that each state shall determine the matter for itself by action of its legislature. At the

---

per cent, was less accurate, although in the congressional elections of 1946 the Gallup margin of error was less than one per cent. On the general subject, see L. H. Bean, *Ballot Behavior; A Study of Presidential Elections* (Washington, D. C., 1940), Chap. x, and V. O. Key, Jr., *Politics, Parties, and Pressure Groups*, Chap. xx. Criticisms of polls as having little trustworthiness or utility are directed mainly to tests of opinion on particular issues or questions rather than to tests of voters' attitudes toward candidates. Cf. L. Rogers, "Do the Gallup Polls Measure Opinion?," *Harper's Mag.*, CLXXXIII, 623-632 (Nov., 1941).

It goes without saying that there are many forms of campaign activity in addition to those here mentioned, such as getting voters registered, house-to-house canvassing, and the like. More extended reading on the general subject will be found in E. M. Sait, *American Parties and Elections* (rev. ed.), Chap. xxii; R. C. Brooks, *Political Parties and Electoral Problems* (3rd ed.), Chap. xii; P. H. Odegard and E. A. Helms, *American Politics* (2nd ed.), Chaps. xvi-xix; V. O. Key, Jr., *op. cit.*, Chap. xviii; and R. V. Peel and T. C. Donnelly, *The 1928 Campaign; An Analysis* (New York, 1931), and *The 1932 Campaign: An Analysis* (New York, 1935). An interesting bit of reading, although relating to state rather than national politics, is R. L. Neuberger, "I Run for Office," *Harper's Mag.*, CXLIV, 153-159 (Feb., 1947). See also the books by J. A. Farley and Al Smith cited on p. 283 below.

[1] The number of electors on the party list in a given state—whether named on the ballots or merely filed with the secretary of state—corresponds, of course, to the number of electoral votes to which the state is entitled. The electors themselves are usually party leaders or other prominent party members, but, as noted above, may in no case include members of Congress or holders of office under the national government. One may derive some satisfaction from serving as an elector, but it will have to be enjoyed in obscurity.

[2] On the forms of ballots used in presidential elections, see S. D. Albright, *The American Ballot* (Washington, D. C., 1942), Chap. v.

outset, the legislature itself elected in a majority of states, and the people took no direct part at all. As democratic sentiment grew, however, popular election was substituted in one state after another, with the result that after 1832 the legislature elected only in South Carolina, and there only until the Civil War.

In states in which the electors were from the first chosen by the people, it was at one time not unusual to employ a district system, under which one elector was chosen by the voters of each congressional district and two were elected by those of the state at large. The competition of political parties, however, caused this plan to lose favor. Under the district system, the electoral vote of a state was likely to be divided among two or more candidates; to win the full vote, it was necessary for a party to carry every district. The alternative was, of course, a general ticket system, under which a party could make a clean sweep merely by securing a plurality throughout the state as a whole. Enhancing as it did the importance of a state in national politics, this plan won the support both of party leaders and of public sentiment. In 1832, only four states retained the district system; and they soon gave it up. Michigan reverted to it in 1891, but only temporarily.[1] In every state, therefore, each voter votes for as many electors as his state is entitled to, e.g., forty-seven in New York, twenty-eight in Illinois.

A majority in the electoral college is necessary to victory—unless achieved through election by the House. But this does not prevent us from having "minority" presidents, i.e., presidents who (speaking strictly, the electors who chose them) received fewer than half of the total popular vote cast; as a matter of fact, we have had seven such—two of them at two different times each.[2] Lincoln, in 1860, obtained more popular votes than did any one of his competitors, but nevertheless polled half a million less than a majority of the whole number recorded. Wilson, in 1912, received two million more popular votes than did his nearest competitor, Theodore Roosevelt, yet only forty-two per cent of the total.[3] In both of these cases, the opposition was unusually divided. But the same thing can happen even if there are only two major tickets in the field. Hayes was elected over Tilden in 1876, although his popular vote

Margin notes: District and general ticket systems; "Minority" presidents

[1] A Democratic legislature of a state which was normally Republican sought in this way to insure that in the approaching presidential election the Democrats would secure a share of the electoral votes. The plan succeeded; nine Republican and five Democratic electors were chosen. But when the Rpublicans regained control of the legislature, they lost no time in restoring the earlier law. The act of 1891 was upheld by the Supreme Court in McPherson v. Blacker, 146 U. S. 1 (1892).

[2] The list, with dates of election, is: Buchanan (1856), Lincoln (1860), Hayes (1876), Garfield (1880), Cleveland (1884 and 1892), Harrison (1888), and Wilson (1912 and 1916).

[3] Wilson's six million popular votes were so distributed as to yield 435 electoral votes; Roosevelt's four million were so distributed (involving pluralities in only six states) as to yield only 88; Taft's three and one-half million curiously contained only two pluralities, i.e., in Vermont and Utah, and yielded only eight electoral votes. With a million and a half fewer popular votes than his opponents combined, Wilson, in terms of electoral votes, was overwhelmingly triumphant.

was about three hundred thousand smaller; and Harrison triumphed over Cleveland in 1888, although with one hundred thousand fewer votes. All that a candidate needs in order to obtain the full electoral vote of a state is a plurality of the popular vote; and popular pluralities, no matter how small, in a sufficient number of states—no very great number if the list includes populous states like New York, Pennsylvania, and Illinois— insure election. An opposing candidate may have swept the states which he carried by sufficiently heavy majorities to give him top rating in terms of popular votes. But, lacking the requisite number of electoral votes, he nevertheless goes down to defeat.[1]

With the entire electoral vote of a state falling to a candidate polling a bare plurality of the popular vote,[2] parties naturally are induced to concentrate their campaign efforts upon border-line states (especially if having a big block of electoral votes), in the hope of edging through to a plurality count. New York is commonly such a state; and party managers are never likely to forget that in 1884 fewer than six hundred popular votes swung that state's thirty-six electoral votes to Grover Cleveland, and that it was these votes that made him a victor over the Republican candidate. Importance of the prize under such circumstances may tempt to vote-buying and other corrupt or dubious practices.

Casting the electoral vote

The theory of the constitution is that the electors are officers of their respective states, and it was on this account that the states were left free to determine how they should be chosen. The place where each group meets within its state is fixed by the legislature thereof (being, naturally, the state capital); and if the electors receive any remuneration

[1] The arithmetic of our presidential elections presents no end of curious features. In 1928, 1,067,586 Democratic votes in Pennsylvania and 2,089,863 in New York failed to yield a single electoral vote for Al Smith. On the other hand, it would have required a shift of only 416,055 votes in certain close states, out of a total presidential vote of over thirty-six millions, to make Smith president instead of Hoover. In 1936, 27,476,872 popular votes (60 per cent of the total) yielded President Roosevelt 523 electoral votes (98 per cent of the total); 16,679,983 popular votes yielded Governor Landon only eight electoral votes. Each Roosevelt electoral vote represented the preferences of 53,000 voters; each Landon electoral vote, those of 2,085,000. In 1940, 27,243,466 popular votes yielded President Roosevelt 449 electoral votes, and 22,304,755 yielded Willkie only 82. In 1944, 25,602,646 popular votes yielded Roosevelt 432 electoral votes, and 22,017,592 yielded Dewey only 99; in Illinois, for example, 2,080,000 votes gave Roosevelt the state's 28 electoral votes, while 1,940,000 (a difference of only 140,000) gave Dewey none. For an interesting exposition of how the 1928 election would have worked out under a proposed constitutional amendment leaving each state its existing allotment of electoral votes but distributing them, in each state, among the candidates in proportion to their popular votes, see *Proportional Representation Rev.*, 3rd ser., No. 94 (Apr., 1930). Under such a plan, Roosevelt in 1936 would have received approximately 322 electoral votes and Landon 194. Complete data (with helpful maps) on eleven presidential elections ending with that of 1936 are presented in E. E. Robinson, *The Presidential Vote, 1896-1932* (Stanford University, 1934), and *The Presidential Vote, 1936* (Stanford University, 1940). The U. S. Bureau of the Census, too, has published a report entitled *Votes Cast in Presidential and Congressional Elections, 1928-1944* (Washington, D. C., 1946).

[2] It is possible for the voters so to split their votes that electors supporting different candidates will win in the same state. But this has happened only four times in the last half-century—in Maryland in 1904 and 1908, in California in 1912, and in West Virginia in 1916.

for their services, it must come out of the state treasury. A federal statute of 1934, however, requires that they meet in the respective states and cast their ballots on the first Monday after the second Wednesday in December following their election. And the Twelfth Amendment to the constitution enjoins that the voting be by ballot; that presidential and vice-presidential candidates be voted for separately; that distinct lists be made up showing all persons supported for either office, with the number of votes received by each; and that these lists, signed and sealed in duplicate, be transmitted to the president of the Senate at the seat of the national government.[1] As evidence of their power to act, the electors transmit also their certificates of election, bearing the signature of the governor.

The constitution is explicit enough on most matters, but curiously vague on the counting of the electoral vote. The Twelfth Amendment says that "the president of the Senate shall, in the presence of the Senate and House of Representatives, open all the certificates and the votes shall then be counted." But who shall make the count? The constitution is silent. If conflicting returns are sent in from a state, who shall decide which shall be received and which rejected? Again, the constitution does not say. For nearly a hundred years, no particular difficulty arose from these omissions; for counting the votes, the natural device of tellers representing both houses was employed, and there were no serious cases of conflicting returns from a state. In the Hayes-Tilden contest of 1876, however, two sets of electoral certificates—one favorable to Hayes and the other to his Democratic opponent—were sent to Washington from South Carolina, Florida, and Louisiana, with also one vote in Oregon in dispute. With the outcome of a close race dependent on the twenty-one votes involved, and with the Republicans controlling one branch of Congress and the Democrats the other, a crisis of the first order was presented; and only after the two houses agreed to set up an extraordinary electoral commission (consisting of five senators, five representatives, and five members of the Supreme Court), and to accept its rulings on the certificates in dispute, was a way out of the trouble discovered. Whether or not because eight of the fifteen members of the commission were Republicans (or of Republican antecedents), all twenty-one contested votes were allotted to Hayes, who thereupon was declared elected (185 to 184), without a vote to spare. The country was kept in suspense until within two days of the time for the new president to be inaugurated.[2]

When the excitement died down, public-spirited men of both parties began looking for some way of preventing similar trouble in the future.

Counting the electoral vote

[1] An act of 1887 requires that two copies of the lists be transmitted also to the secretary of state (at Washington). Formerly, all were sent from each state by special messenger. Under the terms of an act of 1928, however, they began in that year to be sent by registered mail.

[2] A. C. McLaughlin, *A Constitutional History of the United States,* Chap. XLVIII; P. L. Haworth, *The Hayes-Tilden Disputed Presidential Election of 1876* (New York, 1906).

The
Electoral
Count
Act
(1887)
The problem, however, was a thorny one, and a decade passed before any agreement could be reached. Finally, in 1887, an Electoral Count Act supplied at least a partial solution.[1] Recognizing that presidential electors are state officers whose right to act is certified by the governor, and who meet and perform their sole task within the state boundaries and under state authority, the new law placed responsibility for settling disputes as far as possible upon the states themselves. Any determination of a dispute (it provided) in accordance with a state law covering the subject, and arrived at not less than six days before the time fixed for the meeting of the state's electors, should be accepted as conclusive. Manifestly, however, the authorities of a state might fail to arrive at a settlement and conflicting returns still make their appearance at Washington. In such event, the two houses of Congress, acting separately, were to decide which certificates should be accepted. If, however, as might easily prove the case, the houses could not agree, any returns having the advantage of being certified by the governor of the state should be accepted; and if none came with such endorsement (and the houses still could not agree), the state involved should lose its vote in that particular election.

Although imperfect, this legislation went perhaps as far toward solving the problem as was feasible. There was doubt about the power of Congress under the constitution to exercise control over such aspects of presidential elections, and there was still no guarantee against a state's vote being forfeited because of inability of both the state itself and Congress to resolve a conflict. To be sure, it might be held that if a state cannot settle its own electoral disputes, it may reasonably be expected to accept the consequences; and it must be added that to this day only a few of the states have provided by law for handling controversies of the kind. Disfranchisement under any conditions is, however, undesirable.[2]

The
electoral
count as
now
carried
out
With rare exceptions, of course, the counting of the electoral votes is a mere formality; the country knows weeks in advance exactly what the figures will be. On the day fixed by law—formerly, the second Wednesday in February, but now the sixth day of January—the members of the two houses gather in the hall of the House of Representatives, with the president (or president *pro tempore*) of the Senate in the chair, and with four previously designated tellers—a Democrat and a Republican from each house—ready to tabulate and count. Starting with Alabama, and proceeding in alphabetical order, the presiding officer opens the certificates transmitted by the several electoral bodies and hands them one by one

---

[1] 24 *U. S. Stat. at Large*, Pt. II, 373-375. The act was passed by a Congress dominated by the Democrats, who always contended that they had been defrauded in 1876.

[2] Even when there is no dispute, Congress may scrutinize the electoral vote of any state to determine whether it has been "regularly given," *i.e.*, cast, counted, and reported in the manner prescribed by the constitution and laws. If in any instance either house decides that there has been irregularity, the state's votes are not counted.

to the tellers; the latter read the contents aloud and set down the numbers of votes; and the presiding officer announces the totals, which in due time are entered, with a list of the votes by states, in the journals of the two houses. The person receiving the largest number of votes for president, provided the number is a majority of the whole number of electors chosen, *i.e.*, a minimum of 266 out of a total of 531, is declared elected; and similarly in the case of the vice-presidency.

In the event that no candidate for president receives a majority, the election is, of course, thrown into the House of Representatives, where each state has one vote, to be bestowed as the majority of the state delegation determines. Until 1804, the choice of the House in such a contingency was to be made between the candidates who were tied, if there was a tie, or among those highest on the list (up to five) if there was simply lack of a majority. The Twelfth Amendment, however, provided for selection among "the persons having the highest numbers not exceeding three;" and of course that is now the law—the winner being any one of the three receiving the votes of a majority, *i.e.*, nowadays at least twenty-five, of the states. Since 1801, the president has been chosen by the House only once, *i.e.*, in 1825, when John Quincy Adams emerged victor over Jackson, Crawford, and Clay. If no candidate for the vice-presidency obtains a majority of the electoral vote, the Senate—the members voting in this case as individuals—choose from the highest two, the victor being required to receive the votes of a majority of the whole number of senators. Vice-President Richard M. Johnson was elected in this way in 1837.

Notwithstanding all the constitutional and statutory regulations on the subject, it is still possible for the country to come up to the expiration of a presidential term with no president-elect ready to be inaugurated. Not only may the choice itself still be hanging fire, but a man duly elected may have died before the inauguration date, or may have failed to qualify (as, for example, by refusing to serve). Providing belatedly for such contingencies, the Twentieth Amendment, adopted in 1933, stipulates (1) that in case of the death of a president-elect, the vice-president-elect shall become president, and (2) that if at the time for inauguration a president-elect has not been chosen or has failed to qualify, the vice-president-elect "shall *act as president* until a president shall have qualified." Conceivably, however, the same situations might arise as to both president-elect and vice-president-elect; and for this contingency the Amendment authorizes Congress to make provision by law—which, in a Presidential Succession Act of 1947, it has done.[1]

Provision in case of lack of a majority

Some recent safeguards

---

[1] See pp. 436–438 below. In the contingency indicated, the speaker of the House of Representatives, and if none were available, the president *pro tempore* of the Senate, would become "acting president." With a new Congress meeting and organizing nearly three weeks before a new presidential term begins, a speaker would be almost certain to be at hand; and in any case the Senate (when there is no vice-president) always has a president *pro tempore*.

Proposed Changes in the Method of Electing the President and Vice-President

The
problem
deeper
than
merely
that
of the
electoral
college

Proposals for altering the method of electing the president and vice-president have been discussed from time to time throughout our national history. The Twelfth Amendment remedied certain defects; the Twentieth corrected others; and various statutes, notably the Electoral Count Act of 1887 and an act of 1934 passed in pursuance of the new calendar introduced by the Twentieth Amendment, improved matters still farther. But the chief anomaly remains. On being asked, the average person would probably reply at once that this anomaly is the electoral college; and there is no denying that that device has never, except at the beginning, functioned as intended, or that, so far as its formal acts are concerned, it could readily be dispensed with. The actual anomaly, however, is not so much the electoral college itself as the practice of translating popular votes into electoral votes and then awarding all electoral votes of a state to candidates receiving a mere plurality of the popular vote; the electoral college is merely a recording machine—the issue is rather as to the method of arriving at the results which it perfunctorily records; and the plausible suggestion, often heard, that the electoral "row of ciphers" simply be abolished touches a matter not so simple as it sounds.

Some
possible
changes

What are the principal possibilities in the situation—aside from simply going on with our present system? At least five can be discerned. (1) Obviously, one would be to do away with the system of indirect election altogether, throw the entire country into one great constituency, and elect directly by plurality or majority vote, with no reference to state lines. Few people, however, are so naive as to favor this. Not only would the plan defy all considerations of state interest and pride, with less populous states tending to lose electoral power,[1] but it could hardly be operated at all except on the basis of a uniform national suffrage and election law—which, however, assuredly could not be obtained. (2) Another possibility would be to let voting continue on state lines as at present, the people, however, voting directly for presidential (and vice-presidential) candidates, with victory going to the candidate polling a popular plurality in a majority of the states. This, however, would be clearly objectionable, because it would enable a number of the smaller states to swing an election by means of only a minority of the nation-wide popular vote; although it is not to be forgotten that the present system overweights the small states[2] and that we have had no fewer than seven "minority"

---

[1] Thus Nevada, which, with three electoral votes, now has 1-177th of the total electoral power, would, on a population basis, have only 1-1040th.

Debarring Negroes from voting as they do, the Southern states would likewise be at a disadvantage.

[2] Because Senate as well as House seats figure in the apportionment of electoral votes.

presidents under it. The foregoing plans—both apparently impracticable or undesirable or both—involve not only no "electoral college," but no "electoral" votes. Other proposed schemes contemplate electoral votes, though no electoral college. Under one of these, results would be determined, not by the immediate votes of the people, but by electoral votes into which, under some formula, popular votes would be translated. And the formula might be of three widely differing sorts. On the one hand, (a) the popular vote in a state might be translated as now into electoral votes and all of the state's electoral votes awarded to the presidential candidate receiving simply a popular plurality in the state as a whole; or (b) the translation might be on the same state-wide basis, but with electoral votes awarded to different candidates in proportion to their share of the total popular vote, or (c) the translation might be, not on a state-wide basis, but on that of districts equal to the number of the state's electoral votes, given candidates receiving the electoral votes of only those districts in which they had achieved pluralities. Under these last three plans, the president and vice-president would be chosen, not in terms of the popular vote as such, but in terms of electoral votes only; and while the electoral college might be maintained as a formal device for recording such electoral votes, there could perfectly well be a simple, automatic, mathematical procedure for declaring the equivalent of popular votes in terms of electoral votes, with no intervention by presidential "electors" at all.

A constitutional amendment on the lines of plan (a) above, and sponsored by the late Senator George W. Norris of Nebraska, twice narrowly failed to secure the necessary two-thirds vote in the Senate in May, 1934. Greater gains, however, would flow from adoption of either plan (b) or plan (c) above, *i.e.*, one under which the electoral vote of a state would be computed and allotted on a proportional rather than a general ticket basis and a state's entire electoral vote thus would be prevented from going to a given candidate simply because he happened to obtain a plurality of the total popular vote, and notwithstanding that he might have run a poor second, or even third, in important sections of the state.[1] As Michigan's experience with her law of 1891 reminds us, there is, even now, nothing to prevent a state from independently adopting the proportional principle (the Michigan plan based it on districts)— although the formality of choosing electors could not, of course, be abandoned without amending the federal constitution. But here again the great obstacle is state interest and pride; New York will be a far weightier factor politically if all of her forty-seven electoral votes unfailingly go to the same candidate than if her votes could be divided and scattered; and so with every other state. The same considerations, therefore, that originally influenced one state after another to give up the

Desirability of abandoning the state-wide plurality system

[1] A constitutional amendment on these lines received the endorsement of the House judiciary committee in March, 1948.

district plan may be counted upon to block any attempt to revive it or anything resembling it, except perhaps locally and sporadically; and one is bound to conclude that, although the way in which we choose our chief executive could undoubtedly be improved in a number of respects, the outlook for reform—beyond a possible discontinuance of the electoral college, which would be relatively unimportant unless the state-wide plurality system were abandoned with it—is not promising.[1]

Results of Popular Election in Terms of Presidential Fitness

Under the procedures described earlier in this chapter, thirty-two different men have attained the presidency—twenty-five by being elected directly to the office and seven by succeeding a deceased chief executive. In exercising their electoral function, what sort of a record have the people achieved? How do the presidents that they have chosen measure up in terms of capacity, vision, diligence, and other qualities of statesmanship?

An uneven record

Some sixty years ago, Mr. (later Lord) Bryce included in his widely influential book, *The American Commonwealth*, a chapter entitled "Why Great Men Are Not Chosen President."[2] He did not mean to imply that none such is ever chosen. But, looking back over a line of twenty presidents who had served the nation in its first hundred years, our friendly English critic could not see that the people had shown any consistent disposition to elevate even their strongest men (leaving aside the question of actual "greatness") to the highest office in their power to bestow. Nor do they seem to have developed any strong inclination of the kind in later days. Through a century and a half, American presidents, another foreign observer affirms, have for the most part been mediocre when compared, for example, with British prime ministers during the same period.[3] The judgment seems a trifle severe; there have been British prime ministers of inferior caliber. But it has enough validity to be disturbing.

Party responsibility for the choices made

Some people believe that if the plan of election originally adopted—with the choice quietly made by men bearing individual responsibility for their decisions—had been adhered to, the general level would have been higher. Perhaps it would; though there is no way of proving it. In any event, the early rise of political parties and of such party machinery as the national nominating convention doomed that system to collapse and brought into play a wholly different one under which the president became the choice, not (except in form) of the electoral college, nor yet, in any very exact sense, of the people as a whole, but essentially of a political party which, having made a candidate its standard-bearer, went on to

---

[1] On the general subject, see J. E. Kallenbach, "Recent Proposals to Reform the Electoral College System," *Amer. Polit. Sci. Rev.*, XXX, 924-929 (Oct., 1936); L. Rogers and W. Y. Elliott, "Shall We Abolish the Electoral College?," *Forum*, XCVII, 18-22 (Jan., 1937); "Should the Electoral College Be Abolished?" [Symposium], *Cong. Digest*, XX, 67-96 (Mar., 1941).

[2] Vol. I, Chap. VIII.

[3] H. J. Laski, *Parliamentary Government in England* (New York, 1938), 243.

amass enough votes to carry him to victory. To be sure, such a party
candidate is initially named by a gathering of delegates presumed to
reflect the sentiments of a large section of the voters. To be sure, too, he
cannot reach the White House unless the voters support him in sufficient
numbers. But at election time they have opportunity to choose among
only two or three or half a dozen candidates picked and put before them;
and whoever becomes president does so because of having been chosen
initially by a party as an "available" candidate. This is not to say that
if a big democracy is going to have an elective chief executive at all,
there is any better method of choosing him; nor certainly to imply that
parties do not play an indispensable rôle in our present electoral process.
It is merely to state a basic fact, *i.e.*, that the few persons who ever have
a chance under our system to become president get it only when, and
because, parties give it to them.

Unfortunately, the considerations and circumstances making a man
available as a party candidate are not always—perhaps not usually—
such as to guarantee that he will attain high rating as president if
elected. There is, of course, no single formula, or pattern, for presidential
timber; the same person might be wholly acceptable to a party under one
set of conditions and not at all so under another; everything depends on
the character of the times, the prevailing public temper, and many other
things. But at all events, to be favored for selection as a candidate a
man will do well (1) to have the confidence of party leaders in his vote-
getting ability; (2) to have a winsome, human personality; (3) to be
well enough known to have a place in the popular mind, without being
too closely identified with any particular school of thought, sect, or
"cause"; (4) to hail from a "pivotal" state or section which his candidacy
might be expected to swing into the victory column; (5) to be no novice
in politics, yet clear of the antagonisms and enmities likely to be accumulated during a long and vigorous political career; (6) to have, behind the
scenes, some clever and well-financed person or group devoted to advancing his interests in quarters where such effort will count—perchance a
"king-maker" like William McKinley's Mark Hanna, Woodrow Wilson's
George B. Harvey, or Franklin D. Roosevelt's Al Smith and James A.
Farley. One with aspirations may safely be in private life, as was Wendell
Willkie, who, indeed, came into the presidential race in 1940 quite unexpectedly and only a few weeks before the nominating conventions; he
may be a not too aggressive or pugnacious member of Congress, as were
Harrison, McKinley, Harding, and Truman; he may have been a cabinet
member like Taft and Hoover; but perhaps he would do best to be, or
to have been, the governor of a state (preferably an important one), as
were Cleveland, both of the Roosevelts, Wilson, Smith, Coolidge, Landon,
and Dewey.

But the exigencies of party politics bring men to the presidential nomination, and perchance election, in devious ways—sometimes almost as

Some factors in "avail-ability"

A game
of luck
and
chance

if by the workings of a lottery. A candidate with apparently little chance gathers unexpected momentum and emerges a victor; another for whom a carefully nursed "boom" has been built up falls completely out of the running; a deadlocked convention turns in desperation to a "dark horse;" bosses in hotel hideouts reach decisions which become virtual mandates to harassed delegates; the necessity for carrying some large, close state tips the scale to the advantage of a "favorite son" against better known, and perhaps abler, candidates from less strategic parts of the country. And so it goes—with these only a few of the hazards and accidents attending the game. In Britain, a prime minister invariably advances to his post of prestige and power along a rugged line of accumulating experience in the House of Commons and in successive higher executive posts;[1] our presidents sometimes have had no legislative experience at all, save perhaps in a state legislature, and rarely have had much contact with executive and administrative branches of the government over which they are called to preside.

Some
results

Under conditions such as these, the rough and tumble of party politics kept Hamilton, Gallatin, Marshall, Clay, Calhoun, Webster, Seward, Sumner, Hay, and Root from the presidency, while bringing into the office mediocrities like William Henry Harrison, Fillmore, Pierce, Buchanan, Johnson, and Harding. Of course, it is only fair to remember that the system, within three-quarters of a century, gave us Lincoln, Cleveland, the two Roosevelts, and Wilson; also that a good many presidents— Hayes, Arthur, McKinley, and Taft, among more recent ones—while lacking any special claim to distinction, nevertheless proved of at least good average capacity. Perhaps, after all, as Lord Bryce commented in a later book, "things have on the whole gone better than might have been predicted."[2]

Qualities
to be
sought
in a
president

Certain qualities, it is manifest, a president must have if he is to be successful; with rare exceptions, he will realize the possibilities of his high office only in the degree to which he possesses them. He must be able; he must be diligent; he must be honest; he must be courageous; he must be tactful; he must be capable of making large decisions promptly, intelligently, and in clear-cut fashion; above all, one is tempted to say, he must be a good politician, adept at working with men, managing them, and inspiring their confidence. Not all presidents, of course, have fully measured up to these requirements. The office has happily been preserved unsullied by personal turpitude; but some incumbents have been too lenient toward self-seeking and corrupt men surrounding them. No president has been wanting in patriotism; but some have lacked courage and decision, and one or two have been notably deficient in tact. Strange as it may seem, two within the recollection of the present genera-

[1] F. A. Ogg, *English Government and Politics* (2nd ed.), 130-133.
[2] *Modern Democracies* (New York, 1921), II, 73. For an interesting study of the professional backgrounds of American presidents, see S. Herbert, "The Premiership and the Presidency," *Economica*. No. 17 (June, 1926).

tion (Taft and Hoover) were not clever enough at politics for either their own comfort or the country's good.[1]

REFERENCES

The Federalist, No. LXVIII.

E. S. Corwin, *The President: Office and Powers; History and Analysis of Practice and Opinion* (New York, 1940), Chap. II.

V. O. Key, Jr., *Politics, Parties, and Pressure Groups* (2nd ed., New York, 1947), Chaps. XIII-XV.

E. M. Sait, *American Parties and Elections* (3rd ed., New York, 1942), Chaps. XX-XXII.

R. C. Brooks, *Political Parties and Electoral Problems* (3rd ed., New York, 1933), Chaps. XI-XII.

P. H. Odegard and E. A. Helms, *American Politics; A Study in Political Dynamics* (2nd ed., New York, 1947), Chaps. XVI-XXI.

H. W. Horwill, *The Usages of the American Constitution* (London, 1925), Chap. II.

J. H. Dougherty, *The Electoral System of the United States* (New York, 1906), Chaps. I-V, IX-XIII.

L. T. Beman, *The Abolishment of the Electoral College* (New York, 1926).

L. Overacker, *The Presidential Primary* (New York, 1926).

C. Becker, "The Unit Rule in National Nominating Conventions," *Amer. Hist. Rev.*, V, 64-82 (Oct., 1899).

C. A. M. Ewing, *Presidential Elections* (Norman, Okla., 1940).

H. L. Mencken, *Making a President* (New York, 1932). A flippant but informing analysis of the Democratic convention of 1932.

J. A. Farley, *Behind the Ballots; The Personal History of a Politician* (New York, 1938).

————, *Jim Farley's Story; The Roosevelt Years* (New York, 1948).

A. Smith, *Up to Now; An Autobiography* (New York, 1929).

H. Agar, *The People's Choice* (Boston, 1933).

M. Josephson, *The President-Makers* (New York, 1940).

F. Kent, *The Great Game of Politics* (New York, 1924).

R. V. Peel and T. C. Donnelly, *The 1928 Campaign; An Analysis* (New York, 1931).

————, *The 1932 Campaign; An Analysis* (New York, 1935).

E. E. Robinson, *The Presidential Vote, 1896-1932* (Stanford University, 1934).

————, *The Presidential Vote, 1936* (Stanford University, 1940).

————, *They Voted for Roosevelt; The Presidential Vote, 1932-1944* (Stanford University, 1947).[2]

U. S. Department of Commerce, Bureau of the Census, *Vote Cast in Presidential and Congressional Elections, 1928-1944* (Washington, D. C., 1946).

[1] Significant biographies or autobiographies of American presidents include Theodore Roosevelt, *Autobiography* (New York, 1913); Calvin Coolidge, *Autobiography* (New York, 1929); A. Nevins, *Grover Cleveland; A Study in Courage* (New York, 1932); H. F. Pringle, *Theodore Roosevelt* (New York, 1931), and *The Life and Times of William Howard Taft* (New York, 1939); W. E. Dodd, *Woodrow Wilson and His Work* (Garden City, N. Y., 1920); R. S. Baker, *Woodrow Wilson; Life and Letters*, 8 vols. (New York, 1927-39); W. A. White, *A Puritan in Babylon; The Story of Calvin Coolidge* (New York, 1938); W. F. Dexter, *Herbert Hoover and American Individualism* (New York, 1932); F. Perkins, *The Roosevelt I Knew* (New York, 1946).

[2] This volume and the two preceding ones present for the first time a complete county-by-county record of presidential election returns for all parties throughout the United States during the last fifty years.

L. H. Bean, *Ballot Behavior; A Study of Presidential Elections* (Washington, D. C., 1940).

————, *How to Predict Elections* (New York, 1948).

P. F. Lazarsfeld, B. Berelson, and H. Gaudet, *The People's Choice; How the Voter Makes Up His Mind in a Presidential Campaign* (New York, 1945).

J. B. Bishop, *Presidential Nominations and Elections* (New York, 1916).

W. J. Bryan, *A Tale of Two Conventions* (New York, 1912).

W. F. McCombs, *Making Woodrow Wilson President* (New York, 1921).

A. S. Link, *Wilson; The Road to the White House* (Princeton, N. J., 1947).

G. E. Mowry, *Theodore Roosevelt and the Progressive Movement* (Madison, Wis., 1946).

K. C. MacKay, *The Progressive Movement of 1924* (New York, 1947).

K. H. Porter, *National Party Platforms* (New York, 1924).

G. J. Shulz, *Election of the President of the United States by the House of Representatives*, 68th Cong., 2nd Sess., Sen. Doc. No. 227 (1925).

Official Report of the Proceedings of the Republican National Convention, issued quadrennially; *ibid., Democratic National Convention.*

Campaign Textbooks, issued by the various parties at election time.

PART II

THE NATIONAL GOVERNMENT

1. ORGANIZATION, POWERS, AND PROCEDURES

CHAPTER XIV

THE STRUCTURE OF CONGRESS

Preceding chapters have dealt with various features of the American plan of government considered as a whole—constitutional foundations, federalism, the separation of powers, citizenship, civil rights, suffrage, political parties, the electoral process. We now turn to government as organized and operated on each of the three great levels characteristic of our system, (1) national, (2) state, and (3) local.[1] To be sure, governments on these various levels do not function in water-tight compartments, but rather are interrelated, and at a good many points interlocked. Certainly the national and state governments are solidly tied together, state and local governments still more so; and in these later days even national and local governments have developed new and significant contacts. Fundamentally, however, each of the three occupies a field of its own; and each will stand out in clearer relief and be more readily understood if made the principal focus of attention through a separate series of chapters. We start with the government to be chiefly emphasized in this book, i.e., the national.

Once more, however, a break-down of subject-matter becomes necessary. In accordance with what Madison termed "a fundamental principle of free government," the framers of our national constitution wrote into the document three well-known "distributing clauses" as follows: (1) "All legislative powers herein granted shall be vested in a Congress of the United States;" (2) "The executive power shall be vested in a president of the United States;" and (3) the judicial power of the United States shall be vested in one Supreme Court, and in such inferior courts as the Congress may from time to time ordain and establish." [2] And in taking up the government thus envisaged, we of necessity fix attention, in order, upon the three great resulting branches or establishments—first, the legislature, i.e., Congress, then the executive, i.e., the president (and simultaneously the executive departments, the "independent establish-

Three branches of government

---

[1] The treatment of state and local government is omitted from the National Government edition of this book.
[2] Art. I, § 1; Art. II, § 1; Art. III, § 1.

ments," the civil service, and the agencies of administration generally), and finally the judiciary. In considering the separate branches, however, we must steadily keep in mind the multifold interrelations of the three, and especially the "checks and balances" interposed to promote integration and prevent one branch from gaining too great ascendancy over the others.[1]

The legislative function   We start with the legislative branch for the same reason that the constitution not only starts with it, but devotes upwards of half of its original space to it. Legislative, executive, and judicial branches, to be sure, are bracketed in the fundamental law as equals, and in the books are commonly described as coördinate; and in form they undoubtedly are such. The legislative function, however, involving as it does the framing of public policy and assertion of it in the form of enactments enforceable at law, really is primary, with the others only secondary, in the obvious sense at least that there must first be laws before laws can be executed or cases heard and decided under them. A difficulty with the Articles of Confederation was that, although providing for a "Congress," they contemplated a government almost wholly lacking in substantial legislative functions; and it is not strange that the makers of the new constitution not only rectified this error, but gave first place in the new basic law to creating a true national legislature and endowing it generously with power. It is not meant to imply that executive and judicial branches have nothing to do with determining policy, nor that Congress gives our laws form and meaning singlehandedly. Nevertheless, the basic relationships of the three branches, as indicated, point unmistakably to Capitol Hill as the place for starting any study of our national system.

The Bicameral Form

Why two houses were provided for   One of the first questions confronting the Philadelphia convention of 1787 was whether to provide for a national Congress of two houses or of only one. The Congress then existing had but a single house, and the New Jersey plan contemplated continuing that arrangement. On the other hand, English precedent pointed in the direction of two houses; and of the new Revolutionary state constitutions, all except two (those of Pennsylvania and Georgia) provided for two houses. When, however, decision was eventually reached—and almost unanimously—for the bicameral form, two practical considerations undoubtedly outweighed any mere precedents. One of these—very influential with people of substance, such as the convention chiefly represented—was that the broad powers about to be conferred ought not to be intrusted to any single body elected by the people generally, but rather should be shared by a body so constituted

---

[1] The relations of the twin principles of separation of powers and checks and balances, as viewed by the constitution's makers, were discussed illuminatingly by Madison in *The Federalist*, No. XLVII. Cf. H. L. McBain, *The Living Constitution* (New York, 1927), Chap. V; C. B. Swisher, *The Growth of Constitutional Power in the United States* (Chicago, 1947), Chap. III.

as to be more cautious, deliberate, and conservative. In other words, a second chamber was desired as a check upon democracy. And the other consideration, although of different sort, fitted in well with this. From the outset, it will be recalled, the large states insisted that representation be proportioned to population, the small ones that it be on a basis of state equality; and the only method that could be discovered for harmonizing two points of view resolutely adhered to was the one embodied in the Connecticut Compromise, *i.e.*, that of giving the large states their way in one legislative branch and the small states theirs in a second branch—a solution that of itself, even if there had been no supporting motivations, would have made two houses necessary. An incidental advantage seen in the arrangement was also a certain balancing off of major economic interests, since the more populous states were mainly commercial and the less populous ones mainly agricultural. Hence, in the outcome a House of Representatives was provided for, elected directly by the people and in proportion to numbers, and a Senate elected indirectly, with all states equally represented, and indeed conceived of as essentially a council of the states.

On the whole, the decision was a wise one. To be sure, two legislative houses have the disadvantage of facilitating deadlocks and delays, duplication of effort, and diffusion of responsibility. A municipality or other local area, having only limited powers, has little need for one house as a check upon another; and most of our cities, large and small, have done away with their former cumbersome two-chambered councils.[1] Indeed, the plan has been challenged in connection with state legislatures as well; and in 1934 Nebraska pioneered by adopting a constitutional amendment under which, since 1937, the legislature of that state has consisted of but a single house.[2] In the domain of the national government, however, policies and measures frequently involve such fundamental matters, *e.g.*, the protection of civil rights, or the declaration of war, that it is a good thing for them to be weighed and shaped and checked by two legislative bodies, approaching them separately, and perhaps from quite different angles, rather than by only one. Few people seriously suggest that we give up bicameralism at Washington, although plenty of proposals are aimed at overcoming some of its admitted defects.

A wise decision

The House of Representatives

The constitution's authors intended the president to be chosen, actually as well as nominally, by a college of electors, and senators by state legislatures. The House of Representatives, however, was designed to spring directly from the people, and accordingly the constitution has from the first provided that its members shall be elected every two years "by the people of the several states," defined as including all persons

By whom elected

[1] See pp. 891-892 below (in complete edition of this book).
[2] See pp. 886-887 *ibid.*

qualified to vote for a member of the "most numerous" branch of their state legislature.[1] Restricted only by the Fifteenth and Nineteenth Amendments prohibiting denial of the right to vote on grounds of race, color, or sex, the different states regulate the suffrage for their inhabitants as they choose, primarily for their own legislative and other elections, but incidentally for congressional, senatorial, and presidential elections as well.

Apportionment of seats   Although a broadly national, popular body, the House is still further constructed with reference to state lines. Every representative is elected within a given state, and every state has, as such, a definite quota of members.[2] Provisional quotas were assigned in the constitution, as originally adopted, to serve until a census could be taken; and thereafter representatives were to be apportioned among the several states "according to their respective numbers," which were to be computed by "adding to the whole number of free persons, including those bound to service for a term of years, and excluding Indians not taxed, three-fifths of all other persons."[3] The "other persons" referred to were, of course, slaves; and this provision became one of the important compromises of the constitution. When slavery was abolished, the three-fifths clause was rendered obsolete, and the constitution now provides simply, in the Fourteenth Amendment, for apportionment among the states "according to their respective numbers, counting the whole number of persons in each state, excluding Indians not taxed."[4] As we have seen, it provides also (though in a clause never enforced) for a reduction in the representation of any state which withholds voting privileges from adult male citizens of the United States "except for participation in rebellion, or other crime."[5]

[1] Art. I, § 2, cl. 1. The Seventeenth Amendment, under which senators are now likewise chosen by direct popular vote, contains this same provision.

[2] By courtesy, Hawaii and Alaska are allowed to send one "territorial delegate" each, and Puerto Rico a "resident commissioner." Although permitted to speak on matters pertaining to their constituencies, and also to serve on committees (beginning in 1946, all are added in any case to the committees on agriculture, public lands, and armed services), these persons are not full members of the House and consequently are not entitled to vote.

[3] Art. I, § 2, cl. 3.

[4] The Supreme Court having held (in Superintendent v. Commissioner, 295 U. S. 418, 1935) that all Indians are subject to federal taxation, all were included in the population basis for the apportionment of 1941. It has frequently been proposed that aliens be excluded from the population figures on which apportionments are based— as indeed they are in the case of legislative apportionments in ten states. For this, a constitutional amendment would be required; and one introduced in 1941 by Senator Capper of Kansas was advocated by him on the ground that it is "unfair to American citizens" for states containing numerous aliens to have more votes in Congress on that account. A full discussion of this matter, with a recommendation that the basis of apportionment be made, not population, but votes cast in the last previous presidential election (which, of course, would automatically eliminate aliens), will be found in L. F. Schmeckebier, *Congressional Apportionment* (Washington, D. C., 1941), Chap. VI. An effect of shifting to the basis of votes cast might be to stimulate voting; but states in which a substantial share of the potential electorate is deprived of the suffrage by either legal or extra-legal means would suffer loss of representation, and altogether the change is not likely to be made.

[5] See pp. 195-196 above.

The constitution does not expressly say that representation in the The problem of an increasing membership House shall be reapportioned after each decennial census, but that is clearly what it means; and until the enumeration of 1920, Congress never failed to take the necessary action—usually after an interval of not more than one or two years. The procedure followed varied somewhat on different occasions, but in any case Congress scrutinized the census figures, decided how many members the House should have during the ensuing decade, and, having allotted these among the states as equitably as it could (so that each state would have at least one seat—in accordance with constitutional requirement—and as many more as its population entitled it to), passed an act putting the new arrangements into effect. It is curious to observe that one of the grounds on which the constitution was opposed during the debates on ratification was that, since the number of representatives was not to exceed one for every 30,000 people, the House of Representatives would be too small; one of the best-known papers in *The Federalist* was devoted entirely to answering that objection.[1] No longer is there any apprehension on that score; on the contrary, the House has grown to such size (435) that, although it still is not the largest among the world's legislative bodies, there is wide agreement that it contains too many members for the most effective transaction of business.[2] Partly as a result of the expansion of the country, partly because of the reluctance of states to see their quotas reduced to make room for increased representation of faster growing states, and partly on account of the natural unwillingness of members to legislate themselves or their colleagues out of districts, every reapportionment in our history down to 1930, except one, *i.e.*, in 1842, resulted in a substantial increase.[3] Following the census of 1920, no plan could be devised that would not either reduce the representation of as many as eleven states or increase the membership of the House considerably beyond 435. Unwilling to do either, Congress simply drew back from the problem and allowed the country to drift along a full decade without any reapportionment at all.[4]

Only in 1929 was the situation remedied—and then only by an act pro- Present method of apportionment viding for reapportionment under the coming 1930 census, and at decennial intervals thereafter.[5] In accordance with this legislation (as amended in 1941), reapportionment proceeds as follows: (1) the membership of

[1] No. LVII (Lodge's ed., 350-355).
[2] Cf. p. 416 below.
[3] It must not be inferred that a state's quota was never reduced. Had the ratio been so maintained that no state would ever have lost representatives, the House would now be two or three times as large as it is.
[4] The House did, indeed, pass a bill raising the membership to 470, but the Senate refused to concur. It would always, of course, have been possible to offset an increase resulting from a general reapportionment by enforcing the penal clause of the Fourteenth Amendment, under which the Southern states alone would have lost thirty or more seats. But such action has never been politically feasible. There is no judicial process by which Congress can be compelled to take such a step—just as there has never been any by which it could be forced to enact a reapportionment law.
[5] 46 *U. S. Stat. at Large*, 26.

the House remains fixed "permanently" at 435;[1] (2) after each census, the Census Bureau in the Department of Commerce prepares for the president a table showing the number of inhabitants of each state and the number of representatives to which each state would be entitled under either of two alternative methods of computation;[2] (3) the president transmits the information to Congress as soon as the next regular session after the census begins; and (4) the reapportionment according to the method of computation employed in the last previous reapportionment goes into effect unless within sixty days Congress itself works out and enacts a different one. Under this general plan (which has the obvious advantage of preventing the matter from again going by default), a reapportionment based on the 1930 census resulted in a gain of from one to nine seats by eleven states and a loss of from one to three by twenty-one; and another, ten years later, enabled eight states to gain a total of ten seats while ten others were losing one apiece.[3]

General ticket and district systems

Except for requiring direct popular vote, the constitution leaves the "times, places, and manner" of choosing representatives to be determined by the legislatures of the several states—although with superior authority in Congress to make or alter regulations on the subject.[4] For half a century, elections were in some states in single-member districts, in others on a general, or state-wide, ticket. But the apportionment act of 1842 required every state populous enough to be entitled to more than one representative to be divided by the legislature into districts "composed of contiguous territory," each returning one member; and the apportionment acts of 1901 and 1911 added the qualifying term "compact."

---

[1] A Congress, however, cannot bind its successors; hence, notwithstanding its declared "permanency," the number is not to be regarded as necessarily final.

[2] I.e., the method of "equal proportions," employed in the reapportionment of 1941 and that of "major fractions" in vogue for some time previously. These alternative methods have stirred much controversy, among statisticians and political scientists as well as in Congress, but are too mathematically technical to be described here—though it may be observed that the results, when the two are applied, are never very different, and sometimes not different at all. Not only the methods just mentioned, but three other possible ones which have at different times been advocated, are explained in detail, with discussion of their relative merits, in L. F. Schmeckebier, Congressional Apportionment, Chap. IV. Cf. Z. Chafee, "Congressional Reapportionment," Harvard Law Rev., XVII, 1015-1047 (June, 1929), and E. V. Huntington, Methods of Apportionment in Congress, 76th Cong., 3rd Sess., Sen. Doc. No. 304 (1940). The whole difficulty arises, of course, from the fact that after each state has been allotted the one seat to which it is entitled in any case and the task of allotting the remaining 387 seats is taken up, it invariably is found that dividing a state's population by the number of people entitled to a seat (i.e., the "quota of representation") leaves a fractional quota remaining, perhaps a "major" fraction, i.e., more than half enough for an additional seat, perhaps only a "minor" fraction; and the apportionment methods mentioned above differ on the ways in which these fractions are handled. In the reapportionment taking effect in 1932, the country-wide ratio (i.e., total apportionment population divided by 435) was 278,376; in that effective in 1942, it was 301,164.

[3] Gains (in 1941): Arizona, Florida, Michigan, New Mexico, North Carolina, Oregon, and Tennessee, one seat each, and California, three seats. Losses: Arkansas, Illinois, Indiana, Iowa, Kansas, Massachusetts, Nebraska, Ohio, Oklahoma, and Pennsylvania, one seat each. For tabulation, see Cong. Record, 77th Cong., 1st Sess., Vol. 87, Pt. I, p. 81.

[4] Art. I, § 4, cl. 1.

Curiously enough, the act of 1929 failed to use any of the terms "contiguous," or "compact," or "equal;" and when, three years afterwards, an effort was made to have a redistricting law in Mississippi set aside on the ground that the seven congressional districts provided for were not composed of contiguous and compact territory, the federal Supreme Court held that the failure to repeat the requirements in the 1929 act by implication repealed them.[1] In legal circles, there had been much doubt. on the point; and the country at large was hardly aware of what had happened. In the opinion of the Court, however, the omission had not been inadvertent, but intentional; and since new legislation in 1941 was silent on the subject, the former requirements seem no longer to apply. It may be added that even when federal law on the subject was entirely explicit, Congress made no effort to enforce it upon the states, and that federal district courts holding state reapportionment acts contrary to law because of creating districts lacking in compactness or in equality of population were usually reversed.[2]

For reasons to be explained presently, the district system is decidedly superior to the general ticket plan. It, however, has drawbacks—in addition to making it practically impossible for congressmen to be chosen from outside of limited geographical areas. To begin with, there is the difficulty of laying out districts fairly and equitably. In each state, the job falls to the legislature, which, if that body does its duty, will, every time that the state becomes entitled to more or fewer representatives, reconstruct the pattern of districts accordingly. But even when intentions are the best, the task is not easy. In order that a citizen's vote may count for as much in one district as in another, it is desirable that districts be as nearly equal as possible in population. It is also advantageous not to split counties between two or more districts, and likewise not to partition municipalities except in the case of those, like New York and Chicago, too populous to comprise a single district. But often the constructing of a district becomes a sort of jig-saw puzzle, with perhaps several different groupings of counties about equally plausible geographically, but with widely differing political implications.[3]

Problems raised by the district system:

1. Difficulties of redistricting

---

[1] Wood *v.* Broom, 287 U. S. 1 (1932).

[2] A state receiving an increase in its quota of representatives when a reapportionment is made may, until a new districting is carried out, elect its additional representatives at large; and a state suffering a decrease may, similarly, elect its entire quota at large. Hence the congressmen-at-large of whom one occasionally hears. In four states (Delaware, Nevada, Vermont, and Wyoming), too, congressmen are elected at large for the reason that the state is entitled to only one seat. All told, there are thirteen congressmen-at-large in the Eightieth Congress (1947–49).

[3] In 1931, when thirty-two states were confronted with the necessity of redistricting, disputes arose in Missouri, Minnesota, and New York which, in the first two states, were settled only after being carried to the federal Supreme Court, and in the third prevented any reapportionment at all during the ensuing decade, and indeed until 1944.

For a thorough discussion of the districting of states, see L. F. Schmeckebier, *op. cit.*, Chap. ix. Cf. V. O. Key, Jr., "Procedures in State Legislative Apportionment," *Amer. Polit. Sci. Rev.*, XXVI, 1050-1058 (Dec., 1932). Maps showing the arrangement of congressional districts in the various states, as existing in 1948, will be

Furthermore, the redistricting of a state can never be carried out in the rarefied atmosphere of mathematical abstraction. On the contrary, it is beset, both in and out of the legislature, by all manner of personal, community, regional, and partisan interests and motivations. In particular, there is—in all too many instances—the well-known practice of gerrymandering. This term dates from 1812, when Governor Elbridge Gerry of Massachusetts inspired, or at all events condoned, a notorious piece of partisan districting in his state; [1] the practice itself goes back even farther. The principle behind the gerrymander is simple: "In districting a state or city, spread the majorities of your own party over all or over as many districts as possible. If you have not enough votes to control every district, concentrate the strength of your opponents in as few districts as possible, so that it will do them the least good." [2] Plenty of laws have been enacted to curb the practice; but, human nature and party motivations being what they are, the temptation offered politicians who find themselves in a position to control the redrawing of political boundary lines is usually too strong to be resisted. Even the statutory requirement before 1929 that states be divided into districts composed of "contiguous and compact territories" seldom deterred legislative majorities from mapping out "shoe-string," "saddle-bag," and "dumb-bell" districts ingeniously contrived to yield the controlling party the largest possible number of seats at ensuing elections. If the Republicans were in control, they would seek to concentrate the most formidable Democratic strength in a few districts, and to cancel out the remainder by distributing their own strength in such a way as to yield small, but reasonably safe, pluralities in the others. If the Democrats gained the upper hand, they would in turn be likely to shift things around to their own advantage. The courts, too, seldom intervened; while as for the present, all federal regulation having been terminated, only such restraints remain as are imposed by public opinion and by a very limited number of provisions (as in Virginia) in state constitutions.

A final difficulty with the district system is that the legislature of a state may fly in the face of propriety, and even of plain constitutional mandate, by neglecting or refusing to redistrict at all. It may do this because the party in power stands to gain by keeping things as they are, or because the dominant rural portions of a state do not want to admit large urban populations to more power, or because of simple inertia. Three states have not redistricted since 1912 and 1913, one not since 1911, one (Maryland) not since 1902, one (Arkansas) not since 1901, and

---

found in *Official Congressional Directory* (2nd ed. corrected to June 11, 1947), 779-829.

[1] One of the resulting districts had the shape of a lizard. "Why, this district looks like a salamander," remarked an observer. "Say rather a Gerrymander," replied an opposition editor, thereby coining a political term which has ever since been current. For a map showing this historic gerrymander, see J. Winsor, *Memorial History of Boston* (Boston, 1880), III, 212.

[2] R. C. Brooks, *Political Parties and Electoral Problems* (3rd ed.), 475.

one (New Hampshire) not since 1881. With population constantly shifting, the result of such negative, or "silent," gerrymandering is often gross
inequality of population among congressional districts, with manifest
frustration of one of the most basic principles of our democracy.[1]

Under the general ticket system prevailing in many states before 1842, *The question of fuller representation for minorities*
a party polling a bare plurality of the popular votes for congressman
captured the entire state delegation, notwithstanding that in some sections of the state the candidates of a different party might have been
far in the lead;[2] and the main object of Congress in making the district
system obligatory was to open a way for parties with such localized
strength to win at least a handful of seats. In a very rough sort of way,
the district plan undoubtedly makes for the representation of minorities;
a Republican state is likely to have a few Democratic congressmen, and
vice versa. The proportions which result are, however, very rough indeed.
The strength of a minority party may be fairly impressive in the aggregate, yet so distributed throughout a state as to yield no district majorities whatever; as, for example, when, in Indiana in 1932, the Republicans
cast 683,517 votes for congressman, but the Democrats, with 849,821,
made a clean sweep of the twelve seats.[3] From this as well as from inequalities in the total, as also in the voting, populations of districts, it
comes about that no House of Representatives, even when newly elected,

---

[1] This "silent gerrymander" is practiced also notoriously in connection with wards
of cities and with state legislative districts.
  An interesting chapter in the history of congressional reapportionment has been
written of late in Illinois—a state in which no reapportionment had taken place
since 1901 and in which disparities had reached a stage where one district had
only 112,116 people but another 914,053 (both curiously in the Chicago area). Repeated efforts to compel action by resort to the state courts having failed, a suit
was begun in a federal district court (by a professor of political science at Northwestern University, a professor of law at the University of Chicago, and a Chicago
attorney) to secure a declaratory judgment against the governor and other officers
composing the state primary certifying board, the effect of which would be to
"declare" the existing congressional apportionment invalid and require the election
of all of the state's twenty-six representatives on a state-wide ballot until such time
as the legislature should enact a valid redistricting statute. Among arguments employed was that as matters stood people were being deprived of the equal protection
of the laws and of their right as citizens of the United States to have their votes
in congressional elections counted at full value. The district court, however, dismissed the suit; and when the petitioners carried the matter to the federal Supreme
Court, it was only to be told (in a four-to-three ruling) that what they asked was
beyond the Court's competence to grant, since the question was "of a peculiarly
political nature and therefore not meet for judicial determination." Colegrove *v.*
Green, 328 U. S. 549 (1946). The effort, however, proved by no means fruitless. An
atmosphere had been developed in which the matter could no longer be trifled with
locally; and under leadership of the governor, plans were laid (to quite an extent
on bipartisan lines) for redistricting legislation which in June, 1947, was placed on
the statute-book. Under the new arrangement, Cook county (Chicago and environs),
with 4,049,331 people in 1940, obtained thirteen of the total twenty-six congressional
seats to be disposed of, and the remainder of the state, with 3,824,824 in 1940, was
assigned an equal number. On the legal stages of the affair, see F. L. Burdette, "The
Illinois Redistricting Case," *Amer. Polit. Sci. Rev.*, XL, 958-962 (Oct., 1946).
[2] This is, of course, what still happens in the choice of presidential electors.
[3] A clean sweep, indeed, occurred five times in the state mentioned between 1910
and 1932, and never did the majority party polling more than 55.6 per cent of the
votes cast. See L. E. Lambert, *The Congressional District System in Indiana* (Bloomington, Ind., 1943).

can claim to mirror the political opinion of the country in more than a very general sort of way.[1] And one will not be surprised to learn that those who deplore this situation bring forward as a remedy the device of proportional representation, under which, if adopted for congressional elections, there would be a return to the general ticket plan, coupled, however, not with plurality election, as in earlier days, but with some method of allotting seats (in multi-member districts or on a state-wide basis) in proportion to the numbers of popular votes polled by the various tickets. Congress could, of course, in some future reapportionment act, require the states uniformly to elect according to the proportional plan. There is no present prospect of this being done; but short of it, existing law might be changed so as to offer an option of election either by districts or otherwise, thereby opening a way for individual states to experiment with a proportional system if they so desired.[2]

Further congressional regulation of elections

Congress has gone farther, in regulating congressional elections, than merely to require use of the district system. In 1872, it enjoined that all such elections be by secret ballot;[3] in 1873, that they be held throughout the country on the same day, namely, the Tuesday following the first Monday in November of every even-numbered year[4] (previously, voting was in some instances *viva voce*, and elections were held at widely varying dates); and in 1910-11 and 1925, that candidates should not permit their expenditures to exceed $2,500, or under an alternative rule, $5,000. Candidates are nominated as the laws of the several states provide; for although, as has appeared, Supreme Court decisions of recent years clearly open a way for congressional regulation of nominating procedures, no national legislation on the subject has as yet been enacted. In most cases, the direct primary is employed; but in several states nominations are still made by district nominating conventions composed of delegates representing counties, towns, or other subdivisions.

Contested elections

The constitution makes the House of Representatives the judge of the "elections, returns, and qualifications" of its members,[5] and accordingly every dispute involving a seat is decided by the House itself. If a candidate is unwilling to concede his defeat, he may ask for and obtain a local recount of the votes as provided for in the state election laws; and if

---

[1] In the elections of 1942, Republican congressional candidates throughout the country polled 1,267,000 more votes than did their Democratic opponents. Yet the Democrats won 224 seats, the Republicans only 207, and Democratic control of the House remained intact.

[2] For a comparison of the party complexion of Congress after the 1930 election with what it would have been under proportional representation, see *Proportional Representation Rev.*, 3rd ser., No. 99, p. 46 (July, 1931); and for a similar comparison based on the 1932 election, G. H. Hallett, "Is Congress Representative?," *Nat. Mun. Rev.*, XXII, 284-288 (June, 1933). In the latter instance, the Democrats would have come off with 268 seats instead of 313, and the Republicans with 159 instead of 117. Cf. V. Torrey, *You and Your Congress* (New York, 1944), Chaps. v-vi.

[3] This does not preclude the use of voting machines.

[4] Unless the constitution of a state fixes a different date, as is true in Maine, where, as noted elsewhere, congressmen are elected the second Monday in September.

[5] Art. I, § 5, cl. 1.

still dissatisfied, he may carry his case to the House, where formerly it would be referred to one of three standing committees on elections, but since 1946 it has been handled by one of the new committees—that on House administration. In its turn, the committee weighs the evidence, hears the rival claimants and their counsel, takes other testimony if desired, and prepares a report recommending that one candidate or the other be declared elected; and such a report the House commonly accepts. Party considerations are not unlikely to color the decision, and the English plan of turning over such cases to a non-partisan and disinterested board selected from the judiciary is to be preferred.[1] Fortunately, the number of contests in this country is small—rarely more than half a dozen resulting from any given election.

Four qualifications, including one of a negative nature, are required of a representative by the constitution. He [2] must be twenty-five years of age or over (if not when elected, at all events when he takes his seat); he must have been a citizen of the United States at least seven years (not necessarily immediately preceding election); he must be, at the time of his election, an inhabitant of the state in which he is chosen;[3] and he cannot, while a member of the House, hold any "office under the United States." [4] The last-mentioned restriction is construed to debar Army and Navy officers, as well as holders of civil office; and it is hardly necessary to point out that, in disqualifying heads of executive departments, it contrasts sharply with the unwritten rule in Great Britain which requires ministers to have seats in Parliament.[5]

Qualifications of members

On sundry occasions the question has arisen whether qualifications in addition to those specified in the constitution can be imposed. The answer is both no and yes. On the one hand, plenty of court decisions lay it down as a principle of law that neither the states nor Congress can add to or subtract from the qualifications enumerated.[6] On the other hand, usage, as every one knows, has decreed almost inexorably—notwithstanding complete silence of the constitution on the matter—that members shall be residents of the *districts* which they represent.[7] Furthermore, in passing upon the qualifications of newly chosen members, the

Can other qualifications be required?

---

[1] V. M. Barnett, Jr., "Contested Congressional Elections in Recent Years," *Polit. Sci. Quar.,* LIV, 187-215 (June, 1939).

[2] Women are eligible on the same terms as men, and a considerable number have been elected. See p. 183 above.

[3] Art. I, § 2, cl. 2. In practice, the last-mentioned requirement is construed to mean a legal resident for voting purposes.

[4] Art. I, § 6, cl. 2. A state office does not disqualify. The purpose of the prohibition of federal office-holding is to uphold the principle of separation of powers by keeping the legislative and executive branches apart. A member of Congress may accept appointment to a federal office, provided it is not one which has been created, or the emoluments of which have been increased, during the term for which he was elected, and provided, of course, he forthwith resigns his congressional seat. A federal officer may be elected to Congress, but must resign his office when taking his seat.

[5] Officers under the Crown, other than ministers, are, however, debarred from the House of Commons. See F. A. Ogg, *English Government and Politics* (2nd ed.), 135.

[6] *E.g.,* Thomas v. Owens, 4 Md. 189 (1853).

[7] See p. 406 below.

House may also, as a matter of practice, make additions; at all events it did so in 1900, when it refused to seat Brigham H. Roberts of Utah on the ground that he was a polygamist, and again in 1919, when Victor L. Berger of Wisconsin was excluded because of having been judicially convicted of sedition and disloyalty.[1] To be sure, these decisions were of doubtful constitutionality. The proper procedure would seem to be to seat an objectionable person and then expel him. But the actions taken in the cases mentioned stand on the record as evidence that, regardless of both the theory and the law of the matter, the House can actually impose a test for admission of which the constitution makes no mention. Some states, too, on their part, have translated into law the custom requiring members to be residents of the districts which they represent.[2]

The Senate

Equal representation of the states

With its members not only chosen by direct popular vote but distributed among the states in proportion to population, the House of Representatives is—as the constitution's framers intended it to be—a broadly national body, with state boundaries merely incidental to its structure. The Senate, on the contrary, was designed to rest on the purely geographical and federal basis of states as political entities; and not only were its members to be chosen by state legislatures, rather than by the people directly, but all states were given equal representation, regardless of size or population. Each state was allotted two senators; and none might be deprived of its equality in this respect except with its own consent.[3] To be sure, the federal principle was not carried as far as some of the small-state people desired: senators were to vote as individuals and not by states, and their salaries were to be paid out of the national treasury rather than by the states individually. But equal representation and voting power for all states, large and small, populous and otherwise, made the Senate a truly federal body; and such it remains today, notwithstanding that in one important respect, i.e., direct popular election of its members, its position has since 1913 come to be more like that of the other branch.

Criticism of the arrangement

To many people in all periods of our national history, this equality of unequals has seemed unreasonable, and even indefensible. To begin with, Alexander Hamilton has been proved right in his contention—contrary to prevailing opinion in his time—that, once the new government was in operation, there never would be a conflict of interests between large states and small states as such. Throughout our history, cleavages have run on quite different lines. They have been regional, or sectional, e.g.,

[1] The Supreme Court eventually cleared him, and after being elected a third time by his district, he was seated.

[2] In so far as merely declaratory of existing practice, such state regulations are harmless enough; if judicially tested, they, however, would almost certainly be declared unconstitutional.

[3] Art. V.

between parts of the country that were mainly agricultural and other parts devoted chiefly to industry and trade. Whether a state was large or small has made little or no difference in its political attitudes and alignments. And so it very well can be argued that the precaution taken by the constitution's authors for the protection of the small states is unnecessary and need not be perpetuated.

In the second place, the spread between the smallest and largest state populations has grown far greater than was ever anticipated, with equality of representation correspondingly more incongruous, at least as a matter of mathematics. New York, with 13,479,142 population (in 1940), has two senators; Nevada, with 110,247, also has two senators. Pennsylvania has about a million and a half more inhabitants than all New England; but New England has twelve senators and Pennsylvania two. The six states of New York, Pennsylvania, Illinois, Ohio, Texas, and California have over fifty million inhabitants, or nearly forty per cent of the total population of the continental United States. Yet, in a Senate of ninety-six members, they have only twelve, *i.e.*, about twelve per cent. A Senate majority could, indeed, be made up to represent not more than one-fifth of the people of the country. More significant, too, than this mere disproportion of numbers is the distorted representation given major economic and social interests. Industry and commerce preponderate in only a few, but usually densely inhabited, states; agriculture preponderates in many states, more sparsely populated; and equality of state representation in the Senate inevitably gives rural interests disproportionate influence in that body.

People who have been troubled about this situation have suggested various remedies, among them that a state be allowed an additional senator for every million inhabitants in excess of some fixed number. This would not result in an exact proportioning such as is presumed to apply in the case of the House of Representatives, but it would materially alleviate the existing inequalities; and at first glance the proposal seems plausible. If carried out, it would tend to correct the present overweighting of the less populous agricultural portions of the country, mainly the West and South. There are, however, several things to be noted before conclusions are reached. In the first place, the number of senators would be greatly increased, and such efficiency as the Senate now shows as a deliberating and revising body might be seriously impaired. In the second place, the change—added to popular election of senators, as already provided for in the Seventeenth Amendment—would tend to make both houses representative of the same people in the same proportions (instead of one being representative of numbers and the other of areas), and hence would remove a main reason for having a second chamber at all. In doing this, too, it would tend to enable a comparatively small number of populous states to dominate both houses and in that way control national policy, whereas now a few such states may dominate the popular

Proposed changes

branch but in the Senate the votes of half or more are required for finally enacting legislation. Furthermore, much of the criticism of existing arrangements springs from the mistaken idea that there can be no true representation without proportioning to numbers. Plenty of times, the president single-handedly better reflects the opinions and desires of the people of the country than do several hundred locally elected congressmen; and even if senators be thought of as representing people in the same manner as members of the other branch, there is no reason why some may not represent eight or ten millions quite as adequately as others represent one-tenth of the number. Even congressmen represent constituencies today ten times more numerous than when Congress was first organized. Finally, the entire notion of giving some states more senators than others is hardly more than academic, for the reason that such an innovation, requiring not only a constitutional amendment, but the express consent of every state whose representation would become less than that of some other state—would be practically impossible to bring about.[1]

Original mode of election Five or six different ways of choosing senators were considered by the constitution's framers, and election by the state legislatures was finally hit upon as the least objectionable, with the proviso that a vacancy arising in any state, by resignation or otherwise, when the legislature was not in session should be filled by temporary appointment by the governor.[2] Certain distinct advantages were, indeed, expected to flow from this method of selection. Members of legislatures, it was thought, would be most likely to know the qualifications of senatorial candidates, and, being themselves men of substance and responsibility, would choose persons of superior character, experience, and judgment. Elected by the legislature, a senator would feel himself the representative, not of a faction or group or section, but of the entire state. The national and state governments would be geared together in a significant way, and people who were troubled lest the strengthening of the former might lead to eventual extinction of the latter (such fears have not been confined to the days of the New Deal) would find ground for reassurance.

Movement for direct popular election These considerations were plausible, and in the testing period of the Republic they had genuine weight. Later on, they seemed less important; and as government became progressively more democratic, the conviction grew that senators, like representatives, ought to be chosen by the people directly. This view was not based merely upon theory. Legislative election developed many practical drawbacks and abuses—deadlocks leaving

---

[1] Some redistribution of voting power in the Senate might conceivably arise in future from setting off metropolitan areas, such as New York, Chicago, and Detroit and their respective environs, as separate states. Cf. p. 81 above. The constitution guarantees equal representation of the states in the Senate, but imposes no barrier to the partitioning of states, beyond requiring the consent of the legislature of any state affected.

[2] Art. I, § 3, cl. 2.

senatorial seats vacant for years at a time,[1] control of elections by bosses and corporations, virtual purchase of seats, absorption of the legislatures in senatorial elections to the neglect of other business. As early as 1826, proposals for direct popular election were heard, and after the Civil War the matter became a theme of frequent discussion. Between 1893 and 1912, the House of Representatives five times passed resolutions submitting a constitutional amendment on the subject; and though the Senate invariably refused to concur, political parties endorsed the reform in their platforms and two-thirds of the state legislatures went on record for it.

Meanwhile, a number of states, chiefly west of the Mississippi, worked out a plan under which popular election was attained, to all intents and purposes, regardless of the fate of the proposed amendment. The means employed was the direct primary. By state law, the voters of each party might be authorized to indicate at the polls which of the party candidates for a senatorship they preferred, all nominations so made being formally reported to the legislature. Usually that body was trusted, without any special precaution, to execute the public will by electing the designated candidate of the majority party. Oregon and Nebraska, however, introduced a plan under which candidates for the legislature were asked to pledge their support in advance to the "people's choice," irrespective of party. In either case, there was, as with presidential electors, no obligation other than moral; legally, the legislature remained free to elect whomsoever it would. But the popular will was almost invariably carried out. By 1912, senators were nominated popularly in a total of twenty-nine states, scattered throughout the country, and election by legislatures was coming to be quite as much a fiction as is the choice of the president by the electoral college. *Rise of nomination by direct primary*

Under these circumstances, resistance in the Senate weakened. Many members recognized that they already were, in effect, elected by the people; and over the opposition of most party leaders and bosses, the Seventeenth Amendment, in 1912, passed both houses of Congress, and in 1913 was proclaimed in force. Under the new arrangement, senators are chosen directly by the people of the several states, after nominations in primaries or conventions; and, as in the case of the House of Representatives, the electors include all persons qualified to vote for members of the "most numerous branch of the state legislature." If a vacancy arises, the governor of the state normally issues a writ of election to fill it for the remainder of the unexpired term. The legislature may, however, empower him to make temporary appointments; and nearly all legislatures have done this. *The Seventeenth Amendment*

---

[1] Notable deadlocks of the kind included one in Pennsylvania in 1899, when a successor to Senator Quay was to be elected, and one in Delaware, where J. E. Addicks kept up a running fight for a senatorship from 1895 to 1903. An act of Congress passed in 1866 provided that if the two houses of a legislature, voting separately, should find themselves unable to elect a senator, they should meet in joint session and elect by majority vote. Even in joint session, however, it might be difficult or impossible for any candidate to emerge with a majority.

The effects of the change to direct popular election cannot be measured with precision. Liberation of the state legislatures from the distractions entailed by senatorial elections has been a genuine gain. Deadlocks have been made impossible, and a state's full representation at all times (except for brief intervals following the death or resignation of a senator) has been assured. The consequences for the Senate itself are not so clear. Since 1913, several hundred senators have been elected or reëlected. But whether they have been of higher caliber than they would have been under the old method of election, no one can say. Certainly the amendment produced no abrupt shift of personnel. Practically every senator who could have expected to be continued in office at the hands of his state's legislature was continued on the popular basis; indeed, contrary to expectation, reëlections have consistently been more numerous under the popular system than before.[1] Furthermore, abuses arising from the lavish use of money in senatorial nominations and elections did not disappear, as is evidenced by the Newberry controversy of 1918-22, the cases of William S. Vare of Pennsylvania and Frank L. Smith of Illinois in 1926-29, and other somewhat less noted instances.[2] Money is employed in a different way, because it is now the state-wide electorate that has to be reached; and in this situation considerable outlays become not only inevitable, but justifiable. Speaking broadly, however, senatorial politics tends to remain a game for the well-to-do, or at all events for those able to muster strong financial support. Certain undesirables, e.g., self-seeking plutocrats and virtual appointees of avaricious capitalistic interests, are now pretty well excluded; but others, e.g., the demagogue, the whirlwind campaigner, and especially the shrewd manipulator of federal patronage,[3] have perhaps better chances than before. Popular election is of

[1] R. E. McClendon, "Reëlection of Senators," Amer. Polit. Sci. Rev., XXVIII, 636-642 (Aug., 1934).

[2] In winning a senatorial seat in Michigan in 1918, Truman H. Newberry spent something like $195,000—an amount far in excess of that recognized as a legitimate electoral outlay by Michigan law, i.e., $1,875, as also by the federal statute of 1910, which fixed the figure at $10,000. Most of the amount was poured out in securing the nomination in a primary in competition with Henry Ford. Convicted under the federal law in a lower court, Newberry appealed to the federal Supreme Court, which in 1921 set aside the conviction, four of the nine justices being of the opinion that Congress lacked power to regulate nominations and a fifth concurring for a different reason (Newberry v. United States, 256 U. S. 232). When finally seating the defendant by a close vote in 1922, the Senate passed a resolution declaring his outlay in quest of his nomination excessive, contrary to sound policy, and dangerous to free government; and in the end, Newberry decided that his seat would not be comfortable and resigned. A full account of the affair will be found in S. Erwin, Henry Ford vs. Truman H. Newberry (New York, 1935). By votes of 53 to 28 and 56 to 30, on December 7 and 9, 1927, the Senate refused to seat Vare and Smith, respectively, on charges of improper receipt and use of large sums of money in securing nomination and election; and prolonged subsequent investigations and controversies failed to bring a reversal of the decisions. See C. H. Wooddy, The Case of Frank L. Smith; A Study in Representative Government (Chicago, 1931). Campaign expenditures of Senator Joseph R. Grundy of Pennsylvania, and of Mrs. Ruth Hanna McCormick of Illinois, stirred much comment in 1930, and in the latter case were subjected to an official investigation.

[3] Developments in the civil service have, however, narrowed the possible scope of such activities. See Chap. XXIII below.

itself no guarantee of fitness; and whether, over a prolonged period under that system, the upper house will show a higher level of ability, integrity, and achievement than in the days of Webster, Clay, and Calhoun, or of Allison, Spooner, and Hoar, remains to be determined. The prospect that it will do so is not particularly flattering.

The term of senators is six years. Some of the framers of the constitution favored a longer period; indeed, a few advocated election for life. But to most persons six years seemed sufficiently long to insure the desired stability and continuity. A term of such length puts a senator in a very different position from a representative. Unlike the latter, he has time in a single term to acquire experience, and even to attain a certain degree of leadership; and he can devote himself for several years to public affairs without too much distracting anxiety over reëlection. Most senators, furthermore, have more than one term, and periods of service running to eighteen, or even twenty-four, years are not uncommon.[1] Continuity of personnel arising from long terms and numerous reëlections is further secured by an arrangement under which the terms of one-third of the members expire biennially, with the result that the Senate never finds itself in the position in which the House of Representatives is found every two years—a new body, with greatly altered membership, obliged to organize from the ground up.[2] On the contrary, it is continuous and always organized. Considerably more than two-thirds of its members at any given time have served at least as long as two years; leadership develops slowly and as a rule changes gradually; precedents and traditions are carried along on the current of a never-ending stream. *Term and continuity of service*

Senators must be at least thirty years of age, and must have been citizens of the United States at least nine years. Otherwise, their constitutional qualifications are identical with those of representatives. They must be inhabitants of the states that elect them, and during their tenure they may not hold any office under the United States. Like representatives, too, they may not at any time be appointed to a civil office under the authority of the United States which shall have been created, or the emoluments of which shall have been increased, during the time for which they were elected.[3] Equally with the House, the Senate is judge of the *Qualifications*

---

[1] In 1944, Senator E. D. Smith of South Carolina, failing of renomination, retired from the body after thirty-six years of continuous service, and Senator Arthur Capper of Kansas has now served thirty years. The average turnover in the Senate from 1790 to 1924 was 27.2 per cent. In the Fifty-first Congress (1889-91), it fell to the low figure of 10 per cent. The average turnover in the House between 1790 and 1924 was 44 per cent. Cf. the study by McClendon cited above.

[2] The original senators were divided into three classes, with terms expiring in two, four, and six years, respectively. In no case were both senators of a state placed in the same class, and the senators of states admitted later were always assigned, by lot, to different classes. Hence, barring vacancies arising from death or resignation, only one senator is elected in a state in any given year.

[3] In 1909, President Taft appointed Senator Philander C. Knox secretary of state, notwithstanding that the salaries of heads of executive departments had been increased while the appointee was in the Senate. The constitutional difficulty was got around, somewhat equivocally, by an act of Congress reducing the stipend of the

elections, returns, and qualifications of its members; [1] and here also the question has arisen whether qualifications can be imposed in excess of those prescribed by the constitution. We have seen that the House once took the doubtful course of refusing to seat a member-elect because he was a polygamist. Asked, in 1903, to seat a senator-elect (Reed Smoot) who, although not a polygamist, was known to be an adherent of the Mormon Church, the Senate took what seems to be the better constitutional ground, namely, that any person duly elected and having the qualifications required by the constitution must be received, even though he may subsequently be expelled. In refusing in 1927-29 to seat Frank L. Smith of Illinois and William S. Vare of Pennsylvania, who, although duly certified as elected, had allowed too much money to be spent in behalf of their respective candidacies, the upper house seemingly receded from its previous more correct position—although effort was made to justify the course taken on the ground that improper receipt and use of funds had invalidated the election of both men. However, when, in 1941, it seated William Langer of North Dakota, elected regularly enough, but charged (by a group in his own state) with being unworthy of membership, it reverted to its earlier more defensible practice. [2] Expulsion of a senator or representative requires a two-thirds vote and may be for any cause. But neither senators nor representatives are regarded as civil officers of the United States in the meaning of the constitution, and consequently they are not subject to impeachment.

Status of Members of Congress—Other Aspects

Privileges and immunities

Members of both houses have certain privileges and immunities, based on hard-won English usages, and aimed at protecting freedom of attendance, speaking, and voting. A senator or representative may be arrested at any time for treason, felony, or breach of the peace—which, as construed, means indictable offenses of every sort; [3] so that he enjoys no exemption from the processes of the criminal law. But while attending a session, or going to or returning from a session, he cannot be arrested

---

secretary of state, during Knox's incumbency, to the earlier figure. On questions raised by the appointment of Senator Hugo L. Black as associate justice of the Supreme Court in 1937, see D. O. McGovney, "Is Hugo L. Black a Supreme Court Justice De Jure?," Calif. Law Rev., XXVI, 1-32 (Nov., 1937).

[1] Contested elections are investigated and reported upon by the standing committee on rules and administration, succeeding in 1947 a former committee on privileges and elections.

[2] The charge against Langer was that, when attorney-general and later governor of his state, he had allowed his official actions to be influenced by his interest in various business deals. The Senate committee on elections (as then existing) recommended that he be unseated, but the recommendation did not finally prevail. In January, 1947, a recently reëlected senator, Theodore G. Bilbo of Mississippi, was not officially refused his seat, but confirmation of his right to sit was held up pending his recovery from an operation. Various charges had been brought against him relating to improper dealings with war contractors and inciting racial hatred in his primary campaign. During the following summer he died, and his status was never cleared up.

[3] Williamson v. United States, 207 U. S. 425 (1907).

on civil process or compelled to testify in a court or serve on a jury. Moreover, "for any speech or debate in either house" he cannot "be questioned in any other place." [1] That is, he cannot be proceeded against, outside of the house to which he belongs (it, of course, may censure or even expel him), because of anything he may have said in the course of debate, committee hearings, or other proceedings properly belonging to the business of the house. He cannot, for example, be sued for libel or slander by a person whom he may have criticized. The exemption is sometimes used as a shield for unwarranted personalities, and even for downright scurrility, but it is fundamentally justifiable. If a member knew that he might be proceeded against at law by any person taking offense at his remarks in the exercise of his proper functions, he would speak and act (in view of the general publicity of congressional proceedings which now prevails) under an altogether undesirable sense of restraint. The immunity relates, of course, to legal proceedings only, and quite properly confers no protection against criticism by press and public on grounds of public interest and policy.

One other constitutional right of members is that of receiving compensation for their services, at a rate fixed by law (of their own making) and paid out of the national treasury. Until 1855, they contented themselves with a small per diem allowance, but at that time a salary of $3,000 was authorized, which in 1865 was increased to $5,000, in 1907 to $7,500,[2] and in 1925 to $10,000 (in the case of the speaker of the House of Representatives, and likewise the president *pro tempore* of the Senate when there was no vice-president, $15,000). In later years, demand arose for further increase. Senators and representatives testified plausibly that living costs in Washington, combined with unavoidable expenses incident to their station, made it impossible for them to get along on what they were paid; and disinterested observers, supporting the contention, urged that something be done to correct the situation. A new salary figure most commonly in mind was $15,000, and in 1946 the Senate passed a comprehensive legislative reorganization bill [3] carrying provision for that amount. Approving the measure in somewhat emasculated form, the House of Representatives cut the figure to $12,500, coupling with it, however, provision for an additional tax-free $2,500 for incidental expenses; somewhat reluctantly, the Senate concurred in the amendment; and therefore, since the date indicated, compensation for all members has been on this basis.[4] When, in 1942, a somewhat unfortunately-timed bill was passed to improve the financial outlook of members by assuring them retirement annuities on a graduated scale after fifteen

Pay and perquisites

---

[1] Art. I, § 6, cl. 1.

[2] This level was first reached under a "salary grab" act passed by a "lame-duck" Congress in 1873, but public disapproval was so strong that the next Congress restored the previous figure.

[3] See p. 412 below.

[4] Members of the two houses have always been paid at the same rate. The speaker of the House and president *pro tempore* of the Senate, however, receive $20,000.

years of service, a storm of public disapproval caused the measure to be repealed within two months. The legislation of 1946, however, gives all members opportunity to qualify, on a contributory basis (six per cent of salary), for entry into the general federal retirement and pension system,[1] with annuities starting (after at least six years of service) at the age of sixty-two. In addition to salary, funds for incidental expenses, and provisions for retirement allowances, members are entitled to perquisites including (1) a travel allowance for one round trip each session between the member's home and Washington at the liberal rate of twenty cents a mile—intended, however, to help meet the cost of transporting his family; (2) an allowance of $9,500 a year for representatives and of $20,000 a year for senators for clerk hire; and (3) the franking privilege, enabling members to send free through the mails personal correspondence and other materials stamped with their names.

Congressional Personnel

What kinds of men and women do the voters send to Washington to represent them in the House and Senate? One might reply, "Nearly all kinds;" for the 531 representatives and senators constitute in many ways (although not in all) a good cross-section of the nation itself. A recent careful study of a particular Congress (the Seventy-seventh, 1941-43), brought to view characteristics that can safely be regarded as fairly typical under present-day conditions;[2] and a few of them may be noted here. To begin with, the average age of representatives was fifty-two and of senators fifty-eight—which is far beyond the average adult age (forty-three). Nearly all were firmly rooted in the states, and even in the localities (in the case of representatives), which they represented, by virtue either of having been born there or of having become resident there at an early age. Different religions were represented in rough proportion to their numbers of communicants throughout the country. In other ways besides age, the situation was less typical of the general body politic. Eighty-eight per cent of the representatives and senators had attended a college, professional school, or both—which, of course, is a far higher proportion than among people generally. As one would expect, a disproportionate number had held previous public positions of one kind or another; for example, 156 had served in state legislatures and 109 as prosecuting attorney. Vocationally, the outstanding fact was the preponderance of lawyers—although not all of the 311 members listed as such were actively practicing at the time of their election. Other professions—agriculture, journalism, education—were represented more sparingly, and along with them, a variety of business and financial interests. Although "dirt farm-

---

[1] See p. 517 below. The standard pension is two and one-half per cent of the average annual salary during service multiplied by the years of service, but in no case exceeding three-fourths of salary received at the time of retirement.

[2] M. M. McKinney, "The Personnel of the Seventy-seventh Congress," *Amer. Polit. Sci. Rev.*, XXXVI, 67-75 (Feb., 1942).

ers" were not numerous, agriculture claimed approximately one-tenth of the membership—with, of course, all members from agricultural states counted upon to be sensitive to agricultural interests. The man most conspicuously absent was the manual laborer: only a single member listed himself as a factory worker, although probably a few others had at one time or another been such. Hardly any interest is more vocal around the Capitol than labor. But those who speak for it do so either as lobbyists from the outside or as members concerned about labor-employer relations and policies without themselves ever having riveted a girder or stood at the assembly line. And at this point, Congress contrasts sharply with the British House of Commons, which for more than a generation has contained sizable numbers of members (since the election of 1945, a large number) not only belonging to trade unions and the Labor party, but drawn directly from labor ranks.

REFERENCES

The Federalist, Nos. LII-LXIII.

D. S. Alexander, *History and Procedure of the House of Representatives* (Boston, 1916), Chaps. I, XVI.

W. Wilson, *Constitutional Government in the United States* (New York, 1908), Chaps. IV-V.

W. W. Willoughby, *Constitutional Law of the United States* (2nd ed., New York, 1929), II, Chap. XXXIX.

W. F. Willoughby, *Principles of Legislative Organization and Administration* (Washington, D. C., 1934), Chaps. XV-XIX.

R. Luce, *Legislative Assemblies* (Boston, 1924).

V. Torrey, *You and Your Congress* (New York, 1944). Concerned primarily with electoral aspects.

E. C. Griffith, *The Rise and Development of the Gerrymander* (Chicago, 1907). Covers the subject to about 1850.

C. O. Sauer, "Geography and the Gerrymander," *Amer. Polit. Sci. Rev.*, XII, 403-426 (Aug., 1918).

L. F. Schmeckebier, *Congressional Apportionment* (Washington, D. C., 1941).

G. H. Haynes, *The Election of Senators* (New York, 1906).

————, *The Senate of the United States; Its History and Practice* (Boston, 1938), I, Chaps. III-IV. This two-volume work is now the standard treatise on the Senate.

C. H. Kerr, *The Origin and Development of the United States Senate* (Ithaca, N. Y., 1895).

G. J. Schulz, *Creation of the Senate* (Washington, D. C., 1937). Legislative Reference Service, Library of Congress.

L. Rogers, *The American Senate* (New York, 1926).

C. H. Wooddy, "Is the Senate Unrepresentative?," *Polit. Sci. Quar.*, XLI, 219-239 (June, 1926).

————, *The Case of Frank L. Smith; A Study in Representative Government* (Chicago, 1931).

S. Erwin, *Henry Ford vs. Truman H. Newberry; A Study in American Politics, Legislation, and Justice* (New York, 1935).

C. A. M. Ewing, *Congressional Elections, 1896-1944; The Sectional Basis of Political Democracy in the House of Representatives* (Norman, Okla., 1947).

L. Overacker, *Money in Elections* (New York, 1932).

M. M. McKinney, "The Personnel of the Seventy-seventh Congress," *Amer. Polit. Sci. Rev.,* XXXVI, 67-74 (Feb., 1942).

"The 150th Anniversary of the U. S. Congress" [Symposium], *Cong. Digest,* XVIII, 97-128 (Apr., 1939).

Biographical Directory of the American Congress, 1774-1927, 69th Cong., 2nd Sess., House Doc. No. 783 (1928).

Official Congressional Directory. Two or three editions a year, obtainable through the Superintendent of Documents, Washington, D. C.

CHAPTER XV

THE ORGANIZATION OF HOUSE AND SENATE

The two-year period for which a House of Representatives is elected fixes the duration of "a Congress;" at its expiration, a new Congress, with changed membership and organization, begins. Since the first one assembled in 1789, Congresses have been numbered consecutively; and the sessions of each—whether regular or special—are identified officially as the first or second (or third) as the case may be. The Congress elected in November, 1946, and organized in January, 1947, was the eightieth in the series. "Congresses"

Every Congress has at least two sessions, because the constitution requires that Congress "assemble at least once in every year."[1] In addition, it may, "on extraordinary occasions," be called into special session by the president.[2] Until 1933, the terms of members of the House of Representatives and of a third or more of the senators, elected in a given November, did not begin until the following March 4; and, unless earlier called into special session, the new Congress did not meet until the first Monday of the following December—thirteen months after election. Starting at that time, its first regular session might continue indefinitely through the next twelve months, and commonly lasted at least until late summer. And this would be known as its "long" session. Starting the next December, its second regular session could last only until the terms of members expired (and with them the Congress itself) on the next March 4; and, with limits thus fixed, this would be the "short" session. Sessions: 1. The old arrangement

The arrangement was not a good one. By the time a Congress reached its short session, a new Congress had been elected. Many members of the old one had become "lame ducks" by being defeated for another term; there might even have been a shift in the party complexion of one or both of the houses. Nevertheless, with a Congress fresh from the people simply waiting its turn, the old Congress would go through another entire (and often rather perfunctory and futile) session. A change of calendar to obviate such overlapping was long advocated, notably by the late Senator George W. Norris of Nebraska; and at last, in 1933, a constitutional amendment on the subject—the Twentieth—was placed before the states, whose alacrity in ratifying it showed that the country was more than ready for it. As a result, the terms of all representatives (and of one-third or more of the senators) nowadays begin on January 3 follow- 2. The present plan

---

[1] Twentieth Amendment, § 2, replacing (but not in this respect differing from) Art. 1, § 4, cl. 2.
[2] Art. II, § 3.

ing election,[1] with the first regular session of a new Congress starting on the same day unless the two houses have agreed upon a slightly different date, *e.g.*, to avoid Sunday. The second regular session operates on a similar schedule the next year; and both sessions may run as long as desired within a twelve-month period—although the Legislative Reorganization Act of 1946 provides that, except in time of war or of national emergency proclaimed by the president, the two houses shall adjourn *sine die* each year not later than the end of July "unless otherwise provided by Congress." [2] "Lame-duck" sessions are a thing of the past, and the need for special sessions has been considerably reduced.[3]

Adjournment

Unlike certain national legislatures that the world has known, Congress is not obliged to remain in session during any fixed portion of a year. Conversely, it cannot be dissolved, after the manner of parliaments in cabinet-government countries like Great Britain. Every Congress is entitled to fill out its full two years, meanwhile regulating its adjournments practically as it pleases. Neither house may adjourn without the consent of the other for a period longer than three days, or to any other place than that in which the houses are at the time sitting. Otherwise, the matter is left to arrangement between the houses themselves, save only that when they cannot agree as to the time of adjournment, the president may intervene and adjourn them to "such time as he shall think proper." [4] No occasion for exercise of this particular presidential authority has ever arisen.

How a New Congress Organizes for Work

Need for organization in legislative bodies

Whatever its numbers, its tasks, or its powers, a deliberative assembly such as the House of Representatives or the Senate can make headway only by means of some plan of organization that will transform an

---

[1] The date for inaugurating a new president was simultaneously shifted from March 4 to January 20, so that every fourth year both the legislative and executive branches make a fresh start practically together. Incoming presidents with legislative programs which they desired to press used to be obliged to call into special session (after March 4) a new Congress which otherwise would not meet until December. Nowadays, a new Congress is already in session when they take office.

[2] Under pressure of defense preparations and of war, the sessions of 1940 to 1945 inclusive lasted either a full year or nearly so, although in some cases with recesses of a few weeks. With congressional elections impending, the final session of the Seventy-ninth Congress was hastened to a conclusion in early August, 1946. The first session of the Eightieth Congress, however, after a lengthy recess beginning July 26, 1947, was resumed on November 17, by call of the president, and finally closed on December 19.

[3] Either house, it should be observed, may be called into special session without the other, and in practice the Senate occasionally is so convoked to act upon executive appointments and treaties—matters with which the House of Representatives, as such, has nothing directly to do. There would be little that the House could do independently, and it has never been convened separately. A special session of a single house is not, of course, a special session of *Congress*. For a list of special sessions of the Senate from 1791 to 1933, see *Official Congressional Directory*, 2nd ed. corrected to June 11, 1947, p. 242. Unlike state legislatures, which, when called into special session, usually can deal only with matters specified by the governor in the call, Congress, when so convened, is in full possession of all its constitutional powers.

[4] Art. II, § 3. Cf. Art. I, § 5, cl. 4.

amorphous crowd of members into an integrated working body. There must be officers to direct proceedings, maintain order, and keep records. There must be commonly accepted rules of procedure. There must be facilities, chiefly committees, for parcelling out tasks too numerous, intricate, or otherwise exacting to be performed in their entirety by the membership as a whole. The constitution requires the House to have a speaker as its presiding officer, makes the vice-president of the United States the president of the Senate, and requires the latter body to have a president *pro tempore* to serve in the absence of the vice-president.[1] Beyond this, however, each branch is at liberty to provide itself with such officers, set up such committees, adopt such forms of procedure, and impose upon itself such rules as it sees fit, subject only to the limitation that "it may not by its rules ignore constitutional restraints or violate fundamental rights."[2] By the same token, each has enjoyed virtually unrestricted scope for acquiring, by deliberate decision or, more commonly, by gradual and more or less casual growth, a rich equipment of informal mechanisms and unwritten customs which quite as often account for what the observer hears and sees on Capitol Hill as does anything to be found in the official code of rules.

One who would understand the machinery with which Congress carries on its work will do well to begin by observing how a newly assembled Congress organizes. In the Senate, to be sure, not a great deal happens. Because of overlapping terms, that body has a continuous existence and has never been without organization since it started operations in 1789. At the opening of a new Congress, there is accordingly no occasion for organizing the Senate from the ground up; about all that is necessary is to swear in the new members, fill vacant offices (if any), and revise the committee lists in accordance with changes in personnel and in the number of seats held by the different parties. *What happens when a new Congress meets*

1. In the Senate

The situation in the House is quite otherwise. All of the members of that body reach the end of their terms at the same time, and with them disappear all officers, all committees, and even all rules; when a new Congress convenes, the House is merely a group of unorganized members-elect. Some one must, of course, take responsibility for getting action started, and by long-established usage (now embodied in a statute) this duty falls to the person who has been clerk of the preceding House. Taking the chair, he calls the assembly to order and reads the roll of members-elect by states alphabetically, using a list made up from certificates of election placed in his hands by the proper state officials. If it appears that any seat is claimed by a person other than the one holding a certificate, the matter is referred for investigation and report (after the House has fully organized) to the standing committee on House administration. In the meantime, the person named in the certificate is presumed to have *2. In the House of Representatives:*

(a) Reading of the roll

[1] Art. I, § 2, cl. 5, and § 3, cls. 4-5.
[2] United States *v.* Ballin, 144 U. S. 1 (1892).

been duly elected, and he participates both in the organization of the House and in its regular work after organization until such time as it is determined that he is not entitled to a seat.

(b) Election of officers

The roll having been read, the work of organization proceeds. As a rule, it is completed quickly—sometimes in a single sitting—although a close balance of political forces may precipitate a deadlock extending over days, and even weeks. The first important step is the election of a regular presiding officer, *i.e.*, a speaker, who forthwith takes the chair. After that, a clerk is chosen, and also a sergeant-at-arms, a doorkeeper, a postmaster, and a chaplain. While the constitution explicitly provides that all of these officials shall be elected by the House, what actually happens is that the House merely ratifies a slate previously agreed upon by a caucus of the majority members.[1] The speaker is voted for separately; the others usually as a group.[2] None of the officials named, not even the speaker, is required by law to be a member of the House; and, as a matter of fact, only the speaker ever is a member. Each appoints all of the subordinates connected with his office; and all are subject to removal by the House, although no speaker has ever thus been dispossessed.

(c) Taking the oath

The speaker-elect is escorted to the chair by the defeated candidate and sworn in, usually by the member of longest service. In turn, the speaker administers the oath to the members as a body, except those whose qualifications have been challenged; such persons are obliged to stand aside, and the oath is not administered to them until their right to membership has been established. Having once taken the oath, a member can be cut off from official connection with the House (in advance of the expiration of his term) only by death, by resignation, or by expulsion by a two-thirds vote of his fellow-members.

(d) Adoption of rules

After officers have been elected and the oath administered, it is customary for one of the older members of the majority party to move adoption of the rules of the House in the preceding Congress. If—as is usually the case—any members think that these rules ought to be changed, this is the time for them to try to get action; for, once the old rules have been readopted, they are almost certain to stand throughout the remainder of the session without significant amendment. The past quarter-century has witnessed several spirited attempts to introduce amendments at this stage, and a few have been successful.[3] Regardless of party, the older and more "regular" members—especially the leaders—commonly prefer, however, to keep intact the procedures under which they perchance have risen to power; most new members are too inexperienced to have strong opinions one way or the other; and insurgent groups

---

[1] See p. 325 below.

[2] The death of a speaker during his term of service is usually followed by an election carried out without a contest, as when Speaker William B. Bankhead was chosen in 1936 and Speaker Sam Rayburn in 1940.

[3] Notably at the opening of the Sixty-eighth Congress in December, 1923; the Seventieth, in December, 1927; the Seventy-second, in December, 1931; and the Seventy-fourth, in January, 1935.

bent upon change usually lack the votes necessary to attain their purpose. The old rules having been readopted, all further proposals for change are automatically referred to the committee on rules—a group dominated by leaders of what is commonly called the House "machine," and even more disinclined to innovation than the general run of members. Any suggested departure which in any way threatens the continued control of these men in House affairs is likely to be smothered promptly by the committee and never heard of again, at least until the next Congress organizes.

The sources from which the rules, as they stand today, have been drawn are: (1) the constitution, in so far as a rather limited number of its provisions are pertinent; (2) concurrent actions of the two branches of Congress, illustrated chiefly by Title 1 of the Legislative Reorganization Act of 1946 amending House and Senate rules concerning committees;[1] (3) the *Manual of Parliamentary Practice* prepared by Thomas Jefferson for use of the Senate when he was its presiding officer;[2] (4) the regulations adopted by the House itself from the beginning of its existence, and in early days based largely on the practice of the colonial legislatures and of the British House of Commons; and (5) the decisions of successive speakers and chairmen of the committee of the whole—decisions which bear much the same relation to the rules that court decisions bear to statutes. Originally, the rules were few and easily learned; today, the formal regulations alone (quite apart from the *Manual,* and also leaving out of account the exceedingly numerous decisions of speakers and chairmen[3]) number forty-three, fill upwards of two hundred printed pages, and form "perhaps the most finely adjusted, scientifically balanced, and highly technical rules of any parliamentary body in the world"—certainly a code so elaborate and complicated that few members ever succeed in mastering it completely.[4] Steeped in House

How the rules have developed

[1] See p. 413 below. A word of explanation, however, is necessary here. All portions of the act referred to except Title 1 were statutory in the full sense that they could be modified or rescinded only by some regular act of Congress. Title 1 was statutory also, but in the qualified sense that in enacting it each house was regarded as simply subscribing to new rules which it might have adopted separately, and which it was recognized as having full power to change or abandon later by its own independent action. With the ultimate principle of control over their own rules thus preserved to the two houses, both promptly put their new committee systems into operation when the Eightieth Congress was organized in January, 1947.

[2] Jefferson's *Manual* is printed in 70th Cong., 2nd Sess., House Doc. No. 629, and in various editions of the *House Manual and Digest* and of the *Senate Manual, e.g.,* in the 1947 edition of the latter, at pp. 291-403. In 1937, the provisions of the *Manual* were adopted *en bloc* as governing House procedure "in all cases to which they are applicable, and in which they are not inconsistent with the standing rules and orders of the House."

[3] Collected and edited by Asher C. Hinds (long a clerk at the speaker's table) under the title of *Parliamentary Precedents of the House of Representatives,* 5 vols. (Washington, D. C., 1907). In 1919, a supplement and index-digest, prepared by Clarence Cannon, House parliamentarian, was published; also in 1935 a new supplement, continuing Hinds, and entitled *Cannon's Precedents of the House of Representatives of the United States* (3 vols., numbered on the exterior VI, VII, and VIII).

[4] Among the matters dealt with are the duties of officers; the number, nature, and kinds of committees; committee procedure and reports; the daily order of business; the "calendars;" priority of motions; questions of privilege; etc.

regulations and general parliamentary law as he is, and must be, the speaker requires the assistance of a parliamentarian and an assistant parliamentarian, both prepared to advise when a difficult (it can no longer often be a wholly unprecedented) situation arises.

The growth of the rules has not, in the main, resulted from periodic revisions, or from wholesale additions or renovations; such general overhaulings have been few. Rather, it has come about chiefly by gradual adjustment and accretion—old rules being cautiously revised and perhaps eventually discarded, new ones occasionally finding places in the list. Most obvious and significant throughout has been the trend toward concentration of control over the time and business of the House in the hands of the leaders of the majority party—the speaker, the majority members of the rules committee, the chairmen of the other great committees, the "floor leader," the "steering committee"—with a corresponding narrowing of the opportunities left open to minority elements to interfere with carrying out the purposes of the majority, either by frontal attack in debate or by resort to obstructive or dilatory parliamentary tactics, known as filibustering. Minorities complain; but, after all, it is consistent with the basic principle of representative government that majorities shall not be unduly obstructed in attaining their objectives.[1]

(e) Election of committees A final principal stage in the organization of a new House of Representatives is the election of committees—a procedure to be explained, however, when the committee system comes up presently for consideration.

We accordingly are ready to turn to a closer view of the machinery with which a completely organized House carries on its work—first, and most fully, that operating in the House of Representatives, and afterwards (for distinctive features only) that employed in the Senate. In both cases there will have to be mention not only of formal agencies known to the rules, but also of instrumentalities not so recognized yet equally important to the picture.

The Speaker of the House of Representatives

Powers and functions The constitution touches upon the internal organization of the House only to the extent of providing that the body shall choose its speaker and other officers;[2] all of the power and prestige that the speaker has

---

[1] The rules of the House will be found in successive editions of the *House Manual and Digest*, which is always kept strictly up to date. Mr. Robert Luce, long a congressman from Massachusetts, and a prolific and scholarly writer on legislation, is authority for the statement that a simplification of the rules would enable "a session to be reduced in length one quarter, or a quarter more work could be turned out, and in either case the product would be better." *Legislative Procedure* (Boston, 1922), 19-20. When, however, in 1945, the Joint Committee on the Reorganization of Congress, on whose recommendations the Legislative Reorganization Act of 1946 was based (see p. 412 below) was set up, it was enjoined from proposing any general revision of rules of procedure—although in the end it did suggest the greatly modified form of House Rule X providing for the present scheme of committees. A convenient guide to House procedure in all its aspects is *Cannon's Procedure in the House of Representatives* (4th ed.), 78th Cong., 2nd Sess., House Doc. No. 675 (1944).

[2] Art. I, § 2, cl. 5. The office of speaker originated in the English House of Com-

gained through the years have flowed, not from constitutional grants of authority, but from rules made by the House itself, from accumulating usage and precedent, and perhaps most basically from the need of the House, in the absence of other provision, for official leadership and command. Notwithstanding a partial eclipse two score years ago when he was removed from the committee on rules and when the right to appoint all standing committees was taken from him, the speaker is still the most conspicuous figure in the House, and as such he has many important things to do. He takes the chair at the hour appointed for a sitting of the House, sees that the journal of the preceding sitting is read, preserves order and decorum, and, in case of disturbance or disorderly conduct, causes the galleries or lobbies to be cleared. He "recognizes" members desiring the floor. He signs all acts, addresses, joint resolutions, writs, warrants, and subpoenas ordered by the House; interprets and applies the rules; decides questions of order, with no really effective appeal to the House; puts questions to a vote; and appoints such select and conference committees as from time to time are authorized. As a member of the House in full standing, he has the same right to speak and to vote that other members have, although under the rules he is not required to vote except when his vote would decide the issue, e.g., by creating or breaking a tie, producing a necessary two-thirds majority, or establishing a quorum; and of course taking the floor in debate is optional, with all speakers doing so occasionally, but not often. The speaker, furthermore, may appoint any other member to serve as presiding officer in his place

---

mons many centuries ago, was transplanted to the colonial legislatures, and naturally was envisaged by the constitution's framers as a device designated by all experience for use in the national House of Representatives.

The speakership alone will be treated here, but a few facts may be noted concerning the less important House officials. (1) The clerk is responsible for keeping an accurate record of the proceedings of the House—in other words, the journal which the constitution requires to be kept and to be published from time to time (Art. I, § 5, cl. 3). Copies of the printed *Journal* are furnished to every member, and are also sent to designated officials in every state. The clerk issues, at the direction of the House, all writs, warrants, and subpœnas; he certifies to the passage of all bills and joint resolutions; he makes contracts for supplies or labor required by the House; he keeps and pays the stationery accounts of members, and pays the officers and employees of the House their monthly salaries. (2) The sergeant-at-arms is required to be present in the House during its sittings, and to assist, if need be, in maintaining decorum, under the direction of the speaker or chairman of the committee of the whole. If for any reason the office of clerk is vacant, the sergeant-at-arms makes up the temporary roll used at the organization of a new House. He also executes the commands of the House, by summoning absent members, serving subpœnas for witnesses, and in other ways; and it is from him that members obtain their salaries and mileage allowances, as provided by law. (3) The doorkeeper enforces the rules regulating admission to the floor and galleries of the House, and is required to file with the committee on accounts, at the beginning and end of each session of Congress, an inventory of all furniture, books, and other public property in the committee and other rooms under his charge. (4) The postmaster superintends the post-offices maintained in the Capitol and the House office-buildings for the accommodation of members and employees. (5) The chaplain is required to be present at the beginning of each day's sitting (unless he provides a substitute) and to open it with prayer. All of these offices, and the many subordinate positions attached to certain of them, fall to supporters of the dominant party in the House. See L. Rogers, "The Staffing of Congress," *Polit. Sci. Quar.*, LVI, 1-22 (Mar., 1941).

for a period not to exceed three days (in case of illness, ten days) ; and in practice he often calls upon other members to occupy the chair temporarily.[1] Chosen in the first instance by a caucus of the majority party members,[2] and thereupon formally elected by the House (usually in competition with a minority nominee), a speaker may ordinarily expect to be reëlected at the beginning of each succeeding Congress as long as he remains a member and his party continues in control. If the party balance is overturned, the incoming majority is likely to elevate to the post the man who previously was minority floor leader.

The "revolution" of 1910-11

Forty years ago, one would have put high in the list of powers enjoyed by the speaker that of appointing all standing (as well as special and conference) committees, together with their chairmen, and including the most privileged and influential committee of all, namely, the committee on rules—of which, indeed, the speaker himself served as chairman. This power, however, added to all of the others, made of strong-willed speakers like James G. Blaine (1869-75), Thomas B. Reed (1889-91 and 1895-99), and Joseph G. Cannon (1903-10) virtual autocrats, without whose assent practically no legislation could be enacted, or even considered; and a House "revolution," sponsored in its earlier stages by a coalition of insurgent Republicans and Democratic minority leaders, culminated, in 1910 (after one of the most spectacular parliamentary battles in the history of the House), in the removal of the speaker from the rules committee, and eventually, in 1911, in the transfer of the selection of all standing committees from him to the House itself.[3] This was a hard blow, and the speakership has never since been quite the same. But plenty of important prerogatives remain—granting or refusing members the floor, declining to put motions regarded as dilatory, ruling members out of order, deciding vital questions of procedure—together with, as observed above, a certain amount of appointing power, and sometimes also the important power of reference, i.e., of deciding to what committee a public bill shall be referred when the clerk of the House (who normally makes the assignments in accordance with the nature of the bill) is in doubt. All told, if the speaker no longer rules with the rod of a "Czar" Reed or a Cannon, he nevertheless is still a force of the first magnitude in the actual work of legislation.[4]

---

[1] The foregoing and other regulations will be found in House Rule 1, §§ 1-7. The speaker spends less time presiding than might be supposed, the reason being that he does not occupy the chair when the House is sitting as committee of the whole—in most sessions a good deal more than half of the time. See pp. 358-359 below.

[2] Indeed, the choice may actually have been made by agreement among rival candidates and their supporters before the caucus met, as in the case of Speaker Rainey's selection in 1933. On sectionalism as a factor in the election of speakers, see *Amer. Polit. Sci. Rev.,* XXIX, 985-986 (Dec., 1935).

[3] C. R. Atkinson, *The Committee on Rules and the Overthrow of Speaker Cannon* (New York, 1911). In theory, the power to appoint its standing committees had always belonged to the House; but in earlier and simpler days it had been turned over to the speaker.

[4] Along with the president of the Senate and the majority floor leaders of the two houses, he is often called to the White House to discuss legislative programs and

Take, as a single illustration, the power of recognition. Much of the time, the only way in which any member can gain the ear of the House is by being formally "recognized," *i.e.*, given the floor, by the speaker;[1] and this opens up considerable opportunity for that official to control the course of debate in such a manner as practically to determine the fate of any measure to which he cares to extend, or from which he prefers to withhold, his favor. To be sure, he is bound to follow the rules of the House; and the rules give fixed precedence to some committees or to their chairmen, and require some distribution of time between members favoring and those opposing a pending measure. But, with all due allowance for these and other limitations, the speaker still has a good deal of leeway for exercising his own discretion in granting the floor to members; and in this way he often has frustrated the introduction or consideration of motions to which he personally, or the party with which he was identified, was opposed.

A favorite expedient of members who want to obstruct the adoption of a measure, or to wear down opposition, is to offer motions designed solely to use up time. Confronted with a situation in which an obstreperous Democratic minority seemed likely to make legislation practically impossible, Speaker Reed, in 1890, hit upon the plan of refusing to entertain motions which he regarded as dilatory; and before the end of the year the House, agreeing with him that "the object of a parliamentary body is action, not the stoppage of action," embodied the new policy in a formal rule which is still in force.[2] Such a rule cannot prevent members from slowing up business by exercising their constitutional right to demand the yeas and nays,[3] even though the purpose be plainly dilatory. But the adoption of it by the House illustrates how the speaker not only may recognize or refuse to recognize, very much as he likes, in the daily course of proceedings, but may even influence the House to

---

strategy with the chief executive. Indeed, he was always a main figure in the Monday morning conference utilized for years by President Franklin D. Roosevelt. With a different party from the president's in control of the House, and therefore of the speakership, he is still likely to be invited to White House conferences, although in the company (following President Truman's practice) of both majority and minority leaders.

[1] The statement's qualification is required by the circumstance that in certain instances when a bill is called up for consideration, the committee chairman and the ranking minority member have control of the floor and may allot time to members without regard to the speaker; and of course the speaker's power of recognition does not apply when the House is sitting as committee of the whole, for then he is not even in the chair.

[2] House Rule XVI, § 10. Another familiar obstructive device of minority groups in a closely divided House in earlier times was to leave the House short of a quorum (*i.e.*, a majority present) by refusing to answer to a roll-call designed to determine whether a quorum was present, or by not participating when a vote was being taken. In 1890, when the same Democratic minority threatened to make legislation impossible by resorting to these tactics, Speaker Reed, with characteristic forthrightness, overcame the difficulty of the "disappearing quorum" by instructing the clerks to count as present all members physically present, whether they answered to their names or not; and this clearly reasonable procedure, although violently protested at the time, also found a permanent place in the rules (House Rule XV, § 3).

[3] Art. I, § 5, cl. 3.

accept as fixed practice a principle or plan of recognition which he has himself devised.

Though often enough swayed by partisan considerations in earlier centuries, the speaker of the British House of Commons—prototype of parliamentary speakers throughout the English-speaking world—long ago became a wholly disinterested and impartial moderator, unidentified with any party organization or movement inside or outside of the body over which he presides. He attends no party gatherings, contributes to no party funds, makes no campaign for reëlection in his constituency, refrains from so much as setting foot in a political club.[1] The American speakership, both in Congress and in the state legislatures, has developed on very different lines. It is, and has been almost from the beginning, frankly partisan. "I believe it to be the duty of the speaker," declared a past incumbent on taking the chair, "standing squarely on the platform of his party, to assist in so far as he properly can the enactment of legislation in accordance with the declared principles and policies of his party, and by the same token to resist the enactment of legislation in violation thereof."[2] This very well expresses the prevailing view. To be sure, the speaker must not be swerved by party considerations from faithful enforcement of the rules of the House. If he is wise, he will strive to be fair in his treatment of the opposition. He may even win encomiums from his political opponents—as did Mr. Longworth—for protecting their interests and rights. But, wholly unlike his British counterpart, he is actively and openly identified with his party's organization in the House—an indispensable cog in the majority machine. In the days of Reed and Cannon, he was a party figure second only to the president himself; even yet, he must usually be accorded front rank not merely in legislative influence, but in politics as well.

With few exceptions, the speakers of the House (there have been forty-seven in all, including speakers *pro tempore*) have been men not only of well-tested ability, industry, and tact, but also of sufficient aptitude for leadership to have brought them to the fore in their respective parties even before their elevation to the speakership; in proof of which one needs only to glance at the long list of persons who have held the office and observe the names of Henry Clay, James K. Polk, Robert C. Winthrop, Schuyler Colfax, James G. Blaine, Samuel J. Randall, John G. Carlisle, Thomas B. Reed, Joseph G. Cannon, Champ Clark, and John N. Garner. Despite, however, the high political importance attaching to the position in times past, only one speaker (Polk) ever reached the presidency, although Blaine missed it narrowly. This circumstance has

---

[1] On the English speakership, see F. A. Ogg, *English Government and Politics* (2nd ed.), 379-384, and especially M. MacDonagh, *The Speaker of the House* (London, 1914). Historically, the speaker was so termed (in days before the House of Commons gained full legislative power) because his main function was to "speak for" the body when petitioning the king.

[2] Nicholas Longworth, in *Cong. Record*, 69th Cong., 1st Sess, p. 382 (Dec. 7, 1925).

not been altogether fortuitous; for whoever holds the speakership runs grave risk of arousing antagonisms within his party, as happened notably in the cases of Blaine, Reed, and Cannon; and this, of course, makes attainment of the presidency difficult or impossible.[1]

The Committee System in the House of Representatives

Legislative bodies the world over save time and otherwise promote efficiency by referring most matters that come before them to committees for examination and report; and nowhere is an extensive committee system more indispensable than in the American House of Representatives, confronted as it is every biennium with thousands of different legislative proposals, to say nothing of other items of business that require its attention. In early days, each bill or other proposal was likely to be referred to a committee created for the particular purpose and promptly discharged when its task was completed; and such "select," or "special," committees are still employed for studying designated subjects or sometimes investigating departments, services, or activities of the government.[2] Of a temporary nature also, although serving a different purpose, are conference committees, set up as needed to confer with similar committees of the Senate with a view to ironing out differences in the form and content of bills as separately passed by the two houses. As we shall see, too, the House very frequently resolves itself into committee of the whole for considering revenue, appropriation, and other important measures; and occasional committees, temporary or standing, are maintained jointly with the Senate, good examples today being a congressional joint committee on atomic energy and a similar committee on labor-management relations. Finally, early in the history of the House, standing committees made their appearance, and for a long time past all members have been assigned, at the opening of each Congress, to one or more of these "miniature legislatures" charged with receiving, examining, and presumably reporting upon measures of a given class or type referred to them during the two years of their existence, and with perhaps taking the initiative also in framing and introducing bills.

Although small in earlier days, the number of standing committees

(marginal note: Kinds of committees)

---

[1] A sketch of the varying fortunes of the speakership between 1910 and 1927 will be found in P. D. Hasbrouck, *Party Government in the House of Representatives* (New York, 1927), 1-25.

[2] One of the best known (and most criticized) special committees of the House in recent times was the "committee to investigate un-American activities," headed from 1938 to 1944 by Representative Martin Dies of Texas. See A. R. Ogden, *The Dies Committee* (Washington, D. C., 1944). At the opening of the Seventy-ninth Congress, in January, 1945, this committee, which had lapsed, was not only unexpectedly revived (with different personnel), but transformed into a standing committee; and since the committee reorganization of 1946 it has retained that status, under the name of "committee on un-American activities." See "Constitutional Limitations on the Un-American Activities Committee," *Columbia Law Rev.*, XLVII, 416-431 (Apr., 1947); and for an unfavorable discussion of the committee's activities by one of its members, J. Voorhis, *Confessions of a Congressman* (Garden City, N. Y., 1947), Chap. xv.

mounted to the amazing total of sixty-one before a reorganization in
1927 brought it down to forty-seven (increased in 1945 to forty-eight [1]).
Even when this reduction took place, it should have been carried farther,
because many committees survived which had little or nothing to do,
important fields of legislation were split between rival groups, jurisdictions overlapped, and confusion continued. Committees, however, and
especially committee chairmanships, represented vested interests; and
not until 1946 was it found possible to "streamline" the overgrown structure (in both houses) on the greatly altered pattern later (January,
1947) put into operation. In a subsequent chapter devoted principally to
the general problem of improving Congress, the background of this significant step will come more fully to view,[2] and for the present it must
suffice to observe simply that the number of standing committees—reduced to nineteen—has been rather more than cut in half, and that
whereas formerly membership ranged from two to forty-three (in the
case of the old committee on appropriations), with twenty-one the commonest number, the present range is from nine to forty-three, with
twenty-five or twenty-seven the most usual figure.

The present complete list of committees, with number of members, is
as follows:

Agriculture, 27

Appropriations, 43

Armed Services, 33

Banking and Currency, 27

District of Columbia, 25

Education and Labor, 25

Expenditures in the
    Executive Departments, 25

Foreign Affairs, 25

House Administration, 25

Interstate and Foreign
    Commerce, 27

Judiciary, 27

Merchant Marine and Fisheries, 25

Post-Office and Civil Service, 25

Public Lands, 25

Public Works, 27

Rules, 12

Un-American Activities, 9

Veterans' Affairs, 27

Ways and Means, 25

Thirteen of the list passed over into the new plan with names unchanged; three, i.e., armed services, education and labor, and post-office
and civil service, represent in each case a union of two former committees;
the remaining three are more or less new; and the statute enumerating the
series [3] undertakes to define with some logic and precision the range of
matters to be referred to each.

[1] Forty-six if three then existing committees on elections be viewed as, in effect,
one committee organized in three branches. Lists of House committees, with the
names of members, have long been printed in successive issues of the *Official Congressional Directory.*

[2] See pp. 411-413 below.

[3] 60 *U. S. Stat. at Large*, 812.

Under previous arrangements, congressmen might be assigned to only one major committee, although also to any number of lesser ones, and the average member rarely served on fewer than three or four. In the new system, with committees less than half as numerous, members uniformly serve on only one, except that members of four committees likely to be less hard-pressed, *e.g.*, on the District of Columbia, may serve on a maximum of two. Previously, somewhat over a third of the more important committees met regularly on a certain day (or days) each week throughout a session, while others met, if at all, only on call of their chairmen. Under the new scheme, all committees have a good deal to do and ordinarily find it necessary to meet at least once a week;[1] in any event, all are required by the legislation of 1946 to "fix regular weekly, biweekly, or monthly meeting days;" and if a chairman refuses or fails to call a special meeting requested by three or more members, there is a procedure by which they may themselves call one. Without special leave, however, no committee except that on rules may sit while the House is in session.

As we have seen, standing committees, since 1911, have been elected by the House itself, even though what that body actually does when a new Congress opens is merely to ratify lists of committee assignments prepared in advance by committees of selection set up by the respective party forces having claim to be represented. With only rare representation of third parties, the committees consist of Republican and Democratic members, in proportions fixed by the committee of selection of the majority party so as to reflect, at least with reasonable accuracy, the relative number of seats possessed.[2] Thus in the Seventy-ninth Congress (organized in January, 1945), with 243 Democrats and 190 Republicans in the House, the quotas (in the then typical committee of twenty-one) were twelve Democrats and nine Republicans; while in the Eightieth Congress (organized in January, 1947), with 246 Republican and 187 Democratic members, the ratio on most committees (with total membership increased to usually twenty-five or twenty-seven) was fifteen or sixteen Republicans to eleven Democrats. Each party, of course, is free to determine for itself who of its members shall represent it on each of the committees. The committee of selection, or "committee on committees," to which the Republicans intrust the drawing up of their lists is named by the party caucus, or conference, and consists of one member from each state having Republican representation in the House—each

---

[1] There is also more extensive use of subcommittees than formerly. See p. 413, note 1, below.

[2] This bipartisan basis of the committees is highly significant, in the first place because it enables all larger sections of the country to be represented at practically all times on all of the committees, and in the second place because it encourages the committees to look upon themselves as organs not so much of a party as of the House itself. In making assignments, a congressman's personal preferences are taken into account, although of course they cannot always be met. It is an important asset to any congressman to be a member of a committee having to do with matters, *e.g.*, agriculture or interstate commerce, of large concern to his district.

such member having, however, as many votes as there are Republican congressmen from his state.[1] The Democrats, in caucus, first select their quota of members of the prospective ways and means committee,[2] and then delegate to this group, as a committee of selection, the task of preparing the Democratic lists for all of the remaining committees. With majority and minority lists (approved by the respective party caucuses) before it, the House rarely consumes much time in carrying out the formality of election.

Committee chairmanships and the principle of seniority

Each committee is therefore composed of majority and minority members, with the majority always holding the chairmanship and (except in rare instances in which party lines break) completely in control, yet significantly with the minority almost always in a position to obtain a hearing for its views. Whether or not the ablest member of a committee, the chairman is easily the most important. It is he who calls committee meetings (presumably, however, since 1946 in accordance with a regular calendar), prepares the agenda for such meetings, guides and directs deliberations, reports their results to the House, leads in debate on the measures so reported, and not infrequently sees outstanding legislation sent down into history with his name attached, either alone (e.g., the McKinley Tariff Act, the Clayton Anti-Trust Act, the Newlands Reclamation Act, the Taylor Grazing Act, etc.) or jointly with that of the chairman of the corresponding Senate committee (e.g., the McDuffie-Tydings Act, the Norris-LaGuardia Act, the Smith-Connally Act, the Taft-Hartley Act, etc.) It is he, too, who is officially consulted on matters pertaining to his committee; and, all in all, he enjoys superior status with Congress, in official circles, and with the public. In view of all this, the method of his selection is curious. "At the commencement of each Congress," say the rules, "the House shall elect as chairman of each standing committee one of the members thereof;"[3] and the formality of election is, to be sure, proceeded with when the committee slates are ratified. Except, however, on rare occasions when questions of party regularity are involved,[4] chairmanships are awarded on a basis of seniority; that is to say, the majority member of longest continuous service on a committee will almost as a matter of course be put up by the party nominating authority for the chairmanship.[5] Indeed, the same seniority

[1] Thus in the Eightieth Congress (1947-49) the representative of New York's Republican delegation had twenty-eight votes, while the solitary Republican congressman from Montana had but one. In that Congress, a total of thirty-five states had one or more Republican congressmen, and hence the committee of selection contained that number of members.

[2] Numbering ten in the Eightieth Congress.

[3] Rule X.

[4] As, for example, in the case of the nominally Republican members who supported the elder Senator LaFollette for the presidency in 1924.

[5] The general practice is to continue members on the same committees from Congress to Congress; and this is wise, because many legislative projects of major importance carry over for several sessions and require for their proper handling a large accumulation of knowledge of subject-matter as well as prolonged acquaintance with the individuals, groups, and administrative personnel concerned. When the

principle applies to the ranking of all committee members: majority members are listed according to their periods of service, minority members likewise; and all move up on the respective lists as members nearer the top drop out by death, failure to secure reëlection, or possibly withdrawal in order to accept membership in a different committee. A new congressman, therefore, regardless of how eminent or able he may be, has no chance at all to secure the chairmanship of a committee, or usually even a very high place in any committee's rank and file. Indeed, he counts himself fortunate if he draws assignment to a lowly position on a committee of first- rather than second-rate importance—on ways and means, for example, rather than on expenditures in the executive departments.[1] Starting (as a majority member, let us say) at or near the bottom of his party's quota, he will, of course—if the people back home send him to Washington often enough—gradually make his way up toward the chairmanship as members ahead of him drop out. Arriving finally at second place, he will become known as "ranking majority member;" and when the next vacancy occurs in the chairmanship, his claim will be held superior to that of any other member (providing his party is still in control of the House), even though he may be out of step with and *persona non grata* to the bulk of his party. Capture of the House by the opposing party will, of course, leave him high and dry, as simply ranking minority member, who, however, if party fortunes change soon enough, will yet step into the chairmanship. If worse calamity befalls and he drops out entirely for a term or two, he must—no matter how experienced or competent—start again at the bottom.

Manifestly disregarding substantially all qualifications except length of continuous committee service, this method of allotting chairmanships has naturally come in for a good deal of criticism; as we shall see, failure to make any change in it has been charged up as a serious shortcoming of the legislative reorganization carried out in 1946. In logic, there is little to be said for the plan. To be sure, it insures chairmen who have had long experience with and knowledge of their committee's field and function; and that is worth something. It also averts the conflicts, intrigues, and deadlocks that probably would occur if chairmen were to be chosen anew every two years under some wide-open system; it affords some chance for members to rise to positions of power regardless of the importance of their state, or of their record for party regularity; and while it yields occasional misfits, it has brought to the chairmanship of the greater committees many men of ability and distinction. This conceded, however, the system still leaves a good deal to be desired. If men rising to signifi-

Seniority criticized

Democrats have a congressional majority, a disproportionate number of committee chairmen are likely to be Southerners because of having been kept in office by uninterrupted Democratic control in their section. This was notably the situation in the later Democratic Congresses of the New Deal period.

[1] There have, however, of late been scattered instances of new members winning assignment to committees of major importance, notably that on foreign affairs.

cant chairmanships prove high-minded, industrious, competent, and statesmanlike, Congress and the country are simply lucky. For the system itself affords no guarantee of such a result; on the contrary, it holds back men of taste and capacity for committee leadership, thrusts forward others of little aptitude or ability, and asks nothing of a man on the way to the top other than that he simply keep on living, get himself reëlected regularly, and remain on the same committee. Plenty of times, congressional leaders, and even the committees concerned, would prefer chairmen different from those brought to the top by seniority. There are, however, arguments both ways; as well-intentioned a group as the Joint Committee on the Organization of Congress (1945) could make no recommendation on the subject because of inability to agree on any alternative plan; and with the practice as deeply ingrained in the congressional structure as it is, any early shift to a different method seems improbable—especially since finding some method incontestably better would be no easy task.[1]

The committee on rules

Of the numerous House committees, only one calls for special comment here, i.e., the highly privileged and decidedly powerful committee on rules; certain others, e.g., the ways and means committee and the committee on appropriations, will receive attention at later points.[2] For upwards of a hundred years, the rules committee was merely a special committee set up at the opening of each Congress to offer the customary motion that the old rules be readopted, with such changes, if any, as the committee cared to propose. Even after it was added permanently to the growing list of standing committees in 1880, its potentialities as an agency of unified and centralized control of House business were not immediately realized. In the next thirty years, however, successive rulings of the speaker and orders of the House invested it with prerogatives of little less than dictatorial character. Consisting, until 1910, of the speaker and two majority and two minority members appointed by him, it was, of course, dominated by the three majority representatives—actually by the speaker himself; and it was this arrangement in particular that enabled the vigorous and picturesque Cannon to determine almost single-handedly what might and what might not be considered by the House and therefore to wield almost absolute control over all important legislation.[3] The speaker's removal from membership in the committee, the

---

[1] For a fuller statement of the pros and cons of the question, see R. Young, *This Is Congress*, 108-114; and for a thoughtful defense of the seniority principle, J. K. Pollock, "The Seniority Rule in Congress," *No. Amer. Rev.*, CCXXII, 235-245 (Dec., 1925-Feb., 1926). The plan is followed in the Senate as in the House, and with the same advantages and disadvantages. An instance of its disadvantages, in Senate experience, was the elevation, in 1941, to the chairmanship of the committee on military affairs of a senator (Reynolds of North Carolina) who had opposed substantially every defense measure advocated by the Administration, supported by the bulk of his party, and adopted by broad bipartisan vote.

[2] See Chaps. xxv-xxvi below.

[3] Since two of the majority members counterbalanced the two minority members, Mr. Cannon was accustomed to say that the committee on rules consisted of "myself and one assistant."

transfer of the selection of its members to agencies of party caucuses, and the increase of these members to ten, later to twelve, still later (1937) to fourteen,[1] left the speaker with perceptibly diminished power, but did not of themselves lessen the control of the committee over the legislative work of the House. As we shall see, that control has in later days been cut down somewhat in actual practice by the rise of two new agencies of the majority caucus, the steering committee and the majority floor leader, with the result that, aside from the chairman, the members of the committee no longer rank, as they once did, among the dominant personalities of the House. Inasmuch, however, as the rules committee is commonly the medium through which these guiding agencies achieve their objectives, the committee is still to be regarded as an instrumentality of considerable potency and importance.

To begin with, once the general body of rules has been readopted at the opening of a Congress, all proposals for amendment are referred to the rules committee, which is likely to hold up action in any event, but certain to do so if the changes suggested would tend to impair control of business by the majority "machine." More important, however, is the committee's power to present to the House, at almost any time, *special* rules or orders requested by the majority management and fixing the sequence in which pending measures shall be considered, or limiting the time allowed for debate on a given matter, or indicating the sections of a bill that may and those that may not be amended, or specifying the number and even the nature of permissible amendments, or in other ways vitally determining the conditions under which the work of the House in a given situation shall proceed;[2] and usually the regimented House majority votes whatever the committee proposes.[3] Specially privileged in obtaining the floor, the committee may at any time (except only when a conference committee's report is being considered or the House has voted to go into committee of the whole) interrupt debate by introducing a special rule thrusting forward some entirely different bill or resolution irrespective of the regular order of procedure. Insurgents now and then catch the majority managers napping, and succeed in getting a bill before the House contrary to the managers' intentions. But in such an emer-

How the committee functions [marginal note]

[1] Reduced again in January, 1945, to twelve (eight Democrats and four Republicans), and continued in the same form in the Eightieth Congress, organized in January, 1947, except with the party quotas reversed.

[2] For example, the special rule under which the tax bill of 1943 was considered in the House limited general debate to two days, after which no amendments were to be in order except such as might be offered by direction of the ways and means committee, and such amendments being themselves not amendable. Even more drastic was a "gag" rule under which, in 1940, debate on a complicated and abstruse excess profits tax bill (no copy of which was available to congressmen until the day before the rule was adopted) was restricted to two hours. In extenuation, it was explained that no congressman could have understood the measure anyway!

[3] The speaker, however, retains an important check on the committee, in that, if he desires, he can prompt some willing congressman to make a point of order against a rule to which he objects, and then sustain it, thereby stifling the rule before it can be adopted.

gency, the rules committee can always be hurriedly convened and a special order to meet the situation devised and reported, not only interrupting consideration of the rebel measure, but indefinitely sidetracking it in favor of other business. Furthermore, the committee may itself draft a bill overnight, introduce it in the House the next afternoon, and force its passage the same day, without opportunity for. so much as reference to a "subject" committee.[1] Small wonder that House minorities are all the time crying out against "gag rules"! Their only hope of relief, however, lies in transforming themselves into majorities—which, irrespective of party, could be depended upon, in their turn, to employ exactly the same tactics! Reliance on special rules as a means of expediting and controlling proceedings has in later years been growing steadily, and nowadays hardly any important legislation is enacted without the aid of them.[2]

Party Instrumentalities

The speaker and other officers, the committees and their chairmen— even the resourceful rules committee—are agencies of the House as such, designed to enable it to carry on business in an orderly and effective manner. This formal machinery, however, is only part of the actual organization employed in the day-to-day conduct of proceedings. There are also agencies which exist quite outside of the rules and on that account are sometimes termed the "invisible government" of the House—although their activities may be, and usually are, quite as open and "visible" as those of any regular officer or committee. Of such nature are chiefly the majority caucus (Republican congressmen prefer the term "conference"[3]) and certain instrumentalities through which it works, especially the steering committee, the floor leader, and the whip and his assistants. The minority has a caucus, too, a floor leader, whips, and even sometimes a steering committee, although naturally these are not ordinarily in a

---

[1] The rules committee is itself, of course, a "procedural" committee. In a recent instance, the committee even substituted another measure (the Case labor bill of 1946) for one that the regular labor committee had reported out for consideration.

[2] During the memorable special session of 1933, called by President Franklin D. Roosevelt to deal with the banking crisis, special orders emanating from the rules committee governed the consideration of all important matters by the House except in the case of certain emergency measures for which a procedure was invoked so direct and speedy that not even the rules committee had a chance to function. See *Amer. Polit. Sci. Rev.*, XXVIII, 70-83 (Feb., 1934), and cf., on an earlier period, *ibid.*, XXVI, 43-57 (Feb., 1930). In the first session of the Seventy-seventh Congress, opening January 3, 1941, the House broke all precedents in its use of special rules. Sixty-seven were introduced and voted on, all but three calling for immediate consideration of the measures to which they applied and limiting the time to be allowed for debate. Of the sixty-seven, fifty-eight were adopted. In the two succeeding sessions, the numbers of special rules introduced were forty-three (forty-one adopted) and forty-nine (forty adopted), respectively. In the first session of the Eightieth Congress (January 3-December 19, 1947), seventy special rules were introduced, and fifty-eight were adopted. Not all special rules requested by the majority managers are actually introduced, but the exceptions are few.

[3] The Democrats use this term also, but only to designate a caucus that does not seek to bind the participants to a given course of action. For purposes of simplicity, the traditional name "caucus" may, however, be adhered to in the present discussion.

position to have much to do with running the House at any particular time. The speaker is of the majority party, and the committees are dominated by members of that party as well. Nevertheless, as already indicated, they are agencies of the House as a whole. The informal, or so-called "invisible," agencies mentioned are, however, *party* agencies pure and simple—majority or minority as the case may be. Combined with the speaker and committees in their party aspects, these agencies, on the majority side, round out the machinery by which a given party at a given time controls and manages the House.

A caucus consists of the members of the House belonging to the majority or minority party as the case may be, and functioning either directly through privately held meetings or indirectly through agencies such as those mentioned above. From the fact that nowadays both parties convoke their caucuses far less frequently than formerly and leave decisions to be made more largely by a few leaders, it has been deduced that the caucus is no longer a significant factor in the legislative process; and certainly it is true that the device has waxed and waned through the years. The emphasis placed upon the point by some observers is, however, exaggerated. In the first place, the caucus still functions actively in organizing a new House of Representatives. It prepares the slate of officers (including the speaker) which a new House unfailingly elects. Through the medium of its "committee on committees," it designates the majority members (and the chairmen) of all standing committees, subject, of course, to House election. Directly or indirectly, it names the majority steering committee, floor leader, and whips. It considers whether changes in the rules of the House are desirable, and decides what ones, if any, to instigate the rules committee to propose for adoption. On its part, the minority caucus similarly nominates officers, makes committee assignments, and sets up "invisible" machinery; and any party crisis involving the members, or any necessity for significant changes of official or committee personnel during a session, may bring into action the caucus of the party concerned.[1]

In the second place, the caucus may be convoked (and occasionally is) to consider policies or measures and to formulate plans for united party action. In earlier days, both Republicans and Democrats made frequent use of such meetings, with the form and fate of much legislation virtually determined in them. The broad outlines of proposed or pending measures might be debated and decisions reached concerning them; the majority members of important committees might be directed to see that com-

1. The majority caucus or conference

---

[1] Thus when, in April, 1946, numerous Democratic members resented criticism directed against them from the office of the chairman of the party's national committee, Postmaster-General Hannegan, they convoked a meeting of the Democratic caucus to consider the matter. In the Senate (where party caucuses also prevail), a good illustration was afforded in February, 1944, when the Democratic floor leader, Alben W. Barkley, abruptly resigned in protest against criticisms of Congress voiced by President Roosevelt in vetoing a tax bill and a caucus reëlected him to the post by acclamation.

mittee reports were presented first to the majority caucus and only afterwards to the House as a whole; decisions might be reached upon what
measures to press, what ones to hold back, what ones to prevent from
ever being debated at all. For reasons not altogether clear, the caucus no
longer functions so actively in this way. Whereas, during the first administration of President Wilson the Democrats considered every important
measure in caucus, with obvious effect upon the remarkable legislative
record of that period, during their long tenure from 1933 to 1946 they
held almost no caucuses at all; [1] and the Republicans, although keeping
their "conference" more alive, have of late convoked meetings only very
irregularly. Even as a deliberative device, the caucus is not, however,
dead. Rather, it stands silently in the background always capable of
being called into action; and if a handful of managers seem to be running
the party's affairs in the House and making its decisions for it, closer
examination will show that they, after all, serve only as caucus agents
and presumably spokesmen.

2. The steering committee   Two principal instrumentalities through which the caucus, whether
majority or minority, operates are the "steering committee" and the floor
leader. With the Republicans in control of the House at the date of
writing (1947), the majority steering committee consisted of ten members
selected by the Republican committee on committees, the eight Republican members of the committee on rules, and four other members serving
ex officio—a total of twenty-two, and with the floor leader as chairman.
At the same time, the minority steering committee contained the minority
leader, the caucus chairman, and one representative from each of fifteen
districts into which for Democratic purposes the country is divided—a
total of seventeen. Strictly unofficial, working behind the scenes, and not
formalized even to the extent of having printed stationery, the Republican committee, as in effect an executive committee of the majority
conference, keeps the parliamentary situation in hand, whips faltering
members into line, and in sundry ways sees that the will of the majority—
perchance of the conference if it has expressed itself—is carried out.
Including as it does the majority members of the powerful rules committee, it selects from the great mass of bills encumbering the House
calendars those which the majority managers wish to advance to final
consideration, and, after these have been decided upon, utilizes the rules
committee in keeping the tracks clear for favorable action upon them.
Its busiest moments are likely to be in the last crowded days of a session.
When the Democrats were in control of the House after 1933, their
steering committee was almost as inactive as their caucus, seldom even
meeting. Everything was left to the leaders.

3. The majority floor leader   Acting under general direction of the steering committee, of which he
is chairman, the majority floor leader is almost equal in power to the
speaker, from whom, indeed, he has inherited some of his prerogatives,

[1] Except on matters relating to House organization.

and to whose office he may reasonably aspire to succeed.[1] He keeps informed on the drift of opinion among the majority members, persuades and admonishes in the interest of party harmony, plans the course of debate and indicates to the speaker what members are to be given the floor on particular measures, directs the activities of the whips, confers with the minority floor leader on the length to which debates shall be allowed to run and the times at which votes shall be taken, and convokes his party members in caucus or conference as need arises. If one were asked to indicate the two individuals wielding most power in House affairs, he would not go far wrong in naming the speaker and the majority floor leader.

The majority whip, if a Republican, is named by his party's committee on committees, and if a Democrat, by the majority floor leader; and he may appoint any number of assistant whips up to a dozen or more, commonly selected with a view to wide geographical distribution. A familiar duty of the whips is to see that the party members are at hand when significant votes are likely to be taken; but equally important is the canvassing of members to find out their attitudes on issues and policies, for the guidance of the floor leader and the speaker.

4. The whips

From all this it is obvious that a person who views House organization and procedure merely through the medium of official machinery and formal rules will gain only a very imperfect understanding of how the work of Congress is actually performed. Speaker, rules committee, other committees, function—not as agencies or authorities apart—but as cogs in a larger machine which includes also the extra-legal party instrumentalities mentioned. Back of all else stands the majority caucus, whether continuously active and assertive or intermittently dormant; because even the speaker owes his position to caucus selection and is expected to lend himself loyally, in so far as the rules give him leeway, to seeing that opportunity is provided for decisions made by the caucus, directly or by its agents, to be carried out. Even in its greatest periods of activity, the caucus, of course, does not concern itself with everything coming before the House; no more do its agents such as the steering committee. There is no point to stirring party machinery to action on the many pieces of business on which party lines will not be drawn.[2] Furthermore, in their present mood, most congressmen prefer to be free agents, voting as they please rather than under caucus or other directives; many indeed do not hesitate to identify themselves with bipartisan *blocs*, to which they indeed may regard themselves as owing first al-

The power of the party leadership

[1] As did Floor Leaders Byrns in 1935, Bankhead in 1936, Rayburn in 1940, and Martin in 1947.

[2] During the second session of the Seventy-ninth Congress (Jan. 14-Aug. 2, 1946), 900 of the 1,200 bills and resolutions passed by the House were passed under unanimous consent procedure after little or no discussion. Only 113 measures were debated to the extent of three or more pages of the *Congressional Record*. The record in the first session of the Eightieth Congress (January 3-December 19, 1947) was not materially different.

legiance. Recognizing this situation, the Republicans seldom attempt to bind their members even when a caucus is held and a line of action laid down; while the Democrats, although making caucus action on a question of policy or principle binding if supported by a two-thirds vote (provided the two-thirds constitutes a majority of the full Democratic membership of the House), nevertheless obligate no one on a question of constitutional construction or on a matter on which the member has received instructions from or made pledges to his constituents. Whether or not caucus action is involved, members of both parties are, however, in general, *expected* to support the decisions reached by their accepted party leadership in the House (whether approving of them or not), and habitual failure to do so can usually be depended upon to have unpleasant consequences.

The System Criticized

Needless to say, the power of the interlocking majority-party agencies enumerated—caucus, steering committee, floor leader, speaker, and chairmen of rules and other key committees—and the ways in which that power is sometimes employed stir much discontent. Stifling of individual initiative, penalizing of independence, relentless use of the "steam roller," drive spirited members to insurgency and inspire attempts to build up *blocs* cutting across caucuses and party lines. The simple fact is that, although the effective functioning of such a body as the House of Representatives imperatively demands leadership, no provision whatsoever for congressional leadership is made in the constitution or the laws. Under parliamentary systems of government, such as the English, legislative leadership devolves naturally upon the cabinet. But our government is not of that sort. To be sure, the president supplies a good deal of leadership on larger matters; certainly such chief executives as Woodrow Wilson and Franklin D. Roosevelt have done so.[1] The president, however, is at the White House, not on Capitol Hill, and such leadership as the House must have within its own ranks it has been obliged to develop for itself. This it has done according to no preconceived plan, but largely as the exigencies of party politics have determined. The results have been different in different periods. Once it was the speaker who dominated. Again (after the rules committee became elective), the speaker and that committee, sharing control. Still again, it was the majority caucus. Nowadays—as for a good while past—control is perhaps to be regarded as potentially in the caucus, but actual, practical leadership as being largely rather in the speaker, floor leader, and the chairmen of rules, ways and means, and other major committees—which, of course, means that it is considerably dispersed and not always easy to locate, although in any event gathered in the hands of an interlocking, majority, managerial

The need for leadership

---

[1] On presidential leadership in legislation, see Chap. XVIII below (especially pp. 378-380, 392-397).

directorate.[1] In all periods there has been dissatisfaction on the part of individuals and groups that have found themselves with less independence and power than they believed they ought to have; revolt against "dictatorship" has followed revolt, only—speaking broadly—with the result, at best, of transferring supreme control from one point in the system to another.

The present mechanisms of control do not, of course, lack apologists, and some of the arguments employed have a good deal of validity. There must, we are told, be not only routine rules and procedures, but people who will assert themselves as leaders, and means by which those who lead can get things done. To members whose policies and desires meet with frustration, such leaders will inevitably seem arbitrary and their methods harsh. But, once in power, these same members would most likely develop a leadership of precisely the same character. The system as it stands must therefore be regarded as reflecting the general will of the membership. At all events, a dissatisfied majority can change it at any time. An arbitrary speaker can be overruled, or even deposed, by a majority vote. Any special order brought in by the rules committee can be thrown out in the same way. Either this committee or any other one can be compelled to report upon any matters referred to it. Majority or minority could, if it chose, decide to have no caucus, no steering committee, no floor leader. Therefore, runs the argument, since the full mechanism, in both its official and unofficial—its legal and its extra-legal or party-made—aspects, goes on with little change from Congress to Congress, it must be regarded as fairly satisfactory to all save a few unreasonable members who are unable to adapt themselves to the ways of majorities.

Justification for the existing arrangements

The argument is plausible, yet it does not quite cover the case. The difficulty is that, upon analysis, the alleged majority may very well turn out to be no majority at all. A speaker, for example, mounts the tribune because a majority of a party majority has agreed to vote for him. But such a majority may easily fall short of being a majority of the whole House. Similarly, if polled individually, the bulk of the House membership well might, as suggested above, be found to prefer quite a different grouping, and quite different chairmen, in the great committees. By the same token, measures approved in caucus and voted on the floor because members of the majority party, even though really opposed to them, feel obligated, either by caucus actions or by other pressures, to give them

But what of majority rule?

---

[1] "The distribution of power in Congress is in many respects similar to the game of button, button, who has the button? One knows that someone has the button, but it is at times difficult to tell precisely where it is. The responsibility for action lies in many hands and in many groups. As soon as you think you know where the responsibility lies, where the button is, it is slipped to someone else. The internal organization of Congress is so involved and so complicated that very few men, and they specialists in the legislative process, know who are the individuals and the groups concerned with any specific piece of legislation...." R. Young, *This Is Congress* (New York, 1943), 81-82.

their support, may become law with the actual approval of what is numerically only a House minority. In other words, legislation tends to be only in form by House majority; in reality, it is often by mere *majority-caucus* majority.

Government by majority is, however, a tricky concept. We fondly suppose that we have it in this country, and at times we actually do so. Congressmen and senators, nevertheless, are often elected by mere pluralities; several of our presidents have had only a minority of the popular vote behind them; and decisions in Congress by something less than over-all majorities are merely part of an order of things which may be faulty but is capable of being corrected only by procedures too drastic to stand much chance of being undertaken.[1]

Organization of the Senate

Officers: the president

Crossing over to the opposite end of the Capitol, one finds in the Senate both a formal organization and a superimposed mechanism of party instrumentalities broadly resembling those in the House, yet in some respects working quite differently. To begin with, the officers are much the same, except that the "president" of the Senate occupies a position decidedly unlike that of the speaker of the House. Being, by terms of the constitution, the vice-president of the United States, he is, of course, not chosen by the body over which he presides; hence, partisan and factional contests over filling the chair, such as have punctuated the parliamentary history of the House, have no place in the annals of the Senate—save as occasionally stirred by election of a president *pro tempore* to preside when the president is absent or when the office is vacant.[2] Furthermore, the president of the Senate has no such control over legislative procedure as that which the speaker wields in the House; sometimes he is not even a member of the party having a majority in the chamber. As a moderator, he maintains decorum, recognizes members, decides points of order, puts questions to a vote, and announces the results. His power of recognition is, however, exercised with less partisan motivation than in the House; and not only are his decisions on points of order always subject to appeal to the Senate itself, but especially difficult questions of order are frequently put up to the body before being ruled on by the presiding officer at all. As a non-member, he never participates in debate and votes only when necessary to break a tie. Unless a person of unusual force, which he rarely has been, and also of high standing in

[1] For conveniently assembled current information on the machinery of the House and its workings, see articles by A. W. Macmahon, E. P. Herring, O. R. Altman, and F. M. Riddick, dealing with successive sessions and published yearly in the *American Political Science Review*. The *Official Congressional Directory* also is useful.

[2] Under a resolution of 1890, a president *pro tempore* serves until his successor is chosen. At the opening of the first session of the Seventy-second Congress (December, 1931), the Senate failed to elect. The incumbent, George H. Moses, therefore served throughout that Congress without reëlection.

the councils of his party, the figure ensconced in the Senate chair seldom seeks to exercise any sort of leadership or to influence the course of legislation.[1]

Like the House, the Senate has a set of formally adopted rules, carrying over from session to session except as changes are made at rather lengthy intervals. For reasons already explained, they do not have to be adopted *in toto* at the beginning of each Congress; and, reflecting the smaller numbers, the more intimate traditions, and the special functions of the body, Senate rules are fewer, simpler, and more easily mastered than those of the House [2]—likewise better fitted to protect the rights of minorities and promote free discussion.[3] There is, of course, in the Senate also no lack of parliamentary precedents, forming the basis for a rich endowment of unwritten custom or usage.

Rules

Needless to say, there are committees—special and conference committees as in the House, and fifteen standing committees, many of them corresponding closely to, and bearing the same names as, committees in the other branch.[4] Prior to 1946, the number of standing committees— thirty-three [5]—was relatively as excessive as in the House, and with the same disadvantages. The Legislative Reorganization Act which streamlined the House committee structure, however, performed the same service for the Senate; and beginning with the first session of the Eightieth Congress (organized in January, 1947), the list has been:

Committees

Agriculture and Forestry	Finance
Appropriations	Foreign Relations
Armed Services	Interstate and Foreign Commerce
Banking and Currency	Judiciary
Civil Service	Labor and Public Welfare
District of Columbia	Public Lands
Expenditures in the	Public Works
Executive Departments	Rules and Administration

[1] Vice-President Garner went directly from the speakership of the House to the presidency of the Senate in 1933, and although exerting a good deal of influence in a quiet and informal way, nevertheless accommodated himself successfully to the traditions of his new environment. Henry A. Wallace, when vice-president, was a prominent figure in wartime government circles, but the traditional sort of presiding officer in the Senate—except for the very unusual experience of breaking a tie vote no fewer than five times during his first eighteen months (on four occasions staving off defeat for the Administration). Harry S. Truman stepped immediately from a senatorial seat to the presiding officer's chair (January, 1945), but in three months became president of the United States through the death of Franklin D. Roosevelt. A president *pro tempore,* of course, remains a senator with full privileges and prerogatives.

[2] Even so, when the late Dwight W. Morrow—an expert in unraveling intricacies in other fields—was senator from New Jersey, he sadly confessed that after six months of faithful attendance on the floor he still was often unable to fathom the parliamentary situation of the moment.

[3] The Senate's rules will be found in *Senate Manual, Containing the Standing Rules, Orders, Laws, and Resolutions Affecting the Business of the United States Senate,* 80th Cong., 1st Sess., Sen. Doc. No. 11 (1947).

[4] In 1930, the Senate discontinued use of the committee of the whole except (unless decided otherwise) in considering treaties.

[5] Before a reorganization of 1921, the number had mounted to seventy-four.

Nearly all represent survivals, with in some cases broadened functions, from the committee list as existing before the reorganization; and in contrast with the former régime, under which committee memberships ranged from three to twenty-five, all (except in the single case of appropriations, with twenty-one members) are now fixed at thirteen. Much reshuffling was required when the new plan went into operation in 1947, but, once the scheme was instituted, it again became true, as theretofore, that, like the Senate itself, senatorial standing committees never die, new members being infused into them biennially, but the bulk of the membership always carrying over from the preceding Congress. Committee positions are divided between the two major parties in about the same proportion as in the House; [1] and, whereas formerly it was not unusual for a senator to serve on as many as five, or even more, committees, under the new plan he may not serve on more than two.[2]

How committees are made up

The method of making up committee lists in the Senate is practically the same as that prevailing in the House. At the opening of a new Congress, the leaders of each party appoint a "committee on committees" to distribute vacant positions among newcomers, to settle questions of seniority (for the seniority principle operates substantially as in the House), and, in the case of the majority party, to name the various chairmen. When these party agencies have completed their work, the slates are reported back to the respective caucuses for approval and afterwards go to the Senate as lists of majority and minority nominees. Election on the floor of the Senate usually follows on a single ballot, without hesitation or discussion.

Party instrumentalities

The Senate is, of course, hardly less responsive to considerations of party than is the House, and special party instrumentalities—caucuses or conferences, steering committees, whips—are scarcely less in evidence. Like the machinery known to the rules, these extra-legal agencies work, however, under limitations imposed by the differing nature and traditions of the smaller body. The House is a highly integrated mechanism, with power concentrated in few hands. Perhaps its numbers and its susceptibility to waves of emotion or passion require it to be so. The Senate is a relatively small conclave of older and more experienced men, with more marked individuality, more respect for tradition, and considerably less willingness to be herded and controlled. The presiding officer is, of course, in no position to dominate. The committee on rules—now "rules and administration"—is but a pale image of the rules committee of the House. Although choosing leaders and whips, and occasionally deciding upon a concerted course of action, a party caucus rarely amounts to more than a sort of informal conference; insurgents or irregulars often refuse

[1] In the Eightieth Congress, commonly either eight Republicans and five Democrats or seven Republicans and six Democrats.
[2] Three in the case of majority members of the committees on District of Columbia and expenditures in the executive departments. The complete list of committee assignments will be found in successive issues of the *Official Congressional Directory*.

to go into caucus at all. In short, senators insist upon maintaining their own individuality and upon delegating control to no committee or other agency. Proceedings are leisurely; debate is most of the time practically unrestricted; coercive force is virtually unknown.

REFERENCES

G. B. Galloway, *Congress at the Crossroads* (New York, 1946), Chap. IV.

J. P. Chamberlain, *Legislative Processes: National and State* (New York, 1936), Chap. V.

W. F. Willoughby, *Principles of Legislative Organization and Administration* (Washington, D. C., 1934), Chaps. XXI-XXV, XXXII-XXXIII.

F. M. Riddick, *Congressional Procedure* (Boston, 1941), Chaps. I-VII.

D. S. Alexander, *History and Procedure of the House of Representatives* (Boston, 1916), Chaps. II-VII, X, XII.

S. W. McCall, *The Business of Congress* (New York, 1911), Chaps. II, III, VIII, X.

E. Kefauver and J. Levin, *A Twentieth-Century Congress* (New York, 1947), 114-142.

M. P. Follett, *The Speaker of the House of Representatives* (New York, 1904).

C. W. Chiu, *The Speaker of the House of Representatives Since 1896* (New York, 1928).

G. H. Haynes, *The Senate of the United States; Its History and Practice* (Boston, 1938), I, Chaps. V-VII.

R. Luce, *Congress—An Explanation* (Cambridge, Mass., 1926), Chap. IV.

————, *Legislative Procedure* (Boston, 1922).

————, *Legislative Assemblies* (Boston, 1924).

————, *Legislative Problems* (Boston, 1935).

P. D. Hasbrouck, *Party Government in the House of Representatives* (New York, 1927).

A. C. Hinds, "The Speaker of the House of Representatives," *Amer. Polit. Sci. Rev.*, III, 155-167 (May, 1909).

C. R. Atkinson and C. A. Beard, "The Syndication of the Speakership," *Polit. Sci. Quar.*, XXVI, 381-414 (Sept., 1911).

J. G. Cannon, "Powers of the Speaker," *Century Mag.*, LXXVIII, 306-312 (June, 1909).

L. W. Busbey, *Uncle Joe Cannon* (New York, 1927). An autobiography recorded by a private secretary.

S. W. McCall, *Life of Thomas B. Reed* (Boston, 1914).

W. A. Robinson, *Thomas B. Reed, Parliamentarian* (New York, 1930).

L. G. McConachie, *Congressional Committees* (New York, 1898).

B. L. French, "Sub-Committees of Congress," *Amer. Polit. Sci. Rev.*, IX, 68-92 (Feb., 1915).

E. E. Denison, *The Senate Foreign Relations Committee* (Stanford University, 1942).

A. C. F. Westphal, *The House Committee on Foreign Affairs* (New York, 1942).

J. K. Pollock, "The Seniority Rule in Congress," *No. Amer. Rev.*, CCXXII, 235-245 (Dec., 1925-Feb., 1926).

Official Congressional Directory, previously cited.

CHAPTER XVI

THE POWERS AND FUNCTIONS OF CONGRESS—A GENERAL VIEW

We shall need to look more closely into the workings of the congressional machinery described, including the relations between Congress and other branches of the government. Before doing this, however, it will be useful to get an over-all picture of the functions falling to one house or both to perform. To be sure, Congress is commonly thought of as our national lawmaking agency; and such, indeed, it is.[1] But the enactment of legislation is only one of its many tasks, and not always the one making heaviest demands upon its time and energy. No fewer, indeed, than seven principal forms of activity occupy one house or both from time to time: (1) constituent, *i.e.*, having to do with constitutional revision, (2) electoral, (3) executive, (4) judicial, (5) directive and supervisory, (6) investigative, and (7) legislative—an enumeration which of itself is sufficient to indicate that, although established with a view to a separation of powers, Congress, like the presidency, deviates from that principle widely and often in its actual functions and workings.

Non-Legislative Functions

1. Constituent

Some of the functions mentioned are dealt with fully enough at other points in this book, and are cited here only in order that the total range of congressional activities be not lost to view. When considering the method of amending the national constitution, we saw that, while Congress cannot under any circumstances independently make a change in the fundamental written law, not a syllable of that document can be altered without congressional action in some form.[2] When viewing the mode of electing the president and vice-president, we saw that Congress

2. Electoral

acts as a board to canvass the electoral vote and declare the results; and that, in the event of failure of an electoral majority, the House of Representatives chooses the president and the Senate the vice-president.[3] When discussing the executive functions of appointment and treaty-making,

3. Executive

we presently shall observe how they are shared by the president with the Senate.[4]

---

[1] Not, however, our *only* such authority, notwithstanding what Art. I, § 1, of the constitution seems to say; for treaties and executive agreements have the force of law, judicial decisions declare law and in doing so may in effect make it, and rules and regulations laid down by the president, heads of departments, and administrative bodies are in effect laws and are treated by the courts as such if made in pursuance of authority validly "delegated" by Congress. See pp. 343-346 below.

[2] See p. 41 above.

[3] See pp. 275-277 above.

[4] See pp. 451-454, 786-787 below.

The remaining four major functions enumerated, *i.e.*, judicial, directive and supervisory, investigative, and legislative, call for some attention here.

The constitution endowed the president and Senate with broad powers of appointment; and in practice a general power of removal soon developed in the hands of the president and of appointing officers responsible to him. But how could an unfit official be got rid of if the appointing officer failed to act? How could the president himself, in case of abuse of power or other official delinquency, be put out of office before the end of his elective term?

4. Judicial

The answer lay within easy reach in the historic device of impeachment; and with little division of opinion, the constitution's makers wrote into the document the well-known provision that "the president, vice-president, and all civil officers of the United States shall be removed from office on impeachment for, and conviction of, treason, bribery, or other high crimes and misdemeanors." [1] Two points in this clause are especially to be noted. First, only civil officers are subject to impeachment: military and naval officers are liable to trial by court-martial, but cannot be impeached; and members of the legislative branch, although "civil," are construed not to be "officers" in the meaning of the impeachment provision.[2] Second, the grounds on which impeachment proceedings (more or less equivalent to indictment by grand jury) can be brought are specified—as definitely, perhaps, as is feasible. Bribery is self-explanatory, and treason is defined by the constitution.[3] "High crimes and misdemeanors" is a flexible phrase, but commonly construed to include only offenses of a grave nature involving something more than mere incompetence or partisanship.

Impeachment

The process of impeachment starts in the House of Representatives, where, upon charges being preferred against a given official, a committee is appointed to investigate. The committee reports to the House; and if, upon consideration of the findings, the majority so votes, the charges, in the form of "articles of impeachment," are sent to the Senate (which has no option but to hear the case); at the same time a committee of "managers" is named by the House to conduct the trial. The Senate furnishes the accused with a copy of the charges against him, fixes a date for the trial to begin, and when the time arrives converts itself into a court under the chairmanship of its regular presiding officer, unless the president of the United States is on trial, in which event—and because

Impeachment procedure

---

[1] Art. II, § 4. Provisions for the impeachment of state officers likewise found their way into most state constitutions.

[2] The unsuccessful attempt to impeach Senator William Blount of Tennessee, in 1798, is the only instance on record of any effort to impeach a member of Congress. After the House had brought charges against Blount, on the ground that he had participated in a conspiracy to stir up trouble in Florida and Louisiana (at that time belonging to Spain), the Senate expelled him and then declared him exempt from impeachment and dismissed the charges for want of jurisdiction.

[3] Art. III, § 3, cl. 1.

the vice-president would have a personal interest in the outcome—the chair is occupied by the chief justice of the United States.[1] The accused is allowed counsel, and he may appear and give testimony in person; and witnesses for and against him are brought in and questioned. At the close of the proceedings, which may last through many weeks, the galleries are cleared and the Senate votes. A two-thirds vote is necessary to convict; anything less results in acquittal. The penalty in case of conviction is removal from office, to which may be added disqualification for ever holding "any office of honor, trust, or profit under the United States;" and the president's power of pardon and reprieve does not apply. Once retired to private life, furthermore, the convicted person, if he has committed an indictable offense, may be proceeded against in the ordinary courts like any other offender.

Past impeachment cases   In the entire history of the country, impeachment proceedings have been brought against only twelve federal officers, mainly judges; and only four have been convicted and removed from office.[2] On charges based chiefly upon open violations of a Tenure of Office Act, passed over his veto in 1867 (and later held unconstitutional), President Johnson came within one vote of being convicted in 1868. The only cabinet member impeached was also acquitted. All of the four officers actually convicted belonged to the judiciary; three were district judges, and one, tried in 1913, was a judge of a special Commerce Court which no longer exists.

5. Directive and supervisory   Another congressional function, and one which people sometimes confuse with lawmaking in the proper sense, is that of direction and supervision. Acting directly, or by delegating authority to the president to act for it, Congress creates administrative agencies and services, fixes their powers and functions, and to some extent regulates their procedures; and while, once they have been established, funds for maintaining them are requested by the president, on the basis of estimates approved by the Bureau of the Budget, Congress alone can make the appropriations necessary to their existence and operations. When considering such appropriations, it can scrutinize and criticize the work of any agency, and, if it chooses, curtail its activities or even, in effect, abolish it by leaving it without funds.[3] At any time, too, it can direct that certain

[1] A plan for removal of high federal officers, including judges, through a special court, such as Congress would have power to establish, is advocated in E. L. Bennett, "A Court of Qualifications as a Forum of Removals and Retirements," *Amer. Polit. Sci. Rev.*, XXXIII, 47-52 (Feb., 1939).

[2] The cases involving judges are listed on p. 552 below; the others involved Senator William Blount (1798), President Andrew Johnson (1868), and Secretary of War William W. Belknap (1876). Secretary Belknap sought to evade impeachment proceedings by resigning his office, but the Senate was not deterred from hearing his case.

[3] It was in this way, for example, that two notable depression-time agencies—the Civilian Conservative Corps and the National Youth Administration—were brought to an end in 1943 and 1944, respectively; also the National Resources Planning Board in 1943.

The Legislative Reorganization Act of 1946 (see p. 411 below) expressly charges all

things be done, or impose entirely new duties; and at any time it can institute inquiries into the policies, actions, and procedures of offices, bureaus, or other establishments, through the medium of investigating committees which, serving somewhat after the manner of grand juries, have on various occasions been instrumental in exposing inefficiency or corruption, and sometimes have brought about remedial action. Not only in connection with such investigations, but at other times, Congress can call upon administrative establishments for information and reports, to be transmitted either directly or through the president; and its relations with the great regulatory commissions like the Interstate Commerce Commission and the Federal Trade Commission are especially close. In establishing agencies, defining their functions, and making rules governing their activities, Congress employs the same machinery and procedures as when enacting measures having the character of law. In doing these things, it is, however, not making law, but only taking actions involved in running the government, somewhat as a board of directors acts in running a great business establishment; and attending to matters of this sort absorbs a surprisingly large amount of the time and energy of the two houses.

The investigative function may properly receive a further word of comment; for, although resting only upon implied power, it has attained an importance approaching that of the control of finance, and indeed of legislation itself. Its development in connection with administration is to be explained largely by our form of government. Under a cabinet system like the English, the heads of departments and other ministers sit in the legislature and are always available for questioning and eliciting information. With us, legislature (in this case Congress) and administration are far more separate; and while much information is forthcoming through the normal channels of reports and of appearance of administrative officials before regular congressional committees, there remain gaps which frequently can be filled only by systematic investigations carried on by special committees authorized by resolution and provided with necessary funds—although it is not to be forgotten that investigations may be, and often are, carried on also by subcommittees of the regular standing committees.[1] A proper function of a representative assembly is to watch and control the government and throw the light of publicity upon its acts; and under our system, legislative investigations become a major technique for holding the executive and administrative agencies to

6. Investigative

House and Senate standing committees with exercising continual vigilance over the execution of any and all laws falling within their respective jurisdictions. In unusual cases, the two houses may set up a joint committee to perform this function, as was done with respect to the Labor-Management Relations [Taft-Hartley] Act of 1947. See p. 743, note 3, below.

[1] Not all investigations of administrative agencies, furthermore, are animated by suspicion or hostility. Some (especially if sponsored by a friendly Congress) are intended to vindicate or otherwise support, rather than to harass or embarrass, the agencies affected.

strict accountability.[1] Over the years, the War Department has been investigated most frequently, but the Treasury Department, the Interior Department, and other departments, divisions, and independent establishments have had their share of attention.

Congressional investigating committees are set up, however, not only to probe into the workings of administration. Of the more than five hundred, in all, created at one time or another between 1789 and 1946, many—especially in later years—have been charged with inquiring into lobbying, expenditures in campaigns, immigration, industrial relations, the manufacture and sale of munitions, the operation of stock exchanges, the conservation of wild animal life, the interests of small business, postwar economic policy and planning, and what not. In early times, most investigating committees, of whatsoever sort, were House committees; in later years, the larger proportion have been Senate committees;[2] some two dozen have been joint committees; and several notable ones, e.g., the Industrial Relations Commission of 1912, the Commission on Law Observance and Enforcement of 1931, and the Temporary National Economic Committee of 1938 (eventually producing some sixty volumes of hearings and monographs, besides more than thirty research reports) have included not only representatives of both branches of Congress, but members (usually appointed by the president) representing the executive branch or even the general public. Investigations may, of course, be animated by personal or partisan motives. As a rule, however, they are conducted on a loftier plane: many are honestly aimed at bringing to light the full facts about some government activity or some national problem or experience; many, at securing information for the intelligent drafting of laws, at shaping general governmental policy, or even at molding public opinion. Some prove futile; some, prejudiced and abusive; but from many flow important remedial actions.[3]

Persons from whom information or testimony is sought are not always disposed to coöperate. Gradually, however—and with full backing from the courts—Congress has assumed authority to employ compulsion;[4] so that nowadays any duly constituted investigating committee has ample power not only to subpoena witnesses and administer oaths, but to require the production of books, papers, correspondence, contracts, and

[1] In 1927, a Supreme Court decision held the power of investigation to be "an essential corollary of the legislative function." McGrain v. Daugherty, 273 U. S. 135.
[2] In the past decade, however, the House has resumed considerable activity, as illustrated by an extensive investigation of the National Labor Relations Board completed in 1940 and by a protracted inquiry into subversive influences (in government circles and outside) carried on by the Dies committee to investigate un-American activities—converted in 1945 into the present standing committee of the House on that subject. Cf. A. R. Ogden, *The Dies Committee* (2nd ed., Washington, D. C., 1945).
[3] As passed in the Senate, the Legislative Reorganization Act of 1946 confined future congressional investigations to regular committees; but the House did not agree.
[4] As early as 1821, the Supreme Court upheld the power of Congress to punish for contempt. Anderson v. Dunn, 6 Wheaton 204.

records deemed relevant to any inquiry, and, if necessary, to invoke judicial aid in securing them.[1]

The Legislative Function—Basis and Scope

But, after all, Congress is primarily a legislature; and from here on, in this chapter and the succeeding one, it will be considered in that aspect. To it, indeed, the constitution assigns "all legislative powers herein granted." [2] Two or three things, however, are to be observed at the outset. The first is the significant qualifying effect of the last two words, "herein granted." As has been emphasized so many times, our national government is a government of limited, enumerated powers; and the principle holds for Congress no less than for every other part of the establishment. Not only do the House and Senate have no power not expressly delegated, or legitimately implied in some express delegation, but the section of the constitution (Art. I, § 8) conferring a lengthy list of powers is balanced off with a section immediately following in which numerous powers are just as definitely denied—in addition to which many prohibitions are laid down in the earlier amendments and at other points in the document.

A primary function —but not unlimited

Fundamental, indeed, to our system is the fact that Congress has not full and unrestricted legislative power, like the British Parliament, but only the legislative power *herein granted.* In other words, every exercise of legislative power by Congress must be based upon some authorization in the constitution. When, therefore, legislation is proposed or demanded, its advocates must be able to point to some clause (or clauses) of the constitution which, either expressly or by fair implication, grants the necessary authority. If, on their part, opponents can show that constitutional sanction is lacking, or at least can point to Supreme Court decisions so indicating, it will probably be useless to enact a proposed measure; for, once a test case is brought, the Supreme Court—the final

---

[1] So great was the wartime impetus to congressional investigations that in 1944 the Senate had twenty special committees of inquiry at work and the House thirty-one, often duplicating each other's efforts or otherwise poorly coördinated. Most useful among the number were a Senate Committee to Investigate National Defense, headed by Senator (now President) Harry S. Truman—later known as the Mead-Kilgore Committee—and a House Committee on National Defense Migration, headed by Representative John H. Tolan, both credited with much constructive work in behalf of efficient preparation for and conduct of the war. Important later investigations included those carried on by a Joint Committee on Investigation of the Pearl Harbor Attack (with hearings filling thirty-nine volumes aggregating 25,000 pages) and a Joint Committee on the Organization of Congress, whose findings eventuated in the Legislative Reorganization Act of 1946 (see pp. 411-415 below). In addition to standard works on the general subject listed on p. 346 below, the following discussions are pertinent: D. Lynch, *The Concentration of Economic Power* (New York, 1946), Appendix on "The Rôle of Congressional Investigations;" M. N. McGeary, "Congressional Investigations During Franklin D. Roosevelt's First Term," *Amer. Polit. Sci. Rev.,* XXXI, 680-695 (Aug., 1937); and L. W. Koenig, *The Presidency and the Crisis* (New York, 1944), Chap. v, dealing with congressional investigations during the recent war. Cf. W. McCune and J. S. Beale, "The Job That Made Truman President," *Harper's Mag.,* CXC, 616-621 (June, 1945).

[2] Art. I, § 1.

judge of congressional powers—will almost certainly rule that Congress has exceeded its constitutional authority. This restricted scope of congressional power easily explains why debates on the constitutionality of proposed laws occupy so much time and attract such wide attention in connection with congressional proceedings.

In the second place, notwithstanding what seems to be the explicit assertion of the constitution, Congress does not actually possess *the whole* of such national legislative power as there is. In a chapter soon to follow,[1] we shall see how the president, by equally explicit constitutional provision, shares in the work of lawmaking, and indeed often takes a leading part in it. We have already seen, too, how the courts, in their task of construing and applying the laws, often necessarily bend and amplify them, in effect adding to, and actually making, law. We shall find, also, that not only treaties and executive agreements but also rules and regulations laid down by the president, or even by heads of departments and by administrative officers or bodies, are in effect laws and, as indicated above, are treated by the courts as such if made in pursuance of authority validly conferred by Congress.[2]

Express grants The situation, in a nutshell, regarding the scope of congressional legislative power is that (a) such power is defined positively by numerous express grants, (b) it is defined negatively by almost equally numerous express prohibitions, and (c) between these two fields lies a broad, ill-defined, disputed domain of implied and resulting powers. Upon many matters there can be no question as to general congressional power (however much there may be as to practical applications of such power), because power has been conferred in definite and unmistakable terms. In this connection, one has only to recall the long list of subjects already referred to as enumerated chiefly in the eighth section of Article I, including taxation, borrowing, currency, patents, copyright, bankruptcy, postal service, naturalization, the regulation of foreign and interstate commerce, the maintenance of an army and navy, and the declaring of war. As already suggested, however, express grants hardly go farther than to make it clear that Congress has authority over the specific subjects enumerated; a swarm of questions will commonly arise as to how a given power is to be exercised, what are its limits, and the like. And when one encounters a grant of such obviously indefinite scope as that of providing for the "general welfare" of the United States,[3] he will not be surprised to find differing interpretations which, in the case mentioned, produce wide rifts among our best authorities on constitutional law. Express grants are a great help in determining what the powers of Congress, and of the government generally, are; but they also become points of departure for argument and conflict.

---

[1] Chap. XVIII below.
[2] See pp. 460-462 below.
[3] Art. I, § 8, cl. 1.

Most of the powers expressly conferred upon Congress are permissive; that is to say, the two houses are constitutionally free to exercise them or not, in whole or in part—however necessary in practical fact it may be to make use of certain of them, *e.g.*, taxation. Some grants, however, are mandatory. For example, it is made the duty of Congress to call a convention of the states to amend the constitution whenever the legislatures of two-thirds of the states so request;[1] likewise to provide for taking the census every ten years,[2] to reapportion seats in the House of Representatives after each census,[3] and to make regulations for carrying appeals from the lower courts to the Supreme Court.[4] In no instance of the kind, however, is there any way in which Congress can be compelled to act if it fails to obey the constitutional mandate—as indeed it did fail to reapportion the House of Representatives after the census of 1920. The courts will not intervene, for manifestly they would have no means of exercising any compulsion. The sole remedy lies with the electorate, and consists in choosing congressional majorities prepared to observe the constitution's requirements.[5]

Permissive and mandatory powers

When there are express grants or express restrictions, the authority of Congress to legislate on a given subject, or its lack of power to do so, is likely to be sufficiently clear. On many subjects, however, the authority, if possessed at all, must be derived by implication or inference from some of the powers granted in express terms. That legislative power may legitimately be derived in this manner, the constitution itself practically asserts in the "implied powers" clause, which gives Congress authority to "make all laws which shall be necessary and proper for carrying into execution" the powers expressly vested by the constitution in Congress or in any other branch of the government.[6] Likewise, five of the last nine amendments expressly state that Congress shall have power to enforce them by "appropriate legislation." Sharp differences of opinion over what measures may, and what ones may not, fairly be deemed "necessary and proper," or "appropriate," for carrying into effect the delegated powers of the national government have made the powers of Congress "the great battleground of the constitution." The Supreme Court, however, early adopted a liberal interpretation of the clauses involved, to the general effect that if it can be shown that Congress has been given authority to deal with any specific subject, the two houses, in exercising that authority, are free to select any means or instrumentalities whatsoever which are not prohibited by the constitution, are appropriate, and are consistent

Implied powers

---

[1] Art. V.

[2] Art. I, § 2, cl. 3.

[3] *Ibid.*

[4] Art. III, § 2, cl. 2.

[5] It may be observed in this connection that, like other legislative bodies, Congress can pass no irrepealable act. Any measure put on the statute-book by one Congress is legally subject to abrogation, or to any degree of amendment, by any subsequent Congress.

[6] Art. I, § 8, cl. 18.

with the spirit as well as the letter of that instrument.[1] Furthermore, whether a given law is "necessary," within the meaning of the constitution, is a "political" question for Congress alone to answer; the courts will not rule upon it.[2]

Resulting powers

The scope of congressional authority has been considerably widened, too, by decisions of the Supreme Court to the effect that it is not necessary for Congress to trace back every one of its powers to some single grant of authority, direct or implied, but that such authority may be deduced from a number of the specified powers taken collectively, or from all of them combined.[3] Powers derived in this way are commonly called "resulting powers." The criminal code of the United States affords a good illustration. The constitution gives the national government express power to punish only five kinds of crime. Congress, however, unquestionably has power to provide for punishing the violation of any national law and for safeguarding the constitutional rights of persons under accusation, even though the authority exercised in a particular case is neither expressly granted nor inferable from any single express grant in the constitution.

So-called "emergency powers"

In enacting a good deal of the legislation aimed at overcoming the depression of the thirties, and also legislation during the two world wars, Congress was often represented as making use of its "emergency powers;" and the impression was thus conveyed that the constitution confers some special class of powers designed to be invoked by Congress only in time of great national stress. The fact is, however, that Congress has no power or group of powers labeled "emergency powers." To be sure, there has been more than one great national emergency in our history; and the existence of such has been recognized officially by both president and Congress, as also by the courts. Nor can there be any denying that in times of economic and international crisis Congress has enacted laws which it would not have passed under ordinary circumstances. Neverthe-

---

[1] This was the purport, and in part the language, of Chief Justice Marshall's classic statement in McCulloch v. Maryland (1819). See pp. 68-69 above.

[2] In recent years, the phrase "federal police power" has come into common use; and in this connection it calls for a word of explanation. The police power in general has been defined as the power to restrict the rights of liberty and property in the interest of the public health, safety, morals, or general welfare. No such broad power is conferred upon Congress in the constitution, and the most common instances of its exercise are found in state legislation and municipal ordinances. Such police powers as Congress may be said to have are legally only special or peculiar forms of some express or implied power in which the protection of the public health, morals, safety, or general welfare is prominently involved. But in practice they are very great, the sources from which they spring being principally the power to lay taxes, to appropriate money, to establish post-offices and postroads, and to regulate interstate and foreign commerce. Illustrations of police authority emanating from the last-mentioned source are afforded by the Fair Labor Standards Act of 1938 regulating wages, hours, and child labor, a variety of meat inspection and pure food and drugs laws, the Mann white-slave act, the anti-crime acts of 1934, and the Social Security Act of 1935. See W. W. Willoughby, *Constitutional Law of the United States* (2nd ed.), II, Chaps. XLI, XLIV; R. E. Cushman, *Studies in the Police Power of the National Government* (Minneapolis, 1920).

[3] Cohens v. Virginia, 6 Wheaton 264 (1821).

less, as the Supreme Court has definitely said, "emergency does not create power;" nor does it increase power already granted in the constitution; nor does it diminish the restrictions imposed upon the exercise of power.[1] At most, an emergency may merely require new applications of powers already in use, or bring into play powers never before, or at all events only rarely, used. The constitutional basis for what are popularly called emergency powers must, therefore, be sought among the clearly granted powers; and it is to be found chiefly in the power to regulate foreign and interstate commerce and the currency, in the power to tax, to borrow, and to appropriate money, and in the power to provide for the national defense. In stimulating national recovery after 1932, and in promoting national defense after 1940, Congress invoked and applied these basic powers in many novel ways, creating a popular illusion—but only an illusion—that some special reservoir of "emergency powers" had been tapped.

The mere fact that Congress has been invested with authority to legislate upon a given subject does not necessarily mean that the states are thereby deprived of the right to legislate upon the same subject. Naturally, in all instances where the power has been expressly prohibited to the states, as, for example, with respect to coining money and laying duties on imports, Congress alone may legislate; and in such instances its power is said to be exclusive. These are instances, too, in which, even without any express prohibition upon the states, a power by its very nature, belongs exclusively (or almost so) to Congress, e.g., the regulation of interstate and foreign commerce.[2] But in practically all matters which do not fall within the two categories indicated, Congress and the state legislatures are said to have concurrent power; so that acts of Congress and state statutes relating to the same subject may be in full force at the same time. Thus, there may be both national and state control over congressional elections; and both Congress and the states may levy taxes on the same property or incomes. The term "concurrent power" covers also certain powers which may be exercised by a state only until Congress exercises the same power. On bankruptcy, for example, every state originally was at liberty to make its own laws; and such laws had full force and effect until Congress (in 1898) chose to exercise its own right to legislate on the subject. Once Congress had acted, any "concurrent" state bankruptcy laws, even though not formally repealed, fell into a state of suspended animation. *Exclusive and concurrent powers*

One further aspect of congressional legislative power hinges upon an interesting question: must Congress exercise its legislative authority *Delegation of legislative power*

[1] Home Building & Loan Assoc. v. Blaisdell, 290 U. S. 398 (1934). Cf. J. P. Clark, "Emergencies and the Law," *Polit. Sci. Quar.*, XLIX, 268-283 (June, 1934).

[2] Regulation of the naturalization of aliens, originally regarded as a concurrent power, was placed by the Supreme Court, in Chirac v. Chirac (2 Wheaton 259), in 1817, in the category of exclusive national powers—even though state as well as federal courts are still employed in naturalization work.

exclusively by its own direct action, or may it hand over portions of such authority to be exercised by the president, an executive department, a board or commission, or some other branch or agency of the government? The query is an old one, and the constitutionality of many a federal statute has hung upon the way in which the Supreme Court, at a given time, has answered it. On the one hand, the constitution, as we have seen, vests in Congress "all legislative powers herein granted"—which might seem to set up a presumption against any right to "farm out," or delegate, any powers of the kind. On the other hand, such delegation is nowhere prohibited; and the "sweeping," or "implied powers" clause, authorizing Congress to make all laws "necessary and proper for carrying into operation" powers vested in Congress or in any department or office of the government, might be construed to open a way for Congress to decide that the most effective use that it could make of some of its powers would be to delegate the exercise of them to the president or, through him, to some regulative or administrative agency. The latter is the view that has commonly prevailed; and the Supreme Court has sustained many delegations of the kind.

Illustrations

When, sixty years ago, it was proposed to vest in an expert independent commission the regulation of railway freight and passenger rates in interstate commerce, it was objected that this would be an unconstitutional delegation of legislative power. Nevertheless, Congress, convinced of the impossibility of dealing satisfactorily with such complicated matters by direct and detailed legislation, passed the Interstate Commerce Act of 1887, simply prescribing that all rates and services should be reasonable, and then delegating to the new Interstate Commerce Commission the duty of determining the reasonableness or unreasonableness of rates in specific cases.[1] For similar reasons, powers of like nature have been conferred upon the Federal Trade Commission, the Federal Communications Commission, and a long list of other regulative bodies, as well as also upon departments or establishments therein.[2] The president, too, has been the direct beneficiary of many such delegations, as when, in 1934 (with later renewals), he was given authority to conclude trade agreements with foreign states altering tariff rates by as much as fifty per cent, thereby operating in a field, i.e., tariff-making, traditionally regarded as of a legislative nature. Numerous as such delegations are in ordinary peacetime, too, they become vastly more imposing in time of war, when to the chief executive's manifest authority as executive and as commander-in-chief must invariably be added many and great powers

[1] See pp. 630-633 below. Eventually the Commission's powers were extended to include actually fixing rates.

[2] During the recent period of price control, the Office of Price Administration furnished another good example. Congress could not itself fix and readjust exact prices, any more than railway rates. What it did was rather to enact an underlying statute —the Emergency Price Control Act of January, 1942—providing for price regulation, and requiring prices to be "fair and equitable," but leaving determination of specific price levels to the administrative body set up for the purpose.

essential to unified and effective direction of the war effort—powers, furthermore, which Congress alone is competent to confer. In World Wars I and II, Presidents Wilson and Roosevelt, respectively, attained their lofty pinnacles of authority largely by virtue of powers bestowed (usually for limited periods) by Congress.[1]

In upholding such delegations, however, the Supreme Court has insisted upon a restrictive and significant distinction: powers, it has said, that involve merely making detailed applications of law (in other words, decisions and acts properly to be regarded as administrative) may be delegated; powers involving the general determination of policy (in other words, true acts of legislation) may not.[2] It is of the essence of legislation to lay down the rules, fix the standards, or specify the conditions by which those in charge of administration shall be guided; and these things only Congress is constitutionally competent to do. But after Congress has prescribed the general framework of regulations within which railroad rates, for example, shall be determined, it is proper enough (and indeed quite necessary) for it to pass on to a more specialized agency (in this case the Interstate Commerce Commission) the task of approving, or even fixing, the exact rate on a ton of steel shipped from Pittsburgh to New York—though, of course, any power so delegated can be modified or even withdrawn at any time.[3] It was this distinction between delegation of basic legislative authority and delegation of supplementary administrative authority—or rather the failure to recognize the distinction—that brought to grief much of the legislation associated with the earlier stages of the New Deal. Various "recovery" laws of 1933-34 undertook to confer upon the executive a sort of "roving commission" to make laws in the form of codes and regulations for trade and industry, but in doing so, failed to set up definite standards, or "yard-sticks," to govern in exercising the powers bestowed. As a consequence, the Supreme Court, in case after case, overthrew the legislation.[4] As differently constituted in these more recent years, the Court undoubtedly would view similar measures more tolerantly. Indeed when,

Marginal note: Limitations upon delegation

---

[1] Congress, in a given situation, may have virtually no alternative to making a given delegation, yet may have misgivings about it; and, as indicated elsewhere, during the recent war period it sometimes attached specifications opening a way for independent recall of delegated powers by concurrent resolution. See p. 381, note 3, below.

[2] It should be added in this connection that Congress may not delegate its essential legislative power to the states, as by authorizing them to regulate interstate commerce. Nor may Congress delegate its essential legislative function to the people, by authorizing them to make, through referenda, binding decisions upon matters of legislative policy. Congress might, however, authorize an *advisory* referendum, as an aid in ascertaining the wishes of the voters—although it has never done so. See W. W. Willoughby, *Constitutional Law of the United States* (2nd ed.), III, Chap. LXXXXIX.

[3] Withdrawn without reference to the president if the power has been granted subject to recall by concurrent resolution; otherwise, by means of an act of legislation subject to possible presidential veto.

[4] On the judicial decisions growing out of the recovery acts—especially the National Industrial Recovery Act of 1933—see pp. 658. 680 below.

in 1944, it sustained the Emergency Price Control Act mentioned above,[1] it was regarded as having taken a very significant step in liberalizing the nature and extent of the powers which may legitimately be delegated to the executive or to administrative agencies. The principle still holds that a delegation of power, to be upheld, must go no farther than to confer discretion in administering laws which themselves cover the essentially *legislative* aspects of the subjects with which they deal. But the content of the term "legislative" is now construed less strictly than it used to be.

REFERENCES

J. M. Mathews, *The American Constitutional System* (2nd ed., New York, 1940), Chap. IX.

W. W. Willoughby, *Constitutional Law of the United States* (2nd ed., New York, 1929), III, Chaps. LXXXV-LXXXVII.

A. W. Macmahon, "Congressional Oversight of Administration; The Power of the Purse," *Polit. Sci. Quar.*, LVIII, 161-190, 380-414 (June, Sept., 1943).

G. B. Galloway, "The Investigative Function of Congress," *Amer. Polit. Sci. Rev.*, XXI, 47-70 (Feb., 1927).

————, *Congress at the Crossroads* (New York, 1946), Chap. I.

J. M. Landis, "Constitutional Limitations on the Congressional Power of Investigation," *Harvard Law Rev.*, XL, 153-221 (Dec., 1926).

E. J. Eberling, *Congressional Investigations* (New York, 1928).

M. E. Dimock, "Congressional Investigating Committees," *Johns Hopkins Univ. Studies in Hist. and Polit. Sci.*, XLVII, 1-182 (1929).

M. N. McGeary, *The Development of Congressional Investigative Power* (New York, 1940). On developments since 1928.

J. F. Lawson, *The General Welfare Clause; A Study of the Power of Congress Under the Constitution* (2nd printing, Washington, 1934).

T. W. Cousens, "The Delegation of Federal Legislative Power to Executive Officials," *Mich. Law Rev.*, XXXIII, 512-544 (Feb., 1935).

L. L. Jaffe, "An Essay on Delegation of Legislative Power," *Columbia Law Rev.*, XLVII, 359-376, 561-593 (Apr., May, 1947).

A. Simpson, Jr., *A Treatise on Federal Impeachments* (New York, 1917).

————, "Federal Impeachments," *Univ. of Pa. Law Rev.*, LXIV, 651-695, 803-830 (May, June, 1916).

Extracts from the Journal of the U. S. Senate in All Cases of Impeachment,...1789-1904, 62nd Cong., 2nd Sess., Sen. Doc. No. 876 (1912).

[1] Yakus *v.* United States, 321 U. S. 414.

CHAPTER XVII

CONGRESS AT WORK—THE LEGISLATIVE PROCESS

The Capitol building in which Congress meets is a monumental sand- The
stone and marble structure situated at a jog in Pennsylvania Avenue physical
setting
about a mile from the White House, and on the brow of a low hill over-
looking downtown Washington, the broad Potomac, and the heights of
Virginia beyond. Since 1857, the House of Representatives has occupied
a large rectangular hall in the south wing of the building; the Senate,
transferred in 1859 from a room later used (though since vacated) by
the Supreme Court, sits in a similar but smaller chamber in the north
wing. As in legislative halls of Continental Europe, although not in
England, the seats in each room are arranged in concentric rows, theater-
fashion, facing the marble platform on which the presiding officer sits;
and deep galleries provide space for six or eight hundred spectators—
press, diplomatic, members' relatives, and general public. Formerly, the
hall of the House of Representatives was fitted with separate desks for
the members; and the Senate chamber is still so equipped. But the
growth of numbers in the lower branch made it necessary, after the reapportionment of 1911, to remove the desks, leaving only the seats, in
close proximity, as in a theater. Two large tables are, however, conveniently placed for the use of floor leaders and of committees whose
reported bills are up for consideration—one on each side of the center
aisle, near the aisle and well toward the front. At one of these, the majority members of the reporting committee take their station; at the other,
the minority members. So far as practicable, Republican members of the
House sit together on one side of the chamber and Democratic members
on the other.[1] The seats of individual representatives are assigned, at
the beginning of a session, by lot; although in point of fact they are not
occupied regularly, and a member entering the hall while business is
going on is likely to take any seat, not then in use, that happens to strike
his fancy. In the Senate, where there is never a general vacating of
places, a newcomer establishes his right to any seat not already belonging
to a member, and as a rule occupies it regularly. The physical equipment
of the legislative branch further includes numerous committee rooms in
the Capitol building, an immense marble office-building for the members
of the Senate, two such buildings for those of the House, a library in the

[1] In both cases, the Democrats to the right and the Republicans to the left of the
presiding officer, although the arrangement (unlike the location of "right," "center,"
"left," and various intermediate shadings in European parliaments) has no political
significance.

347

Capitol, and the separately housed Library of Congress, which is the largest library not only in the United States but also in the world.

General aspect of congressional business

Although each branch of Congress is intrusted with certain tasks which the other does not share,[1] the two spend most of their time at the same sort of thing, *i.e.*, considering bills which, to become effective, must be passed in identical form at both ends of the Capitol[2]—or resolutions, which may be (1) joint resolutions tantamount to bills and, like them, submitted to the president, or (2) concurrent resolutions, which, relating merely to internal congressional housekeeping, or being mere expressions of attitude or opinion, are not so submitted, or indeed (3) simple House or Senate resolutions, declaring a policy or purpose of one house only. Some of the measures on which the two bodies deliberate are designed to make or declare new law; others, merely to amend, clarify, or consolidate existing law; many do not make or modify law at all in any proper sense, but rather appropriate money, confer powers, formulate rules, give directions, or even, as has been indicated, merely express attitudes or opinions. Speaking broadly, however, whenever matters are up which call for formal proposal, discussion, and decision in both of the houses, the same machinery is, or may be, employed, and likewise the same basic plan of procedure, however frequently the "regular order" may be, and is, deviated from in particular cases. Accordingly, a reasonably adequate understanding of how Congress carries on its work will be obtained if we briefly trace the steps that normally are taken between the time when a legislative proposal is put into the form of a bill or joint resolution and the final publication of the measure (if it has emerged successfully) as a completed statute.[3]

Introduction, Authorship, and Number of Bills

How bills are introduced

Nothing is easier than to give a bill its start, *i.e.*, to "introduce" it. Whether a measure be "public," *i.e.*, of general application, or "special" (or "private"), *i.e.*, applying only to specified persons, objects, or places, all that is required in the House of Representatives is that a copy of it, endorsed with the name of the introducer, be dropped into a box on the clerk's table; in the Senate, there is only the additional formality of getting recognition from the presiding officer before sending a bill to the secretary's desk. Any bill may make its first appearance in either house, except only that bills for raising revenue are required by the constitution to "originate" in the House of Representatives.[4] Indeed, through its right

[1] For example, confirmation of appointments and consideration of treaties by the Senate and preparation of impeachment proceedings by the House.

[2] The two houses meet in joint session (in the chamber of the House of Representatives) only (1) to witness the count of the presidential electoral vote, (2) to receive oral messages from the president, and (3) to hold formal ceremonies such as state funerals and receptions for distinguished visitors to the country.

[3] Finance legislation, involving somewhat specialized procedures, falls within the scope of later chapters dealing with national revenues and expenditures. and accordingly is treated at that point.

[4] Art. I, § 7. cl. 1.

to amend revenue bills, even to the extent of substituting new ones, the Senate may, in effect, originate them also.[1] Once introduced, a bill continues "alive" throughout the duration of the existing Congress or until sooner disposed of; in a succeeding Congress, however, it can get on a calendar only by being reintroduced.

Nothing would be farther from the truth, however, than to suppose that some member of the House or Senate, or some group of members, is the actual author of every measure presented. Congress, we are assured by a former member of long experience and high standing, is "not to any material extent an originating body." [2] In the first place, a large proportion of all major public bills introduced emanate—sometimes in fully drafted form—from the executive branch of the government, *i.e.*, from the White House or from one of the executive departments or independent establishments. To be sure, contrary to the situation in countries having a cabinet system of government, no member of the executive branch can directly introduce a bill. This, however, imposes no serious impediment; a senator or representative, or a committee, can always be found to take care of the simple ceremony—what usually happens being that a bill coming from "down-town" is placed in the hands of the appropriate standing committee and introduced through it, normally by the chairman.[3]

In the second place, bills originate with (or at least are inspired by) persons, groups, or organizations entirely outside of government circles; and often these are presented by members individually. Here we come upon a main reason for the flood of bills that descends upon Congress at every session. Senators and congressmen themselves, sometimes sharing the great American illusion that the way to cure any ill is to "pass a law," originate a certain number. But to a far greater extent they are merely the purveyors of proposals from the outside. Judging it worth while to please those with interests or "causes," and at the same time to have their own names in the newspapers (in their home districts, at all events) as the authors of bills, senators to some extent, but especially representatives, usually are willing to introduce any number of measures, however ill-considered and fantastic, at the request of persistent lobbyists or constituents with "a grievance, an ambition, or a hope." They need not personally favor, or even fully understand, everything they introduce; hundreds of bills every session bear "by request" labels, often enough indicating that the members formally presenting them disclaim any personal responsibility for their contents. But not a whit less on that account, such bills inundate the clerk's desk and help clutter up the calendars,

Authorship

---

[1] See p. 366, note 1, below.

[2] R. Luce, *Congress—An Explanation*, 3. In his *The President, Congress, and Legislation* (New York, 1946), L. H. Chamberlain assigns somewhat greater weight to congressional initiative and leadership in the legislative process.

[3] This matter of administrative initiative in lawmaking is discussed lucidly in E. E. Witte, "Administrative Agencies and Statute Lawmaking," *Pub. Admin. Rev.*, II, 116-125 (Spring, 1942). On the president's rôle, see pp. 378-380 below.

sometimes turning up with clock-like regularity in session after session for twenty or thirty years. Formerly, a very large proportion of these bills coming from the outside were special or private—relating to pensions, claims for damages, and the like, and usually contemplating expenditure of federal money; and a good many are still such, notwithstanding limitations imposed in the Legislative Reorganization Act of 1946.[1] Many bills originating outside, however, are of a public character—measures sponsored or urged by business, labor, farmer, railroad, liquor, or other groups or interests, and sometimes looking to the enactment of extensive laws; and the stream of these shows no sign of drying up.[2]

Multiplicity

The number of bills and resolutions introduced at every session used to be amazing, as many as 2,500 having been known to make their appearance in the House of Representatives alone on an opening day; and even counting pension bills only as grouped in omnibus measures, the total for most Congresses ran from ten or twelve thousand to upwards of fifteen thousand—about two-thirds of the number, as a rule, being introduced first in the House and the remainder in the Senate. Of the

---

[1] See pp. 411-415 below.

[2] Administration bills are almost invariably drafted by experts in the departments (with more or less consultation with the chairmen or other members of the appropriate committees), and bills originating with private individuals or interests will often have been put into shape by hired counsel or otherwise before being intrusted to a member or a committee. For example, the memorable Logan-Walter bill of 1940, aimed at curbing the powers of the great regulatory commissions, and finally killed by presidential veto, was drafted by the American Bar Association's committee on administrative law (see pp. 487-488 below). Senators and representatives—whether as individuals or as committees—desiring assistance in preparing measures can always get it from a service known as the Office of Legislative Counsel, carried on in the Library of Congress since 1918 by a non-political chief draftsman and assistants who are officers of Congress, and reënforced by a staff of unheralded but extremely useful research and drafting experts (besides a few clerks), each specializing in a field such as taxation, banking, agriculture, or commerce. See F. P. Lee, "The Office of Legislative Counsel," *Columbia Law Rev.*, XXIX, 381-403 (Apr., 1929). Cf. *State Government*, V, 6-9 (July, 1932). Not a few important measures, *e.g.*, revenue, appropriation, and currency bills, are finally worked out and written by the appropriate standing committee, with Legislative Counsel aid if desired.

Needless to say, the drafting of a bill of even comparatively limited scope is a difficult and delicate undertaking. Every detail of the proposal must be coördinated with the great mass of statute and case law already existing; words must be chosen with care so as to convey the meaning intended; powers and agencies of enforcement must be prescribed in full recognition that upon them will depend final attainment of the object sought; and always must be borne in mind the fact that the legislation, if of a restrictive nature, will meet opposition from the start and will almost certainly collapse unless drawn on such lines that the courts will sustain it. The Office of Legislative Counsel worked eighteen months on the draft of the tariff act of 1930.

In addition to the Office of Legislative Counsel, there is in the Library of Congress a Legislative Reference Service broadly comparable in function to such services in many of the states, and prepared to assist not only congressional committees, but also individual members by collecting and placing at their disposal publications, compilations, and other informational materials. See J. P. Chamberlain, *Legislative Processes: National and State*, Chap. xiv, and especially W. B. Graves, "Legislative Reference Service for the Congress of the United States," *Amer. Polit. Sci. Rev.*, XLI, 289-293 (Apr., 1947). Under provisions of the Legislative Reorganization Act of 1946, both the Office of Legislative Counsel and the Legislative Service are now more adequately financed and supported than formerly, and the latter has added to its earlier somewhat meager force a dozen "senior" specialists in a variety of economic and political fields.

yearly grist, the best that one could say was that few of the measures offered contained possibilities of wise legislation, fewer still received attention, and fortunately still fewer ever passed. With private-bill legislation curtailed, the number of measures introduced may be expected hereafter to be somewhat smaller. In the first session of the Eightieth Congress (January 3-December 19, 1947) alone, however, the figure for the House of Representatives was 5,658 (bills and resolutions) and for the Senate 2,312, with 526 finally adopted (395 public and 131 private).[1]

Committee Stage in the House of Representatives [2]

All bills introduced are given a number (becoming, for example, H.R. 144 or S. 177) and referred to one or another of the standing committees.[3] Such private bills as still may be presented are turned over automatically to the committee suggested in each case by the sponsor of the bill as the appropriate one for handling it; public bills are sorted out and assigned according to the subjects with which they deal, nominally by the speaker, actually as a rule by the clerk or one of his assistants. Sometimes, however—indeed, fairly often in these days of long and complicated laws— a bill is of such a nature that it might be referred with almost equal propriety to any one of two or more committees; and in this event, as indeed in all cases of doubt, and also in the case of all bills received from the Senate, the speaker is likely to decide personally what shall be done —perchance having regard for the composition of the committee almost as much as for the nature of the bill. Sometimes a bill, after being referred to one committee, is recalled and sent to a different one; but only very rarely is a measure divided between two or more committees. The fate of a proposed piece of legislation may well be determined at this initial stage by the bill being referred to a committee likely to be friendly or, on the other hand, to one likely to be unsympathetic; and at this point the speaker may still wield the power of life or death. Authors or sponsors of a bill that is being held up in committee may maneuver to get it transferred to another committee likely to be more favorable. Thus, after being stifled in the ways and means committee for several Congresses, an oleomargarine tax bill was, in 1902, finally turned over to the committee on agriculture, reported favorably, and duly passed. To achieve this end, however, it may become necessary to rewrite the bill.

Reference to committee

---

[1] During the first session of the Seventy-ninth Congress (January 3-December 21, 1945), 5,995 bills and resolutions were introduced in the House and 2,118 in the Senate; during the second session (January 14-August 2, 1946), 2,128 in the House and 977 in the Senate. In the first session, the House passed 1,184 and the Senate 1,005; in the second, the House passed 1,183 and the Senate 1,098. The final product, however—i.e., passed by both houses in the same form—was 658 (293 public and 365 private) in the first session and 967 (440 public and 527 private) in the second.

[2] To avoid repetition, the legislative process will here be outlined for the House only, with significant Senate variations noted.

[3] In this initial stage, procedure is on the principle that all bills are created free and equal. All start on the same footing. Once the race for enactment has begun, however, the vast majority are found to have been left at the post.

After being stymied by refusal of the House labor committee and the Senate education and labor committee to report it out, the highly controversial War Labor Disputes [Smith-Connally] bill of 1943 [1] was so recast as to enable it to be referred in the Senate to the judiciary committee and in the House to the committee on military affairs, both of which reported it favorably and so cleared the way for its eventual passage. Reassignment can be forced upon an unwilling speaker only by a majority vote of the House; and committees from whose custody it is proposed to remove a bill can usually be counted upon to resist—as the two labor committees did (ineffectually) in the case of the Smith-Connally bill. Obviously, if bills were to be tossed about freely among committees, much confusion would result; and in practice reassignments are rare. In any case, a bill, after being referred, is printed and distributed to all House members.[2]

Committees at work

Each standing committee now has a commodious room in the Capitol or in one of the two large office-buildings provided for the use of members, with books, pamphlets, records, and whatever stenographic service is needed; and there it holds meetings as required, using forenoons for the purpose in order to avoid conflict with sittings of the House (starting regularly at noon).[3]

Even with minor committees now eliminated, some have relatively light loads. Others, however, receive scores, and even hundreds, of bills every session, or have unusually long and complicated measures to handle (perchance, as in the case of finance bills, to write), and accordingly find themselves crowded for time. To expedite matters, these create subcommittees (usually of five members) to which particular measures or classes of measures are assigned, or even individual sections of the same measure if it be one of exceptional complexity and importance; and reduction of the number of standing committees in 1946 has resulted in even more use of subcommittees than before. At all events, it is in the committees, and more or less behind the scenes, that much of the actual record of Congress—especially in the case of the House of Representatives—is written. "Congress in its committee rooms," declared Woodrow Wilson, "is Congress at work."[4]

Sources of information

On receiving a bill, a committee has first to inform itself on the measure's nature and contents, and then to decide what to do with it. For the great majority of bills, this means nothing more than a cursory

---

[1] See p. 735 below.

[2] Sections of presidential messages recommending legislation are similarly referred to the appropriate committees.

[3] The Legislative Reorganization Act of 1946 requires every standing committee to have regular weekly, biweekly, or monthly meeting days, and to adhere to its schedule, with special meetings also as needed. As already observed, only the rules committee is privileged to meet during a House sitting, unless by special leave. In 1947, the Senate tried the experiment of meeting only three or four days a week in order to leave more time for committees, but as the session wore on the plan could not be maintained.

[4] *Congressional Government* (Boston. 1885), 79.

glance, revealing that the proposal has little or no merit (or at any rate no present interest for the committee), and summarily condemning it to a lingering death in the committee files. A bill here and there, however, will be recognized as having some genuine claim to attention; and if time permits, it probably will receive consideration. In the case of such a measure, the first requisite is information from which to judge whether legislation on the subject really is needed, whether the bill in hand is calculated to meet the need, and what results and implications would follow if it were passed. The committee—at least some of its more experienced members—may already know a good deal about the subject. But usually more will have to be learned. And the needed information is, or may be, obtained in a variety of ways. Availing themselves of the resources of the committee library, of the Library of Congress (including the Legislative Reference Service), and of official files, committee members may study the proposal at first hand and come to a conclusion as to what action to take. Specified portions of the measure (or even the whole of it) may be assigned to subcommittees for more intensive study. Under the reorganization legislation of 1946, furthermore, all committees are entitled to the services of as many as four persons qualified to assist in carrying on research. Either by request or on their own initiative, interested officials, too, may appear in person to give testimony and present argument; heads of departments, indeed, have been doing this increasingly in later years. And of course lobbyists can usually be depended upon to volunteer information or materials, however biased.

Enough has been said, however, about the ways in which bills originate to suggest that most measures of large importance—certainly most Administration measures—reach Congress only after extensive investigations of the subjects dealt with have been made. Congress itself, or one of the houses, may have sponsored such an inquiry, by either a standing or a special (sometimes a joint) committee. Again, Congress may have caused an investigation to be made by the Department of Labor, the Interstate Commerce Commission, or some other department or establishment. Still again, Congress may have arranged for a study by a commission consisting of a certain number of senators and representatives, together with persons drawn from the general public and selected by the president. Or, the president may himself have found funds or secured an appropriation with which to carry on an investigation through the medium of a commission appointed by himself, and with a view to proposing legislation based on the data brought to light. Thus when, in 1934, President Franklin D. Roosevelt decided upon a national program of social insurance, he created an *ex officio* committee on economic security which, through a staff of experts, brought together most of the facts and recommendations on which the great federal Social Security Act of 1935 was based. Similarly, when in 1935 he turned his attention to a general reorganization of the executive branch of the national government, he appointed a committee (of expert private citizens) on administrative management to conduct studies without which a well-considered scheme could not have been devised.[1] All materials assembled in such ways are, of course, placed at the disposal of the Senate and House committees through whose hands the resulting bills will pass; although naturally the committees may themselves gather such further or different information as they desire.

Public hearings

Finally, if a bill deals with a highly controversial subject, or will seriously affect large numbers of people, the committee having it in charge will almost certainly hold public hearings on it. That is to say, arrangements will be made for interested individuals or spokesmen of organizations having something at stake, or presumed to be in possession of useful information, to appear before the full committee or a subcommittee designated for the purpose and give testimony while the members listen and perhaps draw them out with questions. Certain persons are commonly invited to appear, but opportunity will usually be offered others who desire to do so, including paid attorneys engaged to support or oppose the measure, or particular clauses of it. On a great tariff bill, hearings—usually conducted by subcommittees visiting different sections of the country—may extend over many weeks, the stenographic reports running into thousands of pages of print.[2] Both House and Senate use the device increasingly, as also do most of the state legislatures; and although briefly experimented with in one or two European countries, it may be looked upon as a characteristic feature of the American legislative process.

Possible courses of committee action

Notwithstanding varying amounts of publicity in the earlier stages of its deliberations, the committee eventually goes into executive session on a bill and reaches its conclusions in private.[3] Any one of several results may follow. It may report the bill unchanged, which is, of course, tantamount to recommending its passage. Or it may strike out some sections, add others, or alter the phraseology, and report the measure in this amended form. Or it may frame a bill of its own and present it as a

---

[1] See p. 483 below.

[2] On a similar scale have been hearings on other types of bills in recent years, e.g., the Senate judiciary committee's hearings of 1937 on the President's court reorganization bill (see p. 546 below). Extended hearings take place also in connection with congressional investigations (see pp. 337-339 above); but in this instance the persons who appear are chiefly those whom the committee desires to question and summons for the purpose.

[3] It is considered a breach of good faith for members to disclose what went on in the committee while in executive session, even though they may be sorely tempted to do so; and the votes taken in committee are never made a matter of public record. It is easy to condemn (as some have done) the secrecy surrounding committee deliberations. But there is another side to the matter. In the executive sessions of committees, writes an experienced former member already quoted, falls "the most interesting, important, and useful part of the work of a congressman, and the part of which the public knows nothing. Indeed, the ignorance of the public about it is one of the causes of its usefulness. Behind closed doors nobody can talk to the galleries or the newspaper reporters. Buncombe is not worth while. Only sincerity counts." R. Luce, Congress—An Explanation, 12.

substitute. In all of these cases, the report is likely, although by no means certain, to lead to favorable action by the House, especially if the committee (or even the majority group, in instances where party lines are drawn sharply) has come to its decision by a unanimous vote; and thus (to the dislike of some) legislation tends to be, in effect, by committee—by a *series* of separate committees—with the House acting only as a ratifying agency. The committee has, however, one other possible course: it may make no report at all—in other words, may "pigeonhole" the bill; and this, as we have seen, is the fate that befalls three-quarters or more of all measures introduced. The decision to make no report may come after, and as a result of, investigations and hearings; but in the great majority of instances it arises from agreement (tacit or otherwise) at the very beginning not to take up the bill at all.

The ease with which a committee can kill a bill by simply not reporting it has always been a sore point, and controversy on the subject has filled many pages in the annals of the House.[1] To be sure, committees are only agents of the House, and as such are subject to orders and instructions; if the House desires to discharge a committee from the further custody of a bill—in other words, require it to report—there is nothing to prevent it from doing so. The matter is, however, less simple than it sounds, because it is usually a minority, rather than a majority, that wants to get a bill out of a hostile or lethargic committee; and as the rules stand (dating originally, on this point, from 1910), there is no means by which anything less than a majority (218) can—after a bill has been in a committee's hands as long as thirty days—force a vote on a "discharge" question. In 1931, the House did adopt a rule under which as few as 145 members (one-third instead of one-half) could force such a vote; but on the ground that this gave too much scope to pressure groups and compelled the House to call back bills which only a minority wanted to have considered, the plan was abandoned in 1935.[2] Consequently, it remains true that almost any measure can be killed in its initial stages by simple failure of the committee having it in charge to report.[3] Committees serve as agents of the House to investigate and make recommendations, and the House expects normally to be guided by their conclusions. Should they refuse to recommend action, that is ordinarily the end of the matter. Without, indeed, the rigorous sifting of bills in this

Forcing a committee to report

---

[1] Of course, a committee may report a bill adversely. But this is rarely done; if it cannot report favorably, recommending passage, it commonly does not report at all.

[2] The new rule was both introduced and repealed by a Democratic House, and repeal was motivated largely by the desire to make it less easy for a Republican minority to force reporting, for consideration on the floor, of measures palpably out of line with the New Deal program. To be sure, the Republicans could at the time muster only 102 out of the required 145 votes; but enough Democrats sometimes joined them to make the rule operative.

[3] It has sometimes happened that a bill definitely approved by a committee failed to reach the floor because the chairman did not report it. The Legislative Reorganization Act of 1946, however, makes it the duty of a chairman to report any approved bill "promptly."

way, the House would be hopelessly swamped with work, and it would become necessary to place severe restrictions upon the number of measures that members may introduce. Occasionally, a committee fails to report a meritorious bill for the simple reason that the majority members are personally or politically prejudiced against it. But most measures that come to their end because of failure to report deserve no better fate.[1]

The Handling of Bills After Committee Stage

The cal-
endars

Having been returned to the clerk of the House, a reported bill is placed in one of three series, or lists, known as "calendars." If a revenue bill, an appropriation bill, or a bill relating to government property, it goes on the Calendar of the Whole House on the State of the Union, commonly known as the Union Calendar; if a public bill not relating to revenue, appropriations, or property, it finds a place on the House Calendar; and if a special or private bill, on the Calendar of the Committee of the Whole House, sometimes called the Private Calendar.[2] Bills go on the respective calendars strictly in the order in which they are reported; and once there, they remain for the period of a Congress (not merely a session) unless taken off.

Selection
of bills
for con-
sidera-
tion

It must not be supposed, however, that bills are invariably called up from the calendars in the order in which they are listed—still less that all calendared bills are actually debated and voted on. With nearly a score of standing committees reporting bills, the calendars grow congested, and the best that the House can do is to pick off a bill here and one there for adoption by simple consent procedure, or, in the case of more controversial ones, for fuller consideration, making sure that the most essential measures, *e.g.*, appropriation bills, are included, but letting the others take their chances. No House rule, indeed, is more frequently set aside than that which directs that bills shall be taken up in their calendared order; and no power of the majority steering committee is more

[1] In the two sessions of the Seventy-eighth Congress (1943-44), there were twenty-one motions to discharge committees from further consideration of particular bills, but only three received the necessary 218 votes. In the first session of the Seventy-ninth Congress (1945), the rule was invoked only once, *i.e.*, to get out of the rules committee an anti-poll tax bill which the House subsequently passed, but without concurrence by the Senate. In the second session of the Seventy-ninth Congress (1946), seventeen discharge petitions were filed, but only two received the necessary 218 votes. The number of bills forced to the floor in this way is always small, but in the past decade it has included a few measures of major importance—as, for example, the Fair Labor Standards ["Wages and Hours"] bill in 1938 and anti-poll tax bills on three or four different occasions. For the illuminating history of the finally successful effort to bring the discharge rule to bear against the rules committee in the case of the Fair Labor Standards bill, see *Amer. Polit. Sci. Rev.*, XXXII, 1102-1107 (Dec., 1938). On the discharge rule in general, see F. M. Riddick, *Congressional Procedure,* Chap. XIII. How bills are occasionally salvaged from committee cold storage by being transferred to different committees has been indicated above (see p. 351).

[2] There are, in addition, two "special" calendars. On one—a Consent Calendar—are eventually placed bills (usually minor and unopposed) which can be called up on the first and third Mondays of each month and considered under unanimous consent. On the other—a Discharge Calendar—are placed motions to discharge a committee from further consideration of a bill.

important than that by virtue of which it decides when, and in behalf of what bills, the committee on rules shall bring in for adoption by majority vote a special rule or order making a given bill the regular business of the House forthwith or at whatever later time the order may specify, and attaching such time limitations on debate and restrictions upon amendments as the committee may stipulate. Most weightier measures—and some not so weighty—are thus lifted out of their sequence on the lists and put in a preferred position; otherwise, they would never be reached. Hundreds of measures "die on the calendars" in every Congress.

There is, to be sure, a daily order of business, duly prescribed in the rules. But, as would be inferred from what has been said, this "regular" order is so frequently departed from as to have comparatively little significance. In the first place, certain days are set aside for the consideration of (1) certain classes of measures, *e.g.*, the first and third Mondays of each month for bills transferred from the Union or House calendar to the special "Consent Calendar,"[1] and the second and fourth Mondays for business relating to the District of Columbia; and (2) measures called up under special procedures, *e.g.*, "calendar Wednesday," when standing committees having in their custody various sorts of "unprivileged bills" may be given a chance to report. Again, at any time after the journal has been read, it is in order to move that the House go into committee of the whole to consider revenue or general appropriation bills. A number of standing committees, too, have the privilege of reporting at practically any time, and—what is more important—asking for immediate consideration of their reports. Bills introduced at the instigation of the president or of a department head, or for any other reason regarded as Administration measures, are often given right of way. From the rules committee may come at any time proposed orders which, if adopted, will turn proceedings in an entirely different direction. Finally, on specified days, the House may, by two-thirds majority, suspend all rules and depart as widely as it likes from the regular procedure, even to the extent of passing a major bill through all of its stages at a single vote, or at all events on the same day.[2] Under these circum-

Regular
order of
business
not ad-
hered to

---

[1] If when such bills are called up, there is no objection, they are passed without debate, and of course without amendment. If objection develops, and more than three members continue to oppose when a bill is later called a second time, the measure goes back to the calendar from which it came. In point of fact, much minor legislation is enacted by "consent."

[2] Ordinarily, the two-thirds rule serves to protect the interests of the minority. It fails in this respect, however, when, as during most of the period from 1933 to 1946, one party has so large a majority that the rules can be suspended by a vote of the members of that one party alone. An interesting example of summary legislation is afforded by an emergency banking bill introduced by Majority Floor Leader Byrns on March 9, 1933, allowed forty minutes of debate, passed by the House without a record vote and before printed copies were available, passed by the Senate a few hours later, and promulgated by the president the same evening (see *Amer. Polit. Sci. Rev.*, XXVIII, 70, Feb., 1934). A bill urged by President Truman, and empowering the chief executive to draft strikers in basic industries into the armed services in case other methods of settling strikes failed, was passed in this same fashion on May 25, 1946, but despite such speed, was permitted to die on the

stances, the process of legislation in the House has been likened to the running of trains on a single-track railroad. "The freight gives way to a local passenger train, which sidetracks for an express, which in turn sidetracks for the limited, while all usually keep out of the way of a relief train. Meanwhile, when a train having the right of way passes, the delayed ones begin to move until again obliged to sidetrack." [1]

Committee of the whole

Mention has been made of the committee of the whole; and inasmuch as the sessions of this committee occupy the greater part of the time of the House,[2] something more should be said about it. In reality, there are two committees of the whole: (1) the Committee of the Whole House, which considers private bills, and (2) the more important Committee of the Whole House on the State of the Union, which handles public bills for raising revenue, for appropriating money, and indeed for most other purposes as well. Both are, of course, simply the House of Representatives sitting in a different guise. A member moves that the House resolve itself into committee of the whole for the consideration of a designated bill; the motion is put and passed; the speaker yields the chair to a special chairman whom he designates; one hundred members constitute a quorum, instead of the majority required when the House is in regular session; debate proceeds, very informally, under a rule allowing only five minutes to each speaker at a time, unless with unanimous consent; there are no time-consuming roll-calls, divisions being taken only *viva voce*, by a rising vote, or by tellers, with no record kept of how members vote; motions to refer or to postpone are not permitted; and when discussion is completed the committee votes to "rise," the speaker resumes the chair, the mace (the symbol of the speaker's authority) is restored to its place on a marble pedestal at the right of the chair, and the chairman of the committee reports the decisions reached. The House must, of course, act upon the committee's report in order to give it effect. This very useful device enables all finance, and most other important, bills to be considered for amendment under circumstances such that, as a rule, every member of the House who desires to do so can be heard; it permits large numbers of amendments to be presented, explained, and disposed of speedily; it facilitates rapid-fire, critical debate which commonly shows the House at its best; and the absence of recorded yeas and nays

speaker's table after refusal by the House to concur in Senate amendments. On suspension of the rules, see J. Q. Tilson, *Parliamentary Law and Procedure*, Chap. XII. As Mr. Tilson remarks (p. 107), some of the most important bills ever enacted into law by the American Congress have been passed under a motion to suspend the rules.

[1] D. S. Alexander, *History and Procedure of the House of Representatives* (Boston, 1916), 222.

[2] "Under our rules today, ninety-five per cent of all the business that we transact is transacted in committee of the whole, and ninety-five per cent of the votes cast in this body are cast in committee of the whole...." H. A. Cooper, in *Cong. Record*, 68th Cong., 1st Sess., p. 8. In 1930, the Senate discontinued the device except for the consideration of treaties; and, curiously, it is employed but little in our state legislatures.

enables members to register their sentiments without check or restraint such as published votes sometimes impose.

A bill or joint resolution can be adopted only after three readings. Of these, the first is by title only; speaking strictly, it no longer is a "reading" at all, for the requirement is deemed to be met by printing the title in the *Congressional Record* and the *Journal*. Then the measure goes to committee and, if reported back, is placed upon its calendar for a second reading. The second reading—which (provided it is ever reached) takes place in committee of the whole or, for bills not there considered, in the House itself—is an actual reading in full [1] (unless dispensed with by unanimous consent or suspension of the rules), with opportunity for debate and for amendments to be offered; [2] and this is followed by a vote on the question, "Shall the bill be engrossed [*i.e.*, reprinted as amended] and read a third time?" If this stage is passed successfully, the third reading takes place (by title only unless a member—probably to the disgust of his colleagues—demands a reading in full), with a vote then taken on final passage. If the result is favorable, the bill or resolution, duly signed by the speaker, is ready to be sent to the Senate, or, if that body has already enacted it in identical form, to the president. *The three readings*

Normally, debate takes place only on the question of ordering a bill to a third reading, although, if not cut off by the "previous question" (explained below), it may be renewed on the question of final passage. When a measure reaches the stage at which it can be discussed on the floor, the chairman (or other designated representative) of the committee which has reported it favorably speaks in its behalf, being followed by a minority member of the committee if, as is usually the case, the report has not been unanimous. Other members of the committee speak alternately for and against the bill, and finally members of the House who do not belong to the committee are recognized—provided any time remains. And this matter of time presents problems. A rule dating from 1841 forbids a member to speak longer than one hour, except with unanimous consent. [3] This alone, however, would not keep debate within desirable bounds, and two additional, more drastic, devices are employed: (1) advance agreements between the opposing leaders—frequently embodied in special orders brought in by the rules committee—fixing the length of time (in terms of days, hours, or even minutes) that discussion shall be permitted to run, and perhaps indicating how the time shall be allotted, and (2) a practice (mentioned above and borrowed in modified *Closure*

---

[1] The reading of bills by a reading clerk—long ago abandoned in the British Parliament and in several of our more progressive state legislatures—entails a serious waste of valuable time. Mr. Luce estimates that something like a month of every session is thrown away in mere "clerical enunciation." *Congress—An Explanation*, 27. The custom was started in days before bills were printed.

[2] If a bill is being considered under suspension of the rules, no amendments are permissible, and if under some special order of the committee on rules, none (usually) except within limitations specified in the order.

[3] A member in charge of a bill is allowed an additional hour to close debate.

form from the British House of Commons) known as the "previous question." At any stage of discussion (except in committee of the whole), any member of the House may "move the previous question"; and if the motion carries, a quorum being present, debate is closed (with forty minutes allowed if there has as yet been none), no more amendments can be offered, and a vote is taken on whatever is pending.

Checks
on ob-
struction
Formerly, opponents of bills under discussion employed all manner of expedients to kill time and prevent action. Dilatory motions were made; unnecessary roll-calls were forced; efforts were put forth to stop proceedings by leaving the House without a quorum; time-consuming amendments were offered; and as a result much time was wasted. Rulings of vigorous speakers,[1] duly incorporated into the standing regulations, have considerably reduced the effectiveness of such tactics, although ways of slowing up business (chiefly demanding incessant time-consuming roll-calls [2]) are still within the reach of members disposed to employ them.

Methods
of voting
Upon conclusion of the consideration of a bill or resolution, or an amendment thereto, a vote is taken. In regular sittings of the House, four, and in the committee of the whole three, modes of voting are used. The first, and most common, is a division by simple sound of voices, i.e., a *viva voce* vote. If any member is dissatisfied with the announced result of this, he may demand a rising vote; whereupon the supporters of each side of the question stand and are counted. Again, if one-fifth of a quorum demands it, a vote is taken by tellers: a teller is designated for each side; the two take their places in front of the speaker's desk; the members in favor of the measure pass between them and are counted, and then those opposed; and the result is declared by the tellers and announced by the chair. Or, finally (in the House as such, though never in committee of the whole), if one-fifth of those present demand it, the "yeas and nays" are ordered: the clerk calls the names of the members, who respond with "aye" or "no"; these individual votes—sometimes different (since they are to be put permanently on record) from those previously cast *viva voce*—are recorded; and the result is duly announced. The yeas and nays may be demanded before any one of the other methods has been employed, and, if ordered, are taken forthwith.[3] Effort used

[1] Notably those of Speaker Reed in 1890 refusing to entertain motions regarded as dilatory and instructing the clerks to count as present all members observed to be within the chamber, whether responding to roll-calls or not.

[2] Under existing regulations, the House has no way of protecting itself against waste of time in this manner. By express constitutional provision, one-fifth of the members present can demand a yea and nay vote whenever they so desire (Art. I, § 5, cl. 3). A roll-call requires some forty-five minutes, and in the session of 1935 it was estimated that the 203 roll-calls taken (either on demand for the yeas and nays or to determine the presence of a quorum) consumed approximately five of the thirty-three weeks of the session. A great deal of such time could be saved by the introduction of electrical voting, as advocated in a lucid discussion of the general subject in E. Kefauver and J. Levin, *A Twentieth-Century Congress* (New York, 1947), Chap. v, and as now employed in the legislatures of thirteen states.

[3] When the question is one of passing a measure over a presidential veto, the constitution requires the yeas and nays to be taken and recorded. Art. I. § 7. cl. 2.

to be made to compel all members present to vote, but this has been given up as impracticable.[1]

Procedure in the Senate—Filibustering and Closure

After a bill is passed in the House, it is certified by the clerk and carried by him to the Senate chamber. Procedure there, being in most respects like that in the House, need not be described in detail. Whether sent over from the other end of the Capitol or originating in the Senate itself, a bill is referred by the presiding officer to one of the standing committees; if acted upon favorably, it is reported; if reported, it is placed on the calendar,[2] from which it may be called up either in or out of its turn; three readings must be passed, the second one, at which amendments are offered, being usually the critical test; votes are taken substantially as in the lower house; and in the end the bill may be adopted as it stands, or adopted with amendments, or rejected.

There are, nevertheless, some important differences between Senate and House procedure. For one thing, whereas the Senate formerly made more use of the committee of the whole than does the House, it abandoned the device altogether in 1930 except only in dealing with treaties. In the second place, with the exception that appropriation bills enjoy a certain priority, there is virtually no privileged business in the Senate, leaving the calendar to be followed almost automatically.[3] More important still is the absence of any very effective arrangements for limiting debate. There are no restrictions on the length of speeches, except such as are occasionally agreed upon in advance with respect to a particular measure; nor any upon their number, except that a senator may not, without consent, speak more than twice on the same subject in a single day; and—save for (1) occasional resort to a "unanimous consent" procedure (under which the members agree to a specified restriction of debate), and (2) the very infrequent use of a closure rule adopted in 1917—debate proceeds with less restraint than in any other important legislative body in the world. The comparatively small number of members has made this possible; and it cannot be denied that such liberty has some genuine advantages. The knowledge that ordinarily debate will not be cut off as long as any member, majority or minority, has something to say stimulates discussion and encourages the consideration of measures from

Differences between Senate and House procedure

The rules require this method of voting also when the question is one of submitting a constitutional amendment to the states.

[1] In 1941, the Columbia University Press announced the forthcoming publication of a stupendous work entitled *The Atlas of Congressional Roll-Calls; An Analysis of Yea-and-Nay Votes* (41 vols.), with maps showing the geographical distribution of the vote in every one of the 54,000 roll-calls in both branches of Congress from 1789 to 1932; and the first volume, in point of fact covering the previous years 1777-1789, appeared in 1944.

[2] Unlike the House, the Senate has but one calendar—although it is supplemented by orders of business which are, in effect, special calendars.

[3] This is the more possible because of the smaller number of bills introduced in the Senate than in the House.

all angles. It operates, too, as a wholesome check, not only upon party autocracy, but sometimes upon tendencies to executive dictatorship as well. At all events, the Senate has been adamant in its refusal to adopt anything resembling the one-hour rule prevailing at the other end of the Capitol.

Obstruction in the Senate—filibustering

Unfortunately, liberty is sometimes abused. In the Senate, the commonest form of such abuse is boresome garrulity—wasting time by sheer talkativeness, as often as not on some subject entirely foreign to that supposed to be under discussion.[1] To be sure, an injunction of Jefferson's *Manual* is presumed to apply: "No person is to speak impertinently or beside the question, superfluously or tediously." But empty seats on the floor and yawning spectators in the galleries bear testimony to the fact that this restriction—the latter part of it, at all events—is frequently ignored. More troublesome, however, is the practice of deliberately taking advantage of freedom of debate with a view, not to throwing light on the topic in hand or to converting the opposition, but to delaying and perhaps preventing action. This procedure, commonly termed "filibustering," and taking many forms—dilatory motions, demand for quorum roll-calls, reading from books or articles, and mere irrelevant *talking*—was by no means unknown in earlier times (there was an instance of it in the first session of the First Congress in 1789), but has been brought into play most spectacularly and successfully in the last sixty years, and especially since about 1910. A filibuster may be organized and conducted by a group of two or three, or more, members, working in carefully arranged relays,[2] or it may be carried on by a member singlehandedly; and it may have as its object to defeat a measure by "talking it to death," to compel it to be amended, or to force the majority to agree to tack on some provision or to pass some other measure, perhaps quite unrelated, in which the filibusterers are interested.[3] At best, valuable time is wasted; in addition, useful measures are sometimes defeated and needed appropriations held up. A favorite time to launch a filibuster used to be the closing weeks or days of a "short" session, since all that was necessary in order to achieve the purpose in mind was to hold out until an unalterable hour for adjournment of the session (noon of March 4) arrived. The Twentieth Amendment put an end to short sessions; yet senatorial filibustering is by no means a lost art.[4]

[1] It has been remarked that in the Senate "a controversy may be raised about any question, and at any distance from that question"!

[2] A filibustering senator, growing weary, may yield the floor to another filibustering member for a question, which may take several hours, and then the first speaker may resume.

[3] Sometimes, too, a Senate filibuster is employed to put pressure on the House of Representatives—as, for example, when, in 1936, a Senate group held up action on a postal appropriation bill, itself innocent enough, until the House had been coerced into drastic modification of a pending ship subsidy bill.

[4] In point of fact, Senator Huey Long carried on a memorable filibuster against the National Industrial Recovery Bill in the very first Congress after the Twentieth Amendment took effect. An anti-lynching bill was killed by a Southern filibuster in

The only positive restraint thus far imposed upon the practice took the form of a rule adopted in 1917, following defeat by filibuster of a bill ardently desired by President Wilson for the arming of American merchant ships. The procedure prescribed is as follows.[1] First, a petition to close debate on a specified measure must be signed by one-sixth (sixteen) of the senators. On the second calendar day after this petition has been filed, the roll of senators is called on the question: "Is it the sense of the Senate that the debate shall be brought to a close?" If there is a two-thirds vote in the affirmative, the pending measure becomes the "unfinished business" of the Senate until disposed of, to the exclusion of all other business; and thereafter no senator is permitted to speak for more than one hour in all on the measure itself, on amendments to it, or on motions relating thereto. Furthermore, no amendments may be presented except with unanimous consent; no dilatory motions or amendments are permissible; and all points of order are decided by the chair without debate.

The closure rule of 1917

This is closure in rather a mild form; the stipulated two-day delay gives the opposition a chance to mobilize its forces, and the required two-thirds is a high hurdle for the supporters of the effort to surmount. In the first nine years, the device was successfully invoked only twice, *i.e.*, in the debates on the Versailles Treaty in 1919 and on adherence to the World Court in 1926, and in the entire period 1917-47 only twenty-five closure petitions were voted upon and only four received the necessary two-thirds majority.[2]

Rare use of the device

When taking the chair as president of the Senate in 1925, Vice-President Charles G. Dawes lectured the members on the folly of trying to

The problem still unsolved

1938, and in 1942-46, an anti-poll tax bill, duly passed in the House, was several times prevented from coming to a vote in the Senate by Southern filibuster or threat of such (see p. 193 above). The second session of the Seventy-ninth Congress, in 1946, witnessed several filibusters, one of them lasting twenty-two days and aimed (successfully) by Southern senators against a bill making a Fair Employment Practice Committee a permanent government agency. The most noted filibuster in the first session of the Eightieth Congress (January-December, 1947) was conducted by an "irregular" Republican senator, Wayne L. Morse of Oregon, and a handful of Democratic collaborators in an effort to stave off a vote on the question of overriding President Truman's veto of the Labor-Management Relations [Taft-Hartley] Bill until the veto message could have had time to produce repercussions in the country and perhaps change some senatorial votes. The Senate was kept in session continuously from noon, June 20, until 4:30 P.M., June 21, when agreement was reached to take the vote two days later. During the delaying action, a Democratic filibusterer (Glen H. Taylor of Idaho), fortified with a glass of water, a box of cough drops, and a container of milk, discoursed eight hours and a half on fishing, Wall Street, baptism, and his children. Being a past tent-show performer may have helped. Morse had breakfast while taking one of his turns, talking between bites.

[1] *Senate Manual,* Rule XXII.

[2] Efforts in 1942 and 1946 to invoke closure against the anti-poll-tax legislation filibusters were uniformly unsuccessful. Senators definitely favorable to the proposed legislation, when put to a test, drew back from forcing its opponents to stop talking. Very few of long service had not themselves engaged in filibustering at one time or another. One of the more notable recent attempts to apply the closure rule was made by Administration forces in May, 1946, when, however, an effort to limit debate on a $3,750,000,000 loan to Great Britain failed by a vote of 41 to 41, *i.e.,* 23 votes short of the necessary two-thirds.

carry on their work under archaic rules that sometimes permit a single individual to defeat important legislation favored by an overwhelming majority; [1] and when retiring four years later, he referred reproachfully to the Senate as being, among modern deliberative bodies, the only one that has "parted with the power to allot its time to the consideration of subjects before it in accordance with their relative importance." Not even so vigorous a critic as Mr. Dawes, however, could stir much response either at Washington or throughout the country; and while the Senate has lately accepted a drastic reorganization of its top-heavy committee system, there is no assured prospect of any early change of heart on the use (or misuse) of time on the floor. [2] The weight of argument, indeed, is by no means entirely on one side of the question. Quite to the contrary, senators and others who honestly believe the existing lack of restraint to be on the whole advantageous bring forward a number of contentions, all of considerable validity: (1) that under the rules as they stand, the Senate (as Mr. Dawes was obliged to concede) contrives to transact a very creditable amount of business—in five recent Congresses, for example, passing 182 more bills and resolutions than did the House; [3] (2) that the present oft-used device of "unanimous consent," by which the members agree in advance to limit speeches on a given measure after a certain day and to take a vote at a specified hour, serves all necessary purposes, being indeed itself a species of closure; (3) that by far the greater portion of the measures killed by filibuster are not favored by the country and are never revived; and (4) that the vigorous protests against filibustering sometimes voiced on the Senate floor come frequently from members whose pet projects have suffered, but who, with circumstances reversed, would be quite ready to plan and launch filibusters of their own. It is perhaps utopian to suggest that the best solution for the problem would lie in an extension of "senatorial courtesy" [4] to include a decent respect for the right of one's colleagues to vote on a legislative proposal.

[1] *Cong. Record,* 69th Cong., Spec. Sess. of Senate, Vol. LXVII, pp. 1-2. Cf. Democratic Majority Leader Barkley's remarks, on somewhat more general lines, in 1938: "I agree that the rules of the Senate are the most archaic conglomeration of contradictory decisions that ever prevailed in any parliamentary or legislative body ... I think the rules of the Senate ought to be revamped. They ought to be modernized. They ought to be so changed as to make the Senate a self-governing body, which it is not now." "When a senator once takes the floor," admitted Democratic Floor Leader Robinson in 1932, "nobody but Almighty God can interrupt him—and the Lord never seems to take any notice of him."

[2] It is only fair to mention, however, that in 1946 both Democratic and Republican leaders evinced more interest in curbing filibustering than for some time past. Cf. *Amer. Polit. Sci. Rev.,* XL, 15-16 (Feb., 1947).

[3] It is capable, too, of keeping debate on a high plane, as it did when considering the lend-lease bill of 1941 and the Charter of the United Nations in 1945.

[4] See pp. 453-454 below.

Conference Committees

A bill which passes both branches of Congress in identical form is sent Resolving differences between the houses to the president and becomes law if it receives his signature or is repassed by two-thirds majorities over a veto. The Senate may, however, amend a House bill, and the House may amend a Senate bill; and unless the first body forthwith accepts all of the amendments added by the second one, or the second one recedes from its position (neither of which will often happen in the case of an important measure), some means must be found for overcoming the disagreement. The device regularly employed to bring the houses into harmony is the appointment of "committees of conference;" and statistics show that, on the average, from one-tenth to one-twelfth of all the bills and resolutions that Congress adopts— including almost all more important ones, *e.g.*, on taxation, commerce, agriculture, labor relations, etc.—are referred to such mediating agencies.

A bill having been passed in two differing forms, either house may ask for a conference; and the request having been agreed to (very rarely is it refused), the presiding officer of each house names as a rule three or five, but occasionally, for very significant bills, seven; or even nine, "managers" to represent it, including almost invariably in each case the chairman, the ranking majority member, and the ranking minority member of the committee having the bill in charge.[1] The House occasionally instructs its conferees on certain points, *e.g.*, not to yield on this or that particular provision; the Senate is less inclined to give instructions, yet now and then does so; and in so far as instructed, the managers can compromise only after going back to the body which they represent and obtaining permission. But as a rule the conference is "free"; that is to say, the managers are at liberty to discuss all features of the bill upon which there is disagreement and to exercise their own judgment in whipping it, by process of give and take, into a form which both houses will accept. They are not supposed, however, to change anything upon which the two houses have previously agreed.

Sometimes the task is easy and is performed in a few hours—for example, if it becomes a matter simply of splitting the difference between two sets of figures in appropriation or other finance bills. More often— especially if questions of basic policy are involved—it is difficult and

---

[1] Normally this will send to the conference those members of the respective houses who have had chief responsibility for managing—perhaps also for framing—the measure to be discussed. Occasionally, however, a bill is so transformed at one end of the Capitol that the committee chairman and majority ranking member no longer approve of it and can hardly be expected to put up a spirited fight for it. Under these circumstances, they ought not to be appointed, or, if appointed, to accept service, as conferees. The number of conferees from the two houses on a given bill may differ; but this does not greatly matter since agreements are reached, not by majority vote of the group, but by concurring majorities of the two sets of conferees acting separately. Although objection has sometimes been raised to the presence of nonmembers, both Senate and House conferees frequently take along with them to conference outsiders who can furnish expert information and advice.

entails days, or even weeks, of hard work.[1] If in the end it proves impossible, the bill fails, unless other conference committees are appointed and have better luck. As a rule, however, a consensus is arrived at; and the reported bill is almost always accepted or rejected by the houses without further attempt at amendment. Ordinarily, the house which has insisted on amendments recedes less from its position than the one which first passed the bill.

Defects of conference committee procedureAs a device for oiling the machinery of legislation, committees of conference are, under American conditions, manifestly indispensable.[2] Nevertheless, they have shortcomings. Without exception, they work behind closed doors, hold no hearings, and give their proceedings no publicity. Doubtless it would be difficult for them to make headway if they did otherwise. Nevertheless, in view of the power which they wield, strong objection can be, and is, raised. For while, as observed, the committees are supposed to deal only with actual differences between the houses and to stay well within the bounds set by the positions which the two have taken, respectively, they often work into measures, as reported, provisions of their own devising, even going so far as to rewrite entire sections with the sole purpose of incorporating the views which the majority members happen to hold. Log-rolling enters in, as in the work of the houses separately; and sometimes the compromises reached embody rather the worst than the best features of the two contending plans.[3] Conference committee reports are likely to reach the houses near the close of a session; under the rules, they are highly privileged, especially in the House of Representatives; and while either house may disagree to a report and call for another conference, there is usually a strong presumption in favor of adoption. There may be little time for critical scrutiny or debate; and failure to act—especially if financial provisions are involved—might seriously interfere with the operation of the govern-

[1] Scores, and even hundreds, of changes may have been introduced by the house which last considered the measure, and indeed the whole of the bill following the enacting clause may have been stricken out in favor of a new bill. Even in revenue legislation—despite the constitutional provision that all bills for raising revenue shall originate in the House—the Senate sometimes goes that far. Thus in 1883 the upper house struck out everything after the enacting clause of a tariff bill and wrote its own measure, which the House felt obliged to accept. It likewise added 847 amendments to the Payne-Aldrich tariff bill of 1909, dictated the schedules of the emergency tariff act of 1921, rewrote an extensive tax revision bill in the same year, and recast most of the permanent tariff bill of 1922.

[2] They are the more necessary under our American system, because, in the first place, our national and state legislatures—unlike the British Parliament, for example—are organized on the principle of strict law-making equality of the two houses, so that no bill or joint resolution can prevail unless agreed to in precisely the same form by both; and in the second place, because, whereas in cabinet-governed countries the ministers, who in a sense constitute a continuous conference committee of the two houses, are in a position to promote harmonious decisions, our system of divided government tends to leave the legislative branches isolated and devoid of coördinating machinery except such as the houses themselves create.

[3] There is the classic example of a tariff bill of several years ago in which the House imposed a duty of twenty-five cents a ton on coal, the Senate increased it to fifty cents, the House demanded a conference, and the conferees "compromised" on seventy-five cents!

ment. In practice, this often results in the adoption of important provisions, more or less surreptitiously added, without consideration by either house—in other words, legislation nominally by Congress but actually by conference committee. Any remedy found will probably take the form of reducing the need for using conference committees at all; and the principal suggestion to that end is that bills and resolutions be referred not, as now, to separate committees of the two houses, but to joint committees, which not only would hold single sets of hearings, but might deliberate and report back bills to the two houses in such agreed form that further significant differences would not be likely to develop. Arrangements of this nature yield good results in the legislatures of Massachusetts, Connecticut, and Maine. There are obstacles, however, to adoption of the plan for Congress, not the least of them being a natural aversion of House members to joint committees likely to be dominated by senators; and the streamlining of the committee structure provided for in the Legislative Reorganization Act of 1946 made no approach to such a solution beyond providing for joint functioning by the financial committees of the two houses in framing a "legislative budget," [1] and for optional joint hearings by House and Senate committees dealing with the same subject.

Other Aspects of Procedure

When a bill has been passed in identical form by both houses, it is "enrolled," i.e., written or printed on parchment, and thereupon is signed by the presiding officers and sent to the president. If it is approved, or if it becomes law without presidential action, it is transmitted to the Department of State to be deposited in the archives, and also to be published. If it receives a "messaged" veto, it goes back to the house in which it originated and becomes law only if, upon reconsideration, it is passed in both houses by a two-thirds vote. If it is pocket-vetoed, it simply dies. [2]

On the ground that parts of its work, e.g., the consideration of treaties, *Publicity of proceedings* was of such a nature as to require secrecy, the Senate at first sat exclusively behind closed doors; indeed, even the House of Representatives occasionally barred the public. Strong objection, however, arose; and in 1793 the Senate adopted the wiser plan of opening its doors whenever engaged in ordinary legislative business and closing them only during "executive" sittings, i.e., sittings in which only business directly shared

[1] See p. 565 below. There are, to be sure, some two score joint committees or "commissions," but most of them are either committees having only relatively unimportant "housekeeping" functions, e.g., supervision of congressional printing, or more or less temporary special committees such as that which, in 1945, reported the plan for congressional modernization adopted in 1946, or that set up in 1947 to watch over the operation and administration of the Labor-Management Relations [Taft-Hartley] Act. Standing joint committees of considerable importance, however, include one on internal revenue legislation, one on the president's economic report, and one on atomic energy.

[2] On the various forms of presidential veto, see pp. 381-387 below.

with the executive, *e.g.*, appointments and treaties, was considered. The last closed meeting of the House was held not long afterwards, in 1811. On the theory that the Senate should be free to discuss treaties, appointments, and sometimes other matters, without publicity being given to anything said, privacy for executive sessions was maintained for nearly a century and a half. Eventually, however, it broke down, partly because in later decades enterprising press correspondents found ways of ascertaining practically everything that was said and done in private sessions, but especially because of growing opinion, both in and out of the Senate, that, save under very exceptional circumstances, the public is quite as much entitled to know the views expressed and the position taken by individual senators on appointments and treaties as on anything else. The matter was brought to a head in 1929 by unauthorized publication of senatorial votes on the hotly contested confirmation of a judge of the Court of Customs Appeals, and the outcome of an exciting debate was the adoption of a new rule under which all business previously handled behind closed doors might thenceforth be considered in "open executive session" if so decided by majority vote. The House still has a rule permitting closing the doors for the purpose of receiving confidential information from the president; and the Senate not only is likely to take similar action when important treaties are under consideration, but did so in June, 1942, when hearing the chairman of the naval affairs committee explain plans for new naval construction, and again in October, 1943, when listening to a detailed report by five members lately returned from a visit to areas abroad in which American armed forces were engaged.

Published records:

The constitution requires both houses to keep a journal and to publish it "from time to time."[1] The journals are, however, bare records of bills introduced, reports presented, and votes taken—that is, minutes of official actions, not records of debates. For a long time, debates in the House of Representatives were not reported except in a haphazard way in some of the better newspapers; and Senate debates were practically not reported at all, although general accounts of what took place in that branch were frequently printed, as were occasional speeches.[2] In 1833, the *Congressional Globe*, presenting the debates verbatim, was started as a private venture; and in 1873 its place was taken by the present *Congressional Record*, prepared by officers of Congress and printed by the government. Published daily during sessions, the *Record* purports to give an exact stenographic reproduction of everything said on the floor of the two houses—save, of course, during closed sessions of the Senate. This,

1. Proceedings

---

[1] Art. I, § 5, cl. 3.

[2] The collections entitled (a) *Debates and Proceedings in Congress, 1789-1824* (42 vols., 1834-56)—commonly cited as *Annals of Congress*—and (b) *Register of Debates in Congress* (14 vols., 1825-37) bring together these fugitive materials from newspaper, pamphlet, and other sources. There is, of course, nothing official about these publications, and the reports on which they are based are very incomplete and sometimes highly partisan.

however, it does not actually do, partly because members sometimes edit their remarks in such a way as to make important changes in them, and also because, in the case of the House, speeches are frequently printed, under special leave, which were never delivered by word of mouth at all. The Senate does not permit the inclusion of undelivered speeches, but is quite as liberal as the House in allowing members to put into the *Record* correspondence, editorials, public documents, speeches of members on public occasions (even at party gatherings), magazine and newspaper articles, and selections from books, which have not been read in debate.[1] These practices go far toward explaining why the *Record* has grown so voluminous as to be practically useless to non-members except, of course, for historical or research purposes. Anywhere from twenty to twenty-five thousand of its generous triple-columned pages are filled every biennium—enough matter, such as it is, to make up a library of perhaps a hundred ordinary volumes.[2]

2. Statutes

All acts and joint resolutions, when the process of enactment is completed, are transmitted to the Department of State and printed by it in the form of separate "slip-laws," which are commonly obtainable on application;[3] and at the close of each session, the texts are collected, indexed, and published under the title of *Statutes at Large of the United States*—one volume containing all public acts and joint resolutions and a second being devoted to private acts and resolutions, concurrent resolutions, treaties, and presidential proclamations.[4]

Relative Importance of Senate and House

Although the framers of the constitution attached great significance to the Senate as a checking and revising body, and as a medium for preserving the dignities and powers of the states, the legislative center of gravity for a generation or more was clearly the House of Representatives. After about 1830, however, the Senate steadily came forward, numbering in its

An unstable equilibrium

---

[1] A proposal from the floor of the House of Representatives in 1937 to restrict the pages of the *Record* to actual proceedings (at a saving of $173,000 a year) met with a decidedly chilly reception. The present cost of publishing the *Record* is approximately a million dollars a year.

[2] Of 5,400 pages devoted to House proceedings in the second session of the Seventy-eighth Congress (1944), 3,089 recorded actual debates on bills and resolutions; in the case of the Senate, 2,284 pages out of 4,500. These proportions were fairly typical. It must be remembered that a very large portion of the bills and resolutions considered are not controversial and are not debated at all. In the session mentioned, only eighty-six out of 953 passed by the House stirred any real debate, and only forty-seven out of the 931 passed by the Senate.

In the spring of 1947, a "Daily Digest" was added as a special feature of the *Record*. The Senate intended it to be published also separately, but the House failed to act on the matter.

[3] They can be subscribed for also through the Superintendent of Documents at three dollars a year.

[4] A complete compilation of the "general and permanent laws" currently in force will be found in *Code of the Laws of the United States*, 4 vols. (Washington, D. C., 1940), with supplements covering the laws enacted in later sessions. A convenient general manual is L. F. Schmeckebier, *Government Publications and Their Use* (rev. ed., Washington, D. C., 1939).

ranks most of the outstanding men of the day (Webster, Clay, Calhoun, to mention but a few), and becoming, indeed, the principal forum of legislative activity in the generation leading up to secession and the Civil War. From about 1870, the House recovered ground, partly because of a natural reaction against the Senate's lofty assertions of authority (especially in the domain of foreign relations), partly because of abuses associated with "senatorial courtesy," but mainly because of the increasing proportion of senators whose principal claim to distinction was wealth, corporate backing, or cleverness in political manipulation. But again, noticeably after about 1912—after senators began to be elected directly by the people, and after ultra-conservatives and spokesmen of the vested interests began (for whatever reason) dropping out—the pendulum swung back; and today the Senate, if not actually predominant, is at all events of greater weight than two or three decades ago, and probably still gaining.[1]

The Senate's advantages   Nor is present senatorial ascendancy a mere matter of luck or chance; substantial reasons for it can be found in various advantages which the upper house enjoys as compared with the lower. Its members are, on the average, somewhat older, have wider knowledge of public affairs, and, in particular, have more legislative experience because of longer terms, more numerous reëlections, and continuous recruiting of vigorous members from the lower house. Its members, too, are commonly more important as party leaders within their states (and in some cases nationally) than are representatives. Their smaller number gives men of talent a better chance to show their mettle and become known to the country at large. With rare exceptions, senators enjoy far more patronage than do representatives; and the Senate's special powers of confirming appointments and assenting to the ratification of treaties place in its hands weapons which can be employed formidably in relation to other matters as well. Finally, while it unhappily remains true, as Lord Bryce remarked many years ago, that neither branch of Congress attracts the best talent of the nation,[2] the upper house tends to absorb, sooner or later, the best that enters political life. Certainly the Senate today contains fewer men of wealth, and decidedly fewer political bosses of the Hanna-Quay-Platt type, than forty or fifty years ago. By the same token, it is less conservative than formerly; indeed, an examination of the records would probably give it a claim to be regarded as more liberal and progressive than the other branch. On the average, debate is on a higher plane;

[1] Responsibility for sharing directly in the building of the new postwar world—accepting United States membership in the United Nations, assenting to the peace treaties, and the like—lends special importance in our time, although of course in other ways the responsibility is shared by the House as well.

[2] *Modern Democracies*, II, 52. Lord Bryce's discussion of the reasons makes illuminating reading. In brief, they are: (1) the dullness of congressional duties; (2) the scant opportunities for attaining distinction; (3) the requirement of residence in the member's state and district; and (4) the exceptional opportunities which America offers for careers in other directions.

greater interest has been manifested in curbing the abuses of lobbying; support for the legislative modernization of 1946 was more wholehearted —support, indeed, for more reorganization than the House was willing to accept. To be sure, under the existing rules of procedure, demagogues run riot and bring the body into disrepute and even contempt. To be sure, too, the Senate as a whole is sometimes swayed by partisan passion and prone to "play politics," as is the House; its record on the spoils system is clearly inferior. By and large, however, it contains a larger proportion of members whose speeches and votes show independence of spirit and judgment; and, while handicapped by the propensity of mediocre members to stand stiffly on their rights under the rules and try the patience of the country with their obstinacy or buffoonery, it is composed, in at least as large degree as the House, of men who are able, industrious, fair-minded, sparing in speech, and anxious to get on with the public business.[1]

REFERENCES

J. P. Chamberlain, *Legislative Processes: National and State* (New York, 1936), Chaps. VI-IX, XIII.

H. Walker, *Law-Making in the United States* (New York, 1934), Chaps. X, XII-XIV.

F. M. Riddick, *Congressional Procedure* (Boston, 1941), Chaps. VIII-XV. New edition in preparation (1948).

S. W. McCall, *The Business of Congress* (New York, 1911), Chaps. III-VII, IX.

G. B. Galloway, *Congress at the Crossroads* (New York, 1946), Chaps. VI-VIII.

D. S. Alexander, *History and Procedure of the House of Representatives* (Boston, 1916), Chaps. XI-XV, XVII.

W. Wilson, *Congressional Government* (Boston, 1885), Chaps. II-IV.

W. F. Willoughby, *Principles of Legislative Organization and Administration* (Washington, D. C., 1934), Chaps. XXVI-XXXVI.

R. Luce, *Congress—An Explanation* (Cambridge, Mass., 1926), Chaps. IV-V.

————, *Legislative Procedure* (Boston, 1922).

E. Kefauver and J. Levin, *A Twentieth-Century Congress* (New York, 1947).

L. Rogers, *The American Senate* (New York, 1926), Chaps. IV-V, VII-VIII.

G. H. Haynes, *The Senate of the United States; Its History and Practice*, 2 vols. (Boston, 1938).

P. D. Hasbrouck, *Party Government in the House of Representatives* (New York, 1927), Chap. XII.

J. Q. Tilson, *Parliamentary Law and Procedure* (Washington, D. C., 1935).

R. Young, *This Is Congress* (New York, 1943). In several respects, the best general book on the subject.

T. V. Smith, *The Legislative Way of Life* (Chicago, 1940).

J. Voorhis, *Confessions of a Congressman* (Garden City, N. Y., 1947). A vivid account of ten years' service in the House of Representatives.

G. H. E. Smith and F. M. Riddick, *Congress in Action; How a Bill Becomes a Law* (Washington, D. C., 1948). An elementary but accurate outline.

L. G. McConachie, *Congressional Committees* (New York, 1898).

A. C. McCown, *The Congressional Conference Committee* (New York, 1927).

F. L. Burdette, *Filibustering in the Senate* (Princeton, N. J., 1940).

---

[1] An interesting and suggestive characterization of Congress by a well-informed former member of the House will be found in a book already mentioned a number of times, *i.e.*, R. Luce, *Congress—An Explanation*, Chap. v.

G. W. Pepper, *In the Senate* (Philadelphia, 1930).

Manual of the United States Senate and *Manual and Digest of the House of Representatives* (Washington, D. C., recent editions).

Congressional Record. Published daily during sessions by the Government Printing Office at Washington, D. C. (obtainable through members of Congress or by subscription through the Superintendent of Documents).

Governmental Affairs (Washington, D. C.). A daily summary of congressional business, listing bills introduced, committee meetings, hearings held, and with occasional digests of bills. Published by the Chamber of Commerce of the United States.

United States News (Washington, D. C.). Presents unofficial weekly comment on congressional proceedings, as well as on other significant operations of the national government.

American Political Science Review. See annual articles by L. Rogers, A. W. Macmahon, E. P. Herring, O. R. Altman, and F. M. Riddick on successive sessions of Congress during the past thirty years.

CHAPTER XVIII

THE PRESIDENT AND CONGRESS

When the framers of our national constitution decided to distribute "Presidential" and "cabinet" government federal powers among three coördinate sets of authorities—president, Congress, and courts—they, in effect, ordained that we should have a "presidential," rather than a "cabinet," or "parliamentary," form of government; and in later times our presidential plan became a model for most countries in the Western Hemisphere, just as the cabinet system, maturing first in Great Britain, spread throughout the British Empire and most of Western Europe. In a cabinet, or parliamentary, system [1] there is commonly a king or other titular chief executive; he may even be called a president, as in France under the Third and Fourth Republics. Conversely, in a presidential system there is likely to be a cabinet, as in the United States. The difference between the two, however—and it is a basic one—is that in a cabinet system the actual operating executive consists of ministers (functioning together as a cabinet) who are at the same time members of and leaders in the legislature, and responsible to it (at least to the more popular branch), whereas a presidential executive not only is outside of the legislature, but draws his authority from the same source as the legislature itself, *i.e.*, popular election, and in his relations with the legislature is not "responsible" but rather coördinate; and with the further logical difference that whereas under a cabinet system the responsible ministers remain in office only so long as they continue to enjoy the confidence and support of a legislative majority, a presidential executive has a fixed term and during it can be ousted from office only by the extreme and unusual procedure of impeachment.

A manifest advantage of the cabinet system is that the executive Advantage of the cabinet system and legislature can never long be at odds on important matters of policy. Ministers losing legislative support give way, almost automatically, to others at least presumed to have such support; [2] and harmony again prevails, at any rate for a time. Under the presidential form, on the contrary, there is much possibility of protracted discord, division, and frustration, with no assurance of relief until fixed terms of office expire; [3] and for this

---

[1] The two terms are used interchangeably, according as one is viewing the system primarily from the side of the executive or from that of the legislature.

[2] Before they do so, however, they may obtain a parliamentary dissolution, in the hope that new elections will yield a majority with which they can work.

[3] This situation, of course, arises chiefly when one party is in control at the White House and a different one in one or both branches of Congress, as has been the case in twenty-eight of the eighty Congresses in the country's history, with the House of Representatives differing politically from the chief executive fourteen times, the

373

reason, as well as others, a good many people regard it as unfortunate that we started off with such a system, and consider that, if it were at all practicable to win the necessary public approval, it would be desirable for us to go over to the cabinet plan, even at this late day.[1]

Executive and legislature actually interlocked

However that may be, the point for emphasis in the present chapter is that, even under the system we have, the national executive and national legislature, *i.e.*, the president and Congress, are not, in practice, completely isolated from each other, but on the contrary—while constituting far more distinct and separate *foci* of political power than are to be found in a cabinet government, do actually maintain many close contacts and, by and large, become jointly the architects of most of our national legislation and public policy. To be sure, a glance at the constitution might lead one to suppose that the president is important only as an executive. "The executive power" is expressly vested in him; on the other hand, "all legislative powers" granted are conferred upon Congress. Actually, however, the president is far more than merely an executive— just as Congress is considerably more than merely a legislature. Steadily growing authority to issue orders and regulations makes him, to all intents and purposes, a legislator in his own right; and not only the constitution, but practical necessity as well, assigns him a weighty share in the legislative work of Congress. By availing himself, indeed, of his constitutional authority to convoke Congress in special session, to transmit messages, to recommend measures, and to veto bills, and equally by utilizing his extraconstitutional opportunities to consult with congressmen, to direct the preparation and introduction of bills, to work for the fulfillment of his party's legislative promises, to appeal to the country on legislative programs, and to wield the leadership in policy-framing which under our system is seldom forthcoming on Capitol Hill, the president has tended more and more to become, in addition to chief executive, our chief legislator as well; so that while there is not, and under our constitution cannot be, such an integration of authority as a cabinet system affords, the results attained need not always be, and sometimes are not, materially

---

Senate six times, and both houses eight times, including the recent Eightieth Congress. After the elections of 1946, in which the Republicans captured both the House of Representatives and the Senate, a Democratic senator from Arkansas (J. William Fulbright), speaking as a warm supporter of the President but also as a student of American history and government, seriously suggested that the Democratic president resign—after appointing a Republican secretary of state who, there being no vice-president, and as the law of succession then stood, would forthwith become president. The idea was to obviate what otherwise would be an interval of division and discord between the two branches, such as, in a number of respects, the period 1946-48 certainly proved. The people had spoken; they had declared for Republican rule; the unity and responsibility of such rule should not be thwarted by the presence of a chief executive of different persuasion in the White House. The proposal was somewhat on the fantastic side, and there never was any chance of its adoption. From a theoretical viewpoint, however, it had some merit.

[1] The cabinet and presidential types are compared in W. H. Taft, *Our Chief Magistrate and His Powers* (New York, 1916), Chap. 1; H. L. McBain, *The Living Constitution* (New York, 1927); and W. Wilson, *Congressional Government* (Boston, 1885).

different. To comprehend, therefore, what the presidency really means in this country, as well as the process by which our national laws are made and national taxes and expenditures authorized, one must look carefully into this matter of the chief executive's relations with Congress—and first of all into an imposing list of ways in which, notwithstanding our vaunted separation of powers, he may participate in, and even dominate, the work of the two houses.[1]

Presidential Control Over Legislation

By constitutional provision, a Congress lasts two years and has one regular session each year, beginning in the first week of January. Over the beginning and ending of regular sessions, the president has no absolute control, except that he may adjourn the houses "to such time as he shall think proper" if they find themselves unable to agree on a time of adjournment.[2] Practically, however, he may wield a good deal of influence upon the length of sessions, either by insisting upon legislation that would keep the houses at work—a "must" program, it is sometimes termed [3]—or, conversely, by withholding proposals which, if submitted, would have the same effect. Almost invariably, the date of adjournment is a matter of more or less amicable agreement between the president and the Senate and House leaders.[4] Furthermore, the president may, at his discretion, convene the houses, or either of them, in special session. In former times, when a new Congress would not otherwise meet until thirteen months after election, special sessions were by no means infrequent, and much important legislation was enacted in them—notably in sessions convoked by President Taft in 1909, President Wilson in 1913, President Harding in 1921, President Hoover in 1929, and President Roosevelt in 1933, with a view to getting a new Administration's legislative program under way (and incidentally securing confirmation of appointments) without waiting the many months that must elapse before the opening of the first regular session. Nowadays, however, a different situation obtains. Under the Twentieth Amendment, a new Congress meets as soon as the terms of its members begin; its two regular sessions start in January of consecutive years and run into the summer, with July 31

1. Control over sessions of Congress

---

[1] It seems desirable to bring the president into the picture at this point, while our attention is centered primarily on the legislative process, even though doing so means to postpone speaking of some general aspects of the office—term, compensation, succession, and the like which otherwise might have priority. The presidency in general, the president and his cabinet, and the president as chief executive will later tie in with our study of the executive and administrative side of the government.

[2] Art. II, § 3. This power of adjournment has never been exercised, although in October, 1914, President Wilson was urged to make use of it. In the early summer of 1940, President Franklin D. Roosevelt strongly desired that the third session of the Seventy-sixth Congress be terminated; but Congress, impressed with the growing urgency of national defense, and apparently backed by public opinion, was of a different mind, and the issue was not forced.

[3] Illustrations are afforded by the prolongation of sessions through the summers of 1934, 1935, and 1937 to act on matters urged by President Roosevelt.

[4] On the new rule since 1946 relating to adjournment by July 31 of each year, see p. 308 above.

fixed as a normal but not absolute deadline; and for special sessions there is likely to be little need—unless in an emergency like that created by the outbreak of a major war in Europe in the autumn of 1939, when such a session was called to repeal our embargo on the export of arms to belligerent states, and in other respects to amend the Neutrality Act of 1937.[1]

2. Messages   The constitution's requirement that the president give Congress information on "the state of the Union" and recommend for its consideration "such measures as he shall judge necessary and expedient"[2] is entirely logical. His peculiar vantage ground enables him to know many things about both foreign and domestic affairs that are beyond the ken of the members of the legislative branch; he can speak from an over-all view, and commonly with authority, in pointing out defects and needs, and can suggest remedies in line with actual executive and administrative experience; and he is no less under obligation than is Congress itself to put information and ideas at the country's service.

How frequently the president shall communicate with Congress by message, at what times, at what length, and in what way, the constitution does not specify; and, within limits, each president exercises his own discretion. It long ago became customary, however, to transmit at the opening of each regular session a comprehensive "state of the union" message summarizing the situation of public affairs, calling attention to matters requiring early consideration, and perhaps indicating definite legislation which, in the president's judgment, ought to be enacted. Under present practice, too, this is followed—usually within three or four days—by a message transmitting the annual budget.[3] And under terms of the Full Employment Act of 1946 there must come to Congress also near the opening of a regular session a "national production and employment budget," or economic budget, based on studies by the Council of Economic Advisers and setting forth the policies which in the chief executive's judgment must be pursued in order to maintain high-level production and full employment.[4] Nowadays, therefore, these three messages may be counted upon whenever a new session starts. In addition, shorter messages—sometimes scores of them during a session, each usually dealing with some specific subject or project—are transmitted as occasion demands or the president desires. Sometimes these ask Congress for a grant of some power (or powers) of which the president finds himself in need—power, for example, such as President Roosevelt requested

---

[1] Even in this case, the President had tried to get the desired legislation during the preceding regular session. From 1940 to 1945 inclusive, the regular sessions of wartime Congresses ran completely or substantially through successive calendar years, leaving no possible room for special sessions.

[2] Art. II, § 3.

[3] On January 21, 1946, President Truman departed from custom by submitting to Congress his state of the union and budget messages as a single document, 25,000 words in length.

[4] See pp. 723-724 below.

in 1933 to deal with a banking crisis. Sometimes they transmit a report or other body of material on the basis of which new legislation is asked, as, for example, when in 1937 President Roosevelt laid before the two houses the challenging report of his Committee on Administrative Management on the broad subject of administrative reorganization. Sometimes, indeed, they not only ask for legislation, but submit the text of a fully drafted bill (or at all events the broad outlines of one), as in 1937 when President Roosevelt asked for legislation reorganizing the federal judiciary,[1] or in 1947 when President Truman asked for unification of the armed forces under a new over-all national defense establishment.[2] Or, of course, a message (in this case addressed only to the house in which the measure originated) may be devoted to explaining the reasons for vetoing a bill already passed.

Washington and John Adams appeared in person before the two houses in joint session and delivered their messages orally. Jefferson, however, transmitted his messages in writing; and this practice prevailed until 1913, when, somewhat to the consternation of Congress, the oral form was revived by President Wilson. Oral messages were employed by President Harding; and, with the aid of the radio, President Coolidge read his first two annual messages to both Congress and the country. President Hoover reverted to the written message; President Franklin D. Roosevelt employed first one form and then the other;[3] and President Truman has most commonly, but not invariably, employed the written form.[4] The oral message has some advantages: it is likely to be more concise than the written one, which, if the truth be told, has in plenty of instances been diffuse and uninteresting;[5] it gives the president a chance to make his personality felt, not only in Congress, but (by means of the radio) throughout the country; and, even if only momentarily, it brings the executive and legislative branches into a closeness of touch which under a presidential form of government is too often lacking. On the other

Oral and written messages

---

[1] See p. 547 below. On this occasion, mimeographed copies of the bill were attached to copies of the message and in that form distributed to members immediately before the message was read. Such a bill must, however, be formally introduced by a committee chairman or other member of Congress.

[2] See p. 824 below.

[3] His decision to deliver the "state of the union" message of January 3, 1936, orally, with a nation-wide radio hook-up, and in the evening rather than during the day, aroused partisan criticism on the ground that a solemn constitutional function was being turned into a key-note speech in a campaign for reëlection. The complaint was hardly justified, although some portions of the message would probably have been more appropriate in a "fireside" talk addressed to the people directly.

[4] Six times in the country's history the president has appeared before the Senate alone on official business, the most recent being President Truman's visit of July 2, 1945, in behalf of assent to ratification of the Charter of the United Nations.

[5] That presidents sometimes labor hard to achieve brevity and force is indicated by the fact that the initial draft of President Hoover's first general message ran to 60,000 words and the final draft to only 12,000. As would be surmised, a president does not simply sit down and write a message (at all events one of wide coverage) as a piece of original composition. Many, if not most, parts of it will, in effect, be drafted in the executive departments or other agencies; and his task becomes one of assembling, assorting, and rephrasing the raw materials and deciding for how much, and for what, he will take responsibility.

hand, the oral message may solidify opposition and precipitate conflicts which a written communication would hardly arouse.

The effects of messages

How influential the general run of presidential messages are is a matter upon which it is difficult to generalize. Certainly they receive more publicity than does any other government document. Except, however, in the case of the two messages transmitting the fiscal and "economic" budgets, Congress is under no obligation beyond giving a respectful hearing; even the two mentioned may not eventuate in all of the actions desired; while as for the rest, the two houses may act quite out of line with the recommendations made, or may refuse or neglect to act at all. Much depends, of course, upon whether the president's party is in control of both houses. But even if it is, there is no guarantee that his advice will be followed.[1] Sometimes, it may be added, a message is really aimed at the country, or even at the world at large, rather than at Congress. The president may desire to stimulate public interest in and discussion of a given subject, with or without a view to legislation, and may use the congressional message as a means to that end. Theodore Roosevelt did this repeatedly. Or he may want to make his Administration's attitude known to a foreign state or group of states without incurring the embarrassments that might flow from resort to the customary diplomatic channels; as, for example, when Monroe, in 1823, slipped into his annual message to Congress statements serving notice to the European Powers that the American continents were no longer open to new colonization, thus laying the basis for the significant national policy ever since known as the Monroe Doctrine. In numerous oral messages during the first World War, President Wilson summed up and unified the thought of the country on submarine warfare and other challenging aspects of the international situation; likewise, in his message of January 2, 1918, he set forth, virtually on behalf of the Allied and Associated Powers, and in the form of his famous "Fourteen Points," the major terms or conditions deemed indispensable to a peace settlement. From Franklin D. Roosevelt's messages during his second and third administrations, one could arrive at a tolerably complete picture of the country's developing foreign policy in a period of growing tension and ultimate war.

3. Initiating and promoting legislation

By requiring the president to recommend to Congress "such measures as he shall judge necessary and expedient," the constitution in effect confers upon him the power, and indeed the duty, of legislative initiative; and, as we have seen, a very large proportion of the public bills that crowd the calendars of Congress emanate from the branch of government for which the president is primarily responsible. To be sure, many of these measures are of more or less routine character—extending, inter-

[1] During his first year in the White House, President Truman made more than twenty-five major proposals to Congress, practically all of them through the medium of messages. Although the Democrats controlled both houses, however, not more than ten of the number prevailed; and of these, half were revised to include features of which the President disapproved.

preting, or modifying statutes to meet needs that administrative experience has brought to light; and with these the president personally may have little or no connection. But others are of first-rate importance—breaking new ground, introducing new policies, providing for actions that will vitally affect large numbers of people. Even these may originate with executive departments or independent establishments; indeed, most of them do so. But either they will have been inspired or encouraged by the president, or at least his support for them will have been sought; because an administrative agency going to Congress for legislation will always want to do so with the advantage of presidential backing. Some such measures win their way into the chief executive's legislative program, others do not. But in any event there commonly *is* a presidential program; and in it will be found not only projects which have been brought to the White House by the administrators, but others, and perhaps larger ones, for which the president personally bears primary, if not sole, responsibility. The chief executive may be deeply concerned about far-reaching changes and reforms, as was Theodore Roosevelt about the regulation of corporation procedures, or Woodrow Wilson about the improvement of banking and trade practices. National difficulties may press upon him, as they did upon Herbert Hoover. A national crisis may confront him, as a disastrous banking situation confronted Franklin D. Roosevelt when he first took office in 1933, and again an international threat, when, in 1940, the world situation suddenly thrust upon the country the necessity of embarking upon a stupendous program of defense. Or it may be a crisis such as confronted President Truman, when, in May-June, 1946, a series of great strikes had tied up the country's railroad transportation and paralyzed its industry, and when the President appeared before a joint session of Congress to ask for immediate adoption of an emergency strike-control bill by which his message was accompanied. But whether or not such special conditions exist, the chief executive will find it incumbent upon him to meet public expectation in at least some degree by thinking about laws that ought to be passed, by working with the appropriate subordinates and advisers in formulating suitable measures, by seeing that the proposals are duly introduced in the House or Senate, and by using his influence to get them on the statute-book. And this influence is not confined to the president's personal and party connections on Capitol Hill, but includes what has aptly been termed "the most powerful lobby in Washington," consisting of the administrative personnel and agencies at the chief executive's disposal for amassing information and arguments and bringing these to bear upon the committees and members of the two houses.[1]

[1] W. B. Munro, *The Government of the United States* (5th ed., New York, 1946), 174. On occasion, the president not only may suggest or request legislation, but may adopt a strong tone in demanding it. As an extreme illustration may be cited an occurrence of September, 1942, when, with a view to averting the disaster of inflation, President Franklin D. Roosevelt bluntly told Congress and the country that unless

It may be true, as a recent writer maintains, that a close analysis of major national legislation in the past half-century will show more congressional, and less presidential, initiative and control than is commonly supposed; and it certainly is true that legislation in this country is "characteristically a collegial process in which the rôle of the Congress is no less important than that of the president." [1] But even the authority mentioned is bound to concede that "the emergence of the chief executive as a force in the initiation and formulation of legislation is...a twentieth-century phenomenon;" [2] and, making all due allowance for the fact that conditions, influences, forces, and demands external to governmental agencies of any kind lie back of and heavily influence the entire operation of the legislative process, the president's rôle within that framework is assuredly one of the most significant features of our political system. [3]

4. Guidance in finance

In the domain of finance, the president's relations with Congress are particularly close. Never (at all events until the Legislative Reorganization Act of 1946 introduced certain new procedures [4]) having developed any very effective agency of its own for attaining coöperation between the two houses, or for formulating policy, with respect to the budget as a whole, the legislative branch depends heavily upon the executive for leadership; and, as indicated elsewhere, the Budget and Accounting Act of 1921 made the president, through the director of the budget, virtually the general business manager of the government. [5] In that capacity, he annually transmits to Congress full information concerning the national finances, together with a coördinated fiscal plan for the coming year; as occasion requires, and particularly in special situations such as constantly arose during the recent period of defense preparations and war, he

---

by October 1 there should be legislation repealing a provision of the Emergency Price Control Act of the previous February 2, prohibiting ceilings on food products until farm prices had gone, on the average, sixteen per cent beyond "parity prices," he would fall back upon his powers as commander-in-chief and take whatever action he deemed necessary. Under the threat thus held over it, Congress grudgingly complied.

[1] L. H. Chamberlain, *The President, Congress, and Legislation* (New York, 1946), 11. The author of this excellent book analyzes the legislative history of ninety-six major laws passed by Congress in the past fifty years and comes off with the conclusion that twenty per cent of the number are to be ascribed primarily to executive influence, forty per cent to congressional influence, thirty per cent to influence divided equally between the executive and Congress, and ten per cent to influence from private interests. Chap. I presents a convenient epitome of the study.

[2] *Ibid.*, 11.

[3] Of course, not all presidents have been equally vigorous in promoting legislation. Washington and Jefferson were moderately influential (although primarily through certain of their cabinet members, *e.g.*, Hamilton). Thereafter none, except to a degree Jackson, Lincoln, and Cleveland, concerned themselves actively with the matter until Theodore Roosevelt's dynamic and aggressive spirit was injected into the picture. With Roosevelt, the philosophy of executive dominance in legislation clearly came to the fore, where it remained under Wilson, the second Roosevelt, and Truman. Taft, Harding, Coolidge, and Hoover were content with lesser rôles.

[4] See p. 565 below. Even the new plan bringing together the revenue and appropriations committees of the two houses for collective action provides only a device for fixing a ceiling for expenditures *after* the president's budget recommendations have been received.

[5] See p. 563 below.

transmits supplementary requests for appropriations; and while the two houses are not obliged to meet his demands in full, or, on the other hand, to stay within the limits of expenditure which he recommends, they are likely to hear from him in no uncertain terms if they fail to do either. There was a time when the president's influence was exerted mainly to keep Congress from playing fast and loose with the nicely adjusted plans which his budget agency, in conference with the revenue and spending authorities, had worked out. In the depression-war decade of unprecedented spending, it fell rather to economy-minded leaders in the two houses to apply brakes to spending programs of which the president had approved; and in the early postwar period the chief executive's spending plans were still outrunning the ideas of an opposition Congress.[1]

The Veto Power

Next in the list of presidential controls over legislation we encounter the power to disapprove bills and resolutions passed by Congress. Recollection of experience with later colonial governors and their absolute vetoes had left the executive veto in no very high favor with the generation that saw the constitution adopted. The designers of the new federal system had in mind, however, a balanced government in which each branch should be prevented from encroaching upon the rights or absorbing the powers of the other branches; and the most feasible means of defense for the executive against encroachments by the legislature seemed to be the power of veto. Furthermore, as Hamilton urged in *The Federalist*, the veto would "furnish an additional security against the enaction of improper laws."[2] Accordingly, the constitution requires that every bill which shall have passed the two houses of Congress shall, before it becomes a law, be presented to the president, who, if he approves, shall sign it, and if he disapproves, shall return it, with his objections, to the house in which it originated, and it shall then become law only if both houses, by two-thirds vote, again pass it.[3] To be sure the veto, under this proce-

Constitutional basis

---

[1] See pp. 570-572 below.

[2] No. LXXIII (Lodge's ed., 458).

[3] Art. I, § 7, cl. 2. The ensuing clause goes on to say that "every order, resolution, or vote" (except on a question of adjournment) to which the assent of both houses is necessary shall be presented to the president and be subject to the same veto procedure as a bill; and joint resolutions, regarded as tantamount to bills, are so treated except those submitting constitutional amendments for action by the states. Not only is this latter exception made in the face of what seems a plain constitutional requirement, but rather frequent resolutions of another type, *i.e.*, concurrent resolutions, are never submitted. Often such concurrent resolutions are merely declaratory of an attitude or opinion, but sometimes they have to do with the publication of documents or with other matters not too easily distinguished from subjects of legislation. When, in April, 1937, the Senate was about to pass a concurrent resolution condemning sit-down strikes as "illegal and contrary to sound public policy," the Republican leader sought in vain to have the form of joint resolution substituted in order that the President might be forced to take a position on the subject. During the later Roosevelt administrations, when large discretionary powers were being delegated more or less reluctantly to the president, the concurrent resolution took on a new and more important aspect, in that legislation granting powers to the chief executive sometimes reserved the right of Congress to nullify or terminate presi-

dure, is not absolute, but only suspensive.[1] It makes necessary a reconsideration of a disapproved bill or resolution; it gives the president an opportunity to present a formal argument against the measure; and the two-thirds requirement makes a second passage more difficult than the first. But such a veto does not kill a measure for which a sufficient amount of legislative support can be mustered.

Courses open to the president on a bill or resolution

When a bill or resolution is passed by the two houses and presented to the president, any one of four things may happen. (1) The president may promptly sign it, whereupon it becomes law.[2] (2) He may hold it without either signing or vetoing it, in which case it becomes law at the expiration of ten days (Sundays excepted), without his signature, provided Congress is still in session.[3] He may adopt this course because he dislikes the measure and is unwilling to put his name to it, although recognizing that a veto would be useless or politically inexpedient; or because he is undecided about its constitutionality or general merit and prefers not to commit himself. (3) He may hold the measure on his desk —figuratively, tuck it in his pocket—and by so doing quietly kill it if Congress adjourns within ten days.[4] Because of obviating the necessity of making a formal explanation to Congress (sometimes politically disadvantageous), a "pocket" veto may, from the president's point of view, be preferable to a direct, "messaged," veto;[5] and many bills come to grief in this way, particularly by reason of the fact that as a rule considerable numbers of measures are rushed through Congress in the closing days of a session and require only to be "pocketed" by the president to be kept off the statute-book. Formerly, it was considered that no bill might be signed after Congress had adjourned. Backed by

dential action under such legislation, and to do so by *concurrent resolution*—a technique giving the president no opportunity to reverse the congressional decision by veto. The Reorganization Act of 1939, the first Lend-Lease Act of 1941, the First War Powers Act of 1941, the Emergency Price Control Act of 1942, and several other measures contained provisions of this nature. See H. White, "The Concurrent Resolution in Congress," *Amer. Polit. Sci. Rev.*, XXXV, 886-889 (Oct., 1941); cf. *ibid.*, XXXVI, 895-900 (Oct., 1942).

[1] As explained below, if the president fails to return a bill and Congress adjourns before the measure has been on his desk for ten days, the effect is that of an absolute veto.

[2] Ordinarily no message to Congress is called for, although when approving an anti-racketeering bill in 1946 and a "portal to portal" bill in 1947, President Truman transmitted a message explaining how he and his legal advisers interpreted various provisions thought likely to be contested in the courts.

[3] The fact that the ten-day period is reckoned from the presentation of the bill—not its passage—became of much importance when President Wilson went abroad in 1919 to participate in negotiating the Treaty of Versailles, and again in January-February, 1945, when President Franklin D. Roosevelt was absent from the country some five weeks in connection with wartime conferences abroad.

[4] In the case of Okanogan Indians *v.* United States (279 U. S. 655), often referred to as the Pocket Veto case, the Supreme Court held in 1929 that this means ten calendar, not legislative, days. It held also that the rule applies to any congressional adjournment, not merely final adjournment at the end of a Congress—although the practice had always been on the latter assumption. See *Amer. Polit. Sci. Rev.*, XXIV, 67-69 (Feb., 1930).

[5] President Franklin D. Roosevelt, however, initiated the practice of attaching an explanatory memorandum to each bill pocket-vetoed.

the opinion of his attorney-general, President Wilson in 1920, however, signed a number of bills after adjournment; and the right to do so (within a ten-day period after presentation of the bill) has been unanimously affirmed by the Supreme Court.[1] Finally (4), a bill may be vetoed outright. That is to say, the president may, by positive act, disapprove it, in which case it goes, with a message giving his reasons, to the house in which it originated.[2] As has appeared, a pocket veto, even though arising from mere inaction, is the strongest veto of all, because there is no opportunity for Congress to reverse it. A direct veto has the effect, rather, of starting a reconsideration of the bill, first in the house of its origin, and afterwards, if successful there, in the other house; and if the hurdle of a two-thirds vote can be surmounted at both ends of the Capitol, the measure becomes law notwithstanding the president's disapproval.[3]

In the *Federalist* paper quoted above, Hamilton ventured the prediction that the veto would "generally be employed with great caution," and that there would be more danger of the president "not using his power when necessary, than of his using it too often, or too much." For many decades at least, this forecast was borne out. Not until Andrew Johnson's administration did any president deem it necessary to resort to a veto in defense of his own constitutional rights; and altogether it has been used for this purpose no more than a dozen times. Indeed, there were only fifty-one vetoes, all told, before the Civil War. The first six presidents vetoed bills only on the ground that they were unconstitutional or technically defective.[4] Jackson, who in sundry ways made the presidency something different from what it had been before, gave the veto a new twist by employing it to stifle measures conceded to be constitutional and technically correct, but considered objectionable in their aim and content.[5] Yet Jackson, in eight years, vetoed only twelve bills. In the turbu-

Frequency of vetoes

[1] Edwards *v.* United States, 286 U. S. 482 (1932). The present plan is preferable, because instead of the president waiting anxiously, with pen poised, in his room at the Capitol to sign bills as fast as rushed to him in the closing hours of a session, he can take time to study them. When, in July, 1947, the Eightieth Congress supposedly closed its first session (it was later reconvened), some 250 bills, important or otherwise, awaited President Truman's attention.

[2] In Wright *v.* United States (302 U. S. 583), the Supreme Court held, in 1938, that a vetoed bill can validly be returned to a branch of Congress at a time when it has recessed and only the other branch is in session. In such a situation, said the Court, "Congress" is still in session.

[3] When, on May 22, 1935, President Franklin D. Roosevelt appeared before a joint session of Congress to deliver a veto message in person, he introduced a new and dramatic feature of veto procedure—though one not again encountered later.

Another variation from the procedures described arose in 1934 when, an equal-rights nationality bill having been presented to President Roosevelt, he conferred with the legislative sponsors of the measure and induced the houses to recall the bill by concurrent resolution for amendment along specified lines.

[4] Except that Madison vetoed two measures on grounds of policy.

[5] He also claimed and exercised the right to veto bills which he thought unconstitutional notwithstanding that the Supreme Court had ruled to the contrary. The best illustration is the veto, in 1832, of the bill to renew the charter of the second United States Bank. There can be no doubt that in his broader interpretation and use of the veto power Jackson was entirely within his rights. The constitution says simply that if the president "approves" a bill he shall sign it, and if not he shall return it. "No better word," former President Taft once observed, "could be found

lent era of Reconstruction, the veto was employed more freely, and later presidents have not taken the conservative attitude of their remoter predecessors. Except in the cases of Grover Cleveland and Franklin D. Roosevelt, however, the number of vetoes has rarely averaged more than five or six a year; between them, those two presidents are responsible for more than two-thirds of all presidential vetoes in the country's history— in the case of Cleveland a total of 414 (largely vetoes of pension and other private bills), in that of Roosevelt a total of 631 (371 direct and 260 "pocket," and including vetoes of the widest variety of measures, both public and private [1]). Of eight presidents who made no use of the veto power at all, the most recent was Garfield—though it should be added that Congress was never in session during his brief tenure.

General expansion of the veto power

The most significant thing is not, however, the tendency toward increase in the number of vetoes. The really important matter is the freedom with which presidents, as one writer has put it, "offset their own judgment against that of Congress, not merely on great questions involving the public welfare, and on disputed constitutional questions, but on trivial matters whereon their means of information are not greater or better than those at the command of Congress, and whereon their individual judgment does not appear to be superior to that of the average congressman or senator." [2] In other words, the veto power has been so expanded by usage as to become a general revising power, applicable

in the language to embrace the idea of passing on the merits of the bill." *Our Chief Magistrate and His Powers*, 16.

[1] G. C. Robinson, "The Veto Record of President Franklin D. Roosevelt," *Amer. Polit. Sci. Rev.*, XXXVI, 75-78 (Feb., 1942). Professor Robinson (of Iowa State Teachers College) is in possession of very complete and reliable data on presidential vetoes throughout the country's history. Full information for the period after 1889 can be obtained from R. L. Baldridge [comp.], *Record of Bills Vetoed and Action Taken Thereon by the Senate and House of Representatives, Fifty-first Congress to Seventy-sixth Congress, Inclusive, 1889-1941* (Washington, D. C., 1941).

It is interesting to notice that President Franklin D. Roosevelt's 631 vetoes constituted more than a third of the total number (1,852) in the country's history to January, 1948. Of course, Roosevelt occupied the presidency about four years longer than any of his predecessors. On the other hand, his own party was continuously in control of Congress.

By vetoing a total of 91 bills during his first two and one-half years in office, President Truman started what promised to be a veto record quite commensurate with those of Cleveland and Franklin D. Roosevelt. In the early summer of 1947, he was locked in combat with the Republican majority in Congress, twice successfully vetoing a bill of wide popular interest for the reduction of federal taxes, and unsuccessfully vetoing the Labor-Management Relations [Taft-Hartley] Bill, of at least equally wide concern. In the latter instance, he not only interposed a sharply-worded veto, but tried hard to keep the Senate (where there seemed some chance of averting a two-thirds vote) from overriding the veto—to this end broadcasting his objections to the measure, calling senators to the White House for conference, and addressing an appeal through the Democratic minority leader, Senator Barkley. With both the tax and labor bills supported by heavy majorities in both branches of Congress, only a few months after national elections, and with many members of the President's own party favoring both, these vetoes gave the country a vivid demonstration of the very great legislative power which the veto carries with it— power, indeed, to cancel out, by the fiat of one man, the collective will of very nearly three-quarters of 531 senators and representatives.

[2] E. Stanwood, *History of the Presidency from 1898 to 1916* (new ed., Boston, 1928), 324.

to all legislation, whether important or not, and whether relating to public matters or to private and personal interests. The result has been to make the president a far more active and potent factor in legislation than he originally was or was intended to be.

This does not mean, however, that the veto power has, in these later days, been used loosely and irresponsibly. On the contrary, it has commonly been employed reluctantly and with due discretion. Most vetoes of measures important enough to have attracted popular attention have been supported by public sentiment, and comparatively few have been overridden by subsequent action of Congress. Not until Tyler's administration did any vetoed bill receive the two-thirds vote in both houses necessary to make it law. Wilson was reversed six times, and Cleveland seven, but Coolidge only four times; Hoover, three times; Truman (to April, 1948), twice; Harrison, Theodore Roosevelt, and Taft, once each; and McKinley and Harding not at all. Even Franklin D. Roosevelt's reversals numbered only nine.[1] In practice, therefore, the direct veto tends to become almost as absolute as the "pocket" variety; only rarely and with great difficulty can sufficient votes be mustered in the two houses to override an unfavorable presidential decision. This has led to the suggestion that the veto power be weakened by making it possible for a vetoed measure ultimately to prevail by being repassed in the two houses by a simple majority (as is the rule in a number of states), rather than the present two-thirds. On the other hand, it has been suggested that the veto be strengthened by requiring that a bill, to be carried over a veto, be repassed by an affirmative vote of two-thirds of the entire membership of each house, instead of, as now, by two-thirds of a quorum in each.[2]

Another, and more important, proposal looking to strengthening the veto power is that authority be conferred to veto individual items of a bill while nevertheless approving the measure as a whole. As matters stand, the president must assent to or veto a bill in its entirety; he cannot approve part and reject part. When anyone of the regular annual or deficiency appropriation bills is placed on his desk, he may find that, although ostensibly based on estimates prepared by his budget bureau,

Marginal notes: Few vetoes overridden by Congress / The question of the veto of items

---

[1] Among the most noteworthy measures to become law over the veto in the last thirty-five or forty years are the Webb-Kenyon Act of 1913, vetoed by Taft; the Volstead Act of 1919 and an immigration act providing for a literacy test, vetoed by Wilson; the Soldiers' Bonus Act, vetoed by Coolidge; the Bonus Loan Act and the Philippine Independence Act of 1933, vetoed by Hoover; three measures vetoed by Franklin D. Roosevelt, i.e., the Bonus Act of 1936, the War Labor Disputes [Smith-Connally] Act of 1943, and (on the occasion of the first veto of a measure of the kind in our national history) the Revenue Act of 1943; and the Labor-Management Relations [Taft-Hartley] Act vetoed by Truman in 1947.

[2] Effort has sometimes been made to show that this higher requirement is already the law. Thus in a case decided by the Supreme Court in 1919, the plaintiff contended that the Webb-Kenyon Act was not a valid piece of legislation, since, after veto of it by President Taft, it was passed in the Senate by a vote of merely two-thirds of the senators present rather than two-thirds of the total membership. The Court refused to take this view. Missouri Pac. Ry. Co. v. State of Kansas, 216 U. S. 262 (1910).

the measure as passed contains clauses slipped in by Congress interpolating additional expenditures or altering the amounts requested for particular purposes; and it might be in the public interest for him to strike these out. This, however, he cannot do; and, rather than leave important services without funds or inflict hardship by preventing salaries from being paid, he is practically certain to sign the bill as it stands. The situation is not as bad as it used to be before the Budget and Accounting Act of 1921 became law; [1] because under the operation of that statute, appropriation acts usually follow fairly closely the specifications transmitted by the executive. Indeed, if only there could be incorporated into the budget system, by law or practice, the salutary English plan under which the legislature adds no new items of expenditure to those requested by the executive, and makes no increases in the amounts asked, the problem would be solved. There being, however, little prospect of this being done, the item veto in connection with expenditures remains an unsettled question. All but nine of the states have empowered their governors to veto appropriation items—in some instances also to reduce the amount carried by an item; and similar power for the national executive has been advocated for many decades. When, however, President Roosevelt, in 1938, urgently requested a grant of such authority and the House assented, the Senate refused to concur, on the ground that the item veto would constitute an invasion of congressional authority, and that in any event it could properly be authorized only by a constitutional amendment. The general objections have been raised, too, (1) that the power would enable a president, if he were so minded, to discriminate unfairly between appropriations favored by his supporters and others of concern mainly to his opponents, and (2) that, with the power known to be in the president's hands, Congress might fall into the habit, as have some state legislatures, of gratifying departments and pressure groups by voting extravagant appropriations and deliberately saddling the executive with the burden of whittling them down and with the unpopularity likely to arise from doing so.

It would likewise be useful to the president to be able to veto specific provisions of bills other than appropriation measures. President Wilson, in 1920, felt constrained to veto an entire bill providing for a national budget system in which he thoroughly believed, rather than approve what he conceived to be an unconstitutional clause relating to the method of removing the comptroller-general.[2] President Coolidge would have liked to veto a provision of the immigration act of 1924 which he well knew would give deep offense to Japan. In 1943, President Roosevelt would have been glad to apply the knife to a section in a bill authorizing an increase of the national debt limit, for the reason that the offending section annulled a ceiling of $25,000 after payment of taxes which in the previous year he

[1] See p. 563 below.
[2] *Ibid.*

(under terms of a Stabilization Act, but contrary to the intent of Congress) had ordered to be imposed on salaries; but there was no way of doing so without frustrating a new loan which the government needed immediately.[1]

Other Presidential Weapons and Techniques

Convening Congress in special session, sending messages (or delivering them orally), initiating bills, transmitting budget proposals, and wielding the veto power by no means exhaust the president's resources in influencing legislation. By letting it be known (publicly or privately) that he will veto a pending bill unless certain features are added to or withdrawn from it, or other changes made in it, he may be able virtually to determine the form which the measure will finally take, or even to prevent it from being passed at all; indeed, he may thus head off a bill before it has even been introduced. When Theodore Roosevelt gave Congress public warning that he would veto certain measures if sent to him, loud protest was raised against such virtual use of the veto in advance. No one, however, could find anything in the constitution or laws to prevent a chief executive from making his views and intentions known whenever he desires, and in later days, as the leadership of the White House in legislation continued to grow, threat of veto became one of the most familiar of presidential weapons. Sometimes the expedient serves its purpose instantly by causing a bill to be abandoned, especially if there is no reason to suppose that the majorities necessary to overcome a veto could be obtained. Sometimes, however, Congress persists in passing a measure, in confidence of eventual triumph, even though well aware that a veto message is ready to be transmitted the moment the bill reaches the president's desk.[2] Sometimes, indeed, congressmen who want to stand well

1. Threat of veto

---

[1] A practice which has exposed Congress to valid criticism and frequently created antagonism between the legislative and executive branches is that of attaching "riders" to appropriation and other bills, i.e., provisions on wholly or essentially extraneous matters, inserted because of little hope of getting them through in any other way. The last instance cited above affords, indeed, an illustration—another being a section written into an appropriation bill of 1945 breaking up the national system of employment offices (a proposal so objectionable to President Truman that he vetoed the entire bill); and still another being clauses tacked on to various appropriation measures of 1946 forbidding salaries to be paid to any persons advocating, or belonging to organizations advocating, overthrow of the government by force. In the House, such riders can usually be thrown out, under the rules, if a point of order is made against them. In the Senate, there is freer scope for them, although in pursuance of the Legislative Reorganization Act of 1946 a new rule has greatly improved the situation by putting an end (if it is actually enforced) to riders on appropriation bills. Riders to other sorts of measures, however, are not outlawed; and the president is still without power to single them out for veto.

[2] The Logan-Walter bill of 1940 (relating to judicial procedures of regulatory commissions) was passed in full knowledge that a veto awaited it; and after the veto, it very narrowly failed to become law. When the two houses sent the Revenue Act of 1943 to the president's desk, they were prepared for a veto, even if not for the vigorous language in which it was couched; and the measure became law notwithstanding the veto. With President Truman on record against its objectives, the tax-reduction bill of 1947 was passed in the face of a probable veto; and when, after being killed, it was introduced again with only the starting date changed, the President publicly announced that he would veto it a second time—which he did,

with their constituents vote for a dubious measure with an easier conscience because they have every reason to believe that the chief executive is going to kill it.

2. Use of patronage

A less obstrusive and rather commoner means of presidential influence on legislation is the distribution of patronage. To be sure, there is less to distribute now than formerly, but nevertheless, in the aggregate, still a good deal. Candidates for offices filled by the president and Senate are usually brought to the chief executive's attention and urged upon him by senators (sometimes representatives) from states in which positions have become available; and success or failure in securing appointments invariably goes far toward determining a member's standing with his party in the home bailiwick. In his dealings with senators and congressmen of his party, the president therefore holds the whip hand; if they fail to support policies and measures in which he is interested, he has only to turn a deaf ear to their pleas for patronage in order to subject them to back-fire from office-hungry constituents. To be sure, overt threats and definite bargains on the subject are not often made.[1] But members can hardly be expected to be oblivious to the practical advantages of being numbered among the supporters upon whom the president will feel that he can depend; and we have the word of a former president that the control over legislation arising from this source is very great.[2] Naturally, it will be at its peak when a new Administration, of different political faith, has come in, with plenty of offices at its disposal, and in a session taking place immediately, i.e., before appointments have been made. Since the Twentieth Amendment took effect, every new Administration starts almost simultaneously with the first regular session of a new Congress, so that the maximum of opportunity for presidential influence through patronage is bound to arise the moment a president of different political complexion enters the White House. An incoming chief executive who wishes to make full use of his power of patronage will naturally be slow about distributing the loaves and fishes, keeping his followers in a state of expectancy as long as he can while the more important parts of his program are being translated into law. Thus it is generally understood that Franklin D. Roosevelt's appointments in 1933 were systematically held back in order to keep wavering senators and representatives in line while novel, and sometimes startling, measures for national recovery were being enacted. Congressmen may fret and fume,

thereby ending all chance for such legislation during the session. In none of the situations mentioned did threat of veto sway Congress from the course on which it had embarked; rather, it only stiffened the determination of those favoring the legislation to go ahead. Under less tense circumstances, however, such threat sometimes acts as a deterrent; and at all times, of course, it may do so in the case of some individual members.

[1] An historic case is President Cleveland's direct and open threat to withdraw patronage from Democratic senators failing to support the repeal of the Silver Purchase Act in 1893.

[2] W. H. Taft, Our Chief Magistrate and His Powers, 27.

but this is part of the price they pay for perpetuating patronage in the upper brackets of the national service.[1]

A variant of this procedure appears when, in addition to withholding patronage, the president tries to influence party members not to reëlect senators or representatives who have opposed his legislative measures or whose general attitude on public policy is out of line with his own. This he may do by quietly but none the less significantly abstaining from any word of endorsement or approval; but he also may openly oppose a candidate and appeal to the electorate against him. The most notable recent instance of resort to this latter technique (and on a large scale) was President Franklin D. Roosevelt's unsuccessful attempt in the elections of 1938 to "purge" Congress of Democratic members who had opposed his court reorganization bill and other measures.[2]

3. Intervention in elections

Still another source of influence is personal contact, conference, and persuasion. To be sure, the president does not appear on the floor of either branch of Congress to take part in debate, or indeed for any purpose other than to read an occasional formal message.[3] But this does not prevent him from discussing measures and policies with large numbers of members, individually and in small groups, in his office or his study at the White House, over the griddle cakes and sausages at the breakfast table (a well-known Coolidge custom), or even in the room set apart for him at the Capitol. From early in his first administration, Franklin D. Roosevelt made systematic use of a Monday morning conference participated in by the vice-president, the speaker of the House, the Democratic leaders in the House and Senate, and chairmen of varying committees having major bills pending; and every one around Washington knew that this weekly meeting, at which the chief executive received a report on the status of the legislative program and told the conferees what he wanted done, was frequently of more significance than meetings of the cabinet. There are occasions, too, when a president calls into conference

4. Personal conference and persuasion

---

[1] They realize, too, that they may personally stand in need of presidential favor if, failing of reëlection, they later seek consolation in the form of a federal appointment.

[2] See "What Flows from the Purge?" [Symposium], *Cong. Digest*, XVII, 225-256 (Oct., 1938). In advance of the congressional elections of 1946, President Truman was under some pressure to proscribe Democratic members (mainly Southern) who had not gone along with the Administration. He refrained from any blanket purge, but openly opposed the renomination of one Missouri congressman who, as a member of the House committee on rules, had opposed his measures, and who went down to defeat in the primary. One may generalize to the extent of saying that, although no active purges may be involved, presidents are always in politics—some more deeply, however, than others.

[3] He probably loses nothing by this, because if he participated in debate on the floor, what he said would soon come to be looked upon as of little more significance than if uttered by a senator or representative; and this would both lower the dignity of his office and lessen his influence with the people. Anyway, few votes are ever changed by debate. President Hoover's appearance before the Senate in 1932 to argue for a sales tax which would have aided in balancing the budget was a very exceptional occurrence, and in the outcome it yielded no practical result—except to stir resentment among the senators. *Cong. Record*, 72nd Cong., 1st Sess., Vol. 75, p. 11732.

the chairman and other influential members (perhaps including representatives of the minority quota) of a standing committee; and at such times he may urge or demand that a given measure be postponed, or that it be speeded up, or that it be amended in specified ways. When confronting congressional groups of these sorts, he may employ arts ranging all the way from genial encouragement or gentle persuasion to bold ultimatum, *e.g.*, a threat to hold Congress in session until it does what he desires," or, conversely, to veto a pending or proposed bill if passed. On the other hand, he may be induced to accept amendments to bills in which he is interested, or even to make important changes in his general legislative program. In any event, his views, promptly carried back to the two houses by the conferees, are likely to exert a good deal of influence. Executive control over legislation by this method was exercised conspicuously by Presidents Cleveland, Wilson, and the two Roosevelts.[1]

5. Cultivation of popular support   In the long run, nothing is so useful to the president in his dealings with Congress as the backing of public sentiment. Members cannot afford to fly in the face of their constituents, and if the president is strong in city and countryside, he commonly has little to fear. Realizing this, every president courts popular approval for himself and his policies. Some are more adept at cultivating the public than are others; some more fortunate in occupying the White House at times when public support is easy to win. But all have unmatched opportunities for publicity; and all can utilize messages to Congress, addresses on carefully chosen public occasions, greetings (in person or otherwise) to organizations and meetings, press conferences,[2] conferences with key citizens and with delegations, letters addressed to private individuals but intended for the public, and in later years heart-to-heart talks to the people by radio (in the fashion so successfully employed by the mellifluous-voiced

[1] To supplement personal conferences, some recent chief executives, notably Hoover and Franklin D. Roosevelt, at times employed a "contact man" charged with serving as a general *liaison* between the White House and the Capitol. In his earlier years, President Wilson did not utilize face-to-face conferences as much as some other presidents, but he made heavy use of the telephone.

[2] The practice of meeting a hundred or more representatives of American (and some foreign) press associations and leading newspapers at the White House at regular intervals, giving them information and comment, and answering such questions as he chose, was instituted by President Wilson, although abandoned after the United States entered World War I. While relying heavily on the radio, Franklin D. Roosevelt had a sense of publicity which made him quick to capitalize on the public-relations possibilities of the press conference, and for years his semi-weekly conferences (more than a thousand all told) were known as the "biggest single show in Washington." Instead of seeing the press representatives regularly twice a week, President Truman has seen them only when he considered that he had something to give out; and conferences have become briefer, with less presidential discourse and sometimes banter than under Roosevelt. J. E. Pollard, *The Presidents and the Press* (New York, 1947), tells the story of the press conference from its beginnings; and other accounts include L. C. Rosten, *The Washington Correspondents* (New York, 1937), and "President Roosevelt and the Washington Correspondents," *Pub. Opinion Quar.*, I, 36-52 (Jan., 1937); L. Rogers, "President Roosevelt's Press Conferences," *Polit. Quar.*, IX, 360-372 (July-Sept., 1938); and J. H. Crider, "The President's Press Conference," *Amer. Mercury*, LIX, 481-487 (Oct., 1944). Cabinet members (notably the secretary of state) and other high officials hold occasional press conferences also.

Franklin D. Roosevelt), to build and maintain a public opinion which congressmen will hesitate to antagonize or ignore.[1] If all else fails, a president may appeal directly to the nation against Congress, and both Theodore Roosevelt and Woodrow Wilson did so;[2] although such a course is risky, and hardly to be undertaken save by a president of genuine stature and having a decidedly good case.[3]

One further form of presidential activity requires mention in this connection, *i.e.*, the appointment of temporary commissions charged with investigating specified subjects or problems and reporting data and conclusions which may be made the basis of recommended legislation. Congress creates committees of its own members for similar purposes; but the commissions here referred to are initiated, appointed, and instructed by the president, with or without appropriations from Congress to cover their expenditures (salaries are never provided), and their reports are presented directly to the president for such use as he may care to make of them. The object may be to bring to light full data on some broad subject on which legislators, administrators, educators, and indeed the public at large, need to be better informed—good illustrations being afforded by President Taft's Commission on Industrial Relations created in 1912, President Hoover's Commission on Law Observance and Enforcement (the Wickersham Commission) appointed in 1929, his Commission on Social Trends appointed in 1930, and President Franklin D. Roosevelt's Temporary National Economic Committee set up in 1938. Or the purpose may be to pave the way for legislation in a given field, as when President Roosevelt's Committee on Economic Security, appointed in 1934, was given the task of making studies preliminary to what turned out to be the momentous Social Security Act of 1935, or when President Truman's Advisory Commission on Universal Training,

6. Appointment of fact-finding and opinion-guiding commissions

---

[1] President Roosevelt's appeals to the people in his numerous radio talks during his first administration were not those of a champion against Congress, which, on the whole, was tractable enough, but rather those of a national leader reporting on what was being done and why, and seeking to sustain public morale. Without employing the radio directly to build back-fires against refractory senators and congressmen, he in later years made clever appeals over the air for popular support of the greater measures and policies to which he was devoted; and from time to time during the defense effort of 1940-41 and the war effort of 1941 and after, he talked to the country about the situation as currently developing and stressed the need for understanding and coöperation on the part of all of the people. The presidential secretary then in charge of public relations is authority for the statement that some of the President's wartime talks were heard by as many as 61,500,000 people, or some seventy-nine per cent of the country's adult population. President Truman likewise has made considerable use of radio, on at least one notable occasion going on the air to denounce a measure (the Taft-Hartley Labor-Management Relations Bill of 1947) passed by Congress, and to explain and justify his veto of it.

[2] One of the most famous of direct presidential appeals to the country was that of Wilson in 1919 in behalf of American membership in the League of Nations. Perhaps the effort was foredoomed to failure, but in any event it was cut short by a physical collapse in the course of a transcontinental speaking tour.

[3] An interesting analysis of "presidential propaganda" will be found in L. Rogers, *The American Senate*, Chap. VII, although radio-broadcasting has added a technique of major importance since Professor Rogers wrote. Cf. H. W. Stoke, "Executive Leadership and the Growth of Propaganda," *Amer. Polit. Sci. Rev.*, XXXV, 490-500 (June, 1941).

was appointed in 1946. Or the intent may be to lay the foundation for extensive administrative reforms, as in the case of President Roosevelt's Committee on Administrative Management, appointed in 1936, and making recommendations summarized in a later chapter,[1] and also his Committee on the Improvement of the Civil Service (the Reed Committee), appointed in 1939. As a rule, Congress does not take altogether kindly to the creation of such agencies, preferring (often in a futile sort of way) to do its own investigating.[2] However—notwithstanding that it would be difficult to show that much actually happened after certain investigations were made—a great deal of useful fact-finding and opinion-guiding work has been done, large amounts of useful information have been amassed (some of it, to be sure, soon going out of date), some significant administrative changes have resulted, and a considerable amount of desirable legislation has been given an impetus without which it might never have been enacted.[3]

Circumstances Favoring Presidential Leadership in Legislation

1. The president as party leader

Certain practical situations operate to the president's advantage in employing the constitutional powers and extraconstitutional techniques enumerated. First of all is his position as leader of his party. Originally, the chief executive was not a party man; Washington thought of himself as identified with no party and chief of no faction. When, however, parties came into the field and presidents began to be elected as party representatives, party leadership became as truly a function of the president as it is of the British prime minister; and it is nowadays a hardly less important source of power than is the authority conferred in the constitution itself. Chosen as a party man to head a government operated frankly under the party system, the president surrounds himself with advisers of his own political faith, consults chiefly his fellow-partisans in Congress on proposed appointments, confers mainly with them on the framing of policy, and depends primarily on their loyalty and support for realization of his legislative program. He represents the party throughout the entire country, as members of Congress do not; and the country looks to him, even more than to Congress, for fulfillment of the pledges which his party has made. Everything affecting the well-being and prospects of his party has relevance for the success of his administration, and hence is of concern to him personally. One therefore will not be surprised to find him usually claiming supreme direction of his

[1] See p. 483, note 2, below.

[2] An illustration of this short-sighted attitude is afforded by the cutting off of all appropriations in 1943 from President Roosevelt's National Resources Planning Board (see pp. 710-711 below).

[3] Reports of presidential commissions are usually printed and thus made available to members of Congress as well as to other people in the government. Sometimes, however, the Administration has the advantage, when its bills are being considered, of having the information while its opponents have only theories and emotion. A full survey of the general subject will be found in C. Marcy, *Presidential Commissions* (New York, 1945).

party's affairs. While still only a presidential candidate, he picks the chairman of the national committee of the party; after assuming office, he may take a hand in the selection of congressional and other candidates, and may appeal to the voters to give them support, as did Theodore Roosevelt in the congressional elections of 1906 and Woodrow Wilson, less successfully, in those of 1918; [1] he may suggest, and even dictate, planks to be included in party platforms, both national and state; he may, indeed, to all intents and purposes decree his own renomination (as did Franklin D. Roosevelt in 1940 and 1944) or the nomination of the man whom he favors as his successor (as Theodore Roosevelt forced the nomination of Taft by the Republicans in 1908). Jefferson, Jackson, Lincoln, McKinley, Wilson, and the two Roosevelts may be enumerated as presidents who in a preëminent degree dominated their respective parties.[2]

It goes without saying that the president's relations with Congress, including his control over legislation, depend very largely upon the party situation at a given time, and upon the vigor and skill with which he capitalizes on his position as party leader. The most favorable circumstance is one in which a new president, with a definite and attractive program, comes into office along with a Congress containing substantial majorities of his own party in both houses, as was the fortune of Woodrow Wilson in 1913 and Franklin D. Roosevelt in 1933. If to this situation be added a national emergency requiring prompt and drastic action—as certainly was the case in 1933—opportunity is proportionately increased. Under such conditions, the limits of leadership and control are, speaking broadly, fixed only by the president's own competence, energy, and persuasiveness. The least favorable circumstance, on the other hand, is, of course, one in which a chief executive, with perhaps his own initial zeal somewhat dulled, has seen his party's majorities melt away, in one house or both.[3] To be in supreme command of his party the country over is a

Effects on relations with Congress

---

[1] Or, as we have seen, he may throw his influence *against* the election or reëlection of certain candidates.

[2] An English or Canadian prime minister going out of office with his party remains the recognized party leader, but not so an American president, whose position in a more or less leaderless opposition party is at best only that of nominal chief, as illustrated by the rôle of Herbert Hoover in the Republican party after 1933. This matter of the leadership of a minority party is, indeed, something that American political ingenuity has never worked out. Especially is there uncertainty about the status of a defeated presidential candidate who has not held the presidency. After his defeat in 1940, Wendell Willkie prepared to go on as leader of his party ("leader of the loyal opposition"), as the thrice-defeated Bryan had done after 1896, 1900, and 1908. But the effort was not wholly successful. Likewise, after Thomas E. Dewey's defeat in 1944, he did not continue to be generally recognized as Republican leader.

[3] The nadir used to be reached in the closing session of a Congress taking place after the president himself had been defeated for reëlection. Under the calendar introduced by the Twentieth Amendment, this situation—last witnessed in the case of Hoover in the winter of 1932-33—cannot arise again (unless in the extremely unlikely event of a special session being called by a defeated president after an election). In general, however, a president's grip will be relaxed whenever it becomes known that he will not be a candidate for reëlection. This was the experience, for example, of Theodore Roosevelt in 1906-08. In addition to the limitations imposed

mighty asset when that party has the votes on Capitol Hill to put through whatever measures the White House desires. But when it is the opposition party that has the votes—even in only one of the houses— leadership of a minority is of little avail. In such a situation, a president is forced back upon the arts of persuasion and compromise, with only the threat of veto and of appeal to the people to help him; and sometimes little can be accomplished.[1] There is no mystery about the fact that most great pieces of legislation are enacted in the first half of presidential administrations. To a degree, the explanation is, of course, that a new president (or even one newly reëlected), coming into office with what he inevitably construes as a popular mandate in behalf of the policies which he and his party have espoused in the campaign, naturally turns promptly to getting those policies carried out. But a main reason is that if they are not carried out during the first two years, they probably will not be carried out at all. For rarely is a president in as strong a position after the Congress which was elected with him goes out of office and the new Congress elected in the middle of his term comes in. His party will usually have a reduced majority in one or both branches; indeed, he is fortunate if he does not find the opposition in control of the House, perhaps also of the Senate. His patronage, too, will have lost much of its bargaining value, because nearly all of the important posts will have been filled. The time for a president to translate his party leadership into legislative performance is normally when party loyalty and spirit are running strong and party votes are plentiful as a result of recent victory at the polls. Later on, his leadership will probably have to be directed principally to repairing damage wrought by defeats, schisms, and other set-backs.[2]

by election for a fixed term, presidential leadership sometimes suffers from the choice of a president not fitted for leadership (*e.g.*, Taft, Harding, and Hoover), and at all times encounters obstacles arising from the difficulty of maintaining a clear and honest line of demarcation between the president as party leader and the president as head of the government of all the people. During the famous "purge" of 1938, aimed at defeating in the primaries and elections Democratic senators and representatives who had opposed his measures, Franklin D. Roosevelt professed to be campaigning against the delinquents, not as president of the United States, but as "head of the Democratic party, charged with responsibility for carrying out its principles;" and during the campaign of 1940 he labeled some of his speeches "political" and others "non-political" (those made during the campaign of 1944 being without exception frankly "political").

[1] A notable instance of an effort to handle such a situation was President Wilson's dealings with a Republican Senate in 1920, especially with respect to the Treaty of Versailles.

[2] The strengthened position of the Roosevelt Administration as a result of the sweeping Democratic victory in the elections of 1934 stands out as a notable exception to the foregoing observations. The elections of 1938 and 1942, however, yielding heavy Republican gains, ran true to form. On the first of these latter occasions, the Administration's previous majorities had been so overwhelming that, although now diminished, they remained entirely adequate; on the second, the still heavier losses, combined with growing defection of Southern Democrats, left only majorities that were thin (at least in the House) and not too dependable; and the elections of 1946 put both houses under control of the opposition. In half a century prior to 1948, the opposition party failed at mid-term elections to increase its representation in the House only once and in the Senate only four times.

A second circumstance strongly favorable to presidential influence upon legislation is the need on Capitol Hill for leadership and direction from some outside source. Experience shows that Congress, when left to its own devices, tends to disintegrate into minority, partisan, and sectional elements and to flounder in a bog of contrary purposes. Even if there is capable and recognized leadership in the houses singly, there is usually no one save the president to bring the two branches together in effective support of great policies and measures. On plenty of occasions, senators and representatives show resentment when exhorted, advised, or requested from "downtown;" yet when a new path is to be hewed, they almost invariably hesitate and show confusion until and unless a directing hand points the way and a commanding voice urges to action.[1] In other words, Congress works well only under stimulus and pressure, which may, of course, come ultimately from public opinion, or even from considerations of party welfare, but in any case usually needs to be transmitted or applied by the president. With a president of different party in the White House, congressional majorities are, of course, less responsive to executive leadership; and—as illustrated by the delays and futilities characterizing the early months of the Republican-dominated Eightieth Congress in 1947—then is when legislation is likely to move most haltingly. *[margin note: 2. The need of Congress for outside leadership]*

Finally, there is the circumstance that, more and more, the people look to the president, not simply to coördinate and direct the national administration and to speak for the country in dealings with foreign governments, but to develop well-conceived lines of domestic policy, to propose the legislation necessary for carrying out such policy, and to exert enough pressure upon Congress to get this legislation enacted. They expect him, indeed, to "manage" Congress; and if through lack of political skill, or because of adverse circumstances too difficult to be overcome, he does not do so, they (justly or unjustly) pronounce him a failure. In other words, they regard him as "head of the government" (legislative branch as well as executive) and hold him responsible accordingly—a situation from which he draws grave perils but also high challenge and inspiring opportunity. *[margin note: 3. Popular demand for presidential leadership]*

"The nation as a whole," once wrote a scholar who himself later attained the presidency, "has chosen him [the president], and is conscious that it has no other political spokesman. His is the only national voice in affairs. Let him once win the admiration and confidence of the country, and no other single force can withstand him, no combination of forces

---

[1] An excellent illustration is supplied by the stumbling fashion in which the Burke-Wadsworth Selective Service Bill of 1940 was handled. Unlike most important bills of our day, this one did not originate at the White House. Although known to favor it "in principle," the President did not put himself squarely behind it, or exert himself actively in its behalf—with the result that, although the measure finally became law, Democrats who otherwise would have lined up pretty solidly for it and Republicans who would have felt it their duty to oppose it spent precious weeks in hedging, equivocating, and seeking safety first by doing nothing while awaiting a great light.

will easily overpower him. His position takes the imagination of the country. He is the representative of no constituency, but of the whole people. When he speaks in his true character, he speaks for no special interest. If he rightly interpret the national thought and boldly insist upon it, he is irresistible; and the country never feels the zest of action so much as when its president is of such insight and caliber. Its instinct is for unified action, and it craves a single leader." [1]

An illustration of presidential leadership in legislation There are times when ordinary legislative leadership, and even the leadership of party, merges into a broad national leadership transcending all political and other dividing lines. Naturally, these are most likely to be periods of grave national stress. Such a leadership was Lincoln's in the earlier stages of the Civil War and Wilson's while the United States was engaged in the first World War. Such a leadership also was that of Franklin D. Roosevelt in the first two years of his presidency—easily the most remarkable that the country has known in days of peace, although of course rivaled by the same chief executive's leadership in the defense effort of 1940-41 and in the later war. Taking office at a time when long accumulating economic maladjustments had come to a head in a banking crisis of major proportions, Mr. Roosevelt struck a bold note in his inaugural address by declaring not only that there must be quick action, but that, while it was to be hoped that the "normal balance of executive and legislative authority" would prove adequate to the situation, he was prepared, in the event that Congress should fail to do its part, to ask that body "for the one remaining instrument to meet the crisis—broad executive power to wage a war against the emergency as great as the power that would be given me if we were in fact invaded by a foreign foe."

The new Congress having been convoked in special session, the president became chief lawmaker to a degree certainly never before witnessed in the country's history. A rapid fire of messages descended upon Capitol Hill; and when each was presented, a supporter of the Administration stood ready to introduce a bill (originating also in, or at all events sponsored by, the White House) covering the proposals made. In a session lasting a hundred days, only one important measure was passed which did not have such a history. To be sure, some bills encountered opposition within the president's party and were amended in committee, or even on the floor. By and large, however, the function of Congress was merely to agree; on as far-reaching a measure as the Farm Relief

---

[1] W. Wilson, *Constitutional Government in the United States*, 68. "The power and prestige of the presidency comprise the most valuable political asset of the American people; they are, moreover, in a very true sense the creation of the American people." E. S. Corwin, *The President: Office and Powers*, 306. For an illuminating study of presidential leadership and of the unfortunate consequences when it is lacking (*e.g.*, in years immediately following both the Civil War and World War I), see E. P. Herring, "Executive-Legislative Responsibilities," *Amer. Polit. Sci. Rev.*, XXXVIII, 1153-1165 (Dec., 1944). Cf. W. E. Binkley, *President and Congress* (New York, 1947).

Bill (giving rise to the memorable Agricultural Adjustment Administration), only four hours of debate were allowed in the House, with no amendments permitted. Messages and proposals were strategically timed; telephone calls from the White House admonished or warned the hesitant; radio talks to the nation reassured the troubled and inspired sentiment that no congressman could ignore. And all was done with manifest public approval. A frightened people wanted action, and a bold president was prepared to see that they got it.

As was to be expected, popular applause later died down, and a hesitant or frankly critical attitude developed toward much that had been done; the Supreme Court, indeed, declared important parts of the recovery legislation unconstitutional. But the matter of interest to us here is the height to which presidential leadership ascended and the techniques by which it was sustained. It is important to note, too, that legislative leadership from the White House did not abdicate when the first round of remedial measures had been passed. On the contrary, many of those more or less temporary measures were dovetailed into schemes for far-reaching and permanent rehabilitation and reform—schemes, *e.g.*, that for a nation-wide system of social security, which later were relayed to Congress in the form of urgent recommendations or of fully drafted bills, and in part were later enacted into law.

A General View of Presidential Power

"The waters of democracy," Woodrow Wilson once wrote, "are useless in their reservoirs unless they may be used to drive the wheels of policy and administration." And it is the experience of practically all democracies not only that leadership is the only means by which latent power can be turned to account, but that the requisite leadership can be supplied only by the executive. In Great Britain, Canada, and other countries having cabinet systems, this means the ministers; in the United States, it means the president. At the stage which our study has now reached, it must be sufficiently obvious that the salient fact about the presidency is its prolonged accumulation of power—by constitutional endowment, by legislative delegation, by judicial construction, by custom and practice—in the enforcement of law, in the conduct of foreign relations and of war, in the use of the veto, and even in the shaping of public policy as controlled ostensibly by the legislative branch. The earliest chief executives, being "just about what the framers of the constitution expected the incumbents of the office to be,"[1] took a comparatively modest view of their own authority. Jackson, however, brought to the White House not only a resolute disposition, but an impatience with restrictions, and with conservative traditions, which was characteristic of the section from which he came and of the generation in which he lived. In his hands, the presidency became a far more potent instru-

[margin note: A hundred years of cumulative development]

[1] W. B. Munro, *The Government of the United States* (rev. ed.), 130.

mentality than before; and although after his day the office had its ups and downs, as it passed from stronger to weaker hands and back again, and as the times demanded of the chief executive a vigorous rôle or permitted a more inactive one, hardly any later incumbent ever willingly gave up a particle of power once successfully asserted.[1] On the contrary, every fresh advance became, in turn (perhaps after an interval of inaction), a point of departure from which still more exalted claims to authority were projected; and under Franklin D. Roosevelt, notwithstanding occasional set-backs, a peak was reached overtopping all that had gone before.[2]

Basic factors involved

The reasons for this extraordinary development are not to be found in motivations springing from personal pride and ambition. Most of the presidents, being human, have found pleasure in the exercise of authority; but few, if any, have coveted power for its own sake. Presidential preeminence has reached its present proportions for reasons obvious enough to every reader of these lines. One is the tremendous growth of the functions and activities of the federal government, and of the administrative machinery (falling within the president's particular province) required for carrying on the government's work. Another is the development of what is to all intents and purposes direct popular election, giving the chief executive a rightful claim to be regarded as no less a spokesman of the national will than is Congress. Still another is the decline rather commonly regarded as having taken place in the past half-century in the resourcefulness and efficiency of Congress,[3] opening the way for greater presidential initiative and control. A fourth, related to the foregoing, is the oft-demonstrated, ever-growing, and increasingly imperative need for the leadership and direction in legislation and general policy-framing which in a cabinet system are exercised preëminently by the prime minister and his advisers, but for which our system makes no provision— a need which there is no possible way of meeting except primarily through the president. A contributing factor of tremendous importance, too, has been, of course, a succession of great national crises—the Civil War, World War I, the depression of the thirties, the perilous international situation created by the Nazis and the Fascists, and finally World War II

---

[1] Except, of course, special wartime powers of a manifestly temporary character.

[2] In the opinion of Professor Edward S. Corwin, about one in three of the thirty-one individuals who have held the presidency have contributed to the development of its powers. Washington, Jefferson, Jackson, Polk, Lincoln, Hayes, Cleveland, Wilson, and the two Roosevelts form his suggested list. *The President: Office and Powers*, 29. The opening chapter of the volume cited presents an excellent analysis of the varying conceptions of the presidential office that different chief executives in different periods have held (see also pp. 309-316); and for a fuller historical analysis, W. E. Binkley, *President and Congress* (New York, 1947). In the seventies and eighties of the last century, the presidency suffered a perceptible sag, which is reflected interestingly in Woodrow Wilson's *Congressional Government* and James (later Lord) Bryce's *American Commonwealth*, published in 1885 and 1889, respectively. On the other hand, Henry Jones Ford's *Rise and Growth of American Politics* and Woodrow Wilson's *Constitutional Government in the United States*, published in 1898 and 1908, respectively, portray the office as once more on the up-swing.

[3] See p. 402 below.

—all of them inevitably making national leadership a topmost concern and forcing executive power to new levels.

The president not a dictator

Plenty of people do not like what has been going on; and there is no denying that the balance contemplated by the makers of the constitution has been, to a considerable extent, upset. Even in Jefferson's day, the ugly charge of dictatorship was hurled in the president's direction. Jackson, Lincoln, the first Roosevelt, and certainly the later Roosevelt, incurred similar criticism. Thinking only, however, of the times through which we ourselves have lived, those who view with alarm the heights to which the presidency has soared would have great difficulty in showing how important things needing to be done could have been done otherwise than through presidential initiative, direction, and drive. They would have to admit, too, that many of the powers complained of have been expressly voted to the chief executive by the people's representatives in Congress—who also could recall them (in some cases by mere concurrent resolution) if so minded. And, whether or not the critics could be argued into admitting it, the fact remains that strong and unified government does not necessarily mean arbitrary government, nor a powerful chief executive a dictatorial one. Despite all, the president is still a responsible servant of the people; and such he will remain as long as the ultimate popular and congressional controls inherent in our representative system endure.[1]

Control Over the President by Congress

The emphasis thus far placed upon the president's lofty rôle must not be allowed to obscure the fact that, as between executive and legislature, influence and control do not flow in only a single direction; for the president, in his turn, is subject to considerable restraint, and in the final analysis to a good deal of direct control, from Congress. Few indeed of his powers can be exercised without spending money; and for money he is absolutely dependent upon Congress. Few, likewise, can be exercised except through departments, boards and other agencies, for the establishment and maintenance of which he is similarly dependent. For enactment of the legislation he desires, he must rely upon Congress. He must get senatorial consent to his appointments and his treaties. He can wage war only if Congress declares it. His vetoes can be overridden in the two houses. His every act (personal or through subordinates) can

Constitutional specifications

---

[1] The special aspect of presidential powers under the impact of wartime conditions will be considered in a later chapter (see pp. 811-814 below).

The fullest and most authoritative recent analyses of presidential powers will be found in E. S. Corwin, *The President: Office and Powers*, Chaps. III-VII (pp. 297-308 especially on "dictatorship"), and C. P. Patterson, *Presidential Government in the United States* (Chapel Hill, N. C., 1947), Chaps. IV, VI-IX. Cf. L. Rogers, "Presidential Dictatorship in the United States," *Quar. Rev.*, CCXXXI, 127-148 (Jan., 1919), and "The American Presidential System," *Polit. Quar.*, VIII, 517-529 (Oct.-Dec., 1937); "The Increasing Power of the President" [Symposium], *Cong. Digest*, XII, 257-288 (Nov., 1933). See also materials presented in J. E. Johnsen [comp.], *Increasing the President's Power* (New York, 1934).

be looked into and criticized, and some of them can be reversed. If worst comes to worst, he can be impeached and removed from office.

Practical restraints   In the give and take of personal relations with senators and representatives, furthermore, he may be argued into changing his views or modifying his policies. Defeat of his measures or refusal of his requests may compel him to give up a program in which he firmly believes: witness Franklin D. Roosevelt's enforced relinquishment in 1937 both of his favorite plan for administrative reorganization and of his cherished project for reconstruction of the Supreme Court; his reversal in 1943 on a $25,000 ceiling for salaries; and the involuntary abandonment, in 1943-44, for lack of funds, of three agencies dear to his heart, the National Resources Planning Board, the Civilian Conservation Corps, and the National Youth Administration. Either house, or both, may make "requests" (not—at least in form—*demands*) upon him for documents or information which he cannot well withhold, however much he might prefer to do so,[1] or, as indicated above, may institute investigations of executive or administrative work for which he is directly or indirectly responsible. Congress may pass laws imposing new duties upon him or his subordinates, and may limit the discretion of heads of departments or other officers and require them to do given things in a given way, irrespective of the president's wishes.[2] Even a supposedly friendly Congress may flout the Administration's policy again and again during a session, the Senate, in particular, being prone to assume an attitude best described as "baiting the president." [3]

REFERENCES

J. P. Chamberlain, *Legislative Processes: National and State* (New York, 1936), Chap. xv.

W. Wilson, *Constitutional Government in the United States* (New York, 1908), Chap. iii.

————, *Congressional Government* (Boston, 1885), Chap. v.

H. L. McBain, *The Living Constitution* (New York, 1927), Chap. iv.

G. B. Galloway, *Congress at the Crossroads* (New York, 1946), Chap. vii.

H. Hazlitt, *A New Constitution Now* (New York, 1942), Chaps. ii-v.

G. Cleveland, *Presidential Problems* (New York, 1904), 3-78. A discussion of executive independence by an ex-president.

E. S. Corwin, *The President: Office and Powers; History and Analysis of Practice and Opinion* (New York, 1940), Chap. vii.

C. P. Patterson, *Presidential Government in the United States; The Unwritten Constitution* (Chapel Hill, N. C., 1947), Chaps. vi-vii, x.

H. J. Laski, *The American Presidency* (New York, 1940), Chap. iii.

[1] Such requests, when relating to the negotiation of treaties or to other aspects of foreign relations, usually recognize the necessity of discretion in this domain by incorporating the phrase, "if not incompatible with the public interest."

[2] A good recent illustration of the president being obliged to assume responsibility for enforcing a complicated and controversial act of Congress to which he was opposed is afforded by the Labor-Management Relations [Taft-Hartley] Act of 1947. See pp. 740-744 below.

[3] Practically all of the matters referred to in this paragraph have been, or will be, discussed elsewhere, and hence are merely mentioned here.

E. P. Herring, *Presidential Leadership; The Political Relations of Congress and the Chief Executive* (New York, 1940), especially Chaps. II-IV, VII.

——————, "Executive-Legislative Responsibilities," *Amer. Polit. Sci. Rev.,* XXXVIII, 1153-1165 (Dec., 1944).

R. Young, *This Is Congress* (New York, 1943), Chap. II.

A. Hehmeyer, *Time for Change* (New York, 1943), Chaps. VI-VII, X.

H. C. Black, *The Relation of the Executive Power to Legislation* (Princeton, N. J., 1919), Chaps. III-V.

W. E. Binkley, *President and Congress* (New York, 1947).

G. F. Milton, *The Use of Presidential Power, 1789-1943* (Boston, 1944).

J. E. Johnsen [comp.], *Increasing the President's Power* (New York, 1934).

E. C. Mason, *The Veto Power* (New York, 1891).

C. A. Berdahl, "The President's Veto of Private Bills," *Polit. Sci. Quar.,* LII, 505-531 (Dec., 1937).

L. H. Chamberlain, *The President, Congress, and Legislation* (New York, 1946); also article on same subject in *Polit. Sci. Quar.,* LXI, 42-60 (Mar., 1946).

W. E. Dodd, *Woodrow Wilson and His Work* (Garden City, N. Y., 1920), Chaps. VI-VII.

F. D. Roosevelt, *On Our Way* (New York, 1934).

——————, *Public Papers and Addresses,* 5 vols. (New York, 1938). Also: 1937 Vol., "The Constitution Prevails"; 1938 Vol., "The Continuing Struggle for Liberalism"; 1939 Vol., "War—and Neutrality"; 1940 Vol., "War—and Aid to Democracy" (all New York, 1941).

CHAPTER XIX

THE IMPROVEMENT OF CONGRESS AND OF LEGISLATIVE-EXECUTIVE RELATIONS

Some
extreme
charges

It long has been a familiar experience to hear Congress criticized, censured, ridiculed—by editors, columnists, radio commentators, publicists, and occasionally even by congressmen themselves. In endless chorus, we have been told that the two houses are inefficient, irresponsible, dilatory, extravagant, provincial, aimless, wanting in vision, and suffused with demagogy. If the situation is half as bad as some people would have us believe, the heart has indeed gone out of our American representative system and our plight is assuredly unhappy, particularly in an era when perhaps our greatest national need is intelligent and effective democratic government.

The
situation
not as
bad as
painted

Fortunately, the heedless and indiscriminate criticisms dinned into our ears are not supported by the facts. To be sure, Congress, as it operates, shows plenty of imperfections;[1] and undoubtedly it has suffered some decline in public esteem, especially since its failure to cope with the depression of the thirties except as a rubber-stamp in the hands of a more resourceful and vigorous chief executive. But there is no reason to believe that the character and caliber of its members are any lower than fifty or a hundred years ago;[2] many among them will risk political defeat rather than vote contrary to their convictions; and of corruption, in at least its grosser forms, there is little or none. Times have changed, and the ponderous oratory that once resounded through crowded halls has given way to less ornate discussion; but, as an eminent authority has remarked, the quality of serious speeches in both houses, considering the increased complexity of most of the problems that have to be dealt with, is still "amazingly high."[3] Much of the complaint that one hears is merely partisan, captious, and abusive. Much of it springs from the disappointment or exasperation of people whose pet projects have come to grief (often deservedly), or whose notions of what ought to be done have not happened to coincide with those of the congressional majority. No Congress, however efficient, could hope to please everybody—nor,

---

[1] Unquestionably, the Legislative Reorganization Act of 1946 (already mentioned many times, and to be considered further in the present chapter) has remedied some of these, at least to a degree. But even after the experience of an initial session under the new law, the full and lasting consequences of the changes introduced remained to be disclosed; besides, a good many shortcomings went largely or wholly untouched in the legislation.

[2] "About the same proportion of outstanding, average, and lesser people," says an experienced member, "as in any individual community." E. Kefauver, in E. Kefauver and J. Levin, *A Twentieth-Century Congress* (New York, 1947), 15.

[3] C. A. Beard, in *Amer. Mercury*, LV, 531 (Nov., 1942).

indeed, in all respects to please anybody. Do what they may, or do nothing at all, the members are bound to encounter disapproval and complaint. The truth is that, notwithstanding frequent waste of time and misdirection of effort, a vast amount of careful and intelligent work is done on Capitol Hill, especially in the great committees, and that, notwithstanding the increasingly complicated and critical matters with which they have to deal, the two houses somehow succeed in placing on the statute-book numerous measures representing honest attempts to promote the public well-being and backed by a great volume of favorable public sentiment. A stream does not rise higher than its source; by and large, Congress is no better, and no worse, than the people from which it springs.[1]

This said, however, certain shortcomings have also to be recognized; and three, out of many, may be mentioned.

Nevertheless some shortcomings:

Too much business is transacted—too many bills of deep concern to the people are passed—without the full debate that would familiarize members with what they are voting on and acquaint the country with the issues involved. No doubt it is true—particularly in view of the multiplicity of matters pressing for attention, together with the complicated character of many modern legislative problems—that most of the work on important bills is, and must be, performed in the committee rooms. When, however, measures of the magnitude of the Labor Relations Act of 1935 and the Fair Labor Standards Act of 1938 can slip through the House of Representatives with only three hours and six hours, respectively, of discussion on the floor, one is justified in believing that a basic purpose of wide popular representation is to a serious extent failing to be realized. In the more leisurely Senate, to be sure, there is genuine debate (when not blocked by a filibuster); but the mechanized procedures of the overgrown and over-regimented House have practically left that body without opportunity or incentive to debate large measures (except sometimes financial bills) in a large way. As matters go in the House, the fate of most important bills is predetermined by decisions and actions of the majority leaders, with perhaps the aid of the majority caucus, or conference, and certainly the assistance of the rules committee. Bills reported from a standing committee are explained briefly by the committee chairman, and perhaps other majority members in an agreed order, and spokesmen of the minority are allowed a chance to present their views. But, with rare exceptions, no one expects votes to be changed by the arguments on either side. The general run of members have not studied

1. Inadequacy of debate

[1] On "What Congress Is Supposed To Do" and the difficulty of doing it, see R. Young, *This Is Congress* (New York, 1943), Chap. i. Cf. C. A. Beard, "Congress Under Fire," *Yale Rev.*, XXII, 35-61 (Sept., 1932), and "In Defense of Congress," *Amer. Mercury*, LV, 529-535 (Nov., 1942); J. Voorhis, "Stop Kicking Congress Around!," *ibid.*, LVIII, 647-655 (June, 1944); H. S. Pritchett, "What's Wrong with Congress?," *Atlantic Mo.*, CLV, 288-294 (Mar., 1935); E. S. Bates, "Is Congress So Bad?," *Curr. Hist.*, XLIII, 595-600 (Mar., 1936); J. H. Topkis, "How Bad Is Congress?," *Polit. Sci. Quar.*, LXII, 531-551 (Dec., 1947).

the measure; they assume that the committee majority (or minority, as the case may be) has gone into the matter and knows what it is talking about; they hesitate to involve themselves in a discussion in which they might be worsted, and still more to incur suspicion of party irregularity or disloyalty. Accordingly, they usually vote almost automatically to uphold their fellow-partisans on the committee, in pursuance of whatever program has been mapped out by the party leaders.[1]

2. Excess of party motivation and bickering

Congress is an assemblage of politicians; by and large, if members were not politicians, they would not be in Congress. That is quite all right, too—unless as legislators they fail to rise above the politician-complex. There need be no criticism of party regularity on the part of members, of sharp divisions on party lines, of legislation enacted by a party majority and opposed by a party minority; these are of the essence of party government and party responsibility, which, on the whole, have justified themselves in all democratic countries fortunate enough to have them. Where criticism is rightly lodged is against the bickerings, delays, distortions, and futility displayed by Congress in periods when politics is allowed to dominate the scene and no word can be spoken or move made without suspicion of partisan motivation. Naturally, such periods are most likely to ensue when a congressional or presidential election is in the offing; and at such times—no matter how critical the state of the country—the two houses are likely to be seen at their worst. In the spring and early summer of 1946, for example, Congress played fast and loose with tremendously vital matters such as price control and inflation, the recruitment of the armed services, and housing for veterans, simply (or at least mainly) because Democrats and Republicans were sparring for advantage in the fall elections.

3. Division of responsibility

Another difficulty is diffusion of responsibility. This, of course, brings the president into the picture, because responsibility for what is done or not done on Capital Hill is inevitably divided between Congress and the White House—an awkward but inescapable situation touched upon in the previous chapter. Enough has been said at other earlier points to make it clear that within Congress itself, however, there is no effective concentration of responsibility. Matters can be tossed back and forth between the two houses; both houses are splintered into committees, not so many now as formerly, but still functionally overlapping and duplicating as between the two houses, and even at some points within a single house. In the House of Representatives especially, the "managers" presumably direct proceedings. But often one is moved to ask who among them can be held responsible for given decisions or acts; with party lines often shattered by *blocs* and other unorthodox groupings, *e.g.*, the in-

---

[1] As long ago as 1884, Woodrow Wilson wrote: "The theater of debate upon legislation [has shifted] from the floor of Congress to the privacy of the committee-rooms," and "the House sits, not for serious discussion, but to sanction the conclusions of its committees as rapidly as possible." *Congressional Government* (21st impression), 79, 81.

formal but effectual alliance of conservative Northern Republicans and even more conservative Southern Democrats in the Seventy-ninth and Eightieth Congresses (1945-49), even party responsibility becomes attenuated and at times hardly more than a fiction.

Some Handicaps Under Which Congress Works

It is only fair to recognize that Congress operates under a number of disadvantageous circumstances, for some of which it is responsible and for others not.[1] The size and regional diversity of the country multiply and complicate the tasks to be performed. The federal nature of the government raises serious problems of constitutional law and policy, as does also the principle of separation of powers. Absence of the sort of leadership supplied by cabinets in countries like Great Britain and Canada forces the houses to seek leadership where they can find it, and sometimes to submit to a presidential leadership (as during President Franklin D. Roosevelt's earlier years) reducing Congress to hardly more than a rubber-stamp.

Still other disadvantages are perhaps less obvious.[2] One of them is the short term of members of the House of Representatives. When the constitution was framed, it was the fashion to argue that "where annual elections end, tyranny begins;" and the authors of *The Federalist* found it necessary to devote one of their papers to a defense of a term as lengthy as two years.[3] Nowadays, many consider the term not too long, but too short. The average person elected to the House for the first time has no acquaintance with the prevailing methods of doing business, has had no legislative experience (except possibly in a state legislature or a city council), and has only a superficial knowledge of most matters with which Congress is called upon to deal. Elected for two years only, he cannot progress far toward becoming a useful member, much less a leader, before his mandate expires. Many congressmen, to be sure, are reëlected at least once or twice, and are thus enabled to accumulate knowledge and experience. Indeed, a computation in 1929, based on the then existing Seventy-first Congress, showed that the average period of service of all members of the House at that time was 8.45 years. The figure was as high as this, however, only because of the exceptionally long stretches of service of certain members—thirty-five years, in one case—and the fact remains, not only that many members serve for only one or two terms,

1. Two-year term for congressmen

---

[1] As already mentioned, some impediments connected with organization and procedure have to a degree been removed by the Legislative Reorganization Act of 1946; but the disadvantages here enumerated remain.

[2] One former handicap, *i.e.*, the biennial "lame-duck" session, has been removed (see p. 307 above). Never again will we have a situation like that existing in the dark winter of 1932-33 when a Congress containing 158 members who had been repudiated by the voters was functioning precariously under the discredited leadership of a defeated president, yet with a grave national crisis at hand.

[3] No. LIII (Lodge's ed., 333-339). Under the original Revolutionary state constitutions, the members of the state legislature were elected annually in every state except South Carolina, and there biennially.

but that from one-seventh to one-third of the names on the roll of every newly elected House were never there before. Furthermore, a member cannot get far into a two-year term without being obliged to turn his thoughts to reëlection, particularly if he comes from a "close" district. This distracts his attention and divides his energies. Still another practical disadvantage of the two-year term is that, while it provides a perhaps desirable opportunity midway during a president's four years for a canvass and registration of popular opinion, in doing so it frequently brings the House of Representatives into the control of a party opposed to the president (as in the second Wilson administration, the Hoover administration, and the Truman administration), thereby tending to produce friction and paralyze action. A constitutional amendment fixing the term at four years has been introduced many times, but neither Congress nor the country has ever manifested much interest in the matter.

2. Insistence upon residence of a member in his district
Another disadvantage arises from the insistence of our politicians and people that a congressman be a resident of the district which he represents; and this brings us to another interesting contrast between American and British usage. In Britain, a man aspiring to enter Parliament, but finding no opportunity in his own district, "stands" in some other district, wherever there is an opening and the party authorities will accept him as a candidate; or a member, defeated in the district which he has represented, tries his luck in another and, if successful, goes ahead with his career. There is nothing in the national constitution or laws to prevent a person doing the same thing in the United States, save that he cannot, of course, become a candidate in any district outside of the state in which he lives; and there have been a few congressmen from New York and Chicago who dwelt in a section of the city not included in their respective districts. In general, however, if a man were to seek election in a district in which he did not live, he would make little headway against the voters' assumption that only one of their own number can safely be trusted to look after their interests. The results are sometimes unfortunate. Good men who happen to live in districts not dominated by their own party are cut off from any chance to serve the country in Congress; valuable members are forced to drop out simply because defeated in their home constituency; and the pernicious concept is fostered of the congressman as merely the district's official agent—errand-boy, one is tempted to say—for procuring appointments, buildings, relief allotments, and anything else that can be got when the plum-tree is shaken.

3. Lack of intelligent and sustained public interest
Most of the time, Congress suffers, too, from a dearth of interest in its work in quarters where such interest ought to be keen, and an excess of interest in other quarters where it is likely to have harmful effects. Considering that the two houses every twelve months enact hundreds of laws which operate throughout the entire United States and authorize the spending of multiplied billions of the people's money, it might be ex-

pected that their work from year to year, and almost from day to day, would command the attention of the general mass of citizens. That it commonly fails to do so is not open to argument. Only when some unusual fight over the rules, or some sensational investigation, or a filibuster, or a particularly tense debate, is to be recorded does the average small-town newspaper—on which, notwithstanding the radio, most people still depend for what they know about affairs at Washington—give much prominence to congressional proceedings; and even the metropolitan press no longer finds news value in congressional debates such as, in earlier days (particularly before the Civil War), were reported extensively, analytically, and with full recognition of the public interests involved. To be sure, more of the work of Congress is nowadays done in committee rooms, and with less open and spectacular discussion. But it loses nothing in importance on that account; and if the press does not report it as it once did, the only reason is the apparent lack of popular demand. If, however, the people do not take a continuous, discriminating, and appreciative interest in what their representatives say and do at the national capital (as well as, of course, at state capitals and local seats of government), they have themselves to blame if things go wrong.[1]

There are, of course, those whose interest is unflagging. But to a regrettable extent they turn out to be men and women with an axe to grind—persons who want a constitutional amendment proposed or killed, a statute passed, defeated, or amended, a favorable or an unfavorable committee report made, an appropriation voted, or some other benefit conferred; and another of the handicaps under which Congress works is the inescapable, and sometimes improper, pressure brought to bear by these "lobbyists."[2] It is to be observed that the lobby of which one so

4. "Pressure groups" and lobbying

---

[1] On August 15, 1944, Senator Pepper of Florida introduced a joint resolution authorizing the broadcasting of congressional proceedings (78th Cong., 2nd Sess., Sen. Joint Res. 145). The proposal did not meet with much favor in Congress, and the public's response to such broadcasting would be problematical. Even the gallery spectator is rewarded only now and then by spirited half-hours amid dreary stretches of dull routine.

[2] Shading off into direct and systematic lobbying, yet more or less to be distinguished from it, are the incessant demands upon the congressman's time and attention from axe-grinding constituents who ply him with letters and telegrams and bombard him with requests for personal favors. Letters, former Vice-President Garner once observed, "are a congressman's bread and butter." The daily grist is appalling; and most of the writers are not simply sending friendly greetings—they want something, perchance information, a government document, settlement of a pension claim, a commission in the Army or Navy, an adjustment of income taxes, relief from a burdensome federal regulation, an appointment for a personal conference. And while many of the requests can be shunted off to some other government agency, the congressman with an eye on reëlection, or merely conscientious about serving his constituents, will feel obliged to give personal attention to a heavy proportion of them. This is only one of the many ways in which a congressman's time is so used up that little remains for studying matters of national importance. Senator Tydings of Maryland once reported that his typical day included sixty interviews, three hundred letters, one to five committee meetings, and a meeting of the Senate; and Congressman Estes Kefauver of Tennessee has furnished an equally terrifying exhibit of an average day's activities in his own experience (E. Kefauver and J. Levin, *A Twentieth-Century Congress,* 190-194). As the logical link between the people back home and the vast impersonal bureaucracy of Washington, the congressman cannot, and should

frequently hears in Washington—the "third house" of the paragraphers
—consists not so much of persons seeking favors directly for themselves
as of professional paid agents (sometimes ex-congressmen and ex-
senators, who are presumed to know the right lines of approach) of great
interests or organizations, whose business it is to haunt the legislative
halls and members' offices [1] and work unceasingly for whatever objects
their clients have in view; although a more refined technique, now increasingly employed, takes the form of prompting a congressman's
constituents to write or wire their representative in behalf of a given
project or proposal. Especially active in these ways are the lobbyists of
the American Legion, the Veterans of Foreign Wars, the Chamber of Commerce of the United States, the American Farm Bureau Federation, the
American Association of Railway Executives, the A. F. of L. and the
C. I. O., the Joint Committee of National Utility Associations, American Coal Distributors, the American Gas Association, the National
Petroleum Association, the United States Savings and Loan League, the
National Association of Real Estate Boards, the interests centered in the
woollen, cotton, meat-packing, sugar, leather, steel, and other great
industries, and even the National Federation of Federal Employees, the
Federal Council of Churches, the League of Women Voters of the United
States, and the National Education Association. There is even an organization working for various causes conceived to be in the interest of the
general public, and known as "People's Lobby, Inc." [2]

Magni-
tude of
lobbyists'
opera-
tions

Not all lobbying, be it noted, is reprehensible, either in object or in
method. There are lobbyists for the most worthy causes as for the least
worthy; and their work may be entirely open and above-board, and may
have desirable educational results, just as it may follow devious courses,
by dubious means, toward mercenary, or even corrupt, ends. The fact
remains, however, that the footsteps of every congressman are dogged
by men—increasing numbers of women too—whose flattering attention
is aimed exclusively at influencing him, by entreaty, promise, or threat,
to vote for or against this or that particular bill, tariff schedule, subsidy,
or privilege. Upwards of four hundred national organizations maintain a
total of eight hundred to a thousand liberally paid legislative agents per-

---

not, wholly escape the service function referred to. It has been suggested, however,
that for his relief a congressional service bureau might be set up, manned with
competent persons who could take care of a vast share of the queries and requests
that daily clutter up every congressional desk.

[1] The offices, too, of commissions, boards, department heads, and even that of the
president; because, although lobbying is usually thought of only in connection with
legislative bodies, a vast amount of the same sort of thing is directed toward other
agencies of government as well. Obviously, it will not be necessary to lobby against
a bill if an interested department can be persuaded not to have it introduced.
Pressure-group activities in relation to parts of the government other than Congress
are discussed at length in E. P. Herring, *Public Administration and the Public Interest* (New York, 1936).

[2] In April, 1946, it became necessary for President Truman to admonish naval
officers to desist from lobbying against a bill for merging the War and Navy Departments and unifying the country's armed forces.

manently at the capital; and hundreds more are likely to be represented from time to time when measures affecting their interests are under consideration. Scarcely an important bill passes without complaint arising in some quarter that an importunate and lavishly paid "locust swarm" of lobbyists has had a hand in enacting it; and often as not the complaint is fully justified.[1] Sometimes, indeed, the pressure group behind the lobby is only one side of a triangle, with (a) a labor *bloc* or a farm *bloc* in Congress and (b) administrative agencies serving the same cause or interest constituting the other two; and thus a pressure-group economy or society may give rise to (changing the figure) "government by whirlpools of special interest groups," with the national interest in danger of being lost to view.[2]

Lobbyists have long infested the state capitals no less than Washington, and all but thirteen of the state legislatures have enacted laws designed to place limits on their operations—usually by requiring persons engaged in lobbying to acknowledge the fact by registering with some designated official, by forbidding the legislative floor to such persons, and by requiring them to make their expense accounts a matter of public record. In perhaps no more than half a dozen states, however, are such regulations consistently enforced, and nowhere are they fully effective. At Washington, the matter has long received intermittent attention, with the Senate from time to time sponsoring committee investigations and even passing bills requiring lobbyists to register and to reveal by whom they were employed and to what end. In the lower house, however, such measures long invariably perished—partly because of honest doubt (inspired to some extent by the not too impressive experience of the states) as to how effective any general attempt at regulation would prove; partly by the manifest difficulty of getting at and prohibiting improper practices without also interfering with legitimate ones; partly by the helpfulness attributed by many congressmen to the information and materials supplied to them by lobbyists; and partly, if the truth be told, by the fear of many congressmen that any law enacted might place

The problem of regulation

[1] A random illustration of the power of "pressure groups" in legislation is afforded by the measures of 1933-34 providing for Philippine independence. See G. L. Kirk, *Philippine Independence* (New York, 1936), Chaps. iv-v. The Hawley-Smoot tariff act of 1930—for that matter, almost any tariff act—affords another good example. Occasionally, too, the "locust swarm" is really only an influential individual, as when the demagogue Father Coughlin compassed the defeat of the World Court bill of 1935 almost single-handedly.

The power of the lobbyist would be sharply reduced if congressmen would but realize (1) that frequently he is engaged in promoting his own special interest rather than the interest of the people for whom he claims to speak, and (2) that often as not lobbyists cannot deliver the votes they promise or threaten.

[2] The most important treatise on the general subject is E. P. Herring, *Group Representation Before Congress* (Baltimore, 1929), but a more recent and very informing one is S. Chase, *Democracy Under Pressure; Special Interests vs. the Public Welfare* (New York, 1945). For additional references see p. 423 below. A large amount of interesting information will be found in *Lobby Investigation; Hearings Before Sub-Committee*, 71st Cong., 2nd Sess., Pursuant to Sen. Res. 20 (Washington, D. C., 1930).

obstacles in the path of lobbying activities in which they themselves might want to engage after going out of office. As a result, until of late federal regulation never went farther than to require public utility lobbyists to register and workers in behalf of foreign interests and of shipping interests both to register and to place on record the nature and objects of their activities. In some quarters, there was a rather futile hope that mere airing of the subject in frequent discussion, combined with the publicity forced upon the particular groups of lobbyists mentioned, would operate measurably as a corrective.

The Federal Regulation of Lobbying Act of 1946

To any one familiar with the maze of influences and pressures amidst which Congress works, it must, therefore, have come not only as somewhat of a surprise, but also as a cause for gratification, when the Legislative Reorganization Act of 1946 was found to contain, as Title III, a Federal Regulation of Lobbying Act, poorly drafted, but at least giving the country its first general law on the subject. Like the main body of the statute, the lobbying section originated in the Senate; and its acceptance there was perhaps to be expected. Reversing earlier attitudes, however, the House also accepted it; and in January, 1947, its provisions went into effect. The salient features of the new regulatory system (applying to lobbying by every sort of interest on every sort of subject [1]) are: (1) every person receiving any form of compensation for attempting to influence the passage or defeat of any legislation by Congress must, before he begins operations, register with the clerk of the House and secretary of the Senate; (2) in doing this, he must disclose by whom he is employed, in whose interest he works, and how much and by whom he is paid and for how long, both as salary and for expenses; (3) every three months, he must report in detail and under oath all monies received, and the ways in which they have been spent; (4) every person soliciting or receiving contributions to any organization or fund for lobbying purposes must keep an exact account of all contributions received, the name and address of every contributor of as much as five hundred dollars, all expenditures made by or on behalf of such organization or fund, and the name and address of every person to whom money has been paid out; and (5) full and detailed reports covering these matters must be filed yearly with the House and Senate officials mentioned, and for two years must be kept open for public inspection. [2] Violators of any of these provisions are liable to a fine of five thousand dollars or imprisonment for a year, or both, and are debarred from further lobbying activities for a period of three years after conviction.

[1] But defined to exclude mere appearance before congressional committees, activities by any public official in his official capacity, and news or editorial comment published by any newspaper or other regularly issued periodical.

[2] From requirements (4) and (5) are exempted state and local committees of any political party, and any other political committee as defined in the Federal Corrupt Practices Act of 1925. Contributions to party and other political committees are, of course, regulated to some extent by the act mentioned and by other separate legislation. See pp. 224-225 above.

Within two weeks after the new legislation was approved, registration forms were supplied to more than four hundred individuals and organizations; and this was a mere beginning.[1] Many border-line cases existed in which there was uncertainty as to whether the law applied. By January 1, 1948, however, the number of registrations exceeded one thousand, with compensation reported up to sixty-five thousand dollars a year for men and seven thousand for women. The volume and vigor of lobbying would seem to have been reduced but little, if at all; certainly the real estate lobby, the wool lobby, the sugar lobby, and plenty of others were sufficiently in evidence in the 1947 congressional session. On the other hand, lobbyists have to a greater extent been forced into the open; and altogether some improvement appears to have resulted.[2]

Congressional Self-Improvement

For the impediments thus far mentioned, Congress, speaking broadly, is not itself to blame; even lobbying (which, of course, has both its good and bad sides) will go on, perhaps undiminished, in spite of the new regulating legislation, and certainly can never be completely suppressed. Not so long ago, however, one would have been obliged to add that Congress labored also under impediments of its own making, or at all events of such a nature that it could, by its own action, remove or alleviate them; and it is gratifying to be able to record that in the summer of 1946 the two houses finally capped a vast amount of talk about self-improvement with action in the form of a statute deserving to rank with the most important one, e.g., the Budget and Accounting Act of 1921, ever as yet passed for bettering the character of federal legislation and the conditions under which legislative work is carried on. Several features of this Legislative Reorganization Act [3] have necessarily been mentioned in earlier connections, and it remains here merely (1) to explain the circumstances under which the measure was passed, (2) to summarize its major contributions, and (3) to indicate a few problems which it failed to solve.

Long ago it became obvious that if Congress was in future to hold its own in growing competition with executive power, to meet the challenges of difficult times, to serve the nation in the fashion which its basic function in our political system presupposes, and to recover lost popular confidence and prestige, it would have to be liberated from various conditions and methods operating to shackle it in the performance of its work. And equally obvious was the fact that—at many points at least—such improvement lay entirely, or almost so, in the members' own hands. Perhaps wartime exigencies were required to drive the challenge home.

The Legislative Reorganization Act of 1946

[1] The first lobbyists actually registered represented the People's Lobby and the W.C.T.U.

[2] For a full analysis of the new law and of its workings during the first year, see B. Zeller, "The Federal Regulation of Lobbying Act," *Amer. Polit. Sci. Rev.,* XLII, 239-271 (Apr., 1948).

At all events, during the two years covered by the Seventy-eighth Congress (1943-45), more than fifty proposals for particular reforms, or in some instances for a general program of reform, were introduced in the two houses; and while none prevailed, a joint resolution of February, 1945, took the significant step of setting up a bipartisan Joint Committee on the Organization of Congress, composed of six members of each branch (Senator Francis Maloney, and after his death Senator Robert M. LaFollette, chairman; Representative Mike Monroney, vice-chairman), and charged with making a study of the subject and recommending plans "with a view toward strengthening Congress, simplifying its operations, improving its relationships with other branches of the United States Government, and enabling it to meet its responsibilities under the constitution." Taking its task seriously, the committee held hearings (on thirty-nine different days) and carried on studies for more than a year, until finally, early in 1946, it was ready with a report going to the root of many organizational difficulties and proposing far-reaching changes.[1] Meeting at first a somewhat cool reception—especially from committees that did not want to be abolished and from committee chairmen who did not want to be legislated out of their positions of prestige and their perquisites—and encountering numerous obstacles of a parliamentary nature, an omnibus bill incorporating the recommendations appeared for a time to have an uncertain prospect. Clever handling of the measure, however, brought it eventually to a vote in both branches; and although the House of Representatives was responsible for deleting a number of worth-while provisions, the amended bill became law as the Seventy-ninth Congress closed its last session. It so happened that before the new measure could take effect (in the Eightieth Congress, organized in January, 1947), the congressional and senatorial elections of 1946 sharply reversed the political complexion of both houses; and apprehension arose lest this result in the intended reorganization (especially of the committee system) being only partially or half-heartedly carried out. Notwithstanding misgivings, and even protest, in some quarters, however, the new Republican leadership affirmed its intention to give the reforms a fair trial; and in most particulars, although not all, the legislation has since been in full effect.

In summary, the principal features of the reorganization are as follows: [2]

---

[1] Joint Committee on the Organization of Congress, *Organization of the Congress,* 79th Cong., 2nd Sess., Sen. Rep. No. 1011 (1946). Influential in preparing the way for this move in Congress was a committee of the American Political Science Association which from 1942 met frequently with senators and representatives for discussion of the subject. For the report of this committee, with recommendations, see *The Reorganization of Congress; A Report of the Committee on Congress of the American Political Science Association* (Washington, D. C., 1945). Contributing also to the discussion was R. Heller, *Strengthening the Congress* (Washington, D. C.. 1945), published under the sponsorship of the National Planning Association.

[2] Most of the matters mentioned have been, or will be, touched upon at appropriate points in other chapters, but it may be useful to bring them together briefly

1. *Simplification of the committee structure.* Hardly any one, in Congress or out, used to discuss congressional improvement without stressing the need for a drastic overhauling of the sprawling aggregation of standing committees, which had hardly changed in a hundred years except for increases in number. There were far too many committees (eighty-one in the two houses, with two hundred or more subcommittees); many overlapped or were otherwise useless; many bore no logical relation to recognized areas of public policy and of administrative jurisdiction. Members of the House served on as many as five or six, and senators sometimes on as many as seven or eight. And although some committees met rarely or not at all, it still was true that the average member had so many committee obligations that he could not possibly discharge them all; even with lax attendance, there was continual interference with other phases of legislative work, including service on important special committees which further taxed the member's time. To correct these glaring evils, (1) the former forty-eight standing committees in the House were reduced to nineteen, and the thirty-three in the Senate to fifteen; (2) committee jurisdictions were redefined with a view to eliminating overlapping and duplication and assigning each committee a definite sphere of activity; and (3) with slight exceptions, each representative was restricted to a single committee and each senator to two.[1]

2. *Improvement of committee operations.* With fewer committees, and many charged with widened jurisdictions, it was assumed that all would need to maintain regular schedules of meetings; and all (except the appropriations committees in the two houses) are required to fix regular weekly, biweekly, or monthly meeting days, with special meetings called by the chairman (or under certain conditions by members themselves) as deemed desirable. Each committee is required to keep a complete record of its proceedings; persons appearing at hearings are expected, so far as practicable, to file in advance written statements of their testimony and to present orally only brief summaries thereof; and every committee chairman is required to report promptly all bills approved by his committee, instead of using his discretion about the matter, and perhaps killing a bill by failure to report, as formerly.

3. *Assistance to committees.* To handle committee correspondence and stenographic work, especially for the chairman and ranking minority member, each committee is empowered to employ a clerical staff of not more than six clerks; and to assist in research and other activities, each (except the appropriations committees) may utilize the services of up to

---

here. Cf. R. M. LaFollette, Jr., "Systematizing Congressional Control," *Amer. Polit. Sci. Rev.*, XLI, 58-68 (Feb., 1947).

[1] After the legislation became effective, surprise was expressed and criticism at least implied in the press (see, for example, *N.Y. Times*, Apr. 14, 1947, p. 1) because of the "rash" of subcommittees that had broken out, with accent on specialization. The number, however (146 in the House), was not much larger than it had been; and with most of the basic committees charged with broadened jurisdiction, the development was natural and not particularly harmful.

four "professional staff members," again assigned primarily to the chair-man and ranking minority member.[1] This represents a more liberal allow-ance of committee aid than in the past, the main shortcoming being the failure of the act to put selection of the various assistants on a merit basis.

4. *Curtailment of petty business.* For a long time, Congress was under fire for permitting multitudes of bills adjusting claims, granting pensions, authorizing bridges over navigable streams, and for other comparatively minor purposes, to clog its proceedings and use up time better spent on more important things;[2] and a special message of President Roosevelt in 1942 urging assignment of much of this work to other agencies elicited no response. At last, however, the two houses saw the light, at least dimly; and in the legislation of 1946, some significant remedies were applied. To be sure, a careless reader of the reorganization law, noting a provision which on its face seems categorically to prohibit all private-bill legisla-tion, might get an exaggerated impression of the extent of the reform; and, looking over the laws enacted in the first session after the measure took effect and finding numerous private acts (131 in fact) among them, he well might be puzzled. For, as indicated, private bills are still intro-duced and passed. In the matter of claims, for example, while those arising after January 1, 1945, are handled only by administrative agencies or in the courts (depending on whether the amount involved exceeds one thousand dollars), any arising earlier than the date men-tioned are still adjusted through private-bill legislation; and several were so adjusted in the session referred to. Other exceptions will be found in the law also. Nevertheless, a general presumption against private bills is established; bridge-building proposals are now taken care of, not by Congress, but by specified officials in the Department of the Army; indi-vidual pension claims go only to the Veterans Administration; and, altogether, the field for private-bill legislation is sharply restricted—with even damage claims (except of certain specified types) promising to require no further attention after those of longer standing shall have been liquidated.

5. *Regulation of lobbying.* Provisions of this first federal legislation of general scope ever enacted on the subject, and following closely the rec-ommendations of the Joint Committee, have been reviewed in full above.[3]

6. *Improvement of financial procedure.* A significant new stage in han-dling the president's budget proposals, involving joint studies and deci-

---

[1] On account of the peculiar burdensomeness of their work, the appropriations committees are left free to engage more assistance if needed.

[2] A subcommittee of the House judiciary committee used to handle, every session, three thousand or more bills arising from people wanting the government to pay them for every imaginable sort of injury alleged to have been suffered at the hands of federal officials or employees. On the general subject, see R. Luce, "Petty Business in Congress," *Amer. Polit. Sci. Rev.,* XXVI, 815-827 (Oct., 1932); C. A. Beard, "Squirt-Gun Politics," *Harper's Mag.,* CLXI, 147-153 (July, 1930).

[3] See p. 410.

sions by the revenue and appropriations committees of the two houses, is introduced; although comment on it must be postponed to a later chapter dealing with budgetary matters.[1]

7. *Strengthening supervision over administration.* In pursuance of the duty of Congress to see that the measures which it enacts are carried out in the spirit intended and that money voted to put policies into effect is spent properly, and with a view to assisting the two houses in keeping track of the administration of the laws and in considering desirable changes in them, all committees are admonished to exercise continuous watchfulness over the execution of any and all laws falling within their respective jurisdictions.

8. *Provision of better pay and of retirement allowances.* Salaries of members are raised from $10,000 to $12,500 a year; a special expense allowance of $2,500 a year is provided; and members are made eligible for contributory pensions after six years of service and at the age of sixty-two. It was a sad commentary on public comprehension of problems of national legislation that people commonly saw in the Reorganization Act when passed only a "salary grab;" and, by and large, the press did not help them to a more adequate understanding of the measure's true significance.[2]

All in all, the reorganization of 1946 was the most extensive that Congress has undergone at any given time in the nearly one hundred and sixty years of its history. The Joint Committee, however, did not, in its report, touch upon all of the improvements that might have been, and were, suggested; the LaFollette-Monroney bill as introduced did not embody all of the Joint Committee's recommendations; and Congress did not write into the new law everything in the bill as introduced, or even as passed by the Senate. Room therefore remains for further change; and effort will continue to be made—if not at any early date within Congress itself, at all events by interested individuals and groups outside—to bring about completion of the task.[3] A word may be added about some further improvements deserving of consideration.

Some problems remaining

---

[1] See pp. 565-566, 571-572 below.

[2] The foregoing enumeration by no means exhausts the contents of the legislation of 1946, but further matters are relatively minor. Two things (among others) embraced in the original plan, and included in the bill as passed by the Senate, were eventually left out. One was provision for employment by each member of an expert and well-paid "administrative assistant" to take care of a large amount of the correspondence with and services for constituents—a task which at present takes up so much of a member's time that he often has little remaining for what is really his most important function, *i.e.*, studying and making up his mind on proposed legislation. The second omission was a clause prohibiting the future use of special committees—the theory of this revolutionary proposal being that functions now performed by special (including investigating) committees might better be kept in the hands of the standing committees or of subcommittees set up by them. Use of special committees has been considerably reduced since the legislation of 1946 was passed, but the general problem remains.

[3] Some writers express the opinion that the job is seventy-five (some say hardly fifty) per cent done—although such matters hardly lend themselves to exact measurement. In December, 1946, a bipartisan National Committee on Strengthening Congress, representing business, agriculture, labor, and the press, was formed under the

1. *Reduction in the size of the House of Representatives.* To begin with, the membership of the House of Representatives (435) is too large. This is not so serious a drawback as some others that have existed, but it is generally agreed that something like 300 (first exceeded under the reapportionment of 1881) would be a figure more compatible with efficient conduct of legislative business. Congressmen at present represent, on an average, ten times as many constituents as in the early days of the country; and, with adequate assistance, they could just as effectively represent twice as many as now. A reduction in the number of members is improbable; but it could, of course, be accomplished by simple legislative act in connection with any decennial reapportionment.

2. *Transfer of District of Columbia business.* From a dozen to twenty days of every session in each house are given to matters relating to the District of Columbia—detailed matters of "petty business," often of a sort which in every city of the land except Washington is handled by the locally elected council.[1] To be sure, the constitution requires Congress to "exercise exclusive legislation in all cases whatsoever" over the area containing the seat of the national government. But everyone recognizes that this need not be construed so literally as to prevent turning over District legislative work to the existing commissioners or perhaps a newly created council, with merely a veto by Congress upon more important measures.[2] The reorganization of 1946, however, did not touch this situation; on the contrary, it retained in the abridged committee lists of both houses a committee solely for the consideration of District legislation.

3. *Improvement of parliamentary procedure.* In setting up the Joint Committee which brought forth the reorganization bill, Congress expressly withheld the right to recommend any changes in the parliamentary rules governing proceedings in either house. This was not because these rules stand in no need of improvement, but only because neither house wanted its ways of transacting business made a subject of inquiry and criticism by any agency even partly outside of its own membership. No student of the legislative process can fail to perceive points at which congressional procedure could be bettered; indeed, plenty of members of both houses would like to see changes made. For such improvement, however, the country will have to wait for action by the houses singly, and perhaps a considerable time.

---

chairmanship of Robert Heller, Cleveland industrial engineer and author of *Strengthening Congress* mentioned above, to uphold the gains already made and to agitate for completion of the reform. Convenient analyses and diagrams will be found in R. Heller, *Strengthening the Congress; A Progress Report* (Washington, D. C., 1946), issued by the National Planning Association. Cf. E. Kefauver, "Did We Modernize Congress," *Nat. Mun. Rev.*, XXXVI, 552-557 (Nov., 1947).

[1] And so it comes about that the Congress of the United States is found solemnly passing bills to tax dogs in the District, to fix the number of taxicabs to be licensed, or to reinstate policemen ousted from the force.

[2] On the present government of the District, see pp. 861-863 below.

4. *Introduction of a system of joint committees.* In another connection, it has been pointed out that Massachusetts, Connecticut, and one or two other states derive distinct advantage from a plan under which, instead of duplicating and rival committees on given subjects in the two legislative houses, unity and dispatch are brought to committee work by a system of joint subject-matter committees, each having integrated jurisdiction in a given area. No plan of this sort, however, was proposed to Congress in 1946, and of course none was adopted. The only approach made—in addition to authorization of joint hearings by Senate and House committees when desired, as a means of saving time—was a provision of the law (already mentioned) for joint meetings of the committees of the two houses having to do with revenue legislation and appropriations, with a view to studying the president's budget recommendations and agreeing on a "legislative budget" to be reported for House and Senate consideration.[1] If this device for coöperative action eventually succeeds (it did not work well at its first trial), it may suggest the wisdom of applying the principle to other legislative fields like banking and currency or interstate and foreign commerce, with even the substitution of a single joint committee in a given field for separate ones.[2]

5. *Termination of the seniority system.* Next may be mentioned the obvious problem of seniority in connection with committee chairmanships. To be sure, as we have seen, there are arguments both for and against the prevailing practice (for it is only a practice, not a rule). Nearly all students of the legislative process, however, agree not only that mere length of continuous service on a committee is an illogical basis for promotion of a member to a chairmanship, but that many times the results are highly unfortunate. The Joint Committee reporting the reorganization measure of 1946 could not, however, agree on the subject; the ensuing legislation was silent upon it; and in so far as it offers a genuine challenge to change, developments are for the future.

6. *Introduction of a scheme of "policy committees."* There is no lack of party machinery and activity in Congress, but many students of our national legislative process believe that certain new party instrumentalities would yield a desirable increase of party responsibility and usefulness. Aiming in this direction, the Joint Committee put forward a plan for a set of four well-staffed "policy committees"[3] (one for the majority and one for the minority in each house), all consisting of seven members appointed by the appropriate party caucus (or conference) at the opening of each new Congress; all concerning themselves within their respective spheres with formulating over-all party legislative policy; and the two majority committees acting, in addition, as a council to meet reg-

---

[1] See p. 565 below.

[2] This last-mentioned plan (on the analogy of Massachusetts legislative arrangements) is advocated by R. Luce, former Massachusetts congressman, in his *Congress —An Explanation*, 30-32.

[3] Not to be confused with regular committees of the two houses.

ularly with the president and some or all members of the cabinet to facilitate the formulation and carrying out of national policy, and to improve relationships between the legislative and executive branches. Although promising useful service, not only in opening an avenue for better legislative-executive relations, but in clarifying party positions and policies at both ends of the Capitol in terms of national welfare rather than sectional or special interests, the House of Representatives rejected the proposal; and the legislation of 1946 contained no provision on the subject. The Senate, however, was not deterred from later voluntarily authorizing such committees for the 1947 session on an experimental basis.

The Improvement of Legislative-Executive Relations

Significant as has been the partial reform of Congress, an even more fundamental problem is that of improving the relations between the legislative and executive branches. By no one's planning, but by the logic of practical experience and necessity, those relations have become far more numerous and intimate than the makers of the constitution anticipated. Under our system of separated powers, they continue, however, to be relations between two distinct authorities, Congress and president, occupying "two islands of separate and jealous power;" and hence they often result in delays, deadlocks, weak compromises, and divided responsibility. Perhaps these disagreeable consequences are the price we have to pay for a basic safeguard which most people still consider a virtue of our constitutional system. But they are often impediments to smooth operation of the government, and much thought has been devoted to methods of obviating, or at least minimizing, them. It must suffice here to call attention briefly to some suggestions that have been offered.

Proposal for adoption of a cabinet system

Of course, the boldest way of seeking harmony and unity between Congress and the executive would be to abandon our historic principle of separation of powers and frankly go over to a cabinet system like the British. This done, the president would become a mere titular chief executive, with only formal and ceremonial functions. The actual executive would become the cabinet, which, with its members seated in Congress, would function as the supreme agency of policy-framing and of leadership in legislation. The cabinet would be responsible to Congress, and would remain in office only so long as enjoying majority support in that body. Failing such support, it would give way to a new cabinet more to the legislature's way of thinking. Conversely, if the cabinet were to become convinced that one or both houses of Congress had got out of step with the country, it could cause one or both to be dissolved and a new election held. This, truly enough, would be a way of largely obviating the tension, friction, and futility now too often characterizing legislative-executive relations in Washington; and interesting books have been written advocating the plan or at all events something approaching it.[1] The proposal has only to be mentioned, however, to be dismissed as visionary. No sensible person really supposes that our people are prepared for so momentous a step in the foreseeable future; and even if they were, it does not follow that cabinet government would work as well here as in countries having different traditions. More than a hundred years of accumulating experience were required to bring the system to maturity in the land of its birth.

But there are other proposals, more practicable even if enjoying scarcely more prospect of adoption. One is that, while the president should continue appearing before Congress only, as now, to present messages, the heads of executive departments should be extended the privilege of the floor in both houses for the purpose of giving information, answering questions, and engaging in general debate. As civil officers of the United States, department heads are ineligible to membership in either house. But for the purpose mentioned, it would not be necessary to make them members. Already they and other higher administrators are sometimes seen mingling with senators and representatives in the corridors and cloakrooms of the Capitol. With increasing frequency, too, they appear before congressional committees to supply information, answer questions, or urge the passage of bills in which the Administration is interested. Would it not be better, it is asked, to give the entire membership of either house, or of both houses, a chance to hear what they have to say and to question them in the same direct manner in which ministers are questioned in the British House of Commons? The administrators, on their part, would be afforded opportunity to get clearer notions of what Congress meant when passing a law, to explain the difficulties and problems that have arisen in carrying it out, to answer charges, and to justify their policies; and the plan could be adopted by simple revision of the rules of the two houses. Advocates of the idea seem, however, not to have given sufficient consideration to the danger that, instead of expediting business, the effect might be rather to slow it up, because of the disposition of members hostile to the Administration to ply its spokesmen with questions provocative of debate—although, as British experience shows, there might be ways of screening the questions asked (at least the written ones) so as to prevent time being consumed with queries definitely irrelevant or merely partisan.[2]

Other proposals:

1. Admitting heads of departments to the floor in Congress

---

[1] A quick change-over to the cabinet system is advocated in H. Hazlitt, *A New Constitution Now* (New York, 1942), as it also was a generation ago in W. MacDonald, *A New Constitution for a New America* (New York, 1921). Even if such a step were practicable, it would be at the sacrifice of at least one very great asset of our present system, *i.e.,* the presidency as a unifying and energizing force in our national life. Removing the presidency as the focal point in our national politics, it also would tend to open the way for fragmentation and sectionalization of political parties, with all the disadvantages accruing from a multi-party system.

[2] In the First Congress, it is interesting to observe, department chiefs not only appeared on the floor of both houses, but took part in debate. The practice died out, however, and numerous attempts in later periods to revive it proved unavailing. A

2. Using
members
of Con-
gress as
depart-
ment
heads
A more radical plan, which had the support of President Taft, would
be for the president, in selecting his heads of departments, to take them,
or at any rate most of them, from the members of his party in Congress,
the persons so chosen remaining members of the legislative branch entitled to participate in debate, to introduce bills, to serve on committees,
and to vote. This would be a step in the direction of a cabinet system,
yet stopping a long way short of it. But in any case it raises doubts. To
begin with, a constitutional amendment would be required. And if this
hurdle could be surmounted, there would still be the rather anomalous
position in which a president—retaining his present constitutional powers
and prerogatives, yet surrounded by chief agents and advisers whose
political fortunes were more or less independent of his own—would find
himself. In so far as the plan would make for greater harmony between
the executive and legislative branches, it doubtless would prove advantageous. But there is no clear guarantee that it would do this.

3. Insur-
ing
priority
for
Adminis-
tration
measures
Most public bills of major importance now come to Capitol Hill from
the other end of Pennsylvania Avenue (the White House, the departments, or other agencies), and the legislative success of a session depends
largely on the fate of these measures.[1] Why not, it is asked, frankly
accept this situation and, by suitably amending the rules of the two
houses, definitely guarantee Administration bills priority such as is
assured Government (i.e., cabinet) bills in Great Britain? If executive
leadership in legislation is inevitable (and presumably desirable), why
not freely and wholeheartedly clear the way for it? Without necessarily

---

history of proposals on the subject through more than one hundred years, and an
able presentation of the favorable arguments, will be found in 63rd Cong., Spec.
Sess. of Senate, Sen. Doc. No. 4, *Privilege of the Floor to Cabinet Members; Reports
Made to the Congress of the United States* (1913).

In October, 1943, Congressman Estes Kefauver of Tennessee introduced in the
House of Representatives a resolution amending the rules of the House to provide
that, on at least one day in every two weeks, heads of departments and independent
agencies should appear in the House by request to answer orally written and oral
questions put to them by members—such question period to occur not oftener than
once a week and to consume not more than two hours. The proposal won hearty
support from younger members and in the press, but was frowned on by the House
leadership, and never stood much chance of adoption. Interest in the plan when proposed was whetted by Secretary Hull's appearance, by invitation, before the House
and Senate, meeting jointly, to give a confidential report on the results of an international conference at Moscow in which he had participated. The occurrence was
noteworthy, because never in a century and a half had a cabinet member addressed
Congress in such a fashion. But it was not the sort of thing contemplated in the
Kefauver resolution. See E. Kefauver, "The Need for Better Executive-Legislative
Teamwork in the National Government," *Amer. Polit. Sci. Rev.*, XXXVIII, 317-325
(Apr., 1944); E. Kefauver and J. Levin, *A Twentieth-Century Congress* (New York,
1947), Chap. vi; W. P. Armstrong, "The Kefauver Resolution," *Amer. Bar Assoc.
Jour.*, XXX, 326-329 (June, 1944). The Kefauver proposal was reintroduced in the
House of Representatives in January, 1945, but without result.

[1] In the domain of high policy, this is, of course, less true when the Administration
lacks the advantage of majorities in the two branches of Congress. In the first session of the Eightieth Congress (1947), for example, the two top measures passed by
Congress—a bill for reducing federal taxes (passed twice with different beginning
dates) and the Labor-Management Relations [Taft-Hartley] Act—not only did not
emanate from the White House, but were vetoed there, in one case successfully, in
the other not. Most of the time, however, the same party dominates at both ends of
Pennsylvania Avenue and the statement made above holds true.

condemning the general idea, three things are, however, to be said: first, that when the Administration has the advantage of a working majority in the two houses (as throughout the period 1933-46), it even now can count with great assurance upon highly preferential treatment (not always acceptance, but at least attention) for its bills; second, that when it has no such majority, its bills are not likely to prevail in any case; and third, that, so long as Congress clings to its still important function of legislative initiative, it will certainly not be willing to tie its hands by any general rule relegating measures of its own devising to the notoriously unfavorable position occupied by private members' bills in the Government-led and -controlled House of Commons at Westminster.

Several students of the legislative-executive problem have suggested supplementing existing machinery with some sort of a council that might be of service in tying the two branches more closely together. We have had a proposal that the chairmen of standing committees in each house (reduced to ten) be organized into a "legislative" or "congressional" cabinet, with responsibility for mapping out programs of legislative business, and with continuous contact with the president in formulating public policy.[1] We have had the suggestion of a "joint legislative council," to consist of eleven senators and eleven congressmen, with three additional members appointed by the president, to serve as a central legislative policy committee through which all proposed legislation would have to pass, and as an agency for organized consultation between Congress and the president.[2] We have had a plan for a congressional cabinet to consist of the chairmen of about nine *joint* Senate-House committees (if such were ever to supersede the present separate committees of the two houses), and to be combined with an equal number of members of the executive cabinet in a joint executive-legislative cabinet, to serve as a bridge between the two branches and link them in harmonious action.[3] And most recently, as we have seen, the Joint Committee on the Organization of Congress proposed (and the Senate approved), to the same end, a plan under which a majority "policy committee" of each house—not necessarily composed entirely of committee chairmen—be joined with the president and his cabinet to constitute a legislative-executive council.[4]

4. Setting up a joint legislative-executive council

[1] R. Young, *This Is Congress* (New York, 1943), Chap. VIII. The suggested "cabinet" would bear a good deal of resemblance to legislative councils developed in Kansas and some other states. See p. 918 below.

[2] A. Hehmeyer, *Time for Change* (New York, 1943), Chap. IX.

[3] T. K. Finletter, *Can Representative Government Do the Job?* (New York, 1945), Chap. XI; and cf. E. S. Corwin, *The President: Office and Powers* (New York, 1940), 303-306. An interesting step in the direction indicated was taken early in 1944, when, at the suggestion of Secretary Hull, an informal committee on foreign policy, linking the Department of State and the foreign affairs committees of the two houses of Congress, was instituted. Mr. Finletter goes on to propose still more drastic measures, *e.g.*, amendment of the constitution to provide for election of president, senators, and congressmen for identical terms, with power in the president to dissolve both House and Senate (he also retiring simultaneously) and order new elections in case of deadlock between Congress and the joint cabinet. *Ibid.*, Chap. XII.

[4] Something like this is proposed by C. A. Beard in his *The Republic* (New York, 1944), 256-258.

"Fourteen members of Congress," says a principal author of this last suggestion, "would sit around the council table with the president and his ten cabinet members. Cabinet members for the first time would have an opportunity to participate directly in the discussion of a unified legislative program. Legislative leaders could avoid head-on clashes with the president over much legislation if a better understanding were secured of the point of view of the executive branch, and *vice versa*."[1] With policy committees thus far set up only in the Senate, there has as yet been no opportunity to organize the joint council contemplated; and no other plan or device of the kind has been offered from any quarter.

The immediate outlook

Indeed, the outlook for adoption of any of the several proposals reviewed is not, at the time of writing (1948), particularly bright. Everyone agrees that, under our system of government, there are few if any matters of greater importance than the working relations between the legislative and executive branches; nearly everyone concedes that the objective to be sought is not the further building up of two separate and powerful authorities, confronting and battling each other, but rather the development of two complementary and interlocked agencies capable of serving the interests of the country through common consultation, planning, and action. At present, the most promising means of promoting such a relationship would seem to be a mediating legislative-executive council on one or another of the different lines suggested, perhaps preferably the kind of a council envisaged by the Joint Committee. Congress, however, has lately emerged, with a deep sense of satisfaction and even exultation, from a decade or more of unprecedented executive domination. It furthermore has surprised, and to a degree over-strained, itself in adopting the partial reorganization of 1946. And it is hardly in a mood either to undertake right away any further overhauling of its own machinery and procedures or to enter into new "entangling alliances" with the White House. Since the 1946 elections, there has been the fact, too, that with one party controlling the two houses and a different party the presidency, any step toward tying the legislature and the executive more closely together would be fraught with peculiar difficulty—even though it is in precisely such a situation that the need for bridging the legislative-executive gap may be greatest. When, eventually, presidency and Congress again come under the same party control, the task may be easier—although in that more normal situation it might easily go by default as not seeming urgent.[2] Sooner or later, remedial measures will likely be taken. But for the present they lie in the uncertain future, with the circumstances prompting them remaining to be disclosed.

[1] Ex-Senator R. M. LaFollette, Jr., in *Amer. Polit. Sci. Rev.*, XLI, 64 (Feb., 1947).
[2] Such a view would, however, be fallacious, because even the closest party harmony at any given time between the president and congressional majorities in no wise obviates the need for improved integration of discussion, planning, and leadership.

REFERENCES

R. Young, *This Is Congress* (New York, 1943), Chaps. v-vi, viii.

J. T. Flynn, *Meet Your Congress* (New York, 1944), Chap. xiv.

T. K. Finletter, *Can Representative Government Do the Job?* (New York, 1945), Chaps. x-xii.

A. Hehmeyer, *Time for Change* (New York, 1943), Chap. ix.

H. Hazlitt, *A New Constitution Now* (New York, 1942), Chap. xii.

C. P. Patterson, *Presidential Government in the United States; The Unwritten Constitution* (Chapel Hill, N. C., 1947), Chap. x.

G. B. Galloway, *Congress at the Crossroads* (New York, 1946), Chap. x.

E. Kefauver and J. Levin, *A Twentieth-Century Congress* (New York, 1947).

E. P. Herring, *Presidential Leadership; The Political Relations of Congress and the Chief Executive* (New York, 1940).

————, *Group Representation Before Congress* (Baltimore, 1929).

H. L. Childs [ed.], "Pressure Groups and Propaganda," *Annals of Amer. Acad. of Polit. and Soc. Sci.,* Vol. XLXXIX, 1-239 (May, 1935)

D. C. Blaisdell, "Government Under Pressure," *Pub. Affairs Pamphlets,* No. 67 (New York, 1942).

K. C. Crawford, *The Pressure Boys; The Inside Story of Lobbying in America* (New York, 1929).

S. Chase, *Democracy Under Pressure; Special Interests vs. the Public Welfare* (New York, 1945).

P. H. Odegard, *Pressure Politics; The Story of the Anti-Saloon League* (New York, 1928).

B. Zeller, "The Federal Regulation of Lobbying Act," *Amer. Polit. Sci. Rev.,* XLII, 239-271 (Apr., 1948).

W. McCune, *The Farm Bloc* (Garden City, N. Y., 1943).

E. E. Schattschneider, *Politics, Pressures, and the Tariff* (New York, 1935), Pts. iii-v.

J. Daniels, *Frontier on the Potomac* (New York, 1946).

"Economic Power and Political Pressure," Temporary National Economic Committee Monograph No. 26 (Washington, D. C., 1941).

Committee on Congress of the American Political Science Association, *The Reorganization of Congress* (Washington, D. C., 1945).

Joint Committee on the Organization of Congress, *Organization of the Congress,* 79th Cong., 2nd Sess., Sen. Rep. No. 1011 (1946).

R. Heller, *Strengthening the Congress* (Washington, D. C., 1945)

P. S. Broughton, "For a Stronger Congress," *Pub. Affairs Pamphlets,* No. 116 (New York, 1946).

J. A. Perkins, "Congressional Self-Improvement," *Amer. Polit. Sci. Rev.,* XXXVIII, 499-511 (June, 1944).

J. P. Harris, "The Reorganization of Congress," *Pub. Admin. Rev.,* VI, 267-282 (Summer, 1946). Discounts and criticizes the Legislative Reorganization Act of 1946.

C. A. Beard, "In Defense of Congress," *Amer. Mercury,* LV, 529-535 (Nov., 1942).

L. Rogers, "The Staffing of Congress," *Polit. Sci. Quar.,* LVI, 1-22 (Mar., 1941).

J. Voorhis, *Confessions of a Congressman* (Garden City, N. Y., 1947).

W. R. Tansill [comp.], *The Organization of Congress; A Select Annotated Bibliography . . . ,* 79th Cong., 1st Sess. (1945).

CHAPTER XX

PRESIDENT AND CABINET

In preceding chapters, focussed on the legislative branch of the national government, the president has appeared only in so far as he shares in or influences the workings of that branch. After all, however, his primary position in the government is as an executive; in him, indeed, the constitution tersely vests "the executive power." And we now turn to the executive side of our system—the president as chief executive, the heads of departments as his top-ranking advisers and agents, and afterwards the ramifying controls through which the executive powers of management and enforcement are carried down the avenues of administration to the people of every community in the land.

The problem of the executive in 1787

When the constitution's framers made bold to plan a really new system of government for the country, they found little difficulty in deciding that there should be a national executive. The precise form to be given it, however, provoked controversy. Should supreme executive power be intrusted to a single official, or should it be vested in a board or commission? How should the executive be chosen? What should be the term, and should more than one term be permitted? In case a single executive were provided for, should a council be associated with him, on the analogy of the governor's council in the states? Above all, what should be the executive's powers, and what relations should the executive have with other branches of the governmental system? No problems coming before the Philadelphia convention, indeed, aroused greater differences of opinion than some of these. On twenty-one different days, the general subject of the executive was under discussion; on the method of election alone, more than thirty separate votes were taken.[1]

A single executive decided upon

A decision in favor of a single rather than a plural executive was, however, reached with no great difficulty. Most foreign precedents pointed in this direction, and every one of the American states had a single executive, *i.e.*, a governor or a "president." The plan offered the obvious advantages of prompter action and more concentration of responsibility; and while it might seem to open the way for executive tyranny, and even for monarchist maneuvers, fear of such miscarriages was allayed by prescribing a fixed term, restricting powers, and providing for removal by impeachment. If the executive, as some members desired, had been made nothing more than an agency to carry into effect the will of the legislature, the plural form probably would have been adopted; and this might

[1] M. Farrand, *The Framing of the Constitution* (New Haven, 1913), Chap. XI.

have left matters in such a position that a cabinet system like the English would have resulted. But after it was decided that the executive should constitute a coördinate branch, drawing authority independently from the people and charged with many duties besides enforcement of the acts of Congress, it was both natural and wise to concentrate power and responsibility in the hands of a single person.

Presidential Term, Qualifications, and Emoluments

One of the consequences of a presidential system like ours is a fixed term of office for the chief executive; and although a few members of the Philadelphia convention were willing that the president should hold office during good behavior, the question narrowed down to (1) a seven-year term without eligibility for reëlection or (2) a four-year term with no such restriction. At one stage, the seven-year plan was adopted. But when it became clear that the president was not to be chosen by Congress, the main objection to reëligibility disappeared, and the briefer term, without restriction as to reëlection, was substituted.[1]

Term and re-eligibility

In the course of time, it became a tradition that a president should not have more than two terms. Washington's advanced age and dislike of party strife led him to refuse to be a candidate for a third term. Jefferson, who originally favored a single seven-year term, could doubtless have been elected a third time, but he also declined. Jackson's popularity would probably have insured him a third election; but he publicly commended the decisions of his predecessors[2] and in 1836 threw his support to Martin Van Buren. General Grant, in 1880, was induced to break with precedent by seeking a nomination for a third, although non-consecutive, term. But the public disapproved, and the effort failed. In 1912, Theodore Roosevelt also sought a third term, after being out of office for four years. President Taft received the regular Republican nomination; whereupon the Roosevelt following organized a new party, nominated their leader, and launched a campaign which won many more electoral votes than were received by the regular candidate. The third-term contestant was, however, not elected. President Coolidge's coy announcement in 1927 that he did not "choose to run" for reëlection in 1928 did not prevent a large amount of third-term talk as campaign time approached; and a skeptical opposition element in the Senate (both Democrats and Republicans) induced that body to adopt a resolution declaring any departure from the no-third-term principle "unwise, unpatriotic, and fraught with peril to our free institutions." This rather extravagant pronouncement was, of course, a mere expression of opinion, wholly devoid of legal effect. Naturally, the point was made by Coolidge

Precedents against a third term

---

[1] An incidental effect of the Twentieth Amendment, adopted in 1933, was to shorten the first term of President Roosevelt (and of Vice-President Garner) by a month and a half, by terminating it on January 20 instead of March 4, 1937.

[2] Indeed, in messages to Congress he six times advocated a constitutional amendment limiting the president to a single term of four or six years.

supporters that even if the incumbent were renominated (as he very likely could have been) and reëlected, he would have had only two full, elective terms in office.[1] But an amendment to the resolution making it applicable only to presidents who had served "two elected terms" was rejected.[2]

Hardly a textbook on American government down to 1940 failed to cite the no-third-term tradition as a choice illustration of the way in which the actual, working constitution grows through usage or custom. Then, however, came a shock: a president—Franklin D. Roosevelt—was elected to a third term! There will always be differences of opinion as to the motivation of this third-term candidacy. At the time, charges were flung about that the two-time president preferred to shatter national tradition rather than surrender leadership in carrying the New Deal program through its later stages, and even that he was animated by sheer love of power. It is fairer, however, to accept his own explanation (as given by radio to the Chicago convention that renominated him), namely, that until after the outbreak of war in Europe in the autumn of 1939 he thought of no course other than retiring at the end of his second term, but that in the meantime the situation of the United States in the world had grown so critical that it had become his duty to offer the country the advantage of continuous presidential experience and leadership during the emergency.[3] With the third term as a major issue, the campaign of 1940 called forth argument (1) that no man ought to be subjected to the physical strain of the presidency for longer than eight years, (2) that the powers of the office have come to be such that intrusting them to the same hands for more than eight years would be dangerous to our republican institutions, (3) that no man in any office is indispensable to the well-being of a great nation, and (4) that with the barrier to a third term once broken down, the way would be open to a fourth and a fifth, and indeed to an indefinite prolongation of power. On the other hand, it was contended (1) that—as was true—the constitution's framers had contemplated indefinite reëligibility, (2) that there was nothing sacred about the no-third-term tradition, (3) that the people have means of protecting themselves against too long tenure or other abuse of the presidency, and especially (4) that in the existing emergency it was to the nation's interest to retain in the White House a president having the personal qualities, the long experience, and the superior information undeniably possessed by the then incumbent. By keeping the country, and even his

[1] He had succeeded to the presidency upon the death of Harding in 1923 and had been elected to the office only once, i.e., in 1924.

[2] See W. B. Munro and W. Lippmann, "Shall We Break the Third-Term Tradition?," Forum, LXVIII, 162-173 (Aug., 1927). It is thought that, but for the state of his health, Woodrow Wilson, viewing the presidency as the American equivalent of the British premiership, would have been favorably inclined toward a third term. E. S. Corwin, The President: Office and Powers, 36.

[3] For an intimate view of Roosevelt's state of mind while deciding that he must forego retirement, see R. T. McIntire, White House Physician (New York, 1947), Chap. IX.

personal friends, in the dark as to his intentions throughout the pre-convention period, Mr. Roosevelt cleverly prevented the development of any serious rival candidacies; [1] and although his renomination at Chicago was not by the acclamation hoped for, it fell not far short of it, and four months later the country ratified it—not overwhelmingly in terms of the popular vote, but by an electoral vote of 449 to 82.[2]

As indicated above, there were those in 1940 who considered that, in the words of Professor Corwin, "If the anti-third-term taboo [was] once set aside, it [would] take a long time for an anti-fourth-term or anti-fifth-term taboo to develop. In a word, the presidential term [would] become indefinite—just what in 1787 it was expected to be." [3] As the year 1944 approached, with the country straining every sinew in a global war and enmeshed in a multitude of operations and commitments with the United Nations, indications grew that President Roosevelt could, and would, expect another nomination at the hands of his party. Once more, by keeping silent substantially to the date of the nominating convention, he fostered the presumption of such a nomination, frustrating any possible development of rival candidacies; and when finally he spoke, it was to say in the same breath that while on every personal ground he would prefer to retire, the country's need for continuity of leadership in so critical a period would influence him to remain at the helm if again nominated and elected. The renomination that quickly followed (again at Chicago)—although, as in 1940, not unanimous—was merely a bit of routine; and anything resembling a no-fourth-term tradition was scotched before it had time to begin to form. The outcome, after a spirited campaign, was still another reëlection; and, times and situations being what they were, and all precedent having been shattered in any event, the matter of a fourth term weighed more lightly with the voters than had the third-term question in 1940.

Naturally enough, the third- and fourth-term battles of 1940 and 1944 called forth proposals for limiting presidential tenure by constitutional amendment; and although a Democratic Congress could hardly have been expected to initiate or sanction an action which by implication would have repudiated the decisions of the party in the years mentioned, a Republican Congress—the first in sixteen years—was no sooner organized in January, 1947, than plans for an amendment were eagerly launched. In earlier times, proposals on the subject had commonly looked to restricting the chief executive to a single term, perhaps lengthened to six years. There always had been people who considered that a president

Marginal notes: A fourth term also

Proposals to limit presidential tenure: 1. By prohibiting any reëlection

---

[1] As a matter of plain fact, a principal reason why the leaders of his party became so enthusiastic about his renomination was that they had no other strong candidate.

[2] The popular vote was 27,243,466 for Roosevelt and 22,304,755 for Willkie. Contemporary literature on the third-term issue includes W. Thornton, *The Third-Term Issue; Hot Potato of American Politics* (New York, 1939), and F. Rodell, *Democracy and the Third Term* (New York, 1940). Cf. C. W. Stein, *The Third-Term Tradition; Its Rise and Collapse in American Politics* (New York, 1943).

[3] E. S. Corwin, *The President: Office and Powers,* 38.

eligible for reëlection could hardly escape, or perhaps seriously resist, temptation to make appointments, wield the veto power, and otherwise shape his course with an eye to continuance in office, and who therefore believed that it would be better if there were no reëligibility to even a second term; and single-six-year-term proposals began making their appearance in Congress as early as 1828.[1] Reflecting the stir created by Theodore Roosevelt's third-term candidacy in 1912, Woodrow Wilson was chosen to the presidency in that year on a platform advocating an amendment making the chief executive ineligible for reëlection;[2] and in 1913 the Senate adopted a resolution offering an amendment lengthening the term to six years and forbidding any person who had held the office by election or under operation of the law of succession to hold it again "by election." Although reported favorably by the judiciary committee, this proposal did not come to a vote in the House; and revival of it in the next Congress was similarly barren of result. During the 1940 campaign, a Senate judiciary subcommittee held hearings on a single-six-year-term amendment proposed by a disaffected Democratic senator, Edward R. Burke; but Administration and party leaders naturally frowned on the proceeding, and the effort came to nothing. It is a matter of record that at least two former presidents favored an amendment of the kind;[3] and during the 1940 campaign a former Democratic candidate for the office (John W. Davis) took a similar position.

2. By permitting only two terms

Many persons favoring restriction in principle have, however, considered that prohibition of any reëlection at all would be unnecessarily drastic; and to the six-year term it has been objected that, if (as seems probable) the House of Representatives continues to be chosen for only two years at a time, the likelihood of wasteful legislative-executive discord would be enhanced, since there would be *two* interim congressional elections instead of only one as now. For these and other reasons, proposals in later days have been more likely to aim at imposing upon every president a limit of two terms, or at all events prohibiting as many as three. The Republican candidate in 1940 (Wendell L. Willkie) pledged that, if elected, he would, in his first message to Congress, urge an amendment limiting the tenure of any president to "eight years or less"; and in 1943 committee hearings took place in the Senate on such an amendment, introduced and somewhat liberally supported by Democratic members not too cordial toward President Roosevelt—although no action of any kind resulted.

[1] In all, no fewer than one hundred constitutional amendments of this purport have been introduced.

[2] The candidate did not himself endorse this plank. On the contrary, in a letter written early in 1913 (although not made public until 1916), he declared that a "fixed constitutional limitation to a single term of office" would be "highly arbitrary and unsatisfactory from every point of view" (*Amer. Year Book*, 1916, 34); and, as has been indicated, he apparently would not have been averse to trying for a third term if his health had permitted.

[3] Jackson and Taft. For Taft's views, see his *Our Chief Executive and His Powers* (New York, 1916), 4.

Standing high on the Republican program when the Eightieth Congress began operations in 1947, the matter was brought to prompt decision. By a vote of 285 to 121 (more than the necessary two-thirds), the House of Representatives, on February 6, and after but one day's debate, adopted a resolution submitting to the states an amendment limiting a president to two terms, whether or not consecutive, and so defined that even a portion of an unfinished term served by a vice-president succeeding to the office would count as one of his "terms." Five weeks later, the Senate, by a vote of 59 to 23, similarly approved an amendment identical with that adopted in the House, except that any fraction of a term not exceeding one year was to be disregarded, thus making it possible for a president to serve a maximum of nine years instead of eight.[1] The differing forms taken by the resolutions in the two houses made it necessary to invoke the services of conference committees, as did also the fact that whereas the House resolution contemplated action in the states by legislatures, the Senate proposal provided for ratification by state conventions, after the manner of the Twenty-first Amendment repealing prohibition; and in the end an amendment was agreed upon and referred to the states (to be acted on by legislatures) forbidding any person to be elected to the presidency more than twice, but making eligible to a second election any person who had occupied the office not more than two years while filling out an unexpired term, *i.e.*, as vice president succeeding to the position in mid-term.[2] In other words, the maximum tenure was to be ten years— two full terms and not more than one-half of a third. The situation was complicated by the fact that President Truman, incumbent when the discussions were going on, was filling out an unexpired term; and with a view to not penalizing him, a proviso was added exempting him from the amendment's operation.[3]

The "Twenty-second Amendment" submitted

In the course of debates on the amendment, both Republicans and Democrats professed to desire to exclude party politics; and a good deal of the discussion actually was on somewhat academic lines, emphasizing historical precedents. Notwithstanding considerable Democratic support, the Republicans, however, supplied the driving force; and in arguing against prolongation of presidential tenure beyond two terms, they plainly had in mind chiefly the recent experience with Franklin D. Roosevelt and his four successive elections. Contending that more than two terms tended to aggravate the evils of overgrown executive power and of centralization, and threatened dictatorship—moreover, that the majority party was interested merely in getting the question squarely before the people—the defenders were met principally with the arguments that their

Some arguments pro and con

---

[1] The House resolution received the support of all 238 Republicans and of 47 out of a total of 197 Democrats; the Senate resolution, that of 48 Republicans out of 51 and 11 Democrats out of 45. In both branches, the South provided the bulk of the opposition.

[2] For the full text of the proposed amendment, (see Appendix).

[3] So far as the amendment (if finally ratified) is concerned, he therefore might be elected not only in 1948, but also in 1952 and even 1956.

proposal amounted to a vindictive assault upon the memory of a deceased president, that the people ought always to be free, in time of national emergency, to keep a chief executive in the White House longer than eight, or even ten, years if the interests of the country demanded, and that the future of the nation ought not to be "mortgaged to the dead hand of the past." To the charge that the Democratic opposition had reversed its own position of 1912 and 1928, there was, and could be, no effective reply.[1]

Outlook for the amendment's adoption

Persons easily deceived by appearances might have got the impression that the amendment was going to sweep quickly through the state legislatures and become law of the land; starting with Maine, eight ratifications were recorded within a month—eighteen (half of the required number) within the first five months. But no such pace could be maintained. Numerous legislatures concluded their 1947 sessions before there was opportunity to act, or at all events adjourned without acting; few would be in session in 1948; it was at least doubtful whether any solidly Democratic legislatures in the South would act favorably (the South alone could very nearly frustrate the proposal[2]); in short, not only was it certain that the earliest opportunity for securing the requisite three-fourths would be 1949 (with most legislatures then in session), but doubt could easily be entertained as to whether the amendment would ever become effective at all. In any event, the outcome was likely to be determined more largely by politics than by sober reflection on constitutional principles.

Presidential qualifications

Whatever additional qualifications a president may be expected to have, he must meet three tests explicitly imposed by the constitution: (1) he must be at least thirty-five years of age; (2) he must have been a resident of the United States for at least fourteen years (not necessarily —as illustrated in the case of Hoover—the last fourteen before election); and (3) he must be a "natural-born" citizen. Inasmuch, too, as the vice-president may at any time be called upon to take up the duties of the presidency, he is expected to have all of the qualifications required for that office.

Salary and allowances

Benjamin Franklin argued in the Philadelphia convention that, since wealth and power are the corrupting allurements which human nature finds it hardest to resist, the president should be allowed nothing whatever from the public treasury beyond his expenses. But though the famous Pennsylvanian had the reputation of being the wisest man of his day, his proposal was not even put to a vote; and by constitutional provision the president receives a salary, with the safeguard that it may

---

[1] For a summary of the debates (though principally with reference to the mode of ratification), see E. S. Brown, "The Term of Office of the President," *Amer. Polit. Sci. Rev.*, XLI, 447-452 (June, 1947). Cf. "Should the United States Constitution Limit the Terms a President May Serve?" [Symposium], *Cong. Digest*, XXVI, 14-23 (Jan., 1947).

[2] The Virginia and Mississippi legislatures, however, ratified after the above lines were written, and to April 1, 1948, only the Oklahoma legislature had definitely rejected the proposal. The total of ratifications at the date mentioned was twenty-one.

be neither increased nor diminished during the period for which he has been elected. He is forbidden to receive any other emolument, either from the United States or from any state. But this is construed not to prevent the United States from providing him with a dignified colonial mansion (the White House), a suite of executive offices, a secretariat, and special allowances for automobiles, furniture, repairs, entertainment, and travel, amounting to some $450,000 a year.[1] Originally fixed at $25,000 annually, the president's salary was raised in 1873 to $50,000, and in 1909 to $75,000—on which, however, he pays income taxes like any other citizen.

Presidential Burdens and Provisions for Assistance

Some presidents put in longer hours and work harder than others, but for none is the office a sinecure; few are as fit when they leave the White House as when they entered it. There is, first of all, a vast amount of administrative routine. Much can, of course, be turned over to subordinates; but much also is of such a nature that the president cannot escape it. The daily grist of correspondence is exacting and time-consuming. Heads of departments, members of Congress, party leaders, spokesmen of business interests, and a wide variety of other people must be given personal interviews. Delegations, official and unofficial, must be welcomed. State receptions and dinners must be held. Appointments to public office make heavy demands. When Congress is in session, there are bills to be studied, programs of legislation to be mapped out, innumerable conferences to be held; and even during legislative recesses, much may need to be done for the furtherance of legislative projects which the chief executive has at heart. Foreign relations call for much—in periods of stress like the past decade, almost constant—attention. Even with the spadework done by other officials or by "ghost writers," preparation of messages and of public addresses chains the president to his desk; cabinet meetings, official entertainment of foreign and other guests, press conferences, radio talks, and participation in public ceremonies take their toll of energy and time. And as if all this were not enough, the president is expected to exercise a general watchfulness over the state of the country and at times of crisis—such as the stock-market crash of 1929, the great droughts of 1930 and 1934, the banking *débâcle* of 1933, and the paralyzing strikes of 1946—to devise, guide, and lead in carrying out measures of relief and remedy. Though assisted by a White House secretariat considerably increased in numbers and improved in efficiency, President Hoover found even less leisure than did most of his predecessors, not simply because by nature he was a "twelve hour a day man," nor even because the last two and a half years of his administration proved a

The president at work

---

[1] W. Hard, "The White House Plant," *World's Work*, LVIII, 46-53, 106-116 (Jan., 1929). The cost of unofficial entertaining is borne by the president himself, but that of official functions is met out of a fund of $30,000 given the chief executive every year to spend at his discretion. Custom has it that if adherents of more than one political party are present, a function is "official," otherwise not.

peculiarly trying time in the life of the nation, but because the volume of even the normal work to be done mounts from year to year and almost from day to day. With a titanic program of national recovery and social rehabilitation on his hands, later an equally stupendous program of national defense, and eventually a global war of staggering proportions (with the White House the focal point of the combined stresses of a dozen military fronts), President Roosevelt—although temperamentally fitted to carry a great load with a minimum of strain—much of the time lived and worked under pressure that could not fail to take heavy toll.[1]

In a significant report submitted early in 1937, the President's Committee on Administrative Management in the Government of the United States (composed of three outstanding students of government, and appointed by President Roosevelt to consider desirable improvements in the national administrative system [2]) asserted that, because of the increasing work to be done, the president's "immediate staff assistance" was "entirely inadequate" and proposed that not to exceed six new administrative assistants be provided, to serve as "direct aids in dealing with the managerial agencies and administrative departments of the government." Fully endorsing this suggestion, but considering that it did not go far enough, President Roosevelt developed a more ambitious plan for strengthening the "management arms" of the chief executive; and—the six assistants having in the meantime been authorized and appointed—a new framework of executive correlation was introduced by order of September 8, 1939, in pursuance of powers conferred in the Reorganization Act of the previous April 3.[3] Into a new Executive Office of the President were gathered a number of establishments previously scattered and in some instances only imperfectly developed; and all—although bearing little relation to one another—were made directly dependent upon and responsible to the chief executive, without connection with any of the regular executive departments.[4]

---

[1] Vice-Admiral Ross T. McIntire, President Roosevelt's personal physician throughout his twelve years in the White House, might demur, but the plain implication of his *White House Physician* (New York, 1947) is that the President's life was materially shortened by the strain of office, especially as experienced during the last two or three years.

For "human interest" accounts of the president at work, one may turn to I. H. Hoover, *Forty-two Years in the White House* (Boston, 1934), by a shrewd observer who served under several presidents as chief usher at the White House; W. Irwin, "Portrait of a President [Hoover]," and "The President's Job," *Sat. Eve. Post*, CCIII (Jan. 17, Mar. 7, 1931); and D. Pearson and R. S. Allen, "How the President [Franklin D. Roosevelt] Works," *Harper's Mag.*, CLXXIII, 1-14 (June, 1936). Cf. biographies of various presidents.

[2] See p. 483 below.

[3] See pp. 482-484 below. In taking this step, the President said: "[It] has been common knowledge for twenty years that the president cannot adequately handle his responsibilities; that he is overworked; that it is humanly impossible, under the system which we have, for him fully to carry out his constitutional duty as chief executive because he is overwhelmed with minor details and needless contacts arising directly from the bad organization and equipment of the government."

[4] We have a General Staff for the Army; the Executive Office of the President may be regarded as in a sense a General Staff for the president on the civilian side

Establishments included

Shifted from time to time as need arose, the establishments now (1948) embraced are: (1) the White House Office, including the presidential secretaries, clerks, and administrative assistants, and serving the president in the performance of the many detailed duties incident to his daily routine; (2) the Bureau of the Budget, charged not only with drawing up the annual budget, but with the improvement of management, planning, and statistical services throughout the entire national administration;[1] (3) the Liaison Office for Personnel Management, assisting the president in coördinating personnel-management policies throughout the government;[2] (4) the Office for Emergency Management, dating from 1940 and comprising a framework within which most of the great civilian war agencies of 1940-45, like the War Production Board and the Office of Defense Transportation, were set up and operated, and in which a few, in fields like housing and economic stabilization, survive today;[3] and (5) the Council of Economic Advisers, created under terms of the Full Employment Act of 1946 and charged with assisting the president in preparing an annual "economic report" for submission to Congress.[4]

The Vice-Presidency and Arrangements for Presidential Succession

Since presidential elections take place only at regular four-year intervals, some arrangement is necessary for filling out a term in case the president dies, resigns, or is removed by impeachment; and the constitution provides for a vice-president, who is to take up the duties of president whenever the office falls vacant or the president is himself unable to discharge them.[5] No president has resigned;[6] none has been removed, although the impeachment proceedings against Andrew Johnson failed by a single vote; and no president has been incapacitated to such an extent or for so long a period as to lead to the assumption of presidential functions by the vice-president, although such a transfer of authority was seriously discussed after the wounding of President Garfield by an

—a widely ramifying mechanism superimposed on the departments and other agencies for the promotion of administrative "housekeeping."

[1] See pp. 563-565 below.

[2] See p. 505 below.

[3] See pp. 816-819 below.

[4] See p. 376 below. An informing symposium on the Executive Office of the President (before various changes were made in it) will be found in *Pub. Admin. Rev.*, I, 101-140 (Winter, 1941). Cf. M. R. Eiselen, "Work Relief for Presidents," *Social Sci.*, XII, 201-205 (Apr., 1937); N. M. Pearson, "A General Administrative Staff to Aid the President," *Pub. Admin. Rev.*, IV, 127-147 (Spring, 1944); D. K. Price, "Staffing the Presidency," *Amer. Polit. Sci. Rev.*, XL, 1154-1168 (Dec., 1946); and F. M. Marx, *The President and His Staff Services* (Chicago, 1947).

[5] Under the language of the original constitution, the vice-president succeeds only to the "powers and duties" of the office, not to the office itself, and hence in 1927 it was argued that another term for Mr. Coolidge would not be a third term as *president*. The Twentieth Amendment, of later date (1933), however, says that if a president-elect dies before taking office, the vice-president-elect "shall become president."

[6] On the way in which a president or vice-president may resign—a matter unprovided for in the constitution—see note by E. S. Brown in *Amer. Polit. Sci. Rev.*, XXII, 732-733 (Aug., 1928). One vice-president has resigned, *i.e.*, John C. Calhoun in 1832

assassin's bullet in 1881, and also during the earlier stages of President Wilson's illness in 1919-20.[1] Seven presidents, however, have died in office, and a like number of vice-presidents have in consequence assumed the duties of the presidency. Since Van Buren, no vice-president has been elected president unless he had first succeeded to the office by the death of the incumbent.

The vice-president's share in the work of government

Unless an emergency makes it necessary for him to assume the powers and duties of president, the vice-president (with salary of twenty thousand dollars) has no constitutional function except to preside over the Senate; even there he is not a member and has no vote except in the case of a tie. He is, in reality, an executive officer, with, however, only potential, rather than actual, powers and functions. But he may at any moment be called upon to take the helm of the government, and it goes without saying that he will do well to keep informed on the state of public affairs and on the policies and plans of the Administration. From the vantage point of the presiding officer's chair in the Senate, he will, of course, learn much of what is going on in legislative circles. He needs also, however, to be in close touch with the executive side of the government; and an obvious means to this end is attendance at meetings of the cabinet. Somewhat curiously, however, Calvin Coolidge, John N. Garner, Henry A. Wallace, and Harry S. Truman, are the only vice-presidents in the country's history who have sat with the cabinet with any regularity.[2]

---

[1] J. Kerney, "Government by Proxy," *Century Mag.*, CXI, 481-486 (Feb., 1926). No definition of presidential inability is laid down in the constitution or the laws, and there is no specification of who is to decide when the president's disablement is so serious and prolonged that an "acting president" is needed. The commonest opinion in 1919-20 was that the decision lay with the vice-president, with or without ratification by Congress.

Likewise, no provision is made for a substitute when the president is temporarily absent from the country, as was Woodrow Wilson during the Paris Peace Conference of 1919 and as was Franklin D. Roosevelt repeatedly in connection with wartime conferences such as those at Casablanca, Cairo, Teheran, and Yalta. Modern means of communication, however, enable a president to keep in close touch with Washington wherever he may be.

[2] C. O. Paullin, "The Vice-President and the Cabinet," *Amer. Hist. Rev.*, XXIX, 496-500 (Apr., 1924). Although lukewarm, or even hostile, toward some of the policies of the Roosevelt Administration, Vice-President Garner's strong sense of personal and party loyalty, together with his exceptional familiarity with congressional business (acquired in part as a former speaker of the House of Representatives), made him more of a power in the government of his day (1933-41) than vice-presidents commonly have been. See current newspapers for the rôle which he played during an interval of party and congressional confusion in the last two weeks of July, 1937 (*e.g., N. Y. Times,* July 20). Having himself originated some of the basic principles of the New Deal—marshaling also the data and ideological argument for defending them—and seeing eye to eye with his chief at practically every point, Vice-President Wallace (1941-45) likewise could be depended upon to invest the vice-presidency with unusual vitality. Quite unprecedented, indeed, was his active service, from the summer of 1941, as chairman of the Economic Defense Board (later the Board of Economic Warfare), consisting of various cabinet members and charged with coördinating the actions and policies of defense agencies and with developing integrated defense plans. In 1943, however, he was rebuked by the President for quarreling publicly with the secretary of commerce and was removed from his chairmanship by conversion of the Board of Economic Warfare into the Office of Economic Warfare under another chairman; and in 1944 the doubtful support given him by the President, combined with conservative (especially Southern) disapproval of his affiliations

If occasion arises, the duties of the presidency devolve upon the vice-president. But, obviously, there is no guarantee that at any given moment there will be a vice-president; this official may himself have died, resigned, been removed, or become incapable of attending to public business.[1] Moreover, after a vice-president has assumed the presidency, there would be no one—unless further arrangements were made—to step into the highest office should it again fall vacant. Accordingly, the constitution empowers Congress to provide for the case of removal, death, resignation, or inability both of the president and vice-president, "declaring what officer shall then act as president." [2] The first legislation on the subject, dating from 1792, provided that the president *pro tempore* of the Senate should succeed, or in case no such official were available, the speaker of the House of Representatives. The plan, however, was open to various objections. It might result in the government passing under the direction of a chief executive belonging to a different party from that to which the president and vice-president had belonged, entailing an abrupt break in the continuity of executive policy. By bringing a legislator into executive office, it might weaken the principle of separation of powers. More serious, if both the president and vice-president should die during the interval between the expiration of one Congress and the meeting of the next, there might be no president *pro tempore* of the Senate, and there certainly would be no speaker of the House. Nevertheless, the law stood unchanged for almost a hundred years. In 1881, the death of President Garfield, some weeks before a newly elected Congress was to convene (and with no vice-president remaining after Arthur moved to the White House, nor any president *pro tempore*, nor any speaker) brought the situation afresh to the country's attention; and five years later a new presidential succession act [3] withdrew the officers of the legislative houses from the succession and substituted a plan under which, after the vice-president, the heads of the executive departments then existing (all present ones except Agriculture, Commerce, Labor, and Air) were to succeed—in a sequence stipulated in the law, and beginning with the secretary of state—due regard being paid, of course, to the constitutional qualifications of age, citizenship, and residence. Never as yet, however, has the succession actually passed beyond the vice-president.

Upon Harry S. Truman's elevation to the presidency in April, 1945, the vice-presidency, of course, once more fell vacant; and the hazards entailed by long presidential air journeys contemplated in connection with

Marginal notes:
Further provisions for succession

The Presidential Succession Act of 1886

President Truman's proposal for change

---

with some of the more radical elements in the country's politics, cost him a nomination for a second term.

[1] In point of fact, seven vice-presidents have died in office, but luckily not one, as it turned out, who would have been called upon to assume the duties of a deceased president. As mentioned above, one vice-president (John C. Calhoun) has resigned. Including successions to the presidency, the vice-presidency has thus become vacant fifteen times in the country's history.

[2] Art. II, § 1, cl. 6.

[3] 24 *U. S. Stat. at Large,* 1.

conferences on international affairs gave both the President himself and many other people grave concern about the situation that would arise in the event of any casualty. Legal provision was, of course, perfectly clear: the secretary of state (then Edward R. Stettinius, Jr.) would succeed. But there was doubt whether he would prove well fitted by previous experience, including loose party connections; and in the President's mind there was still more serious misgiving about the propriety of any arrangement under which, in appointing a possible later secretary of state,[1] he would in effect be selecting his own successor in case of his own death or incapacitation. Starting from Washington on the first of his long air trips, he accordingly transmitted to Congress a special message (June 19, 1945) urging that the law of 1886 be amended so as to place the speaker of the House of Representatives (then Sam Rayburn) at the top of the list, after him the president *pro tempore* of the Senate (then Kenneth McKellar), and only then the heads of departments in the specified order—any such successor, however, to serve only until the next congressional elections, when, under some special arrangement, a president might be elected to fill out the unexpired term.[2] The main object was to avert a successor chosen in effect by the president, although there would be the additional advantage that a new incumbent (at least in the case of the speaker and president *pro tempore* of the Senate) would be—as under the law of 1792—a person *elected* to a position of service in the national government; and the speaker was given priority (contrary to the arrangement before 1886) because, being newly elected to Congress every two years, he would be closest to the people, and, having been chosen speaker by the majority party in the House, might be presumed to be an acknowledged leader of the party to which the president, in the normal situation, had belonged.

The Presidential Succession Act of 1947
Omitting only the provision for a special election to fill out an unexpired term, the House of Representatives promptly and enthusiastically approved a bill incorporating the President's recommendations. The Senate, however, was more cautious. To start with, an able and popular former senator, James F. Byrnes, had (as noted above) become secretary of state, and his former colleagues had no interest in seeing him sidetracked. In the second place, the Senate did not like the provision of the proposed legislation giving the speaker precedence over the president *pro tempore*. In the third place, it was considered quite possible that the 1946 elections would bring the Republicans into control of the House (as they actually did)—in which event a Republican speaker would stand next in

---

[1] A new secretary, in the person of former Senator James F. Byrnes, was in fact soon appointed. Of course any similar successor from farther down the cabinet list would equally be a presidential appointee.

[2] *Cong. Record*, 79th Cong., 1st Sess., p. 6272. The law of 1792 had provided for a special presidential election following the accession of any one other than a vice-president to the presidential office, but the act of 1886 had omitted any provision on the subject beyond requiring that Congress, if not already in session, should be convoked within twenty days.

line to a Democratic president; and it was anticipated that this would provoke a Democratic drive for revision or repeal and throw the entire matter again into confusion. A speaker, too, might be notoriously unfit for the presidency—might, indeed, even be a woman! In addition, there was a constitutional worry. Back in 1792, James Madison had objected to the legislation then enacted on the ground that, whereas the constitution provided for specification by Congress of what "officer" should act as president in the case of no vice-president being available, the speaker and president *pro tempore* were not "constitutional officers," both being (as members of Congress) not national but state officers. Constitutional lawyers in the Senate raised the same objection to the House bill of 1945. The Supreme Court has never ruled on the definition involved, and it is possible to cite precedents both ways.[1] At all events, the point (though some thought it unimportant) proved a senatorial stumbling-block; and for the various reasons indicated, as well as on the general ground that the subject called for further study, the Senate for the time being shelved the House bill.

Although opposed on the issue by many members of his own party, President Truman revived his proposal in his annual message of January, 1946, and (to the surprise of some) reiterated it in February, 1947, when, with the Republicans in control of Congress, the first two officials in the contemplated order of succession would be of that party. At last, too, he had the probably somewhat mixed satisfaction of seeing his plan prevail, over the opposition of most of his own party and through the support of political opponents now having something immediately to gain from it. In June, 1947, a bill putting the speaker first in line of succession (after the vice-president, of course, if there be one), the Senate's president *pro tempore* next, and heads of executive departments next (in the traditional order [2]) was passed by the Senate (50 to 35); during the next month it was approved by the House (365 to 11); and the resulting Presidential Succession Act [3] is now the law on this troublesome subject.[4]

By placing the speaker and president *pro tempore* (though in reversed

---

[1] An incident frequently invoked was Senator Blount's contention in 1797, which the Senate upheld, that he could not be impeached because he was not an officer of the United States. The ruling, however, was that of the Senate, not of the Supreme Court. The point was often made also that the main reason for repealing the original statute in 1886 was the belief of Congress at that time that the president *pro tempore* and speaker, not being officers of the United States, were ineligible to the succession. For a summary of most of the arguments, see "The Question of Amending the Presidential Succession Act; Pro and Con [Symposium], *Cong. Digest*, XXV, 67-96 (Mar., 1946).

[2] Except that the secretaries of agriculture, commerce, and labor were added to the list. A speaker or president *pro tempore* succeeding to the presidency fills out the unexpired term, but a cabinet officer elevated to the office serves only until a speaker or president *pro tempore* becomes available. Any one (except a vice-president) succeeding to the post is, under the new legislation, merely "acting president."

[3] *Pub. Law 199—80th Cong., 1st Sess.*

[4] Accordingly, at the date of writing (January, 1948) the line of succession to President Truman (there being no vice-president) stood: Speaker Joseph W. Martin, President *pro tempore* Arthur H. Vandenberg, Secretary of State George C. Marshall, and thereafter other cabinet members in the designated order.

order) next in line after the vice-president, the new legislation substantially restores the plan prevailing from 1792 to 1886; and the resulting arrangement is subject to most of the criticisms advanced against that plan, and in part indicated above. There is still doubt about whether the speaker and president *pro tempore* can be regarded as meeting the constitutional requirement that the succession shall devolve only upon an "officer" of the United States; [1] the arrangement agreed upon contravenes the principle of separation of powers (something like it was expressly rejected by the Philadelphia convention of 1787 on that ground, and adopted in the law of 1792 only over strenuous opposition); the contention that the plan is more "democratic" because the speaker and president *pro tempore* have been elected by some segment of the national electorate and chosen to their special legislative posts by the respective houses is not clearly convincing; fortuitous replacement of a chief executive of one party by a speaker or president *pro tempore* of a different party, with the continuity of executive policy broken and no opportunity given for the people to express themselves, seems not wholly desirable.[2] In rejecting President Truman's proposal to restore the device of a special election for choosing a president to fill out an unexpired term, Congress quite possibly negatived the most useful part of the original scheme. At all events, the new system does not solve all problems, and further legislation at some future time is not unlikely.[3]

The Cabinet

The early question of an advisory council

As early as 1781, when the first executive departments were created by the Continental Congress, it was suggested that their principal officers consult together as an advisory council, and in the convention of 1787 several plans for a council—a council of appointment, a council of revision, or a general advisory council—were considered. No proposal on the subject, however, was adopted, and it remained for an informal advisory group, consisting of the heads of the then existing departments, to form around the president, not in response to any constitutional or statutory provisions, but as a mere matter of convenience and usage. To this day, the "cabinet" is, as such, quite unknown to the formal constitution and recognized only casually in the statutes.

How the cabinet arose

From the beginning of his first administration, Washington, in addition to calling on the heads of departments for written opinions, as authorized in the constitution, discussed matters orally with various principal officers, including the department heads; and in 1793, the disturbed interna-

---

[1] For an attack from this viewpoint on the legislation's constitutionality (by Senator Carl A. Hatch), see *Cong. Record,* 80th Cong., 1st Sess., pp. 7932-7936.

[2] This is, of course, what would happen today if a mid-term successor to President Truman should become necessary.

[3] For fuller discussions, see J. E. Kallenbach, "The New Presidential Succession Act," *Amer. Polit. Sci. Rev.,* XLI, 931-940 (Oct., 1947); R. S. Rankin, "Presidential Succession in the United States," *Jour. of Pol.,* VIII, 44-56 (Feb., 1946); L. Wilmerding, Jr., "The Presidential Succession," *Atlantic Mo.,* CLXXIX, 91-97 (May, 1947).

tional situation—more concretely, the crisis with France—caused these consultations, with what was already beginning to be called a cabinet, to become relatively frequent. Some people shook their heads and predicted that from this "cabinet conclave," unknown to the constitution, would flow all manner of abuses. We can easily enough see now, however, that some such development was inevitable. In common with other public men of the day, Washington originally supposed that the Senate—small in numbers and constitutionally associated with the executive in appointments and treaty-making—would serve substantially as an executive council, after the manner of upper chambers in most of the colonial governments. But when he appeared on the floor of that house to consult about certain Indian treaties, the demeanor of the members clearly showed that they did not take this view of their functions, and the expected relationship did not develop. Furthermore, deviating from practice both in England and in the colonies, the Supreme Court, in 1793, informed Washington that it did not consider itself as having power to give opinions on questions of law, even to the president, except in deciding actual cases; hence the need for consultation could not be met in that direction. Finally, the House of Representatives discouraged—in time virtually prevented—heads of departments from appearing on the floor in person in order to submit reports, answer questions, and participate in discussion.[1] As a consequence of all these more or less independent but contemporary developments, the president and heads of departments were together forced into the relatively isolated position characteristic of our American scheme of "divided" government, and compelled to rely upon one another for opinions and advice to an extent originally unanticipated. The upshot was the cabinet.[2]

To this day, the cabinet has remained what it was at the outset—a purely advisory body. The president can make much use of it, or little, or none at all, as he chooses. Looking upon the heads of departments as mere administrative officers, and preferring the advice of his personal friends, official and otherwise, Jackson early discontinued cabinet meetings altogether; and some other presidents, e.g., Grant, much of the time Wilson, and in his first years Franklin D. Roosevelt, have leaned but

Varying relations with the president

[1] We have seen that nowadays there are proposals that both houses adopt a different policy. See p. 419 above.

[2] The beginnings of the cabinet are described fully in H. B. Learned, *The President's Cabinet* (New Haven, 1912), Chap. v.

The heads of departments as chiefs of separate branches of the administrative mechanism are dealt with on pp. 474-477 below. Since the creation of the Federal Security Agency, the Federal Works Agency, and the Federal Loan Agency in 1939, there have been administrative establishments in Washington, even in peacetime, larger in personnel and perhaps more important in function than at least one or two of the departments; and their "administrators" frequently sit with the cabinet. Anyone, in fact, may so sit if invited by the president. The regular cabinet members are, however, the department heads—except that, under the National Security Act of 1947 unifying the country's defense establishments, heads of the Departments of the Army, the Navy, and the Air Force are not cabinet members, but only the secretary of defense, an over-all administrator, heading what is known as the National Military Establishment. See pp. 824-826 below.

lightly on their cabinet advisers. On the other hand, certain presidents, *e.g.*, Pierce and Harding, have consulted their cabinets at every turn and have usually followed the advice received. An able cabinet can go far toward making up for the deficiencies of a weak president, and can also give added strength to a strong one.

Meetings
and in-
fluence

Nowadays, the cabinet meets ordinarily once a week (except during vacation and campaign periods), though naturally oftener in time of war or other stress.[1] Ranging widely over problems and policies of the Administration (not omitting their party aspects [2]), discussions are directed mainly to matters, large or small, which the president himself introduces, although others may be brought up—usually with consent secured in advance—by the department chiefs.[3] Proceedings are decidedly informal. There are no rules of debate; free interchange of opinion takes place in a conversational manner; only rarely is there a vote; no minutes or other official records are kept, and sometimes differences of opinion develop afterwards as to whether a given subject was considered at all.[4] Furthermore, such decisions as are reached are mere recommendations. Just as the president is free to submit or not submit a matter for consideration,[5] so is he free to make any final disposal of it that he likes. Ordinarily, he will be influenced by the views of the men whom he has chosen to be his principal advisers. But if he thinks that their advice is not sound, he is under no compulsion to follow it. It is he, not they,

[1] Much of the time—as recently as Franklin D. Roosevelt's earlier years—there have regularly been two meetings a week. No one is entitled to call a meeting except the president. During Wilson's illness, Secretary of State Lansing incurred his chief's displeasure by taking it upon himself to call meetings, and his forced retirement soon followed.

[2] Frank Knox, a Republican appointed secretary of the navy by President Roosevelt in 1940, was accustomed to slip discreetly out of cabinet meetings when discussions assumed a partisan tone.

[3] Because of lack of confidence in his advisers' competence, or because of a desire to proceed strictly according to his own ideas and meanwhile to keep even the cabinet in the dark, the president may (as Wilson sometimes did) withhold completely from discussion some of the weightiest matters of the hour.

[4] A good deal of interesting information about cabinet meetings can be gleaned from published correspondence, memoirs, and autobiographies of ex-members, such as *The Letters of Franklin K. Lane* (Boston, 1922); W. C. Redfield, *With Congress and Cabinet* (Garden City, N. Y., 1924); and D. F. Houston, *Eight Years with Wilson's Cabinet*, 2 vols. (Garden City, N. Y., 1926). The above description holds true generally, but actually the atmosphere of cabinet meetings differs under different presidents. Under Franklin D. Roosevelt, meetings were long and leisurely, sometimes lasting two hours, with everyone given plenty of time to say what was on his mind—though with the President sometimes more or less monopolizing the conversation, and often largely with stories of the past. Under Truman (at least in earlier days), meetings have been short and crisp, rarely lasting more than an hour, and with the President watching the clock and not hesitating to rise from his chair, even with a member speaking.

[5] When President Roosevelt and two or three intimate advisers worked out the plan for the famous court bill of 1937 (proposing, among other things, to add up to six new justices to the Supreme Court), the measure was shown to the attorney-general only in order that he might prepare a supporting letter, and was communicated to the cabinet only a few minutes before it exploded in Congress and touched off a barrage of bitter discussion throughout the country. See p. 546 below. It is only fair to add, however, that the President had publicly given indication that his mind was running along the lines of the bill.

who will have to bear ultimate responsibility before the country for whatever is done. "Seven nays, one aye—the ayes have it," announced Lincoln, following a cabinet consultation in which he found every member against him. Cabinet discussions bring out useful information and opinion, clarify views, and promote morale in the Administration. They help the president pick his course in both international and domestic affairs. But they do not culminate in decisions upon policy by mere show of hands.[1]

Department heads—that is to say, cabinet members—are selected with both their administrative and advisory functions in mind. Several other considerations, however, enter in. First, the appointees must normally be of the president's party. Washington made Jefferson secretary of state and Hamilton secretary of the treasury. But friction arose, and it soon proved desirable to bring the chief offices into the hands of men who saw eye to eye in political matters. Since 1795, the principle of party solidarity has been adhered to rather closely. To be sure, Cleveland appointed as secretary of state a man who had been thought of as a Republican candidate for the presidency. But the appointee (Walter Q. Gresham) had supported Cleveland in his electoral campaign. McKinley appointed a "gold" Democrat secretary of the treasury; Theodore Roosevelt and Taft each appointed a Democrat secretary of war; Hoover made a Democrat attorney-general. But in all of these instances, except possibly the first, the appointee had not been prominent in national politics. The same was true of Henry L. Stimson, appointed secretary of war by Franklin D. Roosevelt in 1940; although another Republican (Frank Knox) simultaneously made secretary of the navy had only four years previously been his party's candidate for vice-president.[2] Regard for party affili-

The selection of members:

1. Party status

---

[1] No president, of course, relies upon his cabinet alone for advice; some, indeed, e.g., Jackson, have notoriously preferred other sources. Members of Congress (especially the majority leaders), old friends and associates, bankers, business men, labor leaders, experts on social and economic problems—these are only a few of the people who will be found wending their way to the White House, either by invitation or on their own initiative. During the earlier years of Franklin D. Roosevelt's presidency, the cabinet was, on the one hand, pretty much submerged in a "super-cabinet," known as the National Emergency Council, and consisting, in addition to the heads of departments, of some two dozen heads of new recovery agencies and persons brought in as experts from outside of government circles, and, from a different direction, pushed into the background by the so-called "little cabinet," a galaxy of "intellectual"—largely professorial—experts and reformers (Moley, Tugwell, Corcoran, Rosenman, Cohen, Berle, and others) appointed, for the most part, to under-secretaryships and assistant-secretaryships and comprising the group popularly dubbed the "brain trust." As conditions became more normal, the regular cabinet emerged in something like its full stature, although outsiders continued to have much influence and the professional brain-trusters merely gave way to non-academicians, chiefly young lawyers. The President's principal adviser for a number of years (Harry Hopkins) was not a cabinet member except for a brief period; and in general—apart from wartime necessities—Mr. Roosevelt preferred to have "idea" men (Henry A. Wallace was for a good while in favor as such) around him rather than administrators. Certainly it was chiefly the former who imparted slants to his attitudes, decisions, and policies.

[2] When appointed secretary of agriculture in 1933, Henry A. Wallace was a registered Republican, but he had been supporting Democratic candidates since 1926. Secretary of the Interior Ickes, also, was at least of Republican antecedents.

ation does not mean, however, that only party leaders are appointed. The tendency to look upon the cabinet as a council of party leaders has pretty much come to an end. Appointees normally belong to the party in power at the White House; but as a rule half or more of them are not party leaders in any proper sense of the term, and some have taken no active part in politics at all.[1]

2. Other factors

Other practical considerations more or less influencing the president's selection are geographical distribution, the representation of various wings or factions of the party, and obligations incurred for political support. It will not do to take all of the cabinet members from the East, or from the West, or from any other single section of the country. Appointment of representatives of different elements in the president's party is designed, of course, to conciliate opposition and to promote solidarity. A good illustration is President Wilson's appointment of William Jennings Bryan as secretary of state in 1913, with a view to winning for the Administration the support of the more radical wing of the Democratic party.[2] Selections must frequently be made, too, with a view to rewarding individuals (or groups behind them) who have aided conspicuously in the president's election. Still another powerful factor is personal friendship and favor. Every president takes into his official family men whom he knows but slightly; but he is likely to include also one or two men who, whatever other claims they may have, are first of all personal friends, e.g., Harry M. Daugherty in Harding's cabinet, Ray Lyman Wilbur in Hoover's, and William H. Woodin in Franklin D. Roosevelt's original group. All told, however, a steadily increasing proportion of cabinet officers are chosen for their special knowledge and experience or their administrative ability, proved or presumed. Frequently they are persons who have attained eminence in the professional or business world. The secretary of the treasury is very likely to be of this type, as, for example, William G. McAdoo and Andrew W. Mellon; the secretaries of commerce and agriculture also, as in the instances of Herbert Hoover, David F. Houston, and Henry A. Wallace; and perhaps one may add the secretary of labor, as in the case of the first woman to receive a cabinet appointment, Frances Perkins. The attorney-general is at least always a lawyer. Rarely is a member encountered, however, who has ever had any connection with the work of the department over which

[1] On the other hand, of course, members are occasionally chosen mainly or solely because of their services as party leaders or officers. Examples include the selection of Will H. Hays, Walter Brown, James A. Farley and Frank C. Walker, for the postmaster-generalship by Presidents Harding, Hoover, and Franklin D. Roosevelt, respectively, whose campaigns the appointees as national committee chairmen had managed. Cf. D. G. Fowler, *The Cabinet Politician; The Postmaster-General, 1829-1909* (New York, 1943). The Senate commonly assents to the president's cabinet selections without much opposition or hesitation. But see p. 452, note 5, below.

[2] An even better one is Lincoln's effort to give representation to as many as possible of the discordant elements embraced in the then young Republican party—resulting, it has been said, in "the most uncongenial and contentious group ever assembled beneath the White House roof."

he is called to preside; and, contrary to earlier practice, few heads of departments are now carried over from one administration to another, even when a new president is of the same party as his predecessor.[1] For the experience, as well as the technical competence, essential to satisfactory performance of its work, a department is dependent mainly upon subordinate officers who do not come and go with changes at the White House.

REFERENCES

E. S. Corwin, *The President: Office and Powers; History and Analysis of Practice and Opinion* (New York, 1940), Chap. II.

H. J. Laski, *The American Presidency* (New York, 1940), Chap. II.

W. W. Willoughby, *Constitutional Law of the United States* (2nd ed., New York, 1929), III, Chaps. LXXXI, LXXXIII.

C. C. Thach, "The Creation of the Presidency, 1775-1789," *Johns Hopkins Univ. Studies in Hist. and Polit Sci.*, XL, 415-596 (Baltimore, 1922).

J. W. Perrin, "Presidential Tenure and Reëligibility," *Polit. Sci. Quar.*, XXIX, 423-437 (Sept., 1914).

C. W. Stein, *The Third-Term Tradition; Its Rise and Collapse in American Politics* (New York, 1943).

C. S. Hamlin, "The Presidential Succession Act [of 1886]," *Harvard Law Rev.*, XVIII, 182-195 (Jan., 1905).

H. H. Sawyer, "The Presidential Succession," *Amer. Mercury*, XVI, 129-135 (Feb., 1929).

R. S. Rankin, "Presidential Succession in the United States," *Jour. of Politics*, VIII, 44-56 (Feb., 1946).

J. E. Kallenbach, "The New Presidential Succession Act [of 1947]," *Amer. Polit. Sci. Rev.*, XLI, 931-940 (Oct., 1947).

L. C. Hatch, *A History of the Vice-Presidency of the United States*, rev. and ed. by E. L. Shoup (New York, 1934).

O. P. Field, "The Vice-Presidency of the United States," *Amer. Law Rev.*, LVI, 365-400 (May-June, 1922).

C. G. Dawes, *Notes as Vice-President, 1925-1929* (Boston, 1935).

K. Young and L Middleton, *Heirs Apparent; The Vice-Presidents of the United States* (New York, 1948). A series of popular sketches.

H. B. Learned, *The President's Cabinet* (New Haven, 1912).

M. L. Hinsdale, *History of the President's Cabinet* (Ann Arbor, Mich., 1911).

W. H. Smith, *History of the Cabinet of the United States* (Baltimore, 1925).

J. A. Fairlie, "The President's Cabinet," *Amer. Polit. Sci. Rev.*, VII, 28-44 (Feb., 1913).

B. J. Hendrick, *Lincoln's War Cabinet* (Boston, 1946).

[1] Except that a vice-president succeeding to the presidency in mid-term usually continues the cabinet of his predecessor, at least for a time. There was an unusually rapid turnover within a few weeks after President Truman took office in April, 1945 —four changes in the first forty-one days.

Departments for whose chiefs the president often goes farthest afield are those of War (since 1947, "the Army") and Navy. Restriction of these posts (by unvarying usage) to civilians is likely to mean in any case that appointees will not know much about the work to be performed. "I know," said Elihu Root when made secretary of war by President McKinley, "nothing about war; I know nothing about the Army." For a survey of the more recent secretaries of war from this point of view, see E. P. Herring, *The Impact of War* (New York, 1941), Chap. IV. Henry L. Stimson, who headed the War Department during World War II, served in the same office from 1911 to 1913 under President Taft and also had military experience in World War I.

D. G. Fowler, *The Cabinet Politician; The Postmaster-General, 1829-1909* (New York, 1943).

L. Brownlow *et al.*, "The Executive Office of the President: A Symposium," *Pub. Admin. Rev.*, I, 101-140 (Winter, 1941).

F. M. Marx, *The President and His Staff Services* (Chicago, 1947).

W. E. Dodd, *Woodrow Wilson and His Work* (4th ed., New York, 1921).

F. Perkins, *The Roosevelt I Knew* (New York, 1946).

President's Committee on Administrative Management in the Government of the United States, *Report, with Special Studies* (Washington, D. C., 1937).

CHAPTER XXI

THE PRESIDENT AS CHIEF EXECUTIVE

General Features of the Federal Executive Power

After the framers of the constitution decided to provide for a distinct executive branch of government, and to place a president at its head, they had the difficult task of determining what powers this novel official should have. Bitter experience with an essentially headless government under the Articles of Confederation suggested that such powers should be ample. On the other hand, all history testified to the danger that an individual raised to a pinnacle of authority might develop the traits of an autocrat or dictator. The men of 1787 wanted neither weakness and futility nor dictatorship; and they tried hard to devise a presidency that would be strong and effective, yet sufficiently circumscribed to be safe. They had no idea that they were creating an office destined to become the most powerful ever known in a democracy; disliking and fearing executive absolutism as they did, they would have been frightened at the very thought of such a thing. That, nevertheless, is precisely what they were doing; and the gratifying thing is that the presidency which they planned could be magnified as it has been through the years with never a threat of the sinister consequences which they certainly would have deplored.

The quest for a strong but not dangerous president

Of the three branches into which our national government is divided, the executive has indeed advanced farthest from the point at which it started. The judiciary has considerably more than held its own—mainly because of its power to review legislation and executive actions. The legislative branch has run a poor third; and for this the remarkable development of the presidency has been primarily responsible.

Whatever else he may be—guide and collaborator in legislation, party leader, general custodian of national interests—the president is first of all an executive; in him, the constitution expressly vests "the executive power," [1] and from him neither Congress nor the courts can take such power away.

The president as executive

In defining the president's executive power, however, the constitution falls somewhat below its customary level of clarity. In one place, it unequivocally bestows on him "the executive power," certainly suggesting that whatever executive power there is belongs to him alone. Later on, however, it separately grants him certain specific powers of an executive nature, *e.g.*, those of appointment (with the advice and consent of the

Does all executive power reside in him?

[1] Art. II, § 1, cl. 1.

445

Senate), treaty-making (also with the Senate's approval), and pardon and reprieve; and people have sometimes wondered why, if *all* executive power is conferred, the constitution's framers should have thought it necessary to provide in this way for particular powers of the kind, and whether, after all, there may be executive powers which, not being expressly granted, are to be regarded as withheld.[1] Another point that has troubled some students of the subject is that, while the president is charged with taking care that "the laws be faithfully executed,"[2] the actual task of executing them inevitably falls mainly to other people, who, therefore, might be looked upon as sharing in a power nominally possessed by the president alone. Still again, when Congress discharges its constitutional function of making "all laws which shall be necessary and proper for carrying into execution" the powers of the national government,[3] the question might arise whether the two houses are sharing in the executive function. Many of these laws bestow powers and duties on the president. Are these *executive* powers, and if so, how did Congress come by them if *the* executive power is lodged in the president? Or is such legislation to be regarded as merely indicating that such and such executive powers are to be exercised, and under conditions more or less definitely specified?

The actual sources of executive power

Abstruse questions such as these are mentioned here, not for debate, but only to give some idea of how complex our system of divided government really is, and to make clear why presidential powers should so often have stirred controversy and furnished issues for adjudication in the courts. In practical fact, the sources from which presidential executive powers are derived are simply two: (1) constitutional clauses directly conferring them (as interpreted by the president—often on advice of his attorney-general—and as further interpreted, when challenged, by a usually generous Supreme Court), and (2) acts of Congress passed in pursuance of the "necessary and proper" clause, or of other direct or implied authority. When, for example, Congress establishes a new executive department, a new diplomatic post, or a new administrative commission, it automatically enlarges the president's power of appointment and removal. When it passes a tariff act, such as the Hawley-Smoot Act of 1930, authorizing the president to readjust tariff rates up or down as recommended by the Tariff Commission, it puts into his hands an important power over foreign commerce. When it goes farther (as in 1934, with later renewals), and authorizes the president to conclude international trade agreements independently of the Tariff Commission, it still further extends this power. When, as in the Reorganization Act of 1939, it em-

[1] Certain of the executive powers individually bestowed would no doubt have required special mention because of the connection with them assigned to the Senate. But this cannot account for the mention of others, *e.g.*, pardon, with which the Senate has nothing to do.

[2] Art. II, § 3.

[3] Art. I, § 8, cl. 18.

powers the chief executive to rearrange the administrative machinery of the national government in the interest of economy and efficiency (with only a right of disallowance reserved to Congress), it bestows significant new discretionary authority. And when, in time of war, it authorizes him to draft all eligible men into the armed services, to establish a censorship over all communications by mail, cable, radio, and other means passing between the United States and countries to be specified by the president, to requisition machinery and materials for war production, and to take over and operate mines and factories affected by strikes, it bestows powers of truly immense proportions.

A question which has stirred considerable difference of opinion, even among presidents themselves, is that of whether the president has inherent, as well as conferred, executive power. That is, has he power, outside of the constitution and laws, simply because he is the chief executive? Alexander Hamilton and Andrew Jackson thought so; on one occasion, the Supreme Court inclined to the same view; [1] and Theodore Roosevelt, after going out of office, recorded that as president he had "insisted upon the theory that the executive power was limited only by specific restrictions and prohibitions ...," and that he had "declined to adopt the view that what was imperatively necessary for the nation could not be done by the president unless he could find some specific authorization to do it." [2] The basic characteristic of our national government is, however, that it is a government of limited powers—of only such powers as are delegated in the constitution or can properly be inferred from that instrument, which clearly means that no executive power (or power of any other sort) is inherent, in the sense of antedating and transcending the constitution. "The true view of the executive function is, as I conceive it," wrote President Taft, "that the president can exercise no power which cannot be reasonably and fairly traced to some specific grant of power or justly implied or included within such express grant as necessary and proper to its exercise. Such specific grant must be either in the constitution or in an act of Congress passed in pursuance thereof. There is no undefined residuum of power which he can exercise because it seems to him to be in the public interest." [3] President Roosevelt was politically-minded, President Taft legally-minded; and the view of the latter seems clearly the more correct—even though most of the time in the past the Supreme Court has been willing to allow the president very wide latitude in interpreting his constitutional powers, and in that qualified sense has

[1] *In re Neagle,* 135 U. S. 1 (1890). See W. H. Taft, *Our Chief Magistrate and His Powers,* 88-91. In the Neagle case—turning on the question of whether the president had any right to assign a federal deputy marshal to protect a federal judge who had been threatened—the Court defined the executive power as including (without express provision) the protection of all rights, duties, and obligations growing out of the constitution or out of our international relations—in short, extending "all protection implied by the nature of the government under the constitution."

[2] *Autobiography* (New York, 1913), 388-389.

[3] *Our Chief Magistrate and His Powers,* 139-142.

sometimes been said to have recognized the chief executive as having "inherent" powers.[1]

Viewed in the large, the president's powers and functions, as conferred in the constitution and laws, fall into two general groups: (1) those that are mainly or wholly executive, and (2) those that involve sharing in the work of legislation. Unknown to the constitution and laws, although of course related to the two categories mentioned (especially the second), is a third set of functions, *i.e.*, those arising from the president's position as principal leader of his party. Executive powers (with which we are here concerned) fall, in turn, into six main groups: (1) enforcement of the laws and preservation of domestic order; (2) appointment and removal of civil and military officers; (3) supreme direction of administration, including the function of issuing orders and regulations; (4) pardon, reprieve, and amnesty; (5) management of foreign relations; and (6) control, as commander-in-chief, of the military and naval establishments, together with the conduct of war. The last two of these will necessarily be dealt with in later chapters devoted to foreign relations and defense;[2] the other four must engage our attention here.[3]

Enforcement of the Laws and Preservation of Order

The most solemn obligation laid upon the president by the constitution is to "take care that the laws be faithfully executed."[4] His oath of office expressly requires him to "protect and defend" the highest law of all, *i.e.*, the constitution; and by logical deduction his function extends not only to enforcing all federal laws (including treaties), but protecting all federal instrumentalities and property. For discharging this lofty responsibility, he has ample facilities—first of all, the vast array of federal officials and employees engaged in carrying on the routine work of the departments and other agencies (collecting taxes, operating the postal system, and what not); and afterwards, in so far as its services may be

---

[1] Curiously, the rôle played by Taft as chief justice in later days, notably in the Myers case (see p. 455 below), contributed to promoting the concept of inherent powers. As a rule, however, when the president is regarded as performing some executive act by virtue of inherent power, a close examination of the constitution and laws will show that authority for what has been done can be inferred from some provision in them. Congress has no monopoly of implied powers; the president has them also.

As mentioned in a different connection (see p. 769, note 1, below), in the case of United States *v.* Curtiss-Wright Export Corporation, 299 U. S. 304 (1936), the Supreme Court said that if the power to conduct foreign relations had not been conferred in the constitution, the national government would have possessed it anyway; and since the conduct of foreign relations is by nature an executive function, this assertion of the Court has sometimes been construed as tantamount to attributing at least potential inherent power to the president. Actually, of course, the president's authority to manage the country's foreign relations has to rest on no such inferential basis, for it is expressly conferred; and in 1942 (significantly in the midst of war) the Court asserted unequivocally that "Congress *and the president*, like the courts, possess no power not derived from the constitution." *Ex parte* Quirin, 317 U. S. 1, 25-26 (1942).

[2] Chaps. xxxiv-xxxv below.

[3] Legislative and party functions were considered in Chap. xviii above.

[4] Art. II, § 3, cl. 1.

needed, a particular branch of the executive establishment having as its main, though not exclusive, purpose the over-all enforcement of law where something more than routine operations of other agencies are required. This special machinery of law enforcement consists, of course, of the Department of Justice, with a staff in Washington headed by the attorney-general, and with a field organization embracing principally the district attorneys and marshals and their deputies. Not even all of this, however, exhausts the chief executive's law-enforcing resources; because he has the help also of the courts, and, if need arises, may make full use of the Army and Navy, and likewise of the National Guard when called into federal service. Congress has passed numerous measures authorizing the use of both national and state forces for the purpose [1]—even though, so far as the Army and Navy are concerned, the president would have the necessary power in any event. "The entire strength of the nation," the Supreme Court has said, "may be used to enforce in any part of the land the full and free exercise of all national powers and the security of all rights intrusted by the constitution to its care.... If the emergency arises, the army of the nation, and all its militia, are at the service of the nation to compel obedience to its laws." [2]

The obligation of law enforcement permits of no exceptions. The president may consider a given law undesirable (as President Truman considered the Labor-Management Relations Act of 1947) or even unconstitutional (as President Taft considered the Webb-Kenyon law of 1913 on shipments of liquor into dry states); but this gives neither him nor any other official any license to wink at its non-enforcement. In practice, however, there is some latitude. To begin with, in enforcing laws it is necessary to interpret them—to determine what they mean and to what extent they are applicable to particular situations; and the president's construction of a law (always reviewable by the courts) may be different from that which Congress intended when passing the measure—with enforcement perhaps following less rigorous lines. Moreover, some presidents, because of personal views or of disinclination to a more active course—or perchance in response to influential opinion in their party, or even to public indifference—may be more lax in pressing enforcement procedures than are others. More or less the same anti-trust laws have been on the books under all of the presidents for a quarter of a century. But periods in which the attorneys-general were encouraged or prodded to prosecute offending corporations relentlessly have been followed by others in which little happened; and for wartime reasons such prosecutions were at one stage deliberately slowed up by President

Some practical deviations

---

[1] The series began with (1) a militia act of 1792, which authorized the president to call forth the militia whenever the execution of the federal laws was obstructed by combinations too powerful to be suppressed through the ordinary course of judicial proceedings, and (2) an act of 1807 authorizing use of the Army and Navy under similar circumstances.

[2] *In re Debs,* 158 U. S. 564 (1895).

Roosevelt. There are laws also which, by their nature, offer peculiar difficulties and can never be enforced in full. Such was the Volstead Act of 1919, designed to give effect to the Eighteenth Amendment.[1]

Repression of domestic disorder As we have seen, the constitution specifies that the United States shall guarantee to every state a republican form of government, and shall protect the states against both invasion and domestic violence. If the republican form of government in a state is threatened or danger of an invasion arises, the president may act without awaiting any request from the state authorities. If, however, the situation involves merely domestic disorder, he cannot act until he is asked to do so, unless the execution of national law, the carrying on of a national activity, the safety of national property, or the flow of interstate commerce is imperiled; in this contingency, he may intervene independently, as did President Cleveland, over the protest of the governor of Illinois, when, in 1894, the carrying of the mails and the flow of interstate commerce were obstructed by the Pullman strike at Chicago.[2] A request for national assistance in repressing domestic violence is made by the legislature of the state if it is in session, otherwise by the governor. The president is not under compulsion to comply; indeed, he is not likely to do so unless, after investigation, he considers that the authorities of the state have reached the limit of their capacity to handle the situation. When first asked by Governor Cornwell to aid West Virginia in curbing disorders produced in that state by protracted strikes of bituminous coal miners in 1921, President Harding refused, although later developments led him to take the desired action.[3]

---

[1] Laxity in law enforcement (federal, state, and local)—aggravated by, but not solely traceable to, the adoption of national prohibition—led President Hoover, in 1929, to appoint a commission on law observance and enforcement; and the resulting Wickersham Commission's voluminous (although not particularly influential) report was published in 1931.

[2] Governor Altgeld protested vehemently against the use of federal troops in the state unless he or the legislature requested it. But the President stood firmly on his right and duty to execute the national laws with all the force at his command, and in the Debs case previously cited his position was sustained unanimously by the Supreme Court, on the ground that it was justified by interference by the strikers with the transportation of the mails and the flow of interstate commerce. See Cleveland's own account of the affair in his *Presidential Problems* (New York, 1904), Chap. II. Cf. B. M. Rich, *The Presidents and Civil Disorder* (Washington, D. C., 1941), Chap. VI; A. Lindsey, *The Pullman Strike* (Chicago, 1943); W. R. Browne, *Altgeld of Illinois* (New York, 1924), Chaps. XII–XVI; A. Nevins, *Grover Cleveland; A Study in Courage* (New York, 1932), Chap. XXXIII.

[3] A race riot in Detroit in June, 1943, led President Roosevelt to issue a proclamation calling upon the rioters to "disperse and retire peaceably to their respective abodes;" and when the governor of the state, having imposed a modified form of martial law on the Detroit metropolitan area, requested the aid of federal troops, some six thousand were moved in as a means of restoring order. The state was the more helpless in the situation, of course, because its National Guard units had been called into wartime federal service. See E. Brown, "The Truth About the Detroit Riot," *Harper's Mag.*, CLXXXVII, 488-498 (Nov., 1943).

Appointment and Removal

Except for the members of Congress, only two officials connected with the national government are elected by the people, namely, the president and vice-president. All others are appointed.[1] Basically, the power to appoint is vested in the president; and notwithstanding that he literally and personally appoints only a very small fraction of the people nowadays on the federal payroll, no authority intrusted to him is, year in and year out, of greater practical importance. With it goes not only control over the work of administration in its larger aspects, but also considerable influence upon legislation as a result of the conferment, or withholding, of offices sought by importunate senators and representatives for their constituents. A president's appointments may go far toward making or breaking him as head both of the government and of his party.

Even in early days, when federal officials were few, it was not expected that the chief executive would appoint them all; nowadays it would be inconceivable that he do so, even through some purely formal procedure. In the constitution, we read that Congress "may by law vest the appointment of such inferior officers as they think proper in the president alone, in the courts of law or in the heads of departments,"[2] and this has opened a way for relieving the president of the great bulk of appointments to be made. To be sure, the constitution neither defines the term "officer" nor indicates who are to be considered "inferior" officers. It does specify ambassadors, other public ministers or consuls, and judges of the Supreme Court as officers who are to be appointed by the president and Senate. But aside from this brief list, it leaves Congress free to indicate who are "inferior" officers, and to assign the appointment of such to the president acting independently, to the courts, or to heads of departments—all not thus assigned being presumed, as superior officers, to be appointed only by the president and Senate. The congressional power referred to has been exercised repeatedly; indeed, whenever Congress establishes a new position or class of positions, it fixes its status by prescribing how appointments shall be made—whether by the president and Senate or in some other way. A limited number of appointments have been intrusted to the president independently; the courts have been given authority to choose their clerks and other staff members; and as for the host of lesser officers and employees comprising the nation-wide civil service, the heads of departments (or of other establishments) have been given the appointing power, limited only by the competitive examination system now widely prevailing.

The range of presidential appointing power

How far this dispersion of the appointing power has gone is indicated by the fact that, in a total federal civil personnel of 1,999,431 near the

[1] Strict accuracy requires it to be observed, however, that each house of Congress chooses its own officers, except that the vice-president of the United States is *ex officio* president of the Senate.

[2] Art. II, § 2, cl. 2.

close of 1947, only some 16,000 were put in their positions by the president and Senate,[1]—even including postmasters of the first, second, and third classes who, although still appointed by the president and Senate, have since 1938 been included in the classified civil service, rendering presidential selection hardly more than a formality.[2] The proportion is smaller than most persons realize. But, significantly, it includes the people in most of the top levels of the official hierarchy (heads of departments; under secretaries, assistant secretaries, and many bureau chiefs; members of the numerous federal commissions and boards; collectors of customs and of internal revenue; district attorneys and marshals; and of course ambassadors, ministers, consuls, and judges); and this is why his appointing power is still ample to give the president the whip-hand in administration—indeed more than ample, since many groups of officials still appointed by him, *e.g.*, collectors of customs and of internal revenue, could easily be provided for in some other way without detracting at all from his effective headship of the administrative system. In truth, burdened as he is with multifold other tasks, the chief executive is still charged with many more appointments than he ought to be called upon to make; a couple of hundred, in the topmost levels, would be quite enough.

Limitations under which the power is exercised:

Important, and even momentous, as the president's appointing power unquestionably is, within the range indicated, it is hedged about with restrictions, some of a legal nature, others arising merely out of practical conditions. To begin with, by constitutional provision the chief executive appoints, not independently (except in a few instances as indicated above), but "by and with the advice and consent of the senate;" to speak with complete accuracy, he *nominates,* the Senate *confirms* (by a majority vote of the members present[3]), and he thereupon *appoints.* As was explained by Hamilton in *The Federalist,* this arrangement was adopted, not to relieve the president of responsibility for appointments, but to check any spirit of favoritism that he might manifest and to prevent the appointment of "unfit characters from state prejudice, from family connection, from personal attachment, or from a view to popularity."[4]

1. Advice and consent of the Senate

It long ago became customary for the Senate to assent almost as a matter of course to the president's selections for the highest positions in the executive departments. The heads of departments serve, at least ostensibly, as his principal advisers; besides, as chief of the executive branch, he bears full responsibility for their official acts. On both grounds, it is only fair that in choosing them he shall normally have complete freedom; and only six nominees for such posts have ever been rejected.[5]

---

[1] In addition, of course, many military offices are filled in this way.

[2] See p. 500, note 2, below.

[3] Confirmation or rejection must be absolute, without any conditions attached.

[4] No. LXXVI (Lodge's ed., 474).

[5] R. B. Taney, for secretary of the treasury, in 1834; Caleb Cushing, for secretary of the treasury, in 1843; David Henshaw, for secretary of the navy, in 1844; J. M.

Nominations. to judgeships and diplomatic positions have been refused assent—or at all events strongly opposed—with somewhat increased frequency in later decades, yet as a rule are not seriously challenged.[1] In other fields and on lower levels, the power to confirm or reject is employed freely;[2] and the president must be prepared, in case one nomination fails, to offer another or to see the office stand vacant for a time. During a Senate recess, however, a temporary or "recess" appointment may be made, lapsing at the close of the next session unless confirmed—although there is nothing except considerations of expediency to prevent another recess appointment of the same man the moment the Senate adjourns.[3] The number of senatorial rejections naturally varies with circumstances. If the president and Senate are on good terms, and especially if the president's party enjoys the advantage of a loyal senatorial majority, nominations are likely to be approved almost automatically.[4] If, however, there is lack of harmony, rejections or refusals to act will be relatively numerous.

The president may anticipate trouble, too, if he presumes to nominate a person to a collectorship of customs or other office in a particular state

2. "Senatorial courtesy"

Porter, for secretary of war, in 1844; Henry Stanberry, for attorney-general, in 1868; and Charles B. Warren, for attorney-general (rejected twice), in 1925. Occasionally, however, nominees are confirmed only over considerable opposition. Thus a Democratic Senate, in 1940, divided on confirming Henry L. Stimson as secretary of war and Frank Knox as secretary of the navy (both being Republicans) by votes of 56 to 28 and 66 to 16, respectively; and early in 1945—even after the post had been stripped of important financial powers which a Senate majority did not want to see intrusted to him—Henry A. Wallace was confirmed as secretary of commerce only by a vote of 56 to 32. In 1877, Republican leaders in the Senate, indignant because the incoming president, Rutherford B. Hayes, had made up his cabinet list (an exceptionally excellent one) without deferring to their wishes, held up confirmation; but they were soon overborne by strong expressions of public disapproval, and in the end all of the nominees were confirmed almost unanimously.

[1] President Hoover's nomination of Charles E. Hughes to be Chief Justice of the United States, in 1930, met with sturdy opposition, although the outcome was a favorable Senate vote of 56 to 20.

[2] President Roosevelt's nomination of Aubrey W. Williams to be administrator of the Rural Electrification Administration was rejected in 1945, and in 1946 President Truman was compelled by Senate opposition to withdraw Edwin W. Pauley's nomination to be under-secretary of the Navy. The most dramatic recent contest over the confirmation of a major nomination came in 1946 in connection with the proposal of David E. Lilienthal, a former chairman of the board of directors of the Tennessee Valley Authority, for chairman of the recently established and important United States Atomic Energy Commission. With the Commission already organized, the President sent the nominations of the five members to the Senate on January 15; a joint congressional committee on atomic energy held hearings lasting five weeks, in the course of which violent opposition to Mr. Lilienthal was manifested by Senator Kenneth McKellar, on largely personal grounds, and with hostility developing also among Republican senators; on March 10, the Senate section of the joint committee (which alone had jurisdiction to report officially to the Senate) approved the nomination by a vote of 8 to 1; and, after prolonged and heated debate on the floor, the nomination received senatorial confirmation, April 9, by a vote of 50 to 31.

[3] Against persistent Senate opposition, Theodore Roosevelt in this way kept a Negro in the office of collector of customs at the port of Charleston, S. C., from 1902 to 1904. With the Senate in session, a recess appointee draws no salary until confirmed.

[4] As, for example, during the second session of the Seventy-eighth Congress (January 10-December 19, 1944), when of 10,119 nominations to civil and military posts submitted to the Senate, 10,073 were confirmed, four were rejected, eighteen were withdrawn, and twenty-four were not acted upon.

without first ascertaining that the nominee is acceptable to the senators (especially the senior senator) from that state—provided, of course, such senators are of the president's party. If he does this, and the senator or senators object, "Courtesy of the Senate" requires all members of the body to vote against confirmation. So inflexible is this tradition that hardly any president will now challenge it by offering a nomination of the kind without first assuring himself that the senators having an immediate interest are agreeable.[1]

3. Other practical restrictions

In making appointments, the president is limited by still other conditions of a highly practical nature. He cannot simply pick men for thousands of posts "out of the air," so to speak. Rather, he must depend upon other people to bring candidates to his attention and make clear their claims; and this opens a way for the great majority of presidential appointees actually to be chosen by senators or representatives belonging to the president's party—the principal rôle being played by senators, yet with representatives often making proposals in the case of federal officials operating entirely within a congressional district, or indeed in the case of more important ones when the state has no senator belonging to the president's party.[2] Finally, appointments are often virtually dictated by the necessity of placating a wing of the party, meeting a demand of a particular section of the country, or keeping some influential politician in line. Small wonder that every president finds his appointing power—in other words, his "patronage"—one of his greatest burdens! Every time he appoints to an office, former President Taft used to say, he makes nine enemies and one ingrate. The worst of it is that, under the pressures exerted, a good many poor appointments result.

Removals—the question of concurrence by the Senate

The constitution makes all civil officers of the United States liable to removal by impeachment, but only upon conviction of treason, bribery, or other high crimes and misdemeanors. Obviously, there must be removals for incompetency, neglect, and other reasons which have no relation to the specified grounds for impeachment; and the question of how such removals should be made forced itself upon the attention of Congress almost immediately after the new government under the constitution was set up. Two opposing views appeared. One was that, since the constitution was silent on the subject (except as to impeachment), the power to remove

---

[1] Another form of senatorial courtesy, working in reverse, comes into view when, the president having nominated a *senator* to an office, the Senate confirms the nomination immediately and as a matter of course, without referring it to any committee. Departure from this practice in the case of the nomination of Hugo L. Black to an associate justiceship of the Supreme Court in 1937 stirred much interest. See K. Cole, "Mr. Justice Black and 'Senatorial Courtesy,'" *Amer. Polit. Sci. Rev.*, XXXI, 1113-1115 (Dec., 1937).

[2] A prominent senator (Carl A. Hatch) observed in the course of debate in 1943 that when appointments have to be confirmed by the Senate, senators from the states affected actually make them, leaving the president with only a veto power. "The right to reject, which the constitution vests in the Senate, has become the right to select." The coveted influence of members of Congress in selecting appointees furnishes the main reason, of course, why the president continues to have thousands of appointments to make.

was to be regarded as implied in the power to appoint, and therefore should be exercised by the same authorities that were associated in making appointments—which in the case of "presidential" offices would mean the president and Senate. Alexander Hamilton was strongly of this opinion; and in earlier days even the Supreme Court seemed to agree with him. The other view was that, since the president was to be directly responsible for the efficiency of all national administration, it would be unfair to tie his hands by requiring the Senate's consent to removals. Madison argued convincingly for this opinion, and it finally won general acceptance.

For three-quarters of a century, the matter seemed settled. In 1867, however, it was reopened dramatically when Congress, inspired by hostility to President Johnson, passed over his veto a Tenure of Office Act providing that, while the president might *suspend* a civil officer when the Senate was not in session (and therefore unable to act on the matter), he should definitely *remove* no such officer—not even a member of his cabinet—if appointed with the advice and consent of the Senate, except with the approval of that body. To be sure, this startling measure was repealed in part in 1869 and completely in 1887. To be sure, too, most people believed, with Johnson, that it was unconstitutional.[1] Before it disappeared from the statute-book, however, an act passed in 1876 re-affirmed the disputed principle by providing that postmasters of the first, second, and third classes should be appointed, and might be *removed*, by the president by and with the advice and consent of the Senate. Notwithstanding doubts, therefore, it seemed that, while normally the president might make removals freely and without consulting the Senate, Congress could go as far as it liked in prescribing exceptions.

The famous Tenure of Office Act of 1867 never, while still in force, came before the courts in such a way as to lead to a decision upon its validity; and the statute of 1876 likewise ran for fifty years without effective challenge. In 1920, however, President Wilson, without consulting the Senate, removed Frank S. Myers, first-class postmaster at Portland, Oregon, whom he had appointed in 1917; and when, Myers himself having died in the meantime, the administratrix of his estate carried to the Supreme Court a suit for the salary lost through removal, that tribunal held that in so far as the act of 1876 attempted to place restriction upon the power of the president to remove officers appointed by him with the consent of the Senate, it was unconstitutional.[2] This meant that the

The
Myers
case
(1926)

---

[1] The President's refusal to abide by the measure was a main reason for his impeachment.

[2] Myers *v.* United States, 272 U. S. 52 (1926). Up to now, the Supreme Court had always succeeded in side-stepping any ruling on the nature and location of the removal power. In the course of its decision, too, it vindicated President Johnson's veto of the statute of 1867 by pronouncing that measure unconstitutional *post mortem*. Incidentally, the Myers case marked the first time in history that the federal government, through the Department of Justice, appeared in the Supreme Court to attack the constitutionality of an act of Congress.

removal of Myers without the matter being referred to the Senate was constitutionally and legally proper, and that, after all, it is not within the power of Congress to limit the president's discretion by making removals contingent upon senatorial assent.[1]

No one, of course, ever argued that the president's power of removal is absolutely unlimited. By express constitutional provision, federal judges (except in the territories and dependencies) hold office during good behavior; and this is construed to mean that they can be removed only by impeachment.[2] Furthermore, officials who secure appointment under the merit system (usually directly or indirectly from heads of departments representing the president) are removable only "for such causes as will promote the efficiency of the service," even though, in practice, this restraining clause is so elastic as to make it possible for the appointing officer to remove almost any merit appointee for insufficient reason as well as otherwise.[3]

The Humphrey case (1935)

But, beyond this, can any restraints be imposed? Until somewhat over a decade ago, the outcome of the Myers case would presumably have indicated an answer in the negative. In 1935, however, the matter was given a new slant by another significant Supreme Court decision. This time the official removed was William E. Humphrey, a Republican member of the Federal Trade Commission (originally appointed by President Coolidge), who, because of not seeing eye to eye with President Roosevelt upon questions of public policy, was asked in 1933 to hand in his resignation, and, upon refusing to do so, was summarily ejected from office. Once more, a suit for recovery of lost salary was carried to the highest court by an executor; and this time the case was won.[4] In writing the Myers decision, Chief Justice Taft had voiced the *dictum* that the considerations which debarred Congress from interfering with the president's power to remove an executive officer, such as the Portland postmaster, applied equally to removals from independent regulatory commissions, even though performing quasi-legislative or quasi-judicial, rather than truly executive, functions. The Court now, however—doubtless to Mr. Roosevelt's consternation—unanimously held otherwise. When establishing the

---

[1] E. S. Corwin, "Tenure of Office and the Removal Power Under the Constitution," *Columbia Law Rev.*, XXVII, 353-399 (Apr., 1927); H. L. McBain, "Consequences of the President's Unlimited Power of Removal," *Polit. Sci. Quar.*, XLI, 596-603 (Dec., 1926); J. Hart, "The Bearing of Myers v. U. S. upon the Independence of Federal Administrative Tribunals," *Amer. Polit. Sci. Rev.*, XXIII, 657-673 (Aug., 1929), and reply by A. Langeluttig, *ibid.*, XXIV, 57-66 (Feb., 1930). The briefs, oral arguments of counsel, and opinions of the Court in the Myers case will be found in 69th Cong., 2nd Sess., Sen. Doc. No. 174 (1926).

[2] During a period of bitter partisan conflict (in 1801), sixteen judges of circuit courts established by a "lame-duck" Federalist Congress were ousted by having their posts abolished at the hands of a Republican Congress. But of course these were not removals in the ordinary sense; and the action was that of Congress, not of either the president and Senate or the president alone.

[3] See pp. 509-510 below.

[4] Rathbun [Humphrey's executor] v. United States, 295 U. S. 602 (1935). On the same day, the Court administered another blow to the President by holding the National Industrial Recovery Act unconstitutional. See p. 658 below.

Federal Trade Commission,[1] Congress had given the members seven-year terms and had made them removable by the president only for "inefficiency, neglect of duty, or malfeasance in office." No charge on any of these grounds had been brought against Mr. Humphrey; his removal—which he protested vigorously until his death shortly afterwards—was based solely and frankly upon the President's dislike of his views; and on that account the Court found it unlawful. The right to remove a purely executive officer, it said in substance, derives from the inherent nature of the executive power, and under our system of separation of powers is protected against congressional interference. But the Federal Trade Commission is a non-partisan and essentially non-executive agency set up by Congress to carry specified congressional enactments into effect, and the same principle of separation of powers forbids the president to remove its members for reasons other than those which Congress, in the proper exercise of its legislative authority, has prescribed. The decision was of no avail to the now deceased commissioner, but it placed a new and desirable limitation upon the presidential removal power. Thenceforth, members of the numerous great independent regulatory commissions were presumed to be secure against dismissal for reasons of a "political" character.[2]

[1] See p. 655 below.

[2] Professor E. S. Corwin sums up the situation since 1935 as follows: "(1) As to agents of his own powers, the president's removal power is illimitable; (2) as to agents of Congress's constitutional powers, Congress may confine it to removal for cause, which implies the further right to require a hearing as a part of the procedure of the removal." *The President: Office and Powers*, 96. For full discussion of the Humphrey case, see W. J. Donovan and R. R. Irvine, "The President's Power to Remove Members of Administrative Agencies," *Cornell Law Quar.*, XXI, 215-248 (Feb., 1936). In 1937, President Roosevelt sponsored a reorganization measure which would have given the chief executive full power to make such removals as that attempted in the case of Humphrey, but Congress refused to pass it.

The removal of Dr. A. E. Morgan, in 1938, as chairman of the Tennessee Valley Authority, because of his refusal to produce evidence in support of charges which he had made against his fellow-directors, presented a different angle. The T.V.A. is not a "regulatory commission," but rather a government corporation. Besides, Congress had given the president authority to remove its officials, even if not for precisely the reason for which the removal was actually made. Hence, when Dr. Morgan contested his removal, the Supreme Court refused to support him. Morgan *v.* United States, 312 U. S. 701 (1941).

The subject should not be dismissed without observing that by law of 1921 creating the General Accounting Office (see p. 568 below), one principal official of that Office, the comptroller-general, although appointed by the president, is removable only by joint resolution of the two houses of Congress. Regarding this arrangement as unconstitutional, President Wilson vetoed the original Budget and Accounting Bill of 1920 providing for it. A statute of 1945 undertook to justify it by declaring the General Accounting Office "a part of the legislative branch of the government" (59 *U. S. Stat. at Large*, 616).

A further fact to be noted is that Congress can (as in the case of the judges in 1801) separate officials from their posts by abolishing the posts themselves. Thus when, in 1943, provision was made for liquidating the National Youth Administration, persons engaged in managing that service were legislated out of jobs unless others could be found for them. In 1943, Congress, however, over-reached itself by, in effect, attempting to remove three officials (Robert M. Lovett, secretary of the Virgin Islands, and Goodwin B. Watson and William E. Dodd, Jr., of the Foreign Broadcast Intelligence Service of the Federal Communications Commission), not by abolishing their positions, but by attaching a rider to a deficiency appropriation measure stipulating that the three, charged with subversive activities as affiliates of

If the Senate cannot legally prevent a removal (except in so far as the principle of the Humphrey case is applicable), it also cannot compel one to be made. This principle—never really doubted by any constitutional lawyer—received forceful illustration in February, 1924, when the Senate called upon President Coolidge to ask for the resignation of his secretary of the navy, on the ground that the latter had been remiss in the performance of his official duties. Affirming that "the dismissal of an officer of the government, such as is involved in this case, other than by impeachment, is exclusively an executive function," the President explained in a public statement that no official recognition could be given the resolution; and legal opinion and popular sentiment alike strongly supported the position taken.[1]

Direction of Administration—Issuing Orders and Regulations

Quite as important as the president's authority to appoint and remove officials is his power to direct them in performing their duties. As exercised today, this power is the outcome of long and somewhat hazardous development. The idea of the constitution's framers was that the control of executive and administrative work should be divided between the president and Congress; and when the first executive departments were established, it was prescribed that the former should have power to direct two of them, i.e., State and War, but that the head of the third, i.e., the

---

Communist organizations, should not continue on the federal payroll beyond a specified date unless in the meantime renominated by the president and reconfirmed by the Senate. The president dared not veto the entire measure, but in approving it he condemned the rider as being to all intents and purposes a bill of attainder and therefore unconstitutional, as well as an encroachment upon the executive branch of the government. See F. L. Schuman, "Bill of Attainder in the Seventy-eighth Congress," *Amer. Polit. Sci. Rev.*, XXXVII, 819-829 (Oct., 1943). In a suit for back pay brought by the three men (who had continued in their posts), the Supreme Court later concurred with the president, pronouncing the rider a bill of attainder and therefore void. United States v. Lovett, 328 U. S. 303 (1946). For a full account of the affair, see R. E. Cushman, "The Purge of Federal Employees Accused of Disloyalty," *Pub. Admin. Rev.*, III, 297-316 (Autumn, 1943).

[1] Another angle of the relations of president and Senate in the matter of appointments and removals was presented in 1931, when the Senate, after confirming three persons nominated by the president for membership in the reorganized Federal Power Commission, changed its mind and attempted to recall the confirmation. President Hoover took the position that the confirmations represented completed acts, that the commissioners were duly in office, and that the only way—aside from removal by the president—in which they could be ousted was by impeachment. "I cannot admit the power of the Senate," he asserted, "to encroach upon the executive function by removal of a duly appointed executive officer under the guise of reconsideration of his nomination." The Senate's answer was to order the names restored to the executive calendar; and although when the question of confirmation was brought up again, two of the three were endorsed by narrow margins, the third, George Otis Smith, was rejected. Backed by the President, Smith was already at work as chairman, and the Senate's next move took the form of *quo warranto* proceedings to test his right to continue. The outcome was a decision of the Supreme Court unanimously upholding the President's contention and denying the Senate's right to recall the confirmation of a nominee, once the latter's commission has been issued by the president. United States v. Smith, 286 U. S. 6 (1932). In 1939, President Franklin D. Roosevelt refused to yield to a request of the Senate that he return its resolution assenting to a given appointment to a district judgeship in Tennessee. On the other hand, a president is not obliged to go through with an appointment simply because the Senate has assented to it.

Treasury, should report directly to Congress. The earlier presidents used their directing power sparingly, and the courts viewed it as substantially limited to the fields in which it was expressly conferred.[1]

Notwithstanding the spectacular growth of executive power in these later days, Congress still wields a good deal of control over the administrative machinery and operations of the government. It is Congress that creates the executive departments and, as a rule, their more important subdivisions—the independent establishments, too—and determines what their functions shall be. It is Congress that says, in many situations, what shall be done and—in so far as it likes—how it shall be done. Congress alone can provide the requisite funds, and it can investigate, criticize, and suspend or permanently stop many, if not most, kinds of administrative activity, regardless of the wishes of the president and his administrative associates. Moreover, many lines of responsibility and control run directly from administrative agencies to Congress, with in fact "a maze of criss-crossing relationships between the president, Congress, and the departments, independent commissions, public corporations, and other agencies composing the federal establishment."[2] Nevertheless, Congress does not, and cannot, itself *administer;* day in and day out, it is the president—personally or through his higher subordinates—that exercises direction and control; and Congress not only accepts this fact, as it must, but—even while tying the president's hands by creating independent regulatory commissions, imposing its own regulations upon administrative agencies, requiring the president to exercise his supervisory powers through some particular channel, and in other ways— steadily contributes to exalting the executive power of direction by providing new governmental machinery to be operated by the president, and by assigning all manner of directive duties and tasks to him.

Diffusion of control over administration

In point of fact, the directing power is one which must have developed in a large way in any case. Not only does the power to remove necessarily involve the power to direct,[3] but the latter power has a clear con-

Basis and extent of the power of direction

---

[1] The Treasury Department still reports to Congress as well as to the president; but in point of fact all department reports are intended for use of both the president and Congress, and the distinction originally set up has little or no present significance.

[2] As a recent writer has remarked, it is a common error to picture the lines of administrative control and of responsibility as uniformly running vertically from subordinate to superior up through agency channels converging in the chief executive as the top of the hierarchy. In the large, they do this. But the complete picture is far from being so simple—which, of course, is only one more illustration of the artificiality of our vaunted theory of separation of powers. See E. P. Herring, "Executive-Legislative Responsibilities," *Amer. Polit. Sci. Rev.,* XXXVIII, 1159 (Dec., 1944). Cf. L. D. White, "Congressional Control of the Public Service," *Amer. Polit. Sci. Rev.,* XXIX, 1-11 (Feb., 1945).

[3] This was illustrated clearly when President Jackson ordered the deposits of government funds in the United States Bank to be withdrawn, and ousted two secretaries of the treasury before obtaining one who would give the necessary instructions. Armed with the power of removal, he could keep on commanding until some one was found to obey. The incident was important, because if Jackson had yielded, a precedent would have been established which, if followed, would have made it possible for the departments to carry on their work without full responsi-

stitutional basis in the injunction that the president shall "take care that the laws be faithfully executed," and, in his inaugural pledge, that he will "faithfully execute" the office of president and "preserve, protect, and defend the constitution." His foremost duty, indeed, is to see that the laws are enforced—not only the acts of Congress, but treaties, decisions of the federal courts, and all other national instruments having back of them the authority of the constitution; and to this end he must be regarded as endowed with power to direct his administrative subordinates, even as he is authorized to use the armed forces if such a course becomes necessary. To be sure, acts required of heads of departments and other executive officers by law, *i.e.*, acts which are "ministerial" in character rather than political, are theoretically outside of the president's jurisdiction; in case of neglect, there are recognized judicial procedures for compelling performance of them. Nevertheless, even here the president may assert himself; he may, in fact, go so far as to threaten removal of an officer for performing an act required of him by Congress, thereby forcing upon him a disagreeable choice between incurring judicial action and losing his position.

The power to issue orders   Closely related to the power of direction is the power to issue commands and regulations in the form of executive orders. The nature and scope of the government's multifarious activities are defined, at least broadly, in the constitution and in acts of Congress, but the details of organization, the forms of procedure, and, in general, the *minutiœ* of administration are, and must be, left to be worked out and put into effect by those who stand closer to the work to be done. Thus, an immigration law, in seeking to debar paupers and criminals from admission to the country, will declare general policy and may specify rather fully the means and manner by which the policy is to be carried out, yet it will remain for the executive branch of the government to prescribe most or all of the detailed regulations covering the work of inspection, the handling of appeals from the decisions of the examining authorities, the detention of applicants refused admission, and similar matters; and such regulations are normally to be regarded as having the full force of law. Most of this "subordinate," or "administrative," legislation is formulated and issued by the heads of departments, or even by their inferiors. A considerable amount, however, comes also from the president—although even in this case it is likely to be prepared by the head of a department, or under his direction, on matters pertinent to his field. In any event, of course, ultimate responsibility for all regulations and orders issued rests with the chief executive, who himself promulgates (among other things) the Consular Regulations and the Civil Service Rules, together with rules

---

bility to the president; and the result of this probably would have been a situation somewhat like that existing in the states, where the governor usually has but little control over the other principal officials. See p. 928 below (in complete edition of this book).

for the Patent Office and the customs and internal revenue services. In some cases, he acts by virtue of powers inherent in his constitutional position, *e.g.*, as commander-in-chief of the armed forces;[1] in other instances, *e.g.*, in fixing the duties to be paid on imported goods under our trade agreement legislation, he acts by express statutory authority; in still others, he proceeds on the basis of powers inferred from the nature or tone of the law to be executed.[2]

Of course there is the principle of separation of powers to be reckoned with. As traditionally interpreted, legislation is the function of Congress. Yet many executive orders have the appearance, nature, and effect of law; and when their sole warrant is to be found in acts of Congress, they raise the question whether Congress has not, to all intents and purposes, handed over some of its legislative authority to be exercised by the executive—a thing which numerous judicial decisions deny it the right to do. To be sure, the Supreme Court has many times taken refuge in the position that in conferring ordinance-making powers Congress is not violating the principle of separation, for the reason that what is delegated is not lawmaking power, but only authority to "fill in the details" of legislative policy already laid down by the legislative branch. There came a time, however, when the Court, as then constituted, felt it necessary to call a halt; and a series of decisions, chiefly in 1935-36, invalidated the National Industrial Recovery Act, the first Agricultural Adjustment Act, and other measures passed to combat depression, on the ground that they had devolved purely legislative powers upon the chief executive and consequently were unconstitutional.[3] As a result, the delegation of regulatory authority to the president suffered a set-back, and with it the power to issue orders having the force of law. Yet the recession was more apparent than real. Death or retirement of Supreme Court justices opened a way for appointment of others disposed to look more tolerantly upon the expansion of executive regulatory authority. The tightening of the international situation led, in 1940, to the launching of a stupendous program of national defense, inviting legislation conferring upon the executive wide discretionary powers. And when, in December, 1941, the country was plunged into war—a situation that in any event would have magnified executive authority—sweeping powers of regulation by executive order (carried over in part from the First World War) found expression in a multitude of controls which no American who lived through those difficult years needs to have described.[4] Even yet, this situation has

The constitutional issue involved

---

[1] As when in 1942 an order was issued reconstructing the entire organization of the Army.

[2] A total of 2,570 executive orders, besides 416 proclamations, were issued during Franklin D. Roosevelt's first two administrations.

[3] See pp. 658-659, 678-681 below. A well-reasoned explanation and defense of the discretionary provisions of the acts in question will be found in J. Dickinson, "Political Aspects of the New Deal," *Amer. Polit. Sci. Rev.*, XXVIII, 197-209 (Apr., 1934).

[4] On presidential ordinance powers in wartime, see, however, p. 812 below.

not been fully liquidated; while, as for the future, there is little reason to doubt that executive ordinance-power, judicially curbed only in more extreme and dubious cases of congressional delegation, will continue at a high level.[1]

Pardon, Reprieve, and Amnesty

Finally (with foreign relations and war powers reserved for discussion in later chapters), there is the president's power, as chief executive, to grant pardons and reprieves.[2] The effect of a full pardon, the Supreme Court has said, is to make the offender, in the eye of the law, "as innocent as if he had never committed the offense."[3] A reprieve, of course, is only a postponement of the execution of a sentence. In wielding the pardoning power, the president acts in complete independence of Congress and of the courts; it is for him alone to say who shall be pardoned, at what time, and under what circumstances, subject only to two constitutional limitations: he cannot pardon a person who has been convicted by impeachment and thus restore him to office; and he can pardon only in cases in which the offense has been against the authority of the United States as distinguished from that of a state. An application in behalf of a convicted person may have any one of several results: (1) full and unconditional pardon; (2) pardon qualified by conditions, and revocable if the beneficiary fails to live up to them; (3) parole without pardon; (4) commutation of sentence, having the effect of shortening a period of imprisonment, substituting a fine for imprisonment, substituting life imprisonment for death, or otherwise reducing a penalty; (5) reprieve, or mere delay of punishment; and (6) refusal to take any action at all. Every application received is looked into by the pardon attorney in the Department of Justice; the district attorney and presiding judge in the district where the petitioner's trial was held are likely to be consulted; the attorney-general makes a recommendation; and usually the president's rôle is largely confined to carrying out the recommendation made. Ultimate responsibility for what is done is, however, the president's; and while he commonly does not personally hear persons pressing a case, he may do so in instances where grave doubts exist or important questions of public policy are involved. In the interest of impartial justice, he and every one having to do with pardons must be prepared to withstand

---

[1] Congress itself may, of course, recall a delegated power, or may legislatively annul any order issued which in its opinion constitutes an abuse of such a power. On the concurrent resolution as a device in this connection, see p. 381, note 3, above.

Formerly, much inconvenience arose from the lack of any provision for systematic assembling and publication of current executive orders and administrative regulations. The defect, however, was remedied in 1936 by the establishment of an official daily *Federal Register* in which all significant orders are printed as soon as issued.

[2] Art. II, § 2, cl. 1.

[3] It does not, however, have the effect of restoring money that has been paid as a fine or as court costs, property that has been forfeited, or office that has been vacated. H. Weihofen, "The Effect of a Pardon," *Univ. of Pa. Law Rev.*, LXXXVIII, 177-193 (Dec., 1939).

touching appeals and powerful influences.[1] A modified form of pardon is amnesty, which is a sort of blanket pardon extended to numbers of people who, without having been individually convicted, are known to have violated federal law, as by engaging in rebellion. Amnesties may be declared by act of Congress; but the usual method is that of presidential proclamation.

REFERENCES

The Federalist, Nos. LXIX-LXXII, LXXVI-LXXVII.

W. W. Willoughby, *Constitutional Law of the United States* (2nd ed., New York, 1929), III, Chaps. LXXXIII-LXXXIV.

W. H. Taft, *Our Chief Magistrate and His Powers* (New York, 1916), Chaps. III-V.

E. S. Corwin, *The President: Office and Powers; History and Analysis of Practice and Opinion* (New York, 1940), Chaps. I, III-IV.

————, *The President's Removal Power Under the Constitution* (New York, 1927).

C. P. Patterson, *Presidential Government in the United States; The Unwritten Constitution* (Chapel Hill, N. C., 1947), Chap. VIII.

H. W. Horwill, *The Usages of the American Constitution* (London, 1925), Chaps. III-IV, VII.

H. J. Laski, *The American Presidency* (New York, 1940), Chaps. I, IV.

G. F. Milton, *The Use of Presidential Power, 1789-1943* (Boston, 1944).

W. E. Binkley, *The Powers of the President; Problems of American Democracy* (Garden City, N. Y., 1937).

L M. Salmon, "History of the Appointing Power of the President," *Amer. Hist. Assoc. Papers,* I, No. 5 (Washington, D. C., 1886).

C. E. Morganston, *The Appointing and Removal Power of the President of the United States,* 70th Cong., 2nd Sess., Sen. Doc. No. 172 (1929).

A. W. Macmahon, "Senatorial Confirmation," *Pub. Admin. Rev.,* III, 281-296 (Autumn, 1943).

J. Hart, *Tenure of Office Under the Constitution* (Baltimore, 1930).

————, *The Ordinance-Making Powers of the President of the United States* (Baltimore, 1925).

F. F. Blachly and M. E. Oatman, *Federal Regulatory Action and Control* (Washington, D. C., 1940).

W. H. Humbert, *The Pardoning Power of the President* (Washington, D. C., 1941).

N. J. Small, *Some Presidential Interpretations of the Presidency* (Baltimore, 1932).

B. M. Rich, *The Presidents and Civil Disorder* (Washington, D. C., 1941).

F. D. Roosevelt, *On Our Way* (New York, 1934).

---

[1] The number of applications for a presidential pardon run to about 1,600 a year. In some states, courts have the right to suspend the sentence of a convicted offender. No federal court, however, enjoys such power, for under the constitution clemency is exclusively an executive function.

CHAPTER XXII

NATIONAL ADMINISTRATION—FUNCTIONS AND AGENCIES

The Nature and Importance of Administration

Politics and administration

One does not have to be an expert on government to recognize two basic activities as very nearly summing up everything: (1) deciding upon policy, and (2) carrying policy into effect—the first broadly a matter of politics, the second a matter of administration. By "politics" is meant, of course, a great deal more than mere party conflict. Included in it is the birth and growth of ideas, the development of principles, the formation and expression of opinion, the organization and techniques of parties, propaganda, electoral procedures, and especially legislation— in short, the entire range of activities and processes through which ideas crystallize into policies and policies are translated into law. By administration is meant the processes and procedures by which policies laid down in statutes, rules, orders, and the like are put into effect, the business and "housekeeping" activities of government are carried on, and the personnel requisite for performing such work is recruited, assigned its tasks, disciplined, and directed. Policy-making is concerned primarily with ends or objectives, though often incidentally also with means; administration, primarily with machinery, methods, and techniques. To be sure, even under a system of separation of powers, the agencies performing the two great functions are not walled off rigidly from one another; on the contrary, they are firmly meshed together. In our national government, Congress is presumed to be the supreme policy-making authority; yet it creates much of the machinery of administration, provides the money for maintaining it, prescribes administrative duties and sometimes methods, and in so far as it likes investigates and criticizes results—although it does not itself, and cannot, *administer*. In their turn, the administrators supply information, develop plans, submit proposals, assist in drafting laws and orders, make and remake policy even in the very process of administration, and in other ways contribute directly and heavily to the work of legislation—so heavily, indeed, that the complaint is sometimes heard that Congress and other legislatures have abdicated their most important task, that of deciding policy. As chief executive and at the same time active collaborator in lawmaking, the president himself is a major connecting link between politics and administration. Nevertheless, although the two go hand in hand, their dual aspect persists; and every intelligent student of our system of government must begin by recognizing it—by grasping the fact also that few, if any, problems transcend that of how public decisions arrived at by policy-determining agencies can most effectively be put into operation by public servants.

There must be recognition, too, of the intrinsic importance of administration in the governing process. Hardly more than sixty years have elapsed since Woodrow Wilson pioneered with the earliest systematic discussion of the subject in any language.[1] But subsequently, and especially since about 1920, administration, on all levels of government, has come in for vastly increased attention, having, indeed, become of itself a major field of research, instruction, and experiment.[2] After all, notwithstanding its long neglect, administration is, as Wilson emphasized, "the most obvious part of government;" it is, as he bluntly added, "government in action." Certainly it is administration that day by day brings government closest home to the people. Congress may deliberate through long months in Washington (likewise a legislature in a state capital) and enact laws by the score without touching the citizen or his pocketbook unless these laws are applied and enforced throughout the length and breadth of the land by administrative authorities.

It is, indeed, the quality of administration that mainly conditions the effectiveness of the democratic process; democratic government means democracy in administration—the gearing of administrative machinery to the liberal principles underlying the state—no less than democracy in legislation. To no small degree, the ill-fated Weimar Republic in Germany proved a failure for the reason that an ostensibly democratic constitutional system was clogged and frustrated by administrative machinery still pervaded by the aristocratic, officious, and arbitrary attitudes characteristic of the old Imperial régime—an administrative mechanism frequently admired abroad for its technical efficiency, but lacking in the most essential aspect of all, i.e., conformity with the democratic principles on which the government as a whole was supposed to be based. Even where, as in the United States, administration is, on the whole, permeated with the democratic spirit, the character of government, as a going concern, still depends heavily on administrative quality and capacity. Good laws are, of course, desirable, and justice through the courts is indispensable. But it is easier to get good laws and impartial court decisions than to secure uniformly economical and efficient administration. The legislature has only to declare its will in an act of broad and general scope, and thereupon its work is finished—save as it may later watch what happens and perchance launch an investigation if it considers that things are not going right. But in any case the big task remains, i.e., to fit

The significance of administration

---

[1] "The Study of Administration," *Polit. Sci. Quar.*, II, 197-222 (June, 1887).

[2] Growing recognition in this country of the importance of administration was reflected in the formation, in 1939, of a national Society for Public Administration, whose quarterly journal, the *Public Administration Review,* should be known to all students of the subject. Cf. F. M. Marx [ed.], *Elements of Public Administration* (New York, 1946), Chap. II (by A. Leiserson) on "The Study of Public Administration."

the terms of the measure to the existing public situation; to select the officials who are to interpret the law and apply it; to instruct, supervise, and discipline these officials; to settle innumerable questions of detail (many of them highly technical, many involving important matters of principle); to prevent laxity, favoritism, and fraud. It has been an American failing to assume naïvely that all that is necessary in order to cure an evil or achieve some other desirable end is to "pass a law." As a people, we are only beginning to understand that, even when a law is well conceived and in good form, the vital test comes in the administering of it. And such administration is no mere mechanical process; on the contrary, it is a very human affair, coming close to the people, and dependent for its effectiveness quite as much upon the people's attitudes and reactions as upon the competence and diligence of the administrators themselves. By its very nature, too, administration must be in full operation all of the time, day and night, fifty-two weeks a year. Congress sometimes goes a good many months without being convened, and the courts are accustomed to lengthy recesses between terms. Administrative management and operation, however, must be kept up ceaselessly; individual administrators may take vacations, but administration is never adjourned.

Growing magnitude and complexity   Whether in nation, state, or city, the work of administration tends to grow ever more varied, complicated, and exacting. Government stretches its regulating arm in new directions, adding every time that it does so to the activities to be carried on or supervised by its agents. Technological advances continually give rise to new tasks and introduce fresh elements of complexity into old ones. Ill-equipped to make provision in detail for the application of principles and policies embodied in the laws which they enact, legislatures increasingly leave it to administrative authorities to supply rules and regulations as necessity arises, with more and more people needed for carrying the regulations into effect. All of these tendencies were strikingly in evidence long before the days of the New Deal, when, as we shall see, programs of recovery and reform were undertaken on lines such that, for the time being, government—at least on the federal level—seemed to have become almost entirely a matter of administration. In the later thirties, Congress and the state legislatures (with some aid from the courts) regained a certain amount of the ground lost; administration did not seem quite so completely to hold the field. After 1940, however, large-scale defense preparations opened new avenues for administrative expansion; and later participation in a global war, while of course giving rise to waves of empowering and to some extent regulatory legislation, nevertheless made government once more mainly a gigantic administrative enterprise. With combat ended, the pendulum again swung back somewhat: on the one hand, federal and state controls were relaxed, wartime agencies terminated or curtailed, the numbers of officials and employees (especially on the federal level) sharply reduced;

on the other hand, multitudes of questions of policy in an era of reconversion and reconstruction—concerning labor and employment, taxation,
national defense, social security, dealings with needy nations and peoples,
and what not—challenged the legislative branch to augmented activity.
Administration, none the less, remains, and certainly will continue, by all
odds the principal segment of government activity. In point of numbers
employed, volume and variety of functions performed, and cost to the
taxpayer, the country's "big government" of which we hear much, pro
and con, is primarily "big administration." [1]

Some Fundamental Features of the National Administrative System

National and state legislatures and legislative processes are entirely
separate from each other, and so are the systems of national and state
courts. In the field of administration, however, there is a good deal of
interlocking, extending indeed to all three major levels of government—
federal, state, and local. Thus, federal elections are managed by state and
local officers acting under state law, and state courts as well as national
courts naturalize aliens under national law. Offenders against national
laws may be apprehended by state and local police, as well as by United
States marshals and other federal agents. State and local officials were
drawn deeply into the enforcement of the Volstead Act when national
prohibition was in effect, and still help enforce federal pure food and
drugs acts, federal wild-life and game laws, the federal plant quarantine
law, and federal public health measures. In the area of agriculture, such
inter-relationships are particularly abundant; county agricultural agents,
for example, although usually appointed locally, are in effect agents of
federal, state, and local governments alike, and all contribute to their

*1. The
national
govern-
ment
basically
self-
sufficing*

---

[1] Not only so, but, in the words of an able student of our government, "... if Congress and the president continue to establish and expand administrative agencies
and endow them with sweeping powers, the task of disciplining such agencies and
keeping their conduct in line with our fundamental conceptions of justice will be
one of the most difficult and important that the government and the people have
to face." C. B. Swisher, *The Growth of Constitutional Power* (Chicago, 1946), 153.
Cf. M. J. Pusey, *Big Government—Can We Control It?* (New York, 1945); P. H.
Appleby, *Big Democracy* (New York, 1945); C. Edison, "The Case Against Big
Government," *Amer. Mercury*, LIX, 283-289 (Sept., 1944).

On the general subject of administration as a function of government in the
United States, see F. M. Marx [ed.], *Elements of Public Administration* (New York,
1946), Chaps. i-v; C. E. Merriam, *On the Agenda of Democracy* (Cambridge, Mass.,
1941), Chap. ii; and M. E. Dimock, *Modern Politics and Administration* (New
York, 1937), Chap. ix.

Professor John M. Gaus has suggested that an illuminating commentary on the
growth of public administration, and of attitudes toward it, in this country is supplied
by four essays, widely separated in time and circumstance: (1) Henry Adams, "Civil
Service Reform," *No. Amer. Rev.*, CIX, 443-475 (Oct., 1869); (2) Woodrow Wilson,
"The Study of Administration," *Polit. Sci. Quar.*, II, 197-222 (June, 1887), reprinted
in *ibid.*, LVI, 481-506 (Dec., 1941); (3) C. A. Beard, "Administration in a Great
Society," *American Government and Politics* (4th ed., New York, 1924), Chap. iii;
and (4) L. D. White, "Public Administration," in *Encyclopaedia of the Social
Sciences* (New York, 1930), I, 440-450. See J. M. Gaus, "The Present Status of the
Study of Public Administration in the United States," *Amer. Polit. Sci. Rev.*, XXV,
120-134 (Feb., 1931); and cf. the same writer's *Reflections on Public Administration*
(Univ. of Alabama, 1947).

pay.[1] The defense and war effort of a few years ago saw federal selective service legislation carried out largely through state and local agencies, and state and local defense councils used extensively by most of the federal defense and war agencies—for example, by the Office of Price Administration in the rationing program. Some people even consider that the states may end by becoming hardly more than administrative areas and agencies of the government at Washington. Notwithstanding all this, however, the first major fact about the national administrative system is that the national government is still basically self-sufficient in the sense that its laws are, as a matter of principle and to a very great degree in practice, carried out and its other work performed by its own separate administrative personnel.

2. The pattern of administrative organization

A person unfamiliar with the machinery of our national administration might naïvely suppose that it could rather readily be diagrammed as a vast but simple pyramid, with the president at the apex, branches ramifying symmetrically downwards through various layers or levels, and every agency fitting neatly into its appointed position. A closer view would, however, dispel any such illusion. For in truth the system (if such it can be called) displays no such integration; on the contrary, it is loose, disjointed, *unsystematic*. To be sure, its dominating feature is a group of more or less coördinate executive departments created by act of Congress and serving directly as administrative arms of the president.[2] The constitution itself does not provide in so many words for such departments, nor, of course, say how many there shall be or what they shall be called. It, however, plainly assumes that departments will exist: [3] it authorizes the president "to require the opinion, in writing, of the principal officer of each of the executive departments;" it also empowers Congress "to vest the appointment of inferior officers in the heads of departments;" and a large share of the burden of administrative work today is carried by the eleven departments thus far set up—State, Treasury, War (now Army), Navy, Air Force, Post-Office, Interior, Justice, Agriculture, Commerce, and Labor.[4] There is, however, a great deal of administrative

[1] Federal aid, of course, has contributed to closer inter-governmental relationships in many fields; although in most instances administration of the services federally assisted remains with the states, the federal government retaining only rights of inspection and supervision.

[2] Even in official usage the terms "executive" and "administrative" are employed very loosely. In the strictest sense, the president and vice-president are the only *executive* officers in the national government; the departments, and even the heads thereof, are *administrative*. As being attached to the executive branch of the government, however, the departments are known as "executive departments," and the civil service as the "executive civil service."

[3] Under the Articles of Confederation, Congress had established departments of foreign affairs, war, navy, treasury, and post-office, and their usefulness had been so clearly demonstrated that the constitution's makers simply took their continuance for granted. In or after 1789, each department was, however, reëstablished, by congressional act and with various changes, the department of foreign affairs becoming, for example, the later Department of State.

[4] The War Department was renamed, the Department of the Air Force was created, and the three Departments of the Army, the Navy, and the Air Force were coördinated under a secretary of defense in 1947. See pp. 824-825 below.

machinery which has never been placed in any department. Beginning, in effect, with the creation of the Civil Service Commission in 1883 and of the Interstate Commerce Commission four years later, "independent establishments"—provided for in most instances directly by act of Congress, but sometimes set up by executive order in pursuance of power delegated or otherwise possessed—so multiplied that even before the launching of the Roosevelt Administration's recovery program in 1933 their number had reached a score or more; and the New Deal, the national defense program instituted in 1940, and the later war, gave rise to a bewildering array of additional ones, some of which have disappeared because of time limitations or by direct abolition, some by reason of consolidations, and some (e.g., the famous National Recovery Administration) on account of judicial invalidation of the legislation on which they rested, but many of which—certainly at least forty—survive, in one form or another, today. As will be explained later, several of the separate agencies encountered—particularly the boards and commissions—have functions that are rather more legislative and judicial than administrative. But some are largely or wholly administrative. And further to expand the picture (although serving usefully for purposes of integration), a variable list of twenty or more of the number have since 1939 been grouped under the entirely autonomous Executive Office of the President, or under one or another of three coördinating "agencies" (Federal Security, Federal Loan, and Federal Works), each hardly if any less important than some of the departments themselves, and with their "administrators" commonly invited to sit with the cabinet.[1] Finally,

[1] In 1946, President Truman announced his intention to ask Congress to transform the Federal Security Agency into a department. At the date of writing (1948), however, no action had been taken and the three "agencies" embraced the following principal units:

1. *Federal Security Agency:*
   United States Office of Education
   United States Public Health Service
   Social Security Administration
   Food and Drug Administration
   Office of Vocational Rehabilitation
   Bureau of Employees' Compensation

2. *Federal Loan Agency:*
   Reconstruction Finance Corporation
   Federal National Mortgage Corporation
   RFC Mortgage Company
   Rubber Development Corporation

3. *Federal Works Agency:*
   Public Buildings Administration
   Public Roads Administration
   Federal Fire Council
   Federal Real Estate Board

There is also a National Housing Agency (containing a Federal Home Loan Bank Administration, a Home Owners' Loan Corporation, a Federal Housing Administration, and a Federal Public Housing Authority), which, however, is classified as an "emergency" agency rather than as a permanent feature of the administrative system.

A brief report submitted in 1948 by the Senate committee on expenditures in the executive departments has as its principal feature a chart (approximately 3 x 5 feet in dimensions) entitled "Organization of Federal Executive Departments and Agencies"

forming the substructure of both the departments and the "establish-ments" are "the men (and women too) in the trenches," *i.e.*, the host of lesser officials and employees constituting the "executive civil service," operating partly in Washington but in far larger numbers under district and regional offices scattered over the country.

Going from one great department to another in Washington, one would find plenty of variation in structural arrangements, arising partly from dissimilarity of work to be performed, partly from the as yet unfinished reorganizations undertaken in recent years, partly, too, from the flexi-bility and capacity for quick readjustment made necessary by the very nature of administration, *i.e.*, the employment of practical means (which must be readily adaptable) to definite ends (which themselves may also change). Nevertheless, there are also common features. To begin with, all of the departments are organized under single heads, known in every instance, except for the attorney-general and the postmaster-general, as a "secretary." Furthermore, nearly all of the departments have from one to four assistant secretaries and a chief clerk; and all except two or three (*e.g.*, Justice and Post-Office) have also an under-secretary. Assistant secretaries are usually in charge of specified groups of departmental agencies and functions; the under-secretary is more on the order of a general sub-head, relieving the pressure upon the secretary and on occa-sion acting as his substitute. Like their chiefs, assistant and under-secre-taries have traditionally been political appointees, serving only so long as the president who chose them remained in the White House. There have been instances, however, of appointees continuing in office through several administrations, the most notable being that of Alvey A. Adee, who achieved the extraordinary record of serving as an assistant secretary in the Department of State from 1882 until his death in 1924. On the analogy of the department head, the under-secretary may very properly be a "political" official. It would be an improvement, however, if assistant secretaries were to come to be regarded as in all cases entitled to retain their office during good behavior, after the maner of permanent under-secretaries in government departments in Great Britain.

It goes without saying that in every department the work to be per-formed is parcelled out among numerous sections or branches; and while, in general, the traditional bureaucratic pattern prevails, with the secre-tary at the apex of the pyramid and with successive levels of officials beneath him, ramifying downwards to the lowest grades of civil servants, there is not always evidence of complete symmetry or logic. One encoun-ters divisions, bureaus, "offices," and "services," headed by commissioners, directors, comptrollers, chiefs—with no very clearly fixed meaning for some of the terms employed. On the personnel side, the significant fact

and showing literally every establishment and agency within the executive branch, together with its component parts down through the "division" level, and as of January 1, 1948—a total of 2,169 entries. 80th Cong., 2nd Sess., Sen. Report, Com-mittee Print No. 3.

is, however, to be observed that, whereas in times past the heads of bureaus and other such branches were almost invariably appointed and removed on political grounds, there is now more acceptance of the principle that they should be selected on grounds of fitness alone and, even when originally appointed for political reasons, should be left undisturbed as long as they give good service. To them it falls, in particular degree, to keep the individual administrative agencies going and to supply the needed continuity of knowledge and experience. Twenty years ago, a student of the subject was able to show that in several of the major departments—especially those, like Agriculture, which carried on work of a technical and scientific character—most bureau chiefs (or their equivalents) enjoyed substantial permanence of tenure; and, notwithstanding occasional lapses, the situation is more favorable today, not so much because of civil service requirements as because the increasingly complex and technical nature of nearly all governmental operations makes it, almost from year to year, more obviously absurd and impossible to intrust bureau chiefships and similar positions to mere office-seekers.[1]

The more important independent establishments generally take the form of boards or commissions (of three, five, or often seven members), with all of the members sharing equally in authority and the chairman serving merely as a general manager of operations; although auxiliary to the board itself will be found, in cases like the Interstate Commerce Commission and the Federal Trade Commission, a structure of secretaries, counsellors, bureaus, divisions, and the like, quite comparable to those found in the departments. The tendency is to employ boards and commissions when the work to be done is not wholly, or perhaps even primarily, administrative, but involves also making regulations analogous to legislation and reaching decisions of a judicial nature—in other words, when what is needed is not so much instant action as consultation, deliberation, and considered decision shared in by several minds. The members are likely to be so selected as to represent different political parties and varied social and economic interests; long terms make for development of expertness, and arrangements for overlapping prevent a complete change of personnel at any given time. *(b) Independent establishments*

Still another organizational type appears when, for carrying on activities publicly planned and undertaken but similar in nature to private business, Congress sets up a government corporation, owned (*i.e.*, most or all of the capital provided) by the government, presided over commonly by a general manager acting under authority of a board of directors, and either attached to a department or left independent, but in any case enjoying a freedom of action—in buying, selling, borrowing, loaning, managing—that makes it, as some one has remarked, the most independ- *(c) Government corporations*

---

[1] The organization of all of the departments will be found outlined in any recent issue of the *United States Government Manual*, and in more detail in the chart mentioned in the immediately preceding foot-note.

ent of the independent establishments.[1] Best known, perhaps, among the literally scores of such agencies (approximately one hundred in 1945) are the Reconstruction Finance Corporation, the Federal Deposit Insurance Corporation, the Inland Waterways Corporation, and the Tennessee Valley Authority.[2]

(d) Field services

Most people think of the national government as "carried on" simply in Washington. To be sure, they know that post-offices and revenue-collectors' offices are widely scattered; but they have little conception of the extent to which the federal government is everywhere throughout the country, and not only its laws and courts, but its agencies of management and enforcement. The truth is that from Maine to California, the familiar pattern of states, counties, cities, and the like is overlaid with criss-crossing patterns of federal administrative jurisdiction (regions, sections, districts, areas, zones, centers, and what not), less conspicuous, and often quite unknown to the layman, yet indispensably linked as operating areas to the great central establishments in the national capital; in 1946, a bare list of such federal geographical units filled fifty-five pages of print, while individual cities like New York, Boston, Philadelphia, Chicago, and Los Angeles were the locations of literally hundreds of regional or other subordinate offices.[3] In the Treasury, War, Justice, Agriculture, Interior, Commerce, and Labor Departments, almost every service of a nature requiring it to operate locally (and the majority are such) has its own set of administrative regions or districts with directors, boards, or other authorities heading up divisional machinery. Even independent establishments like the Civil Service Commission, the Interstate Commerce Commission, the Federal Reserve Board, and the Veterans Administration are similarly equipped. It will not be surprising, therefore, to discover, in the next chapter, that of the entire federal civil service, only 195,000 is located in Washington and all the remainder elsewhere in the country.[4]

4. Types of functions

So vast and varied are the functions performed by the agencies of these different sorts that one could find a score of ways of classifying them. Obvious enough from what has already been said would be a classification as investigating, administrative, and quasi-legislative and quasi-judicial. Another grouping would throw them into three other categories,

[1] A Government Corporation Control Act of 1945 (59 *U.S. Stat. at Large,* 597), however, imposed a number of new financial and other limitations on such corporations. See C. H. Pritchett, "The Government Corporation Control Act of 1945," *Amer. Polit. Sci. Rev.,* XL, 495-509 (June, 1946). For good brief discussions of government corporations in general, see F. M. Marx [ed.], *Elements of Public Administration* (New York, 1946), Chap. XI, and M. Fainsod and L. Gordon, *Government and the American Economy* (New York, 1941), Chap. XIX.

[2] See Chaps. XXVII, XXXI below. Current information about the organization and activities of all branches of the administrative system will be found in the *United States Government Manual,* which one has only to leaf through to be impressed with the magnitude of the present establishment.

[3] In 1947, some 1,200 in New York City, 1,000 in Chicago, and 500 each in Philadelphia and Los Angeles.

[4] J. W. Fesler, "Federal Administrative Regions," *Amer. Polit. Sci. Rev.,* XXX, 257-268 (Apr., 1936); E. Latham, *The Federal Field Service* (Chicago, 1947).

as follows: (1) those that involve, not service to or regulation of the public directly, but rather service to other agencies of the government, such as is rendered by the Treasury Department, the Bureau of the Budget, the Civil Service Commission, and various authorities having to do with purchasing and distributing supplies; (2) those that consist, at least primarily, in rendering services directly to the people, and including the great bulk of the work of such departments as Agriculture, Commerce, Labor, Post-Office, and Interior, and of establishments like the Office of Education; and (3) those that are, to be sure, for the ultimate benefit of the people, but which consist immediately in the regulation and restraint of private individuals and corporations, good examples being the work of the Department of Justice, the Interstate Commerce Commission, the Federal Trade Commission, and the Securities and Exchange Commission. Still another, though related, way of viewing the matter would be to think of the functions of a department, for example, as falling into (1) "overhead," or "staff," functions, having to do with personnel, equipment, funds, and other means by which the department's work is carried on—a matter of departmental housekeeping—and (2) "direct service," or "line," functions, having to do with the services rendered or regulations imposed in relation to the public. Needless to say, the latter functions constitute an agency's sole reason for existence; all others are only means to an end.

By its nature, administration is the work of subordinates; even the heads of departments are subordinate to the president. Consequently, all administrators are subject to control from some source. In point of fact, members of the national administration are subject to control from a number of sources. To begin with, they are controlled by and responsible to their immediate superiors; and this applies to heads of departments no less than to every one else. Under cabinet systems, department chiefs, as ministers, are responsible to the popular branch of the legislature. But not so under our presidential system; here, whatever such officials do is considered as done by the president; he takes responsibility for their acts before Congress and the country, and, fortified with the power not only of direction but of removal, he naturally will hold them answerable directly to himself. At the same time, Congress also has a place in the picture, because, after all, it not only has set up the departments and directly or indirectly authorized virtually all of the other agencies, but often has fixed their duties and functions; and, defined in this way by law, such duties and functions are normally beyond the power of the president to curb or countermand—except in so far as he may take the dubious course of neglecting or refusing to see that they are performed. Congress, furthermore, controls through the power of the purse, through its right to demand reports and conduct investigations, and, in extreme cases, through its power of impeachment. Finally, there is a possibility of control also by the courts. The general principle is that when an

5. Lines of responsibility and control

administrative officer is carrying out a provision of law which manifestly leaves room for discretion, he is performing a political act and cannot be called to account for it in a court, but that, on the other hand, when a duty or action is so defined by law as to allow no latitude for choice, it is *ministerial* and subject to judicial review. As compared with administrators in the departments, independent establishments (some of which, as has been observed, are only incidentally administrative, or not such at all) sustain somewhat varying, and even uncertain, relationships. Some are clearly responsible to the president; others, rather to Congress; still others are more or less answerable to both, or even occasionally to neither; and the confusion that may arise at this point furnishes one of the arguments sometimes employed against the multiplication of such bodies.

Department Heads as Administrative and Advisory Officers

Rather than inject a wearisome catalogue of departments and independent establishments here or at any other point in this book, our plan will be to call attention to the organization and functions of the more important ones when later discussing such topics as foreign affairs, finance, defense, commerce, agriculture, and labor. It will be helpful, however, at the present point, to take note of some principal tasks and duties which heads of departments have in common—apart from their cabinet membership, which has been touched upon in another place.[1]

1. Appointing and removing subordinates

To begin with, the great bulk of subordinate officials and employees in the departments are appointed, directly or indirectly, by the department chiefs—acting, of course, as always, in the president's name. One must hasten to add that by far the larger proportion of the positions filled in this way have now been placed in the classified service, which means that the appointments must be made under the restrictions laid down in the civil service laws and regulations. This, of course, greatly narrows the appointing officer's discretion and leaves him with relatively little "patronage" of a strictly political character. The power is, nevertheless, an important one; and with it goes a power of removal, likewise restricted, to be sure, by civil service regulations, yet also decidedly substantial.

2. Directing the work of the department

Subject to the supreme directing power of the president and to varying amounts of control by Congress (and, if the truth be told, by more experienced and often better informed subordinates), each department head guides and supervises the work of all bureaus, divisions, offices, and other agencies in the department under his care. How much he will himself be directed by the president will depend upon circumstances, *e.g.*, how strongly disposed a given president may be to assert himself, how much confidence the president has in the secretary's capacity and judgment, and the degree to which decisions of major importance are required

[1] See pp. 438-443 above.

by special conditions existing at a given time. But in any event it falls to the department head to wield a general power of direction and control (including discipline) over the branch of administration intrusted to him, as also to represent the department's interests in procuring appropriations, additional personnel, increases of pay, and better working conditions.[1]

Another highly important function is that of issuing rules and regulations. The far-reaching and ever-expanding ordinance power of the president has been commented on in another connection.[2] Many "executive orders" relating to the functioning of a department, however, are actually prepared by the department head or under his direction. Moreover, in many instances, administrative regulations are not only prepared in the departments, but promulgated in their name, or even in the name of a bureau or division. Good examples include the voluminous regulations under which the postal service is carried on and patents granted. Indeed, each department head is authorized by statute "to prescribe regulations, not inconsistent with law, for the government of his department, the conduct of its officers and clerks, the distribution and performance of its business, and the custody, use, and preservation of the records, papers, and property appertaining to it," and also to make rules appropriate for securing proper examination of accounts. Furthermore, broad regulatory powers covering important matters have been conferred on particular department heads, bureau chiefs, and the like, as well as upon commissions and other agencies outside of the departments. For example, the secretary of the treasury has been authorized to prescribe regulations for enforcing the customs and internal revenue laws, and for ferreting out the counterfeiting of the currency of the United States; and the secretary of agriculture has been authorized to make rules governing the importation and interstate movement of animals and plants, the protection of forest reservations and of migratory birds, and the execution of acts of Congress relating to meat inspection. The reasons for the remarkable growth of "subordinate," or "administrative," legislation in the departments and independent establishments are, of course, similar to those accounting for the steady widening of the ordinance power of the president himself—boiling down to the sheer inability of Congress, when legislating, to anticipate and provide for the thousand and one detailed situations that have to be met when a law is being brought home to the people in terms of day-to-day enforcement.[3]

3. Issuing rules and regulations

[1] On the position of the department head as director, see P. H. Appleby, "Organizing Around the Head of a Large Federal Department," *Pub. Admin. Rev.*, VI, 205-212 (Summer, 1946).

[2] See pp. 460-462 above.

[3] The legislative activities of heads of departments are, of course, by no means confined to issuing rules and regulations. As pointed out elsewhere, such officials furnish legislative information, appear before congressional committees, advise with the president on legislative measures and programs, and have much to do with initiating and preparing bills for the consideration of Congress.

4. Decid-
ing ap-
peals
Still another important thing that the department head has to do is to decide disputes arising out of acts of his subordinates. In the administration of the laws governing such matters as immigration, conservation, the postal service, taxation, and social security, great numbers of controversies inevitably develop. Persons affected unfavorably may feel that an official has exceeded his powers, or that he has reached a decision not warranted by the facts in the case; and fairness demands that opportunity be afforded for a reconsideration of the decision or action. Conceivably, all such questions might be carried to the courts. But the federal Supreme Court itself has explained that, while appeal to the courts is proper enough when the construction of a statute is involved, such appeal, if permitted in the multitude of disputes arising out of the ordinary field operations of the departments, would so swamp the courts as to "entail practically a suspension of some of the most important functions of government."[1] Hence, except when decision hinges upon an interpretation of law, appeal normally lies only to higher administrative officials or boards, including in the later stages the heads of departments; and in many kinds of cases—for example, appeals against closure of the mails to persons and concerns alleged to be engaged in fraudulent transactions —the verdict of the department head is final, although in a limited number there is appeal to the president himself.[2] "Administrative adjudication" on these lines comes in for a good deal of criticism from people who consider that functions of a judicial nature ought to be performed only by courts. Like administrative legislation, however, it is not only inevitable, but, under suitable safeguards, entirely proper.[3]

5. Sup-
plying
informa-
tion and
giving
advice
The statutes creating the State, War, and Navy Departments expressly made the heads of those establishments responsible to the president; those creating the Treasury and Interior Departments did not do this, specifying rather that the department head should "report" to Congress. Manifestly, the first-named departments are more immediate organs of the president in carrying out his constitutional functions than are the others. In actual practice, however, all department heads are alike responsible to the chief executive; and all submit reports and recommendations which quickly become common property at both ends of Pennsylvania Avenue. Both president and Congress, furthermore, may at any time make requests of department heads for information, with or without opinions and advice. The president usually asks informally and orally for such data as he desires, although of course he may ask in writ-

[1] American School of Magnetic Healing v. McAnnulty, 187 U. S. 94 (1902).

[2] If it be wondered how the rather famous postal-censorship case of Hannegan v. Esquire (237 U. S. 146, 1946) got into the courts, the answer is supplied by the fact that the case turned on basic interpretation of the postal statutes. In its decision, the Supreme Court sustained an injunction restraining the postmaster-general from enforcing an order revoking the second-class permit of Esquire magazine.

[3] For further consideration of this matter, in relation principally to the independent regulatory commissions as distinguished from the executive departments, see pp. 486-489 below.

ing. Congress, or either house, normally makes its requests through the medium of resolutions. Armed with the power of removal, the president is able to enforce compliance. But Congress is in a different position; if a department head refuses to respond to a request, and is upheld in doing so by the president, it is helpless unless willing to resort to the extreme expedient of impeachment. The Supreme Court has held, furthermore, that when the head of a department is required to give information, he may do so through subordinates, rather than in person.[1]

Finally, all heads of departments, but especially those of such departments as the Treasury, Interior, Agriculture, and Labor, are called upon to serve *ex officiis* as members of various supervising or coördinating boards and committees. In some instances, duties are only nominal, but in others there is important work to be done.

6. Serving on boards and committees

The Growth of Independent Establishments

At the close of the first hundred years under the constitution, there were still only seven executive departments, concerned almost entirely with the old-line, primary functions of government such as foreign relations, finance, justice, and defense. Not long thereafter, however, three additional departments, having to do with agriculture, commerce, and labor, made their appearance, and along with them, as indicated above, the earliest important independent establishments. Later on, proposals for still more departments were plentiful. Aside from a new Air Force Department instituted under the reorganization of national defense in 1947,[2] none of these prevailed; but this did not prevent separate administrative and regulatory agencies from continuing to multiply. On the contrary, they sprang up like mushrooms—some (like the Federal Trade Commission in 1914 and the United States Tariff Commission in 1916) as products of the vigorous regulatory policies of the first Wilson Administration, others in years of readjustment (especially 1920-21) following World War I, and ever so many more in the era of the New Deal, when, in furtherance of the steadily broadening recovery and reform program of the Roosevelt Administration, Washington became a veritable labyrinth of new "alphabetical" establishments, a few of them attached more or less loosely to a department, but the majority having no such connection. In a constantly changing scene, some agencies, of course, disappeared because of time limits, some on account of shifts of policy, some because of judicial decisions overthrowing the legislation on which they rested, still others by consolidations or other forms of reorganization. But many dropped out only to be replaced by more or less similar sub-

Stages

---

[1] Miller *v.* Mayor of New York, 109 U. S. 394 (1883). One department head is charged in a particular degree with giving advice, namely, the attorney-general, from whom the president habitually solicits opinions upon the constitutionality or legal propriety of contemplated executive actions or of legislation which he has in mind or which is before him for signature.

[2] See pp. 824-825 below.

stitutes; entirely new ones—like the Social Security Board in 1935—kept thrusting themselves into the picture; and, altogether, an official committee which surveyed the situation in 1936 [1] was able to find—entirely apart from the bewildering array of agencies inside several of the larger departments—not fewer than ninety different federal establishments.[2] One would not need to be told, too, that after 1940 the defense effort and the later war gave rise to a maze of new establishments of the kind (many loosely appended, as on a peg, to the Office for Emergency Management in the Executive Office of the President), although in a number of instances destined to be only temporary.[3]

Reasons How is this remarkable development (paralleled, too, in the states) to be accounted for? Why so great multiplication of activities? And why, in so many cases, activities assigned to independent establishments rather than to the regular departments? One can understand that in wartime or in depression emergency, government must embark upon many novel and improvised activities; also that the shortest cut to arranging for carrying them on may easily seem to be to assign them to agencies especially created for the purpose. But how account for the great establishments like the Interstate Commerce Commission, the Federal Trade Commission, and many more that have been set up in normal times with a view to permanence and endowed, as the years have passed, with ever-growing powers? The answer is to be found in (1) the overflowing of state boundaries by trade and business, and by programs of social amelioration, requiring that state regulation be supplemented by national control, and (2) the inability of Congress—on account of the technical character, the ceaseless fluctuations, and the widening scope of the problems involved—to supply the needed regulation on other than very broad and general lines. But why assign the resulting functions to an independent establishment rather than to a department? There is no single reason. Sometimes the decision has been made for no good reason at all—because of personal or political considerations, or even sheer carelessness. Sometimes Congress (or the president acting under the authority of Congress) has been reluctant to impose upon a department still more heterogeneous tasks than it already had. Often it has been considered that the work to be provided for would be performed more satisfactorily (a) by officials appointed directly by the president and Senate, for relatively long terms, than by subordinates in a department, and (b) by a non-partisan (or more truly bipartisan) board bringing several minds to

---

[1] The President's Committee on Administrative Management. See p. 483 below.

[2] For a tabulation as of 1933 (at the beginning of the New Deal), see L. F. Schmeckebier, "Organization of the Executive Branch of the National Government of the United States," *Amer. Polit. Sci. Rev.,* XXVIII, 952-956 (Dec., 1933). All changes from that date to 1942 are recorded in supplementary lists compiled by Mr. Schmeckebier and published from time to time in later issues of the same journal. Current lists nowadays will be found in the *United States Government Manual.*

[3] See pp. 816-819 below. All this, of course, was in addition to much expansion of machinery within the departments.

bear upon the problems of policy-making involved, than by officials acting singly. Occasionally, decision has been dictated by the convenience of
carrying on some important enterprise of the government through the
instrumentality of a corporation, chartered under the laws of one of the
states or of the District of Columbia. Often influential, too, has been a
desire to assign functions to agencies, particularly boards and commissions, less directly under the control of the president, and more responsible to Congress, than are bureaus or services within a department.[1]

Viewing the independent establishments as a group, some are discovered to be merely fact-finding agencies, with no power to do anything
except carry on inquiries and make reports. Of such nature is the United
States Tariff Commission, charged with studying the administration,
operation, and effects of the tariff laws and reporting its findings to the
president and Congress. A few are found to be primarily investigative,
but with authority also to use their influence, in more or less direct ways,
to promote definite ends, conditions, or interests. Increasing numbers,
however, are charged with administrative duties; many, too, with making
regulations to apply and supplement the broadly phrased acts of Congress, on lines which, even though the courts may shrink from admitting
it, are clearly legislative; many, in addition, wield weighty judicial—or
again to speak by the book, *quasi*-judicial—powers. In certain instances,
legislative and judicial work quite transcends administration in any exact
sense of the term, bringing the establishments closer functionally to Congress or the courts than to the president. Indeed, nearly all of the greater
commissions, *e.g.*, the Interstate Commerce Commission, the Federal
Trade Commission, the Federal Communications Commission, and the
Federal Securities and Exchange Commission, defy the principle of separation of powers by being at one and the same time administrative,
legislative, and judicial, and indeed also investigative and advisory. It
goes without saying that service with agencies of this nature presupposes
both ability and experience; and it is gratifying to observe that while
practically all commissioners are on a political basis in the sense of being
appointed by the president and Senate, a large proportion of them bring
to their tasks both of the qualifications mentioned, often including experience in other, and sometimes similar, federal or state positions.[2]

Kinds of power exercised

---

[1] In pursuance of this objective, members are usually given longer terms than the
president (often seven years), and also overlapping terms, so that no chief executive
will likely be able to determine the entire personnel of the agency. We have seen,
too, that the president's power to remove members of boards and commissions
created by Congress is limited. See pp. 456–457 above.

[2] This aspect is treated fully in E. P. Herring, *Federal Commissioners; A Study of
Their Careers and Qualifications* (Cambridge, Mass., 1936). The best treatise on the
general subject of independent establishments is R. E. Cushman, *The Independent
Regulatory Commissions* (New York, 1941).

Structural and Functional Reorganization

Growing criticism of earlier conditions

It was, no doubt, inevitable that an administrative structure built up over the years largely without plan or design, "like the barns, shacks, silos, toolsheds, and garages of an old farm," should come to have serious defects; and far back in the present century criticism of it began to be heard, not only from members of Congress, writers, taxpayers, and administrators themselves, but from a rising generation of professional students of public administration as a science and an art. Administration is the costliest part of government, and the taxpayer was stirred by the rapid multiplication of agencies to be supported, each naturally bent upon consolidating its position, expanding its activities, fattening its payrolls, and each tending to become a sort of parent stem from which other newer agencies and services continually sprouted.[1] Much criticism was motivated also by dislike, in principle, of the extension of government control over business and other aspects of economic and social life—tantamount, we were told, to paternalism, and bordering dangerously on socialism—as well as by hostility to the projection of national regulation into fields traditionally regarded as provinces of the states. In other words, what many critics had in mind primarily was the functions performed rather than the machinery employed. Yet persons—especially professional students of the administrative process—who fixed their attention upon the latter also found plenty of grounds for complaint.[2]

Some cardinal principles of good administrative organization

Careful consideration of what is involved in efficient and economical administration in city, state, or nation has brought agreement on certain rather definite principles. (1) The multifold tasks to be performed should be grouped according to their nature and each group assigned to one of a relatively small number of fairly large and more or less coördinate departments. (2) The grouping should be on a carefully considered functional basis, so that each department will occupy and have full control over a definite and integrated field. (3) Every agency and every official should stand in some definite relation to some superior agency or authority, the lines of control running downward, sharply and clearly, and those of responsibility just as sharply and clearly upward. (4) All personnel except policy-making officials at the top should be organized in a civil service, classified according to the nature of the duties to be performed, recruited by a civil service commission (or similar authority) employing suitable tests, and enjoying security of tenure. Other principles, relating for example to budgeting, might be mentioned; but the foregoing are chiefly of concern here and in the chapter to follow.

[1] "The nearest approach to immortality on earth is a government bureau," J. F. Byrnes, *Speaking Frankly* (New York, 1937), 7.
[2] The point of view is represented, though with some over-emphasis, in J. M. Beck, *Our Wonderland of Bureaucracy* (New York, 1932); also in L. Sullivan, *The Dead Hand of Bureaucracy* (Indianapolis, 1940), and *Bureaucracy Runs Amuck* (Indianapolis, 1944).

Tested by standards such as these, the organization of national administration a decade or two ago disclosed at least three major shortcomings. First and most obvious was the lack of coherence and integration inevitably flowing from the circumstances under which the system had been built up. Many offices and bureaus, to be sure, upon being created to meet some definite administrative need, had been fitted into the scheme in a manner entirely appropriate. But in perhaps equally numerous instances a new unit or service had been simply tacked on at any point seeming at the moment convenient, or dictated by political or other questionable considerations. In many instances, no new unit or service ought to have been created at all; an existing one ought merely to have been enlarged or otherwise fitted to the purpose. As a consequence, not only did independent establishments spring up on all sides, but some of the executive departments (notably the Treasury) became literally jungles of unrelated units and services. Administrative and regulatory work in great fields like public health and conservation of natural resources was parcelled out among half a dozen different agencies, scattered through three or four departments or in no department at all—a situation from which could result only confusion, duplication, and waste, accentuated by jealousies and disputes among department heads and bureau chiefs as to who should control particular activities.[1]

Former violations of these principles:

1. General looseness and planlessness

A second main 'defect, closely connected with the foregoing, was the lack of effective responsibility to, and of control by, the chief executive. The fault was not the president's; agencies were so numerous and their relationships so confused that no man could possibly keep an eye on all of them. As a result, however,—asserted President Roosevelt's Committee on Administrative Management (to be mentioned again shortly)— there had grown up, without plan or intent, "a headless fourth branch of the government, responsible to no one, and impossible of coördination with the general policies and work of the government as determined by the people through their duly elected representatives." As indicated above, good administration presumes direct and simple lines of authority and responsibility. The lines running between many of the federal agencies and the president were, however, both devious and obscure. Indeed, many boards and commissions were so far removed from presidential control that their performance of administrative functions con-

2. A "headless fourth branch of the government"

---

[1] A survey made by Herbert Hoover as secretary of commerce in 1925 revealed that at that time four different bureaus, in two departments, had to do with public health; eight agencies, in five departments, were charged with the conservation of resources; fourteen agencies, in nine departments, were engaged in public works construction and engineering; another group of fourteen, in six departments, administered merchant marine laws; and the purchasing of some two hundred million dollars' worth of supplies was carried out through no fewer than forty agencies in Washington and thirty-four in other parts of the country. On a later occasion, Mr. Hoover commented facetiously upon having found that the brown bears were under the jurisdiction of the Department of Agriculture, the grizzly bears under the guardianship of the secretary of the treasury, and the polar bears under his own protection as secretary of commerce!

stituted a positive invasion of the president's rights and responsibilities as over-all manager of national administration.

8. Boards and commissions unfitted for administrative work

And this matter of the performance of administrative functions by boards and commissions entailed a deficiency of still more serious character. As the President's Committee freely conceded, for purposes of consultation, discussion, advice, and reflection of diverse views and citizen opinion, such plural agencies are "extremely useful and necessary." But, as the Committee also said emphatically, they are too slow and cumbersome to serve acceptably as agencies of administration. Many, nevertheless, had been charged with important administrative duties; and the error, in the Committee's opinion, urgently needed correction.

Obstacles to reorganization

For a long time, the idea of overhauling the national administrative structure was paid lip-service in government circles, but with action paralyzed. Manifestly, many arrangements would be involved which rested upon acts of Congress; so that authority to proceed must come from that body. Indeed, there were members who contended that reorganization was a legislative function which Congress could not constitutionally delegate. Most students of the problem, however, agreed that Congress was not fitted or equipped for the task, that any worth-while reorganization would have to be planned rather by the executive branch itself and put into effect by presidential order, and that, at most, Congress ought merely to confer the necessary blanket authority and reserve some right of veto upon changes proposed. Doubtful, nevertheless, about many of the issues involved, and hesitant to intrust so much discretion to the chief executive, Congress was inclined to shy away from the subject and, when finally induced to act, to confer power only rather grudgingly and with strings attached. As would be surmised, too, commissioners, bureau chiefs, and other officials and agencies, entertaining a strong sense of their own importance, coveting a maximum of independence, and unwilling to be "abolished" or perchance even transferred, were commonly predisposed against any reorganization program, which, once launched, might place them in peril. The pros and cons of the various suggested changes, also, were generally rather technical, and people at large, although certainly standing to profit from increased efficiency and economy, were neither much acquainted with the concrete issues involved nor interested in them. Even among the well-informed, there was honest doubt as to whether some of the changes most often advocated—especially those looking to the gathering of scattered agencies into existing or new executive departments—would not lead to undesirable extensions of national control, with corresponding weakening of the states. Fear was expressed, likewise, lest reorganization be found to have had the effect of throwing some of the services or agencies into politics.

The Reorganization Act of 1939

Presidents Taft, Wilson, and Harding gave their support to reorganization proposals that eventually came to nothing; and although, under an act signed by President Hoover a few hours before he went out of office, President Franklin D. Roosevelt was able, by executive orders in 1933-34, to introduce a number of changes, the field was still largely untouched when he, in 1936, appointed his Committee on Administrative Management to make a full survey of the situation and submit proposals. Reaching Congress at a time, in 1937, when feeling was running high over the President's project for reorganizing the Supreme Court,[1] bills aimed at carrying out the resulting recommendations encountered rough sailing.[2] At length, however, in the spring of 1939, a Reorganization Act of major importance, giving the president much, although not all, of the authority urged by the Commission, was placed on the statute-book.[3] No change might be made in the number or names of the executive departments; fifteen additional specified agencies, including the principal regulatory commissions and certain other independent establishments, were to be left untouched; and the Commission's suggestions for extending the merit system in the civil service "upward, downward, and outward" found no reflection in the law.[4] Outside of these limitations, however, the president was authorized, until January 20, 1941, to "reduce, coördinate, consolidate, and reorganize" the various agencies of the government, employing for the purpose, not executive orders, but rather proposed "plans," which should become effective sixty days after being transmitted to Congress unless in the meantime disapproved in their entirety—by a sort of veto in reverse—by concurrent resolution of the two houses.[5] The objects of all changes were to be (1) to reduce

[1] See pp. 546-549 below.

[2] The report proper was published under the title of *Administrative Management in the Government of the United States* (Washington, D. C., 1937); the report, together with various supporting studies, under the title of *Report of the Committee* [on Administrative Management], *with Studies of Administrative Management in the Federal Government* (Washington, D. C., 1937). Supporting studies made by experts under the Committee's direction were published separately under appropriate titles.

Bracketing "good administration" with "consent of the governed" as a prime requisite of good government, the report recommended, in addition to other things, (1) that substantially all independent establishments, including the great commissions, be placed by presidential order in some one of the executive departments; (2) that after being placed in a department a commission be divided into an administrative section and a judicial section, the one to form a regular bureau or division of the department, the other to be in the department only for purposes of "administrative housekeeping" but otherwise wholly independent both of the department and of Congress; (3) that the Department of the Interior be renamed Department of Conservation and two new departments—Social Welfare and Public Works—be created; (4) that a National Resources Board be set up to serve as a permanent central planning agency under the president; (5) that the merit system be extended "upward, outward, and downward" to include all positions in the executive branch of the government except those of a policy-determining nature; and (6) that administrative reorganization be thenceforth viewed, not as something to be accomplished once for all and at a stroke, but as a continuous activity aimed at meeting changing needs and conditions.

[3] 53 *U. S. Stat. at Large,* 56.

[4] Various independent actions of 1938-40 (both legislative and executive) nevertheless vastly extended the merit system. See p. 500 below.

[5] The device of the "plan," rather than of executive order, was specified on the theory that the president would act in the matter in his legislative, rather than his executive, capacity, and also because there was doubt whether Congress can constitutionally nullify an executive act of the president by a mere concurrent resolution.

expenditures, (2) to increase efficiency, (3) to group agencies "according to major purpose," (4) to reduce the number of agencies, and (5) to "eliminate overlapping and duplication of effort."

Resulting changes   Under terms of this legislation, President Roosevelt, at intervals during 1939-40, submitted to Congress five successive "plans," or groups of proposals; although all evoked opposition, none was blocked; and together they gave the government's administrative organization a widely different appearance from before. Some agencies were abolished outright; several were shifted from one department to another; quite a number of those hitherto unattached were placed within some department; and a lengthy list of scattered ones were grouped under the three new coördinating "agencies" named above,[1] each headed by an administrator, and constituting a new level in the administrative set-up comparable in importance to the departments themselves.[2] The financial saving alone, Congress was assured, would amount to fifteen or twenty million dollars a year.

Wartime developments   There was still more to be done when 1941 arrived and the president's authority expired. For the time being, Congress refused to renew the grant. With the country plunged into war, however, a wholly new situation arose. On the one hand, the effects of the changes already made were blurred and rendered difficult to appraise by abnormal conditions; on the other, it became imperative that, for purposes of war efficiency, the president should continue to have powers (beyond those possessed as general executive, and even as commander-in-chief) to make readjustments. Congress, therefore, in the First War Powers Act, approved less than two weeks after Pearl Harbor, empowered the chief executive, during the continuance of the war and for six months thereafter, to make such redistributions of functions among administrative agencies as he should find desirable, so long as restricted to "matters relating to the conduct of the present war;" and under this authorization a multitude of new administrative agencies arose, accompanied by many transfers, consolidations, redistributions, and other changes, even in branches of the service ordinarily thought of as purely civilian.

A new Reorganization Act (1945)   In the summer of 1945, actual combat with the Axis powers finally came to an end. To be sure, the president's reorganizing authority was not immediately affected; legally, the United States remained at war, even with hostilities formally declared terminated on December 31, 1946. No sooner was the fighting over, however, than it became apparent that there would have to be new arrangements and new powers for reorganization. Special wartime administrative machinery began to be dismantled; sooner or later, the president's emergency authority would lapse; when this occurred, agencies transferred or consolidated under it would, unless

---

See J. D. Millett and L. Rogers, "The Legislative Veto and the Reorganization Act of 1939," *Pub. Admin. Rev.*, I, 176-189 (Winter, 1941).

[1] See p. 469 above.

[2] As indicated earlier, it was in one of these plans also that provision was made for the Executive Office of the President.

other provision were made, revert to their former positions, however desirable it might be that they should not do so; manifestly, after all that had happened to the administrative structure during nearly four years of war, extensive review and readjustment for peacetime would be a necessity. In this situation, President Truman asked Congress for a fresh grant of reorganizing authority; and the upshot was another general Reorganization Act (approved December 20, 1945),[1] bearing resemblance to the prewar measure of 1939 in again exempting specified agencies,[2] chiefly regulatory boards and commissions (although the President wanted all included), in giving Congress sixty days in which to veto any proposed plan, and in placing a time limit, contrary to the President's request, on the powers delegated—in the present instance, April 1, 1948. Instructing the director of the Bureau of the Budget to consult with the departments and establishments and prepare reorganization plans, the Chief Executive thereupon set forth boldly upon a course not unlike that traversed by his predecessor under the act of 1939. Three plans providing for some twenty-eight transfers, consolidations, and other changes (chiefly in the areas of housing, agriculture, welfare, and public lands) were laid before Congress in May, 1946; and although all met with flat rejection, by large majorities, at the hands of the House of Representatives, two escaped defeat in the Senate, with the result that they automatically became effective after the sixty-day period of suspension. Still further plans, relating chiefly to labor and housing, were submitted in 1947, with varying results.

From the foregoing outline, administrative reorganization may appear a problem or task that runs on and on, without end; and such indeed it is. Four times since 1933, statutory authority to reorganize has been conferred upon the executive; and the number of agencies abolished or consolidated, or functions transferred, exceeds three hundred. Even with all this, however, need for further and continuous readjustments stretches out ahead; and, with the president's delegated authority soon to expire (in 1948), Congress in 1947 projected a fresh start by creating a bipartisan and widely representative Commission on Organization of the Executive Branch of the Government, charged with investigating the existing organization and methods of operation of all departments, bureaus, agencies, boards, commissions, and the like in the executive branch and reporting to the two houses promptly after the first meeting of the Eighty-first Congress in January, 1949—significantly, after the turmoil of the 1948 elections was over.[3] From the able group made up for this

A continuing task

---

[1] 59 *U. S. Stat. at Large,* 613.

[2] Twelve, however, this time, instead of fifteen. Indeed, proposals relating to five of the twelve might be made if presented apart from any others.

[3] With twelve members in all (six from each of the two leading parties), the Commission consists of four persons appointed by the president, four by the president *pro tempore* of the Senate, and four by the speaker of the House of Representatives —in the respective instances, two being selected from the executive branch, two from the Senate, and two from the House. with two also from private life. Included in

ambitious undertaking may be expected the most thorough and impartial over-all study of reorganization problems since that carried out by President Roosevelt's Committee on Administrative Management in 1936-37; and in all probability the submission of its report will start a fresh round of reorganization effort—presumably through new grants of authority to the chief executive to carry out recommendations made.[1] As observed above, the earlier President's Committee urged a conception of administrative reorganization as being, not a task to be performed at a stroke and thereupon considered finished, but rather an activity to be carried on substantially all of the time; and this point of view is now coming to be widely shared.

Some results achieved

The general record of the reorganizations of the past ten or fifteen years justifies a few major conclusions. One is that the president's position as chief executive has been strengthened by improved integration of the agencies for whose functioning he is responsible. A second is that Congress has in no way suffered from its grants of reorganizing authority: no reorganization thus far has impaired congressional control over administration. On the contrary, with the agencies better coördinated, Congress has been put in an improved position to review their work and to enact needed legislation. Significantly, there have been only one or two instances in which Congress has ever seriously considered undoing an administrative change. Lastly, however, it must be added that, notwithstanding high hopes and large promises, administrative reorganization has not resulted in substantial reductions in the cost of government. Savings on a rather insignificant scale have no doubt flowed from some curtailments of personnel and some consolidations of effort. Programs of activity have, however, commonly expanded as machinery was reconstructed; and the rewards of reorganization must normally be looked for, not in terms of dollars and cents, but in better correlation and direction of such programs and in strengthened capacity of the government to meet critical situations thrust upon it.

The Special Problem of the Regulatory Commissions

Peculiar functions and status

Congress, as we have seen, has habitually refused to allow the Interstate Commerce Commission, the Federal Trade Commission, and several other agencies of that nature to be tampered with by the president in

the Commission's membership are ex-President Herbert Hoover, Secretary of Defense James Forrestal, ex-Ambassador Joseph P. Kennedy (first chairman of the Security and Exchange and Maritime Commissions), Mr. Dean Acheson, former under-secretary of state and experienced in investigating the work of the independent establishments, Civil Service Commissioner Arthur S. Flemming, and Professor James K. Pollock of the University of Michigan. On the Commission and its task, see F. Heady, "A New Approach to Federal Executive Reorganization," *Amer. Polit. Sci. Rev.,* XLI, 1118-1126 (Dec., 1947). Ex-President Hoover was chosen Commission chairman.

[1] While the bill was pending, both the comptroller-general of the United States and the director of the Bureau of the Budget expressed skepticism about any significant results being attained through this new approach to the problem. But Congress was not deterred from passing the measure unanimously in both houses.

his reorganization plans. And for this there is a reason, although by some regarded as inadequate. To a degree, these major independent establishments administer and enforce, and accordingly are parts of the administrative system. But they do much more than simply administer and enforce. Far beyond most mere administrative agencies, they interpret broadly-phrased acts of Congress, supplement them, amplify them, and in effect add to them—so that, regardless of the theory that legislative power cannot be delegated, they become to all intents and purposes little legislatures, at all events legislative arms of Congress. At the same time, they also receive complaints, take evidence, hear counsel, study briefs, and make decisions—which, if this does not transform them into courts, certainly makes them at times almost indistinguishable from such to the naked eye. The commissions, therefore, stand closer to Congress and to the judiciary than to the president; to protect them against being "packed" by a president on coming to office, their members, as we have seen, are given longer terms than his (frequently seven years) and also overlapping terms; and Congress jealously guards them against presidential maneuverings that might eventually land them in one or another of the executive departments, where they would come under full control from the White House. If anything is to be done about them, Congress wants to do it.

This does not mean that nothing has needed to be done. On the contrary, some of the commissions were until lately under a heavy crossfire of complaints. Prominent among the criticisms voiced were (1) that, combining administrative, legislative, and judicial powers as they did, they defied the principle of separation on which our liberties are supposed to be to a considerable extent dependent, and (2) that they had been allowed to become too literally *independent* establishments, self-contained and operating almost as if in air-tight compartments. But more particular exception was taken to various procedures which, in the almost total absence of earlier regulation in the statutes, the commissions built up over a long period of years. Rules and regulations vitally affecting the rights of persons and property, it was charged, were often made without the people concerned being allowed opportunity to be heard; findings and decisions of a judicial nature were arrived at and enforced without a chance for injured persons to appeal to the courts.[1] There *was* some public access to the commissions, and there *was*, under certain conditions, appeal to the courts. The complaints mentioned, however, and others like them, once had enough foundation to stir lively discussion; and in 1940 a drastic measure for applying correctives (the Logan-Walter bill[2]) failed to become law only because of a sharply worded presidential veto.[3] As

Criticisms and proposals

[1] On the development of administrative justice, see C. B. Swisher, *The Growth of Constitutional Power in the United States* (Chicago, 1946), Chap. VI.

[2] Entitled: "A bill to provide for the more expeditious settlement of disputes with the United States, and for other purposes."

[3] The severer features of this measure (drafted by a Committee on Administrative

an alternative to this rather badly conceived proposal, a milder plan was, however, brought forward by a Committee on Administrative Procedure, appointed by President Roosevelt, presided over and indeed originally suggested by Attorney-General Francis Biddle, and hence generally known as the Attorney-General's Committee—a group of lawyers who worked long and hard on the subject; and after the matter had been side-tracked for a number of years by the war, Congress finally, in 1946, passed an Administrative Procedure Act [1] based largely on the Committee's recommendations and promptly approved at the White House.

The Administrative Procedure Act of 1946

The measure referred to is a complicated piece of legislation, and only a few of its provisions of broadest import can be indicated here. In general, it deals with the procedures to be followed by government agencies in performing quasi-legislative and quasi-judicial functions, and with the relations of such agencies to the courts through the channel of judicial review; and the agencies covered are not simply the regulatory commissions, mainly responsible for the problems involved, but, by definition of the act itself, all "authorities" embraced within the national government except Congress, the courts, and the governments of territories, possessions, and the District of Columbia. Principal requirements imposed on the agencies are: (1) that they shall give full publicity to the machinery and methods by which they work and to the ways in which persons desiring to bring proposals and requests to them may do so; (2) that when they contemplate making a rule they shall give ample notice, personally or through the *Federal Register,* to all individuals or corporations that might be concerned, at the same time indicating the authority by which they plan to act and specifying the terms of the proposed rule, or at least the subjects and issues involved; (3) that officers or employees investigating and presenting cases for adjudication shall be allowed no part in deciding them, *i.e.,* the functions of prosecutor and judge shall be kept separate; [2] (4) that, so far as the orderly conduct of business will permit, any interested person shall be allowed to appear before any agency or its officers or representatives for the presentation and determination of any issue, request, petition, or controversy; (5) that persons compelled to appear (and there is full power to subpœna witnesses) shall be permitted to be accompanied by counsel or other qualified representatives; and (6) that any relevant information or testimony, documentary or oral, shall be received, with any interested party entitled to present rebuttal evidence and to cross-examine witnesses. Another

---

Law set up by the American Bar Association in 1933) were inspired by a particular dislike of lawyers for the procedures of the Federal Labor Relations Board and the Federal Securities and Exchange Commission. Some of the old-line commissions were, indeed, expressly exempted from the bill's provisions.

[1] 60 *U. S. Stat. at Large,* 237.

[2] That this safeguard was not immediately made effective in all agencies is illustrated by the provisions of the Labor-Management Relations [Taft-Hartley] Act of 1947 transferring prosecuting functions under the Labor Relations Board to a new "general counsel." See p. 742 below.

stipulation was that after a year every agency should appoint and employ, under civil service regulations, as many competent "examiners" as might be needed for carrying on investigations, preparing cases, and doing general "spade work" preparatory to agency action.[1]

Moreover, to clear up the hitherto frequently obscure matter of appeal to the courts against agency actions, it is provided that every such action made reviewable by statute, and every other final action for which no other adequate remedy in any court is otherwise provided, shall be subject to judicial review, thus establishing the right of a person unfavorably affected by an agency action to go into court in quest of redress.[2] And the court so appealed to is required to set aside any agency action, finding, or conclusion discovered to be arbitrary or entailing abuse of discretion, or in excess of statutory or constitutional authority, or arrived at without observance of regular lawful proceedings, or unwarranted by the facts (in so far as the facts are reviewable *de novo* by the reviewing court). Pending court action, also, any agency may, in the interest of substantial justice, postpone the date for any of its actions to take effect.

New provisions for judicial review

Although applicable to other federal establishments besides regulatory commissions, the new law is of importance chiefly in connection with them—for the obvious reason that it is principally they that carry on activities of the kinds envisaged. So long as the commissions remain independent establishments, there will be people to criticize them on that score; and others will continue troubled about the fusion in them of administrative, legislative, and judicial functions, although one would be hard put to it to say how this could be wholly avoided. The safeguards, however, set up in 1946 should go far toward remedying procedural defects of which there had been just complaint; and improvements at points where the actions of such bodies impinge upon the rights and liberties of the people are immensely more significant than any mere readjustments of structure or machinery that might be undertaken.

REFERENCES

L. D. White, *Introduction to the Study of Public Administration* (rev. ed., New York, 1939), Chaps. XXXIII-XXXVIII.

M. E. Dimock, *Modern Politics and Administration; A Study of the Creative State* (New York, 1937), Chap. IX.

————, *The Executive in Action* (New York, 1945).

L. M. Short, *Development of National Administrative Organization in the United States* (Baltimore, 1923), Chaps. II-XIX, XXIII.

A. N. Christensen and E. M. Kirkpatrick, *The People, Politics, and the Politician; Readings in American Government* (New York, 1941 and 1947), Chaps. XVII-XVIII.

[1] In the legislation as enacted, one important recommendation of the Attorney-General's Committee found no place, *i.e.*, that a permanent Office of Administrative Procedure be created and assigned the task of continually studying problems in this field and proposing solutions.

[2] Except where statutes expressly preclude such review, or where an agency is by law given full and final discretionary authority.

P. Appleby, *Big Democracy* (New York, 1945).

H. D. Smith, *The Management of Your Government* (New York, 1945).

C. H. Wooddy, *The Growth of the Federal Government, 1915-1932* (New York, 1934).

R. E. Cushman, *The Independent Regulatory Commissions* (New York, 1941).

E. P. Herring, *Federal Commissioners; A Study of Their Careers and Qualifications* (Cambridge, Mass., 1936).

————, *Public Administration and the Public Interest* (New York, 1936).

A. W. Macmahon and J. D. Millett, *Federal Administrators; A Biographical Approach to the Problem of Departmental Management* (New York, 1939).

S. Wallace, *Federal Departmentalization* (New York, 1941).

E. Latham, *The Federal Field Service* (Chicago, 1947).

F. F. Blachly and M. E. Oatman, *Administrative Legislation and Adjudication* (Washington, D. C., 1934).

————, *Federal Regulatory Action and Control* (Washington, D. C., 1940).

J. P. Chamberlain, N. T. Dowling, and P. R. Hays, *The Judicial Function in Federal Administrative Agencies* (New York, 1942).

J. M. Landis, *The Administrative Process* (New Haven, 1939).

W. Gelhorn, *Federal Administrative Proceedings* (Baltimore, 1941).

J. M. Gaus, L. D. White, and M. E. Dimock, *Frontiers of Public Administration* (Chicago, 1936).

J. M. Gaus, *Reflections on Public Administration* (Univ. of Alabama, 1947).

L. D. White *et al.*, *New Horizons in Public Administration* (Univ. of Alabama, 1945).

L. Meriam and L. F. Schmeckebier, *Reorganization of the National Government; What Does It Involve?* (Washington, D. C., 1939).

F. M. Marx [ed.], "Federal Executive Reorganization: A Symposium," *Amer. Polit. Sci. Rev.*, XL, 1124-1168 (Dec., 1946), XLI, 48-84 (Feb., 1947).

————, [ed.], *Elements of Public Administration* (New York, 1946).

G. Warren [ed.], *The Federal Administrative Procedure Act and the Administrative Agencies* (New York, 1947).

F. H. Sherwood, "The Federal Administrative Procedure Act," *Amer. Polit. Sci. Rev.*, XLI, 271-281 (Apr., 1947).

President's Committee on Administrative Management, *Report of the Committee, with Studies of Administrative Management in the Federal Government* (Washington, D. C., 1937).

U. S. Attorney-General, Committee on Administrative Procedure, Report of, entitled *Administrative Procedure in Government Agencies*, 77th Cong., 1st Sess., Sen. Doc. No. 8 (1941).

J. Hart and E. E. Witte, *The Exercise of Rule-Making Power;* and *The Preparation of Proposed Legislative Measures by Administrative Departments* (Washington, D. C., 1937). Studies for the President's Committee on Administrative Management.

Service Monographs of the United States Government. A series of some seventy volumes dealing with various federal bureaus, commissions, and other administrative agencies, prepared under the auspices of the Institute for Government Research, and published in earlier years through the Johns Hopkins Press, Baltimore, and subsequently by the Brookings Institution, Washington, D. C. The series does not cover agencies created in later years, and in the case of older ones the volumes are often badly out of date.

Annual reports of the heads of the several departments, and reports of independent establishments, transmitted at the convening of Congress in regular session in January, and obtainable on application to the chief clerk of the department concerned or through the Superintendent of Documents, Washington, D. C.

United States Government Manual (Washington, D. C.). Published twice a year.

CHAPTER XXIII

THE EXECUTIVE CIVIL SERVICE

To the present point, our system of national administration has been viewed mainly on the higher managerial levels, and as operating principally in the national capital, although with plenty of branch agencies scattered over the country. But president, heads of departments, undersecretaries and assistant secretaries, division directors, bureau chiefs, and members of boards and commissions form only an insignificant fraction of the multitude of men and women who, year in and year out, carry on the civilian activities of the national government. For every one such official, literally thousands of others (officers and employees[1]) are found in the far-flung force known as the executive civil service—"executive," as being attached to the executive rather than the legislative or judicial branch of the government, and "civil" as differentiated from the Army, the Navy, the Marine Corps, the Coast Guard, and other establishments of a military character. Under our federal system, all of the states, together with their subdivisions such as counties and cities, have civil services of their own; and in the aggregate the personnel on these levels, in normal times, heavily outnumbers that on the federal level.[2] Starting with only some three hundred in 1789, the federal service, however, mounted to 208,000 by the close of the nineteenth century; rose to above 900,000 under impact of the First World War; ran along between 500,000 and 600,000 during the ensuing decade and a half; passed the million mark for the first time during the defense effort of 1940-41; stood at 1,545,131 when Pearl Harbor plunged the country into war; reached an

Scope and numbers

[1] In discussions of the administrative system, the terms "officer" and "employee" are often used rather loosely and even interchangeably. There is, however, a distinction—an officer being properly a person appointed to a public position *created by law* and involving responsibility for the enforcement of law, an employee a person merely *hired* by an officer or official body to do certain work and without any responsibility fixed by law. The difference is that between, for example, a collector of internal revenue and a stenographer in his office. For the federal Supreme Court's interpretation of the matter, see Burnap *v.* United States, 252 U. S. 512 (1920).

[2] Thus in 1941, when the federal service numbered 1,150,000, state and municipal services together numbered 3,240,000 (including, of course, teachers in public schools). During the ensuing war years, the federal service was almost tripled, and temporarily passed the state-municipal figure, which actually declined three and one-half per cent on account of loss of employees to the federal government, to the armed forces, and to war industries, and because of curtailment of state and local services. With peace restored, state and municipal services began to be rehabilitated; a total of 400,000 employees were added in 1946 alone; and nowadays the state and local again outnumber the federal. At the beginning of 1945, when the federal service stood at 3,375,000, combined state and local services numbered 3,135,000—a total of perhaps one-ninth of the nation's entire labor force. In October, 1947, the proportions were approximately 3,775,000 state and local and 2,000,000 federal. State and local increase is to be attributed to a number of factors, but especially to resumption and expansion of services curtailed by the war and to the wartime growth of cities.

all-time peak of 3,375,000 on January 1, 1945, and after tapering off somewhat during the later war months, and more rapidly after hostilities ceased, stood at the still huge figure of 2,285,570 at the end of December, 1946. Expansion of activities and controls in wartime invariably results in a greatly increased government personnel; but nothing like the enlargement of the federal service in 1941-43 was ever experienced in this country or elsewhere. In 1947, economy-minded Republican majorities in the new Eightieth Congress launched a drive (supported by some Democrats) for further sharp curtailments, and by the end of the year the total was brought down, as indicated above, to two millions. There was, however, little expectation that the normal peacetime figure would ever again fall below a million and a half.

During the war, at least a million and a quarter of the vast army of civilians on the federal payroll were employed in arsenals, shipyards, and other establishments normally under private control. Contrary to popular impression, however, the federal civil service, even in peacetime, is not made up simply of "government clerks" or "workers" engaged in dull routine. There are, of course, hundreds of thousands such. But there are also thousands of men and women of scholarship, professional training, and technical expertness, such as the nature of much modern governmental work requires: *e.g.*, chemists, biologists, meteorologists, physicians, sanitation authorities, foresters, geologists, agronomists, live-stock experts, entomologists, hydrographers; engineers (civil, electrical, hydraulic, mining, highway, etc.); economists, statisticians, and accountants; numerous lawyers; a great body of professional administrators.[1] Only a small proportion of the total force live and work in the national capital—in October, 1947, only 195,000, as compared with the 1,805,000 then constituting the field services, the latter performing duties in all parts of the land, including the dependencies, and, in the case of the diplomatic and consular establishments, in foreign countries as well. For many years before the war, the proportion of women in the service remained fairly constant at around nineteen per cent. Under wartime conditions, however, it rose to thirty-seven per cent, and in October, 1947, was still almost twenty per cent.[2]

[1] As far back as 1928, a Personnel Classification Board needed 1,300 pages of print to describe the more than two thousand types of positions then existing in the field service alone. Twenty-three different kinds of engineers were enumerated.

[2] Until 1932, the Civil Service Commission kept men and women eligibles on separate lists, and certified to appointing officers from one list or the other as requested. In the year indicated, however, an amended rule authorized the Commission to merge the existing registers, and thenceforth to certify eligibles without regard to sex unless the nature of the duties was such that, in the Commission's opinion, they could be performed only by men or by women, as the case might be. In normal times, the preference given men who have been in military service (see p 507 below) operates to keep the proportion of women lower than it otherwise might be. Since 1933, one of the three members of the Civil Service Commission has been a woman, first Lucile F. McMillin, widow of a former Tennessee congressman and governor, and afterwards (since 1946) a former secretary of labor, Frances Perkins.

Obviously it is the civil servants who—collecting the taxes, spending The crucial matter of personnel the money, carrying out the laws, handling the mails, protecting natural resources, inspecting mines and packing plants, mediating labor disputes, developing housing, operating agricultural programs, handling veterans' affairs, and what not—bring the national government close to the people (as close often as local governments themselves) and largely determine the public's ideas as to how efficient and useful that government is. To be sure, they are subordinates. But the service to which they belong is no mere piece of power-driven machinery—no mere collection of robots in a mechanized, impersonal "bureaucracy." On the contrary, it is a vast array of human personalities, with all the virtues and frailties, wants, and ambitions, of other people; and while the efficiency with which it discharges its functions depends to a degree upon the wisdom of the laws given it to administer, the intelligence of the supervision over it exercised from above, and the adequacy of financial provisions made for it, the matter of greatest importance is the fitness of the civil servants themselves for the jobs assigned them. For our purposes, discussion of the federal civil service therefore resolves itself largely into a survey of different aspects of civil service personnel. How are civil servants recruited? Are they selected and appointed for reasons of demonstrated merit, or on merely personal and political grounds? How are they classified and paid? How is their work evaluated, and under what conditions are they promoted? How are removals made, and why? What arrangements are there for retirement? What opportunities have civil servants for bettering their condition? What facilities are there for preparing young people to become civil servants? To what extent does the service offer opportunity for a career?

The Era of Spoils

For a generation or more after the national government was organized Generally satisfactory appointments, 1789-1829 under the constitution, the selection and appointment of administrative officers and employees left little to be desired. Washington placed the matter at the outset upon a high plane by announcing his intention to "nominate such persons alone to offices ... as shall be the best qualified;" and although the rise of political parties led his successors to give more weight to political considerations when filling posts as they fell vacant or as new ones were created, there were not many removals for partisan reasons—except perhaps during the first two years of Jefferson's first administration. There was as yet, of course, no system of competitive examinations. But with relatively few appointments to be made, it was possible to exercise vigilance and secure generally satisfactory results.

Then came the election of Andrew Jackson, and with it a new theory Jackson paves the way for the spoils system and practice as to personnel in the national government. Already, a Tenure of Office Act of 1820 had helped set the stage for a spoils system by fixing a four-year term for district attorneys, collectors of customs, and other groups of officials, and thus giving every incoming president a large number of positions to fill without the inconvenience of dis-covering reasons for removing competent incumbents.[1] Out of Tennessee came Jackson with the conviction, first, that any man of average intel-ligence and industry ought to be able to master the duties connected with practically any public office, second, that "more is lost by the long con-tinuance of men in office than is generally to be gained by their experi-ence," and, third, that up to then the offices had been altogether too generally monopolized by the seaboard states and should be shared much more liberally by the new frontier democracy which he represented. Putting his views into practice, the new chief executive did not indeed make the clean sweep of anti-Jacksonian office-holders for which many of his supporters clamored, but nevertheless filled substantially all vacancies as they arose with men who thought as he did, and in addition removed, in his first year alone, officers and employees of all grades to the then unprecedented number of some seven hundred.

The blame for fastening the spoils system upon the country is, however, not to be laid entirely, or even mainly, at Jackson's door. In the first place, removals and appointments on partisan grounds were already common in several of the older as well as newer states,[2] and in cities—the practice now being merely carried over in a large way into the domain of the national government. In the second place, the tightening up of party machinery, and the intensification of party politics, following the so-called "era of good feeling," would almost certainly have led in any case, under conditions then existing, to an increased use of public offices as rewards for party service. Finally, Jackson's views on office-holding, while of course deplored by many people, were warmly concurred in by those forces of the new democracy, especially in the West and South, that had been mainly responsible for his election. When, in 1832, Senator William L. Marcy of New York summed up the viewpoint of Jacksonians in the remark, "To the victors belong the spoils," he coined a phrase that readily passed into general currency; already, removal as well as ap-pointment for party reasons was becoming part of the accepted order of things in nation, state, and city.

Some points of view about spoils

Nor must the surrender to the spoils idea be ascribed to mere per-versity. We are accustomed to regard it as almost axiomatic that the hundreds of thousands of civil servants who administer our laws and spend our money should be selected solely on the basis of fitness, as shown by competitive examinations or other tests. And undoubtedly it is true that the practical politicians of all generations have been lukewarm

[1] Until this measure was passed, it was customary for federal officials, except of course the president, vice-president, and heads of executive departments, to hold office during good behavior. Additional groups were brought under the terms of the act in later years, *e.g.*, postmasters in 1836.

[2] Notably New York and Pennsylvania. See H. L. McBain, "DeWitt Clinton and the Origins of the Spoils System," *Columbia Univ. Studies in Hist., Econ., and Pub. Law*, XXVIII (New York, 1907).

toward, or openly opposed to, what we call the merit system, for no more exalted reasons than that they wanted to be able to secure appointments for their relatives, friends, and henchmen, and also to be in a position to influence and control appointees beholden to them. In Jacksonian days and since, however, there have been arguments for the spoils principle (or at any rate *against* its opposite) which, while often specious, and frequently representing nothing more than lame attempts to rationalize attitudes really motivated by selfishness and greed, nevertheless were sometimes sincere and even worthy of respectful consideration. It has been contended, for example, that we operate our national and state (and often local) governments through a party system, that parties are indispensable in a democracy, and that parties cannot thrive, or even endure, without the invigoration that comes from having offices and jobs to dispense to the faithful. There is the point of view, too, that when the people elect a new president and he very properly gathers about him a corps of top administrators of his own political persuasion, the change should go all down the line, so that higher officials will not find themselves compelled to work with subordinates with whom they may not be in sympathy. In the long run, it is argued, the best results will be attained by placing squarely upon appointing authorities full and unfettered responsibility for selecting the personnel with which they choose to work. Jackson thought, and so do some people today, that, just as no one has any *right* to be appointed to a public position, so no appointee has any vested right to be continued in his post indefinitely; otherwise, other people are denied opportunity. And this suggests the Jacksonian concept also of rotation as being not only calculated to keep the government service vigorous through the infusion of fresh blood, but indispensable to the equality of opportunity presumed to prevail in a democracy. On top of all this, it is seriously argued nowadays by some reputable students of the subject that, after two generations of trial of appointments and removals under a controlled merit system, so many shortcomings have been revealed that it would be better to abandon the system altogether and frankly go back to the old plan of spoils.[1]

Notwithstanding such lines of argument—to all of which there are, of course, convincing answers—people after Jackson's day could not wholly close their eyes to the unfortunate consequences of the orgy of spoils amidst which they lived. On all sides, experienced and worthy public officials were being ousted to make room for political henchmen. The public services were thrown into demoralization every time a change of administration took place. The president was harassed almost beyond

Beginnings of civil service reform

[1] For a vigorous defense of this idea, see J. Fischer, "Let's Go Back to the Spoils System," *Harper's Mag.*, CXCI, 362-368 (Oct., 1945); and cf. K. Cole, "The 'Merit System' Again," *Amer. Polit. Sci. Rev.*, XXXI, 695-698 (Aug., 1937); W. F. Davies, "Why I Believe in the Patronage System," *Nat. Mun. Rev.*, XIX, 18-21 (Jan., 1930); and W. Turn (a political boss), "In Defense of Patronage," *Annals of Amer. Acad. of Polit. and Soc. Sci.*, CLXXXIX, 22-28 (Jan., 1937).

endurance by place-seekers and their friends. Senators and representatives (like legislators in the states) found themselves pursued day and night by importunate constituents, with much of their time and energy diverted from more important tasks. Administration fell to a generally low level; politics itself grew more mercenary and corrupt. As early as 1853 and 1855, Congress undertook, in a feeble way, to improve conditions by requiring that some thousands of clerkships in Washington be classified on a basis of compensation, and that candidates be appointed to these positions only after examination by the head of the appropriate department. Even on this limited scale, the reform came to nothing; and an act of 1871, under which a civil service commission was set up and a broader scheme of competitive examinations introduced, proved almost equally barren of results.

The Pendleton Act (1883)

Happily, the cause was not lost. Able men turned their best energies to its support; national and state civil service reform associations were organized;[1] recent reforms in Great Britain were studied and made familiar to American readers.[2] *Harper's Weekly, The Nation,* and other influential journals took up the fight; the assassination of President Garfield by a disappointed office-seeker in 1881 supplied dramatic impetus; and the new president, Arthur, confounded the prophets by vigorously espousing the cause. The upshot was that, early in 1883, Congress passed a well-considered civil service measure[3]—modeled on the English order in council of 1870 and commonly known as the Pendleton Act—which from that day to this has, as progressively applied to increasing numbers, been the fundamental law governing admission to the national civil service.[4]

[1] Notably the National Civil Service Reform League, founded in 1881, renamed in 1945 the National Civil Service League, and today one of the most vigilant and influential agencies for promoting the application of merit principles in national, state, and local civil services. On the League and its work during the period covered, see F. M. Stewart, *The National Civil Service Reform League* (Austin, Tex., 1929). *Good Government,* published bimonthly at 67 W. 44th St., New York City, is the League's official organ.

[2] Especially through a scholarly book entitled *The Civil Service in Great Britain* (New York, 1880), written by an ardent reformer, Dorman B. Eaton, whom President Hayes commissioned to study the British system with particular reference to its adaptation to conditions in the United States. After ineffectual earlier efforts, Great Britain adopted, by order in council of 1870, a comprehensive merit plan which forms the basis of what recently has been the most carefully selected, and perhaps the most efficient civil service in the world, though now somewhat upset by the impact of the Labor government's nationalization program. See F. A. Ogg, *English Government and Politics* (2nd ed.), Chap. x.

[3] 22 *U. S. Stat. at Large,* 403.

[4] Similar legislation soon followed in Massachusetts and New York, and by this time, one can say, the reform movement in American public administration was definitely under way. Three score years, however, have left it short of complete success in the national domain; while even yet only twenty of the states have enacted service-wide merit laws.

Progress and Present Status of the Merit System

Two main lines of action were contemplated in this epoch-marking measure. One was the progressive classification of clerks and other employees—first in the Treasury and Post-Office Departments, and afterwards, as the president should direct, in other departments as well. The second was the extension to all such classified positions of the plan or principle of recruitment by competitive examination. At the outset, the reform did not extend far. In the first year, the number of positions affected did not exceed 14,000 out of a total of some 110,000. Gradually, however, the number grew, in Washington and by extension also to some of the field services; so that by 1933, on the eve of Franklin D. Roosevelt's assumption of the presidency, it exceeded 450,000, or some eighty per cent of the entire federal service at that time. Much of the increase, of course, was automatic, arising from the expansion of staffs in branches of the service already on the classified basis. Other gains flowed, however, from occasional acts of Congress placing specified groups of positions, whether new or old, in the classified service,[1] e.g., an act of 1902 classifying the employees of the Bureau of the Census; and still others from executive orders issued in pursuance of discretionary authority conferred in the Pendleton Act or in supplementary statutes—as, for example, when President Cleveland brought into the classified service numerous positions in the internal revenue service and in the Department of Agriculture, or when President Theodore Roosevelt brought in the rural free-delivery employees and all fourth-class postmasters north of the Ohio and east of the Mississippi. Perhaps chiefly because of the burdens which political appointments imposed upon them and upon their heads of departments, the presidents always outran Congress in their desire to see the competitive system extended; Congress, indeed, the Civil Service Reform League bluntly declared as recently as 1937, was always the chief obstacle to progress.

The assertion is borne out not only by repeated failures of the two houses, when enacting legislation entailing large numbers of additional appointments, to place the new positions in the classified service, but by actual retrenchments for which Congress, or at all events members hungry for spoils, must be held responsible. Every new presidential administration saw advances on some sectors, but retreats on others— retreats forced on even such sterling friends of the merit principle as Presidents Cleveland, Wilson, and Hoover. Retrogressive pressure was, of course, heaviest at times when a party long out of power suddenly found itself in control, e.g., when the Democrats took over in 1885, 1913,

The classified service and its earlier growth

Difficulty of holding ground gained

---

[1] The term "civil service" is often employed loosely, and by people who should know better, as synonymous with "classified service" or "competitive service." The classified service (under the "merit system") forms, of course, only a fraction— although today a very large one—of the civil service viewed correctly as embracing all civilians in the public employ.

and 1933, and the Republicans in 1897 and 1921. And it proved effective, not because presidents and other appointing officers enjoyed the worries that go with spoils politics, but simply because an apathetic public permitted patronage-mongers in Congress, abetted sometimes by heads of departments who at heart were primarily politicians, to push the merit system back from hard-won positions.

The problem of extension to the higher levels

It goes without saying that despite significant advances to be noted below, the pattern presented by the classified service continued decidedly irregular. Extensions were rarely in accordance with any fixed plan, and recessions introduced further incongruities. For decades, the most obvious need was a general leveling up whereby all branches and grades of the service comparable with others to which the merit system had been extended should be brought under it likewise. Along with this, however, was the urgent need also for extending the merit principle to higher levels of the service than had as yet been reached except at a few scattered points. To be sure, certain higher officials, including many chiefs of bureaus and divisions, had for a good while been selected for their professional standing and retained in office during good behavior. Even these, however, were protected by no legal guarantees against removal at pleasure; and large groups of intermediate and higher offices long remained (as some still do) on a frankly political basis—notably in the postal service, the customs service, the internal revenue service, the mint and assay services, the public lands service, the reclamation service, the immigration service, and the field services of the Department of Justice. Every one concedes that officers having to do in any important way with policy-framing ought to be selected with a view to harmonious representation of public opinion—which normally means on a party basis; and, admittedly, candidates for higher posts as a rule cannot be tested, and would not submit themselves for testing, in the same way that clerks and typists are examined. In our entire federal executive and administrative system, however, there are—in peacetime—at the most not above perhaps one thousand officials who really have to do significantly with determining policy;[1] there are well-known and adequate modes of ascertaining the fitness of candidates, no less for places of heavy responsibility in the government service than for positions of trust in great banking and business establishments; and—as has so often been urged by the Civil Service Commission, the National Civil Service League, and other interested and informed people—the whole number, with only the exceptions mentioned, properly belong in the non-political competitive system.

Obstacles   Chief obstacles to reform on these lines were—and to a degree still are: (1) reluctance of politicians, especially in Congress, to see so much

---

[1] No exact figure can be given; obviously, much depends upon the content read into the terms "significantly" and "policy." Technically, the only officials in federal agencies who actually *determine* policies are the agency heads. But many others have at least some share in policy-formulation. For present purposes, the exact number is of no consequence: the point is that in any case it is small.

valuable patronage cut off, (2) fear that the party in power would be able to "freeze" the existing situation, assuring permanent tenure for its appointees, and (3) the fact that in the case of some 15,500 "presidential offices," appointment was made by the president and Senate, so that they could not be brought under the merit system, on the regular lines, without legislation abrogating the Senate's "advice and consent." More than one president (including Taft in 1912 and Coolidge in 1924) recommended removal of the last-mentioned difficulty by legislation vesting appointment to the offices in question in the president alone or in heads of departments—along with abrogation of the four-year term (or other fixed term) where such limitation persisted. But politicians, particularly in the Senate, were always pretty solidly against the proposal.

Franklin D. Roosevelt's accession to the presidency in 1933, followed by the launching of the New Deal, opened the way for the merit system to be dealt some heavy blows. The Democrats were back in power after twelve lean years, and the rank and file were hungry for offices. Swift creation of new agencies of recovery and reform sharply multiplied the number of positions to be filled. And in the great majority of cases Congress exempted from the competitive system the hordes of new and transferred employees, leaving the way open for spoils at a juncture in the national life when nothing could have been less desirable. The president himself issued the first executive order on record withdrawing from the classified service positions (in the Bureau of Foreign and Domestic Commerce) placed therein by a predecessor. To be sure, a few of the sixty or more new agencies created—notably the Tennessee Valley Authority and the Farm Credit Administration—voluntarily decided to operate in accordance with merit principles. But as a result of wholesale exemptions by law, and of spoils raids in a good many of the older establishments as well, the service as a whole so far slipped back that the proportion on a merit basis sank from some eighty per cent early in 1933 to hardly more than sixty-three per cent at the middle of 1937. An atmosphere developed in which the merit system was challenged and endangered as in few earlier periods of its history; indeed, in some states there were efforts to repeal civil service laws outright.

Retrenchment in 1933-38

Of course, things could not go thus badly without stirring protest. Outside of government circles, the Civil Service Reform League, the Civil Service Assembly of the United States and Canada, the National League of Women Voters, and other organizations—and inside such circles, the National Legislative Council of Federal Employee Organizations and the Civil Service Commission—campaigned not only for a reversal of the trend, but for an extension of the merit system to include every non-policy-framing group or grade. In 1937, the President's Committee on Administrative Management declared for extension of the competitive system, not only "upward and outward," but also "downward," so as to include skilled workmen and laborers; and in the same year, the President

Renewed agitation for reform

himself, who all along had assured the reformers that the system was in no danger at his hands and would be "extended and improved" during his administration, urged upon Congress that all except policy-making positions be placed on a merit basis.

Progress in 1938-40—the Ramspeck Act

At the opening of 1938, one would hardly have surmised that the merit system in the federal service was on the eve of its greatest triumphs; yet so it proved. To begin with, the President himself, in that year, not only overhauled and modernized the existing civil service rules, but ordered into the classified service all previously exempt non-policy-determining positions—some one hundred thousand—over which he had the necessary power. More important, Congress, in 1940, made up for a good deal of past dereliction by passing the Ramspeck Act [1] authorizing inclusion in the service, at presidential discretion, of *all* positions remaining exempt except those subject to presidential appointment with Senate confirmation and a few other limited groups; and in the following year, 182,000 were brought in by a single order. Except in so far as Congress might weaken in the case of future groups, or withdraw existing ones, the way was open for throwing the now widening boundaries of the merit system around substantially all of the federal service, aside, of course, from that portion of it appointed by the president and Senate, including many officials having to do with making policy. [2]

Wartime experience

One of the gravest problems raised by the defense preparations started in 1940, and especially by the ensuing war, was that of manpower—for the armed services, for industry, for agriculture, and likewise, one hardly need add, for the federal civil service. Even the multiplying activities incident to the defense effort necessitated within a year an increase of federal personnel by upwards of half, and from the outset there was fear (although, if the truth be told, hope among some politicians) that the

---

[1] 54 *U. S. Stat. at Large*, 1214.

[2] A word should be added about the special case of postmasters. Early in the century, fourth-class postmasters, postal clerks, letter-carriers, and other minor postal employees were placed in the classified service, postmasters of the first, second, and third classes, however, being left outside, partly at least because they could be appointed only with confirmation by the Senate. President Wilson bettered the situation by instructing the Civil Service Commission to hold examinations for such postmasterships and by undertaking to nominate in every case the candidate receiving the highest rating, regardless of politics. President Harding let down the bars to political appointments by reverting to the earlier practice of nominating one of the *three* standing highest, though in 1936 President Roosevelt reverted to the procedure of President Wilson. Finally, two years later, in the Ramspeck-O'Mahoney Postmaster Act (52 *U. S. Stat. at Large*, 1076), Congress gave the examination system a statutory basis by placing the then 14,800 first-, second-, and third-class postmasters in the classified service—on a special footing, to be sure, since incumbents continued to be appointed by the president and Senate, yet with indefinite tenure, and with only candidates examined by the Civil Service Commission, and certified as having one of the three highest ratings, eligible to appointment. Even yet, however, congressmen and senators have a good deal of influence upon selections made from the highest three (the practice of appointing not necessarily the highest, but one of the highest three, has been resumed); and persons without such backing are likely to consider it useless to take the examinations. Both the National Civil Service League and the Civil Service Commission urge the elimination of senatorial confirmation and advocate appointment in all cases of the candidate standing highest.

machinery for recruiting, testing, and grading potential employees would not prove equal to the task. The burden thrown upon the Civil Service Commission was, indeed, staggering, the more by reason of heavy losses of existing personnel both to military service and to competitive private industry. Not only, however, did the Commission for a time contrive to meet the demands upon it—by employing every possible channel of publicity to attract capable recruits, by streamlining its procedures, and by drawing upon state and municipal rosters of eligibles placed at federal disposal [1]—but it succeeded reasonably well in maintaining the merit standards of the past, the competitive system proving stronger in the emergency than either friend or foe had anticipated. Even before the end of 1940, however, concessions had to be made in an executive order authorizing the Commission to suspend the competitive provisions of the Civil Service Act in relation to any given position or class of positions, appointments under such suspensions to be without civil service "status" and only for the duration of the emergency; and, with the service doubling in numbers even before Pearl Harbor, such suspensions became numerous as the only means of keeping the defense activities supplied with adequate manpower.

Then came the war, and with it, in time, still another doubling of federal civilian personnel—most largely workers in arsenals, navy yards, and similar establishments of military significance. More and more, it became necessary to subordinate, or entirely suspend, age limits and experience requirements, and, in the more congested sectors of the service, to waive various examination procedures completely. And when such expedients failed to meet the insatiable demands of the employing agencies, a new executive order of February 16, 1942, opened a way for "war service" appointments to many entire categories of positions, with only "pass" (as distinguished from competitive) examinations, and without reference to classified status at all, yet carrying tenure, at the Commission's discretion, for the duration of the war and for six months thereafter. Keeping its hand on the situation as best it could, the Commission nevertheless was obliged to see some departments and special wartime establishments run wild with selection and use of much of their personnel; and in 1943 an investigation by the House civil service committee under Representative Ramspeck brought to light abuses—especially in the form of over-staffing—which an act of Congress required the director of the budget to seek to remedy, even to the extent of fixing personnel ceilings for given establishments. Combined with a restraining influence exerted by the findings and recommendations of a joint committee on the reduction of non-essential federal expenditures, the remedies applied contributed to a tapering off in 1943 of the rate at which

---

[1] Authority to certify eligibles from state registers to fill federal positions, in cases in which the Commission had coöperated in conducting the state examinations, was acquired in 1938.

new federal personnel was being recruited; and of course this enabled the Civil Service Commission to recover some of its lost control.

For the time being, the looser practices made necessary by the emergency undeniably weakened the merit system; standards sagged, and the quality of recruits deteriorated. The concessions made, however, were designed to be only temporary; and one will hardly doubt that in so critical a situation it was more important to secure indispensable manpower (if not the best, then such as could be got) than to insist uncompromisingly upon standards capable of being realized only under more normal conditions. The saving feature was that, in so far as there was a let-down, it was dictated, not by the interests of partisanship, but solely by the existing state of the labor market; and it is significant that this was the first major national emergency during which large groups of positions were not exempted outright from merit-system requirements by act of Congress. Unmarred by breakdown or scandal, the wartime adjustment merely demonstrated the flexibility and adaptability of a civil service structure sometimes criticized on the ground of excessive rigidity.[1]

With hostilities ended, the task arose of getting the service back on a peacetime basis; and it could not be other than slow and difficult. Even if in future the service were to number the predicted million and a half, fully as many more members must in the meantime be discharged and returned to private employment, including the many who had been given tenure for the duration and six months after. At the same time, the government was pledged to receive back former civilian employees who had been drawn into military service, notwithstanding that their former agencies might have been abolished, absorbed, or their functions redistributed. As pointed out above, the total remaining on the payroll had, in one way or another, by December 31, 1946, been lowered to 2,285,570, leaving three-quarters of a million still to be "terminated." Spurred by the Republican economy drive in the Eightieth Congress, the number, as previously indicated also, was further reduced in 1947 to two millions. The other side of the matter was the reinstatement of regular methods of recruitment; and in February, 1946, President Truman issued an order directing the Civil Service Commission to "resume operations under the Civil Service Rules," although as yet modified to some extent by special

[1] The federal civil service in wartime is discussed in L. V. Howard and H. A. Bone, *Current American Government* (New York, 1943), Chap. IV; L. V. Howard, "War and the Federal Service," *Amer. Polit. Sci. Rev.,* XXXVI, 916-930 (Oct., 1942); A. S. Flemming, "Emergency Aspects of Civil Service," *Pub. Admin. Rev.,* I, 25-31 (Autumn, 1940); and L. D. White [ed.], *Civil Service in Wartime* (Chicago, 1945). Of course the war period was not entirely without assaults upon the merit system motivated by political considerations. Included among these were efforts to secure legislation subjecting to senatorial confirmation all appointments and promotions in designated agencies, or even all appointments and promotions whatsoever, carrying salaries above some stipulated amount. Indeed, in 1943 the Senate actually passed a bill to this effect (fixing $4,500 as the dividing line), although the House of Representatives rejected it.

regulations for the period of transition. War-service appointments were to end and normal competitive examinations to be revived "at the earliest possible date," and war-service appointees (constituting approximately two-thirds of federal personnel on V-J Day) were to be dropped if they failed to compete, or to qualify, in examinations given for permanent appointment. After all, merit as a basis for appointment had not been abandoned during the war; the standards for measuring it had merely been relaxed; all that remained was to restore them under the regular competitive-examination procedures; and today the system is back substantially where it was.

Notwithstanding, therefore, the let-down made inevitable by the war, the merit system, over a period of years, has realized truly remarkable gains. Of course, the fight to maintain and extend it has to be unremitting. In 1944, for example, there was a serious threat that some 8,500 legal positions, brought into the classified service by executive order of 1941, would be withdrawn from it by congressional action; as indicated above, in 1943 a determined effort was made to promote the interests of patronage by subjecting to senatorial confirmation all appointments and promotions carrying salaries above $4,500 (a then total of some 28,000 positions); in 1944, Congress passed a Veteran's Preference Act which, although from one point of view merely perpetuating a long-established policy on veteran preference,[1] relaxed qualifications standards in a very dubious manner; in 1946, it enacted without a dissenting vote, and the president approved, a measure exempting from civil service regulations all positions in the medical unit of the Veterans' Administration. Such retrogressive efforts are to be expected, and some will succeed, at least temporarily. Nevertheless, the greatly enlarged proportion of regular civil servants now having classified status (including most of the wartime increment, and amounting in all to at least ninety per cent), combined with the authority enjoyed by the president to add still further to the number, marks an achievement of the first order in the fight for good government in this country. Notwithstanding all that has happened, the nation faces the postwar era with the merit system more solidly entrenched than at any earlier time in its history.

An over-all advance

Recruitment Under the Merit System

The primary object of the Pendleton Act and of the long line of later statutes and executive orders extending its provisions to additional groups of civil servants is, of course, to promote appointment on a basis of demonstrated fitness and to assure appointees security of tenure during good behavior. And to assist appointing authorities in finding persons qualified for places in the classified service, the law provides for a Civil Service Commission of three members, unattached to any executive department or other agency, and appointed by the president with the

Personnel agencies:

1. The Civil Service Commission

[1] See pp. 507-508 below.

advice and consent of the Senate (for no fixed term) under the limitation that not more than two of the members may be "adherents of the same political party." As time passed and conceptions of personnel administration broadened, the Commission's functions grew, until nowadays it is found not only framing and administering competitive examinations and certifying lists of eligibles (once considered its sole duty), but classifying civil servants, making rules and regulations providing for in-service training, investigating charges of political activity, keeping service records reported to it by the establishments, administering the efficiency-rating system and also the retirement law, and doing numerous other things related to the upbuilding and improvement of the federal service—serving withal as a top agency for providing leadership to the departments in improving their personnel management and for furnishing guidance to the president and Congress in the formulation of enlightened personnel policies for the building of a genuine career service. Within the limits of its powers and resources, the Commission has served the country usefully as a central personnel agency over a long period of years; and with powers and resources considerably increased (although sometimes without too much assurance of adequate financial support), it gives promise of still greater service in times ahead. A staff of some 1,775 rose to one of 6,900 during the war, later receding to some 3,500 (in October, 1947); and under a wartime reorganization of 1942, functions are distributed among divisions such as personnel classification, examining and personnel utilization, retirement investigations, appeals and review, service records, budget and finance, information, investigations, and inspection. For purposes of general recruiting, there are, in principal cities throughout the country, fourteen regional offices (each under a regional director) and also various branch offices; and the general field organization is completed by (1) some 5,000 "local boards," made up of postmasters, collectors of revenue, and other national officers who as needed are called into special service for this purpose by the Commission, without extra pay, and who, in some seven hundred cities, from time to time hold "assembled," i.e., group, examinations at first- and second-class post-offices (every such post-office has a board) or in other federal buildings, and (2) a growing number of "establishment," or rating, boards which formerly conducted chiefly "unassembled," i.e., individual, examinations designed for lower-grade clerical, trades, and labor positions, but now are found recruiting, examining, and certifying applicants in the professional, semi-professional, technical, and administrative fields as well. Both types of boards are, of course, field agencies of the Civil Service Commission and function under supervision of that body's regional directors.[1]

[1] See R. J. Jouno, "Establishment Boards in the Federal Civil Service," *Amer. Polit. Sci. Rev.*, XLI, 955-962 (Oct., 1947). In 1937, the President's Committee on Administrative Management, animated by doubts about the suitability of boards and commissions for top administrative work, urged (see *Report*, 9-11) that the Civil Service

For the better management of their staffs, various executive departments and establishments began a good while ago to appoint personnel directors and other such officials of their own; and an executive order of 1938 (accompanying a general revision of civil service rules) prescribed, among other things, that thenceforth a division of personnel supervision and management, under a director, should be maintained in every department and major independent establishment, each director to be appointed, under the merit system, by the department or establishment head. Still further to encourage coördinated attack upon personnel problems, these several agency directors, along with representatives of the Civil Service Commission and the Bureau of the Budget, and such additional persons as the president may name, are linked up in a Federal Personnel Council which in 1940 became a unit of the Civil Service Commission itself.[1] Finally, with a view to tying the personnel system more directly to the chief executive, another order, in 1939, established a Liaison Office of Personnel Management, thereafter a constituent unit of the Executive Office of the President.

2. Other coördinating agencies

With the exception of relatively few posts filled through non-competitive, or "pass," examinations, "classified" appointments are made only on the basis of the showing of candidates in competitive tests. These tests are, in general, arranged by the examining and personnel utilization division of the Civil Service Commission, announced in advance in newspapers and on placards displayed in post-offices and other public places, and administered in various cities throughout the country by the examining boards. They may be either written or unwritten, or both. Candidates for the great bulk of positions of a clerical or other subordinate nature

Examinations

Commission be replaced by a single executive officer, to be known as a civil service administrator, and supplemented by a civil service board of seven members, selected to represent business, education, labor, agriculture, and similar interests, and charged with observing, investigating, planning, and advising in the name of the general public. Although renewed from various quarters in later times (see, for example, "Better Bureaucrats," *Fortune,* Supp., Pt. IV, pp. 10-12, Nov., 1943), the proposal has never been acted upon. In point of fact, the Commission ably performed an almost impossible task during the war; and the record achieved not only seems to insure its continuance, but gives promise of a permanently strengthened position with respect to financial support, staffing, and relations with personnel machinery in states and municipalities.

On the Commission and its peacetime work, at all events in earlier days, see D. H. Smith, "The United States Civil Service Commission," *Service Monographs,* No. 49 (Baltimore, 1928); also, for the entire period of its existence, the Commission's annual reports, and for later developments, J. McDiarmid, "The Changing Rôle of the United States Civil Service Commission," *Amer. Polit. Sci. Rev.,* XL, 1067-1096 (Dec., 1946). For complete text of Executive Order No. 7915 of June 24, 1938, revising the rules under which the Commission normally operates, see *Annual Report of the U. S. Civil Service Commission* (1938), 48-58. Most of the new features were aimed at improving the Commission's examining procedures and promoting in-service training for employees. The rules were again revised somewhat by executive order of February 24, 1947.

[1] The chairman of the Council is Mr. Frederick M. Davenport, head of the National Institute of Public Affairs, a private organization which every year places forty or fifty college and university graduates as unpaid interns in various federal establishments. On the activities of the Council, see *Good Government,* LXI, No. 3 (May-June, 1944).

are examined in groups, and exclusively in writing; those seeking positions which call for scientific, technical, legal, or other special attainments are rated, either competitively or otherwise (by the regular Commission boards or by the newer examining agencies above mentioned), in respect to experience, education, training, and fitness, as ascertained usually by interviews and testimony rather than by formal written examination. In the preparation of examination questions, the Commission often enlists the aid of experienced persons in the several departments, and occasionally of academic and other outside experts.

Contrast
of Amer-
ican and
British
systems

The law requires examinations to be "practical in their character," and, so far as possible, to "relate to those matters which will fairly test the relative capacity and fitness of the persons examined to discharge the duties of the service into which they seek to be appointed." Herein our American system differs considerably from the British. In Great Britain, the competitive principle operates more consistently in the higher levels of the official hierarchy than with us; public service is looked upon to a greater extent as a profession, and even a career; and the main object of examinations is to recruit the service (especially that portion of it embraced in the "administrative class," open only to graduates of leading universities) from young men and women who expect to spend their lives in public employment, and whose education and native ability make it probable that they will rise from one grade to another and steadily grow in usefulness as administrators. Hence, British examinations are framed mainly with a view to broadly testing the candidate's general attainments and capacity. Mathematics, history, philosophy, the classics, natural science—these and other branches of higher learning receive much emphasis. Even the examinations for positions of a purely clerical nature are framed on these lines, although naturally confined to more elementary subjects. Under the American plan, the object, in the majority of cases, is not primarily to test general attainments and capacity; rather, it is to ascertain the applicant's technical proficiency and present fitness for the kind of work that he seeks. And since there is a very great variety of kinds of work to be sought, the Commission is under the necessity of providing an equally great variety of different examinations—no fewer than 1,700 when a count was made a few years ago. "There is something to be said, of course, for both systems. The American is more democratic; it exacts little of the beginner in the way of general knowledge, and it affords a haven for men and women of all ages who are attracted by its pecuniary rewards, modest though they are. This, however, is about all that can be said for it. The British system is less democratic. But it attracts to the public service men and women who, on the average, not only are younger and more energetic than American appointees, but better fitted by education, and probably native capacity as well, to become increasingly able, useful, and responsible officials." [1] That we occasionally

---

[1] F. A. Ogg, *English Government and Politics* (2nd ed.), 231-232.

veer cautiously in the direction of the English system is illustrated by the action of the Civil Service Commission, beginning in 1934, in setting up limited "registers" (*e.g.*, for junior professional assistants after 1939) with examinations of general rather than specific nature and open only to graduates of colleges and universities.[1] But by and large our system still suffers from aiming no higher than at merely attracting recruits who have crammed up on the requirements for some particular and probably routine job—without regard for the mental acquirements and capacities that would fit a candidate, once appointed, to go on to larger responsibilities.

On the registers of the Civil Service Commission, at Washington and in the offices of the regional directors, are kept the names of all persons who have passed the various examinations with a grade of seventy or above. Appointment, of course, withdraws a name from the list; and since 1939 the list itself, however many names of persons in waiting may remain on it, lapses at the end of a year—unless, as sometimes happens, the Commission decides to prolong its life another year rather than order a new examination. When a clerk or stenographer or other employee in the classified service is needed by a department, the Commission supplies the appointing officer with the names of three persons who stand highest in the appropriate list of eligibles. The officer normally appoints one of the three, and the other two resume their places on the waiting list.[2] If no one of the three is appointed, the officer must be prepared to assign some good reason when asking for more names. By way of a check, too, upon the judgment of the examiners and appointing authority, every appointee is placed on probation for a period of formerly six months but now one year. During this time, he can be removed summarily, with no reason assigned except that his work is unsatisfactory. If retained longer, however, he gains "civil service status," with all the security of tenure for which the law provides. Removals during the probationary period are extremely few—fewer, one may add, than they should be.

The free working of the arrangements described is, however, obstructed by certain special provisions. From as far back as the Civil War, honorably discharged, or retired, veterans, and wives or widows of such, have,

Making appointments

Veteran preference

---

[1] See F. M. Davenport, L. B. Sims, *et al.*, "Political Science and Federal Employment," *Amer. Polit. Sci. Rev.*, XXXV, 304-310 (Apr., 1941).

Formerly, aliens who had declared their intention to be naturalized were permitted to take the examinations, and occasionally they received appointment. Examinations nowadays, however, are open only to citizens, except in the rare event of a lack of citizen applicants. There is no fee.

During the fiscal year ending June 30, 1940 (the last before the defense and war effort created the abnormal situation described above), a total of 839,112 persons were examined; 374,890 of the number received a passing grade; and 102,366 obtained appointment. *Annual Report of the U. S. Civil Service Commission* (1940), 131.

[2] The "rule of three," making it possible for the candidate highest on the list to be passed over in favor of the second or third, is characteristic of the American system. In Great Britain, only one name is submitted and the candidate standing highest can be sure of appointment, barring very unusual circumstances. Of course, it sometimes happens under any system that a person to whom appointment is offered no longer wants it, because, perhaps, of having secured more desirable employment. In such a case, the appointing authority simply turns to another eligible.

under varying regulations, been eligible for civil service positions on terms easier than those applying to others; and even before 1941 more than one-fifth of all new federal appointments went to "preference eligibles" on this veteran basis. In anticipation of employment difficulties for discharged veterans after the recent war, President Roosevelt, early in 1944, reaffirmed the general principle of civil service preference for ex-servicemen; and at his request, Congress, in the following summer, passed the Scrugham-Starnes (Veterans' Preference) Act,[2] not only giving veterans—whether or not they had seen active service—a monopoly of specified kinds of minor civil service jobs (as guards, messengers, etc.) and empowering the president, for five years after the war, to add to the list, but providing also for (1) arbitrarily adding ten points to the earned examination ratings (conditioned by no minimum educational requirement) of honorably discharged ex-servicemen and women with service-connected disabilities, wives of disabled ex-servicemen, and unmarried widows of ex-servicemen; (2) placing all such persons whose earned rating plus preference is above seventy at the top of the appropriate registers ahead of all other eligibles, except in the case of professional and scientific positions with entrance salary of over $3,000 à year; and (3) adding five points to the earned examination ratings of honorably discharged ex-servicemen and women not disabled, and giving such persons preference in appointments over all others rating equally high.[2] The idea that the nation should suitably compensate those who have risked their lives in its defense, and should take care of those who have incurred physical or mental injury in doing so, is sound. From the point of view of good administration, it is, however, unfortunate that we have fallen into the habit of discharging this obligation, not alone by pensions, "bonuses," hospitalization, and the like, but by permitting the civil service to be permeated with persons whose claim to *some* kind of compensation is indisputable, but who can be edged into public positions (often over persons better qualified) only by disregarding considerations which clearly ought to govern when public employees are being selected. The service promises in future, nevertheless, to be heavily pervaded with veteran-preference appointees, capable and otherwise.[3]

Appor-
tionment
according
to popula-
tion

Another restriction arises from a requirement of the Pendleton Act which has always had a particular appeal for members of Congress with a weakness for patronage, namely, that "as nearly as the conditions of good administration warrant," appointments in the departments and independent offices at Washington shall be apportioned among the several states and territories and the District of Columbia on a basis of population. The rule is not applied in the case of veterans, and in any event it

[1] 58 *U. S. Stat. at Large,* 387 (1944).
[2] More or less similar arrangements prevail in many of the states.
[3] The principles and problems involved in veteran preference are discussed at length by J. F. Miller in C. J. Friedrich *et al., Problems of the American Public Service* (New York, 1935). 243-334.

can be followed in only a rough sort of way, for the reason that eligibles from many Southern and Western states are not sufficiently numerous. Even so, it is responsible for the appointment of many persons of inferior qualification.

Discipline, Removal, Promotion

The merit system was introduced not only to improve the methods by which civil servants are selected, but also to afford a security of tenure never enjoyed under the sway of spoilsmen. Opponents of the reform sought to discredit it by arguing that protected employees, feeling themselves safe, would grow careless and inefficient. There was no intention, of course, that such results should be permitted to follow; and while it is probably true that governments are, on the whole, more lenient with those who serve them in civil capacity than are private businesses with persons on their payrolls, the regulations applying to our national service (both classified and otherwise) contemplate full powers of discipline and removal—so long, in the case of the classified service (says one of the rules), as "like penalties shall be imposed for like offenses, and no discrimination shall be exercised for political or religious reasons." Every member of the service is liable to disciplinary action at the hands of some superior authority; and such action may range all the way from mere reprimand to suspension (not to exceed seventy days), reduction in rank and pay, and, in extremer cases, removal. *No lack of disciplinary control*

For it must be observed that development of the merit system has in no wise abrogated the judicially established principle that the power to appoint normally carries with it the power to remove. What the rules (statutory or otherwise) do is merely to give merit appointees security against arbitrary and unreasonable removals, a protection which officials outside the classified service have no legal ground for claiming. In the main, this protection consists in requiring that removals shall be made only—as an act of 1912 puts it—"for such cause as will promote the efficiency of the service;" that refusal to contribute time or money to a political party (or, on the other hand, making a contribution, of money at all events) shall in no case be ground for removal; and that removals shall be made in a manner essentially fair to the employee involved. Fairness is construed to require that the employee be furnished with a written statement of the charges against him and that he be allowed reasonable time in which to make a written reply.[1] Unlike employees under most state and municipal civil service systems, however, he has no right to an oral hearing or trial before dismissal takes effect, although he may be allowed one as a matter of grace; nor can he expect any court to intervene in his behalf. Within the substantive and procedural limitations thus *Removals*

---

[1] For full discussion, see H. C. Westwood, "The 'Right' of an Employee of the United States Against Arbitrary Discharge," *Geo. Washington Law Rev.*, VII, 212-232 (Dec., 1938).

imposed, the appointing authority (the head of a department in the majority of instances) can sever from that part of the service within his jurisdiction any person whom he judges to be negligent, incompetent, dishonest, disloyal, or otherwise a hindrance to good administration. The power, however, is exercised all too sparingly.[1]

[1] The international situation of recent years, and particularly the war, inevitably brought to the fore the matter of disloyalty and subversive activities within the service. To begin with, Congress, in the Hatch Political Activities Act of 1939, made it unlawful for any person employed and paid by the federal government to have membership in any political party or organization advocating the overthrow of our constitutional form of government. Proceeding on lines of much more doubtful constitutionality, the two houses later tried their hand at purging the service of members alleged to be guilty of subversive activities, but ended with only a dubious action undertaking to separate three persons from the federal payroll (see p. 457 above). Two successive interdepartmental committees carried on laborious inquiries into large numbers of charges made against individual employees, but came out with results of so negative a character that the committees themselves pronounced their work not worth while. Throughout the war period, too, the Civil Service Commission looked into numerous cases involving persons admitted to the service on a temporary basis subject to later investigation and certification, and at one stage set up a loyalty rating board to investigate applicants whose loyalty was called in question. The problem was not solved with the close of the war. On the one hand, many continuing charges of disloyalty within civil service ranks were palpably irresponsible and hysterical. On the other hand, an impartial commission, after long study of the situation, was compelled to conclude that there was enough evidence of such disloyalty to justify a concerted effort to ferret it out and eject the guilty.

With Congress pressing for action (and meanwhile, in 1946, attaching riders to several appropriation acts forbidding funds to be used in paying salaries to persons advocating, or belonging to organizations advocating, overthrow of the government by force), the upshot was a somewhat startling executive order of March 22, 1947, in which President Truman instructed the attorney-general to list all "totalitarian, Fascist, Communist, or subversive" groups seeking to change our form of government "by unconstitutional means;" declared membership in, or sympathetic association with, any such group sufficient to stamp a federal official or employee, civil or military, as disloyal; called upon the Civil Service Commission, working through the departments and other agencies, and checking with the F.B.I., to investigate for loyalty all existing civil servants not already checked and also all new appointees, and instructed every department and agency to maintain one or more loyalty boards to hear disloyalty charges against employees, and the Commission to set up a "loyalty review board" to act as a court of final appeal. Not content with the president's action, and charging that it was not being followed up energetically, the House of Representatives, on July 15, passed a measure ordering a loyalty investigation throughout the entire service. Simultaneously, however, the Civil Service Commission announced that 811 federal employees found disloyal were being discharged, and that the service-wide inquiry ordered by the president was about to start; and consequently the House bill was not acted upon in the Senate.

The delayed general investigation was launched on August 18, 1947, with every federal employee required to be fingerprinted and to fill out a "loyalty identification" form for checking against F.B.I. files of persons suspected of subversive tendencies. If an employee's loyalty was brought into question, the F.B.I. was to conduct an inquiry and report to the Civil Service Commission; the Commission, in turn, was to report to the employing agency; the agency was to hold a trial before a departmental loyalty review board; if this board cleared the employee, the case and the board's action on it would be reviewed by a panel of a central twenty-member Loyalty Review Board set up by the Commission; if, on the other hand, the departmental board decided that the employee ought to be dismissed, the recommendation would go to the employing agency, but with right of the employee to appeal to the central board and to employ counsel, submit evidence, and produce witnesses or affidavits. All new appointees after October 1, 1947, were to be checked against F.B.I. files and in any event to be investigated by F.B.I. agents if any question was raised. Such arrangements for wholesale investigation (barely beginning to operate when these lines were written) represented, of course, a rather startling new development in our civil service procedures.

Included in the protection thrown around members of the classified Immunity from partisan pressures service is immunity from pressures of a partisan nature. By terms of the Pendleton Act, no classified officer or employee may be solicited for political funds by a congressman, senator, or federal office-holder—or indeed by any person whatever within a building used by the federal government. There is nothing to prevent such solicitation by non-office-holders, so long as they do not invade a government building for the purpose, and sometimes officers and employees are in this way practically coerced into making contributions. No one, however, may be removed, demoted, or even threatened, by his superior either for making or for refusing to make a political contribution.

In return, members of the service—although, of course, permitted to Restraints upon partisan activities vote,[1] and likewise to express privately their opinions on political issues— are required to abstain from activities of a partisan character. From 1907, a rule, based on an executive order, has forbidden members of the classified service to take any "active part in political management or in political campaigns"—a regulation construed by the Civil Service Commission to debar them from membership in party conventions, addressing party gatherings, participating in the preparation of party resolutions or platforms, serving on party committees, assisting in getting out the voters on election day, serving as election officers, distributing campaign literature or emblems, arranging party meetings or demonstrations, publishing anything in the interest of a particular candidate or party, and a long list of other activities having a partisan aspect—although not including mere passive attendance at party meetings or making contributions to party funds through persons not connected with the federal government. And, although the Commission (itself without power to remove any one having civil service "status"[2]) long complained that infractions which it looked into and reported were frequently ignored by the authorities having power to remove, partisan abuses at the hands of federal civil servants in times past must, in the main, be laid at the door, not of the classified service, but of that portion of the service remaining on a political basis.

To meet this situation, Congress, in 1939, passed the first Hatch Polit- The Hatch Act of 1939 ical Activities Act,[3] designed to prevent "pernicious political activities" on the part, not only of classified federal employees, but of all federal employees except only those occupying policy-determining positions. To be sure, restrictions upon soliciting political contributions from classified

---

[1] Many, however, are non-voters because of having no residence except in the District of Columbia. See p. 862 below.

[2] Except in the case of its own employees. A widespread impression that the Commission has general power to dismiss civil servants is erroneous. Employees admitted temporarily and subject to later investigation can be discharged by the Commission if the results of the investigation prove unsatisfactory. But once a person is in the service with permanent status, the Commission cannot, of its own motion, get him out—unless it can show that he secured status by misrepresentation or other fraudulent means.

[3] 53 U. S. Stat. at Large, 1197.

civil servants were not made applicable to the unclassified. But aside from this, all officers and employees of the United States, classified and unclassified alike, were forbidden to take any active part in political management or political campaigns, or to use their official authority with a view to affecting in any way "the election or nomination of any candidate" for a federal office.[1] Officials in the non-classified service may, to be sure, publicly voice their opinions on political subjects and candidates, provided (the attorney-general has ruled) they do it not as "part of an organized campaign;" members of the classified service may express such opinions only privately. And the act is construed to forbid any civil servant to whom it applies to become a candidate for any elective state, territorial, or municipal office—at all events if campaigning is involved.

The Hatch Act of 1940

When approving this legislation, President Roosevelt called attention to the fact that it applied to officers and employees of the federal government only, and recommended that it be extended to cover "state and local government employees participating actively in federal elections." The upshot was a second Hatch Act,[2] in 1940, (1) forbidding employees of state and local governments, if engaged in full-time activities financed wholly or in part by federal funds, to use their official authority in such ways as to "interfere with" any presidential or congressional nomination or election, and (2) forbidding any persons whose *principal* employment is in a federally aided activity (a) to use their official authority or influence for the purpose of interfering with any nomination or election, (b) to coerce, command, or advise any other such employee to make a political contribution or loan, and (c) to take any active part in political management or a political campaign.[3] Not so long ago, the number of persons affected by legislation on these lines would not have been large. The enormously increased interlocking personnel of federal, state, and local governments as developed in later years has, however, brought hundreds of thousands of state and municipal employees into a position to feel the force of the restrictions imposed.[4]

To regard either the foregoing or any other "clean politics" legislation as capable of completely eliminating "pernicious political activities" would, of course, be naïve; and, not only have there been violations of the new laws, but efforts have several times been made to weaken them

[1] As observed elsewhere, the notoriously heavy participation of federal office-holders in national and state party conventions—always a great advantage to any party in power, and to the "Administration" as against other interests in the party—now became a thing of the past. More than fifty per cent of the members of the Democratic national convention which renominated President Roosevelt at Philadelphia in 1936 were postmasters, marshals, revenue collectors, district attorneys, and other federal officials. Some votes in Congress for the Hatch legislation were motivated by no loftier purpose than to make it more difficult for Mr. Roosevelt to control the 1940 convention and win a nomination for a third term.

[2] 54 *U. S. Stat. at Large,* 767.

[3] The second Hatch Act was noteworthy also for the new regulations which it sought to impose upon the collection and use of campaign funds. This feature, however, has been considered elsewhere (see pp. 224-225 above).

[4] Even at the date of the legislation, some 300,000 were estimated to be affected.

by qualifications and exemptions, with the more or less openly avowed purpose of eventually bringing about their repeal. When, however, one recalls the scandalous political activities of federal office-holders in the elections of 1934, 1936, and 1938 (especially in the form of seeking to herd relief-workers to the polls), and likewise the brazen public assertions of certain among them that people on the federal payroll must "stick together" and "keep their friends in power," one realizes that in the past decade a notable new chapter in the history of American political reform has been written. It is to be hoped that reactionary and self-seeking politicians will not be permitted to erase it.[1]

In the business and professional world, it is recognized that nothing contributes more to the efficiency and morale of a staff than reasonable assurance of advancement in rank and pay, not according to mere seniority, but under flexible arrangements placing a premium on meritorious service. The same holds true in public administration, even though the fact has not always been so clearly perceived. Few problems of our American civil service (national, state, and local) have, however, proved more baffling. Upon what qualities or attainments of the civil servant should promotion be based? How are these qualities or attainments to be measured? Should promotion be by formal examination or simply on the basis of some one's judgment? Should higher positions in a given branch of the service be filled only by promotion, or should outsiders also be allowed to compete for them? In the Pendleton Act we read that no classified officer or employee shall be promoted "until he has passed an examination," or is shown to be specially exempted from such examination;" and a long-standing rule promulgated by the president enjoins that "competitive tests or examinations shall, as far as practicable and useful,

Promotion and transfer

---

[1] In February, 1947, the Supreme Court handed down two simultaneous decisions holding the Hatch legislation constitutional. In one case, the United Public Workers of America (C. I. O.), acting in behalf of twelve federal employees accused of political activity, charged that the act violated constitutional rights of freedom of speech, press, and assembly. But the Court, in United Public Workers of America *et al. v.* Mitchell *et al.* (330 U. S. 75, 1947), held the law a proper congressional safeguard of "the integrity and competency of the service"—although the only one of the twelve persons adjudged actually to have violated the law was a roller in the United States mint at Philadelphia who had served as a Democratic ward committeeman and had worked at the polls in the 1940 election. The other case involved a member of the Oklahoma highway commission who for two years had acted as Democratic state chairman. In accordance with the law, the state had been penalized by the withholding of $10,800 (the amount of the commissioner's salary for the two years) in federal road aid funds, and the state had challenged the law's validity. In Oklahoma *v.* United States Civil Service Commission (330 U. S. 127, 1947), the Supreme Court held that although the federal government had no power to regulate the local political activities of state officials, it was entirely competent to fix the terms on which the money allotment to states should be disbursed. Cf. F. Heady, "The Hatch Act Decisions," *Amer. Polit. Sci. Rev.*, XLI, 687-699 (Aug., 1947). For a fuller analysis of the Hatch Acts and some of the questions arising under them, see L. V. Howard, "Federal Restrictions on the Political Activity of Government Employees," *Amer. Polit. Sci. Rev.*, XXXV, 470-489 (June, 1941), and J. R. Starr, "The Hatch Act—An Interpretation," *Nat. Mun. Rev.*, XXX, 418-425 (July, 1941). Cf. V. O. Key, Jr., "The Hatch Act Extension and Federal-State Relations," *Pub. Personnel Rev.*, I, 30-35 (Oct., 1940); U. S. Civil Service Commission, *Interpretation of the Hatch Act and Regulation of Political Activity* (Washington, D. C., 1940).

be established to test fitness for promotion in the classified service." Both regulations obviously recognize the possibility of promotions without examination, and until within the past decade, while examinations were more or less irregularly employed, the selection of persons for advancement, in the staffs at Washington as well as throughout the country, was commonly at the discretion of administrative chiefs, guided presumably by such efficiency ratings as might be available, although always with opportunity also to be swayed by personal or political considerations. An executive order of President Roosevelt in 1938, however, tightened up the procedure considerably. The Civil Service Commission was instructed to work out and put into operation a general service-wide promotion system, and since that time the Commission itself has been conducting promotion examinations for positions common to more than one department or establishment, while, under the supervision of the Commission's promotion division, individual departments and establishments have been holding examinations for promotion within their respective jurisdictions; and the Commission's direct examinations open avenues not alone for simple promotions, but also for transfers from one branch of the service to another. Efficiency records, too, are kept more systematically than formerly, with ratings (under terms of the Ramspeck Act) reviewed in every department and establishment by a board of review (composed of one member appointed by the Commission, one by the agency head, and one by the employees) and reported in full to the Commission. Actual promotions are likely to be determined by the results of examinations, checked against candidates' efficiency ratings.[1]

Classification, Pay, Retirement

The slow progress of classification

The only way in which a million or two of federal employees can be brought into orderly arrangement and dealt with according to plan is to group them into classes or categories; and the most obvious basis for such grouping is the nature of the function performed or work done.[2] Different and appropriate examinations can then be devised for each group or sub-group, and likewise compensation fixed on a corresponding graduated scale. Notwithstanding, however, that this seems elementary, Congress long neglected to make the arrangements called for. Different departments or agencies had different classifications, or virtually none

---

[1] It is hardly surprising that the situation relating to promotions and transfers became demoralized, and almost chaotic, during the recent war. At no point, perhaps, did the Civil Service Commission more completely lose its grip. Promotions, in great numbers, were speeded up, and often quite independently, by hard-pressed departments; employees were shunted in droves from agencies that needed them less to others needing them more; large numbers even negotiated their own transfers with no regard for any supervising machinery. Nowadays, however, the regular procedures are again in operation.

[2] Classification for this purpose is not to be confused with the "classified service" in the sense of the portion of the civil service under the merit system. Much of the classified service in the latter sense has never yet been classified in the sense here contemplated, i.e., as to function and for purposes of pay.

at all; examinations were given with little reference to uniformity in nature or difficulty of tests; and compensation was provided with little attention to orderly salary schedules, with persons doing the same kind of work equally well receiving different pay, holders of superior positions in one department or bureau receiving less than inferiors in a different one, and women usually paid less than men for doing the same kind and amount of work. In 1923, a Salary Classification Act was belatedly passed, under which a classification board inventoried the competitive service in the District of Columbia, grouping into classes all positions involving the same types of work, and assigning appropriate salary ranges (with equal pay for men and women), within limits fixed by the act, to each grade or class. The great bulk of the service—outside of the District—was left untouched (except as classified locally or regionally by office heads, more or less on the pattern of the District classification); and so it remained—except, under special statutes, in the foreign and postal services—until 1940, when the Ramspeck Act authorized the president, operating through the Civil Service Commission, to start the service-wide task afresh. Hardly was the job under way, however, before the defense effort and the war so disrupted the normal situation that any classifications made could be on only a more or less temporary basis; and even yet a large part of the undertaking remains to be carried out.

So far as it has gone, however, general classification works out some- *The classification in effect* what as follows. Some twenty-two hundred different types of positions recognized by the Civil Service Commission are thrown into five classes, or "services," each subdivided into grades. At the top is the "professional and scientific service," consisting of positions requiring professional, scientific, or technical training equivalent to graduation from a college or university. Next comes a "subprofessional service," requiring training of the same sorts but less of it, and entailing duties subordinate to those of the first class. Below this is a "clerical, administrative, and fiscal service," bringing together minor positions having to do with office, business, or financial activities. Still farther down the scale is the "custodial service," having duties associated with the care of public buildings, the transportation of persons or property, and the like. And at the bottom is the "clerical-mechanical service," including all positions, outside of recognized trades or crafts, involving skill or experience in machine operation, or merely counting, assorting, and similar duties.

In its report of 1937, the President's Committee on Administrative *Scales of pay* Management laid great stress on the need for raising the then prevailing levels of compensation, not only for officials such as department heads and bureau chiefs, but for the rank and file as well. With matters as they were, the Commission said, people of large ability steered clear of the service because the top salaries were too low; competent men were continually being drawn off into private employment; and poorly paid officials were tempted to cater to special interests in the hope of opening up better opportunities. In the lowest levels, to be sure, compensation compared rather well with that to be secured at the hands of private business; a study made in 1932 showed that the average remuneration in the federal government was about $1,500 a year, while in the whole of industry it was about $1,200. But from perhaps the $2,500 level, the comparison became increasingly unfavorable; and in the higher professional and technical branches the differential was wide. No one would expect the government to match the salary scales of great banks and corporations; and it can always capitalize on certain advantages of public employment which tend to offset lower pay. The point seems well taken, however, that considerations both of efficiency and of prestige require it to reward talent generously enough to attract and hold it as the highest sort of investment in the public interest.[1]

Wartime adjustments

In the national emergency starting in 1940, the problem became especially acute. With private industry reaching out for literally millions of new employees and paying them generously, high-grade civil servants proved increasingly difficult to obtain and experienced older ones hard to hold. To meet the situation, Congress, in 1941, passed a Salary Adjustment Act opening the way for periodic salary increases for substantially all federal officials and employees occupying permanent positions within the scope of the compensation schedules fixed by the Classification Act of 1923, and not having attained the maximum rate of pay for the grade to which their positions were allocated;[2] and under this legislation many thousands of salary readjustments took place. Some of the difficulties encountered in recruiting the enormously increased numbers of civil servants required after war began have been mentioned elsewhere. Among them, of course, was low pay in a period of rising living costs, which at the same time was stirring discontent among people already in the service. While demands mounted, Congress marked time. But at length, in December, 1942, a temporary measure was passed lengthening the workweek of an estimated million and a half civil servants to forty-eight hours and providing for either (a) time and a half over-time compensation for work in excess of forty hours a week (the over-time to be based on that part of the employee's salary below $2,900 a year, with total compensation not to exceed $5,000), or (b) in the case of employees whose work did not lend itself to an over-time schedule, a flat ten per cent increase. On the basis of a forty-eight-hour week, the effect of the over-time provisions was to yield approximately a twenty per cent pay increase. By its own terms, the measure expired in April, 1943; but, with the war still in progress, a new Permanent War Pay Act was placed on the statute-book,

---

[1] "A man primarily interested in making money has no business in public service, and to men who belong in it, its intangible rewards are sufficient to compensate for extra money sacrificed. But an able public servant should be paid enough to support his family on a scale reasonably commensurate with the importance of his position. And his pay should be high enough to serve as a mark of public respect for his profession." *Fortune,* XXVIII, 11 (Nov., 1943).

[2] The Salary Adjustment [Ramspeck-Mead] Act, 55 *U. S. Stat. at Large,* 613.

removing the $5,000 limitation mentioned above and giving employees not under the over-time system an additional fifteen per cent, instead of ten. All in all, however, Congress refused during the war to recognize the need for general and permanent revision of Classification Act pay-scales; and at the end, levels of compensation did not average much higher than at the beginning.

With living costs promising to remain high, nothing was clearer than that further and more lasting increases would have to be made. Almost immediately, indeed, after V-E Day, and following an intensive con-sideration of the matter by congressional committees and other agencies concerned, a Federal Employees Pay Act [1] was placed on the statute-book, giving substantial permanent advances to a large proportion of the members of the service,[2] and supplemented almost simultaneously by a Postal Field Service Pay Act giving 400,000 postal workers a flat increase of $400 annually (in the case of fourth-class postmasters, a twenty per cent advance). Moreover, in the spring of 1946, additional legislation further raised the pay of a million employees (not including postal work-ers) by fourteen per cent or $250 a year, whichever was greater—though at the same time requiring that three-fourths of the increased charge on the national budget otherwise entailed should be averted by reduction of personnel by at least 750,000 by July 1, 1947. The effect of these develop-ments was to remove much uncertainty and discontent and to make federal personnel feel that it was working for a considerate and progres-sive employer. In 1945, too, the forty-eight-hour work-week instituted during the war was reduced, in most branches of the service, to the standard forty hours.

Postwar increases

Under any scale of compensation thus far prevailing, or likely to be adopted, the great majority of civil servants cannot be expected to put aside much for a rainy day—still less to provide in any adequate manner for old age; and the only satisfactory way of enabling them to be sepa-rated from the service, after they have passed their prime, without be-coming dependents or public charges is to make them beneficiaries of a system of retirement pensions. From early in the country's history, Con-gress was generous, and sometimes prodigal, in pensioning war veterans and their dependents. On the other hand, it did not get around to making provision for civil service pensions until less than thirty years ago. Under a Civil Service Retirement Act of 1920 (amended in 1926, 1930, 1942, and 1948), however, we now have a compulsory part-contributory pension system applying originally to members of the classified service only, but later extended to substantially all of the unclassified service (unless otherwise provided for) as well. Under the normal arrangement,

Retire-ment and pensions

[1] 59 *U. S. Stat. at Large*, 295.
[2] The increase amounted to twenty per cent on base pay up to $1,200; ten per cent on that portion of pay between $1,200 and $4,600; and five per cent on any pay in excess of $4,600. This was the first general increase in base rates since passage of the Classification Act of 1923.

six per cent of the salary or other pay of any person covered is deducted; as the "retirement and disability" credit accumulates, the government adds to it interest compounded annually at three percent; and from the fund thus built up the retired employee receives an annuity in a form and on a scale determined by law. The beneficiary may, if he likes, pay in more (up to ten per cent of his salary), assuring himself of a larger annuity. But under a normal plan introduced in 1948, his annuity (if his best five years' pay averaged $5,000 or more) is one-half of one per cent of salary multiplied by years of service; or (if his salary average was less than $5,000), it is one per cent of salary plus $25.00 multiplied by years of service. Even in its regular form, the system gives beneficiaries reasonable assurance against dependency in ill-health and old age, and brings the United States abreast of the more advanced countries in making provision for the multitude of men and women who spend their lives doing the government's routine work, many of them with little or no prospect of promotion or other betterment.[1]

The Organization of Federal Employees

The right to organize conceded

As the country's largest employer, the national government encounters questions of labor relations and labor policy not unlike those confronting private industry; and among these are problems raised by the unionizing of civil servants for purposes of betterment through collective action. Organizations of federal employees first appeared some sixty years ago, and rather naturally in the postal service, closely resembling a private business and notorious for its long hours, low pay, and otherwise unfavorable working conditions. Letter-carriers organized nationally in 1889, post-office clerks in 1890, railway mail clerks in 1891, rural letter-carriers in 1903. At first, the resulting associations, having chiefly a fraternal aspect, were encouraged, indeed largely controlled, by the superior officers of the Post-Office Department. When, however, about 1898, they began trying to put pressure upon Congress to raise the level of pay throughout the service, they lost favor with the authorities; and in 1902 President Theodore Roosevelt issued an executive order forbidding all federal

---

[1] Formerly, the retirement age for railway postal clerks and certain other groups was sixty-two; for city and rural letter-carriers, post-office clerks, and other specified groups, sixty-five; and for other employees, seventy. In line with a long-standing recommendation of the Civil Service Commission, however, Congress in 1942 fixed seventy as the uniform age limit for compulsory retirement. After thirty years' service, employees may retire voluntarily at fifty-five, and after fifteen years' service, at sixty or sixty-two (for different groups). The government may retire them at these ages without their consent, but with right of the employee to ask for a review of his case by the Civil Service Commission. Special retirement arrangements exist for certain groups, e.g., in the foreign service. Dating from 1916, a workmen's compensation act authorizes compensation for employees killed or injured in the discharge of their duties. For some years, the Civil Service Commission has been urging that federal employees be made eligible also for unemployment compensation benefits.

A clear, although necessarily technical, analysis of the civil service retirement system as it stood before changes made in 1948 will be found in L. Meriam, *Relief and Social Security* (Washington, D. C., 1946), Chap. VII.

officers and employees, on penalty of dismissal, "either directly or indirectly, individually or through associations, to solicit an increase of pay or to influence or attempt to influence, in their own interest, any other legislation whatever ... save through the heads of departments under or in which they serve." [1] Even after being made more stringent in 1908, this "gag" order proved only partially effective. Nevertheless, it stirred so much complaint that in 1912 Congress passed an act, strongly backed by the American Federation of Labor, freely recognizing the right of federal employees to petition Congress or any member thereof for increased pay or improved working conditions, forbidding membership in employee organizations having these objectives to be made a ground for dismissal or demotion, and conceding the right of the organizations to affiliate with labor unions outside of the public service, so long as such relationship did not impose any "obligation or duty ... to engage in any strike or ... to assist ... in any strike against the United States." [2] Framed with reference primarily to the postal service (for it was only in the period of the First World War that federal employees outside of that service began to organize on any considerable scale), this measure voices the policy of the national government in connection with all parts of the civil establishment today.

In the last thirty years, the unionizing of federal employees has gone forward fairly rapidly. Nine different groups of postal workers now have their own nation-wide organizations, enlisting in some instances as much as nine-tenths of their potential strength.[3] A National Federation of Federal Employees, dating from 1917, links up more than six hundred local unions of federal employees, composed of persons engaged in various services outside of the separately organized postal branch; an American Federation of Government Employees, originating in a secession from the National Federation in 1932, and inclined toward the C.I.O. without being affiliated, has grown rapidly, especially among employees of agencies of New Deal antecedents; the same is true of the United Federal Workers of America (affiliated with the C.I.O.), which came into the picture in 1937; and, notwithstanding the opinion of many people that such relationships should not be permitted (they were forbidden in Great Britain in 1927), thousands of employees engaged in mechanical trades, *e.g.*, printers, carpenters, and plumbers, belong to the regular unions maintained by their privately employed fellow-craftsmen.

Existing organizations and their activities

Naturally, the service associations are concerned first of all with salary scales, hours, retirement rights, and other matters relating to the status of their own members; undoubtedly they have helped secure better working

Pros and cons of employee organization

---

[1] *Nineteenth Annual Report of the U. S. Civil Service Commission* (1902), 75.
[2] 37 *U. S. Stat. at Large,* 555.
[3] Toward the close of 1946, postal officials and employees recovered their earlier position as the largest functional group in the federal service (465,048 by January, 1948, compared with the next largest group, 381,384 civilians in the Department of the Army).

conditions for many groups of employees, the National Federation contributing heavily, for example, to adoption of the Retirement Act of 1920 and the Classification Act of 1923. Of course the demands which they make sometimes seem out of line with the public interest, and hence stir resentment. Many people, indeed, fear that they will grow so powerful as virtually to hold a club over the government, threatening paralysis of its activities unless they get what they want. In the long run, however, they have an interest, not only in promoting the general efficiency of the service to which they belong, but in keeping the public favorably disposed; and as a rule they can be counted upon to support merit principles, promote employee morale, and help raise the quality of work performed by their members.[1] The things for which they are most frequently criticized are their lobbying activities in Washington,[2] their occasional excursions into politics (chiefly by way of working covertly against unfriendly congressmen seeking reëlection), and their relations with labor organizations outside of the service—although it must be added not only that the National Federation severed all connection with the A. F. of L. in 1931, but that the no-strike pledge contained in the constitutions of most of the federations has been kept faithfully, so that our government has almost wholly escaped defiance of its authority by its own regular employees such as has at times seriously embarrassed the governments of France, Italy, and other European countries.[3]

[1] The National Federation of Federal Employees and the American Federation of Government Employees warmly supported the efforts leading up to the Ramspeck Act of 1940.

[2] See E. P. Herring, *Group Representation Before Congress*, Chap. ix.

[3] In several appropriation bills for the ensuing fiscal year, Congress in 1946 stipulated that before receiving pay-checks federal employees in the services concerned should execute affidavits that they were not members of any organization of federal employees sanctioning strikes against the government of the United States; and the Labor-Management Relations [Taft-Hartley] Act of 1947 (see pp. 740-744 below) generalized the principle by declaring it unlawful "for any individual employed by the United States or any agency thereof ... to participate in any strike," and provided further that any person so employed and taking part in a strike "shall be discharged immediately ... and shall forfeit his civil service status, if any, and shall not be eligible for reëmployment for three years by the United States or any such agency."

In the sentence to which this footnote is appended, the word "regular" is used advisedly, because of course strikes have been engaged in by workers in the employ of the government temporarily. A notable instance was a strike late in 1946 involving the full membership of the United Mine Workers of America, at a time when nearly all bituminous coal-mines had been taken over, and were being operated, by the federal government as an expedient for overcoming stoppages arising from strikes against private operators.

Full discussion of the organization of public (including federal) employees will be found in G. R. Clapp *et al. Employee Relations in the Public Service*, cited on p. 524 below. See also S. D. Spero, *The Labor Movement in a Government Industry; A Study of Employee Organization in the Postal Service* (New York, 1924); E. L. Johnson, "General Unions in the Federal Service," *Jour. of Politics*, II, 23-56 (Feb., 1940); D. Ziskind, *One Thousand Strikes of Government Employees* (New York, 1940), relating chiefly to strikes in local-government areas; R. N. Baldwin, H. E. Kaplan, and S. D. Spero, "Have Public Employees the Right to Strike?," *Nat. Mun. Rev.*, XXX, 515-528 (Sept., 1941).

Continuing Civil Service Problems

The United States has the distinction of being the first large nation in **An un-finished task**
the Western world to develop a public service based, not on class or caste,
but on broad principles of democracy. For this, however, it has paid a
price, in the form of the spoils system with all its resulting inefficiency
and waste. In the last sixty years, we have been trying to rid ourselves
of this incubus; and the gains realized, in the federal field and in many
states and cities, have been impressive. Nationally, we have advanced
from a situation in which practically all appointive positions were dispensed as spoils, with little or no regard for competence and experience,
to one in which nine out of every ten appointees get on the payroll only
by proving their worth, usually through competitive tests. No one would
maintain that the sifting procedures employed could not be improved, or
that they keep out all incompetents. Under the law's requirement of
"practical" examinations, they leave the door open for many people of
very narrow preparation and of little general capacity. Nevertheless, they
do presuppose *some* standards—which is more than the spoils system ever
did. Even a hasty reading of the foregoing pages, however, will suggest
that a long road remains to be travelled before civil service in this country can be regarded as in an entirely satisfactory condition. For one thing,
the spoils system has not yet been completely eliminated on the federal
level, and every now and then it threatens to recover ground that it has
lost; while in any case the battle can in no sense be considered won so
long as the system remains entrenched in over half of the states and in a
far larger proportion of counties and cities. On the federal level, too, we
have still a great deal to do in carrying to completion the long lagging
functional classification of field employees, in getting the pay structure
on a logical and flexible basis in relation to fluctuating living costs, in
improving the techniques of efficiency-rating, in further developing a
defensible general plan of promotions, and in solving problems of man-
agement-employee relations hardly less pressing in government service
than in private industry.

Effective handling of matters such as these would help meet the great-   **The civil service as a career**
est need of all, *i.e.*, that for surrounding the service with conditions still
more favorable for attracting into it talented young men and women
aspiring to make it a career. Our experience with spoils politics caused us
for half a century to think of civil service reform in hardly more than a
negative sort of way, *i.e.*, in terms of frustrating the spoilsman and excluding the most obviously unfit from the public services, while the more
positive objective of enabling the services to get their full share of really
superior recruits was pretty much lost to view. The same experience, too,
has been largely responsible for the prevalent, but essentially false, concept of the public employee as a "tax-eater," a "payroller," as inefficient
and perhaps corrupt, as an overpaid and underworked parasite. The

battle with the spoilsman cannot be relaxed; for he is still with us. But the road to opportunity in the federal and other services must be made smoother and more alluring—by more positive and effective education pointed in that direction, by better examining techniques, by higher pay, by a system of promotions inspiring greater confidence, by transferring higher positions now on a political basis to the classified service so that the competent civil servant may aspire to go all the way up the ladder, and in other ways occurring to any discriminating observer. Studies made some years ago indicate that the "prestige value" of the federal service, while still low enough, is higher than that of state and municipal services—in other words, that the public has more respect for and confidence in the national service than the others.[1] Too long, however, the impression prevailed (and not without reason) that appointment to even the federal service led nowhere and, except as a makeshift, was to be shunned by young people of energy, ambition, and capacity. Today, the situation is changing. A rich variety of newer types of positions, calling for novel skills, hold out inducements; opportunities are open for advancement to higher levels in the service (even if not always the highest); the challenge of public administration as a profession is being widely felt—nowhere more than in the colleges and universities; indeed, from an almost uniform attitude of indifference, often openly encouraged by vocational advisers, the collegiate youth of the country is being stirred to genuine interest, not only in administration as a subject of academic study, but in public service as a personal opportunity and even duty. And there is no more hopeful sign than this latter; for it is the young men trained at Oxford, Cambridge, London, and more recently the provincial universities, who have brought the British civil service to its recognized position as, all in all, the best that the world has known. The greatest need of our American service is a larger proportion of recruits well trained before they enter, fit for steady advancement, and happy in careers achieved in the public employ.

Civil service training

At one time, George Washington dreamed of a national university that would train young men for the federal service, and often afterwards an institution was suggested that would do for the civil service what the academies at West Point and Annapolis do for the Army and Navy. Nothing of the kind has been provided; in the days of the spoils system, neither the politicians nor the people for whom they got jobs would have had any interest in such facilities; and with the service as large as it is nowadays, and its activities as varied as they have become, no single training establishment could go far toward serving the purpose. Under a merit system, the need for training none the less exists; and fortunately it is met today, in considerable measure, by the opportunities provided in

[1] L. D. White, "Politics and Public Service," *Annals of Amer. Acad. of Polit. and Soc. Sci.*, CLXIX, 87-90 (Sept., 1933). Cf. the same author's *Prestige Value of Public Employment* (Chicago, 1929), and *Further Contributions to the Prestige Value of Public Employment* (Chicago, 1932).

colleges and universities (besides many professional and other more or less specialized schools) in every part of the land. The most basic preparation thus afforded commonly takes the form of courses on the principles and techniques of public administration in general, supplemented often with courses treating more particularly of administration in states or cities, and perhaps courses on such cognate subjects as administrative law. And for the candidate of serious purpose, a general grounding on these lines is useful, if not indispensable. When, however, he confronts his examination for entrance into the service, he will find himself tested, not on administrative theory, but on one or more concrete subjects germane to the kind of employment that he seeks, i.e., accounting, statistics, taxation, public health, forestry, some branch of law or of engineering, and the like; and those responsible for training and guiding young people in academic institutions for entry into public service are now directing their work far more than formerly into such substantive fields. Particularly is this true in the lengthening list of institutions in which special programs have been organized and facilities provided.[1]

In many branches of the federal service, too, one's systematic training need not stop upon appointment. Just as most large private establishments provide their employees with opportunities for continued training, with a view to increasing their efficiency and preparing them to assume larger responsibilities, so there have been developed in Washington extensive facilities for "in-service" training for personnel officers, income-tax officials, and many other groups in various departments (notably Agriculture) and agencies. During the recent war, when departments were thronged with hastily gathered recruits largely or totally unfamiliar with the work assigned them, such programs were multiplied beyond all precedent, with the Civil Service Commission itself setting up a training division in 1942 to render assistance. For serious-minded persons weighing the pros and cons of entering upon a civil service career, the prospect of having opportunity, after entrance, to obtain training enhancing the chances of advancement is often an added inducement.[2]

REFERENCES

C. R. Fish, *The Civil Service and the Patronage* (New York, 1904), Chaps. x-xi.
W. D. Foulke, *Fighting the Spoilsmen; Reminiscences of the Civil Service Reform Movement* (New York, 1919).

[1] This aspect of public-service training receives appropriate emphasis in J. W. Fesler, "Undergraduate Training for the Public Service," *Amer. Polit. Sci. Rev.*, XLI, 507-517 (June, 1947). Various conferences on the general subject have been held, notably one at the University of Minnesota in 1931, resulting in a volume entitled *University Training for the Public Service* (Minneapolis, 1932). Cf. G. A. Graham, *Education for Public Administration* (Chicago, 1941); M. B. Lambie, *Training for the Public Service* (Chicago, 1935); L. Meriam, *Public Service and Special Training* (Chicago, 1936), discounting emphasis on university training; and *University Education and the Public Service*, Princeton University Bicentennial Conferences (Princeton, N. J., 1947).

[2] E. Brooks, *In-Service Training of Public Employees* (Chicago, 1939).

D. H. Smith, "The United States Civil Service Commission," *Service Monographs*, No. 49 (Baltimore, 1928).

J. McDiarmid, "The Changing Rôle of the U. S. Civil Service Commission," *Amer. Polit. Sci. Rev.*, XL, 1067-1096 (Dec., 1946).

W. E. Mosher and J. D. Kingsley, *Public Personnel Administration* (rev. ed., New York, 1941). Contains full bibliography.

F. W. Reeves and P. T. David, *Personnel Administration in the Federal Government* (Washington, D. C., 1937).

L. Meriam, *Personnel Administration in the Federal Government; An Examination of Some Pending Proposals*, Brookings Institution Pamphlet Series, No. 19 (Washington, D. C., 1937).

————, *Public Service and Special Training* (Chicago, 1936).

————, *Principles Governing the Retirement of Public Employees* (New York, 1918).

Commission of Inquiry on Public Service Personnel, *Better Government Personnel* (New York, 1935).

L. Gulick [ed.], "Improved Personnel in Government Service," *Annals of Amer. Acad. of Polit. and Soc. Sci.*, CLXXXIX, 1-198 (Jan., 1937).

L. Wilmerding, *Government by Merit* (New York, 1935).

C. J. Friedrich *et al.*, *Problems of the American Public Service* (New York, 1935).

M. B. Lambie, *Training for the Public Service* (Chicago, 1935).

L. D. White, *Introduction to the Study of Public Administration* (rev. ed., New York, 1939).

————, *Government Career Service* (Chicago, 1933).

———— [ed.], *Civil Service in Wartime* (Chicago, 1945).

J. M. Pfiffner, *Public Administration* (New York, 1935), Chaps. VIII-XII.

O. P. Field, *Civil Service Law* (Minneapolis, 1939).

G. R. Clapp *et al.*, *Employee Relations in the Public Service; A Report Submitted to the Civil Service Assembly of the United States and Canada* (Chicago, 1942).

L. F. McMillin, *Women in the Federal Service* (3rd ed., Washington, D. C., 1941).

F. M. Davenport *et al.*, "Political Science and Federal Employment," *Amer. Polit. Sci. Rev.*, XXXVI, 304-310 (Aug., 1942).

S. Greer, *A Bibliography of Civil Service and Personnel Administration* (New York, 1935).

A. D. Brown, *List of References on Civil Service and Personnel Administration in the United States: Federal, State, Local* (Washington, D. C., 1936).

Civil Service Act, Rules, and Regulations, Annotated [Amended to October 31, 1943] (Washington, D. C., 1943).

Annual Reports of U. S. Civil Service Commission (Washington, D. C., 1883 ff.).

U. S. Civil Service Commission, *A Brief History of the United States Civil Service* (Washington, D. C., 1933).

Good Government (New York, 1881—). Published bimonthly by the National Civil Service League.

The Federal Employee (Washington, D. C., 1916—). Published monthly by the National Federation of Federal Employees.

Public Personnel Review. Published quarterly by the Civil Service Assembly, Chicago.

CHAPTER XXIV

THE NATIONAL JUDICIARY

The crowning defect of the government under the Articles of Confederation, wrote Alexander Hamilton in *The Federalist,* was "the want of a judicial power."[1] To be sure, the states had their individual sets of courts, carried over from colonial days. But there was no system for the country as a whole; and so keenly was the deficiency felt that every plan of revision submitted to the Philadelphia convention provided some method for meeting it. In the end, the new constitution not only emphasized the establishment of justice as one of its major purposes, but contained an article devoted entirely to instituting a system of courts resting exclusively on national authority. The reasons why such a national judiciary is needed in this country are fairly obvious. To start with, the federal constitution and the laws and treaties made under it are declared the "supreme law of the land." If, however, there were only state courts to construe this supreme law, almost as many different interpretations might result as there are states, leaving the law in the absurd position of meaning one thing here and another there; and to prevent this, interpretation is, and must be, vested in courts belonging to a nation-wide system established and maintained by the same authority that makes the law itself. In the second place, under a federal system there are certain to be controversies over boundaries and other matters between two or more states; and national courts may be relied upon to provide more impartial tribunals than state courts for deciding such. The same holds true for disputes between citizens residing in different states; while if the national government itself becomes a party to a law-suit with its own citizens, it can hardly be expected to leave matters in the hands of a state court. Inasmuch, too, as the control of foreign relations is vested exclusively in the national government, controversies concerning the status or rights of ambassadors and other representatives of foreign governments may best be adjudicated in courts created by the same authority that would be held responsible by those governments for any infractions of the law of nations, namely, the national government, rather than in courts deriving their authority from state governments, with which foreign nations can have no direct dealings.

For these and other reasons, the makers of the federal constitution therefore wrote into the document the well-known third, or judiciary, article, providing for a system of national courts. Almost the only point

Why a system of national courts

The judiciary article

[1] No. XXII (Lodge's ed., 132).

on which they disagreed was as to whether there would be need for a full set of such tribunals, both higher and lower. Madison thought so, Hamilton thought not; and the matter was wisely left for later decision. As ultimately adopted, Article III provided simply that the national judicial power "shall be vested in one supreme court and in such inferior courts as Congress may from time to time ordain and establish."[1] Specifying further that the judges of supreme and inferior courts shall hold office during good behavior and that their salaries shall not be reduced during their period of tenure, the article concludes with a remarkably concise and lucid statement of the nature and limits of national judicial power (with special safeguards prescribed in connection with treason)—a matter so obviously basic as to furnish the natural starting point for any study of the system.

Scope of the Federal Judicial Power

Federal jurisdiction:

In the domain of justice, as in all others, the national government has only delegated powers—which means that the national courts have jurisdiction over only those classes of cases specified in the constitution, or implied in it, while the state courts have jurisdiction over all others. As a glance at the judiciary article will show, the federal judicial power[2] extends to some cases because of the nature of the matter in controversy, and to others because of the status or residence of the parties concerned. The first of these two classes of actions includes (1) all cases in law and equity arising under the constitution, laws, and treaties of the United States, and (2) all cases of admiralty and maritime jurisdiction. That is to say, whenever, in any lawsuit, a right is asserted which is based upon

1. On the ground of nature of controversy

some provision of the national constitution, laws, or treaties, or when it is asserted that some right secured by the national constitution, statutes, or treaties has been violated by the enactment of a state law or municipal ordinance, the case may be commenced in, and decided by, the federal courts; or, if commenced in a state court, it may, before final decision, be transferred to the federal courts. In other words, whenever it becomes essential to a correct decision of a lawsuit to obtain an interpretation or application of the national constitution, laws, or treaties, the case comes within "the judicial power of the United States." Cases of "admiralty and maritime jurisdiction," also falling in this class, have to do with offenses committed on shipboard, and with contracts which by their

---

[1] In the Judiciary Act of 1789, Congress not only set up the Supreme Court as required, but supplemented it with courts of two other grades—thirteen district courts and above them three circuit courts.

[2] "Judicial power," as defined by Professor Edward S. Corwin, is "the power to decide 'cases' and 'controversies' in conformity with law and by the methods established by the usages and principles of law." *The Constitution and What It Means Today* (10th ed., Princeton, N. J., 1948), 117. Among other things, it involves the interpretation of existing law, the right to have a decision reviewed only by a *higher court,* and the right to enforce authority by punishment for contempt. It does not necessarily include determination of questions of fact or passing upon questions of a political nature.

nature must be executed partly or wholly on the high seas or "navigable waters of the United States," *e.g.*, contracts for the transportation of passengers and freight, marine insurance policies, contracts for ships' supplies and seamen's wages, and actions to recover damages for torts and other injuries. In time of war, prize cases, too, are included.

The second class of cases comes within the scope of the federal judicial power because of the character or residence of the parties, and includes (1) all cases affecting ambassadors and other public ministers and consuls; [1] (2) controversies to which the United States is a party; (3) controversies between two or more states; (4) controversies between citizens of different states; (5) disputes between citizens of the same state claiming lands under grants from different states; and (6) controversies between a state or its citizens and foreign states, citizens, or subjects. Included in the list in the original constitution were also controversies between a state and citizens of another state. When, however, in 1793 the Supreme Court sustained an action brought against the state of Georgia by a citizen of South Carolina,[2] the decision stirred protest as being derogatory to the dignity of a sovereign state; and five years later, as we have seen, the Eleventh Amendment forbade federal courts to take cognizance of any suit brought against a state by the citizens of another state or of a foreign state. Any citizen of a state desiring to bring suit against it may do so only in the state's own courts—and then only if the legislature of the state has sanctioned such actions—which sometimes is done. In the federal courts, a state may be sued only by the United States, by another one of the states, or by a foreign state.

The mere fact, however, that certain classes of cases are mentioned in the constitution as falling within the judicial power of the United States does not necessarily mean that they are thereby wholly removed from the jurisdiction of the state courts—because the constitution gives the federal courts no *exclusive* jurisdiction whatever. Congress alone determines what classes of cases shall be handled exclusively by the federal courts; and all others may be tried in state courts as well. Under existing national statutes, the federal courts have *exclusive* jurisdiction over all civil actions in which the United States or a state is a party, except those between a state and its own citizens; also over all cases involving crime against the United States, and all admiralty, maritime, patent-right, copyright, and bankruptcy cases arising under either the national constitution or national statutes. Over practically all other kinds of cases to which the federal judicial power extends, federal and state courts have concurrent jurisdiction, with the party instituting a case (the plaintiff) enjoying the

Marginal notes:
2. On the ground of status of the parties

Exclusive or concurrent jurisdiction?

---

[1] In point of fact, under international law diplomatic representatives of foreign governments are immune from prosecution in the courts of the country to which they are accredited. For committing a criminal offense, they may be sent home, or their recall may be requested; but they are exempt from legal process.

[2] Chisholm *v.* Georgia, 2 Dallas 419 (1793).

[3] See p. 46 above.

option of commencing his action in a court of his own or the defendant's state, or of bringing it in a federal court.

How cases get into the federal courts

The existence at all times of thousands of cases on the dockets of the federal courts may be accounted for in one or another of three different ways. By far the greatest number are cases begun and ended in a federal court because that is the only forum in which they can be tried at all. Other cases have been commenced in a state court, but have been transferred, at the request of the defendant, to a federal court to be finally disposed of there. Such removal is permissible (1) when the parties reside in different states, and (2) when, even though they reside in the same state, the case raises a "federal question"—in other words, involves some right or immunity claimed under the national constitution, laws, or treaties. In either event, the removal must take place before the state courts have rendered final judgment. Such removals are permitted in order to place the defendant on an equal footing with the plaintiff (who had the choice between the federal and state courts when he brought his suit), and especially to protect the defendant against the effects of local prejudice. Lastly, cases get into the federal courts as a result of appeals from decisions of the highest court of the state where action started, or in consequence of the Supreme Court voluntarily undertaking to review them. If, in deciding a case the highest state court upholds a state law alleged by one of the parties to violate the federal constitution, laws, or treaties, that party normally can get the case carried on appeal to the federal Supreme Court. If, on the other hand, the state court finds the statute in conflict with the federal constitution, laws, or treaties, the defeated party has no *right* of appeal, although since 1914 the Supreme Court may at its discretion call up the case by a process known as writ of *certiorari* and review it.[1]

Kinds of Cases Tried

1. Criminal law and cases under it

The cases appearing in the federal courts in one or another of the ways just mentioned fall into two great divisions, criminal and civil.[2] The only criminal jurisdiction belonging to the federal courts is such as has been conferred by act of Congress; and Congress, of course, has no authority to define crimes and fix penalties except as derived, directly or

---

[1] Before congressional legislation of 1925, appeals from the decisions of state courts, when authorized, were by a procedure known as "writ of error," under which the Supreme Court had no option but to hear the case involved. In the year mentioned, however, writs of error were superseded completely by writs of *certiorari*, issued as a matter of choice by the Supreme Court to the state or federal court concerned and calling up a case for review.

[2] In the domain of *civil* law, the function of government consists principally in laying down the rules which are to guide individuals and corporations in their relations and dealings, and in providing tribunals in which controversies may be adjudicated, although government officials may have to do in various ways with seeing that the results of adjudications are carried out. In the field of *criminal* law, government lays down prohibitions, prescribes penalties, ferrets out infractions, provides courts for trying accused persons, and in addition bears sole responsibility for executing judicial findings.

indirectly, from the constitution. In only five kinds of cases has that instrument directly conferred this authority, namely, (1) piracies and felonies committed on the high seas; (2) offenses against the law of nations, or international law; (3) counterfeiting the securities and current coin of the United States; (4) treason against the United States; and (5) offenses committed in the District of Columbia, in any other place wholly under national control (such as a fort or an arsenal), or in the territories and dependencies, where Congress has full authority to define crimes and determine their punishment.[1]

If the criminal dockets of the federal courts contained only cases falling within these five classes, the criminal jurisdiction of these tribunals would be rather unimpressive. Congress, however, may add indefinitely to the constitutional list as given above. Nothing is more natural than, when enacting a law, to declare any violation of it a criminal offense; and this is done in large numbers of instances. The power to establish post-offices, for example, manifestly carries with it power to make it a crime to rob the mails. In 1934, indeed, Congress invoked its authority over interstate commerce to extend federal criminal jurisdiction even to cases initially falling to the state courts but assuming a federal aspect by reason of the flight of persons involved, *e.g.*, kidnappers, from one state into another.[2]

Statutory crimes

All courts operate under rules of procedure covering such matters as the nature of evidence, the use of juries, and carrying appeals; and in the case of the federal courts the constitution leaves all such rules to be made by or under the authority of Congress except in so far as the constitution itself touches the matter.[3] For procedure in civil cases, the constitution goes no farther than to require trial by jury when the amount in controversy exceeds twenty dollars.[4] On procedure in criminal cases, however, the first ten amendments contain a number of provisions

Criminal procedure

---

[1] The federal criminal code will be found in *Code of the Laws of the U. S.* (1940), Title 18. There are nine principal federal crime-control agencies: the Bureau of Investigation (F.B.I.) and the Immigration Border Patrol (both in the Department of Justice) ; the United States Secret Service, the Intelligence Unit of the Bureau of Internal Revenue, the Enforcement Division of the Alcohol Tax Unit, the Customs Agency Service of the Bureau of Customs, the Bureau of Narcotics, and the United States Coast Guard (all in the Treasury Department) ; and the Office of Chief Inspector of the Post-Office Department. But of course federal district attorneys may prosecute crimes against the United States, whether or not brought to light by any of the agencies named.

[2] With jurisdiction restricted to their respective states, state authorities have often been handicapped by lack of any right to cross state lines in pursuit of persons accused or suspected of crime. Federal penal legislation of the sort mentioned above has aided in bringing about a closer coördination and coöperation of state and federal criminal authorities.

[3] Congress began laying down rules in the Judiciary Act of 1789 and in later days added to or amended them as they accumulated. The work, however,—grown increasingly technical—can more appropriately be performed by experienced jurists than by the ordinary run of legislators; and in recognition of this, power to make rules governing civil procedure has several times been delegated to the Supreme Court, and in 1940 power to make rules for criminal procedure also. See p. 553, note 2, below.

[4] Seventh Amendment.

designed to surround accused persons with safeguards against arbitrary and irregular prosecutions—provisions carried over largely from the English common law and in several cases embodied in the English Bill of Rights of 1689. No civilian, for example, may be put to trial for a federal offense (except a misdemeanor) unless he has been indicted by a grand jury, nor be compelled to testify against himself, nor be deprived of life, liberty, or property without due process of law. Persons accused of crimes are entitled to a speedy and public trial by an impartial jury;[1] to a trial in the vicinity where the crime was committed, in order to facilitate the obtaining of witnesses; to be furnished with an exact copy of the indictment; to have witnesses subjected to cross-examination in their presence; to have compulsory process for obtaining witnesses; to have the assistance of counsel for their defense; and to be admitted to bail in a reasonable sum, pending their trial. Furthermore, no person may again be subjected to trial in a federal court for the same offense if he has once been acquitted on the charge.[2] The same offense, however, may be punishable by state authorities in the state courts and by federal authorities in the federal courts—as, for example, in cases involving the passing of counterfeit money, in cases of fraud when use has been made of the mails, and in cases of theft from freight-cars moving in interstate commerce. The fact that a person has been successfully prosecuted for such an offense in a state court is no bar to prosecuting and convicting him in a federal court; for in such instances the defendant is being tried in different jurisdictions for offenses against different sovereignties. Situations of the sort were particularly numerous during the days of national prohibition.

Criminal prosecutions are instituted and trials conducted, on behalf of the federal government, by district attorneys appointed by the president, on recommendation of the attorney-general, for each of the eighty-four districts into which the states are now divided; and the territories have their district attorneys serving in a similar capacity. In exceptionally important and complicated cases, a special district attorney may be appointed to represent the government.

2. Civil cases:

(a) Cases at law

A second and more numerous category of actions tried in the federal courts is cases of a civil character; and on the basis of the law administered, three distinct types of such cases must be distinguished—cases at law, cases in equity, and admiralty cases. Cases at law comprise mainly actions arising out of civil wrongs, called torts, and actions based upon contracts, either express or implied. They rest upon some principle of the old common law carried over from England, or upon some state or federal

---

[1] The right to trial by jury does not extend to petty offenses, and under certain circumstances may be waived, even in felony cases. See Schick v. United States, 195 U. S. 65 (1904); Patton v. United States, 281 U. S. 276 (1930); and especially Adams v. United States, 317 U. S. 269 (1942). For the guidance of persons drawn to serve on juries in federal courts, the Judicial Conference of Senior Circuit Judges has prepared a small *Handbook for Petit Jurors* (1944), which explains in language readily understood the functions of jurymen in such courts.

[2] Cf. pp. 166-173 above.

statute; and they are tried in accordance with the rules of the English common law, or modifications thereof provided for by state or federal statutes.[1] In most actions at law, the redress sought is money damages, and the remedy is granted only after the wrong has been committed or the contract has been broken. There are many cases, however, in which the granting of money damages to the injured party is an inadequate remedy, for the very good reason that the defendant may refuse to pay the judgment obtained against him and has no property which can be seized and sold to satisfy the judgment. Or it may be impossible to estimate the amount of damages that would result from the non-fulfillment of an agreement. In still other cases, a contract may be involved—for example, a deed conveying title to real estate—which is perfectly regular and legal on its face and is executed with due formality, although the circumstances surrounding its execution may have been tainted by fraud, intimidation, or undue influence.

In order to do "equity," or "substantial justice," in such cases as these, the "equity jurisdiction" of English and American courts has been built up through the centuries as a supplement to the usual law remedies. Industrial strikes often result in injury or destruction of property for which no adequate money damages can be collected; at all events, regular legal action can do nothing more than make awards after the damage has been done. In equity proceedings, however, a federal court may, by issuing a writ of injunction, command strikers and their sympathizers to refrain from injuring or destroying property, thereby preventing damage from taking place. And any violation of the terms of an injunction constitutes an offense known as contempt of court, which may be punished severely and summarily by the court whose jurisdiction has been disregarded, in many cases without benefit of jury trial for the offending parties.[2] Again, when it is impossible to estimate the amount of damages that might result from a breach of contract, as when the owner of a valuable race-horse has agreed to sell that horse—the only one the purchaser wants—a court, in equity proceedings, will, by a decree of "specific performance," order the owner to carry out the agreement. In a third type of cases, a court, in equity proceedings, may entirely set aside a deed for the transfer of property on the ground of fraudulent or other improper circumstances surrounding the execution of the instrument.

(b) Cases in equity

The rules and remedies peculiar to equity practice and procedure are enforced by the same federal judges who administer the principles and rules of the common law and of statute;[3] and it is always necessary

No separate equity courts

[1] In the decision of many cases based upon diverse citizenship of the parties, the courts are called upon to interpret or apply no provisions of national law, but merely those of state laws. For example, if a suit is brought between citizens of New York and of Pennsylvania regarding land in Pennsylvania, the only law involved in the case and applied by the federal court is the local law of Pennsylvania.

[2] On the use of injunctions in labor disputes, see pp. 731-732 below.

[3] In most states also, law and equity are administered by the same justices; but eight (mainly in the South) have separate equity, or "chancery," courts.

in equity proceedings, before a judge will grant the appropriate equity relief, to establish the fact that the party seeking equity has no adequate remedy at law. In its long history in England and in this country, equity has come to have its own elaborate and highly technical code of rules and precedents parallel to the complicated rules and procedures operating in actions at law; and such equity rules as are observed and enforced in our federal courts are drawn up, and at extended intervals revised, by the justices of the Supreme Court.

(c) Admiralty cases

Lastly, the same federal judges who administer common law and equity also administer admiralty and maritime law in cases of tort and contract connected with shipping and water-borne commerce on the high seas or "navigable waters of the United States." Such cases are tried and determined in accordance with the highly technical and peculiar rules of an admiralty code inherited from England and modified by acts of Congress. In prize and piracy cases, the judges sitting in admiralty courts also administer international law.

The courts as business managers

In their handling of cases at law and in equity, the federal courts in recent decades have increasingly become the managers of important businesses, through their right to appoint receivers to take charge of and manage property, pending litigation, for the benefit of the owners, stockholders, or creditors. As a result, the courts have found themselves indirectly engaged in the operation of railways, municipal transportation systems, mines, factories, and various other business enterprises; and in so doing they are required to pass upon questions of business administration, service, and personnel, supervise accounts, authorize bond issues and sales of property, and intervene in controversies between employers and labor unions over wages and working conditions. In this capacity, "they are as truly the business managers of the properties or enterprises which they are judicially guarding as if the judges bore the title of president or superintendent." [1]

Structure of the Federal Judicial System

From the nature and scope of the national judicial power, we turn to the system of courts in which this power is exercised, finding as we do so three major facts: first, that the "federal judicial system," in the proper sense, comprises three grades or levels of tribunals; second, that (as already indicated) only the Supreme Court at the top is directly provided for in the constitution; and third, that all courts on the lower levels have been established and their jurisdictions defined by Congress in statutes starting with the Judiciary Act of 1789, which is still the basic law underlying the system's organization. We find also that no federal judges are elected, but rather that all are appointed by the president with the advice and consent of the Senate,[2] and that all except some

---

[1] W. MacDonald, *A New Constitution for a New America*, 192.
[2] In February, 1939, the Senate refused to confirm the nomination of Floyd H.

in a special category of "legislative courts" (to be mentioned below) hold office during good behavior and are removable only by impeachment.

The hierarchy starts at the bottom with district courts, of which eighty-four are distributed over the country (with several also in the overseas territories [1]), in order to bring them within reasonably easy reach of litigants. A small state, such as Vermont or New Hampshire, may constitute a district by itself; larger or more populous states may be divided into two or more districts; and in still other cases, a district may consist of parts of two or more states. And the number of judges attached (totalling some 180 for the country as a whole) varies from one to as high as thirteen, according to the volume of business to be handled. Where there is more than one judge, the court holds its sessions in different "divisions" simultaneously, each with a single judge sitting. Attached to every district court, moreover, is a district attorney to conduct prosecutions, a United States marshal to serve writs and execute orders and judgments, and a commissioner to hold preliminary hearings in criminal cases. [2]

1. District Courts

Cases triable in a district court are of many different sorts. All federal crimes are prosecuted there, and all proceedings instituted under the anti-trust laws. Included also are admiralty cases, suits arising under the internal revenue, postal, copyright, patent, and bankruptcy laws, or under any law regulating commerce, as well as cases removed from a state court before final judgment and cases between citizens of different states and between citizens of a state and a foreign state or its citizens if the value in controversy exceeds $3,000. [3] In some instances, appeals may be taken directly to the Supreme Court; but as a rule they go first to a circuit court of appeals. The district court itself has no appellate jurisdiction (except in a qualified sense on rulings of their commissioners); the common impression that cases may be appealed from a highest state court to a federal district court is quite erroneous.

Their jurisdiction

Until 1911, the next level of courts above the district courts consisted of a series of nine circuit courts, so-called because to each of the large

2. Circuit courts of appeals

Roberts to be district judge in western Virginia, because his nomination was "utterly and personally obnoxious" to both senators from Virginia. This rejection of a person whose qualifications for a judgeship were generally conceded revived discussion of the defects of the present system of naming federal judges, and of possible substitute methods. For earlier discussions, see W. D. Mitchell, "Appointment of Federal Judges," *Amer. Bar Assoc. Jour.*, XVII, 569-574 (Sept., 1931); B. Shartel, "Federal Judges—Appointment, Supervision, Removal," *Jour. of Amer. Judic. Soc.*, XV, 21-30, 46-51, 79-88 (June-Oct., 1931).

[1] One each in Alaska, Hawaii, Puerto Rico, the Virgin Islands, and the Panama Canal Zone.

[2] See pp. 555-556 below.

[3] This "diversity of citizenship" jurisdiction long proved troublesome because of the proneness of corporations doing business in various states besides the one in which they are incorporated, and of which they are "citizens," to take advantage of it to evade the jurisdiction of the courts of states in which cases arise, or, in the instance of public utilities, to get injunctions against orders of state rate-making authorities. Recognizing the abuse, Congress, in 1934 and 1937, enacted legislation forbidding district courts to make diversity of citizenship a reason for taking jurisdiction in taxation, rate-making, and certain other kinds of cases when it can be shown that state courts are prepared to act. 48 *U. S. Stat. at Large,* 775; 50 *ibid.,* 738.

areas or circuits into which the country was divided was assigned one member of the Supreme Court, who in early times when the Supreme Court had little business often actually visited his circuit and held court either alone or in conjunction with the circuit judge. In 1891, an additional judicial level or layer, consisting of circuit courts of appeals, was interposed above the circuit courts,[1] which, however, in the interest of simplification were abolished twenty years later,[2] leaving the circuit courts of appeals, as today, the only courts of intermediate status. One such court is now found in each of ten circuits, with also a court of equivalent status in the District of Columbia, comprising in effect an eleventh circuit; and each Supreme Court justice is still assigned to a circuit (in two instances, to two), even though none ever finds time actually to "ride circuit" as legally he still might do. The object of creating the circuit courts of appeals was to relieve the Supreme Court of appellate business which even half a century ago was getting out of hand; and the purpose of them still is to take pressure off that hard-pressed tribunal and, in so doing, to speed up the processes of justice.

Nature and functions

District judges not too fully occupied may be called upon to help with circuit-court work; but a circuit court of appeals regularly consists of from three to six circuit judges; and, in contrast with the district courts, in which the judges sit singly, at least two circuit judges must hear every case, with certification of a case to the Supreme Court for instructions or for final decision if the circuit judges hearing it divide equally upon it. The work of circuit courts of appeals is confined entirely to hearing appeals from district courts within the respective circuits, together with reviewing and enforcing orders issued by certain administrative bodies, notably the Interstate Commerce Commission, the Federal Trade Commission, and the National Labor Relations Board. In many kinds of cases—e.g., those between aliens and citizens, those between citizens of different states where no federal issue is involved, and those arising under the patent, copyright, bankruptcy, and revenue laws, or the law of admiralty (except prize cases), when the amount in controversy does not exceed one thousand dollars—decisions are normally final. In most instances, however, the Supreme Court may, upon petition of either party, and before final action, order a case transferred to itself for review and decision. And any case in which a circuit court declares a state law unconstitutional may, as a matter of right, be carried on appeal to the highest tribunal; indeed, practically any case may be so appealed if that tribunal recognizes in it a question of construction of the federal constitution or laws and on that ground chooses (as it usually does) to accept jurisdiction. On this basis, cases growing out of enforcement of the anti-trust laws or orders of the Interstate Commerce Commission, or turning upon the constitutionality of state legislation, almost invariably go di-

[1] 26 *U. S. Stat. at Large,* 826 (1891).
[2] 36 *U. S. Stat. at Large,* 1167 (1911).

rectly from district courts to the Supreme Court, by-passing the circuit courts altogether.[1]

At the top of the system—in a sense, at the head of the entire judicial organization of the United States—stands our most august tribunal, the Supreme Court, first organized under the Judiciary Act of 1789 with a chief justice and five associate justices.[2] Since then, the total number of justices, as fixed by Congress, has once been as high as ten, although for a long time past—notwithstanding a presidential proposal in 1937 to increase it to a possible fifteen—it has been nine.[3] Appointed, of course, by the president and Senate, all hold office during good behavior,[4] with removal only by impeachment; like judges in the lower federal courts, all have salaries fixed from time to time by Congress, subject only to the restriction that no salary may be reduced during a judge's period of service; and all who have served at least ten years may retire at the age of seventy. Sitting, too, in a splendid new building not far from the Capitol,[5] the Court regularly has one session, or "term," a year, beginning on the first Monday in October and commonly ending by the close of the following May. During an average eight-month term, something like a thousand appealed cases are likely to be heard and considered—a far cry from the state of things when John Marshall, assuming the chief justiceship in 1801, found only ten cases on the Court's calendar and had difficulty in arranging for a small committee room in which the Court could sit.

3. The Supreme Court

Although receiving slightly higher compensation,[6] the chief justice has, in reality, no more weight or influence in deciding cases than any of the associate justices. He is simply the presiding judge at sessions of the Court, acting further as a sort of chairman in assigning to his associates the task of writing the Court's decisions in cases that have been heard and discussed. His position in this respect does not, however, exempt him from performing his share of this kind of work. He also appoints members of the Court to serve on committees which now and then revise the

The chief justice

[1] In December, 1946—on petition of the federal government and with the assent of the defendants—the Supreme Court agreed to take jurisdiction at once over an appeal by the United Mine Workers and its president, John L. Lewis, against a decision of the federal district court for the District of Columbia finding the defendants guilty of contempt of court. Normally, the case would have gone first to a circuit court of appeals; but it was considered that, in the critical situation existing, this would involve undesirable delay. See p. 732, note 1, below.

[2] C. Warren, "The First Decade of the Supreme Court of the United States," *Univ. of Chicago Law Rev.*, VII, 631-654 (June, 1940).

[3] The number—originally six—was reduced to five in 1801, increased to seven in 1807, to nine in 1837, to ten in 1863, reduced to seven in 1866, and again increased to nine in 1869.

[4] In the Philadelphia convention of 1787, it was proposed that, following English analogy, federal judges be made removable by action of the two houses of Congress. But the plan was decisively defeated—unwisely in the later opinion of Thomas Jefferson.

[5] For more than seventy years prior to 1935, the sessions of the Court were held in the old Senate chamber in the Capitol. See T. E. Waggaman, "The Supreme Court; Its Homes, Past and Present," *Amer. Bar Assoc. Jour.*, XXVII, 283-289 (May, 1941).

[6] $25,500 as compared with $25,000.

rules governing equity procedure and the rules of practice in actions at law, and which also have drafted rules of criminal procedure. In all, thirteen chief justices have presided over our highest judicial tribunal since its creation.[1] The outstanding figure in the list is John Marshall, whose tenure covered more than thirty years (1801-35), and who, because of his forceful and winsome personality, his firm and clear convictions in favor of a liberal construction of the powers of the national government, and the masterful logic and lucidity of style with which those convictions were expressed in many a notable decision during the formative period of our national institutions, is justly regarded as "the second father of the constitution"—even though some of the constitutional interpretations for which he is famous are not in favor with the Court as it stands today.[2] There have been associate justices also whose personality and influence upon our constitutional history entitle them to mention—notably James Wilson (1789-98), Joseph Story (1811-45), Stephen J. Field (1863-97), John M. Harlan (1879-1911), and Oliver Wendell Holmes (1902-32).

Juris-
diction

Cases come before the Supreme Court in one of two ways—by original suit and by appeal; but the two are of very unequal importance. In the constitution, we read that "in all cases affecting ambassadors, other public ministers, and consuls, and those in which a state shall be a party, the Supreme Court shall have original jurisdiction."[3] Hence the Court is not, as are the circuit courts of appeals, exclusively appellate. Two things are, however, to be observed: first, that Congress may not enlarge the scope of the Court's original jurisdiction—as it attempted to do in the Judiciary Act of 1789 by conferring such jurisdiction in mandamus cases[4]—since that would be tantamount to amending the constitution in an unconstitutional manner; and second, that even as to the cases specified, the Supreme Court does not have exclusive jurisdiction except (as ordained by Congress) where the case is against an ambassador, minister, or consul, or where, in a case to which a state is a party, the other party is the United States, a foreign state, or another state of the Union. Cases of the latter sort are likely to be significant, but they are not numerous

[1] In chronological order, they are: John Jay, 1789-95; John Rutledge, 1795-96; Oliver Ellsworth, 1796-1800 (resigned); John Marshall, 1801-35; Roger B. Taney, 1836-64; Salmon P. Chase, 1864-73; Morrison R. Waite, 1874-88; Melville W. Fuller, 1889-1910; Edward D. White, 1910-21; William H. Taft, 1921-30; Charles E. Hughes, 1930-41; Harlan F. Stone, 1941-46; and Fred M. Vinson, since 1946.

[2] On the influence of Marshall, see series of addresses delivered at the centennial celebration of his appointment, *John Marshall; Life, Character, and Judicial Services,* 3 vols. (Chicago, 1903); W. E. Dodd, "Chief Justice Marshall and Virginia," *Amer. Hist. Rev.,* XII, 776-787 (July, 1907); E. S. Corwin, *John Marshall and the Constitution* (New Haven, 1919); and A. J. Beveridge, *Life of John Marshall,* 4 vols. (Boston, 1916-19). There is also a two-volume edition of the last-mentioned work (1929).

[3] Art. III, § 2, cl. 2.

[4] In 1803, this portion of the Judiciary Act was held void in the famous case of Marbury *v.* Madison, 1 Cranch 137. A mandamus is a writ issued by a court commanding a public officer, a corporation, or an inferior court to perform some specified ministerial duty (one not involving the exercise of any discretion). The right to issue the writ, as also a number of others, is enjoyed by both federal and state courts.

enough to occupy much of the Court's time. Far otherwise is it with cases brought to the court on appeal. Many come from some lower federal court; many from the highest court of some state; and hundreds have to be heard every year. To be sure, the Court has a good deal of discretion as to what cases it will, and what ones it will not, hear; and the tendency of later congressional legislation touching the matter—notably the important Judiciary Act of 1925—has been to widen this discretion in a variety of ways.[1] Deluged with petitions for writs of *certiorari* calling up for review and decision cases still pending in lower courts, it can pick and choose, complying only when it comes upon a case which it thinks it should handle. Doubly deluged with requests for the writ looking to appeals against decisions already handed down in lower federal or highest state courts, it again often can accept or refuse jurisdiction very much as it likes. Disappointed litigants frequently declare warmly that they will carry appeal right up to the Supreme Court! But even if they actually set out to do so, most of them will fail to arrive. For unless their appeal springs from a situation in which a highest state court has (a) held valid some state law alleged to be contrary to the federal constitution or to a federal law or treaty, or (b) has held invalid some federal law or treaty, there is no ground on which it can be asserted as a right; and with the Supreme Court more and more focussing its attention, not upon mere adjudication of law suits in the manner of the regular law court that it was designed to be and long was, but rather upon constitutional interpretation and policy, especially in social and economic fields, appeals lacking in these latter interests are likely to encounter no very warm reception. Constitutionally and legally, the jurisdiction of the Court may still be largely what it long has been; but, as actually exercised, it has come to be rather highly selective (outside of certain fields of definite obligation), and with the emphasis always on cases involving interpretation and policy.

Expanding use of discretion

When the Court sits, the black-robed justices occupy a row of high-backed black leather chairs on the "bench," the chief justice flanked on either side by four associates. Behind them are marble columns and rich red velour drapes; in front, seating arrangements for some three hundred spectators, with tables for attorneys and directly before the mahogany bar shielding the justices a lectern on which those who address the Court may rest their documents and notes. A case is an action between two parties, who may be private individuals, corporations, or governments; and invariably the parties will be represented by attorneys, who not only argue their clients' side of the controversy, but supply the justices with briefs and other materials to be studied at leisure.[2] In the old days, oral

How the Court works

---

[1] It will be remembered that *all* of the Court's appellate power comes to it from acts of Congress, which therefore can freely expand or contract it.

[2] Any lawyer who has practiced before the highest court of his state may be admitted to practice before the Supreme Court by being presented by a sponsor and paying a small fee.

arguments were interminable; Webster and Calhoun went on, not for hours, but for days. Cases were fewer and the Court had more time. In 1849, a two-hour limit on each individual effort was set; today, under all ordinary circumstances, the limit is a single hour, which must include the answering of questions with which the justices sometimes ply those addressing them.[1] As arguments on batches of cases are concluded, the justices devote Saturdays in their conference room to reviewing and discussing them, and also the documents, eventually arriving at conclusions on each case which can be supported by at least four of the "quorum" of six which must be present when any case is argued.[2] If fewer than this minimum can concur in a given instance, a rehearing is likely to be ordered; although if a decision of a lower court is involved, an even division simply means that the decision will stand.[3] Assuming concurrence by at least four justices, it then falls to the chief justice to designate some majority member—perchance himself—to write the Court's opinion; and after the resulting document has been discussed and possibly amended, the opinion is read—to sometimes an eager audience and perhaps an anxious country—at an ensuing Monday sitting of the Court.

Concurring and dissenting opinions

The opinion thus prepared and made public will ordinarily set forth not only the conclusion reached, but also the line of reasoning followed, with also supporting citations. One or more justices, however, may have arrived at the same goal, but by a different route; and any such will be permitted to present "concurring" opinions (concurring in the result, but not the grounds for it). Still other justices may have found themselves unable to go along with the majority on either the result or the reasoning; and any such have the privilege of presenting single or joint "dissenting" opinions—which, indeed, not infrequently are considerably more challenging and cogent than the majority opinion itself, and which, attracting hardly less attention from lawyers, become subjects for thought and discussion, with often a chance eventually of winning acceptance and turning our federal jurisprudence into some new channel.[4] In

---

[1] The Court convenes at noon on all weekdays except Saturdays and usually rises about 4.30.

[2] From 1789 to 1863, a minimum of five justices, constituting a majority, sufficed for the hearing of a case. With the Court's membership raised to ten, the majority principle was preserved by increasing the "quorum" to six. When, however, the total again became nine, the quorum rule was (inadvertently it seems) left unchanged. Situations have arisen in which the Court could not take jurisdiction of a case because as many as four justices were disqualified to participate, by former connection with the Department of Justice or some other circumstance; and bills have been introduced in Congress to restore the quorum to a simple majority of five. See H. E. Cunningham, "The Problem of the Supreme Court Quorum," *Geo. Washington Law Rev.*, XII, 175–189 (Feb., 1944).

[3] In this way, the federal income tax law of 1894 was held unconstitutional in 1895 (Pollock *v.* Farmers' Loan and Trust Co., 158 U. S. 601), and an Oregon minimum wage law and a New York unemployment insurance law were held constitutional in 1917 and 1936, respectively.

[4] This is the more true because sometimes dissents represent the views of as many as four of the nine justices and therefore have fallen short of controlling the decision

his day, John Marshall considered that, as head of the Court, it was his business to take care of the reading of all opinions in a case, even those in dissent. For now more than a hundred years, however, the practice has been for all justices to read their own opinions—first the justice who has written the majority opinion, then the concurrers, and finally the dissenters. And all opinions are published by the government, for the benefit of the legal profession and of the general public, in a series of volumes prepared under the editorial supervision of a reporter appointed by the Court, and entitled *United States Reports*.[1]

In eleven states, the constitution authorizes the governor or legislature to call upon the state's highest court for an advisory opinion upon the constitutionality of any existing law (not as yet actually tested in a case) or of any law contemplated or in process of being enacted. Early in its history, however, the federal Supreme Court took a stand against performing any such service in behalf of the president or Congress; and while a good deal might be gained if the Court were to reverse this policy, opening a way for a sort of preview of the attitude which it probably would take on a legislative provision or executive action *if* a case were to arise under it, there is doubt whether it would do so even if Congress were expressly to authorize, or even require, advisory opinions to be rendered. An advisory opinion would not *bind* the Court to a given course of action if and when later confronted with an actual case; but it would set up presumptions which might avert the confusions resulting from

No advisory opinions

---

by only the narrowest of margins. A famous dissenting opinion was that of Mr. Justice Holmes in Hammer *v.* Dagenhart in 1918, becoming in United States *v.* Darby, in 1941, the majority opinion of the Court (p. 51 below). See E. A. Evans, "The Dissenting Opinion; Its Use and Abuse," *Missouri Law Rev.,* III, 120-142 (Apr., 1938); C. H. Pritchett, "Division of Opinion Among Justices of the United States Supreme Court, 1939-41," *Amer. Polit. Sci. Rev.,* XXXV, 890-898 (Oct., 1941); *ibid.,* "The Voting Behavior of the Supreme Court, 1941-42," *Jour. of Politics,* IV, 491-506 (Nov., 1942); *ibid.,* "Ten Years of Supreme Court Voting," *Southwestern Soc. Sci. Quar.,* XXIV, 12-22 (June, 1943); *ibid.,* "The Coming of the New Dissent; The Supreme Court, 1941-43," *Univ. of Chicago Law Rev.,* XI, 49-61 (Dec., 1943); and *ibid.,* "Dissent on the Supreme Court, 1943-44," *Amer. Polit. Sci. Rev.,* XXXIX, 42-54 (Feb., 1945). In the last-mentioned article, Professor Pritchett comments on the increasing proportion of "dissents" in later years—rising from usually ten to twenty per cent of the cases decided in earlier days to a clear majority of them in 1943-44. This recent record of vacillation and disagreement, in a Court supposed to have been rendered more homogeneous and harmonious by the "liberalizing" appointments of 1938-41 (see p. 548 below), has disturbed a good many people, who, in trying to find reasons for it, are likely to include among them the rather astonishing fact that of the present nine members of the Court (1948), six were, when appointed, totally devoid of judicial experience, and one other had served only as a police judge. For detailed analyses of the "voting behavior" of the Court throughout the period 1937-47, see Pritchett references on p. 558 below.

[1] Reports of Supreme Court decisions before 1882 are usually cited by the name of the reporter who prepared them for publication, as follows: Dallas, 4 vols., 1790-1800; Cranch, 9 vols., 1801-15; Wheaton, 12 vols., 1816-27; Peters, 16 vols., 1828-42; Howard, 24 vols., 1843-60; Black, 2 vols., 1861-62; Wallace, 23 vols., 1863-74; and Otto, 17 vols., 1875-82. Since 1882, the *Reports* have been designated by serial number only, beginning with Volume 108 and cited as 108 U. S., etc.

The Court Reporter Act of 1944 (58 *U. S. Stat. at Large,* 5) insures a verbatim record of all federal court proceedings, unless expressly dispensed with. *Annual Report of the Director of the Administrative Office of United States Courts* (1944), 7-9.

enactment of a law, enforcement of it for a year or two (or even longer), and eventual discovery that it had never been a valid law at all—as, for example, in the case of the federal income tax law of 1894 and the National Industrial Recovery Act of 1933.[1]

The Supreme Court and the Function of Judicial Review

Judicial review a basic feature of American government

By far the most significant function of the Supreme Court is performed (and, as we have seen, the one upon which it concentrates its best effort) when it passes upon the validity of state constitutional provisions or of state and federal legislation; for in so doing it serves as protector of the supremacy of national law, defender of the reserved powers of the states, and guardian of the constitutional system in general. Of course, the Supreme Court is not our only tribunal possessing the power of review: the topmost court in each state has the last word on whether state laws conform with the state's constitution; and both federal district courts and courts of appeals may declare any state constitutional provision or state law or federal law incompatible with the federal constitution and refuse to enforce it. When, however, any question of constitutionality on the federal level is involved, it usually may be carried from a state supreme court or a lower federal court to the Supreme Court of the United States, whose verdict upon it is final—at least so long as the Court does not change its mind.

How and why judicial review arose and the significance of it for the building of a strong national government have been touched upon at an earlier point in this book.[2] The fact was noted that the federal constitution nowhere expressly confers the function upon any federal court, and that there have always been people who looked upon the exercise of it— particularly as developed by the Supreme Court—as sheer usurpation. But it was observed, also, that no less authorities than Alexander Hamilton and John Marshall believed that, in hearing and deciding cases, the courts must necessarily have an eye to the constitutional validity of any state or federal laws (or indeed executive actions) involved; and the opinion was asserted, not only that under a divided system of government such as ours court review of legislation was historically inevitable, but that it is entirely consistent with the spirit of the constitution and indeed, in our situation, indispensable. At all events, such review is an established and generally accepted fact, sharply differentiating our government from systems like the British in which every parliamentary enactment is *ipso facto* constitutional—although our American usage is significantly paralleled in various countries like Australia and Switzerland having a federal form of organization. And while it is common enough to hear complaint of discord between president and Congress, "encroachments"

---

[1] E. F. Albertsworth, "Advisory Functions in the Federal Supreme Court," *Georgetown Law Rev.*, XXIII, 643-670 (May, 1935); F. R. Aumann, "The Supreme Court and the Advisory Opinion," *Ohio State Univ. Law Jour.*, IV, 21-55 (Dec., 1937).

[2] See pp. 67-70 above.

of the federal government on the states, and other conflicts and confusions, one well might shudder before the spectacle of disunity and frustration which the United States would present, save for the harmonizing and integrating controls that the courts have been able to exercise through their power to review the actions of legislatures and officials and invalidate those found inconsistent with constitutional mandates and meanings.

For a more vivid impression of the way in which judicial review operates, let us take two concrete illustrations and consider what actually happens. (1) In 1897, the legislature of New York, relying on the state's police power, passed a statute limiting employment in bakeries to sixty hours a week and ten hours a day. After several years, an employer by the name of Lochner was indicted for violating the law, and in both lower and higher state courts was convicted. The courts having held the law consistent with the federal constitution, the defendant's attorneys then seized upon his right to have the case further reviewed and sued out a writ of error taking it to the federal Supreme Court, which had no option but to hear it. The question for decision was, of course, whether the bakeries law was in any manner inconsistent with the national constitution or with a federal statute, and consequently no law at all because of conflicting with the "supreme law of the land." Four of the nine justices found no inconsistency. But five thought that bakery employees had been deprived of their freedom of contract as guaranteed by the Fourteenth Amendment; and by this narrow margin the law was set aside and the defendant given final victory.[1] (2) In 1916, Congress, seeking to curb child labor, enacted a law prohibiting goods to be transported in interstate commerce if children under fourteen or sixteen years of age (under varying specified conditions) had been employed in producing them. On behalf of two minor sons employed, in disregard of the terms of the act, in a cotton mill at Charlotte, North Carolina, a certain Dagenhart brought suit against Hammer, district attorney, alleging that Congress lacked power to pass the act in question and asking that enforcement of it against the two youths be enjoined; and when a federal district court upheld the suit and pronounced the act unconstitutional, the government appealed the case to the court of last resort. In this instance, the Supreme Court justices had to lay a federal, rather than a state, statute alongside the federal constitution and decide whether the two were compatible, and in so doing either sustain or reverse the previous finding, not of a state, but of a federal, court. In the outcome, and again by a five-to-four vote, the decision was against the legislation questioned. This was in days before the Court had broadened its conception of commerce to include manufacturing, mining, and the like if the product enters the channels of interstate commerce; and the verdict was that, while ostensibly regulating such commerce (which of itself would have been proper enough),

How judicial review operates

Some illustrations

---

[1] Lochner *v.* New York, 198 U. S. 45 (1905). The majority held the law also to be not a legitimate exercise of the police power.

Congress had sought primarily to regulate matters constitutionally reserved for control by the states—wherefore the child labor statute could not be enforced against the Dagenhart youths.[1]

What it
means to
pronounce
a statute
unconsti-
tutional
Although directed to particular situations in individual cases—in one of the instances cited to an unknown baker, and in the other to two even less known boys working in a factory [2]—decisions like the foregoing have, of course, a generalized effect; at once they gain universal application. Either a state or a federal statute held unconstitutional by the highest court may go unrepealed for years. But everyone knows that if similar cases were to arise, the Court would, in all probability, reach the same conclusion; and hence, for all practical purposes, the "statute" becomes a dead letter.[3] The common notion, however, that the Court vetoes or annuls laws is entirely erroneous. What the Court does is simply to pronounce unconstitutional, and therefore unenforceable, measures which in its eyes have never been valid *laws* at all, even though (as in the case of the New York bakeries statute) they may have been in operation for years.[4] By the same token (although there is much misunderstanding of this also), the Court does not flaunt or frustrate the public will. "It is sometimes said," observed Mr. Justice Roberts in delivering the Court's opinion when the first Agricultural Adjustment Act was held unconstitutional in 1936, "that the Court assumes a power to overrule or control the action of the people's representatives. This is a misconception. The constitution is the supreme law of the land ordained and established by the people. All legislation must conform to the principles it lays down. When an act of Congress is appropriately challenged in the courts as not conforming to the constitutional mandate, the judicial branch of the government has only one duty—to lay the article of the constitution which is involved beside the statute which is challenged and to decide whether the latter squares with the former. All the Court does, or can do, is to announce its considered judgment upon the question.... This Court neither approves nor condemns any legislative policy. Its difficult and delicate task is to ascertain and declare whether the legislation is in accordance with, or in contravention of, the provisions of the constitution; and, having done that, its duty ends." [5] Plenty of times, decisions holding acts of Congress unconstitutional have encountered strong public disapprobation; they did so in the bakeries and child labor cases mentioned above. If, however, in a given case the Court has scrupulously lived up to the standard of performance outlined by Mr. Justice Roberts,

[1] Hammer *v.* Dagenhart, 247 U. S. 251 (1918), later overruled by a differently constituted Court in United States *v.* Darby, 312 U. S. 100 (1941). See p. 619 below.

[2] Although their names are now immortalized in the annals of our constitutional law.

[3] Certainly this was true of the child labor law mentioned; and although, as indicated, a reoriented Court eventually took a different position on congressional regulation of manufacturing, twenty-three years elapsed before it did so.

[4] O. P. Field, *The Effect of an Unconstitutional Statute* (Minneapolis, 1935).

[5] United States *v.* Butler, 297 U. S. 1 (1936), at p. 62.

no fault properly attaches to it. Perhaps in enacting a law later invalidated, Congress should have been more careful about constitutional proprieties; perhaps there really was no proper basis for the law at all without a constitutional amendment. On the other hand, one cannot be too sure; the Court itself is not infallible, nor its view of constitutional limitations unalterable. Times change; justices die or resign; new presidents nominate new justices who, being human, have their own particular slants on things; and sometimes these new justices reverse the rulings of their predecessors, imparting to some constitutional clause a meaning wholly different from that previously attributed to it and rendering a statute outlawed yesterday valid enough if enacted tomorrow. All that one can say is that, in reaching decisions, the Court at any given time endeavors to declare impartially what legislation is, and what is not, compatible with the federal constitution as the justices *then* understand the relevant clauses of that instrument.

Without doubt, the most appropriate agency for construing the division of powers between the nation and the states, and for authoritative determination of the constitutional powers of both the legislative and executive branches of the national government, is the judiciary. In the area of national power, the constitution has placed numerous restrictions upon both Congress and the executive in the interest of the rights and liberties of the people. If either of these authorities were permitted to fix the measure of its own powers, especially in times of public stress, such restraints might be violated or even ignored in the very emergency situations (*e.g.*, during war) which they were largely designed to meet. Furthermore, the judiciary is in some respects the weakest of the three branches of the national government. It controls neither the purse nor the sword. Acting alone, it is unable directly to encroach upon either of the other branches, or to do mortal injury to political or civil liberty. Its members are less likely to be influenced by momentary passion than are the members of Congress—perhaps than the president also. All in all, with the judges possessed of their negative, yet effective, check upon Congress and the executive, the limitations of the constitution unquestionably have been more scrupulously observed and strictly enforced than otherwise they would have been.[1]

The Supreme Court the safest arbiter

There is, however, another side to the picture. When interpreting and applying the language and spirit of the constitution, Supreme Court justices are acting not merely, nor chiefly, as a judicial body settling lawsuits; on individual suits adjudicated, they hang, as from pegs, broad determinations of public policy—even though decisions of that nature are supposed to come rather from the political branches of the government.

The Court also a maker of policy

[1] It is not to be overlooked that even a constitutional amendment may be brought to judicial test, as was the Eighteenth. On the other hand, rulings of the Supreme Court invalidating legislation may prompt the launching of an amendment—as in the case of the Sixteenth, conferring on Congress taxing powers considered by the Court as not previously existing.

Thus when, after Congress has passed an act and the president has approved it, the Court intervenes in a case brought under the measure and overthrows it, the effect is to rule that the policy embodied in the act shall not, after all, be the policy of the country—at least not until a perhaps differently constituted Court sometime later takes a different view; and the ground for such intervention is that, in the Court's opinion, the constitution does not mean what Congress and the president thought it did. In other words, the actual, effective constitution at any given time is the constitution *that the judges recognize*. "We are under a constitution," remarked former Chief Justice Hughes many years ago, "but the constitution [and therefore what can lawfully be done under it] is what the judges say it is." [1] Mr. Justice Frankfurter has put the matter even more tersely by saying: "The Supreme Court is the constitution."

This certainly is attributing to the Court an immensity of power; little need is there for purse or sword. [2] Of course, the Court has been responsible for invalidating only a very small percentage of the thousands of measures passed by Congress and the state legislatures since 1789—some seventy acts of Congress and two hundred or more pieces of state legislation between 1865 and 1935. In a good many instances, however, the laws stricken down have been of major importance, *e.g.*, the federal income tax law of 1894, the child labor laws of 1916 and 1919, and a stream of New Deal statutes of 1933-35. Frequently, too, the measures involved have arisen out of, or been surrounded with, bitter political controversy. And while it is no longer worth any one's breath to argue against the authority of the Court to exercise the function of review, and while, too, a great deal of deference has been shown the Court (particularly in its heyday of power and prestige between 1865 and 1930), it has always remained open to people who did not like what was happening to criticize the manner in which the Court performed its functions, to attack the point of view and philosophy animating various groups of justices, and even to cast aspersions upon the motives and discernment of presidents in selecting the justices in the first place.

Grounds of complaint
Complaints have been lodged on many grounds. Among the most frequently heard have been those directed against decisions by five-to-four majorities. In the Court's early history, there were not many hair-line decisions of this sort. In later years, however, they have multiplied (although still, of course, exceptional); and some have had the effect of overthrowing laws in which large numbers of people were interested. [3]

---

[1] *Addresses* (New York, 1908), 139. Mr. Hughes was governor of New York and not a member of the Court when he said this.

[2] Shortly before he retired from the bench in 1932, Mr. Justice Holmes observed that he could discover "hardly any limit but the sky" to the Court's asserted power to invalidate state acts; and in 1936 Mr. Chief Justice Stone asserted that the only check upon the Court is its own "sense of self-restraint." To be sure, both of these remarks were made somewhat querulously in the course of dissenting opinions.

[3] The total of laws *overthrown* by five-to-four decisions nevertheless does not exceed twenty. It will be recalled that if the Court divides equally, *e.g.*, four to four,

From one point of view, it may seem absurd that a single justice out of nine should have the power to bowl over a measure passed by two houses of Congress, signed by the president, perhaps strongly supported by the people, and given a clean bill of health by four of his colleagues; and to prevent such a thing from happening, it has many times been proposed that some larger proportion of the justices (perhaps two-thirds) be required for overruling a statute or any part thereof.[1] To this suggestion, however, it may be countered that very few significant measures ever come to grief in the manner indicated (as a matter of statistics, more five-to-four decisions go in favor of a measure than against one), and that in a country devoted to the principle of majority rule there is no more reason for insisting upon something *exceeding* a majority in court decisions than, for example, in enacting legislation.[2]

Until a decade or more ago, the most general and basic criticism of the Court was that in an age increasingly sensitive to needs for social and economic reform, the justices clung to old legalisms and rigidities and made the path of progress difficult. Too often, it was charged, they allowed the conservatism and caution of the elderly and the well-fixed to blind them to the significance of new viewpoints and aspirations. For it must be remembered that what the Court says and does at any given time depends very largely upon who the justices are, upon their temperaments, and upon their characteristic attitudes and views. To be sure, they are supposed to be above personal animus, partisan or otherwise; and to this end they are assured all possible independence and security. But they remain human beings, and bring to their posts strong political, social, and economic predilections—to which they, indeed, sometimes owe their appointment. And in interpreting and applying words and phrases—"regulate," "commerce," "due process of law"—which have come down in some instances from the eighteenth century, they can hardly fail to be swayed, consciously or unconsciously, by their social philosophies and general outlook on affairs.[3] When, therefore, in past times they were found denying to national or state governments authority to deal with public prob-

---

the effect is to sustain a state or federal decision against which there has been an appeal.

[1] Numerous amendments on this line have been proposed in Congress, but without result. A former member of the Court (John H. Clarke) once urged that the Court itself voluntarily adopt a two-thirds (or similar) rule.

[2] R. E. Cushman, "Constitutional Decisions by a Bare Majority of the Court," *Mich. Law Rev.*, XIX, 771-803 (June, 1921).

[3] C. G. Haines, "Political Theories of the Supreme Court from 1789-1885," *Amer. Polit. Sci. Rev.*, II, 221-244 (Feb., 1908); C. A. M. Ewing, "Geography and the Supreme Court," *Southwestern Polit. and Soc. Sci. Quar.*, XI, 26-46 (June, 1930); R. E. Cushman, "What's Happening to Our Constitution?," *Pub. Affairs Pamphlets*, No. 70 (New York, 1942). When selecting persons for appointment to the Supreme Bench, the president, in his turn, may deliberately give a slant to the Court's probable decisions by choosing appointees of particular background and experience and of known political and economic views. See p. 548 below. Cf. J. P. Frank, "The Appointment of Supreme Court Justices; Prestige, Principles, and Politics," *1941 Wis. Law Rev.*, 172-210, 343-379 (Mar., May, 1941).

lems on which action was desired and attempted, they were blamed not only for exalting their own views of sound public policy above those of the constitutionally ordained policy-determining organs of government, but for preventing a living constitution from realizing its possibilities in terms of social and economic well-being. And from various quarters proposals were heard—as far back as fifty years ago—not only to do away with five-to-four decisions, but (1) to amend the constitution so as to provide that any measure invalidated by the Court might none the less be made law by being reënacted by two-thirds majorities in both branches of Congress [1] (precisely as in the case of a presidential veto), and even (2) to extinguish the Court's power of review altogether.

The Court Reorganization Controversy of 1937

The most recent period in which feeling on the subject was deeply stirred was the first half of Franklin D. Roosevelt's second administration (1935-37), eventuating in the most heated controversy over judicial matters in our history, and with the Supreme Court as the principal focus of attention. A Court on which the youngest member was sixty-one and the oldest eighty (with an average of seventy-two), and on which five justices represented a school of thought grounded upon the principles of *laissez faire,* individualism, and free competition,[2] was striking down one New Deal regulative measure after another—the National Industrial Recovery Act of 1933, the Agricultural Adjustment Act of the same year, the Railroad Retirement Act of 1934, the Bituminous Coal Conservation [Guffey] Act of 1935, and others; [3] and in circles of more liberal persuasion strong demand arose that something be done to curb such obstruction and clear the way for the newer legislative programs.

President Roosevelt's plan

Various possibilities were open. The Court might be stripped of its power to declare acts of Congress unconstitutional, and this was advocated by some. But President Roosevelt, who felt as strongly as any one that the Court, as constituted, was badly out of touch with social and economic realities ("living in horse and buggy days") and had become an impediment to the solution of pressing national problems, approached the issue from a different angle, looking rather to Court rejuvenation and liberalization through the infusion of younger and more flexible-minded members—making, as he said in a startling message to Congress on February 5, 1937, "the judiciary as a whole (and the Supreme Court in

[1] Theodore Roosevelt and Senator Robert M. LaFollette, Sr., for example, advocated this.

[2] Van Devanter, McReynolds, Sutherland, Butler, and a little less certainly Roberts. The other four—Hughes, Brandeis, Stone, and Cardozo—were products of an urban environment (as Roberts also was) and inclined to less conservative and rigid attitudes on governmental functions and powers, especially when large social and economic issues were involved. Party politics was a secondary consideration; there was a Wilson appointee and a Coolidge appointee in each group.

[3] Eleven, in all, in 1935-36. For a general survey, see B. Rauch, *The History of the New Deal, 1933-1938* (New York, 1944), Chap. xi. Cf. C. P. Curtis, *Lions Under the Throne* (Boston, 1947), Chap. x.

particular) less static by the constant and systematic addition of new blood to its personnel." [1] There were at the time in the entire federal judiciary thirty judges who were over seventy years of age, and in the Supreme Court six. Congress, it was proposed, should authorize the appointment of an additional judge for every federal judge who, having served as long as ten years, and having reached the age at which such judges may retire, *i.e.*, seventy, should fail to retire within six months— the new judges to serve concurrently with the old. Should none of the Supreme Court justices over seventy accept the thinly-veiled invitation to retire, the total number on the bench would become fifteen, which in any case was to be the maximum.

The proposal entailed no constitutional difficulties; the power of Congress to regulate the number of judges in all federal courts, and of the president and Senate to appoint them, is incontestable. Its wisdom and expediency, however, as well as the motives behind it, became subjects of stormy discussion in press, on platform, over the radio, in bar association meetings and state legislatures, and especially in Congress. The President was sharply charged with planning to "pack" the Supreme Court with new members of his own way of thinking, and thereby in future to control its decisions, which, in turn, it was alleged, would lead to the reversal of earlier decisions restricting national and state powers and, in effect, to amending the constitution and reconstructing the system of government in an unconstitutional manner, with the states deprived of any opportunity to express themselves on the changes involved. [2] To the contention that the Supreme Court had already overturned the intended balance in our scheme of government by developing its powerful, and some said arbitrary, veto on acts of Congress and the executive, it was retorted that the President's plan would destroy whatever was left of the system of "checks and balances" by making the Supreme Court

Charges and counter- charges

[1] A weakness of the President's proposal lay in the fact that although the appointment of different and younger justices might lead to immediate "liberalization" of the Court, and thus hasten the solution of national problems that admitted of no delay, there could be no assurance that ten or fifteen years later these same justices would not be found practically as conservative as those whom they were intended to assist or supplant. Experience shows that work on the Court often "makes liberals of conservatives and conservatives of liberals," and that presidents have more than once been mistaken in the men they have appointed. In order to insure full realization of the end sought, the plan needed to be supplemented with a constitutional amendment providing for compulsory retirement of all federal judges upon reaching a specified age; and such an amendment was introduced in the Senate in 1937, although not adopted.

On the President's plan, see D. O. McGovney, "Reorganization of the Supreme Court," *Calif. Law Rev.*, XXV, 389-412 (May, 1937); A. T. Mason, "Politics and the Supreme Court; President Roosevelt's Proposal," *Univ. of Pa. Law Rev.*, LXXXV, 659-677 (May, 1937); and C. Fairman, "The Retirement of Federal Judges," *Harvard Law Rev.*, LI, 397-443 (Jan., 1938). Cf. C. G. Haines, "Judicial Review of the Acts of Congress and the Need for Constitutional Reform," *Yale Law Jour.*, XIV, 816-856 (Mar., 1936).

[2] It is interesting to observe that, in his *American Commonwealth*, first published in 1888, James (later Lord) Bryce placed his finger on the possibility of influencing and controlling the Court by juggling the number of justices, and pronounced it "a joint in the Court's armor." I, 276.

completely subservient to the president, or at any rate to the president and Congress.[1]

Legis-
lative
failure
but actual
Court
transfor-
mation

After exciting days, a bill embodying the main features of the presidential plan failed to pass; and no new and younger judges were authorized. There was, however, remedial legislation relating to the functioning of the lower federal courts.[2] And concurrently the Supreme Court itself underwent significant changes, even if not by the method urged—changes which enabled the President and the country to get what they wanted, yet without legislative action at all (eating their cake, so to speak, and still having it). In the first place, whatever the reason (and the main factor was a shift of position by Mr. Justice Roberts), the Court, even while the controversy was going on, showed a change of heart, not only by handing down a series of decisions upholding certain New Deal measures such as the Railway Labor Act (1934), the National Labor Relations [Wagner] Act (1935), and notably the Social Security Act (1935),[3] but also by completely reversing the position it had taken in the District of Columbia case (Adkins v. Children's Hospital) on the constitutionality of minimum-wage legislation.[4] Moreover, within the space of hardly more than a year, three "conservative" justices retired or died, opening a way for the appointment of "liberals" in their places. In 1941, the most stalwart anti-New-Dealer of all (Justice McReynolds) retired; by 1943, all but two of the nine justices (Roberts and Stone) were Roosevelt appointees; and between 1936 and 1946, not only was only one act of Congress declared unconstitutional (and it not an important one), but no fewer than two dozen earlier restrictive decisions were overruled or modified.[5] In this situation, even the President's interest in Court reorganization through legislative action waned; and almost before the country was aware, the controversy passed into history—although not without reverberations in the form of an effort of Mr. Roosevelt in the congressional elections of 1938 to "purge" his party of candidates who had been active in opposing his plans.

The
"New
Deal"
Court

For now the better part of a decade, the country has had a Supreme Court with a New Deal background and orientation. To some people, this is a source of gratification, to others quite the reverse. The period

[1] Although certain Democratic members of Congress, as well as party leaders and lawyers outside, openly opposed the President's plan, the line-up of supporters and opponents in the country at large closely followed the alignment of "New Dealers" versus "Anti-New Dealers" prevailing in the presidential campaign of 1936. This was the point at which the deteriorating relations between President Roosevelt and Congress, characteristic of later years, really began.

[2] 50 U. S. Stat. at Large, 751-753. The act creating the Administrative Office of United States Courts (1939) was also a direct result of the President's recommendations in 1937. See p. 552 below.

[3] See pp. 726, 733, 757 below.

[4] West Coast Hotel Co. v. Parrish, 300 U. S. 379 (1937).

[5] Perhaps the most notable of these was the Schechter decision of 1935 invalidating the National Industrial Recovery Act. In Yakus v. United States (321 U. S. 414, 1944), sustaining the constitutionality of the Emergency Price Control Act of 1942, that decision was expressly reversed.

has not been one of great jurists on the Court; few of the newer appointees had ever attracted attention for their legal learning; few even brought to their task significant judicial experience.[1] The period has been notable for divided opinions and sometimes sharply-worded dissents. And in 1946 bickering among the members—although no novelty, as historians are aware—attained the proportions of a national scandal. Nevertheless, the Court in this period (perhaps for the very reason that it was so devoid of profound jurists) significantly modernized its methods of constitutional interpretation, and by the same token the constitution itself; and this modernization consisted essentially in replacing a traditional legalistic and almost mechanistic method of deducing decisions from the facts in a case, with little or no consideration of social and economic factors, by an approach based on the idea that the constitutionality of a law may properly depend, not solely upon the words and phrases of the constitution as meticulously weighed and dissected by the justices, but at least equally upon perception and understanding of the social or economic conditions that led the legislature to pass the law in the first place. An occasional earlier justice of the Court had this less legalistic, more practical, approach; Oliver Wendell Holmes and Louis D. Brandeis, famed as dissenters, did so. But its adoption by substantially the full Court has come only in the last few years; and the resulting freshness and flexibility in attitudes and actions will make the decade a notable one in Court history after most of the relatively obscure justices have personally been forgotten. After all, a main responsibility of the Court is to keep the law abreast of the times.[2]

[1] Chief Justice Stone (who died in 1946) and Mr. Justice Frankfurter had legal learning, but no previous judicial experience. Mr. Justice Rutledge had important earlier judicial experience, and Chief Justice Vinson (appointed in 1946) had served for six years on the circuit court of appeals for the District of Columbia.

[2] See C. B. Swisher, *The Growth of Constitutional Power in the United States* (Chicago, 1947), Chap. IX, "New Horizons for the Judiciary;" C. P. Curtis, *Lions Under the Throne* (Boston, 1947), Chaps. XI-XIII; R. E. Cushman, "What's Happening to Our Constitution?," *Pub. Affairs Pamphlets*, No. 70 (New York, 1942); M. J. Pusey, "The Roosevelt Supreme Court," *Amer. Mercury*, LIX, 596-603 (May, 1944); K. C. Davis, "Revolution in the Supreme Court," *Atlantic Mo.*, CLXVI, 85-95 (July, 1940); and T. R. Powell, "Our High Court Analyzed," *N. Y. Times*, June 18, 1944. For President Roosevelt's opinion that the Court fight of 1937 "marked a definite turning point in the history of the United States," see an article published under his name in *Collier's*, CVIII (Sept. 13 and 20, 1941). Whether or not such significance is properly to be attached to the Court controversy in and of itself, few if any developments in recent decades have higher importance than infusion into the Supreme Court of a personnel responsible since 1937 (1) for tearing away the old constitutional barriers which left business and private enterprise relatively free from federal control, and (2) by the same token for emphasizing the use of federal powers in behalf of the rights of the individual as well as for the protection of property and corporate interests. In feeling their way toward a determination of the proper limits of the increased controls over property and business exercised by federal agencies, the members of the new Supreme Court, however, find themselves holding widely differing views; and this is one of the reasons for the numerous clashes of ideas mentioned above and notoriously characterizing decisions and opinions during the last few years. See the articles by C. H. Pritchett cited above (p. 538, note 4); and for full studies of the agreements and disagreements of the justices in cases decided during 1937-47, the same author's "The Roosevelt Court: Votes and Values," *Amer. Polit. Sci. Rev.*, XLII, 53-67 (Feb., 1948), and *The Roose-*

The Judiciary and the Other Branches of Government

The
judiciary
inde-
pendent,
and yet
not so

By providing that federal judges should hold office "during good behavior," and by forbidding Congress to reduce their compensation during
their period of service, the framers of the constitution sought to free
the judiciary from any sense of dependence upon, or undue influence
by, either the executive or Congress; and in this they were completely
successful, so far as the judges individually are concerned. In performing their official duties, federal judges, personally, are considerably more
immune from outside influences than are most state judges, elected or
appointed for relatively short terms. Nevertheless, even the federal
judiciary enjoys no such independence of the other branches of the
government as either of them enjoys with respect to the other and to
the judicial branch; and the reasons are not hard to find. In the first
place, the constitution directly provides for only one federal court, the
Supreme Court, leaving all inferior courts to be created and their jurisdictions to be defined by the joint action of Congress and the executive.
Second, even in the case of the Supreme Court, Congress and the president have to coöperate in maintaining it, in determining the number of
judges, in fixing their compensation, and in regulating its appellate jurisdiction. Third, all federal judges are appointed by the president and
Senate.[1] Finally, the assistance of the executive may become indispensable to the enforcement of the decrees or other processes which the
courts issue.

Possi-
bility of
partisan
inter-
ference

As a result of one or more of these circumstances, it is legally possible
for Congress and the president to increase the number of judges in any
federal court, and, by filling the new positions with judges whose views
upon questions of public policy coincide with those of the president and
a majority of the Senate, to overcome or counteract the influence of what
would otherwise be a majority of judges holding different views. Or, to
take another possible instance, Congress may reduce the size of the
Supreme Court, or of any other federal court, by enacting that vacancies
shall not be filled until the number of judges reaches a certain lower point.
Congress may even go so far as to deprive the Supreme Court of its appellate jurisdiction over a given class of cases, as once happened during
the Reconstruction period when an unfavorable decision on the constitutionality of certain acts was anticipated. Only rarely, however, has

---

velt Court; A Study in Judicial Politics and Values, 1937-1947 (New York, 1948. Cf.
W. F. Dodd, "The United States Supreme Court, 1936-1946," *Amer. Polit. Sci. Rev.*,
XLI, 1-11 (Feb., 1947).

[1] In nine instances, presidential appointments to the Supreme Court have met
with outright rejection by the Senate, and in twelve others a presidential nomination
has been rejected indirectly, as by failure to act or by indefinite postponement of
action. These cases are listed in the 5th (1935) edition of this book, p. 436, note 2.
Cf. F. R. Black, "Should the Senate Pass on the Social and Economic Views of
Nominees to the United States Supreme Court?," *St. John's Law Rev.*, VI, 257-271
(May, 1932); C. W. Smith, Jr., "President Roosevelt's Attitude Toward the Courts,"
Ky. Law Jour., XXXI, 301-315 (May, 1943).

there been clear evidence of any intention on the part of a president to "pack" the Supreme Court in order to dominate it, or on the part of either a president or Congress to influence its decisions in particular cases—even though a series of scattered appointments may, as in the case of the Roosevelt Court of the late thirties, admittedly aim at injecting a new point of view and ultimately securing decisions in accord with a president's political philosophy. During one brief period early in the country's history, the record with regard to the inferior courts was less satisfactory; in 1801, a Federalist Congress created new circuit judgeships expressly in order to enable a Federalist president to fill them with Federalist judges; and a few months later, a Jeffersonian-Republican Congress, for equally partisan reasons, abolished the new positions.[1] Happily, however, these instances of frankly partisan interference with the judicial system stand practically alone; when the circuit courts of appeals were created in 1891, the older circuit courts were abolished in 1911, the short-lived Commerce Court was discontinued in 1913, and the Judiciary Act of 1925 was passed, partisan motives were almost completely absent.[2]

In extreme situations where enforcement of court processes is resisted by combinations too strong to be overcome by United States marshals and their deputies, the federal courts are obliged to call upon the president for the aid of the armed forces. If he is unsympathetic toward the court's attitude, he may refuse to act; in which event the court is helpless and its orders or decrees may be completely nullified. An instance occurred in the administration of President Jackson, when the Supreme Court upheld certain claims of the Cherokee Indians, while the President sided with the Georgia authorities, who forcibly and successfully resisted the execution of the Court's decision.[3]

Enforcement of court processes

Finally, it is legally possible for Congress, from partisan motives, to attack members of the federal judiciary through impeachment proceedings charging individual judges with treason, bribery, or "other high crimes and misdemeanors;" and since impeachment is the only possible method of getting a judge out of office against his will, there doubtless is potential danger of it being resorted to when the actual motive is political. In all, however, impeachment proceedings have been brought against only nine members of the federal judiciary; only four have been convicted

Impeachment of judges

[1] M. Farrand, "The Judiciary Act of 1801," *Amer. Hist. Rev.*, V, 682-686 (July, 1900); W. S. Carpenter, "Repeal of the Judiciary Act of 1801," *Amer. Polit. Sci. Rev.*, IX, 519-528 (Aug., 1915).

[2] In making judicial appointments, however, presidents have generally favored members of their own political party. An official count of federal judges appointed during 1933-48 shows that in this period of fifteen years, 183 Democrats and only nine Republicans were named to judgeships, exclusive of territorial courts and the lower courts in the District of Columbia. All told, there were, early in 1948, 288 federal judgeships, all of which were filled. Of these, it was estimated that not more than sixty were held by Republicans.

[3] This incident arose in connection with the cases of The Cherokee Nation *v.* Georgia, 5 Peters 1 (1831), and Worcester *v.* Georgia, 6 Peters 515 (1832).

and removed; and the only instances in which partisan considerations ever played a major rôle were the impeachments of Judges Pickering and Chase during the presidency of Jefferson.[1]

Improved Administration of the Federal Judicial System

The
Federal
Judicial
Conference

Until 1922, the district courts, and likewise the circuit courts of appeals, were virtually independent units, without a supervising or unifying head. When work grew excessive in one district or circuit, the usual remedy was for Congress to create a new judgeship or two, although there might be a dozen judges in other districts or circuits with comparatively little to do. In the year mentioned, however, Congress passed an important act opening the way for the long-needed unification and equalization of court work.[2] The chief justice of the United States now became, in some degree, a supervising and directing head of the entire federal judicial system, and provision was made for a federal judicial conference or council, convoked annually, presided over by the chief justice, and composed of all the senior circuit court judges of the ten circuits, with occasionally other federal judges and officials attending. To this conference it fell (1) to make comprehensive surveys of business in the federal courts; (2) to prepare plans for assignment and transfer of judges to or from circuits and districts as circumstances might make desirable; (3) to submit suggestions to the various courts "in the interest of uniformity and expedition of business"; and (4) to recommend remedial measures to Congress. For a decade or more, these and other newer arrangements imparted a degree of unity and flexibility in handling court business which had been conspicuously lacking.

The
Administrative
Office of
United
States
Courts

Later on, however, the system seemed to stand in need of further renovation; and in his famous message of February 5, 1937, relating to judicial reorganization,[3] President Franklin D. Roosevelt recommended that the Supreme Court be authorized to appoint a proctor to assist the Court in supervising the conduct of business in the lower courts. No action resulted at once. But in 1939 Congress set up the Administrative Office of United States Courts, with a director at its head, appointed by the Supreme Court and holding office during the pleasure of that body. One division of the new agency—that of business administration—looks after the housekeeping needs of the lower courts and helps generally in the management of their administrative affairs; a second—

---

[1] The successful impeachment proceedings were those against John Pickering (1803-04); West H. Humphreys (1862); Robert W. Archbald (1912-13); and Halstead L. Ritter (1936). The unsuccessful cases were those against Samuel Chase (1804-05); James H. Peck (1830-31); Charles Swayne (1904-05); and Harold Louderback (1933). In April, 1926, the House of Representatives adopted articles of impeachment against George W. English, judge of the district court for the Eastern District of Illinois; but on the eve of the trial Judge English resigned, and the proceedings were discontinued. Cf. J. tenBroek, "Partisan Politics and Federal Judgeship Impeachments Since 1902," *Minn. Law Rev.*, XXIII, 185-204 (Jan., 1939).

[2] 42 *U. S. Stat. at Large*, 837.

[3] See p. 546 above.

that of procedural studies and statistics—furnishes the Supreme Court with information concerning the state of judicial business and makes recommendations looking to increased efficiency and speed.[1]

The annual conference of senior circuit court judges continues to function, and to it the director of the Administrative Office is required to submit annual reports on the state of business in, and the material needs of, all the courts. In addition to attending this conference, the senior circuit judge in each circuit holds, at least twice each year, a council composed of all the circuit judges for the circuit; and this council considers plans for the effective and expeditious transaction of business in the district courts—plans which it becomes the duty of every district judge to help carry out. In addition, a conference of both circuit and district judges is held annually, to review the state of business in the courts and to discuss means of improving judicial administration; and since practicing lawyers, as well as judges, are vitally concerned with such matters, the law wisely permits the appointment of a limited number of members of the bar to sit with the judicial members of this conference.[2]

Other conferences and councils

Legislative Courts

The courts thus far described form what is technically known as the "federal judicial system;" and, inasmuch as they are provided for expressly or by implication in the judiciary article, they often are called the "constitutional courts," in order to distinguish them from certain special courts established by Congress under powers derived mainly from other parts of the constitution, and therefore called "legislative courts." In creating and organizing these courts (which include all of the federal courts in the territories), Congress has a very free hand with respect to the tenure, compensation, and appointment of judges, as also the scope of jurisdiction and methods of procedure; indeed, it is bound by none of the limitations found in the judiciary article. It may, for example, provide that the judges shall serve for only limited terms instead of during good behavior, and in several instances it has done so.

"Constitutional" and "legislative" courts

Under the power to appropriate money to pay the debts of the United States, Congress created, in 1855, a Court of Claims, primarily for the

Some examples

---

[1] H. P. Chandler, "The Place of the Administrative Office in the Federal Court System," *Cornell Law Quar.*, XXVII, 364-373 (Apr., 1942); J. J. Parker, "The Integration of the Federal Judiciary," *Harvard Law Rev.*, LVI, 563-575 (Jan., 1943).

[2] F. W. Morse, "Federal Judicial Conferences and Councils; Their Creation and Reports," *Cornell Law Quar.*, XXVII, 347-363 (Apr., 1942).

One other aspect of the operation of the federal judicial system, touched upon above, is the authority conferred from time to time by Congress upon the Supreme Court to prescribe rules of procedure to be followed by the lower federal courts. Until 1940, this authority was largely restricted to cases of a civil nature; and resulting rules covered chiefly such matters as bankruptcy proceedings, admiralty cases, copyright cases, and the like. In the year mentioned, however, it was extended to the trial of all criminal cases in district courts; and rules have now been promulgated for this broad field. In formulating rules for both civil and criminal procedure, the Court relies heavily on advisory committees consisting of eminent lawyers and jurists.

purpose of adjudicating claims against the government and reporting its findings to Congress or to the Department concerned.[1] Under the power to regulate commerce and to grant patents, Congress, in 1909, authorized a Court of Customs Appeals to hear and decide appeals from rulings made by a United States Customs Court (dating from 1890) in applying the tariff laws, and in 1929 broadened the tribunal into a Court of Customs and Patent Appeals, with the right to review also rulings of the commissioner of patents in administering the patent laws. The Revenue Act of 1942 transformed a United States Board of Tax Appeals into the Tax Court of the United States, with authority to adjudicate disputes over alleged deficiency in or over-payment of income, estate, excess profits, and some other taxes, with review by a federal circuit court of appeals. Dealing as they do with questions between private individuals or corporations on the one hand and agencies of the government on the other, all of the courts named are of the type or variety commonly known as administrative courts, and their jurisdiction is by way of exception to the general rule under our American system that cases of the kind shall be handled by the regular constitutional tribunals.[2] But there are also legislative courts of the more conventional sort. Under expressly granted power to govern territories, such courts have been created in all of the territories and major dependencies; and the constitution's grant of exclusive authority over the District of Columbia has opened the way for Congress to provide the people of the District with a court of appeals, a supreme court (inferior to the former), and several subordinate municipal courts. Territorial courts do not exercise "judicial power of the United States," but only a special judicial power conferred by Congress. Appeals, however, may be taken to a circuit court of appeals and in some instances to the Supreme Court.

The Department of Justice [3]

Origins

Following English and colonial precedent, Congress provided in the Judiciary Act of 1789 for an attorney-general who should advise the executive branch of the government on legal matters and represent it in

[1] Under an act of 1887, the United States consents to be sued in the Court of Claims on all claims founded upon any contract "express or implied;" and by the Federal Tort Claims Act of 1946 (a section of the Legislative Reorganization Act), it consents to be sued for injuries "caused by the negligent or wrongful act or omission of any employee ... acting within the scope of his office or employment." Of course, wartime operations of the armed services are excluded; and there can be no suit for damage from loss of mail.

[2] In 1936, a committee of the American Bar Association brought forward a plan for an integrated federal administrative court with general jurisdiction over business of the kind; but no action has resulted. See L. G. Caldwell, "A Federal Administrative Court," *Univ. of Pa. Law Rev.,* LXXXIV, 966-990 (June, 1936); R. M. Cooper, "The Proposed United States Administrative Court," *Mich. Law Rev.,* XXXV, 193-252 (Dec., 1936). On the general subject, see W. G. Katz, "Federal Legislative Courts," *Harvard Law Rev.,* XLIII, 894-924 (Apr., 1936).

[3] This establishment is an *executive department,* and not a part of the judiciary. Its functions and operations, however, warrant bringing it into any discussion of the federal system of administering justice.

judicial proceedings. The officer was not expected to give all of his time to the work, and he was not made the head of a department, although as soon as the cabinet developed he became a member of that group. With the growth of the country and of the government's activities, the duties of the position naturally increased. Solicitors and other assistants were provided; the attorney-general gave up private practice; and at last, in 1870, under pressure of the great volume of legal work flowing from the Civil War and Reconstruction, Congress belatedly established a Department of Justice in which the government's legal business was for the first time concentrated and systematized.

In number of officers and employees, the Department is among the two or three smallest.[1] But it performs exceedingly important functions, and no other one, except perhaps the Treasury, is so interlocked with the others. The principal officers in Washington are the attorney-general, who gives his time mainly to studying legal questions referred to him by the president or heads of departments and rendering opinions on them, with occasional (though now very rare) appearances before the Supreme Court in cases of exceptional importance; a solicitor-general (with also an assistant solicitor-general), who commonly represents the government before the Supreme Court, and sometimes other federal courts; an assistant to the attorney-general, who has supervision over all of the major subdivisions of the Department and over the district attorneys and marshals; and six assistant attorneys-general, each in charge of a main division of the Department, *i.e.*, anti-trust, tax, claims, criminal identification, land, and customs. Included in the Department are also three bureaus: the Federal Bureau of Investigation (the famous F.B.I.) with its force of special agents and other personnel, and with functions paralleling and supplementing those of the secret service in the Treasury, including, of course, the crime-detection work of the highly efficient "G-Men;" an Immigration and Naturalization Service, which, in 1940, was transferred from the Department of Labor to the Department of Justice; and a Bureau of Prisons. The list of principal agencies is completed by a Board of Immigration Appeals and a Board of Parole. *Washington organization*

Outside of the national capital, the Department has, of course, such machinery as the sixteen district headquarters of the Immigration and Naturalization Service, with many scattered stations under each; also field representatives of the anti-trust and other divisions. But the most important field force consists of the district attorneys and United States marshals, who, although operating primarily in connection with the federal district courts, belong to the executive rather than the judicial establishment and are under direct supervision of the attorney-general and his staff. There is a district attorney and a marshal in each of the eighty-four judicial districts into which the states are divided, besides others in Alaska, Hawaii, Puerto Rico, the Virgin Islands, and the *Field force*

[1] Some 26,000 persons were on its payroll in 1948.

Panama Canal Zone. Both offices date from 1789, and their incumbents are appointed by the president and Senate for four-year terms, on recommendation of the attorney-general. A district attorney presents to a grand jury all violations of national laws coming to his attention within his area; and if that body brings an indictment, it falls to him to conduct the government's case against the accused. In nature, his work therefore corresponds rather closely to that of a county prosecuting officer acting under state authority. Marshals and their deputies are charged with arresting and holding in custody persons accused of crime, summoning jurymen, serving legal processes, executing the judgments of federal courts, and protecting federal judges from personal violence when engaged in the performance of their official duties.[1]

Principal functions Speaking broadly, the Department of Justice has two main functions. The first is to give opinions to the president and heads of departments on questions touching their duties and involving construction of the constitution or the laws. The courts will answer such questions only in deciding actual cases, and, as we have seen, cannot be looked to for advisory opinions on constitutional and legal matters coming up almost daily in the carrying on of the government's work. For these, the officials concerned are dependent upon the attorney-general and those who may advise with him in the Department. In many instances, the opinions rendered prove final and conclusive, and hence determine the law; and sometimes they profoundly influence the political, as distinguished from the purely legal, policies of the government. The "Opinions of the Attorney-General" are published, after the manner of judicial decisions, and acquire weight as precedents in a similar way. Opinions are not furnished, however, to Congress or its committees, but only to the executive authorities. Executive orders are invariably scanned before being issued; but mere departmental regulations are not scrutinized, nor are abstract or hypothetical questions answered.

The second main function of the Department is to supervise or conduct suits to which the United States is a party and to prosecute offenders against the revenue, currency, commerce, banking, postal, and other national laws. Suits begun by the government are brought before a district court or the Supreme Court, according to the nature of the case; and while suits against the government are not allowed as a matter of right, they are in fact permitted, and are instituted in a district court or in the Court of Claims. In the lower courts, the government, whether

---

[1] The duties of district attorneys and marshals are set forth more fully in *Code of the Laws of the U. S.* (1940), Title 28, §§ 481-511. Cf. R. H. Jackson, "The Federal Prosecutor," *Jour. of Amer. Judic. Soc.*, XXIV, 18-20 (June, 1940). It may be added that in each judicial district the district judge appoints one or more United States commissioners empowered to administer oaths, issue warrants for the arrest of persons accused of violating federal laws, subpœna witnesses, conduct preliminary hearings of accused persons, and discharge them or admit them to bail. Such commissioners are, however, attached to the judiciary, and not to the executive as represented by the Department of Justice.

plaintiff or defendant, is commonly represented by the district attorney of the district in which the action is begun; in the Supreme Court and Court of Claims, by the solicitor-general or his assistant.[1]

REFERENCES

1. THE JUDICIAL SYSTEM

B. F. Wright, *The Growth of American Constitutional Law* (Boston and New York, 1942), Chaps. VII, IX, XI.

C. B. Swisher, *The Growth of Constitutional Power in the United States* (Chicago, 1947), Chap. IX.

A. N. Christensen and E. M. Kirkpatrick, *The People, Politics, and the Politician; Readings in American Government* (New York, 1941 and 1947), Chaps. XIX-XXI.

C. P. Patterson, *Presidential Government in the United States; The Unwritten Constitution* (Chapel Hill, N. C., 1947), Chap. IX.

C. E. Hughes, *The Supreme Court of the United States; Its Foundation, Methods, and Achievements* (New York, 1928).

R. H. Jackson, *The Struggle for Judicial Supremacy* (New York, 1940).

R. E. Cushman, *The Supreme Court and the Constitution* (New York, 1938).

————, "What's Happening to Our Constitution?," *Pub. Affairs Pamphlets*, No. 70 (New York, 1942).

————, *Leading Constitutional Decisions* (8th ed., New York, 1946).

C. A. Beard, *The Supreme Court and the Constitution* (New York, 1912).

E. M. Eriksson, *The Supreme Court and the New Deal* (Los Angeles, Calif., 1940).

C. G. Haines, *The American Doctrine of Judicial Supremacy* (2nd ed., Berkeley, Calif., 1932).

————, *The Rôle of the Supreme Court in American Government and Politics, 1789-1835* (Berkeley, Calif., 1944).

E. S. Corwin, *The Doctrine of Judicial Review* (Princeton, N. J., 1914).

————, *The Twilight of the Supreme Court; A History of Our Constitutional Theory* (New Haven, 1934).

————, *Court Over Constitution; A Study of Judicial Review as an Instrument of Popular Government* (Princeton, N. J., 1938).

H. L. Carson, *The Supreme Court of the United States; Its History and Centennial Celebration, February 4, 1890* (Philadelphia, 1891).

C. Warren, *The Supreme Court in United States History*, 3 vols. (Boston, 1922).

K. B. Umbreit, *Our Eleven Chief Justices; A History of the Supreme Court in Terms of Its Personalities* (New York, 1938).

C. A. M. Ewing, *The Judges of the Supreme Court, 1789-1937* (Minneapolis, 1938).

F. Frankfurter and J. M. Landis, *The Business of the Supreme Court* (New York, 1927).

E. R. Nichols [ed.], *Congress or the Supreme Court: Which Shall Rule America?* (New York, 1935).

R. K. Carr, *Democracy and the Supreme Court* (Oklahoma City, 1936).

C. P. Curtis, *Lions Under the Throne* (Boston, 1947).

[1] Two minor, although not unimportant, functions of the Department are advising the president on requests for pardons and administration of the federal penitentiaries at Atlanta, Leavenworth, Lewisburg, Pa., McNeil Island, and Alcatraz Island in San Francisco Bay, and of the jail and reform schools in the District of Columbia.

An excellent account of the operations of the Department of Justice, prepared in part by a former attorney-general, is H. S. Cummings and C. McFarland, *Federal Justice* (New York, 1936). Cf. J. A. Fairlie, "Law Departments and Law Offices in American Governments," *Mich. Law Rev.*, XXXVI, 906-934 (Apr., 1938).

J. M. Henry, *Nine Men Above the Law; Our Supreme Court* (Pittsburgh, 1936).

D. Lawrence, *Nine Honest Men* (New York, 1936).

W. McCune, *The Nine Young Men* (New York, 1947).

C. H. Pritchett, *The Roosevelt Court; A Study in Judicial Politics and Values, 1937-1947* (New York, 1948).

R. E. Cushman [ed.], "Ten Years of the Supreme Court: 1937-1947," *Amer. Polit. Sci. Rev.*, XLI, 1142-1181 (Dec., 1947), XLII, 32-67 (Feb., 1948).

D. Alfange, *The Supreme Court and the National Will* (New York, 1937).

R. J. Harris, *The Judicial Power of the United States* (Baton Rouge, La., 1940).

W. S. Carpenter, *Judicial Tenure in the United States* (New York, 1918).

C. B. Swisher, *Stephen G. Field, Craftsman of the Law* (Washington, D. C., 1930).

B. R. Trimble, *Chief Justice Waite; Defender of the Public Interest* (Princeton, N. J., 1938).

C. Fairman, *Mr. Justice Miller and the Supreme Court, 1862-1890* (Cambridge, Mass., 1939).

F. Frankfurter, *Mr. Justice Holmes and the Supreme Court* (Cambridge, Mass., 1938).

F. Biddle, *Mr. Justice Holmes* (New York, 1942).

A. T. Mason, *Brandeis; A Free Man's Life* (New York, 1946).

J. P. Pollard, *Mr. Justice Cardozo—American Lawyer* (New York, 1940).

S. J. Konevsky, *Chief Justice Stone and the Supreme Court* (New York, 1945).

Readers who do not have access to a law library will find convenient summaries (through 1948, by R. E. Cushman) of significant Supreme Court decisions, year by year, in the *Amer. Polit. Sci. Rev.*, commonly in the April issue.

2. THE DEPARTMENT OF JUSTICE

H. B. Learned, *The President's Cabinet* (New Haven, 1912), Chap. VII.

L. M. Short, *Development of National Administrative Organization in the United States* (Baltimore, 1923), Chap. XV.

H. S. Cummings and C. McFarland, *Federal Justice* (New York, 1936).

A. Langeluttig, *The Department of Justice of the United States* (Baltimore, 1927).

J. M. Beck, "The World's Largest Law Office," *Amer. Bar Assoc. Jour.*, X, 340-342 (May, 1924).

A. J. Dodge, "Origin and Development of the Office of Attorney-General," 70th Cong., 2nd Sess., House Doc. No. 510 (1929).

S. Key, "The Legal Work of the Federal Government," *Va. Law Rev.*, XXV, 165-201 (Dec., 1938).

C. B. Swisher, "Federal Organization of Legal Functions," *Amer. Polit. Sci. Rev.*, XXXIII, 973-1000 (Dec., 1939).

A. Robb, *Biographical Sketches of the Attorneys-General* (2nd ed., mimeo., Washington, D. C., 1946).

A. C. Millspaugh, *Crime Control by the National Government* (Washington, D. C., 1937).

J. J. Floherty, *Inside the F.B.I.* (Philadelphia, 1943).

F. L. Collins, *The F.B.I. in Peace and War* (New York, 1943).

Annual report of the attorney-general.

2. FUNCTIONS AND SERVICES

CHAPTER XXV

NATIONAL EXPENDITURES—THE BUDGET SYSTEM

In the foregoing group of chapters, the national government has been considered primarily from the viewpoints of structure, powers, and modes of operation. But this leaves its really most significant aspect still largely unexplored, namely, the services which it renders in great substantive fields of national concern like commerce, business, currency and banking, credit, agriculture, conservation of resources, labor, social welfare, defense, foreign relations; and to this challenging phase—constituting, of course, the principal reason for maintaining the government at all—we now turn.

One prime prerequisite for virtually everything that the government does, however, is money; as the harassed government under the Articles of Confederation quickly found out, little can be done without access to funds. To be sure, money is required merely for operating the machinery earlier described—for equipment, salaries, wages, pensions, and the like. If that were all, however, the national budget would be small indeed compared with what it now is. Aside from interest on the swollen national debt, the really large outlays go for *services*—agricultural aids, conservation of resources, social security, defense, and others—and for the facilities, materials, labor, subsidies, and what not which they entail. And before trying to bring these services into the picture, one by one, it will be logical to look into the financial arrangements by which they are supported, including how the government decides what to spend and on what, and how it gets the money. A prudent individual first calculates his resources and then trims his outlays so as to keep within them. A government, too, cannot be indifferent to its flow of income. Since, however, a government can accelerate that flow indefinitely, chiefly by increasing taxes and by borrowing, it can, and often under the driving force of public demand and necessity must, decide upon expenditures first, and shape its plans later, or at all events as it goes along, for obtaining the necessary funds. Taking our cue from this fact, we start with national expenditure, and afterwards look into the matters of revenue and debt.

Money as a prerequisite

The Federal Spending Power

The constitution has rather more to say about raising revenue than about spending it: authority to tax, as well as to borrow, is expressly conferred; and various limitations upon the taxing power are carefully prescribed. A government, however, that could not spend money would

Constitutional basis

be no government at all; and in the case of the national government, power to spend not only is expressly granted in a clause of the constitution authorizing Congress to "pay the debts and provide for the common defense and general welfare of the United States,"[1] but clearly is implied in numerous provisions conferring authority to do things that could not possibly be done without spending money, *e.g.*, raise and support armies, provide and maintain a navy, establish post-offices and post-roads, and maintain a system of courts. If necessary, spending power could be deduced also from the granted powers to tax and borrow, since manifestly there would be no point to raising money in such ways if it could not be used. Only three specific restrictions are imposed: (1) that appropriations for the support of the Army shall not be "for a longer term than two years;" (2) that "no money shall be drawn from the Treasury but in consequence of appropriations made by law;" and (3) that "a regular statement and account of the receipts and expenditures of all public money shall be published from time to time."[2]

Some broad interpretations

Nevertheless, throughout much of our national history the spending power of Congress has been a prolific source of constitutional controversy. Primarily, the question has been whether the power to spend is limited to purposes connected with the exercise of *other* powers delegated in the constitution, or whether it is a power independent of, and in addition to, other powers and properly to be exercised for *any* purpose so long as having to do with "common defense and general welfare."[3] In early days, strict constructionists like Madison took the first view, loose constructionists like Hamilton the second; and, remembering the drift toward broad construction as the decades passed, one will not be surprised to learn that the more liberal interpretation gained wide, though by no means universal, acceptance, or that Congress gradually fell into the habit of regarding its spending power as to all intents and purposes limited only by broad and indefinite defense and welfare objectives. Nay more: no appropriation made on this basis was ever—simply as an act of spending—successfully challenged in the courts. And not only so, but in its memorable decision of 1936 overthrowing the Agricultural Adjustment Act of 1933,[4] the Supreme Court—while condemning the processing taxes for which that measure provided, and invalidating it on that sole ground—went out of its way to assert that "the power of Congress to authorize the expenditure of public moneys [or to tax] for public purposes is not limited by the direct grants of legislative power found in the constitution" (which is precisely what Hamilton in his day contended), and further that such expenditure is constitutionally legitimate so long as the welfare at which it is aimed can be plausibly represented as na-

[1] Art. I, § 8, cl. 1.
[2] Art. I, § 8, cl. 12, and § 9, cl. 7.
[3] There has been the same question also with respect to taxation. See pp. 577-580 below.
[4] United States *v.* Butler, 297 U. S. 1, 66 (1936). See p. 680 below.

tional rather than local, with Congress the judge, subject only to judicial veto if discretion is exercised arbitrarily or unreasonably.[1]

A good while before these principles were so securely established judicially, the spending power was brought into fresh controversy by the rise of the grant-in-aid system. Not unnaturally, when Congress began appropriating funds to states for promoting education and public health, building roads, and performing other functions traditionally regarded as state rather than federal, taxpayers sometimes objected to diversion of their contributions to such purposes; and in 1923 the Supreme Court was confronted with not only a case brought by a taxpayer, but also one brought by the state of Massachusetts, challenging the constitutionality of a measure of 1921 (the Sheppard-Towner Act) on the ground that by appropriating federal money to aid states in reducing maternal and infant mortality the act was serving purposes not national but only local and invading the sphere of self-government reserved to the states under the Tenth Amendment. No direct affirmation of the measure's constitutionality resulted. But in a consolidated decision of the two cases the Court (1) brushed aside the contention of Massachusetts by pointing out that under the act no state was obliged to accept the federal grant unless it wished to do so, and (2) set aside the taxpayer's protest on the ground that her share of the federal funds granted under terms of the legislation was too inconsequential to give her reasonable ground to maintain a suit.[2] And from that day onward, the swelling stream of federal funds flowing into the states in the form of grants-in-aid found sanction in these considerations—although nowadays supplemented by the Court's broad ruling, mentioned above, that Congress has power to appropriate money, to states or otherwise, for any purpose comprehended within "common defense and general [i.e., national] welfare." For a good while, federal officials were fearful lest such undertakings as slum clearance and housing projects be regarded judicially as "out of bounds;" but a decision of 1945 allayed the apprehension. So long, therefore, as a general-welfare purpose can be shown (and this usually offers little difficulty), the field for federal grants to states seems wide open. Nor is it essential that grants be matched from state funds; and, as for the regulatory power commonly going along with grants, the Supreme Court itself has said that it is natural and proper for the federal government "to regulate that which it subsidizes."[3]

The matter of grants-in-aid

How Appropriations Are Made—The Budget System

Not a dollar of federal money can be expended legally except in pursuance of authorization, direct or indirect, by Congress; and passing

The rôle of Congress

[1] R. L. Post, "The Constitutionality of Spending for the General Welfare," *Va. Law Rev.*, XXII, 1-30 (Nov., 1935); E. S. Corwin, "The Spending Power of Congress," *Harvard Law Rev.*, XXXVI, 548-582 (May, 1923).

[2] Massachusetts *v.* Mellon and Frothingham *v.* Mellon, 262 U. S. 447 (1923).

[3] Wickard *v.* Filburn, 317 U. S. 111, 131 (1942).

the great appropriation bills becomes one of the most important tasks of that body at every regular session. In these measures, Congress, in effect, instructs the Treasury to supply the executive departments and other spending agencies with stipulated sums, according to specifications set forth in great detail. Indeed, one of the chief means by which Congress exercises control over administration is this minute and itemized allocation of money, cutting off an activity here by leaving it without financial support, adding an activity or agency there by making the necessary fiscal provision, and in these and other ways predetermining far more than do some foreign parliaments the lines on which the government's work shall be carried on.[1]

For many years before the adoption of the present budget system in 1921, appropriation bills were drafted and introduced by no fewer than nine separate House committees—the bills themselves regularly numbering fourteen—and in the Senate were handled by as many as fifteen different committees. Based upon more or less inflated requests made by the various spending agencies, and merely swept together and transmitted to Congress in an undigested mass by the secretary of the treasury, these bills were not only framed, but considered and reported by the several committees, in little or no relation to one another—and, what was worse, in little or no relation to the condition of the Treasury or to the outlook for revenue. With no single guiding hand to exercise restraint, they were likely to emerge in even more swollen form than when they first made their appearance; and although the president might warn and admonish, he as a rule could do nothing in the end except affix his signature, since to do otherwise would mean to halt essential government activities. Under such division of responsibility, log-rolling became a fine art, the "pork-barrel" an inexhaustible resource.

In days when expenditures were relatively modest and revenues (chiefly from high protective tariffs) usually adequate to meet them, criticism of such haphazard procedures had little or no effect. The startling upswing of national outlays during the First World War, however, lent new force to a growing demand for reform; and in 1921 a national budget system, such as had long been talked about, became a reality. The essence of a sound budget system consists in careful planning of the expenditures of a given period in relation to anticipated income, by a single authority, which not only will achieve the necessary correlation but shoulder responsibility for results; and while the plan

---

[1] In Great Britain, Parliament is content to vote lump sums for various departments and services, and to leave the executive—which in effect means the Treasury —to make detailed allocations, including the fixing of salaries and wage-scales. Accuracy requires it to be said not only that early appropriations in the United States took the form of lump-sum grants, but that of late a good many such grants have been made—for example, during the depression for public works and relief, and during the recent war, for the Army and Navy. The prevailing procedure is, however, otherwise; and it constitutes one of the most important restraints on the executive branch, and particularly the president.

introduced by the Budget and Accounting Act of 1921 [1] left, and still leaves, a good deal to be desired, it in general meets this basic prerequisite.

The planning and coördinating agency set up by the act is the Bureau of the Budget, originally attached loosely to the Treasury Department, although in effect an independent establishment. As supreme director of national administration, the president is, however, the logical authority to bear primary responsibility for preparing integrated programs of spending and revenue-raising; and after Franklin D. Roosevelt became chief executive, the Bureau was drawn into closer relations with the White House, until eventually, under authority conferred in the Reorganization Act of 1939, it was absorbed outright into the Executive Office of the President, thereupon becoming definitely the arm of the chief executive for all contacts and dealings with the financial side of the government. More adequate financial support was thenceforth received, and under the management of an able "career man," the late Harold D. Smith, as director, the Bureau quickly became one of the most vigorous and effective establishments in Washington. [2]

The Bureau of the Budget

There has been, also, a remarkable expansion of functions. From an agency concerned with little more than coördinating requests for funds in relation to expected revenues and putting them into coherent shape for transmission to Congress, the Bureau has developed into the principal aid to the president in planning and guiding the operations of the entire executive branch of the government. Conceptions of the budgetary process itself have been broadened to include not only the formulation of well-defined financial programs for the various departments and establishments, but also supervision of and control over the execution of such programs, including continuous study of problems of administrative organization and business methods. Resulting in part from the enlargement of governmental activities in fighting the depression of the thirties, the Bureau's new rôle arose to an even greater extent from situations created by the more recent defense effort and war, when greater responsibilities than ever before were thrust upon the president, and when, in passing them along, as he must, to departments and other agencies, he found the Bureau the handiest and most serviceable medium for maintaining the supervision and responsibility incumbent upon him. [3] To a division having

The Bureau's expanded rôle

---

[1] 42 *U. S. Stat. at Large*, 20.

[2] The director is appointed by the president alone, and for an indefinite term.

[3] Such service the Bureau is able to render through the basic power given the director to "revise, reduce, or increase" the estimates of the several departments and agencies—a power from which flows broad discretion over the substance of department programs, not only in the planning stage but also later; because after the programs have received Bureau approval, and after Congress has voted the necessary appropriations, the departments and establishments must still obtain the Bureau's approval for their financial procedures in carrying out their programs, including the periodic (usually monthly) allotment of funds and the maintenance of reasonable reserves for contingencies. In addition, since 1939 a division of legislative reference in the Bureau has examined and reported upon all measures pending in Congress which, if enacted, would impose a charge upon the public treasury or otherwise affect

to do with receiving, reviewing, and preparing estimates are added others charged with coördinating departmental proposals for legislation with the established policies of the president, studying fiscal programs in relation to the state of the national economy, supervising the statistical work of government agencies, and advising and assisting on problems of administrative organization, procedure, and management. It was perfectly natural that when in 1945 Congress gave President Truman authority to reorganize the national administration on a permanent peacetime basis, his first step should have been to call on the Budget Bureau for the formation of plans.[1]

Preparing the budget

Although the government's tax year, *e.g.*, the year for which taxable income is computed and in which most taxes are paid, corresponds to the calendar year, and therefore starts on January 1, its "fiscal" year, *i.e.*, the year for which expenditures are planned and accounts made up, opens on July 1;[2] and a given fiscal year is hardly entered upon before work on the financial arrangements for the ensuing year is started. First of all, every spending agency is asked by the Budget Bureau to compile detailed estimates of the funds that it will need in the next fiscal year and to submit such estimates not later than September 15. In larger agencies, this is done by special budget officers, in lesser ones by members of the staff detailed for the purpose; and for many weeks conferences go on between these or other agency representatives, on the one hand, and Budget Bureau officials, on the other—the former commonly pressing for as generous allotments as they can hope to get, the latter raising questions, offering objections, and seeking to whittle down requests sometimes regarded as extravagant.[3] On larger matters, the budget director is brought into the discussions; and, subject only to reversal by the president, his word is law for every department, bureau, board, and commission as to what expenditures (and in what amounts) shall be recommended to Congress and what ones shall not. Meanwhile, the Treasury Department, on its part, has been asked not only for data concerning interest charges on the national debt, but also for detailed estimates of the revenues that may be expected in the period, together with proposals for increasing

---

the president's fiscal policy, the purpose being to determine the relation of such measures to the "financial program of the president;" indeed if the Bureau does not think well of a measure passed, it may, and sometimes does, prepare a veto message and advise the president to sign it.

[1] The workings of the Budget Bureau are discussed at first hand by a former director, Harold D. Smith, in his *The Management of Your Government* (New York, 1945). Other excellent accounts will be found in N. M. Pearson, "The Budget Bureau; From Routine Business to General Staff," *Pub. Admin. Rev.*, III, 126-149 (Spring, 1943), and F. Morstein Marx, "The Bureau of the Budget; Its Evolution and Present Rôle," *Amer. Polit. Sci. Rev.*, XXXIX, 653-684, 869-898 (Aug. and Oct., 1945).

[2] A fiscal year, therefore, runs from July 1 to the following June 30, and is designated by the year in which the last six months fall. Thus "fiscal 1948" is the period from July 1, 1947, to June 30, 1948.

[3] In August, 1947, the chairmen of the House and Senate appropriations committees asked that a representative of each committee be permitted to be present at all conferences (starting the next month) preliminary to framing the executive budget for fiscal 1949.

such revenues in case they promise to be insufficient. With all of the estimates and other information finally in hand (ordinarily by December 1), Bureau officials total up the amounts, arrange data in logical order, and work the whole into a volume of several hundred pages—*i.e.*, the "budget"—which, by the close of the calendar year, is placed on the desk of the president. At this last moment, that official can revise or strike out items. But usually he has already assented to most of them; and, with Congress coming into regular session normally on January 3, he, commonly within a few days after transmitting his "state of the union" message, submits a special message presenting the budget as a balanced fiscal plan for which he assumes full responsibility, and covering not only appropriations but revenue proposals and, if necessary, proposals for deficit financing.[1]

In 1920, with the adoption of a budget system imminent, the House of Representatives prepared for the new order of things by enlarging its general appropriations committee to thirty-five (now forty-three) members, giving it jurisdiction over all appropriation proposals, and authorizing it to employ as many as fifteen subcommittees (the present number is twenty-one) for handling proposals relating to particular departments or agencies.[2] Received in the House, a budget's revenue proposals are turned over at once to the committee on ways and means, and its far bulkier proposals for expenditure to the appropriations committee; and formerly the two committees and their subcommittees worked independently from this point, with the Senate commonly waiting more or less patiently until after bills had been passed in the House. With a view, however, to more coördination, the Legislative Reorganization Act of 1946[3] interposed a new procedural stage by requiring that, upon the president's proposals being received, the House committees on ways and means and appropriations and the corresponding Senate committees (on finance and appropriations), or duly authorized subcommittees thereof, shall form themselves into a joint committee and, with the president's recommendations before them, work out a "legislative budget" to be reported to the two houses by February 15 for adoption by concurrent resolution; and while touching so far as necessary upon matters of taxation and debt, this budget is to have as its primary feature the stipulation

The budget before Congress

---

[1] As observed elsewhere, President Truman, on January 21, 1946, varied the usual procedure by transmitting the "state of the union" message and the budget for the ensuing year as a single document. The budget message will usually be found in the *N. Y. Times* of the following day. See, for example, the issue of January 13, 1948.

If unanticipated necessity arises, supplementary and deficiency estimates may be presented to Congress after submission of the regular budget; and "deficiency" appropriation bills are passed at almost every session. It is hardly necessary to add that in a period like the recent war years, special—and huge—appropriations become necessary without much reference to the regular calendar.

[2] The corresponding Senate committee now (1948) has twenty-one members. In 1940, the Brookings Institution recommended that the separate House and Senate appropriations committees be replaced by a single joint appropriation committee of the two houses, equipped with a permanent staff of budget and fiscal experts.

[3] See p. 411 above.

of maximum, or "ceiling," figures for expenditures for different purposes, as well as a figure for the year's total outlay.[1]

Framing
appropri-
ation
bills
When turning to their separate tasks of enacting finance legislation, the two houses therefore have before them not only the integrated budget transmitted by the president, but in a sense an alternative budget, framed by their own joint committee against the background of the executive budget and perhaps differing considerably from it; and if by joint resolution they adopt the latter, they then have it to work from in framing and enacting appropriation measures, with at least a presumption that such measures will be trimmed to keep within the ceiling figures which the legislative budget proposes—although there is no compulsion whatever that this be done. At all events, from this point on, procedure is substantially as before. Appropriations subcommittees in the House work out bills covering appropriations in their several fields of jurisdiction; these bills—twelve in number—are reported to the general appropriations committee, and by it to the House; as separate measures, they are transmitted to the Senate, where again they are considered by subcommittees, by the main committee, and finally on the legislative floor; and, as individually emerging (usually after conference committees have been called into play), they eventually are sent, one by one, to the White House, where almost invariably they are signed.[2] Hitherto, no attempt has been made to gather all of the separate bills into a single grand appropriation measure, as is done in Great Britain. But during the 1947 session, the Senate rules committee endorsed a proposed amendment to the Legislative Reorganization Act under which, beginning in 1948, such a consolidation would be required; and the proposal was expected ultimately to be adopted.

Some
benefits
realized
During the quarter-century since the federal budget went into operation, it has abundantly proved its worth. Under the relatively normal

---

[1] With no fewer than 102 members, this joint committee is, of course, unwieldy for effective work, and on the single occasion (January-February, 1947) on which the committee had functioned down to the date of writing, its study of the president's budget and preparation of a report were delegated to a subcommittee composed of five members (three Republicans and two Democrats) of each of the four component committees, and reporting ultimately to the full committee.

On the new plan's unsatisfactory results at its first trial, see p. 571 below.

[2] Appropriation measures, like others, are, of course, subject to veto. Seldom, however, can they be disapproved without risk of disrupting some branch of the government's activities, even when they include provisions to which the chief executive objects. As we have seen, there is no "item veto."

The various stages in preparing and handling appropriation bills are indicated above in a few lines. But this should not be allowed to obscure the fact that, in addition to sharing in the activities of the joint committee as described, the House appropriations committee and its subcommittees are working diligently throughout almost the whole of a session—weighing proposals, conferring with Budget Bureau and administrative officials, holding hearings, and the like. Frequently, most of the appropriation bills are not ready to be passed—at all events are not passed—until a session is drawing toward a close. The congestion was particularly severe near the presumed end of the first session of the Eightieth Congress in July, 1947 (actually, the session was resumed during the following November), when more than half of the major appropriation measures had not reached the White House at the beginning of the final week.

conditions prevailing in the earlier part of the period, it enabled the president to hold the spending agencies reasonably in leash and to effect substantial economies; and even in the years of extraordinarily lavish expenditure associated with the New Deal and the later defense and war effort, when the executive rather than Congress was taking the lead in planning huge outlays, it imparted unity and responsibility which otherwise would have been lacking. Not only does the system open a way for thorough and impartial review of the estimates of all spending agencies, and for reduction of those found questionable, before they are sent to Capitol Hill, but it enables Congress to act with fuller information concerning not only pending proposals, but the state of the country's finances generally, recent and current trends, and the outlook for at least a brief period to come; and when the President's Committee on Administrative Management appraised the system in its report of 1937, it gave full credit for these and other gains.

There is, however, room for improvement. It would be advantageous, *Possible further improvements* for example, if department heads and the director of the budget were given the privilege of the floor in Congress, so that they might explain budgetary proposals (or omissions) to the general membership of each house, as they now explain them to individual leaders, committees, and subcommittees. Appropriation bills of general character are no longer introduced except by the regular appropriations committee. But representatives and senators freely exercise their privilege of introducing bills calling for the expenditure of money for particular projects—building a post-office, constructing a dam, dredging a harbor, or "improving" a river —in which they (at all events the voters back home) are interested. Although the Legislative Reorganization Act of 1946 amended the rules of the Senate so as to forbid any increase by that body of amounts specified in reported appropriation bills, or the insertion of any new items, unless to carry out provisions of some existing law, or unless moved on authority of some standing or select committee, even this far from airtight restriction was not applied to the House. Furthermore, adoption by joint resolution of the new joint committee's figures for expenditure as proposed in its legislative budget is, as we have seen, purely tentative, not precluding subsequent enactment of bills appropriating far larger sums. It would save taxpayers millions of dollars a year if Congress were to emulate the example of the British Parliament, and, as a matter of regular practice, refrain from voting money for any purposes, or in any amounts, not specified in the carefully considered plans of the executive, or at all events add or increase items only with executive endorsement. At the least, if present usage is to continue, it would be helpful if, by constitutional amendment, the president were given power to veto separate items of appropriation bills, as governors in all but nine states have been authorized to do.[1]

[1] See pp. 385-387 above and p. 934 below (in complete edition of this book).

Execut-
ing the
budget—
the Gen-
eral Ac-
counting
Office
In its report of 1937, the President's Committee on Administrative Management criticized the Budget Bureau for concentrating too much upon the preparation of budgets and not giving enough attention to "supervision over the execution of the budget by the spending agencies." As the committee was frank to recognize, the Bureau had never up to that time been given sufficient staff or money to enable it to perform this added task. The situation has now been measureably corrected; and much is done by way of checking up on the use actually made of funds voted and supervising the transfer of funds from one agency to another. There is need for such work, notwithstanding the existence of another agency—the General Accounting Office—created, in point of fact, by the same act of 1921 which brought the Budget Bureau into existence. In addition to auditing the accounts of spending agencies, this independent establishment—independent because its head, the comptroller-general, is appointed by the president and Senate for a fifteen-year term and is removable only by impeachment or, for cause, by joint resolution of Congress—has as a main function the validating of payments for services, supplies, etc., as a means of seeing that all such outlays fall within the purposes and limits of appropriations as made by Congress; without the comptroller-general's approval, money for such purposes cannot be drawn from the Treasury, or, if drawn and paid over, must be refunded. After 1933, the General Accounting Office became a focus of vigorous controversy, partly because the then comptroller-general, personally hostile to the New Deal, held up numerous payments in connection with New Deal enterprises as lacking proper authorization in congressional appropriations; and in 1937 the President's Committee made recommendations, eagerly accepted by the President himself, looking to abolition of the Office, transfer of "pre-audits" to the Treasury Department, and retention of post-audits in a new agency to be headed by an auditor-general. Sharply clashing views developed, however, in various responsible quarters; and the suggested changes have not been made. Meanwhile, President Roosevelt's opportunity to select a comptroller-general of more sympathetic disposition eased the situation, though without ending the problem.[1]

Growth and Present Pattern of National Expenditures

The
rising
cost of
govern-
ment
A cardinal feature of the past forty or fifty years in this country has been the steep rise in the cost of government, sharply accelerated in

[1] The Committee's discussion of the subject will be found in its report, *Administrative Management in the Government of the United States*, 20-24. Later on, the Brookings Institution submitted a report to a Senate committee on government reorganization which in some respects opposed the recommendations of the President's Committee. See *Report to the* [Senate] *Select Committee to Investigate the Executive Agencies of the Government* (Washington, D. C., 1937), No. 5, pp. 79-102. Cf. J. McDiarmid, "Reorganization of the General Accounting Office," *Amer. Polit. Sci. Rev.,* XXXI, 508-516 (June, 1937); also D. T. Selko, *The Administration of Federal Finances* (Washington, D. C., 1937), in which the President's Committee and Brookings views are compared, to the advantage of the latter.

periods of depression and war, yet by no means confined, on any level, to emergency times. In 1913, national, state, and local governments together spent only a little over three billion dollars; by 1932 (before large spending for depression purposes started), the figure had risen to almost fourteen billions, and in 1941 (with national defense making heavy demands, but before we were at war), it mounted to twenty-seven billions. To this inexorable trend, several factors have contributed. One is the steady growth of population, requiring government to serve ever larger numbers of people. Another, even more significant, is increasing urbanization; for it costs more to supply the services required, and according to the standards demanded, by people in cities and towns than in rural areas. A third is the effect of inventions and technological advance; witness the billions spent on highways since the motor car came into common use and the rising outlays on airports since aviation entered the transportation field. A fourth is the rising price level; in 1941, governments paid for what they bought at prices on the average fifty-four per cent higher than in 1932 and eighty-eight per cent higher than in 1913. Transcending all else, however, is the enormous expansion of services which governments of all kinds undertake to render. The point need not be elaborated here, for illustrations of it occur in almost every chapter of this book. Suffice it to say that between 1913 and 1932 new or enlarged services accounted for practically one-third of all government expenditures of the period, and between 1932 and 1941, for considerably more than one-half. Taken together, the various factors enumerated would have raised federal (as well as state and local) expenditures to unprecedented heights even if there had been no depression and no World War II.[1]

Some reasons

Back in 1889-91, the Fifty-first Congress achieved considerable notoriety by authorizing federal expenditures aggregating somewhat over a billion dollars for the biennium; and during the first decade of the present century, total federal outlays rarely exceeded half a billion a year.[2] World War I naturally pushed the figure much higher. But afterwards the country settled down to a more or less normal peacetime expenditure routine, with outlays devoted principally to interest and retirement of the national debt, veterans' pensions, maintenance of the executive, legislative, and judicial establishments, support of the Army and Navy, and relatively modest enterprises in such domains as reclamation, river and harbor improvement, and highway construction. Even so, by the begin-

National expenditures in recent decades

---

[1] Exclusive of special costs entailed by the defense effort launched in 1940, the federal share of total governmental expenditures in 1941 was approximately one-third, the states' share somewhat over one-fifth, and the share of local governments somewhat over two-fifths. With defense costs figured in, the federal share was fifty-six per cent. For a full analysis of governmental expenditures in general, see F. Dewhurst *et al.*, *America's Needs and Resources* (New York, 1947), Chap. xx.

[2] In 1790, Alexander Hamilton compiled an initial federal budget of less than four millions and worried about how to get the money. Today, Chicago alone spends more than eight times as much.

ning of Franklin D. Roosevelt's presidency in 1933, outlays had reached four billions a year; and from that point the pattern was warped almost beyond recognition—first, by new forms of expenditure (on work relief, aid to agriculture, assistance to youth, social security, and what not) introduced in an effort to get the country out of depression and to improve the general social and economic order, and afterwards, in far greater measure, by outlays entailed by the defense program and the ensuing war. Three years of fighting the depression pushed the figure for fiscal 1936 to over nine billions. Some improvement of the national situation permitted a drop to about eight billions the next year. But economic recession in 1937-38, combined with growing outlays for defense (especially naval), carried the figure steadily upward to $12,710,000,000 in fiscal 1941, exclusive of debt retirement. Even this was only the beginning of a leap to heights which a few years previously would have been considered fantastic. Within the first six months of the following fiscal period, the fast-expanding defense effort merged into war effort on the most gigantic scale ever known to the country; and the total outlay for that year (fiscal 1942) reached the astonishing figure of $32,396,000,000— more than World War I cost us altogether. This too, however, was merely a prelude to more stupendous outlays later; in fiscal 1943, they rose to seventy-eight billions (almost double the total national income in the depression year 1932), and in 1944 to almost ninety-four billions; while in fiscal 1945, the last year of the war, expenditures exceeded a hundred billions—or almost exactly half of the "gross national product" (total production of goods and services) for that year.[1] With hostilities ended, outlays for fiscal 1946 dropped to slightly less than sixty-five billions, and for fiscal 1947 to approximately forty-two and one-half billions.

The post-war problem of reduction   Heavier federal taxation than the country had ever before known naturally served to take care of only a fraction of the wartime expenditures outlined, and, as we shall see, the national debt mounted from forty-two billions in 1940 to the amazing total of 279.5 billions in 1946; fiscal 1947, indeed, became the first year in eighteen in which outlays did not outrun receipts. Most people who saw in newspaper headlines the mounting figures of wartime expenditure were merely benumbed, or at most were led to wonder how such sums could ever be raised or the borrowings entailed by them paid off. There were those, however, who called loudly for reductions in non-defense outlays; and, between them, the Budget Bureau and a joint congressional committee on "non-essential" expenditures contrived reductions which saved a billion or two a year. The difficulty was, however, that no one could figure out any really large savings without cutting deeply into major undertakings like agricultural aid, pensions, and social security; and with not only sturdy opposition

[1] During the year ending June 30, 1940, eighteen per cent of the total national outlay went for defense; in the following year, about forty-nine per cent; in the next year, eighty per cent; and in each of the next three (1943-45), more than ninety per cent.

voiced by the vast numbers of people who would have been affected, but the government itself committed to leading the nation to victory abroad without material sacrifice of hard-won social and economic gains at home, the limits of budgetary trimming were soon reached. With hostilities terminated in 1945, demobilization of armed forces and suspensions or curtailments of wartime activities almost automatically brought federal expenditures down to the figures for 1946 and 1947 indicated above. But, in view of the burden imposed by the swollen national debt, and of wide-spread demand for tax relief, they still were appallingly high; and a Republican Congress elected in 1946 stood pledged not only to reduce taxes but also to cut expenditures by perhaps as much as five or six billions.

Now it was, when the Eightieth Congress organized in January, 1947, and the president's budget for fiscal 1948 was received, that the new joint-committee plan introduced by the Legislative Reorganization Act of 1946 had its first trial; and the experience was not particularly heartening. Not only did the huge "town-meeting" committee have to break new ground, but—with Republicans controlling Congress and a Democrat seated in the White House (and with, in addition, the 1948 elections beginning to loom)—legislative-executive relations were too suffused with politics to permit of the careful and dispassionate work needing to be performed. The committee's Republican leadership, furthermore, was caught between extravagant promises of economy on the one hand and fixed obligations impossible to evade on the other. The president's budget called for an expenditure of $37,528,000,000.[1] When analyzed, however, nearly forty per cent was found to be represented by three items (interest on the national debt, tax refunds required by law, and veterans' benefits) in which little or no cutting was possible, and another thirty per cent to be for national defense, hardly susceptible of much reduction under existing international conditions—leaving only thirty per cent (for items like costs of operating the executive, legislative, and judicial establishments and outlays on agriculture, conservation, social security, and the like) offering any real latitude for downward revision. And for weeks the committee (more accurately, its subcommittee of twenty as indicated above) juggled figures and floundered in an effort to achieve substantial savings in this last-mentioned sector.[2]

The outcome, enveloped in a fog of partisan controversy, will always be a matter of difference of opinion; but certainly it left campaign promises (which might better not have been made) unmatched by performance. To be sure, the joint committee, dividing sharply on party lines, reported a legislative budget cutting the president's recommended expenditures by

The new joint committee and its experience in 1947

---

[1] Later increased by $165,000,000.

[2] Cuts in appropriations for activities of the State and Interior Departments stirred vigorous protests from agencies affected and from interests outside, *e.g.,* Western people concerned about the progress of reclamation projects.

six billions.[1] To be sure, too, the House of Representatives passed a concurrent resolution approving it. On its part, the Senate, however, reduced the cut to four and one-half billions; and in the upshot the plan became so mired down in log-rolling and sniping at the Administration that when the twelve essential appropriation measures at last emerged (most of them, as already observed, only when the session seemed about to end [2]) several of the number bore little clear relation either to the joint committee's figures or to the president's. After it was all over, Republican leaders laid claim to "real" reductions aggregating as much as four and one-half billions; on the strength of the approximately 34.8 billions voted, the figure seemed nearer two and three-quarter billions; while Budget Bureau officials put it at from a billion and a half to two billions, with President Truman never conceding any wider margin. In point of fact, as fiscal 1948 started, the prospect of additional outlays was such (particularly if the projected European Recovery Program for assistance to European rehabilitation were approved in time to begin operating before the middle of 1948) that no saving at all might remain; quite apart from the European program, the budget message of January 12, 1948, estimated the current year's total expenditures at 37.7 billions—very close to the sum originally requested, and three billions in excess of the amount voted.

The budget for fiscal 1949

In 1942, President Roosevelt thought that the national outlay after the war, even including interest on the national debt, would not normally exceed ten billions a year; in 1946, financial experts were estimating the figure at from twenty to twenty-five billions; nowadays, there is small prospect of it falling far below thirty-five billions. The budget for fiscal 1949 transmitted by President Truman on January 12, 1948, contemplated an expenditure of $39,669,000,000—the largest sum ever asked for a peace year except fiscal 1947; and although a Republican-controlled Congress received it with threats of vigorous pruning, there was little reason to expect a final outcome materially different from that of the preceding year.

The pattern of present expenditures summarized

Meanwhile, the budget message referred to disclosed a pattern of actual expenditures in fiscal 1947 (July 1, 1946, to June 30, 1947) as follows:

Objects of Expenditure	Amount in Millions
National defense	$14,280
Veterans' programs	7,369
International affairs and finance	6,540
Interest on the national debt	4,958
Tax refunds	3,897
Social security and welfare	1,379
General costs of government	1,317
Aids to agriculture	1,247

[1] The report, transmitted to Congress on February 14, will be found in the *N. Y. Times* of the following day.

[2] *I.e.*, in July. As indicated above, the session was resumed in November.

[3] As approved during the spring of 1948, outlays were to start in fiscal 1949.

Objects of Expenditure	Amount in Millions
Conservation	627
Transportation and communications	587
Housing and community facilities	402
Finance, commerce, and industry	237
Labor	119
Education and general research	75
Total	$42,505

In this tabulation, the towering fact is, of course, that somewhat over three-quarters of our total national outlay relate directly to war, the effects of war, or our efforts to prevent future war: [1] thirty-four per cent for the maintenance of our defenses, eighteen per cent for veterans' services and benefits, twelve per cent for interest on a national debt largely resulting from war, and over fifteen per cent for support of international programs and activities in the interest of world peace. The cost of running the entire government (equipment, salaries, wages, civil pensions, and the like) comes to but an insignificant three per cent; and while in later chapters we shall be reviewing activities and services that appear large and expensive in fields like agriculture, conservation, and social security, all of them combined drain the Treasury of hardly more than eleven per cent of the total funds paid out. Only if and when the top-heavy outlays incident to war can be sharply curtailed is the government likely to be able to keep pace with demands that undoubtedly will multiply for fuller and richer general services to the people.

REFERENCES

R. Young, *This Is Congress* (New York, 1943), Chap. VII.

D. T. Selko, *The Federal Financial System* (Washington, D. C., 1940), Chaps. IV-X, XXIII-XXIX.

——————, *The Administration of Federal Finances* (Washington, D. C., 1937).

H. M. Groves, *Financing Government* (rev. ed., New York, 1945), Chaps. XXII-XXIV.

H. L. Lutz, *Public Finance* (4th ed., New York, 1947), Chap. IV.

W. F. Willoughby, *The National Budget System* (Baltimore, 1927).

——————, *The Legal Status and Functions of the General Accounting Office* (Baltimore, 1927).

A. E. Buck, *The Budget in Governments of Today* (New York, 1934).

H. D. Smith, *The Management of Your Government* (New York, 1945).

E. E. Naylor, *The Federal Budget System in Operation* (Washington, D. C., 1941).

R. H. Rawson, "The Foundation of the Federal Budget," in C. J. Friedrich and E. S. Mason [eds.], *Public Policy* (Cambridge, Mass., 1941), Chap. IV.

J. A. Maxwell, *The Fiscal Impact of Federalism in the United States* (Cambridge, Mass., 1946).

L. Wilmerding, *The Spending Power; A History of the Efforts of Congress to Control Expenditures* (New Haven, 1943).

[1] In the budget for fiscal 1949, transmitted on January 12, 1948, seventy-nine per cent was so allocated.

P. W. Ellis, *The World's Biggest Business; American Public Spending, 1914-1944* (New York, 1944).

H. C. Mansfield, *The Comptroller-General; A Study in the Law and Practice of Financial Administration* (New Haven, 1939).

E. F. Bartlett, *Accounting Procedure of the United States Government* (Chicago, 1940).

D. H. Smith, *The General Accounting Office* (Baltimore, 1927).

C. Shoup, *Federal Finances in the Coming Decade* (New York, 1941).

President's Committee on Administrative Management, *Administrative Management in the Government of the United States* (Washington, D. C., 1937), 15-24.

[Brookings Institution], *Report to the Select* [Senate] *Committee to Investigate the Executive Agencies of the Government*, 75th Cong., 1st Sess., Sen. Doc. No. 5 (Washington, D. C., 1937).

Annual Report of the Secretary of the Treasury on the State of the Finances.

CHAPTER XXVI

NATIONAL REVENUES—THE TAX SYSTEM

Sources of Federal Funds

Our governments, on all levels, habitually live in part on borrowed money. In a given year, they may take in as much as they spend and thus have the comfort of a balanced budget. But hardly ever are they out of debt; and in periods of stress their borrowings may mount to impressive totals. To be commented upon at some length below, this matter of government borrowing is mentioned as we start merely to remind ourselves that the national revenues now to be considered do not account for all of the federal government's usable funds. Borrowings are not revenue. A man borrowing a thousand dollars from a bank may have the money in his pocket, but he is not taxed on it as income; for of course it is *not* income. At some specified rate of interest, he may have the use of it for a while. But he will have to pay it back. — 1. Loans

Furthermore, not all true national revenue is derived from taxation. To begin with, the government carries on business, or quasi-business, enterprises and pockets the receipts from them as any private businessman or corporation would do. One thinks instantly of the postal service, from which in 1946 the government drew more than one billion and a quarter dollars—not *profit* to be sure, but that is beside the present point. There are receipts also from the mints, the Government Printing Office, the Tennessee Valley Authority, the Alaska Railroad, the Panama Canal, the Inland Waterways Corporation, and other such diversified sources. In the second place, there is income from fees charged for services or privileges, as when a patent is applied for, a book copyrighted, or a lawyer admitted to practice before the Supreme Court. Third, there are fines levied in the courts, penalties for non-payment of taxes, and forfeitures of property taken from transgressors (*e.g.*, liquor or tobacco on which the required excise taxes have not been paid) or liquor, jewelry, perfumes, and the like (a million and a half dollars' worth in 1947) confiscated from smugglers or from importers, or even travellers, making fraudulent declarations. There are sales of property, too—public land or surplus war equipment. There are rentals from grazing lands and irrigated lands. There is interest on loans to farmers and to homeowners. There are even gifts, as the National Gallery of Art in Washington (presented by the Mellon estate) eloquently testifies. Relatively, the national government enjoys less non-tax revenue than do many of the — 2. Non-tax revenues

575

states, especially with their heavy federal subsidies in the form of grants-in-aid. But the total easily amounts to a billion and a half dollars a year.

3. Taxes   Nevertheless, the federal government lives principally from taxes;[1] and a major difference between the government under the Articles of Confederation and that under our present constitution is that, whereas the former could raise money only (aside from borrowing) by making requisitions upon more or less negligent states, the latter can reach down past the state governments to the individual citizen, levy on his property or business or income, and enforce payment, if necessary, by seizing and selling his possessions. Very appropriately, the long list of powers given Congress in the eighth section of the constitution's first article starts off with the power "to lay and collect taxes, duties, imposts, and excises." Nor was it simply by chance that the constitution's framers employed all of these different terms. To them, "taxes" meant primarily levies, like poll taxes and land taxes, falling *directly* on persons or property, and with the burden incapable of being shifted to other shoulders; "duties" and "imposts" referred to levies on imports and exports, respectively (what we commonly call tariff or customs duties [2]); and "excises" were levies on the production, distribution, or use of commodities— "internal revenue," as we early fell into the habit of terming this form of tax in distinction from revenue derived from foreign trade and collected at the ports. Moreover, in contrast with "taxes," duties, imposts, and excises are *indirect*, in that, while of course imposed directly enough upon importers, manufacturers, distributors, and the like, they can be, and commonly are, passed on to the consumer in the form of higher prices for goods, so that it is really he who pays the duty or excise, even though likely enough not to realize that he is doing so. The various terms employed in the taxing clause are therefore not without significance, even though in everyday usage it is customary to lump all of the different levies together under the general heading of "taxes"—which indeed we shall do in the present chapter.

A tax (in the broad sense indicated) is, of course, a levy or charge imposed normally to raise money for public purposes [3]—"an exaction," the Supreme Court has said, "for the support of the government." [4] It may be assessed upon individuals or upon corporations or other groups. It may take any one of many forms (not all employed by the national government)—property taxes, income taxes, excise taxes, sales taxes, license taxes, inheritance taxes, poll taxes, tariff duties, and still others. It may be direct or indirect. Always, however, a tax is compulsory; one

---

[1] Except, of course, in wartime, when far more may be raised by borrowing than by taxation.

[2] Although (in the clause cited) using terms broad enough to include levies on exports, the constitution elsewhere forbids any such to be laid. Art. I, § 9, cl. 5.

[3] The qualified form of statement is made necessary by the circumstance that, as we shall see, taxes are occasionally designed primarily for regulative purposes and only incidentally to raise revenue.

[4] United States *v.* Butler, 297 U. S. 1 (1936), 61.

may choose whether to pay rent or wages or prices, but not whether to pay taxes. Furthermore, while justified solely as a contribution in return for government service rendered (in at least some broad sense), tax burdens necessarily are apportioned among payers according to their property, income, business transactions, and the like, and not at all on the basis of benefits individually received—although it may be presumed that when tax money is employed for police or military protection, for example, the big taxpayer has more to be protected and in that sense gets service in some proportion to what he pays.

The Federal Taxing Power

Under the constitution's taxing clause, Congress has general freedom to tax persons and objects within the national jurisdiction; and if the people think themselves taxed excessively or unfairly, they will find remedy, not in the courts, but in electing a Congress—perchance also a president—pledged, or at least predisposed, to a different tax policy. Notwithstanding, however, that the federal government has far more effective powers of taxation (borrowing also) than do the state governments, there are limitations, both express and implied. To begin with, Congress is not free to levy taxes for any conceivable purpose whatsoever, but only (as the constitution plainly says) "to pay the debts and provide for the common defense and general welfare of the United States." "Debts" (manifestly including current obligations) and "defense" are sufficiently definite terms. "General welfare," however, is so broad that, as we saw when discussing expenditures, there have always been differences of opinion as to what activities and objectives may be read into it. In practice, however,—especially of late—it has not furnished much of a hurdle for tax-planners to surmount. Any taxation (or appropriation) for a purpose regarded by Congress (backed by the Supreme Court) as falling within the boundaries marked out by the constitution for the federal government can be justified under it; and not only Congress, but the Court as at present constituted, is rather easily satisfied on the point.

Down to World War I, the greatest part of the national revenue always came from indirect taxes; and, as we shall see, a large share is still derived from that source. In laying taxes of this kind, Congress, however, is bound by the constitutional provision that "all duties, imposts, and excises shall be uniform throughout the United States." [1] The requirement does not prevent tobacco excises, for example, from falling more heavily upon sections where tobacco products are manufactured extensively than upon others where there is little industry of the kind; it means merely that, in general, all cigars or cigarettes of a given kind or condition must be taxed at the same rate in all parts of the country. A tax may fall with very different weight on different areas, on different businesses, or on different classes of people. But—save for the exceptions regarding tariff duties to

Restrictions:

1. Purpose

2. Uniformity of indirect taxes

[1] Art. I, § 8, cl. 1.

be mentioned in the following paragraph—it must bear with the same weight on the same objects of taxation wherever found.

3. Uniformity among ports of entry

To reënforce this principle, the constitution further enjoins that in regulating commerce Congress shall not authorize customs duties to be collected at one rate at one port and at a different rate at another, or to be computed according to different rules.[1] At one time, this meant absolute uniformity at all ports as to any given kind or class of imports, whatever their place of origin. Under Supreme Court decisions since 1901, however, rates on commodities coming from the insular dependencies may differ from those on imports from other areas;[2] and under the trade agreement system instituted in 1934[3] there is much additional variation, according to the foreign country from which given commodities are received. The constitutional restriction mentioned, however, is fully preserved; the duty on a box of cigars from Puerto Rico may differ from that on a box from Brazil, but each will be uniform at all ports.

4. Other express restrictions

The taxing power is further limited (1) by a constitutional provision forbidding duties to be imposed on exports, although Congress is authorized to regulate export trade in every way other than by taxation; and (2) by a requirement that direct taxes shall be apportioned among the several states according to population.[4] As interpreted in earlier days—to include only poll or capitation taxes and taxes on land (and at one time slaves)—direct taxes have been laid by Congress only four times in our history, most recently in 1861.[5] Taxes on incomes laid in 1862 were held by the Supreme Court not to be direct taxes. When, however, the validity of a new income tax law was challenged in the last decade of the century, the Court ruled differently;[6] and ultimately, as we have seen, the obvious impossibility of taxing incomes in accordance with any mathematical apportionment among the states led in 1913 to adoption of the Sixteenth Amendment, brushing aside the entire question of whether income taxes are or are not direct taxes and simply authorizing Congress to "lay and collect taxes on incomes, from whatever source derived," without apportionment.

5. Implied restrictions

Finally may be mentioned restrictions nowhere specified but up to now regarded, with judicial support, as implicit in the nature of the federal union, *i.e.*, restraint from taxing (a) the property or essential functions of state governments or their subdivisions[7] and (b) securities issued by such jurisdictions or incomes derived therefrom.[8] As pointed out elsewhere, the restriction relating to securities will in all probability be

---

[1] Art. I, § 9, cl. 6.
[2] DeLima *v.* Bidwell, 182 U. S. 1 (1901); and for a more recent decision, Cincinnati Soap Co. *v.* United States, 301 U. S. 308 (1937). See p. 842 below.
[3] See p. 584 below.
[4] Art. I, § 2, cl. 3.
[5] C. J. Bullock, "The Origin, Purpose, and Effect of the Direct-Tax Clause in the Federal Constitution," *Polit. Sci. Quar.*, XV, 217-239, 452-484 (Sept., June, 1900).
[6] Pollock *v.* Farmers' Loan and Trust Co., 158 U. S. 601 (1895).
[7] Affirmed in Collector *v.* Day, 11 Wallace 113 (1870).
[8] Affirmed in Pollock *v.* Farmers' Loan and Trust Co., as cited.

terminated before long by Congress, with Supreme Court backing, as a similar one relating to the taxation of state and local salaries already has been.[1] As yet, however, it belongs in the list.

Most laws imposing taxation can readily be classed as revenue measures, *i.e.*, measures in which the primary, if not sole, purpose is to produce income for the government. As intimated above, there are, however, measures which, although tax laws in form, are intended mainly for regulative purposes and, if yielding revenue at all, do so only incidentally. A good example is tariff schedules planned for the protection of American industries against foreign competition. In so far as goods affected find their way to our ports notwithstanding heavy duties attached to them, revenue results. But high productiveness is not expected. Indeed, Congress has at times gone so far as to impose taxes with the avowed purpose of destroying a business enterprise altogether—taxing it out of existence and thereby rendering it wholly unproductive. A case in point, mentioned in other connections, is an act of 1865—in form a tax measure pure and simple—imposing so onerous a levy on notes issued by state banks that, as was the intention, it became unprofitable to issue them and their issuance ceased. By taxation, too, the sale of oleomargarine colored to resemble butter, dealing in sawed-off shot-guns, and manufacturing white phosphorus matches have been almost or completely stopped. In general, measures of the kind have been sustained whenever the courts considered that the taxing power was being used in pursuit of a purpose expressly or impliedly within the scope of congressional authority. When, in 1922, the Supreme Court invalidated an act imposing a special tax on the profits of manufacturers employing child labor, it did so, not because the measure was not primarily for raising revenue, but because the regulation of child labor (the sole purpose of the tax) was regarded by the justices then sitting as a function reserved to the states. The same was true when, in 1936, the Court objected to the "processing taxes" laid by the Agricultural Adjustment Act of 1933 as a means of raising money for a program of curtailing agricultural production. Protective tariffs have commonly been upheld, quite apart from the taxing power, on the basis of the power to regulate foreign commerce.

Is a tax constitutional, however, when not clearly either a revenue measure or a device for rendering effective some delegated or implied power, but rather is aimed solely, or principally, at promoting the "general welfare"? This question was raised pointedly by a law of 1902 laying a prohibitive tax upon colored oleomargarine, by an act of 1912 placing a similar tax upon the manufacture of poisonous phosphorus matches, by narcotic-drug laws of 1914 and 1919 imposing taxes on registered dealers, and by an act of 1919 laying a special tax on the profits of concerns employing children under the age of sixteen, the sole purpose being to discourage the use of child labor. In cases coming before it at different

Taxation not primarily for revenue

Taxation and "general welfare"

[1] Graves *v.* New York, 306 U. S. 466 (1939). See pp. 88-89 above.

times, the Supreme Court upheld both the oleomargarine and the narcotics law as revenue measures, refusing to inquire into the legislative intent.[1] The constitutionality of the phosphorus match law has never been judicially tested. But when the child labor law was challenged, the Court fixed attention on the motive animating Congress, and held the measure not a valid exercise of the taxing power.[2] For similar reasons, it invalidated the processing taxes levied under the first Agricultural Adjustment Act (1933) and a tax on producers of bituminous coal (1935), on the ground that the former were for the purpose of regulating agricultural production and the latter only a penalty for non-compliance with regulations affecting the business of coal-mining, neither of which fields was then regarded by the Court as within the bounds of congressional control.[3] As previously indicated, however, a Court now oriented to more liberal viewpoints has shown greater tolerance in such matters; and the presumption is that to the many occasions on which the federal taxing power has already been used with impunity in advancing social and economic ends, with considerations of revenue wholly secondary, will in future be added still others of major significance. In much of our income and inheritance taxation during recent decades, the purpose of curbing "swollen fortunes" can be discerned almost as clearly as that of obtaining revenue; and in messages to Congress in 1935 and on other occasions, President Franklin D. Roosevelt, pushing farther ideas advanced by Presidents Theodore Roosevelt, Wilson, and Hoover, warmly advocated such a policy, with a view to more equitable distribution of wealth and economic power.

The Enactment of Tax Measures—Newer Arrangements for Tariff-Making

Origins and frequency of tax legislation

Appropriations are generally made for some specified and limited period, most commonly a year, and consequently a sheaf of appropriation bills must be passed every twelve months, with deficiency measures interspersed as needed. Measures imposing or readjusting taxation, on the other hand, are usually without time limits; a given tax once levied, or a given rate once established, continues operative as long as not repealed or amended. This, however, does not mean that many years go by without new revenue legislation. Every annual budget transmitted to Congress by the president contains estimates of the revenue to be anticipated from existing sources; and along with these will almost invariably be submitted proposals for increasing the inflow by new or amended taxation if the yield does not promise to be sufficient, or for decreasing it if (as rarely happens any more) it promises to exceed needs, or for main-

[1] McCray v. United States, 195 U. S. 27 (1904); United States v. Doremus, 249 U. S. 86 (1919); Nigro v. United States, 276 U. S. 332 (1928).
[2] Bailey v. Drexel Furniture Co., 259 U. S. 20 (1922).
[3] United States v. Butler, 297 U. S. 1 (1936); Carter v. Carter Coal Co., 298 U. S. 238 (1936).

taining the yield but redistributing tax burdens if, as President Truman contended in his "state of the union" message of January, 1948, such change is dictated by considerations of public policy.[1] On its part, Congress, too, may—as in the case of two tax-reduction bills killed by presidential veto in 1947 and one passed over a veto in 1948—initiate revenue measures quite outside the executive's budget plans. Accordingly, tax legislation—if not in the form of a comprehensive revenue act, at least in that of a more or less significant amending measure—is to be anticipated with substantially the same yearly regularity as appropriation acts.

All measures for raising national revenue are required to originate in the House of Representatives;[2] and all portions of the president's annual budget message relating to revenue are forthwith referred to the ways and means committee of that body. Formerly, this committee would then immediately address itself to framing a tax bill for consideration by the two branches. Under the Legislative Reorganization Act of 1946, however, it now first participates in the deliberations of the large joint committee charged with formulating a legislative budget. Nevertheless, since contemplated expenditures are likely to emerge from that super-committee somewhat reduced rather than increased, no new or greatly altered tax plans are likely to be offered; and this means that in proceeding to frame tax legislation to be reported to the House the ways and means committee can usually start with the president's proposals substantially as it always did. Occasionally, although not often, the president will have had little to propose; such was the situation in 1947, when, with President Truman having no new taxes to recommend, and firmly of the opinion that circumstances did not warrant repealing or reducing existing ones, the budget message suggested practically no revenue legislation at all. Even so, the ways and means committee, responding to congressional opinion, party promises, or perchance public demand, can be depended upon to formulate plans for at least some new revenue legislation, even if only, as in 1947, for tax reduction; and in the upshot, as indicated above, hardly any regular congressional session fails to produce its revenue bill.

The handling of revenue bills

Working for weeks (through subcommittees when necessary), with normally the president's proposals before it, and with help from conferences with the chief executive, budget director, Treasury officials, bankers, business-men, and others, the committee finally emerges with its measure, which for further weeks absorbs much of the time and energy of the House. Passed by that body, the bill goes to the Senate, where, notwithstanding that the House was originally intended to enjoy substantial primacy in controlling the national purse, most revenue measures are more or less drastically altered, either in the finance committee or on the floor.

---

[1] The President's proposal on this occasion was that in the next fiscal year each taxpayer be given a "cost of living" tax credit of forty dollars (with the same amount also for each dependent), and that the three and one-fifth billions lost in this way be made up by higher taxes on corporate earnings. The plan did not prevail.

[2] Art. I, § 7, cl. 1.

There is, indeed, nothing to prevent the Senate from amending a House revenue bill by striking out all parts after the enacting clause and inserting an entirely new bill; and occasionally something of the sort has happened. It is even possible for a bill which in effect, and almost in technical form, is a bill to raise revenue to be passed in the Senate before the House has taken any action at all. In any case, a major tax bill, after passing the Senate, will unfailingly have to "go to conference;" and it is, of course, in the form in which it emerges from conference that the two houses finally enact it and the president signs it.[1] Throughout the entire procedure, the country—especially the business element—watches with interest, and even anxiety, to see what new taxes will be decided upon and what increases, decreases, or other changes will be made in existing ones.

The special case of tariff legislation

In earlier days, Congress from time to time turned its attention to enacting a revenue measure (though usually having non-revenue objectives as well) of a type raising special difficulties and problems, *i.e.*, a general tariff law prescribing the duties to be paid on articles imported from foreign countries and also, under varying conditions, from certain of the insular dependencies; and the country's history is punctuated with voluminous and controversial statutes of this nature—in later decades, the McKinley Act of 1890, the Wilson-Gorman Act of 1894, the Dingley Act of 1897, the Payne-Aldrich Act of 1909, the Underwood Act of 1913, the Fordney-McCumber Act of 1922, and, most recently, the Hawley-Smoot Act of 1930.[2] A generation ago, however, tariff-making by unassisted effort of Congress—never very satisfactory—was found no longer tolerable, and changes began to be introduced under which, although with ultimate control still vested in Congress (as constitutionally it must be), actual tariff-making passed progressively, by congressional delegation, into the hands of the executive, where most of it now is. People suspicious of the growth of executive power, and especially those clinging to a protectionist philosophy, do not relish the newer arrangements arrived at, and a reaction against them may some time prevail. The probability, however, is that the country will never again see vast omnibus tariff laws enacted as in the old days.[3] The defects of such tariff

[1] Until 1947, the only presidential veto of a general revenue bill in the nation's history was President Franklin D. Roosevelt's strongly worded, although unavailing, disapproval, February 22, 1944, of a measure providing for hardly more than one-fifth of the additional revenue of ten and one-half billion dollars urgently advocated by the Administration—a bill objectionable to the President also on other grounds. In both houses, the veto was overridden by heavy majorities. In June and July, 1947, President Truman successfully vetoed two major revenue bills (differing only in dates for taking effect)—both providing for a substantial lowering of income-tax rates, and both framed and introduced in Congress over strong presidential objection. See p. 587, note 2, below. In April, 1948, he vetoed another such bill, but this time unsuccessfully.

[2] For a history of the enactment of these measures, see L. H. Chamberlain, *The President, Congress, and Legislation* (New York, 1946), Chap. III.

[3] When in those times a general overhauling of the tariff system was contemplated, the House ways and means committee commonly assembled in Washington some weeks, or even months, before Congress was to meet, dividing itself into subcom-

legislation were many and grave. Responsibility for decisions was too much diffused between the two houses; special interests and their lobbyists exerted too great influence; general tariff bills became such labyrinths of facts and figures that even the most conscientious congressman could not inform himself on more than a minor fraction of the provisions on which he was expected to vote. Furthermore, regardless of how well-considered any set of schedules might be when first adopted, fluctuations of prices in the world market might render it inadequate almost before the ink was dry on the statute. Obviously, the need was not only for tariffs based on more comprehensive, exact, and up-to-date information, but for tariffs that would be more flexible—capable of quicker adaptation to changing situations.

In 1916, a good start toward reform was made when a United States Tariff Commission was set up, composed of six members representing both leading parties and charged with continuous investigation of all economic matters bearing upon tariff policy, and with reporting in full to both the president and Congress.[1] Of itself, this did not really go very far. Naturally, the Commission had no independent power to make changes in the tariff laws or in their administration; and at first it did not even have power to supplement the information which it imparted with recommendations except of very general character. In the tariff acts of 1922 and 1930, however, another long step was taken. Thereafter, not only was the Commission to investigate differences in the cost of production of any domestic article and any like or similar foreign article, but it was required to recommend to the president, on the basis of its findings, specific increases or decreases in tariff rates; and the president, in turn, was authorized to readjust rates, either up or down, within a range of fifty per cent, with no intervention from Congress. The effect was to give us for the first time a flexible tariff—one that enabled differentials be-

Flexible tariff arrangements

---

mittees for the preparation of different portions of a bill and holding public hearings. The majority members alone would do most of the work, with little opportunity for the minority except to sit in at final meetings and hear what had been decided upon. If, however, the minority was inactive, the lobbyists were not. Urging higher rates here and lower ones there, as the interests which they represented might dictate, these assiduous servants of economic and other pressure groups had a field-day indeed whenever a tariff bill was in the making. The full committee having taken formal action, the resulting bill sometimes was discussed in the majority party caucus (the Underwood Tariff of 1913 was so handled), although normally it went at once to the House, where in any case it was likely to become the most important subject for debate during the session. Having passed the House, it went to the Senate, where, indeed, the finance committee might have been doing exploratory work simultaneously with the House committee. On rare occasions, the Senate accepted the House bill with only minor modifications; as a rule, it introduced extensive changes, sometimes practically writing a new bill. At all events, the measure would be "sent to conference," where effort would be made to work out a reasonable compromise; and the measure that emerged could usually be counted upon to be accepted by both houses without further change. For an excellent study of pressure-group politics in the heyday of congressional tariff-making, see E. E. Schattschneider, *Politics, Pressures, and the Tariff* (New York, 1935).

[1] 39 *U. S. Stat. at Large,* 756. The Commission was provided for in the general revenue act for the next fiscal year.

tween costs of production here and abroad to be counterbalanced without awaiting the slow and uncertain results of ordinary legislation.

More, however, was to come. Tariff revision by the procedure described was still cumbersome: the president could act only on recommendation of the Commission; like most such bodies, the Commission was prone to move slowly; and its recommendations could apply only to specific articles, without embodying any general program. Moved by these limitations, and by the urgency of stimulating our foreign trade as the depression deepened, President Roosevelt asked for, and Congress in 1934 passed, a Reciprocal Trade Agreements Act [1] giving the chief executive broad authority to bargain with foreign countries for mutually advantageous trade agreements, with no intervention by the Tariff Commission or any other agency, except that the Commission might serve as a source of information and advice. Articles on the dutiable list might not be transferred to the free list, or *vice versa;* no rates might be lowered by more than fifty per cent; the "most-favored-nation" principle must be preserved; and before any agreement with a foreign government was concluded, interested parties must be given opportunity to present their views. Otherwise, the president might act freely. Renewed in 1937, 1940, 1943, and most recently in 1945, the plan went far toward achieving its purpose, with trade agreements in operation by 1945 (notwithstanding wartime interruptions) with twenty-eight different nations and the effective general level of our tariffs down almost to that prevailing under the low-tariff Underwood Act of 1913. Every renewal of the legislation, none the less, was vigorously contested by interests believing themselves injured, or at least threatened, as well as by elements in Congress and outside opposed in principle to such surrender of historic protectionist policy; and in 1947—a year before the existing law was to expire (June 12, 1948), congressional opposition threatened not only a peculiarly bitter partisan fight over renewal in the following session, but piecemeal scuttling of the system in the meantime—as, for example, by a wool tariff bill passed with almost no public attention and very little congressional debate, and authorizing the president to give added protection to American wool-growers by raising duties on foreign wool by fifty per cent or by barring as much as half of the normal shipments from abroad, notwithstanding obvious inconsistency with trade-agreement objectives. The wool bill was killed by an anticipated presidential veto, but in the meantime the agreement system was weakened somewhat by an executive order [2] under which all agreements made in future were to contain an "escape clause" providing that negotiated concessions might be modified or withdrawn if resulting imports attained such volume as to threaten

[1] 48 *U. S. Stat. at Large,* 943 (1934). Technically, the measure was an act to amend the tariff act of 1930.

[2] Significantly based on proposals offered by two Republican senators (Vandenberg and Millikin) as a compromise between their high-tariff colleagues and the Administration.

serious injury to domestic producers, with the Tariff Commission authorized to inquire into all such situations and make recommendations.[1] Even with these concessions, the question of renewal was expected to stir much controversy in 1948. On the other hand, the plan in general enjoys substantial support; the world situation calls for keeping international trade at the highest possible level; in October, 1947, the United States became a party to a series of agreements concluded at a Geneva Trade Conference by twenty-three nations and providing for all-round tariff reductions for three years ranging up to fifty per cent; and it seems safe to assume that, in one form or another, the reciprocal trade agreement will remain the predominant device, in lieu of old-style tariff laws, for determining under what conditions the goods of foreign countries may be brought in at our ports.[2]

The Pattern of Federal Taxation

As indicated above, the federal government started off by relying principally upon indirect taxation, chiefly duties on imports; and so satisfactorily were the country's tax needs met from this source that until the Civil War direct taxes were brought into play only three times and excise taxes only in two brief periods, 1791-1802 and 1813-18. The exigencies of the conflict between the states, however, not only forced a temporary reversion to direct taxation, but brought excise taxes again into use; and from that time onwards the latter always had a place in the tax structure, although with tariff duties (designed to protect the country's industries as well as to yield revenue) still dominant. Sometimes the argument was heard that people would be more tax-conscious, and therefore more concerned about economy and efficiency in government, if taxation were less disguised. But politicians commonly preferred to keep federal tax burdens more or less hidden, and the indirect forms were consistently adhered to. Only toward the end of the century did new currents of social

Trends since early times

[1] The Commission, of course, continues to exercise its functions under the earlier flexible tariff legislation with respect to all rates not made the subject of agreements with foreign countries.

[2] Some opponents of tariff-reduction have contended that the agreements are in reality "treaties," requiring assent in each case by the Senate. Long ago, however, somewhat similar agreements made in pursuance of the tariff acts of 1890, 1922, and 1930 were sustained by the Supreme Court in Field v. Clark, 143 U. S. 649 (1892), Hampton v. United States, 276 U. S. 394 (1928), and other decisions.

On the trade agreement program, see works cited on p. 595 below, and, in addition, S. Welles, "Trade Agreements in a New World," *Atlantic Mo.*, CLXXI, 41-44 (Mar., 1943); H. P. Whidden, "Reciprocal Trade Program and Post-War Reconstruction," *For. Policy Reports*, XIX, No. 2 (Apr. 1, 1943); H. H. Hutcheson, "Foreign Trade Policy of the United States," *ibid.*, XXIII, No. 1 (Mar. 15, 1947); J. D. Larkin, "The Trade Agreement Act in Court and in Congress," *Amer. Polit. Sci. Rev.*, XXXI, 498-508 (June, 1937); H. C. Hawkins, "Administration of the Trade Agreement Act," *1944 Wis. Law Rev.*, 1-14 (Jan., 1944).

On March 1, 1948, President Truman asked Congress to extend the Trade Agreements Act for another three years, *i.e.*, until June 12, 1951, characterizing it as "an essential element of United States foreign policy." A month later, a joint resolution meeting the request had not yet come up for consideration. Vigorous opposition from Republican majorities in both houses was anticipated.

and economic opinion bring to the surface concepts of a radically altered tax pattern—one in which, while tariffs and excises should not be discarded, a major place should be assigned to a tax based upon ability to pay as measured in terms of individual and corporate incomes; and, constitutionally validated by the Sixteenth Amendment, the new form of levy established itself firmly in our system (1913) shortly before we became involved in World War I.[1] One of the advantages of income taxation is its flexibility—the ease with which, by juggling a few rates and brackets, it can be made to yield vastly more or vastly less as may be desired; and under the impact of then unparalleled wartime expenditures in 1917-18 the national revenue from this source was pushed to topmost place—a position which it consistently maintained until 1933. Even in the memorable depression year 1932, more than half of the government's tax revenue was obtained in this way. With depression conditions continuing and deepening, however, taxes on personal and corporate incomes yielded steadily diminishing returns; and once more the bulk of national revenue began to come from customs duties and excises, even though here, too, yields were reduced by languishing commerce and slackened business. Some measure of prosperity having been regained, the income tax stream began rising again in 1937; and under wartime tax legislation after 1941 it became a veritable torrent, completely dwarfing all other tax sources.

Taxes and tax yields today

As submitted to Congress in January, 1946, the president's budget for fiscal 1947 (July 1, 1946-June 30, 1947) estimated receipts from all sources at forty-one and a half billions; actually, they amounted to forty-three and one-fifth billions, which, with expenditures held to forty-two and one-half billions, yielded the first surplus that the country had known in upwards of two decades.[2] Not all of this revenue, of course, came from taxes; but the great bulk of it did so, and the main sources from which it was derived can be indicated briefly as follows:

1. Income taxes

Towering above all others (in fiscal 1947) were personal and corporation income taxes—the former yielding over twenty billion dollars and the latter more than 9.7 billions, an aggregate of over thirty billions, or almost three-fourths of the total tax receipts. In the taxation of yearly incomes of individuals, the following main features appear:[3] (1) complete exemption of all income below a figure ($500) supposed to represent the minimum requisite of a bare existence, and somewhat larger ($1,000)

---

[1] There had been some earlier experience with federal income taxes. A wartime tax of the kind, laid in 1861, lasted, in one form or another, until 1872; a tax of the sort imposed in 1894, with a view to compensating for loss of revenue caused by reduction of tariff rates, was in the following year pronounced unconstitutional; and a tax laid in 1909 on the income of corporations was to all intents and purposes an income tax, although evasively termed an *excise* tax on the privilege of doing business.

[2] In January, 1947, budget receipts for fiscal 1948 were estimated at 37.7 billions; but a year later the figure was raised to 45.2 billions, which, with expenditures estimated at 37.7 billions, promised a surplus of 7.5 billions. In January, 1948, receipts in fiscal 1949 were estimated at 44.5 billions and expenditures at 39.7 billions.

[3] The system is here outlined as it stood in 1947. Some changes introduced in 1948 are indicated in note 2 on the following page.

in the case of married persons; (2) additional modest amounts of income exempted, or "deductible," for children or other dependents ($500 for each); (3) further deductions covering such matters as interest paid, contributions to charities, and state and local taxes; and (4) a graduated tax on other income, rising to as lofty a level as some $156,000 on an income of $200,000. Non-profit organizations, *e.g.*, churches, colleges, lodges, coöperative associations, and labor unions are exempt; and corporations and other organizations for profit have their own system of exemptions, normal taxes, surtaxes, and the like, capped during the war by an "excess-profits" tax rising by stages to a point where ninety-five per cent of such profits went to the government, although this particular levy has since been repealed. Lowering personal exemptions to the figures indicated above for single and married persons in 1943 brought millions of people for the first time within the ranks of federal income-tax payers, presumably diffusing tax-consciousness more widely than ever before; [1] although for a very large proportion of small taxpayers the tax is figured by the employer and paid by him after being "withheld" from wages, with opportunity for recovery by the worker of any amounts paid in excess of what is due. Salaried persons find twenty per cent deducted from their pay checks, the contribution thus credited figuring (as in the case of wage-earners) in the final reckoning which determines whether the taxpayer still owes something or perchance is entitled to a rebate.[2]

On a number of occasions from the Civil War onwards, the federal government imposed some form of tax on estates of deceased persons or on inheritances of portions thereof, and since 1916 an estate tax has been a regular feature of the federal tax pattern. Formerly, exemptions

2. Estate and gift taxes

[1] Because of high exemptions, there were only between three and four million payers of personal income taxes in the twenties. Wartime extensions brought the number to seventeen millions in 1941 and forty-three and one-half millions in 1944, with, however, some twelve millions in the lowest brackets taken off the tax-rolls in 1945.

[2] Taxes on income not derived from wages or salaries are payable in quarterly installments starting March 15 of the tax year—not of the following year, as before 1943.

At the last moment before releasing these pages for printing (April, 1948), it became possible to include a word on income-tax changes just introduced. After being twice thwarted by President Truman's vetoes in 1947, the Republican and some Democratic forces in the House and Senate, bent upon immediate tax reduction, renewed their efforts in the second session of the Eightieth Congress. The House of Representatives passed a bill designed to cut income-tax yields for the calendar year 1948 by $6,500,000,000; the Senate reduced the figure to $4,800,000,000; and in the latter form the bill was sent to the President. A veto followed (April 2); the House immediately overrode it by a vote of 311 to 88, the Senate by a vote of 77 to 10; and the measure became law. Significant changes introduced included: (1) raising the personal exemption to $600, with double the amount in the case of blind persons and persons sixty-five years of age or over, thereby entirely removing an estimated 7,400,000 individuals from the tax rolls (with an estimated 47,000,000 remaining); (2) permitting family income to be split equally, for tax purposes, between husband and wife, opening a way for substantial tax savings in higher income brackets; and (3) reducing taxes by (in the case of a single person with no dependents) from 56.3 per cent in the lowest income bracket inversely to 5.6—8.35 in the highest brackets.

ran as high as $100,000, and rates in lower brackets were relatively moderate, although high in upper ones. Naturally, under wartime taxation, exemptions were reduced (to $60,000) and rates stiffened. In order to reach wealth that might escape estate taxation by being given away by the possessor with that end in view, a federal gift tax (on a graduated scale approximately three-fourths as heavy as estate taxation) was introduced in 1924, repealed in 1926, and reintroduced in 1932. Here again, rates were increased in wartime; and in 1947 estate and gift taxes together yielded about two billions, or somewhat over five per cent of total tax receipts. Combined with "progressive" income taxes, estate and gift taxes operate powerfully to check the growth and transmission of large fortunes, thereby promoting a socially desirable distribution of wealth.

3. General excise taxes

Then there are the taxes paid in some small way even by persons too poor to be reached by the income tax and on a larger scale by more lavish spenders, i.e., the excises falling on tobacco, liquor, motor-fuel, theater-admissions, cosmetics, and scores of other objects, many of them luxury articles to be sure, but including everyday necessities for at least a good many people. No one needs to be told how greatly the list of articles taxed was lengthened, or how sharply rates were pushed upward, under wartime revenue legislation; as recently as 1947, too, wartime rates were continued indefinitely by Congress. The aggregate yield in the year mentioned was in the neighborhood of 7.3 billion dollars.

4. Payroll taxes

A special form of excise is the tax levied upon employers for the maintenance of unemployment compensation under the federal security program.[1] This tax is different from others in that, although the federal government levies it, only ten per cent of it is federally collected, the remainder being collected and eventually paid out in benefits by the states. The portion federally collected in 1947 amounted to about two billions.

5. Customs duties

Finally comes a form of tax which as recently as 1910 topped all others in productiveness, i.e., customs duties. Reflecting the generally reduced level of such taxes under the trade-agreement program, the yield in 1947 was only $494,000,000.

Complexity of the general tax structure

Throughout a long period of our history, the country's tax structure was relatively stable, and, for the times, relatively satisfactory; state and local governments lived principally from the proceeds of the general property tax, the federal government principally from the yield of customs duties. In the past thirty or forty years, however, the situation has changed greatly. Mounting expenditures, increasing inadequacy of the general property tax, tempting new resources for revenue like motor cars and gasoline, and newer tax ideas and objectives, have attracted the states to numerous forms of taxation rarely or never employed previously; while, on its part, the federal government has revolutionized its

[1] See pp. 750-753 below.

tax pattern, with the tariff relegated, as we have seen, to an almost insignificant position, and reliance now placed mainly upon levies on incomes, inheritances, and the distribution and consumption of goods. As a result, the tax structure, whether of the federal government or of almost any individual state, has become so diverse and complicated that only experts can fully understand its ramifications. Few operations of government, too, are more prolific of legislation and of administrative and judicial rulings than is taxation; so that even if a tax pattern is mastered in all of its details at a given time, one coming back to it only a little later must be prepared to find new turns and twists imparted to it.

The close of World War II naturally left the country most immediately concerned about some reduction of the extraordinarily heavy tax burden carried over from the war years; and efforts to that end which failed in 1947 proved moderately successful in 1948—although with warning simultaneously sounded that need for strengthening the national defenses might make it necessary to reimpose tax remitted or even to levy higher ones. No one pretending to any grasp of the country's financial problems supposed for a moment, however, that any mere lowering of federal income-tax rates or repeal of excise levies would meet the national need. Long before the war, there had been urgent questions concerning tax methods, policies, and objectives, and many of these had been made more urgent and difficult by the tax experience of the war period, as also by the national government's certain requirement for the future, and permanently, of revenues vastly exceeding any that had served its purposes until within the past decade or two. Accordingly, it was widely taken for granted that for purposes of the years ahead the entire existing federal tax system, including the interrelations of federal and state systems, must be given thorough study, preparatory to an extensive overhauling; [1] and no sooner did its tax-reduction plans of 1947 collapse than the House ways and means committee, with the aid of an advisory group of experts, set about such a study, even though in a thickening atmosphere of politics leaving one apprehensive about the thoroughness and objectivity with which the undertaking would be carried out. In any event, one could safely predict that questions of tax policy would hold the center of the stage for a good while to come.

It is not feasible to enter here upon any analysis, or even enumeration, of the many issues likely to be involved; some of them quickly run into technicalities with which we cannot have to do.[2] But any reader of this book can readily surmise what a few of the number will be. Should any existing federal taxes be abandoned—as a heavy wartime tax on excess

Need for revision

Some questions to be considered

[1] In his message of June 16, 1947, vetoing the first of two tax-reduction bills, President Truman called for such study and revision.

[2] One such issue is whether estate and gift taxes should be combined into a single "transfer" tax, as recommended in a recent Treasury Department study. It may be added that the Revenue Act of 1948 eased estate and gift taxation by applying to such taxes the plan of splitting between husband and wife made applicable to income taxes.

business profits already has been? Should any new forms of taxation be introduced—for example, federal taxation of income from state and local securities, so warmly advocated by President Roosevelt?[1] Should the tax base be broadened by terminating exemptions now enjoyed by a lengthy list of interests and enterprises, such as farm and consumer co-operatives, mutual insurance companies, rural electrification undertakings, and surplus funds of labor unions? Should the taxation of incomes be deliberately kept at levels, in the higher brackets, making accumulation of wealth difficult or impossible?

The problem of "double taxation" Calling for attention, too, whenever the general tax structure is under consideration is always the question of "double taxation." With both nation and states reaching out in later years for new sources of revenue, it naturally has come about that frequently they are found taxing the same objects; in fiscal 1946, indeed, no less than ninety per cent of federal and state receipts came from the same sources. To be sure, the federal government leaves the general property tax entirely to the states (principally for local use) and, as we have seen, relies for the major part of its revenue upon personal and corporate income taxes, estate and inheritance taxes, and consumption taxes of many different kinds, notably on liquor, tobacco, and gasoline. But all of these objects are taxed by some or all of the states as well;[2] indeed, apart from the general property tax, there are few if any important forms of taxation to which both the national and state governments do not lay claim, each without much regard to the other or to the taxpayer; and often (indeed almost invariably in these days) the sums collected by the national government within a state from a given tax exceed the amounts collected from that tax by the state itself.[3] Persons finding their salaries or the gasoline they buy taxed twice sometimes harbor an idea that such double imposition is unconstitutional. In this, they are wrong. Not only does the constitution have nothing to say against double taxation; it in effect presupposes it by leaving broad and general taxing powers to two largely independent governments, both resting directly upon the people. Even though not unconstitutional, however, the existing situation imposes handicaps on business and industry and sometimes excessive burdens on individual taxpayers, and one will not be surprised to learn that a good deal of thought has been devoted to it not only by tax experts but by business organizations, taxpayer associations, and state officials; the 1947 conference of governors, for example, devoted a substantial part of its

[1] A federal sales tax like that employed in several states was proposed during the war. A Congress and people that would have none of it in emergency would hardly, however, be won over to it in more normal times. Cf. E. R. Nichols and C. Wallis [comps.], *A Federal Sales Tax* (New York, 1942); R. G. and G. C. Blakey, *Sales Taxes and Other Excises* (Chicago, 1945).

[2] Individual incomes, for example, by twenty-nine states, corporate incomes by thirty-eight, tobacco products by thirty-eight, and gasoline sales by all.

[3] Even triple taxation results when corporations pay taxes on their net profits and then, such profits having been distributed to stockholders as dividends, both federal and state governments tax the stockholders on such income.

program to the subject. Sometimes it is suggested that the federal government withdraw from gasoline taxation (a field which it entered only in 1932), while the states give up taxing tobacco and its products; or that, in return for a monopoly of taxing liquor, the states give up taxing incomes. A recent extensive staff study in the federal Treasury Department, however, stops short of any definite recommendations on these or related lines; and in a period when all governments instinctively shy away from proposals looking to drying up sources of revenue, solutions are not in sight.[1]

Borrowing Money—The National Debt

When expenditures and revenues are approximately equal, a government is said to have a "balanced" budget. If, on the other hand, expenditures exceed receipts, there is a deficit, and the budget is said to be out of balance. In ordinary times, and for ordinary purposes, income derived from taxation, supplemented by receipts from non-tax sources, ought to be, and usually has been, sufficient to meet the federal government's needs. In time of war, however, or other unusual strain, such as a period of business depression, or to meet the cost of some special undertaking like the Panama Canal, borrowing must be resorted to; and the accumulated obligations thus incurred give rise to the national debt. The power to borrow is expressly conferred in the constitution,[2] being indeed one of the very few powers granted absolutely without restriction; and as a consequence Congress may borrow from any lenders, for any purposes, in any amounts, on any terms, and with or without provision for the repayment of loans, with or without interest.[3]

The power to borrow

Borrowing may take any one of several forms. By authority of Congress, the Treasury may sell notes or certificates having attractiveness for banks and other financial institutions because of short terms and exceptionally low interest rates; and this is constantly being done. To accelerate tax receipts, it may issue "tax anticipation" notes to large

Methods

[1] On the general subject, see W. Kilpatrick, "Neglected Aspects of Intergovernmental Fiscal Relations," *Amer. Polit. Sci. Rev.*, XLI, 452-462 (June, 1947); also three articles by J. W. Martin: "The Problems of Duplicating Federal and State Taxes," *State Government*, XVII, 287-289 (Mar., 1944); "Functions of Intergovernmental Administrative Coöperation in Taxation," *ibid.*, XVII, 327-332 (May, 1944); and "Federal-State Tax Coöperation," *Nat. Mun. Rev.*, XXXIV, 21-26 (Jan., 1945). In February, 1933, an interstate commission on conflicting taxation was set up by the Interstate Legislative Assembly of the American Legislators' Association, and in 1935 it published at Chicago a volume entitled *Conflicting Taxation*. This, however, is now largely superseded by the Treasury Department study mentioned above (Division of Tax Research, Treasury Department, *Federal-State Tax Coördination*, mimeo., Washington, D. C., 1947).

[2] Art. I, § 8, cl. 2.

[3] The United States operates under no *constitutional* debt limit, such as is fixed for many of the states in their constitutions, and such as states commonly establish for counties and cities. For some time, however, a federal debt limit has been maintained by act of Congress, the figure being raised by gigantic leaps during the late war until in March, 1945, it reached 300 billions. In June, 1946, an act of Congress reduced it to 275 billions.

taxpayers, to be turned in by the corporation or individual at tax time at face value plus interest received on what has been in effect a loan.[1] Of far greater importance, however, is the sale of long-term interest-bearing bonds in large denominations to banks, insurance companies, administrators of trust funds, and the like, and in smaller denominations (down to twenty-five-dollar savings bonds) to individual savers and investors;[2] and such securities rate high in the money markets, not only because they usually pay attractive interest as conservative investments go, but because the national government (unlike some of the states) has never repudiated a debt.[3] If, however, in time of special need the investment motive, reënforced by patriotic appeals and high-pressure salesmanship, fails to bring about voluntary purchases in sufficient amounts. the government may compel purchases by "deferred-savings" devices of one kind or another.

The national debt since 1916:

1. After World War I

In the past decade and a half, the United States has been added to the long list of countries laboring under the burden of a huge national debt. As recently as 1916, on the eve of our involvement in World War I, we were paying interest, as a nation, on less than a billion dollars.[4] Three years of war financing—in the course of which upwards of twenty billion dollars' worth of Liberty and Victory bonds were disposed of to literally millions of purchasers—raised the figure to above twenty-five billions. Peace restored, extensive borrowing ceased; and, in a period of what was looked upon as unparalleled prosperity, national revenues, notwithstanding lowered tax rates, exceeded national expenditures, year after year, permitting substantial debt retirement. By the end of 1930, we owed only a trifle over sixteen billions. With a little more sacrifice during lush days, the whole of this might have been liquidated; and, as we are now situated, it is a pity that we did not put forth the effort.

2. During the depression

Already, however, at the date mentioned, the effects of the great depression were being felt widely, both by governments and by private persons and corporations. Revenues fell off sharply; outlays for relief and related purposes mounted to new heights; under a policy of "borrowing itself into prosperity," the country went on from a national debt of twenty-nine billions in 1935 to one of forty-two billions on June 30,

---

[1] During the Civil War, there was borrowing even by inflating the currency. The government issued "greenbacks" covered by no adequate reserve of gold or silver, and then used them in paying for goods and services; any one accepting them in effect held simply government promises to pay, supported merely by a good reputation for integrity.

[2] Opportunity to lend the government money on an even more modest scale is afforded by the postal savings system.

[3] When conditions become more favorable, the government is not unlikely, however, to refund a loan, i.e., to retire it and substitute another at lower interest rates. Commercial interest rates have been prevailingly low in the past decade and a half, and in the recent war period the government had the advantage of being able to borrow at rates distinctly below those that it had to pay during World War I—on the average, about two per cent as contrasted with four and one-fourth per cent.

[4] This, of course, takes no account of very substantial debts of states and their subdivisions.

1940, when for the twelfth successive time the government closed a fiscal year with a formidable deficit.[1]

But worse was yet to come. In the autumn of 1939, a major war broke out in Europe, accompanied by grave developments in the Far East; and for two years each succeeding month brought the conflict nearer to our own shores—until, finally, in December, 1941, we found ourselves actually at war with the three principal totalitarian states. Regardless of deficits, therefore, the country was compelled to tighten its belt and undertake, first, a *defense* program (on land and sea and in the air) which alone would have removed all possibility of a balanced national budget for years to come, and afterwards a *war* effort whose cost and resulting liabilities mounted, as we have seen, to fantastic heights. Notwithstanding heavily increased taxation, fiscal 1941 showed a deficit of over five billions and the debt soared to $48,961,000,000—an increase of nearly six billions in a single year. And that was while we were still at peace. Within two months after Pearl Harbor, the sixty-billion mark was passed; on December, 1942,—with the country at war only a year—the figure was close to one hundred billions; by June 30, 1943, it topped 140 billions; in December, 1944, it stood at 231 billions; and at the end of February, 1946 (though half a year after the surrender of our last totalitarian foe), it reached a peak of 279.7 billions, entailing an annual interest charge of almost five and one-half billions.

3. During World War II

People who thought seriously about such matters were not all of one mind about the possible consequences of such a situation for the country's future. Some considered that if the national income continued at a high level after the war the burden could be carried and the debt gradually reduced without serious interference with our standard of living; and such persons naturally derived satisfaction from the circumstance that we "owed the debt to ourselves," and not to foreign lenders.[2] On the other hand, many viewed the situation with alarm, believing that a debt of such proportions could not prove otherwise than a dead weight from which our people would long suffer retardation; and adding to such apprehension was not only the indisputable fact that no one could foresee whether there actually would be a high national income over a prolonged postwar period,[3] but also the consideration that owing the debt to ourselves would not prevent the burden of it from falling very unequally and disproportionately upon different segments of the population. In theory, at least, several different courses were open to us. (1) We might simply repudiate the debt completely, as the Soviet government

4. The long road to liquidation

---

[1] Only once before (immediately before and during the Civil War) had the government ever gone for any comparable period—eight years in that case—with an unbalanced budget.

[2] From this point of view, the debt in essence constitutes a claim of our multiplied millions of holders of federal bonds upon the future productive capacity of the country.

[3] A wartime study of the possibilities was J. Mayer, *Postwar National Income; Its Probable Magnitude* (Washington, D. C., 1944).

repudiated the old Tsarist national debt in Russia. But that was not the American way (even though debts of quite a number of our states— including practically all of the Southern states after the Civil War—have been liquidated in that manner). (2) We might go into default on the debt, *i.e.*, simply not pay the interest on it to the holders of government securities. But this would be totally out of line with all previous national policy (even though there has been a good deal of defaulting on municipal and other local debts). (3) We might "monetize" the debt, *i.e.*, convert bonds into money, which would terminate interest obligations. (4) We might simply "maintain" the debt, paying interest scrupulously, but not making much effort to reduce the principal—a procedure by no means uncommon in European countries.[1] Or (5) we might do what, after all, was taken for granted as the only thing we could and should do, *i.e.*, maintain the debt and whittle it down as we could in periods when revenues permitted.

The outlook for debt reduction

Upon this last honorable but difficult course we have now embarked. As yet (1948), the national income has remained on a very high level; and after deficits which reached their peak at 55.5 billions in fiscal 1943 had been whittled down, even in the later war years, and still further to 20.7 billions in 1946, the president, as indicated above, was able to report for fiscal 1947 the first budget surplus in seventeen years. Furthermore, use for debt purposes of funds borrowed late in 1945 but not needed for current spending (together with other fiscal operations not to be described here) had enabled enough to be shaved off the debt to bring it down, by March 1, 1948, to 254 billions. How rapidly liquidation could proceed from that point was, of course, problematical. On the one hand, debt-reduction could be depended upon to loom large in all budgetary planning. On the other, national expenditures were certain to continue on a high level; to protect the economy against repression and stagnation, taxes must be reduced; an economic recession might at any time seriously affect tax yields; another war might start the government borrowing again; and even if calamity were averted, return to more normal conditions—with only the ordinary sort of moderate prosperity—easily might bring national income and outgo to a ratio permitting little beyond merely "servicing" the debt, *i.e.*, paying interest, with no headway toward reducing the principal. Financial experts have computed that, starting in 1947, approximately five and a quarter billions a year would have to be paid on principal to wipe out the debt in fifty years. No one expects such a schedule to be carried out; few, indeed, expect the debt ever to be paid, in the sense of the country becoming literally debt-free. Fortunately, such a consummation is not essential to the national well-being; barring such wholesale disasters as may possibly be threatened by atomic

---

[1] Behind this policy might be the deliberate purpose to manage the debt by "letting the country grow up to it," *i.e.*, attain such population and wealth that, proportionally, the debt burden would be materially reduced.

warfare, a country of the population, resources, skills, and expanding potentialities of the United States can support a debt, even a large one, without fatal consequences. Generations as yet unborn will, however, feel the weight of debt burdens which we in our time have piled up; and the most elementary dictate of common sense is that, from here on, no opportunity be lost to reduce these burdens whenever, and as rapidly as, circumstances will permit.[1]

REFERENCES

I. NATIONAL REVENUES—THE TAX SYSTEM

D. T. Selko, *The Federal Financial System* (Washington, D. C., 1940), Chaps. I-III, XI-XXII.

H. M. Groves, *Financing Government* (rev. ed., New York, 1945), Chaps. VII-XIV, XVI-XVIII.

————, *Postwar Taxation and Economic Progress* (New York, 1946).

R. G. and G. C. Blakey, *The Federal Income Tax* (New York, 1940).

P. J. Strayer, *Taxation of Small Incomes* (New York, 1939).

C. Shoup, "The Taxation of Excess Profits," *Polit. Sci. Quar.*, LV, 535-555 (Dec., 1940), LVI, 84-106 (Mar., 1941).

R. Magill, *The Impact of Federal Taxes* (New York, 1943).

———— et al., *A Tax Program for a Solvent America* (New York, 1947).

A. G. Hart, E. G. Allen, *et al.*, *Paying for Defense* (Philadelphia, 1941).

W. Warren *et al.*, *Financing the War* (Philadelphia, 1942).

S. Ratner, *American Taxation; Its History as a Social Force in Democracy* (New York, 1942).

P. Studenski [ed.], *Taxation and Public Policy* (New York, 1936).

M. S. Eccles *et al.*, *Curbing Inflation Through Taxation* (New York, 1944).

S. Chase, *Where's the Money Coming From? Problems of Postwar Finance* (New York, 1943).

P. A. Bidwell, *Tariff Policy of the United States; A Study of Recent Experience* (New York, 1936).

————, *The Invisible Tariff* (New York, 1939).

J. D. Larkin, *The President's Control of the Tariff* (New York, 1936).

————, *Trade Agreements; A Study in Democratic Methods* (New York, 1940).

F. B. Sayre, *The Way Forward; The American Trade Agreements Program* (New York, 1939).

A. Isaacs, *International Trade; Tariff and Commercial Policies* (Chicago, 1948).

C. Kreider, *The Anglo-American Trade Agreement* (Princeton, N. J., 1943).

"Should Legislation be Enacted by Congress Taxing State and Municipal Securities?" [Symposium], *Cong. Digest*, XXI, 69-96 (Mar., 1942).

"Federal, State, and Local Government Fiscal Relations; A Report by a Special Committee Designated to Conduct a Study on Intergovernmental Fiscal Relations in the United States," 78th Cong., 1st Sess., Sen. Doc. No. 69 (Washington, D. C., 1943).

Taxes: The Tax Magazine. Published monthly by the Commerce Clearing House, Inc., Chicago.

---

[1] A. H. Hanson and G. Greer, "The Federal Debt and the Future," *Harper's Mag.*, CLXXXIV, 489-500 (Apr., 1942); J. T. Flynn, "That Postwar Federal Debt," *ibid.*, CLXXXIV, 180-188 (July, 1942); S. Chase, *Where's the Money Coming From? Problems of Postwar Finance* (New York, 1943). See also a series of recent graphic studies issued by the Committee on Public Debt Policy (New York, 1947).

II. The National Debt

H. M. Groves, *Financing Government* (rev. ed., New York, 1945), Chaps. XXVI-XXVII.

H. M. Lutz, *Public Finance* (4th ed., New York, 1947), Chap. XXXII.

S. E. Harris, *The National Debt and the New Economics* (New York, 1947), Chaps. I-III, XIII, XVII-XXIV.

C. C. Abbott, *Management of the Federal Debt* (New York, 1946).

W. Withers, *The Public Debt* (New York, 1945).

H. G. Moulton, *The New Philosophy of Public Debt* (Washington, D. C., 1944).

A. E. Hart *et al., Debts and Recovery* (New York, 1938).

P. W. Stewart and R. S. Tucker, *The National Debt and Government Credit* (New York, 1937).

CHAPTER XXVII

MONEY, BANKING, AND CREDIT

The Currency System

If one wishes to acquire a piece of property, he may do it in three prin- _{The na-} cipal ways: he may trade another piece of property for it, by a process known as barter; he may pay for it in "cash," i.e., money; or he may give a promissory note for the amount due—in other words, buy "on credit" with a piece of paper not itself money but calling for payment of money later. Primitive peoples commonly employ barter, and the practice has by no means died out in our more advanced society; the used car market, for example, is a modern form of barter. Nearly everywhere, however, money and credit have now become the usual means of exchanging goods and services, with money the more basic, inasmuch as credit is merely a device for deferring money payments. One asked to define "money" might well be in the dilemma of the man asked to define "elephant": he could offer no satisfactory definition, but he would know an elephant when he saw one. Broadly, money is any officially recognized and generally acceptable symbol of value available for the purchase of goods or payment for services. Its place may be taken by instruments of credit—promissory notes, bank checks, drafts, or bills of exchange; but these have value only as standing for money. Money therefore serves as a measure of price and a convenient medium for exchange of goods and services. Universally, its unitary values have been fixed in some relation to the precious metals; to avert confusion, these values must have some uniformity over a wide area, at least an entire country, and must have stability; this can be attained only if coins (or paper representing them) are issued by some central authority; hence, regulating the currency becomes a major function of every modern government.

During the Revolution and under the Articles of Confederation, this country had sorry experience with everything relating to currency. Even in colonial days, when the regular English system of pounds, shillings, and pence prevailed, much difficulty had arisen from rather wide circulation of Spanish and other foreign coins of uncertain and fluctuating values; and when, after 1776, both the newly formed states and the Continental Congress undertook to overcome money scarcity by starting the printing presses and issuing large quantities of paper currency backed by no gold or silver, conditions became chaotic. People hoarded such "hard money" as they could get hold of; little was left to circulate except paper

597

of dubious value; prices went skyward; business was demoralized; inter-state trade became almost impossible; different states added to the confusion by all manner of hand-to-mouth monetary expedients. Small wonder, therefore, that the constitution's framers in 1787 considered one of the first needs of the new nation to be a sound and uniform currency system; or that they wrote into the document two significant clauses directed to that end—one giving Congress full authority to "coin money [and] regulate the value thereof;"[1] the other forbidding the states to "coin money, emit bills of credit, or make anything but gold and silver coin legal tender in the payment of debts."[2] Regulation of the currency was not to be among governmental functions shared by nation and states.[3]

Earlier experience with a national coinage— the gold standard   When providing in 1792 for the contemplated uniform currency system (as yet in the form of coinage only), Congress wisely discarded the cumbersome English pattern in favor of our simpler decimal plan with its eagles, dollars, dimes, and cents, and, in line with existing market values, fixed the ratio between silver and gold at fifteen to one. It was easier, however, to say that fifteen ounces of the white metal were equal to one ounce of the yellow than to keep them so. In fact, with the two metals constantly fluctuating in the world market, they could not be kept equal at all; and for a hundred years questions relating to changes in the ratio, in terms of the amount of gold and silver to be contained in dollars of the two varieties, furnished fuel for political controversy. With silver declining in value, silver dollars became "cheaper" and gold dollars tended to be hoarded; on the other hand, with the number of grains of gold in a gold dollar reduced by Congress, gold dollars became the favorite with people who had to buy anything or pay a debt, and silver went out of circulation. In 1873, Congress "demonetized" silver altogether—that is, suspended the coinage of silver dollars. But in mining and agricultural areas especially, this stirred vigorous opposition, with "remonetization," at sixteen to one—"free coinage of silver"—becoming a political issue on which eventually the exciting presidential campaign of 1896 was waged almost to the exclusion of everything else. With their sixteen-to-one candidate, William Jennings Bryan, the Democrats, however, lost; and in 1900 a Republican Congress settled matters by placing on the statute-book a Gold Standard Act[4] making the gold dollar the unit of value and requiring that all other money be maintained on a parity with gold, so that a silver dollar or a paper dollar might be taken to the Treasury at any time and exchanged for a dollar 25.8 grains gold, nine-tenths fine.

[1] Art. I, § 8, cl. 5.
[2] Art. I, § 10, cl. 1.
[3] In the course of time, it was found that states were chartering banks with the power to issue notes which were, in effect, bills of credit; and the Supreme Court sustained them in doing so (Briscoe v. Kentucky, 11 Peters 257 (1837). To stop this, Congress in 1865 imposed a ten per cent tax on such notes, making it unprofitable to issue them; and in Veazie Bank v. Fenno, 8 Wallace 533 (1869), the Supreme Court sustained the tax and its purpose.
[4] 31 U. S. Stat. at Large, 45 (1900).

Between them, the government and the banks were supposed to maintain gold reserves adequate to back up all other money in this way.

With silver still coined and circulated but only gold a standard of value, the system instituted at the turn of the century operated for more than thirty years, and one might have supposed that it was going to be permanent. A person cherishing such an assumption, however, would have been reckoning without foreknowledge of the great economic and political upheaval wrought by the depression of the thirties, when, with a view— so it was maintained by President Roosevelt and those who shared responsibility with him—to imparting reasonable inflation to the currency, raising prices, reducing the burden of debts, and thus contributing to recovery, a swift series of actions put an entirely new face on our monetary system. To begin with—and hastened by a crisis in March, 1933, requiring a temporary closing of all banks—all holders of gold coin, gold bullion, and gold certificates issued by the federal reserve banks were required to turn them over to the national government, receiving in exchange various forms of paper currency. Next, under executive order of April 20, based on an Emergency Banking Act [1] of a few weeks earlier, the gold standard was formally abandoned and the free movement of gold in international trade stopped; holders of silver or paper currency no longer could have it converted into gold. Following on, Congress, by joint resolution of June 5, canceled the "gold clause" commonly written into long-term bonds and other contracts, both public and private, and calling for the payment of principal and interest in "gold coin of the present weight and fineness"—which meant, among other things, that the government's own obligations and those of private persons alike, even though specifying payment in gold coin, were thenceforth to be payable in any form of legal tender. [2]

The system revolutionized in 1933-34

More, however, was to follow. In the Agricultural Adjustment Act of 1933, the president had been given power to "devalue," i.e., to cheapen, the dollar by not more than sixty nor less than forty per cent; and on January 31, 1934, an executive order reduced the gold content of the dollar from 23.22 grains to 15⅝₂₁, or something like forty-one per cent (actually 40.94)—with the result of giving the country, in effect, a fifty-nine-cent dollar. [3] Next, under a Gold Reserve Act [4] of the same month,

[1] 48 *U. S. Stat. at Large*, 162 (1933).

[2] 48 *U. S. Stat. at Large*, 112. This action was criticized sharply on both legal and ethical grounds. See R. L. Post and C. H. Willard, "The Power of Congress to Nullify Gold Clauses," *Harvard Law Rev.*, XLVI, 1225-1257 (June, 1933). In 1935, however, it was fully sustained by the Supreme Court as to private contracts in Norman *v.* B. and O. Ry. (294 U. S. 240), and as to government bonds in Perry *v.* United States, 294 U. S. 330.

[3] Presidential power over the value of the dollar was extended a number of times, but in 1943 was allowed to lapse. The objectives were (1) to bring the American dollar more nearly into line with foreign currencies which had been devalued, and (2) to stimulate a rise of prices calculated to help restore national prosperity. The first was not fully attained, since many foreign governments devalued still further; and the effect on prices is at least debatable, since in practice the dollar's purchasing power continued much as before.

[4] 48 *U. S. Stat. at Large*, 337.

and with a view to accumulating a stock of gold ample to serve as a metallic base for the paper currency, the government was authorized to buy all gold remaining in possession of the federal reserve banks, and also to buy abroad; and as a result of this "nationalizing" policy, some twenty-five billion dollars' worth of bullion (more than half of the world's supply) has been acquired and stored, principally in vaults buried deep in the ground at Ft. Knox, Kentucky. No more gold is coined, of course, or circulated in that form. Finally, a Silver Purchase Act [1] of June, 1934, passed at the insistence of farming and silver-producing interests, "nationalized" the white metal also by authorizing purchases (as in the case of gold, at prices above the current market level) up to a point where the total metallic reserve would be three-fourths gold and one-fourth silver; and in pursuance of this, a stock of bullion valued at more than two billion dollars has thus far been acquired from our own producers and by import, and likewise stored in vaults, principally at West Point. In general, the object of all of the depression-time measures reviewed was a "managed" currency which, with increase of the volume of money but decrease of its value, would raise the price-level of commodities. In periods like that in which we have recently been living, the effect of cheap money is, of course, to push high prices still higher.

Paper money introduced

If money were in the form of coin only, gold and silver would have to be minted instead of buried in the earth. But most money, as we see and use it today, is paper, with gold and silver merely held in reserve as security. The constitution speaks only of coining money, without a word about paper currency—except to forbid the states to issue it. Such currency, nevertheless, was in circulation after 1789 as before. The first and second Bank of the United States [2] (while existing) issued notes, and, as we have seen, state banks did likewise, even though their issues were often of shifting and uncertain value. Even before the Civil War, there was some demand that responsibility for paper money be centralized in the national government; and when difficulty was encountered in floating loans for carrying on that conflict, Congress took the momentous steps of (1) authorizing, in 1863, the government itself to issue paper currency (later known popularly as "greenbacks"), and (2) instituting, in the same measure, our later system of national banks, with power to issue notes up to ninety per cent of their holdings of United States bonds.[3] Although not redeemable in gold or silver, greenbacks were declared legal tender for every use, public and private, except payment of customs duties and interest on government bonds, and for a good while the right of Congress to authorize such currency, and particularly to make it legal tender for private debts, was sharply challenged. At the first test, the Supreme

[1] 48 *U. S. Stat. at Large*, 1178 (1934).
[2] See p. 602 below.
[3] 12 *U. S. Stat. at Large*, 665. B. and L. P. Mitchell, *American Economic History* (Boston, 1947), Chap. XXIII.

Court upheld a private citizen in refusing to accept the new legal tender in discharge of a debt.[1] But, with membership somewhat changed, and upon two other pending cases being reargued, the tribunal, in 1871 (although by a slender margin) pronounced the "legal tender acts" an exercise of constitutional authority properly to be implied from the power to borrow money.[2] The net effect of the "legal tender cases" was, therefore, to open the door wide for federal issues of and control over paper currency, and for such currency in future to have the field to itself; already, in 1865, as we have seen, Congress, with full judicial sanction, had placed a ten per cent tax on notes of state banks designed to prevent them from longer being issued.

As a consequence of its rather tortuous history, the American currency system is more complicated (with, for example, more forms of paper) than some of those abroad. Nevertheless, with certain varieties, *e.g.*, gold coins and gold certificates, eliminated, and certain others, *e.g.*, notes of national banks, nearly all called in, it is simpler than it used to be; and— what is more important—since 1933 all forms have been legal tender and on a parity with one another, so that no one need hesitate to accept payment for goods or services in whatever type of currency is offered. Currency now in general circulation consists of (1) three principal forms of paper: (a) United States treasury notes, in no very large quantity, (b) silver certificates backed by silver bullion held by the Treasury, and— by far the most important—(c) federal reserve notes, issued by federal reserve banks in denominations of five dollars and upwards; (2) silver dollars, not much used (with paper dollars available) except in the West; and (3) "fractional" currency, facilitating small transactions and making change: (a) silver half-dollars, quarters, and dimes, and (b) subsidiary or token coins in the form of nickels and pennies.[3]

Present forms of currency

Development of the National Banking System

Banks as authorized by state legislatures were familiar enough when the federal constitution was adopted, but a proposal in the Philadelphia convention that the new national government also be given power to create and regulate them was expressly rejected; and from the absence of any such provision, strict constructionists in early days naturally deduced that no power of the kind existed. The first secretary of the treasury, Alexander Hamilton, however, took a different view; and, with

Early experi- ence

---

[1] Hepburn *v.* Griswold, 8 Wallace 603 (1870).

[2] Knox *v.* Lee, Parker *v.* Davis, 12 Wallace 457 (1871). Two vacancies on the Court had meanwhile been filled with persons known to disapprove of the 1870 decision.

[3] Paper money (as also postage stamps, revenue stamps, savings bonds, and other government paper) is manufactured in a bureau of engraving and printing in Washington; coins are made at mints located in Philadelphia, Denver, and San Francisco, with assay offices, where precious metals are received, tested, evaluated, and paid for, in New York and Seattle. Appropriate bureaus in the Department of the Treasury are in charge. See W. A. DuPuy, "How Our Money is Manufactured," *Curr. Hist.*, XXIV, 236-241 (May, 1926).

Federalist backing, he not only drew up a plan for a central national bank that would be a help to the government in collecting revenues, holding funds, and floating loans, but in 1791 induced Congress to charter such an institution for a twenty-year period, with the government owning one-fifth of the stock. Although managed competently and serving usefully the purposes intended, this first Bank of the United States incurred the jealousy of state banks, as well as hostility from people opposed in principle to centralization, and in 1811 it was allowed to lapse. Almost immediately, however, the government became involved in financial difficulties incident to the War of 1812, and the upshot was the chartering in 1816—again for twenty years—of a second Bank of the United States, generally similar to the first one and in its time serving similar purposes no less effectively. But opposition continued, especially in the Western parts of the country; indeed, much of the political controversy characterizing the so-called "era of good feeling" centered in the Bank and its influence on financial policies and practices. And when, in 1828, the political forces supporting Andrew Jackson swept into power, the Bank was foredoomed. In 1832, Jackson, as president, vetoed a bill that would have renewed its charter; in 1833, he withdrew all federal deposits from it; and, thus repudiated, it in 1836 fell to the status of a mere state bank and, after languishing for a time, closed its doors.[1]

The constitutionality of national banks established

This second bank had, however, the distinction of furnishing occasion for the Supreme Court's memorable decision in McCulloch v. Maryland not only sustaining the constitutionality of the Bank itself, but, as we have seen, affirming the broad principles on which national power in this country has ever since been based.[2] Ostensibly, the question at issue was only whether the state of Maryland had any right to tax notes issued by the Bank's Baltimore branch. But that could not be decided without inquiring into the right of the Bank itself (and its branches) to exist. And *this* could be determined only as a matter of fundamental constitutional interpretation—specifically as involving the legitimacy, nature, and limitations of implied and resulting powers. The tests applied by Chief Justice Marshall in rendering the Court's opinion were (1) that a power claimed have a legitimate end, (2) that this end be within the scope of the constitution, and (3) that the means employed be "appropriate," plainly adapted to the end in mind, and consistent with the constitution's letter and spirit; and when the second Bank was measured by these criteria—in the light of the government's conferred powers "to lay and collect taxes," "to borrow money," and "to make all laws necessary and proper for carrying into execution the foregoing powers"—the result, in the Court's judgment, was a complete vindication of the authority of

---

[1] The principal works on the two Banks are J. T. Holdsworth, *The First Bank of the United States* (Philadelphia, 1910), and R. C. H. Catterall, *Second Bank of the United States* (Chicago, 1903). Both banks had headquarters in Philadelphia, but with branches scattered over the country.

[2] See pp. 67-69 above.

Congress to create the Bank, and, by implication, national banks of any type and in any number.

From the time when the second Bank of the United States ceased to operate (as such) until the Civil War, the field was left entirely to state banks. Chartered under widely varying laws, these institutions, however, left a good deal to be desired; in particular, as we have seen, the paper money which they issued, often inadequately backed by reserves of gold and silver, was likely to be of shifting and uncertain value. To the growing need for a uniform currency was added other considerations and pressures when the Civil War came on. With a wartime psychology prevalent, people not only wanted to withdraw their money from banks, but demanded gold or silver—which the banks did not have in sufficient quantities. And when the federal government needed to float loans to meet military necessities, the banks were helpless to give much assistance, with the Treasury forced to turn to a private banker, Jay Cooke, to help sell its bonds on favorable terms. In acts of 1863 and 1864, inspired by such wartime experiences, Congress therefore came to a step which well might have been taken long before, *i.e.*, the establishment, not of a single bank as in 1791 and 1816, but of a national banking system, comprising banks throughout the country chartered, regulated, and inspected by national authorities and empowered to issue notes designed to circulate as money. A state bank might become a national bank by buying a prescribed amount of federal bonds and holding them as security for the redemption of its paper issues, and of course accepting federal regulation; or new national banks might be established outright. At all events, the object was to bring into existence banking institutions which could distribute government bonds, lend money to the government, and render other services, and that at the same time would contribute to nationalizing and stabilizing the currency.

A national banking system established

The banking system thus introduced not only proved its worth at the time, but in later years preëmpted much of the banking field. State banks, of course, continued to exist; and, numbering some 10,000, they in the aggregate still carry on a large amount of business.[1] But more than five thousand national banks now dot the country—some in large cities with deposits running into the billions, others in county-seats or other smaller towns with deposits of but a few hundred thousand—all, however, private in character, all with capital subscribed by their stockholders, but all nevertheless chartered by the federal government, operating under numerous regulations laid down by that government, and closely supervised by the comptroller of the currency in the Treasury Department, who

National banks today

[1] Federal land banks, federal home loan banks, and the like—designed to extend credit to particular categories of borrowers—stand outside of the regular system of "commercial" banks here in mind. See pp. 607 and 685 below. Still another special class of banks, although serving people of all sorts without discrimination, is the government's own nation-wide chain of banks operated in connection with the postal savings system.

from time to time sends out examiners to visit and inspect them, and to whom they make full reports of their condition at least three times a year.[1]

The federal reserve system

A good while ago, however, oscillations between nation-wide prosperity and depression brought to light grave defects. One was excessive rigidity not only of rules requiring the same reserves to be maintained regardless of business conditions, but also of restrictions forbidding notes to be issued beyond the total of government bonds held, notwithstanding that the volume of business might call for considerably larger issues. Another shortcoming was the circumstance that the banks were so many entirely separate institutions, with no more means for coming to one another's relief in time of stress than railroads or merchandising establishments. Experience with panics in 1893 and 1907 led Congress to look into the matter; and a comprehensive and highly beneficial Federal Reserve Act [2] was passed in 1913 creating a federal reserve system which, operating as a largely autonomous establishment, has ever since been a major feature of national banking arrangements.

Its organization

The object of the federal reserve system is to link up the whole number of national banks—such state banks also as care to join—in an integrated structure and to impart greater elasticity to their operation. To this end, important special machinery is employed. First of all, the country is divided into twelve federal reserve districts, in each of which is located a federal reserve bank, usually in the district's principal city.[3] In each case, all or nearly all stock (the minimum being four million dollars) is subscribed by the member banks within the district, and control is vested in a board of nine directors, three named by the general management of the reserve system in Washington, six by the member banks.[4] The general management referred to consists of a board of governors (the Federal Reserve Board) of seven members appointed for fourteen-year terms by the president and Senate, with due regard for both geographical distribution and representation of financial, agricultural, industrial, and commercial interests; and this board, quartered in an imposing building in Washington and endowed with broad supervisory powers, bears full responsibility for formulating monetary policies and exercising general

---

[1] J. G. Heinberg, "The Office of Comptroller of the Currency," *Service Monographs,* No. 38 (Baltimore, 1926).

[2] 38 *U. S. Stat. at Large,* 251. In view of the Democratic party's reputation for monetary unorthodoxy during the preceding quarter-century, it is interesting that this legislation should have been enacted when that party was in control of both the presidency and Congress. The person most responsible for the legislation's enactment was President Wilson; and the one most responsible for the form taken by it was Representative (later Senator) Carter Glass of Virginia.

[3] The federal reserve cities are Boston, New York, Philadelphia, Richmond, Atlanta, Cleveland, Chicago, St. Louis, Minneapolis, Kansas City, Dallas, and San Francisco.

[4] Of the six directors chosen locally, three may be bankers, but three must be actively engaged in business or agriculture. The chief executive of each district bank —known as the president (formerly the governor)—is chosen by the board of directors for a five-year term, is eligible for reappointment, and must be approved by the central board of governors.

direction of the system. All national banks must belong to and hold stock in the federal reserve bank of their district; state banks may do so if they meet the requirements and find membership to their advantage—as most of them do.

The federal reserve banks—often referred to as "bankers' banks"— do not carry on a general banking business with individuals and corporations, but instead perform services, directly at least, only for the federal government and the member banks of their respective districts. Services to the government are many and various. Proceeds of revenue collections are deposited in them, and in general they have custody of government funds which in earlier days were left idle in sub-treasuries; they make transfers of such funds according to directions; and they serve as fiscal agents in selling securities and paying government checks and coupons. For member banks, they act as clearing houses for the handling of checks and other financial instruments, serve as depositaries for surplus funds, store gold and silver held as reserves, and, more important, provide rediscounting facilities enabling the needs of customers to be met and a greater volume of business to be done. What happens in this latter connection can be explained briefly. A national or state bank loans money to individuals and corporations, taking the borrowers' notes—"discounting" them, as the phrase goes. If demand is heavy, the bank may reach a point where it has no more money at its disposal; and in the old days that would end matters—the bank would simply have to give further applicants a refusal. Nowadays, however, what a bank in this situation would almost certainly do would be to transmit at least a large part of its accumulated "commercial paper" (which may include mortgages and various forms of collateral) to the federal reserve bank to which it belongs and get it "rediscounted," *i.e.*, borrow money on it just as the original borrower did; and with this money it could make new loans and of course earn new profits. But this is not all. On the basis of the commercial paper thus pouring in—although also with at least a forty per cent backing of gold certificates based on the government's stock of gold [1]—the reserve bank can issue paper money with which to perform its rediscounting operations (the national banks themselves can no longer do this); and in this way arise the federal reserve notes which, as we have seen, constitute the largest share of paper currency circulating in the country today. When times are good and business active, the transactions involved are accelerated, with the resulting greater volume of currency tending to meet the increased demand; when business is slack, credit is in less demand or at any rate cannot be financed, discounting and rediscounting proceed at a slower pace, and reserve notes pile up in the vaults of the reserve banks until reviving demand calls them forth. One of the ways in which the Federal Reserve Board seeks to stabilize the credit structure of the country and control cyclical tendencies to alternating

Its workings

[1] The percentage is subject to rather frequent change.

prosperity and depression is by expanding or contracting the credit facilities of commercial banks by lowering or raising the rediscount rate; a lower rate will give the commercial banks easier access to funds and encourage them to help business by lending at moderate interest rates, a higher rate of course having the opposite effect (which may become desirable in periods of over-speculation or inflation). Stabilization is sought also through employment of an "open-market committee," dating from 1935, consisting of the board of governors and five representatives of federal reserve banks, and empowered to control the open-market buying and selling of commercial paper and of government bonds and other securities by the reserve banks—large purchases of commercial paper naturally having the effect of supplying member banks with more free funds and, in the case of government bonds, strengthening the market and keeping up prices—both of which may prove desirable in depression-time.

The banking crisis of 1933 and some remedial measures

As set up under the legislation of 1913, the federal reserve system served useful purposes and indeed seemed to have solved our major banking problems. Certainly it helped greatly to carry the country through the expansion of its economy and later contraction, incident to World War I. In the "roaring twenties," with their pseudo-prosperity and gross over-extension of credit, however, it failed to furnish a sufficient brake. After the stock-market crash of 1929, our banks proved unable to weather the storm in any such fashion as did those of Great Britain, Canada, and some other countries; and not only did many collapse, but it became necessary for President Roosevelt, immediately upon taking office in 1933, to bring into play a half-forgotten wartime grant of presidential power and temporarily close every bank in the land. A stop-gap Emergency Banking Act, mentioned above, was rushed through Congress liberalizing the conditions under which reserve banks might issue notes and applying other remedies, and in a short time banks able to demonstrate their soundness were permitted to reopen, with others—provided with additional capital by purchases of stock by the Reconstruction Finance Corporation or aided in other ways—eventually restored also. The experience, however, was a harrowing one, and it is small wonder that a good deal of remedial banking legislation of permanent character (too complicated and technical to be reviewed here) was enacted in the next two years. Now it was—in a Banking Act of 1935 [1]—that the federal reserve system was given its first systematic overhauling, leaving it in the general situation already described as existing at the present day. Now it was, too,—in the Glass-Steagall Act of 1933 [2]—that speculative temptations to which large numbers of banks had succumbed in the past were at least partially removed by requiring that thenceforth banking establishments should not engage in both commercial, i.e., general, banking and

[1] 49 *U. S. Stat. at Large,* 684.
[2] 48 *U. S. Stat. at Large,* 162.

"investment" banking—if they insisted upon continuing the latter, they must give up the former. And now also it was that (in the same measure), in the hope that if depositors could be assured that their money would be safe in banks, they would be willing to leave it there, thus averting bank "runs" and resulting bank closings (such as produced the banking crisis of 1933), a plan of guaranty of bank deposits was introduced temporarily in 1933 and permanently in 1935. Under this latter plan, deposits in all banks included within the federal reserve system, federally authorized trust companies, and all non-member banks applying and meeting certain specifications, are insured through a Federal Deposit Insurance Corporation (an independent establishment) up to a maximum of $5,000.[1] North Dakota, Nebraska, and one or two other states which in earlier days experimented with bank-deposit insurance were never able to keep their systems solvent. The federal system is more broadly and adequately based—although another banking *débâcle* like that of the early thirties would subject it to a severe, and possibly disastrous, test.[2]

Credit Facilities and Operations

A major function of national and state banks is the loaning of money, on suitable security, to individuals, businesses, and corporations; and without such service—even though supplemented by lending operations of independent capitalists, insurance companies, and many miscellaneous institutions—the national economy could not operate. A good while ago, however, need became apparent in some vital fields of activity for credit facilities which banks and other existing agencies could not, or at all events did not, fully supply; and to meet the deficiency, the federal government has itself built up a vast and complicated credit structure, furnishing facilities particularly in the fields of agriculture, housing, and general business. In almost no instances is money loaned directly out of the federal Treasury to individual borrowers. To be sure, much of that dispensed comes truly enough from the Treasury. As a rule, however, it reaches borrowers only through the medium of some intervening agency which receives and sifts applications, makes and manages loans, and bears responsibility for getting the money back again; and the agency employed may be a bank or other corporation specially authorized by act of Congress, with capital subscribed largely or wholly by the government, and answerable to the government for all its operations. Thus, in the field earliest entered, *i.e.*, agriculture, we find a series of twelve government-

The federal government becomes a money-lender

---

[1] Somewhat over one-half of the stock of this Corporation was subscribed by the Treasury and the remainder by the federal reserve banks. The necessary insurance reserve comes from an annual assessment, at the rate of one-twelfth of one per cent, upon the average deposits of each insured bank. On December 31, 1946, a total of 13,550 commercial banks and trust companies were covered—7,088 as federal reserve members and 6,462 (state banks and trust companies) as non-members. Twelve district offices are scattered throughout the country.

[2] For titles of several special treatises on the federal reserve system, see p. 615 below.

maintained regional land banks, with various auxiliary banks and fiscal agencies, making both long-term and short-term credit available to farmers and farm coöperatives on conditions usually more favorable than can be obtained from commercial banks.[1] Sometimes—as in the cases of the Reconstruction Finance Corporation and the Export-Import Bank of Washington, to be mentioned again presently—the lending agency is a single corporate establishment operating on government capital or at all events with the government backing any bonds that it may issue. Sometimes, indeed, the intervening institutions do not actually lend money at all, but, as in the case of the Federal Housing Administration, simply stimulate credit by insuring building and loan associations, banks, or other private lenders against part or all of any losses that they may incur on approved loans. Again, as in the case of a Home Owners' Loan Corporation established during the depression of the thirties to stem the tide of mortgage foreclosures, the method may be that of taking over mortgages or other private obligations, satisfying the holders with government-guaranteed bonds, and afterwards recovering on the debts as far as conditions permit.[2] Manifestly, at some points, the government's operations compete with those of regular banks and other private lending agencies; at others, they stimulate and assist them.

The Reconstruction Finance Corporation:

1. Background

With agricultural and housing credit left to be touched upon again in appropriate later chapters,[3] something may be added here concerning a federally-maintained credit agency which, from a relatively modest start, developed into the largest banking enterprise—indeed, one of the largest public enterprises of any kind—in the country, i.e., the Reconstruction Finance Corporation. One hardly will be surprised to learn that this huge establishment's beginnings were associated with the depression. In the dismal days when it arose, not only commercial banks, but thrift institutions like savings banks, insurance companies, and building and loan associations, found themselves almost unable to function because of "frozen loans," perhaps good enough eventually but not immediately collectible from hard-pressed borrowers; railroads and other corporations, even though with plenty of assets, could not carry on their customary financing operations; municipal and other local governments were similarly embarrassed; multitudes of farmers and home-owners, unable to meet payments on mortgages, faced foreclosure and disposses-

[1] A Federal Home Loan Bank system is operated on substantially the same plan, with eleven regional federal home loan banks scattered over the country and the government owning part of the stock.

[2] Since discontinuing its lending operations in 1936, this Corporation (now in the National Housing Agency) has been engaged solely in administering the mortgages remaining in its hands; and it expects finally to liquidate its work with no net loss to the government. A new chapter in the history of federal assistance to home-ownership was, however, opened in 1944, when the Servicemen's Readjustment Act (popularly known as the "G.I. Bill of Rights") created opportunity for honorably discharged veterans to obtain government-secured loans for twenty years to buy or build homes or to acquire farms or business property.

[3] See Chaps. xxx and xxxiii below.

sion; and from harassed individuals, business interests, and corporations the country over appeals flowed in upon the national government for assistance in tiding over the period of stress.

Responding to the demand, and upon recommendation of President Hoover, Congress early in 1932 created the Reconstruction Finance Corporation, patterned after the War Finance Corporation of 1918, and placed under the management of a board of seven directors, three *ex officiis* and four appointed by the president and Senate.[1] The new agency was endowed with a capital of $500,000,000, all subscribed by the Treasury, and eventually (being continued and utilized on even a larger scale during the Roosevelt administrations) with far greater sums, with the result that it became a vast super-credit institution, holding a key position in nearly every phase of the government's recovery program. Authorized from the first to make properly insured loans to banks, to trust and insurance companies, to building and loan associations, to agricultural and live-stock credit associations, and to railroads, it in time was permitted to extend assistance to ordinary private industry, and within a period of less than three years (1932-35) it disbursed the stupendous sum of almost seven billion dollars. Some of this money went for purposes of relief, but the bulk of it was allocated to institutions and businesses for assistance in reviving commercial, industrial, agricultural, and transportation activities—"priming the pump" of national prosperity. On the whole, the results were excellent, and many of the loans were repaid in a surprisingly short time.[2] By 1937, however, the agency was widely thought to have served its purpose; and at that date Congress passed an act to facilitate its gradual withdrawal from lending activities by authorizing the president to suspend or terminate its operations in any field of lending whenever he should find that credit for borrowers in that field was "sufficiently available from private sources to meet legitimate demands."

2. Depression and wartime activities

Before the R.F.C. could wind up its activities, however, Congress gave it a fresh lease on life by authorizing it, in 1938, to make further private loans to combat a current recession in business; and, with the defense effort and later war presently ensuing, the agency, far from being liquidated, entered upon a new and even more vigorous period of activity. In the critical years 1940-41, it not only played an extremely important rôle in financing defense industry by making loans and investments that private capital could not take the risk of making, but it brought into existence various subsidiary government corporations, such as the Rubber Reserve Company, the Mineral Reserve Corporation, the Defense Plant

---

[1] 48 *U. S. Stat. at Large,* 162, and 52 *ibid.,* 212.

[2] On the R.F.C.'s early operations, see J. H. Jones (chairman of the board of directors until 1945), "Billions Out and Billions Back," *Sat. Eve. Post,* CCIX, 5-7, 23 ff. (June 12, 26, 1937). Cf. *Fortune,* XXI, 42-51 ff. (May, 1940). In the first few years, more than eighty different pieces of legislation extended the scope of the agency's activities in one direction or another, until eventually almost every sector of the American economy was embraced.

Corporation, the Defense Supplies Corporation, and the Defense Homes Corporation, thereby assisting in the accumulation of reserve supplies of rubber, tin, manganese, and other raw materials indispensable in wartime, aiding industrial plant expansion, and helping provide housing facilities for defense workers.[1]

3. An uncertain future

Looked upon as strictly an emergency device, the R.F.C. was originally limited to a single year, subject to extension by the president for an additional two years. Congress, however, has prolonged its life a number of times—most recently, by act of 1947, to June 30, 1948.[2] People inclined to deplore large concentrations of financial power have always found fault with the agency, sometimes even pronouncing it a national menace; and there can be no denying that many times it practically has held the power of life and death over numerous large financial and business institutions and interests. Banks and other private lending institutions, too, although warmly supporting the Corporation's creation in their days of dire need, have grown critical because of the competition which it now offers them; and as a result—while fair-minded people concede its great usefulness in both the depression and war periods—the agency is now on the defensive, with Congress unwilling in 1947 to extend it for more than a single year, and also (when prolonging it for this period) curtailing the scope of its operations, as by limiting its lending authority on new business to two billion dollars and terminating most of its war finance activities. The principal center of hostility in Congress is the Senate,[3] where in June, 1947, the committee on banking and currency decided upon a full investigation of the agency's competition with private lending institutions, its methods of accounting,[4] and its financial condition, with certainty of finding that it has made money on its loans but on the other hand has incurred deficits through financing subsidy programs and warplant construction for which Congress made no appropriations. As matters stood early in 1948, the Corporation's future was at least in doubt.[5]

[1] Under authority granted by 54 *U. S. Stat. at Large,* 572, 897, 961 (1940), and four other acts, with amendments.

[2] *Pub. Law 132—80th Cong., 1st Sess.*

[3] As first passed in the House, the 1947 bill for extension provided a two-year authorization. In his budget message of January 12, 1948, President Truman recommended extension beyond the expiration date indicated above. To the following March, however, no such action was taken.

[4] The R.F.C. is exempt from regular audits by the General Accounting Office, though a special investigation of its accounts was carried out in 1945-46, resulting in a report sharply criticizing them as in need of basic changes. In 1945, Senator Byrd of Virginia termed the R.F.C., with its numerous subsidiaries, "the most colossal banking institution the world has ever known, either public or private ... [and] virtually immune from the control of Congress ... actually, as it now operates, a fourth branch of the government." *N. Y. Times,* Jan. 23, 24, 25, 1945. As chairman of its board of directors, Mr. Jesse H. Jones once said that the Corporation could "make loans in any amount, for any length of time, at any rate of interest, to anybody."

[5] Set up originally as an independent establishment, the R.F.C. was placed in 1942 in the Department of Commerce—only, however, to revert to its earlier status when, early in 1945, the Senate manifested unwillingness to confirm Henry A. Wallace as

There is, however, another and very different side to the federal government's lending operations; from the period of World War I, it has been deeply involved in foreign as well as domestic financing. In connection with the conflict mentioned, loans aggregating ten billion dollars were made to Great Britain, France, and half a dozen other countries with which we were associated, on the theory that they would be repaid out of reparations exacted from the defeated Central Powers. The reparations program, however, broke down; most of the countries that owed us money fell into chronic financial difficulty, aggravated by the depression of the thirties; and no one of the number except Finland ever paid us anything substantial on principal in addition to interest. Some people thought that the debts ought simply to be wiped off as having been incurred in a common cause; others considered that they might as well be forgotten, since they would never be paid in any case. Irked by the experience, Congress, in 1934, passed an act declaring mere "token" payments unsatisfactory and cutting off all defaulting nations from floating further loans in this country.[1]

The federal government also a lender abroad:

1. During World War I

With Europe again at war after 1939, it was inevitable that the United States should once more be approached for help; indeed, during the critical period before we were ourselves drawn in—when we still hoped for an Allied victory to which we should not be obliged to contribute under arms—we decided that it would be good insurance to bolster the Allied cause by extending material aid. This time, however, the method employed was not direct loans of money, but instead the adoption, in 1941, of a scheme of "lend-lease" under which, throughout the later war years, goods and services were exchanged among the Allies on the understanding that repayment of balances due would eventually be made, if made at all, in such other goods as might be agreed upon by the parties involved;[2] and the upshot was that after the end of hostilities, various of our associates in the war, but chiefly Great Britain, Russia, France, and China, were obligated to us in varying amounts which may or may not ever actually be liquidated—difficulties entailed including not simply the unfavorable economic condition of the debtor countries, but our own hesitation about upsetting our economic balance by accepting the requisite goods, even if offered. For the reasons mentioned—although probably the default will be rationalized in terms of a common war effort to which

2. Since 1941

---

secretary of commerce unless the R.F.C. were exempted from his jurisdiction. The present board of directors consists of five members serving full time.

Another federal lending agency that should not go unmentioned is the Export-Import Bank of Washington, established in 1934, with all stock owned by the government, and designed to facilitate trade with foreign countries, the territories, and the insular possessions. Its range of operations has, however, been broadened to include loans to savings and loan institutions and for assistance in the rehabilitation of war-torn countries. A good deal of the money which the Bank has handled has been borrowed from the R.F.C.

[1] Johnson Debt Default Act, 48 *U. S. Stat. at Large,* 574.

[2] China, however, sharing somewhat meagerly in lend-lease, received a number of direct loans.

all participants were morally bound to contribute everything they could —it is not unlikely that the story of lend-lease will end very much as did that of World War I loans.

Meanwhile, with hostilities ended, the United States has been drawn into not only heavy direct outlays upon relief for war-stricken peoples, but new and expensive lending operations for the rehabilitation of war-devastated countries and economies—for the sake of improving world conditions, promoting monetary stability, and encouraging the world trade on which our own prosperity to no small extent depends. In the summer of 1946, Great Britain was given a loan of three and three-quarter billion dollars for aid in restoring her economy and relaxing restrictive trade practices forced upon her by the war and its drain on her financial resources; in 1947, four hundred millions were placed at the disposal of the president for loans, credits, or grants to Greece and Turkey in an effort to stabilize those countries and fend off domination by Soviet Russia; several foreign governments have been granted large credits for the purchase of surplus war property; as indicated above, the Export-Import Bank of Washington has been authorized to make loans for reconstruction of war-torn countries and for foreign development projects; under the Bretton Woods Agreements Act of 1945,[1] the United States participates heavily in an International Bank for Reconstruction which makes or guarantees loans to member countries for programs of economic and financial reconstruction, and in an International Monetary Fund which similarly gives temporary assistance to member countries in financing deficits incurred in monetary-stabilization operations.[2] In the summer of 1947, indeed, our government boldly brought forward a project—originally known as the Marshall Plan, but later officially termed the European Recovery Program—under which, if reasonable coöperation abroad could be assured, the United States would take the leading rôle in a concerted effort to get all Western and Central Europe on its feet by means of loans, credits, and outright contributions.[3] Surely, if other evidence were lacking of the country's deep commitments in world affairs, our present and potential lending operations abroad—as indeed our rôle in international financing generally—would fill the gap.

[1] 59 *U. S. Stat. at Large,* 512 (1945).

[2] The government's subscription to the $9,100,000,000 capital of the International Bank was $3,175,000,000, and its contribution to the International Monetary Fund of $8,800,000,000 was $2,750,000,000.

[3] A figure originally mentioned by the plan's sponsors for the American outlay was three billion dollars during each of three years. Conferences at Paris during the summer of 1947, participated in by sixteen European nations, however, fixed $22,440,-000,000 as the sum that would be required over a period of four years, with $15,810,000,000 indicated as the amount to be expected from the United States. For the full report, see *N. Y. Times,* Sept. 24, 1947. That this country would have to share heavily in some effort of the kind was virtually taken for granted by our people, regardless of party. The extent and conditions of such participation, however, offered plenty of questions for the government, and especially for Congress, as 1948 opened. When these pages were closed (during the following March), Congress seemed on the point of voting four or five billions for the program's initial year.

The Treasury Department

The vast volume of fiscal business destined to arise out of the financial powers (especially the power to tax) conferred upon the new government in 1789 was not, of course, foreseen. Nevertheless, one of the first requisites was machinery for the collection of taxes, the care of funds, and the keeping of accounts; and the resulting Treasury Department has developed into a huge administrative establishment, employing more people (some 85,500 in 1948) than the majority of other departments and performing tasks, great and small, of highly varied character. On the policy side, the Department's position is relatively weak—certainly as compared with that of the British Treasury. Before the present budget system arose, congressional committees framed finance bills, with some regard, of course, for information and advice from Treasury officials, yet also with jealously guarded independence; while today, the Bureau of the Budget, performing functions constituting the very heart of public finance, is not even in the Department and finance bills, however originating, are at all events not measures to which the Department has contributed more than statistical data (especially as to revenues and debt) along with recommendations.[1] Our system provides for no finance official with the vast powers of initiative, planning, and decision possessed by the British chancellor of the exchequer; certainly the secretary of the treasury is no such official. In a fashion, the purposes are served by the Budget Bureau as an arm of the president, but with the great difference that not even the budget director nor the president himself—still less the Treasury Department's head—can carry the great finance bills of a fiscal year to the legislature, introduce them, explain them, and drive them through to enactment. Separation of executive and legislative powers is still too real for anything like that.

In the field of administration and management, however, the Department's activities are numerous and essential. Foremost among them is collection of the tax revenues, chiefly through a bureau of customs and a bureau of internal revenue. The bureau of customs collects the duties on imports provided for by the tariff laws and trade agreements, the work being performed at some three hundred main or subsidiary "ports of entry" located on the Pacific and Atlantic coasts, on or near the Canadian and Mexican borders, or in Alaska, Hawaii, Puerto Rico, and the Virgin Islands, and grouped in fifty-one customs collection districts.[2] The bureau of internal revenue collects the personal and corporation

Scope and limitations

Financial functions:

1. Collection of revenue

---

[1] The Department's principal activities on the policy side relate to taxation, on which it has maintained a research division since 1938. Since the same date, there has also been a division of monetary research.

[2] In the interior of the country, there are ports of entry also, where duties are collected on imports shipped under bond. In addition to the collectors, deputy collectors, surveyors, and appraisers employed at all ports of entry, each customs district has a customs patrol, charged with preventing illegal entry of merchandise and with protecting the customs revenues.

income taxes, estate and inheritance taxes, capital stock taxes, liquor, tobacco, and amusement taxes, and a wide variety of other imposts; and for this purpose, the country, including Alaska and Hawaii, is divided into sixty-six districts, each in charge of a collector, with the requisite staff of deputy collectors, revenue agents, and other assistants.[1]

2. Custody of funds
A second main Department function is that of keeping the government's money and paying its bills in accordance with appropriations duly made. In the Treasury Building in Washington is a treasury (in the physical sense), in whose vaults large sums are held; and until 1921 there were sub-treasuries in nine other principal cities. Government money has also long been placed in banks; and since the discontinuance of the sub-treasuries most of it is so deposited, principally in federal reserve banks. The custodian of the government's monies and also of its stocks of gold and silver bullion is an official known as the treasurer of the United States.

3. Control of the currency
A third important function is control of the currency. As already stated, a bureau of engraving and printing prepares all of the paper money, as well as bonds and other securities, of the national government, and a bureau of the mint supervises the mints and assay offices. In addition, a bureau of the comptroller of the currency supervises the national banks, directs periodic inspections of them, and sees to the issuance and redemption of federal reserve notes and federal reserve bank notes; and a United States Secret Service guards the currency and securities against counterfeiting—although charged also with protecting the president, his family, and a president-elect from possible injury.

4. Management of the national debt
Finally may be mentioned the Department's management of the national debt, concentrated since 1940 in a bureau of the public debt, located in a division known as the Fiscal Service. Once it has been decided by the proper authorities to make a new offering of public debt securities, *e.g.*, savings bonds, the bureau prepares the necessary documents, directs the handling of subscriptions and allotments, and plans and issues the securities themselves. It also attends to the retiring of securities, and is responsible for all public-debt accounting and auditing.

Non-financial functions
Early in its history, the Department began to be assigned functions which had little or nothing to do with finance, and until after World War I it served as a dumping ground for offices and activities that Congress did not know how to dispose of otherwise. In recent years, however, such non-financial functions have been gradually reduced by transfers to other departments or agencies, until today the only important units of the kind still included are a bureau of narcotics, charged with enforce-

---

[1] Collectors of customs and internal revenue collectors have long been political appointees. The same is true of deputy collectors, who, although at one time selected under merit rules, were by act of 1913 placed outside the classified service. Being subject to senatorial confirmation, all of the officials mentioned fall outside the range of those who, under the Ramspeck Act of 1940, may be included in the classified service by presidential order.

ment of the anti-narcotic laws; a procurement division, which determines policies and methods relating to purchase, warehousing, and distribution of supplies for all agencies of the federal government except the armed services; and the United States Coast Guard, which, after operating as a service under the Navy from late in 1941, was transferred back to the Treasury Department on January 1, 1946.

REFERENCES

L. H. Chamberlain, *The President, Congress, and Legislation* (New York, 1946), Chaps. vii-viii.

L. F. Schmeckebier, *New Federal Organizations* (Washington, D. C., 1934), Chap. i.

S. C. Wallace, *The New Deal in Action* (New York, 1934), Chaps. iii-vii.

L. M. Hacker, *A Short History of the New Deal* (New York, 1934), Chap. iii.

F. D. Roosevelt, *On Our Way* (Washington, D. C., 1934), Chaps. i, iii, v.

B. and L. P. Mitchell, *American Economic History* (Boston, 1947), Chaps. xxv-xxvi, xxxiv.

D. R. Dewey, *Financial History of the United States* (12th ed., New York, 1934).

A. B. Hepburn, *History of Currency in the United States* (rev. ed., New York, 1924).

J. S. Lawrence, *Banking Concentration in the United States* (New York, 1930).

T. J. Anderson, Jr., *Federal and State Control of Banking* (New York, 1934).

J. P. Dawson, "The Gold Clause Decision," *Mich. Law Rev.*, XXXIII, 647-684 (Mar., 1935).

T. E. Gregory, *The Gold Standard and Its Future* (rev. ed., New York, 1935).

E. W. Kemmerer, *The A B C of the Federal Reserve System* (11th ed., Princeton, N. J., 1938).

————, *The A B C of Inflation* (New York, 1942).

P. M. Warburg, *The Federal Reserve System; Its Origin and Growth* (New York, 1930).

S. E. Harris, *Twenty Years of Federal Reserve Policy*, 2 vols. (Cambridge, Mass., 1933).

R. L. Weissman, *The New Federal Reserve System* (New York, 1936).

E. A. Lewis [comp.], *The Federal Reserve Act of 1913, with Amendments and Laws Relating to Banking, Dec. 23, 1913—July 31, 1946* (Washington, D. C., 1946).

The Federal Reserve System; Its Purposes and Functions (2nd ed., Washington, D. C., 1947). Published by the Federal Reserve System.

A. W. Crawford, *Monetary Management Under the New Deal* (Washington, D. C., 1940).

G. Greer, "This Business of Monetary Control," *Harper's Mag.*, CLXXI, 169-180 (July, 1935).

C. Warburton, "Monetary Control Under the Federal Reserve Act," *Polit. Sci. Quar.*, LXI, 505-534 (Dec., 1946).

L. Pasvolsky, *Current Monetary Issues* (Washington, D. C., 1934).

J. McDiarmid, *Government Corporations and Federal Funds* (Chicago, 1938).

H. Spero, *Reconstruction Finance Corporation's Loans to Railroads, 1932-1937* (Cambridge, Mass., 1939).

[Brookings Institution], *Report to the Select* [Senate] *Committee to Investigate the Executive Agencies of the Government*, 75th Cong., 1st Sess., Sen. Doc. No. 5, pp. 6-42 (Washington, D. C., 1937). Describes the organization of the Treasury Department.

C. K. Shaw, "Supervision of Field Services in the United States Revenue Administration," *Amer. Polit. Sci. Rev.*, XXVII, 930-942 (Dec., 1933).

G. G. Johnson, *The Treasury and Monetary Policy, 1933-1938* (Cambridge, Mass., 1939).

I. Crump, *Our United States Secret Service* (New York, 1942).

United States Government Manual, section on "Department of the Treasury" in any late edition.

Annual Report of the Secretary of the Treasury on the State of the Finances; quarterly reports of the Reconstruction Finance Corporation; annual reports of the Federal Deposit Insurance Corporation, the Home Owners' Loan Corporation, etc.

CHAPTER XXVIII

FOREIGN AND INTERSTATE COMMERCE

As illustrated by preceding chapters dealing with taxation, spending, Government and economic affairs banking, currency, and credit, there is a very close connection in this country between government and economic life; itself influenced in a multitude of ways by economic interests and forces, government in turn is occupied mainly with tasks and problems relating in one way or another to the national economy. From the field of finance, we turn to other broad areas in which federal power is brought to bear upon economic affairs—first of all, that of commerce, embracing not merely trade in the ordinary sense but all forms of transportation and communication by which trade and intercourse are carried on. In the succeeding chapter, the relations of government with general business will be considered; here, however, we take up commerce in particular, because (although, of course, most commerce *is* business) our national government's control over business flows, to a large extent, from its authority to regulate commerce.

Lack of any central power to control the conditions under which commerce was carried on with foreign countries and among the several states was a principal defect of the Articles of Confederation; and, as we have seen, it was a controversy between certain of the states over conflicting commercial interests and policies that set in motion the train of events leading to the convention of 1787. It is not strange, therefore, that the delegates assembled at Philadelphia should have sought to supply a remedy; and this they did by writing into the new constitution a brief but fertile clause giving Congress power to "regulate commerce with foreign nations, and among the several states, and with the Indian tribes." [1] Indeed, this power stands second in the list of those conferred; and while no one at the time could have foreseen such a result, it is doubtful whether any other of the constitution's provisions (except those relating to taxation and expenditure) has prompted an equal amount of legislation and debate or contributed so much to the vigor of the national government as we know it today. Certainly none has had so much to do with developing the close relation long existing between government and business—a relation steadily growing closer and more significant as the commercial enterprises of our people increasingly transcend state and national boundaries.

At the outset, the power conferred really had no very extended scope.

[1] Art. I, § 8, cl. 2.

All commerce carried on wholly within the bounds of any state was left to be regulated exclusively by the state concerned; and this, of course, is still true, even though, as we shall see, Congress, in controlling interstate commerce on the broader lines now prevailing, sometimes prescribes regulations that necessarily affect intrastate commerce as well. To be sure, federal power over all other commerce was granted in broad and general terms; and of four express limitations imposed, only one—that forbidding Congress to lay any tax or duty on exports—ever proved of much significance.[1] But to men of pack-horse and sailing-ship days, commerce meant only the literal exchange of goods—buying and selling, importing and exporting; and while even on this basis interstate regulation was a novel and challenging undertaking, its scope was insignificant in comparison with that later developed. The floodgates for expansion were first opened in 1824, when, in delivering a Supreme Court opinion in the famous case of Gibbons v. Ogden,[2] Chief Justice Marshall not only affirmed full

authority of Congress to maintain the free flow of interstate and foreign commerce within the individual states, but declared commerce to consist not only of *traffic* (buying, selling, and transporting commodities), but of *intercourse* as well, thereby giving it an entirely new content and meaning. The name of Marshall is associated with many nationalizing decisions of this period, but hardly with any of greater potential consequence than this. Immediately, the carrying of persons (not simply goods) from one state to another, or to a foreign country, became "commerce," subject to congressional regulation; and as forms and methods of intercourse later multiplied, the field for control correspondingly expanded. In time came the railroad; then the steamship; then the telegraph; then the telephone; then the motor vehicle; then "wireless;" then radio-broadcasting; then the airplane. And to all these the regulative authority of Congress was progressively extended, with the Supreme Court coming close behind with decisions validating most of the powers asserted and sometimes hinting at even broader ones that might be assumed.

Indeed, the Court not only kept pace with Congress in pursuit of the newer forms of interstate and foreign commerce arising from an expand-

---

[1] Art. I, § 9, cl. 5. The other three limitations (contained in the same article and section) are: (1) the foreign slave-trade might not be prohibited before 1808; (2) no preference may be given by any regulation of commerce or revenue to the ports of one state over those of another; and (3) vessels bound to or from one state may not be obliged to clear, enter, or pay duties in another state. The first of the three was only temporary, and the second and third have operated merely to prevent discrimination against the commerce of any state or group of states. The prohibition of federal export taxes was a concession to the Southern exporters of agricultural products, designed to shield them from a tax burden supposed to fall on the exporter himself. Export taxes, if freely allowed, might have been employed at times not only to obtain revenue but to conserve natural resources by checking shipments of lumber, oil, coal, and other products out of the country. There is, however, nothing in the constitution to prevent regulation of export trade by Congress in any way other than taxation, *e.g.*, by imposing embargoes.
[2] 9 Wheaton 1.

ing technology; animated by the new philosophy dominating it since Newer judicial interpretations since 1937 1937, it has found ways of enlarging the concept of commerce in other directions as well—sometimes sharply reversing an earlier position in order to do so. Two examples may be cited. On many earlier occasions, the question had arisen as to whether Congress had authority to legislate concerning conditions under which manufacturing and mining were car- Two examples: ried on when such conditions were more or less related to interstate commerce. For a long time, the Court replied emphatically in the nega- 1. Manufacturing and other production tive, saying that manufacturing and commerce were two quite different matters and that federal regulative authority extended only to commerce, or at all events to matters affecting commerce *directly*. When, for example, in 1916, Congress passed the first child labor law, forbidding shipment in interstate commerce of products of any factory, shop, or mine employing children under specified ages, the Court—although closely divided, and with Mr. Justice Holmes registering a celebrated dissent—overthrew the measure as being aimed (as indeed it was) pri- marily at regulating, not commerce, but manufacturing and mining.[1] Against a rising tide of contrary opinion, this point of view was main- tained for another quarter of a century. Then, however, it gave way. Beginning in 1933, numerous statutes enacted to promote national re- covery proceeded from the bold assumption that, properly construed, the commerce clause gives Congress authority to regulate substantially the entire business structure of the country, including wages, hours, and other working conditions, prices, volume of production, the buying and selling of securities—in short, anything that affects interstate commerce *directly or indirectly*. And although most of the earlier acts in the series were overthrown judicially on the ground of being too free in their delegations of power or pushing the commerce power to unjustifiable lengths, or both, in 1937 a majority of the Court unexpectedly swung around to the opin- ion that, nearly all manufacturing and other production being, under present-day conditions, carried on with a view to the interstate or na- tional, or even the international, market, the commerce clause may properly be construed to empower Congress to promote the health of interstate and foreign commerce by any measures improving the health of business in general.[2] From this revolutionary concept, it was but a step to holding, more specifically, that all manufacturing, mining, lumber- ing, and other productive enterprises in which raw materials and finished products are carried in interstate commerce are inseparable from such

---

[1] Hammer *v.* Dagenhart, 247 U. S. 251 (1918).

[2] This newer view was developed and discussed (a good while before the Court itself adopted it) in E. S. Corwin, "Congress's Power to Prohibit Commerce; A Crucial Constitutional Issue," *Cornell Law Quar.*, XVIII, 477-506 (June, 1933), and "Some Probable Repercussions of 'Nira' on Our Constitutional System," *Annals of Amer. Acad. of Polit. and Soc. Sci.*, CLXXII, 139-144 (Mar., 1934). Cf. J. T. Ganoe, "The Roosevelt Court and the Commerce Clause," *Ore. Law Rev.*, XXIV, 71-147 (Feb., 1945); R. L. Stern, "The Commerce Clause and the National Economy, 1933-1946," *Harvard Law Rev.*, LIX, 645-693, 883-947 (May, July, 1946).

commerce, and therefore within the scope of congressional regulative power; and it was on this basis, as we shall see, that the National Labor Relations Act of 1935 and the Fair Labor Standards ["Wages and Hours"] Act of 1938—both relating primarily to industry, but both gaining judicial acceptance because of their commercial implications—were sustained, in 1937 and 1941, respectively.[1]

2. Insurance

Another illustration of the same sort of thing is supplied by extension of the sphere of congressional control to include the business of insurance. In 1869, the Supreme Court had held private insurance companies not to be engaged in interstate commerce, even when most of their business was carried on across state lines,[2] and on this understanding, such companies and their business had from then on been regulated solely by the states. In 1943, however, some two hundred private fire insurance companies and over a score of individuals identified with the Southeastern Underwriters Association were indicted collectively for violating the Sherman Anti-Trust Act[3] by conspiring to fix arbitrary and non-competitive premium rates and to maintain monopolistic controls by boycotts and other means; and when the case was argued before the Supreme Court, four of the seven justices then sitting refused to be bound by the decision of seventy-five years earlier and, on the contrary, held interstate insurance operations to be interstate commerce.[4] It was shown that, when the only regulation to be feared was from the states, insurance companies had themselves sought to evade such regulation by maintaining that their business was interstate; and the conclusion at which the Court arrived (four to three) simply was: "No enterprise of any kind which conducts its activities across state lines has been held to be wholly beyond the regulatory power of Congress under the commerce clause.[5] We cannot make an exception of the business of insurance."[6]

[1] See pp. 726, 728 below.

[2] Paul v. Virginia, 8 Wallace 168 (1869). There were other early decisions of similar purport.

[3] See pp. 651-652 below.

[4] United States v. Southeastern Underwriters Association, 322 U. S. 533 (1944).

[5] This, of course, was after the decisions bringing manufacturing and other forms of production under the clause mentioned.

[6] The decision's effect was two-fold: (1) to make the defendants liable to prosecution under the Sherman Act, and (2) to open the way for Congress to take over from the states, partly or wholly, the regulation of all private insurance business having an interstate aspect. The interests affected pressed earnestly for a chance to reform, and the upshot was an act of Congress in 1945 (59 U. S. Stat. at Large, 33) making the insurance business substantially immune from prosecutions under the anti-trust laws until January 1, 1948, and postponing federal regulation indefinitely, with a view to enabling the companies to mend their ways and also to giving the states an opportunity to take care of the situation if they could by making their own regulations more effective; and a number of states have since been enacting legislation on the subject—based in some instances on model bills drawn up by the insurance industry itself. See Council of State Governments, Revision of State Systems for Insurance Regulation (Chicago, 1946). The point to the episode for present purposes is, however, the extension of congressional regulating authority (however little it may actually be exercised) to the insurance business by a Court not above changing its mind. On the general subject, see E. W. Sawyer, Insurance as Interstate Commerce (New York, 1945).

Constitutionally, "commerce" today therefore includes not only the exchange of commodities, but the transportation of them, and of persons and live-stock, by land, water, or air; the transmission of intelligence by telegraph, telephone, wireless, radio, and newspapers; [1] manufacturing, mining, fishing, and logging when having interstate aspects commercially; and the writing of insurance policies—and all are subject to congressional regulation in so far as involving interstate or international operations. Even agriculture is drawn in, not only as its products flow through the channels of trade, but in such extraordinary ways as the exclusion of products from interstate commerce as a means of controlling production and the fixing of prices for products "in the current" of interstate commerce.[2] To be sure, there are processes and transactions which, at least to the layman, seem quite as closely related to commerce as do some of the things which have been held to be included, but which nevertheless the Supreme Court has thus far regarded as only incidents or aids to commerce and not as themselves commercial acts or instrumentalities. For example, the buying and selling of bills of exchange has been construed not to be commerce. From time to time, however, by congressional act or judicial construction, new activities, as in the case of insurance, are brought within the meaning of the term; and no man can say what the ultimate limits will be.

The term "regulate" has likewise undergone judicial interpretation and expansion. From having denoted power merely to permit and control commerce under certain conditions, it has come to include authority to protect, encourage, and promote it, and on the other hand, to limit it, or even prohibit it altogether, when considered in the national interest. Furthermore, Congress not only may regulate existing instrumentalities of interstate and foreign commerce, but under the power to promote

[1] Newspapers were brought in by a Supreme Court decision of 1937 in Associated Press v. National Labor Relations Board (301 U. S. 103). In protesting the constitutionality of the National Labor Relations Act as applied to it, the Associated Press contended that it was not engaged in commerce and that subjecting it to the provisions of the act amounted to violating the First Amendment by restricting freedom of the press. By five-to-four, the Court, however, held that the gathering and dissemination of news is commerce and that no constitutional freedom was jeopardized by applying the act.

[2] Indeed, federal price control in general, so extensively employed during the recent war—and applying not only to commodities sold in interstate commerce but to those sold locally as well if interstate prices can be regarded as in any way affected—rests entirely on the commerce power.

The Supreme Court has gone so far as to bring within the scope of the regulative authority of Congress employees engaged in the maintenance and operation of buildings occupied by tenants engaged "in commerce or in the production of goods for commerce," i.e., engineers, watchmen, elevator operators, and others. The work of such employees has "so close and immediate a tie with the process of production for commerce" that they are to be regarded as engaged in "an occupation necessary to the production of goods in interstate commerce." Kirchbaum v. Walling, 316 U. S. 517 (1942). Even employees of an electrical concern engaged in commercial and industrial wiring for customers carrying on interstate commerce have been held to be included. Roland Electric Co. v. Walling, 327 U. S. 657 (1946). See M. M. Davisson, "Coverage of the Fair Labor Standards Act," Mich. Law Rev., XLI, 1060-1088 (June, 1943); ibid., XLIII, 867-900 (Apr., 1945).

may charter new corporations, *e.g.*, railroads, to serve as such instrumentalities.[1] In short, as a result of the commerce clause and of judicial decisions based upon it, Congress has authority to enact any legislation appropriate for not only the control but also the advancement of commerce in its interstate and foreign aspects—"to adopt measures to promote its growth and insure its safety, to foster, protect, control, and restrain." [2]

Branches of the commerce power

Along with the power to regulate foreign and interstate commerce, Congress is given authority to regulate commerce with the Indian tribes. Of some importance in our early history, this phase may now be passed over with the barest mention. Of major significance today are those aspects of congressional authority having to do with the regulation of commerce (a) with foreign nations and (b) among the several states; and to each of these attention will be given in the remainder of this chapter.

The Regulation of Foreign Commerce

Scope

In its provision for congressional regulation, the constitution brackets foreign commerce and interstate commerce in the same phrase. Authority over foreign commerce is, however, really the broader, for the reason that the national government has exclusive, and practically unrestricted, jurisdiction over our relations abroad, this having the effect of reënforcing and supplementing the authority specially conferred in the commerce clause; foreign commerce, too, may be regulated by treaty as well as by congressional act.[3] The authority to regulate foreign commerce, furthermore, extends to every act of transportation or communication cutting across our national boundaries, no matter how deep in the country's interior may be the point of beginning or of termination. A cablegram to England sent from Chicago is foreign commerce from the time it is first placed on the wires; a consignment of ladies' gowns from Paris to Cleveland is foreign commerce not simply until it is unloaded from a ship or airplane at New York, nor even simply until it reaches Cleveland, but until the importer has sold the original package or at least broken it for the purpose of selling its contents. Only (ruled the Supreme Court more than a hundred years ago) when imports—the original package or its contents—have "come to rest," and are commingled with the general property of the people of a state, does the controlling authority of Congress end and that of the state begin.[4]

[1] Thus the Inland Waterways Corporation was created by Congress in 1924 to carry on the operations of the government-owned river and coastwise waterway transportation system.

[2] Chief Justice Hughes, in Texas and New Orleans Ry. *v.* Brotherhood of Railway and Steamship Clerks, 281 U. S. 548 (1930).

[3] Indeed, there is possibility of conflict between congressional regulation and treaty regulation; for example, a treaty may contain stipulations inconsistent with existing tariff laws, at least until one or the other is changed. Federal control over foreign commerce is further conferred in a clause of the constitution authorizing Congress to define and punish piracies and felonies on the high seas (Art. I, § 8, cl. 10).

[4] Brown *v.* Maryland, 12 Wheaton 419 (1827).

Regulations of foreign commerce which Congress has enacted (or possesses authority to enact) may be divided into (1) those aimed at promoting trade, or at all events American shipping,[1] (2) those aimed at restricting or preventing trade, and (3) general rules looking to safety and convenience.

It would be difficult to name any national policy which the government of the United States has pursued longer and more consistently than that of protecting and promoting the foreign trade of our people. The very first Congress passed acts with this in view; and to a considerable extent the legislative and diplomatic history of the country from that day onwards could be told in terms of efforts to open new markets for American goods abroad, to secure and maintain equal opportunity for American traders, and to build up relations and agencies calculated to promote these ends. The diplomatic and consular services have been, and are, used to assemble and transmit needed information; with active congressional support, the Department of Commerce—especially through its bureau of domestic and foreign commerce—built up, in the later twenties, a world-wide corps of special commercial agents, though later in part withdrawn; the entire international policy of President Franklin D. Roosevelt, although far transcending the interests of commerce, was designed, along with other and even greater objectives, to make the United States more of a trading nation than ever in the past.

The promotion of trade and shipping

As even this brief enumeration suggests, the encouragement of foreign trade is the business of no single branch or agency of the government; the president, several of the executive departments, many bureaus and services, and of course Congress, are heavily involved. Thinking here, however, primarily of the rôle of Congress, we find promotional and regulatory activities including the following: (1) legislation and appropriations supporting trade-promotion personnel and efforts of the executive branch; (2) exemption, by the Webb Act of 1918,[2] of American export companies from the restrictions of the anti-trust laws, so long as certain conditions are met; (3) authorization in 1913 of national banks having a capital and surplus amounting to a million dollars to establish branches in foreign countries to facilitate business relations, together with assent to an executive order of 1934 establishing a special bank in Washington—the Export-Import Bank—"to facilitate exports and imports and the exchange of commodities between the United States and other nations;" and (4) enactment of a reciprocal trade agreement law in 1934 (four times renewed since) conferring on the president wide latitude in stimulating trade by reducing tariff duties.[3] Important legislation, too, has been aimed not only at increased exports and imports, but at encouraging the transportation of them in American ships; and this effort

The rôle of Congress

[1] In relation to both foreign and domestic commerce, the power to *regulate* has always been construed to include the power to *promote*.
[2] 40 *U. S. Stat. at Large,* 516.
[3] See p. 584 above.

has taken two main forms: (1) tonnage duties or taxes based on the cubical capacity of vessels arriving in American ports from foreign countries, and graduated so as to fall more heavily on ships built or owned abroad than on American vessels (or, in lieu of such taxes, higher duties on foreign goods imported in any but American vessels [1]); and (2) laws for the encouragement of an American merchant marine. Under impetus supplied by World War I, Congress in 1916 created a United States Shipping Board for the purpose of developing a greatly needed naval auxiliary and merchant marine; and in 1920 and 1928, the board's powers were expanded along lines more directly related to the promotion of peacetime commerce. Direct subsidies to private steamship lines—such as have been common enough in foreign lands—have generally been strongly opposed in this country. Nevertheless, between 1928 and 1936, substantial subsidies, in disguise, were provided, chiefly in the form of lucrative contracts for carrying the mails overseas; and in the last-mentioned year direct and heavy subsidization was introduced under terms of a Merchant Marine Act in which the government engaged to bear up to half of the cost of constructing merchant ships, and to make up to ship owners and operators the full difference between the cost of operating American and foreign vessels competing for the same business. [2] World War II left the country with a merchant marine out of all proportion to any foreseeable need, and ways and means of reducing it has been a later problem.

Restriction or prohibition of trade

Of congressional regulations restricting or prohibiting foreign trade, three types need only be briefly mentioned. One is general tariff laws which, when having as their principal object, not the production of revenue, but the protection and stimulation of home industries, find their constitutional justification at least as much in the power of Congress to regulate foreign commerce as in the taxing power. Notwithstanding the trade agreement system, designed to promote trade by lowering tariffs, the policy of the country, subscribed to by both leading political parties, is still that of protecting American industry and agriculture by a system of duties on imports from abroad; and of course this means that a protective tariff law is by intention a measure for restricting foreign trade— imports directly and exports indirectly, since foreign peoples cannot buy

---

[1] The constitution expressly forbids the states to levy tonnage duties without the consent of Congress. Such permission was, however, granted in numerous instances in the early history of the country for the purpose of enabling states having harbors to improve them. When the national government assumed the work of harbor improvement, construction of lighthouses, buoys, etc., the main motive for granting such privileges disappeared.

[2] This act of 1936 also replaced the United States Shipping Board with a United States Maritime Commission, under which ship construction was pushed to new heights during the recent war, chiefly in government-owned plants operated by private concerns. In 1937, the Commission submitted to Congress a comprehensive *Economic Survey of the American Merchant Marine* (Washington, D. C., 1937). Cf. C. D. Lane, *What Citizens Should Know About the Merchant Marine* (New York, 1941).

in the American market unless they can also sell.[1] A second type of restrictive regulation takes the form of limiting (or in the case of persons not eligible for naturalization, forbidding outright) the immigration of aliens into the United States. Immigration is commerce and could be controlled by Congress on that basis even if the regulation of it were not also an incident of the power of a sovereign government to manage its foreign relations. Finally, and of more drastic nature, are embargoes such as have been laid several times in our history (*e.g.*, in 1794, in 1812, and during World War I) suspending commerce completely with all or specified countries or (under some exports-licensing plan) in specified commodities. Sometimes the object has been to lessen the likelihood of the United States being drawn into a foreign war, or to serve as a weapon in a war actually going on; sometimes, to prevent aid being given to revolution or aggression in a foreign country; sometimes—as amidst the defense effort preceding the recent war—to conserve materials and products urgently needed for this country's own security;[2] sometimes—as during the period of industrial reconversion after 1945—to prevent undue drain upon the domestic supply of given commodities.[3] But in any case the power to impose the ban resides in Congress—although the president may be permitted to exercise it (as in 1940) under delegated congressional authority.

Perhaps the largest and most varied class of congressional regulations relating to foreign trade is that consisting of navigation or inspection laws, enacted by the first Congress and on numerous occasions since, and now enforced by a bureau of marine inspection and navigation in the Department of Commerce.[4] Objects in mind have been the protection of American shipping, the stimulation of shipbuilding, safeguarding the health and safety of passengers, and promoting the well-being of seamen. Notable among measures having the last-mentioned purpose was the LaFollette Seamen's Act of 1915.[5]

Regulations in the interest of safety or convenience

---

[1] Tariff legislation and reciprocal trade agreements have been considered elsewhere (see pp. 580-585 above).

[2] The Neutrality Act of 1937, under which the president would have had power to cut off shipments of munitions to Japan and China during the war starting in that year, was never invoked; but the National Defense Act of 1940, authorizing a scheme of exports-licensing, became the basis for drastic restrictions by executive order on the export of war supplies of nearly every character to not only Japan but other countries apart from Great Britain.

[3] By March, 1947, the wartime list of items subject to export control had been reduced from a peak of over 3,000 to approximately 500. In the following July, however, Congress, at President Truman's request, extended controls over exports and imports in critical short supply here and abroad, in order to "protect the economy of the United States as well as discharge our international responsibilities." See *N. Y. Times,* July 16, 1947. Exports of gasoline and oil to Russia were among the newly restricted items.

[4] Most of these regulations apply also to coastal vessels and to shipping on the Great Lakes when involved in interstate or foreign commerce. See J. G. B. Hutchins, "One Hundred and Fifty Years of American Navigation Policy," *Quar. Jour. of Econ.,* LIII, 238-260 (Feb., 1939).

[5] 38 *U. S. Stat. at Large,* 1164.

The Regulation of Interstate Commerce

The pro-
motional
aspect

The national government has a long record of promoting interstate as well as foreign trade. To be sure, the emphasis is somewhat differently placed in the two cases. With respect to trade abroad, effort is directed primarily to expanding the outlets for American goods—to influencing or inducing peoples of other countries to buy our products. In the interstate field, the effort is not, at least directly, to swell the volume of trade, but rather to expand and improve the facilities with which trade (or more properly commerce in all its forms) is carried on. Many indeed are the activities which in one way or another contribute to this end—certainly such basic ones as maintaining the currency system, the banking system, and the postal system, but also, in earlier days, promoting Western railroad building by grants of land, and, in our own time, aiding the states in the development of a nation-wide network of motor roads, creating the Inland Waterways Corporation for the stimulation and operation of inland water traffic, equipping the major airways of the country with operating and safety devices (also furnishing financial assistance in the form of lucrative air-mail contracts), providing facilities needed for coastwise traffic and excluding foreign vessels from participating in such traffic, and many other services that might be mentioned. Interstate commerce could never have attained its present proportions without the national government's help in a score of ways.

The reg-
ulative
aspect

What
interstate
commerce
includes

Turning, however, rather to the regulative aspect, we have first the question of precisely when commerce becomes interstate (and hence subject to congressional regulation) and how long it remains such. With slight qualifications to be mentioned presently, the regulation of commercial transactions begun, wholly carried on, and completed within a single state falls exclusively to the authorities of that state.[1] The moment, however, such a transaction crosses a state boundary it ceases to be intrastate, and becomes interstate, commerce. Not only does the interstate character attach to a shipment of goods, under such circumstances, as soon as it is delivered by the shipper at the freight-office, warehouse, or depot of a common carrier, *i.e.*, a railroad, steamship line, or express company, but, by judicial interpretation, it continues to adhere to the transaction throughout the entire journey and until the goods have been delivered to the consignee. Only then do the authorities of the state in which they have arrived have a right to tax them or regulate their sale or use.

The
scope of
congres-
sional
control

Again with slight qualifications pointed out below, Congress has *exclusive* authority to regulate whatever falls within the broad range of interstate commerce—whether commerce carried on by land or by water,

---

[1] For the enforcement of its own regulations relating to commerce, practically every state has some administrative board or commission, variously called a railway commission, a public utilities commission, or a commerce commission. See p. 954 below (in complete edition of this book).

partly by land and partly by water, by air, or in any other manner. And the wide sweep of this power is well illustrated by the situation as to water-borne traffic. Wherever navigable waters form, either in their natural condition or by artificial union with other waters, a continuous highway over which commerce is carried on between two or more states, or with a foreign country, they become "navigable waters of the United States," whose use Congress may control as an incident of the power to regulate foreign and interstate commerce. Even though a river is not navigable naturally and no improvements are contemplated, the Supreme Court has held that it may be classified as navigable if it can be made so by "reasonable improvement." And the commerce power is not restricted to considerations of navigation. "Flood protection, watershed development, recovery of the cost of improvements through utilization of power, are likewise parts of commerce control.... The authority of the government over the stream is as broad as the needs of commerce." [1]

Moreover, even in the immediate field of transportation, congressional power over interstate commerce does not stop with the mere movement of persons, commodities, livestock, or intelligence from state to state; it includes also the relations of those engaged in such transportation with their employees. Thus Congress may legally require railway companies to equip their trains with safety appliances, to reduce the number of hours a day which their employees work, to grant employees compensation when injured in the course of their employment, to bargain collectively with employees' representatives, and to institute retirement or pension systems; and all of these things it has actually done.

In addition, just as there may be embargoes upon foreign commerce, so there may be limitations upon, or even outright prohibitions of, commerce among the states; the original constitution explicitly recognized this by forbidding Congress to put a stop to the slave trade prior to 1808. The principle now governing in the matter was laid down by the Supreme Court in 1925 as follows: "Congress can certainly regulate interstate commerce to the extent of forbidding and punishing the use of such commerce as an agency to promote immorality, dishonesty, or the spread of any evil or harm to the people of other states from the state of origin. In doing this, it is merely exercising the police power, for the benefit of the public, within the field of interstate commerce." [2] In accordance with this view, Congress has prohibited the transportation from state to state of lottery tickets, "filled" milk, stolen property, and women for immoral purposes; in the Webb-Kenyon Act of 1913, it prohibited shipments of intoxicating liquor into "dry" states (a prohibition later written into the constitution in the Twenty-first Amendment); in 1929, it divested prison-made goods of their interstate aspect when shipped in interstate commerce and made their admission into a state a matter for state deter-

---

[1] United States v. Appalachian Electric Power Co., 311 U. S. 377 (1940).
[2] Brooks v. United States, 257 U. S. 432 (1925).

mination; in the so-called "Lindbergh Law" of 1932, it made kidnapping a federal offense when the victim is taken across state lines; in the Securities Act of 1933, it closed the channels of interstate commerce (as well as the mails) to dealers in securities neglecting or refusing to register under the law; and all of these actions, where challenged judicially, have been fully upheld. In attempting in 1916 to curb child labor by debarring from interstate commerce commodities produced with the aid of such labor, it was balked by the decision in Hammer *v.* Dagenhart. But, as noted elsewhere, the power then denied won full acceptance twenty-three years later when the Fair Labor Standards Act, with its child labor restrictions, was fully sustained.[1]

Relations of federal and state power   Of a vast number of commercial transactions and operations, it is easy to say that they are wholly subject to state control, and of others it is equally easy to say that, being clearly of an interstate nature, they are entirely removed from such control; and if all could be classified so readily, few if any doubts about the respective jurisdictions of state and federal authorities in this field would arise. Many commercial transactions and operations, however, cannot be made to fit into either of two such mutually exclusive categories, and a good deal of confusion and of litigation has resulted, with some overlapping of state and federal laws. In the realm of taxation, the situation is fairly clear; the states may tax property (*e.g.*, railroads) within their bounds even though employed for interstate purposes, but may not tax transactions in either interstate or foreign commerce, or the gross receipts derived from them, or the sale of goods intended for shipment into a different state, or indeed impose any financial burden on interstate commercial *business* as distinct from property. In a different direction, however, there is more difficulty. The states have a broad and basic police power, entitling them to regulate almost everything in the interest of public health, safety, morals, and general well-being. The power, of course, extends to transportation; and some regulations in that field can hardly be kept from affecting interstate, as well as purely intrastate, commerce. Moreover, within limitations, regulations having such application have been sustained by the courts— although plenty of others have been overthrown. Thus, while a state may not limit the length of trains running in interstate traffic or apply a "Jim Crow" law to interstate bus passengers,[2] it may require all engineers operating within its borders, even on through trains, to be tested for color-blindness. If in reviewing a state's police regulations impinging upon interstate commerce and on that account challenged, the Supreme Court finds their main purpose to be the protection of the health or safety, or promotion of the convenience, of the state's own inhabitants, or that they are primarily of only local application, they are likely to be

[1] See p. 728 below. The action mentioned also prohibits interstate transportation of goods produced under conditions of hours and wages not conforming to standards specified in the legislation.

[2] Morgan *v.* Virginia, 328 U. S. 373 (1946).

upheld as not amounting to any substantial invasion of the authority of Congress. If, however, they are regarded otherwise, they will almost certainly be overruled.[1] And the upshot is to place all instrumentalities of interstate commerce, even though employed in intrastate commerce as well, within the almost exclusive federal jurisdiction indicated above. Not only so, but the federal government can reach down into the states and impose controls upon their own instrumentalities if and when deemed essential to making its control over interstate transportation fully effective. For example, if cars employed only in local transportation are hauled as part of a train along with cars used in interstate transportation, they must be equipped with safety appliances required by the federal Safety Appliance Act, lest they impede or endanger interstate transportation;[2] and to guard against low intrastate rates that might throw an undue burden on interstate traffic (as well as to save carriers the trouble of simultaneously administering two or more sets of rates), state-made railroad rates lower than interstate rates are invariably invalidated.[3]

Aside from land grants to railroads and appropriations for the improvement of rivers and harbors, little national legislation relating specifically to interstate commerce was enacted until some sixty years ago; and the first form of such commerce to challenge serious attention was railroad transportation. Railroads naturally took on an interstate character at an early stage of their development. While, however, federal lands and subsidies were lavished upon them, regulation of their operations was long left entirely to the states, and it was only after the Civil War, when railway-building set in on a greatly increased scale and the inadequacy of state regulation was forced upon public attention, that demand arose for control by national authority. By the later seventies and the eighties, abuses calling for remedy were many and glaring. Railroad stocks and bonds, often issued without adequate backing, fluctuated wildly in the money markets; bankruptcies engineered by speculators involved honest investors in disaster; despite such efforts as the states could make within their restricted spheres, passenger and freight rates were pushed to the

Federal regulation of railroads

---

[1] The subject of interstate trade barriers is pertinent here, but has been considered on pp. 124-126 above. In general, the courts have not interfered with such barriers, as being indirect rather than direct burdens on interstate commerce.

[2] Southern Ry. Co. v. United States, 222 U. S. 20 (1911).

[3] After interstate rates were raised in pursuance of the Transportation Act of 1920, many states sought to preserve a lower level of rates within their boundaries. In Wisconsin R. R. Commission v. C. B. and Q. R. R. Co., 257 U. S. 563, the Supreme Court ruled that this could not lawfully be done. In the famous Shreveport case of 1914, the Supreme Court held that a state rate-making authority may not discriminate against an out-of-state commercial center by authorizing disproportionally low freight rates in behalf of such centers within the state (Houston, East and West Texas Ry. Co. v. United States, 234 U. S. 342 (1914)—arising out of an effort of the Texas railway commission to maintain rates eastward from Dallas to other Texas points a third lower than those from Shreveport, La., to the same points, notwithstanding that the distances from Shreveport were in some instances less). In this same case, the Court, indeed, laid down the broad and general principle that "whenever the interstate and intrastate transactions of carriers are so related that the government of the one involves the control of the other," Congress has full power to regulate both classes of transactions.

highest levels that the traffic would stand; special favors, in the form of preferential rates or of rebates, were shown certain shippers as against others; altogether, the business was carried on with little responsibility to the public, and with plenty of discriminative and other dubious, if not clearly fraudulent, practices.

The Interstate Commerce Act (1887) and its expansion

The upshot of rising popular protest was the passage by Congress, in 1887, of an Act to Regulate Commerce,[1] forbidding excessive charges, discriminations, and other unfair practices, and creating a special agency —the Interstate Commerce Commission—to administer and enforce the principles and rules laid down. Much additional legislation was required later, as railroad transportation raised new problems and as regulation was extended to other and newer forms of commerce. There was a Hepburn Act of 1906, an Esch-Cummins Transportation Act of 1920, a Motor Carrier Act of 1935, a Transportation Act of 1940, and a long line of other statutes. Moreover, all of the laws underwent amendment and expansion; and of course much was added by judicial interpretation. The heart of the vast regulatory system built up over two full generations remains, however, the pioneer act of 1887, to which, indeed, most later legislation was assimilated as, in both form and effect, amending annexes. Under it and the laws and decisions supplementing it is now regulated all interstate commerce carried on by railroads, by common carriers by water (both inland and coastal), by express companies, by sleeping-car and other private-car companies, by motor-bus companies, and by pipe lines except those for the transportation of gas and water; likewise, bridges, ferries, car-floats, and lighters, and indeed terminal and other facilities of whatsoever character when used in the interstate transportation of persons or goods. Until 1934, the act applied also to instrumentalities and facilities used for the transmission of intelligence by means of electricity, such as telegraph, telephone, cable, and wireless systems. These, however, are now provided for in a separate Communications Act of the year mentioned; and, as we shall see, air-borne commerce and radio-broadcasting likewise have their separate laws and distinct administrative authorities.[2]

Restrictions imposed

Upon railroads—and, so far as applicable, upon all other instrumentalities of public service subject to the basic law—are imposed numerous restrictions, each prompted by some earlier abuse. Thus, (1) rates for the transportation of persons and freight must be just and reasonable, and calculated to yield a "fair return" on the value of the property employed; (2) rebating, directly or indirectly, and undue discrimination or preference between persons, corporations, or localities are prohibited under severe penalties; (3) charging a higher rate for a short haul than for a long one over the same line in the same direction is forbidden, except in certain special instances when authorized by the Interstate Commerce

---

[1] 27 *U. S. Stat. at Large,* 379.
[2] See pp. 634-636 below.

Commission; (4) free transportation may be granted only to narrowly restricted classes of persons; (5) railroads are forbidden, except in a few special cases, to operate, own, or control, or to have any interest in, any competing carrier by water; (6) except under strict supervision of the Commission, competing lines may not combine, merge their receipts, and apportion resulting profits; (7) carriers may not transport commodities (except timber and its products) in which they have a direct property interest; and (8) they may issue long-term securities, purchase or build additional lines, or abandon old lines, only with the Commission's consent.

In addition to these restraints, numerous positive duties have been imposed. For example, (1) printed schedules of rates must be kept open for public inspection, and changes in them may be made only after permission has been granted by the Interstate Commerce Commission; (2) full and complete annual reports must be made to the Commission, covering such matters, and arranged in such form, as the Commission prescribes; (3) all accounts must be kept according to a uniform system authorized by the Commission; (4) in case of injury to any of its employees, a carrier must grant pecuniary compensation, unless the accident was caused by the willful act or negligence of the injured party; (5) the standard or basic work-day for railway employees engaged in the operation of trains is eight hours, and carriers must conform their wage schedules to this standard, and grant overtime pay; (6) all trains engaged in interstate commerce must be equipped with automatic safety appliances; and (7) all railway companies so engaged must maintain compulsory retirement and pension systems for their superannuated employees.[1] *Duties imposed*

The Interstate Commerce Commission—the regulating agency charged with enforcing the regulations indicated and innumerable minor ones as well—consists of eleven members appointed by the president and Senate for seven-year terms, and has a staff of some 1,600 clerks, attorneys, examiners, statisticians, investigators, and technical experts, organized in sixteen major bureaus, each under a director or chief who reports directly to a commissioner or to the full Commission. The commissioners work largely in divisions, or panels, of not fewer than three members each; and a decision of a division has the same force and effect as a *The I.C.C.*

[1] A Railroad Retirement Act of 1934, requiring railroads to contribute to a pension fund for superannuated employees, was invalidated by the Supreme Court in 1935 as "in no proper sense a regulation of interstate transportation." R. R. Retirement Board *v.* Alton R. R., 295 U. S. 330. Eventually, under encouragement from President Franklin D. Roosevelt, the roads and their organized employees themselves worked out a retirement plan under which both are taxed to create a fund from which the latter receive annuities, death benefits, and unemployment compensation; and laws of 1937 and 1938 embodying the resulting arrangements were never challenged judicially. Employees of common carriers other than railroads are not covered, but instead come under the system of old-age and survivors insurance described in a later chapter. See pp. 754-756 below. Railroad employers and employees have to pay higher payroll taxes than do employers and employees under the old-age and survivors system, but the benefits paid are substantially larger. See L. Meriam, *Relief and Social Security* (Washington, D. C., 1946), 141-163.

decision of the Commission itself—subject to the entire Commission granting a rehearing, and finally to court appeal. Any person, corporation, municipality, or other private or public group may lodge with the Commission a complaint concerning any alleged infraction of the interstate commerce laws, and the Commission, acting ordinarily through one of its panels, must institute an inquiry. If preliminary investigation discloses that the complaint may be well founded, a hearing follows, on lines not unlike those to be observed in a court of justice: plaintiff and defendant are represented by attorneys; books, papers, and other materials (which the Commission has full power to order produced) are placed in evidence; witnesses are examined; and at the end the Commission embodies its conclusion or finding in an order enforceable in the federal courts, although also with right of appeal to those courts by the party affected adversely. Orders may relate to rates, quality or conditions of service, or any one of literally scores of other things falling within the scope of the laws; and disobedience renders the offender liable to prosecution.[1]

Control over rates

Under the original law, the Commission did not have power to make rates, either upon its own initiative or upon complaint of shippers that existing rates were unreasonable. Ultimately, however, although only after a vigorous campaign of popular education, and in the face of persistent opposition from the carriers—the necessity of conferring extensive rate-making power was brought home to the national mind; and under laws passed in 1906 and 1920, the Commission is authorized, on complaint and after hearing, not only to fix "just and reasonable" rates, regulations, and practices, but also to prescribe definite maximum or minimum, or both maximum and minimum, charges. The resulting burden, although inevitable, is indeed a heavy one; for rate-making is no simple operation, and the Commission finds itself much of the time under cross-fire from shippers and other interests clamoring for lower charges, and, on the other hand, carriers insisting that rising operating costs or other factors call for rate increases. On the theory that to compel property "affected with a public interest" to be used without suitable compensation would amount to confiscation, it is, in general, conceded that rates should be such as to insure a "fair return" on the "value" of the property involved.[2] But upon what constitutes "fair return," and especially as to how "value" is to be determined, there can be, and is, a great

---

[1] The Commission's dependence upon the assistance of outside people in carrying on its work, and the methods employed by special interests to influence its policies and decisions, are brought out in E. P. Herring, "Special Interests and the Interstate Commerce Commission," *Amer. Polit. Sci. Rev.*, XVII, 738-751, 899-917 (Oct.-Dec., 1933). For a full summary of the duties of the Commission, see any recent edition of the *Official Congressional Directory* or of the *United States Government Manual*.

[2] Smyth v. Ames, 169 U. S. 466 (1898). Two Supreme Court decisions of 1942 and 1944, however, considerably weakened the principle and completely overturned a rate-making formula laid down in Smyth v. Ames. See Federal Power Commission v. Natural Gas Pipe Line Co. of America, 315 U. S. 575 (1942), and Federal Power Commission v. Hope Natural Gas Co., 320 U. S. 591 (1944).

variety of opinion. The matter is too involved to be discussed here, but it may be observed that, whereas until later years the Supreme Court was inclined to support valuation based (for example, in the case of a railroad) on what it would cost currently to reproduce the road and its facilities, less an allowance for depreciation, the present tendency is rather to favor valuation in terms of the amount of money actually put into constructing and developing the road from its beginning, again of course with deduction for depreciation.

Some Newer Areas of Regulation

Historically, the regulation of interstate commerce has, until later years, been largely a matter of regulating railroads. A good deal of such commerce, however, has always been water-borne—in vessels plying the coastal waters of the country or its rivers and lakes. Notwithstanding that the power of Congress to control such water-borne commerce was perfectly clear, for a long time such regulation (more properly promotion) as was undertaken took the form almost entirely of federal planning and expenditure for the improvement of rivers and harbors; and over the years billions of dollars have been spent for this purpose, sometimes legitimately and wisely, but often from motives that had more to do with politics than with navigation—river and harbor bills having traditionally been a favorite source of congressional "pork." Only in the Transportation Act of 1940[1] did Congress get around to instituting a genuine system of regulation of rates, services, and management for trade carried on by water (or partly by water and partly by rail), on lines broadly similar to those long applying to railroads. Already aptly termed "the economic supreme court of the American transportation world," the Interstate Commerce Commission now found itself with a considerably widened jurisdiction.[2]

1. Inland and coastwise water transportation

Meanwhile, however, that jurisdiction had been enormously extended also in another direction. The automobile had been introduced, and trucks and buses had come into use. For a good while, distances covered were usually limited and no regulation was deemed necessary beyond state or local provisions concerning licensing and safety. As truck and bus business developed, however, on something approaching its present huge scale, serious difficulties and abuses arose—cut-throat competition between companies and between them and the railroads, under-payment of employees, laxity about accident insurance, dubious financing; and although remedial measures were instituted by some states, it became apparent that the business had so largely assumed an interstate charac-

2. Motor transportation

---

[1] 54 *U. S. Stat. at Large,* 898.

[2] It may be mentioned again that all commerce on inland waters, as well as all coastwise trade, is, by act of Congress, restricted to American vessels, and that a considerable share of it in the central portions of the country is in the hands of a self-supporting government establishment, the Inland Waterways Corporation (in the Department of Commerce), operating the Federal Barge Lines.

ter that, as the Interstate Commerce Commission long urged, the problem
was fundamentally one for the national government. In 1935, therefore,
Congress passed a Motor Carrier Act [1] bringing all interstate truck and
bus lines within the pale of federal law and making the I.C.C. the
regulating authority. If intending to operate across state boundaries, a
truck or bus company must initially secure a certificate of convenience
and necessity from the Commission; and thereupon its financing, rates,
hours of labor, safety appliances, and general level of service become
subject to that body's supervision almost exactly as in the case of
railroads.[2]

3. Electrical communications

As illustrated by motor transport (and indeed, if one goes back far
enough, by the railroad and the steamship), science and technology are
responsible for many new modes of transportation, progressively expanding the scope of "commerce," and adding by so much to the problem of
regulating it. In the field of communications (which no less than transportation is embraced in "commerce"), they have added, if possible,
even more. In most European countries, the telegraph, the telephone, and
radio are government-owned and operated, directly or through auxiliary
corporations. Apart from some limited ownership and operation of facilities for its own use by the national government, all of these instrumentalities in the United States have been developed and are owned and
operated privately; and since all more important ones are necessarily
interstate in scope, all come within the range of federal control over
commerce. Originally, telegraph and telephone regulation fell to the
Interstate Commerce Commission; although when, in 1927, it was belatedly recognized as necessary to institute similar regulation of radio-
broadcasting, that function was assigned rather to a separate Federal
Radio Commission, charged with issuing licenses, assigning wave-lengths,
and exercising some supervision over advertising. This latter arrangement
did not work well; and in 1934 the desirability of a new plan for radio
control, combined with a conviction that the Interstate Commerce Commission was expending its time and energies on transportation matters
to the neglect of problems connected with interstate electrical communications, led Congress to pass a comprehensive Communications Act [3] (a)
abolishing the Radio Commission and transferring its work to a new
Federal Communications Commission, and (b) withdrawing telegraph
and telephone regulation from the I.C.C.[4] and vesting it in the new
agency, which therefore now has for its province the entire field of interstate (and to a more limited extent foreign) communications by both

[1] 49 *U. S. Stat. at Large*, 543-547; W. H. Wagner, *A Legislative History of the
Motor Carrier Act of 1935* (Washington, D. C., 1935).
[2] Excepted from provisions of the law are trucks carrying newspapers, those belonging to farmers' coöperative associations, taxicabs, and certain other classes of vehicles
[3] 48 *U. S. Stat. at Large*, 1064.
[4] Regulation of cable lines to foreign countries also, although control over these
has always been to a considerable extent in the president.

wire and radio.[1] Speaking generally, the powers, functions, and procedures of the Communications Commission are similar to those of the
I.C.C., with, in the case of radio, the allotment and control of use of the
air lanes in accordance with "public interest, convenience, and necessity"
one of its most formidable tasks. The new arrangement for telegraph,
telephone, and cable regulation in 1934 marked the only instance in over
sixty years of the jurisdiction of the I.C.C. being narrowed.[2]

Shortly after World War I (which imparted a considerable impetus to
aviation), a standing interstate conference having as its object the
promotion of uniformity in state legislation [3] brought forward a Uniform
State Law for Aëronautics; and numerous states adopted it. As time
went on, however, much, if not most, flying became interstate; and in
1926 Congress passed an Air Commerce Act applying to all interstate
aviation and giving a bureau of air commerce in the Department of
Commerce power to fix standards of safety, to test and license aviators,
and to make rules governing air traffic. This agency has since been superseded, and (after a somewhat bewildering succession of changes) there
have come to be, since a Civil Aëronautics Act [4] was passed in 1938, two
main interrelated federal agencies with functions of the kind: a Civil
Aëronautics Administration and a Civil Aëronautics Board—the former
concerning itself principally with mapping, lighting, and marking interstate airways, providing regular and emergency landing fields, licensing
planes and pilots, and fostering aviation research; the latter, principally
with the quasi-legislative and quasi-judicial functions of controlling
rates for the transportation of passengers, mail, and goods, promulgating
safety regulations, investigating aircraft accidents, and suspending or

*4. Avia-
tion*

[1] The states, however, retain some control over telephone companies, especially
their local rates.
[2] The Communications Commission has seven full-time members, appointed by
the president and Senate for seven-year terms. For a full account of it and its work,
see H. H. Trachsel, *Public Utility Regulation* (Chicago, 1947), Chap. x. On the earlier
agency of radio regulation, see L. F. Schmeckebier, "The Federal Radio Commission," *Service Monographs*, No. 65 (Baltimore, 1932); and cf. "The American *v.* the
British System of Radio Control" [Symposium], *Cong. Digest*, XII, 202-224 (Aug.-
Sept., 1933). For later discussions, see C. J. Friedrich and E. Sternberg, "Congress and
the Control of Radio-Broadcasting," *Amer. Polit. Sci. Rev.*, XXXVII, 797-818, 1014-
1026 (Oct., Dec., 1943); M. J. McManus, "Federal Legislation Regulating Radio,"
So. Calif. Law Rev., XX, 146-171 (Feb., 1947); T. P. Robinson, *Radio Networks and
the Federal Government* (New York, 1943); and especially L. White, *The American
Radio* (Chicago, 1947), an excellent study forming part of the report of the Commission on Freedom of the Press (see p. 161, note 2, above).
As an amendment to the Communications Act of 1934, Congress, in April, 1946,
passed an "anti-Petrillo" act (60 *U. S. Stat. at Large*, 89), aimed at curbing arbitrary demands and edicts of James C. Petrillo, president of the American Federation
of Musicians, by establishing criminal penalties for "coercive practices affecting
radio-broadcasting." Under the measure, broadcasters may not be coerced (1) to hire
more employees than they need; (2) to pay for services not performed; (3) to pay
unions for using phonograph records; (4) to pay a second time for broadcasting a
transcription of a previous program; or (5) to halt programs originating outside of
the United States, or any type of non-commercial, educational, or cultural program
in which the participants receive no pay for their services. Tested in the courts, the
act was upheld in United States *v.* Petrillo, 67 Sup. Ct. 1538 (1947).
[3] See pp. 921-922 below.
[4] 52 *U. S. Stat. at Large*, 973.

revoking licenses. Although placed in the Department of Commerce for "housekeeping" purposes, both are more truly independent establishments—in form, branches of a Civil Aëronautics Authority, even though this "Authority" is merely a name, all of its functions being performed either by the Civil Aëronautics Administrator or the Civil Aëronautics Board. In a domain in which strict uniformity of rules and practices is peculiarly desirable, the states have in most instances risen to the need by incorporating all federal-made regulations into their own aviation codes.

To insure more adequate airport facilities throughout the country, Congress in 1946 passed a Federal Airport Act [1] appropriating five hundred million dollars for the continental United States and twenty millions for Alaska, Hawaii, and Puerto Rico, over a period of seven years, the federal allotments to be matched by local funds. Direction of the federally-aided program falls to the Civil Aëronautics Administration, which, through its Office of Federal Airways, is charged also with the planning, construction, maintenance, and operation of the Federal Airways System, now extended throughout Alaska, Hawaii, the Panama Canal Zone, and other United States possessions and totaling more than 43,000 miles of airways.[2]

The Department of Commerce

Origins   Impressed with the growing urgency of problems of commerce and industry, and acting on strong recommendation of President Theodore Roosevelt, Congress in 1903 added to the then eight executive departments a Department of Commerce and Labor. Ten years later, Labor was set off as a separate department. Commerce was left, however, with a field of activity already broad, and in later times so expanded that any survey of the Department's present eighteen or twenty principal offices and services would take one over an enormous area of government enterprise.[3] Besides the department head, principal personnel consists chiefly of an under-secretary, two assistant secretaries, a solicitor, and various directors of divisions and other officials of comparable rank; and a field service charged with keeping in touch with trade and business

[1] 60 *U. S. Stat. at Large,* 170.

[2] M. W. Willebrandt, "Federal Control of Air Commerce," *Jour. of Air Law,* XI, 204-217 (July, 1940); D. H. Green, "Coöperative Efforts of Federal, State, and Local Governments under a Federal-Aid Airport Plan," *State Government,* XVIII, 75-78 (May, 1945); "The States and a National System of Airports," *ibid.,* XI, 81-84 (May, 1945); W. C. Green, "The War Against the States in Aviation," *Va. Law Rev.,* XXXI, 835-864 (Sept., 1945); "Aviation Transport," *Law and Contemporary Problems,* XI, 429-630 (Winter-Spring, 1946).

Another form of federal regulation of interstate commerce which might be spoken of here is that applying to the transmission of electric energy across state lines. The subject of water-power will, however, be touched upon later in connection with the conservation of resources. (See pp. 706-707 below.)

[3] It will be noted, however, that, in general, *regulating* functions are not included, but rather are assigned to independent quasi-legislative, quasi-judicial establishments like the Interstate Commerce Commission and the Federal Communications Commission.

throughout the country and making the resources of the Department readily available is organized under fourteen regional and sixty-two district offices operating from principal cities.[1]

Central to the departmental structure is the Bureau of Foreign and Domestic Commerce, dating from 1912 and sometimes described as "the business man's representative in government." As developed notably during Herbert Hoover's tenure as secretary of commerce (1921-29), the bureau was for many years vigorously engaged not only in compiling statistics and otherwise advancing commercial interests at home, but in studying business trends throughout the world, promoting American export trade, and rendering services of many kinds to American business-men abroad. As a result of having perhaps somewhat overreached itself as a promoter, and also of drastic curtailment of foreign-trade oppor-tunities in the war years after 1939, activities on the foreign front were sharply reduced, and in the years mentioned a Foreign Commerce Service which the bureau had built up was transferred to the Department of State. Strong desire to recover and expand foreign trade after the war led, however, in 1945, to some reorganization directed to that end, and an Office of International Trade is now one of the bureau's principal divisions. At home, the bureau continues to compile and publish statistical information, direct the departmental field service and through it main-tain helpful relations with local organizations like chambers of commerce and boards of trade, assist industry in its relations with government agencies and in solving its problems of production, distribution, trans-portation, and marketing; and in line with growing concern over the outlook for small business in the face of tendencies to industrial con-solidation, an Office of Small Business is maintained for studying the problem and doing what it can to protect and promote small-scale manu-facturing and other enterprise.

The Bureau of For-eign and Domestic Commerce

Other branches and activities of the Department, which in most instances can merely be mentioned, include (1) a Coast and Geodetic Survey, which assists mariners by charting the coastlines of the United States and its dependencies, as well as lake and river beds and ocean currents, and which also makes seismological observations with a view to reducing earthquake hazards; (2) a Weather Bureau (transferred from the Department of Agriculture in 1940), operating the basic national system of meteorological observations, analyzing the resulting data, and preparing and distributing weather forecasts and warnings; (3) a Patent Office (about which something will be said in the next chapter) admin-istering the patent laws enacted by Congress; (4) the Civil Aëronautics Administration mentioned earlier; (5) the board administering the Inland Waterways Corporation, also noted; and finally two agencies—(6) the

Other divisions and services

[1] A full view of the department's organization and activities will be found in any recent edition of the *United States Government Manual*. Cf. latest annual report of the secretary of commerce.

National Bureau of Standards and (7) the Bureau of the Census—on each of which a word of comment may be offered.[1]

Established in 1901, the National Bureau of Standards was originally designed primarily to compare and test standards of measurement (dimension, weight, temperature, and the like) employed in scientific investigation, industry, commerce, and educational institutions with standards adopted or recognized by the government, and thus to promote uniformity of usage in fields in which precision is required or at least useful. With the passing years, however, the bureau has developed into a general laboratory for fundamental research in physics, chemistry, and engineering—the greatest of its kind in the country and certainly not surpassed abroad. Much of its work, although not without practical applications, proceeds in the somewhat rarefied atmosphere of pure science. But much also—especially in relation to the testing of materials like minerals, rubber, paper, leather, and plastics, the development and evaluation of new products, and the formulation of commercial standards for manufactured goods—is strictly applied science and as such comes close home to the public. A great deal is done at the request of, or in collaboration with, other agencies of the national government; but the bureau coöperates also with state and local officials, with business and professional groups, and, as indicated (e.g., through sponsorship of quality-guaranteeing labels) with the public itself. A staff numbering more than two thousand—mostly highly-trained scientists and technicians— is employed.

Finally, there is the Bureau of the Census. Charged with carrying out the decennial enumeration required by the constitution, this "greatest fact-finding and figure-counting agency in the world" is responsible also for various supplementary enumerations provided for by statute—for example, a census of agriculture every five years and a census of manufactures every two years. Until a few decades ago, decennial censuses were taken by a force of supervisors and enumerators specially organized on each occasion for the purpose, and when the task was completed the machinery was dismantled, to be set up anew at the next census period. A permanent census office, under a director, was, however, established in 1902,[2] partly with a view to developing an experienced staff, but mainly in order to permit one phase or another of the work—supplementary enumerations and compilations, and classification and interpretation of data—to be carried on continuously. The range of census inquiries has increased greatly, now covering not only population, occupations, wealth, agriculture, and manufactures, but also crime, wholesale and retail trade,

---

[1] In 1942, the functions of a bureau of marine inspection and navigation were distributed between the bureau of customs (Treasury) and the U. S. Coast Guard (then in the Navy Department).

[2] In the Interior Department, but transferred to the Department of Commerce and Labor in 1903, and included in the Department of Commerce since the separation took place in 1913.

foreign trade, state and city finances, and housing;[1] and the resulting published reports, although at first glance sometimes dry and forbidding, yield the student who refuses to grow discouraged comprehensive and illuminating exhibits of the country's social and economic conditions and trends.[2]

REFERENCES

M. Fainsod and L Gordon, *Government and the American Economy* (New York, 1941), Chap. IX.

H. D. Koontz, *Government Control of Business* (Boston, 1941), Chaps. I-XII.

F P. Hall, *Government and Business* (2nd ed., New York, 1939), Chaps. III-V.

H H. Trachsel, *Public Utility Regulation* (Chicago, 1947), Chaps. IX-XI, XIX-XX.

W. W. Willoughby, *Constitutional Law of the United States* (2nd ed., New York, 1929), II, Chaps. XLIII-LX.

E. S. Corwin, *The Constitution and What It Means Today* (10th ed., Princeton, N. J., 1948), 31-48.

————, *The Commerce Power versus States' Rights* (Princeton, N. J., 1936).

G. C. Reynolds, *The Distribution of Power to Regulate Interstate Carriers Between the Nation and the States* (New York, 1928).

V. M. Barnett, Jr., "The Power to Regulate Commerce," *Amer. Polit. Sci. Rev.,* XLI, 1170-1181 (Dec., 1947).

E. R. Johnson, *Government Regulation of Transportation* (New York, 1938).

C. Crumbaker, *Transportation and Politics* (Eugene, Ore., 1940).

B. C. Gavit, *The Commerce Clause of the United States Constitution* (Bloomington, Ind., 1932).

J. E. Kallenbach, *Federal Coöperation with the States Under the Commerce Clause* (Ann Arbor, Mich., 1942).

F. D. G. Ribble, *State and National Power Over Commerce* (New York, 1937).

C. D. Drayton, *Transportation Under Two Masters* (Washington, D. C., 1946).

F. Frankfurter, *The Commerce Clause Under Marshall, Taney, and Waite* (Chapel Hill, N. C., 1937).

I. L. Sharfman, *The Interstate Commerce Commission,* Parts I-IV (New York, 1931-37).

————, "The Interstate Commerce Commission—An Appraisal," *Yale Law Jour.,* XLVI, 915-954 (Apr., 1937).

Geo. Washington Law Rev., V, 289-461 (Mar., 1937). Series of articles on the Interstate Commerce Commission.

E. P. Herring, *Public Administration and the Public Interest* (New York, 1936).

————, *Federal Commissioners; A Study of Their Careers and Qualifications* (Cambridge, Mass., 1936).

S. Chase, *Tomorrow's Trade; Problems of Our Foreign Commerce* (New York, 1945).

P. M. Zeis, *American Shipping Policy* (Princeton, N. J., 1938).

[1] In 1946, the bureau's functions relating to vital statistics were transferred to the Federal Security Agency.

[2] W S. Holt, "The Bureau of the Census," *Service Monographs,* No. 53 (Baltimore, 1929); L. F. Schmeckebier, *The Statistical Work of the National Government* (Baltimore, 1925). On the taking of the sixteenth decennial census in 1940, see *Report of the Secretary of Commerce* (1940), 37-60. Cf. S. Chase, "What the New Census Means," *Pub. Affairs Pamphlets,* No. 56 (New York, 1941).

Because of its gathering and sifting of financial data, the bureau has become, in effect, a national clearing house for information on state and local governmental organization, activities, and finances; indeed, for students of state and local problems its annual reports on state, municipal, and county finances are indispensable.

C. C. Rohlfing, *National Regulation of Aëronautics* (Philadelphia, 1931).

C. E. Puffer, *Air Transportation* (Philadelphia, 1941).

J. H. Frederick, *Commercial Air Transportation* (Chicago, 1942).

G. Goodman, *Government Policy Toward Commercial Aviation* (New York, 1944).

W. Beard, *The Regulation of Pipe Lines as Common Carriers* (New York, 1941).

T. P. Robinson, *Radio Networks and the Federal Government* (New York, 1943).

H. L Elsbree, *Interstate Transmission of Electricity* (Cambridge, Mass., 1931).

C. J. Friedrich and E. Sternberg, "Congress and the Control of Radio-Broadcasting," *Amer. Polit. Sci. Rev.*, XXXVII, 797-818, 999-1013 (Oct., Dec., 1943).

Annual reports of the secretary of commerce, the Interstate Commerce Commission, the Federal Communications Commission, etc.

CHAPTER XXIX

GOVERNMENT AND BUSINESS

The American colonies had experience with the regulation of business and trade by Parliament and to some extent also regulated such matters for themselves. Subsequently, the states took over the function, gradually developing controls now exercised over transportation, banking, insurance, public utilities, and indeed business activities of almost every nature, except as conducted by the national government or involving transactions in interstate or foreign commerce. For a long time after 1789, it was considered that, in general, the field was not one to be occupied by the federal government. To be sure, that government might and should remove impediments to, and otherwise promote the flow of, private business enterprise; and it is not to be forgotten that in the first decade under the constitution the federal government laid business under heavy obligation by putting the national credit on a secure basis, establishing a sound monetary system, chartering a United States Bank, and creating other favorable conditions so notoriously lacking under the Articles of Confederation. Even the measures required for these purposes, however, encountered sturdy opposition, on constitutional or other grounds; and that the federal government should undertake any general regulation or control of business interests, operations, and practices would to most people have seemed altogether undesirable. Later on, it appeared proper enough for national authority to provide roads, build canals, and even lay protective tariffs, thus furnishing facilities, assistance, and encouragement. But even then its function was not to interfere, restrain, or regulate. In so far as restriction was required, the states might provide it. They, too, however, should proceed with moderation; for the country's development, it was believed, would best be served by allowing free scope for competitive private enterprise.[1]

A century and half, however, has brought a remarkable change. Not only does the federal government nowadays encourage and promote business in a multitude of ways not conceived of in Hamilton's and Jefferson's time, but it has swept a mighty regulating arm over virtually the entire field of commercial, industrial, and financial activity, fixing conditions of competition, forbidding practices held socially undesirable, and, under copious legislation associated initially at many points with

Earlier points of view

The different situation today

---

[1] Much of the earlier opposition to federal regulation, while ostensibly directed toward safeguarding the rights of the states, was actually motivated by a desire for no regulation at all.

the New Deal, controlling production, prescribing minimum wages and maximum hours, requiring collective bargaining, and prohibiting false or misleading advertising of commodities and securities. In the recent war period, a peak was reached when industrial establishments were, in effect, told what they might manufacture, when access to necessary materials was scaled according to priorities, and when the prices at which products might be sold were placed under ceilings prescribed from Washington; and even though such wartime controls are now a thing of the past, business continues under broader peacetime federal regulation than in any earlier period of our history. Moreover, a topmost national concern in postwar years, rivalled only by international security, has been the maintenance of business prosperity and the rôle that the federal government ought to play in promoting that objective.

Reasons for the change

At some risk of over-simplification, the main factors in bringing about this vastly augmented control by the federal government over the nation's business may be reduced to four. First of all is the vast expansion of business entailed by the rise of modern industry. As late as the Civil War, American society was still predominantly agrarian. Only sixteen per cent of the people lived in places of eight thousand or more; industrial production was limited and largely of the household type; industrial units outside of the home were mostly small mills and factories, owned by individuals or small companies, and independently operated; "business" consisted largely of trade, transportation (by turnpikes, canals, and later railroads), banking, land deals, and some mining. After the Civil War, however, the country moved rapidly into its present industrial era, characterized by the modern factory system, with its power-driven machinery, its assembly-lines and other mass production techniques, its standardization of products, its wage system, its growth of cities; and business became predominantly the manufacturing and distribution of goods. A second factor leading to increased federal control inevitably followed; and this was the rise of large—eventually huge—business corporations. Before 1870, the industrial corporation hardly existed outside of textile manufacturing in New England; after that date, as enterprise expanded and the economies and other advantages of the corporate way of doing business were more clearly perceived, corporations multiplied in a score of fields and mounted to amazing size and power— familiarly illustrated by the great structures associated with the names of Carnegie and Rockefeller in the domains of steel and oil. From days of small and isolated business enterprises, with little or no pyramiding of managerial authority, the country moved into a period of vast concentrations of enterprise and capital, with corresponding consolidation of management and with all of the possibilities of manipulation and monopoly inherent in such a situation.

Even if these huge businesses had operated only within particular states, they would hardly have been susceptible of adequate regulation by state action alone. But of course they operated far more widely; and a third factor in influencing the national government to expand its control of business was the ramifying interstate and foreign economic empires resulting from the developments described. The great corporations (and indeed many lesser ones) drew their capital from investors all over the country, shipped their products to every state and foreign land, maintained branches and plants in different states and territories, and over the years developed business undertakings and procedures of such scope and character that if they were to be regulated at all, it could be only by a government with nation-wide authority. Finally, the national government's broadened control over business is in these later days accounted for to no small extent by the Supreme Court's newer view in the past decade of the range and scope of federal regulative jurisdiction. After long insisting upon a rigid line of separation between commerce and manufacturing, with the commerce power denied any application to the latter, the justices, as we have seen, finally brought all manufacturing, mining, lumbering, and the like, in so far as having any interstate aspect, within the scope of federal control—with the consequence of sharply increasing the potential range of business regulation from Washington.[1]

The upshot is that, just as in the cases of labor and agriculture, the federal government now controls, as well as assists, business in ways unheard of only a generation or two ago. Before certain of these ways are pointed out, however, two further background factors must be mentioned—first, the solidarity of business as a force in our national life, and second, the influence of business upon government itself. There is no way of knowing precisely how many people in this country are now engaged in business. The number has been estimated at between six and eight millions, depending upon what is considered "business." But at all events the gamut runs all the way from the independent corner grocery to the industrial or financial corporation counting its assets in hundreds of millions, or even billions, of dollars.[2] At first glance, there is little unity in the picture. Small business struggles against big business; independent dealers fight the chains; railroads do battle with bus and air lines; high-cost producers seek political protection against low-cost producers; manufacturers want protective tariffs, importers want none; New England textile interests combat newer similar interests in the South; competition is bitter within industries, and between industries; scores of trade associations do whatever they can to get favors and advantages for their own industries, localities, or regions.

There is, nevertheless, more solidarity than appears. Business interests, large and small, have, as is often said, a "business-man's point of view;"

The unity of business interests

---

[1] See pp. 619-620 above.

[2] In a bulletin of June, 1947, the Committee for Economic Development reported that in 1939, when the latest federal census of business was taken, ninety-eight per cent of all business establishments in the country were small—a million and a half with no employees at all and only 52,000 with more than fifty.

large over-all organizations like the National Association of Manufacturers and the United States Chamber of Commerce encourage and
express this point of view, consolidating sentiment and speaking for the
business community as a whole; although often rivals, textile interests,
iron and steel interests, transportation interests, have common ground
and may work together for common purposes; at many points, big business pulls little business along with it; interlocking directorates and
financial relationships blur the pattern of separateness and harmonize
conflicting interests and objectives. Representatives of "big business"—
bankers, insurance men, corporation executives, newspaper publishers,
and the like—"have their internecine battles and rivalries, but on the
larger issues of public policy they form a solid phalanx of opinion. Inti-
mately knit together by social and financial ties, sitting on the same
boards, exercising the same general responsibilities, they easily develop a
common point of view and a common outlook. Differences there may be
on details of tactics and strategy, but on ultimate objectives there is a
natural and understandable consensus." [1] And solidarity of opinion does
not stop here. Big bankers influence lesser ones, and they still lesser ones
within their radius of contact. So, too, with corporations and industries
of other sorts—influence radiating downwards, indeed, through all levels,
and certainly not excluding the millions of people who, having investments in General Motors or the Pennsylvania Railroad or any one of
thousands of other enterprises, large or small, instinctively incline toward
the viewpoints of those bearing responsibility for operating the business
to the advantage of all concerned. Notwithstanding incessant internal
clashes of interest and policy, therefore, the American business world, by
and large, presents a common front of immense prestige and potentiality.

Business
in
politics

Furthermore, this common front is utilized powerfully for political
purposes. Back of it lie many millions of votes; and while we hear less
of the business vote than of the labor or farmer vote, no one can fail to
perceive that at every presidential and congressional election it is thrown
heavily to some particular presidential candidate, or to the congressional
candidates of a particular party, as against the rest—on some occasions
impressively so, as in favor of the gold-standard McKinley in 1896 or
against Franklin D. Roosevelt in 1936. But it is not through nominations
and elections alone that business seeks to guide national policy. There
are also broad avenues of influence upon the president by advice and
persuasion, upon department heads in their work of administration, upon
the great regulatory commissions like the Federal Trade Commission,
and especially upon Congress in connection with legislation. Here we
enter, of course, the labyrinth of pressure-group activity, including lobbying; and the fact has already been stressed that among the scores of
groups and interests assiduously endeavoring to influence senators and

[1] M. Fainsod and L. Gordon, *Government and the American Economy* (New
York, 1941), 24-25.

representatives to support or oppose given legislative proposals, a prominent place must be given business organizations and groups, from the National Association of Manufacturers down. To be sure, business interests do not always see eye to eye; one may be found pressing for a piece of legislation strongly opposed by others. Representatives of importing concerns will hardly coöperate with representatives of manufacturers' organizations in a campaign for a new protective tariff law. All in all, however, there is a good deal of concerted effort, with even diverse and independent efforts contributing to the development of an attitude or atmosphere favorable to the business point of view in general. There is the technique, too, of utilizing radio, newspapers, motion-pictures, billboard advertising, and pamphlets, not alone to interest the public in buying goods or services, but to create good-will which in turn may transmit itself to lawmakers and administrators and eventuate in the adoption of measures and policies which business, or some segment of it, favors. One of the major lessons which business has learned in the past generation is the folly of ignoring or defying public sentiment—the wisdom, indeed, of cultivating such sentiment in every possible way.

In the relations of government and business in this country today, almost everyone has an interest, indeed something directly at stake—all persons, of course, directly engaged in business activities; all who have money invested in any form of business enterprise; all labor, organized and unorganized, employed in establishments that do business; farmers who buy and sell and borrow, and who often themselves are directly engaged in business, *e.g.*, in coöperative marketing associations; people anxious in any way about government policy in relation to the distribution of wealth; all property owners and users; indeed, the entire mass of consumers—which makes the matter one of truly universal concern.

Some Government Aids to Business

In the previous chapter, we examined the commerce clause of the constitution (which, as emphasized, supplies the constitutional basis for most regulation of business in general) and looked into the ways in which commerce as such is regulated under it. In the remainder of the present chapter, we shall be concerned with (1) some ways, not already touched upon, in which the federal government assists business, as well as individuals not directly engaged in business enterprise; (2) the development of business regulation in general from the later nineteenth century; (3) some newer forms of regulation introduced during the fight for recovery from the depression of the thirties; (4) some more or less temporary forms of regulation accompanying our participation in World War II; and (5) a few aspects of the government's own direct participation in business.

In point of fact, there is not much that the national government undertakes that does not actually or potentially, directly or indirectly, encourage, protect, or otherwise serve the interests of business. The maintenance of friendly intercourse abroad, the stationing of consuls in foreign cities, the upkeep of the Army and Navy for national defense, the preservation of domestic law and order, the regulation of commerce, the subsidizing of shipping interests and of air carriers, the provision of a currency system, the control of banking, the operation of a postal service, even the taxing of earnings, helping to make the other activities possible—all contribute to conditions obviously indispensable if the business interests of the country are to thrive. Protective tariffs in some ways restrict business, and certainly are not to be considered indispensable to it, yet are presumed also to have fostered business, at least in the domain of manufacturing. Three activities, however,—validated by express grants of power in the constitution—may be singled out for mention here: (1) maintaining a system of weights and measures, insuring the definiteness and stability of standards which business relations require, (2) granting copyrights and patents, and (3) regulating bankruptcy.

1. Weights and measures

The authority given Congress to "fix the standard of weights and measures"[1] is so unrestricted that it can be, and has been, exercised in respect to all manner of measurements—length, weight, volume, temperature, strength, quality, and others; and to aid in determining such standards, the Bureau of Standards elsewhere mentioned is maintained in the Department of Commerce. Along with the familiar units taken over from old English usage—the pound, yard, gallon, bushel, etc. (with their derivatives), the metric system employed in Continental countries, and having some decided advantages, has been given official status, even though as yet but little actual use is made of it outside of scientific circles. So far as developed to the present time, the function of the national government is merely to "fix" standards, keep models in the Bureau of Standards, and furnish models or copies to the states, leaving it almost entirely to state and local governments to require conformity to the appropriate standards in business and other transactions in so far as they choose to do so. Congress might not only *fix* standards, but set up machinery for enforcing them nationally. This, however, it has not done, with the result that in day-to-day practice there is not entire uniformity the country over.

2. Copyrights and patents:

The constitutional basis of our laws and regulations relating to copyrights and patents is a grant of authority to Congress "to promote the progress of science and the useful arts" by securing to authors and inventors, for limited periods, "the exclusive right to their respective writings and discoveries."[2] The exclusive right conferred is by way of

a. Copyrights

exception to the common-law rule against monopolies, the purpose being, of course, to reward talent and encourage creative effort. The privilege of copyright extends not only to books, but to periodicals, paintings,

[1] Art. I, § 8, cl. 5.
[2] Art. I, § 8, cl. 8.

charts, maps, dramatic and musical compositions, cartoons, lectures, sermons, motion pictures, and photographs; and the period covered is twenty-eight years, with in most cases option of one renewal for an equal length of time. Included is the exclusive privilege of translating, dramatizing, and presenting a work; and in the case of a musical composition, the right also to perform it publicly for profit and to exact a royalty for any reproduction of it by mechanical instruments. A grant of copyright is made to everyone seeking it and depositing one or more copies of his work, with payment of a two-dollar fee; copyright, too, is property and transferable as such. On the other hand, the Copyright Office in the Library of Congress, which administers the law, makes no effort to ascertain whether any infringement of a previously copyrighted publication or production is involved; if such is alleged, the party considering himself injured can seek redress only through a suit for damages, or injunction proceedings, in a federal court.[1]

Through a Patent Office in the Department of Commerce, a patent **b. Patents** may be granted to any person who has invented or discovered "any new and useful art, machine, manufacture, or composition of matter, or any new and useful improvements thereof, not known or used by others in this country ... and not patented or described in any printed publication in this or any foreign country ... and not in public use or on sale in this country for more than one year" prior to the filing of the application.[2] As suggested by this phraseology, patents, unlike copyrights, are not granted to every one who applies; on the contrary, the Patent Office is supposed to do its best to find out whether the machine, device, or process for which a patent is sought is actually new and whether a patent for it would infringe upon rights under some patent previously granted; and the period for which a patent runs is only seventeen years, with, in general, no right of renewal. Appeals against decisions of the patent examiners in the Patent Office may be taken to a board of patent appeals in the Office, and thence to the Court of Customs and Patent Appeals or to a federal district court. Moreover, while in general the monopolistic rights carried by a patent are not challengeable, the uses made of patents, especially by big industries, singly or in combination, sometimes bring

[1] In order to receive the protection of our copyright laws, books printed in the English language must be type-set in the United States. On the general subject, see Z. Chafee, Jr., "Reflections on the Law of Copyright," *Columbia Law Rev.*, XLV, 503-529, 719-738 (July, Sept., 1945). On the many complicated aspects of international copyright, see M. M. Kampelman, "The United States and International Copyright," *Amer. Jour. of Internat. Law*, XLI, 406-429 (Apr., 1947). In June, 1946, a significant convention for uniform copyright protection was signed at Washington by representatives of the American republics.

[2] To promote seed-breeding and afford agriculture the same opportunity to participate in the benefits of the patent system that has been given to industry, Congress, in 1930, enacted a Plant Patent Act (46 *U. S. Stat. at Large*, 376) under which any person who has "invented or discovered and asexually reproduced any distinct and new variety of plant, other than a tuber-propagated plant," may receive a patent. From 1931, when Plant Patent No. 1 was awarded for a climbing rose, 701 plant patents had been awarded by 1946.

the holders into conflict with the laws prohibiting contracts in restraint of trade.[1] Slightly over a hundred years ago, a commissioner of patents soberly recommended to Congress that his office be abolished because "everything had been invented." How far wrong he was is indicated by the fact that upwards of fifty thousand patents are in our times granted every year, the 2,436,705th in the country's history being, in fact, recorded at the close of February, 1948.[2]

3. Bankruptcy

Bankruptcy is one of a number of matters over which the national and state governments have concurrent legislative power; and for more than a hundred years (except for three brief intervals) it was left entirely to state control. In 1898, however, Congress passed a general bankruptcy act;[3] and thereupon former state laws on the subject either were repealed or fell into a condition of suspended animation. It is still permissible for a state to legislate on bankruptcy. But in all cases of conflict the national law takes precedence; and this law is so comprehensive that little need or room for state action survives. Proceedings in bankruptcy cases come under the jurisdiction of the federal district court of the district in which the bankrupt resides; and after a bankrupt's assets have been inventoried and equitably distributed among his creditors, the judge enters a decree discharging him from all further legal liability for debts incurred prior to the commencement of proceedings.[4]

The extraordinary number of bankruptcies occurring during the depression decade of the thirties led to much new legislation supplementary to existing bankruptcy law, notably (1) an act of 1933 opening the courts

[1] Much testimony was presented to the Temporary National Economic Committee of 1938-41 (see p. 654 below) concerning the close relationship often existing between the possession of patent rights and the development of monopolies, and the Committee recommended a number of changes in the patent laws as a corrective. To study the subject further, a National Patent Planning Commission was created in 1941, from which came, two years later, a report upholding the existing system as a whole, but proposing a number of additional safeguards such as (1) compulsory recording in the Patent Office of all agreements between American and foreign patentees; (2) shortening to twenty years the possible time between application for a patent and the patent's expiration (although patents run for only seventeen years, it has been possible to keep an application pending over a long period of years, thus in effect indefinitely prolonging the protection enjoyed); and (3) establishment of a court having to do only with patent appeals. Legislation on these, or related, lines remains to be enacted. See O. R. Barnett, *Patent Property and the Anti-Monopoly Laws* (Indianapolis, 1943); W. T. Kelley, "Restraints of Trade and the Patent Law," *Georgetown Law Jour.*, XXXII, 213-233 (Mar., 1944); A. E. Kahn, "Fundamental Deficiencies of American Patent Law," *Amer. Econ. Rev.*, XXX, 475-491 (Sept., 1940); and A. M. Smith, "Recent Developments in Patent Law," *Mich. Law Rev.*, XLIV, 899-922 (June, 1946).

[2] A simple explanation of the patent system will be found in W. R. Ballard, *There Is No Mystery About Patents* (New York, 1946). Charging each applicant a fee of forty dollars, the Patent Office actually makes money for the government.

In addition to granting patents, the Patent Office registers trade-marks and labels for use on goods distributed through channels of interstate and foreign commerce. Registration is for twenty years, is indefinitely renewable, and can be protected through appeal to the courts. A new and more adequate trade-mark law (the Lanham Act, 60 *U. S. Stat. at Large,* 427) was enacted in 1946.

[3] 30 *U. S. Stat. at Large,* 544.

[4] Most of the details of bankruptcy proceedings are attended to by a referee in bankruptcy, appointed by the judge and reporting to him from time to time.

to persons (especially farmers) and railroads with assets exceeding liabilities yet unable to pay their debts as they matured, and facilitating settlements between such "debtors" (not "bankrupts") and their creditors without the stigma of bankruptcy; (2) an act of 1934 permitting corporations in general to reorganize as "debtors" (not "bankrupts") with the consent of a majority of their creditors; (3) a municipal bankruptcy act of 1934 (held unconstitutional in 1937, but forthwith replaced with a law excluding counties [1]), extending to counties, cities, and other local "taxing districts" privileges similar to those conferred on individuals and railroads in 1933; and (4) a farm mortgage moratorium act of 1935, duly upheld by the courts after an earlier measure of the kind had been overthrown. Taken together, these measures (which are still operating in the liquidation of old debt situations) proved of substantial importance in speeding up business and agricultural recovery, especially by permitting prompt readjustment, on a sound basis, of debts owed by railroads and other corporations. At the same time, the opprobrium of bankruptcy was entirely obviated in the case of any company whose affairs were sufficiently sound to be susceptible of reorganization. Finally, in 1938 and 1946, Congress enacted general revisions of the bankruptcy laws calculated to coördinate and unify the expanded system.[2]

Federal Regulation of Business Combinations and Practices

Business in this country attained its present immense proportions mainly by the growth of corporations and the welding of corporations, in turn, into combinations or associations of still greater size and power. Corporations may be given their legal status as business units by act of Congress—both private corporations, such as railroads and banks, and government-owned and operated corporations, like the Reconstruction Finance Corporation and the Tennessee Valley Authority. As a rule, however, they obtain their charters from a state (Delaware being a favorite because of the easy terms permitted), with legal rights ostensibly restricted to the state of incorporation, but in practice extending to other states as well by virtue of some simple formality of registration. Their owners are the people (often numerous and widely scattered) who hold shares of stock; capital is obtained also from those who lend them money, receiving certificates of indebtedness in the form of bonds; and the officers and directors who operate them are largely immune from personal responsibility, with the organizations, as such, also sustaining only limited liability at law. Sixty or seventy years ago, corporations began forming combinations based upon agreements among otherwise independent establishments to fix prices, divide sales territory, limit production, and share profits. There presently appeared also "trusts," in which the stocks

Corporations, trusts, and holding companies

[1] Nevertheless with counties and special assessment districts brought back under the legislation in 1940.
[2] 52 *U. S. Stat. at Large*, 840; 60 *ibid.*, 323. Cf. E. A. Lewis [comp.], *Bankruptcy Laws of the United States* (Washington, D. C., 1946).

of a group of corporate units were gathered into the hands of a single company acting as trustee, with of course control over all of the affiliates. In time, too, arose "holding companies," with assets consisting solely of the stocks of operating companies whose affairs they controlled, and developed particularly in the field of gas, electric, and other public utilities.[1] On such a scale were these developed that in 1933 our two hundred largest industrial units (corporations, trusts, holding companies, and other combinations), with assets aggregating almost a hundred billion dollars, controlled not only nearly half of the country's industrial wealth, but a fifth of the national wealth all told.[2]

The problem of monopoly

From such concentration of economic power, evils long ago began to flow—over-capitalization, "watered" stock, and the like, but chiefly monopoly, with its attendant strangulation of smaller competitive enterprises, its complete domination of an economic function or group of functions, its independent and irresponsible control over services and prices. In certain fields, to be sure, monopoly is hardly to be avoided. Speaking generally, it is not practicable for two or three gas and electric companies to operate in the same city; and in such cases monopolistic abuse has to be prevented by direct public regulation, as for example of rates. From England, however, America inherited a deep-seated antipathy to monopoly in general, and the common law as brought across the Atlantic (and still basic to our legal system) made unlawful any monopolistic powers and practices unreasonably obstructing trade—in other words, interfering with the freedom of competing businesses, large and small, to organize and operate on equal terms. And this free scope for individual initiative and enterprise, leaving the way open for failure and disaster, but also for opportunity and success, and insuring the consuming public the benefits of quality and price flowing from a competitive quest for markets and profits, has remained the most treasured feature of our American economic system. By the same token, the protection of this national heritage—in other words, the curbing of monopolistic abuses— has been, increasingly in this latter half-century of big business, a major public concern and a topmost task of government.

State regulation becomes inadequate

For upwards of a hundred years—while the Supreme Court continued to regard Congress as having no power to regulate interstate commerce except as to matters involved *directly* in commerce—the states were left to deal alone with monopolistic and other practices interfering with the free flow of trade; and whatever correctives they brought to bear rested either simply upon the old common-law principle that all combinations operating to restrain trade *unreasonably* were illegal, or upon statutes defining or modifying that principle's applications. In earlier and simpler

---

[1] The largest earlier holding company to appear was the Standard Oil Company, starting as a trust in 1879 but reorganized as a holding company in 1899. The United States Steel Corporation followed shortly (1901).

[2] National Resources Committee, *The Structure of the American Economy* (Washington, D. C., 1939), 105.

days, no great amount of difficulty was experienced; business was for the most part on a small scale, and state regulation served most essential purposes. When, however, the era of big business dawned, and of business operating over wide interstate areas, something more became urgently needful; despite all that the states could do, large industrial combinations ruthlessly crushed out competitors, established monopoly in their respective fields, and raised profits to fantastic levels by arbitrary increases of prices.

In 1890, therefore, Congress, taking a view of its commerce power then somewhat novel, risked judicial disapproval by passing a notable measure—the Sherman Anti-Trust Act—aimed at protecting trade and commerce "against unlawful restraints and monopolies," and to that end declaring, in sweeping terms, every contract, combination, or conspiracy in restraint of trade or commerce among the several states or with foreign nations to be illegal, and providing heavy penalties for violations.[1] The law was amply stiff. Congress, however, made the mistake of providing no agency definitely charged with administering it. To be sure, it might be, and was, assumed that the measure would be enforced by the attorney-general and his representatives, the district attorneys, throughout the country. But the Department of Justice showed little zeal for such action; a Supreme Court decision in the Sugar Trust case of 1895 [2] severely narrowed the scope of the law by ruling that although the defendant produced all but two per cent of the sugar used in the United States, its business was primarily *manufacturing*, rather than *commerce*, and therefore subject to regulation only by the states; and for a decade thereafter virtually nothing happened—with most of the great industrial "trusts" of later days in the meantime getting their start.

"Trust-busting" was one of President Theodore Roosevelt's prime interests, and successful prosecution of the Northern Securities case [3] by the government in 1904 gave him fresh impetus. Notwithstanding government victories in other cases, however, the Supreme Court again weakened the law by setting up a distinction between combinations which, in the Court's opinion, involved only a "reasonable," and those which amounted to an "unreasonable," restraint of interstate or foreign trade. In cases in 1911 against the American Tobacco Company [4] and the Standard Oil Company,[5] for example, the Court applied this "rule of reason" and in effect read into the law declaring illegal "every" combination, etc., in restraint of trade, the word "unreasonable," after the word "every." The effect was practically to reverse or overrule not only the probable intent of Congress, but earlier decisions in which the Court had

Marginal notes:
Federal control introduced— the Sherman Act (1890)

The "rule of reason"

---

[1] 26 *U. S. Stat. at Large*, 209.
[2] United States *v.* E. C. Knight Co., 156 U. S. 1 (1895).
[3] United States *v.* Northern Securities Co., 193 U. S. 197 (1904). The defendant was a holding company charged with monopoly in the railway field.
[4] United States *v.* American Tobacco Co., 221 U. S. 106 (1911).
[5] Standard Oil Co. of New Jersey *v.* United States, 221 U. S. 1 (1911).

held that *all* such combinations in restraint of trade came within the limits of the statute.

Experience of this sort naturally suggested that if the law applied only to "unreasonable" combinations and contracts, some means should be provided by which well-intentioned combinations might know definitely whether they would be regarded by the government as "reasonable," and therefore lawful, without first being subjected to a criminal prosecution to determine their status. Demand arose, too, for clarification as to the kinds of arrangements that the government would look upon as unreasonable restraints upon trade, and as to the corporate practices that it would regard as constituting unfair competitive methods. The upshot was (1) the passage, in 1914, of the Clayton Anti-Trust Act [1] to reënforce and supplement the Sherman Act of 1890, and (2) the simultaneous creation of the Federal Trade Commission as an agency to coöperate with the Department of Justice in the enforcement of "anti-trust" laws, new and old, and especially to curb unfair competitive practices in the conduct of business.

The
Clayton
Anti-
Trust
Act
(1914)

Earnestly sponsored by President Wilson as a "new law" to meet "conditions that menace our civilization," though opposed with equal vigor by business interests, the Clayton Act (1) forbade price-cutting to drive out competitors, granting rebates, making false assertions about competitors, limiting the freedom of purchasers to deal in the products of competing manufacturers, and a long list of other abuses, discriminations, and restraints of trade; (2) forbade corporations to acquire stock in competing concerns if the effect would be to lessen competition, and outlawed interlocking directorates in the case of larger banks, industrial corporations, and common carriers; (3) made officers of corporations personally liable for violations of the act; and (4) made it easier for injured parties in cases arising under either this act or the original anti-trust law to prosecute their suits.[2]

---

[1] 38 *U. S. Stat. at Large*, 730.

[2] Labor had been disturbed because in certain anti-trust cases, notably the Danbury Hatters' case of 1908 (Loewe *v.* Lawlor, 208 U. S. 274) the Supreme Court had taken the position that boycotts instituted by labor unions obstructed the flow of commerce among the states and therefore came within the inhibitions of the Sherman Act. To meet this situation, the Clayton Act specified that nothing in the anti-trust laws "shall be construed to forbid the existence and operation of labor, agricultural, or horticultural organizations ... or to forbid or restrain the individual members of such organizations from carrying out the legitimate objects thereof; nor shall such organizations, or the members thereof, be held or construed to be illegal combinations or conspiracies in restraint of trade, under the anti-trust laws." Although hailed by the labor leader Samuel Gompers as "labor's charter of freedom," this part of the law proved disappointing to organized labor because of the manner in which the courts interpreted and applied it in specific cases, *e.g.,* United Mine Workers *v.* Coronado Coal Co., 259 U. S. 344 (1921). On some later cases involving labor unions, see C. O. Gregory, "The Sherman Act *v.* Labor," *Univ. of Chicago Law Rev.,* VIII, 222–245 (Feb., 1941); D. F. Cavers, "Labor *v.* the Sherman Act," *ibid.,* 246–257 (Feb., 1941), and "And What of the Apex Case Now?," *ibid.,* VIII, 516–520 (Apr., 1941); L. B. Boudin, "Organized Labor and the Clayton Act," *Va. Law Rev.,* XXIX, 272–315 (Dec., 1942), 395–439 (Jan., 1943). Cf. M. Woll, *Labor, Government, and Industry* (New York, 1945).

A quarter-century of irregular enforcement

The object of the new legislation of 1914 was to close the gaps in the Sherman Act, and President Wilson hailed it as supplying "clear and sufficient law to check and destroy the noxious growth [of monopoly] in its infancy." Notoriously, however, it proved less effective than had been hoped. In interpreting "unfair methods of competition," the courts grew increasingly tolerant; to a dead-weight of opposition from large business interests was added honest doubt of disinterested persons, including some federal officials, as to whether the entire program was practicable, or even desirable, and especially as to whether ameliorative regulation of trusts and other combinations was not preferable to attempts to break them up completely; efforts to make directors personally liable for the acts of corporations almost completely broke down. During World War I, the entire body of legislation was, to all intents and purposes, suspended; through ensuing Republican administrations, it was seldom invoked; and when the National Recovery Act of 1933 was passed, in an effort to rescue the country from a great depression which the anti-trust laws had manifestly not availed to prevent, those laws were expressly suspended for so long as the Recovery Act should remain in force.[1] This period of suspension proved, however, of only two years' duration, and thereupon the laws came back into at least nominal operation. Presently, too, they acquired some actual vigor. In 1938, a former professor of law at Yale University, Thurman W. Arnold, was placed in charge of the anti-trust division of the Department of Justice, and forthwith became the most assiduous "trust-buster" that the country had known since Theodore Roosevelt, instituting in five years forty-four per cent of all proceedings started under the anti-trust laws between 1890 and his retirement in 1943.[2] There was, however, some shift from the old idea of "trust-busting" as an object in itself to that of simply defending a free market in the necessities of modern life; and with this broader social end in view, prosecutions were directed primarily against private groups that had established themselves in strategic positions of control—against "bottlenecks of business" that blocked the distribution of products anywhere along the line from the raw-material stage to purchase by the ultimate consumer.[3] In 1938, also, under President Roosevelt's initia-

---

[1] For a long time, even when an Administration honestly tried to inject new life into anti-trust-law enforcement, it was compelled to operate within a very narrow compass because of the failure of Congress to provide adequate funds for properly staffing the anti-trust division of the Department of Justice, leaving it possible to prosecute only the most flagrant cases in a few large industries.

The government does not go out and hunt situations capable of being made grounds for anti-trust cases. When a complaint looking plausible comes in, the anti-trust division simply decides whether to make it a basis for instituting proceedings against the accused.

[2] In the fiscal year 1940 alone, 345 suits were instituted and 280 terminated; and of the latter, the government won 265. Mr. Arnold was succeeded by another aggressive prosecutor, Wendell Berge (1943-46).

[3] Some idea of the range of anti-trust prosecutions may be gathered from the fact that outstanding cases in the past ten years have involved charges against upwards of two hundred Southeastern fire insurance companies, the Associated Press, the

tive, Congress provided for a Temporary National Economic Committee charged with looking deeply into the entire problem of concentration of wealth and economic control, and the effects of it on American life.

The situation during World War II

While, however, the new enforcement campaign was in progress, the country was plunged into World War II. The Committee had reported voluminously in 1941, piling up impressive evidence of the tremendous concentration of wealth and economic power that had taken place, but offering only divided recommendations for remedial action—even if the times had been favorable for any action at all.[1] And in wartime, proceedings under existing laws had to be slowed down, the President announcing in 1942 that, while every effort would be made to protect the public interest, with no violation of law escaping ultimate punishment, prosecutions would be postponed whenever it could be shown that such a course would tend to promote the production of materials for war use; in the same year, indeed, Congress expressly exempted from prosecution at any time any acts or omissions "deemed in the public interest" and approved by the chairman of the War Production Board after consultation with the attorney-general. There was not complete cessation of anti-trust activity: in 1943, fifty-two suits were instituted, forty-three were concluded, and 152 investigations were started; and in 1944 the "largest anti-trust suit in history" was filed against the Association of American Railroads and various individual railroad companies and investment banking houses, aimed at breaking an alleged rate-making monopoly in the transportation field. In general, however, the war years were a period of slackened effort.

Pullman Car Company, four large chemical corporations and their foreign affiliates, fifteen of New York City's largest department stores, two of the largest chain grocery-store companies, the American Waxed Paper Association, the Aluminum Company of America (ALCOA), the American Can Company, the Diamond Match Company and eleven associated concerns, eight major motion picture companies and their affiliates, eighteen major oil companies and others (often called the Madison oil case), eighteen leading automobile tire manufacturers, Chicago milk dealers and related labor unions, optical and other glass manufacturers, the General Electric Company, contractors and labor unions in building industries, the Fashion Originators Guild of America and the Millinery Creators Guild, the American Society of Composers, Authors, and Publishers, German- and British-controlled borax corporations, eighteen major producers engaged in selling stainless steel, the Association of American Railroads, its officers and bankers, and forty-seven Western railroads, and (late in 1947) the Investment Bankers Association of America and seventeen leading investment banking partnerships and corporations.

Among almost innumerable books and articles relating to the general subject may be cited: T. W. Arnold, *Anti-Trust Law Enforcement, Past and Present* (Washington, D. C., 1940), and *The Bottlenecks of Business* (New York, 1940); series of articles on "The Sherman Anti-Trust Act and Its Enforcement" in *Law and Contemporary Problems*, VI, 1-160 (Winter, 1940): C. D. Edwards, "Thurman Arnold and the Anti-Trust Laws," *Polit. Sci. Quar.*, LVIII, 338-355 (Sept., 1943); and P. E. Hadlick, *Criminal Prosecutions Under the Sherman Anti-Trust Act* (Washington, D. C., 1939).

[1] *Final Report and Recommendations of the Temporary National Economic Committee*, 77th Cong., 1st Sess., Sen. Doc. No. 35 (Washington, D. C., 1941). A full analysis of the testimony presented before the Committee will be found in D. Lynch, *The Concentration of Economic Power* (New York, 1946). More recent information on the same general subject is contained in a report of the Federal Trade Commission, "The Present Trends of Corporate Mergers and Acquisitions," 80th Cong., 1st Sess., Sen. Doc. No. 17 (1947).

The war ended with large numbers of suits pending or postponed, and with others needing to be instituted; and the Department of Justice soon gave evidence of renewed activity.[1] On the other hand, President Roosevelt's aggressive concern was no longer in the picture, and the overshadowing problem of reconversion of industry to a peacetime basis served as an unsettling and deterring factor. In any event, it was clear that, by and large, the story of anti-monopolistic regulation in this country had not been one of highly impressive achievement. A limited number of great concerns—chiefly the Standard Oil Company and the American Tobacco Company as earlier constituted—had been broken up; others had been brought to book and penalized; many minor punishments had been inflicted along the way. Basic obstacles, however, remained, and probably will always remain. Among these, one was, and is, the dependence of the laws for vigorous enforcement upon the economic predispositions and personal inclinations of successive presidents; another, more serious, was the lingering uncertainties, despite all the legislation, as to what constituted "unfair competition," "unreasonable" restraint of trade, and the like; still another was the wavering support which enforcing authorities could expect from the courts; and weightiest of all was the inescapable economic fact that large-scale production, calling for large-scale organization, makes for economies, and therefore sometimes for more and cheaper goods and services for the consuming public. Under these circumstances (and others that might be mentioned), the effort to maintain equity and opportunity for business of *all* sorts, small as well as large, needed, to be sure, to be kept up, yet could be expected, at best, to yield only somewhat modest results.[2]

A continuing dilemma

Accompanying the Clayton Act of 1914 was a twin measure substituting for a bureau of corporations which Theodore Roosevelt had persuaded Congress to set up in the Department of Commerce a new enforcing agency known as the Federal Trade Commission; and, like its prototype, the Interstate Commerce Commission, this later body (consisting of five members appointed by the president and Senate for seven-year terms,

The Federal Trade Commission: 1. Functions

---

[1] In the summer of 1947, a reorganized anti-trust division under John F. Sonnett embarked upon an intensified program, including actions against suspected conspiracies in the food and clothing fields, and against tire and tube manufacturers, color-film producers, and various segments of the steel, chemical, building materials, and Western oil industries. Some suits represented merely a resumption of prosecutions abandoned or suspended during the war. In the more recent cases, however, the emphasis has been on alleged price-fixing in fields where the consumer is pinched, and on new and broader use of *criminal* prosecutions where price-fixing is evident. J. D. Morris, "Trust Busters Plan Speed-up Campaign," *N. Y. Times,* Aug. 22, 24, 1947.

[2] The Truman Administration's efforts in April, 1947, to persuade the nation's manufacturers, wholesalers, and retailers to enter into agreements to lower prices of their commodities to the general public, as a means of fighting inflation and reducing the cost of living, met an unexpected obstacle in an interpretation of the anti-trust laws. For fifty years the Supreme Court has consistently adhered to the principle that *price-fixing* agreements are unlawful. Lawyers now contended that the *price-cutting* agreements urged by the Administration would be price-fixing, and therefore legally hazardous. *N. Y. Times,* Apr. 6, 1947.

with not more than three drawn from any one political party) has throughout its history been a major independent establishment, with a staff now numbering more than five hundred. Designed fundamentally for guarding against and correcting unfair competitive practices in business conducted on an interstate level (*e.g.*, combinations or agreements keeping trade out of the hands of competitors, excluding competitors from access to materials, controlling prices, granting discounts or rebates, or compelling merchants to buy only from some one dealer), the Commission not only aids the Department of Justice in carrying out provisions of the original Sherman and Clayton Acts, but is especially charged with applying a Webb-Pomerene Act of 1918 exempting concerns engaged exclusively in foreign trade from certain stipulations of the anti-trust laws, and with enforcing (1) an amendment of 1936 to the Clayton Act known as the Robinson-Patman Anti-Discrimination Act, and designed to prevent sellers from arbitrarily giving advantages to some buyers, as against others, through disguises such as advertising allowances and brokerage fees,[1] (2) a Wheeler-Lea Truth-in-Advertising Act of 1938,[2] applying especially to the food, drug, and cosmetics businesses, and (3) a Wool Products Labeling Act of 1940,[3] which seeks to protect producers, manufacturers, and consumers against the presence of unrevealed substitutes and mixtures in wool products.

2. Activities

In pursuance of its many duties, the Commission is found (1) enforcing the laws against unfair competitive practices on the part of corporate and other businesses participating in interstate commerce (except banks, common carriers, broadcasting companies, and other enterprises whose regulation is provided for through different channels); (2) working out lists of unfair practices and holding conferences in which representatives of industry are encouraged to agree to avoid such practices (although the line between lawful and unlawful agreements, even on such matters, is not always easy to fix); (3) issuing "cease and desist" orders when violations of law are discovered and the violators are not disposed to desist of their own accord; (4) requiring corporations to submit reports covering aspects of their business on which the Commission desires information; (5) advising with corporations on organizational and other matters with a view to helping them avoid running afoul of the law;

---

[1] 49 *U. S. Stat. at Large*, 1526. Under this measure, it is unlawful for any person or firm engaged in interstate commerce "to discriminate in price between different purchasers of commodities of like grade and quality, where such commodities are sold for use, consumption, or resale ... and where the effect of such discrimination may be substantially to lessen competition, or tends to create a monopoly in any line of commerce." The measure was both defended and opposed in Congress as a means of protecting "independent" merchants against the competition of chain stores, and often is referred to as the "Chain-Store Act." See W. Patman, *The Robinson-Patman Act* (New York, 1938); B. Werne [ed.], *Business and the Robinson-Patman Law* (New York, 1938); and G. H. Montague, *The Robinson-Patman Act and Its Administration* (Chicago, 1945).

[2] 52 *U. S. Stat. at Large*, 111.

[3] 54 *U. S. Stat. at Large*, 1128.

(6) guarding against unlawful acquisitions of stock by corporations and against prohibited interlocking directorates; (7) investigating trade conditions and practices in and with foreign countries where combinations or practices may affect the foreign commerce of the United States; and (8) recommending to Congress new legislation calculated to uphold the principle of fair competition in the interest of both business itself and the public.

In enforcing the laws against unfair practices, the Commission may act on its own initiative, on direction of the president or of Congress, or at the suggestion or request of the attorney-general. As a rule, however, action in a particular situation starts with a complaint lodged with the Commission by some individual, group, firm, or corporation having a grievance against a specified business concern because of some practice which it is pursuing; and hundreds of such complaints are filed every year. If, upon preliminary investigation, the Commission finds a complaint groundless or trivial, or relating to something over which the Commission has no jurisdiction, nothing happens. If, however, the protest is believed to have merit, the offender is called upon to explain—often with the result that all parties consent amicably to a "stipulation," or agreement, under which the practice complained of is to be abandoned. If, finally, the concern under attack is not prepared to yield so readily, and the Commission considers it clearly in the wrong, a "cease and desist" order will command the offender to discontinue within sixty days the practice or practices in question; and failure to comply with such an order subjects the violator to suit brought by the attorney-general, unless in the meantime an appeal has been taken to a federal circuit court of appeals, which may find the order unjustified or technically deficient and declare it of no effect. *3. Procedures*

In addition to obstacles arising from the inherent difficulty of construing such terms as "unfair practice," and from gaps and vaguenesses in the law on the subject, the Commission has encountered many serious impediments to its work. It has not always had adequate financial support from Congress; its members have been shifted rapidly and often have been selected primarily on political grounds; although supposed to be final judge of the facts in a case, it frequently has found the courts insisting upon making their own inquiries into facts, and many times has seen its cease-and-desist orders overthrown. All in all, however, it has done much to raise the standards of American business; and not only smaller business but the consuming public has profited heavily from the various forms of protection which it affords.[1] *4. Difficulties encountered*

---

[1] E. P. Herring, "Politics, Personalities, and the Federal Trade Commission," *Amer. Polit. Sci. Rev.,* XXVIII, 1016-1029 (Dec., 1934), and XXIX, 21-35 (Feb., 1935), is an illuminating analysis of the "atmosphere" in which the Commission carries on its work. Cf. the same author's *Federal Commissioners; A Study of Their Careers and Qualifications* (Cambridge, Mass., 1936). On the Commission activities, see any recent edition of *United States Government Manual.*

Some Special Fields of Business Regulation

Supplementary to the regulation of general business under such basic statutes as the Sherman Act and the Clayton Act, with their amendments, are many restrictive arrangements applying to particular branches or areas of business. An older illustration is the system of regulations imposed by a Packers and Stockyards Act of 1921 [1] on packers, commission men, and stockyard operators for the protection of farmers and stock-raisers against arbitrary price manipulations, discriminatory charges, and other unfair practices from which they long had suffered. Administered by the bureau of animal industry in the Department of Agriculture, in conjunction with state departments of agriculture or live-stock commissions, this measure was upheld by the Supreme Court as a legitimate exercise of the federal commerce power. [2]

Fields occupied during the depression

Many of the special fields of regulation, however, were first occupied by the federal government in connection with its efforts during the thirties to overcome the depression of that period and to prevent its recurrence. Those efforts, to be sure, went far beyond the mere regulation of particular types of business. In the National Industrial Recovery Act of 1933, [3] based on the assumption that the federal commerce power involves full authority to remove burdens from commerce and obstructions to its flow, attempt was made virtually to revolutionize the pattern of industry and of industrial relations with a view to increasing production, spreading work among the unemployed, raising wages, stimulating purchasing power, abolishing child labor, promoting collective bargaining, and curbing wasteful competition. [4] On the ground, however, that Congress had stretched the commerce power unwarrantably to include manufacturing, and had been too free in delegating powers of an essentially legislative nature to the president, the Supreme Court invalidated the act after two years of operation; [5] and, except for being preserved, as the so-called "Little N.R.A.," for business concerned with furnishing supplies to the federal government under contract, the entire

---

[1] 42 *U. S. Stat. at Large,* 159.

[2] Stafford *v.* Wallace, 258 U. S. 495 (1922).

[3] 48 *U. S. Stat. at Large,* 195.

[4] Almost equally important parallel legislation aimed at agricultural recovery will be mentioned in the next chapter. See pp. 678-681 below.

The essence of the new industrial scheme was a system of "codes of fair competition," covering hours, wages, and other matters—codes which, after being drawn up for different industries and trades by representatives of their own choosing and approved by the president, were to be binding on all persons engaged in the given industry or trade, with heavy fines for violation. General direction was vested, under the president, in a National Recovery Administration; and at the end of the first year some five hundred codes were in operation, with two hundred more in process of adoption. The plan was intended only for the period of national recovery, although hope was entertained that some of its more ameliorative features would survive afterwards on a voluntary basis.

[5] Schechter *v.* United States, 295 U. S. 495 (1935). The majority argument ran largely on the lines of that advanced in the Sugar Trust case of 1895. (See p. 651 above.)

structure collapsed.[1] Other remedial measures of the period, however, proved more acceptable to the Court and became the basis for business regulation that has survived and expanded to this day. Three particular areas so covered may here be mentioned: the issue and sale of securities, public utility holding companies, and the sale of agricultural commodities.

Millions of Americans own shares of stock in medium-sized or larger businesses; many others hope to do so; millions also have, in effect, lent money to such businesses by purchasing and holding their bonds or debentures. Only in this way could our gigantic industrial machine be financed; only in this way, too, could great numbers of thrifty people find profitable outlets for the bulk of their savings. Such distribution of stocks, bonds, and other securities, however, opens a very wide field for fraudulent practice. The average investor is in no position to know the actual financial condition, the prospects, or even the reliability and integrity, of many of the businesses to which he is solicited to intrust his money; and if he is at all gullible, he stands large chance of being "taken in" by the high-powered salesmanship of dishonest, or at least unscrupulous, promoters and agents. To be sure, the common law can be invoked against persons perpetrating fraud. But against slippery vendors of securities, it is not likely to prove of much avail. To be sure, too, the national government stands ready to prosecute persons using the mails for fraudulent purposes. But most sales of securities are not made by mail. And so notorious did abuses become, with people swindled out of millions every year, that Kansas, in 1911, led off in a belated effort of the states to make life uncomfortable for sellers of "blue sky" by placing all traffic in stocks and bonds within the state under public regulation. Other states followed suit, with the result that nowadays virtually all of the forty-eight have "blue-sky" laws, commonly requiring securities offered in the state to be registered and purveyors of them to be licensed, and enforced by a securities commissioner or similar official, usually with authority to prohibit the sale of a given security issue in the state unless investigation (in case of doubt) reveals that there is nothing fraudulent about it.

Control over securities—inadequacy of state action

Here again, however, state regulation, although beneficial, could not fully meet the need. Machinery was inadequate for the complicated investigations required; more serious, promotors and salesmen freely operated across state lines, in a business that to a large extent was interstate in character. When the depression developed in the thirties, it was considered that a main contributing cause had been the unloading upon the public of worthless or dubious securities through misrepresentation

Federal control introduced

---

[1] The National Labor Relations [Wagner] Act of 1935, however, salvaged practically the whole of one section of the Recovery Act guaranteeing the right of collective bargaining. See p. 724 below. For good general histories of the period, see B. Rauch, *The History of the New Deal, 1933-1938* (New York, 1944), and A. M. Schlesinger, *The New Deal in Action, 1933-1939* (New York, 1940). Cf. L. Lyon *et al., The National Recovery Administration; An Analysis and Appraisal* (Washington, D. C., 1935).

and other fraud [1]—"a traffic," as President Roosevelt characterized it, "in the social and economic welfare of our people;" and the experience brought home forcibly the need for stricter and more uniform regulation by national authority. The upshot was the enactment by Congress of two carefully drawn statutes—in 1933, a Securities Act focussed on the issuance of new securities, and in 1934, a Securities Exchange Act, applying to the buying and selling of securities generally.[2]

The Securities Act of 1933

The basic purpose of these two interlocked pieces of legislation is to protect investors against every sort of fraudulent practice in the issuing and handling of securities offered for sale in interstate commerce. To this end, the act of 1933 begins by requiring all issues of stocks, bonds, or other securities, if to be offered in interstate commerce or by mail, to be registered with originally the Federal Trade Commission but since 1934 the Securities and Exchange Commission set up in that year.[3] Every such registration must be accompanied by a "registration statement" containing full financial and other information, and also by the "prospectus" intended to be used in soliciting purchases by the public, and containing all information which an investor ought to have when making a decision; and selling or offering to sell to the public in interstate commerce or through the mails any security not properly registered with the Commission is made a penal offense. Not only so, but heavy civil liability is laid upon any corporation, including its directors and principal financial officers, for any untrue or only partly true declaration of a material fact in a registration statement or prospectus. To the ancient rule, therefore, of *caveat emptor*—"let the buyer beware"—is added the complementary injunction, *caveat vendor,* "let the seller beware." It is not the business of the Commission, any more than that of a state securities commissioner, to pass upon the inherent value of securities issued or upon the outlook for prosperity of the corporation issuing them; and no action by the Commission is to be construed as a recommendation of any security to potential purchasers. The agency's only function, up to this point, is to see that complete information concerning a security is made available to the public, that this information is accurate, and that no fraud is practiced in connection with sales.[4]

[1] Losses from this source were estimated in 1933 to have aggregated twenty-five billion dollars in the preceding ten years, or about $200 for every man, woman, and child in the United States. 73rd Cong., 1st Sess., Sen. Rep. No. 17, p. 2 (1933).

[2] 48 *U. S. Stat. at Large,* 74, and 48 *U. S. Stat. at Large,* 881.

[3] This Commission consists of five members appointed by the president and Senate for staggered five-year terms. Excepted from the provisions of the act are securities issued by the national, state, and local governments, by national and state banks, by religious, educational, and other corporations not organized for profit, by railroads and other common carriers, and by building and loan associations.

[4] C. C. Rohlfing *et al., Business and Government* (4th ed.), Chap. VII; "The Federal Securities Act of 1933" [Symposium], *Cong. Digest,* XIII, 136-156 (May, 1934). Cf. "Three Years of the Securities Act," *Law and Contemporary Problems,* IV, Nos. 1-2 (1937). The constitutionality of the Securities Act was upheld by the Supreme Court in Electric Bond and Share Co., *v.* Sec. and Exch. Commission, 303 U. S. 419 (1938).

To aid in promoting this general end, the Securities and Exchange Act The Securities Exchange Act of 1934 of 1934 went an important step farther. A large proportion—perhaps the major part—of the securities registered with the Commission are bought and sold on stock exchanges found in twenty or more of our principal cities, the largest and best known being that in New York. Formerly, however, transactions in securities in these markets were subject to little regulation beyond the few restrictions which the exchanges themselves saw fit to impose upon their members; and these provided little protection for the investing public. All manner of unsavory and dishonest practices grew up—"wash sales," matched orders, "rigging the market," "jiggles," pools, and other manipulations—by which prices were pushed up or forced down for the benefit of insiders, while innocent investors were led like lambs to the slaughter. Speculation "on margin," too,—i.e., paying only a certain percentage in cash for what is bought—reached scandalous proportions, notably in the frenzied market operations shortly preceding the crash of 1929, and threatened to precipitate the entire national credit structure into chaos.

To remedy this situation, the transactions of all exchanges engaged in interstate commerce are declared by the act of 1934 to be "affected with a national public interest" which makes it necessary to provide for their regulation and control "in order to protect interstate commerce, the national credit, the federal taxing power, to make more effective the national banking system and the federal reserve system, and to insure the maintenance of fair and honest markets in such transactions." Annual and other reports are required to be filed with the exchanges and the Commission by all corporations or companies having securities listed, and any deviations from material fact constitute grounds for suspending or withdrawing the security from trading. Various provisions outlaw sundry objectionable practices of the past, and, all in all, the measure seeks to make the exchanges fair and open market-places for investors rather than mere rendezvous for conspiring speculators. One will not be so naïve as to suppose that all stock-market operations have since been, or will in future be, beyond reproach. Exceedingly timely and useful safeguards have, however, been supplied.[1]

[1] The powers of the Securities and Exchange Commission have been extended by successive acts of Congress, until it now (1948) administers four important statutes in addition to the two mentioned in the text: the Public Utility Holding Company Act of 1935 (see p. 662 below), the Trust Indenture Act of 1939 (53 *U. S. Stat. at Large,* 1149), the Investment Company Act of 1940 (54 *ibid.,* 789), and the Investment Advisers Act of 1940 (54 *ibid.,* 857). In addition, the Commission advises federal district courts under the bankruptcy laws in connection with reorganization proceedings for debtor corporations. See M. Fainsod and L. Gordon, *Government and the American Economy,* Chap. xii; H. H. Trachsel, *Public Utility Regulation* (Chicago, 1947), Chap. xi; E. Stein, *Government and the Investor* (New York, 1941); B. Shaw, "Investigation Powers of Federal Commissioners—the Securities and Exchange Commission," *Mich. Law Rev.,* XXXVI, 786-801 (Mar., 1938), H. V. Cherrington, *The Investor and the Securities Act* (Washington, D. C., 1942); J. Frank, *If Men Were Angels* (New York, 1942).

In June, 1946, the Securities and Exchange Commission asked for extension of its jurisdiction so as to cover the securities of all corporations having assets of over

A problem of growing importance in later years has been that of the public utility "holding company"—a corporation chartered in some particular state, holding the majority stock in operating companies scattered over the country, and able, as matters formerly stood, to evade any great amount of regulation, and therefore to indulge in shady practices of many descriptions. Some of the abuses, indeed, which the Securities Act and the Securities Exchange Act were designed to remedy attained their greatest seriousness in connection with the marketing and distribution, through stock exchanges, of the securities of such holding companies. To deal with the matter, Congress, in 1935, passed a significant measure under two "titles," one a Public Utility Holding Company Act and the other a Federal Power Act.[1] In the first portion of the statute, the Securities and Exchange Commission is given jurisdiction over holding companies engaged in the production of gas and electricity [2] and either participating in interstate commerce or making use of the United States mails—which, manifestly, means virtually all of them. All holding companies [3] have been forced to register with the Commission, and to file with it a registration statement giving full information concerning the company itself and its subsidiaries; securities can be issued and properly acquired only with the Commission's consent; other sorts of transactions, too, must have similar sanction. In these and other ways too numerous to mention, the national government has been given substantially the same control over public utility holding companies that state authorities have for years been exercising over operating companies. If President Roosevelt could have had his way, all such holding companies would have been doomed to extinction. Conviction, however, that a holding company may be both legitimate and socially useful, reënforced by large-scale lobbying by the interests concerned, influenced Congress to reject the drastic "death sentence" clauses of the original bill and to go no farther than to stipulate that after the beginning of 1938, the operations of a holding company should be confined to a single integrated utility system, so as to be easier to inspect and control. In pursuance of this provision, and under the vigilant supervision of the Federal Power Commission, a number of large holding companies, such as Associated Gas and Electric and Electric Bond and Share, have in recent years been

---

three million dollars and with more than three hundred security-holders, though no action has as yet (March, 1948) been taken. The effect would be to add about a thousand to the two thousand already included, and among them would be such large enterprises as the Aluminum Company of America and the Great Atlantic and Pacific Tea Company. The total number of corporations and companies filing federal tax returns in 1947 was 475,000. But the great majority were very small, and a good many were entirely in the hands of particular families or of employee groups.

[1] 49 *U. S. Stat. at Large*, 803.

[2] The regulation of rates, facilities, and business practices of electric and gas companies doing an interstate business (as distinguished from matters relating to their security issues) has been vested in the Federal Power Commission, dating from 1930. See p. 706 below.

[3] Except such as hold less than ten per cent of the stock of any subsidiary.

divesting themselves of operating companies and connections held not to be appropriate elements in an integrated system.[1]

Based also upon the commerce power is the Commodities Exchange Act of 1936,[2] which seeks to prevent and remove obstructions upon interstate commerce arising from market manipulation and excessive speculation upon exchanges dealing in agricultural commodities. After various administrative shifts, a Commodity Exchange Authority in the Department of Agriculture is now in charge of enforcement, with wide discretionary power over exchanges trading in wheat, rice, corn, and other grains, cotton, butter, eggs, and other commodities; and the agency is empowered to fix the limits to "futures" trading and to speculative trading done by any one person upon exchanges, to curb excessive speculation and market manipulation, and, in general, to fix trading rules and fair trade practices.

Regulation of the sale of agricultural commodities

The Government, Business, and World War II

The new system of increased control by government over business as outlined in the preceding pages was hardly in full operation before the country turned to the stupendous defense and war effort of 1940 and after; and hardly a business establishment or operation failed to be affected, if not indeed transformed, by subsequent developments. The great objective throughout was "economic mobilization," with the prevention, or at all events the curbing, of inflation coming in, by 1942, as an objective of hardly secondary importance; and the means employed ranged all the way from encouragement of voluntary effort to the imposition of the most rigid and far-reaching controls. At the outset, the problem was chiefly one of stimulating the production of materials needed by the Army and Navy. Even this soon entailed a scheme of priorities compelling producers to give right of way to Army and Navy orders as against orders from private dealers or consumers; also arrangements for allocation, under presidential order, of goods and materials, so as to avert shortages and keep all essential industries going at top speed. Before long, prices began to mount; and an Office of Price Stabilization and Civilian Supply (renamed in August, 1941, Office of Price Administration[3]) was given the task of preventing price spiraling and checking inflation, with power to determine fair and reasonable maximum prices, *i.e.*, price "ceilings."[4] An executive order of August, 1941, introduced a system

Wartime mobilization

---

[1] See L. S. Lesser, "Constitutional Powers of the Securities and Exchange Commission Over Public Utility Holding Companies," *Geo. Washington Law Rev.*, VIII, 1128-1147 (June, 1940); J. F. Davisson, "Death Sentences for Public Utility Holding Companies," *ibid.*, VIII, 1148-1164 (June, 1940). The constitutionality of the modified "death sentence" provisions of the law was upheld by the Supreme Court in North American Co. *v.* Sec. and Exch. Commission, 327 U. S. 686 (1946).

[2] 49 *U. S. Stat. at Large,* 1941. This act was in form an amendment of the Grain Futures Act of 1922 (42 *U. S. Stat. at Large,* 998).

[3] See p. 817 below.

[4] In May, 1942, a general "price-freezing" plan went into operation, with the highest prices of the preceding March serving as ceilings.

of control over the huge instalment credit business carried on through the nation's banks, stores, and personal finance companies. As early as June, 1940, the Navy Department was authorized to take over and operate private plants when unable to come to agreement with the managers on defense contracts; and the power to requisition (with compensation, of course) both plants and materials was extended by stages until by October, 1941, the president had authority to take over any military or naval equipment or the machinery, tools, or materials necessary for the manufacture or operation of such equipment, provided such articles were needed for the country's defense and could not be obtained otherwise. On the basis of authority somewhat indirect, but none the less effective, the entire automobile industry was asked in January, 1942, to turn all of its resources to the production of war materials; a month later, the radio-manufacturing industry was given three months in which to do the same thing; and by rapid stages practically all other consumers' durable-goods industries were similarly put in process of "conversion." From this, it was but a step to rationing retail sales to consumers. Even in 1941, gasoline was rationed to dealers; and in 1942 it was rationed to consumers (first in seventeen Eastern states, and later throughout the entire country), while automobiles, tires, fuel oil, coffee, sugar, and eventually numerous other commodities, were rationed the country over. Shortage of plant capacity became a problem also, and gradually the government was drawn into financing plant expansion, with a total authorized expenditure of more than eight and one-half billion dollars by the summer of 1942.[1]

Postwar "reconversion"

These are merely a few of the many ways in which government and business were rapidly brought into new or altered relations by the national emergency. Others included the slowing up of enforcement of anti-trust regulations, as already mentioned. As the end of war approached, the staggering problem loomed of "reconversion," i.e., getting industry back into its normal channels and loosening the iron grip of wartime government upon the country's business; and—carried forward for more than a year, after hostilities ended, under general supervision of a Civilian Production Administration, successor to the War Production Board of previous years [2]—the task was gradually accomplished.[3] The government curtailed its own business operations; priorities disappeared; price control was in time abandoned; and in general something like the traditional scope for free enterprise was restored, subject, of course, to surviving and reinvigorated prewar regulation through agencies dealt with earlier in this chapter. No one was so naïve as to suppose that everything could be put back where it was in 1940. But—again speaking generally—the relations of government and business promised, after the entire

---

[1] Cf. pp. 813-814 below.
[2] See p. 816 below.
[3] The Civilian Production Administration was abolished in December, 1946.

experience was over, to look, in their broader outlines, a good deal as described in foregoing pages.

The Federal Government's Direct Participation in Business— The Postal Service

So strong has been the tradition of private initiative and management in American business that governments, whether national, state, or local, have invaded the field far less extensively than in a number of other countries.[1] More or less incidental to its strictly governmental functions, however, every one of the states not only buys supplies but sells products; a state university, for example, marketing live-stock and foodstuffs produced on the experimental farms of its agricultural college is as truly engaged in business as is any private purveyor of such commodities. Numerous municipalities, too, own and operate waterworks, electric light plants, gas works, street railways, airports, bridges, tunnels, and other utilities. From the earliest days, the national government also has been in business; indeed, the postal system which it took over from the old Confederation in time developed into one of the largest business enterprises in the world. Nowadays, the United States buys and sells real estate; manufactures munitions, currency, ordnance, and many other things; builds ships; constructs buildings, highways, and other public works; loans money through a multitude of channels; operates the largest printing establishment in the world; carries on, through the wholly-owned Inland Waterways Corporation, an extensive transportation business on the Mississippi and other inland waterways; owns various other operating corporations (like the huge Reconstruction Finance Corporation) and directly operates the Alaska Railroad and the Panama Canal. During World War I, the national government took over temporarily the management of all railroads and telegraph and telephone systems, and at various times during World War II coal mines and even certain mercantile establishments. Since the end of hostilities in 1945, it has been engaged in marketing numerous industrial plants and great quantities of supplies representing surplus property left over from the war. In all, or nearly all, of these undertakings, it competes directly with private business.

One national enterprise which, in the main, is not thus competitive is the postal service;[2] and in view of its high importance, a word in conclusion may be said concerning it. So intimate is the connection between the postal service and commerce that, had the constitution been entirely silent on postal matters, Congress easily might have established a postal

Various lines of activity

The postal service:

Constitutional basis

[1] Notably, in recent years, Great Britain, where, since the installation of a socialist Labor government in 1945, a broad program of "nationalization" of industry (coal, transport, etc.) has been carried into effect.

[2] Even here, however, the parcel-post system competes with express companies and the money-order and postal savings systems to some extent with the operations of banks.

system under powers implied in the commerce clause. One finds, however, in the list of powers expressly conferred that of establishing "post-offices and post-roads;"[1] and the only serious constitutional issue which has ever arisen in connection with the subject has been that of whether, as strict constructionists for a good while contended, the power conferred extended only to designating which of existing routes should be used for transmission of the mails, or whether, as broad constructionists argued, it included the right to build and operate roads especially designed for the purpose. As has usually happened, the more liberal interpretation prevailed, and in later decades the improvement of the postal service has repeatedly been employed as a justification for federal aid to highway construction and development of airlines, even within individual states. The postal power belongs exclusively to Congress, and the postal service that has arisen under it is, in the strictest sense, a government monopoly.

Growth and func-tions

Although nation-wide postal establishments operated by government authorities do not go back very far historically, the services rendered by such agencies are nowadays considered prime necessities; and the postal system of the United States has become, not only the most extensive in the world, but probably the largest single peacetime business enterprise in which any government has ever been directly concerned.[2] Indeed, a person desiring to portray the amazing development of the United States in the past hundred and fifty years could hardly do so more effectively than in terms of the growth of the postal system. He could cite the 41,751 post-offices and 32,161 rural delivery routes in operation on June 30, 1946, the latter serving over twenty-nine million people; the receipts of $1,224,-572,173 (the second largest in the history of the service) in the same year,

---

[1] Art. I, § 8, cl. 7.

[2] Benjamin Franklin laid the foundations of our postal system when deputy post-master-general of the colonies during the twenty years before the Revolution, and also postmaster-general in 1775-76. The Post-Office Department, by which the present system is administered, came into existence in a roundabout way. It was not recognized by statute as a coördinate executive department until 1874. But to all intents and purposes it enjoyed that status from 1825, when the term "post-office department" was first used in the title of an act of Congress; and even more definitely from 1829, when, on the initiative of President Jackson, the postmaster-general became a member of the cabinet. The Department is headed by a postmaster-general, who, for obvious reasons, is often selected with a view to his experience in managing a great business, e.g., John Wanamaker, or, at all events, in conducting large enterprises, not excluding (as in the case of Will H. Hays, James A. Farley, and others who could be mentioned) national political campaigns. Each of four assistant post-masters-general has charge of a bureau of the Department, which in turn is organized in divisions under superintendents or chiefs; and there are other general departmental officers, including special assistants to the postmaster-general. The bulk of the Department's work is done, of course, throughout the country, in collecting, assorting, transporting, and delivering mail (including parcels of merchandise), receiving and caring for savings, transferring money under the money-order system, and enforcing the laws against lottery schemes and swindlers. Development of motorized rural delivery service has enabled post-offices to be reduced from a top figure of 76,945 in 1901 to the present 41,751. Of four classes into which they are divided on the basis of annual receipts, the first (with receipts exceeding $40,000) includes some 2,200 and the fourth (with receipts below $1,500), 19,630, or almost one-half of the total.

The political side of the postmaster-generalship is dealt with in D. C. Fowler, *The Cabinet Politician; The Postmaster-General, 1829-1909* (New York, 1943).

compared with $280,000 in 1800; the million and more letters mailed every hour of the day from one end of the year to the other; the forty billion pieces of mail handled in a year; the more than 460,000 regular and temporary employees, a number equivalent to two-thirds of the entire executive civil service not so many years ago. But even more striking would be the facts relating to the expansion of functions and activities which has made the Post-Office the department whose operations come closest home to the great mass of the people. High points in the recital would be the introduction of the registration system in 1855, the beginning of urban free delivery in 1863, the establishment of the money order system in 1864, the starting of rural free delivery service in 1896, the introduction of the postal-savings system in 1911, the starting of the parcel-post system in 1913, and the launching of air-mail service, now operated on a large scale under contracts with private aviation companies, in 1918.

It is not in the nature of public services to make money, and hardly any of them do so. To be sure, conducted essentially as a business enterprise, with the people paying for the service they get, the postal establishment has commonly been looked upon as one that ought at least to pay its own way. Rarely, however, in the past hundred years has it been able to do this; when, in certain recent years, enormously increased war-time business enabled it to report a sizable profit, the showing stood out in bold relief against an almost unbroken succession of annual deficits.[1] And the reasons for deficits are not difficult to discover. One is the heavy cost of handling and transporting vast quantities of printed matter for the entire federal establishment—all going, of course, postage free.[2] Another is the necessity of maintaining service over large rural areas where the outlays entailed are bound to be out of all proportion to the returns. A third is the over-payment—from a purely business point of view—of air carriers. A fourth is the especially low rates allowed on educational, scientific, religious, and fraternal publications, the free distribution of country newspapers within the county of publication, and free carriage of books, pamphlets, and other reading matter in raised characters for use of the blind. Finally comes also substantial increases of pay and reduction of hours for postal employees, over against the practical impossibility of pushing postal rates much above their existing levels.[3]

Some of the policies referred to are aimed at promoting the public well-being, and on that ground may be, and probably are, defensible.

The financial aspect

[1] Surpluses reported in various years between 1934 and 1940 were fictitious because arrived at only by ignoring heavy subsidies granted to steamship and air lines for carrying mail.

[2] Mail covered by the franking privilege of members of Congress is another item, but not so large as commonly supposed. In 1946, when it cost the Post-Office Department more than one hundred million dollars to handle the materials mentioned above, the outlay on congressional franked mail was only some $846,000. Cf. E. Stern, *History of the Free Franking of Mail in the United States* (New York, 1936).

[3] In reporting a deficit of $263,000,000 for the fiscal year 1947 (the largest then on record), the postmaster-general ascribed it principally to wage increases.

A business run on such lines is not, however, likely to make ends meet; and in the case of a business of a public-service nature like the postal establishment, operating in a country of continental proportions, it probably ought not to be expected to do so. The Post-Office could reasonably be expected to pay its way only if free to cut off—as a private business undoubtedly would do—any branch or operation demonstrating its inability to be self-sustaining. A postal service ministering to a twentieth-century civilization cannot, however, be conducted on the simple dollars-and-cents basis of a chain store or a motor plant.

REFERENCES

B. and L. P. Mitchell, *American Economic History* (Boston, 1947), Chaps. xxvii-xxviii.

M. Fainsod and L. Gordon, *Government and the American Economy* (New York, 1941), Chaps. viii-xvi.

L. H. Chamberlain, *The President, Congress, and Legislation* (New York, 1946), Chap. ii.

H. D. Koontz, *Government Control of Business* (Boston, 1941), Chaps. xiii-xx, xxix-xxxi.

F. P. Hall, *Government and Business* (2nd ed., New York, 1939), Chaps. xxiii-xxvii.
————, *The Concept of Business Affected with a Public Interest* (Bloomington, Ind., 1941).

E. P. Herring, *Public Administration and the Public Interest* (New York, 1936), Chaps. vii-viii, xviii-xix.

R. E. Cushman, *The Independent Regulatory Commissions* (New York, 1941), Chaps. iii-vi.

F. F. Blachly and M. E. Oatman, *Federal Regulatory Action and Control* (Washington, D. C., 1940).

C. C. Rohlfing *et al., Business and Government* (4th ed., Chicago, 1941).

L. S. Lyon, M. W. Watkins, V. Abramson, *et al., Government and Economic Life; Development and Current Issues of American Public Policy*, 2 vols. (Washington, D. C., 1939, 1940).

M. W. Watkins *et al., Public Regulation of Competitive Practices in Business Enterprises* (rev. ed., New York, 1940).

D. Richberg, *Government and Business Tomorrow; A Public Relations Program* (New York, 1943).

T. C. Blaisdell, Jr., *The Federal Trade Commission* (New York, 1932).
————, *Economic Power and Political Pressures,* Monograph No. 26, T.N.E.C. (Washington, D. C., 1941).

A. A. Berle and G. C. Means, *The Modern Corporation and Private Property* (New York, 1933).

Economic Principles Commission of the National Association of Manufacturers, *The American Individual Enterprise System; Its Nature, Evolution, and Future,* 2 vols. (New York, 1946).

J. P. Miller, *Unfair Competition* (Cambridge, Mass., 1941).

T. W. Arnold, *The Bottlenecks of Business* (New York, 1940).
————, *Democracy and Free Enterprise* (Norman, Okla., 1942).

National Resources Committee, *The Structure of the American Economy* (Washington, D. C., 1939).

D. Lynch, *The Concentration of Economic Power* (New York, 1946).

W. E. Atkins, G. W. Edwards, and H. G. Moulton, *The Regulation of the Security Markets* (Washington, D. C., 1946).

E. Frazer, *The Securities Business Comes of Age* (Leonia, N. J., 1946).

M. E. Dimock, *Government-Owned Enterprises in the Panama Canal Zone* (Chicago, 1934).

————, *Developing American Waterways* (Chicago, 1935).

J. H. Thurston, *Government Proprietary Corporations in the English-Speaking Countries* (Cambridge, Mass., 1937).

C. Warren, *Bankruptcy in United States History* (Cambridge, Mass., 1935).

Report of the Attorney-General's Committee on Bankruptcy Administration, 1940 (Washington, D. C., 1941).

L. Rogers, "The Postal Powers of Congress," *Johns Hopkins Univ. Studies in Hist. and Polit. Sci.*, XXXIV, 149-337 (1916).

E. W. Kemmerer, *Postal Savings; History and Critical Study of the Postal-Savings System of the United States* (Princeton, N. J., 1917).

J. A. Dienner, *The United States Patent System* (Cleveland, 1940).

O. R. Barnett, *Patent Property and the Anti-Monopoly Laws* (Indianapolis, 1943).

H. G. Fox, *Monopolies and Patents; A Study of the History and Future of the Patent Monopoly* (Toronto, 1947).

B. Currie [ed.], "The Patent System," *Law and Contemporary Problems*, XII, No. 4 (1947).

U. S. Department of Justice, *Investigation of Government Patent Practices and Policies* (Washington, D. C., 1947).

United States Government Manual (Washington, D. C.), current edition.

Annual reports of the Federal Trade Commission, the Securities and Exchange Commission, the postmaster-general, etc.

CHAPTER XXX

ASSISTANCE TO AGRICULTURE

Agriculture in the American economy The United States started as an almost purely agricultural country, and such it remained for upwards of a hundred years. Ninety-five per cent of its population was rural in 1790, and as late as 1860 the proportion was still above eighty per cent. In his first annual message, President Jackson referred to agriculture as connected with every other interest of the people and "superior to them all," and it was to farmers and planters that the political parties of the day made their primary appeal. After the Civil War, however, the situation changed. Industry and trade expanded, and over a period of two generations the national economy assumed the diverse and complicated aspect which it presents today. By 1920, the urban-rural balance had been tipped in favor of the urban; and since then urban population has risen to seventy-seven per cent of the total and rural fallen to twenty-three per cent—not far from an exact reversal of the proportions in 1860.[1] The farmer is still important politically and his well-being the object of much concern in government circles; but the industrial worker has been crowding him for attention from the politician and for first consideration in the shaping of public policy.

Some significant changes Upon the greatly diminished proportion of our people now engaged in agriculture rests, however, the major responsibility for feeding the country (likewise of late no small part of a hungry postwar world) and supplying its fibers and other raw materials; and this it does from a total of 5,900,000 farms (1,100,000,000 acres), of which hardly more than half produce anything over and above what is consumed by their occupants.[2] Even so, over-production, with accompanying low prices, has been a source of much difficulty in the past, notably preceding and during the depression of the thirties, and in time may become such again. The explanation of the capacity thus developed lies to some extent in improved crops and breeds (for example, hybrid corn), but mainly in the revolutionizing of farming in later years—never more rapidly than during the recent war—by mechanization, enabling fewer workers to produce more with less effort; between 1940 and 1944, food output, aided by favorable

---

[1] The census of 1940 showed the rural farm population numbering approximately thirty millions. In 1947, however, the Bureau of the Census and the Bureau of Agricultural Economics agreed on an estimate of only 27,550,000 for the farm population on January 1 of that year—a gain of 2,400,000 over the wartime low of January 1, 1945, but 9.8 per cent below 1940. The urban-rural percentages (for 1940) given above are therefore subject to some present revision.

[2] In 1944, the top tenth of the country's farms produced half of the total agricultural output (in terms of dollar values).

weather, was pushed upwards by thirty-five per cent, with farm laborers reduced by two and one-half or three millions and, altogether, hardly more able-bodied men engaged in farming than in 1875. In the last quarter-century, the size of farms has been increasing and the number decreasing; farms of more than a thousand acres (113,000 in all in 1945) now account for forty per cent of the total of farm land as compared with twenty-five per cent in 1920; more than half of the total is in farms of over five hundred acres as compared with one-third in 1920; and in 1945 the average farm for the country as a whole (175 acres) was fifty acres larger than in 1920.[1] The explanation is to be found largely in mechanization; and undoubtedly the tendency will continue. On the other hand, tractors, combines, corn-pickers, cotton-strippers, and other power-driven machinery capable of being used economically on small acreage are being developed; and it is fair to conclude that, at all events for some time to come, the moderate-sized family farm will continue to be the backbone of the country's agriculture, if not indeed, as Thomas Jefferson so ardently believed, of its democratic institutions and general well-being.[2]

To be sure, there is a darker side to the agricultural picture, quite apart from the absorption of smaller farms into larger ones (if that be regarded as definitely undesirable). In 1940, two-fifths of all farms in the country were operated, not by owners, but by tenants—"share-croppers" in the South and also large numbers of renters in even such favored areas as the Middle West.[3] There are the hazards of weather, of pests and scourges, of competition of foreign products, of marketing costs, of heavy taxes, and what not. The proportion of agricultural income to total national income is surprisingly low—in 1940, only about eight per cent. Periods of prosperity, too, such as prevailed during and after World War II, seem inevitably to be followed by periods of over-production and depression; and, despite prolonged and prodigious efforts of the federal government to bring the industry to a stabilized parity with the other great economic interests of our people, it still is not at all points satisfactorily meshed with the general national economy.[4]

Unfavorable aspects

[1] The growth of large farms and ranches has naturally been heaviest in the farther West, but has also been characteristic of the "Corn Belt." See P. S. Taylor, "Goodbye to the Homestead Farm," *Harper's Mag.*, CLXXXII, 589-597 (May, 1941).

[2] See A. W. Griswold, "The Agrarian Democracy of Thomas Jefferson," *Amer. Polit. Sci. Rev.*, XL, 657-681 (Aug., 1946).

[3] Agricultural prosperity, however, reduced the proportion by 1948 to thirty per cent.

[4] Factors in the growing tendency to over-production—in addition to those already mentioned—include the decline of export markets, the reduced need for feedstuffs resulting from the replacement of millions of horses and mules by motor machinery on farms, the increased use of commercial fertilizers and of insecticides, more careful selection of seeds, the changing food habits of the people, especially in the cities (cereals declining in demand, with orchard and garden products gaining), the turning of Western grass-lands to tillage (notably in the period of World War I), and the opening of new lands to cultivation by reclamation projects making water available. Altogether, agricultural productivity is increasing at a rate several times faster than the rate of population growth—although if the standard of living of large masses of the population could be brought up to desirable levels, the problem of surpluses would largely, if not wholly, disappear.

Government and Agriculture

State and local activities Although by nature and tradition the most highly individualistic form of enterprise in which our people have engaged, agriculture, like both industry and labor, long ago turned to the halls of government for encouragement and assistance. Nor has the quest been in vain. From early days, local governments contributed by providing roads, enforcing fencing regulations, exterminating pests, supporting fairs and exhibitions, maintaining schools, and in other ways promoting rural welfare; and nowadays county boards have agricultural functions, and the interests of the farmer are in numerous ways served by an official known as the county agent [1] (with also often a female home-demonstration agent), sometimes appointed by the board and in any event—although responsible to both state and federal authorities—acting as a principal promoter of agricultural improvement within his county. A hundred years ago and more, state legislatures, too, were passing laws and making appropriations for the farmer's benefit; and this they continue to do, not usually by virtue of express constitutional provisions, but in pursuance of reserved powers liberally construed by the courts. Nearly every state also has an agricultural college engaged in instructional and advisory work both on the campus and in the field, and likewise a department or board of agriculture endowed with inspecting, licensing, certifying, and other administrative authority, as well as with general advisory and educational functions.

Responsibility of the federal government The nature of agriculture and its problems is, however, such that neither local nor state action can fully meet the farmer's needs. Basic to all such needs is that of being able to market grain, tobacco, cotton, live stock, and other products at prices yielding a fair return on property employed and labor expended. Yet prices are determined largely or entirely by competitive conditions quite transcending the control of any single state. Products must be transported, too, through channels of commerce cutting across state, and even national, lines. And although even the national government is in no position to do all that the farmer's interests might seem to require, manifestly it can reach farther, and with more effect, than can any state. To be sure, the federal constitution makes no mention of agriculture. But no more does it speak directly of industry or labor. And Congress has many powers, e.g., raising and appropriating money, regulating interstate and foreign commerce, and providing postroads, from which broad federal authority for regulating and assisting agriculture can be, and has been, deduced. Beginning with proposals heard as early as Washington's first administration, and gaining momentum as agricultural interests and problems took on more of a national, and eventually international, aspect, the conviction grew that primary responsibility for ministering to the needs of agriculture in a large and

[1] For a graphic account of the activities of a typical county agent (in Texas), see N. M. Clark, "Grassroots Bureaucrat," *Sat. Eve. Post,* CCXVI, 26 ff. (Oct. 23. 1943).

coherent way rests with the federal government; and a systematic account of the activities flowing from this conception in the past three-quarters of a century—and particularly since 1933—would fill a book.[1] Nor could the long story be brought to any end; for in the face of constantly changing agricultural conditions and needs, the federal government's task steadily grows more complicated and exacting, with problems of adjustment of production to consumption, of stabilization of farm income, of land use, of soil erosion, of farm tenancy, of resettlement of handicapped rural populations, of rural electrification, and the like, still only partially solved—even though the generally prosperous state of the farmers in the recent war and postwar period has, for a time at least, rendered some of the challenges less pressing.[2]

Speaking broadly, the significant rôle of agriculture in state and federal government today is a result of farmer-planter, stock-raiser, fruit-grower influence exerted through political channels. In earlier times, farmers and planters were generally too isolated, as well as too individualistic, to permit of much effective organization. But even then the bulk of members of Congress represented rural states or areas and in their approach to public problems were instinctively sympathetic toward the interests of such areas. Today, not only does the equal representation of the states in the Senate still insure a majority from rural states in at least one branch of Congress, but the bringing of people closer together by improved means of transportation and communication (notably the motor-car, the telephone, and radio-broadcasting) has made it easier for farmers to organize and work together—almost equally with urban business-men and workingmen; and as a result, agriculture not only still

The politics of agriculture

---

[1] Such a book indeed (or the closest approach to it) is J. M. Gaus and L. Wolcott, *Public Administration and the United States Department of Agriculture* (Chicago, 1940).

[2] If problems such as those mentioned above have not been solved, it is not for lack of an impressive executive department at Washington to give attention to them; for the Department of Agriculture is not only one of the largest government establishments in the world, but one of the best organized and conducted. It was not by chance that the same year (1862) which saw the Homestead Act and the Land Grant College [Morrill] Act (see p. 677 below) placed on the federal statute-book yielded also a third statute creating a "department of agriculture;" and although for a time the new agency was only a unit within the Department of the Interior and presided over merely by a commissioner, pressure from increasingly vocal agricultural interests finally, in 1889, influenced Congress to raise it to coördinate rank with the seven executive departments then existing—agriculture thus becoming the first great occupational interest to win a seat in the cabinet. The story of the Department in these last fifty or sixty years has been not simply one of swiftly multiplying functions and activities and rapidly growing staff; it has been a record also of systematic, persistent, and fruitful research, making the Department today an outstanding example of useful association of science and government. The Department, indeed, contains more persons of scholarly attainment and fewer appointed for political reasons than any other; and it deserves credit for developing a thoroughly modern personnel system, including liberal provision for in-service training, long before any other major federal establishment. On the Department's historical development, see H. B. Learned, *The President's Cabinet* (New Haven, 1912), Chap. xi, and J. M. Gaus and L. Wolcott, *op. cit.*, Chaps. i-v. A full picture of present organization and functions will be found in any recent issue of the *United States Government Manual*.

has heavy representation in legislative halls, but it has elaborately developed machinery of its own for formulating principles and programs and for urging acceptance of these wherever policies are made and executed—the main obstacle being diversity of interests among agricultural groups such as grain-growers, cotton-growers, sheep and cattle raisers, dairy farmers, and fruit-growers, who, in such matters as the tariff, do not always see eye to eye.

Farmer organizations

From as far back as the seventies and eighties of the last century, farmer organizations like the National Grange of the Patrons of Husbandry and at least two Farmers' Alliances are heard of, and in 1892 the experiment of a Populist party was launched. Springing up naturally in periods of farm depression and discontent, such movements commonly made headway only while the difficulty lasted, and afterwards evaporated. Although not originally inspired by depression, a largely agrarian Nonpartisan League, organized in North Dakota and spreading to adjoining states, similarly declined—partly as a result of internal dissension— leaving as its principal residue a Farmer-Labor party which, joining farmers with city-workers, and now merged with the Democrats as the Democratic-Farmer-Labor party, has remained a political force in Minnesota. Nation-wide farm organization as existing today, however, dates mainly from within the period since World War I. With the collapse of a wartime agricultural boom in 1920, there was no return to the idea of organizing a farmer political party; rather, effort was concentrated upon electing to Congress sympathetic members of the two major parties and welding them, in both Senate and House, into a disciplined farm *bloc* to advance agrarian interests. For three or four years, too, the resulting *bloc* showed considerable vigor, with several pieces of remedial legislation to its credit; and although in later times it found difficulty in holding together, at intervals ever since it has made its somewhat shadowy existence felt.[1] More important, however, has been the building up of three major nation-wide farm organizations which today constitute the main channels of farmer influence on policy-making at Washington. One—the National Grange, with an aggregate membership of some 800,000, and representing principally fruit and vegetable growers and dairy and poultry men, with an admixture of non-farmers attracted by its social activities—dates back to the Granger movement of seventy-five years ago, and is relatively conservative. A second—the Farmers' Educational and Coöperative Union of America—with strength mainly in the plains areas which suffered most from the droughts and related disasters of the thirties—is a more radical group, with somewhat socialistic inclinations. The third—an American Farm Bureau Federation, dating originally from 1919 and strongest in the Midwest and South, although well represented in states like New York and California—is a middle-of-the-road organization, with county farm bureaus federated into state

[1] W. McCune, *The Farm Bloc* (Garden City, N. Y., 1943).

bureaus as its constituent units, and with a total popular membership (doubled during the war) of more than a million. The Federation is private rather than public. But it has been built up locally largely by county agents (who are public officials); state colleges of agriculture have fostered and worked with it; its relations with the Department of Agriculture are close; and one will not be surprised to learn that in such periods as the early years of the New Deal it has had an influential hand in the formulation of government policy—notably in connection with the Agricultural Adjustment Act of 1933.[1] All such organizations, indeed, are well represented in Washington by agents and lobbyists; and any student of pressure-group activities and influences in the American scene will do well to put farmer granges, unions, federations, bureaus, and the like near the top of his list of exhibits.

Production and Marketing

As a factor in an expanding national economy, agriculture has developed in such a manner that the farmer normally finds himself confronted with three main sets of problems, pertaining respectively to (1) production, (2) marketing, and (3) credit. On the production side, the federal government has sometimes intervened to curb surpluses and sustain prices by curtailing output, as notably under the New Deal program for national recovery in the earlier thirties. As a rule, however, the objective has rather been increased and better assured production; and to this end a number of policies have more or less consistently been pursued: (1) making arable land available, in earlier days by liberal parcelling out of public land,[2] and more recently by stimulating the removal of farmers from exhausted or otherwise substandard land to areas of greater productiveness; (2) imposing tariffs on farm products from abroad, with a view to larger home markets for American products and at better prices—a policy, however, never too effective for the reason that in the case of most staple crops, such as cotton and grain, the American farmer himself normally produces an exportable surplus; (3) scientific research aimed at introducing new crops, improving varieties and breeds, increasing soil productiveness, combatting pests and diseases, and applying sound principles of economics to all stages and forms of the agricultural process; and (4) disseminating the results of research and otherwise promoting popular education on agricultural subjects. A word may be said about each of the last two policies mentioned.

Encouragement of production

[1] See p. 678 below. There are, of course, numerous more specialized farmer organizations, *e.g.*, the National Livestock Producers Association and the American Dairy Federation.

[2] Notably under the Homestead Act of 1862, by whose terms any person could acquire 160 acres from the public domain by paying a modest registration fee and actually occupying the "homestead" for at least five years. As observed by Professor W. B. Munro, this act "set the pattern of land ownership in much of the West—the farm of moderate size cultivated by its owner." *The Government of the United States* (5th ed., New York, 1946), 462.

Scientific
research

The medium through which research of direct significance to agriculture is carried on is mainly a series of bureaus and services in the Department of Agriculture. The earliest function of the Department was, indeed, scientific investigation and dissemination of the information gained therefrom; and notwithstanding later multiplication of activities in other directions, the Department is still by all odds the greatest research establishment of its kind in the world. Of bureaus devoted particularly to investigation (and coördinated under an Agricultural Research Administration), seven of principal importance have to do with (1) agricultural and industrial chemistry, (2) animal industry, (3) dairy industry, (4) entomology and plant quarantine, (5) plant industry, soils, and agricultural engineering, (6) human nutrition and home economics, and (7) agricultural economics.[1] From these terms, one can easily infer the general nature of the inquiries and experiments conducted by the various agencies, even though only an expert can completely understand and appreciate the technical procedures and objectives frequently involved. Still other units devoted not quite so exclusively to research, yet continually carrying on studies of significance, include (1) a Forest Service, which not only investigates forestry problems, but takes care of as many as 152 national forests (comprising over 179,000,000 acres) in forty states and territories, and shares responsibility with the Land Office and the Reclamation Service in the Department of the Interior for carrying out and extending the national conservation program gradually developed since 1900; and (2) a Soil Conservation Service, dating from 1935 and concerned with bringing about physical adjustments in land use with a view to protection of resources and development of a better balance in agriculture. Agricultural research, however, is carried on not only by federal agencies, but also by state and territorial experiment stations; and federal assistance to these is provided from funds pledged by various acts of Congress and administered by an Office of Experiment Stations in the Department of Agriculture, which, in a supervisory capacity, lends unity and consistency to the programs undertaken.[2]

Agricultural
education

The object of the investigative activities of the foregoing agencies is practical assistance to farmers; and this necessitates facilities for popularizing the results obtained.[3] Such information, of course, is conveyed

---

[1] Good summaries of the work of these bureaus will be found in any recent issue of the *United States Government Manual*. Detailed treatises (although out of date, and not always dealing with units as at present constituted) include G. A. Weber, "The Bureau of Chemistry and Soils," *Service Monographs,* No. 52 (Baltimore, 1928); F. W. Powell, "The Bureau of Plant Industry," *ibid.,* No. 47 (Baltimore, 1927), and "The Bureau of Animal Industry," No. 41 (Baltimore, 1927); J. Cameron, "The Bureau of Dairy Industry," *ibid.,* No. 55 (Baltimore, 1929).

[2] A Research and Marketing Service Act of 1946 (60 *U. S. Stat. at Large,* 1082, 1087) placed new stress on agricultural research and authorized increased appropriations over a five-year period. See *Report of the Secretary of Agriculture, 1946,* pp. 113-116; and H. K. Thatcher, "Agricultural Research and Marketing Under Public Law 733," *State Government,* XIX, 282-285 (Nov., 1946).

[3] See T. S. Harding, "Informational Techniques of the Department of Agriculture," *Pub. Opinion Quar.,* I, 83-96 (Jan., 1937).

directly through the medium of widely distributed bulletins, reports, and other printed documents. In these days of radio-broadcasting, a good deal—notably such things of immediate concern as market reports and weather predictions—is put on the air. But the federal government (in common with the state governments) has also committed itself to an ever-widening program of agricultural education in the stricter sense of the term. To begin with, the Land Grant College [Morrill] Act of 1862 [1] and certain supplementary legislation bestowed upon the states, in proportion to their representation in Congress, some 10,840,000 acres of public land, with the stipulation that the proceeds of sales be used in each case for the support of one or more colleges devoted primarily (although other subjects might be taught) to instruction in "such branches of learning as are related to agriculture and the mechanic arts." From this arrangement arose the "land-grant colleges" which dot the country today—in many states, *e.g.*, Indiana, Iowa, and Michigan, separate "agricultural and mechanical" colleges, in others, *e.g.*, Illinois, Wisconsin, and Minnesota, colleges forming divisions of the state university. Some states parted with their land at absurdly low prices, and in 1890 a generous Congress started the practice—ever since maintained—of making direct appropriations from the federal treasury for additional aid to the institutions that had grown up. Simultaneously, steps were taken to see that the colleges carried out the purposes for which the grants were made; and out of this has developed substantial federal control over curricula and other features.

In such a domain as agriculture, research involves experimentation; and not only are first-hand investigations carried on at Washington, but as long ago as 1887 every land-grant college was required to maintain an experiment station, devoted particularly to inquiries conducted with respect to the conditions of climate, soil, and markets of the region adjacent to the given station. Under the Smith-Lever Act of 1914, furthermore, various forms of extension work were instituted with a view to bringing information directly to the farmer and his wife in their home; indeed, every one of the agricultural colleges now maintains a distinct division for such work in both agriculture and home economics, with federal supervision supplied by an Extension Service in the Department of Agriculture, and with the county agent serving as the principal channel through which the contributions of federal and state research are made available locally. All in all, in no field of government activity is there more federal-state-local interlocking and coöperation than in that of agriculture.

Having shown the farmer how to "make two blades of grass grow where one grew before" and how to raise live stock more efficiently, the government found that it had created for itself a new and even greater problem. More farmers now had produce to sell; more had come to be

The problem of marketing

[1] *12 U. S. Stat. at Large*, 503

dependent upon receipts from "cash crops;" any obstruction to the transportation of commodities to distant markets, or to the handling of such commodities in the increasingly intricate processes by which they reached the consumer—any piling up of surpluses and depression of prices—was of deep concern. And when, after an over-extension of agricultural production incident to World War I, difficulties at these points began to multiply, the farmer turned to his government for aid, especially in developing markets, sustaining prices, and minimizing the effects of market manipulations engaged in by speculators and others for their own advantage. Down to 1929, such assistance took the form, chiefly, of (1) furnishing full, exact, and up-to-the-minute information concerning crop and marketing conditions and prospects, both at home and abroad; (2) establishing and maintaining uniform grades and standards for commodities handled through the channels of interstate and foreign commerce; (3) regulating bonded warehouses and stockyards, licensing commission merchants, brokers, and others who handled or dealt in perishable farm products, and in other ways protecting the producer against discrimination and fraud; and (4) protecting him against the operations of "bearish" speculators dealing in "futures," *i.e.*, engaging to deliver specified quantities of a given commodity on a given date at a given price, and depending for profit upon forcing down the buying price—the price received by the farmer—in the meantime. All measures taken on these lines,[1] however, failed to yield farmers as a class a proportional share of the prosperity which the country considered itself to be enjoying in the period 1921-29; and a comprehensive Agricultural Marketing Act of the last-mentioned year, designed to promote and finance coöperative marketing and stabilize prices through the instrumentality of a Federal Farm Board authorized to encourage the formation of farmers' coöperatives and in other ways to assist in promoting effective marketing, brought no better results—principally because there was no power to do the thing that the situation most obviously required, *i.e.*, curb overproduction. Accordingly, the problem of outlets and prices was no new one when the Roosevelt Administration took it over, in a period of dire distress not only in industry and business but in agriculture as well.

The first Agricultural Adjustment Act (1933)

The National Recovery Act of 1933, touched upon in the preceding chapter, was designed primarily to stimulate revival of trade and industry. Not only, however, did agriculture stand in at least equal need of assistance, but without improvement of its situation, commercial and industrial revival could not go far. Accordingly, under impetus supplied by the newly installed Administration, Congress—invited by the Presi-

[1] Among them were a Meat Inspection Act of 1890, an Animal Quarantine Act and a Grain Standards Act of 1901, a Food and Drugs Act of 1906, a Plant and Quarantine Act of 1912, a Cotton Futures Act and a Federal Warehouse Act of 1916, a Packers and Stockyards Act of 1921, a Grain Futures Act of 1922—all designed to extend the use of federal standards and inspection services, and all initiated largely as marketing aids to farmers, although obviously of importance for consumers as well.

dent to enter "a new and untrod path"—boldly bracketed with the Recovery Act a novel Agricultural Adjustment Act designed to benefit the farmer through a program of crop curtailment and drastic marketing controls.

The new legislation had various objectives, but its basic aim was clear and simple, *i.e.*, to increase the farmer's purchasing power by raising the prices which he received for his products—prices which at the time were so depressed by accumulated surpluses that frequently they did not even cover the cost of production.[1] More specifically, the objective was "parity," that is, a price level at which farm products would have the same purchasing power as in the arbitrarily selected but favorable base period 1909-14;[2] and the goal was to be attained by inducing farmers to cut production to a point sufficient to cause prices to rise to the intended level. The farmer, however, could not be asked to curtail the output on which he depended for income without being compensated financially for doing so, and it became necessary to decide from what source the requisite funds should be obtained. They might simply, of course, have been allocated from the federal treasury; and, as it turned out, a substantial share of them actually were. But it was considered that—at least in the main—they ought to be contributed somewhat more definitely by the people for whom the farmer raised crops, *i.e.*, by the consumers of such crops; and when it was realized that a tax directly on consumers would be difficult to collect, decision was reached to impose the levy instead upon "processors" of commodities, *i.e.*, cotton manufacturers, millers, meat-packers, and others who prepared agricultural products to which the act applied[3] for public use—it being understood and intended that the burden would, in turn, be passed along in the form of higher prices to consumers.

General purport

Asserting that the depressed condition of agriculture had "burdened and obstructed the normal currents of commerce," the authors of the act sought to give it a valid constitutional foundation by putting it forth as a measure by which such burdens and obstructions might be removed. And the task of carrying out the terms stipulated was assigned to the appropriate executive department—more specifically to the secretary of agriculture,[4] to whom was given unprecedented authority to reduce the market supply of enumerated agricultural commodities through volun-

Crop reduction features

[1] Unlike industrial establishments, farms cannot simply close down when markets are glutted, or change in a few months to some other form of production. Once in operation, a farm must be kept going, and when prices fall, the tendency of the farmer—unless relief is afforded in some other way—is simply to increase his production in order to maintain his income, thus contributing to a further decline of prices.

[2] In the case of tobacco, the base period was August, 1919, to July, 1929.

[3] Originally seven, *i.e.*, wheat, cotton, field corn, rice, tobacco, hogs, and milk and its products. Later additions were beef, dairy cattle, peanuts, barley, flax, grain sorghums, sugar beets, sugar cane, and potatoes.

[4] To administer the law, an Agricultural Adjustment Administration, in several divisions, was organized in the Department, although on a largely autonomous basis.

tary agreements by farmers (for a consideration) to reduce acreage planted, to plow under a percentage of crops already growing, to kill surplus sows and pigs, and otherwise to curtail production—the consideration, of course, being the receipt of government-paid cash subsidies graduated according to the potential productiveness of the land involved. Following enactment of the law, the system went into operation, and after a year the administrator was able to report that three million farmers, considering that they at least had nothing to lose, had signed production-control contracts withdrawing from surplus production a total of some forty million acres of grain, cotton, tobacco, and dairy land; that the farmer's cash income, including benefit payments, had risen by thirty-nine per cent; and that the buying power of farm commodities had improved by twenty per cent.[1] Full parity prices were never realized; but by 1935 the average of farm prices was up sixty-six per cent, and the farmer's outlook appeared brighter than for years.

Marketing arrangements

Along with production, the act dealt also with marketing; and here, too, the secretary of agriculture was endowed with new and far-reaching authority, i.e., to enter into marketing agreements with processors and others engaged in handling any agricultural commodity "in the current of interstate or foreign commerce;" and entering into such agreements was declared to be not a violation of the anti-trust laws. Of even greater importance was the power conferred to issue, or to refuse, revocable licenses (and to fix their terms) permitting processors and others to handle, in the currents of interstate or foreign commerce, any agricultural commodity or "any competing commodity." The object, of course, was to enable the secretary to prevent—or eliminate—unfair prices and practices.[2]

The A.A.A. declared unconstitutional (1936)

Almost from the day of enactment, the constitutionality of the Agricultural Adjustment Act was questioned, attacks centering chiefly upon the processing taxes—"the heart of the law." Hundreds of cases appeared in the federal courts challenging the right of the government thus to employ the taxing power as a means of bringing about national regulation of agricultural production, and in a six-to-three decision rendered early in 1936,[3] the Supreme Court pronounced the taxes unconstitutional,

---

[1] S. C. Wallace, The New Deal in Action, Chap. XI; H. A. Wallace, New Frontiers, Chaps. XIII-XVI; L. M. Hacker, "Ploughing the Farmer Under," Harper's Mag., CLXIX, 60-74 (June, 1934).

[2] By fixing prices, establishing quotas for producers, providing rules of fair competition, and setting up boards of control, marketing agreements under the act brought into existence a far greater amount of coöperative marketing than previously existed. Closely related to the Agricultural Adjustment Act were the Bankhead Cotton Control Act of 1934, the Kerr-Smith Tobacco Control Act of 1934, and the Warren Potato Act of 1935.

[3] United States v. Butler, 297 U. S. 1 (often referred to as the Hoosac Mills case). The case arose out of the refusal of the receivers of a bankrupt New Hampshire textile establishment to pay taxes still due on the processing of cotton. A federal district court had ordered them to pay the sum; a circuit court of appeals had told them not to pay it because the levy was unconstitutional; and the government had taken the case to the Supreme Court.

asserting that they were not taxes in the true sense (that is, levies for support of the government), but rather exactions from one group of people to provide benefits for another group—a device, too, by which Congress had presumed to invade a field, *i.e.*, agricultural production, reserved to the states under the Tenth Amendment, and therefore outside the sphere of the national government.[1]

A New Approach to "Parity"

Although the plan described had cost taxpayers and consumers nearly twice as much as the processing taxes had brought in,[2] it had contributed heavily to increasing farm income, and invalidation of the taxes was a blow to farmers, who could no longer hope to receive the benefits, or bounties, which the taxes had provided. Manifestly, farm income would drop sharply unless some substitute were devised; manifestly, too, such a substitute would have to be based upon some constitutional authority other than the taxing power. With little delay, a new starting point was found in the long-recognized right of Congress to provide for conservation of the country's natural resources; indeed, in a Soil Erosion Act passed in 1935, following widespread devastation and distress caused by floods and dust-storms, Congress had unwittingly provided a foundation upon which a new farm-aid and crop-control program could be constructed.[3]

The quest for a substitute plan

Believing that an indirect production-control plan, if tied in with this soil conservation measure, would pass the test of constitutionality, Congress, in February, 1936, passed a Soil Conservation and Domestic Allotment Act[4] erecting a new edifice of farm relief, but making production control *incidental* to soil conservation. As in the first A.A.A., restoration of the pre-World War I purchasing power of the farmer was the end sought; but the goal was now to be reached by a new route—soil conservation rather than acreage control. Instead of direct bounties for curtailed production, benefit payments were to be made to farmers voluntarily coöperating with the government in the work of soil protection, especially by shifting land from soil-depleting crops such as corn, cotton, tobacco, and wheat to soil-conserving or soil-building crops such as alfalfa and clover, with soil-building payments due also for planting specified acreages of legumes or turning cultivated land into pasturage.[5] In protecting

The Soil Conservation and Domestic Allotment Act (1936)

---

[1] The marketing provisions of the law were not affected by the decision, and Congress promptly reënacted them (50 *U. S. Stat. at Large,* 246). But the production features, centered in the processing taxes, went out of the window.

[2] Some $1,700,000,000, as compared with receipts of $900,000,000.

[3] 49 *U. S. Stat. at Large,* 163. The act—administered by the Soil Conservation Service in the Department of Agriculture—had declared it "the policy of Congress to provide permanently for the control and prevention of soil erosion and thereby to preserve natural resources, control floods, prevent impairment of reservoirs, maintain the navigation of rivers and harbors, protect public health and public lands, and to relieve unemployment." See Anon., "Saving Our Soil," *Pub. Affairs Pamphlets,* No. 14 (New York, 1937).

[4] 49 *U. S. Stat. at Large,* 1148.

[5] No special taxes were introduced for meeting soil-conservation payments. Appropriations made from the government's general funds were presumably to be justified

the productiveness of their soil, farmers, it was hoped, would so reduce their output of staple crops that surpluses would disappear.

Agricul-
tural
Adjust-
ment
Act
(1938)

Perhaps this expectation was too optimistic; at all events, 1937 proved an especially good crop year, and the old vicious spiral of commodity surpluses and sharply declining prices set in again. Accordingly, in 1938—with staggering surpluses promising to be still further swollen by bumper crops—Congress passed a new Agricultural Adjustment Act,[1] scrupulously avoiding processing taxes and any other devices likely to encounter judicial disapproval, but nevertheless contemplating, like the ill-fated measure of 1933, direct control of agricultural production. Continuing the conservation program of 1936 for what it was worth, the measure sought to achieve the desired control by additional arrangements briefly as follows: (1) if in any year the production of wheat, corn, cotton, rice, or tobacco threatened to create a surplus that would break the price, the new Agricultural Adjustment Administration now set up was to take a referendum among the producers of a given crop on the desirability of imposing limitations;[2] (2) if two-thirds voted favorably, the A.A.A. was to allot to each producing county, on the basis of the average acreage seeded during the preceding ten years, the number of acres that might be planted to the given crop; (3) within each county, and with the coöperation of local committees, an allotment was to be made, in turn, to each producing farmer, of a maximum acreage from which he might market his product without restriction; (4) the producer might raise more acres of the crop if he insisted, but if he marketed products from such excess acreage during a period of surplus, he was to be subject to fine; (5) on surplus crops so produced, a farmer might receive loans from a Commodity Credit Corporation in amounts calculated according to "parity" prices; (6) such surplus crops should be stored under government seal in elevators or warehouses until such time as a scarcity might arise, when the farmer might sell them at the parity price and repay his loans—such sales operating to prevent the market price from ever rising far above parity; and (7) when the price of a given commodity should fall below parity, the producer should be entitled to receive from the government payments sufficient to make up the deficiency. In short, surplus crops were to be stored in years of superabundance, without the farmer being left short of cash, and then would be available to be thrown on the market in years of shortage from drouth or other cause—with prices held always close to parity levels, and with in any event the farmer guaranteed a return (price plus subsidy if necessary) not below such levels. To this system of an "ever-normal granary" was added, too, a provision for wheat-crop insurance (extended in 1941

(and still are) on the basis of the power to tax and appropriate money for promoting the general welfare.

[1] 52 *U. S. Stat. at Large*, 31.
[2] L. V. Howard, "The Agricultural Referendum," *Pub. Admin. Rev.*, II, 9-26 (Winter, 1942).

to cotton), undertaking to protect producers against depleted yields due
to drouth, flood, insect infestation, and plant diseases—insurance costs
(*i.e.*, premiums) being payable by the insured to the government either
in cash or in surplus wheat (or cotton), and the latter becoming an additional reserve of the ever-normal granary.[1] Completing the structure of
the New Deal farm program, and fully sustained as constitutional by a
now reconstructed Supreme Court,[2] the legislation of 1938 proved both
successful and popular during the brief period that elapsed before conditions were sharply altered by World War II.

Some Wartime Developments

Little did the authors of the various crop-restriction and surplus-
reduction programs dream that the day was near when the country's
main problems in agriculture would be those of increasing production and
building up surpluses. But so it turned out. Even before the United States
entered the war, the expanding need for American foodstuffs in the war-
torn democracies, the generous assistance provided under "lend-lease"
legislation, and the growth of consumer demand in our own country arising from our defense effort, impelled the Department of Agriculture to
announce a farm program for 1942 calling for "the largest production in
the history of American agriculture."[3] The increases mainly contemplated were in what had previously been considered non-basic commodities—chiefly such foodstuffs as poultry, eggs, milk and other dairy
products, meat, vegetables, and sugar. Basic crops with a long record of
surpluses—wheat, cotton, tobacco, and rice—continued under somewhat
restricted production and marketing until 1943; although corn acreage

New emphasis on production

[1] A Federal Crop Insurance Corporation was set up in the Department of Agriculture to administer the insurance system, and in later years the plan was extended
to flax and some other crops.
Independent of the new A.A.A., but designed to reënforce its provisions for reducing surpluses, were three other expedients: (1) export subsidies for wheat, cotton,
and cotton goods; (2) provision of free lunches for several million under-nourished
school children; and (3) the distribution of food stamps among eligible low-income
families, to be used in exchange for specified surplus commodities (including cotton)
at local stores—a device, however, terminated under wartime conditions in 1943.
Provision for free lunches for school children was continued by the National School
Lunch Act of 1946, "as a means of national security and to safeguard the health and
well-being of the nation's children." 60 *U. S. Stat. at Large*, 230.
[2] Chiefly in Mulford *v.* Smith, 307 U. S. 38 (1939), upholding the marketing provisions as applied to tobacco, and Wickard *v.* Filburn, 317 U. S. 111, approving the
imposition of a penalty for wheat produced in excess of a prescribed quota,
even though the excess was consumed on the farm where it was raised. In the
latter case, the Court held that the excess wheat, though grown for home consumption, "exerts a substantial economic effect in interstate commerce," because "it
supplies the need of the man who grew it, which would otherwise be reflected by
purchases in the open market. In this sense, the Court held, home-grown wheat
"competes with wheat in commerce." It will be observed that whereas the act of
1933 was aimed directly at limiting production, that of 1938 was aimed only at keeping surpluses out of the interstate and foreign market, and that therefore the Court
had to test the latter statute only in terms of interstate and foreign commerce—
which made full acceptance of it a matter of no particular difficulty.
[3] The reasons why agriculture "entered defense and war with less fuss and fury
than any other section of the national economy" are explained in J. L. McCamy,
"Agriculture Goes to War," *Pub. Admin. Rev.*, II, 1-8 (Winter, 1942).

(corn being a feed grain) was allowed to be considerably increased, and the 1943 crop proved the largest in a decade. As a result of heavy feeding of wheat also to livestock, and of its use in the production of alcohol, that grain was, by 1943, fast moving from a surplus to a deficit situation; and early in the year the War Food Production Administration removed all wheat-acreage and marketing restrictions, with the result that the 1943 crop became the second largest on record. Not only so, but in midsummer the same authority asked wheat-growers to step up their 1944 acreage to sixty-eight million, as compared with somewhat over fifty-four million seeded the previous year. Finally, in 1944, all effort to control food production, save by voluntary means, was for the time being abandoned, although restrictions were retained upon the production and marketing of tobacco.

Curbing farm prices

Within a year after Pearl Harbor, the well-being of the people and the prosecution of the war itself were menaced by rising prices and by a growing danger of runaway inflation; and agriculture was deeply involved. Early in 1942, a powerful farm *bloc* in Congress contrived to write into a basic Emergency Price Control Act [1] a provision prohibiting ceilings on food products until farm prices had gone, on the average, sixteen per cent beyond "parity prices"—parity, it will be recalled, being a level of prices at which farm products would have the same purchasing power as during the five-year period preceding the First World War. Thus shielded, farm prices mounted steadily; and in September President Roosevelt informed Congress that with a view to keeping the cost of living within bounds, the recent prohibitory clause would have to be repealed, and, further, that if it were not repealed by October 1, he, acting under his authority as commander-in-chief, would disregard its restrictions and proceed independently to carry out an anti-inflationary program entailing both wage stabilization and fixing of farm prices considerably below "parity." Amid loudly voiced protests against this threatened suspension of national law by independent executive action, Congress went to work on bills ostensibly aimed at accomplishing the desired purpose; and presently an act was passed authorizing the chief executive to stabilize not only farm prices but wages and salaries. In the case of farm prices, however, the measure went only half-way; because ceilings might not be fixed below either parity or the highest market levels between January 1 and September 15, 1942, whichever was higher. Thenceforth, the consumer had better protection against skyrocketing food costs, yet with the farmer enjoying a prosperity limited only by an inadequate labor supply.[2]

[1] 56 *U. S. Stat. at Large*, 23.
[2] On June 30, 1946, the Emergency Price Control Act of 1942 expired and agricultural prices began rising. A month later, however, new legislation reimposed controls in part for a period of one year. The agricultural policies of the New Deal accustomed farmers to subsidies in exchange for regulations. During the war and earlier postwar years, however, they were impatient with regulation, especially of prices; they were doing well and wanted no interference.

Credit Facilities

When, in earlier days of more diversified agriculture, a farmer wanted A growing need to acquire additional land, make improvements, or perhaps carry over a crop in the hope of a better market, he normally must turn for funds to a regular commercial bank; and of course a considerable amount of such borrowing still goes on. Commercial banks, however, have always been interested primarily in serving the needs of industry and commerce, and, if loaning money at all to farmers and stock-raisers (regarded as greater risks), have been likely to do so only on less favorable terms, including higher rates of interest. Moreover, in recent decades a steadily increasing proportion of agriculture has ceased to be diversified and become specialized. Cotton farmers there always were, but now we have, in addition, wheat farmers, corn and hog farmers, dairy farmers, fruit farmers, ranchers, and what not; and while some of these, especially dairy farmers, may have proceeds coming in more or less all of the time, it is characteristic of most of them to have little income except at one or two periods of the year when cash crops are ready for marketing. To normal farmer needs for credit on favorable terms are therefore added special demands arising from this newer situation.

The upshot has been the building up, over the past thirty-five years, A farm loan system instituted of a country-wide system of credit institutions—a network of banks and other agencies—authorized, supported, and regulated by the federal government, and operated exclusively for service to the farmer. The development started in 1916, when, after commissions appointed by Presidents Taft and Wilson had looked into the needs existing even in that day, Congress passed the first piece of federal credit legislation in our history, a Federal Farm Loan Act,[1] looked upon in some quarters as dubiously "radical," yet with objectives endorsed by all major parties in the campaign of 1912. A Federal Farm Loan Board was set up in the Treasury Department as manager, and in a leading city of each of twelve districts into which the country was divided for the purpose was established a federal land bank, with capital subscribed mainly by the United States, and endowed with power to issue tax-exempt bonds to raise money with which to make loans secured by mortgages on landed property. These land banks lent money, however, not directly to individual farmers, but to groups of ten or more organized voluntarily in what were known as national farm loan associations. An association received applications from its members, approved or rejected them, took and endorsed mortgages on the applicant's property, and, on the basis of these, secured from the banks funds which it passed out in the form of loans to its members.[2] To broaden the service, the same act of 1916 also authorized

[1] 39 *U. S. Stat. at Large*, 360.
[2] R. J. Bulkley, "The Federal Farm Loan Act," *Jour. of Polit. Econ.*, XXV, 129-147 (Feb., 1917); G. E. Putnam, "The Federal Farm Loan Act," *Amer. Econ. Rev.*, VI, 770-789 (Dec., 1916).

the formation of joint-stock land banks, with capital stock subscribed by private individuals, and enjoying about the same privileges and performing the same functions as the federal land banks. And to complete the structure, an Agricultural Credits Act of 1923 [1] instituted a series of twelve intermediate credit banks designed particularly to serve the farmer who wanted, not long-term credit, but loans for a few months or a year, and loans secured, not on land, but on live stock, corn, wheat, or other commodities.

Depression-time developments   After the depression of the thirties—bearing perhaps more heavily upon farmers than upon any other group—had harassed the country for some time, with little promise of abating, it became apparent that still larger credit facilities would have to be provided; by 1933, a tenth of the country's farms had been sold at public auction to satisfy creditors, and the number of such sales was steadily increasing.[2] To be sure, the act creating the Reconstruction Finance Corporation in 1932 had empowered that agency to organize regional agricultural credit corporations in the twelve federal land-bank districts, with a capital in each case of not less than ten million dollars subscribed by the Corporation; and loans made by these institutions had helped. But need remained; and the years 1933-34 saw additional legislation, with various new borrowing facilities introduced. An Emergency Farm Mortgage Act of 1933 [3] (constituting a distinct section of the Agricultural Adjustment Act of that year) opened up ways for the farmer to borrow directly from a fund of two hundred millions [4] administered by a farm-loan commissioner (later land-bank commissioner) in a Farm Credit Administration now superseding the Federal Farm Loan Board, and in particular made borrowings available for the redemption or repurchase of farm property lost under foreclosure proceedings during the previous two years. A Farm Credit Act [5] of the same year (a) set up twelve production credit corporations, one in each city having a federal land bank, to provide short-term credit for all types of farm and ranch operations and (b) instituted a system of banks to serve twelve thousand or more coöperative buying and selling associations among farmers of the country—a central bank for coöperatives and regional banks operating in the same twelve cities. A Commodity Credit Corporation was brought into existence by executive order of 1933, with power to buy, hold, sell, lend upon, or otherwise deal in such agricultural commodities as might be designated from time to time by the president. And a Federal Farm Mortgage Corporation, created by Congress in 1934 in an act amplifying the Emergency Farm Mortgage Act of the previous year, was empowered to issue tax-exempt bonds

[1] 42 *U. S. Stat. at Large*, 1461.
[2] Most farms thus sold passed into the possession of banks, insurance companies, mortgage companies, and other financial institutions. In Iowa, for example, one-tenth of all farm land was by 1935 held by corporations.
[3] 48 *U. S. Stat. at Large*, 41.
[4] Provided by the Reconstruction Finance Corporation.
[5] 48 *U. S. Stat. at Large*, 257.

(guaranteed by the government) which might be exchanged for others held or issued by federal land banks, thereby increasing the resources of those banks available for the refinancing of farm mortgages.[4]

The upshot of the entire series of measures reviewed (and substantially all are still in effect) is that in each of the twelve farm credit districts into which the country is divided there is now a federal land bank, a federal intermediate credit bank, a production credit corporation, and a bank for coöperatives—the four forming a coördinated administrative unit, and the whole comprising a truly gigantic framework of agricultural credit institutions.[2] How serviceable the system will prove in the long run remains to be disclosed; the problems of the farmer, under modern national and international conditions, are too complicated to be solved by mere access to loan funds. If, however, it be agreed that a prime essential is to enable the farmer to retain possession of his land, and to continue supporting his family from it notwithstanding ups and downs in general agricultural conditions, it would seem that facilities to that end could hardly have been provided more generously by an anxious government, constantly prodded, as of course it has been, by a powerful farm lobby. Long-term loans on land are readily obtainable at reasonable rates of interest and on easy terms of repayment; short-term loans on crops or stock are similarly accessible; indeed, there is hardly any important type of farm or ranch operation for which, under specified conditions, a loan of some kind is not to be had. Management of the entire system, excluding the Commodity Credit Corporation, has been gathered into the hands of a single coördinating authority, the Farm Credit Administration, dating from 1933, incorporated into the Department of Agriculture in 1939, and now constituting one of the major agencies in that department.

The present system summarized

Rural Betterment

From activities directed to the scientific and economic aspects of farming, the Department of Agriculture has moved on in later years, especially since 1933, to what may be termed broadly the human, or social, aspects of the occupation. Impelled to do this by rural backwardness and distress brought sharply to view by the economic depression of the thirties, and by the exclusion even yet of farmers and agricultural laborers from the benefits of existing social insurance systems (though not from public *assistance* programs), the Department now regards as part of its regular task the systematic promotion of better living condi-

[1] After one act of Congress providing for moratoria on the foreclosure of farm mortgages was pronounced unconstitutional by the Supreme Court in 1935 (Louisville Joint-Stock Land Bank *v.* Radford, 295 U. S. 555), another on somewhat different lines was upheld (Wright *v.* Vinton Branch Mountain Trust Bank, 300 U. S. 440) in 1937. As a result, large numbers of farmers were enabled to procure adjustments with their creditors and retain their land.

[2] On June 30, 1945, the various lending agencies involved had outstanding loans aggregating nearly six billion dollars.

tions in rural communities.[1] Only a few outstanding services of this nature can, however, be mentioned here.

The agricultural credit institutions described above are designed primarily to benefit farmers who own, or have an ownership interest in, the land they cultivate. There is another large agricultural class that cannot avail itself of these credit agencies, for the reason that those who are numbered in it own no land and little, if any, other property that might serve as a credit basis for loans. These less fortunate people are the tenant farmers, share-croppers, and farm laborers, who since 1880 have been steadily increasing in proportion to the number of farm-owners, and now comprise upwards of half of the total number tilling the soil. They are the people who give rise to what is called the farm tenancy problem; and the areas where large numbers of them live, notably the Southern and Southwestern states, form our "rural slums." Following a penetrating, and fairly startling, report in 1937 on the conditions and outlook of these submerged elements, submitted by a committee on farm tenancy appointed by President Franklin D. Roosevelt, Congress in the same year passed the Bankhead-Jones Farm Tenant Act,[2] under which the government, operating through state and local machinery terminating in county committees of farmers, not only makes outright grants to meet emerging situations, but offers forty-year loans on easy terms to farm tenants, farm laborers, and share-croppers to enable them to acquire homes and lands of their own, and likewise "rehabilitation loans" for the purchase of live stock and farm equipment, for refinancing indebtedness, and for family subsistence. Under the direction of a Farmers Home Administration set up in the Department of Agriculture in 1946 (and taking over the functions of a previous Farm Security Administration and certain other agencies), the arrangement has achieved substantial results during the ten years of its operation.[3]

The depression of the thirties focussed attention upon three or four million "economic refugees," many of whom dwelt in the hard-hit mining and manufacturing regions of the East and Middle West, although the majority were extracting a meager living from dying cotton lands in the South, from the dry and exhausted arable and grazing lands of the West and Southwest, and from the cut-over timber areas of the North and Northwest. To remove these people from public relief rolls, and keep them off, the national government launched in 1935 (1) a "land-use

[1] This function it shares, of course, with establishments such as the Department of Labor, the Public Health Service, and the Office of Education; and all have drawn inspiration and guidance from private agencies such as the Country Life Commission appointed by President Theodore Roosevelt some forty years ago. For a broad treatment of the subject, see J. M. Gaus and L. Wolcott, *op. cit.,* Chap. XI.

[2] 50 *U. S. Stat. at Large,* 522.

[3] R. B. Vance, "Farmers Without Land," *Pub. Affairs Pamphlets,* No. 12 (New York, 1937); *Law and Contemporary Problems,* IV, 423-575 (Oct., 1937), series of articles on farm tenancy. During the decade mentioned, forty-year loans were made to some 41,500 farm tenants, share-croppers, and farm laborers unable to get credit elsewhere.

program," aimed at taking some ten million acres of substandard or sub-marginal land out of crop production and turning it to more suitable uses, *e.g.*, forest or pasture; (2) a "resettlement program," looking to the re-moval of toilers on substandard land to land of better quality; (3) a "rehabilitation program," emphasizing reëstablishment of credit for indigent farmers living on reasonably satisfactory land; and (4) a "sub-urban program," contemplating the development of "model" communities on the outskirts of urban areas for the benefit of low-income city work-ers and suburban farmers.[1] Management of these various enterprises was at first (1935) intrusted to an independent Resettlement Administration; in 1937, it was transferred to the Farm Security Administration in the Department of Agriculture; and in 1946, with the Farm Security Admin-istration terminated as such, it was placed under the new Farmers Home Administration, in the same department, with instructions that liquida-tion of all resettlement and rehabilitation projects be completed as soon as possible.[2]

Until a decade ago, the United States lagged behind several other countries in bringing electrical energy within the reach of rural popula-tions, and even today more than forty per cent of the nation's farms are still without electric light and power. In 1936, however, Congress passed a Rural Electrification Act[3] launching a long-term program under which considerable progress has been made toward providing farms with cheap light and power, relieving the drudgery of the farmer and his wife, and adding to the farm's income-producing equipment. Management of the undertaking is vested in a Rural Electrification Administration, at first independent but since 1939 a unit within the Department of Agriculture; and it consists principally in making long-term self-liquidating loans up to one hundred per cent of cost (1) to associations (often farmers' co-operatives organized for the purpose), corporations, states, or local-government bodies, to enable them to build transmission lines and buy generators for furnishing electrical energy to people in rural areas for whom central-station services are not available, and (2) to individuals or firms engaged in wiring farm buildings and installing electrical and plumbing appliances and equipment—no loans being extended directly to consumers. Down to July, 1946, funds to a total of $825,000,000 (bor-

3. Rural electrifi-cation

---

[1] Greenbelt, Maryland, seven miles from Washington, became in October, 1937, the first of these communities to be opened for occupation. Not many others on a similar scale were actually developed, but about 150 smaller "farm projects" were launched.

[2] A full study of the nation-wide tenancy problem is presented in *Report of the President's Committee* [on Farm Tenancy], published by the National Resources Committee at Washington, D. C., in 1937. For a readable survey, see R. B. Vance, "Farmers Without Land," *Pub. Affairs Pamphlets*, No. 12 (New York, 1937). Cf. C. Larson, "Greenbelt, Maryland; A Federally Planned Community," *Nat. Mun. Rev.*, XXVII, 413-420 (Aug., 1938).

[3] 49 *U. S. Stat. at Large*, 1936. A Rural Electrification Administration had, however, been created during the previous year by executive order. For a full account of rural electrification, see H. H. Trachsel, *Public Utility Regulation* (Chicago, 1947), Chap. XXI.

rowed by the R. E. A. principally from the Reconstruction Finance Corporation) were allocated to substantially one thousand borrowers in forty-five states, Alaska, and the Virgin Islands. Almost 475,000 miles of line were in operation and a million and a half families were served. In some places, private utility companies have been extending their lines to discourage government-financed enterprises from being started. But the field for further public financing remains large.[1]

REFERENCES

M. Fainsod and L. Gordon, *Government and the American Economy* (New York, 1941), Chap. v.

S. C. Wallace, *The New Deal in Action* (New York, 1934), Chaps. ix-xv.

B. Rausch, *The History of the New Deal, 1933-1938* (New York, 1944), Chaps. xi, xiv.

L. H. Chamberlain, *The President, Congress, and Legislation* (New York, 1946), Chaps. vi-vii.

L. Meriam, *Relief and Social Security* (Washington, D. C., 1946), Chap. x.

D. C. Blaisdell, *Government and Agriculture* (New York, 1940). The best brief survey.

J. M. Gaus and L. O. Wolcott, *Public Administration and the Department of Agriculture* (Chicago, 1940).

C. R. Ball, *Federal, State, and Local Administrative Relationships in Agriculture*, 2 vols. (Berkeley, Calif., 1938).

A. C. True, *A History of Agricultural Experimentation and Research in the United States, 1607-1925* (Washington, D. C., 1937).

G. Baker, *The County Agent* (Chicago, 1939).

C. B. Smith and M. C. Wilson, *The Agricultural Extension System of the United States* (New York, 1930).

E. S. Sparks, *History and Theory of Agricultural Credit in the United States* (New York, 1932).

E. L. Butz, *The Production Credit System for Farmers* (Washington, D. C., 1944).

J. C. Clendenin, *Federal Crop Insurance in Operation* (Palo Alto, Calif., 1942).

R. H. Skilton, *Government and the Mortgage Debtor, 1929 to 1939* (Philadelphia, 1946).

P. S. Wager, *One Foot on the Soil; A Study of Subsistence Homesteads in Alabama* (University, Ala., 1945).

H. A. Wallace, *America Must Choose* (New York, 1934).

————, *New Frontiers* (New York, 1934).

W. Gee, *The Social Economics of Agriculture* (New York, 1932).

C. T. Schmidt, *American Farmers in the World Crisis* (New York, 1941).

W. H. Clark, *Farms and Farmers; The Story of American Agriculture* (Boston, 1945).

W. McCune, *The Farm Bloc* (Garden City, N. Y., 1943).

F. M. Muller, *Public Rural Electrification* (Washington, D. C., 1944).

A. F. Oehman, "The Agricultural Adjustment Act of 1938," *Georgetown Law Jour.*, XXVI, 680-694 (Mar., 1938).

H. Walker and W. R. Parks, "Soil Conservation Districts; Local Democracy in a National Program," *Jour. of Politics*, VIII, 538-549 (Nov., 1946).

---

[1] A further phase of rural betterment in which, if growing demand for federal aid eventually prevails, the national government will in future share more actively than at present is the improvement of rural schools, attended by a heavy proportion of the country's children. Cf. pp. 112-113 above.

J. D. Lewis, "Democratic Planning in Agriculture," *Amer. Polit. Sci. Rev.*, XXXV, 232-249, 454-469 (Apr., June, 1941).

Department of Agriculture, *Miscellaneous Publications*, No. 88 (1934), "The U. S. Department of Agriculture; Its Structure and Functions."

Service Monographs, as cited in footnotes above.

Farmers in a Changing World: The Yearbook of Agriculture (Washington, D. C., 1940).

Annual reports of the secretary of agriculture, the administrator of the Farm Credit Administration, the administrator of the Farmers Home Administration, the administrator of the Rural Electrification Administration, etc.

CHAPTER XXXI

THE CONSERVATION OF NATURAL RESOURCES

Earlier
wasteful-
ness

Perhaps it is inevitable that an energetic and growing people taking over a virgin continental expanse richly endowed by nature should be guilty of extravagance and waste. So, at all events, it has been in the United States, where for a hundred years good land was so abundant, and forest, mineral, and other resources so apparently inexhaustible, that no generation felt any concern about economical use in its own time or possible shortages later on. On the theory that the quickest and surest way to develop the country was to get its resources into the hands of people who would settle new areas, promote new industries, and expand national production, the federal government for a long time (state governments also within their more restricted spheres) systematically sold or gave away agricultural land, mineral lands, forest lands, and whatever else was available, to substantially any private individuals, railroads, or other interests desiring them. For a long time, too, when good grass land was put to the plough and exposed to ruinous soil erosion, or noble forests were devastated by rapacious lumber companies, or petroleum, gas, coal, and other mineral deposits were wastefully used, there were few to protest.[1]

The con-
servation
move-
ment

Toward the close of the nineteenth century, however, warnings began to be sounded, not only that the supply of available public land was fast diminishing, but that continued heedless exploitation of forests, minerals, and other natural wealth would one day leave the country impoverished. Sharing in this apprehension was President Theodore Roosevelt and a small group of persons surrounding him (notably his intimate friend, Gifford Pinchot, who in 1898 became chief of the federal Bureau of Forestry); and measures for protecting and developing the country's resources became one of that chief executive's principal concerns, along with the not wholly unrelated objective of curbing trusts and monopolies.[2] A new gospel of conservation was preached with crusading zeal; a national commission was set to work surveying conditions and needs; the governors of the states were called into conference at the White House; and for the first time the nation became to some degree "conservation

[1] "It was once said by Mr. Henry A. Wallace ... that 'no civilization has ever builded in so short a time what our forefathers builded in America;' but it may equally well be suggested that no civilization has in so short a time consumed and destroyed so much of the resources of the earth." H. Finer, *The T. V. A.; Lessons for International Application* (Montreal, 1944), 3.

[2] T. Roosevelt, *An Autobiography* (New York, 1913), 393-422.

conscious." The entire idea, however, ran sharply counter to a century-old tradition, and not only did powerful interests with something to lose resist it, but people generally had difficulty divesting themselves of the notion that there was plenty of everything. Only as, during the next quarter-century, the fact was gradually brought home that we already had used up more than half of our known petroleum supply, the larger part of our natural gas, more than a third of our high-grade coal, most of our best iron, an alarming share of our copper, lead, and zinc, and an amazingly large proportion of our forest reserves—to say nothing of having exhausted millions of acres of our soil—did the country really awaken to the urgent importance of conserving resources and, where possible (as in the case of forests and perhaps soil) restoring some part of what had disappeared. During this quarter-century (roughly 1905-30), laws were passed, agencies of enforcement and supervision set up, and land, forests, minerals, water supply, and water-power sites given at least moderately effective protection. As yet, however, the resources involved were almost exclusively those in the publicly, rather than privately, owned parts of the country; and while the public domain was extensive, it was next perceived that if the nation was to be assured the benefits of conservation on the scale required for its future well-being, controls would have to be extended, so far as constitutionally possible, to privately owned areas as well. Such expansion—helped along by the depression of the thirties (inspiring programs of public works with a strong conservational slant), by the recurring droughts, dust-storms, floods, and other disasters of the same period, and eventually by the necessity for maximum utilization of our resources (the "sinews and muscles of our defense machinery"[1]) for national defense and war—became the contribution of the era of the second Roosevelt. Now for the first time were undertaken really complete surveys of the resources and potentialities of every great section of the country.[2] Now (as pointed out in the previous chapter) farmers everywhere were invited and urged to participate in a federally-managed program of soil rebuilding and conservation. Now, too, the idea of specially fostering land use, forestry, water-power, and "a more abundant life" in selected river valleys (beginning with the Tennessee Valley) was launched. Now also closer relations were developed between nation and states in conservation matters, and public perception quickened that squandering and dissipating resources constituting so large a part of the national wealth would be the surest way of inviting national impoverishment and decline. Now, furthermore, it was responsibly proposed that conservation be officially recognized as a major national function by converting the Department of the Interior into a Department of Conservation, or otherwise somehow pro-

---

[1] *Annual Report of the Secretary of the Interior* (1940), p. xxxi.
[2] By the National Planning Board instituted in 1933 and its successor establishments. See pp. 710-711 below.

viding for such a co-equal branch of the federal executive establishment.[1]

What
conserva-
tion
means

During the long course of this development, the concept of conservation underwent significant expansion. At the outset, it was largely limited to maintaining in adequate supply resources like forests which, as used, could be renewed, and to eliminating avoidable waste of others, such as oil and gas, not capable of replenishment. It still includes these things, of course, and is applied to many kinds of resources not originally envisaged. But to these somewhat negative concepts of simple replacement or avoidable depletion where replacement is not possible has been added the notion of conservation as a more positive policy of building up and utilizing resources for the satisfaction of maximum social needs. As the Department of the Interior put it in a report of a decade ago, conservation now means "the management and wise use of the natural assets to prevent their depletion and at the same time *to produce wealth*." [2] Hence it means not only preventing existing farms from being ruined by soil erosion, but making new farms available through provision of water for irrigation; not only protecting existing forests from devastation, but developing means for their wise use, with additions meanwhile from lands too worn-out or otherwise marginal to be worth much for other purposes; not only keeping oil and gas from burning in the fields, but restricting output in the interest of coming generations. Broadly, as stated by two recent writers, it means adjusting the entire natural environment—forbidding here, restricting there, developing yonder—to human requirements and achieving a reasonable balance between the present and future needs of society.[3]

Federal-
state
relations

Even in its narrower aspects, conservation is appropriate for governmental action, and indeed quite dependent upon it. The rugged individualists who developed the country in pioneering days proceeded on the principle of taking and using what they found; and, left to themselves, their more sophisticated but hardly less individualistic descendants would probably have not much more regard for the interests of posterity. Moreover, the tasks involved, and particularly the planning entailed, could be undertaken on the necessary scale only by government. Like so many others of our enterprises, however, the work of conservation is greatly

---

[1] How appropriately the Interior Department (dating from 1849) might be renamed as suggested is evidenced by the following list of its major bureaus and other divisions: (1) Bureau of Land Management (formed in 1946 by merging a long-existing General Land Office and a Grazing Service); (2) Bureau of Reclamation; (3) Geological Survey; (4) Bureau of Mines; (5) Fish and Wildlife Service; (6) Bureau of Indian Affairs; (7) National Park Service; (8) Oil and Gas Division; (9) Division of Power; (10) Bonneville Power Administration; (11) Southwestern Power Administration; and (12) Division of Territories and Island Possessions. For full description, see latest issue of the *United States Government Manual*. The origins and earlier history of the Department will be found treated in H. B. Learned, *The President's Cabinet*, Chap. x, and L. M. Short, *Development of National Administrative Organization in the United States*, Chap. IX.

[2] *Why a Department of Conservation*, 75th Cong., 3rd Sess., Sen. Doc. No. 142 (1938), 3.

[3] M. Fainsod and L. Gordon, *Government and the National Economy*, 735.

complicated in this country by our federal system. Up to a point, to be sure, the national government has free scope. As we shall see, more than one-fifth of the country (mainly but by no means exclusively west of the Mississippi) is owned outright by the nation as a whole; and on this "public domain" the national government, as proprietor, can lease grazing lands, restrict access to minerals, regulate the use of forests and plant new ones, control the use of water-power, protect wildlife, and, speaking broadly, do anything else it likes, with no constitutional questions or embarrassments raised. And here, of course, is where conservation activities have been pursued most vigorously and effectively. The greater part of the country's resources, however, are in areas over which the national government has no control as owner; and in these it falls mainly to the states and their subdivisions to do whatever is done. The results are very uneven. Some states have well-developed programs covering forest protection and extension, control over water resources, regulation of oil and gas production, promotion of drainage and irrigation projects, and protection of fish and other wild life, according as such activities are appropriate to particular states. Other states are lax; twenty-five do not even have a department of conservation, or other such administrative agency. In any case, plenty of room is left for national authorities to help out—which indeed they must do if there is to be any approach to effective conservation the country over. Nor in spite of constitutional limitations are means for such participation lacking. Through discussion and published information, the federal government can educate the people on the subject; through grants-in-aid, it can join with the states in financing and controlling conservation activities; its commerce power can be invoked in regulating the development and use of navigable streams and the sale of commodities and services, *e.g.*, hydroelectric energy, and its treaty-making power in protecting migratory wildlife; through voluntary arrangements, carried out in conjunction with states, it can enlist farmers in programs of soil conservation, and from these in turn derive means of controlling crop production. All of these things not only can be, but are being done; and it is reasonable to expect that as time goes on conservation, like many other activities cutting across federal-state lines, will more and more be nationalized.

Land and Land Use

Federal conservation activities have to do, first of all, with the most _{Public land} basic of natural resources, *i.e.*, land, and on two principal lines—safeguarding the public domain and protecting the soil of arable land wherever threatened by depletion through erosion. Of the total 1,900,000,000 acres contained in the continental United States today (exclusive of Alaska and the Canal Zone), upwards of one and one-half billion acres, or eighty per cent, have at one time or another been "public land," *i.e.*, land nationally owned. Of this, more than a billion acres have been sold or given away, leaving a present national domain of somewhat over 430,000,000 acres—greatly reduced from what it once was, to be sure, but still considerably exceeding one-fifth of the total national area. Even now, it is as if all that part of the country east of the Mississippi river less only the states of Mississippi, Alabama, Georgia, and Florida were public land; several states, indeed, *e.g.*, Arizona, Nevada, Idaho, and Utah contain more land publicly than privately owned. Of lands disposed of, vast quantities were in earlier times granted to the states for sale in aid of education and internal improvements; later on, much was bestowed upon transcontinental railroads; a great deal was allotted to soldiers and sailors; large tracts were sold to speculating land companies; and under terms of the Homestead Act of 1862—offering 160 acres to any one who would pay a registration fee of ten dollars and perform a limited amount of work on his holding during a period of five years—millions upon millions of acres were parcelled out among pioneering home-seekers.[1] Prodigality and fraud often went hand in hand; yet vast areas passed into the possession of thrifty populations which helped make the country what it is today.

With the national domain shrinking, however, to something approaching its present proportions, and with the newer idea of conservation developing, the government thirty or forty years ago grew less prodigal. Restrictions were imposed on free entry; large areas were set off as permanent national holdings; and finally, after a decade of virtual suspension, allotments were entirely stopped in 1935. In 1946, to be sure, President Truman, by executive order, reopened certain remaining lands to entry (except any containing deposits of thorium, uranium, or other "fissionable materials for the release of atomic energy"), under carefully guarded conditions. But with the government also embarked, from a good while past, upon a policy of acquiring land by purchase, condemnation, cession, or gift from private (or sometimes even public) holders, and adding such land to public forests or utilizing it for park development, water-power development, or other purposes, the expectation is that henceforth there will be little net loss of acreage. Such acquisitions, indeed, sometimes raise problems for the states affected; because, once the title to land is vested in the federal government, such land becomes immune from state and local taxation. And in response to demands for recompense, Congress has enacted legislation requiring some of the federal undertakings to make contributions to units of government most affected in lieu of taxes.[2] Of the more than 430,000,000 acres comprising the public domain today, 219,000,000 are included in national forests,

---

[1] In 1909, homestead grants in arid and semi-arid areas were increased to 320 acres; and in 1916 grants in other areas to 640 acres, in the interest of stock-raising.

[2] On such contributions by the Tennessee Valley Authority, see p. 708, note, 3, below. In lieu of taxes on national forest lands, the federal government turns over twenty-five per cent of its receipts from such lands to the states in which they are situated, and in the case of mineral lands, thirty-seven and one-half per cent of all royalties received.

some 55,000,000 in more or less permanent Indian reservations, and more than 11,000,000 in national parks, wild-life refuges, reclamation projects, military and naval reservations, and holdings for a wide variety of other purposes.[1]

Large stretches of the earlier public domain, located chiefly in the Western states, were arid or semi-arid—much of the land fertile enough, but unproductive unless supplied with water; and since 1902 a Bureau of Reclamation in the Interior Department has been charged with conservation of the limited water resources of seventeen Western states—largely by dams, reservoirs, aqueducts, pumping stations, and the like—for irrigation, power development, and domestic and industrial uses. In 1947, fifty-seven projects had been completed and were in operation; thirty more had lately been started; and, in all, nearly twelve million acres of land were encompassed in projects either under construction or authorized. Many projects, notably such huge ones as Hoover (formerly Boulder) Dam and Grand Coulee, not only supply water for municipal consumption, for irrigation, and for the development of electric power for the use of industries, but afford sorely needed flood protection as well. The matter, however, is pertinent at the present point because the original and still dominating purpose of reclamation is to make land usable for those who need it. In recent years, crops valued at four hundred million dollars have been produced on lands watered by reclamation systems.[2]

Reclamation

In the previous chapter, we observed how Congress sought to rationalize and validate the crop control features of the Soil Conservation and Domestic Allotment Act of 1936 by tying them up with the provisions of a Soil Erosion Act of 1935.[3] Immediate motivation for this latter statute was supplied by disastrous floods and dust-storms of recent years. But for a good while it had been realized that the country's most precious resource of all (apart from water), *i.e.*, soil, was being depleted wherever land was ploughed, and in great regions of the West and Southwest with

Soil conservation

---

[1] On public land history and policy, see B. H. Hibbard, *A History of Public Land Policies* (New York, 1924); R. S. Yard, *Our Federal Lands; A Romance of National Development* (New York, 1928); R. M. Robbins, *Our Landed Heritage; The Public Domain, 1776-1936* (Princeton, N. J., 1941); Committee on the Conservation and Administration of the Public Domain, *Report to the President of the United States* (Washington, D. C., 1931); W. L. Knous, "The Use of Public Lands—A National Problem," *State Government*, XX, 209-211 (Aug., 1947).

[2] In 1947, the Bureau of Reclamation mapped out a seven-year plan estimated to cost two billion dollars and aimed at the building of enough new dams, pumping plants, canals, and related works to irrigate an additional four million acres and to create 40,000 to 50,000 large new farms, besides adding greatly to the existing output of hydroelectric power. Largest among individual projects was the irrigation of a million acres in Oregon with water carried by canals and tunnels from Franklin D. Roosevelt Lake, behind Grand Coulee Dam. An economy-minded House of Representatives undertook to cut the appropriation requested for the first year by more than half. In response to a storm of protest from the Western parts of the country, the allotment, however, was eventually increased, although left considerably below the $145,702,000 asked. Reclamation is a fruitful source of sectionalism in politics. For a general survey of federal power projects, see H. H. Trachsel, *Public Utility Regulation* (Chicago, 1947), Chap. XXII.

[3] 49 *U. S. Stat. at Large,* 163. See p. 681 above.

startling rapidity. Yellowed rivulets and turbid major streams alike, after every rain, testified mutely—as did also clouds of powdery dust borne eastward across the country by air currents in periods of drought—to the irrecoverable wealth that was being lost; fields once productive grew barren and useless; farm after farm went to ruin. In 1936, the Soil Conservation Service, starting its work under the act of the preceding year, reported that, throughout the country as a whole, a total of 735,000,000 acres of land (enough to make twenty states the size of Illinois), once splendidly adapted to cultivation, grazing, or forest culture, had been seriously impaired or totally destroyed by either water or wind erosion, or both. Ten years later, the same authority still was obliged to say that half a million acres were being ruined by erosion every year, at a direct and indirect cost to the country of three billion dollars.

To 1935, little was done to encourage and help farmers to fight this deadliest of all their enemies, except for some studies made and local projects undertaken by state experiment stations. Under legislation of that year, however, a broad federal program was instituted, with the Soil Conservation and Domestic Allotment Act of the following year adding emphasis by making subsidies to farmers expressly contingent on the employment of soil conservation practices. Under the law of 1935, responsibility for carrying on research and for working with states, localities, and individual farmers in bringing about physical adjustments in land and introducing soil-conservation methods (contouring, strip-cropping, terracing, crop rotation, farm drainage, and the like) is vested in the Soil Conservation Service in the Department of Agriculture; every state has enacted laws under which soil conservation districts may be set up; and 1,700 such districts, embracing two-thirds of all the farms in the country, have been organized. Land-owners within any district have a right to help and guidance from field offices of the Conservation Service, or from county agents; and the service undertakes to send technicians to advise with anyone in need of them. Before the war, the Service also bought up submarginal agricultural land, improved it, and issued permits for its use by farmers and stock-raisers; and this activity is expected to be resumed.[1]

Forests—Minerals—Petroleum

Forests

As a deliberate program, conservation in this country really had its beginning fifty or sixty years ago in an effort to preserve and extend the

---

[1] An informing little publication is M. S. Stewart, "Saving Our Soil," *Pub. Affairs Pamphlets*, No. 14 (New York, 1937).

By way of concrete illustration, the facts may be noted that in Wisconsin (not a chief sufferer from erosion, but yet with a quarter of the top soil lost from nearly half of the total land area), 43 soil conservation districts have been organized, embracing about 89 per cent of the farms in the state; Conservation Service technicians have helped formulate 14,480 individual farm plans for acre-by-acre treatment of 2,286,000 acres; and not long ago 485 representative farmers who kept strict records reported an increase in production, as a result of conservation farming, of 28.7 per cent for all major crops.

nation's forests. Theodore Roosevelt not only perceived the immense value to the people of forests yielding timber for building, fostering wild life, furnishing recreational facilities, stabilizing the distribution of moisture, and preventing soil waste, but deplored the rapidity with which forest wealth was disappearing at the hands of lumber companies and other private exploiters. As early as 1891, Congress had empowered the chief executive to set aside suitable portions of the public domain as national forests; and, starting with Roosevelt, successive presidents made liberal use of this authority. Naturally, forests provided for in this manner were restricted largely to the West, where nearly all of the public domain lay. But in 1911, Congress, envisaging a forest program applicable to the entire country, provided for extensive purchases of land for forest purposes on the watersheds of navigable streams wherever situated;[1] and later still other purchases were authorized, including large submarginal stretches better fitted for forest development than for cultivation. The upshot is that the United States today has a total of 152 national forests, situated in some forty different states and territories, and with an aggregate area (219,000,000 acres) over two-thirds as extensive as the state of Texas.[2] Many states, too, have set apart forests or created extensive parks of their own; so that of the country's present aggregate of wooded areas (630,000,000 acres), not far from one-third in terms of acreage benefit from direct federal or state protection. To be sure, these public forest areas are not simply walled off as reserves for the future. A forest is not harmed by, but rather benefits from, judicious use, *e.g.*, removing fully matured trees in order to clear the way for younger growth. Accordingly, in the national forests (and usually in state forests as well), timber is cut and marketed by private companies, under government supervision; selected tracts are leased for grazing purposes; and nearly every portion is open to campers and other recreation-seekers, under regulations permitting no damage to the wooded growth. The first consideration, however, is the preservation of the forests as *forests;* and to this end they are given all possible protection against fire, insects, disease, soil erosion, flood, and damage from indiscriminate grazing, as well as from destructive cutting.[3] In areas that require it, systematic planting of young trees is carried on, whether as reforestation of lands that have been denuded or as afforestation of lands not previously wooded but likely to be useful only if made so. Over two-thirds of the forest resources

[1] At the time, the development of what came to be the present splendid Shenandoah National Park in the Blue Ridge Mountains was particularly in view.

[2] Administration of some 179,000,000 acres is in the hands of a Forest Service placed appropriately enough in the Department of Agriculture, although a person not familiar with the history of the arrangement might expect to find it in the Department of the Interior. Other forested areas are administered by the National Park Service and the Bureau of Land Management in the Department of the Interior.

[3] One of the earlier forms of federal grants-in-aid was introduced in 1911, when the national government began subsidizing the states in the interest of forest-fire protection. Whereas before that date only eleven states appropriated any money for the purpose, nearly all are now doing so.

of the country remain in private hands, and much is utilized wastefully; indeed, there is so great private opposition to the marketing of lumber produced on the public domain that less is permitted to be produced there than would easily be possible. Taken as a whole, however, our nation-wide forest situation is decidedly better than it would have been if the enlightened federal and state policies of recent decades had not been followed.[1]

Minerals   Mineral resources on the public domain are conserved, too, by a policy developed since 1910 under which the government expressly reserves for itself any mineral wealth that may be found to exist, and merely leases mineral lands for exploitation by private interests operating under government supervision and paying royalties into the national treasury, a portion being turned over to the states concerned. Mineral resources are studied and reported upon by the Geological Survey in the Department of the Interior; and mining methods, prevention of mine accidents, and treatment and utilization of ores, the country over, are dealt with similarly by a bureau of mines in the same department. So far as mineral resources are in private hands (and most of them are so), the main problem presenting itself to governments, both state and national, is that of relieving the long-depressed bituminous coal industry. Except temporarily during the recent war emergency, too much soft coal is mined; the high-grade deposits are showing signs of depletion; the business was operated at a huge loss for many years, and the condition of the workers, although now improved, has often been deplorable. The states, however, cannot—in any event, do not—act sufficiently in concert to make any headway with the problem. And when the national government sought in some degree to solve it, first through an N.R.A. coal code in 1933, and later through a "little N.R.A." set up by the Bituminous Coal Conservation [Guffey] Act of 1935, the effort was frustrated by Supreme Court decisions.[2] A new Bituminous Coal [Guffey] Act, omitting all features of the earlier measure to which the Court had objected, was passed in 1937

---

[1] R. A. H. Thompson, "What's Happening to the Timber," *Harper's Mag.*, CXCI, 125-133 (Aug., 1945); B. DeVoto, "The West Against Itself," *ibid.*, CXIV, 1-13 (Jan., 1947), especially on the competition between grazing and forest interests.

Wildlife—fish, wild animals, and birds—is by no means confined to public forests, or indeed to forests of any kind. This, however, may be an appropriate point at which to call attention to the fact that wildlife is another resource which both federal and state governments seek to safeguard. The national government first actively entered the field with an act of Congress in 1900 forbidding the shipment in interstate commerce of wild animals and birds taken in violation of state laws. In 1929, a Migratory Bird Conservation Commission was created to plan land purchases for the establishment of refuges; in 1937, the Pittman-Robertson Act earmarked excise taxes on fire-arms, shells, and cartridges for apportionment among the states in aid of wildlife conservation projects; and in 1940, miscellaneous agencies (mostly transferred from other departments) were consolidated into the Fish and Wildlife Service now forming one of the most important conservation divisions of the Interior Department.

[2] The 1935 act was declared unconstitutional (Carter *v.* Carter Coal Co., 298 U. S. 238, 1936) by a Supreme Court that had not yet recognized manufacturing and mining as partaking of the character of interstate commerce.

and later upheld.[1] Expiring, however, in 1943, the measure was not renewed; and in later days the industry has gone along much as before, except in so far as new terms and conditions for the miners have been wrested from the operators by strikes like that occurring in the spring of 1946.[2] The coal problem—still unsolved, and likely to grow more acute as substitute sources of heat and energy are increasingly employed—has many aspects besides that of conservation; but protection of diminishing high-grade deposits is still involved in it.[3]

Only two per cent of the oil produced in the United States today comes from the public domain; and although the amount produced on state lands is larger, the great bulk of the aggregate output is yielded by lands that have passed into private ownership—which means that whatever is undertaken by government in the interest of conservation must proceed by public regulation rather than by management of a resource still in the public possession. For a long time, little or nothing was accomplished. To be sure, in 1909 President Taft withdrew from entry such limited national oil lands as existed; and the chief effect of reopening them to lease in 1920 was to precipitate the Teapot Dome affair, one of the scandals of the century.[4] A Federal Oil Conservation Board set up by President Coolidge came off with no more helpful contribution than an assertion that the confusions of a singularly erratic industry would in time be overcome by the industry itself; and it was only after discovery of the vast eastern Texas fields in 1930-31, catapulting output and shattering prices, that either the states or the federal government attempted significant action. Texas, Oklahoma, and Kansas tried, by compact, to discourage over-production by forbidding shipments exceeding fixed quotas from the respective states, but in spite of all they could do, "hot oil" streamed into other parts of the country, production continued at extravagant levels, and demoralization prevailed, especially after the federal Supreme Court held that governors of states might not resort to martial law in order to police production controls with the aid of militia.

Petroleum: 1. Slow development of regulation

The excess oil was, however, shipped in interstate commerce; and this gave the federal government an opening. Accordingly, in the National Industrial Recovery Act of 1933, the president was authorized, with a view to helping the states out of their dilemma and reënforcing their efforts at control, to prohibit the transportation in interstate or foreign commerce of any petroleum or its products produced or withdrawn from storage in excess of amounts permitted by state law or regulation; and

2. Federal and state activities

[1] Sunshine Anthracite Coal Co. v. Adkins, 310 U. S. 381 (1940).

[2] As a consequence of this strike, the federal government took over management of the mines, which it retained until June 30, 1947. See p. 732, note 1, below.

[3] G. L. Parker, *The Coal Industry* (Washington, D. C., 1940); E. V. Rostov, "Bituminous Coal and the Public Interest," *Yale Law Jour.*, L, 543-594 (Feb., 1941); W. H. Hamilton, "Coal and the Economy—A Demurrer," *ibid.*, 595-620 (Feb., 1941).

[4] Albert Fall, secretary of the interior, was proved guilty of accepting bribes from prominent oil men to lease the Teapot Dome reserve (in Wyoming) without competitive bidding.

a code for the oil industry, with the secretary of the interior as administrator, was duly put into operation. Tested in the courts, however, the arrangement collapsed: in the "Hot Oil" cases of 1935, the highest federal tribunal ruled that Congress had exceeded its constitutional authority by delegating to the chief executive power which by its nature was tantamount to making laws; [1] and later in the year, it invalidated the N.I.R.A. as a whole, [2] leaving the oil code in ruins. The damage, nevertheless, was not irreparable. To begin with, the states returned with fresh vigor to the policy of coöperative state regulation; and, with authorization from Congress given in advance, four of them entered into a new compact prorating volume of production and of allowable interstate or foreign shipments, with in time most others adhering to the plan. [3] Moreover, Congress followed up its rebuff from the Supreme Court by passing the Connally ["Hot Oil"] Act of 1935 [4] (for two years, but later renewed) *directly* forbidding the shipment in interstate or foreign commerce of oil produced in excess of quotas fixed by state laws, with no authority in the president except to suspend the restriction if he should find a disparity between supply and demand. Even at the time, the judges could hardly have found anything in this to which to take exception; and after their change of mind in later cases concerning the relation of manufacturing and mining to interstate commerce, they assuredly could not have done so. Aside from state controls, the interstate compact and the supporting act of Congress furnish today, therefore, the country's only effective guarantees of reasonable husbanding of its rich but not inexhaustible oil resources.

3. Present situation   The entire fabric depends on coöperation in good faith by the oil-producing states. They regulate production by restricting the quantities of locally-produced oil that may leave their bounds for other states or foreign countries; aside from controlling production on the public domain, the federal government goes no farther than to back them up by invoking its commerce power against shipments which they themselves have forbidden. Undoubtedly the arrangement leaves something to be desired. Some minor oil-producing states are not in the compact at all; any heavy-producing state could demoralize the industry by withdrawing, or by not

---

[1] Panama Refining Co. *v.* Ryan, 293 U. S. 388 (1935).

[2] Schechter *v.* United States, 295 U. S. 495 (1935).

[3] In 1947, Congress gave its consent to renewal of the compact for four years (*Public Law 184—80th Cong., 1st Sess.*). The act contains the text of the compact. Each state, within its own bounds, regulates production by prorating, or allocating, to each producer a maximum number of gallons or barrels which he may produce, usually fixed in proportion to his potential production. An Interstate Oil Compact Commission created by the original agreement, and with headquarters at Oklahoma City, carries on investigations and in other ways promotes the objects of the compact, although without compulsory powers. See W. D. Webb, "The Interstate Oil Compact; Theory and Practice," *Southwestern Soc. Sci. Quar.*, XXI, 293-301 (Mar., 1941); B. M. Murphy, "The Interstate Compact to Conserve Oil and Gas; An Experiment in Coöperative State Production Control," *Miss. Law Jour.*, XVII, 314-346 (Mar.-May, 1946), with text of the compact.

[4] 49 *U. S. Stat. at Large,* 30.

living up to its agreements; the matter is of such national importance that leaving the basic decisions to be made, as they are, by hardly more than half a dozen principal producing states might well seem questionable. And one will not be surprised to encounter the suggestion that full and direct control of production and of commerce in the product be assumed by the national government. Formerly, it would have been considered that this could not be done constitutionally. Since the National Labor Relations Act decisions of 1937, however, this obstacle apparently has been removed; nowadays any industry whose products flow through the channels of interstate commerce, as those of the oil industry extensively do, may be federally regulated under the commerce power. But other obstacles remain—general public satisfaction with the results of the present system in terms of oil and gasoline prices,[1] and, more important, the stout resistance that would arise from the oil-producing states, instinctively hostile to any diminution of control over resources from which they derive heavy income, both private and public.[2]

[1] Apart, at least, from concern about the inflated prices of postwar years.

[2] Considerations of space forbid treatment here of the more or less parallel problem of conservation of natural gas. The main statute applying is the Natural Gas Act of 1938 (52 *U. S. Stat. at Large,* 821) ; and the subject will be found fully covered in F. F. Blachly and M. E. Oatman, *Natural Gas and the Public Interest* (Washington, D. C., 1947).

In 1946-47, there was brought into the open a long-standing controversy over whether rich "tidelands" oil deposits, located along the coast of California and other states between low-water mark and the three-mile limit of American jurisdiction, belong to the United States or to the coastal states. An act giving the states clear title was vetoed by President Truman on the ground that the question was one for the Supreme Court to decide; and in the House of Representatives the veto was sustained. A measure of similar purport was introduced in both branches of Congress early in 1947; but meanwhile a brief claiming possession was filed in the Supreme Court by the federal government, and before legislation resulted a decision was handed down (in United States *v.* California, 67 Sup. Ct., 1658) sustaining the government's contention. "We decide that California is not the owner of the three-mile marginal belt along its coast," bluntly said the Court, "and that the federal government rather than the state has paramount rights in and over that belt, an incident to which is full dominion over the resources of the soil under that water area, including oil." The decision related only to the tidelands of California, but seems equally applicable to those of Texas and other oil-producing coastal states. The amount of oil capable of being obtained from the California coastline alone (notwithstanding millions of gallons that have been withdrawn under lucrative pumping leases bestowed by the state) has been estimated at as much as three billion gallons. See A. B. McGinty, "Oil and States' Rights," *Current Hist.,* X, 227-231 (Mar., 1946) ; W. P. Keeton, "Federal and State Claims to Submerged Lands Under Coastal Waters," *Texas Law Rev.,* XXV, 262-274 (Jan., 1947). Following the Supreme Court ruling, a "purely interim" agreement was entered into between the federal Department of Justice and the state of California (1) permitting continuation of tidelands oil and gas operations under existing leases, and (2) specifying that royalties received by the state should be held in a special fund until final determination of precisely what rights and properties belong to the state and what to the federal government. The agreement, however, might be revoked by Congress at any time, and in any event was not to last beyond September, 1948. It was anticipated that after matters were fully straightened out, all leases would be issued (or reissued) by the federal government, which, however, would pay California thirty-seven and one-half per cent of all royalties received. Meanwhile, on behalf of California and other states, the national association of state attorneys-general registered strong objection to a Supreme Court decree designed to carry the judicial ruling into effect.

Water and Water Power

Hardly less essential to the public well-being than land and its proper use is water and its proper distribution and control. From early times, towns and cities have been concerned with providing water for their inhabitants, and states, counties, and specially organized districts have had to do with protection against floods and with drainage projects, pollution abatement, power development, and irrigation. Almost from the beginning, the federal government likewise has been involved. Important rivers commonly border or flow through a number of states; drainage basins cut widely across state lines; areas requiring water storage and irrigation know no state limits. And constitutional authority to operate in this field is ample. First of all, there is full power over the water resources of the public domain, in whatever states located. In the second place, there is authority to improve and regulate the use of navigable streams as avenues of interstate commerce; and the Supreme Court has said that "navigability...is but a part of this whole [authority]. Flood protection, watershed development, recovery of the cost of improvement through utilization of power, are likewise parts of commerce control."[1] And if other warrant were lacking, there would always be the convenient general welfare clause.

Aside from the navigability of streams, entailing chiefly the removal of obstructions and the regulation of water-power development, the federal government's rôle in connection with water resources presents itself in two main phases—control of situations in which there is danger of too much water, and the conservation and use of meager supplies in areas naturally semi-arid or especially subject to drought. While looking to states and localities to bear primary responsibility for providing levees and other forms of flood protection, the federal government has for seventy-five years or more stood ready to lend financial assistance, especially at times of unusual disaster. More significantly, however, as the concept of conservation has broadened, and as destructive floods have multiplied in the basins of the Mississippi, Ohio, Missouri, Colorado, and other rivers, and in later years also in New England and Pennsylvania, it has extended its activities to include permanent programs of flood prevention, in collaboration with state and local authorities; and on public works connected with such programs it already has spent, since the serious Mississippi Valley flood of 1927, considerably more than a billion dollars, with further liberal outlays authorized. The states, of course, are not absolved from continued responsibility for their own protection, and after Congress, in 1936, authorized any two or more of them to enter into flood-control compacts, four New England states immediately concerned promptly signed an agreement for flood control in the valleys of the Connecticut and Merrimac, and Minnesota and the Dakotas followed

[1] United States *v.* Appalachian Electric Power, 311 U. S. 377 (1940).

with a compact for similar control in the valley of the Red River of the North. The same comprehensive Flood Control Act,[1] however, which authorized such interstate arrangements virtually accepted flood control as in general a federal function, with states and localities hardly obligated beyond seeing to it that necessary land and rights of way are provided; and even this obligation has since been considerably relaxed.[2]

Apart from the irrigation needs of large regions in the West (which the federal government has long been meeting through enterprises carried on by the Bureau of Reclamation mentioned above), scarcity of water, until a decade or two ago, presented no problems sufficiently serious to evoke wide public concern. Destructive droughts and devastating sandstorms occurring in the summers of 1934 and 1936, however, dramatically stressed the need for conserving and enlarging the water resources of a vast expanse—the "dust bowl"—of the Great Plains region.[3] Surveys of the stricken territory revealed that a chronically serious condition had been growing worse; that large stretches of once fertile land were being turned into desert by unscientific farming (over-grazing and especially the ploughing of grass-land); and that good rainfall, far from being a blessing, might only add to the area's impoverishment by carrying away still more of the topsoil. Realization of the situation prompted coöperative efforts by state and federal governments to minimize the effects of droughts, if not actually to prevent them.[4] An act of Congress in 1937 authorized the Department of Agriculture to promote the construction and maintenance of reservoirs, ponds, wells, dams, and pumping facilities, and another in 1939 provided especially for water conservation in districts where farmers were too distressed to assume repayment obligations under the general reclamation laws. Even by 1936, President Roosevelt was able to report: "Thousands of ponds or small reservoirs have been built in order to supply water for stock and to lift the level of the underground water to protect wells from going dry. Thousands of wells have been drilled or deepened; community lakes have been created;

Combatting water scarcity

----

[1] 52 *U. S. Stat. at Large,* 1215.

[2] In the early summer of 1947, the Mississippi Valley experienced its worst flood in more than a hundred years, with Congress appropriating $15,000,000 for repairing and extending flood-control facilities in the area. See *U. S. News,* July 18, 1947, pp. 13-15, "Master Plan for River Control: Guarding the Mississippi Basin"; and President Truman's message of July 16 on flood control, *N. Y. Times,* July 17, 1947. Naturally, the experience lent fresh impetus to proposals for harnessing the Mississippi's greater tributaries, especially the Missouri, on lines similar to those employed by the T. V. A. in the Tennessee Valley. Three dams now (1948) under construction—on the Big Horn, Powder, and Yellowstone rivers—mark a significant beginning.

[3] More specifically, the "dust bowl" of 1934-36 was in the southwestern part of Kansas, the southeastern part of Colorado, the Panhandle region of Oklahoma and Texas, and the northeastern portion of New Mexico.

[4] Following the report of a temporary Great Plains Drought Area Committee in August, 1936, the President appointed a Great Plains Committee, which in December of the same year submitted a report covering every angle of the drought problem in the ten Great Plains states where the major disaster of 1936 occurred. The report was transmitted to Congress early in the following year and printed as 75th Cong., 1st Sess., House Doc. No. 144.

and irrigation projects are being pushed. Water conservation by such means is being expanded ... all through the Great Plains area, the western corn-belt, and the states that lie farther south." [1]

The great river systems with which the United States is favored afford almost limitless opportunities for the harnessing and utilization of water-power; and so long as their policies do not conflict with federal rights, the states may control hydroelectric power generation and transmission as they like. In a number of ways, however, the national government has been drawn into this same field of activity. To begin with, the War Department has full authority over dams and other structures affecting the navigability of inland waters. In the second place, there is full national power to control the construction and use of hydroelectric plants on streams flowing—as many do—through the public domain. A third national prerogative is that of regulating the transmission of electricity across state boundaries, as a form of interstate commerce. And a fourth activity, upheld by the Supreme Court as constitutionally legitimate, is government building of dams in key locations on important rivers, with a view not only to improvement of navigation, flood control, and per-chance irrigation, but also production and sale of power, as witnessed today in the basins of the Tennessee, Colorado, and Columbia rivers.

Recognizing that altogether too loose a policy had been pursued in disposing of power sites on the public domain and on navigable rivers elsewhere, Congress, in 1920, provided for a Federal Power Commission composed of three cabinet members, and ten years later replaced it with a similarly named body of five members (appointed by the president and Senate) with authority—as enlarged by later legislation—to license the construction of hydroelectric plants, to regulate the issuance and market-ing of securities of private utilities engaged in interstate commerce, and to control interstate wholesale electric rates and interstate natural gas rates—in other words, with approximately the same functions in its field that the Interstate Commerce Commission exercises with respect to rail-roads. [2] The Flood Control Act of 1936 [3] extended the agency's authority to include multiple-purpose river-basin planning, and likewise develop-ment of hydroelectric power at flood-control dams constructed by the

---

[1] Another device employed was a Prairie States Forestry Project, entailing the planting of a "belt" of trees about a hundred miles wide and extending nearly a thousand miles from North Dakota to Texas; and under supervision of the Forest Service nearly two and one-half hundred million trees were planted, between 1934 and 1946, partly to serve as protection against wind erosion of soil, and partly (in earlier years) to give employment and relief to needy residents of the stricken area.

[2] 41 *U. S. Stat. at Large,* 1063, upheld as constitutional in 1940 in United States *v.* Appalachian Power Co., 311 U. S. 377. The Court's extremely generous interpretation in this decision of what constitutes a navigable stream—and (as we have seen) of what federal control over navigable streams can be stretched to include—operated to expand the federal government's jurisdiction over water-power even beyond that clearly envisaged in the statute itself. Not only was the New river (in Virginia and West Virginia), concerning which the case arose, not actually navigable; there were not even plans for making it so. The Court held it "navigable" simply because *potentially* it could be made so.

[3] 52 *U. S. Stat. at Large,* 1215.

War Department; and the Natural Gas Act of 1938 [1] made further additions by conferring control over interstate transportation and sale of
another important energy source—natural gas.

The most notable aspect of national hydroelectric activity in recent
years has been the undertaking of great power projects directly by the
government; and in nearly all cases, power production has been planned
to be accompanied by developments in conservation, navigation, flood
control, reforestation, irrigation, and national defense. Under New Deal
leadership, an immediate objective (at all events during the worst stages
of the depression of the thirties) was to supply stimulus to the capital
industries furnishing the materials used. But the larger, long-term objectives have been, of course, to advance the social and economic betterment
of the areas served, to promote the national well-being, and, incidentally,
to help solve the nation-wide problem of cheap electric service for the
masses.[2]

*Develop-
ment of
federal
power
projects*

The Tennessee Valley Authority

Our review of federal conservation policies and measures may, perhaps, be most fittingly concluded with some special mention of a group
of enterprises—the "keystone of the New Deal arch"—undertaken during
the past decade and a half in the valley of the Tennessee River. Developments at Muscle Shoals (on the middle Tennessee) during the First World
War, and designed for the extraction of nitrogen from the air for use in
manufacturing explosives, left the national government the owner of 2,300
acres of land, two nitrate plants, a power house, and Wilson Dam. Later
years saw much controversy over the use, if any, to be made of this
property; and little progress toward a solution was attained until, at the
request of President Roosevelt, Congress in 1933 passed a Tennessee
Valley Authority Act,[3] aimed at improving the navigability and promot-

*Origin
and
purpose*

---

[1] *52 U. S. Stat. at Large,* 821.

[2] "The magnitude of the Commission's responsibilities in connection with the
licensing of water-power projects is suggested by the fact that forty per cent of all
the generating capacity installed in non-federally owned hydroelectric plants in the
United States is operating under Commission license." *Report of the Federal Power
Commission, 1946,* p. 3. See *Geo. Washington Law Rev.,* XIV, 1-272 (Dec., 1945),
"Federal Power Commission Special Issue."

Few government agencies are under heavier pressure from private interests (in
this case, the great utility companies) than is the Federal Power Commission.
Although coming upon the scene somewhat belatedly, the Commission has stood
guard in a useful way over the nation's water-power and gas resources, and in addition has served a good purpose in preparing well-considered plans for developing
such resources in the future. See R. D. Baum, *The Federal Power Commission and
State Utility Regulation* (Washington, D. C., 1942); and for the results of an extended expert survey of the relations between the federal and state governments and
the power industry, E. E. Hunt [ed.], *The Power Industry and the Public Interest*
(New York, 1944). Cf. also O. Ryan, "Federal and State Coöperation Under the
Federal Power Act," *State Government,* XI, 139-140, 154-155 (Aug., 1938), and especially the survey report, *Electric Power and Government Policy* (Twentieth Century
Fund, New York, 1948).

[3] 48 *U. S. Stat. at Large,* 58. For amendments to the act, see 49 *U. S. Stat. at Large,*
1075 (1935); 53 *ibid.,* 1083 (1939); 54 *ibid.,* 626 (1940); and cf. C. H. Pritchett, "The
Development of the Tennessee Valley Authority Act," *Tenn. Law Rev.,* XV, 128-141
(Feb., 1938). Indispensable to any study of the project's documentary history is A.

ing flood control of the Tennessee, providing for reforestation and proper use of marginal lands in the Tennessee Valley, encouraging the Valley's agricultural and industrial development, assisting national defense by operating government-owned nitrate plants, and indeed pointed toward other objectives not at the time fully specified. Over an area of 41,000 square miles (four-fifths the size of England), embracing portions of seven states,[1] and having a population of about three millions (two-thirds rural), agriculture and industry were to be reconstructed, forests restored, soil erosion checked, mineral resources developed, cheap power and chemical fertilizers produced, and the inhabitants in general assured the benefits of a "more abundant life;" and to carry out the plan, the Tennessee Valley Authority was set up as a government corporation, under a board of three directors appointed by the president, and with a capitalization of fifty million dollars provided at once by Congress and authority to issue bonds on the credit of the United States up to a like amount.[2] As envisaged by President Roosevelt and by the T.V.A. itself, the project was a supremely significant undertaking in democratic management and in the relatively new art of regional planning, blazing the way, it was hoped, for enterprises of similar nature and scope in other suitable sections of the country. As viewed by people of contrary opinion, it constituted a venture in subsidized governmental competition with private utility and other business which would be unfair, uneconomical, and a flagrant abuse of federal powers.

The Authority's power development

Although by no means neglecting conservation and development of the region's soil, forest, and mineral resources or promotion of the health, industry, and general well-being of the residents, the Authority has quite naturally focused its efforts thus far mainly upon taming the unruly Tennessee river, thereby promoting navigability, reducing flood hazards, and, in particular, providing great quantities of electric power. Twenty-one huge dams on the main river or its larger tributaries have been built or acquired; others may be added; and arrangements have been concluded and are in operation for selling surplus power to states, counties, cities, corporations, and individual consumers, with a view not only to recovering some portion of the huge expenses incurred, but also to providing the much-discussed "yardstick" for measuring the justice of rates charged consumers by private utility companies.[3] Contracts with purchasers

---

M. Norwood [comp.], *Congressional Hearings, Reports, and Documents Relating to T.V.A., 1933-1946* (Knoxville, Tenn., 1946), a full chronological check-list of materials.

[1] Tennessee, Virginia, North Carolina, Georgia, Alabama, Mississippi, and Kentucky.

[2] By 1946, the actual federal outlay on the project was about $760,000,000, including $460,000,000 for facilities for the production of electric power.

[3] The T.V.A. Act prescribes that preference in the disposition of power shall be given to coöperative associations and municipalities. On June 30, 1946, the Authority had contracts for sale of power at wholesale with ninety-two municipalities, forty-six coöperatives, and twenty-two privately owned utility companies, besides nine large industrial concerns and a number of projects and plants of federal agencies. In the fiscal year 1944, the Authority returned $14,116,000 net income to the United States

require the resale of electricity at exceptionally low rates controlled by the Authority; and from 1934 until its liquidation in 1943 as a wartime anomaly, an auxiliary corporation, the Electric Home and Farm Authority, concerned itself with educating potential consumers to an appreciation of the advantages of electrical power and financed them in purchasing electrical appliances at low prices. Agreements entered into with leading private power companies, too, have enabled the Authority to extend its market considerably beyond its own immediate area, and several private utility properties have been purchased outright.[1]

Serving incidentally as a means of furnishing much employment, and to that extent contributing directly to the war upon depression, the Tennessee Valley undertaking was from the outset more than merely one more measure for national recovery. As observed by a recent writer, the vital question to which it attempts an answer is "whether an industrious and capable people, though settled in a region which contains substantial natural resources, must continue to endure a low living standard," and "by what means it is feasible, if at all, to assist a people fairly rich in primary resources and available skills to achieve higher productivity and an increase in their level of consumption and possessions?"[2] The enterprise may or may not be followed through on all of the lines originally projected; and for a final assessment of its success and significance, it will be necessary to wait still somewhat longer. In its first fifteen years of operation, however, the gigantic project has afforded a remarkable spectacle of a philosophy developing into a fact, and has inspired at least a vision of a country refurbished throughout its length and breadth by means of similar enterprises undertaken in appropriate areas.[3]

Significance of the experiment

Treasury out of a gross power revenue of $35,200,000, and after paying various jurisdictions $2,168,798 in lieu of taxes lost from properties taken over for T.V.A. purposes. On the interrelations of T.V.A. and the jurisdictions within its area, see M. H. Satterfield, "T.V.A.-State-Local Relationships," *Amer. Polit. Sci. Rev.,* XL, 935-949 (Oct., 1946), and "Intergovernmental Coöperation in the Tennessee Valley," *Jour. of Politics,* IX, 31-58 (Feb., 1947).

Another extensive activity of the T.V.A. has come to be the manufacture and distribution of chemical fertilizers. Distribution is made first of all to agricultural experiment stations throughout the country for controlled tests on various types of soil, but in addition, to coöperatives and other farmer organizations for experimental use under the guidance of the federal Agricultural Extension Service.

[1] The Supreme Court has handed down two main decisions bearing upon the constitutionality of the T.V.A. Act. In Ashwander *v.* T.V.A., 297 U. S. 288 (1936), the Court held that, having the right to build dams needed for national defense or for the improvement of navigation, the federal government may sell any resulting power, and in order to facilitate such sale, may acquire private transmission systems. Later, in a case in which eighteen private power companies lodged complaint against T.V.A. competition and sought an injunction to end it, the Court upheld the right of the government, through its agent, the T.V.A., to engage in competition with private enterprises. Tennessee Electric Power Co. *v.* T.V.A., 306 U. S. 118 (1939).

[2] H. Finer, *The T.V.A.; Lessons for International Application* (Montreal, 1944), 1.

[3] Good brief discussions of the T.V.A. will be found in H. H. Trachsel, *Public Utility Regulation* (Chicago, 1947), Chap. xxiii, and M. Fainsod and L. Gordon, *Government and the American Economy* (New York, 1941), Chaps. x, xix. The literature of the subject is very extensive. Four excellent recent books are listed on p. 712 below.

Soil conservation, forest conservation, flood control, conservation of water, oil, and natural gas, and the development of hydroelectric power sites present a series not of isolated, but of closely interrelated and overlapping, problems affecting the entire country; and adequate solution of them is conditioned upon planning on a nation-wide scale. To the leadership of the New Deal must go credit for a keen awareness of this fact; and, starting with the establishment of a National Planning Board in July, 1933, comprehensive studies of land use, stream use, mineral resources, and related matters were carried on over a period of a decade; while practically all of the states were influenced or induced, on their

---

Convinced of the high value, both local and national, of the Tennessee Valley development, President Roosevelt, in September, 1944, recommended the creation of a Missouri Valley Authority along the lines of the T.V.A. to control and develop the water and other resources of large portions or all of eleven Western states, and at the same time renewed pleas previously made, for setting up similar arrangements for the Arkansas and Columbia river basins. In 1946, no fewer than ten bills were before Congress proposing "valley authorities" for different areas of the country, although none became law. See W. C. Clark, "Proposed 'Valley Authority' Legislation," *Amer. Polit. Sci. Rev.*, XL, 62-70 (Feb., 1946). In 1947, an M. V. A. (Missouri Valley Authority) bill, introduced by Senator James E. Murray, and in some respects going even beyond T.V.A., received warm endorsement from President Truman, who naturally drew upon the Middle West's current flood disasters to give point to his argument. The measure did not come to a vote, but was considered far from dead—although throughout the area concerned (constituting one-sixth of the entire country) there was considerable opposition to setting up any such over-all authority as T.V.A., with a good deal of preference instead for regional development through coöperative and coördinated activities of different federal and state agencies (the Army Corps of Engineers, the Bureau of Reclamation, the Department of Agriculture, the Federal Power Commission, and four state governors) represented in a Missouri Basin Inter-Agency Committee already organized and at work, with congressional approval of some of its flood-control plans secured. See, however, R. Terral, *The Missouri Valley* (New Haven, 1947), for a favorable argument by a St. Louis journalist.

On the clashing views of those advocating a unified "Valley Authority" and those favoring development by various agencies coördinated under the Inter-Agency Committee, see W. Price, "What You Can Believe About the M. V. A.," *Sat. Eve. Post*, CCXVIII, 22 ff. (Jan. 19, 1946); E. R. Abrams, "The Missouri Valley Authority," *Public Utilities Fort.*, XXXV, 201-213 (Feb. 15, 1945); J. K. Howard, "Golden River," *Harper's Mag.*, CXC, 511-523 (May, 1945); R. Lasch, "Why an M.V.A.?," *Atlantic Mo.*, CLXXV, 72-76 (May, 1945); M. L. Cooke, "Plain Talk About a Missouri Valley Authority," *Iowa Law Rev.*, XXXII, 367-390 (Jan., 1947). Among opponents of a unified "Authority" are agencies like the Bureau of Reclamation that do not want to give up their own functions in the region.

It may be added that, through executive action, a Federal Inter-Agency River Basin Committee composed of representatives of the Departments of War, Interior, and Agriculture and the Federal Power Commission has been set up to work on the nation-wide problem; also a Columbia Basin Inter-Agency Committee, similarly composed, which seems not unlikely to prepare the way for another "Authority" of the T.V.A. type.

Of somewhat similar nature is the St. Lawrence deep waterway and power project, for which President Roosevelt repeatedly sought authorization. A treaty on the subject with Canada was rejected by the Senate in 1934; an executive agreement on similar lines was refused approval in 1941; and the latest repulse of the project came in February, 1948, when, by a vote of 57 to 30, the Senate returned a bill on the subject to committee as a polite way of killing it. The project, of course, could not be carried out without congressional appropriations. See "Should the United States Congress Approve the Present Proposal for a Great Lakes–St. Lawrence Seaway?" [Symposium], *Cong. Digest*, XXV, 225-256 (Oct., 1946).

part, to set up planning boards or commissions for similar work.[1] From the federal Planning Board evolved, in 1939, a National Resources Planning Board (in the Executive Office of the President), with three members appointed by the president and Senate;[2] and in promoting the ensuing defense and war effort, this board coöperated actively with the Office of Production Management, the War Production Board, and other agencies on studies related to the location of war industries, and with state planning boards and defense councils on special community problems. It also devoted much attention to the postwar period, with a view to developing plans for necessary readjustments, and in 1942-43 presented to the president two illuminating reports (climaxing a lengthy list of earlier publications)—one entitled *National Resources Development Report for 1943,* in which were outlined some of the major problems to be faced and some of the steps which would need to be taken in effecting an orderly transition from war to peace and for the longer-range development of an expanded economy, and the other bearing the challenging title of *Security, Work, and Relief.* The latter document received considerable attention from the press and public, but both encountered an unfortunately frigid reception in Congress; and, moved by political animus against an activity regarded as preëminently "New Dealish," Congress not only terminated the Board in 1943 by cutting off its funds, but barred the president from utilizing any substitute for it by rather childishly stipulating that the functions previously exercised should not be transferred to any other agency or performed "except as hereafter provided by law." Fortunately, the great amount of useful material assembled and published after 1933 by the Board and its forerunners remains available to those, including Congress itself, who, after all, cannot escape wrestling with many of the very problems to which the Board thoughtfully addressed itself.[3]

REFERENCES

M. Fainsod and L. Gordon, *Government and the American Economy* (New York, 1941), Chaps. x, xix-xx.

J. A. Maxwell, *The Fiscal Impact of Federalism in the United States* (Cambridge, Mass., 1946), Chap. xii.

[1] See list in Council of State Governments, *The Book of the States* (Chicago, 1943), V, 225. It is but fair to recognize that something in the nature of the National Planning Board was suggested by President Hoover's Committee on Recent Social Trends, reporting in 1933.

[2] The members in later years were Frederic A. Delano, Professor Charles E. Merriam of the University of Chicago, and George F. Yantis.

[3] C. E. Merriam, "The National Resources Planning Board; A Chapter in American Planning Experience," *Amer. Polit. Sci. Rev.,* XXXVIII, 1075-1088 (Dec., 1944). On the general subject, see G. B. Galloway and Associates, *Planning for America* (New York, 1941); J. W. Van Sickle, *Planning for the South; An Inquiry into the Economics of Regionalism* (Nashville, Tenn., 1943); "A Symposium on Regional Planning," *Iowa Law Rev.,* XXXII, 193-406 (Jan., 1947); and for a more popular treatment, S. Chase, *Goals for America* (New York, 1942). The National Planning Association (800 21st St., N.W., Washington, D. C.) issues *Planning Pamphlets* and other useful publications.

L. H. Chamberlain, *The President, Congress, and Legislation* (New York, 1946), Chap. x.

J. M. Gaus and L. Wolcott, *Public Administration and the United States Department of Agriculture* (Chicago, 1940), Chap. viii.

R. M. Robbins, *Our Landed Heritage; The Public Domain, 1776-1936* (Princeton, N. J., 1942).

G. Pinchot, *Breaking New Ground* (New York, 1947). An account of the growth of the conservation movement by one of its principal leaders.

A. F. Gustafson *et al., Conservation in the United States* (Ithaca, N. Y., 1944).

H. E. Flynn and F. E. Perkins, *Conservation of the Nation's Resources* (New York, 1941).

G. T. Renner, *Conservation of National Resources; An Educational Approach to the Problem* (New York, 1942).

E. G. Cheyney and T. Schantz-Hanzen, *This is Our Land; The Story of Conservation in the United States* (St. Paul, Minn., 1940).

C. R. Van Hise and L. Havemeyer, *Conservation of Natural Resources* (New York, 1930).

O. E. Parkins and J. R. Whitaker, *Our National Resources and Their Conservation* (New York, 1936).

J. Cameron, *The Development of Governmental Forest Control in the United States* (Baltimore, 1936).

S. W. Holbrook, *Burning an Empire; The Story of American Forest Fires* (New York, 1943).

V. W. Breever, *Forestry Activities of the Federal Government* (Washington, D. C., 1946).

J. Ise, *United States Forest Policy* (New Haven, 1920).

————, *United States Oil Policy* (New Haven, 1928).

N. Ely, *Oil Conservation Through Interstate Agreement* (Washington, D. C., 1933).

E. V. Rostow, *A National Policy for the Oil Industry* (New Haven, 1948).

L. M. Fanning [ed.], *Our Oil Resources* (New York, 1945).

M. W. Watkins, *Oil: Stabilization or Conservation* (New York, 1937).

F. F. Blachly and M. E. Oatman, *Natural Gas and the Public Interest* (Washington, D. C., 1947).

D. H. Smith, "The Forest Service," *Service Monographs*, No. 58 (Washington, D. C., 1930).

E. H. Graham, *The Land and Wildlife* (New York, 1948).

D. Lampen, *Economy and Social Aspects of Federal Reclamation* (Baltimore, 1930).

S. Chase, *The Economy of Abundance* (New York, 1934).

————, *Rich Land, Poor Land* (New York, 1936).

A. D. Frank, *The Development of the Federal Program of Flood Control on the Mississippi River* (New York, 1930).

State Government, XIX, 215-240 (Sept., 1946), "Managing Our Rivers." A series of articles.

P. L. Kleinsorge, *The Boulder Canyon Project; History and Economic Aspects* (Palo Alto, Calif., 1941).

R. L. Duffus and C. Krutch, *The Valley and Its People; A Portrait of T.V.A.* (New York, 1944).

D. E. Lilienthal, *TVA—Democracy on the March* (New York, 1944).

C. H. Pritchett, *The Tennessee Valley Authority; A Study in Public Administration* (Chapel Hill, N. C., 1943).

H. Finer, *The T.V.A.; Lessons for International Application* (Montreal, 1944).

J. L. Fly, "The Rôle of the Federal Government in Conservation and Utilization of Water Resources," *Univ. of Pa. Law Rev.*, LXXXVI, 274-294 (Jan., 1938).

E. E. Hunt [ed.], *The Power Industry and the Public Interest* (New York, 1944).

R. D. Baum, *The Federal Power Commission and State Utility Regulation* (Washington, D. C., 1942).

H. L. Elsbree, *Interstate Transmission of Electricity* (Cambridge, Mass., 1931).

M. E. Dimock, *Regional Factors in National Planning* (Washington, D. C., 1935).

J. D. Millett, *The Process and Organization of Government Planning* (New York, 1947).

Annual reports of the secretary of the interior (1946 report entitled "National Resource Problems"), the Tennessee Valley Authority, etc.

CHAPTER XXXII

GOVERNMENT AND LABOR

Labor
becomes
an or-
ganized
force in
American
society

Under the common law as carried over from England into America, supplemented by a vast growth of newer statutory law, labor involves a relationship between a worker who performs a stipulated service and an employer who compensates him for it in money or in goods. The relationship is of a contractual nature, and traditionally one of the precious heritages of every American has been his freedom to enter, whether as worker or as employer, into such relationship if and when he chooses—in other words, his "freedom of contract." To be sure, in these later times of highly developed labor organization this freedom has, in various ways, been sharply curtailed. Even yet, however, it is in principle basic to the American labor system.

In early days, when most people worked only for themselves, such hired laborers as there were bargained individually with employers and obtained such terms on wages, hours, and the like as they could. Even before 1789, however, mechanics and artisans in a few of the larger cities began drawing together in unions, and as industry expanded and workers multiplied, especially after the Civil War, consciousness of a weak bargaining position without organization, combined with growing desire for improvement of labor conditions in a multitude of directions, led to unionization on an ever-increasing scale. Employers naturally objected; public opinion was skeptical; and following early English precedents, American courts long looked askance at unions as constituting, or threatening, criminal conspiracy. The movement, however, went forward, and in time the courts, the public, and even practical-minded employers, accepted unions as not only inevitable, but—so long as they kept within the laws as gradually being liberalized—a legitimate means of enabling a vast segment of the working population to press in an articulate way for higher wages, shorter hours, and other ameliorations. In time, too, unions began drawing together in regional, or even nation-wide, federations. In 1886, the American Federation of Labor became the common spokesman of organized labor the country over; and after it had served in this fashion for half a century, seceding labor forces set up (in 1938) its lusty and more militant rival of today, the Congress of Industrial Organizations, carrying the labor movement more vigorously into the great mass-production industries.

Not all of labor, of course, is as yet organized—indeed hardly more than one-quarter of it; in a total national labor force (including agricul-

tural workers) of over sixty millions, the A. F. of L. claimed in 1947 Economic and political power
somewhat over seven and one-half million members, the C.I.O., six and
one-half million, and other major organizations, including the four separate
railway brotherhoods, considerably beyond one million—or a total of ap-
·proximately fifteen millions. But no one needs to be reminded of the
economic power which the organizations possess, freshly illustrated by
the paralyzing effects of great strikes of coal-miners, railroad employees,
and other groups during the period of reconversion following the recent
war. Political power is impressive, too; for although there has not arisen
(nor is likely to), as in Britain, a labor party contesting elections and
presenting a united front on legislative floors, tremendous political influence is channeled through the two major parties, or sometimes through
blocs cutting across them, expressing itself by supporting or opposing
presidential, congressional, and other candidates, contributing to campaign funds (through indirect channels, such as the C.I.O.'s Political
Action Committee, since unions *as such* may not lawfully make contributions), planning and urging legislation, lobbying on a grand scale in
Washington and in state capitals, and, in general, employing whatever
means and devices give promise of advancing the interests that wage-
earners, or at all events their leaders, have at heart. Of the power of
labor's political voice in later years—even if not always a united voice—
the pages that follow will give abundant evidence.[1]

Labor influences, and sometimes controls, government; government, in Govern-ment's concern with labor:
turn, regulates and otherwise concerns itself with labor—if possible, even
more than with agriculture. Purely local governments, to be sure, have 1. State and local
not much to do directly with the matter, at any rate beyond regulating
working conditions among their own employees; and even here they are
subject to the superior authority of the state. But, as in the case of agriculture, the states can, and do, draw from their wealth of reserved powers
wide latitude for regulative action. To begin with, the employer-employee
relation is, as has been said, a contractual one, and the states have power
of enforcement as in the case of contracts of other kinds. There is nothing,
too, to prevent a state from enacting and administering a wide variety
of laws controlling the conditions under which work is carried on, so
long, of course, as not conflicting with the national constitution and laws;
and from fairly far back, most of the number have built up more or less

[1] It is generally considered, however, that notwithstanding occasional boasts and
threats of labor leaders, the country's "labor vote" (itself a somewhat nebulous
quantity) cannot be swung at all solidly in any given direction in an electoral contest—even though in many cities, notably New York, it undoubtedly holds a balance
of power. Even so masterful a leader as John L. Lewis was unable to switch any large
number of votes away from Roosevelt to Willkie in the 1940 presidential campaign.
After the 1944 elections, the Political Action Committee (P.A.C.), an auxiliary of
the C.I.O. established in 1943 to promote labor activity on political lines, claimed to
have been at least partially responsible for the election of over one hundred congressmen and half of the newly chosen senators, and for several states being carried by
President Roosevelt. The claim, however, would have been difficult to substantiate,
and in the elections of 1946 only seventy-three of the 318 congressional candidates,
and five out of twenty-six senatorial candidates, so supported were victorious.

extensive codes of labor laws, covering such matters as hours, wages, safety devices, compensation for injury, collective bargaining, and the settlement of disputes—statutes, indeed, which (along with the common law) give unions themselves their legal basis. Beginning with Massachusetts in 1869, all likewise have set up a state labor bureau or department charged with compiling statistics, promoting arbitration and conciliation, and enforcing state-wide labor regulations.[1]

2. Federal

Except in its clauses relating to slavery, the federal constitution makes no allusion to labor; and, speaking broadly, in earlier days, whatever was done with reference to the matter—outside of regulating labor by the national government's own employees and, in time, by the employees of contractors doing work for the government—was supposed to be done by the states. As industry grew, however, and labor problems multiplied, ample constitutional grounds were found for steadily expanding action by the federal government with reference to the entire broad domain of labor interests and relations: (1) the power to tax and appropriate money for promoting the general welfare opens a way for the maintenance of a federal department of labor, for investigation of labor conditions and dissemination of information on the subject, and for providing systems of social insurance benefiting chiefly the laboring man and his family; (2) the power to regulate interstate and foreign commerce (with which, under the changes wrought by technology and by ever-widening judicial interpretation, more and more of labor's rank and file is connected) makes possible the protection of the labor market by restriction of immigration and by tariffs curbing the competition of foreign-made goods, and, far more important, the control of conditions, as to hours, wages, safety for workers, settlement of disputes, and the like, under which goods carried in both foreign and interstate commerce are produced; (3) the power to regulate the jurisdiction and procedure of the federal courts opens a way for dealing with the problem of injunctions; (4) jurisdiction over the territories and the District of Columbia carries with it a control over labor in those areas at least as extensive as that of the states within their own boundaries; and (5) as itself the largest employer of labor in the country, the federal government, of course, has full authority to regulate the labor of its own workers, by inherent right and without any need for constitutional authorization, express or implied.

Earlier Federal Protective Measures

The upshot is that for more than sixty years the national government has increasingly supplemented state control with protective and other regulatory activities affecting the nation's wage-earners. As early as 1882, Congress enacted a Chinese exclusion law as a restriction upon the inflow of competitive labor; three years afterwards, another measure

[1] See pp. 946-948 below (in complete edition of this book).

debarred alien laborers, of whatever nationality, if under contract to individuals or corporations; and a long line of immigration restrictions in later times, culminating in the quota system instituted in 1921, have had as at least one of their major purposes the safeguarding of American employment against swamping by foreign-born workers. Creation of a Department of Commerce and Labor in 1903 further reflected federal concern; and ten years later the influence of labor was strong enough to bring about the establishment of a separate Department of Labor designed "to foster, promote, and develop" the welfare of wage-earners of the United States, to improve their working conditions, and to advance their opportunities for profitable employment.[1]

Meanwhile, taking advantage of its commerce power, Congress entered the broad field of legislative action aimed at protecting labor against harmful exploitation. As far back as 1840, the government had become "an ensample to righteousness," when President Van Buren, by executive order, prescribed a ten-hour day for federal employees on public works; and in 1868 Congress had followed by fixing eight hours as a day's work for all "laborers, workmen, and mechanics" federally employed in any way.[2] Regulations of the kind for labor outside of government employment (and employment by government contractors) was not undertaken federally until early in the present century. But in 1907 an Hours of Service Act limited to sixteen the hours of consecutive work of persons having to do with the interstate movement of railway trains, and in 1916 the Adamson Act, passed at the behest of the railway brotherhoods, reduced the working day for all such persons to eight hours. An Employers' Liability Act of 1908, applying to all employees engaged in interstate commerce, drastically amended and liberalized the common-law rules which, under the old doctrines of "contributory negligence" and "assumption of risk," had until then enabled carriers largely to escape liability for injury or death suffered by their workmen in perform-

Protective laws based on the commerce power

---

[1] The principal branches of the Department of Labor today are: (1) the Bureau of Labor Statistics, (2) the Division of Labor Standards, (3) the United States Employment Service, (4) the Wage Adjustment Board, (5) the Wage and Hour Division and (6) Public Contracts Division (under a single administrator), and (7) the Women's Bureau. A Children's Bureau formerly included was transferred in 1946 to the Federal Security Agency, although functions relating to child labor under the Fair Labor Standards Act of 1938 remain in the Labor Department, in a Child Labor and Youth Employment Branch of the Division of Labor Standards. It should be added that at the date of writing (March, 1948), the United States Employment Service was in the Department of Labor only under temporary transfer, but that President Truman had requested consent of Congress to make the arrangement permanent and to move the Bureau of Employment Security—having to do with unemployment insurance (see p. 750 below)—from the Federal Security Agency and place the two establishments under a single commissioner of employment. The Department's principal officers are the secretary of labor, an under-secretary of labor, three assistant secretaries, and a solicitor. For full description, see the most recent edition of the *United States Government Manual*.

[2] In time, this eight-hour day (seven hours for clerical employees) became standard throughout the government service, and in 1936 the Government-Contracts [Walsh-Healey] Act imposed it also upon contractors and subcontractors with respect to any of their employees engaged in work for the government. 49 *U. S. Stat. at Large*, 2036.

ance of duty.[1] A LaFollette Seamen's Act of 1915 extended to a large class of employees previously subjected to almost incredible hardships and deprivations important safeguards such as suitable food, clothing, and living quarters, reasonable hours, and regular payment of wages; and in 1920 the benefits of the Employers' Liability Act were extended to these workers also. Significant, too, were certain clauses of the Clayton Anti-Trust Act of 1914[2] asserting human labor to be not "a commodity or article of commerce," declaring (contrary to the implications of a Supreme Court decision of 1908) unions, as such, to be not illegal combinations or conspiracies in restraint of trade, and restricting the use of injunctions in labor disputes—although to labor itself this legislation proved disappointing when the courts insisted on whittling away most of the benefits expected to accrue from it. Finally, in 1932, a Norris-La-Guardia Anti-Injunction Act,[3] sponsored by organized labor, made "yellow dog" contracts, i.e., contracts by which employees bind themselves not to join a trade union, unenforceable in the federal courts and expressly forbade the courts to issue injunctions against laborers for striking, for using union funds in aid of a strike, or for inciting others to strike, unless the employer could show that he had made "every reasonable effort" to arrive at a settlement or that unlawful acts had been committed or threatened by the strikers.[4]

Failure of measures for women and children

In one or two directions, the protective efforts characteristic of this first quarter of the twentieth century proved less successful, and because of difficulty with the courts. When, in 1916, Congress undertook to restrict child labor in factories and mines by excluding from interstate commerce the products of establishments employing such labor, the Supreme Court held the measure void as regulating manufacturing rather than commerce;[5] when, in 1919, another attempt was made, on the basis of the taxing power, the result was similar, although of course on different grounds;[6] and when, in 1918, a minimum-wage law for women and children in the District of Columbia was placed on the statute-book, it too fell before a judicial ruling that adult women were being deprived of freedom of contract guaranteed them in the constitution.[7]

[1] An act of 1906 on the same subject, warmly urged by President Theodore Roosevelt, was invalidated by the Supreme Court. Howard v. Illinois Central Railroad Company, 207 U. S. 463 (1908).

[2] See p. 652 above. L. B. Boudin, "Organized Labor and the Clayton Act," Va. Law Rev., XXIX, 271-315 (Dec., 1942), and 395-439 (June, 1943).

[3] 47 U. S. Stat. at Large, 70.

[4] M. G. Ratner and N. J. Come, "The Norris-LaGuardia Act in the Constitution," Geo. Washington Law Rev., XI, 428-472 (June, 1943).

[5] Hammer v. Dagenhart, 247 U. S. 251 (1918).

[6] Bailey v. Drexel Furniture Co., 259 U. S. 20 (1922). The point to the decision was that the tax placed on profits from child-made goods was not a bona fide tax, but only a subterfuge resorted to for regulating production.

[7] Adkins v. Children's Hospital, 261 U. S. 525 (1923). Such freedom, nowhere expressly provided for, was construed to be implicit in the due process clauses of the Fifth and Fourteenth Amendments. Much state legislation of similar purport was likewise overthrown as being "arbitrary, unreasonable, or capricious," and therefore incompatible with "due process." As a rule, too, protective legislation, federal or

All in all, the federal government had, by 1933, concerned itself with labor conditions and problems on a number of fronts, and at some points with considerable effect. All that had gone before, however, proved merely a modest prologue to what was to come after, in a decade and a half witnessing the depression of the thirties, the defense effort starting in 1940, four years of global war, and other years of reconversion to ways of peace. Until near the end, the period was that of the New Deal, conspicuously characterized by broader and stricter regulation of business and industry, increased sympathy in government circles for the interests and aims of organized labor, warm support of the Roosevelt Administration by labor and virtual alliance of fast-growing labor organizations with the Democratic party, and (especially under the impetus of depression) a flood of remedial labor legislation such as the country had never before witnessed. So extensively, indeed, were the privileges and powers of labor augmented that many people came to feel that the balance had been tipped too far; and when the Republican party recaptured both branches of Congress in 1946, the political reorientation brought to light was confidently interpreted, by the victors at least, as springing in part from public desire, not that all of the steps of the past ten or twelve years be retraced, but at least that significant checks and correctives be applied. A comprehensive new labor law of 1947, enacted over the veto of a Democratic president, carried out what was construed to be the popular mandate and very well may prove the starting point of a new period of labor history. At all events, it will make for clarity if we first fix attention upon selected developments principally of the years 1933-46, and afterwards consider separately the changes more recently introduced. Three aspects of the period mentioned chiefly call for attention: (1) the efforts made and devices utilized for promoting employment; (2) the improvement of labor standards through collective bargaining and a system of maximum wages and minimum hours; and (3) the expansion of means and methods of preserving industrial peace. Two further developments of concern mainly to the laboring population—the introduction of a nation-wide system of social insurance and efforts in behalf of more and better low-cost housing—will be touched upon in the chapter to follow.

The new situation after 1933

Promotion of Employment

In enumerating the famous "four freedoms" to which he believed people everywhere entitled, President Roosevelt placed high in the list "freedom from want"—the best guarantee of which is, of course, remunerative employment; and it has always been axiomatic, under our American system of free competitive enterprise, that any person needing

Unemployment a perennial problem

---

state, in behalf of particular groups or classes of workers encountered a hurdle in the "equal protection" clause, with the judges requiring convincing demonstration of the reasonableness of setting off one group as against another for special treatment.

to support himself or a family ought to have a chance to do so by honest toil. The ideal is, however, difficult to realize in practice. Even in periods of comparative prosperity, the lag or collapse of some industries, the shifting of others from one part of the country to another, changes in popular tastes and demands, introduction of new labor-saving machinery and other new techniques of production, the flow of young people from country to city in quest of work and wages, and other unsettling developments constantly going on in the national economy, throw people out of work, and at best—even in a time of stepped-up production like the recent war years—there is always a substantial margin of unemployment;[1] while in periods of economic recession and stagnation, the proportion may mount to appalling levels. At the nadir of the depression of the thirties, the number of unemployed in the country rose to thirteen millions or more; and notwithstanding considerable recovery in the meantime, it was still approximately ten millions in 1940 when the defense effort began rapidly to take up the slack. The problem, if not of averting unemployment completely, at least of holding it to a level not seriously damaging to the economy, is, therefore, always with us.

Ways of dealing with it: State and national governments have long concerned themselves with the matter, approaching it on three principal lines: (1) regulations calculated to reserve the labor market for *adults*, and for *citizens;* (2) maintenance of employment agencies and other devices for bringing the worker and the job together; and (3) in times of special stress, programs of public works designed to furnish a livelihood for large numbers of workers otherwise unemployed.

1. Efforts to promote employment of *adults* and *citizens* Efforts to curb child labor, while of course directed primarily toward protecting the children themselves against exploitation, always had the secondary purpose of preserving more jobs for adults. For a long time, not much success attended them. As indicated below, however, the Fair Labor Standards Act of 1938 went far toward solving that particular problem. Efforts to protect the American worker against competition from workers abroad, or alien workers resident in the United States, have taken the form principally of (1) protective tariffs laid partly or wholly with a view to keeping out of the American market commodities produced by cheap labor abroad, and thereby supposedly guaranteeing more work for American laborers and at higher wages; (2) restrictive immigration laws, keeping for American workmen jobs which, under a looser immigration policy, would go in large numbers to foreigners; and (3) laws confining labor on public works to persons of citizen status.[2] In private industry, it has been found impracticable to deny aliens the same right to employment as citizens, because in the view of the courts such

---

[1] Even in June, 1947, when an all-time peak of civilian employment (60,055,000) was reached, the number of unemployed was officially reported at 2,555,000.

[2] Of course, this third expedient does not of itself reduce unemployment; it may mean simply fewer unemployed *citizens*.

denial is tantamount to refusing equal protection of the laws.[1] State laws providing for such discrimination in connection with public undertakings have, however, been upheld; and since 1938 the federal government has also successfully maintained a policy of permitting no aliens to be employed on any federally-aided work project. An additional restriction in the interest of a maximum number of jobs for adult workers dependent upon the general labor market (although not coming under the heading of foreign or alien competition) takes the form of limitations upon the sale of prison-made goods in competition with other goods, by laws enacted in most of the states not only restricting the marketing of such goods manufactured in the state's own prisons, but imposing—under authority conferred by Congress in the Hawes-Cooper Act of 1929[2] (effective in 1934)—the same limiting conditions upon the distribution of goods produced in prisons of other states.

Even when jobs are plentiful, there is the problem of bringing job and worker together; and over so vast a country, with industries so diversified, and with costs and difficulties of seeking work except in one's immediate locality so prohibitive, the problem is indeed a serious one. For meeting it, a bewildering variety of employment agencies have made their appearance—agencies not creating work, of course, but only directing people to it. Some are conducted by individual employers or employer associations; some are maintained by labor organizations; many are private profit-seeking enterprises. Even under regulation, however, private agencies long ago showed serious defects, and as early as 1890 public agencies began to appear in the field. For a time, these took the form chiefly of employment offices set up and operated by states. During World War I, however, an acute labor shortage led to the creation of a U. S. Employment Service (with offices scattered over the country) in the federal Department of Labor; and although after 1919 the agency was poorly supported and did not prove very effective, a New Deal measure of 1933—the Wagner-Peyser Act[3]—gave it a new lease on life, while at the same time introducing matched federal grants-in-aid, in proportion to population, to state employment offices. In 1939—the Social Security Act of 1935 having introduced a nation-wide system of unemployment compensation[4]—the U. S. Service was incorporated in a Bureau of Employment Security under the Social Security Board; and under this arrangement, the agency was charged afresh with developing a national system of employment offices while at the same time assisting in estab-

2. Public employment agencies

---

[1] A good many years ago, a heavy influx of low-paid Mexican labor into Arizona led the legislature of that state to enact a law requiring every employer of five or more persons to give at least eighty per cent of his jobs to American citizens. In Truax *v.* Raich, 239 U. S. 33 (1915), however, the Supreme Court held the measure invalid. On the general subject, see D. Fellman, "The Alien's Right to Work," *Minn. Law Rev.,* XXII, 137-176 (Jan., 1938).

[2] 45 *U. S. Stat. at Large,* 1084.

[3] 48 *U. S. Stat. at Large,* 113.

[4] See pp. 750-753 below.

lishing and maintaining systems of state public employment offices, with
the aid of federal funds matching the expenditures of states and localities.
With a view to more effective mobilization of manpower for war, all state
employment services were, on January 1, 1942, transferred to full national
control. After hostilities terminated, however, strong sentiment developed
in Congress and among the states for a restoration of their employment
services to the states; and although President Truman (recommending
that the consolidation under federal control be maintained at least until
June 30, 1947) tartly vetoed an appropriation measure providing for the
proposed restoration within a hundred days, the bill as it finally became
law [1] fixed November 16, 1946, as the date; and in that form it was reluctantly accepted at the White House. The U. S. Employment Service
survives (temporarily in the Department of Labor), with its own system
of employment offices in some nine states which as yet have no such
offices of their own; and it is expected to go on indefinitely as a coördinating authority. The federal government, moreover, continues to contribute
subsidies to the restored state services.

3. Programs of public works In periods of heavy unemployment, state and federal governments
alike may come to the assistance of the working population by instituting
programs of public works calculated to provide large numbers of jobs—
as well as, of course, by direct grants for relief. The most striking illustrations of this "pump-priming" method of dealing with a slump in
industry were afforded by the programs embarked upon by states, and
especially by the federal government, in battling the depression of the
thirties, when the government at Washington set up (1) a Public Works
Administration, with large funds for initiating public construction and
financing self-liquidating semi-public building, and (2) a Civil Works
Administration (succeeded by a Works Progress Administration, subsequently renamed Work Projects Administration), with further billions at
its disposal, together with (3) two employment undertakings designed
especially for the benefit of the country's youth—a Civilian Conservation
Corps assembling, over a period of ten years, three hundred thousand
young men in upwards of two thousand camps for work on forestry, park,
flood-control, and other conservation projects; and a National Youth
Administration, organized in 1935 as a branch of the Works Progress
Administration and, over a similar period, financing additional hundreds
of thousands of youth, some attending educational institutions and others
not. With the general employment situation sharply reversed after we
entered World War II, all of these agencies were liquidated—the last two
in 1943 and 1944, respectively.[2]

---

[1] 60 *U. S. Stat. at Large*, 679 (1946).
[2] A. W. Macmahon *et al., The Administration of Federal Work Relief* (Chicago,
1941). A good account of the C.C.C. will be found in Captain X, "A Civilian Army
in the Woods," *Harper's Mag.,* CLXVIII, 487-497 (Mar., 1934), and of the N.Y.A.
in L. L. Gorin, *Youth and World Programs; Problems and Policies* (Washington,
D. C., 1941).

One other line of effort, in the federal field, calls for mention. Fearful of unemployment on a disastrous scale after the war, and hopeful that such a calamity could be staved off, both then and later on, President Truman, members of Congress, various economists, and sundry other persons feeling deep concern, threw their support, in 1945, to a "full employment" bill predicated not only on the federal government's responsibility for preventing depression and unemployment, but on the conviction that, by promoting an "expanding economy," the government might be able to assure jobs permanently for substantially all people willing and able to work. The plan was much too complicated to be explained in full here,[1] but the essence of it was (1) that every year the president should transmit to Congress not only his regular fiscal budget, but also a "national production and employment budget," or economic budget, setting forth the policies which in his judgment should be pursued in order to maintain high-level production and full employment; (2) that if storm signals showed, this budget should propose measures necessary to keep the economy on an even keel (*e.g.*, tax reduction as an incentive to business expansion; public works undertaken by state and local governments; if necessary, public works and other employment-making undertakings by the federal government as well); and (3) that it should be just as much the duty of Congress to consider, and so far as possible implement, the economic budget as the fiscal budget. The heart of the scheme was the close study, forecasting, and planning designed to lie behind the president's recommendations, together with the statutory obligation of Congress to act on what was submitted to it. Many people considered the plan well-meant, but naïve; numerous business-men and economists, in particular, were skeptical about the possibilities of the long-range forecasting presumed and apprehensive lest it lead to government schemes and experiments that would only frighten industry and discourage free enterprise; and, despite much urging from the White House, Congress eventually adopted the plan, in the Full Employment Act of 1946,[2] only after whittling it down to provide simply for (1) an "economic report" by the president each year to Congress, covering levels of employment, production, and purchasing power, current and foreseeable trends, the government's "economic program," and recommendations for legislation; (2) a council of three full-time economic advisers to the president to maintain constant watch over the economic situation, keep in continuous touch with the president concerning it, and advise and assist in preparing the annual report; and (3) a joint committee on the economic report, composed of seven members from each house, charged with

[1] For a detailed analysis by one of the authors of the bill, see J. E. Murray, "A Practical Approach [to Maintenance of High-Level Production and Full Employment]," *Amer. Polit. Sci. Rev.*, XXXIX, 1119-1126 (Dec., 1945). The only foreign country in which something approaching full peacetime employment is attained is Russia; and there, of course, only by virtue of a rigorous collectivism wholly alien to the American mind and way of life.

[2] 60 *U. S. Stat. at Large*, 24.

planning ways and means of carrying out the recommendations made and reporting them for action. Dissatisfied though he was with the weakened form in which the measure passed, the President signed it.[1]

Improvement of Labor Standards—Collective Bargaining

Provisions of the National Industrial Recovery Act (1933)

Even before the remarkable outburst of labor legislation in the earlier years of the New Deal, Congress had availed itself of its commerce power to enact many laws aimed at improving working conditions in industry generally or in particular industries—laws fixing maximum hours, prescribing measures for protection of life and limb, requiring compensation for injuries, and even, in the case of seamen, stipulating adequate food, clothing, and living quarters. With improvement of labor standards as one of its many objectives, the National Recovery Act of 1933,[2] however, went farther than any previous measure, requiring, in its famous Section 7(a), all codes of fair competition adopted by the various industries (1) to set minimum wage levels, fix maximum hours, eliminate child labor, and otherwise improve working conditions, (2) to recognize the right of employees "to organize and bargain collectively through representatives of their own choosing," and (3) to protect every employee or other person seeking employment against being required, as a condition of employment, "to join any company union or to refrain from joining." In laying down these and other regulations, the government not only evidenced a new concern about wages and hours for industry as a whole, but unequivocally endorsed labor unions as instrumentalities through which workers might collectively compel employers to abide by adequate wage and hour standards and otherwise maintain proper working conditions. A National Labor Relations Board, too, was set up in 1934 to conduct elections to determine employee representation for collective bargaining and to deal with controversies arising out of Section 7(a)'s operation.

The National Labor Relations Act (1935)

Many of the gains expected to be realized were placed in jeopardy when, in 1935, large portions of the Recovery Act were voided by the Supreme Court. Promptly in the same year, however, Congress, in response to urgent labor demand, and again invoking its commerce power,

---

[1] With Edwin G. Nourse (former vice-president of the Brookings Institution) as chairman and Leon H. Keyserling (former professor of economics at Columbia University) and John D. Clark (a former dean at the University of Nebraska) as associate members (all appointed by the president and Senate), the contemplated Council of Economic Advisers was forthwith set up in the Executive Office of the President and has since been functioning on the intended lines. Its first study of the national economic situation, showing employment to be currently at a very high level, was placed in the President's hands on December 16, 1946; and the President's first "economic report" to Congress was transmitted on the following January 8. An interim report to Congress was made, also, in the summer of 1947, based on current studies of the Advisory Council; and a second regular economic report was transmitted on January 14, 1948 (see summary in *N. Y. Times* of the following day). Cf. *The Economic Reports of the President as Transmitted to the Congress, January, 1948, July, 1947, January, 1947, with an Introduction by the Council of Economic Advisers* (New York, 1948).

[2] See p. 658 above.

passed a National Labor Relations [Wagner] Act salvaging practically the whole of Section 7(a) with its basic guarantee of collective bargaining.[1] To make such bargaining more free and effective, furthermore, "company" unions (ordinarily including all employees in a given establishment, and commonly dominated by the company officials) were outlawed, so that thenceforth all unions might be fully independent employee organizations; employers were forbidden to discriminate between union and non-union workers; and, although one of the objects was to avert strikes, the act forbade its clauses ever to be construed as interfering in any way with the right to resort to such weapons.[2]

For enforcing this measure, a new National Labor Relations Board of three members (appointed by the President and Senate for five-year terms) was created as an independent quasi-judicial agency, and given two important functions: first, to ascertain and declare who, in any particular plant, were bona fide representatives entitled to speak for the employees in collective bargaining; and second, to hear and pass upon complaints against employers for denying or abridging employees' rights to organize, for refusing to bargain collectively, for discharging employees for union activity, or for indulging in other specified "unfair" practices.[3] Both forms of action were, of course, to be initiated, not by the Board, but by employees (or, under certain conditions in election situations, by employers)—the first, by filing a petition for an election to choose representatives or agents, the second, by filing complaints. If after local investigation by an examiner (with perhaps a hearing in Washington), a complaint was sustained, the Board might issue "cease and desist" orders

The National Labor Relations Board

---

[1] The measure was drafted by Senator Robert F. Wagner of New York and, contrary to popular understanding, President Roosevelt had little to do with it except to endorse and sign it.

[2] The principle of collective bargaining—perhaps the most important feature of both Section 7(a) and the Labor Relations Act—was not new. In legislation relating to railway labor, it had been invoked from as early as 1888, and in 1930 the Supreme Court had sustained it in a case involving an attempt by a railroad company (operating, of course, in interstate commerce) to circumvent it by imposing a company union on its employees (Texas and New Orleans Railroad Co. *v.* Brotherhood of Railway and Steamship Clerks, 281 U. S. 548). The principle found recognition also in the Norris-LaGuardia Act. Cf. W. H. Spencer, *Collective Bargaining Under Section 7(a) of the National Industrial Recovery Act* (Chicago, 1935). From first to last, the basic labor policy of the Roosevelt Administration was to promote the extension of unionism throughout the national economy, to expand the use of collective labor agreements, and in every way to increase the power of labor organizations in the bargaining process, to the end of larger income with shorter working hours.

After the act of 1935 became law, several states enacted "baby Wagner Acts," guaranteeing collective bargaining in purely intrastate industry.

[3] Among these practices were: (1) interference with or coercion of employees in collective bargaining; (2) domination or interference by employers in the formation or administration of any labor organization; (3) discrimination in employment with a view to encouraging or discouraging membership in a labor organization; (4) discharging of, or discrimination against, an employee for filing charges under the act; and (5) refusal to bargain collectively with representatives of employees. In 1936, Congress passed a so-called "strike-breakers' act," making it a felony knowingly to transport in interstate commerce "any person with intent to employ such person to obstruct or interfere ... with peaceful picketing during any labor controversy ... or the right of collective bargaining." 49 *U. S. Stat. at Large*, 449.

enforceable in the courts like similar orders issued by the Federal Trade Commission.

A measure as far-reaching as the National Labor Relations Act could not fail to be challenged in the courts; and since, down to this time, the Supreme Court had always held manufacturing, mining, and the like not to be commerce, and therefore not subject to federal regulation under the commerce power, it was widely expected that when the test came the Court would hold the new legislation to be a regulation, not of commerce, but only of labor conditions in manufacturing and other industries, and therefore void. The outcome, however, was far otherwise. Even though the changes of personnel which were about to transform and liberalize the Court had barely begun, three decisions handed down in 1937 [1] took the ground that, although the manufacturing operations of the defendant corporations were, to be sure, carried on locally, the raw materials used and the finished goods produced were objects of interstate commerce, which had the effect of investing even the manufacturing of them with the character of commerce, and therefore of bringing it within reach of the commerce power—wherefore (1) Congress had a right to require collective bargaining and otherwise regulate labor conditions in manufacturing plants so situated; (2) the Labor Relations Act was constitutional, and (3) employers had no alternative but to comply with the statute's provisions. In these crucial decisions, the Court took a long step toward so modernizing its interpretation of the commerce power as to enable the national government to deal freely with the realities of American business today.

The Improvement of Labor Standards—Wages, Hours, Child Labor

With the Labor Relations Act (and also the Social Security Act of the same year) safely validated judicially, makers of policy in the Roosevelt Administration advanced to another major labor amelioration, and one for which the President himself assumed a large share of responsibility. To this time, federal regulation of wages and hours had been confined substantially to government workers and employees of government contractors, and of common carriers; and while approximately half of the states had wage and hour regulations, in nearly every instance these applied only to women or to women and children, and commonly to certain industries only. Even state legislation merely for women and

---

[1] National Labor Relations Board *v.* Jones & Laughlin Steel Corp., 301 U. S. 1 (1937); National Labor Relations Board *v.* Fruehauf Trailer Co., 301 U. S. 49 (1937); and National Labor Relations Board *v.* Friedman-Harry Marks Clothing Co., 301 U. S. 58 (1937). All three decisions were reached by five-to-four votes of the justices. In another case decided at the same time—Associated Press *v.* National Labor Relations Board, 301 U. S. 103 (1937)—it was contended that the defendant was not engaged in interstate commerce, and that applying the provisions of the Wagner Act to it amounted to violating the First Amendment by restricting freedom of the press. By a five-to-four vote, the Court, however, held that the gathering and dissemination of news is commerce, and that restrictions imposed by the act did not amount to any violation of the freedom in question.

children had not fared too well in the courts; more than once, as relating especially to women, it had been overthrown on the ground of interfering with constitutionally guaranteed freedom of contract.[1] And for adequate safeguards of the kind, at the hands of the states, applying to all women and children, and not only to them but also to men, there was little hope, not only because of the judicial hurdle, but by reason of widely prevailing inertia and laxness on the subject. Accordingly, in 1937 President Roosevelt called upon Congress for a federal law that would pick up where the defunct National Recovery Act left off by putting a "floor" under wages (a minimum wage law) and a "ceiling" over hours (a maximum hours law), and also by abolishing child labor; and the upshot was a Fair Labor Standards ["Wages and Hours"] Act of 1938,[2] representing the government's most ambitious attempt as yet to regulate working conditions in industry. Applying in general to workers engaged in manufacturing, mining, processing, or transporting commodities moving in interstate commerce (although not to employees of common carriers—provided for in other statutes—or to various other designated groups [3]), the act laid down regulations on all of the subjects specified by the President—wages, hours, and child labor.

A minimum wage of twenty-five cents an hour was prescribed for the first year following October 24, 1938; thirty cents an hour for the next six years; and after seven years (in 1945), unless sooner brought into operation under specified circumstances, the figure was to be forty cents

1. Wages

---

[1] In 1905, a New York law limiting hours in bakeries had been invalidated (Lochner v. New York, 198 U. S. 45); in 1917, Oregon laws limiting hours fixing minimum wages for women and children had been upheld (Bunting v. Oregon, 243 U. S. 426, and Stettler v. O'Hara, 243 U. S. 629), but, as noted above, in 1923 a women's and children's minimum-wage law passed by Congress for the District of Columbia had been overthrown (Adkins v. Children's Hospital, 261 U. S. 525), with Arizona and Arkansas laws of similar nature later almost automatically going down in its wake; as recently as 1936, a New York measure of similar purport had been invalidated (Morehead v. New York ex rel Tipaldo, 298 U. S. 587)—although in the following year a similar act on the statute-book of the state of Washington since 1913 was upheld (West Coast Hotel Co. v. Parrish, 300 U. S. 379). After the last-mentioned decision, a leading authority wrote that at last the Supreme Court had put itself on record as upholding the constitutionality of such legislation. The wavering indicated in the list of cases here presented seemed rather, however, to afford no firm ground for assurance—at all events, for any longer time than the Court should continue operating in the new atmosphere engendered by the "court controversy" of 1937 (see p. 548 above).

[2] 52 U. S. Stat. at Large, 1060.

[3] Five groups expressly excepted are: (1) agricultural workers, seamen, employees of airlines, street railways, motor-bus lines, interurban railways, and the employees of weekly or semi-weekly newspapers with a circulation of less than three thousand, the major part of which is in the county of publication; (2) persons employed in bona fide executive, administrative, professional, or local retail capacity, or as outside salesmen; (3) persons employed in any retail or service establishment, the greater part of whose sales are within the state where the business is located; (4) persons employed in fishing and the fishing industry; and (5) persons employed in the area of production to handle, prepare, or can agricultural or horticultural commodities, or to make dairy products. In 1941 (on the eve of our entrance into World War II), the total number of persons to whom the law applied was reported to be in the neighborhood of fifteen and one-half millions; by 1948, it was not far short of twenty millions.

an hour, except in special cases; and in point of fact, the forty-cent level was actually arrived at in July, 1944.[1]

2. Hours

Forty-four hours a week were set as the maximum during the first year of the law's operation, forty-two hours the second year, and forty hours after October 24, 1941—with in all cases overtime pay at one and one-half times the regular rate. Within limits, however, the work-week might be extended by collective bargaining agreements, especially in industries requiring speeding up in certain seasons.

3. Child labor

Finally, child labor was placed under drastic restriction by provisions prohibiting goods produced under conditions of "oppressive child labor" to be handled in interstate commerce—such child labor being later defined as including the employment of any children under sixteen in manufacturing or mining, or under eighteen in occupations declared by the Children's Bureau (then in the Department of Labor) to be "particularly hazardous ... or detrimental to their health or well-being." In occupations covered by the law, other than manufacturing and mining, children might be employed in periods not interfering with their schooling and under conditions not injurious to their health and general welfare.

Constitutionality and administration

Although the new legislation encountered much hostility in some quarters, responsible employers, on the whole, fell into line with it and carried out its provisions faithfully; and when challenged constitutionally, it was sustained unanimously by a Supreme Court [2] that already had broken with its own precedents and accepted the regulation of manufacturing and mining having an interstate aspect as within the bounds of the commerce power. During World War II, the strain upon the country's productive capacity led (in 1943) to authorization of a forty-eight-hour week in war industries, but the deviation was only for the period of emergency. Except for its child-labor provisions, enforceable by a "child labor and youth employment" branch of the Labor Department's Division of Labor Standards, administration is vested in the Department's Wage and Hour Division, with which has been consolidated a Public Contracts Division having to do with enforcing similar wage and hour provisions of the Walsh-Healey Act of 1936 applying to labor on government contracts exceeding ten thousand dollars.[3]

---

[1] Under high-cost-of-living conditions of recent postwar years, there has been strong demand for a sharp stepping-up of this figure. In 1946, the Senate, with warm approval of President Truman, passed a minimum wage bill raising it to sixty-five cents, but the House refused to concur. In 1947, the Republican congressional majority's program called for an increase to sixty cents, but again without action resulting. At the opening of 1948, the A. F. of L. and the C.I.O. were demanding an increase to seventy-five cents, and the same figure was being advocated by President Truman and his secretary of labor. In point of fact, it was estimated, however, that of workers to whom the law applied, only some 1,800,000 were actually receiving less than the figure named.

[2] United States *v.* Darby Lumber Co., 312 U. S. 100 (1941)—completely repudiating the conceptualism of Hammer *v.* Dagenhart, 247 U. S. 251 (1918). Cf. H. A. L., "Constitutional Aspect of the Fair Labor Standards Act of 1938," *Univ. of Pa. Law Rev.*, LXXXVII, 91-105 (Nov., 1938).

[3] J. M. F. Donovan, Jr., "The Practical Administration of the Wage and Hour Act," *Georgetown Law Jour.*, XXXI, 115-145 (Jan., 1943).

The Promotion of Industrial Peace

Throughout the years while labor was achieving the substantial gains outlined (and others as well), strikes, lockouts, slowdowns, boycotts, and other interruptions and disorders associated with labor-management disputes persistently inflicted heavy losses upon industry, labor, and the general public alike; and, aside from the provisions of the Labor-Management Relations Act of 1947 bearing on the status of unions, the bargaining process, and the like, most labor legislation of the past decade has been concentrated on the objective of safeguarding and promoting industrial peace.[1] The rôle of government in this connection is extensive and important. First of all, it consists in regulating labor conditions and relations—as to wages, hours, safety precautions, bargaining rights, and what not—on lines of fairness and justice calculated to keep workers contented and quiet; to this extent, it is essentially preventive. In the second place, however, it entails encouragement of prompt and just settlement of disputes that nevertheless arise, with provision of rules and machinery for facilitating such action. In general, there are four ways of dealing with labor disputes: direct negotiation, mediation, arbitration, and litigation. The first usually proceeds without intervention by government; in the second and third, government may or may not have a part, but with strong likelihood in these days of at least providing mediation boards or other conciliating machinery, whether to be employed compulsorily or optionally; in the fourth, government necessarily participates, through the courts. *[The rôle of government]*

Until within the present century, governmental promotion of industrial peace fell almost exclusively to the states, under their reserved powers; and by 1900 most of the number had legislation on the subject, backed in a dozen or more by standing boards of conciliation or arbitration. As, however, industry took on more of a national aspect, and its problems grew in scope and complexity, the federal government was inevitably brought upon the scene; and in later years it has so preëmpted the field that nowadays state agencies for handling labor controversies have relatively little importance except in Kansas, Colorado, and perhaps one or two other jurisdictions. *[Declining activity of the states]*

The powers of the federal government in this domain have clear constitutional foundations. (1) If labor disturbances threaten the enforcement of any federal law or the discharge of any federal function, e.g., operating the postal service, there is self-evident authority to intervene. (2) If a dispute localized within a particular state leads to disorders of such magnitude that the state authorities find it necessary to call for assistance, the president may respond with federal troops, and definitely *[Bases of federal action]*

---

[1] As a whole, the measure mentioned ostensibly had this same objective also, although many of its opponents maintained that it would augment rather than reduce labor strife.

will do so if federal functions are menaced. To be sure, these actions look immediately only to the enforcement of law or to averting community dangers inherent in labor violence. From the power to take them may readily be deduced, however, the right to look behind what has occurred and take measures to prevent it from happening again. (3) But the basic authority of the federal government for concerning itself with industrial peace comes from a different and far more fertile source, namely, the commerce clause of the constitution; any dispute having, actually or potentially, the effect of obstructing the free flow of commerce *ipso facto* becomes a legitimate object of federal attention. At one time, this did not mean much outside of disputes involving railway or shipping employees or other people engaged directly in transportation. With "commerce" now broadened, however, to include all manufacturing, mining, and other productive enterprise having interstate or foreign aspects or connections, not much industry remains in which labor troubles are beyond the federal government's reach.

Some special sources of authority:

1. The anti-trust laws

As we have seen, a major product of the commerce power is the anti-trust laws; and in turn these become a significant potential medium for federal restraint of labor disturbances. When the Sherman Anti-Trust Act of 1890 made illegal every contract and combination in restraint of interstate commerce, there was no mention of labor unions; and there has always been difference of opinion as to whether they were intended to be included. Nevertheless, in prosecuting the famous Debs case arising out of the Pullman strike of 1894 in Chicago,[1] the government invoked the Sherman Act along with its undisputed power to prevent interference with the United States mails; and in the almost equally famous Danbury Hatters case of 1908,[2] the Supreme Court unequivocally took a position which it has ever since maintained, namely, that the Sherman Act applies to activities of unions no less than to those of corporate combinations. To be sure, at the behest of labor, the Clayton Anti-Trust Act of 1914, as we have seen, declared unions not to be illegal combinations or conspiracies in restraint of trade. But, as judicially interpreted, this did not mean that such organizations could not, especially in connection with strikes, commit acts in restraint of trade for which they could be held responsible; and as recently as 1940 the Supreme Court, maintaining (in spite of the Clayton, Norris-LaGuardia, and other acts) that no act had ever been passed exempting unions from the anti-trust laws, unqualifiedly reaffirmed its traditional position.[3] By interpretation, therefore, the federal government is competent to proceed at law against labor unions whenever it can show that strikes, boycotts, slow-downs, or other activi-

[1] *In re* Debs, 158 U. S. 564 (1895).
[2] Loewe *v.* Lawlor, 208 U. S. 274 (1908).
[3] Apex Hosiery Co. *v.* Leader, 310 U. S. 469 (1940). A federal district court's award of strike damages to the hosiery company was reversed, but, as indicated, the principle of liability when interstate commerce is substantially interfered with was reasserted.

ties interfering with the production of goods have the effect of obstructing the flow of trade.

No person, say the Fifth and Fourteenth Amendments in effect (and here, as in other connections, a corporation is a person) shall be deprived of life, liberty, or property without due process of law. But by strikes, boycotts, and the like, labor organizations do undoubted damage to employers and investors (to say nothing of the general public), stopping production, interfering with distribution, impairing income, and otherwise depriving the injured of property, often without legal procedures invoked; and with a view to lessening such losses as far as practicable— losses for which it rarely is possible to get reparation through civil suits— employers long ago, through their lawyers, began applying to federal and state courts for writs of injunction issued in advance of irreparable injury being done by work stoppages or perhaps violence in connection with picketing, and forbidding the acts that would cause it. The courts were generally responsive, and injunctions issued might order a labor organization or group to continue performing specified acts or rendering specified services threatened with interruption, or to desist from practices resulting in wrongs for which there would be no legal remedy, or at least to abide by disputed conditions or practices until regular procedures for dealing with them had been exhausted. And disregarding such injunctions, or restraining orders, constituted "contempt of court," for which those responsible could be tried summarily (formerly without a jury) and punished by fine and imprisonment. Theoretically, injunctions could be brought to bear upon corporations and upon employers generally as well as upon labor. Only rarely, however, were they so employed; and for a long time they have constituted the most potent means of restraining labor from acts and practices judicially regarded as likely to injure property interests without benefit of due process or hope of redress.

The writ of injunction originated far back in English judicial history, without reference, of course, to modern industrial situations. But its use in this country in later days has been principally in connection with labor disputes; and one will not be surprised to learn that labor organizations long were bitterly hostile to it, charging that the judges, with their wide range of discretion, employed the power arbitrarily, and that under it, as Samuel Gompers used to contend, "personal government" had been foisted upon our people "instead of a government by law." Insistent demand upon the two political parties for legislation restricting the power bore fruit in various provisions of the Clayton Act of 1914, but without much change actually resulting, and it was not until 1932, in the Norris-LaGuardia Anti-Injunction Act, passed under pressure from the A. F. of L., that significant restraints became effective. Positively forbidding labor injunctions to be issued except in strict conformity with the spirit and letter of its terms, this latter statute reaffirmed or expanded many of labor's basic rights. sharply curtailed the previously almost wide open

2. In-junctions

list of actions to which injunctions might be directed, forbade any special powers of injunction to be deduced from the anti-trust laws, and threw safeguards around persons accused of contempt, including the right to jury trial. The constitutionality of the legislation was fully sustained; in cases coming before it, the Supreme Court held faithfully to the law's intent; and while, of course, injunctions in labor disputes continued to be issued by both federal and state courts, their rôle was considerably diminished and labor had cause to be reasonably satisfied.[1]

Federal activities and agencies for promoting industrial peace

As considered to the present point, federal promotion of industrial peace has been repressive and punitive, with the courts as the operating arm of authority. There is, however, another side to the matter—the tendering of "good offices," through various channels, but without powers of compulsion, in efforts to adjust labor-management disputes, either before or after strikes or other overt acts have been resorted to; and to this aspect we must briefly turn.

The special case of railway labor

The most obvious place (aside from its own employment relations) for the government to start trying to allay industrial strife was in relation to railroads, both because under the commerce clause there could be no doubt about constitutional authority, and because of the disastrous consequences of breakdowns in the country's transportation services; and over a period of a half-century or more a system for handling disputes in that field has been developed on separate and more or less unique lines, with the result of a nearer approach to full solution of the problem than in any other comparable area. As early as 1888, Congress began legislating on the subject; and one could enumerate a lengthy list of measures—the Erdman Act of 1898, the Newlands Act of 1913, the Adamson Act of 1916, the Transportation [Esch-Cummins] Act of 1920

---

[1] On labor injunctions under the Labor-Management Relations [Taft-Hartley] Act of 1947, however, see p. 737 below. The power of injunction was brought dramatically into prominence by the case of John L. Lewis and the United Mine Workers of America near the end of 1946. Liquidating a strike of the previous May (the eighth such interruption of coal-mining since 1941), and proceeding under the War Labor Disputes [Smith-Connally] Act of 1943 (see p. 735 below), the federal government had taken over the bituminous coal mines, granting the miners' union terms which the operators had refused to concede, and which were understood to be fixed for the duration of government control. Contending that the Department of the Interior had violated its contract, and frustrated in an effort to negotiate new terms, Mr. Lewis, in November, abruptly announced the contract cancelled and ordered some 400,000 miners out on strike; and when an order of the district court of the District of Columbia to call off the strike was ignored, a fine of $3,500,000 was imposed on the union and one of $10,000 on Mr. Lewis, its president, for "contempt." After being out seventeen days, the miners returned to the pits, and, in response to request from the government, the Supreme Court agreed to hear the case directly on appeal, rather than wait for it to follow the regular channel through a federal court of appeals; and on March 6, 1947, after seven weeks of weighing the evidence, that tribunal, by a vote of seven to two, sustained the district court's action, although ordering the union's fine cut to $700,000 in case all court orders were obeyed (United States v. United Mine Workers of America, 330 U. S. 258, 1947). The hard-fighting president of the union had been pitted against the president of the United States, and the latter had emerged victor. On one side, it had been argued that under the Norris-LaGuardia Act the union was exempt from injunction proceedings; on the other, that the law in question was not applicable to situations in which the government of the United States was a party.

—marking stages in the development of railway mediation and conciliation procedures. Devices introduced were by no means uniformly successful; in 1916, a general strike was averted only by the legislation mentioned; and a shopmen's strike of 1922 proved prolonged and costly. Experience was built up, however, which enabled a Railway Labor Act of 1926 to become (with amendments of 1934) [1] not only the basic law in the field to the present day, but possibly the most potent measure for industrial peace in our national history. Predicated on equality of status and mutual respect of carriers and their employees, this legislation forbids company unions, prescribes collective bargaining, encourages the settlement of disputes by voluntary action, and through a number of different instrumentalities made available, tenders the good offices of the government in settling controversies found beyond the capacity of the carriers and their employees negotiating directly—although without attempting to compel either side to abide by decisions arrived at.

The machinery provided need not be described in detail. To begin with, however, either party to an unsettled dispute may invoke the services of a National Mediation Board, an independent agency of the government consisting of three persons appointed by the president and Senate; or the Board may step into the picture by volunteering its good offices. In any case, the body endeavors to get the parties into conference and to bring about a settlement. Unsuccessful in these efforts, it formerly would try to have the controversy referred to some special group or board of arbitrators chosen by the parties. The commoner procedure now, however, is to turn to another federal agency, the National Railroad Adjustment Board, consisting of thirty-six members working in four divisions or panels, each with equal representation of employers and employees, and each exercising jurisdiction over some particular branch of railway employment. If the appropriate panel also fails (with perhaps by this time a strike voted or actually going on), one final step remains: the National Mediation Board may ask the president to appoint an "emergency board" and set it to investigating afresh the merits of the situation with a view to findings and recommendations which, to be sure, will have no binding effect, but may be received with such public approval as to leave the contenders little practical alternative to accepting them. [2] In this fashion, several serious stoppages of railway service have been prevented.

Railway disputes have been by no means uncommon in recent years, but except in the case of a strike by trainmen and engineers in the late spring of 1946 which for a brief time paralyzed the movement of trains,

Machinery employed

---

[1] 44 *U. S. Stat. at Large,* 577, and 48 *ibid.,* 1185. The constitutionality of the Railway Labor Act was upheld by the Supreme Court in a notable decision rendered in March, 1937 (Virginian Railway Co. v. System Federation No. 40, etc., 300 U. S. 515). In 1936, carriers by air were brought under the same statutes.

[2] Formerly, the president selected members of such boards at his discretion. In 1942, however, a National Railway Labor Panel (more recently of thirty members) was created, and from then on the members of a board to act in any particular situation were chosen from the panel by its chairman.

making it necessary for the government to take over the roads, the machinery described has usually availed to avert actual interruptions of transportation. Concessions made on the occasion mentioned, however, are considered to have weakened the legal and moral force of the railway labor laws of 1926 and 1934, previously held up as model statutes for settling disputes without resort to strike. Even if the measures were of such excellence, however, it does not follow that the procedures employed in the railway field could be transferred with equally satisfactory results to industry generally; the situation of an industry so vital to the public that normally neither party will risk the opprobrium of responsibility for a stoppage, except under extreme provocation, is not typical.

2. The labor field in general:

a. The U. S. Conciliation Service and supplementary agencies

The federal government's efforts to maintain industrial peace have not, however, been confined to the field of transportation. As long ago as 1913, a Conciliation Service, in the Department of Labor and functioning through regional offices scattered over the country, was given responsibility, working through "commissioners of conciliation," for promoting peaceful settlement of any and all labor disputes arising in other fields; and, with various changes from time to time, this machinery was maintained until, as we shall see, displaced in 1947. Never meeting, of course, with entire success, the Service was particularly baffled by strikes in vital industries during the national defense effort of 1940 and the ensuing war; and to supplement its efforts a number of other agencies were tried, one after another, although in no instance with greatly improved results. Thus in 1942, President Roosevelt, by executive order, set up a National Defense Mediation Board to take jurisdiction over any dispute certified to it by the secretary of labor as being beyond the capacity of the Conciliation Service to handle; and when this agency shortly, in turn, demonstrated its inability to prevent recurring labor stoppages, another order replaced it with a National War Labor Board, endowed with authority to take jurisdiction on its own initiative as soon as other procedures for adjustment had failed, and to settle any dispute "finally" (without appeal to the courts), employing for the purpose mediation, voluntary arbitration, or arbitration under rules formulated by the Board itself. Working through twelve regional labor boards, each with power to make decisions subject only to appeal to the parent board, this agency, under wartime conditions, became a sort of supreme court for labor disputes; and on various occasions when its findings and orders were disregarded, the president, as commander-in-chief, instructed federal armed forces to take over and operate plants or services until compliance could be achieved or settlement arrived at. At the end of 1945, with peacetime conditions returning, the Board was, in its turn, succeeded by a National Wage Stabilization Board in the Department of Labor, charged primarily with approving or disapproving applications for wage or salary increases or decreases, but also with some responsibility for helping settle labor disputes not successfully dealt with by the Conciliation Service, the National Labor Relations Board (operating under the National Labor Relations Act of 1935), or special fact-finding boards set up for particular situations. Early in 1947, the Wage Stabilization Board was abolished, leaving the Conciliation Service, with some assistance from the National Labor Relations Board, in possession of the field.

In the meantime, another and stormy chapter in the story of wartime efforts to achieve industrial peace had been written—though without the creation of any additional machinery. Agreements of labor leaders not to cripple the war effort by encouraging strikes were sometimes violated; and recurrent stoppages in the coal industry early in 1943 spurred Congress to pass, in June of that year—over strong labor protest and a forceful presidential veto, but nevertheless by heavy majorities—a War Labor Disputes [Smith-Connally] Act,[1] often referred to as the "Anti-Strike Act," since its declared central purpose was to prevent strikes in wartime. Under terms of this highly controversial measure (limited to the duration of the war and six months after), the secretary of labor, the National Labor Relations Board, and the National War Labor Board were required to be given notice of any dispute likely to result in a strike; if, during a "cooling off" period of thirty days after such notice, no settlement was arrived at, the Labor Relations Board was to take a secret ballot among the employees concerned on the express question of whether they approved the threatened "interruption of war production;" and the results of the vote were required to be made public. If the outcome indicated willingness of the workers to fly in the face of public opinion and go ahead with a strike, there was nothing that the government could do to prevent them; once they had gone through the motions required of them, a strike was legal, war or no war; and not only did wartime strikes actually continue, but the government seemed to many people to have been put in the position of actually facilitating them by itself offering a procedure by which they could be decided upon.[2] To minimize strike damage, the legislation empowered the president to take possession of and operate any plant, mine, or facility whenever a labor disturbance affecting it threatened the production of articles or materials needed for the war effort; and so long as government operation continued, any interference with production by strike, lockout, slow-down, or other disturbance, or any form of encouragement or assistance to such interruption, was illegal. Under these provisions, various strike-bound industrial, and even mercantile, establishments were seized and operated for longer or shorter periods during the later war years.[3]

b. The War Labor Disputes Act (1943)

---

[1] 57 *U. S. Stat. at Large*, 163.

[2] It was on this account principally that President Roosevelt sought to kill the measure by veto. Far from discouraging strikes, he said, the bill, if made law, would "stimulate labor unrest and give government sanction to strike agitations." The measure as enacted was of at least doubtful advantage.

[3] The most widely publicized instance of the kind was the taking over of the merchandizing facilities of Montgomery Ward and Company in April, and again in December, 1944.

The next turn of the wheel came with the expiration of the War Labor Disputes Act on June 30, 1947, and the almost simultaneous passage by Congress of the equally controversial Labor-Management Relations [Taft-Hartley] Act; and although that momentous piece of legislation has yet to be discussed, it will be useful to refer to it here in bringing to a close present comment on promoting industrial peace. Devoted to "conciliation of labor disputes in industries affecting commerce; national emergencies," Title II of the measure mentioned starts off by asserting that "the settlement of issues between employers and employees through collective bargaining may be advanced by making available full and adequate governmental facilities for conciliation, mediation, and voluntary arbitration to aid and encourage employers and the representatives of their employees to reach and maintain agreements concerning rates of pay, hours, and working conditions, and to make all reasonable efforts to settle their differences by mutual agreement reached through conferences and collective bargaining or by such methods as may be provided for in any applicable agreement for the settlement of disputes."

There is, of course, nothing revolutionary about this; for decades, it has been an axiom that government may and should help maintain industrial peace by encouraging and providing facilities for conciliation, mediation, and arbitration—even though such efforts have plenty of times proved unavailing. Under the Taft-Hartley Act, however, a fresh start is made. To begin with, new machinery is set up. After thirty-seven years, the Conciliation Service in the Department of Labor is abolished and all of the functions in this field which it or any other agency in the Department has been accustomed to perform are transferred to a new Federal Mediation and Conciliation Service, under a director appointed by the president and Senate and empowered to set up regional offices "convenient to localities in which labor controversies are likely to arise." And supplementing the new Service is a National Labor-Management Panel of twelve members appointed for three years by the president, six from among persons outstanding in the field of management and six from persons similarly prominent in the field of labor, and charged with advising, at the request of the director, on the "avoidance of industrial controversies and the manner in which mediation and voluntary adjustment shall be administered, particularly with reference to controversies affecting the general welfare of the country." In the second place, the entire function is quite thoroughly divorced from the Labor Department, the new Mediation and Conciliation Service being organized as an independent establishment, with the Labor-Management Panel of course also independent.[1] The arrangement may strike one as strange, but belief has long been growing in many quarters that the government's "good offices" in labor disputes

---

[1] The Labor Department is, however, required not only to maintain a file of all available collective bargaining agreements, but to furnish the Service, employers, employees, or their representatives, any data that might be of use in settling disputes.

might best be tendered through instrumentalities not tied up with any regular department. Coming to the way in which the Mediation and Conciliation Service shall function, the statute provides (1) that in any dispute threatening to affect commerce in more than a local manner the Service may offer its aid, either on its own initiative or at the request of one or more of the parties, and (2) that if the Service fails to bring the parties to agreement by conciliation within any reasonable time, it shall try to induce them voluntarily to seek other means of settlement without resort to strikes, lockouts, or other forms of coercion. On their part, employers and employees are required (1) to put forth "every reasonable effort" to make and maintain agreements covering such matters as pay, hours, and working conditions; (2) to stand ready at all times of dispute to confer and to promote prompt settlement; and (3) in case of failure through more direct channels, to participate fully and promptly in any meetings called by the Mediation and Conciliation Service to consider the situation.

Special provision is made, also, for situations in which labor disturb-ances may affect an entire industry or a substantial part thereof and "imperil the national health or safety." In such cases, (1) the president is to appoint a board of inquiry (with full powers to require attendance of witnesses and production of papers) to investigate and make a written report setting forth the issues involved and the positions of the respective parties, although without making recommendations, (2) this report is to be transmitted to the Mediation and Conciliation Service and published for public information; (3) if the report seems to the president to justify doing so, he may direct the attorney-general to petition any federal district court having jurisdiction of the parties to "enjoin" any strike or lockout (threatened or in progress) connected with the given dispute; (4) if the court agrees that the disturbance is sufficient to jeopardize national health or safety, it may issue the requested injunction, although with appeal permitted to a circuit court of appeals and the Supreme Court; (5) with an injunction issued, it becomes the legal duty of both parties to the dispute "to make every effort to settle and adjust their differences," with the aid of the Mediation and Conciliation Service, although without obligation to accept any proposal made by it; (6) the president must then reconvene the board of inquiry, which at the end of sixty days shall report the situation by that time arrived at; (7) in the next fifteen days, the National Labor Relations Board must take a secret ballot of the employees of every employer involved on whether they are prepared to accept their employer's latest offer; (8) on receiving the results of this ballot, or on being informed of a settlement reached, the attorney-general must take steps to have the injunction "discharged;" and, finally, (9) the president must give Congress a full report on the entire affair, with recommendations if he cares to make any.[1]

Disputes imperil-ing national health or safety

---

[1] A coal strike of March-April, 1948, did not require this entire procedure.

A *New Labor Law: The Labor-Management Relations Act of 1947*

With hostilities ended in 1945 and the country confronted with the task of reconversion to a peacetime economy, few domestic questions gripped public interest as did that of the position to be occupied by organized labor in the days ahead. The current labor picture presented many aspects of contrast. On the one hand: (1) Employment was at a high level, and although there was much apprehension about early possibility of a business recession that might turn into a genuine depression, the economy held up well during the next two years, with employment actually touching an all-time peak in the summer of 1947. (2) Labor had made enormous gains in the past dozen years, not only in size and strength of organizations, but in the outlawing of company-controlled unions, in broad rights of collective bargaining, in floors under wages and ceilings over hours, in a very general withdrawal of younger children from the labor markets, in the curbing of injunctions, and in a variety of other ways. (3) Beneficiary of the Roosevelt Administration's unfailingly sympathetic and coöperative attitude through more than a decade, labor, too, was riding a crest of political power (or at least seemed to be doing so), with more influence in the White House, if not also in Congress, than at any earlier day. On the other hand: (1) Labor-management relations were in a sorry state. Hardly had the Axis surrenders taken place before the wave of industrial disputes and disorders that had been feared became a reality, and by the late spring of 1946 the nation was in the grip of the most formidable labor troubles in a generation. Automobile manufacturing, the oil industry, the lumbering business, coal-mining, meat-packing, and in time even the railroads—all were affected on a nation-wide scale, with countless smaller industries and businesses likewise involved,[1] and at a time when the country's paramount concern was an orderly transition from war to peace, with uninterrupted production vital to the fight on inflation. So critical did the situation become that early in 1946 President Truman was impelled to go before Congress with an extraordinary proposal for drafting striking employees into the Army and compelling them to work in industries considered "necessary to the maintenance of the national economy."[2] (2) Outside of labor circles— even in quarters normally friendly—there was much discontent with existing labor laws, focused primarily on the Labor Relations Act of 1935 and its workings. From the moment when that measure was placed on the statute-book, the law itself, and in time the administration of it by the Labor Relations Board, stirred criticism, not only among em-

---

[1] A total of 116,000,000 work-days were lost during the year.

[2] The plan recommended purported to be nothing more than an expedient for overcoming the existing emergency. But the stiffness of a bill embodying it came as a shock not only to labor but to many other people; before the two houses passed the measure (in somewhat differing forms), its harsher features were softened down, the proposed draft into military service being eliminated; and in the end it was left to languish on the speaker's table in the House and did not become law.

ployers, but in the press and among people generally who, however ready to concede the praiseworthiness of the law's objectives, were irked by its failure to lessen strikes and avert other labor disorders.

During the war years, the issue was somewhat obscured. By 1946, however, with industry in turmoil, it was again at the fore. Some of the criticisms of the 1935 legislation sprang from misconception of the act's true purport; some from mere prejudice or partisanship; some were directed rather at alleged faulty administration than at the legislation itself. One charge was pressed with particular vigor, *i.e.*, that, proceeding apparently on the theory that in industry management is strong, has money, holds the whip-hand, and neither needs nor deserves protective guarantees against its employees, while the latter must be backed up with stiff government regulations if they are not to be overborne and exploited, the employer-employee relationship envisaged in the Wagner Act was wholly one-sided, with a long list of practices made "unfair" if engaged in by management, but nothing made unfair if done by labor organizations or their leaders. In the large, too, this idea contained truth. Within the framework of labor-management relations as set up in the law, it was quite possible for misguided labor groups, and especially for aggressive and vindictive labor leaders, to inflict grievous wrongs upon employers left defenseless, and not simply upon them, but also upon workers themselves, especially the considerable numbers choosing to remain outside of unions. And excesses and abuses proved plentiful, with leaders and agitators and racketeers flouting the law, irresponsibly forcing half-willing groups of workers into actions injurious to labor, management, and the public alike, and, with singularly bad judgment, piling up public resentment bound some day to recoil upon their heads.[1] Joined to immunities long enjoyed by unions and their leaders (for example, as against the anti-trust laws), the one-sidedness of the Wagner legislation, the confidence in labor-leader circles that the government could always be swayed to labor's side, and the regularity with which high-handed practices escaped repression, made for irresponsibility and injustice; and it is not strange that through years of frequent and costly labor disturbances (even while the war was still going on) a large segment of the nation should have come to look upon a better balancing of rights and obligations in the employer-employee relationship, and a correction of labor abuses generally, as imperative in the public interest. Something, the conviction was, "would have to be done about labor."

Such was the background of the Labor-Management Relations Act of 1947,[2] in which much existing labor law, and in particular the National

Demand for "equalizing" legislation

---

[1] These harsh observations are not those of the authors alone. See, for example, an editorial of July, 1947, in *International Teamster* (the publication of the A. F. of L. Teamsters Union) by Mr. Dan Tobin, president of the union, the general purport of which is that, by and large, unions by their conduct "asked for" the Taft-Hartley legislation of 1947 which they so warmly resented.

[2] *Pub. Law 101—80th Cong., 1st Sess.*

Labor Relations Act of 1935, was extensively rewritten.[1] In that background was also the circumstance that the Labor Disputes [Smith-
Connally] Act of 1943 was presently to expire, leaving somewhat of a
void.[2] In addition, there had been earlier efforts (apart from the President's somewhat precipitate "draft" proposal of the preceding year) to
bring about remedial legislation. One of these, growing out of a hostile
report of a House investigating committee as far back as 1940, had collapsed in an atmosphere charged with bitterness and vindictiveness.
Another had taken the form of a Labor Disputes Bill of 1946 associated
with the name of Congressman Francis Case of South Dakota, and making unions liable to damage suits for violation of contracts, broadening
judicial powers of injunction, and introducing other changes obnoxious to
labor. Urging that this bill be laid aside as grist to the mill in a suggested
study of proposals for later legislation, President Truman had killed it by
a narrowly sustained veto.[3]

Then came the Republican victory in the congressional and senatorial
elections of November, 1946, with both branches of Congress passing
under the control of new political forces. Probably some labor legislation
of general scope would have been enacted in any event; large numbers
of Democrats (especially from the South) would have favored it, and
the liquidation of war situations might have required it. With a Republican Congress in power, however, and under a national mandate construed to include labor-law reform, such legislation was inevitable; and
the first six or seven months of the new Eightieth Congress saw a number
of bills amending the National Labor Relations Act prepared and introduced and much discussion of the subject carried on, both in Congress
and outside, until finally a measure emerged—sponsored by the chairmen
of the labor committees of the two houses, Senator Robert A. Taft of
Ohio and Representative Fred A. Hartley of New Jersey—on which, after
conference committees had ironed out important differences, the two
branches were able to agree.[4] In June, 1947, the Taft-Hartley bill passed
the lower house by a vote of 320 to 79 and the upper one by 68 to 24; and

[1] The Labor Relations Act continues in effect except as amended.

[2] Limited to the period of the war and six months after, this measure actually did
expire on June 30, 1947—six months after the president's proclamation of the end
of hostilities on December 31, 1946.

[3] Some labor legislation, however, was enacted in 1946, notably a Hobbs Anti-
Racketeering Act (60 *U. S. Stat. at Large*, 420), strengthening earlier legislation
(1934) for the protection of interstate commerce against interference by intimidation,
threats, or coercion. Making it unlawful to interfere with such commerce by extortion
or robbery, this amending measure was aimed particularly at high-handed practices
by which the trucking of commodities had been beset in many parts of the country.

By executive order in 1941, President Roosevelt set up a Fair Employment Practice Committee (succeeded by another of the same name in the Office for Emergency
Management in 1943) designed principally to prevent companies doing business with
the government from practicing discrimination in employment on grounds of race,
creed, color, or national origin. Always stoutly opposed by Southern congressmen,
the agency lapsed on June 30, 1946, and bills to revive it and broaden its scope so
as to cover all business languished on the calendars.

[4] The House bill was considerably more stringent than either the Senate bill or
the completed measure.

after President Truman had vetoed it as a "bad bill—bad for labor, bad for management, and bad for the country," the houses repassed it by majorities requisite to make it law—331 to 83 and 68 to 25, respectively.[1]

The new measure was an omnibus piece of legislation—a composite of bills separately passed in the two branches—and aimed, as had been the Case bill, at a broad overhauling of labor law, not, to be sure, with respect to wage and hour levels, restrictions on child labor, and the like, but with reference to everything pertaining to the status and conduct of unions, the processes of bargaining, the control of strikes, fair and unfair labor practices—in short, as the title of the law indicated, *labor-management relations* as covered in the National Labor Relations Act of 1935. For present purposes, it must suffice merely to summarize some of the act's more significant provisions. To begin with, (1) while the general principle of unionized labor is accepted as axiomatic, the "closed shop" (making union membership a prerequisite to being hired by an establishment) is entirely forbidden and the "union shop" (requiring workers to join a union after they are hired) is placed under additional restrictions. When the measure was passed, thirty per cent of organized employees were operating under closed-shop arrangements, which, however, the new legislation's supporters regarded as contributing to labor-leader high-handedness; hence the ban, tending of itself to revolutionize the union situation. The union shop may continue, but only if demanded by a majority of all workers eligible to vote on the question in an establishment, and only under other restrictions aimed at protecting employer interests. (2) To correct the inequality of labor-organization and employer responsibility inherent in the Labor Relations [Wagner] Act—which, as we have seen, confined unfair practices to those indulged in by employers only—a section of similar scope and severity in the new law bans six unfair practices engaged in by employees. Employees, for example, may not be coerced to join unions; members in a union shop may not be required to pay excessive dues; employers may not, under the practice popularly known as "featherbedding," be required to pay for services not rendered, *e.g.*, to pay a textile worker for operating a single machine when he could equally well operate four or five, or, in the case of a radio station using records, to hire "live" musicians; and whereas previously only employers were compelled to bargain, unions are now forbidden to refuse to do so. For all of these and other practices, unions for the first time become subject

2. Principal provisions

---

[1] That the measure had a great deal of bipartisan support is indicated by the following statistics on the repassage of the bill over the president's veto:

		House of Representatives	Senate
For:	Republicans	225	28
	Democrats	106	20
Against:	Republicans	11	3
	Democrats	71	22
	Amer. Labor	1	0

to suit. (3) Secondary boycotts (in which one party refuses to deal with another unless such other will, in turn, refuse to deal with a third) and jurisdictional strikes (arising, for example, out of conflicts between A. F. of L. and C. I. O. unions, or between any such and independent unions) are forbidden; and the courts may find damages against unions for such action. (4) Employers may make non-coercive statements or express views to their workers or to others (as they previously might not) without having what they say adduced as evidence of unfair labor practice.

(5) The National Labor Relations Board remains, with membership increased from three to five, and with bargaining and the repression of unfair practices still as its field of activity. To meet the criticism, however, that formerly the Board was at the same time "investigator, prosecutor, judge, and jury," the body is now turned into a wholly judicial agency, a "labor court," with all work of investigation and prosecution devolved upon a new official, the "general counsel," with full supervision of regional offices and field staff.[1] (6) The peaceful procedures of the National Labor Relations Act are denied to a union unless all of its officers declare under oath that they are not members of the Communist party and that they do not favor the forceful or unconstitutional overthrow of the government. (7) Notwithstanding that, three months before the act was passed, one of the most bitterly contested disputes in labor-management relations was supposedly settled when the Supreme Court ruled by five to four that unions of foremen and supervisors, linked up in a Foremen's Association of America, were covered by the act of 1935 and that employers must bargain with them on that basis,[2] the new law denies such unions all bargaining rights. (8) A ban on "industry-wide" bargaining, e.g., bargaining on the basis of an industry (like coal-mining) as a whole, was voted by the House, but deleted by the Senate, although not without final agreement upon restrictions which some persons considered likely to render such bargaining in future impracticable. (9) Protection of the "right to work" has long been urged by employers for the benefit of individuals who refuse to join unions and wish to bargain separately. The act affirms the right of every worker "to refrain from . . . concerted activities" and makes it an unfair practice to interfere with such right, although whether the employer becomes entitled to make agreements with employees not to join unions (the old "yellow dog contract," outlawed by the Norris-LaGuardia Act) is not clear. (10) Naturally, the law has something to say about strikes and other coercive labor practices. In general, the right to strike is, of course, not banned. But strikes with certain specified objectives are forbidden; as we have

[1] On July 17, 1947, Robert N. Denham, a Missouri Republican, was appointed general counsel. The Labor Relations Board had at the time a staff of seven hundred, which, instead of being diminished as expected, was actually augmented. The main need thenceforth was for lawyers to decide cases prosecuted before them by other lawyers directed by the general counsel, and involving particularly labor elections and unfair labor or employer practices.

[2] Packard Motor Car Co. v. National Labor Relations Board, 330 U. S. 485 (1947).

seen, the Norris-LaGuardia Act's provisions concerning injunctions are softened; and strikes of federal employees are unequivocally outlawed. (11) Finally, as pointed out in a different connection, the act prohibits, under severe penalties, contributions by labor unions and corporations alike in connection with federal elections, construed to include primaries, caucuses, and conventions.[1]

Seldom has a piece of legislation been as vigorously attacked and warmly defended as this one. Denounced by angry spokesmen of labor as "extreme," "vindictive," "a monstrosity," "a slave bill," its sharply-worded veto by the President rested on the grounds, chiefly, that it would circumscribe collective bargaining with many "bureaucratic procedures," would promote labor-management friction and time-consuming litigation, and would discriminate against workers "in a consistent pattern of inequality." In other quarters, while conceded to be not a perfect measure, but of necessity a product of give and take, the law was praised for making employees as well as employers answerable for unfair practices and subject to suit on contracts, for guaranteeing new and needed protection to union minorities, for giving the worker some assurance that he can pursue his trade whether he joins a union or not, for putting an end to alleged autocratic powers and procedures of the Labor Relations Board, and, in general, for imposing for the first time upon labor unions with their swollen powers responsibilities commensurate with those powers.[2] Criticized for publicly declaring the act unenforceable and thus seeming to invite non-compliance, the President made amends (if fault there was) by also publicly calling upon both labor and management to exercise patience and moderation in accommodating themselves to the new situation. At almost every turn, the legislation left room for questions of interpretation; labor-management differences of view and clashes of interest early began emerging; and nothing was more certain than that for years (assuming that the basic legislation remained on the statute-book) the courts would be kept busy with resulting litigation. As experience accumulated, supplementary and amending legislation would be required;[3] and, with presidential and congressional elections approaching, widespread political repercussions were inevitable. All in all, the Labor-Management Relations Act opened a new chapter, not only in American labor history, but quite possibly in the entire development of

3. Aspects of the new situation

---

[1] Late in March, 1948, the federal Supreme Court agreed to review a district court's verdict holding this provision of the act unconstitutional.

[2] Most features of the legislation were independently proposed and urged in H. W. Metz and M. Jacobstein, *A National Labor Policy* (Washington, D. C., 1947), which therefore is useful as an exposition of the favorable arguments.

[3] In recognition of this, and under terms of the Taft-Hartley Act itself, a congressional joint committee on labor-management relations, composed of seven members designated from the membership of the appropriate standing committee of each house, was set up to watch the operation and administration of the law, to study the entire field of labor-management relations, and to recommend such new or revised legislation as it finds advisable. Senator Taft was made chairman of the committee; and a report was required not later than March 15, 1948.

American economy and life. Confronted with the largest, the most aggressive, and the most powerful labor movement that the world has ever seen, the country will increasingly stand in need of a well-considered basic labor policy favorable to the operation of a free economic system in the framework of a democratic society. Whether the new legislation has supplied such a policy, the future must decide.[1]

REFERENCES

M. Fainsod and L. Gordon, *Government and the American Economy* (New York, 1941), Chap. vi.

L. H. Chamberlain, *The President, Congress, and Legislation* (New York, 1946), Chap. iv.

J. Lombardi, *Labor's Voice in the Cabinet: A History of the Department of Labor from Its Origin to 1921* (New York, 1942).

H. U. Faulkner and M. Starr, *Labor in America* (New York, 1945).

A. L. Bernheim and D. Van Doren [eds.], *Labor and the Government* (New York, 1935).

H. W. Metz, *Labor Policy of the Federal Government* (Washington, D. C., 1945).

———— and M. Jacobstein, *A National Labor Policy* (Washington, D. C., 1947).

J. Rosenfarb, *The National Labor Policy and How It Works* (New York, 1940).

M. Woll, *Labor, Industry, and Government* (New York, 1935).

C. O. Gregory, *Labor and the Law* (New York, 1946).

E. E. Cummins and F. T. DeVyver, *The Labor Problem in the United States* (3rd ed., New York, 1947).

T. R. Fisher, *Industrial Disputes and Federal Legislation* (New York, 1941).

E. E. Witte, *The Government in Labor Disputes* (New York, 1932).

S. H. Slichter, *The Challenge of Industrial Relations* (Ithaca, N. Y., 1947).

N. W. Chamberlain, *Collective Bargaining Procedures* (Washington, D. C., 1944).

C. Eaton *et al.*, "Labor Relations and Labor Law," *Univ. of Chicago Law Rev.*, XIV, 331-454 (Apr., 1947).

F. Tennenbaum, "The Social Function of Trade Unionism," *Polit. Sci. Quar.*, LXII, 161-194 (June, 1947).

R. C. Atkinson *et al.*, *Public Employment Services in the United States* (Chicago, 1938).

D. O. Bowman, *Public Control of Labor Relations; A Study of the National Labor Relations Board* (New York, 1942).

H. Feldman [ed.], "Labor Relations and the War," *Annals of Amer. Acad. of Polit. and Soc. Sci.*, CCXXIV, 1-195 (Nov., 1942).

———— [ed.], "Labor Relations and the Public," *ibid.*, CCXLVIII, 1-198 (Nov., 1946).

T. R. Fisher, *Industrial Disputes and Federal Legislation* (New York, 1941).

[1] Some portions of the legislation—for example, the ban on strikes by federal employees—took effect immediately, but in general the act went into operation on August 22, 1947. Four or five months of experience left the measure hardly less controversial than before it was placed on the statute-book. Significant developments of the period, however, included: (1) some diminution of strikes, as compared with preceding months and especially with the year 1946; (2) a perceptible loss of ground by the Communists in the labor movement; (3) preparation, on the other hand, by numerous labor organizations and leaders to challenge the cardinal features of the law both in the courts and in the elections of 1948. By December, 1947, the officers of 125 national unions and 2,176 local unions (considerably more than half) had filed the non-Communist affidavits required as a condition of access to the services of the National Labor Relations Board.

K. Braun, *The Settlement of Industrial Disputes* (Philadelphia, 1944).

H. S. Kaltenborn, *Government Adjustment of Labor Disputes* (Chicago, 1943).

W. E. Moore, *Industrial Relations and the Social Order* (New York, 1946).

P. S. Foner, *History of the Labor Movement in the United States* (New York, 1947). Covers the subject to about 1880.

Labor Research Association, *Labor Fact Book 8* (New York, 1947).

Annual reports of the secretary of labor, National Labor Relations Board, etc.

CHAPTER XXXIII

GENERAL WELFARE—SOCIAL SECURITY AND HOUSING

Welfare Activities to 1935

Government and public welfare

An ideal society would be one in which every individual had enough to eat and wear, satisfactory shelter against the elements, protection for health, a chance for a good education, and in the case of adults an opportunity to earn a living by moderate toil, with safeguards against worry and want in old age. Such a society never existed, and some people would say that in the troubled world in which we live there is no use dreaming of one. In the United States, to be sure, something of the kind has come nearer to realization than in most other countries. One reason is the vast scope for individual enterprise and advancement afforded by a virgin country of great size and rich resources. Another is the freedom of opportunity characteristic of our political and social democracy. Still another is the exceptional degree to which inventions have found practical applications in the daily life of our people, alleviating drudgery and adding to the conveniences, satisfactions, and rewards of existence. Not even these and other favoring circumstances, however, have availed—or can ever avail—to prevent poverty, misfortune, and insecurity (aggravated from time to time by economic depressions) from marring the social picture; and not only have the more fortunate been called upon from early days to help the unfortunate through private agencies and channels, but to an increasing extent government has been influenced or compelled to accept the promotion of public well-being as one of its topmost responsibilities. In the United States as in other parts of the world, indeed, no development of recent times is more significant than the growth of dependence upon government for assurance of the over-all social and economic security representing (along with international peace) the most poignant desire of the people. To some aspects of the way in which government in this country has met the challenge, we now turn.

Early local and state welfare activities

The earliest activity pointing in the general direction of social security, although falling far short of what we now mean by the term, was the care of the poor. In England, this responsibility, in so far as not discharged by relatives or other private benefactors, early fell to the church parish. Even before the American colonies were founded, however, parliamentary legislation authorized taxation for the purpose, with the parish continuing as the administrative unit; and the colonies inherited the concept of poor relief as a public, tax-supported function. In New England,

746

and some of the middle colonies, the town became the relief agency; farther south, the parish—soon replaced, however, by the county; and to this day, towns and counties throughout the country raise and spend revenue for this purpose. More than a hundred years ago, the states also entered the field—establishing hospitals and asylums for special classes of unfortunates, such as the feeble-minded, the insane, and the blind; setting up boards and other authorities to administer such institutions; in some instances organizing departments of welfare; and more or less effectively supervising local services, encouraging them in broadening their operations and raising their standards (although as late as 1913 twenty-one states still exercised no supervision over local relief in any form). Much was done haphazardly, and in times of stress services sometimes proved pitifully inadequate. On the other hand, deficiencies were to some extent met by the private charities for which our people have traditionally had a commendable record. And in the first quarter of the present century a few states began extending financial aid to persons outside of institutions: Wisconsin, to the blind under a law of 1907; Illinois and Missouri, to mothers under legislation of 1911; and Pennsylvania, Montana, and Nevada, to the aged under statutes of 1923-25.

Aside from taking some responsibility for welfare of the Indians and making various provisions for war veterans and merchant seamen, the federal government long held back from direct activity in this field. There could be little doubt about constitutional power, for one of the things which that government was expressly authorized to do was to raise money "to provide for the ... general welfare of the United States"; [1] and some things not wholly irrelevant were done—certainly the abolition of slavery was, in its way, a contribution. But, in general, the idea for a hundred years and more was that "social work" should be left to states, localities, and private agencies. Even before the great challenge to the federal government precipitated by the depression of the thirties, some change, however, was in evidence. Laws were passed humanizing the conditions attending immigration; the commerce power was employed to curb the transmission of diseases and the distribution of impure food and drugs; safety laws were enacted for rail, water, and air transportation and for mining; various injurious forms of manufacturing (*e.g.*, making matches from white phosphorous) were taxed out of existence; a supervisory public health service was instituted; the circulation of immoral matter through the mails was prohibited; and other things were done for the protection and betterment of large numbers of people. In the field with which we are chiefly concerned in this chapter, however, there were hardly more than two significant developments: in 1912, a children's bureau was established in the then existing Department of Commerce and Labor, although with functions scarcely extending beyond encouraging the states to enact remedial legislation; and in 1921, a [Sheppard-Towner] Act for

Federal contributions

[1] Art. I, § 8, cl. 1.

Promoting the Welfare and Hygiene of Maternity and Infancy [1] made a small appropriation for five years to assist state health departments in carrying on instructional work among expectant mothers, although, even ·after this measure was sustained by the Supreme Court,[2] it was allowed to lapse at the end of its period.

The
shock of
depression The great depression starting in 1929 brought the country a rude awakening, and with it one of the swiftest and profoundest reversals of policy in our history. In a matter of months, millions of workers—eventually ten or twelve millions—were thrown out of employment; and with the bulk of them habitually living on so narrow an economic margin that, once out of work, they were almost immediately in want, social distress became widespread and acute. To be sure, unemployment on some scale was no new thing. But not much had been done about it. Not a state had as yet set up any system of unemployment insurance (although Wisconsin did so early in 1932). Approximately half of the states had introduced some plan of old-age assistance, but usually inadequate; and elsewhere the dependent aged were left to be cared for by their relatives or, in default of that, to become public charges in county or other institutions. Aid to mothers, such as it was, had been cut off, and large numbers of dependent and helpless children were receiving only such more or less casual care as local agencies provided. The longer-term outlook, moreover, was disturbing. Studies by competent authorities showed that, with population growing, the number of available industrial jobs had been declining even before the depression; that, while technological discoveries and inventions opened new avenues of opportunity, they also closed many; that the shifting of once self-sufficient country people to the cities tended to leave them dependent upon industrial ups and downs and in a generally insecure position; that, judging by all experience, periods of prosperity would continue to be followed by periods of recession and adversity; that with life expectancy rising and the birth-rate declining, persons over sixty years of age (many of them with no accumulated savings) would in future constitute a greatly increased proportion of the country's population—one in every eight, it was predicted, by 1980.[3] Unemployment, it appeared, would be permanent and at times heavy— perhaps from three to five per cent even in the best of times; the burden of caring for the needy aged would steadily grow; unless strong measures were taken, the multiplying under-privileged of poorer parts of the country and of congested cities would continue keeping the boasted national standard of living from being fully realized. In short, the problem before the nation was vastly more than merely one of tiding the people over the existing period of calamity.

---

[1] 42 *U. S. Stat. at Large*, 224.

[2] Frothingham *v.* Mellon and Massachusetts *v.* Mellon, 262 U. S. 447. See p. 561 above.

[3] In 1860, only 2.7 per cent of the population was over sixty-five; in 1945, 7.2 per cent. The numbers were, respectively, 860,000 and 9,920,000.

For a time—until the New Deal was launched by the Roosevelt Measures for national recovery Administration in March, 1933—efforts to combat the depression and get a baffled and discouraged nation back on its feet were confined largely to stretching the resources of private charities to their limits, stepping up the activities of city and county relief agencies, voting state appropriations for assistance, encouraging industries to spread work and create jobs, distributing government-owned wheat and other commodities to the needy through the Red Cross, and eventually federal appropriations for public works creating employment, together with loans by the Reconstruction Finance Corporation [1] to state and local governments for public works or direct relief purposes. The "natural" business recovery hoped for by the Hoover Administration, however, failed to materialize, and to the incoming Roosevelt Administration it fell to attack the problem with not only fresh determination, but a new philosophy. States and localities had gone about as far as they could go, except with much more generous federal aid; and it became the policy of the new régime not only to put vast new resources at their disposal, but to act directly, on many different fronts, to create employment and provide relief. Most of the major steps taken have been touched upon at various points in preceding chapters, and no outline of them can be attempted here. Suffice it to say that multiplied billions of dollars were appropriated, piling up a national debt considered extraordinary until dwarfed by that incurred during the later years of defense effort and war; that through a Federal Emergency Relief Administration, a Public Works Administration, a Civil Works Administration, a Works Progress Administration, and other huge agencies that came and went, vast programs of employment and relief were carried forward, by direct action of the appropriate federal establishments, through grants to states, counties, and cities, and in other ways; and that novel measures like the National Industrial Recovery Act of 1933 and the Agricultural Adjustment Acts of 1933 and 1938 were placed on the statute-book (even though in some instances judicially invalidated [2]).

Down to 1934-35, thought and effort were wholly centered on breaking The Social Security Act (1935) the back of the depression. Huge federal outlays for relief and vast loans and gifts to states and localities, however, could not go on forever, even though the conditions now requiring them very well might recur. Moreover, there ought to be ways not only of cushioning the impact of "hard times" when encountered, but of giving large masses of people a new sense of security against hazards having to be faced in both bad times and good. The interest of those having to do with making national policy now turned, therefore, to tapering off the federal government's spending activities and devising ways by which the states, with the help of insurance systems and relatively modest grants-in-aid, could be brought back permanently into the center of the social welfare picture. Federal spend-

[1] See p. 608 above.
[2] See pp. 658, 678-683 above.

ing on employment-making public works and on other forms of relief went on in some degree until after the economic situation was sharply reversed by the defense and war effort of 1940 and after; even for the fiscal year 1941, W.P.A. appropriations aggregated over a billion dollars. But meanwhile, in 1935—after careful studies of the social insurance systems of Europe and of the problem of a permanent program for this country,[1] Congress, by heavy majorities, passed an omnibus Social Security Act which, several times amended in later years, has served to this day as the great charter of our nation-wide social-security system.[2] Conceding that the measure as enacted did not provide complete protection against "the hazards and vicissitudes of life," President Roosevelt, its principal author and sponsor, nevertheless characterized it as "the most useful and fundamental single piece of federal legislation ever enacted in the interest of American wage-earners." Various efforts in recent times to extend its coverage, in terms both of the people to whom it is applicable and of the kinds of protection afforded, have not proved wholly successful. But there is a strong presumption that eventually they will do so; and meanwhile the system as actually operating furnishes truly impressive testimony to the accepted responsibility of government on all levels for maintaining and promoting the public well-being. Some of the system's major features call for comment.

The Social Security System

1. Unemployment compensation:

(a) The federal-state aspect

Towering above all else are the arrangements relating to unemployment compensation and protection for the aged. Loss of their jobs by millions of workers during the great depression sharply emphasized the hazards of layoff and dismissal constantly confronting all industrial and many other employees; and a major objective of the legislation of 1935 was to soften the impact of such disasters by providing—not indefinitely, of course, but for periods varying under different circumstances from fourteen to twenty-six weeks—payments from which workers, usually with

---

[1] Principally by a special Committee on Economic Security appointed by President Roosevelt in 1934, by the National Resources Committee (forerunner of the later National Resources Planning Board), and by the Brookings Institution. See a publication of the Committee on Economic Security entitled *Social Security in America* (Washington, D. C., 1937), and one by the National Resources Committee entitled *The Problems of a Changing Population* (Washington, D. C., 1938). Cf. W. S. Thompson and P. K. Whelpton, "The Population of the Nation," in *Recent Social Trends in the United States* (New York, 1933), Chap. I; W. F. Ogburn, "How Many Old People in the Future," *State Government*, XII, 157-158 ff. (Sept., 1939); and R. Hilton, "Old People; A Rising National Problem," *Harper's Mag.*, CLXXIX, 449-459 (Oct., 1939).

As was to be expected, fantastic schemes were advanced from various quarters, *e.g.*, the "Townsend plan" (which still has numerous adherents), calling for payment of two hundred dollars a month to all persons over sixty on condition only that they stop work and spend their pensions as fast as received; and the "Lundeen plan," calling for weekly payments of not less than ten dollars to all unemployed persons eighteen years of age and over. Cf. M. S. Stewart, "Pensions After Sixty," *Pub. Affairs Pamphlets*, No. 46 (New York, 1940); N. Roosevelt, *The Townsend Plan* (New York, 1939); S. Downey, *Pensions or Penury* (New York, 1939).

[2] 49 *U. S. Stat. at Large*, 620.

meager reserves, could, when laid off or losing their jobs, keep themselves and their families going. Speaking strictly, there is, under the law, no *federal* system of unemployment compensation, uniformly compulsory and federally administered. Such a system was considered by the President's Committee (whose recommendations were largely followed by Congress), but rejected because of fear that it would be held unconstitutional, and because, being wedded to no one of the many forms in which unemployment compensation can be organized, the Committee thought it best to leave the way open for different schemes to be tried in different localities. What the law does is rather to hold out inducements to the several states to devise and set up compensation systems of their own; and these inducements are found, not only in a federal guarantee of the costs of administration, but in arrangements made for raising the huge sums required for operating the system of benefits.

These arrangements require a word of explanation. First of all, the federal government levies a payroll tax of three per cent upon all employers of as many as eight persons during at least twenty weeks of a calendar year, so computing their taxable payrolls, however, as not to include anything paid any employee in excess of three thousand dollars a year. In the second place, the states levy their own payroll taxes—in twenty-eight cases upon the same employers of eight persons, in other instances with certain variations.[1] When, however, an employer pays his federal tax, he is allowed an offset of ninety per cent of it toward the amount which he is paying his state; in other words, he actually pays the federal government only one-tenth of his nominal obligation; and even this, in so far as needed,[2] goes back to his state to meet administrative costs.[3] Should any state elect to stay out of the system, the full federal three per cent payroll tax on its employers would be retained by the national government; and this feature alone (enabling a state to impose a 2.7 per cent payroll tax on employers without actually imposing any additional burden upon them) puts so heavy a premium on state participation that, in point of fact, such participation becomes to all intents and purposes compulsory. All funds collected by the states under the law go into an unemployment trust fund in the federal treasury and are invested in federal securities, subject, of course, to being requisitioned by the states as needed for benefit payments.[4]

(b) Financial arrangements

[1] Ten states started by imposing a tax on employees also, but by 1947 only two were doing this.

[2] The states may employ any agency they like for administering their compensation system. Sometimes they utilize a special unemployment commission, sometimes an industrial or similar body. In any event, benefits are required to be paid through public employment offices.

[3] By no means all is required for the purpose, so that the federal government derives considerable net income from this source—$767,032,000 in 1937-46. There is some criticism of this as unjustifiable.

[4] On April 30, 1946, the trust fund amounted to over six and one-half billion dollars, with money coming in approximately twice as rapidly as it was being paid out.

In operating their individual compensation plans, the states must comply with certain conditions laid down by national law, but it is of the essence of the system that every state shall be at least legally free not only to operate under it or to have no part in it, but also to adopt any particular type or plan of compensation preferred, and, in so doing, to determine the classes of unemployed to be covered and the conditions under which they may participate, as well as the scale of benefits. Under these conditions, while every state (and most of the territories—a total of fifty-two jurisdictions) has been operating under the system since 1937, there is naturally a good deal of difference of practice; and the resulting unevenness has prompted frequent proposals—favored by the top federal administrators and warmly supported by President Roosevelt in his day, although opposed by the states—that the system be taken over and operated on uniform lines by the federal government; and this may yet be done. Already, however, there is substantial uniformity of coverage: nowhere has it been deemed feasible to include all of the gainfully employed; and self-employed persons, agricultural workers, domestic servants, employees of federal, state, and local governments, casual laborers, employees of religious, educational, and other non-profit institutions or organizations, and employees of common carriers in interstate commerce (these last, however, being taken care of under a separate federal scheme instituted in 1939), numbering in all some twelve millions, are everywhere excluded.[1] With respect to other features of the plan, there is also a good deal of similarity from state to state, except as richer states commonly maintain a more liberal scale of benefits than do poorer ones, with an average maximum for the country of approximately sixteen dollars a week, and in all but four states without regard to whether the worker has a family to support.[2] The normal period for which a worker must have been employed in a given establishment before he becomes eligible for benefits is ten weeks, and the length of time during which he can claim payments in case he becomes unemployed varies from fourteen to eighteen weeks, with the latter figure now tending to become most common. Many students of the subject consider that the maximum weekly payment ought in no case to be less than twenty-five dollars, nor the maximum period less than twenty-six weeks; and if the system were to be taken over completely by the federal government, some such standards probably would be adopted. As now existing, the compensation system is available to help more than forty million workers tide over temporary periods of unemployment and mild cyclical recessions; and under the conditions of high employment prevailing much of the time

[1] Even in other groups, the workers must, in general, be regularly "attached to the labor market," able and willing to work, and genuinely unemployed. Persons unemployable because of age or physical handicap are not included—although they may benefit from other social-security arrangements.

[2] The amount received by the individual unemployed worker is determined by his wages earned in a base period, subject to maximum and minimum limitations. The total of benefit payments throughout the country in 1945 was $445,866,000.

since it was instituted, this has served most necessary purposes—except, of course, as large bodies of employees remain unprovided for, and as inflated living costs render benefits less adequate than formerly. For prolonged depression periods of mass unemployment, the system, however, has little to offer; if such times were to come again, there would be no alternative to relief and public works on the pattern of the thirties.[1]

The problem of the aged presents itself in two different although complementary aspects: (1) that of relieving aged persons who, already dependent, cannot be, or are not, adequately cared for by relatives, and (2) that of preventing people not yet old from becoming public charges later on. In earlier times, there usually was little that the aged lacking means of support could do except go to the almshouse. Around 1923, however, some states (Pennsylvania, Montana, and Nevada in the year mentioned) began providing pensions designed to enable such persons to eke out an existence while remaining in their own homes, and by the close of 1934, twenty-eight of the number had enacted legislation on the subject, although in three it was not operative, in only ten was it state-wide, and in most instances the funds available for benefits were small. The depression of the thirties naturally aggravated the plight of large numbers of old people, sweeping away savings and impairing the capacity of relatives to extend help; and, building upon such state systems of aid as existed, the federal Social Security Act of 1935, in its very first title or section, introduced a plan of federal responsibility and coöperation under which assistance for the needy aged has become numerically and financially the most important purely relief program in operation in the country today. The technique employed is the familiar grant-in-aid, on the fifty-fifty principle, with the limitation that the federal contribution to any one person shall in no case exceed a fixed amount per month— fifteen dollars originally, but raised in 1939 to twenty dollars and in 1946 to twenty-five—matching, of course, at least an equivalent amount paid by the state.[2] In one sense, the object was quickly attained: within three years, every state set up an old-age assistance program and qualified to receive federal funds. On the other hand, the arrangement has shortcomings. Only the aged (beyond sixty-five) who can demonstrate genuine need receive benefits—which, of course, is as it should be. But while states that are better off make allotments on a scale necessitating maximum contributions also by the federal government, thus making possible

2. Old-age assistance

---

[1] On the system in general, see L. Meriam, *Relief and Social Security* (Washington, D. C., 1946), 183-242; R. C. Atkinson, *The Federal Rôle in Unemployment Compensation Administration* (Washington, D. C., 1941); and W. Haber and J. J. Joseph, "An Appraisal of the Federal-State System of Unemployment Compensation," *Soc. Service Rev.*, XV, 207-241 (June, 1941). The defects of the present federal-state plan and the advantages that a unified national system would have are set forth in the Social Security Board's *Eighth Annual Report* (1943), 34-40. Cf. H. A. Gray, *Should State Unemployment Insurance be Federalized?* (New York, 1946); G. F. Rohrlich, "Consolidation of Unemployment Insurance and the Problem of Centralization," *Pub. Admin. Rev.*, IV, 43-50 (Winter, 1944).

[2] Needless to say, the beneficiaries make no contribution

monthly benefits rising to eighty dollars, or even more, poorer states are likely to be more niggardly, with total monthly benefits sometimes not exceeding ten or twelve dollars (the over-all average in 1946 was $31.48) ; and, although politics is supposed to play no part, there are credible charges that, in some places, belonging to the right political party helps one to get on the eligible list or to secure a larger rather than smaller allowance. The system is administered by the several states, under federal supervision; and to help carry the cost of administration, an extra federal grant of five per cent is made to each state. In 1946, 2,100,000 persons— about one in five of all those in the country beyond sixty-five—were receiving assistance under the program.

3. Old-age and survivors insurance

Even more imposing are the provisions made in the Social Security Act for old age *insurance*. Applying to substantially the same workers who are reached by unemployment compensation (the principal groups excluded are indicated above), and in 1946 numbering over forty millions, the measure set up a nation-wide contributory retirement system under which annuities or pensions, graduated in amount on the basis of earnings and duration of employment, are payable at the age of sixty-five from a fund built up from money paid in equally by employers and employees,[1] the national government making no financial contribution except to meet the costs of administration, but bearing undivided responsibility for operating the system and playing the combined rôles of collector, bookkeeper, and manager; the states, as such, have no part in the enterprise. In essence, the plan is one for compulsory savings—in other words, for spreading wages over the adult lifetime of the worker rather than over merely his wage-earning years; and on the theory that the employer has a stake in fostering employee frugality and in keeping his workers from eventually becoming dependents requiring public support, he is required to help make the plan workable, as a scheme of "coöperative thrift," by sharing in creating and maintaining the fund. Contributions made by employers and employees alike started at one per cent of the wages paid or received in 1937, and under the original law would have reached a maximum of three per cent in 1949. Because, however, this promised to build up huge reserves long before they would be needed, Congress, from year to year, and usually over presidential objection, "froze" the tax at one per cent, doing this most recently in July, 1947, for the period through 1949, although at the same time specifying that in 1950 the levy shall rise to one and one-half per cent and in 1952 to two per cent.[2] The present reserve (invested in United States securities) exceeds eight billion dollars.

---

[1] The contributions of employees are collected by employers, being simply deducted from wages—as the employers' own contributions may not be—and are sent by the employer (along with his own contributions) to the federal Treasury at Washington.

[2] Since payments are made on only the first three thousand dollars of wages or salaries (the Social Security Administration would have this increased to thirty-six

The amount received by a beneficiary depends to some extent upon the sum that he has paid in, but may in no case exceed eighty-five dollars a month. Of course, people now becoming eligible for payments have not been under the system long enough to have become entitled to any figure approximating the maximum; and at the end of 1946, in point of fact, the average monthly insurance payment to persons quitting work at sixty-five was for men $24.83 and for women $19.83. Contrary to expectation, there were, ten years after the insurance program went into effect, twice as many persons receiving old-age relief as were drawing monthly old-age insurance benefits.[1]

In 1939, the name of this phase of social security was changed to "old age and survivors' insurance," and the scope was broadened to include protection of the family, rather than merely the wage-earner, through the establishment of monthly benefits for aged wives and young children of retired workers, and for widows, orphans, and aged parents of insured workers who die before retirement. The date for the first payment of monthly benefits was advanced from January 1, 1942, to January 1, 1940; monthly benefits during the earlier years of the system were increased; and a few groups previously excluded, and aggregating a million and a half workers, were brought under the terms of the law.[2] Amendments of 1939

Even though as yet not applying to more than two-thirds of the adult population of the country, this old-age insurance system represents a stupendous undertaking, and one that will steadily expand as time goes on, not only by the probable inclusion of additional groups, but by increase in any case of the number of people covered, in the volume of funds required for operation, and, most significantly, in the number of probable beneficiaries, as illustrated by the fact that whereas in 1930 people of sixty-five and over comprised only 5.4 per cent of the country's population, by 1980 their proportion is expected to be as high as thirteen to possibly sixteen per cent. Workers, and especially employers, complain of the contributions they are required to make, and will complain more loudly of the higher ones that will have to be made in the future; sometimes it is argued that a more substantial share of the burden should be carried by the federal treasury. Adoption of the system, however, merely brings us into line with the more advanced foreign countries; and in any event the entire economic and social condition and outlook of the United States makes the scheme, although susceptible of many improvements, an

---

hundred), the maximum yearly contribution of a worker today, and of an employer in his behalf, is thirty dollars.

[1] At the same time, there were 890,000 workers entitled to payments, but preferring to remain at work. No person earning more than fifteen dollars a month may receive social security checks.

[2] 53 *U. S. Stat. at Large*, 1360. See *Fifth Annual Report of the Social Security Board* (1940), 24-54, and D. Waldron, "Social Security Amendments of 1939," *Univ. of Chicago Law Rev.*, VII, 83-111 (Dec., 1939). For an up-to-date collection of the statutes, see *Compilation of Social Security Laws, Including Social Security Act as Amended, and Related Documents Through March 1, 1947* (Washington, D. C., Govt. Prtg. Off., 1947).

elementary matter of common sense and prudence. Future generations will be grateful for it.[1]

Unemployment insurance and old-age assistance and insurance loom largest in the security system set up in 1935, but certain other features also call for mention. (1) On the analogy of assistance to the needy aged, assistance is provided for needy children, in the form of a matched grant (fifty-fifty) to states maintaining an approved program, as all except one or two are now doing. The plan applies only, however, to children living in the home of the mother or other near relative and less than sixteen years of age (if in school, eighteen); and the total benefit to which the federal government will contribute half is twenty-four dollars a month for the first child and fifteen for each additional one.[2] Separately from this plan of direct financial assistance to individuals, the act of 1935 provided the Children's Bureau with a million and a half dollars a year to be used in strengthening state child welfare activities in rural areas and other places of special need. (2) Among causes of permanent and frequently total disability irrespective of age, is, of course, blindness; and even before 1935 some twenty-five states were providing persons so afflicted with modest pensions and facilities for training appropriate to their condition. Under the Social Security Act, the federal government contributes to approved state programs (now maintained in practically all states) to the extent of sharing equally in monthly payments, where need exists, up to a total of originally thirty, but now forty-five, dollars. As a conspicuous form of disability, appealing strongly to people's sympathies, blindness has been singled out for this type of alleviation. Logically, there is no reason why disability arising from heart disease, tuberculosis, paralysis, and other such afflictions should not be dealt with similarly. (3) One of the earlier forms of federal aid (dating from 1920) had as its objective assistance to states in rehabilitating physically handicapped persons and training them for employments within the limits of their capacities. The Social Security Act of 1935 reënforced this kind of service by placing it on a more assured basis, with larger federal grants to states matching them and maintaining satisfactory facilities and management. (4) While no general program of health insurance was included in the 1935 legislation, provision was made for grants (increased in 1939 and 1946) to states for the care of crippled children and for maternal and child health services.[3]

---

[1] Old-age assistance and old-age and survivors insurance are analyzed in full in L. Meriam, *op. cit.*, 22-52, 74-140. At the beginning of 1946, a total of 41,500,000 workers were insured under the latter system.

[2] There is, of course, nothing to prevent a state from *more* than matching the federal contribution, and in a number of cases this is done.

[3] Illuminating articles on all of the foregoing forms of social security and amelioration will be found in *Annals of Amer. Acad. of Polit. and Soc. Sci.*, CCII (Mar., 1939). Services for children are treated fully and authoritatively in E. O. Lundberg, *Unto the Least of These; Social Services for Children* (New York, 1947). Cf. G. Abbott, *The Child and the State*, 2 vols. (Chicago, 1938).

With the single exception of old-age and survivors insurance, every program of security or amelioration touched upon represents a joint federal-state undertaking, with the national government instituting (or validating and expanding) the plan, and offering financial assistance, but with responsibility for organizing the program locally, deciding whether to make it broader than that to which the federal government has committed itself, providing machinery for carrying it out, determining who are to receive benefits and in what amounts, and of course "matching the federal dollar" (or making any other financial provision required), resting upon the states; and within a short time after the 1935 legislation was enacted, all of the states (with respect to certain of the services, or all of them) took whatever action was necessary to qualify for the various forms of aid and coöperation contemplated. Before federal money for any of the joint undertakings becomes available, a state's plans for use of the combined funds must receive the approval of some designated agency of the national government (*e.g.*, the Office of Education in the case of vocational rehabilitation, the Children's Bureau in that of child welfare services) ; and as a rule that agency retains general supervisory functions. To coördinate and supervise the system as a whole, and indeed to administer most parts of it, the act of 1935 provided for a Social Security Board of three members, set up as an independent establishment. When, however, in 1939 a number of appropriate offices and services were brought together in the present Federal Security Agency,[1] the Security Board was included; and under a further reorganization of 1945, the Board was abolished and its functions transferred to the head (administrator) of this agency, who, however, performs them through the medium of a Social Security Administration set up in the Agency with a commissioner at its head and various directors in charge of operating bureaus having to do, respectively, with unemployment security, old-age and survivors insurance, public assistance (old-age, dependent children, and the blind), and other matters.[2] Much of the work to be done can best be, or even must be, done locally, and not only does the Social Security Administration maintain thirteen major regional offices throughout the country, but for carrying on the old-age and survivors program alone, 450 field and branch offices are utilized, along with some 1,700 "itinerant" stations.

Inevitably, the Social Security Act of 1935 was attacked at many points on constitutional grounds, and amidst confusing decisions of lower courts a good deal of doubt arose as to how much of it would ultimately

[1] See p. 469 above.

[2] The Children's Bureau also (transferred from the Department of Labor in 1935) is now appropriately in the Social Security Administration, where its duties include operating the federal-state programs of maternal and child health, services for crippled children, and child welfare services. Under the Taft-Fulbright bill for creation of a federal Department of Health, Education, and Security, pending in Congress in 1947, the functions of the Social Security Administration would be taken over by a Bureau of Public Welfare. A new department bringing together the federal government's welfare activities has been proposed many times and probably will eventually be created.

be sustained. In a series of notable decisions handed down on May 24, 1937,[1] however, the federal Supreme Court—although by narrow margins of five-to-four—took a broader and more liberal view than in earlier decisions such as those involving the N.R.A. and the first A.A.A., and upheld every really vital feature of the basic law, discovering at last, as someone has remarked, "a method for implementing nationalism." Minority justices looked upon the unemployment-compensation (and some other) provisions of the legislation as invading the powers guaranteed to the states by the Tenth Amendment, and therefore as unconstitutional. But the majority considered that the states had been lax about social-security matters, that meanwhile the problem had become national in scope and dimensions, and that therefore Congress was justified in what it had done. "It is too late today," said Mr. Justice Cardozo, "for the argument to be heard with tolerance that in a crisis so extreme the use of moneys of the nation to relieve the unemployed and their dependents [the case which evoked these words was that of the Steward Company, involving the unemployment-compensation features of the law] is a use for any purpose narrower than the promotion of the general welfare"— adding that what constitutes the general welfare in any given situation is for Congress to determine.

Social security in the "G.I. Bill of Rights"

The United States had not long been involved in the recent war before it became apparent that the aids and services provided by the legislation of 1935 and its amendments would need to be considerably broadened in order to meet the situation created by the return of millions of servicemen and women to civilian life; and realization of this led in 1944 to the enactment of a more or less specialized social security measure entitled the Servicemen's Readjustment Act, popularly known as the "G. I. Bill of Rights." [2] For honorably discharged veterans of the late war, the law provided unemployment compensation of twenty dollars a week up to fifty-two weeks of unemployment; federal guaranty of loans up to four thousand dollars for the purchase or construction of homes or the purchase of farms or business properties; subsidies up to five hundred dollars a year, plus subsistence allowances ranging from sixty-five to ninety dollars a month, and for periods up to a maximum of four years, for academic education or professional or technical training; hospitalization and medical care; and other kinds of benefits.[3]

[1] Carmichael *et al. v.* Southern Coal and Coke Co., 301 U. S. 495; Charles C. Steward Machine Co. *v.* Davis, 301 U. S. 548; Helvering *et al. v.* Davis, 301 U. S. 619. These decisions came at a juncture when the controversy over President Roosevelt's plan to enlarge and rejuvenate the Court (see pp. 546-548 above) was at its peak. Just three weeks after they were handed down, the Senate judiciary committee in effect killed the Court proposal by reporting unfavorably a bill in which it was embodied.

[2] 58 *U. S. Stat. at Large,* 284.

[3] "The G. I. Bill of Rights; An Analysis of the Servicemen's Readjustment Act of 1944," *Soc. Security Bull.,* VII, 3-13 (July, 1944). By July, 1946, more than two million veterans were drawing unemployment benefits; almost three million had applied for education and training and about one million were enrolled in courses;

Proposals for Expansion and Reorganization

The over-all objective of the social security system described is one which reformers in all ages and countries have dreamed of, *i.e.*, the abolition of poverty, or at all events the mitigation of its most distressing consequences. To be sure, situations and conditions making for economic want cannot be legislated out of existence: there will always be unemployment; people will go on growing old and incapable of supporting themselves; medical skill and sanitary science have done much for health, yet sickness persists; there will forever be widows and orphans and crippled children and blind and other needy and helpless members of society. What social security seeks to do is to take the economic impact of unemployment or other affliction off the individual, at least partly, and absorb it into a collective burden to be borne by a state-wide or other community. To be sure, in the case of old-age and survivors insurance, the beneficiary himself carries some share of the burden, as funds are built up against the day when he will need to draw upon them. In every other instance, however, assistance is non-contributory; that is to say, the beneficiary, being in present need, does not give, but merely receives.[1] In every case, too, except old-age and survivors insurance (operated on a purely national basis), the unit of organization and administration is the state. The federal government sets up a general framework of action, encourages and in some instances practically compels participation, and often not only reimburses the states for what they spend on administration, but pledges up to half of the funds required for meeting the substantive obligations entailed, provided various specified conditions are met; the grant-in-aid system has of late found its principal expansion in this field. But, in general, activities are state, or at all events federal-state, rather than definitely federal.

Undoubtedly the system has justified itself and is here to stay. In general, it has been well administered; and in the process the standards and techniques of state and local welfare management have received a wholesome toning up. As already indicated, however, defects appear and important changes are likely to be made; and, passing over numerous matters of more or less technical character, two main problems may, in conclusion, be brought into focus. First of all, the system is criticized because of its very incomplete coverage, in two important respects: (1) as to the groups of people to which it applies, and (2) as to the forms of insurance provided. On the first score, the principal deficiency is, of course, the omission from the two basic insurance programs (unemployment compensation and old-age and survivors insurance) of the self-

The funda-
mentals
of the
system

Defects
and pro-
posed
changes:

1. As to
coverage

and borrowings under the loan provisions aggregated $805,000,000. All of these activities have been supervised by the Veterans Administration (see p. 808, note 2, below).

[1] Where there are employer contributions, it may safely be assumed that costs are added to the prices of products, and thus eventually met by the consuming public.

employed, of agricultural workers, of domestic servants, and of other groups previously enumerated—aggregating some twenty million people who, speaking broadly at all events, stand in almost if not quite as much need of protection as do the industrial workers now chiefly covered. On the second score, the most glaring shortcoming is the lack of any provision for broad and general health insurance—almost invariably a conspicuous feature of European systems. For ten or twelve years, leaders of thought on the subject have contended—as Presidents Roosevelt and Truman have repeatedly asserted—that the system now existing constitutes only a good beginning. In 1943, the National Resources Planning Board (soon thereafter abolished), in a 640-page report, reviewed experience to that time, stressed the deficiencies mentioned (along with many others), and suggested ways in which the entire program could be expanded, improved, and geared to postwar national needs.[1] In the same year, and again in 1945, a measure—the Wagner-Murray-Dingell bill—based largely on the Planning Board's recommendations, and aimed at "covering the major economic hazards from the cradle to the grave," was introduced in Congress, with full support from the A. F. of L., the C.I.O., and other groups, though never passed. At frequent intervals (most recently in its report for 1947), the Social Security Board and its successor, the Social Security Administration, has called for a new and greater program, extending to the groups not now covered, plugging another large gap by introducing a nation-wide scheme of disability and sickness insurance, and making numerous other readjustments and extensions in the interest of a balanced and logical system compatible with the American way of life, yet within limits of what the nation can afford.[2]

The vast difficulties involved in working out acceptable plans, the sectional jealousies and rivalries sometimes stirred, the confusion relating to health proposals arising from bitter controversies over "socialized medicine," [3] hesitation over greater expenditures in a period of staggering

---

[1] *National Resources Development Report for 1943* (Washington, D. C., 1943), Pt. 3, "Security, Work, and Relief Policies." Based upon a three-year study, this important document was transmitted to Congress by the President in a letter of March 10, 1943, strongly urging action on the lines recommended. In addition to broadening and extending existing security measures, the Board advocated protection of all youth under twenty-one, more adequate medical care, the expansion of state and local child-welfare services (with federal assistance), free school lunches for all school children, and the unification of all phases of the security program in a single, completely integrated, federalized system. The Board's findings and recommendations will be found summarized in E. M. Burns, "NRPB Proposes Social Security," *Nat. Mun. Rev.*, XXXII, 232-236 (May, 1943), and R. F. Wagner, "Social Security Lifts Its Sights," *Survey Graphic*, XXXII, 283 ff. (July, 1943). The Planning Board report had a significant counterpart in Britain in Sir William Beveridge's *Social Insurance and Allied Services* (Amer. ed., New York, 1942), representing the results of study by a royal commission, and commonly referred to as the "Beveridge Report."

[2] Similar recommendations have been made repeatedly by President Truman, as in his "state of the union" message of January 7, 1948.

[3] In 1947-48, a health bill sponsored by Senator Robert A. Taft was pending in Congress authorizing an annual federal grant of $200,000,000, with state matching on a fifty-fifty basis, to "fill in the gaps in the nation's existing health program." Various features of the plan, especially on the administrative side, were, however, criticized by public health authorities, and the Social Security Administration continued urg-

national debt, and some lingering prejudice against enterprises of New Deal origin, have thus far paralyzed action. There is, however, much to indicate that the situation is gradually shaping toward a general revision and expansion. As the Social Security Board correctly remarked in its final annual report: "Insurance has long been accepted by Americans as a method of guarding against risks to their individual lives and possessions. Social insurance in the United States, at the end of little more than a decade, has proved its feasibility and value as a means of enabling millions of persons to attain a basic minimum of protection that would not have been available to them in any other way."[1]

A second major criticism advanced arises out of the complicated federal-state relationships involved in the existing scheme. As pointed out above, the authors of the act of 1935 seriously considered a completely federal system, but for reasons that seemed sufficient to them rejected it. Except, however, as the states have held out for the present plan, sentiment in later years has shifted heavily in favor of nationalization. The Resources Planning Board recommended it; the Chamber of Commerce of the United States has endorsed it; the Wagner-Murray-Dingell bill provided for it, at least in the area of unemployment compensation; and the Social Security Administration has persistently urged it, pointing out that the present old-age and survivors insurance system could readily be made the basis for a single integrated national program covering all major economic hazards of workers, even though more specialized programs, *e.g.*, for crippled children and the blind, be left separate. Here again, decision remains to be made. Save for state opposition, the change could confidently be predicted. It may come in any case; and if it does, it will almost certainly be accompanied by an expansion of coverage on the lines indicated above. One thing, at least, is clear: our social security system is in no sense a finished product. Rather, we are only feeling our way through its experimental stages.[2]

2. As to federal-state relations

Public Housing

The acute housing shortage experienced by the country during and after World War II, causing untold inconvenience and hardship for great numbers of people, focused attention upon a problem really as old as our present industrial society. Rural housing is often far from what it should be, but when our population dwelt almost entirely on farms or in villages and small towns, people commonly had access to reasonably good houses and there was not much for public authorities to do about

Slow development of state and local control

---

ing a health insurance program financed from contributions by workers and employers on the analogy of old-age and survivors insurance.

[1] *Annual Report of the Federal Security Agency*, § 6, *the Social Security Board, for the Fiscal Year* 1946 (Washington, D. C., 1946), 426.

[2] In 1947, the Senate directed its committee on finance to make "a full and complete investigation" of social security with special reference to coverage, benefits, and taxes. Later, an advisory council of seventeen experts was set up to assist and advise the committee in its inquiry.

the matter. With the rise of great industrial centers, however, the situation changed, and decidedly for the worse. Detached houses gave way to drab tenements; high land values caused crowding and congestion; high rents forced families into pitifully inadequate quarters; immigrant workers congregated in teeming Ghettos, "Little Italy's," and the like; the "slum"—dreary, crowded, and dangerous alike to health and morals— became a blot upon an otherwise fair social economy. Aside from some control over fire hazards and construction methods, the first serious attention given to housing by public authorities was directed to ameliorating the condition of low-income groups in slum areas; and while even in the third quarter of the nineteenth century a few cities bestirred themselves to some extent about the matter, enacting local codes prescribing building regulations and sanitary standards, the effects were slight, and in time reformers turned with more hope to the legislatures of the states. From action in certain of the more highly industrialized states did indeed come measures fixing standards with somewhat beneficial effect. At best, however, the legislation merely imposed regulations on private owners of existing housing or upon private construction, without directly bringing new and better housing into existence. New York, to be sure, went farther by taking action calculated to encourage private enterprise to undertake a good grade of building for people of low incomes, and even by setting up a state housing board charged with planning and promoting slum clearance in the crowded districts of New York City and with supervising the construction of "model tenements." But no other state emulated the example thus set.

The federal government enters the field   Aside from some provision for the housing of war-workers during World War I, the federal government stayed almost completely out of the field until the depression of the thirties. From that time, however, it has been continuously involved, in many different ways and through the medium of legislation and administrative machinery so complicated, and so frequently changed, as to baffle almost any one except a professional student of the subject. As pointed out in an earlier chapter,[1] the first form of federal effort, undertaken at a time when great numbers of people were losing their homes through mortgage foreclosures, was aimed, not particularly at increasing or improving housing, but at enabling hard-pressed home-owners to avoid being dispossessed; and the method consisted in setting up (in 1932) a series of home loan banks under a Federal Home Loan Bank Administration to provide credit for local institutions engaged in home-financing, with, in addition, a Home Owners' Loan Corporation (in 1933) to make direct long-term mortgage loans, out of federal funds and at low interest rates, to distressed home-owners who for one reason or another could not borrow through other channels. Almost simultaneously, however, encouragement of new low-cost building and of renovation of residential properties was undertaken through a

[1] See p. 608 above.

Federal Housing Administration created under a National Housing Act[1] of 1934 and authorized not only to insure lending institutions against possible losses on loans made for the purposes indicated, but itself to make federal loans to these institutions, to be employed in promoting low-rent dwellings. To this point, the objectives had been primarily to enable people to save their homes and to stimulate employment in home building and modernization. Growing appreciation of the permanent social significance of good housing, however, was reflected in a National Housing [Wagner-Steagall] Act[2] of 1937 setting up in the Federal Works Agency a United States Housing Authority charged with making long-term loans (up to eighty per cent of the costs involved) to state or local housing authorities for the construction of low-rent housing and for slum-clearance. The federal government was not to engage directly in the work of construction or demolition, but merely to make loans; municipal or other local authorities directly concerned were to plan projects, furnish such additional funds as might be needed (normally twenty per cent), and execute the different enterprises. Within six years after the legislation was enacted, all but ten of the states qualified for the federal aid by setting up the requisite authorities—sometimes with jurisdiction confined to one or two cities, but often extending to all cities and towns and even to rural areas.

Although fifty-one projects in the eastern part of the country were completed, at a cost of $134,000,000, the plan was hardly in full operation before the national defense effort launched in 1940, and the ensuing war, gave the housing problem a new slant and emphasis. With the rapid expansion of shipyards and of plants for manufacturing airplanes, powder, and other war materials, the building of new plants for such purposes, and the construction of military camps and training quarters, hundreds of thousands of workers and their families flocked to localities not equipped to house them; and partly in order to meet this situation, partly because of scarcity of labor and materials, and partly because Congress virtually cut off supporting appropriations, the general program of civilian construction and slum clearance came almost to a stop. Indeed, under legislation of 1940 federal housing activities were substantially restricted to such as had to do with taking care of the armed forces and of war-plant workers; and between 1940 and the close of 1944, a total of 1,479,502 war-housing units were constructed or reconstructed, about half of the number publicly and about half privately.[3]

Housing and World War II

[1] 48 *U. S. Stat. at Large*, 1246.
[2] 50 *U. S. Stat. at Large*, 888.
[3] An important related federal activity was the control of rents, instituted originally only in connection with dwellings in areas heavily populated by defense-plant workers, but in 1942 made applicable to all real property throughout the country, commercial as well as residential. Because of the continued tightness of the housing situation, this form of regulation was prolonged after the war, and in the early summer of 1947, as applying to housing accommodations, it was extended by congressional act to March 1, 1948, though with modifications embracing authorization of rent increases by fifteen per cent where mutually agreeable to landlord and tenant

Housing
since
the war:

1. Nature
of the
problem
The housing situation confronting the country since the war is a familiar, and for many people a painful, subject. Almost complete cessation of civilian building for five or six years (on top of heavily reduced building during the preceding depression decade), a steady increase of population in the meantime, return from overseas of millions of servicemen looking for homes, and continued deterioration of much older housing long obsolescent—these and other factors easily explain the severe shortage by which every part of the nation has been beset. At the beginning of 1946, competent authorities declared one-third of the country's population ill-housed, and placed the number of dwelling units urgently needed, over and above those of all kinds existing, at not less than three millions. The situation was merely aggravated by depression and war; even earlier, there had not been enough houses and many of those existing had been substandard. The fact was that in the steady progress of our people toward material well-being, housing had lagged: working hours had been reduced by a third to a half; food consumption had increased; education and recreation had advanced; social security had been initiated; even the average span of life had been lengthened. But millions in the low-income groups still lived in slums (both urban and rural), and other millions in homes hardly better fit for habitation. Only about half of the nation's families, too, owned the places in which they dwelt.

The postwar problem, therefore, has been not simply one of providing *additional* housing. It has been one also of replacing poor housing and raising the general housing level. For doing both of these things, conditions have been in some respects favorable. Potentially, we have the land, the labor, the materials. There is keen interest and desire on the part of the public. Precedents are abundant for initiative, planning, and performance by government on all levels. The Supreme Court's concept of the general welfare has been so broadened that the federal government is estopped by no serious constitutional considerations. On the other hand, there have been serious impediments. One is the very magnitude of the country-wide job to be performed; possibly the task is the most stupendous of a domestic character that the nation now has on its hands. Another is the circumstance that while unquestionably a very great rôle must be played by government, strong prejudice against supplanting private with public enterprise is everywhere encountered. Still another is the chronically unstable, disorganized condition of the building industry— a group of quite separate handicrafts unable to work together economically and efficiently. Yet another is the bad consequences of a harsh and

---

and where leases were to run through 1948 or longer. *Pub. Law 129—80th Cong., 1st Sess.* Charging that the rent-increase provision had been prompted by a selfish real-estate lobby, President Truman signed the measure, he asserted, only because the alternative would have been no rent control at all. In February, 1948, rent control was extended by Congress to April 1; and on March 30 the President approved an act (*Pub. Law 464—80th Cong., 2nd Sess.*) prolonging it to March 31, 1949.

burdensome mortgage system. In the immediate situation, too, an almost prohibitive factor has been the high cost of labor and both the cost and scarcity of building materials, as well as, in the background, a pull and haul among federal, state, and local governments over conflicting or interlocking functions and activities.

The record written since 1935 has its bright spots, but on the whole is not one to stir enthusiasm. At Washington, juggling of housing agencies— so incessant and puzzling throughout the war period that the readers of this chapter are being spared an account that could not be otherwise than boresome—went steadily forward, although with possibly some stability arrived at in 1947. Back in 1942, President Roosevelt had sought to bring order out of chaos by consolidating no fewer than seventeen different agencies having to do with the matter in one way or another. In 1947, President Truman found an almost equally colossal operation called for; and although the House of Representatives rejected a plan which he presented under his temporary reorganizing authority, the Senate approved it—with the plan therefore going into effect, since under the current formula of executive reorganization a plan offered by the chief executive became operative unless rejected by both houses. The main feature of the new set-up is a Housing and Home Finance Agency as a sort of roof under which three preëxisting agencies operate—a Home Loan Bank Administration, a Federal Public Housing Authority, and a Federal Housing Administration [1]—although even this coördination was not attained without stiff resistance from real estate boards and other private housing interests which feared that the over-all head of the new establishment would be a "public housing man." 2. Federal housing agencies

As would be expected, the principal assistance rendered by the federal government is financial; and the network of credit agencies developed in this field is hardly less extensive and complicated than that found in the domain of agriculture. Early in chronological order came a government-owned Home Owners' Loan Corporation, established in 1933, in the depth of the depression, to make fifteen-year loans, at low interest rates, to hard-pressed home-owners unable to procure refinancing through normal channels; and although this agency discontinued making loans in 1936 and has since been engaged in cleaning up mortgages which it took over from holders in exchange for government-guaranteed bonds, more than a million home-owners facing dispossession received from it during its brief period of lending loans aggregating more than three billion dollars. Of larger continuing importance, however, are the Home Loan Bank Administration (within which the Home Owners' Loan Corporation is a unit) and the Federal Housing Administration. Originating under a slightly different name in 1932, the Home Loan Bank Administration 3. Financial assistance— credit machinery

---

[1] There is also an advisory National Housing Council, composed of representatives of the three agencies mentioned, the Veterans' Administration, the Reconstruction Finance Corporation, and the Department of Agriculture.

functions through a chain of eleven regional home loan banks located in cities throughout the country, with capital stock owned partly by the government but primarily by building and loan, savings and loan, and other member institutions; and since they specialize in making loans on homes, the banks are particularly available for assistance to veterans under the Servicemen's Readjustment Act of 1944. Operating on a still larger scale is the Federal Housing Administration which since 1934 has —without itself lending money—promoted the building, modernizing, and repairing of homes by insuring banks and other lending institutions against losses on loans made for such purposes. One or more insuring or service offices are maintained in every state and territory, and the number of people whose homes have been beneficiaries of F.H.A. loans of one sort or another runs far into the millions. The Federal Public Housing Authority has the more specialized function of looking after public housing programs directly sponsored and administered by the government— especially emergency housing projects during the war and later years of reconversion, together with low-rent housing and slum-clearance projects for which the Authority makes loans and even grants subsidies in aid of municipal and other local public housing agencies.

Further needs— the Wagner-Taft-Ellender proposal

All this is impressive. Yet room remains for a great deal more to be done—especially in the direction of actual expenditure (not mere loans) by the federal government to speed improvement of a situation still admittedly bad. And this was the objective of a National Housing [Wagner-Ellender-Taft] Bill introduced in and passed by the Senate in 1945, and warmly supported by President Truman, although languishing in a House committee through 1946 and, in somewhat revised form, kept alive, but without adoption, in 1947.[1] Professedly aiming at a decent house and a suitable living environment for every American family, this measure avowed the policy of encouraging the housing needs of the country to be met to the fullest possible extent by private enterprise (directed to the building of moderate-priced homes), but declared also that low-rental needs which could not be met in this way must be served by public action; and to that end it provided for federal expenditure of $143,000,000 a year for ten years through state and local public housing authorities and designed to encourage the construction of fifteen million urban and rural dwellings during the decade. The high hopes pinned to this measure seemed somewhat over-optimistic, but at least they had substance enough to array organized real estate and building interests solidly and successfully against it; and its failure to become law added another chapter to one of the dreariest stories of confusion, frustration, and futility in our recent national history.[2] To be sure, a great deal has

[1] The measure was based on the investigations and findings of a subcommittee on housing and urban redevelopment of a special Senate committee on postwar economic policy and planning.

[2] In April, 1948, the bill, in somewhat amended form, seemed assured of fresh consideration in the Senate, but with the outlook for House approval not bright.

been accomplished. Millions of people are in homes that they would have lost if the federal government had not come to their rescue. Millions more are in better homes than they would have had without government aid in jobs of renovation. Many, too, are in homes that, but for public lending, would not even have been built. All of this once recognized, the situation at the date of writing (1948) nevertheless remained unsatisfactory, with the country still awaiting some sign that a well-considered, genuinely unified, and positively adequate plan was about to be launched and energetically carried out.

REFERENCES

SOCIAL SECURITY

M. Fainsod and L. Gordon, *Government and the American Economy* (New York, 1941), Chap. XXI.

J. A. Maxwell, *The Fiscal Impact of Federalism in the United States* (Cambridge, Mass., 1946), Chaps. VI-XI.

H. M. Groves, *Financing Government* (rev. ed., New York, 1947), Chap. XVI. On social security taxes.

L. Meriam, *Relief and Social Security* (Washington, D. C., 1946). A full critical analysis.[1]

K. de Schweinitz, *People and Process in Social Security* (Washington, D. C., 1948).

G. Abbott, *From Relief to Social Security* (Chicago, 1942).

P. H. Douglas, *Social Security in the United States* (rev. ed., New York, 1939).

M. S. Stewart, *Social Security* (rev. ed., New York, 1939).

L. H. Pink, *Freedom from Fear* (New York, 1944).

A. Epstein, *Insecurity; A Challenge to America* (New York, 1938).

J. P. Harris, "The Social Security Program of the United States," *Amer. Polit. Sci. Rev.*, XXX, 455-493 (June, 1936).

D. S. Howard, *The War and Federal Relief Policy* (New York, 1943).

Committee on Economic Security, *Social Security in America* (Washington, D. C., 1937).

B. E. Wyatt and W. H. Wandel, *The Social Security Act in Operation* (Washington, D. C., 1937).

J. E. Hughes, *The Federal Social Security Tax* (Chicago, 1941).

J. S. Parker, *Social Security Reserves* (Washington, D. C., 1942).

T. Lansdale *et al., The Administration of Old Age Assistance* (Chicago, 1939).

R. Atkinson, *The Federal Rôle in Unemployment Administration* (Washington, D. C., 1941).

"The Proposal for a Federal Compulsory Insurance System of Citizens' Medical Care" [Symposium], *Cong. Digest*, XXV, Nos. 8-9 (Aug., Sept., 1946).

A. J. Altmeyer, "Interstate Problems in Social Security," *Nat. Mun. Rev.*, XXVI, 185-192 (Apr., 1937).

————, "Unemployment Insurance: Federal or State Responsibility?," *ibid.*, XXXII, 237-242 (May, 1943).

P. A. Rauschenbush, "Unemployment Compensation: Federal-State Coöperation," *ibid.*, XXXII, 423-431 (Sept., 1943). A reply to the preceding article.

Council of State Governments, *Unemployment Compensation in the Postwar Period* (Chicago, 1944).

[1] A convenient summary of this large volume can be obtained from the Brookings Institution, Washington, D. C., for fifty cents.

I. G. Carter [ed.], "Appraising the Social Security Program," *Annals of Amer. Acad. of Polit. and Soc. Sci.,* CCII, 1-197 (Mar., 1939).

Social Security Board, Bureau of Research and Statistics, *The Scope of Protection Under State and Local Government Retirement Systems* (Washington, D. C., 1943).

R. M. Ball, *Social Security Reading List, 1947* (Washington, D. C., 1947). A useful bibliography.

R. H. Kurtz [ed.], *Social Work Year Book, 1947* (New York, 1947).

Social Security Bulletin (monthly) and *Social Security Yearbook.* Issued by the Social Security Administration.

Annual reports of the (former) Social Security Board and the Federal Security Agency.

PUBLIC HOUSING

C. Abrams, *The Future of Housing* (New York, 1946). By far the best book on the subject.

E. R. Latty [ed.], "Housing" [Symposium], *Law and Contemporary Problems,* XII, 1-208 (Winter, 1947).

W. Ebenstein, *The Law of Public Housing* (Madison, Wis., 1940).

D. Schaffter, *State Housing Agencies* (New York, 1942).

M. L. Colean *et al., American Housing; Problems and Prospects* (New York, 1944).

D. Rosenman, *A Million Homes a Year* (New York, 1945).

National Housing Agency, *Housing Needs* (Washington, D. C., 1944).

R. B. Vance and G. W. Blackwell, *New Farm Homes for Old; A Study of Rural Public Housing in the South* (University, Ala., 1946).

D. M. French, "The Contest for a National System of Home Mortgage Finance," *Amer. Polit. Sci. Rev.,* XXXV, 53-69 (Feb., 1941).

R. H. Skilton, *Government and the Mortgage Debtor, 1929-1939* (Alexandria, Va., 1944).

CHAPTER XXXIV

FOREIGN RELATIONS

In a world of sixty or more nations, every independent government Nature
and im-
portance must carry on official dealings with other governments; and in this technological age, with distances shortened, points of contact multiplied, and the tempo of life speeded up, "foreign relations" closely rival, and at times overtop, domestic affairs in the difficulties they raise, the attention they require, and the consequences of good or bad management they entail for the public well-being. Foreign and domestic affairs, however, are not, as sometimes supposed, two separate and independent national concerns. On the contrary, they are closely interwoven, domestic affairs being commonly the fount from which foreign interests and policies spring, the matrix or mold in which they are embedded. Under our American system, the authorities chiefly charged with determining and carrying out foreign policies—the president and Congress—are the same as those sharing responsibility for affairs at home; and when, for example, they decide to restrict immigration from European countries or to lower duties on imported goods or to insist upon equality of commercial opportunity in China, they are actuated primarily, not by isolated or theoretical considerations, but by the needs and interests of our economy at home. Even when, a decade ago, they embarked upon the hazardous policy of helping Britain and China withstand the assaults of totalitarian powers, and eventually led us into war in the common cause, their basic objective was to protect our freedom, institutions, and manner of life within our own borders.

One thing that the framers of the constitution in 1787 could take for Constitu-
tional
basis granted was that the new national government would have exclusive control over the country's dealings with governments abroad. Even under the Articles of Confederation, the states had no authority to send or receive ministers and consuls, or to make war, or peace, or treaties, or alliances. Of broad reserved powers retained after 1789, none, therefore, had to do with foreign relations. On the other hand, we have the word of the Supreme Court for it that even if no powers in that field had been expressly conferred on the national government, they would have been vested in it in any case "as necessary concomitants of nationality" [1]—

---

[1] United States *v.* Curtiss-Wright Export Corporation, 299 U. S. 304 (1936). This case turned on the validity of a presidential embargo on the sale of arms to two warring Latin-American nations, Bolivia and Paraguay, in pursuance of a joint resolution of Congress (1934) conferring such power (48 *U. S. Stat. at Large,* 811). Cf. C. P. Patterson, *"In re* The United States *v.* the Curtiss-Wright Corporation," *Texas*

in other words, would have existed independently of any constitutional grant at all. Actually, however, the powers in question were not left on this somewhat tenuous basis. To be sure, there is nowhere a single blanket grant, nor even any mention of "foreign relations" as such. But the president is authorized to "appoint ambassadors, other public ministers and consuls," to make treaties, and to "receive ambassadors and other public ministers;" the Senate is allotted a share in treaty-making, as well as in appointments; and Congress is given power to regulate foreign commerce and to declare war. To clinch matters, the states are forbidden to "enter into any treaty, alliance, or confederation," or into *any* "agreement or compact with . . . a foreign power" except with the consent of Congress, or to engage in war unless actually invaded.[1] In any event, the federal government has sole power—if we are to believe the Supreme Court, *all* power not actually prohibited—to act for us in the international field with or without constitutional authorization, express or implied.[2]

Diffused
responsi-
bility By nature, the conduct of foreign relations is an executive function; and in many countries it is almost exclusively such in actual practice. In the United States, too, it is such a function primarily, yet one also shared heavily with other branches of the government. As chief executive, the president unquestionably is the supreme director of our official international intercourse—both because the powers given him (appointment, direction, negotiation, etc.) are the most basic, and because, as John Jay long ago pointed out, his office enjoys, as compared with Congress, the lofty advantages of unity, continuity, means of secrecy and dispatch, and unique sources of information.[3] Nowhere in the constitution, however, is the president expressly assigned such primacy; on the contrary, he is merely given certain powers, the Senate is given others, and Congress as a whole still others. And while, in outlining here the pattern of control over our foreign relations, the president will have to be assigned the center of the stage, the emphasis will be misleading unless it is at the same time made perfectly clear that what we have in this area of our

---

Law Rev., XXII, 286-308, 445-470 (Apr., June, 1944). On a later occasion, however, the Court stated unequivocally—significantly in time of war—that "Congress and the president, like the courts, possess no power not derived from the constitution." *Ex parte* Quirin *et al.*, 317 U. S. 1, 25-26 (1942).

[1] Art. I, § 10, cls. 1-3.

[2] Of course, under our federal system the control of the states over their internal affairs sometimes raises complications for the federal government in its management of foreign relations. State laws restricting property rights or otherwise discriminating against aliens may conflict with treaty guarantees, prompting protests from governments concerned; as mentioned elsewhere (see p. 137 above), citizens of foreign states may become victims of mob violence in an American city, stirring similar protests, but with local sentiment such that the guilty cannot be brought to justice; the International Labor Organization (of which the United States is a member) may prescribe standards of labor regulation which states are unwilling to meet. In general, the *legal right* of the federal government to see that its international obligations in such matters are fulfilled is clear. But practical difficulties sometimes paralyze action, and the matter is still in an unsatisfactory situation. See H. W. Stoke, *The Foreign Relations of the Federal State* (Baltimore, 1931).

[3] *The Federalist*, No. LXIV (Lodge's ed., 400-406).

government is a responsibility shared by the executive and legislative (and at some points even the judicial) branches [1]—a responsibility considerably more diffused than that prevailing in the conduct of foreign relations in any other important country. The arrangement—resulting from efforts of the constitution's framers to apply the principle of separation of powers in the foreign as in the domestic field—may be justifiable, but we often pay a price for it in terms of unpredictability, delay, confusion, and frustration. Many people regard the dispersion referred to and the lack of an adequately informed public opinion on international matters as the two principal impediments to the most effective conduct of our foreign relations.

With the foregoing basic facts in mind, we turn to the ways in which our foreign relations are managed, starting with the president as supreme director; although, because of the president's functions being exercised largely through the Department of State and its far-flung auxiliary, the Foreign Service, something may well be said about these agencies before the chief executive is brought directly into the picture.

The Department of State

After experimenting unsuccessfully with a "committee of foreign affairs," the Congress of the Confederation created in 1781 an executive department of similar name; and in 1789 this establishment became the first of three or four of like nature to be formally taken over as a unit of the new government under the constitution. Finding it useful, however, to assign the department various duties having little or no connection with foreign affairs, Congress within two months reorganized it as the Department of State; and this more general name and aspect it has ever since retained. The Department's principal function is, and always has been, to carry on, under direction of the president, the official transactions of the United States with foreign governments. Nevertheless, its head, the secretary of state (acting directly or through subordinates), receives the laws passed by Congress, publishes them, and files the original copies for preservation; keeps the great seal of the United States and affixes it to executive proclamations and other official papers; proclaims the admission of new states; transmits to the states constitutional amendments proposed by Congress, receives from the governors official notice of ratifications and rejections, and proclaims amendments when duly adopted; after presidential elections, receives likewise from the governors authentic lists of electors chosen and transmits them to Congress; and performs various other acts as required by law. In other words, notwithstanding that sundry functions of this miscellaneous character have from time to time been transferred to other departments, the State Department remains to a considerable extent a "home," as well as a "foreign,"

Home and foreign functions

---

[1] With also, as will appear, much dispersion even within the confines of the executive branch. See p. 772, note 1, below.

office, charged with keeping archives and proclaiming public acts, and especially with serving as a medium of communication between the president and Congress on the one hand and the authorities of the states on the other. To be sure, most of what is done is purely formal and routine; yet necessary purposes are served.

The great bulk of the Department's activities have to do rather with our government's dealings abroad; and it is with these that we are here concerned. Subject always to presidential direction and control, the secretary of state and his subordinates negotiate treaties and trade agreements; carry on correspondence with foreign states; give instructions to our ambassadors, ministers, and consuls abroad; attend to all matters of extradition; issue passports and visas; make arrangements for international conferences and congresses; gather information about conditions in foreign lands and place it at the disposal of the president, of Congress, or, if suitable, of the public; carry on international cultural activities; and, in general, stand ready to take up any task, in peace or war, which the protection or promotion of American interests beyond our borders entails.[1] Foreign governments and their representatives normally communicate with our government, and in turn receive its communications, only through the Department of State—although the president, on his part, may, and occasionally does, communicate with them through conversations at the White House, through personal agents sent abroad, by transoceanic telephone, and in these later days through personal conferences held at distant points of the earth.[2]

Recent expansion and reorganization

Although still among the smaller departments in personnel, the Department of State, including the Foreign Service, is, in the geographical sweep of its activities, the most extensive of all, being indeed the long arm by which the government reaches out to and deals with matters large and

[1] It would be an error, however, to think of the State Department as the only one of the present eleven having to do, in one way or another, with foreign relations, or even as the only one contributing to the making of foreign policy. Now coördinated under a secretary of defense, the Army, Navy, and Air Force Departments not only have military, naval, and air attachés on the staffs of our embassies and legations, but, working through the new over-all unified defense administration (see p. 824 below), participate in many decisions affecting our relations throughout the world; the Treasury Department takes part in developing programs relating to international finance, *e.g.*, the creation of the international fund and bank operating since 1946 as agencies of the United Nations; the Department of Justice maintains immigration officials in many foreign ports of embarkation and prosecutes anti-trust cases involving cartel arrangements between American and foreign companies; and other departments and agencies could be added to the list. Indeed, in 1943, under wartime conditions, more than thirty different departments and establishments had representatives abroad. See W. H. C. Laves and F. O. Wilcox, "Organizing the Government for Participation in World Affairs," *Amer. Polit. Sci. Rev.*, XXXVIII, 913-930 (Oct., 1944).

[2] See p. 782, note 1, below. Under normal conditions, foreign governments, however, may approach our government only through the State Department. The rule has prevailed ever since Citizen Edmond Gènet, minister plenipotentiary of the French Republic, directed a letter in 1793 to President Washington and was rebuked for doing so. Furthermore, they may not seek to circumvent the Department by appealing directly to the public. For attempting this, Citizen Genêt was recalled by his government at Washington's request.

small, in countries far and near, in every quarter of the globe. No one would need to be told that the explosive international situation during the thirties—followed by the strains and stresses of the greatest war and some of the most formidable diplomatic undertakings in our history—imposed upon the Department the heaviest responsibilities and labors that it had ever known. And one would be prepared to hear that these troubled years brought not only a corresponding multiplication of functions, but much expansion and reorganization of machinery as well. From some 1,100 officers and employees in 1930 or thereabouts (exclusive of the Foreign Service), the Department's force has mounted to more than 8,500—some 6,800 of the number occupying twenty-three different buildings in the national capital. And as for reorganizations, there were two of major scope in 1944, both aimed not only at taking care of wartime needs, but at meeting long-standing criticism of the Department for lacking a sound administrative structure, for failing to keep in touch with congressional and public opinion, and for having neither organization nor personnel adapted to furnishing the kind of leadership in foreign relations which the country had a right to expect. Many circumstances combine to make the Department's internal arrangements exceptionally fluid, and no description is likely to hold true over any very long period of time.[1]

At the Department's helm is, of course, the secretary of state, commonly the most conspicuous cabinet officer, and in any event endowed with a certain primacy by statutory recognition as next after the vice-president, speaker of the House, and president *pro tempore* of the Senate in the line of succession to the presidency. His is the oldest department, with functions of a more delicate nature than those of any other; and usually he sustains more intimate relations with his chief in the White House than does any other department head. So completely and uniquely, indeed, is the Department an agency of the White House that requests made of it by Congress are regarded as made of the president himself; alone among department heads, the secretary of state submits no regular annual report that goes to Congress and the public. Not all secretaries of state have been great men or able administrators, and comparatively few have, like Jefferson and Hay, brought to the office actual experience in diplomacy. The roster of incumbents since 1789 has, however, been adorned with enough honored names—Jefferson, John Marshall, Madison, John Quincy Adams, Clay, Webster, Calhoun, Seward, Blaine, Hay, Root, Hughes, Stimson, Hull, Byrnes, George C. Marshall—to have invested the secretaryship, like the presidency itself, with a lofty tradition.

The secretary of state

[1] The departmental "reorganization order" of January 15, 1944, will be found in the *Department of State Bulletin* of that date, and that of the following December 20 in *ibid.*, Dec. 17, 1944, Supp. The earlier reorganization is described in detail in W. H. C. Laves and F. O. Wilcox, "The Reorganization of the Department of State," *Amer. Polit. Sci. Rev.*, XXXVIII, 289-301 (Apr., 1944), and the later one in the same authors' "The State Department Continues Its Reorganization," *ibid.*, XXXIX, 309-317 (Apr., 1945). A more recent general survey is B. Bolles, "Reorganization of the State Department," *Foreign Policy Reports*, XXIII, No. 11 (Aug. 15, 1947).

From the reorganizations of 1944 (and later lesser ones), a further pattern has emerged showing the following principal features: (1) an under-secretary of state, serving as the secretary's deputy in all matters, and during his chief's absence (as in 1946-47, when Secretaries Byrnes and Marshall spent long periods at international conferences in Europe) becoming acting secretary of state; (2) an under-secretary of state for economic affairs, with over-all responsibility for Department policies and actions in the economic field; (3) a battery of six assistant secretaries of state, each supervising a group of departmental agencies of geographical or functional character; (4) a number of specialized officials such as the counselor, the chairman of policy-planning, and the legal adviser; (5) a total of seventeen "divisions," each responsible for some geographical area, each broken down into sections—called "desks"—with appropriate duties assigned, and all grouped under four major geographical "offices" having to do, respectively, with European, Far Eastern, Near Eastern and African, and American Republic affairs; (6) a director-general serving as administrative head of the Foreign Service; and (7) additional offices concerned with broad functional areas such as international trade policy, economic security policy, transport and communications policy, international information and cultural affairs, intelligence coördination and liaison, intelligence collection and dissemination, public affairs, "controls" (passports, visas, etc.), and budget and finance. Even this brief enumeration will suggest the heavy emphasis now placed upon activities of an informational nature—gathering and sifting data concerning conditions, opinion, and policies in foreign countries, research on methods and standards of intelligence analysis, dissemination abroad of information concerning the United States, furtherance of international exchange of persons, knowledge, and skills—ramifying into a dozen fields like the press, publications, maps, radio-broadcasting, motion pictures, libraries, institutes, exchange of professors, specialists, and students, international conferences, cryptography (development and use of codes), and what not. This, indeed, is the side on which, under conditions and needs brought to the fore by the international situation of the past fifteen or twenty years, the work of the Department has in later times been most notably expanded, except only for activities in connection with the United Nations. It has also been the area of most experimentation and change, as the Department—not always fully supported by Congress—has felt its way in the endeavor both to strengthen the position of the United States and to promote the interests of world peace by cultivating wider knowledge and deeper understanding among our own people and the peoples of the world.[1]

---

[1] For a diagram of State Department organization as it stood after the reorganizations of 1944, see *Department of State Bulletin*, XI, 794-795 (Dec. 17, 1944, Supp.). A full up-to-date outline will be found in the most recent issue of the *United States Government Manual*.

The best account of the history and earlier organization of the Department is G.

The Foreign Service

Under our American practice, the president is responsible for carrying on the country's foreign relations; the secretary of state is his operating agent; the Department of State, the staff; and the Foreign Service, the field agency. Policies are framed primarily by the president and Congress, with the assistance of the secretary of state and his organization, and are executed abroad by ambassadors, ministers, consuls, counselors, secretaries, attachés, and other officers and employees, numbering in all at the present time some 11,000. Formerly, the place of the present highly integrated Foreign Service was occupied by two distinct establishments, *i.e.*, diplomatic and consular, each with not only its own functions, but its separate personnel, system of recruiting and promotion, classification, and salary scale; and, however much aptitude a member of one service might show for work of the kind performed by the other, it was almost impossible for him to be transferred. For many years the feeling grew that the wall separating the two services ought to be broken down, and after numerous proposals had fallen by the wayside, the Rogers Act of 1924 accomplished the desired reform.[1] Diplomatic and consular services were consolidated in a single field force known as the "Foreign Service of the United States;" the diplomatic and consular branches of this service were put on an interchangeable basis, so that transfers might be made from one to the other whenever found advantageous; and provision was made for assignment of new recruits to either branch of the service in which they happened at the time to be needed. Between 1927 and 1939, the experiment was tried of having additional "foreign services" representing the Departments of Commerce and Agriculture. Confusion, however, resulted; and in later years there has been only a single unified service, regulated nowadays in great detail by a comprehensive Foreign

Hunt, *The Department of State of the United States* (New Haven, 1914). On the Department in more recent times, see G. H. Stuart, *American Diplomatic and Consular Practice* (New York, 1936), Chaps. v-vi; L. H. Chamberlain and R. C. Snyder, *American Foreign Policy* (New York, 1947), Chap. vii; and books and articles cited on p. 800 below. For a forward-looking interpretation of the Department's rôle in the changed world of our day, see W. H. C. Laves and F. O. Wilcox, "Organizing the Government for Participation in World Affairs," *Amer. Polit. Sci. Rev.*, XXXVIII, 913-930 (Oct., 1944). The management of foreign relations by secretaries of state down to and including Hughes is dealt with by various writers in S. F. Bemis [ed.], *The American Secretaries of State and Their Diplomacy*, 10 vols. (New York, 1927-29).

The Department carries on an extensive program of publication. First of all, there is the weekly *Bulletin* cited, containing texts of documents, press releases, articles of current interest, and much miscellaneous material. There are serial publications embracing large numbers of bulletins, articles, addresses, and reports. Numerous volumes in the series, *Foreign Relations of the United States*, present selected official papers covering the period from 1861 to the point reached at any given time in the compilation—which at the beginning of 1938 was 1931. In addition, there are special collections, notably on World Wars I and II, the Paris Peace Conference, Russian relations, and Japan. Full lists are obtainable from the Department.

[1] 43 *U. S. Stat. at Large*, 140. See T. Lay, "Foreign Service Reorganization," *Amer. Polit. Sci. Rev.*, XVIII, 697-711 (Nov., 1924).

Service Act of 1946.[1] Under this legislation, the service is administered by a director-general heading an Office of Foreign Service in the State Department, and assisted principally by (1) a board of foreign service (consisting of three assistant secretaries of state, with representatives also of the Departments of Commerce, Labor, and Agriculture, and (2) a board of examiners functioning in connection with recruiting. And personnel is graded into (1) chiefs of mission (ambassadors and ministers), in four ranks or classes on salary levels ranging from $15,000 to $25,000; (2) foreign service officers, in seven classes, with salaries varying from $3,300 to $13,500; (3) foreign service reserve officers (usually specialists), in six classes, with the same scale of salaries; and (4) foreign service staff officers and employees, in twenty-two classes, with compensation ranging from as low as $1,080 to a top figure of $8,820.[2]

Per-
sonnel:

1. The
merit
system

Like other government establishments, the diplomatic and consular services suffered in earlier days from the spoils system; men of ability and experience were sometimes carefully selected for given positions, especially more responsible ones, but by and large appointments were likely to reflect mere personal or political favoritism. In 1895, President Cleveland introduced the rudiments of a merit system in the consular service, and in 1906 President Theodore Roosevelt instituted a plan of competitive examinations and efficiency ratings for the appointment and promotion of consuls of all grades, including consuls-general. In 1909, President Taft started a scheme of competitive examinations in the lower grades of the diplomatic service, with provision for efficiency records as a basis for promotion. This, however, did not affect the members of the service above the rank of secretary, who, accordingly, seldom long outlived the Administrations that appointed them and rarely or never survived a change of the party in power. Furthermore, in both services the reforms rested until 1915 only on executive orders, not on statute. Here again the legislation of 1924 made notable advances, considerably extending the merit system in the newly consolidated service; and later legislation, including the Moses-Linthicum Act of 1931,[3] carried the reform to a point where nowadays recruitment, up to the level of chiefs of mission, is almost entirely on merit principles.

2. Exam-
inations
and
appoint-
ments

Foreign service reserve officers (appointed on only a temporary basis) and foreign service staff officers and employees are not subjected to formal examination. For admission to the more basic category of foreign

---

[1] 60 *U. S. Stat. at Large,* 999. The text of the act, with a good deal of general information, will be found in *The Foreign Service of the United States* (Washington, D. C., Govt. Prtg. Office, 1947); also in J. R. Childs, *American Foreign Service* (New York, 1948), 157-211.

[2] Salaries are supplemented by fairly generous cost-of-living and other special allowances, applicable under widely varying conditions in different parts of the service; and pensions are paid from a retirement and disability fund to which members of the service contribute five per cent of their salaries.

[3] 46 *U. S. Stat. at Large,* 1207.

service officer, however, competitive written and oral examinations are required in all except a few special instances; and the examinations are of such nature that only well-trained college graduates, or persons of equivalent attainments, can hope to pass them. As a rule, the written tests, covering four general and four special fields, and conducted by the Civil Service Commission for the board of examiners, are held in September at various places throughout the country, are taken by from six to eight hundred young men and women, and are successfully passed by from sixty to one hundred; while of the latter number, the rigorous orals conducted the following January in Washington by the board of examiners itself, and stressing character, personality, experience, and proficiency in modern languages, usually eliminate all but twenty-five or thirty.[1] Candidates must be between the ages of twenty-one and thirty, citizens of the United States, and previously designated by the board of examiners for a particular examination. Women are eligible, and since 1922 a few not only have met the tests employed, but later have received appointment. All successful candidates are recommended by the examiners for appointment to the lowest class in the foreign-service-officer bracket (under exceptional conditions, to the next higher class), their names being placed on an eligible list from which the president makes nominations to the Senate as required; and the usual routine is for an appointee to be given a preliminary or preparatory term of a few months as salaried vice-consul at some near-by post (e.g., Mexico City or Ottawa), then to receive some months of intensive instruction in a Foreign Service Institute operated in the State Department at Washington,[2] and only afterwards to be given regular assignment as a full-fledged foreign service officer. Such assignment may carry the title of minister, counselor, first, second, or third secretary, consul-general, consul, or vice-consul, and indeed the appointee is usually commissioned both a diplomatic and a consular officer. All examinations being designed to test intelligence and capacity as well as present knowledge, foreign service appointees are expected to demonstrate fitness to advance from grade to grade; and promotions are based upon merit, with minimum periods of service in each particular grade.[3]

[1] Not only because of this heavy mortality among candidates, but because of the uncertainty of eventual appointment and the possibility of assignment to a succession of unattractive posts, students should very carefully weigh the hazards before deciding, as many ill-advisedly do, to go in for a "foreign service career."

[2] There is also in Washington, closely affiliated with the Department of State but not included in it, a School of Advanced International Studies and Foreign Service Training, established in 1944 to provide advanced instruction for persons looking to employment abroad either by the government or by private industry.

[3] Under regulations dating from 1926, ministers, consuls, and other persons belonging to the Foreign Service may be called to Washington to serve (not to exceed four years) as assistant secretaries or in other posts in which they can give the Department the benefit of their first-hand experience abroad; and, similarly, higher Department officials at Washington may be assigned to duty for limited periods at foreign posts.

Although forming parts of the Foreign Service in the broader sense, ministers and ambassadors [1] are outside the scope of the merit system as described, and are still appointed by the president and Senate on grounds in which political and personal considerations, *e.g.*, reward for party service and for contributing generously to campaign funds, may weigh heavily. Tenure, too, is uncertain, and sometimes brief, especially if the party to which the incumbent belongs soon goes out of power. To be sure, the Rogers Act and the more recent Foreign Service Act of 1946 have as one of their objectives the encouragement of young men of ambition and talent to make the foreign service a career, and to that end both statutes require the secretary of state to give the president from time to time the names of members of the service who have demonstrated their fitness for promotion to the grade of minister; and in recent years a gratifying number of such promotions have been made. Until of late, an obstacle of considerable seriousness arose from restriction of salaries to a range between $10,000 and $17,500, with the result of numerous posts being practically beyond the reach of persons not of independent means.[2] Under the Foreign Service Act of 1946, however, the range is $15,000 to $25,000; and although the increase by no means enables all chiefs of mission to live within their stipends, the situation is better than formerly. There is advantage in a system flexible enough to permit the president to choose our highest diplomatic officers from men of standing and achievement in all professions and fields, and some of our ablest and most successful representatives abroad have been persons without previous diplomatic training or experience. But, also, it is pleasing to know that the rank and file of the service is now so improved that the chief executive cannot find excuse for failing to draw from the "career men" in it with increasing frequency. By and large, our consular establishment has long been as efficient as any in the world. Notwithstanding shining exceptions, our diplomatic service has, in times past, ranked rather low. In so far, however, as our presidents, resisting personal and party pressures, henceforth succeed in filling ministerial and ambassadorial positions, not

---

[1] An ambassador outranks a minister, but is not otherwise different. Historically, "embassies" headed by ambassadors were maintained in the larger foreign countries and "legations" headed by ministers in the smaller ones. In 1893, however, we began sending an ambassador to any country, large or small, that sent one to us; we now have ambassadors in all of the American Republics (even El Salvador and Panama); and nowadays there is no necessary relation between the size or importance of a country and the rank of the diplomatic representative we send to it.

[2] Charles G. Dawes has testified that it cost him $75,000 a year to serve the country as ambassador at London, and John W. Davis that even under careful management the same position cost him between $50,000 and $60,000 a year. The late Professor William E. Dodd of the University of Chicago, appointed ambassador to Germany by President Roosevelt in 1933, seems, however, to have demonstrated over a period of years that, even in a major post, an American envoy *could* live on the salary formerly provided. Even before later revision of the salary scale, the situation was helped materially by a fairly generous system of rent allowances, post allowances equalizing the cost of living at exceptionally expensive posts, pay adjustments in instances where the conditions of exchange would seriously impair the value of the regular official salary, "representation allowances" covering part of the cost of entertainment, and a good system of retirement allowances.

with political appointees, but with men who either have come up with distinction through the secretaryships, counselorships, and similar offices or have attained equally desirable qualifications by experience in other fields, an ancient ground of reproach will have been removed; and it is gratifying to be able to record that of the two score ambassadorial posts which we maintained in 1941, ten were held by career men, and of the thirty ministerial posts, fifteen. In June, 1947, when we maintained forty-four ambassadorial posts (an ambassador to Pakistan has since been added) and twenty ministerial posts,[1] some sixty per cent of the incumbents were appointees from the career service. The commanding position that our nation has gained since 1917 and the ever-growing complexity of our relations abroad, both in peacetime and in wartime, demand not only an extensive but a strong foreign service—strong at the top no less than at the bottom. Appropriately enough, the Foreign Service has been termed our first line of defense.

Asked to indicate the functions of an American diplomatic representative in a foreign country, one might list the more important of them somewhat as follows: (1) to convey messages and inquiries from the home to the foreign government, and to transmit information and replies in return; (2) to cultivate friendly relations with the authorities of the foreign state and keep the way open for prompt and amicable adjustment of controversies; (3) to negotiate agreements and treaties, alone or in collaboration with specially appointed commissioners, and under instructions from the secretary of state; (4) to keep the secretary of state, and through him the president, informed on political conditions and trends abroad, and especially on international developments; (5) to watch legislation and other governmental actions in the foreign state, and make inquiry or lodge complaint if American treaty rights are threatened; and (6) to be of assistance to resident or traveling fellow-citizens, in ways that often tax both ingenuity and patience.[2] Naturally, the burden of responsibility will be heavier in some capitals than in others, and at times of international tension than in days of peaceful routine. But it is never light; and no mere cataloguing of duties, in the foregoing manner, can give a complete measure of it.[3] Associated with each chief of mission abroad is a staff of secretaries, clerks, and interpreters, among whom front rank is taken by the first secretary of embassy (or legation, as the case may be)—a man who must always be qualified to serve as

Diplomatic functions

---

[1] Including three more or less temporarily closed.

[2] Before the outbreak of war in Europe in September, 1939, nearly 400,000 United States citizens resided abroad permanently or substantially so—mainly of course for business purposes.

[3] Exceptionally realistic portrayals of what it means to be an American ambassador to an important country will be found in B. J. Hendrick, *Life and Letters of Walter H. Page* (New York, 1923-24), especially I, 159-161, and W. E. and M. Dodd, *Ambassador Dodd's Diary* (New York, 1941). A full general discussion will be found in J. R. Childs, *American Foreign Service* (New York, 1948), Chaps. VII-XII; and cf. G. H. Stuart, *op. cit.*, Chaps. VII-XVI, a book now being brought up to date.

chargé d'affaires during the absence of his superior or when there is a vacancy.

Consular functions

The primary function of the American consular officer, at least historically, is to promote the interests of American trade abroad; and to this end he observes and reports on economic conditions in his territory, watches for new and larger openings for American goods, sends back information on the most advantageous forms of advertising and the best methods of packing and shipping commodities, and puts himself at the service of the American manufacturer, shipper, or commercial traveler engaged in studying the foreign market on the spot. This, however, is only part of the story. In addition, (1) he certifies the invoices of goods intended for shipment to the United States, and otherwise assists in the administration of our tariff laws; (2) he acts as paymaster (for civilian purposes) of the American government abroad, and also as tax-collector, *e.g.*, in connection with the federal income tax; (3) under certain conditions, he cares for the estates of Americans who die abroad; (4) he witnesses marriage ceremonies when one of the parties is an American citizen; (5) he decides disputes between masters, officers, and men on American ships, provides for stranded seamen, and may discharge seamen from their contracts; (6) he inspects and approves the passports of aliens intending to come to the United States, thus helping enforce our immigration laws; (7) he serves as peacetime business agent in securing fuel and stores for American ships; and, in general, (8) he acts as "guide, philosopher, and friend" to traveling fellow-countrymen. Far less in the public eye than the minister or ambassador, the consular official penetrates corners of the earth where diplomacy rarely or never reaches and is easily the most valuable sort of general utility man that modern government and business have developed.[1]

The President and Foreign Relations

With the Foreign Service as its field organization, the Department of State is the president's regular agency for carrying on our official dealings with foreign governments. Whatever it does is done in the president's name; and we now turn more directly to some activities for which the chief executive, as thus assisted, is responsible.

[1] Consular officers are of various grades—consul-general (in charge of all our consulates in a country), consul, vice-consul, and consular agent. In 1947, we had consular officers in about 250 cities throughout the world. On the prewar consular service, see G. H. Stuart, *op. cit.*, Chaps. XVII-XXI.

Of course, by no means all of our dealings with foreign governments are carried on through the Foreign Service machinery described. As indicated above, other departments besides State have agents functioning abroad; the president often employs special emissaries; and under varying arrangements we participate, through the medium of delegates, councillors, commissioners, and what not, in all sorts of international organizations, from the United Nations down. For a list of these latter organizations, see *United States Government Manual* (2nd ed. revised through June 1, 1947), 113-114; and, with descriptive comment, *International Agencies in Which the United States Participates* (Washington, D. C., 1947), a volume prepared by the Department of State.

In the first place, the president is the official channel of intercourse between our government and governments abroad. On the one hand, subject to the Senate's right of confirmation, he appoints all ambassadors and ministers to foreign countries, and all other foreign service officials (including consuls) stationed therein, with, of course, the full power of direction and removal which the appointing power entails. Indeed, in the belief that they can accomplish more by informal contacts than can be achieved through the formal channels of diplomacy, he may employ "special," "secret," or "personal" agents abroad, who, not being technically public officers, require no senatorial confirmation, and who commonly receive their pay, if any, out of a presidential "contingent fund." [1] Conversely, he receives, on his own responsibility, all foreign ambassadors and other public ministers, with power also, if occasion requires, to break off dealings with them and in effect send them home. Through the State Department, he carries on correspondence abroad, obtaining information, declaring policy, pressing claims, offering settlements, and replying to all manner of inquiries and proposals. Congress, on its part, may not address any foreign power or receive any communication from one; and any private citizen or corporation undertaking, "directly or indirectly,...to carry on verbal or written correspondence or intercourse with any foreign government or its officers or agents [without express authority from the president] designed to influence the measures or conduct of any foreign government...in relation to any disputes or controversies with the United States or to defeat the measures of the government of the United States," becomes liable to penalty.[2] While,

[1] Many times the activities of such agents prove quite as important as those of regular ministers and ambassadors, as, for example, were those of Nicholas Trist in negotiating peace with Mexico in 1848, of Commodore Perry in getting our first treaty with Japan in 1854, and of Colonel E. M. House as roving special emissary of President Wilson in Europe during World War I. Both Presidents Hoover and Franklin D. Roosevelt employed the late Norman H. Davis as an "ambassador-at-large," charged with attending conferences, carrying on discussions, and in general sounding out European authorities on the subjects of disarmament and collective security. From 1940, Myron C. Taylor has appeared intermittently at the Vatican (with which the United States does not maintain regular diplomatic relations) as special representative of the president charged with promoting the interests of peace. Harry Hopkins was dispatched to Great Britain in 1941 to obtain information concerning that country's war needs; and the late Wendell L. Willkie, during a visit to London early in 1941 and later wartime visits to Russia, China, and other lands, executed commissions given him by President Roosevelt. From 1945 until he returned to the United States in 1947 to become secretary of state, General George C. Marshall was occupied in China as a special agent of President Truman in an effort to bring about a reconciliation between Chiang Kai-shek and the Communists. In 1947, indeed, a president employed a predecessor as special agent when Truman sent Herbert Hoover to Germany to investigate the food needs of the population and recommend means of meeting them.

[2] This provision relating to individual activities is quoted from the Logan Act of 1799 (U. S. Code, Title 18, § 5) and was prompted by unauthorized efforts of a Dr. Logan of Philadelphia in Paris to avert threatened war between Napoleon and the United States. When, in 1947, former Vice-President Henry A. Wallace—stoutly opposing President Truman's policy of aiding Greece and Turkey in warding off threatened Communist dominance, and charging that the country's foreign policy in general was pointed toward war—visited Great Britain, France, and other European countries and there gave full expression to his views, strong feeling was aroused in

however, normally using the State Department as his channel, to such a degree that, as we have seen, even foreign governments must ordinarily address the White House not directly but only through the Department, the president may nevertheless go as far as he likes in handling matters directly and personally—even to the extent of managing the country's foreign relations practically from his own desk, as did President Wilson during World War I; or going abroad to lead in the negotiation of a great international settlement, as did the same chief executive when peace was to be made in 1919; or meeting and conferring with representatives of foreign governments at any places selected for the purpose, as President Franklin D. Roosevelt repeatedly met and conferred with Prime Minister Churchill and Marshal Stalin (and on one occasion with President Chiang Kai-shek) during World War II.[1]

2. Recognition

From authority to speak for the nation in its dealings abroad springs a second significant presidential function, i.e., that of determining the attitude to be taken by our government toward newly risen states or newly risen political régimes in existing states. As to who is to decide whether we shall officially "recognize" and have dealings with such states and régimes or, on the other hand, shall simply ignore them, the constitution is silent; and at various times it has been argued that Congress is entitled to participate along with the president. International usage, however, makes the function strictly an executive one; the power to appoint and receive envoys would certainly make it such in the United States; and precedent, backed by judicial opinion, places it wholly in the president's hands, subject only to the discretion of the Senate in confirming diplomatic appointments and assenting to treaties, and to that of both houses in voting foreign service appropriations. Recognition may take the form of welcoming into the family of nations (so far as we can do it by our own action) a state that has lately asserted its independence—as President Monroe, after 1817, recognized a number of newly risen Latin American republics, or as President Theodore Roosevelt in 1903 recognized the republic of Panama, thereby paving the way for the construction of the Panama Canal; and the usual method in such instances is to

---

the United States and there was talk of invoking the Logan Act against him. His activities, however, while of dubious propriety, hardly fell within the scope and intent of the measure, and no official action was taken.

[1] In August and September, 1940, President Roosevelt directly and personally carried on discussions (using trans-Atlantic telephone when necessary) with Prime Minister Churchill looking to the exchange of American over-age destroyers for leases of sites for American naval bases in British possessions in the Western Hemisphere. About the same time, he more than once talked at the White House with Prime Minister King about United States-Canadian coöperation on defense plans. In August, 1941, he met Churchill on the high seas, discussed with him the war situation and the problems of American assistance to Britain, and joined with him in promulgating the Atlantic Charter embodying principles to be adhered to in establishing a new world order after the end of hostilities. On several later occasions, Roosevelt and Churchill met in Washington or Quebec, and three times during the war the President crossed the Atlantic for conferences, on one occasion traveling as far as Teheran, and on another (including the Yalta conference of February, 1945) absenting himself from the country some five weeks).

send and receive diplomatic representatives. Or recognition may take the form of instituting official relations with a new political régime that has taken over in a given country, as when, in 1928, President Coolidge recognized the Nationalist government set up by the Kuomintang in China by concluding a treaty with it, or when, after the U. S. S. R. had waited sixteen years for American recognition, President Roosevelt, in 1933, invited President Kalinin, of the All-Union Central Executive Committee at Moscow, to send a representative to Washington for conference, and followed by concluding a treaty with the emissary, Foreign Commissar Litvinov.[1] Manifestly, the power to recognize carries with it also the power to refuse to recognize; and students of our diplomatic history will recall how President Wilson, in 1915, became primarily responsible for the downfall of the revolutionary president Huerta in Mexico by refusing to have any dealings with the régime which he headed; how Presidents Hoover and Roosevelt stirred Japanese animosity by refusing to recognize the pseudo-state of Manchukuo; and how President Truman, in 1945-46, refused to recognize Communist-dominated governments in Bulgaria, Romania, and Yugoslavia, even though to a degree he was compelled to back down from the position taken. The power of recognition is one to be employed with particular caution, especially when the interests of some strong nation are likely to be affected adversely. If exercised merely to express official acceptance of international situations or facts palpably existing, it cannot properly be challenged. Recognition extended, however, before facts exist is premature and may lead to threat of war.[2]

"Under our system of government," the courts have declared, "the citizen abroad is as much entitled to protection as the citizen at home;"[3] and it falls to the president, as chief executive and director of our foreign relations, to see that such protection is duly extended, whether on the basis of treaty provisions usually covering such matters or otherwise. If an American sojourning in a foreign land or traveling on the high seas is mistreated and cannot obtain justice, the president, acting through the State Department, may make demands in his behalf, and may go to any length short of a declaration of war to obtain redress for him.[4] Similarly, it is the president's duty—up to the limits of national authority—to see that protection is extended to aliens legally domiciled in the United States. He must execute all provisions of the constitution, the national laws, and treaties bearing on their rights; and while he has no way of compelling

3. Protection of citizens abroad and of alien residents

---

[1] Still another form of recognition presents itself when, an insurrection having arisen in a country, the president officially acknowledges the insurgency, or even the belligerency, of the insurrectionists by giving them (so far as the United States is concerned) certain rights which they would not have as mere rebels. President Cleveland thus recognized a state of insurgency in Cuba in 1895.

[2] On recognition in general, see E. S. Corwin, *The President's Control of Foreign Relations*, 71-83; J. M. Mathews, *American Foreign Relations; Conduct and Policies* (rev. ed.), Chap. xxi; and references cited on p. 800 below.

[3] Durand *v.* Hollins, Fed. Cas. No. 4186 (1860).

[4] E. M. Borchard, *The Diplomatic Protection of Citizens Abroad* (new ed., New York, 1927).

state authorities to extend protection in matters, like property-holding, outside the scope of national jurisdiction, he may admonish them to be mindful of alien rights and may instruct district attorneys to lend aliens needed legal aid. In time of war abroad, he may be of assistance to both aliens and citizens by issuing a proclamation of neutrality calling attention to rules of international law and to statutes forbidding various unneutral acts. When the United States is itself at war, however, the rights of aliens of enemy nationality become merely such as international law recognizes in situations of the kind, and the president is not obligated beyond that point.[1]

Treaties and Executive Agreements

The functions thus far reviewed belong to the president quite independently, or at all events are subject to only indirect and limited control by the legislative branch.[2] We come now to two others, of major importance, which again are primarily presidential, yet are also shared to a considerably greater extent by the Senate or by Congress as a whole— (1) treaty-making and (2) shaping foreign policy.

Treaty-making A main instrumentality for regulating and stabilizing international relations is treaties; and the constitution provides that the president "shall have power, by and with the advice and consent of the Senate, to make treaties, provided two-thirds of the senators present concur."[3] Under the Articles of Confederation, Congress made treaties; and the framers of the constitution at first thought of giving the power to the Senate. As, however, the concept of the presidency grew in their minds, the opinion developed that it would be better to assign treaty-making, along with the general management of the country's foreign relations, to the chief executive, associating with him the Senate as an advising and restraining council. The House of Representatives was deliberately omitted from the plan in the interest of "secrecy and dispatch;" and the assent of two-thirds, rather than a simple majority, of the Senate was provided for in order to prevent treaties being made too lightly, and also, and mainly, as a matter of political compromise, to give sectional interests like the New England fisheries added protection against being "sold out."[4]

Presidential initiative The language of the constitution clearly associates the Senate with the president throughout the entire process of concluding and ratifying a treaty; and not only do passages in *The Federalist* indicate that this is what the framers had in mind, but President Washington actually began his treaty-making (with the Southern Indians in 1789) on that basis. A

---

[1] See pp. 139-140 above.

[2] Through its right to confirm nominations to the posts of ambassador and minister, the Senate, to be sure, has some potential control over the channels of diplomacy. But such nominations are almost invariably confirmed.

[3] Art. II, § 2, cl. 2.

[4] R. E. McClendon, "Origin of the Two-Thirds Rule in Senate Action on Treaties," *Amer. Hist. Rev.*, XXXVI, 768-772 (July, 1931).

few years of experience demonstrated, however, that it was more practical and expeditious for the president to "make" the treaty and to seek the Senate's "advice and consent" only afterwards—such consent being simply to a final act of ratification to be performed by the president and making the instrument effective so far as our own government is concerned.[1] To be sure, either branch of Congress, or the two concurrently, may, by resolution, advise or request that a given treaty, or series of treaties, be negotiated; and the president may, in advance or during the course of a negotiation, consult with individual senators, or even the Senate as a whole.[2] But unless the chief executive chooses to set the necessary machinery in motion, no negotiation can be started; he can begin a negotiation regardless of the desire (and even without the knowledge) of either branch of Congress; and rarely indeed is the Senate as a body given any chance to express itself on a proposed treaty until the completed instrument is transmitted to it. Short of flatly withholding

---

[1] On the way in which our treaty-making authority "split into two authorities," see E. S. Corwin, in J. B. Whitton [ed.], *The Second Chance; America and the Peace* (Princeton, N. J., 1944), 143-150.

[2] There are only about a dozen instances in which the Senate as a whole has been so consulted, one of them involving President Polk's securing from the Senate in 1846 of a promise in advance to assent to a convention with Great Britain settling the question of the Oregon boundary; and commonly the president shows much more eagerness to avoid senatorial obstruction than to obtain senatorial advice. On the unpleasant outcome of Washington's attempt to consult with the Senate orally on his Indian treaty, see D. F. Fleming, *The Treaty Veto of the American Senate* (New York, 1930), 16-21. As a matter of expediency, the president and secretary of state usually keep in close touch with at least the members of the Senate foreign relations committee when an important negotiation is in progress, sounding out sentiment in this way on pending proposals and ascertaining how far it is safe or wise to go in this direction or that—a precaution the more necessary because, under the two-thirds rule, a treaty will usually have to have the support of members of both political parties. The president may, indeed, make one or more senators members of a negotiating commission. Thus, three of the five commissioners appointed by President McKinley to negotiate a treaty of peace with Spain in 1898 were senators, one of them being chairman of the foreign relations committee. Two of the four commissioners who, on behalf of the United States, signed the naval limitation treaty concluded with Great Britain, France, Italy, and Japan at the Washington Conference of 1921-22 were senators, one of them again being the chairman of the foreign relations committee. Two of the five commissioners who signed the London Naval Treaty of 1930 were members of the upper house, and so were two of the American delegates to the ill-fated World Monetary and Economic Conference at London in 1933. One will recall also the prominent rôle of two members of the Senate committee on foreign relations, Senators Connally and Vandenberg, not only in framing the Charter of the United Nations at San Francisco in 1945, but in subsequent meetings associated with that organization, as well as in conferences in which the American secretary of state met in Paris and elsewhere with the foreign ministers of the United Nations. President Wilson was widely criticized because he did not include one or two senators in the commission which represented the United States in negotiating the Treaty of Versailles in 1919; and the outcome showed that he at least could not have lost anything by doing so. On the other hand, it should be noted that the plan of including senators in commissions to negotiate treaties has been opposed vigorously, both in the Senate and outside, on the ground that it puts the senatorial members in the position of helping formulate proposals which they will be expected to pass upon later as members of a separate branch of the government, and also on the ground that it is incompatible with at least the spirit of the constitutional stipulation that "no person holding any office under the United States shall be a member of either house during his continuance in office" (Art. I, § 6, cl. 2)—although membership in an international conference can be construed as not properly an "office." Cf. D. F. Fleming, *op. cit.*, 27-32.

assent to ratification, the most that the senators can then do by way of indicating disapproval is to attach amendments making it necessary for the president to renew negotiations with a view to securing the foreign government's acceptance of the proposed changes; or, in the case of a great multilateral agreement on which negotiations could not well be reopened, to assent to ratification but attach reservations designating various features of the agreement as not to be held binding on the United States. In exercising his powers of initiative and direction, the president may work through the rgular diplomatic representative accredited to the foreign government concerned; or he may appoint a special plenipotentiary or commission to go abroad for the purpose; again, he may cause the negotiation to be carried on in Washington through the secretary of state; or, finally, he may undertake, or at least participate in, the negotiation himself, as did President Wilson in connection with the Treaty of Versailles in 1919. When the treaty is completed, he, furthermore, has full freedom to submit it to the Senate, return it to the negotiators for revision, or drop it altogether. He may hold it back because he considers it unsatisfactory, or because he recognizes that submission of it to the Senate would be useless.

The Senate's share in the treaty process

"A treaty entering the Senate," wrote John Hay after six years of experience as secretary of state, "is like a bull going into the arena; no one can say just how or when the final blow will fall—but one thing is certain—it will never leave the arena alive." [1] This statement is much too strong, as is evidenced by two or three major facts: (1) no treaty was rejected outright by the Senate until 1824; (2) the total number so rejected throughout the history of the country to 1935 is only sixty-two; [2] and (3) while the Senate either failed to act upon, or insisted on amendments or reservations to, 152 treaties (to the date mentioned), it unconditionally approved some nine hundred, or more than four-fifths of the entire number presented to it.[3] Quite a number of treaties slip through

[1] W. R. Thayer, *Life and Letters of John Hay* (Boston, 1920), II, 393. Under Senate Rule XXXVI, a treaty received from the president is given a first reading, referred to a committee (naturally that on foreign relations), reported back with or without amendment, considered in committee of the whole (as pointed out elsewhere, this is now the only use made of committee of the whole in Senate practice), reported from committee of the whole to the Senate with or without amendment, and brought to a final vote in the form of a resolution assenting to ratification. Until 1929, the entire procedure was shrouded in secrecy. Not only were all members pledged to divulge nothing concerning a treaty's contents or committee discussions of them, but whenever the project was being considered on the floor the public was rigorously excluded from the galleries. Even yet, there is a certain presumption of secrecy, in that it is to be observed at all stages unless the injunction is expressly removed by Senate action. Since the date mentioned, however (see p. 368 above), it has been customary for treaty discussions to proceed in public. In any event, a treaty is considered only in *executive* session—either "open" or "closed;" and decision to go into open session may come at any stage of the proceedings.

[2] More than one hundred others, however, were so amended that either our own government or the other party (or parties) concerned chose not to go through with them.

[3] D. F. Fleming, "The Rôle of the Senate in Treaty-Making," *Amer. Polit. Sci. Rev.*, XXVIII, 583 (Aug., 1934). In a period of less than six years (Dec., 1924, to

with no opposition at all. Those that stir controversy, however, encounter a genuine hurdle in the two-thirds rule; and it must be admitted that of the treaties that have come to grief in this way a large proportion have been of first-rate importance, *e.g.*, the treaty for the annexation of Texas in 1844, the Olney-Pauncefote, Hay, and Taft-Knox arbitration treaties of 1897, 1904, and 1911-12, the Treaty of Versailles in 1920, the St. Lawrence Waterway Treaty of 1934, and the protocol for adherence to the Permanent Court of International Justice (World Court) in 1926 and 1935; and, further, that many which finally emerge triumphant do so only after a great parliamentary battle, calling into play every sort of pressure from the White House. In numerous instances, too,—beginning with the Jay Treaty in 1794—the Senate's consent to ratification has been qualified by reservations, amendments, and interpretations entailing changes which, if either the president or the foreign government was unwilling to accept them, had the effect of killing the treaty. Arbitration treaties were blocked in this way in 1904 and 1912; likewise the protocol for adherence to the Permanent Court of International Justice in 1926.

At any time while a treaty is pending in the Senate, the president may recall it, either because circumstances have so changed that he no longer favors it or because he perceives that it is doomed to defeat. Even after the Senate has given its consent, a treaty may be held up. It remains for the president to ratify, and, upon being apprised of ratification by the other government (or governments), to promulgate it; and he has the option of refusing to take these final necessary steps, although naturally he will do so only under very unusual circumstances.

For a hundred years or more, the treaty procedure outlined served, on the whole, acceptably. In later days, however, it has given rise to a great deal of dissatisfaction. To begin with, the two-thirds rule, although conceded to have been perhaps defensible under eighteenth-century conditions, is alleged to be out of harmony with our present-day democracy, based as it is upon the principle of government by simple majority.[1] A second objection often voiced is that the rule makes it too easy for special interests to hold up or defeat a treaty to which they take exception. Inasmuch, also, as a very large proportion of senators are elected by predominantly rural populations in thinly peopled agricultural states, the great weight assigned to the Senate in treaty-making gives, in the opinion of some, too much power in this particular domain to populations remote

Dissatisfaction with the existing system

Aug., 1930), the Senate assented to the ratification of 106 treaties, with forty-one different nations. During a day in June, 1934, it approved twelve in a single hour.

[1] Forty-nine senators constitute a quorum with power of life and death over a treaty; seventeen of the forty-nine could prevent a two-thirds majority being obtained; and the seventeen could come from states which by the 1940 census contained only about three per cent of the country's population. No treaty is likely ever to fail because of being opposed by simply the least populous states. It is an historical fact, however, that on one occasion adherence to the World Court was defeated by senators representing decidedly less than one-third of the national population.

from the coasts and more or less provincial in outlook. Yet another complaint is that the House of Representatives is placed in the awkward position of being practically obliged to vote appropriations, and sometimes enact legislation, for putting treaties into effect, although powerless over the making and ratifying of them.[1] Finally may be mentioned the ground-swell of criticism traceable since 1920 to the conviction of many that but for the obstructionist attitude of a Senate minority, the United States would, as a member of the League of Nations and adherent of the World Court, have contributed to international coöperation a degree of vigor that might possibly have changed the entire course of world events in the past unhappy decade.

Proposed
changes

There are, of course, those who would leave matters as they are; and they undoubtedly include a substantial majority of the senators themselves. But a heavy proportion of people who have thought seriously about the subject favor one or the other of two principal proposed changes, *i.e.*, (1) to empower the Senate to assent to the ratification of treaties by simple majority (either of those present or of the total membership) instead of two-thirds, and (2) to make ratification contingent on the assent of such majorities (again either of those present or of the total membership) in *both houses*. Notwithstanding that the latter plan might prove responsible for a good deal of deadlock and delay, it probably is preferable; although neither could be adopted without a constitutional amendment, which, requiring as it would a self-effacing two-thirds vote in the Senate, would be exceedingly difficult to obtain.[2]

Execution and termination of treaties

Once duly ratified by the governments concerned and proclaimed by the president, a treaty becomes, from the international point of view, a contract between the United States and the nation or nations constituting the other parties, and from the domestic point of view, an addition to the law of the land, supreme and enforceable like any other portion of that law. The courts, both federal and state, must give it full effect. Of

---

[1] On this ground, the House early set up a claim to a share in the treaty-making power. In his message on the Jay Treaty in 1796, Washington, however, urged that after a treaty has been duly ratified, Congress is morally, if not legally, obligated to take any action required for enabling the commitments under it to be lived up to; and although the issue was revived in connection with the Treaty of Ghent in 1814 and the treaty for the purchase of Alaska in 1867, the principle thus laid down has consistently prevailed.

[2] Many amendment proposals have been introduced, and in 1945 one of the number, motivated especially at that time by desire to ease the way for American adherence to the contemplated United Nations organization, and in its final form providing for assent to treaty ratifications by majority vote of the total membership in each house, passed the House of Representatives by the requisite two-thirds, without, however, even getting out of the judiciary committee in the Senate. A method already employed roughly approximates the proposed plan in that large matters which very well might have been cast in treaty form are sometimes handled instead as ordinary legislation (bill or joint resolution), requiring only the normal majorities in the two houses. It was thus that Texas and Hawaii were annexed in 1845 and 1898, respectively, and that war with the Central Powers was officially terminated in 1921.

The relations of the president and Senate in treaty-making are discussed at length in W. W. Willoughby, *Constitutional Law of the United States* (2nd ed.), I, Chaps. XXXIII-XXXVI, and in the books by Mathews, Colegrove, Fleming, Wright, Dangerfield, and Holt listed on pp. 799-800 below.

course, not all treaties are, or are intended to be, permanent. Some expressly provide for their own expiration; some are terminated by war; some are replaced by new agreements; some are abrogated by being "denounced" by one or more of the parties. When it is desired in this country to dispense with a treaty, or some portion thereof, our government is likely to seek an agreement to that end with any nation, or nations, concerned. In default of such agreement, however, the president may, on his own authority, simply proclaim the treaty at an end; or he may take such action with the support of a joint resolution of Congress; or Congress itself may make any of the treaty's provisions of no legal effect by enacting legislation inconsistent with them. Although treaties are "law of the land," the Supreme Court has said that they are no more truly such than are acts passed by Congress. Invariably the Court has been reluctant to construe a statute as in violation of a treaty; but when there is manifest conflict, the later in date prevails.[1] Neither a court decision nor a statute can, however, abrogate a treaty as an international contract. Although rendered unenforceable domestically by such means, a treaty preserves its international status until revoked by executive action; and in the meantime the foreign power may construe an adverse judicial decision or statute as a breach of contract entitling it to reparation through an international proceeding.

Often enough, a treaty is of such a nature as to require legislation to make its provisions effective. Can a treaty be made a means of conferring on Congress legislative power not otherwise possessed? Not if one accepts the view of Thomas Jefferson, who contended that the constitutional provision on treaty-making merely sets forth a procedure for exercising granted powers and is not itself a substantive grant. The Supreme Court, however, has ruled differently. In a case decided in 1920, it held that the treaty-making power is a distinct grant of authority to the national government, and broad enough to be applicable to all subjects of national concern and capable of being handled only by international negotiation;[2] from which it follows that federal legislation in pursuance of treaty provisions may properly extend to matters otherwise exceeding congressional competence, even to such as fall clearly within the reserved (including police) powers of the states. In point of fact, legislation of this character has many times been enacted and enforced.

Can treaties confer legislative powers?

Treaties can be ratified and become operative only with the advice and consent of the Senate. But, as already has appeared, not every agreement entered into with a foreign government takes the form of a treaty. Increasing numbers, instead, are "executive agreements," for which—notwithstanding that there is no mention of them in the constitution, and that as a rule they are to all intents and purposes treaties—consent of a two-

Executive agreements

---

[1] Chinese Exclusion Cases, 130 U. S. 581 (1889).

[2] State of Missouri *v.* Holland, 252 U. S. 416 (1920). This decision upheld a statute enacted in pursuance of a treaty with Canada for protection of migratory birds.

thirds senatorial majority is neither sought nor obtained.[1] In some cases, *e.g.*, postal conventions and trade agreements, the "lend-lease" agreements of the recent war period also), such agreements rest upon authority conferred in advance by blanket act of Congress.[2] Many of them, however, are concluded by the president (directly or through agents) without such authorization—sometimes in pursuance of a treaty, sometimes as commander-in-chief of the armed forces, and occasionally purely as chief executive and supreme representative of the country for direct official dealings with foreign states. And if they are submitted on Capitol Hill for approval at all, it is simply to the two houses for majority action. Furthermore, not only are such agreements upheld by the courts as "supreme law of the land," [3] but the limits to which the president may carry them are nowhere defined.[4] Many agreements deal with minor matters which, on their face, do not call for a treaty—for example, petty pecuniary claims of American citizens against foreign governments. But others relate to affairs of prime importance.[5] Indeed, an executive agree-

---

[1] In his *International Executive Agreements* (New York, 1941), W. McClure computes that the total of executive agreements entered into by our government between 1789 and February, 1941, was "well over 1,250—a third more than the number of treaties." From 1929, the texts of such agreements were published in the State Department's *Executive Agreement Series* until 1946, when this Series was merged with a similar *Treaty Series* in the present *Treaties and Other International Acts Series.*

[2] On trade agreements, see pp. 584-585 above.

[3] As in United States *v.* Belmont, 301 U. S. 324 (1937). The federal Supreme Court has never held an international act unconstitutional. An executive agreement, however, binds only the signing executive; his successors are free to continue it or not as they choose.

[4] As a consequence, when the chief executive wants an agreement with a foreign power, he commonly has a three-way choice: to negotiate a treaty and then submit it to the Senate, to secure advance consent of Congress to an executive agreement, or to act alone. His decision upon which course to pursue, at least when the matter at stake is important, will be influenced by the political situation at the time and perhaps by other considerations. But, in general, all three methods are constitutional and valid.

[5] Examples include the Hay open-door notes of 1899; the Boxer protocol with China in 1901; the "Gentleman's Agreement" of 1907 with Japan terminating the immigration of Japanese laborers; the Root-Takahira notes of 1908 on the open door in China; the agreement with Panama in 1914 for enforcing the neutrality of the Panama Canal; the somewhat unfortunate Lansing-Ishii agreement with Japan in 1917; the armistice of 1918 with Germany; the agreement entered into by President Franklin D. Roosevelt with the British government in 1940 under which the United States turned over to Britain fifty over-age destroyers in return for ninety-nine-year leases of sites in British possessions on this side of the Atlantic for the development of American naval bases; the agreements with Denmark's government-in-exile in April and July, 1941, under which the United States acquired the right, in the one case, to establish air bases and other military and naval facilities in Greenland and, in the other, to undertake a naval occupation of Iceland, both aimed at curbing or forestalling German armed operations in the North Atlantic; numerous agreements with allied nations under the Lend-Lease Act of 1941 and the United Nations Relief and Rehabilitation Agreement of 1943-44; and the loan of three and three-quarter billion dollars to Great Britain in 1945. The Rush-Bagot convention of 1817 with Great Britain for the limitation of naval forces on the Great Lakes, and from which developed the policy of the unfortified border between the United States and Canada, was originally an executive agreement, although in the following year it was given a treaty basis. On March 21, 1941, President Roosevelt transmitted to Congress the text of an executive agreement recently signed in Ottawa providing for completion of essential links in the long-contemplated St. Lawrence deep waterway

ment may become frankly a means of evading—temporarily at all events
—the necessity of going to the Senate with a treaty. In 1905, President
Theodore Roosevelt worked out a treaty with Santo Domingo specifying
that the United States should guarantee the integrity of that republic
and take over the administration of the customs with a view to settling
foreign claims and warding off European intervention. The Senate refused to consent to the treaty; whereupon the President entered into a
modus vivendi with the Dominican government on precisely the lines
desired; and for two years the protectorate was maintained on this basis
alone. In 1907, a treaty regularizing the arrangement was at last assented
to and ratified.[1] President Taft, in 1911, entered into a similar agreement
with Nicaragua, which was not superseded by a treaty until 1916,[2]

So far, indeed, was the power of executive agreement carried that in
1941 a responsible State Department official could seriously argue, not
only that the two-thirds rule in the Senate was "a peril to the national
welfare," but that anything that can be done by treaty can also be done
(and the implication was *should* be) by executive agreement.[3] The war
years then dawning, however, saw an uprising on the matter in a quarter
where it was most to be expected—the Senate. Executive agreements of
1940 (mentioned in an earlier footnote) under which the United States
secured from Great Britain long-term leases of sites in the Atlantic for
naval development, and from Denmark the right to take various pre-
cautionary measures in Greenland and Iceland, were so obviously germane to the president's function as commmander-in-chief that they
stirred little protest. When, however, in pursuance of power conferred in
the Lend-Lease Act of 1941, the State Department, under presidential
direction, began concluding agreements with Great Britain, the U.S.S.R.,
China, and other nations involving a network of long-term commitments
running into billions of dollars, dissatisfaction manifested itself. And
when, in 1943, it was learned that a United Nations Relief and Rehabilitation Convention was to be treated as an executive agreement and not

Congress and executive agreements

---

and power project—an agreement essentially in lieu of the treaty on the subject
rejected by the Senate in 1934. This particular agreement, however, could be made
effective only by a congressional appropriation, which was refused. Early in 1948,
President Truman appealed to leaders of both parties in Congress for authority to
conclude a similar agreement, but the proposal was rejected in the Senate by almost
two to one. See p. 709, note 3, above.

[1] *Foreign Relations of the U. S.* (1905), 334-343; T. Roosevelt, *Autobiography*,
551-552. The only substantial difference between the "agreement" and the later
"treaty" was that the latter was ratified by the Senate. Under an executive agreement
of September 24, 1940, the United States finally relinquished the receivership.

[2] Promises, indeed, may be made and understandings reached, fully tantamount to
agreements, without any knowledge on the part of either Congress or the public. A
classic example is President Theodore Roosevelt's agreement with Japan on Far
Eastern policy at the close of the Russo-Japanese war, first brought to light twenty
years later when the Roosevelt papers in the Library of Congress were explored. See
T. Dennett, *Roosevelt and the Russo-Japanese War* (Garden City, N. Y., 1925), 112-
114. More recent examples would include agreements of at least a tentative nature
entered into by President Franklin D. Roosevelt in conferences attended during the
later war years and touching such matters as European postwar national boundaries.

[3] W McClure, *op. cit.*

referred to the Senate, notwithstanding that it entailed "practically illimitable obligations for the United States practically in perpetuity," the State Department was vigorously challenged. Controversy ensued in which the secretary of state was threatened with an official investigation, and in the end a compromise was forced under which, while UNRRA itself was entered into as a matter of executive-legislative action only, and without a treaty, the executive branch promised in future to be more circumspect about observing "constitutional processes." In anticipation, too, of efforts already started to build up a world organization for the preservation of peace, both houses of Congress, in the year mentioned, passed resolutions asserting that American participation must be by such "constitutional processes," which, in the Senate phraseology, were expressly defined as meaning Senate approval by regular two-thirds majority; and in 1945 the Charter of the United Nations was duly submitted to and approved by that body.[1]

Plenty of room for executive agreements remains; and there still is, and can be, no exact definition of their proper limits. Wartime experience has, however, at least vindicated and reëstablished the principle that significant financial commitments may not be made except by treaty, or at all events legislative action of the two houses; that, in general, agreements profoundly affecting the country's foreign interests and policies shall be only by treaty; and, finally, that the dividing line between treaty procedure and some alternative procedure is one to be drawn, in the final analysis, not by the executive, but by the Senate or by Congress as a whole. The chief problem remaining is the tendency to short-circuit the Senate as a treaty-making authority, even on important matters like the Bretton Woods Agreement and the loan to Great Britain, by simple legislation of the two houses either authorizing executive agreements in advance or validating them afterwards.[2]

---

[1] Observing the broad scope of declarations and announcements coming out of conferences like those at Teheran, Cairo, and Yalta, some people at one time wondered whether the international settlements liquidating World War II would not take the form of executive agreements rather than of treaties. President Roosevelt, however, carefully cultivated Senate good-will and coöperation preparatory to treaty action; certainly the majority of senators were prepared to insist that they be given opportunity to perform their constitutional function; and starting, in 1946, with a group of states which had been Axis satellites, a general program of treaty-making has been slowly and hazardously going forward. See W. N. Hadsel, "The Five Axis Satellite Peace Treaties," *Foreign Policy Reports*, XXIII, No. 3 (Apr. 15, 1947).

[2] The fullest treatment of the general subject, although not covering the more recent developments, is W. McClure, *International Executive Agreements*, previously cited. Cf. K. Colegrove, *The American Senate and World Peace*, Chap. v; H. M. Caturdal, "Executive Agreements; A Supplement to the Treaty-Making Procedure," *Geo. Washington Law Rev.*, X, 653-669 (Apr., 1942); Q. Wright, "The United States and International Agreements," *Amer. Jour. of Internat. Law*, XXXVIII, 341-355 (July, 1944); and E. M. Borchard, "Treaties and Executive Agreements," *Amer. Polit. Sci. Rev.*, XL, 729-739 (Aug., 1946). Among the authors cited, McClure favors solving the problem of the Senate's strangle-hold on treaty-making by still wider use of Congress-confirmed executive agreements, and Colegrove inclines to the same view if the two-thirds rule cannot be ended by constitutional amendment, which he thinks most to be desired.

Formulating and Controlling Foreign Policy

In the nature of things, officers and agencies engaged in managing our Has the United States a foreign policy? dealings with foreign governments must feel their way through situations as they arise, make choices and decisions as they go, and leave behind them records of performance not always remarkable for continuity and consistency. In other words, they must not only act, but develop currently a good deal of the policy on which action is based. And, disturbed by the shifts and turns that result, some people impatiently charge that the United States really has no foreign policy, but merely zigzags from position to position as the rough winds of international politics toss the ship of state about. Undoubtedly it is true that our physical isolation in times past, our traditional aloofness from European affairs, and our preference for avoiding long-time commitments seemed for decades to manifest a rather negative attitude on many matters of concern to other nations. But even aloofness, and preference for meeting situations as they arise, represents a policy. Besides, we have not always been aloof; and actually we have had a very respectable number of generally recognized, and sometimes very cogently asserted, foreign policies, among which one has only to mention the Monroe Doctrine, the "open door" in China, abstention (so long as remained possible) from foreign alliances, and, of late, good neighborliness toward Latin America, support for international organization through the United Nations, the "Truman policy" of curbing the expansion of Russian domination in Europe and the Middle East, and the "Marshall plan" for European postwar rehabilitation. The truth is, of course, that while certain basic axioms or attitudes may and should govern, there is, and can be, no single, comprehensive "foreign policy." Instead, there are policies of many sorts, on many different subjects—threads, perhaps, in a skein, but of different color and texture. Moreover, as situations, foreign and domestic, take on different aspects, policies once in the forefront of attention lose interest and significance while others gain new prominence; policies have to be formulated on matters, *e.g.*, the control and use of atomic energy, never before confronted; all in all, the field of policy becomes one of ever-shifting contours.

Furthermore, under our American system, the determination of foreign Who makes foreign policy? policy is not the function of any single branch or department of government, or even exclusively of government at all, since, as emphasized below, public opinion (with the press, the radio, churches and other organizations, playing significant parts) has much to do with it. Within the government itself, the Department of State is naturally a leading contributor; certainly it provides much of the information and advice lying behind all policy-making. But in the past the War and Navy Departments (now gathered under the coördinating secretary of defense) have participated actively, occasionally even fashioning policy independently;[1] and the Treasury, Commerce, Agriculture, and Interior Departments—not to mention independent establishments like the United States Tariff Commission, the Maritime Commission, the Export-Import Bank, and the Atomic Energy Commission—also make contributions. Needless to say, Congress, on its part, takes an active hand—enacting legislation, voting appropriations, declaring war—besides, of course, the special activities of the Senate in connection with foreign-service appointments and treaty-making. Indeed, it would be difficult to mention many agencies in Washington that do not, at some time or other, in one way or another, directly or indirectly, have at least some modest share in providing the information, supplying the incentives, or formulating the plans lying back of one phase or another of the foreign policies developed.

The rôle of the president   The supreme maker of foreign policy remains, however, to be mentioned, *i.e.*, the president; even when not strictly the author of a given policy, he commonly becomes such to all intents and purposes by declaring it to the world and taking the necessary steps to carry it into effect. When Washington proclaimed American neutrality in 1793, and in his Farewell Address warned his countrymen against political entanglements with Europe, he started the country on a course of "isolation" from which in later times only the most extraordinary emergencies ever availed to swerve it completely. Monroe, in 1823, voiced in a message to Congress certain principles concerning foreign political activities in the Western Hemisphere which, under the name of the Monroe Doctrine, developed into one of the most enduring and important of all our foreign policies. When, in 1844, President Tyler's secretary of state, Daniel Webster, instructed Caleb Cushing as our first emissary to China to see to it that the United States received assurance of equal opportunity in that country, he inaugurated a line of policy which, under the more familiar name of "open door," became, and remains, the cornerstone of all American dealings with the Far East. Theodore Roosevelt, Taft, and Wilson brought a number of Caribbean republics under United States supervision and, for better or worse, left us a policy of maintaining Latin American financial protectorates which only a decade or so ago gave way to President Franklin D. Roosevelt's newer "good neighbor" policy. Wilson in 1915 and Hoover in 1932, through their respective secretaries of state, Bryan and Stimson, made it American policy to withhold recognition from international agreements or arrangements in the Far East interfering with the territorial or administrative integrity of China or with equal opportunity for trade and other enterprise in that country. During the earlier stages of World War II, President Franklin D. Roosevelt led in formulating and carrying out the national policy under which the United States first severely strained and later frankly abandoned its neutral position in order to give aid to Great Britain and other fighting nations

---

[1] As when they originated the decree during the war with Japan that no agency of government should make attacks upon Emperor Hirohito personally.

which, in the Chief Executive's opinion, must at all costs be kept from going down. Similarly, he bore full responsibility for the government's unyielding opposition to Japan's proposed "new order" in Eastern Asia, bringing the two countries to the brink of war by 1941, and precipitating them into actual combat before the year ended, with Germany and Italy almost simultaneously declaring war upon us as part of a concerted Axis attack. In the Atlantic Charter of 1941, he joined with Prime Minister Churchill in proclaiming broad postwar international policies to which the United States was solemnly committed on his sole responsibility; and policies were further determined and declared throughout the war, frequently as a sequel of conferences with spokesmen of allied states. Later came a day when, with postwar Europe weakened, divided, and distraught, Soviet Russia seemed to be driving for dominance to the Atlantic, and when to both official and unofficial leaders in this country the well-being of the United States and of the world, perchance the future of Western civilization itself, seemed to demand bold measures for staying the course of ideological conquest and getting disordered European countries back on their feet; and in this situation plans, first for political loans to Greece and Turkey, but presently for coördinated and coöperative reconstruction of much of Europe, were put forward insistently by President Truman's advisers and by him transmitted to Congress for endorsement. When a foreign complication arises, or a new international problem presents itself, it is the president (speaking directly or perhaps through his secretary of state) who has the first opportunity to say what the attitude of the nation shall be; and by the stand that he takes he can so put the country on record that it will be next to impossible for Congress, or even a later president, to change the course that he has set. As we shall see, he may even lead the nation into war; for although he cannot declare war, he can adopt an attitude or create a situation, *e.g.*, by refusing to yield in a controversy with a foreign government, that may make war unavoidable.

Nevertheless, the president does not long play a lone hand, or always have his own way. Rarely can the policies which he formulates or sponsors achieve their purposes unless accepted or financially implemented by Congress; and they may be completely thwarted by lack of congressional support. A zealous Congress forced upon a reluctant chief executive the War of 1812, and likewise the intervention in Cuba in 1898 which led to the war with Spain, the annexation of the Philippines, and a long train of other momentous consequences. An unconvinced Senate balked President John Quincy Adams in his Pan-American policy, Pierce in his Cuban policy, Grant in his Dominican policy, Cleveland in his Hawaiian policy, and Wilson in his endeavor to put the United States into the League of Nations. One of the vigorous and important standing committees in each of the two branches is the committee on foreign relations,[1] in which, in

Congressional limitations and controls

---

[1] "Foreign affairs," in the case of the House of Representatives.

connection with proposed legislation (and, in the Senate committee, with foreign-service appointments and treaties) problems of foreign policy receive extended discussion, sometimes supplemented by lively public hearings.[1] Other standing committees, too,—appropriations, banking and currency, agriculture, merchant marine and fisheries—touch foreign policy at various points; and special committees may be set up to investigate phases or consequences of presidential policy-making. From any of these directions may come criticisms or recommendations eventuating in decisions making it necessary for lines of policy to be abandoned or sharply altered. Finally, too, whatever funds may be required for carrying presidential policies into operation are obtainable only through appropriations voted by Congress. For example, in 1947 President Truman would have been unable even to start doing anything about blocking the expansion of Communist influence in Europe and Asia unless Congress had been willing to appropriate the $400,000,000 requested for aid to Greece and Turkey as the first step in the program. The upshot, therefore, is that, while in foreign relations the president appears to have a singularly free hand, and while he actually does enjoy much liberty of action, our dealings abroad are, after all, controlled by no single branch of the government, but rather are shaped, even if somewhat unequally, at the two ends of Pennsylvania Avenue.[2]

The rôle of public opinion

Back of both president and Congress, however, stand the people; and although the state of popular information on and interest in the affairs of distant nations still leaves a good deal to be desired, in the last analysis no long-term program of foreign policy can be carried out that lacks the support of the voters, evidenced through elections, the press, and in other ways. "No matter," ex-Secretary of State Hull has remarked, "how brilliant and desirable any course may seem, it is wholly impracticable and impossible unless it is a course which finds basic acceptance ... by the people of this country." Here, as in other areas of planning and action, the chief executive must ascertain, scrutinize, and weigh public opinion; failing to do so, he may easily be betrayed into embarking upon

[1] A joint foreign relations committee of the two houses has sometimes been proposed; also some sort of a council on foreign relations composed of cabinet members, senators, and representatives chiefly concerned with foreign affairs. On the influence that an able and experienced chairman of a foreign relations committee may attain, see W. Lippmann, "Concerning Senator Borah," *Foreign Affairs*, IV, 211-222 (Jan., 1926).

[2] On the president, Congress, and foreign policy, see L. H. Chamberlain and R. C. Snyder, *American Foreign Policy*, Chaps. IV-V; B. Bolles, "Congress and Foreign Policy," *Foreign Policy Reports*, XX, No. 21 (Jan. 15, 1945).

In the period from Theodore Roosevelt to Woodrow Wilson, the president held the whip-hand in this domain. Reaction against Wilsonian diplomacy left Presidents Harding, Coolidge, and Hoover in a weakened position. Under Franklin D. Roosevelt, however, international tension and world-wide war, with steadily increasing involvement of the United States, brought the president back into a position of leadership and control equaling, if not surpassing, that which Wilson enjoyed; and while the nation would otherwise have been quite ready after World War II for another period of presidential inaction, the continuing extraordinary difficulties and dangers of the world situation operated to keep President Truman close to the peak which his predecessor had recaptured.

a line of policy leading straight to humiliating frustration at the hands of the people or their elected representatives. Not infrequently, cross-currents of opinion make it difficult to discern what the nation really thinks and wants with respect to a given situation or problem; considerations of self-interest and altruism are often bewilderingly intermingled, and economic, ethnic, or other pressure groups may pull in diametrically opposite directions.[1] But there are ways—in which the president, the State Department, and Congress alike are usually versed—of forming reasonably sure judgments as to how far the country as a whole is prepared to go in supporting a given line of policy or its opposite; and most of the time, planning and action are kept within the limits disclosed—although sometimes, as in the case of the Truman-Marshall project of 1947 for fending off the spread of Russian domination in Europe and the Near East, it becomes necessary to plan (if not also act) first, and cultivate public opinion largely afterwards.[2]

Participation in International Organization

The foreign relations of the United States are by no means confined to direct and separate dealings with nations individually. To begin with, they are operated within a framework of international law, which, originating in ways too complicated to be described here, is at all events a matter of more or less general international agreement or acceptance, and

Some forms taken

[1] As illustrated in the critical years 1940-41 by the propaganda of the [William Allen White] Committee to Defend America by Aiding the Allies, on the one hand, and of the America First Committee and the No Foreign War Committee, on the other.

[2] When, in a speech in Chicago in 1937, President Roosevelt advocated "quarantining" aggressor nations as a means of protecting ourselves against being drawn into armed conflict, press and public reacted unfavorably, in the belief that the effect would be quite the opposite; and the proposal was dropped. The president may, of course, address himself to winning the country to a particular line of policy, as President Wilson sought to win it to membership in the proposed League of Nations. A good example of consulting public opinion was afforded in 1945, when forty-two different organizations were invited to send representatives to San Francisco to advise with American officials participating in working out the plan for the United Nations.

On the rôle of public opinion in our foreign relations, see J. M. Mathews, *American Foreign Relations; Conduct and Policies* (rev. ed.), Chap. XIII; L. H. Chamberlain and R. C. Snyder, *American Foreign Policy* (New York, 1947), Chaps. XII-XIII; V. M. Dean, "U. S. Foreign Policy and the Voter," *Foreign Policy Reports*, XX, No. 13 (Sept. 15, 1944); K. Colegrove, "The Rôle of Congress and Public Opinion in Formulating Foreign Policy," *Amer. Polit. Sci. Rev.*, XXXVIII, 956-969 (Oct., 1944); and W. Johnson, *The Battle Against Isolation* (Chicago, 1944).

The literature on American foreign policy is voluminous. Major titles include S. F. Bemis, *A Diplomatic History of the United States* (New York, 1936); C. A. Beard, *The Idea of National Interest and the Open Door at Home* (New York, 1934); W. Lippmann, *United States Foreign Policy; Shield of the Republic* (New York, 1943); L. H. Chamberlain and R. C. Snyder, *American Foreign Policy* (cited above), containing many documentary materials, as does also R. J. Bartlett, *The Record of American Diplomacy* (New York, 1947), a book of documents and readings; and B. Bolles, *Who Makes Our Foreign Policy?* (New York, 1947), a popular but informing survey in the Foreign Policy Association's "Headline Series." In *Foreign Policy Reports*, published twice a month by the Foreign Policy Association (New York), one will find up-to-date discussions of selected topics; and the fullest account for a very recent period is J. C. Campbell, *The United States in World Affairs, 1945-1947* (New York, 1947).

certainly not a creation of the United States or of any two or three nations alone. In the second place, many treaties which we enter into are not bilateral, but multilateral, *i.e.*, shared in by a considerable number of states, as for example the Versailles Treaty at the close of World War I (which we failed to ratify) or the treaties of 1922 and 1930 on the limitation of naval armaments. Such treaties or conventions are likely to be concluded at diplomatic meetings or conferences in which the United States is represented along with varying numbers of other states; and as world affairs have grown more complex in later decades, their number and importance have tended to increase. Then there is the matter of international associations and organizations to which the United States has become a party (or to which it has contributed financial support)—even before, or at any rate quite apart from, the rise of the problem of world organization posed by the League of Nations and the present United Nations. A recent issue of the *United States Government Manual* lists some one hundred bodies of the kind with which the United States was identified in 1947, established in nearly every instance by multilateral treaty, convention, or agreement,[1] and ranging from a Pan-American Union linking up the twenty-one republics of the Western Hemisphere for closer coöperation, or the Hague Tribunal of Arbitration, to a Universal Postal Union, an International Institute of Agriculture, and a long list of other agencies for investigative, consultative, regulative, and technical purposes. When the League of Nations came into being after World War I, the United States, by Senate decision, refused to become a member. Throughout the ensuing quarter-century it could not, however, hold completely aloof from the organization's activities; and it not only from time to time maintained observers at Geneva, but participated in conferences held under League auspices, ratified various conventions of League origin, took part in the work of several technical and other commissions carrying on League activities, and eventually joined the International Labor Organization closely associated with the League, although persistently refusing to adhere to the World Court which the League set up. All relationships of the kind have added to our personnel occupied with international matters and have given the State Department increased responsibilities for guidance and control; many, too, have entailed legislative work for Congress.

The United States and the United Nations

But the most significant participation of the United States in coöperative international activity has come as a result of the challenging experiences of the recent war decade; and the country now finds itself a leading member of the most pretentious and potentially most important international league or union known to history—the United Nations, born of World War II, projected on its broader lines at the Dumbarton Oaks

---

[1] Many of those existing at the date mentioned were control commissions, tribunals, or other agencies growing directly out of the recent war, and hence to be regarded as more or less temporary. But more than half had existed for some time, quite independently of the war.

Conference of 1944 in Washington, provided with its basic charter or constitution at a later international gathering in San Francisco representing fifty states and dominions, and planned to operate from an American location in the heart of New York City. Not only in the General Assembly and the smaller but pivotal Security Council of this organization is our government represented, but also in a growing list of auxiliary bodies—an Economic and Social Council, a Trusteeship Council, a United Nations Educational and Scientific Organization, an International Court of Justice, and others; [1] and in future (if the new coöperative machinery fulfills the hopes of those who devised it) an increasing proportion of the matters which our State Department and Foreign Service heretofore have handled on the traditional nation-by-nation basis will be dealt with, at least in part, through the United Nations as an over-all medium of world discussion, decision, and action. Diplomatic and consular relations with individual nations will continue, together with probably a good many independent international commissions, unions, and other such agencies. Nevertheless, if the new plan for collective international action succeeds, the pattern and workings of our American foreign-relations machinery may in time undergo considerable change.

REFERENCES

E. S. Corwin, *The President's Control of Foreign Relations* (Princeton, N. J., 1917), Chaps. I-III.

——————, *The President: Office and Powers; History and Analysis of Practice and Opinion* (New York, 1940), Chap. VI.

——————, *Total War and the Constitution* (New York, 1947), Chap. IV.

——————, *The Constitution and World Organization* (Princeton, N. J., 1944).

C. B. Swisher, *The Growth of Constitutional Power in the United States* (Chicago, 1947), Chap. VIII.

J. M. Mathews, *American Foreign Relations; Conduct and Policies* (rev. ed., New York, 1928), Chaps. XII-XXXI.

B. H. Williams, *American Diplomacy; Policies and Practice* (New York, 1936), Chaps. XXI-XXIV. Also Chaps. I-XX for an excellent analysis of American foreign policies before the recent war period.

Q. Wright, *The Control of American Foreign Relations* (New York, 1922), Chaps. XIV-XIX.

R. J. Bartlett [ed.], *The Record of American Diplomacy; Documents and Readings in the History of American Foreign Relations* (New York, 1947).

L. H. Chamberlain and R. C. Snyder, *American Foreign Policy* (New York, 1948). An extensive collection of readings.

J. F. Green, "The President's Control of Foreign Policy," *Foreign Policy Reports*, XV, No. 2 (Apr. 1, 1939).

L. W. Koenig, *The Presidency and the Crisis* (New York, 1944), Chap. II.

[1] By a vote of 89 to 2, and after only six days of debate, the Senate, on July 28, 1945, ratified the United Nations Charter, thereby approving American membership in the organization created by it. On August 2, 1946, it similarly accepted (60 to 2) for the United States compulsory jurisdiction by the International Court of Justice. Membership in the United Nations was finally and officially validated in a United Nations Participation Act of December 20, 1945 (59 *U. S. Stat. at Large*, 619).

C. A. Beard, *American Foreign Policy in the Making, 1932-1940; A Study in Responsibilities* (New Haven, 1946).

————, *President Roosevelt and the Coming of the War, 1941; A Study in Appearances and Realities* (New Haven, 1948).

B. Bolles, *Who Makes Our Foreign Policy?* (New York, 1947).

J. C. Campbell, *The United States in World Affairs, 1945-1947* (New York, 1947).

E E. Dennison, *The Senate Foreign Relations Committee* (Stanford Univ., 1942).

A. C. F. Westphal, *The House Committee on Foreign Affairs* (New York, 1942).

G. H. Stuart, *American Diplomatic and Consular Practice* (New York, 1936).

G. Hunt, *The Department of State of the United States* (New Haven, 1914).

B. D. Hulen, *Inside the Department of State* (New York, 1936).

R. Bendiger, *The Riddle of the State Department* (New York, 1942).

W. H. C. Laves *et al.*, "Emerging Problems in the Conduct of American Foreign Relations" [Symposium], *Amer. Polit. Sci. Rev.,* XXXVIII, 913-969 (Oct., 1944).

W. H. C. Laves and F. O. Wilcox, "The Reorganization of the Department of State," *Amer. Polit. Sci. Rev.,* XXXVIII, 289-301 (Apr., 1944).

————, "The State Department Continues Its Reorganization," *ibid.,* XXXIX, 309-317 (Apr., 1945).

T. Lay, *The Foreign Service of the United States* (New York, 1925).

J. R. Childs, *American Foreign Service* (New York, 1948).

E. Atwater, "The American Foreign Service Since 1939," *Amer. Jour. of Internat. Law,* XLI, 73-102 (Jan., 1947).

W. McClure, *International Executive Agreements; Democratic Procedure Under the Constitution of the United States* (New York, 1941).

E. M. Borchard, "Treaties and Executive Agreements," *Amer. Polit. Sci. Rev.,* XL, 729-739 (Aug., 1946).

————, *The Diplomatic Protection of Citizens Abroad* (new ed., New York, 1927).

H. M. Wriston, *Executive Agents in American Foreign Relations* (Baltimore, 1929).

T. Cole, *The Recognition Policy of the United States Since 1901* (Baton Rouge, La., 1928).

J. L. MacMahon, *Recent Changes in the Recognition Policy of the United States* (Washington, D. C., 1933).

S. B. Crandall, "Treaties; Their Making and Enforcement," *Columbia Univ. Studies in Hist., Econ., and Public Law,* XXI, No. 1 (2nd ed., New York, 1916).

C. C. Tansill, "The Treaty-Making Powers of the Senate," *Amer. Jour. of Internat. Law,* XVIII, 459-491 (July, 1924).

K. Colegrove, *The American Senate and World Peace* (New York, 1944).

R. J. Dangerfield, *In Defense of the Senate; A Study in Treaty-Making* (Norman, Okla., 1933).

D. F. Fleming, *The Treaty Veto of the American Senate* (New York, 1930).

W. S. Holt, *Treaties Defeated by the Senate* (Baltimore, 1933).

"Should the Treaty Authority of the United States Senate Be Curtailed?" [Symposium], *Cong. Digest,* XXII, 227-256 (Oct., 1943).

H. Miller [ed.], *Treaties and Other International Acts of the United States of America* (Washington, D. C., 1931——). Six vols. thus far published. For texts of new treaties as ratified, see *Treaties and Other International Acts Series* (published by the Department of State).

Department of State Bulletin (Washington, D. C.). Published weekly.

International Organization. Published three times a year by the World Peace Foundation (Boston), starting in Feb., 1947, and containing articles, summaries, documents, and bibliography indispensable for keeping abreast of developments in the field.

CHAPTER XXXV

NATIONAL DEFENSE

Until within the past generation, geography assured our country a singularly sheltered position internationally. Even so, modest provisions for defense were always necessary. In little over a century, we engaged in three international wars; and in 1917 we were drawn into the greatest armed conflict that the world had known to that time. Hardly more than a decade ago, however, we still had a comfortable sense of isolation and security. Our Army was small; our Navy, more impressive, yet not pre-eminent; and the national temper was so far removed from militarism as to make it difficult, indeed, to maintain any very substantial defenses at all. Then dawned a period of great change. International turmoil gripped the world; technological advances largely robbed us of the protection afforded by broad oceans; war advanced relentlessly in our direction and at length overtook us. By rapid stages, defense, long a matter of only rather casual interest, became our paramount national concern—and defense no longer confined to mere preparedness, but actualized in deadly combat on land and sea and in the air, in every quarter of the globe. In time, the enemy was defeated and new international machinery set up for keeping the peace. No one supposed, however, that future security was definitely assured any nation; on the contrary, the "absolute weapon" of atomic power raised new and greater fears; and, all in all, defense remains and doubtless will long continue, for us as for other peoples, a problem and challenge of unsurpassed importance. *Defense becomes a major concern*

During the Revolution and the ensuing "critical period," the lack of power of Congress to mobilize the fighting strength and material resources of the country, and to deal promptly and decisively with domestic disorders, gravely imperiled the beginnings of the nation; and the experience put the makers of the constitution in a frame of mind to endow the new government with adequate powers both to make war and to repress insurrection. Into the new fundamental law they therefore wrote upwards of a dozen provisions [1] which, taken together, conferred upon the national government every power at that time deemed necessary for defending the country, whether against Indian depredations, foreign attack, or domestic uprising. [2] Almost equally with the conduct of foreign *Some constitutional principles:* *[1] Defense a responsibility of the national government*

---

[1] At least seven in Art. 1, § 8, alone.

[2] Whether the national government has a general war power over and above these specific grants is a question on which there has been difference of opinion. When, in 1936, the Supreme Court affirmed that there would have been power, "as a concomitant of nationality," to carry on foreign relations even if none had been granted in

relations, defense was made, as it remains today, a national function. To be sure, the states may, and do, maintain militia for use in enforcing their own proper authority. But unless Congress gives permission, they may not "keep troops or ships of war in time of peace" or engage in war unless actually invaded or in such imminent danger as will not admit of delay.[1] Even the state militia may be called into the service of the United States, thereupon passing under the supreme command of the president; and, as is well known, the military establishments of the states have in later times become an integral part of the war machine of the nation.[2] In time of defense emergency, and especially of war, states, counties, cities, and other jurisdictions collaborate with the national government in a multitude of ways. Their efforts, however, are merely phases of an over-all national effort; and full responsibility for that effort rests with the government at Washington.

2. Civil authority supreme over military

A second principle is equally fundamental. While solicitous about providing for defense, the framers of the constitution had no desire to open a way for an overshadowing, and perhaps overweening, military establishment, or for the rise of military dictatorship. To be sure, they did not expressly enjoin in the document—as is done in all of the state constitutions except that of New York—that the military establishment shall in all matters be subject to civil control. But they accomplished the purpose adequately enough by so defining the defense and war powers of Congress and the president (civil branches of the government) as to leave no room for military domination. Congress alone can raise and support armies, make rules for governing them, and declare war; the president is commander-in-chief of all armed forces, whether in peace or in war.[3] As any one conversant with Washington knows, Army and

---

the constitution (see p. 448, note 1, above), it seemed to say the same thing for declaring and waging war; and various leading figures in our history, including Lincoln and Franklin D. Roosevelt, have viewed the war power as a single, integrated power transcending any and all particular grants. In a sense, the matter is of little practical importance; the constitutional grants (together with powers to be inferred from them) have proved ample for all needs. The main significance of the inherent-power theory is that (at any rate if pressed to extreme) it might suggest that when the country is at war the constitution is more or less suspended and the government free to act without reference to the restrictions normally resting upon it. In spite of occasional appearances to the contrary, however, such a deduction would be legally incorrect.

[1] Art. I, § 10, cl. 3.
[2] See p. 110 above.
[3] Quite apart from constitutional provisions, civilian supremacy has been promoted also by the almost unbroken practice of appointing only civilians, not generals or admirals, as heads of the defense departments. The National Security Act of 1947, under which the defense agencies have been reorganized, simply assumes that this will continue as a matter of usage in connection with the heads of the Departments of the Army, the Navy, and the Air Force, but expressly requires that the over-all secretary of defense and his assistants be appointed "from civilian life." Under-secretaries and assistant secretaries in the departments also are uniformly civilians. The president may have had military experience; several incumbents, indeed (e.g., Washington, Jackson, Taylor, and Grant), had previously attained the rank of general. When president, however, all have been civilians. When firmly refusing, in January, 1948, to sanction further use of his name as a candidate for the presidency, General

Navy officers, even in time of peace, exert a good deal of influence upon policies relating to national defense, upon military and naval appropriations, and at times even upon the conduct of foreign relations. But in all such matters the power of final decision rests with civilians.

In few areas are the powers and functions of Congress and the president more interlocked than in that of defense; indeed, as we shall see, the president derives a great deal of his wartime authority from grants, or "delegations," made by Congress. For purposes of a preliminary outline of defense powers, however, each branch may be treated separately; and first Congress.

Defense Powers and Functions of Congress

To begin with, Congress has sole power to "raise and support armies" and to "provide and maintain a navy."[1] These things it does by specifying the number and kinds of troops to be enlisted, prescribing the method of recruitment, fixing scales of pay, authorizing the building and manning of war craft, providing for auxiliary equipment such as forts, arsenals, dockyards, and air services, and of course by raising and appropriating money for the maintenance of military, naval, and air establishments, subject to the constitutional restriction that no appropriation for raising and supporting armies may be made for a longer period than two years.[2] There is no lack of power to take whatever steps are deemed necessary— even to the extent of conscription, as in World Wars I and II—to safeguard the nation in time of peace, and to insure vigorous and effective prosecution of hostilities in time of war. *1. Providing for the Army and Navy*

In the second place, Congress has full authority to prescribe "rules for the government and regulation of the land and naval forces,"[3] and "rules concerning captures on land and water."[4] Resulting regulations for the Army are called the "Articles of War;" those for the Navy, the "Articles for the Government of the Navy;" together, the two are known as the "Military Laws of the United States."[5] Bracketed with the power to make rules concerning captures is authority to "grant letters of marque and reprisal" authorizing private ships in time of war to prey upon the commerce of the enemy. Privateering, however, was abolished by the Declaration of Paris in 1856; and although the United States has never become a signatory of that international instrument, letters of marque and reprisal are no longer issued. Enemy merchant ships, as well as *2. Enacting military and naval regulations*

Dwight D. Eisenhower gave notable expression to the principle of civilian supremacy which ought to govern in a democracy. See *N. Y. Times*, Jan. 24, 1948.

[1] Art. I, § 8, cls. 12, 13.
[2] Art. I, § 8, cl. 12.
[3] Art. I, § 8, cl. 14.
[4] Art. I, § 8, cl. 11.
[5] For further comment, see p. 819 below. If, with the air forces given a new status in 1947 under an additional executive department, an entirely separate body of rules should be found necessary for them, Congress manifestly would have power to enact the requisite "Articles."

neutral vessels carrying contraband, remain, of course, subject to capture by the regular naval forces, with the ultimate disposal of them determined by prize courts sitting in convenient ports and operating under rules of international law, supplemented by regulations laid down by Congress.

3. Exercising control over the National Guard   Congress may provide for as large a standing army as it sees fit; and it is generally agreed that the world situation will in future require a considerably larger one than in the past. Our earlier traditions, however, in common with those of English-speaking peoples everywhere, were opposed to any formidable army in time of peace, inclining rather to the maintenance in each state of a volunteer citizen militia with only such modest training and equipment as would enable it to cope with domestic disorder and to meet other relatively minor needs;[1] and all the states continue to have such militia, even though nowadays linked up with the national defense establishment and bearing the significant name of "National Guard."[2] State contingents of the National Guard are still primarily state instrumentalities, with (so long as not drawn into federal service) appointment of their officers and provision for their training expressly reserved to state authorities. Congress, nevertheless, is authorized to "provide for arming and disciplining the militia," to provide for calling into federal service any and all portions of it required for executing the federal laws, for suppressing insurrections, or for repelling invasions, and to make rules for governing such forces when "employed in the service of the United States."[3] And in pursuance of these broad powers, Congress not only, in an Army Organization Act of 1920, gave the president permanent authority to make use of the National Guard for federal purposes, but has enacted numerous regulations aimed at increasing the establishment's effectiveness and coördinating its organization, training, and equipment with that of the Regular Army—in addition, of course, to contributing heavily to its financial support.[4] When, as a feature of the national defense program launched in 1940, the entire National Guard was drawn into federal service and placed in cantonments for training, Congress stipulated that it might be used only in the Western Hemisphere and in United States territories and possessions, including the Philippines. After war came, however, the restriction was

---

[1] The constitution, indeed, speaks in the Second Amendment of such militia as being "necessary to the security of a free state." There was no need to provide in the original document for *creating* militia; the states already had such establishments, and it was simply assumed that they would continue.

[2] Speaking strictly, the militia includes, under terms of a statute of April 2, 1898, all able-bodied male citizens (and aliens who have declared their intention to be naturalized) between the ages of eighteen and forty-five; and all such are "liable to perform military duty in the service of the United States" (30 *U. S. Stat. at Large*, 361). In ordinary usage, however, the term denotes only the armed establishments maintained by the states, *i.e.*, the organized and trained portion of the militia embraced in the National Guard.

[3] Art. I, § 8, cls. 15-16.

[4] See p. 110 above.

removed, and Guard units, or at all events the men who had composed them, were sent to all overseas theaters of operation.

Congress alone can declare war.[1] Hostilities may, of course, begin without a formal declaration, as in the instance of the Spanish-American War of 1898; indeed, as in the case of the war with Japan, Germany, and Italy beginning in December, 1941, they may be forced upon us by aggressive action of a foreign power, leaving us no alternative. But even in such situations a declaration will promptly be adopted by the two houses, as a means (if for no other purpose) of fixing, for the benefit of neutrals, an exact date from which the rights and liabilities incident to war are to be reckoned. The usual method is a joint resolution, requested and afterwards signed by the president, setting forth the reasons for resorting to arms, and declaring a state of war to exist.[2] Legally, Congress could pass such a resolution without any presidential request, and even over a presidential veto. Such action, however, has never been taken and is inherently improbable. Many times it has been proposed by people anxious to keep the United States out of war that, except when the nation is attacked, the question of going to war should in all cases be put to a country-wide popular vote. Unless the constitution were amended, however, the decision must finally rest with Congress; and it is not clear that a great deal would be gained from the procedure suggested. There would always be the question of the proper stage at which to resort to a referendum, and the people as a whole could not in all situations become sufficiently informed upon the complicated, and often technical, issues at stake to be able to act wisely.[3] As will be emphasized below, the discretion of Congress in the matter is sometimes more theoretical than actual, because the president, in conducting foreign relations, may bring the country to a point where no honorable alternative to war remains; indeed, he can independently take steps leading to actual combat, as when President Roosevelt, before Pearl Harbor, supplied naval escorts

4. Declaring war

---

[1] Art. I, § 8, cl. 11.

[2] For the terse declarations of a state of war with Japan, Germany, and Italy, December 8 and 11, 1941 (55 *U. S. Stat. at Large*, 795, 796, 797), see *Amer. Jour. of Internat. Law*, XXXVI, Supp., pp. 2-3, 24 (Jan., 1942).

Whether the grant of authority to declare war carries with it, as a corollary, the right of Congress to declare the end of a war and the resumption of peaceful relations—as a possible alternative to a proclamation of similar purport by the president —was warmly and exhaustively debated in Congress after World War I, *i.e.*, in 1920-21. Finally, more than two years after the signing of the armistice which marked the actual cessation of hostilities in 1918, a joint resolution was adopted in July, 1921, asserting the war with the Central European Powers to be at an end. In the case of World War II "hostilities" were officially ended for the United States by presidential proclamation of December 31, 1946, but at the date of writing (April, 1948) "the war" was not yet officially over.

[3] With involvement in the steadily mounting European and Asiatic conflagration the uppermost national question in 1941, numerous polls conducted by the Institute of Public Opinion and by newspapers and other agencies undertook to test and measure public opinion on the issue. The results, of course, represented mere samplings, and not only were wholly unofficial, but in some instances worthless because of the slant given the questions asked. Some congressmen polled their constituents in an effort to ascertain their sentiments.

for merchant ships carrying "lend-lease" materials to Great Britain and other countries, resulting in armed clashes between American destroyers and German submarines. And, of course, as already observed, war can come without any option on the part of either Congress or the president. On the other hand, if Congress can declare war, it also can take measures designed to avert it, a good illustration being the Neutrality Act of 1937 authorizing the president, when two or more other nations were at war, to forbid the shipment of arms and munitions to the belligerents, as entailing risk of the United States being dragged into hostilities.[1]

5. Mo-
bilizing
the
nation
for war
effort
There was a time when, except in case of invasion, war was of no great moment to the general mass of the people. Armies were volunteer, taxes indirect, supplies bought in the open market, sacrifice and morale demanded chiefly of the forces in the field. The huge scale on which the mechanized wars of today are waged, however, makes them hardly less of civilian than of military concern. When war comes—and even when merely a threatened war is being prepared for—it is, as President Wilson remarked in 1917, "not an army that we must shape and train; it is a nation." And experience gained both during World War I and in connection with the stupendous defense effort launched in 1940 and merging into the war effort of later days, revealed in startling manner the lengths to which Congress may go in reorganizing and regimenting the national life for purposes of successful prosecution of, or even simply preparation for, war under twentieth-century conditions. As commander-in-chief of the armed forces, the president independently enjoys war powers of impressive magnitude. To Congress, however, it falls, not only to provide the necessary men and money—by conscription acts, revenue acts, and appropriation acts—but to endow the chief executive with much of the broad authority required for turning industry, commerce, transportation, and even science and education, into channels likely to contribute most adequately to successful national effort. The method is commonly that of legislation delegating specified powers for the duration of the war (or other designated period), either with or without creation by Congress of new machinery for exercising them. In each field covered, the resulting system of controls is organized and administered by the executive branch. But the underlying authority comes from Congress; and while the courts have often looked with extreme disfavor upon delegations of power by one branch of the government to another, developments during the first and second World Wars indicated that under wartime stress and excite-

---

[1] Under the United Nations organization, the United States has assumed obligation to engage in international "police" activities ordered by the Security Council which easily might prove tantamount to war, although undeclared so far as Congress was concerned. In the summer of 1947, preliminary consideration was given to the composition and strength of the forces to be placed at the Security Council's disposal, and the United States suggested a total of twenty divisions of ground forces (enough for two field armies), 198 warships, ninety submarines, and 3,800 aircraft, exclusive of air transport, to be contributed on a quota basis by all of the principal powers. The American contributions and all arrangements relating to them are, of course, subject to approval by Congress.

ment Congress can go practically as far as it likes in delegating authority to the president without fear of impediments imposed by the courts. Sometimes grants are made with little hesitation; at other times, only over strong opposition and at urgent presidential request. Occasionally, indeed—as, for example, when in 1944 President Roosevelt asked for power to conscript labor—they are refused.

Except for providing that the writ of *habeas corpus* may be suspended "when in cases of rebellion or invasion the public safety may require it,"[1] the constitution recognizes no distinction between civil rights in peacetime and in wartime. War, however, brings not only an intensity of military activity, but a tenseness of the public mind, requiring and justifying restrictions that would not be undertaken or tolerated in time of peace. And such restrictions may be imposed by the president (commonly through the agency of the Department of Justice), either under his powers as commander-in-chief or in pursuance of authority delegated to him by Congress; or Congress itself may impose them directly by legislative act—going, indeed, to undefined lengths in restraining speech, press, assembly, and other normal rights. Noteworthy statutes of this nature in recent decades include the Espionage Act of 1917, the Sedition Act of 1918, and portions of the peacetime Alien Registration Act of 1940.[2]

6. Regulating wartime civil liberties

Congress, of course, may at all times call for reports from departments or agencies of the government—even from the president himself. Likewise, it may conduct investigations whenever it chooses. With powers concentrated extraordinarily in the executive branch under wartime conditions, reports on how powers are being exercised are likely to be asked for with unusual persistence, and also investigations to be more frequently undertaken. Reports are sometimes perfunctory, and rarely very influential. Investigations, however, are, at least potentially, an important means of exercising control; and of twenty or more ordered during the period 1940-42, and having to do with the defense effort or the management of wartime activities, several proved of genuine significance.[3] Speaking broadly, it is the function of Congress, in addition to providing the commander-in-chief with the powers and sinews of war, to supervise and review the conduct of war, without attempting to take part in managing it.

7. Requiring reports and conducting investigations

Inheriting the practice from English and colonial usage, Congress not only has provided regular pay for soldiers and sailors, but has bestowed land, money pensions, or other special benefits upon the demobilized forces after every war in which the United States has engaged, from the Revolution onwards. The particularly hazardous nature of the service

8. Caring for veterans

---

[1] Art. I, § 9, cl. 2.

[2] The subject is touched upon only briefly here because of having been dealt with in an earlier connection. See pp. 155-156 above.

[3] Among these were the investigation of un-American activities by the Dies Committee, of national defense migration by the Tolan Committee, and of national defense activities in general by the Truman Committee. See pp. 337-339 above.

rendered the country by those who bear arms in its defense has seemed to merit such recognition; persons actually incapacitated, together with their dependents, have been conceded to have an irrefutable claim to the nation's care; powerful political pressure brought to bear upon congressmen by veterans' organizations has often led to grants where the obligation was considerably less clear. So generous, indeed, has been Congress when veterans have been involved that between 1792 and 1930 national outlays on money pensions alone, regardless of land allotments in earlier days and of later heavy costs of hospitalization and medical treatment, reached a total of fifteen billion dollars.[1] Benefits bestowed on veterans of World War II—in addition to the operation of regular pension, rehabilitation, and hospitalization systems, and in recognition of the heavy differential between the relatively low pay of men and women in service and the incomes generally enjoyed by people at home during years of wartime prosperity—have included government aid in carrying protection originating in in-service war-risk insurance; opportunity to acquire on favorable terms surplus war property disposed of by the federal government; increased preferential eligibility for employment in the federal civil service; continued monthly payments for a period after honorable discharge; and, in 1946, terminal leave pay for all wartime furlough periods not actually used—not to mention also the generous provisions of the Servicemen's Readjustment Act ("G. I. Bill of Rights") of 1944 for grants to veterans in aid of education or training, and for government guaranty of loans procured for the purchase of homes, farms, or businesses.[2]

[1] It has never been considered necessary or feasible to pension forthwith *all* persons released from service at the close of a war. Those emerging able-bodied and with unimpaired earning power have normally been expected to take care of themselves, at all events for a considerable time. Beyond this, three main policies or procedures have, in general, been followed: (1) Persons leaving the service with earning power destroyed or reduced by reason of injuries or sickness arising from military duties are pensioned at once, and likewise dependents of persons who have lost their lives. (2) As survivors dwindle in number and lose earning power with advancing age, many are pensioned regardless of the fact that their disability may not be traceable to military service. (3) After the number of survivors has fallen to relatively small proportions, pensions are granted to substantially all, as likewise to widows and other classes of dependents.

[2] The concepts and objectives of this legislation were supplied by a report of the National Resources Planning Board in 1943 entitled *Demobilization and Readjustment; Report of the Conferences on Postwar Readjustment of Civilian and Military Personnel.*

For purposes of more unified and effective administration, a Bureau of Pensions long maintained in the Department of the Interior was in 1930 consolidated by executive order with other scattered agencies having to do with military pensions and veterans relief to form an independent establishment known as the Veterans Administration, which forthwith became one of the most heavily manned branches of the government and also one of those requiring the largest yearly outlays. At the close of 1947, total personnel (201,000) exceeded that of any other federal establishment except only the Departments of the Army, Navy, and Postoffice; and during the 1946 session of Congress alone appropriations amounted to seven and one-third billion dollars. In 1945, Veterans Administration work was so reorganized that most of it could be carried on through branch offices and field stations throughout the country and thus be brought closer to the veteran to be served. Only six per cent, indeed, of the Administration's huge staff now operates in Washington. For

Defense Powers and Functions of the President

The authority of Congress manifestly underlies our entire system of national defense; without it there would be no army or navy, no money, and only imperfect means of mobilizing the nation for a defense effort like that of 1940-41 or for a war effort like that of the ensuing years. This once recognized, however, the central figure in defense, and especially in the conduct of war, is easily found in the president. In its three great wars of the last hundred years, the nation was fortunate enough to have in the White House chief executives—Lincoln, Wilson, and Franklin D. Roosevelt—who would have loomed large in our history in any event. All acquired additional stature from guiding the country's destinies during a supreme war effort; all are thought of primarily as "war presidents." Every president, however, has defense powers and functions in peacetime as well as wartime; and some aspects of these must next engage our attention.

The president as the central figure

Speaking broadly, the sources from which the president derives defense powers are three: (1) his constitutional status as chief executive; (2) superimposed upon this, his rôle as commander-in-chief; [1] and (3) grants, or "delegations," by Congress. The three are not easy to keep distinct; no wartime president ever tried to label every act performed as resting upon authority drawn from some one source to the exclusion of others. President Roosevelt, in particular, rarely considered it necessary to indicate in other than very broad terms the basis of specific war powers as he exercised them, rather leaving it to others to speculate, if they chose, upon whether, in the case of any given act or order, he was relying principally upon his permanent peacetime powers as chief executive, or upon his status as commander-in-chief, or upon statutory grants; and if perchance he made allusion to the latter, he was likely not to cite chapter and verse, but merely to invoke "the war powers acts," or simply, "the statutes."

Sources of his defense powers:

The truth is that, while perhaps distinguishable theoretically, the rôles of chief executive and commander-in-chief are in practice impossible to disentangle—even on a time basis, since the president is commander-in-chief in peace no less than in war. To be sure, it is easy enough to recognize some defense functions as belonging to the president in his capacity as chief executive. Certainly he needs no more authority than that of chief executive to appoint (with Senate confirmation) regular and reserve officers of the Army and Navy; [2] to supervise and direct the Army, Navy, and Air Departments; to enforce military and naval regulations

1. Powers as chief-executive and commander-in-chief

---

a full description of machinery and functions, see latest edition of the *United States Government Manual;* and for a collection of all federal laws on veteran affairs, from 1914 to 1947, *Laws Relating to Veterans* (Washington, D. C., Govt. Prtg. Off., 1947).

[1] Art. II, § 2, cl. 1.

[2] The officers of the National Guard, except when in the service of the United States, are appointed as the several states direct.

laid down by Congress and to supplement them within constitutional limits with others of his own; to initiate and approve or veto general legislation on defense subjects; to present budgets providing for military, naval, and air expenditures; and to employ armed force, when necessary, in seeing that the laws are faithfully executed and in protecting the states (on call from legislature or governor) from domestic violence. On the other hand, it is equally certain that being commander-in-chief adds something—*much*, indeed, although precisely *how much* it would be difficult to say, and undoubtedly more in wartime than in peacetime. What it means to be commander-in-chief, the constitution does not specify; and no definition has been supplied by either Congress or the courts. We know only that, taken in conjunction with powers as chief executive, and viewed in the light of what has actually happened in our major wars, prerogatives as commander-in-chief go far toward raising the president in wartime to a pinnacle unmatched in any democratic country; also that ever-widening interpretations, especially in wartime, provoke plenty of challenges and leave a fringe of uncertainty as to what new reaches of authority may yet be read into the title.

2. Powers delegated by Congress   Neither as chief executive nor as commander-in-chief, however, does the president function in a water-tight compartment; on the contrary, he draws resources and authority from, and acts in coöperation with, Congress. In general, indeed,—whether in peace or in war—Congress provides the money and the men; the president, as chief executive, or as commander-in-chief, or as both, uses them practically at his discretion. Congress, however, not only provides money and men; it also confers powers, even though not always with much discrimination as to whether upon chief executive or upon commander-in-chief. Occasionally, such grants take the form of freeing the president from restrictions which Congress itself has imposed, as for example when, after our involvement in war at the end of 1941, authority was given to employ the National Guard and recruits under Selective Service anywhere in the world, rather than merely in the Western Hemisphere and American overseas possessions. More often, however (at least in wartime), grants involve the delegation of vast discretionary authority to deal with broadly-defined substantive fields—military recruiting, war production, transportation, communications, food and fuel control, prices, and what not—in furtherance of objectives also broadly defined. During World War I, the opinion was advanced by the secretary of war, Newton D. Baker, that such congressional grants not only are superfluous, since the function of commander-in-chief can be construed to carry with it full authority to prosecute a war to the fullest extent, but actually are harmful in that by process of definition they rather narrow than broaden the range of authority possessed. This, however, has never been the view of any wartime president, nor certainly of Congress; and in every war in our history, especially the major ones, the president has been found making many and large requests of the legislative branch for powers in this direction and that, with the two houses sometimes hesitating and delaying, but almost always in the end complying through statutes of appropriate scope and vigor.

With this much said about the bases on which presidential defense powers rest, a word may be added about (1) the president's relation to the beginning of war and (2) the nature and magnitude of his authority once war has commenced. At the outset, there is the now familiar fact that the president may, in effect, start a war going. To be sure, only Congress can declare war. But in his conduct of foreign relations the president may, as suggested earlier, create a situation making war practically inevitable. In the course of stormy negotiations with Mexico in 1846, President Polk ordered American troops to advance into territory then in dispute with that country. The Mexican authorities had made it plain that such a step would be regarded as an act of war, and the soldiers were promptly fired upon. Polk then said that war existed by act of Mexico, and Congress proceeded to a formal declaration. President McKinley ordered the battleship *Maine* to Havana harbor in 1898, notwithstanding that the Spaniards were certain to regard the act as unfriendly. The vessel was blown up, and the Spanish-American War followed. By his handling of relations with Berlin after the sinking of the *Lusitania* in 1915, President Wilson brought the United States to a juncture where the only alternative to a declaration of war upon Germany would have been national stultification. And, more recently, the whole course of policy and action which, over a period of years, led the United States straight to involvement in World War II, while sustained by increasing evidences of broad national support, was projected and carried forward under the sole ultimate responsibility of President Franklin D. Roosevelt.[1]

The president and the beginning of war

In time of peace, the president performs the normal functions of chief executive in connection with defense interests and activities substantially as in relation to other government services; as commander-in-chief, his functions may be virtually limited to a more or less passive headship of the armed establishments.[2] When war comes, however, he rises to a

The president in wartime

[1] As we have seen, his ordering of American destroyers to escort merchant ships carrying supplies to Britain and other countries led to armed clashes even before war began.

Over against the president's capacity for "rushing" Congress and the country into war must, however, be set his power to veto a declaration of war—although no veto of the kind is on record. On a few occasions, too, *e.g.*, in the period leading up to the War of 1812, Congress has been more inclined to war than the president. Cf. S. E. Baldwin, "The Share of the President of the United States in a Declaration of War," *Amer. Jour. of Internat. Law*, XII, 1-14 (Jan., 1918).

[2] A good deal more was, of course, entailed during the year or two preceding our entrance into World War II. With the nation actively pushing its defense program, President Roosevelt, in this period, took many unusual peacetime steps as commander-in-chief, such as sending military observers to European countries, dispatching armed forces to Ireland, British Guiana, and Surinam, leasing naval and air bases from Great Britain in exchange for fifty over-age destroyers (notwithstanding the constitutional right of *Congress* "to dispose of property of the United States"), and, as mentioned above, ordering "lend-lease" cargoes convoyed by American destroyers.

stature supported by all the contributing sources of authority which have been mentioned. Subject to restrictions by Congress (which almost certainly would not be imposed in the midst of conflict), he can send all branches of the armed forces anywhere that he chooses, and use them as he likes.[1] He can take as much part as he likes in mapping out strategy and directing campaigns;[2] indeed there is nothing to prevent him from taking the field in person if he so desires, except, of course, that as a civilian, he would be an amateur—even if he were not pressed to the limit with tasks more properly within his province. Like any other supreme commander, he can terminate hostilities by agreeing to an armistice. He can set up military governments in conquered territory, and, directly or through appointed agents, exercise all executive powers there, and all legislative powers as well until Congress makes different arrangements.[3] Meanwhile, availing himself of broad grants of emergency authority already on the statute-book (even though perhaps long dormant), or voted by Congress in response to White House requests unfailingly made, he can carry out sweeping programs of armed recruitment, civilian mobilization, and economic controls, issue multitudes of administrative regulations, reorganize governmental agencies and create new ones, take over plants in which labor stoppages are interfering with war production or the railroads if transportation difficulties are impeding the war effort, and do such a multitude of other things that the sum-total of authority amassed and exercised almost defies comprehension. Indeed, the object in war being to discover and make effective all national potentialities as speedily as possible, and at the same time to break down the enemy's power of resistance, control over the use of the armed forces inevitably broadens into the general function of taking whatever measures may be found necessary to those ends. As a former secretary of war previously mentioned phrased it, the commander-in-chief's duty is nothing less than to prosecute a war "to the fullest extent." In discharging this responsibility, he, of course, must not violate the constitution or the laws; and, to a degree, he must work in coöperation with Congress, from which much of his high authority has come and to which much of it will return. Out-

---

See C. B. Swisher, "The Control of War Preparation in the United States," *Amer. Polit. Sci. Rev.,* XXXIV, 1085-1103 (Dec., 1940).

[1] The temporary peacetime restriction of 1940-41 in connection with the National Guard and Selective Service recruits has been mentioned. During World War I, the power to send troops abroad before the country was actually invaded was challenged, but in the Selective Draft Law Cases, 245 U. S. 366, 369 (1918) the Supreme Court fully sustained it, asserting that in his capacity as commander-in-chief the president may (in the absence of restrictions imposed by Congress) dispatch forces to any part of the world in which he considers their services needed.

[2] More than most presidents in wartime, President Roosevelt shared, and even led, in planning military and naval strategy and operations during the recent global war. In the summer of 1942, there was some complaint that he and Prime Minister Churchill were trying to exercise too much personal direction. In a later "fireside chat," the President freely conceded the wisdom of leaving military decisions to military men, although without suggesting any relinquishment of his own ultimate power to make them in so far as he chose.

[3] See pp. 821-823 below.

side of these limitations, however, he and his advisers, civil and military, have, and must have, practically a free hand. After all, running a war is, by its very nature, an executive job; it cannot be intrusted to a debating society.[1]

During the Civil War, President Lincoln relied heavily on what he understood to be his prerogatives as commander-in-chief and, although receiving substantial grants of authority from Congress, developed and exercised unprecedented war powers largely on his own initiative and responsibility. Sometimes he later sought validation from the legislative branch, which in most instances was forthcoming, although not in all; frequently he was charged with being a "dictator."[2] During World War I, President Wilson wielded even greater power, but with the difference that (although far from oblivious to his rights as commander-in-chief) he habitually sought and obtained from Congress advance grants of authority deemed necessary for his purposes. In World War II, President Roosevelt predominantly followed the Wilsonian pattern, yet with so keen a sense of the necessity and propriety in wartime of large concentration of authority in the executive that one could never be sure how far he would pursue a line of action deemed essential, whether or not Congress gave its approval. On one notable occasion, in 1942, when Congress showed reluctance to repeal a provision relating to agricultural prices which the president considered dangerously inflationary, he startled the country by, in effect, threatening to set aside the provision by sheer fiat,[3] asserting as he did so that "the president has the power, under the constitution and congressional acts, to take measures necessary to avert a disaster which would interfere with the winning of the war." His general disposition seemed to be to rely heavily on authority delegated by Congress, yet not to consider himself restrained, in the absence of such authority, from going to almost any length, if the matter seemed urgent, under warrant of his constitutional prerogatives as commander-in-chief.

The volume of delegated authority which Roosevelt enjoyed was, however, immense. Much of it, indeed, was accumulated before the war began. To start with, a large residue of special powers conferred on President Wilson, and never taken away, was carried over from the period of World War I. For example, the National Defense Act of 1916 and amending legislation, still on the statute-book, authorized the president in time of war or threatened war to place orders with industrial establishments and compel them to be filled, to require establishments to place

Presidential powers during World War II

Congressional grants

[1] Many times the question will arise as to whether a proposed line of action can be taken without some fresh authorization by law. In such a situation, the president is likely to be guided by opinions received from his attorney-general—who, being a member of the Administration, can usually be depended upon to give the executive the benefit of any doubt.

[2] See E. S. Corwin, *The President: Office and Powers*, 155-189; also J. G. Randall, *Constitutional Problems Under Lincoln* (New York, 1926), Chaps. II, VI-IX, XVI-XVII, XIX-XX, and "Lincoln in the Rôle of Dictator," *South Atlantic Quar.*, XVIII, 236-252 (July, 1929).

[3] See p. 684 above.

their entire output at the government's disposal, and even to requisition and take over for operation by the government "any factory or any part thereof." In the second place, the years of accelerated defense effort, 1940-41—the period of "the war before the war"—were prolific in statutes conferring war powers of colossal dimensions. One was an act of June 28, 1940 (supplemented by another of May 31, 1941) giving the president discretion to require all orders for war equipment to be assigned priority over any deliveries for private account or export. A second was the Selective Training and Service Act of September 16, 1940, authorizing him to institute a system of general conscription. A third was the Lend-Lease Act of March 11, 1941, placing at his disposal ultimate billions which he could turn over, in the form of goods or of credit for the purchase of such, to the governments of any countries whose war efforts he might regard as beneficial to the United States. And other similarly significant legislation of the period—conferring power to prohibit the export of war equipment, to acquire stocks of strategic and critical materials, to arm merchant ships, and the like—could be cited.

Even with all this, room was left for further broad delegations after the war started. And these took the form in the first instance of (1) a First War Powers Act,[1] passed eleven days after Pearl Harbor, and for the most part reviving or broadening various powers earlier granted to President Wilson, including power (a) to establish censorship over all communications by mail, cable, radio, or other means passing between the United States and any country the president might specifiy, (b) to transfer functions—if related to the conduct of war—from one government agency to another, (c) to modify defense contracts and permit them to be entered into without competitive bidding, and (d) to control alien financial transactions and to utilize in the national interest approximately seven billion dollars' worth of alien property in the United States; and (2) an amending Second War Powers Act,[2] passed three months later, and (among other things) enlarging the power to requisition machinery, tools, and materials, and conferring broad rationing and allocating authority. As time went on, still other delegations were made—for example, in the Emergency Price Control Act of January 30, 1942; and before the conflict was half over, the war powers possessed and exercised by President Roosevelt surpassed those known to any of his predecessors.[3]

[1] 55 U. S. Stat. at Large, 838 (1941).

[2] 56 U. S. Stat. at Large, 176 (1942).

[3] In most instances, powers were conferred for specified periods only. Thus the First War Powers Act was limited to the duration of the war and six months after, and the Second, originally to expire December 31, 1944, was eventually given a maximum duration to March 31, 1947. With hostilities ended in 1945 (although the "war" not yet officially terminated), piecemeal whittling away of grants began, and at the end of 1947 little remained except for features associated with certain permanent laws (there are said to be thirty-six of these in all) which by their own terms are operative only during emergencies. At the date of writing (April, 1948), one important survival of wartime legislation was rent control, extended (with some modifica-

Government in Action During World War II

War on the scale of that in 1941-45 requires not only a huge military machine, but a great civilian establishment behind it; and it will be useful to glance at a few aspects of the civilian mobilization achieved in the years mentioned. To be sure, with respect to wartime machinery, the first fact to be observed is that a very large part of the extra work entailed was at all stages performed by the regular agencies of the national government, vastly enlarged in personnel, and of course assisted and supplemented by the governments of states and localities. Congress remained in session most of the time; the president, with vastly increased responsibilities, worked with a new intensity; the War and Navy Departments enormously expanded their activities; the Treasury Department shaped fiscal policy, collected the augmented revenues, and borrowed money from banks and individuals; the Department of Agriculture stimulated and controlled the output of farm products needed in this country and by the allied nations; the Department of the Interior contributed, among other ways, by handling the difficult problem of oil and gasoline supply; the Federal Works Agency supervised defense building; the U. S. Maritime Commission promoted shipbuilding; the Federal Power Commission helped see to it that power was available for munitions plants; the T.V.A. stepped up the production of both power and chemicals; and so on and on. But of course as new activities developed, and earlier ones expanded beyond all previous conceptions, much new machinery became essential; and before long there arose a maze of freshly created federal agencies, so frequently renamed, reconstructed, and replaced as often to bewilder even the close-at-hand observer in Washington. Nearly all such agencies were called into being by executive order, in some cases with, in others without, express congressional authorization, but usually implementing some broad grant of authority that Congress had made; and while some were placed in one executive department or another, many of the more important ones became independent establishments. Anticipating such multiplication, and at the same time the need for tying in the new establishments with the chief executive and commander-in-chief, an executive order as early as May, 1940, set up in the Executive Office of the President a framework known as the Office of Emergency Management, under whose broad roof were later gathered some fifteen major establishments concerned with different basic fields of wartime control, administration, and research. Some of these (and other) emergency creations have now been abolished or absorbed; others still have functions to perform; a few, in one form or another, may prove permanent.[1]

---

tions) in the early summer of 1947 to March 1, 1948; prolonged for an additional month by an act of February, 1948; and in March, 1948, extended further to March 31, 1949. On clauses in wartime acts authorizing the recall of powers by concurrent resolution, see p. 381, note 3, above.

[1] The most convenient guide to the labyrinth of authorities and agencies function-

The task
to be per-
formed The task of getting the nation of 1940 into a state of defense commensurate with the dangers confronting it, and later of tightening and maintaining the mobilization of men, resources, and effort for actual and prolonged war, was stupendous. Nevertheless, by the summer of 1941 industrial production was showing the greatest upsurge ever witnessed in the country; and with war bursting upon us before the year was out, the pace was redoubled. Thenceforth, armed forces, in mounting numbers, were to be equipped and transported to the four corners of the earth; supplies, in staggering quantities, were to be furnished to Britain, Russia, and China, even while our own needs were catapulting to new heights; indispensable materials no longer obtainable from the customary sources were somehow to be provided through other channels; civilian manpower and womanpower were to be turned to their most effective uses; labor was to be kept ceaselessly on the job; prices were to be held in control as a safeguard against run-away inflation; the channels of transportation were to be kept open for maximum war use; public morale was to be bolstered in a multitude of ways; in short, a wartime economy was to be developed, managed, and made to meet the exigencies of a situation in many respects unprecedented. To follow up in detail even a few of the activities involved would require more space than is available here. But half a dozen may be mentioned.[1]

Some
major
fields of
activity:

1. Pro-
duction Aside from recruiting and training men for the armed forces, the topmost necessity in persent-day war is the provision—speedily and in almost incredible amounts—of munitions and supplies; and with a view to assuring itself of ample production of these, some people thought, when war came in 1941, that the government ought to take over any and all private industry whose products were likely to be seriously needed. This idea, however, did not prevail. To be sure, the government did establish numerous munitions plants (usually operated under contract by private corporations) and finance the expansion of old plants of various kinds or the establishment of new ones; and for longer or shorter periods it took over plants here and there to keep operation from being interfered with by labor difficulties. But it did not waver from the policy of relying principally upon mobilizing the products of industry privately operated. The agency most immediately concerned with stimulating and guiding such production was a War Production Board, dating in its later form

---

ing at successive stages of the defense and war effort is the *United States Government Manual* (new edition twice a year); and the defense machinery in its earlier phases is described in J. P. Harris, "The Emergency National Defense Organization," *Pub. Admin. Rev.*, I, 1-24 (Autumn, 1940). Proliferation of agencies became so extraordinary as to give some point to the story of the Japanese spy who is supposed to have sent word to Tokyo in 1942 that it would be a waste of explosives to bomb Washington because no matter what unit of government was hit, two or three others would be left doing the same thing!

[1] Those pertaining to the important matter of labor relations have been touched upon elsewhere. See pp. 734-735 above. For a full treatment, see the volume, *The United States at War*, cited on p. 836 below—an inspiring record.

from 1942; and it was under such direction—resting constitutionally upon provisions of the National Defense Act of 1916, reënforced by a section of the Selective Service and Training Act of 1940—that not only was the manufacture of many consumer goods checked or stopped and the turning out of war supplies pushed from peak to peak, but stockpiles of essential raw materials were built up and priorities established for funneling materials to war industries most in need of them.[1]

2. Man-power

If it had chosen to do so, the national government could have registered all people outside of the armed forces for civilian war work and assigned them to jobs. Despite many proposals in Congress that something like this be done, no policy so far-reaching was ever adopted.[2] After 1942, however, a War Manpower Commission was concerned with promoting the most effective mobilization and maximum utilization of the country's civilian manpower (and to a less extent womanpower as well); and in conjunction with numerous other agencies, such as the Selective Service System, the Department of Labor, and the labor boards functioning in relation to industrial disputes, it served a useful purpose in keeping people at work, and in places and jobs where they were most needed, not only in industry but in transportation and agriculture as well.

3. Price control and rationing

By the end of 1940, dislocations incident to emphasis upon defense industry began to be reflected in a rising cost of living; indeed there was every reason to anticipate that, unless rigorous checks were applied, prices would continue upward as spending power increased and consumer goods grew scarcer, with the result of augmenting the cost of war supplies, stirring discontent in the ranks of labor, pressing hard upon people with fixed incomes, and quite possibly leading to disastrous inflation. Restrictive efforts through an Office of Price Administration established in 1941 proved of slight avail, because of lack of power actually to fix and enforce price-ceilings. An Emergency Price Control Act of 1942, however (later amended to cover rents), provided for an O. P. A. of greater effectiveness; and from that date until the law expired on June 30, 1946, price levels for commodities likely to be affected by prevailing scarcity were kept reasonably well in hand.[3] After a month of confusion, the regulating agency was called back to life for a year, although under a measure leaving wide latitude for progressive curtailment of its coverage; and on June 30, 1947, it was finally liquidated, with the few controls then surviving transferred to other agencies. From early in 1942, broad powers

---

[1] In October, 1945, the War Production Board was superseded by a Civilian Production Administration, whose surviving functions were, in December, 1946, transferred to a new Office of Temporary Controls—itself terminated, in turn, on June 1, 1947. Cf. J. W. Fesler *et al.*, *Industrial Mobilization for War; History of the War Production Board...1940–1945: Vol. I, Program and Administration* (Washington, D. C., Govt. Prtg. Off., 1947).

[2] The closest approach to such a course of action came in 1942, when all men up to sixty-four years of age were registered, with *liability* to call for some kind of duty.

[3] In Yakus *v.* United States, 321 U. S. 414 (1944), the federal Supreme Court held the act's delegation of power to be within constitutional bounds.

(conferred in the Second War Powers Act) to ration commodities among consumers fell also to the O. P.A., being employed, as every one knows, in connection with not only automobiles, tires, gasoline, fuel oil, farm machinery, coffee, sugar, meats, canned goods, and shoes, but numerous other articles for which demand was out of proportion to supply. The last surviving item (sugar) dropped from the list, however, in 1947.[1]

4. Trans-portation   Almost as vital as the production of war materials is the moving of them (and also of troops) to the places where they are needed; and it is not surprising to find that in wartime government exercises special controls over nearly every form of transportation. Less than two weeks after the Pearl Harbor disaster, an executive order set up an Office of Defense Transportation, with jurisdiction (within the general framework of existing transportation controls wielded by the Interstate Commerce Commission and allied agencies) over railroads, inland waterways, air transport, motor transport, coastwise shipping, and pipe lines; and from that time onward the O.D.T. not only controlled railroad traffic so as to get the utmost out of existing trackage and equipment, assure priority for troop movements and for shipments of war materials, and avert terminal congestion at ports, but encouraged greater utilization and conservation of motor trucks and commercial passenger vehicles (under a rationing system), and likewise devices such as group-riding for relieving carriers while also conserving tires and gasoline. Important services, too, were rendered in connection with the transportation of petroleum and its products, and with coastwise shipping. In 1947, President Truman recommended the O.D.T.'s continuance through fiscal 1948; and in the spring of the latter year people were reminded of the agency's existence when it curtailed railroad traffic during a coal strike.

5. Information and censorship   War is waged also in the realm of ideas and their dissemination; and any government in wartime will concern itself not only with getting to its people the information it wants them to have and with cultivating a public opinion favorable to the war effort, but also with keeping from the enemy information that would be useful to him, and with preventing both the enemy and enemy sympathizers from damaging the national morale through open or secret propaganda. The story of our government's efforts after 1940 to keep the nation discreetly informed on the problems, progress, and goals of the defense and war effort would reveal a good deal of fumbling with a difficult problem, leading eventually, however, to a fairly successful integration of responsibility in an Office of War Information established in the summer of 1942.[2] The reverse of the picture took the form of organized effort to prevent dissemination of

[1] P. M. O'Leary, "Rationing and Governmental Organization," *Amer. Polit. Sci. Rev.*, XXXIX, 1089-1106 (Dec., 1945); E. S. Redford, *Field Administration of Wartime Rationing* (Washington, D. C., Govt. Prtg. Office, 1947).

[2] See W. H. C. Laves, "The Face-to-Face War Information Service of the Federal Government," *Amer. Polit. Sci. Rev.*, XXXVII, 1027-1040 (Dec., 1943). The corresponding agency during World War I was a Committee on Public Information, headed by the journalist, George Creel.

information or opinion which might prove of value to the enemy or damaging to the war effort or morale of our own people; and to undertake this responsibility an Office of Censorship was set up almost as soon as we were in the war. In the case of all mail, cablegrams, long-distance telephone calls, radio messages, and other communications going out of (or in the case of mail, coming into) the United States, there was literal censorship in the sense of advance inspection, with decision whether to delete passages or refuse to permit any part to go through. In the case, however, of domestic publications and radio-broadcasting, the method was rather that of securing voluntary compliance with "codes of wartime practices" telling the press and broadcasting companies what they must not print or broadcast—although, of course, with no lack of power to compel compliance where not forthcoming voluntarily.[1]

The conduct of war is definitely a national function, but collaboration by state and local governments, and by voluntary citizen groups as well, is essential to solidarity of effort. During World War II, state and local machinery was employed in operating the selective service system, the rationing system, and to some extent the system of price control; and civilian defense—aimed chiefly, so long as there remained any danger of enemy assault upon our home front, at protecting people and property against the hazards of air raids, but later principally at promoting morale and encouraging productiveness—was organized also largely on a state and local basis. Every state eventually set up a defense council; several thousand cities and counties did likewise; and, in all, millions of men and women rendered various voluntary services. Federal encouragement and supervision were supplied by an Office of Civilian Defense established in 1941, with, however, no final powers of compulsion; and the intelligence, fidelity, and effectiveness with which the state and local agencies functioned naturally showed a good deal of variation the country over.[2]

6. Civilian defense

Military Law, Martial Law, and Military Government

In exercising their defense powers, Congress and the president have certain further jurisdictions requiring a word of comment. One of the number, to be sure, was mentioned earlier when it was stated that Congress has authority to enact "rules for the government of the land and naval forces."[3] As pointed out, too, the resulting regulations for the Army are called the "Articles of War;" those for the Navy, the "Articles for the Government of the Navy;" and together the two are known as

Military law

---

[1] See B. Price, "Governmental Censorship in Wartime," *Amer. Polit. Sci. Rev.,* XXXVI, 837-849 (Oct., 1942). The author was director of censorship throughout the war period. In August, 1945, promptly after the last Axis surrender, the Office of Censorship was liquidated.

[2] A. Miles and R. H. Owsley, *Cities and the National Defense Program* (Chicago, 1941). The Office of Civilian Defense ceased operating on June 30, 1945.

The costs of the war effort in terms of expenditures, taxes, and debt have been touched upon in an earlier chapter. See pp. 569-570 above.

[3] See p. 803 above.

the "Military Laws of the United States." Within their proper spheres, both Army and Navy have "governments" of their own, with the military regulations prescribed by Congress serving as codes of law, with hierarchies of military and naval officers administering such law, with military police and courts-martial [1] aiding in the enforcement of it, and with legal branches under judge advocates general, and likewise legal staffs attached to divisions and corps areas, exercising functions of a judicial nature. The regulations imposed by Congress set forth the powers and duties of officers and men in the military and naval services, define offenses against discipline, provide means and procedures for trying persons accused of such offenses, fix penalties, and otherwise regulate military activities and conduct. While, however, civilians are not subject to military law,[2] soldiers and sailors are by no means exempt from the ordinary law applying to civilians. Breaches of discipline and other minor offenses committed on military or naval reservations are dealt with only by the military or naval authorities. But a case involving serious crime, *e.g.*, murder, is likely to go to a civil court. Moreover, crimes committed outside military reservations may be handled by the military or on the other hand by civil authorities, and in peacetime an offender returning to the reservation where he belongs may be turned over to the proper civil court. In point of fact, almost any civil crime will be found to have been made a serious offense under military law also. Jurisdictional conflicts sometimes arise when state, rather than federal, laws are involved. But the principle is clear that state agents may not interfere with any action or procedure clearly authorized by federal law, military or civil.[3]

Martial
law

Military law should not be confused with *martial* law. The former emanates from Congress and applies only to persons in (or at all events closely associated with) the armed services; the latter emanates from military commanders and normally applies only to the civilian population of a specified area, although members of the military within the area may to some degree be affected also. Furthermore, whereas military law

[1] Courts-martial consist of properly designated officers charged, in particular situations, with hearing cases, rendering decisions, and fixing penalties, which may extend to condemnation to imprisonment or death.

[2] Except to a limited degree in a few instances where auxiliary services are being rendered.

[3] For a good brief discussion of military law and justice, see E. W. Puttkammer [ed.], *War and the Law* (Chicago, 1944). A useful source-book on the subject is A. A. Schiller, *Military Law and Defense Legislation* (St. Paul, Minn., 1941). Cf. L. G. Compton, "Khaki Justice; What Court Martial Means," *Atlantic Mo.*, CLXXIII, 47-52 (June, 1944); Major Gen. A. W. Gullion, "Courts Martial Today," *Amer. Bar Assoc. Jour.*, XXVII, 765-769 (Dec., 1941); Judge Advocate Gen. M. C. Cramer, "Military Justice and Trial Procedure," *ibid.*, XXIX, 368-371 (July, 1943). Experience during World War II gave rise to strong demand for more democratic and less harsh processes of military justice, and in January, 1948, the House of Representatives unanimously approved a comprehensive bill on the subject, with the Senate expected to concur. See K. C. Royall, "Revision of the Military Justice Process as Proposed by the War Department," *Va. Law Rev.*, XXXIII, 269-288 (May, 1947).

takes the form of definite codes which can be read and studied, martial law constitutes no fixed system, but on the contrary consists simply, in any particular situation, of whatever rules and regulations the competent military authority may from day to day impose—the essence of martial law being the replacement for the time being of the ordinary law, and of the courts and other authorities operating under it, by a special régime in which the commander's word becomes the law and special tribunals set up by him (to be distinguished, of course, from courts-martial) handle cases arising under it. There are mixed situations in which civilian authorities may enlist the assistance of the military in executing the regular law, without martial law in the full sense being introduced; and even where full martial law prevails, it is not outside of the constitution and does not of itself abrogate the citizen's constitutional rights—for example, while the privilege of the writ of *habeas corpus* is usually suspended when martial law is in operation, mere proclamation of such law does not of itself suspend the writ. In the great majority of cases, martial law operates under state rather than federal authority, being proclaimed by the governor when he has reason to believe that a disaster like a great fire or earthquake, or disorder growing out of labor troubles, or peril in wartime, has created need in a given area (city, county, or section) for something more than the normal functioning of the regular authorities. In one critical period of our history (the Civil War), however, martial law was proclaimed also by the president; and when Lincoln's actions were judicially challenged, the Supreme Court sustained them as being legitimate applications of his power as chief executive and commander-in-chief.[1] As already observed, suspension of the writ of *habeas corpus*, while usually going along with martial law, is separable from it, both legally and practically; indeed, the constitution has a clause on suspension, while leaving martial law as such unmentioned. Elsewhere it has been pointed out that, while President Lincoln several times suspended the writ on his own authority, the proper view, supported by the courts, now is that only Congress possesses the power, although the president may be authorized to exercise it.[2]

Pertaining as it does to control over conquered territory, military government is something still different from military law and martial law. As commander-in-chief, the president has ample power to institute such government in areas coming under our control, and to maintain it until

Military government

---

[1] The Prize Cases, 2 Black 635 (1863). Cf. *Ex parte* Milligan, 4 Wallace 2 (1866).
[2] See p. 167 above. On the general subject, see the writings of C. Fairman cited on p. 836 below; and cf. E. Warren, "Wartime Martial Control in California," *Calif. State Bar Jour.*, XVII, 185-204 (July-Aug., 1942). On the writ of *habeas corpus:* E. S. Corwin, *The President: Office and Powers*, 176-189; S. G. Fisher, "Suspension of *Habeas Corpus* During the War of the Rebellion," *Polit. Sci. Quar.*, III, 454-488 (Sept., 1888); G. C. Sellery, *Lincoln's Suspension of Habeas Corpus as Viewed by Congress* (Madison, Wis., 1907); G. Anthony, "Martial Law, Military Government, and the Writ of *Habeas Corpus*," *Calif. Law Rev.*, XXXI, 477-514 (Dec., 1943).

such time as Congress may make different arrangements. The necessity for keeping civilian populations out of the way, maintaining supply lines and communications, and preserving at least a semblance of law and order usually requires a certain amount of military government even in territories in which campaigns are going on; after war was carried into Germany in 1945, American and other Allied military-government detachments closely followed Army divisions from region to region and took over control of civilian affairs. The broadest scope for such government comes, however, after conquest has been completed. Puerto Rico, for example, was held under a military régime, directed by the president, from 1898 until 1900, and the Philippines for two years longer. At the close of World War I, we had experience with military government in the Rhineland which did not, of course, leave us with new territory to be provided with civil administration, but from which we at least learned a good deal.

It, however, has been in connection with World War II that military government has enlisted our activities on the largest scale. Foreseeing that this would be true, authorities at Washington planned and carried out preparations on an unprecedented scale: civil affairs sections were set up in the War and Navy Departments; "G-5" staffs were created at different levels in the Army; a School of Military Government for instruction of civilians was organized by the Army at the University of Virginia and a similar school by the Navy at Columbia University; a civil affairs training program was put in operation at ten other universities throughout the country;[1] and some eight thousand men—many of them persons of mature experience in education, engineering, law, and state and municipal administration—were fed into the stream of civilian personnel flowing also from Great Britain, the Soviet Union, and elsewhere into Germany, Austria, Italy, the South Pacific, and eventually Japan proper. Of course the situation was complicated by the fact that the United States was not operating alone, but in conjunction with a number of allied nations; for Europe, there was an over-all Allied Control Council, and for Japan a Far Eastern Commission. Interest and convenience, however, dictated the allocation of particular areas or "zones," notably in Germany, to individual allies; and in that way military government became the almost independent responsibility of the United States in extensive territories, both European and Oriental, occupied to this day (1948) by our armed forces.[2] Except to a limited extent in the South Pacific, no question of ultimate annexation was involved. But the

[1] C. S. Hyneman, "The Army's Civil Affairs Training Program," *Amer. Polit. Sci. Rev.*, XXXVIII, 342-353 (Apr., 1944).

[2] Early in 1946, uniformed and civilian Americans engaged in the occupation of Germany, Austria, and Italy numbered 400,000; in Japan, there were 150,000 more, and in Korea and China, 60,000. These numbers have been gradually reduced—in the case of Europe, by nearly fifty per cent by the middle of 1947. In both Germany and Japan, however, considerable quotas will be required indefinitely.

time at which, and the circumstances under which, our responsibility for the management of affairs in the various areas could be terminated remained at the date of writing (April, 1948) one of the uncertainties of the postwar period.[1]

The Organization of Defense

For nearly one hundred and sixty years, the defense machinery of the United States was conspicuously lacking in integration. To be sure, the president as chief executive and commander-in-chief supplied some unity at the top, as did also the controls exercised by Congress. But the War and Navy Departments were entirely separate; the Army and Navy whose affairs they managed were not only separate, but often uncoöperative and even antagonistic; [2] military and naval interests were treated as two different and essentially unrelated matters. Each branch of Congress had its separate military affairs and naval affairs committee; the appropriations committee in each branch had its separate military and naval subcommittees; and not only all appropriations but substantially all other defense legislation followed sharp lines of division, with Congress rarely in a position to consider both Army and Navy needs and problems at the same time. In earlier and simpler days, the resulting disadvantages were often manifest, but usually not too serious, and little was done toward overcoming them; we emerged from our wars successfully, and with no serious dissipation of energies or waste. Even World War I brought no significant change. World War II, however, was different, not simply in its wholly unprecedented magnitude and complexity and its enormous demands upon coöperative effort of the land, sea, and air forces, but in leaving us with a world situation making it indispensable that the nation maintain not only a far larger armed establishment than ever before in peacetime, but an establishment organized and integrated for the greatest possible efficiency. And the early postwar years have witnessed a defense reorganization outstripping any in all our previous history—even

Former dispersion of defense administration and services

---

[1] It is axiomatic in American military government that local systems of law shall, in general, be maintained and even local agencies of administration left intact, although with changes of personnel if necessary (as in Germany and Japan) for obtaining loyal coöperation from those in office. There is also the task of fostering and assisting efforts to reconstruct machinery of government so as to be acceptable and efficient after the American hand has been withdrawn—to say nothing (as again, for example, in Germany and Japan) of directing a revived cultural life into wholesome channels.

The standard earlier treatise on the subject is D. Y. Thomas, "History of Military Government in the Newly Acquired Territory of the United States," *Columbia Univ. Studies in Hist., Econ., and Public Law,* XX, No. 2 (1904); and a convenient brief historical survey is R. H. Gabriel, "American Experience with Military Government," *Amer. Polit. Sci. Rev.,* XXXVII, 417-438 (June, 1943). On more recent experience, two very informing books are those of H. Holborn and H. Zink cited on p. 837 below. Cf. A. C. Davidonis, "Some Problems of Military Government," *Amer. Polit. Sci. Rev.,* XXXVIII, 460-474 (June, 1944); A. Vagts, "Military Command and Military Government," *Polit. Sci. Quar.,* LIX, 248-263 (June, 1944).

[2] There has traditionally been discord, too, between the Regular Army and the organized militia or National Guard, the former resenting the constitutional status and relatively impregnable political position of the latter.

though still, as recently as the autumn of 1947, mainly a matter of legislative enactment, with the full working out of the plan impossible to foresee.

The National Security Act of 1947On the legislative side, some improvement resulted from the Legislative Reorganization Act of 1946, under which the separate military and naval affairs committees in both branches of Congress were consolidated into single committees on the armed services. But this left quite untouched the main problem of unifying the defense establishments themselves and the machinery for managing their affairs; and the most spectacular new development in the organization of the national government—at all events since the reorganization of Congress—has been the reconstruction of national defense envisaged and outlined in a National Security Act [1] signed by the president on July 26, 1947. From far back, there had been intermittent proposals to merge the War and Navy Departments into some form of defense department, and in some degree to integrate the Army and Navy as well—proposals also that if this were not done, at least the air services of the two departments (along with perhaps civilian aviation) be brought together in a department of aviation on the pattern of air ministries found in Great Britain and some other countries. No approach to action, however, took place until during World War II. Experience in that conflict—evidences of disadvantage arising from Army and Navy independence, evidences also of gain from unified commands in war theaters and notably from operations of the Joint Chiefs of Staff in Washington—prompted new interest in consolidation; and not only did a bill appear in Congress in 1942, but a House committee studied the subject at length in 1943-44. The consensus of opinion was that the change would be too drastic to be undertaken with war in progress. But no sooner were hostilities ended than, with warm support from President Truman (who made achievement of the necessary legislation a major objective of his administration) plans for the contemplated "merger" were revived and actively pressed. In general, the War Department and Army were favorable. Naval interests, however, were opposed, employing as arguments, among others, their fear of the "inertia of size" and their dislike of sacrificing the healthy competition, as they viewed it, existing between the services. Postponed after vigorous discussion in the 1946 congressional session, the proposal was again brought under active consideration in the session of 1947; various compromises having the ultimate effect of reconciling the Navy were worked out; and in midsummer, 1947, the efforts of the legislation's supporters were crowned with success.

National defense as now organizedThe resulting new frame of organization presents several significant features. (1) The War Department (renamed Department of the Army) continues, and likewise the Department of the Navy. (2) Coördinate with these is a new Department of the Air Force, under which all military

[1] *Pub. Law 253—80th Cong., 1st Sess.*

and naval air forces are consolidated into a United States Air Force.[1] (3) Above all three departments (composing the "National Military Establishment"), with their respective secretaries or heads, an under-secretary, and two assistant secretaries, is placed a secretary of defense, symbol of the new coördination and charged with formulating basic policies and programs and exercising general direction and authority over all of the services. (4) As "principal assistant" to the president in all that relates to national security, this "super-secretary" is seated in the cabinet, as the three department secretaries are not. (5) Auxiliary to him, too, are four miscellaneous units, *i.e.*, the Joint Chiefs of Staff; a War Council consisting, under his chairmanship, of the secretaries of the Army, the Navy, and the Air Force and three chiefs of staff; a Munitions Board composed of a chairman and three under-secretaries or assistant secretaries; and a Research and Development Board, with a chairman and two representatives each of the Army, Navy, and Air Force. (6) Finally, directly auxiliary to the president are (a) a National Security Council embracing the secretary of state, secretary of defense, secretaries of the Army, the Navy, and the Air Force, and other persons designated by the chief executive, and designed to help the chief executive integrate domestic, foreign, and military policies relating to defense; and (b) a National Security Resources Board composed of heads or other represen-tatives of departments or other agencies not specified in the law, and charged with preparing plans and programs for the best wartime utiliza-tion of the nation's resources—an agency likely to be only a skeleton organization in time of peace but in wartime discharging substantially the functions exercised during World War II by the War Production Board. Popular interest in the reorganization naturally centered in the rearrangement of departments and the introduction of the over-all secre-tary of defense. Almost equally significant, however, is the galaxy of councils and boards (new or reconstructed) provided for purposes of both long- and short-term study, planning, and advice.

Those responsible for the legislation recognized that, as merely prelim-inary to a vast amount of further reorganization presupposed, it well

---

[1] Thus, in the final compromise, the Army obtained a measure of over-all unifica-tion, the Navy retained a measure of autonomy, and the Air Force won recognition as a distinct service.

Aside from managing a few insular possessions of significance chiefly for strategic purposes, and temporarily administering our new trusteeship for the former Japanese mandated islands (see p. 852 below), the Navy Department has no functions not directly connected with the Navy itself. At different times the War Department has had a considerable variety of non-military responsibilities, including until 1939 super-vision of the administration of Philippine and other insular affairs. These, however, have of late been reduced to only two of substantial importance: (1) construction of public works in connection with river and harbor improvement and flood control, and (2) maintenance and operation of the Panama Canal, together with supervision of the affairs of the Canal Zone. The organization and functions of both depart-ments, now undergoing a good deal of change under the National Security Act, will be found outlined in the latest issue of the *United States Government Manual*. On the former War Department, see especially E. P. Herring, *The Impact of War* (New York, 1941), Chap. IV, and the article by J. D. Millett cited on p. 836 below.

might prove to have opened up as many problems as it solved; indeed, the act itself allowed two years for fully implementing its terms on all levels of the defense system. In turning to some comment on the defense services themselves, it therefore is possible at present to speak of them only as they existed under a former top organization. Changes to which the new administrative and advisory arrangements may lead may prove few or many, but at all events they are for the future to reveal.

The Army of the United States

Component elements

Under terms of the National Defense Act of 1920, the Army of the United States includes (1) the Regular Army, (2) the National Guard, and (3) the Organized Reserve Corps. Defined (at least hitherto) as the "permanent military establishment" in both peace and war, the Regular Army consists of (1) full-time officers and (2) enlisted men and non-commissioned officers, in such numbers as Congress may determine, and ordinarily recruited in peacetime from volunteers serving from one to three years, with optional reënlistments for three-year periods. As indicated at various points above, the National Guard consists of the organized militia of the several states and territories, liberally supported with federal funds, liable to call at any time into federal service, and in 1940 (when numbering 245,000) actually so called. The Organized Reserve Corps consists principally of men who, although engaged in ordinary civilian pursuits, have had training in Reserve Officers Training Corps ("R.O.T.C.") units in colleges and universities—an establishment totalling some 75,000 on the eve of World War II, and constituting a permanent reservoir of officer material on which to draw when need arises, as in 1940.[1]

The Regular Army before 1940

Free from dangerous neighbors on its borders, and far removed from the scenes of Old World conflict (until technological developments brought them near), the United States has traditionally maintained only a small standing army. Active entrance into world politics in the period of the Spanish-American War led to some lasting increase of the forces;

---

[1] On the Women's Army Corps as another at least temporary component, see p. 828, note 1, below.

Under normal conditions, the Regular Army is officered principally by men trained in the United States Military Academy at West Point, and the Navy similarly by men trained in the United States Naval Academy at Annapolis—with some having received, in addition, training of more specialized or advanced nature at an Army War College at Washington, a Naval War College at Newport, Rhode Island, or some one of three or four other auxiliary training centers. Persons to receive basic training are selected in part on a preferential plan—with, for example, special consideration for honor graduates of colleges and universities affording military training under the supervision of Army officers. In the main, however, they are nominees of senators, representatives, and territorial delegates, under a system designed to assure wide geographical, social, and racial distribution and discourage the rise of a military caste, although hardly calculated to insure the best possible selections, since under the rules the young man named in each case as "principal" must be appointed if he passes his examinations notwithstanding that on other than academic grounds —perchance on academic grounds too—some one of the three "alternates" named may be superior.

but even in 1914 the authorized strength of the Regular Army was only 98,000 officers and men, and the actual enlisted strength considerably less. Emergency effort during the First World War brought under arms, chiefly by draft, more than three and one-half millions. As late as 1939, however, the Army's effective strength stood at only 13,814 officers and 174,079 enlisted men—a total of 187,893.[1]

Preparation of the country to meet the dangers looming by 1940 brought, however, a totally different situation. The first moves made were to increase the authorized enlisted strength of the Regular Army and National Guard, to launch intensive campaigns for recruiting volunteers, and eventually to call the National Guard and Organized Reserves in all of the states into federal service. All this, however, was only preliminary to a far more drastic step, i.e., the first *peacetime* resort to selective compulsory military service in the country's history.[2] On September 13, 1940, the president approved a Selective Service and Training Act[3] under which all male citizens and resident male aliens between the ages of twenty-one and thirty-five were required to register, thereupon becoming (except as otherwise provided) liable, as soon as called, to training and service in the land or naval forces of the nation; and chiefly from this legislation, modified and extended in various respects during the next five or six years, resulted the unprecedented force of almost twelve million men which the nation had under arms (in all services) when the Axis Powers collapsed, operating (at one time or another) in more than thirty distinct areas, in nearly all quarters of the globe.[4] Two weeks after the Japanese attack at Pearl Harbor, the draft was broadened to require all men between the ages of eighteen and sixty-four inclusive (except those already registered) to register for conscription in the armed forces or for non-combatant activities. Comparatively few persons beyond military age ever received actual assignments. But the military roster was adjusted to include men of all ages between eighteen and forty-five, with such as fell in class 1A (physically fit, without dependents, and not engaged in an essential industry) subject to first call. Later, various deferred groups between eighteen and thirty-eight were drawn upon, although with monthly payments provided for dependents. As finally developed, the operating machinery consisted chiefly of (1) an inde-

World War II and Selective Service

[1] E. P. Herring, *The Impact of War* (New York, 1941), Chap. III, "The Place of the Army in National Life," is an illuminating interpretation.

[2] A draft act of narrower scope had been passed in 1863 and one resembling the 1940 measure in 1917, but on both occasions the country was at the time actually engaged in war.

[3] 54 *U. S. Stat. at Large*, 885. For the original act and all later amendments, see E. A. Lewis [comp.], *The Selective Service Act as Amended* (Washington, D. C., Govt. Prtg. Off., 1946).

[4] The total number of Selective Service inductions from 1940 to the time of final expiration in 1947 was 10,022,367, or sixty-seven per cent of the entire force ever under arms. Originally, only the Army drew upon the Selective Service lists. Under executive order of December 5, 1942, however, the Navy, Marine Corps, and Coast Guard, previously relying on volunteers, were authorized to recruit from the same source; and the figures mentioned, both above and in this note, include all of these services.

pendent establishment, the Selective Service System, presided over by a director at Washington; (2) the governors of the several states, working through state directors; (3) unpaid local (county or district) boards of three members appointed by the president on recommendation of the governor, and charged with compiling lists of eligibles, keeping them up to date, and managing the actual work of selection within their respective jurisdictions; and (4) local appeal boards to which individuals objecting to their classification or to orders for induction could resort, together with a "government agent" attached to each local board and empowered to appeal on his own part against any registrant's classification or deferment.[1]

The postwar Army

With hostilities finally terminated, demobilization began. Even between V-E Day (May, 1945) and V-J Day (three months later), a top Army strength of 8,300,000 officers and men was cut somewhat, and in ensuing months discharges continued at a pace as rapid as the task of bringing back millions of men from overseas would permit. By January 1, 1946, the number remaining in service was down to approximately half of the earlier figure; by the following summer, to 1,550,000; and by December 1, 1947, to 911,500. Meanwhile, during 1946 General of the Army Dwight D. Eisenhower, Chief of Staff, gave it as his considered opinion that for at least fifteen or twenty years an effective Army strength of 800,000 would be essential, backed by a National Guard of 680,000 (double its prewar strength) and trained officer reserve forces numbering from 100,000 to 150,000; and in the same year Congress, with presidential approval, fixed (at least for some time to come) 1,070,000 as the figure to be maintained for the Army (including 195,000 reserve officers) and 682,114 for the National Guard. So far as the National Guard was concerned, the goal seemed not wholly unattainable; in any case, all of the

---

[1] No cases turning on the constitutionality of the earliest federal draft law—the Conscription Act of 1863—ever reached the Supreme Court, but in a group of actions growing out of the Selective Draft Act of 1917 and protesting the authority of Congress to "raise and support armies" by such a method, that tribunal unanimously found ample justification for it not only in various military clauses of the constitution, but in the "reciprocal obligation of the citizen to render military service in case of need and the right to compel it." Selective Draft Law Cases, 245 U. S. 366 (1918). So convincing, too, were the Draft Law decisions that the Supreme Court was never called upon to pass on any general question of validity of the 1940 legislation, although naturally a number of cases arose involving interpretation and administration. Perhaps the most important conclusion reached in certain of these by-product cases was that determinations made by local draft boards were administrative in nature and not intended by Congress to be appealable to the courts—although without right of appeal, under certain circumstances, being entirely cut off. See Estep v. United States, 327 U. S. 114 (1946).

Detailed accounts of selective service in operation will be found in the works of Boutwell and Duggan listed on p. 836 below.

On May 14, 1942, a bill was approved establishing a Women's Army Auxiliary Corps (W.A.A.C.), designed to utilize the services of women (on a purely voluntary basis) and thereby release soldiers for combat duty. Within a little over a year, 65,000 women were members; and in 1943 the status of the Corps was changed from that of an Army auxiliary to that of a regular component of the Army, with the nickname correspondingly converted to W.A.C. In 1947, the War Department urged that the unit, on a reduced basis, be made permanent.

states accepted the quotas assigned them under the plan, and efforts have since been going forward to recruit up to something approaching the desired strength.[1] The outlook for the Army, however, became a matter of grave concern. On the assumption that all drafted men so desiring could be released and their places taken in sufficient numbers by enlisted volunteers, the Selective Service Act, after being once suspended but later revived, was allowed to lapse on March 31, 1947 (when, indeed, only 100,000 "selectees" remained in service), and on the ensuing June 30 the Army officially went on an all-volunteer basis for the first time since 1940. Already, however, there were misgivings, because the assumption of adequate volunteer enlistments was proving ill-founded; even when the draft law expired, the Army's effective strength had fallen to not much above 900,000; and whereas, to maintain the level agreed on by Congress, the president, and Army authorities, voluntary enlistment must proceed at an average monthly rate of 30,000, it actually was running at 20,000 or less. Notwithstanding various efforts to obtain better results, the situation continued through 1947; and, moved by this as well as by Army budget cuts in Congress, General Eisenhower painted a gloomy picture of American military strength ("a poor second to the Russian"[2]), while speculation mounted as to whether a revival of selective service in some mild form—forecast from the beginning by President Truman in case volunteering should prove an insufficient resource—might not eventually have to be revived.[3] However much we may deplore the fact, the mounting international responsibilities assumed by our country, combined with the sort of a world in which we apparently must live, leave no option to maintaining a degree of military power which even a decade or two ago would have seemed fantastic.

The Navy

A second great defense arm is the Navy, operated through a Navy Department set off from the War Department in 1798 when a conflict with France seemed in the offing, and now one of the three coördinate defense departments for which the act of 1947 provides. Naturally, all funds for "providing and maintaining" a navy must be voted by Con-

[1] Appointment by the secretary of defense, late in 1947, of an interdepartmental committee on reserve components stirred animated discussion of a proposal, often heard, that the National Guard and the Army's organized reserves be merged into a single purely federal militia. Protests from the National Guard Association (official organization of the state militias) evoked the explanation that such a development was not necessarily intended.

[2] In May, 1947, the Soviet Union was supposed to have an armed strength of 3,800,000; even Great Britain had 1,210,000 men under arms.

[3] In the early summer of 1947, Congress passed an act (*Pub. Law 128—80th Cong., 1st Sess.*) designed to stimulate enlistments in various ways. The results were not encouraging; although by early 1948 an aroused public awareness of international dangers was reflected in considerably stimulated recruiting. In a message to Congress on March 18, President Truman called urgently not only for adoption of universal military training, but for a law under which young men might once more be drafted for armed service.

gress—without, however, in this instance any restriction upon the period for which appropriations may be made as in the case of the Army. In Congress, too, is vested full power to regulate naval, as well as military, administration; and of course the president is commander-in-chief of naval and military establishments alike.

From Revolutionary times, the United States maintained a navy of lofty traditions, but of no great size until the close of World War I, when, with an imposing fleet afloat and a still more powerful one under construction, the country found itself, almost as if overnight, with the scepter of sea supremacy within its grasp. At the Washington Conference on the Limitation of Naval Armaments, in 1921-22, agreements were entered into among the leading naval powers under which twenty-eight of our capital ships (including some under construction) were sunk, scrapped, or demilitarized; the London Naval Conference of 1930 provided for still further reductions; and for a time, notwithstanding a certain amount of new building, our naval strength actually declined. Partly as a means of relieving unemployment, a more vigorous building program was, however, entered upon in 1934; and after it became clear not only that other nations (particularly Japan) were rapidly increasing their naval strength by building all types of fighting craft not covered by ratio agreements, but also that the Washington and London treaties would not endure beyond 1936, effort was redoubled, bringing the country once more into a world-wide armament race. Mounting naval appropriations, persuasively urged by President Roosevelt, made possible more building during the later thirties than in any comparable earlier period; and with war breaking out in Europe in 1939 and threatening the destruction of even the British Navy (on which we long had depended heavily), a building program was launched in 1940 aimed at making the United States fleet by 1946 the most powerful that had ever ploughed the seas. The objective now was also a "two-ocean" navy (i.e., a navy capable of being divided between the Atlantic and the Pacific, yet with "command of the sea" in both areas); and since a navy consists not merely of ships, aircraft, shore fortifications, and men, but also of bases, sites for eight well-located bases in or adjacent to the Atlantic were leased from Great Britain for immediate development.

After our own involvement in the war in 1941, the building and launching of naval, as well as merchant, ships—battleships, aircraft carriers, heavy and light cruisers, destroyers, submarines, and all manner of auxiliary craft—was stepped up almost incredibly, proceeding for five years on a scale never before approached in this or any other country, and leaving us at the end with far and away the largest and strongest naval establishment in the world. In July, 1946—five years after inauguration of the two-ocean program—the Navy Department announced that in eight government-owned navy yards and twenty-eight privately owned yards, 1,322 fighting ships had been turned out during the period, and that the United States had a current total of 1,500 combatant ships (with 100,000 auxiliary vessels of all kinds), with 223 additional ones building and to be completed within a year.[1] Corresponding increases took place, of course, in naval personnel, bringing a force of 420,500 officers and men when Pearl Harbor was attacked to the stupendous total of 3,717,000 at the end of 1944.[2] After long trailing Great Britain in naval strength, we had gained parity with that historic maritime power under the agreements of 1921-22, and now had gone so far ahead that there was no close comparison.

From the top figure of personnel mentioned, demobilization proceeded after 1945 as in the Army, with Navy plans contemplating a peacetime "ceiling" of 500,000, in addition to a Marine Corps of 100,000; and in 1946 these quotas were given express statutory authorization. By the end of 1947, the figure for the Navy proper had declined to 399,800, and for the Marine Corps to 83,200. Naturally, new building was largely (although not wholly) suspended. But the country had on its hands (and still has), in active service or in reserve, the huge equipment of ships and other facilities carried over from the war years—more than double the tonnage of Great Britain, and indeed nearly a quarter more than the tonnage of all foreign nations combined.[3] For the long pull ahead, the temper of Congress and people has been favorable to a naval establishment surpassing the total naval strength of the rest of the world—at all events until developments of the Atomic Age shall have shown incontrovertibly that surface craft and operations have become obsolete. With the world situation as it has been, there naturally has come no change of mind on the subject.[4]

Our naval position today

[1] More than 5,000 merchant and cargo ships were built during the same period.

[2] These figures include (1) the Marine Corps, a naval auxiliary dating from 1798 and organized on Army lines to provide the Navy with trained infantry for "amphibious" operations, and (2) the Coast Guard, dating from 1790 and in peacetime attached to the Treasury Department as a sort of maritime police, but during the war absorbed temporarily into the Navy Department.

Significant new units organized during the war included (1) the Construction Battalions ("Seabees") dating from December 28, 1941, and consisting of men trained primarily as construction workers but also as fighters, and (2) the Women Accepted for Volunteer Emergency Service (WAVES), authorized on July 30, 1942, to provide women trained for shore jobs from which men could thus be released for sea duty By 1944, the personnel of the Seabees numbered nearly a quarter of a million, and that of the WAVES some 47,000. In June, 1947, the Navy Department requested Congress to continue the WAVES (by then numbering only 2,500) as a permanent auxiliary, with a maximum strength of 11,000, and also a Marine Corps Women's Reserve, with a strength of 2,200. Early in 1948, action on these lines was pending.

[3] World War II brought the aircraft carrier into recognition as the most important type of capital ship; and with more than one hundred carriers in its possession, the United States is more than twice as well equipped in this respect as any other nation. Future developments in the construction and use of aircraft may, however, take such a course as to diminish the significance of this situation.

[4] At the date of writing (1947), the United States Air Force, under its separate department, had not yet fully taken form in accordance with the terms of the National Security Act, and consequently no attempt can be made to describe it. Potential personnel (as of August 1) included 43,000 officers and 264,000 men; and there were 3,766 first-line combat planes, of which, however, only 1,289 were in commission. A presidential Air Policy Commission had been studying problems suggested by its name (a report was submitted in January, 1948), and in addition Congress had

Some Larger Defense Questions

The
impact of
atomic
power

Our American system of national defense has been outlined at consid-erable length, and space remains for only the barest mention of certain pressing problems, new and old, relating to it, even on the morrow of its greatest tests and triumphs. The major new problem—and quite com-pletely new—is one that, of course, dwarfs all others, *i.e.*, the bearings upon all national defense (our own included) of the release of atomic energy, with all its potentialities for harm as well as help. The dramatic tests conducted at Bikini atoll in the South Pacific in 1946 were designed to reveal, among other things, what the atomic bomb, if employed by an enemy, would do to an American fleet. But it was already manifest that the "absolute weapon" had hurled a challenge at all means and methods of defense employed through the centuries, on land and sea, and that unless its use could somehow in future be kept under rigorous restraint, the nations might as well begin all over again to think through and make provision for the protection of their peoples and possessions in this age of technological revolution. Our first great defense question today is, there-fore, whether we really have any defense at all, or indeed can have, in the new and terrifying situation that has arisen.[1]

The
outlook
for inter-
national
peace

Deeply involved with this is, of course, the question of whether, even though there may turn out to be no really effective defense against the bomb, the new machinery of international peace laboriously built up during and since the recent war will prove so efficacious that defense will become only a more or less academic matter. If there are to be no more aggressions, no more attacks, no more wars, there will be nothing of importance to defend ourselves against, and defense powers, plans, machinery, and expenditures may be allowed to lapse into the limbo of forgotten things. No sensible person, however, can be so naïve or un-realistic as to imagine that any such beatific state of affairs is in store

authorized an Aviation Policy Board charged with reporting by March 1, 1948. Airplane building had fallen off sharply, at a time when it was believed that Soviet Russia was forging ahead rapidly; and in his budget message of January 12, 1948, President Truman asked Congress to earmark for the Air Force almost half of the total recommended defense appropriations and authorization for fiscal 1949.

[1] On August 1, 1946, President Truman signed an Atomic Energy Act (60 *U. S. Stat. at Large,* 756) creating an Atomic Energy Commission of five civilian members charged with providing for the development and utilization of atomic energy "so that it shall, subject to the paramount objective of assuring the common defense and security, be directed, so far as practicable, toward improving the public welfare, increasing the standard of living ... and promoting world peace." Participation by the armed services was restricted to representation in a military liaison committee set up to coöperate with the Commission. The same act provided for a congressional joint committee on atomic energy, composed of nine members of each house.

Non-technical discussions of the bearings of atomic energy upon national and inter-national policy include W. T. R. Fox, "The Struggle for Atomic Control," *Pub. Affairs Pamphlets,* No. 129 (New York, 1947): W. A. Higinbotham and E. K. Lindley, "Atomic Challenge," *Headline Series,* No. 63 (New York, 1947); and H. Hadley, *The United States: Guardian of Atomic Weapons* (New York, 1947). Some-what more thorough analysis will be found in B. Brodie [ed.], *The Absolute Weapon; Atomic Power and World Order* (New York, 1946).

for us. On the contrary, every indication is that, while the United Nations and its auxiliary creations may, as we trust, contribute powerfully to a condition of universal peace in the world, human nature will still be human nature, peoples will still cherish grudges, hatreds, and ambitions, nations will keep on crossing each other's purposes, and governments will continue to fumble opportunities for averting strife and disaster—all of which means that defense unquestionably will remain a problem not to be ignored or side-stepped by the United States any more than by any other nation, large or small.[1]

This being true, the question comes home to us of what kind of a defense system we want, or need, to maintain in coming years—apart from defense against atomic power, certainly not to be ignored, but as yet involved in deep obscurity. And here the main issues are: (1) assuming that the Navy will be kept strong, *how* strong? (2) the same for the air force; and (3) in the case of the Army, shall we fly in the face of tradition and keep permanently a large professional standing army, *or* shall we keep a smaller standing army, but supported by a large reservoir of trained citizen-reserves, *or* shall we revert to our prewar situation, with a small standing army reënforced only by the National Guard and by limited numbers of young men trained, mainly in colleges and universities, for officer duty? On the navy and air-force question, a stand (at least for the time being) has clearly been taken by the services themselves, backed by the president and Congress, in favor of continued superiority to any single or combined force that could be thrown against us.[2] On the army question, Army authorities, warmly backed by Presidents Roosevelt and Truman and by many other prominent civilians, have strongly favored the second of the alternatives enumerated—rejecting the first as violating all our national traditions and the third as being too hazardous, at least until it shall have been established that the nations of the earth have indeed mastered what seems to be the most difficult of all arts for them, *i.e.*, that of living together amicably.

Adoption of the second policy, however,—that of a moderate-sized standing army supported by a large body of citizen-reserves—raises a difficult problem on which public opinion has been divided sharply through years of animated discussion: how shall the training of citizen

What kind of defense system?

Compulsory military training

---

[1] In this country, as elsewhere, recent discussions of ways and means of organizing a lasting peace have evinced significantly little interest in the once-lauded principle of disarmament. We have learned that, while huge armaments may promote wars, the absence of armaments does not insure against them; our own experience of 1940-41 has shown how quickly an unarmed nation can gird itself for combat. We know, moreover, that the world of the past has disappeared, that with the progress of technology the security we once enjoyed is no longer ours, that henceforth, unless heavily guarded, we shall be open to attack from the most distant sources, and by nations which within a few years—perhaps sooner—will have at their command all the terrors of the atomic bomb.

[2] A corollary of this is the retention not only of most or all of the naval and air bases in the Atlantic acquired from Great Britain, but also of various similar vantage points in the South Pacific which fell to us in the course of our war with Japan. See pp. 852-853 below.

reserves be achieved? To the direct question, there is really, of course, only one answer: it would be futile to expect any adequate number of boys and young men to present themselves voluntarily for training, even if facilities were provided; and therefore, if the objective is really to be attained, some form of compulsion will have to be employed. At the close of World War I, President Wilson advocated—as indeed did President Washington in his remote day—a system of compulsory universal military training to provide a backlog of civilian personnel available for active armed service when needed. In turning a deaf ear to this proposal, Congress doubtless merely reflected public opinion. Of late, however, strong support has developed for essentially the same idea, phrased by General George C. Marshall when Army Chief of Staff in 1944 as a permanent policy of keeping the professional standing Army as small as possible, but (it being only a nucleus) buttressed with a very large compulsorily-trained reserve.

The general plan   With various plans brought forward differing more or less in detail, the proposal, concretely, is (1) that all male youth, except those seriously incapacitated physically or mentally, be required to devote one year (probably at about the point of graduation from high school) to special training, under auspices of the Army, and primarily military, although certainly including general physical correction and development, with perhaps other practical instruction of various kinds; and (2) that, following such training, all youth receiving it be retained in reserve components of the Army for some reasonable period, probably five but possibly ten years—although it is alternatively suggested that mere liability to draft would be sufficient. It has been estimated, too, that the number that would come up for training each year would be somewhat more than a million. Bills looking in this direction made their appearance in Congress as early as 1942 and 1944; extensive hearings were held in 1944-45, with a House special postwar military policy committee reporting favorably; and both the Army and the War Department developed plans and strongly supported them. In addition, on June 1, 1947, an able civilian Advisory Commission on Universal Training appointed by President Truman unanimously recommended a plan for a year of training for every physically and mentally normal boy reaching the age of eighteen or completing (or leaving) high school, whichever was later—the first six months to be devoted to basic military training in camp or on shipboard, the second six to further training in service schools or to imparting instruction to a succeeding class of basic trainees.[1] Although favorably reported by the House armed services committee and warmly endorsed by the President, a bill carrying out this proposal was sidetracked in the summer of 1947. Strongly urging, in his message of January 7, 1948, that the measure be made law, the Chief Executive returned vigorously to the

---

[1] *A Program for National Security: Report of the President's Advisory Commission on Universal Training* (Washington, D. C., Govt. Prtg. Office, 1947).

subject in a special message of March 18, in which a limited form of draft was also urged; and although Congress was instinctively hesitant to deal with so explosive an issue before the fall elections, the darkening international situation seemed not unlikely to forbid prolonged delay. Whatever the more immediate outcome, the question promised to remain one of the most troublesome for Congress and the country.

In the eyes of many people, including congressmen, the plan savors too much of the traditional and discredited conscription systems of European countries and Japan, tending to "militarize" and harden rather than to refine youth, and violating American concepts of freedom and democracy. In addition, the objections are voiced (1) that it would not necessarily promote either domestic welfare or international peace, (2) that—and this troubles some military leaders—it would not produce a single man actually ready for service, at home or abroad, and (3) that its cost— estimated by President Truman's commission at one and three-quarter billion dollars a year, and by the War Department at a billion more than that—would prove a serious burden for a debt-ridden nation. On the other hand, it is contended (1) that the training imparted would raise the level of vigorous and effective citizenship; (2) that the plan is "un-American" only in the sense that we have not hitherto tried it; (3) that, as argued by President Truman and by military authorities, it offers the most effective method of maintaining our military strength without incurring the incubus of a huge standing army; (4) that, under the scale of expenditure on which the United States now operates, the cost should be but a minor consideration; and (5) that in the world in which we live our country must, in any event, adjust itself to conditions and procedures not of its own choosing—among them the liability to swift disaster unless large forces, at least partly trained, stand ready to be mobilized instantly. In general, military and naval interests and all sorts of patriotic organizations have been favorable; churches and educational organizations opposed; and organized labor divided, but predominantly opposed.[1]

Some arguments employed

REFERENCES

E. P. Herring, *The Impact of War; Our American Democracy Under Arms* (New York, 1941), Chaps. III-IX.

E. S. Corwin, *The President: Office and Powers; History and Analysis of Practice and Opinion* (New York, 1940), Chap. V.

————, *Total War and the Constitution* (New York, 1947), Chaps. I-III.

W. W. Willoughby, *Constitutional Law of the United States* (2nd ed., New York, 1929), III, Chap. LXXXV.

[1] For a fuller summary of arguments both ways on the general question of policy involved, see J. E. Johnsen [comp.], *Compulsory Military Training* (New York, 1941), and E. C. Buehler [ed.], *Compulsory Military Service* (New York, 1941); and for a sharp attack on the report of the President's commission by a National Council Against Conscription, F. L. Bacon *et al.*, *An Analysis of the Report of the President's Commission on Universal Training* (Washington, D. C., 1947).

C. B. Swisher, *American Constitutional Development* (Boston, 1943), Chap. xxxviii.

War Records Section, Bureau of the Budget, *The United States at War; Development and Administration of the War Program by the Federal Government* (Washington, D. C., 1947).

L. Gulick, "War Organization of the Federal Government," *Amer. Polit. Sci. Rev.*, XXXVIII, 1166-1179 (Dec., 1944).

L. H. Chamberlain, *The President, Congress, and Legislation* (New York, 1946), Chap. v, "National Defense Legislation, 1903-1940."

J. D. Millett, "The War Department in World War II," *Amer. Polit. Sci. Rev.*, XL, 863-897 (Oct., 1946).

C. A. Berdahl, "War Powers of the Executive in the United States," *Univ. of Ill Studies in the Social Sciences*, IX, Nos. 1-2 (Urbana, Ill., 1921).

C. C. Tansill, "War Powers of the President of the United States, with Special Reference to the Beginning of Hostilities," *Polit. Sci. Quar.*, XLV, 1-55 (Mar., 1930).

H. White, *Executive Influence in Determining Military Policy in the United States* (Urbana, Ill., 1925).

L. W. Koenig, *The Presidency and the Crisis* (New York, 1944), Chaps. iii-v.

R. E. Cushman, "The Impact of War on the Constitution," in R. E Cushman *et al.*, *The Impact of War on America* (Ithaca, N. Y., 1942), Chap. i.

C. E. Hughes, "War Powers Under the Constitution," 65th Cong., 1st Sess., Sen. Doc. No. 105 (1917).

W. Whiting, *War Powers Under the Constitution of the United States* (Boston, 1871).

B. Schwartz, "The War Power in Britain and America," *N. Y. Univ. Law Quar. Rev.*, XX, 325-345, 465-498 (July, Oct., 1945).

O. L. Spaulding, *The United States Army in War and Peace* (New York, 1937).

War Department, *The New Army of the United States* (Washington, D. C., 1941).

F. Pratt, *A Short History of the Army and Navy* (Washington, D. C., 1944).

H. and M. Sprout, *Toward a New Order of Sea Power* (Princeton, N. J., 1940). Carries to 1918 the naval history begun in an earlier volume.

————, *America's Problem of National Defense* (Princeton, N. J., 1939).

A. Westcott [ed.], *American Sea Power Since 1775* (Philadelphia, 1947).

N. J. Padelford, *The Panama Canal in Peace and War* (New York, 1942).

G. F. Eliot, *The Ramparts We Watch; A Study of the Problems of American National Defense* (New York, 1938).

————, *The Strength We Need; A Military Program for America Pending Peace* (New York, 1946).

H. J. Tobin and P. W. Bidwell, *Mobilizing Civilian America* (New York, 1940).

W. D. Boutwell *et al.*, *America Prepares for Tomorrow; The Story of Our Total Defense Effort* (New York, 1941).

E. Stein, J. D. Magee, and W. J. Ronan, *Our War Economy* (New York, 1943).

C. O. Hardy, *Wartime Control of Prices* (Washington, D. C., 1940).

B. Brodie [ed.], *The Absolute Weapon; Atomic Power and World Order* (New York, 1946).

J. C. Duggan, *The Legislative and Statutory Development of the Federal Concept of Conscription for Military Service* (Washington, D. C., 1946).

E. L. Bogart, *War Costs and Their Financing* (New York, 1921).

E. R. Stettinius, *Lend Lease; Weapon for Victory* (New York, 1944).

R. E. Dupuy and H. Carter, *Civilian Defense of the United States* (New York, 1942).

A Miles and R. H. Owsley, *Cities and the National Defense Program* (Chicago, 1941).

C. Fairman, *The Law of Martial Rule* (2nd ed., Chicago, 1943).

————, "The Law of Martial Rule and the National Emergency," *Harvard Law Rev.*, LV, 1253-1302 (June, 1942).

A. A. Schiller, *Military Law and Defense Legislation* (St. Paul, Minn., 1942).

H. Holborn, *American Military Government; Its Organization and Policies* (Washington, D. C., 1947).

H. Zink, *American Military Government in Germany* (New York, 1947).

J. T. Shotwell, *War as an Instrument of National Policy* (New York, 1929).

United States Government Manual (Washington, D. C.), current issues for administrative organization and functions.

CHAPTER XXXVI

TERRITORIES, DEPENDENCIES, AND SPECIAL JURISDICTIONS

The terri-
torial
growth
of the
United
States

In the period of the American Revolution, thirteen English colonies along the Atlantic seaboard set themselves up as self-governing states; and from these states the original United States was created. People of that day considered the country large; and since, as defined in the peace treaty of 1783, it included not only the thirteen organized states, but all territory between the Great Lakes and Florida and westward to the Mississippi, it really was so, especially under conditions of communication and transportation then prevailing. Every student of our history knows, however, that this was only a beginning. With the broad trans-Allegheny areas still only sparsely populated, the Louisiana territory was purchased in 1803 and Florida in 1819. Lately separated from Mexico, the wide-sweeping republic of Texas became a state of the Union in 1845. The Oregon treaty of 1846 gave us the forty-ninth parallel as a northern boundary to the Pacific, and the Mexican War of 1846-48 rounded out our dominion to the coast, save only as the southern boundaries of New Mexico and Arizona were fixed by the Gadsden Purchase of 1853. Up to now, only contiguous areas had been annexed. But in 1867—leaping across intervening British territory—we purchased Alaska from Russia. At the end of the century we broke into both the Atlantic and Pacific, adding to a few scattered islets already claimed such larger and richer dependencies as Puerto Rico, the Philippines, Guam, and Hawaii. In 1904, the Canal Zone was acquired from the recently established republic of Panama, and in 1917 the Virgin Islands from Denmark. By 1920, the American flag was flying over considerably more than three million square miles of continental, and more than 700,000 square miles of insular, territory. In the history of territorial expansion in modern times, only that of Great Britain, Russia, and perhaps France, is comparable.[1]

---

[1] Of course, not all of this happened without stirring some suspicion of American motives. So long as we were merely expanding overland westward to the Pacific, European powers might ponder the possible consequences of the rise of a new nation of such proportions, but could hardly fail to perceive how natural and inevitable it was. When, however, our outposts of empire were extended to the West Indies, to the Mid-Pacific, and to the Far East, greater concern was felt; and for fifty years our relations with other "world powers" were complicated by the fact that we, too, had colonial possessions and conceivably might seek to add further to the list. It nevertheless is chiefly in Latin America that our territorial operations have been viewed with apprehension. After all, starting with Puerto Rico, the Canal Zone, and Florida, and advancing westward by way of Texas to California, a very large part of the present United States is of Spanish or Spanish-American antecedents. The circumstances under which some of the areas—notably the Canal Zone—came into our possession left a bad taste in the Latin American mouth which decades of eco-

The Power to Acquire and Govern Territory

When the constitution was drafted, the United States had lately taken over extensive Western lands ceded by certain of the states, and it was with these areas in mind that Congress, as we shall see, was given authority to make rules and regulations for the management of dependent territory. It is not clear that the framers had any intention of authorizing the new national government to acquire additional territory, even though contiguous; certainly they expressly conferred no such power. And Jefferson, in 1803, would have preferred to purchase Louisiana only with the sanction of an empowering constitutional amendment. Nevertheless, repeated decisions of the Supreme Court [1] have settled beyond all question that the right of the United States to acquire territory may be inferred from the power to admit new states, from the power to make treaties, and likewise from the power to carry on war and make peace; and it is by virtue of authority implied in one or more of these express grants that every significant annexation from Louisiana in 1803 to the Virgin Islands in 1917 has been consummated. If these sources of power were insufficient, there still would be the right possessed by every sovereign state, under international law, to acquire territory by discovery and occupation, or indeed by any method compatible with recognized international usage; and it was by discovery and occupation that we possessed ourselves of some of the Guano Islands in the mid-Pacific in 1856 and more recently of certain lands in Antarctica. But the authority implicit in the constitution really needs no reënforcement.

Authority for annexing territory

In the Dred Scott decision of 1857, the Supreme Court voiced the opinion that no power exists to acquire territory "to be held and governed permanently in that character," *i.e.*, to be retained forever as a "colony" rather than in due time admitted as a state (or states) ; and undoubtedly this interpretation was in keeping with the general theory of our constitutional system—so long as newly acquired territory was contiguous, or at all events suitable for eventual statehood on the familiar lines. What the Court of a century ago could not foresee was the country's later expansion into outlying parts of the world, where indeed statehood might in certain situations (*e.g.*, Hawaii) some day become feasible, but where numerous newer possessions (*e.g.*, the Canal Zone and

Eventual statehood not necessary

---

nomic exploitation and "dollar diplomacy" could hardly have been expected to remove; and while the "good neighbor policy" of more recent times has ameliorated the situation, there still is some disposition to look upon the "colossus of the North" as not above land-grabbing when temptation is strong. On more than one occasion, wild talk on this side of the border about annexing Mexico, or even everything to the Isthmus (sometimes Canada as well), has lent color to such mistrust. Most fair-minded Latin Americans nowadays, however, are prepared to accept at face value our protestations that we have no designs on any territories they now possess; and the good faith that we have shown in liberating the Philippines according to promise, and on schedule, should furnish assurance that there are limits to our "imperialism."

[1] Among the earliest, American Insurance Co. *v.* Canter, 1 Peters 511 (1828).

various minor islands) certainly never could be considered for that status. Once the country's expansion began transcending continental boundaries, the test of eventual fitness for statehood began to be quietly ignored, and for fifty years annexations have taken place with little or no reference to it.

Begin-
nings of
terri-
torial
govern-
ment

The United States has had long experience with the government of dependent territories. Created originally from such territories, or "colonies," it in turn found itself, even in the period of the Articles of Confederation, the possessor of far-flung areas requiring arrangements for control. With a view to terminating disputes and promoting national unity, four states—Massachusetts, Connecticut, New York, and Virginia, between 1782 and 1786, ceded to the new nation large domains claimed by them west of the Alleghenies and north of the Ohio river; and easily the most significant single measure enacted during the entire period of the Confederation proved to be a fundamental law known as the Northwest Ordinance, adopted by the old Congress in 1787 for the government of the region north of the Ohio and westward to the Mississippi. Hardly was this act in effect, however, before the new constitution was framed; and primarily to provide for continuing the national authority already asserted, that instrument contained as one of its most cogent clauses a grant of power to Congress to "dispose of and make all needful rules and regulations respecting the territory or other property belonging to the United States.[1] In pursuance of this power, the new Congress under the constitution promptly reënacted the Northwest Ordinance substantially without change.

Signif-
icance
of the
North-
west Or-
dinance

The significance of the Northwest Ordinance lies not only in its liberal provisions for local self-government, for representation in Congress, and for fundamental civil and political rights, but also in the fact that the plan of government provided for fixed a pattern closely adhered to in practically every law thereafter enacted by Congress for the government of our continental possessions; indeed, many of the more essential provisions found in later territorial organic acts were copied almost verbatim from the earlier Ordinance.[2] Of equal, or even greater, import is the express indication in the Ordinance that the people of the Territory were not to be kept in perpetual subjection to congressional authority, but that, on the contrary, the territorial government was to serve simply as a temporary arrangement until the growth of population should warrant the Territory's admission to the Union as a state, or group of states, upon

[1] Art. IV, § 3, cl. 2.
[2] In 1790, for example, Congress authorized for the region south of the Ohio, known as the Southwest Territory, a government very similar to that provided for in the Northwest Ordinance. In territories organized after 1836, however, the appointed council forming the upper branch of the earlier territorial legislature was replaced by a popularly elected senate. C. E. Carter, "Apprenticeship for American Statehood," *Dept. of State Bull.*, XII, 1109-1114 (June 17, 1945), contains an excellent interpretation of our early territorial policy. Cf. *Territorial Papers of the United States*, 12 vols. (Washington, D. C., Govt. Prtg. Off., 1947).

a footing of equality with the older states. In other words, territorial status was to be merely preparatory to statehood—a principle thenceforth adhered to in the case of our contiguous territories, and setting up a certain presumption even in the case of island possessions like Hawaii and Puerto Rico. From the Northwest Territory, five states were subsequently created, *i.e.*, Ohio, Indiana, Illinois, Michigan, and Wisconsin. In similar manner, from the Southwest Territory, organized in 1790, came the states of Kentucky, Tennessee, Alabama, and Mississippi.

In the case of territory acquired by peaceful means, congressional authority to legislate for its government begins the moment the title of the United States is established. During time of war, the president, in his capacity as commander-in-chief, governs, through the Army and Navy, any territory acquired by conquest, whether or not eventually retained.[1] After the establishment of peace, however, his power to govern must be based (a) upon authority granted by the constitution to see that the laws are faithfully executed, or (b) upon some act of Congress for the government of the conquered territory, or (c) in the absence of any act of this nature, upon the implied consent of Congress that the government set up under his military authority be continued. At different times, Congress has temporarily clothed the president with practically absolute authority over an annexed territory. But sooner or later it established, in nearly all of the areas acquired before the Civil War, governments similar to those created in the old Northwest and Southwest Territories; and ultimately all such territories were admitted as states. The only exceptions to the usual procedure were in the cases of Texas and California, which were admitted as states without having passed through the territorial stage.[2]

Presi-dent, Con-gress, and the govern-ment of territory

The organization of territorial governments in those portions of the country not covered by the Northwest and Southwest Ordinances, and also the admission of certain states so covered, furnished occasions, prior to 1860, for many exciting sectional controversies over slavery. At no time, however, has the full power of Congress to fix the form of territorial governments been successfully challenged; and the principle has become firmly established that such governments exist merely as the instrumentalities by which Congress exercises its authority over the territories.

With the exception of Alaska, all territories acquired by the United States before the Spanish-American War not only were contiguous, but had been settled and developed by natives of this country and by European immigrants whose civilization and traditions were not fundamentally different from our own. Consequently, Congress had little or no

New situation after the Spanish-Amer-ican War

---

[1] W. W. Willoughby, *Constitutional Law of the United States* (2nd ed.), I, Chaps. XXIII–XXVIII; L. Reno, "The Power of the President to Acquire and Govern Territory," *Geo. Washington Law Rev.*, IX, 251–285 (Jan., 1941).

[2] A few other states—Maine, Vermont, Kentucky, and West Virginia—were so admitted too; but of course they were formed from original territory of the United States.

hesitation about extending to them a large measure of self-government and all of the civil rights guaranteed by the national constitution.[1] The annexation of Hawaii in 1898, however, and in particular the Spanish-American War, brought under the control of the United States non-contiguous territory lying for the most part in the tropics and inhabited by relatively backward peoples of different race and language, almost totally inexperienced in self-government and enjoying few if any of the civil and political rights which long have been a cherished heritage of our own citizens. Admittedly, the power to govern these new possessions resided in Congress; and at first glance it seemed necessary, in view of earlier Supreme Court decisions, to extend to their inhabitants all of the rights and privileges enumerated in the constitution, including freedom of speech and press, the right to bear arms, and trial by jury. Embarrassing results, however, that might flow from such adherence to legislative and judicial precedents made it desirable to draw some distinction between the legal status of these new acquisitions and that of the older territories on the continent; and in a series of "Insular Cases" decided in 1901 [2] the Supreme Court, after a good deal of wavering, finally developed such a distinction, thereby releasing Congress from some of the restrictions under which it had previously dealt with territorial problems.

"Incorporated" and "unincorporated" territories

The distinction evolved (wholly new to our jurisprudence) was one as between territory "incorporated" in the United States and territory "not incorporated." In the former category were included Alaska, Oklahoma, New Mexico, and Arizona, none of which, at the time the decisions were handed down, had as yet been admitted to statehood. In legislating for such incorporated territories, said the Court, Congress was bound by all limitations specified in the constitution unless plainly inapplicable. Hawaii, Puerto Rico, and the Philippines, on the other hand, were "unincorporated" territories. To be sure, they belonged to the United States rather than to any foreign power; they were appurtenant to, and dependencies of, the United States. But the mere fact of annexation did not make them *parts* of the United States in the sense that all provisions of the constitution automatically became applicable to them. Only if and when expressly "incorporated" into the country by congressional act would they achieve such a position; and meanwhile, in legislating for them, Congress was bound, not by all the constitutional restrictions recognized as applicable to incorporated territories, but only by those contained in parts of the instrument to be regarded as "fundamental" rather than merely "formal."

[1] A useful study of policy and administration in our contiguous territories in a representative period of the nineteenth century is E. S. Pomeroy, *The Territories and the United States, 1861-1890* (Philadelphia, 1947).
[2] Chiefly DeLima *v.* Bidwell (182 U. S. 1), Dooley *v.* United States (182 U. S. 222), and Downes *v.* Bidwell (182 U. S. 244), all turning upon the question of whether the tariff laws of the United States were fully applicable to Puerto Rico. See J. W. Burgess, "The Decisions in the Insular Cases," *Polit. Sci. Quar.,* XVI, 486-504 (Sept., 1901).

Announcement of this interesting doctrine was accompanied, however, Illus-
trations by no enumeration of the constitution's "fundamental" and "formal" parts; and no such listing or definition has ever since been attempted, either by the Court or by Congress. Rather, the policy was pursued of determining the matter as situations arose—as laws were enacted and cases decided under them. On this basis, it was held in the Insular decisions that, in connection with unincorporated territories, Congress is not bound by the constitution's requirement that taxes be uniform throughout the United States, but may impose higher or lower duties upon articles coming from such territories than upon similar articles coming from a foreign country. Similarly, it has been held that the requirement of grand and trial juries for the prosecution of crimes does not apply; also that the mere act of annexation does not make the inhabitants of an unincorporated territory citizens of the United States. Other illustrations could be cited. To be sure, some parts of the constitution *do* apply; for example, Congress certainly could not impose bills of attainder or *ex post facto* laws even upon an unincorporated dependency. And an unincorporated territory may become entitled to the constitution's full benefits by becoming incorporated—as did Hawaii by congressional act of 1900 after an interval of only two years, and as did Alaska as a result of cumulative acts of Congress recognized by the Supreme Court in 1905 as having had that effect. Although resting always on only a rather rough sort of logic—a mere rationalization by an obliging Court of a policy which Congress and the president desired to pursue—the device of unincorporated territory has served usefully to give Congress a relatively free hand in solving many problems arising out of our possession of tropical dependencies inhabited by politically inexperienced peoples.[1]

An exact classification of existing territories and dependencies is Our
terri-
torial
posses-
sions
classified difficult to make, but in general they fall into three categories, as follows: (1) incorporated or fully organized territories, of which there are now the two mentioned, *i.e.*, Alaska and Hawaii; (2) territories unincorporated but with some aspects of incorporated status, *i.e.*, Puerto Rico and the Virgin Islands; and (3) dependencies wholly unincorporated, or "unorganized," *e.g.*, the Canal Zone, Guam, Samoa, Wake, Howland, and a number of other mid-Pacific islands. Outside of this classification fall: (a) certain air and navy bases in the Atlantic and Pacific gained in connection with World War II;[2] (b) a "trusteeship" for the Territory of the Pacific Islands (the former Japanese mandated islands in the South Pacific), assented to by the United Nations in the spring of 1947 and promptly approved by Congress; and (c) certain areas in the Carib-

[1] F. R. Coudert, "The Evolution of the Doctrine of Territorial Incorporation," *Columbia Law Rev.*, XXVI, 823-850 (Nov., 1926).

[2] Eight such bases, scattered from Newfoundland to South America, were acquired from Great Britain in 1940 in exchange for fifty over-age destroyers. Two of the number were bestowed outright and the other six leased for ninety-nine years. On request of Denmark, we agreed in 1947 to relinquish a wartime base acquired in Greenland.

bean—chiefly Cuba, Haiti, and Santo Domingo—in which the United States has assumed limited protective responsibilities, although the several countries concerned (remaining sovereign states) are in no sense "dependencies."

Arrangements for central supervision Corresponding in a rough sort of way to the classification indicated is also the allocation of responsibility for supervising territorial affairs. Most European states having overseas possessions concentrate such supervision in a colonial ministry or other single executive department (although Great Britain has not only a Colonial Office, but also a Dominions Office, and in the past at least has had likewise an India Office). In the United States, however, the responsibility is parcelled out among three different departments, all having to do primarily with other and more or less unrelated matters. Since 1934, the Interior Department's Division of Territories and Island Possessions has had oversight of the incorporated and partly incorporated areas—Alaska, Hawaii, Puerto Rico, and the Virgin Islands, and also of certain small Pacific islands (Baker, Howland, and Jarvis);[1] through its Office of Island Governments, the Navy Department looks after Guam, Samoa, Wake, Midway, and a few other possessions having mainly a strategic or defensive interest; and the Department of the Army supervises the Canal Zone. Detached air and naval bases are in the custody of the Army and Navy Departments; and for the time being (1948) the trusteeship area is under Navy administration, pending transfer to some civilian department or agency.

The Government of Incorporated Territories—Alaska and Hawaii

Executive and legislative machinery In most essential respects, the status of these top-level territories (defined in organic acts which only Congress can amend) is identical with that enjoyed by our newer states when they were passing through the territorial stage. The inhabitants are citizens of the United States; and the constitution and all laws of the United States not locally inapplicable are expressly declared to be in effect as elsewhere in the country. In each territory, the present government consists of distinct executive, legislative, and judicial branches. There is a governor, appointed by the president and Senate at Washington for a four-year term, and paid out of the national treasury, and a legislature consisting of a senate and a house of representatives; and legislative sessions are held biennially. The election of senators and representatives (also of the delegate which the territory sends to Congress) may be participated in by bona fide residents for a year, twenty-one years of age, of citizen status, and able to read and write English (or in Hawaii, Hawaiian). Legislative measures, or items therein, may be vetoed by the governor, and also may be (though very rarely are) disallowed by Congress. A governor's veto may, however, be overcome by a two-thirds vote in both houses.

---

[1] The Philippines, too, from 1939 to 1946.

Judicial power in Alaska is exercised by a federal district court, organized in four divisions. In Hawaii, there are two sets of courts, territorial and federal. The territorial courts correspond rather closely to our state courts, and include a supreme court, circuit courts, and such inferior courts as the legislature may from time to time create. The supreme court consists of a chief justice and two associate justices, all of whom must be citizens of Hawaii. They, and the judges of the circuit courts also, are appointed by the president and Senate for four-year terms, unless sooner removed by the president. Besides these territorial courts, there is a federal district court consisting of two judges, a district attorney, and a marshal—all appointed by the president and Senate for six-year terms and subject to presidential removal.[1]

Both Alaska and Hawaii are active candidates for statehood, and one or the other is likely soon to become the first outlying member of the Union. The case for Alaska is somewhat less convincing than that for Hawaii. Larger than Texas, California, and Montana combined, and endowed with extensive mineral, timber, water-power, and fishery resources, the territory has as yet a population of only some 90,000 (57,000 white settlers and 33,000 native Indians, Aleuts, and Eskimos), and has not a highly developed economy. On the other hand, the present rate of growth will soon bring it abreast of our least populous state (Nevada, with 110,247 in 1940); and, like the present white inhabitants, most of the newcomers will be former residents of other parts of the United States. Pressure for statehood is inspired by a number of practical considerations—desire to share fully in the federal aids (especially for highways) now partly withheld from territories, expectation that much public land would be turned over to the new state, presumed benefits to flow from local control over fisheries, forests, and mining, and freer scope for planning and development as new population comes in; and when, in October, 1946, an advisory referendum was taken, under authority of the territorial legislature, sixty per cent of the voting population declared for the proposed change. Top administrative officials at Washington (including those of the Interior Department) have asserted themselves to be favorable, and enabling measures have been introduced in Congress. On the other hand, a congressional delegation visiting the territory in 1946 was of the opinion that, while eventually statehood should be granted, more time for stabilizing the territory's economy should be allowed; and for the present the outcome remains in doubt.[2]

Hawaii's situation is different in that the territorial population (423,530 in 1940 and in 1947 estimated at 502,000) exceeds that of four existing states[3] and pays more federal taxes than does that of any of

Margin notes: Judicial organization · The question of statehood: · 1. Alaska · 2. Hawaii

[1] United States courts in the territories are, of course, "legislative" courts (see pp. 553-554 above).

[2] E. Gruening, "Why Alaska Needs Statehood," *State Government*, XXI, 31-33 (Feb., 1948).

[3] It is also larger than that of any existing admitted state at the time of its admission except Oklahoma

fourteen existing states, and also in that politically and economically the territory has attained considerably greater maturity than has Alaska. Statehood was vigorously demanded more than a decade ago, and not only did a local referendum in 1939 bring out a favorable vote of more than two to one, but a congressional committee studying the question on the spot reported favorably.[1] In those days, a main impediment was the circumstance that while the Islands formed our primary fortress of defense in the Pacific, more than one-third of their inhabitants were Japanese immigrants (*Issei*) or native-born persons of Japanese ancestry (*Nisei*). The demonstrated loyalty of nearly all such inhabitants during World War II has, however, removed substantially all concern on that score; and the prevailing present disposition is to recognize the territory's claim as unassailable.[2] After extended hearings and inquiry in the Islands in 1946, a congressional subcommittee unanimously recommended prompt statehood; in his annual message of 1947, President Truman (already on record for statehood) supported the recommendation; and in June of the same year the House of Representatives passed an "enabling act" authorizing the territory to proceed with the election of a convention to frame a state constitution. The Senate failed to take up the matter, and it went over to a later session; but favorable action in both branches seemed merely a question of somewhat more time.[3]

The Government of Unincorporated Territories—Puerto Rico and the Virgin Islands

1. Puerto Rico:

(a) Legal status

The most important of our unincorporated territories today, and the least contented and self-reliant of our principal dependencies, is Puerto Rico.[4] For a good while after the island was acquired from Spain in 1898,

---

[1] See Hawaii Joint Committee, *Hearings*, 75th Cong., 2nd Sess. (1938). Cf. W. Matheson, "Hawaii Pleads for Statehood," *No. Amer. Rev.*, CCXLVII, 130-141 (Spring, 1939).

[2] For an illuminating account of the Americanizing of Hawaii's Japanese over a period of fifty years, and especially of the policies pursued amid the stress of the recent war, see A. W. Lind, *Hawaii's Japanese; An Experiment in Democracy* (New York, 1944). Cf. C. H. Coggins, "The Japanese Americans in Hawaii," *Harper's Mag.*, CLXXXVII, 75-83 (June, 1943). The general stability of the Islands, notwithstanding their mixed population, is evidenced by the fact that, with general approval of the white inhabitants, Japanese were not evacuated during the war as from the mainland coastal zones, and by the fact also that, whereas martial law was instituted on the day of the attack at Pearl Harbor, and maintained (with some modifications) until 1944, the Supreme Court, in 1946, held it to have been unjustified and illegally imposed (Duncan v. Kahanamoku, 327 U. S. 304). Cf. E. S. Corwin, *Total War and the Constitution* (New York, 1947), 100-105. For an analysis of the Islands' reasons for demanding statehood, see D. James, "Hawaii's Claims to Statehood," *Amer. Mercury*, LXIII, 330-336 (Sept., 1946). Cf. I. M. Steinbeck, "Statehood for Hawaii," *State Government*, XIX, 243-246 (Oct., 1946); "Should Congress Now Grant Statehood to the Territory of Hawaii" [Symposium], *Cong. Digest*, XXVI, 268-288 (Nov., 1947).

[3] Discussion of the proposal brought out sentiment in some quarters opposed in principle to the admission of any non-contiguous states, on the ground that such a course would prove the beginning of the end of the United States "as we have known it"; former President Nicholas Murray Butler of Columbia University, for example, advanced this argument.

[4] The name of the island, formerly Porto Rico, was changed to Puerto Rico by act of Congress in May, 1932. Down to the establishment of the Philippine Common-

it was governed under a law of 1900 providing for an elective lower house but otherwise allowing little scope for native participation. On the other hand, an organic act of 1917 sought to make up for previous neglect by not only extending larger rights of self-government, but conferring United States citizenship upon the inhabitants, and also giving them a bill of rights covering almost all of the points in the first eight amendments to the federal constitution, with omission of trial by jury and indictment by grand jury. Most statutory laws of the United States not locally inapplicable now apply automatically in the island; and, all in all, the legal situation, as well as the governmental system, is not very different from that found in an incorporated territory like Hawaii. Nevertheless, Puerto Rico remains unincorporated.[1]

"Supreme executive power" is vested in a governor, formerly appointed **(b) The executive** by the president and Senate at Washington and (unlike the governor in an incorporated territory) for no definite term, but, under act of Congress approved by President Truman August 6, 1947,[2] now elected by the voters of the island (beginning in 1948). Seven executive departments were created in 1931, each with a commissioner at its head. The attorney-general and the commissioner of education are appointed by the president and Senate for four years, unless sooner removed by the president; the heads of the other departments are appointed by the governor and senate of Puerto Rico for four years, unless sooner removed by the governor; and the seven department heads collectively form an executive council.[3]

The Puerto Rican legislature is much like the Hawaiian. The senate **(c) The legislature** consists of nineteen members elected by popular vote for a four-year term; each of seven districts elects two senators, and five others are chosen at large. The house of representatives consists of thirty-nine members elected every four years, thirty-five of them chosen from single-member districts and four at large. In electing the senators and representatives chosen at large, each voter is permitted to vote for only one candidate for the senate and house, respectively. Voting qualifications are, for the most part, left by the organic acts to be prescribed by the local legislature, subject to the provision that "no property qualification shall ever be imposed upon or required of any voter." Citizens of the United States who have resided in the island at least one year, and are twenty-one years of age, are voters; and since 1932, women have been included in the electorate. Legislative sessions are held annually; and

---

wealth in 1935, the Philippines also belonged in the "unincorporated" category. From this status, they moved, however, not toward incorporation, but in the direction of independence. See pp. 855-859 below.

[1] A resident commissioner, corresponding to the territorial delegates from Alaska and Hawaii, is elected by the people every four years to represent them in the House of Representatives at Washington, although, like other territorial representatives, without any vote.

[2] *Pub. Law 362—80th Cong., 1st Sess.*

[3] Until 1917, the council, somewhat differently constituted, formed the upper branch of the territorial legislature.

special sessions of the senate, or of both houses, may be called by the governor.

General legislative powers were conferred on the Puerto Rican legislature in 1917 in substantially the same language as in the organic laws of Alaska and Hawaii, but at the same time with a good deal less freedom of action. Legislative organization and procedure are regulated in greater detail than in either of the incorporated territories mentioned, and there is the significant difference with respect to the veto that, whereas in Alaska and Hawaii a vetoed measure repassed by a two-thirds vote in both houses automatically becomes law, in Puerto Rico a vetoed measure so repassed may be referred by the governor to the president at Washington, finally becoming law only if that official approves it or fails to act. As in the incorporated territories also, any legislative act may be disallowed by Congress—although the power is very seldom exercised, and if exercised is subject to presidential veto as in the case of other legislative acts.

(d) The judiciary   As in Hawaii, there are two kinds of courts, territorial and federal. At the head of the former stands the supreme court, composed of five justices appointed by the president and Senate for life or good behavior.[1] Below it are seven district courts, each presided over by a single judge appointed by the governor and insular senate for four years. Finally, there are thirty-four "municipal" courts, in as many judicial districts, with limited jurisdiction in civil and criminal cases. Besides these territorial courts, there is a federal district court with one judge, a district attorney, and a marshal, all of whom are appointed by the president and Senate for four years, unless sooner removed.

(e) The troublesome question of political status   As already indicated, Puerto Rico is dissatisfied with its present lot, although by no means of one mind upon the best method of improving it. The fundamental difficulty is economic; an island only a hundred miles long and thirty-five miles wide, with almost no resources or potentialities except of an agricultural character, and with present-day agriculture based on only a single crop (sugar), is burdened with a steadily increasing population (1,869,255 in 1940 and nowadays approximately 2,175,000) far too large to be supported comfortably, with the result of little prospect for its people except the poverty and squalor in which the masses have always lived. The connection with the United States has proved of some benefit, yet has been by no means an unmixed blessing for either the island or the major country; assimilation is seriously impeded by the insular language being Spanish and the cultural background Latin. Politically, the situation is complicated by the existence of a number of insular parties agreeing only on the desirability of some

---

[1] As passed by the House of Representatives in 1947, the bill giving the Puerto Ricans the right to elect their own governor (see p. 847 above) provided also for appointment of the justices of the insular supreme court by the governor. This feature did not prevail in the Senate, but there is some expectation that it will be taken care of in later legislation.

change in the island's legal status and on the moral right of the inhabitants to decide upon their political future for themselves. Some elements favor complete independence, perhaps after a preparatory period such as the Philippines passed through during the decade 1936-46. Other groups look toward something approaching the autonomous status of a British dominion. The most general demand, however, is for statehood; and several times in the last fifteen years the insular legislature has petitioned Congress on the subject, contending that morally if not legally fifty years of control over the island's affairs commits the United States to such an arrangement. On the side of the United States, however, there well may be hesitation, not only because of the island's backwardness, but because of cultural differences tending to preclude it from ever becoming an integral part of American life. To be sure, both in 1940 and 1944 the platforms of the Republican and Democratic parties declared for statehood "eventually." Such pronouncements, however, are not to be taken too seriously, and in any case "eventually" is an evasive word. With President Truman proposing a plebiscite in which the Puerto Ricans should have a chance to indicate whether they want statehood, dominion status, or complete independence, a joint congressional committee visited the island early in 1947; and from its report was expected to come some action preparing the way for reasonably early determination of the island's future political position.[1]

Acquired from Denmark by purchase in 1917 as a move to forestall possible annexation by Germany, the Virgin Islands (in the Lesser Antilles, and with an area of only 140 square miles) remained under immediate control of the president until 1936, when an amending organic act passed by Congress extended to their 22,000 inhabitants (now about 25,000) a liberal measure of home rule.[2] The insular legislature consists of the popularly elected municipal councils of (a) St. Croix and (b) St. Thomas and St. John, sitting as a single house; executive power is vested in a governor appointed by the president and Senate for an indefinite term, and reporting to the secretary of the interior at Washington; and the judiciary consists of a district court, together with such inferior courts as may be established by law. Measures may be enacted by the legislature only by two-thirds vote, and any which the governor refuses to approve must be transmitted to the president, who has three months in

2 The Virgin Islands

---

[1] On Puerto Rico's economic and social problems, see J. Polk, "The Plight of Puerto Rico," *Polit. Sci. Quar.*, LVII, 481-503 (Dec., 1942); S. B. Heath, "Our American Slum, Puerto Rico," *Harper's Mag.*, CLXXXVII, 56-63 (June, 1943); R. G. and G. F. Tugwell, "Puerto Rico's Bootstraps," *ibid.*, CXLIV, 160-169 (Feb., 1947); and V. Petrullo, *Puerto Rican Paradox* (Philadelphia, 1947). For a Puerto Rican discussion of the political angle, see B. Pagan, *Puerto Rico: The Next State* (Washington, D. C., 1942); and for an excellent over-all survey, O. Holmes, "Puerto Rico; An American Responsibility," *Foreign Policy Reports*, XXII, No. 24 (Mar. 1, 1947). Cf. P. Blanchard, *Democracy and Empire in the Caribbean* (New York, 1947), 209-228.

[2] 49 *U. S. Stat. at Large*, 1807. Somewhat earlier (1927), the inhabitants were given United States citizenship; and all such citizens, twenty-one years of age, may vote if they can read and write English.

which to take action on them; all measures, too, enacted by either a municipal council or the legislative assembly are required to be reported to, and are subject to disallowance by, Congress. In 1947, Governor William H. Hastie (our first Negro territorial governor) urged that the Islands be allowed a resident commissioner in Washington, and that the office of governor be made elective; and in June, 1947, our government reported to the United Nations that an elective resident commissionership was under consideration.[1]

The Management of Wholly "Unorganized" Dependencies

Arrangements for the many wholly unorganized dependencies vary considerably, but with only rudimentary provision for local self-government or none at all. As will be observed presently, proposals were pending in 1947 for extending larger political rights to certain of them (Guam and Samoa); but as yet all are merely possessions, subject to whatever controls may be instituted from Washington.

The Canal Zone

The Panama Canal Zone comprises a strip of territory five miles wide on each side of the Canal, leased in perpetuity from the republic of Panama in 1902, and with a population in 1940 of 51,827. During construction of the waterway, the Zone was governed by the president through a commission. When, however, the work neared completion, Congress, in 1913, authorized the president to discontinue the commission and thenceforth to govern the Zone through a governor and such other officials as he might find necessary. In consequence, a "governor of the Panama Canal," appointed by the president and Senate for four years, now administers the affairs of the Zone, under supervision of the secretary of the army. In the absence of a local legislature, such laws as operate within the area either are made by Congress or take the form of presidential orders. Provision has been made by law also for the establishment of organized towns, and for a system of courts including a district court and beneath it magistrates' courts corresponding to justices of the peace elsewhere; and the constitution's bill of rights has been made applicable in the territory.[2]

Guam and Samoa

Until brought into the limelight by the war in the Pacific beginning in 1941, most of our minor island possessions—Guam, the American (eastern) portion of Samoa, Wake, Midway, Jarvis, Baker, Howland (all located in the mid-Pacific)—were, for the average American, hardly more than names on the map, if even that. In the absence of any arrangements by Congress fixing a definite constitutional status, all are looked

---

[1] H. Cochran, *These Are the Virgin Islands* (New York, 1937); R. G. W., "Rehabilitation of the Virgin Islands," *Foreign Affairs*, XVII, 799-804 (July, 1939); also book by L. H. Evans listed on p. 864 below.

[2] D. H. Smith, *The Panama Canal; Its History, Activities, and Organization* (Baltimore, 1927); N. J. Padelford, *The Panama Canal in Peace and War* (New York, 1942). Legal difficulties continually arise between the United States and the republic of Panama because the latter persists in regarding the Zone as merely a United States leasehold, with sovereignty remaining in Panama.

after by some agency or representative of the executive branch, acting in the name of the president; and none is in any proper sense self-governing or even has civil courts to which the inhabitants may appeal. Guam, largest of the Marianas (225 square miles) and endowed with an excellent harbor, was acquired from Spain in 1898, and long has served usefully as an American naval station and potential naval base. Prior to its conquest by Japan in 1942, the island was governed simply by the president through the commandant of the local naval station, who commonly had little taste or talent for civil administration. There was, to be sure, a locally elected "congress," but only for advisory purposes; and with Japanese control ended in 1944, the previous arrangements were restored.[1] American Samoa became a protectorate of the United States by virtue of an Anglo-German-American agreement of 1899, supplemented by cessions made by native chieftains in 1900 and 1904. Not until 1929, however, did Congress formally accept and recognize the acquisition; and both before and after that date, arrangements for administration, through a naval commandant, were as in Guam.

During the war years, conviction grew that Guam's 24,000 inhabitants and Samoa's 16,000 deserved something better than the rather casual treatment they had received, and in 1947 an investigating civilian committee set up by the Navy Department recommended (1) that full American citizenship be granted to the people of both territories "at the earliest possible date;" (2) that separate organic acts be passed constituting each territory "a body politic with its own bill of rights as its guaranty of personal liberties and establishing a framework for the form of government for each area;" and (3) that, for the immediate future at least, the Navy continue its stewardship within the framework of the proposed organic acts. Another report, compiled at President Truman's request by the secretaries of state, war, navy, and interior, contained similar recommendations; and when Congress adjourned in December, an organic act for Guam, extending United States citizenship and liberal rights of self-government, and earnestly supported by the President, was pending in the House of Representatives, with some presumption that in the next session it would become law, and also one like it for Samoa.[2]

With the development of trans-Pacific aviation, the other islands mentioned (often called the Guano Islands) acquired, even before the recent war, a value apart from their guano, or fertilizer, deposits. Midway and Wake, as well as Guam, are on the direct air route from Honolulu to Manila; Howland and Baker, on the route from Hawaii to Australia; and Jarvis, Samoa, Canton, and Enderbury, on the way to New Zealand.

Other mid-Pacific islands

[1] A detailed study of Guam will be found in L. Thompson, *Guam and Its People* (3rd ed., Princeton, N. J., 1947). Cf. R. E. James, "The Guam Congress," *Pacific Affairs,* XIX, 408-413 (Dec., 1946).

[2] Under terms of the measure, the governor might be a regular, retired, or reserve naval officer, but should perform his duties under supervision of the Interior Department.

In recognition of their resulting importance, the Department of Commerce, and later the Department of the Interior, established small colonizing groups on several of the islands, and Congress voted modest appropriations for maintaining and improving the islands as landing ports for American aviators.[1]

Results of World War II— the new Territory of the Pacific Islands

When the war came, everything west of Midway was lost to the Oriental conqueror. Except for remote points in the Aleutian archipelago, Alaska, however, was never invaded. Much damage was wrought at Pearl Harbor in the attack which touched off the war; but Hawaii was never taken and served throughout the war as a major base for our operations in the central Pacific. The Philippines, of course, were lost, but regained in 1944-45; Guam and Baker Island were recovered in 1944; and in the end not a square foot of the American empire in the Pacific was sacrificed—except, of course, for the independence voluntarily given the Philippines in 1946. Not only so, but the question thrust itself forward of whether, with peace restored, that empire should not be extended to include part or all of the sprays of islets in Micronesia (the Marianas, Marshalls, and Carolines, with a total area of 846 square miles and a population of some 50,000) formerly held by Japan under mandate from the League of Nations, but later taken by American arms—as well as possibly certain other strategically situated South Pacific islands, *e.g.*, Okinawa, Marcus, and the Bonins, in addition. In Army and Navy circles, and in the Department of State, it was virtually taken for granted that, in the case of the former mandated islands at least (certain in any event not to be restored to Japan) American control in some form would be retained; and after President Truman, in November, 1946, transmitted to the Security Council of the United Nations a plan under which the United States should be designated as custodian of the islands under the new United Nations trusteeship system, as an alternative to the outright annexation for which there was a good deal of sentiment, the proposal was, in April, 1947, unanimously accepted.[2] From the later stages of the war, the islands had been in American custody, under a system of military government. After Congress, in July, 1947, ratified the trusteeship arrangement by joint resolution,[3] it, however, became necessary to make some arrangement for civil administration; and with military rule terminated, a plan was introduced by executive order under which the Navy forthwith assumed responsibility, with the commander of the Pacific fleet in charge, but pending transfer to some civilian department or agency as soon as practicable. With these decisions, the United States embarked upon a form of territorial administration entirely new to its experience;

---

[1] By agreement of 1939, Canton and Enderbury islands are under joint control of the United States and Great Britain for a period of fifty years. The Aleutian Islands in the north are an integral part of the territory of Alaska.

[2] *Draft Trusteeship Agreement for the Japanese Mandated Islands,* Dept. of State Pub. No. 2784 (Washington, D. C., 1947).

[3] *Pub. Law 204—80th Cong., 1st Sess.*

and the results will be watched with interest. The archipelagoes affected, with their 50,000 inhabitants, are not American "possessions;" the United States merely controls them, as the "Territory of the Pacific Islands," and administers their affairs under immediate responsibility to the Security Council of the United Nations for promoting the "political, economic, social, and educational advancement of the natives."[1] In sharp contrast with mandated areas under the old League, however, they, as trust territories of a specially defined "strategic area" class (the first such to be approved by the Security Council), may be converted into fortresses of defense; and such use, for our own security and for safeguarding international peace, is, of course, a main reason for desiring to have them in our hands.[2]

The Independence of the Philippines

In earlier editions of this book, a substantial portion of the chapter on territories was devoted to the Philippine Islands, as being the largest and in many respects the most important of our colonial dependencies. From one point of view, the Islands might now go almost unmentioned; for on July 4, 1946, they gained their long-coveted independence and entered the family of sovereign nations as the Philippine Republic. Our relinquishment of them by purely voluntary act had no precedent either in our own experience or in that of other colonial powers. For forty-eight years, how-

[1] Quite apart from this arrangement, the United States has accepted the obligation imposed upon all members of the United Nations to transmit regularly to the secretary-general full information on conditions in all non-self-governing territories for which they are administratively responsible. In August, 1946, our government became the first to comply with this requirement. For full information on the relations between the United States and the United Nations in all that pertains to non-self-governing territories, see *The United States and Non-Self-Governing Territories*, Dept. of State Pub. No. 2812 (Washington, D. C., 1947).

[2] For an argument that, in insisting that this trusteeship be of the strategic class rather than an ordinary non-strategic trusteeship, the United States missed an opportunity to strengthen the concept of collective security as against purely national and unilateral strategic considerations, see J. M. Maki, "US Strategic Areas or UN Trusteeship," *Far Eastern Survey*, XVI, 175-178 (Aug. 13, 1947). At the date of writing (April, 1948), final disposition of other former Japanese possessions in the South Pacific (containing a majority of the most important wartime and postwar bases) remained to be made. Navy plans for maintaining our strategic position in the Pacific contemplated Hawaii and the Guam-Saipan-Tinian area as the hubs of the system, with Kodiak in the Aleutians and Kwajalein in the Marshalls as secondary bases, and with the question still open of building a great base in the Ryukyus more or less in lieu of that at Manila which, by agreement with the Philippine government, had been given up.

Good over-all accounts of the American administrative task in the Pacific area will be found in T. K. Hitch, "The Administration of America's Pacific Islands," *Polit. Sci. Quar.*, LXI, 384-407 (Sept., 1946), and F. M. Keesing, "American Island Territories in the Pacific," in J. C. Vincent *et al.*, *America's Future in the Pacific* (New Brunswick, N. J., 1947), 59-81. Cf. C. H. Gratton, "Our Unknown Pacific Islands," *Harper's Mag.*, CLXXXII, 523-532 (Apr., 1941); B. Orent and P. Reinsch, "Sovereignty Over Islands in the Pacific," *Amer. Jour. of Internat. Law*, XXXV, 443-461 (July, 1941); and D. N. Leff, *Uncle Sam's Pacific Islets* (Palo Alto, Calif., 1940). On the United States trusteeship, see R. R. Robbins, "United States Trusteeship for the Territory of the Pacific Islands," Dept. of State Pub. No. 2850 (Washington, D. C., 1947); F. B. Sayre, "American Trusteeship Policy in the Pacific," *Proceedings of Acad. of Polit. Sci.*, XXII, 46-56 (Jan., 1948); and on the Navy's temporary task in the islands, J. P. Marquand, "Why the Navy Needs Aspirin," *Harper's Mag.*, CXCV, 160-169 (Aug., 1947).

ever, possession of the Islands was a matter of cardinal importance for us;[1] and we are still near enough to the days in which the Philippine problem transcended all other American questions of territorial policy to justify, and even require, bringing the present chapter toward a close with some review of the conditions under which the Islands, following an interval of Japanese domination, achieved their present separate status. As we shall see, the United States is still not wholly without a "Philippine problem."

The development of self-government   The Philippines were acquired by the United States in 1898 as a wholly unexpected result of the war with Spain; and their acquisition gave the United States a new importance in the Far East, where of late its influence had been at a low ebb. Retention of them as an American possession was bitterly opposed by "anti-imperialists," and in assenting to ratification of the peace treaty providing for their transfer, the Senate failed by a margin of only a single vote to declare it the intention of the United States not to annex the Islands permanently, but rather "in due time to dispose of them as dictated by the best interests of the Islands and of the United States." In contrast with British, French, Dutch, and other colonial policy in that quarter of the earth, American policy relating to the Philippines had from the first the two major objectives of (1) systematically preparing the Islands for self-government, and (2) keeping open the question of eventual independence. For nearly three years after the annexation, the Islands had only a military government under direction of the president. In 1901, however, Congress authorized the establishment of a temporary civil government; and in the following year an organic law gave the new dependency a modest start on the road to managing its own affairs. Finally, in 1916, a Philippine Government Act[2]—commonly known as the Jones Act—broadened the suffrage, introduced a legislature of two elective houses, and otherwise provided for a system of insular government which lasted until 1935, and under which self-government was so far attained that by the date mentioned less than three per cent of the public officials, of all grades, were other than Filipinos.

The movement for independence   In its preamble, the Jones Act, moreover, announced the country's intention to give the Islands their freedom as soon as "a stable government" could be established therein; and at once the matter became an

---

[1] Ways in which our interests and policies were affected included the following: (1) our status as a Far Eastern power was naturally enhanced; (2) desire for safety of the Islands led us a good many times before 1941 deliberately to shape our course so as to avoid offending Japanese susceptibilities; (3) by 1940, the Islands ranked fifth as a buyer of American goods and about the same as a source of our imports; (4) approximately a quarter of our total investments in the Far East have been in the Islands; (5) for some time before restrictions were imposed in 1934, enough Filipinos were settling in the United States to impart a new slant to our Oriental immigration problem; (6) the Islands have had a vital place in our sea-power in the Pacific; and, of course, (7) their deliverance from the Japanese constituted a major objective in our war in the Pacific after 1941.

[2] 39 *U. S. Stat. at Large*, 545.

issue of party politics. The act was the work of a Democratic president and Congress, and in its platform of the same year the party endorsed the principle of "ultimate independence." On their part, the Republicans criticized the Democratic position, asserting that the American task in the Islands was but "half done" and talk of independence premature; and the positions thus taken were reiterated in 1920 and 1924, even though without stirring a great deal of interest among the voters. Encouraged by the promise of the Jones Act and by repeated Democratic pronouncements, the insular legislature sent delegation after delegation to Washington in quest of a grant of "immediate, absolute, and complete independence;" and in March, 1934, the demand was met (even though in a somewhat qualified way) in the McDuffie-Tydings bill which became the Philippine Independence Act of the same year.[1] On May 1 following— the anniversary of Admiral Dewey's victory in Manila Bay—the insular legislature unanimously accepted the arrangements offered.

This done, the legislature arranged for an early election of delegates to a convention to draft a constitution for the Islands. The assembly completed its labors in February, 1935, and a month later the new fundamental law received President Roosevelt's approval; whereupon a date was fixed by the Philippine legislature for a popular vote upon the new form of government. With women participating, the decision was for ratification, by the heavy margin of 438,000 to 11,000. The American governor-general thereupon issued a proclamation setting a date for the election of officers; subsequently, the President issued a proclamation announcing the results; and on November 15, 1935, the new government of the Philippine Commonwealth began exercising its powers and functions. *The Philippine Commonwealth established (1935)*

With the launching of the Commonwealth, the Islands entered upon a ten-year period of political and economic readjustment, preparatory to full independence. During this transitional interval, they were to enjoy far greater autonomy than before, yet with plenty of strings attached. They remained part of the United States, even though no longer termed an "insular possession;" their citizens owed allegiance as previously; they could change their constitution only with the consent of the president of the United States—now represented in the Islands by a high commissioner in lieu of the former governor-general.[2] Moreover, all *The ten-year transitional period: 1. Political status*

[1] 48 *U. S. Stat. at Large,* 456. A measure of similar purport passed by Congress in 1933 over a veto by President Hoover had failed to become effective because of rejection of its terms by the Philippine legislature. The drive in Congress which finally made possible the legislation of 1933-34 was engineered primarily by American agricultural interests desiring that Philippine sugar, tobacco, cocoanut oil, cordage, and other products be subjected to tariff duties, instead of admitted duty free as theretofore, and by labor interests wanting Filipino immigration checked or stopped. See G. L. Kirk, *Philippine Independence* (New York, 1936), Chaps. IV-V.

[2] Under the Jones Act, the Islands were represented in the United States House of Representatives by two resident commissioners, chosen by the insular legislature. The Commonwealth had but one such commissioner, appointed by the Commonwealth president.

measures passed by the Commonwealth legislature must be reported to Congress, and certain of them were subject to the president's absolute veto; the president, under certain circumstances, might suspend the operation of any Commonwealth law, contract, or executive order; the United States Supreme Court continued to review cases carried to it from the Philippine supreme court; Philippine foreign relations remained under the "direct supervision and control" of the United States; the United States continued to garrison military posts in the Islands, with authority to call into service all military forces organized by the Commonwealth government; [1] and, finally, the United States might at any time intervene in the Commonwealth's affairs with a view to preserving the established system of government, protecting life, property, and individual liberty, or insuring faithful discharge of the Commonwealth's obligations.

2. Economic relations

In its economic aspect, the status assigned the Commonwealth during the transitional period clearly reflected the motivations, on the American side, chiefly inspiring the Independence Act. In line with the demands of labor, Filipino immigration into the United States was limited to fifty persons a year; while, instead of being admitted duty-free in unlimited quantities, specified Philippine commodities—chiefly sugar, tobacco, cocoanut oil, and hempen products—were admitted free only within specified quotas, all excesses being subject to the same duties as if coming from a foreign country. Subject to revision annually, the quotas agreed upon were, down to 1941, generally large enough to include substantially all of the respective products imported from the Islands. If, however, with the transitional period ended, the quota system were in future to be terminated, the pinch would come; for—although sustaining the highest median standard of living in all Asia—the Philippine economy had for forty years been geared to preferential treatment in the American market and indeed quite dependent upon it. In the spring of 1938, a Joint Preparatory Commission, composed of equal numbers of Americans and Filipinos, recommended that, instead of being terminated abruptly in 1946, trade preferences at that time existing should merely be tapered off over a period extending to 1960, thus enabling the shock to be absorbed gradually. A "cushioning" bill to this effect, however, failed to become law, although the situation for the remainder of the ten-year period was somewhat eased by minor readjustments.

Status when independence attained

Under terms of the legislation of 1934, the Islands were automatically to become independent in 1946, the Commonwealth thereupon emerging as "a separate and self-governing nation." The United States was to be entitled to negotiate for the retention of naval reservations and fueling stations in the Islands; but all military forces were to be withdrawn and all governmental connections severed—one final obligation on our part being to try to arrange with foreign powers for the Islands' future secu-

[1] This, of course, was done when the Japanese invaded the Islands in 1941-42.

rity through perpetual neutralization. And, of course, unless some different agreement were arrived at in the meantime, Philippine products entering the United States would become subject to the same tariff rates as imports from other foreign countries.

It had long been assumed that in the event of war between Japan and the United States, the Philippines not only would be a first object of attack, but could not be saved from subjugation; and after the Pearl Harbor assault in December, 1941, events ran their anticipated course. Despite heroic defense, with such American guidance and aid as difficult circumstances permitted, the Islands fell almost completely under the heel of the invader, with the regular government displaced by a puppet régime and every effort made to persuade the inhabitants that their future, and even their hope for independence, lay, not with the United States, but with Japan. For some time before the catastrophe, the dismal economic outlook associated with the prospect of independence, together with growing threat from Japan's vaunted "new order" for Eastern Asia, had prompted doubts as to whether the program laid down in the Independence Act would ever really be carried out in full—even, indeed, as to whether, in the face of the drawbacks and dangers involved, Filipino sentiment would not itself recoil (as to some extent it actually did) from its earlier objective. But the war removed all such uncertainties. On the one hand, the expulsion of the conqueror and the removal of all further danger from him for at least a long time to come inspired in the Islands a fresh demand for independence at the earliest possible date. On the American side, wartime experience invested the interrupted program with new sanctions and assured its full and early realization. Three weeks after Pearl Harbor, President Roosevelt solemnly promised the stricken Islands that their freedom would be redeemed and their independence established and protected; in 1944, Congress voted him authority to proclaim independence even before 1946 if circumstances should warrant [1]; and, with hostilities ending in the following year, July 4, 1946, was settled upon by general agreement as an appropriate time for the new status to become effective—which curiously meant that, despite all that had happened, independence would be achieved at precisely the time originally contemplated in the legislation of 1934.

On the date fixed, and by proclamation of President Truman, independence became a reality: the transitional Philippine Commonwealth became, and now is, the Philippine Republic, recognized as a sovereign state not only in an American treaty (by which the territory was ceded to the new nation), but by practically all governments, and duly participating as such in the United Nations. Nothing, however, had been clearer than that the United States could not simply give the Islands their freedom and then walk out. More than three years of Japanese domination had left the Islands shattered, with population dispersed, property de-

Margin notes: Independence becomes a reality (1946)

Post-independence economic relations

[1] 58 U. S. Stat. at Large. 625.

stroyed, industries disrupted, communications paralyzed, finances in chaos; and before independence took effect Congress appropriated liberal sums (altogether more than half a billion dollars) for relief for the distressed, compensation for war damage to private property, and aid in restoring and improving public property and essential public services.[1] The matter of trade had likewise to be given attention; and, simultaneously with its grants for rehabilitation, Congress solved that problem by passing a Philippine Trade [Bell] Act[2] guaranteeing Philippine products some degree of preference in the American market for twenty-eight years—the existing duty-free system on a quota basis continuing for eight years (to 1954), and thereafter commodities becoming subject to graduated tariff rates rising by five per cent annually for twenty years, until finally in 1974 all preferential features would disappear. In that no duties at all (within the quotas) were to be paid for almost a decade and some degree of preference to last until 1974 instead of only 1960, these terms were more favorable than those earlier suggested by the Preparatory Commission and supported by President Roosevelt; and, although some people in the Islands as well as in the United States feared that prolonging trade preferences would tend to perpetuate the Islands' artificial export economy and prevent desirable diversification of agriculture and industrial development, the act was made the basis of an executive agreement signed between the two governments on independence day and later declared in force as of January 2, 1947.[3]

One feature of the new arrangements, however, gave considerable trouble. Included in the Trade Act was a clause—inspired by the large rôle that United States capital and enterprise were expected to play in Philippine rehabilitation—guaranteeing equal rights for Americans with Filipinos in the ownership of land in the Islands, the development and exploitation of agricultural, timber, mineral, and other resources, and the operation of public utilities; and on the ground that while the United States was indeed giving political independence with one hand, it was keeping so firm a grip upon economic advantages peculiar to itself with the other that political independence might be rendered a hollow victory, various elements in the Islands, including most of the political parties, raised vigorous objection. To meet the treaty's terms, an amendment to the insular constitution was necessary; and a period of intense discussion and agitation ensued, with American prestige considerably impaired among many segments of the population recently ardent in welcoming our contribution to deliverance from Japanese rule. With President Roxas, however, urging that failure to approve the "parity" proposals would lead to "national disaster and chaos," the people ultimately (on March 11, 1947) approved the amendment by a substantial majority, although

---

[1] The principal measure was a Philippine Rehabilitation Act of 1946 (60 *U. S. Stat. at Large,* 128).

[2] 60 *U. S. Stat. at Large,* 141.

[3] P. E. Abelard, *American Tariff Policy Toward the Philippines* (New York, 1947).

with over half of the voters abstaining; and the proposed economic equality is now in effect.[1]

Meanwhile, there was also the question of military and naval bases to be retained by the United States in the Islands. In all legislation from the Independence Act of 1934 onwards, the right of our government to negotiate with the Philippine government on this matter was scrupulously maintained, and in 1946-47 it fell to our first ambassador at Manila, Paul V. McNutt (a former "high commissioner") to work out arrangements with the proper authorities. The upshot was a ninety-nine-year agreement signed at Manila on March 14, 1947, under which eleven sites scattered throughout the Islands were designated as American military bases and four others as naval "operating areas." Philippine demand that no such base or area be located in Manila or its immediate environs, or indeed near any populous center, was respected; and reassurance was given in the form of official announcement that it would be American policy to keep in the Islands only such armed forces as might be required to man bases and constitute "a small military mission." The principal military establishment is at Fort Stotsenberg, in central Luzon; and in the interest of international peace any of the bases may be made available to the Security Council of the United Nations. The military and naval rights carried by our trusteeship for the former Japanese mandated islands (together with other rights probably to be secured in the final peace with Japan) render the United States less dependent upon the Philippines for facilities for defending its interests in the South Pacific than otherwise would be the case. Continuance of an American military and naval position in the Islands is, indeed, represented as designed no less for the protection of the Islands themselves than for the well-being of the United States; and in pursuance of this idea, an agreement of March 2, 1946, confirmed by Congress in a Philippines Military Assistance Act[2] of the following June 26, provided (among other things) that the insular army should continue to be American-trained.

Military and naval rights retained by the United States

From the Commonwealth, the new Philippine Republic inherited a system of government which, as reëstablished after the interlude of Japanese control, required almost no alterations to fit it for the new stage in the Islands' history. As has been indicated, the national constitution, dating from 1935, and containing full guarantees of civil liberty, was framed by a democratically chosen convention and ratified by heavy popular vote. The Congress for which it provides consists of a senate and

Philippine government

[1] E. W. Mill, *One Year of the Philippine Republic,* Dept. of State Pub. No. 2877 (Washington, D. C., 1947); S. Jenkins, "Great Expectations in the Philippines," *Far Eastern Survey,* XVI, 169-174 (Aug. 13, 1947); W. Wilgus, "Economic Outlook for the Philippines," *Foreign Policy Reports,* XXI, No. 14 (Oct. 1, 1945); E. G. Crossman, "American–Philippine Relations: The Prospect," *Proceedings of Acad. of Polit. Sci.,* XXII, 25-36 (Jan., 1948). In H. J. Abaya, *Betrayal in the Philippines* (New York, 1947), will be found a vigorous Filipino attack upon the United States for supporting "collaborationist" Filipinos (including former President Roxas) in their quest for political power.

[2] 60 *U. S. Stat. at Large,* 315.

house of representatives,[1] elected directly by universal suffrage for two-
and four-year terms, respectively; and the powers conferred upon it (in
many respects broader than the powers of the Congress of the United
States) give it an almost unique position among contemporary legislatures outside of the British Parliament. The chief executive is a president
elected by the people for a four-year term; and his cabinet consists, as
in the United States, of heads of the various executive departments. Interesting variations from our American system are, however, seen in
(1) limitation of the president to eight consecutive years of service;
(2) lack of authority of the Congress to increase appropriations asked
for in the presidential budget, except those for support of the legislative
and judicial branches of the government; (3) possession of the item veto
by the president; (4) action on presidential nominations to public office,
not by the senate, but by a commission of twenty-four members named
in equal numbers by the two branches of the Congress; and (5) definite
authorization for heads of departments to appear and be heard in
either legislative house. Consisting of a supreme court and such inferior
courts as may be established by law, the judiciary has as its most notable
feature for Americans the express authority of the supreme court to
declare statutes and treaties unconstitutional, provided five of the seven
justices concur. For purposes of local government, there are thirty-nine
provinces with an elective governor, and four others with a governor
designated by a bureau of non-Christian tribes.[2]

In anticipation of early independence, and in order that the new
republic might come into being with a government holding "a fresh
mandate from the people," the Philippine Congress, in December, 1945,
passed an act calling a special election on April 23, 1946 (the first since
1941), and empowered the newly chosen officers and members of the Congress, who otherwise, under existing law, would not have taken office
until the following December 30, to assume their posts forthwith. In the
ensuing contest, the presidential incumbent, Sergio Osmeña,[3] was defeated by the incumbent vice-president, Manuel Roxas, who accordingly
was inaugurated on May 28, 1946, as the first president of the independent Philippine nation.

Some Special Jurisdictions

1. Miscel-
laneous
federal
areas or
establish-
ments

In addition to the widespread territories and dependencies dealt with
in earlier portions of this chapter, our national government has extensive
jurisdiction over further areas not forming mere ordinary parts of the
states in which they are situated. To begin with, literally hundreds of
federal military or naval stations, forts, arsenals, dockyards, parks, forest

---

[1] Originally there was only a single house, but the bicameral system was adopted
by constitutional amendment in 1940.
[2] These tribes consist chiefly of the Moros in Mindanao and the Sulu archipelago.
[3] Osmeña had succeeded to the then merely nominal presidency in 1944, on the
death of President Manuel L. Quezon in Washington.

preserves, prisons, hospitals, asylums, post-offices, power sites, and other establishments dot the country; and over all such, by constitutional provision, Congress has exclusive legislative control,[1] with managerial functions also, of course, in federal hands. If the states exercise any functions in these areas or places, e.g., by serving legal processes or taxing private property, they do so only with express congressional assent.

A second and different category of special jurisdictions consists of some two hundred Indian reservations, situated in upwards of twenty states, and with an aggregate population of over 350,000. The gradual establishment of these reservations marked a relatively late stage in the long and troubled relations between white man and red in this country; and the reservations themselves are not necessarily permanent, since sometimes (the inhabitants having become capable of owning their own land and managing their own affairs) a reservation is discontinued and wholly absorbed into the state in which it is located. The constitution merely gives Congress power to "regulate commerce ... with the Indian tribes." But on one basis or another authority has been found not only for gathering most surviving Indians into reservations, but for full federal control over all such areas, however far it may be found desirable to go in particular cases in permitting the inhabitants, under federal supervision, to adopt tribal constitutions and exercise rights of local self-government. An Office of Indian Affairs, in the Department of the Interior, is in general charge, and the necessary field work is carried on by a force of several thousand persons (including many Indians) under regional supervision of five district superintendents. The general theory underlying the system is that the Indians are "wards" of the nation—although the implications of this somewhat nebulous status have not prevented them from also being made citizens.[2]

2. Indian reservations

Finally, for purposes of this brief summary, we come to the area in which the national capital is situated, i.e., the District of Columbia, formed originally from lands on both sides of the Potomac river ceded for the purpose by Virginia and Maryland, but, since the retrocession of Virginia's portion in 1846, consisting of some seventy square miles on the Maryland side of the stream. Over this area—selected only after lively controversy, and first occupied in 1800—the constitution gives Congress power of exclusive legislation,[3] as over any other place transferred to the national government; and while the District has some of the aspects of a state, others of a county, and certainly many aspects of a city, it is legally no one of the three, but simply an area completely and directly controlled by the national government. Devoid of any local leg-

3. The District of Columbia

---

[1] Art. I, § 8, cl. 17.

[2] In Arizona, however, Indians are denied the suffrage as being "persons under guardianship," and in New Mexico they may not vote if not taxed. For a recent full account of Indian administration and affairs, see *Annual Report of the Secretary of the Interior for the Fiscal Year Ended June 30, 1946* (Washington, D. C., 1946), 351-384.

[3] Art. I, § 8, cl. 17.

islature or council, it receives its laws and ordinances exclusively from Congress, subject, of course, to presidential veto as in the case of other legislation. For an executive, it has three commissioners, of whom two are appointed by the president and Senate from among the residents of the District for three-year terms and a third is detailed by the president from the engineer corps of the Army for an indefinite term. As a body, these three commissioners have extensive powers: they appoint to numerous important municipal positions; they have charge of police and fire protection, and make regulations for the safeguarding of life, health, and property; they supervise the local public utilities, including gas, electricity, telephones, transportation, and water-supply. Schools are under a board of education appointed by the judges of the supreme court of the District, and a board of charities and the judges of a municipal court are appointed by the president.[1] For more than forty years prior to 1920, the cost of the District government was divided equally between the national treasury and the taxpayers of the District. In the year mentioned, however, the District's quota was moved up to sixty per cent; and in more recent years the federal government's share has been further reduced, until in fiscal 1947 it amounted to only eight million dollars, or less than ten per cent of the total District budget.[2] Many of the District's upwards of a million inhabitants retain a legal residence in some one of the states and vote there, usually by mail. In the District itself, however, not even taxpayers are voters; there are no locally elected officers, and the District as such has no part in choosing the president or any member of Congress.

The problem of more self-government

That, in general, it is desirable for the national capital to be situated in an area under exclusive national jurisdiction is commonly conceded. In later years, however, opinion—warmly supported in the District—has

---

[1] The District's judicial system, in full, consists of a federal district court, a District court of appeals, the supreme court mentioned, the municipal court, a police court, and a juvenile court.

Actually, government in the District is far more complicated than might be inferred from the above summary. Numerous federal agencies also share in it, some being units in executive departments and others independent agencies. The involved interrelations are shown and explained in a series of charts printed for the House committee on the District of Columbia, 80th Cong., 1st Sess. (1947). Central authority for the District is entirely lacking.

[2] Like state governments, the District collects income taxes, inheritance and estate taxes, incorporation taxes, motor-fuel sales taxes, and unemployment compensation taxes; and, altogether, these "state" taxes bring in about one-fifth of the total municipal revenue. As in other cities, the major source of income is the general property tax. In 1947, the District was running far behind financially and strong demand was rising for a more generous federal contribution, especially in view of heavy increases of federal property (likewise of property used by foreign embassies) which cannot be taxed for District purposes. (Historically, this exemption of government property from taxation is the reason for the federal subsidy.) The tax program is determined entirely by Congress, as also the annual budget of expenditures. The District collects revenue, but the uses to which it is put are subject to the same control as federal funds. See L. B. Sims, "Intergovernmental Fiscal Relations in the Nation's Capital," *Nat. Mun. Rev.*, XXVI, 223-229 (May, 1937); *Fiscal Relations Between the Federal Government and the Government of the District of Columbia* (Washington, D. C., 1937), a report of a study by a committee appointed by the president.

been developing that the inhabitants might well be intrusted with more control of their own affairs (which, indeed, they possessed before Congress took it away in 1878 as punishment for extravagance and inefficiency), and the burden of Congress correspondingly lightened;[1] and recurring agitation against "taxation without representation"—reasonable enough despite generous opportunity given the inhabitants to voice their opinions in committee hearings, and especially through a citizens' advisory council representing numerous local civic organizations—may in time bear fruit, although at present there is no definite prospect of its doing so. Meanwhile, some consolation may be found in the fact that the District has one of the most honest and efficient municipal governments in the world; also in the reflection that, except in the highly improbable event of the national government consenting to taxation of its property for District purposes, or, alternatively, consenting to go on subsidizing the District without managing its affairs, the coveted autonomy would mean a heavier financial burden for the inhabitants than they bear today.[2]

REFERENCES

W. W. Willoughby, *Constitutional Law of the United States* (2nd ed., New York, 1929), I, Chaps. XXIII-XXXII.

J. M. Mathews, *The American Constitutional System* (2nd ed., New York, 1940), Chap. XX.

W. T. Haas [ed.], *The American Empire; A Study of the Outlying Territories of the United States* (Chicago, 1940).

E. G. Arnold, "Self-Government in U. S. Territories," *Foreign Affairs*, XXV, 655-666 (July, 1947).

J. Barber, Jr., *Hawaii; Restless Rampart* (Indianapolis, 1941).

Statehood for Hawaii. Hearings before the Joint Committee on Hawaii, 75th Cong., 2nd Sess. (Washington, D. C., 1938).

R. M. C. Littler, *The Governance of Hawaii* (Palo Alto, Calif., 1929).

W. H. George and P. S. Bachman, *The Government of Hawaii; Federal, Territorial, and County* (Honolulu, 1934).

[1] The congressional reorganization of 1946 (see pp. 411-415 above) afforded a good opportunity to transfer some of the burden of District business from Congress to other agencies, but every proposal to that end failed. Accordingly, the reduced list of standing committees in both houses still contains a committee on the District, and the House of Representatives still allocates the second and fourth Monday of every month to District affairs.

[2] For more than twenty years, one or more proposals to amend the constitution for the benefit of the people of the District have been introduced in practically every session of Congress. One suggestion is to permit residents of the District to vote in presidential elections and to elect their own representatives and senators to sit in Congress. Another goes farther and not only contemplates the election of senators and representatives from the District, but would empower Congress to set up a government modeled upon the state governments, with legislative, executive, and judicial branches. The Democratic platforms of 1940 and 1944 advocated extension of the suffrage to the inhabitants of the District.

A bill providing for a thorough reorganization of the District's government, including the introduction of a council-manager plan, has been reported by a House subcommittee of which Mr. J. C. Auchincloss of New Jersey is chairman. See J. C. Auchincloss, "City Manager for Washington?," *Nat. Mun. Rev.*, XXXVI, 618-624 (Dec., 1947); H. Morrow, "Washington Wants to Join the U.S.A.," *Sat. Eve. Post*, CCXIX, 22 ff. (Mar. 22, 1947).

T. B. Clark, *Hawaii—the Forty-ninth State* (Garden City, N. Y., 1947).

G. W. Spicer, "The Constitutional Status and Government of Alaska," *Johns Hopkins Univ. Studies in Hist. and Polit. Sci.*, XLV, 450-567 (Baltimore, 1927).

T. White, *Puerto Rico and Its People* (New York, 1938).

V. S. Clark *et al.*, *Porto Rico and Its Problems* (Washington, D. C., 1930).

P. T. Homan *et al.*, *Puerto Rican Problems* (Washington, D. C., 1940).

Independence for Puerto Rico. Hearings before the Committees on Insular Affairs and Territories, 79th Cong., 1st Sess. (Washington, D. C., 1945-46).

L. H. Evans, *The Virgin Islands; From Naval Base to New Deal* (Ann Arbor, Mich., 1945).

J. R. Hayden, *The Philippines; A Study in National Development* (New York, 1941) The best work on the subject.

F. Horn, *Orphans of the Pacific: The Philippines* (New York, 1941).

F. M. Keesing, *The Philippines; A Nation in the Making* (London, 1938).

G. L. Kirk, *Philippine Independence; Motives, Problems, and Prospects* (New York, 1936).

Report of the Joint Preparatory Commission on Philippine Affairs, May 20, 1938, 3 vols. (Washington, D. C., 1938).

W. C. Forbes, *The Philippine Islands*, 2 vols. (Boston, 1928).

D. C. Worcester, *The Philippines, Past and Present* (new ed., New York, 1930).

N. Roosevelt, *The Philippines; A Treasure and a Problem* (4th ed., Boston, 1933).

J. P. Laurel, *Local Government in the Philippine Islands* (Manila, 1926).

C. Porter, *Crisis in the Philippines* (New York, 1942).

C. P. Romulo, *I Saw the Philippines Fall* (New York, 1943).

"The Philippines," *Far Eastern Quar.*, IV, 95-181 (Feb., 1945). Eleven excellent articles.

J. I. Brookes, *International Rivalry in the Pacific Islands, 1800-1875* (Berkeley, Calif., 1941).

W. D. McCain, *The United States and the Republic of Panama* (Durham, N. C., 1937).

N. J. Padelford, *The Panama Canal in Peace and War* (New York, 1942).

E. S. Pomeroy, "The Navy and Colonial Government," *U. S. Naval Inst. Proceedings*, LXXI, 291-298 (Mar., 1945).

J. C. Vincent *et al.*, *America's Future in the Pacific* (New Brunswick, N. J., 1947).

T. K. Hitch, "The Administration of America's Pacific Islands," *Polit. Sci. Quar.*, LXI, 384-407 (Sept., 1946).

L. Meriam *et al.*, *The Problem of Indian Administration* (Baltimore, 1928).

J. Collier, *The Indians of the Americas* (New York, 1947).

L. F. Schmeckebier, *The District of Columbia; Its Government and Administration* (Baltimore, 1928).

L. F. Schmeckebier and W. F. Willoughby, *The Government and Administration of the District of Columbia; Suggestions for Change* (Washington, D. C., 1929).

To Provide a Delegate from the District of Columbia. Hearings before the House Judiciary Committee, 78th Cong., 1st Sess. (Washington, D. C., 1943).

National Representation and Suffrage for...the District of Columbia. Hearings before the House Judiciary Committee, 78th Cong., 1st Sess. (Washington, D. C., 1945).

House Committee on the District of Columbia, *Explanation of Charts Showing the Organization of Agencies Providing Governmental Services to the District of Columbia* (Washington, D. C., 1947).

APPENDIX

THE CONSTITUTION OF THE UNITED STATES OF AMERICA

We, the people of the United States, in order to form a more perfect union, establish justice, insure domestic tranquillity, provide for the common defense, promote the general welfare, and secure the blessings of liberty to ourselves and our posterity, do ordain and establish this Constitution for the United States of America.

ARTICLE I

SECTION I

All legislative powers herein granted shall be vested in a Congress of the United States, which shall consist of a Senate and House of Representatives.

SECTION II

The House of Representatives shall be composed of members chosen every second year by the people of the several States, and the electors in each State shall have the qualifications requisite for electors of the most numerous branch of the State legislature.

No person shall be a Representative who shall not have attained to the age of twenty-five years, and been seven years a citizen of the United States, and who shall not, when elected, be an inhabitant of that State in which he shall be chosen.

Representatives and direct taxes shall be apportioned among the several States which may be included within this Union, according to their respective numbers, which shall be determined by adding to the whole number of free persons, including those bound to service for a term of years,[1] and excluding Indians not taxed, three fifths of all other persons.[2] The actual enumeration shall be made within three years after the first meeting of the Congress of the United States, and within every subsequent term of ten years, in such manner as they shall by law direct. The number of Representatives shall not exceed one for every thirty thousand, but each State shall have at least one Representative; and until such enumeration shall be made, the State of New Hampshire shall be entitled to choose three, Massachusetts eight, Rhode Island and Providence Plantations one, Connecticut five, New York six, New Jersey four, Pennsylvania eight, Delaware one, Maryland six, Virginia ten, North Carolina five, South Carolina five, and Georgia three.[3]

When vacancies happen in the representation from any State, the executive authority thereof shall issue writs of election to fill such vacancies.

The House of Representatives shall choose their Speaker and other officers, and shall have the sole power of impeachment.

[1] Altered by the Fourteenth Amendment.
[2] Rescinded by the Fourteenth Amendment.
[3] Temporary provision.

SECTION III

The Senate of the United States shall be composed of two Senators from each State, chosen by the legislature thereof,[1] for six years; and each Senator shall have one vote.

Immediately after they shall be assembled in consequence of the first election, they shall be divided as equally as may be into three classes. The seats of the Senators of the first class shall be vacated at the expiration of the second year, of the second class at the expiration of the fourth year, and of the third class at the expiration of the sixth year, so that one third may be chosen every second year; and if vacancies happen by resignation or otherwise during the recess of the legislature of any State the executive thereof may make temporary appointments until the next meeting of the legislature, which shall then fill such vacancies.[2]

No person shall be a Senator who shall not have attained to the age of thirty years, and been nine years a citizen of the United States, and who shall not, when elected, be an inhabitant of that State for which he shall be chosen.

The Vice-President of the United States shall be President of the Senate, but shall have no vote, unless they be equally divided.

The Senate shall choose their other officers, and also a President *pro tempore* in the absence of the Vice-President, or when he shall exercise the office of the President of the United States.

The Senate shall have the sole power to try all impeachments. When sitting for that purpose, they shall be on oath or affirmation. When the President of the United States is tried, the Chief Justice shall preside; and no person shall be convicted without the concurrence of two thirds of the members present.

Judgment in cases of impeachment shall not extend further than to removal from office, and disqualification to hold and enjoy any office of honor, trust, or profit under the United States; but the party convicted shall, nevertheless, be liable and subject to indictment, trial, judgment, and punishment, according to law.

SECTION IV

The times, places, and manner of holding elections for Senators and Representatives shall be prescribed in each State by the legislature thereof; but the Congress may at any time by law make or alter such regulations, except as to the places of choosing Senators.

The Congress shall assemble at least once in every year, and such meeting shall be on the first Monday in December, unless they shall by law appoint a different day.[3]

SECTION V

Each house shall be the judge of the elections, returns, and qualifications of its own members, and a majority of each shall constitute a quorum to do business; but a smaller number may adjourn from day to day, and may be authorized to compel the attendance of absent members, in such manner, and under such penalties, as each house may provide.

[1] Modified by the Seventeenth Amendment.
[2] Modified by the Seventeenth Amendment.
[3] Superseded by the Twentieth Amendment.

Each house may determine the rules of its proceedings, punish its members for disorderly behavior, and with the concurrence of two thirds, expel a member.

Each house shall keep a journal of its proceedings, and from time to time publish the same, excepting such parts as may in their judgment require secrecy, and the yeas and nays of the members of either house on any question shall, at the desire of one fifth of those present, be entered on the journal.

Neither house, during the session of Congress, shall, without the consent of the other, adjourn for more than three days, nor to any other place than that in which the two houses shall be sitting.

SECTION VI

The Senators and Representatives shall receive a compensation for their services, to be ascertained by law and paid out of the Treasury of the United States. They shall, in all cases except treason, felony, and breach of the peace, be privileged from arrest during their attendance at the session of their respective houses, and in going to and returning from the same; and for any speech or debate in either house they shall not be questioned in any other place.

No Senator or Representative shall, during the time for which he was elected, be appointed to any civil office under the authority of the United States, which shall have been created, or the emoluments whereof shall have been increased, during such time; and no person holding any office under the United States shall be a member of either house during his continuance in office.

SECTION VII

All bills for raising revenue shall originate in the House of Representatives; but the Senate may propose or concur with amendments as on other bills.

Every bill which shall have passed the House of Representatives and the Senate shall, before it become a law, be presented to the President of the United States; if he approves he shall sign it, but if not he shall return it, with his objections, to that house in which it shall have originated, who shall enter the objections at large on their journal and proceed to reconsider it. If after such reconsideration two thirds of that house shall agree to pass the bill, it shall be sent, together with the objections, to the other house, by which it shall likewise be reconsidered, and if approved by two thirds of that house it shall become a law. But in all such cases the votes of both houses shall be determined by yeas and nays, and the names of the persons voting for and against the bill shall be entered on the journal of each house respectively. If any bill shall not be returned by the President within ten days (Sundays excepted) after it shall have been presented to him, the same shall be a law, in like manner as if he had signed it, unless the Congress by their adjournment prevent its return, in which case it shall not be a law.

Every order, resolution, or vote to which the concurrence of the Senate and House of Representatives may be necessary (except on a question of adjournment) shall be presented to the President of the United States; and before the same shall take effect, shall be approved by him, or being disapproved by him, shall be repassed by two thirds of the Senate and House of Representatives, according to the rules and limitations prescribed in the case of a bill.

SECTION VIII

The Congress shall have power to lay and collect taxes, duties, imposts, and excises, to pay the debts and provide for the common defense and general welfare of the United States; but all duties, imposts, and excises shall be uniform throughout the United States;

To borrow money on the credit of the United States;

To regulate commerce with foreign nations and among the several States, and with the Indian tribes;

To establish an uniform rule of naturalization, and uniform laws on the subject of bankruptcies throughout the United States;

To coin money, regulate the value thereof, and of foreign coin, and fix the standard of weights and measures;

To provide for the punishment of counterfeiting the securities and current coin of the United States;

To establish post-offices and post-roads;

To promote the progress of science and useful arts by securing for limited times to authors and inventors the exclusive right to their respective writings and discoveries;

To constitute tribunals inferior to the Supreme Court;

To define and punish piracies and felonies committed on the high seas and offenses against the law of nations;

To declare war, grant letters of marque and reprisal, and make rules concerning captures on land and water;

To raise and support armies, but no appropriation of money to that use shall be for a longer term than two years;

To provide and maintain a navy;

To make rules for the government and regulation of the land and naval forces;

To provide for calling forth the militia to execute the laws of the Union, suppress insurrections, and repel invasions;

To provide for organizing, arming, and disciplining the militia, and for governing such part of them as may be employed in the service of the United States, reserving to the States respectively the appointment of the officers, and the authority of training the militia according to the discipline prescribed by Congress;

To exercise exclusive legislation in all cases whatsoever over such district (not exceeding ten miles square) as may, by cession of particular States and the acceptance of Congress, become the seat of the Government of the United States, and to exercise like authority over all places purchased by the consent of the legislature of the State in which the same shall be, for the erection of forts, magazines, arsenals, dockyards, and other needful buildings; and

To make all laws which shall be necessary and proper for carrying into execution the foregoing powers, and all other powers vested by this Constitution in the Government of the United States, or in any department or officer thereof.

SECTION IX

The migration or importation of such persons as any of the States now existing shall think proper to admit shall not be prohibited by the Congress prior to the year one thousand eight hundred and eight, but a tax or duty may be imposed on such importation, not exceeding ten dollars for each person.[1]

The privilege of the writ of *habeas corpus* shall not be suspended, unless when in cases of rebellion or invasion the public safety may require it.

No bill of attainder or *ex post facto* law shall be passed.

No capitation or other direct tax shall be laid, unless in proportion to the census or enumeration hereinbefore directed to be taken.

No tax or duty shall be laid on articles exported from any State.

No preference shall be given by any regulation of commerce or revenue to the ports of one State over those of another; nor shall vessels bound to or from one State be obliged to enter, clear, or pay duties in another.

No money shall be drawn from the Treasury but in consequence of appropriations made by law; and a regular statement and account of the receipts and expenditures of all public money shall be published from time to time.

No title of nobility shall be granted by the United States; and no person holding any office of profit or trust under them shall, without the consent of the Congress, accept of any present, emolument, office, or title, of any kind whatever, from any king, prince, or foreign State.

SECTION X

No State shall enter into any treaty, alliance, or confederation; grant letters of marque and reprisal; coin money; emit bills of credit; make anything but gold and silver coin a tender in payment of debts; pass any bill of attainder, *ex post facto* law, or law impairing the obligation of contracts, or grant any title of nobility.

No State shall, without the consent of Congress, lay any imposts or duties on imports or exports, except what may be absolutely necessary for executing its inspection laws; and the net produce of all duties and imposts, laid by any State on imports or exports, shall be for the use of the Treasury of the United States; and all such laws shall be subject to the revision and control of the Congress.

No State shall, without the consent of Congress, lay any duty of tonnage, keep troops or ships of war in time of peace, enter into any agreement or compact with another State or with a foreign power, or engage in war, unless actually invaded or in such imminent danger as will not admit of delay.

ARTICLE II

SECTION I

The executive power shall be vested in a President of the United States of America. He shall hold his office during the term of four years, and together with the Vice-President, chosen for the same term, be elected as follows:

Each State shall appoint, in such manner as the legislature thereof may direct, a number of electors, equal to the whole number of Senators and Representatives to which the State may be entitled in the Congress; but no Senator or Representative, or person holding an office of trust or profit under the United States, shall be appointed an elector.

[1] Temporary provision.

The electors shall meet in their respective States and vote by ballot for two persons, of whom one at least shall not be an inhabitant of the same State with themselves. And they shall make a list of all the persons voted for, and of the number of votes for each; which list they shall sign and certify, and transmit sealed to the seat of government of the United States, directed to the President of the Senate. The President of the Senate shall, in the presence of the Senate and House of Representatives, open all the certificates, and the votes shall then be counted. The person having the greatest number of votes shall be the President, if such number be a majority of the whole number of electors appointed; and if there be more than one who have such a majority, and have an equal number of votes, then the House of Representatives shall immediately choose by ballot one of them for President; and if no person have a majority, then from the five highest on the list the said House shall in like manner choose the President. But in choosing the President the votes shall be taken by States, the representation from each State having one vote; a quorum for this purpose shall consist of a member or members from two thirds of the States, and a majority of all the States shall be necessary to a choice. In every case, after the choice of the President, the person having the greatest number of votes of the electors shall be the Vice-President. But if there should remain two or more who have equal votes, the Senate shall choose from them by ballot the Vice-President.[1]

The Congress may determine the time of choosing the electors and the day on which they shall give their votes, which day shall be the same throughout the United States.

No person except a natural-born citizen, or a citizen of the United States at the time of the adoption of this Constitution, shall be eligible to the office of President; neither shall any person be eligible to that office who shall not have attained to the age of thirty-five years, and been fourteen years a resident within the United States.

In case of the removal of the President from office, or of his death, resignation, or inability to discharge the powers and duties of the said office, the same shall devolve on the Vice-President, and the Congress may by law provide for the case of removal, death, resignation, or inability, both of the President and Vice-President, declaring what officer shall then act as President, and such officer shall act accordingly until the disability be removed or a President shall be elected.

The President shall, at stated times, receive for his services a compensation, which shall neither be increased nor diminished during the period for which he may have been elected, and he shall not receive within that period any other emolument from the United States or any of them.

Before he enter on the execution of his office he shall take the following oath or affirmation:

"I do solemnly swear (or affirm) that I will faithfully execute the office of President of the United States, and will to the best of my ability preserve, protect, and defend the Constitution of the United States."

[1] Superseded by the Twelfth Amendment.

SECTION II

The President shall be commander-in-chief of the army and navy of the United States, and of the militia of the several States when called into the actual service of the United States; he may require the opinion, in writing, of the principal officer in each of the executive departments, upon any subject relating to the duties of their respective offices, and he shall have power to grant reprieves and pardons for offenses against the United States, except in cases of impeachment.

He shall have power, by and with the advice and consent of the Senate, to make treaties, provided two thirds of the Senators present concur; and he shall nominate, and, by and with the advice and consent of the Senate, shall appoint ambassadors, other public ministers and consuls, judges of the Supreme Court, and all other officers of the United States, whose appointments are not herein otherwise provided for, and which shall be established by law; but the Congress may by law vest the appointment of such inferior officers, as they think proper, in the President alone, in the courts of law, or in the heads of departments.

The President shall have power to fill up all vacancies that may happen during the recess of the Senate, by granting commissions which shall expire at the end of their next session.

SECTION III

He shall from time to time give to the Congress information of the state of the Union, and recommend to their consideration such measures as he shall judge necessary and expedient; he may, on extraordinary occasions, convene both houses, or either of them, and in case of disagreement between them with respect to the time of adjournment, he may adjourn them to such time as he shall think proper; he shall receive ambassadors and other public ministers; he shall take care that the laws be faithfully executed, and shall commission all the officers of the United States.

SECTION IV

The President, Vice-President, and all civil officers of the United States shall be removed from office on impeachment for and conviction of treason, bribery, or other high crimes and misdemeanors.

ARTICLE III

SECTION I

The judicial power of the United States shall be vested in one Supreme Court, and in such inferior courts as the Congress may from time to time ordain and establish. The judges, both of the supreme and inferior courts, shall hold their offices during good behavior, and shall, at stated times, receive for their services a compensation which shall not be diminished during their continuance in office.

SECTION II

The judicial power shall extend to all cases, in law and equity, arising under this Constitution, the laws of the United States, and the treaties made, or which shall be made, under their authority; to all cases affecting ambassadors, other public ministers, and consuls; to all cases of admiralty and maritime jurisdiction; to controversies to which the United States shall be a party; to controversies between two or more States; between a State and citizens of another State; [1] between citizens of different States; between citizens of the same State claiming lands under grants of different States, and between a State, or the citizens thereof, and foreign States, citizens, or subjects.

In all cases affecting ambassadors, other public ministers, and consuls, and those in which a State shall be a party, the Supreme Court shall have original jurisdiction. In all the other cases before mentioned the Supreme Court shall have appellate jurisdiction, both as to law and fact, with such exceptions and under such regulations as the Congress shall make.

The trial of all crimes, except in cases of impeachment, shall be by jury; and such trial shall be held in the State where the said crimes shall have been committed; but when not committed within any State, the trial shall be at such place or places as the Congress may by law have directed.

SECTION III

Treason against the United States shall consist only in levying war against them, or in adhering to their enemies, giving them aid and comfort. No person shall be convicted of treason unless on the testimony of two witnesses to the same overt act, or on confession in open court.

The Congress shall have power to declare the punishment of treason, but no attainder of treason shall work corruption of blood or forfeiture except during the life of the person attainted.

ARTICLE IV

SECTION I

Full faith and credit shall be given in each State to the public acts, records, and judicial proceedings of every other State. And the Congress may by general laws prescribe the manner in which such acts, records, and proceedings shall be proved, and the effect thereof.

SECTION II

The citizens of each State shall be entitled to all privileges and immunities of citizens in the several States.[2]

A person charged in any State with treason, felony, or other crime, who shall flee from justice, and be found in another State, shall, on demand of the executive authority of the State from which he fled, be delivered up, to be removed to the State having jurisdiction of the crime.

No person held to service or labor in one State, under the laws thereof, escaping into another, shall, in consequence of any law or regulation therein, be discharged from such service or labor, but shall be delivered up on claim of the party to whom such service or labor may be due.[3]

---

[1] Restricted by the Eleventh Amendment.
[2] Extended by the Fourteenth Amendment.
[3] Superseded by the Thirteenth Amendment in so far as pertaining to slaves.

SECTION III

New States may be admitted by the Congress into this Union; but no new State shall be formed or erected within the jurisdiction of any other State; nor any State be formed by the junction of two or more States or parts of States, without the consent of the legislatures of the States concerned as well as of the Congress.

The Congress shall have power to dispose of and make all needful rules and regulations respecting the territory or other property belonging to the United States; and nothing in this Constitution shall be so construed as to prejudice any claims of the United States or any particular State.

SECTION IV

The United States shall guarantee to every State in this Union a republican form of government, and shall protect each of them against invasion, and on application of the legislature, or of the executive (when the legislature cannot be convened), against domestic violence.

ARTICLE V

The Congress, whenever two thirds of both houses shall deem it necessary, shall propose amendments to this Constitution, or, on the application of the legislatures of two thirds of the several States, shall call a convention for proposing amendments, which in either case shall be valid to all intents and purposes as part of this Constitution, when ratified by the legislatures of three fourths of the several States, or by conventions in three fourths thereof, as the one or the other mode of ratification may be proposed by the Congress, provided that no amendments which may be made prior to the year one thousand eight hundred and eight shall in any manner affect the first and fourth clauses in the ninth section of the first article,[1] and that no State, without its consent, shall be deprived of its equal suffrage in the Senate.

ARTICLE VI

All debts contracted and engagements entered into, before the adoption of this Constitution, shall be as valid against the United States under this Constitution as under the confederation.[2]

This Constitution, and the laws of the United States, which shall be made in pursuance thereof, and all treaties made, or which shall be made, under the authority of the United States, shall be the supreme law of the land; and the judges in every State shall be bound thereby, anything in the Constitution or laws of any State to the contrary notwithstanding.

The Senators and Representatives before mentioned, and the members of the several State legislatures, and all executive and judicial officers both of the United States and of the several States, shall be bound by oath or affirmation to support this Constitution; but no religious test shall ever be required as a qualification to any office or public trust under the United States.

[1] Temporary clause.
[2] Extended by the Fourteenth Amendment.

ARTICLE VII

The ratification of the conventions of nine States shall be sufficient for the establishment of this Constitution between the States so ratifying the same.

Done in convention by the unanimous consent of the States present, the seventeenth day of September, in the year of our Lord one thousand seven hundred and eighty-seven, and of the independence of the United States of America the twelfth. In witness whereof, we have hereunto subscribed our names.

[Signed by] [1]

ARTICLES IN ADDITION TO, AND AMENDMENT OF, THE CONSTITUTION OF THE UNITED STATES OF AMERICA, PROPOSED BY CONGRESS, AND RATIFIED BY THE LEGISLATURES OF THE SEVERAL STATES [OR CONVENTIONS THEREIN] PURSUANT TO THE FIFTH ARTICLE OF THE ORIGINAL CONSTITUTION:

Article I. Congress shall make no law respecting an establishment of religion, or prohibiting the free exercise thereof; or abridging the freedom of speech or of the press; or the right of the people peaceably to assemble, and to petition the government for a redress of grievances.

Article II. A well-regulated militia being necessary to the security of a free state, the right of the people to keep and bear arms shall not be infringed.

Article III. No soldier shall, in time of peace, be quartered in any house without the consent of the owner, nor in time of war, but in a manner to be prescribed by law.

Article IV. The right of the people to be secure in their persons, houses, papers, and effects, against unreasonable searches and seizures, shall not be violated, and no warrants shall issue but upon probable cause, supported by oath or affirmation, and particularly describing the place to be searched, and the person or things to be seized.

Article V. No person shall be held to answer for a capital or otherwise infamous crime, unless on a presentment or indictment of a grand jury, except in cases arising in the land or naval forces, or in the militia, when in actual service in time of war or public danger; nor shall any person be subject for the same offense to be twice put in jeopardy of life or limb; nor shall be compelled in any criminal case to be a witness against himself, nor be deprived of life, liberty, or property, without due process of law; nor shall private property be taken for public use without just compensation.

Article VI. In all criminal prosecutions the accused shall enjoy the right to a speedy and public trial, by an impartial jury of the State and district wherein

---

[1] The signatures are omitted here.

the crime shall have been committed, which district shall have been previously ascertained by law, and to be informed of the nature and cause of the accusation; to be confronted with the witnesses against him; to have compulsory process for obtaining witnesses in his favor, and to have the assistance of counsel for his defense.

Article VII. In suits at common law, where the value in controversy shall exceed twenty dollars, the right of trial by jury shall be preserved, and no fact tried by a jury shall be otherwise re-examined in any court of the United States, than according to the rules of the common law.

Article VIII. Excessive bail shall not be required, nor excessive fines imposed, nor cruel and unusual punishments inflicted.

Article IX. The enumeration in the Constitution of certain rights shall not be construed to deny or disparage others retained by the people.

Article X.[1] The powers not delegated to the United States by the Constitution, nor prohibited by it to the States, are reserved to the States respectively, or to the people.

Article XI.[2] The judicial power of the United States shall not be construed to extend to any suit in law or equity, commenced or prosecuted against one of the United States by citizens of another State, or by citizens or subjects of any foreign State.

Article XII.[3] The electors shall meet in their respective States and vote by ballot for President and Vice-President, one of whom, at least, shall not be an inhabitant of the same State with themselves; they shall name in their ballots the person voted for as President, and in distinct ballots the person voted for as Vice-President, and they shall make distinct lists of all persons voted for as President and of all persons voted for as Vice-President, and of the number of votes for each; which lists they shall sign and certify, and transmit sealed to the seat of the government of the United States, directed to the President of the Senate. The President of the Senate shall, in the presence of the Senate and House of Representatives, open all the certificates and the votes shall then be counted. The person having the greatest number of votes for President shall be the President, if such number be a majority of the whole number of electors appointed; and if no person have such majority, then from the persons having the highest numbers not exceeding three on the list of those voted for as President, the House of Representatives shall choose immediately, by ballot, the President. But in choosing the President the votes shall be taken by States, the representation from each State having one vote; a quorum for this purpose shall consist of a member or members from two thirds of the States, and a majority of all States shall be necessary to a choice. And if the House of Representatives shall not choose a President whenever the right of choice shall devolve

[1] The first ten amendments took effect December 15, 1791.
[2] Proclaimed January 8, 1798.
[3] Proclaimed September 25, 1804.

upon them, before the fourth day of March [1] next following, then the Vice-President shall act as President, as in the case of the death or other constitutional disability of the President.

The person having the greatest number of votes as Vice-President shall be the Vice-President, if such number be a majority of the whole number of electors appointed; and if no person have a majority, then from the two highest numbers on the list the Senate shall choose the Vice-President: a quorum for the purpose shall consist of two thirds of the whole number of Senators, and a majority of the whole number shall be necessary to a choice. But no person constitutionally ineligible to the office of President shall be eligible to that of Vice-President of the United States.

Article XIII. [2] *Section* 1. Neither slavery nor involuntary servitude, except as a punishment for crime whereof the party shall have been duly convicted, shall exist within the United States or any place subject to their jurisdiction.

Section 2. Congress shall have power to enforce this article by appropriate legislation.

Article XIV. [3] *Section* 1. All persons born or naturalized in the United States, and subject to the jurisdiction thereof, are citizens of the United States and of the State wherein they reside. No State shall make or enforce any law which shall abridge the privileges or immunities of citizens of the United States; nor shall any State deprive any person of life, liberty, or property, without due process of law; nor deny to any person within its jurisdiction the equal protection of the laws.

Section 2. Representatives shall be apportioned among the several States according to their respective numbers, counting the whole number of persons in each State, excluding Indians not taxed. But when the right to vote at any election for the choice of electors for President and Vice-President of the United States, Representatives in Congress, the executive and judicial officers of a State, or the members of the legislature thereof, is denied to any of the male inhabitants of such State, being twenty-one years of age, and citizens of the United States, or in any way abridged, except for participation in rebellion, or other crime, the basis of representation therein shall be reduced in the proportion which the number of such male citizens shall bear to the whole number of male citizens twenty-one years of age in such State.

Section 3. No person shall be a Senator or Representative in Congress, or elector of President and Vice-President, or hold any office, civil or military, under the United States or under any State, who, having previously taken an oath as a member of Congress, or as an officer of the United States, or as a member of any State legislature, or as an executive or judicial officer of any State, to support the Constitution of the United States, shall have engaged in insurrection or rebellion against the same, or given aid or comfort to the enemies thereof. But Congress may, by a vote of two thirds of each house, remove such disability.

Section 4. The validity of the public debt of the United States, authorized

---

[1] Superseded by the Twentieth Amendment.
[2] Proclaimed December 18, 1865.
[3] Proclaimed July 28, 1868.

by law, including debts incurred for payment of pensions and bounties for services in suppressing insurrection or rebellion, shall not be questioned. But neither the United States nor any State shall assume or pay any debt or obligation incurred in aid of insurrection or rebellion against the United States, or any claim for the loss or emancipation of any slave; but all such debts, obligations, and claims shall be held illegal and void.

Section 5. The Congress shall have power to enforce, by appropriate legislation, the provisions of this article.

Article XV.[1] *Section* 1. The right of citizens of the United States to vote shall not be denied or abridged by the United States or by any State on account of race, color, or previous condition of servitude.

Section 2. The Congress shall have power to enforce this article by appropriate legislation.

Article XVI.[2] The Congress shall have power to lay and collect taxes on incomes, from whatever source derived, without apportionment among the several States, and without regard to any census or enumeration.

Article XVII.[3] The Senate of the United States shall be composed of two Senators from each State, elected by the people thereof, for six years; and each Senator shall have one vote. The electors in each State shall have the qualifications requisite for electors of the most numerous branch of the State legislature.

When vacancies happen in the representation of any State in the Senate, the executive authority of such State shall issue writs of election to fill such vacancies:. *Provided,* That the legislature of any State may empower the executive thereof to make temporary appointments until the people fill the vacancies by election as the legislature may direct.

This amendment shall not be so construed as to affect the election or term of any Senator chosen before it becomes valid as part of the Constitution.

Article XVIII.[4] *Section* 1. After one year from the ratification of this article the manufacture, sale, or transportation of intoxicating liquors within, the importation thereof into, or the exportation thereof from the United States and all territory subject to the jurisdiction thereof for beverage purposes is hereby prohibited.

Section 2. The Congress and the several States shall have concurrent power to enforce this article by appropriate legislation.

Section 3. This article shall be inoperative unless it shall have been ratified as an amendment to the Constitution by the legislatures of the several States, as provided in the Constitution, within seven years from the date of the submission hereof to the States by the Congress.[5]

Article XIX.[6] *Section* 1. The right of citizens of the United States to vote shall not be denied or abridged by the United States or by any State on account of sex.

Section 2. Congress shall have power to enforce this article by appropriate legislation.

[1] Proclaimed March 30, 1870.
[2] Proclaimed February 25, 1913.
[3] Proclaimed May 31, 1913.
[4] Proclaimed January 29, 1919.
[5] Rescinded by the Twenty-first Amendment.
[6] Proclaimed August 26, 1920.

Article XX.[1] *Section* 1. The terms of the President and Vice-President shall end at noon on the 20th day of January, and the terms of Senators and Representatives at noon on the 3rd day of January, of the years in which such terms would have ended if this article had not been ratified; and the terms of their successors shall then begin.

Section 2. The Congress shall assemble at least once in every year, and such meeting shall begin at noon on the 3rd day of January, unless they shall by law appoint a different day.

Section 3. If at the time fixed for the beginning of the term of the President, the President-elect shall have died, the Vice-President-elect shall become President. If a President shall not have been chosen before the time fixed for the beginning of his term, or if the President-elect shall have failed to qualify, then the Vice-President-elect shall act as President until a President shall have qualified, and the Congress may by law provide for the case wherein neither a President-elect nor a Vice-President-elect shall have qualified, declaring who shall then act as President, or the manner in which one who is to act shall be selected, and such person shall act accordingly until a President or Vice-president shall have qualified.

Section 4. The Congress may by law provide for the case of the death of any of the persons from whom the House of Representatives may choose a President whenever the right of choice shall have devolved upon them, and for the case of the death of any of the persons from whom the Senate may choose a Vice-President whenever the right of choice shall have devolved upon them.

Section 5. Sections 1 and 2 shall take effect on the 15th day of October following the ratification of this article.

Section 6. This article shall be inoperative unless it shall have been ratified as an amendment to the Constitution by the legislatures of three-fourths of the several States within seven years from the date of its submission.

Article XXI.[2] *Section* 1. The Eighteenth article of amendment to the Constitution of the United States is hereby repealed.

Section 2. The transportation or importation into any State, territory, or possession of the United States for delivery or use therein of intoxicating liquors, in violation of the laws thereof, is hereby prohibited.

Section 3. This article shall be inoperative unless it shall have been ratified as an amendment to the Constitution by conventions in the several States, as provided in the Constitution, within seven years from the date of the submission hereof to the States by the Congress.

REFERENCES

Department of State, *Documentary History of the Constitution of the United States of America, 1786-1870.* (3 vols., Washington, D. C., 1894-1900).

The Constitution of the United States of America, Annotated to January 1, 1938, 74th Cong., 2nd Sess., Sen. Doc. No. 232.

[1] Proclaimed February 6, 1933.
[2] Proclaimed December 5, 1933.

AMENDMENTS AT PRESENT (1948) BEFORE THE STATES
FOR ADOPTION

Child Labor

Section 1. The Congress shall have power to limit, regulate, and prohibit the labor of persons under eighteen years of age.

Section 2. The power of the several States is unimpaired by this article except that the operation of State laws shall be suspended to the extent necessary to give effect to legislation enacted by the Congress.[1]

Term of Office of the President

Section 1. No person shall be elected to the office of the President more than twice, and no person who has held the office of President, or acted as President, for more than two years of a term to which some other person was elected President shall be elected to the office of the President more than once. But this Article shall not apply to any person holding the office of President when this Article was proposed by the Congress, and shall not prevent any person who may be holding the office of President, or acting as President, during the term within which this Article becomes operative from holding the office of President or acting as President during the remainder of such term.

Section 2. This article shall be inoperative unless it shall have been ratified as an amendment to the Constitution by the legislatures of three-fourths of the several States within seven years from the date of its submission to the States by the Congress.[2]

[1] Proposed to the legislatures of the several states June 2, 1924.
[2] Proposed March 24, 1947.

INDEX

A